# METHODS *of* RESEARCH

# METHODS of RESEARCH
## Educational, Psychological, Sociological

by

## CARTER V. GOOD, Ph.D.

Director of Graduate Studies and Dean
Teachers College, University of Cincinnati

and

## DOUGLAS E. SCATES, Ph.D.

Professor of Education
University of Florida

New York

## APPLETON-CENTURY-CROFTS, INC.

# Preface

THIS BOOK has been written for field workers, graduate students, and members of the senior division of the undergraduate college who would evaluate the quality of conclusions, either as producers or consumers of research. Both the producer and consumer of research literature should know how and by what methods evidence is gathered, analyzed, and interpreted. Knowledge of research techniques and active participation in problem-solving are more likely to stimulate in the student the excitement of learning and of searching for truth than will textbook and lecture materials in the form of ready-made generalizations. Therefore, in this book research is presented as a way of finding answers to questions that make human beings curious or perplexed. Many of our illustrations of research portray scientists and scholars as people, with the joys of discovery and the disappointments or frustrations of wrong hypotheses, inadequate techniques, and physical, psychological, or material handicaps.

The organization of this text follows substantially the steps or sequence of problem-solving: formulation and development of the problem for investigation, and survey of the related literature; selection and use of one or more appropriate methods for gathering evidence, together with analysis and interpretation of the data; and reporting and implementation of the findings. Aspects of analysis and interpretation are treated in the setting of their functional relationships to the methodology of research (historical, descriptive-survey, experimental, case-clinical, and genetic) rather than in the more artificial setting of a separate chapter or section of this book. It is appropriate, however, to point out that Chapter 5, on the descriptive method, is devoted primarily to the concepts and procedures involved in general description, analysis, and classification, together with numerous illustrations of these types of research. The several chapters vary in length and complexity of structure, but so do the steps in problem-solving and the methods of research.

Chapters 5 and 6, on the descriptive-survey methods and data-gathering procedures, are complementary, although in a sense each is internally complete as a unit. Chapter 5 presents a theoretical, rather technical, advanced treatment (together with numerous illustrations) which some college seniors and some beginning graduate students may find in part difficult reading. Chapter 6 is a relatively concrete discussion of the organized forms of descriptive-survey research, together with an elementary treatment of the various data-gathering procedures and instruments used frequently in normative-survey studies. With respect to these chapters and others, the user of the text may find portions in which his immediate interest is not sufficient to warrant careful study; he should select in keeping with his purposes and needs. The content of this text steers a middle course between the concrete details of illustrative investigations and the more abstract concepts and theories of research methodology.

Since there are many specialized graduate courses and texts that deal with the details of educational, psychological, and sociological testing and statistics, these techniques as such will not be treated in the present volume. The psychometric, sociometric, and educational techniques not specifically treated in this book (or mentioned only briefly for illustrative purposes) include the following: intelligence tests and measures of general mental ability, measurement and prediction of special abilities or aptitudes, personality and character tests, measures of attitudes and interests, projective methods and other devices for the study of personality, psychometric and sociometric techniques with standardized testing and statistical emphasis, and educational (accomplishment) tests in or outside of schools and colleges.

This volume is not a "recipe book" of research methods, a "cookbook," a "rule book," or a series of "lesson plans" for problem-solving, reflective thinking, and research; but rather it is a discussion of concepts, principles, and procedures in educational, psychological, and sociological investigations. These intellectual processes do not ordinarily proceed in a succession of orderly steps straight to the goal. This is not the way of research. As has been emphasized and illustrated generally in this book, the sequence of activities in research frequently moves shuttle-like between formulating concepts and gathering of evidence, checking the ideas against the observations, and perhaps collecting new facts.

In many instances in this book the discussion of a particular problem or technique is in the form of a series of questions for the student to think through, with attention directed to the available literature, because the answer may not yet be fully known. The thesis, project, or seminar report of the student is regarded as a functional and appropriate exercise to carry along, paralleling the study of the several chapters of this book, as he engages in developing the problem, reviewing the related literature, selecting and using a data-gathering procedure, analyzing and interpreting the evidence, and preparing the report. This procedure seems preferable to a listing of exercises in the more or less artificial settings at the ends of the various chapters. The student who would achieve intellectual independence through a working knowledge of the research literature will find a reasonably full account of the essential library tools and many illustrative studies. The library aids may be used to bring the bibliographical references of this book up to date at any time in the future.

In the interest of variety, illustrations of two bibliographical (and footnote) forms are given, as explained more fully in Chapter 10: one style in the chapter bibliographies and footnotes at the bottom of the pages, and the other (as examples) in the body of the chapter dealing with technical reporting.

Only moderate use has been made of the term *scientific,* since there is no essential conflict between the procedures of science, philosophy, logic, history, statistics, and case-clinical study. The methods of science (and technology) and of philosophy (and logic) are complementary techniques, perhaps different aspects of the general purpose of a single discipline of inquiry, in the development of problem or concept and in the gathering of evidence with which to test or modify the concept. It is held that science without philosophy is blind, while philosophy without science is empty. Recognition of the importance of theory and philosophy is found especially in Chapter 1 and Chapter 5 (on the descriptive method), which may be regarded in part as a philosophy of research and science.

Because of the increasing interdependence of problems and procedures in certain educational, psychological, and sociological areas, it has been possible to present a common pattern of research methodology, together with numerous illustrations from each special field. Sociology has moved toward integration with social psychology and cultural anthropology. The special aspects of social psychology that have value alike for sociology and for education include problems of personality, the influence of culture and culture patterns and of racial and other groups, the assessment of intelligence and character, the analysis of folk psychology, and the study of political leadership. This trend toward integration of sociology, social psychology, and cultural anthropology, including pertinent applications to educational problems, may be regarded as part of a larger movement toward coöperation in all the human sciences. Evidence of this interdisciplinary approach and of close coöperation between the different areas of behavioral or social science is now found in the literature [1] and in certain graduate programs and research centers which utilize the combined resources of psychology, sociology, anthropology, and education.

While the general outline of the text was prepared after joint planning and discussion between the two authors, each was given primary responsibility for the writing of certain chapters. Good wrote Chapters 2, 3, 4, and 6 through 10, with Chapters 6 and 7 based in large part on examples and memoranda collected by Scates over a period of years. Scates wrote Chapters 1 and 5.

The authors are indebted for advice and assistance to Alice Yeomans Scates, especially in preparing Chapter 7 on experimentation; to Dr. Nathan S. Washton of Queens College for critical reading of the section on classification; to Dr. William H. Burton of Harvard University for editorial assistance; and to a large number of workers in education, psychology, sociology, and other social fields, whose research and writings have provided essential background for this book.

C. V. G.

D. E. S.

[1] Leon Festinger and Daniel Katz, Editors, *Research Methods in the Behavioral Sciences.* New York: Dryden Press, 1953. p. 1-12.

John Gillin and Others, *For a Science of Social Man:* Convergences in Anthropology, Sociology, and Psychology. New York: Macmillan Co., 1954. 296 p.

Howard W. Odum, *American Sociology:* The Story of Sociology in the United States through 1950. New York: Longmans, Green and Co., 1951. p. 445-70.

Florian Znaniecki, *Cultural Sciences:* Their Origin and Development. Urbana: University of Illinois Press, 1952. p. 392-419.

# Contents

# METHODS of RESEARCH

# 1

# Research as a Way of Progress

**Our time is one of rapid progress.** We live in a period of fabulous accomplishment. We cannot fully appreciate this fact, because we ourselves are products of the age and are used to it. Only by means of historical and cultural comparisons, and even then with difficulty, can we gain some sense of the distinctiveness of our own time.

The developments during the first half of this century, when reviewed, are startling. In order to get some pictures of what has been taking place before our eyes, we might imagine ourselves back at the beginning of the twentieth century addressing to scientists, engineers, and industrialists a set of requests representing some of the common wants of mankind. One of these requests undoubtedly would be for an increase in the power of locomotion; we should like to travel over the land with considerable freedom and at a rate far faster than our human body could carry us. The answer fifty years later was an automobile for nearly every family in the United States, in addition to various modes of public transportation. Perhaps in 1900 we should have desired our power of speech magnified untold times and channelled according to our wish, so that we could talk individually to our friends wherever they were. By the middle of the century, in our country there were nearly as many telephones as families. We might have wished in 1900 for power of hearing so sensitive that we could listen to music programs and public addresses while sitting in the comfort of our homes, or in fact wherever we might be. We now have the equivalent of two radio sets for each family for use at home, in our automobiles, in railroad trains, or on the sands of the beach. If we had wished for vision extending across cities, fields, and mountain ranges, so that we could see events at great distance, the answer is that television now brings these happenings to our homes in an instant's time.

These requests, however, leave us earthbound; why not let our fancy range? Should we like to get off the ground and travel with the birds of the air? At present we sail through the air far higher, faster, and farther than birds ever flew. We cross our continent in the light of one day and reach Europe in less than twenty-four hours. Should we like to exceed the speed of sound? We can now stop and wait to hear ourselves coming. Have we often wondered what space was like beyond the "sky"? We can now see more stars than one person could ever count, and by new instruments we obtain evidence of other heavenly bodies which our largest telescope cannot make visible.[1]

Do we wish to know more of the secrets of nature on this earth, so that we could control the very substance of which things are composed? Should we like to change one element into another? We are now doing it. We manufacture new elements which long ago ceased to exist on the earth; we even make elements that probably never did exist on the earth. We can, if we please, even create matter out of mere energy. Man's accomplished mastery in half a century—product of modern thought and method—is the equivalent of a succession of miracles.

There are, however, other wants. Back at the turn of the century, conditions would have justified our saying, "We work too hard. We should like relief from physical labor, so that we may be spared some of the strain and have more time for enjoyment." In answer to this basic want our country now generates enough energy to place at the disposal of each man, woman, and child the mechanical equivalent of 320 slaves to do his work. We enjoy the resultant standard of living and the consequent increase in leisure. The promise for tomorrow is even greater, for we have recently learned how to go beyond chemical reactions and release the great forces in the very heart of the atom itself—we have learned the secret of the sun! [2]

There is one further major request, more basic than all the rest. In 1900 we should undoubtedly have said to the scientists, "We would live longer; pray give us more time on this earth in which to enjoy the many new powers with which you will endow us." The research scientists in biology and medicine have been at work. By mid-century the actuarial statistician could offer this testimony: Man's life had been increased by one-third over that of 1900; and during the whole past century the expected span had risen by nearly two-thirds.[3] We now live twice as long as European man during the Middle Ages—and, if medical men are permitted to continue to experiment, the story has not reached its conclusion.

No golden age of the past in any period, in any land, could approach that in which we now live, and what we have today is but the beginning

[1] Harlow Shapley, "Time and Change in the Metagalaxy." *Scientific Monthly* 67:243-53; October 1948.

[2] It has been predicted that the amount of power developed in the United States in 1953 will be doubled within twenty-five years. See articles in *Life* magazine, January 4, 1954, p. 79-91. For a more complete study, with historical trends, see J. Frederic Dewhurst and Associates, *America's Needs and Resources.* New York: Twentieth Century Fund, 1947. 812 p. See especially p. 589-90, 680-87, 781-87.

[3] "Longevity from Ancient to Modern Times." *Statistical Bulletin,* Metropolitan Life Insurance Company (New York), Vol. 28, No. 10, p. 1-3; October 1947.

See also Hornell Hart and Hilda Hertz, "Expectation of Life as an Index of Social Progress." *American Sociological Review* 9:609-21; December 1944.

of a brilliant future. Through education, each person can be prepared to enter understandingly and appreciatively into this vital, forward-moving, challenging life of the present. But the pace set by the quick changes in the physical and biological worlds heaps unprecedented burdens on man's understanding of himself and his society, so that great amounts of research in the human fields are imperative. The means of conducting these studies, in order that man's understanding of the problems of living may not lag disastrously far behind his understanding of the problems of mechanics, are dealt with throughout the remaining chapters of the present text.

**The rate of progress is still accelerating.** It is the rapidity of increase in tested knowledge and its widespread application to everyday living which distinctively set off the modern era from the past. However, we are not to think of the twentieth century as devoid of all ties with the past. If we produced a curve representing progress, looking backward from the present, it would slope steeply downward across the past few centuries and then round outward into a long undulating course until it disappeared into the obscure millenniums of the dim past. Elements of our modern thought find roots in the life of all the peoples who have contributed from their culture to the richness of Western civilization, and many ideas can be traced back through the intervening years to the ancient dynasties of Egypt, Syria, and Babylonia.

The modern period of intellectual development has its beginning with the Renaissance. It may be dated from about 1300 or about 1600, depending on which phase of the movement one wishes to consider. Tools of modern thought began to be developed and, even more important, basic attitudes that make tested knowledge possible and acceptable were beginning to be formed. The story of the difficult struggles in the early modern period is told elsewhere; for the present, we note simply that, about 1300, historical research and various forms of the humanities began to take on the critical spirit and that astronomy, mathematics, physics, chemistry, and medicine began around 1600 to show similar signs of the modern aggressive, exploratory attitude.

In considering this curve of expanding knowledge, it is not the backward view which should be emphasized so much as the present upward sweep and the prospect for the future. The slope becomes ever steeper. Many elements enter into this growth and there is no single series of data to represent it, but a number of specific traits for which data are available reveal the increasing gradient.[4] The present time is something more than an ephemeral effect in the long history of man's climb; it is an all-embracing upsurge, having behind it the cumulative force of several centuries of progressive growth

4 See the *American Sociological Review*, June 1946, which quotes statements from eighteen sources attesting cultural acceleration.

and having before it the possibility for a new level of life scarcely envisaged even in phantasy.

**Increased amounts of research make progress possible.** When one considers the nature of our present culture, its general dependence on research is clear. The great progress of the recent past has been possible because increased numbers of people were at work on continually increasing numbers of research projects. In the earlier days, when research was done by only a few persons, little intellectual progress could be achieved. It is true that major adaptations to life can be made by the common man, and that convictions can be expanded and declared without benefit of testing, but advances in the refined requirements of technology and clearer insights into the intricate relations of scientific principles call for rigorous training, specialized equipment, and extended, systematic endeavor. The fruits of research will depend upon the number of competent persons engaged in research, and the pace of progress is set accordingly.

Few series of data with which to illumine the point extend back into the last century. We shall have to draw on what is available. There are, for instance, records of the number of patents issued in this country back to 1836. Even though patents are not a thoroughly good index of the amount of research being done, since many patents are based on less study than is research and, on the other hand, much research (in universities and government) does not lead at once to patents, nevertheless an increase in patents does presume a greater concentration of thought and energy devoted to improvements in the area of patentable things. An examination of the data reveals a striking trend. The aggregate number of patents issued in the United States up through 1850 was 18,000. By the end of 1950, the grand total was approximately 2,500,000. One may wish to think of the forward and backward implications of such figures. If man has spent ten thousand centuries achieving his present state, is it not worthy of note that a single century of the ten thousand should contain such a large concentration of effort directed at improvement? Toward the end of this one century (1850-1950), which everyone thought was fairly advanced to start with, man was producing patentable ideas in the United States at an annual rate forty times as fast as at the beginning of this period!

Suggestive evidence on the increasing amount of research is afforded also by the number of persons who obtain the degree of Doctor of Philosophy. Such persons are especially trained to do research. The series of data available extends for less than a century, but it reveals the same tendency as shown by the other curves under consideration.[5]

---

[5] For basic historical data on earned doctor's degrees in all fields, and separately for science fields, see Chapter 2 of Douglas E. Scates, Bernard C. Murdoch, and Alice V.

Actual expenditures for research are the data which would be most significant. They are known, however, for only a few years, and even for those years the figures do not include all research; they relate only to the physical and biological sciences and their applications. The total expenditures for research in the social fields are unknown. The figures which are available support the point that our increasing know-how is based on increasing amounts of research, for they exhibit the same accelerating trend that our technological progress does. In the relatively short space of one decade, from 1920 to 1930, expenditures for research and development in the physical and biological fields more than doubled. Again, in the next ten years they doubled. Growth at this geometrical rate would call for another doubling by 1950, but actually the 1940 expenditures doubled by 1943 and trebled by 1947! The war had ended, but not the rise of research; another doubling (of the 1947 figures) was called for within ten years by a national policy formulating committee.[6]

These rates of expansion are great. If we assume an estimated figure of around $60,000,000 for 1920, the increases are from ten to eighty million dollars each year. This growth is not to be dismissed with the assumption that the increases are military; military research accounted for about half of the actual increase up to 1947. Industry, however, spent eight times as much on research and development in 1940 as in 1920, and the 1947 budget was fifteen times as large as for 1920. None of the figures referred to includes expenditures for atomic energy; those figures might add a great deal to the known increases. Even without the atomic energy research, however, we have in effect increased each year's research and development expenditure by an amount virtually equal to the total amount spent in 1920. That is, if we think of the 1920 figure as representing the highest level of research production to which man had climbed through hundreds of thousands of years of existence, the expenditures in this country since 1920 have on the average *increased each year* over the total of the preceding year by as much as man had increased them above zero in the entire several hundred thousand years prior to 1920. (Rough estimates of expenditures and needs for a program of educational research are presented in Chapter 2.)

Yeomans, *The Production of Doctorates in the Sciences: 1936-1948*. Washington: American Council on Education, 1951. 228 p. (Mimeographed.)

Other data specifically for degrees in education, psychology, and sociology are given in Chapter 2 of the present text.

6 The figures on research and development expenditures in the United States up to 1944 are contained in the report of the Committee on Science and the Public Welfare, Isaiah Bowman, Chairman, and published in Vannevar Bush, *Science, the Endless Frontier*, p. 80. Washington: Government Printing Office, 1945. Some of these figures are reproduced, some are altered, and the 1947 budget figures are given in the President's Scientific Research Board, John R. Steelman, Chairman, *Science and Public Policy*, Vol. I, p. 10, 12, 26. Washington: Government Printing Office, 1947. 5 vols.

**Research can expand indefinitely.** With this astounding record of growth, the question keeps coming to mind, What of the future? It is not a new question; years ago writers were asking, Can the rate of increase keep up? But now we ask, Can the *acceleration* in the increase keep up? What is the impact of these developments on man? Can society stand such a pace?

The answers to such questions depend on a mingling of theoretical, practical, and valuational elements. In the abstract, the answer is yes, research can continue to increase its rate; it can continue to accelerate its increasing rate. How many times in the past have rising curves been exceeded a century later by rates of increase that were incredible at an earlier time! Of all rising curves the trend for research is the most limitless.

Those who say, "What will one find to study next?" do not know research. Those who say, "Will not research ever answer all the questions we need to know—all the really important ones?" do not understand. For research multiplies questions far faster than it answers them. The barriers of ignorance are pushed back but one level at a time, and each new layer of understanding reveals a complexity that was little dreamed of before it was explored. Thus, each achievement brings with it countless new opportunities for further searching—for research is the continuous discovery and exploration of the unknown. And so the penetration goes on and on. Well was the phrase coined, "the endless frontier."

Practically, research will be reduced, either in acceleration or in rate of increase or even in actual amount, when society feels that this course is called for. So far, we have been able to make some assimilation of the host of new products and procedures and understanding which recent research has laid before us; thoughtful persons, however, recognize a tremendous shearing tension between different parts of our culture—our unbelievable enlightenment in the physical fields, our growing control of biological processes, and our much slower grasp of fundamental factors in the field of human behavior. The continuation of rapid research in the future will undoubtedly depend on the extent to which its progress in these different lines can be brought into balance, for no culture can stand indefinitely an increase of shearing stress between its major aspects.

**Do we want research to expand?** Is science man's friend or his foe? Is it a blessing or a curse? Is it man's road to a higher level of existence or is it his certain ruin? To such questions one will get a variety of answers, depending on the variety of backgrounds which color the thinking of the respondents. We have some fears, legitimate fears, of the power that research has placed at our disposal, and equally at the disposal of those who may not be our friends. We have the annoyance of change itself, of having continually to adjust to something different. And we have the irritation of being forced to change our ideas about the world and man as research constantly reveals new facets of nature for which our earlier understanding made no room. Then there are some, perhaps many, who do not like the plain type of thinking which a research point of view emphasizes; they prefer a less factual, more emotional form of reaction to the world.

Some of these ideas will be dealt with more directly in later chapters, where examples from the historical development of science will be given, since attitudes unfavorable to science are not new. In fact the history of modern science is the history of brave men who pursued their investigating, often without the favor of persons in power and probably against the will of the majority of common people. Admittedly, life is filled with compromise; there is no gain except at a price. But how many among us would give up our automobiles and walk—give up the airplane, railroad train, street car, auto bus, truck, and all of their services—because we dislike the factual type of thinking which has made these conveniences possible? How many of us would forfeit the twenty to forty years that science has added to our individual lives, and the greatly increased amount of health and vigor that has been given to us during those extra years, just because we do not want anyone to think of the human body as having machine-like parts, or as carrying on a chain of chemical reactions which make life possible? We are all so greatly indebted to science, we all indulge so heavily in the enjoyment of the fruits of science, that it is thoughtless to condemn science *in toto* because we dislike certain aspects of it.

When we see the power for an increasingly better life, or a stronger, more vigorous and more enduring body, or for a wider diffusion of esthetic enjoyments, we cannot lightly say that we do not want science. To do so would be to deny, not only to ourselves but to millions of others, the things for which man has so long striven—the basic objectives that have been incorporated in his hopes for a better world for himself, his friends, and his children. Now that we have these things within our hands, we encounter the challenge of becoming equal to the task of managing this new estate, turning it to good account, in order that we and our children's children may enjoy the new level of life which research has placed at our disposal.

Perhaps the greatest mistake lies in imputing to science itself qualities and characteristics that are solely qualities and characteristics of human beings. We so often talk, and apparently feel, as though science were animate, as though it carried moral responsibility, as though it were in itself good or bad. There is no more goodness or badness in science than there is in knowledge at large. The applications that man makes of science and the ends for which he employs it are deeply moral, for they fundamentally affect man's welfare. But we must draw a sharp distinction between science and man's use of it. Modern science places in man's hands almost infinite power and thereby places on man a new level of moral responsibility—the choice between an unprecedentedly full life for himself and for his brothers under the sun or, on the other hand, the wholesale destruction of his civilization, his culture, his people, and the land on which they live. If we feel weak in the face of the choice, or inadequate in the discharge of the decision, we must recognize that the path of progress lies not in the direction of damning science, but in the determination to develop the resolute fiber, the essential understanding, and the appropriate methods by which to direct the vast empire of scientific accomplishments toward the realization of those purposes for which man ever strives.

**Science extends the role of intelligence.** We cannot come to a mature conclusion, however, until we have sought a fuller view of research and its functions. We must consider explicitly the question, What is research for? What is its mission in society? Does it destroy the finer qualities of life? Will it dominate mankind?

We must first of all recognize that science is simply a form of knowledge or understanding; it is that portion of knowledge which has been most definitely substantiated. When, therefore, we raise the question of its values and its use, we are in part raising the question of the value and the use of any knowledge and understanding. The role of science is precisely that of intelligence; both derive from the native capacity of humans and animals to learn, to profit by experience, to avoid repeating mistakes endlessly, and, somewhat more broadly, to compare, to generalize, to infer, to predict, to integrate, and thus provide the ideational foundations on which rest evaluational choices, judgment, prudence, wisdom.

Thus science is simply a mature, rigorous, extended, abstracted, and systematized form of experience, of the same basic nature as all other experience. It is true that scientists adopt special safeguards to insure the accuracy of their beliefs, but these precautions in no way change the essential character of science and research as knowledge and as learning. The function of science is to extend man's intelligence, and the function of research is to extend science. Hence, if we wish wisdom, we must expect science; if we wish an increase of wisdom, we must expect research. For science and research are but the accumulated and still accumulating forms of man's most carefully derived understanding, involving appropriate problem-solving methods for gathering and interpreting evidence.

It is common to think of the term *science* as including the many applications of science. For purposes of everyday conversation no harm may result from thus including technology, but for purposes of careful evaluation the greatest possible harm may result—for this amalgamation of concepts identifies science with the ends to which man has put it, and the issue of the value of science becomes confused with the question of whether man has used and directed science in the wisest possible way. The latter question is of the same order as asking whether man has lived well and properly since he inhabited the earth, and we can find no satisfactory answer other than one's own opinion. But the question of the function of science in the mental economy of humanity is of an entirely different order, for science (as a body of substantiated understanding) is but a continuation of the desire of every normal individual to learn by experience, to increase his powers, to refine his ends, and to make choices based on understanding. To doubt the value of science is to bring into question the function of intelligence; and to say that man would be better off without science is in the same direction as saying that man would be better off if he were a brute. Our concern with science, as with intelligence, is not that we have an overabundance of it, but rather that we shall develop it broadly, so that it will deal with the many facets of our existence, and that we shall then apply it to serve all of the ends of man.

**The purpose of research is to serve man.** Concepts of the purpose to which research should be put are at times (perhaps always) enmeshed in the political and social philosophy of a given nation. According to one social philosophy, science is cultivated by a certain economic group for the sake of favoring their position and increasing their earnings. The goals of science, according to this view, are always materialistic. In somewhat the same light other writers have emphasized the historical dependence of research on political and economic interest. For example, when nations desired to expand their overseas trade, instruments of navigation (compass, almanac, sextant, clock, and the attendant conceptual schemes) were developed. We have seen recently in two nations how science has been warped and the findings of current research controlled and directed so as to force scientific principles to accord with political objectives. In the United States, much research is being sponsored by the National Military Establishment in the interests of the security of the nation. After reviewing all such presentations in behalf of special purposes, we are inclined to wonder: Do these constitute a full list? Do they exhaust the possibilities of the service of research to humanity?

If we should turn to the individual scientist and seek an intimate picture of the personal motives which prompt him to pursue his professional labors, we should probably find that he engages in research because of his love for exploration. There is a challenge in the unknown; there is beauty in system. The research scientist loves to wrestle with baffling subtleties and, little by little, bring them into focus and then into regular pattern. He is devoted to his task, often working without regard to hours and without expectancy of material reward. The history of science identifies many who pursued their research at considerable personal sacrifice; some still do so. We have heard of those who faced the ridicule of society because of their peculiar interests and revolutionary ideas; persons who work creatively are ever in this danger. We cannot be unmindful of those who have been persecuted for their scientific investigations; the Renaissance stories have been reënacted within our own lifetimes. Some researchers are actuated by ambition, but more are driven by the urge to find out and by the desire to see order where at first there is only confusion. Their reward is not only the satisfaction of accomplishment; it is an esthetic experience to discover the recurrent rhythms of nature; there is the joy of genuine progress through the creation of something new—but it must not be overlooked that in following these somewhat individual and personal motivations they also add to the intellectual estate of all mankind.[7]

What is the attitude of a democracy toward the purposes of research? In theory, and to a large extent in practice, the attitude found among the democratic peoples will be to further the interests and desires of individuals and to capitalize on these for the welfare of all. An inherent purpose of democracy is to identify, insofar as possible, the social interest with the individual interest. The effort proceeds along two lines: to preserve intact the individual purpose where possible, and in turn to utilize the social product for the common good. Thus the drives of the individual researcher to explore into the unknown, to follow up leads which only he would think were worth following, to seek truth for its sheer beauty—these activities will be safeguarded, since democracy seeks to foster opportunities for the self-expression of its members; and, on the other hand, these activities are likely to be strongly supported, because throughout history the individual thinker and the individual researcher have been the ones who have created science. They have not only contributed the crucial ideas for continuing intellectual progress but have also supplied the stimulation and the criticism necessary to keep the stream of thought flowing and ever self-directing. Democracy is likely to hold that through free competitive research, socially supported but not politically controlled, all mankind—not any one nation nor any single class, but all people—will benefit most. This then is our ultimate democratic purpose for research—the most benefit for the most people.

**Research was born out of man's problems.** Research is now a proved tool of great power. With small and uncertain beginnings, with a heritage which knew not research methods, with tasks of unimagined complexities

---

[7] Statements of purposes and satisfactions in research work, taken from the biographies and other publications of scientists and scholars, are given in Chapter 2.

ahead, and beset with the inertia of ideas already accepted and held by society, what we now know as a vast body of scientific facts and principles was brought into existence through the relentless persevering of men of research. Knowledge of the methodology of research grew with its applications and, with increasing methodological knowledge, the scope of the problems attacked also enlarged. As social interest and demand shifted from mathematics and astronomy to physics, chemistry, geology, biology, and the social fields, so the span of scientific thought was broadened to include an ever increasing array of problems, until today virtually every field of life has been touched by the research approach.

We may ask, What is this powerful tool that has increasingly received the attention of thoughtful men and has so continuously expanded over the range of man's problems? The answer, in outline, is fairly simple. When man faces problems he sooner or later seeks a solution. Solutions to some problems are psychological and take the form of adjustments within the individual—a change of purpose, a new understanding, a different kind of reaction. Other solutions take the form of a change in the external environment, so that a different situation obtains. In any case, rationally derived solutions that give man dependable power over relationships call for an understanding of the nature of the situation and of the factors governing it.

If, in seeking this understanding, man is content to devise and accept intriguing stories based on the ideology of the common lore, he may find explanations that satisfy his surface curiosity, but which are not likely to afford efficient control. What does sound research require? If he questions his explanations, the stage is set for research. If he goes further and challenges the methods by which he arrived at his conclusion; if he critically and systematically repeats his observations; if he devises special tools for taking, recording, and analyzing his observations; if he tests the reliability and the validity of these tools and evaluates his data in other ways; if he scrutinizes the thought processes by which he passes from one step of his logic to another; if he gradually refines his concept of what it is he is trying to explain and considers anew the necessary and sufficient conditions for proof; if at every step he proceeds with the utmost caution, realizing that his purpose is not to arrive at an answer which is personally pleasing, but rather one which will stand up under the critical attacks of those who doubt his answer—if he can meet these criteria and steadfastly hold to his purpose, then he is doing research. The price may be high, the procedure demanding, but the power that results is astounding.

Thus research is born of problems and of man's determination to solve problems. The understandings which result, when integrated into a descriptive, explanatory, and predictive system of concepts, constitute science.

Science is, therefore, the end-product of a long chain of careful effort. This form of endeavor is not restricted to any particular field; born of problems, it is available for problems, as widely in man's experience as they may occur. Its nature is determined not by the content with which the observations and thought sequences are filled, but by man and his purposes—by his needs and his insistence on good answers. The scientific method was forged from the resolute determination to accept nothing short of rigorous solutions, and having been formed, it is available wherever this same resolute purpose may hold. There may be science where there is research, and there can be research wherever there are phenomena that can be known. Research thus becomes man's great ally in the accomplishment of his purposes; where man wills to know, he may bend his effort and find answers.

**Man's major problems demand research.** A tool of such great worth should be put to tasks of no mean order. We come, therefore, to inquire, What are the unsettled forces in man's world today for whose ordering there is strong pressure? What are the great questions, growing out of man's current need, which press to the fore for solution? What are the imperatives, the fundamental "musts" of man's continued existence on this planet? When looked at in terms of what is basic, it is clearly seen that the great problems now lie in the field of man's relations with man. Whereas problems in this realm have always been annoyingly large, they are now made acute, because the knowledge of physical and biological principles which man has acquired has given him great power over life and death, not only of individuals but of entire populations, and this same form of knowledge has so reduced the insulating effects of space that any nation is now the neighbor of every other nation.

For such power and such proximity man is unprepared. His previously accepted controls, inadequate for the past, are puny against forces which can momentarily be unleashed. The relative nearness of all peoples to each other at the present time increases rather than decreases the natural danger of irritation and strong interactions, much as, in the physical realm, compressing a gas increases the collisions among the molecules, adds to their force, and raises the temperature. Much new knowledge, much scientific research, is called for to make our modern world even as stable as it was before society acquired means that threaten its destruction; perhaps as much research in the social realm as has been done in the physical realm; perhaps more research, since the problems are no less intricate and they are of large dimensions.[8]

It is of fundamental importance to recognize that social problems are

<hr>

[8] James B. Conant, "The Role of Science in Our Unique Society." *Science* 107:77-83; January 23, 1948.

to be resolved in the same manner as are physical and biological problems and not directly by volition and emotion. For example, the avoidance of war is not a problem to be solved by wishfulness; it is not to be dealt with by more and more intensity of desire for peace, but rather it must be met by more and more demand for research. We cannot have peace just for the wanting, no matter how hard. The indefinitely recurring experiences of the past should make this plain beyond any trace of question. The long record of interpopulation aggressions that have characterized man's historical period must make us expect social explosions to continue to occur, just as we expect volcanic eruptions or other long established phenomena to persist into the future unless we use adequate means to control those conditions which control the phenomena. Wishing will not of itself accomplish this purpose; wishing is definitely not an adequate means for international control.

Our desire for peace may, however, move us to consider the brilliant record we have made in those areas in which man has most assiduously employed the methods of research. If we follow in the light of these large lessons, we will devote proper amounts of study to the nature, generation, and operation of those forces which produce international tension and conflict, just as we devote time to the study of the nature and control of physical forces that produce strain and possibly destruction. The steam engine and the internal combustion engine, which harness and utilize forces of dangerous potentiality, were produced and perfected by appropriate study and careful research. The development of the means for control (and directing toward useful ends) of the tremendous forces latent in human nature is a problem to be attacked in similar fashion.[9]

In the social field we have unusual difficulty in attaining a scientific or unbiased view, partly because we are participants in our society and our personal fortunes rise and fall with the direction of social movement; and partly because we become used to a world in which we seek to enhance our desires by assertion, by vigorous demand, by some display of emotion, perhaps even by threat. Thus our everyday experiences and our personal perceptions mislead us into thinking of human affairs primarily in terms of the strength and quality of demand. We commonly have little recognition of the conditions and forces (and historical sequences) which have produced our attitudes and orientations, and we may give scant attention to the social forms and interactions that play their part in molding and guiding group decision and action. Scientific study in the human area will, however, free our view from the immediate and obvious, and direct our attention to the underlying and basically controlling factors. When intelligently

[9] Douglas E. Scates, "The Parallel Roles of Physical and Social Science." *Scientific Monthly* 64:14-20; January 1947.

directed, our feelings should serve not as a substitute for research but as a powerful factor in seeing that social research is promoted.

**The goal of research is the good life.** The social goal is positive rather than negative. The avoidance of war, fundamental as that objective is, is not the total good for which man seeks. We must think in broader terms. We must try to envisage man's purposes in their fullness and richness, if we are to see the ways in which research can serve them.

To aid in this purpose we may borrow a classical phrase and speak of "the good life." The concept of the good life has perhaps never been fully defined; probably it cannot be put in specific terms without ruining it, for our goals change rapidly as we approach them and any ideal must be subject to continual reinterpretation, if it is not to be surpassed and forgotten. It may, however, be desirable to mention certain general characteristics which the present writers have in mind, in order to make the concept more meaningful. Our standard for the good life would be the things we would wish for ourselves as individuals, insofar as these are compatible with similar desires by other persons. We would conceptualize a life in which man's needs can be met without undue strain, his suffering reduced to a minimum, and his satisfactions made full and abundant, so that he will regard his life as an enjoyable and dignifying experience. Needs of many diverse kinds— physical, biological, psychological, and social—must be recognized and provided for; there are "hidden hungers" of a psychological nature as well as of a physical nature. Satisfactions graded to the individual's maturing personality and affording a balance between relatively immediate and long-time values must be available within the physical and mental limitations of each person. The individual is entitled to development through education and a rich variety of experiences without his being warped into a fixed mold; the proper recognition of differences among individuals is a necessity. The various freedoms consistent with some security and with the interest of others; the necessity for struggle, the opportunity for creativity, and the reward for effort; the balancing of efficiency and economy with the enjoyment of leisure and esthetics—these and other qualities are involved. But beyond these general qualities the precise interpretation of "the good life" must remain somewhat individual and somewhat variable, subject to progressive reinterpretation.

With some conception of the good life as a goal, it is possible to think more clearly about progress as moving toward that goal and about research as contributing to the movement. Progress may be said to consist of bringing about a more adequate supply, a more equitable distribution, and a more stable enjoyment of those physical, biological, psychological, and social conditions and occurrences which tend to make man's life what he thinks it should be. Progress is a goal to be won; it is not automatic, it is not inevitable, it is not gratuitous. It is something wrested from the passing moments by the impact of a new understanding, by a choice of a new direction, or by the application of a new power. It is essentially novel, something new under the sun. Incorporated into the stream of human activities, it makes tomorrow's routine more effective than today's in the satisfaction of human wants. Progress means more of what we value, less of what we fear. Thus we move toward the goal of the good life.

These characteristics of progress are, however, also the objectives of research. To satisfy man's craving for more understanding, to improve his judgment, to add to his power, to reduce the burden of work, to relieve suffering, and to increase satisfactions in multitudinous ways—these are the large and fundamental goals of research. It is true that there are certain intellectual criteria which research must meet, but this is so only in order that research may satisfy the high demands man has placed upon it; and it is true that there are points at which research is directed not toward any immediate service to society at large, but toward filling in the gaps of scientific theory, although this is merely a delayed form of service through making the whole of science an ever more powerful and dependable resource. In the final analysis, research is justified on the basis of its contributions to better living, its aid to man in his upward climb. It is on this basis that the enormous increases in the support of research have been granted during the present century, and it is because of this increased support that we are now witnessing the greatest advance in knowledge, education, distributed goods, communication, and in other material and immaterial forms of culture. It is the underlying and ultimate purpose of research to create social goods.

It is sometimes thought that research is concerned only with physical things and as such contributes to a view of the world which is materialistic. The research which avowedly has physical phenomena as its domain properly places emphasis on material causes and effects. Much effort has been so devoted and great successes have followed. It is also true that material factors underlie and affect more of man's living than was formerly realized; thus we have physiological mechanisms determining inheritance, mechanical substances contributing heavily to many phases of personality, and mental activity in general being regarded as a functional product of the brain and nervous system. It is natural that we should apprehend and study these physical correlates of life; but it would be unnatural and highly artificial should we stop there, for there are other aspects of life known to every human being and it is the responsibility of research sooner or later to deal with them directly. We may expect further insights into the less tangible aspects of living to flow from a greatly expanded research devoted predominantly to them.

**Research has many values for man.** Lest one disesteem non-social research, it is only proper to note that the results of even purely physical science are not without esthetic and other high value returns. If in the winter we are warmed by modern heating systems, or in the summer we are cooled by mechanical means, are there not thereby possibilities for the greater enjoyment and broadening of life? Is it without rich cultural consequences that we can have ample light in the evening for reading and for various social occasions? Are motion pictures solely physical things? Are they less engaging because we ride to them on a street car, bus, or automobile? Are our sensitivities geared to the universe of physical things when we listen to music from the phonograph and radio, and witness current happenings over television? Is good literature less good when printed and distributed by modern mechanical means? Is oil painting less significant because chemistry has provided colors that will not quickly darken?

As a matter of fact, modern technology has multipled the opportunities for artistic expressions and has increased the wide dissemination of esthetic enjoyment to an extent not imaginable in earlier centuries. Before condemning science as materialistic and as directing our attention toward mean considerations, we should recognize first that not all science is given to material things, and second that from science which is devoted to physical phenomena man has reaped great benefits in the way of increased opportunities for rich living. In fact the time-saving economy of modern technological culture has added more to life in the way of number and variety of rich experiences than have the extra twenty years which have been added to our lives in recent times; both together have extended the scope and fullness of life beyond earlier belief.

It seems necessary to go one step further and point out that sciences which seem to deal with less-than-human matters are not so remote from the individual as they may seem, for even human life is to a very large extent physical. Our entire connection with the outer world is physical. The things we take into our bodies, our food and drink, are composed of the same particles of substance that the physicists and chemists study in their laboratories. The heat which surrounds us, the wind that blows upon us, the light by which we see, the sounds to which we listen, the odors that come to us, the pressures and change of motion which we may feel—all are purely physical phenomena to which our sense organs respond.

Our outgoing responses are of the same character; when we talk, signal, or write, we produce physical phenomena. We have no way of receiving any sensation from the outside world or of communicating any thought or feeling to the outside world save through physical mediums. Add to these considerations the fact that the processes going on within the body are physiological and depend in turn on chemical or physical sequences of reaction, and even those persons who wish to confine their attention to social or psychological phenomena must see our very high dependence on physical substances and activities.

It is not, therefore, a sound basis for objection to say that physical science is subhuman, and without immediate and fundamental relation to the living of every person. We may not, as individuals, wish to give major attention to physical problems, but in all sincerity we must be thankful that there are those specialists who are doing so, for physical problems are intricately interwoven with all of our living. When we do not recognize this, it is because the physical factors are being well adjusted to our needs; but scientists cannot wait till emergency situations occur before giving attention to the understanding and powers of control which will then be called for. Hence scientists, physical as well as physiological and psychological and sociological, study to be ready to serve all who live, so that all may live better.

In considering further the worth of science—science in all fields—we must recognize that there are many outcomes other than the direct increase in useful knowledge. To those who feel that somehow the prosecution of problems of a purely physical nature must sully the soul of man, let it be said that most scientists find esthetic beauty in the phenomena of nature— in the regularities of the far-flung universe that strains credulity as well as sight; the intricate detail of minute systems which tug at the imagination to picture still smaller systems within them. Everywhere there is basic order —pattern, rhythm, balance. Everywhere cause-effect sequences form inter-linking chains. Man's careful observations afford material for wonder, awe, and reverence, as well as for scientific principles and philosophy. Many passages expressing these feelings of admiration and marvel are to be found in the writings of scientists. Perhaps nowhere are the thoughts more tersely and comprehensively given than in the verse of the mathematician Bernoulli, with the expressive translation by Helen Walker: [10]

> Even as the finite encloses an infinite series
>      And in the unlimited limits appear,
> So the soul of immensity dwells in minutia
>      And in narrowest limits no limits inhere.
> What joy to discern the minute in infinity!
>      The vast to perceive in the small, what divinity!

But we do not exhaust the values of research when we cite the enrichment of culture that follows the application of its findings and when we note the

[10] *Mathematics Teacher* 36:87; February 1943.

intellectual beauties of science as viewed by the mind of man; research also has deep-seated psychological aspects. As presented earlier in various settings, the basic claim of research to acceptance is that it is a natural, stimulating, and ennobling aspiration of the human spirit; and without it man feels baffled, frustrated, and weighted with defeat. To stop with what we now have would be to deprive all oncoming humanity of a significant share of living and of an essential element of hope. For research is the open door to a better future; it is the source of faith that man can go forward; it is the challenge that removes the threat of stagnation and decay from all society. So long as there is a strong research program, there can be no decline of Western civilization, for research continuously provides those challenges (and sometimes crises) which drive man forward.

**A science philosophy.** It is the large purpose of education to broaden one's consciousness, to expand one's understanding beyond the horizons of individual experience, and so to add perspective to one's view of the problems of life. In order more perfectly to provide structure and outlook for the thinking of ourselves and of others, we need that more perfect understanding which can come only through continued research. Much of what we now know was obtained in that manner. Because of research in varied fields, we can add many dimensions to thought, so that it will reach backward to encompass the long sweep of past ages, look outward to embrace the diverse cultures of the world, turn inward to focus on invisibly small units of organization, or probe the heavens to study the distant mysteries of space. Thus research enables man to relate himself with the entire universe; it is the means through which man is seen as a living part of the unfolding story of the ages, a superbly balanced organism of magnificent structure, a privileged observer-participant in the drama of civilization.

Though science may at times be narrow, it is also broad—as broad as truth itself. If one be inclined to think of science as a mechanizing influence in his view of the world and of life, perhaps he overlooks the dignifying concept afforded by viewing man as a part of nature—a marvelously complex, delicately sensitive, creatively intelligent, and versatilely able organism, but nevertheless a part of the great plan of the universe which we comprehend as nature. In this view, the existence of an individual takes on extensity in all directions and becomes more than a pinpoint in space and time. He becomes part of the evolving eternity and has connection with everything that has gone before and everything that is to follow. One's life is integrated with the whole story of continuing creation, a story which changes endlessly but never ends. Man may perceive the orderly beauties of the vast interrelated process of existence and say to himself, "I am part of this system for as long as it shall exist. With some mystery behind and some before, all creation moves onward together. We evolve, we develop, we contribute; and recorded in the eternal narrative our individual chapter shall stand."

**Responsibility rests on social science.** The good life makes demands on all fields of science. The problems of producing a good life are in part physical, in part biological, and in part psychological or sociological. Man finds his needs distributed through all areas of knowledge and he likewise finds his satisfactions arising from the meeting of his needs in all areas. Continued study and research progress must, therefore, be maintained over a broad range of interest.

The component of knowledge and understanding to be contributed by social science is a double one. In the physical and biological fields the practical responsibility is to analyze, describe, explain, and discover means of control or work out means of producing a desired effect. In the social fields there are these same problems—identification of factors, study of causation, prediction, the design of means of control, and other aspects of effectiveness and efficiency. But there is also a second line of responsibility in the social sciences, and that is to undertake research which will help man delineate his own purposes.

The responsibility which social science shares with all other sciences (at least in their applied forms) is that of aiding man in obtaining what he has decided he wants. That is, when certain objectives have been chosen, how can they be realized? What means should be employed? What steps taken? In this area of study the problems to be solved relate to effectiveness, feasibility, adequacy, economy, acceptability, and the like. Research along these lines is well known. In education, there is the constant search for more effective methods of instruction, more satisfactory texts and other learning materials, more compatible physical facilities, more efficient administrative organization, and so on. Improvement is sought all along the line in carrying out our society's manifest desire for education.

The second area of responsibility, in which social science characteristically departs from those sciences which do not study human wants, is that of aiding man to determine what he does want. This is the area of decision-making, of analyzing general goals in order to ascertain more specific implications, of appraising likely gains and losses in some venture, of assessing relative interest as it exists in oneself or in a group or a variety of groups, of harmonizing conflicting forces, of choosing from among many attractions, of developing a reasonably consistent yet stimulatingly varied set of objectives, of attaining some dignity while remaining free to adapt. It is a difficult area; it requires the help of all persons studying human nature and human values, whether they be engaged in research in the narrower sense or in more philosophic aspects. Avowedly it is not an area in which research can offer final pronouncements; but such a statement is without significance to those who know research, for research is never final. It is as ongoing as the processes of life itself. In the area of decision, social research can, however, offer aids to man's thinking as it does in all its areas of service.

This second aspect of social research is represented in education primarily through work on the curriculum. The process of selecting those facets of American and world culture which are of most significance in producing future American adults who will have as many as possible of the qualities our society would like for them to have is fundamentally a process of value distillation. As with any other practical activity, it cannot be claimed that the process is wholly scientific, but it can be shown that many aspects of it are. Research in education, in psychology, and in sociology has provided many scientific facts and many scientific principles by which the process of curriculum building is constantly guided.

Perhaps it should be remarked at this point that, if one finds difficulty in establishing a firm dividing line between the first and the second areas of service for social research, as just outlined, the truth is that there is no fixed line. The two areas are but one, seen in different perspectives. Means soon become ends in themselves, and ends are but means to further ends. It is a matter of point of reference, or perhaps of degree of generality. It is convenient, however, for certain purposes, to speak of two areas.

One of the special problems in the field of social decision is that of determining the ends for which all forms of science, physical and social, shall be employed. This is a matter of growing importance. It is one of the problems with which social research is expected to deal. How can research help in deciding about research? One line of study would somewhat naturally be devoted to assessing, historically and currently, the impact of research findings on society. Such facts are an aid to judgment. But another line of research would be devoted to reviewing the processes by which social decisions are made, and to studying new machinery and new criteria by which better decisions might be reached. Such concerns are among the essential problems and goals of social science. They are at present being dealt with, for example, by studies in education (group processes as media of learning), psychology (intragroup and intergroup tensions and interactions), and sociology (the structure and processes of all social groups). As always, the greatest contributions of research come, not through direct answers to practical questions, but from more basic studies of underlying factors which afford an entirely new view of the original question or produce an undreamed of approach to the solution of the problem.

When considering the role of research in practical affairs it is important to distinguish between what is research and what is normal procedure. That is, there is a difference between doing research and utilizing research. Making studies of social problems is one thing; but the views of scientists, whether physical or social, concerning large courses of action are another. Thus, administrators, boards, councils, legislatures, and other deliberative groups may call upon scientists for advice; this practice is becoming increasingly common. The scientist offers his technical knowledge; in addition, he may or may not care to offer social advice. As an individual he is entitled to his social opinions; but as a scientist he may feel that his competence lies more in the area of cause and effect than in arbitrating between the demands of various social groups who want their particular interests protected. This is true even in the case of social scientists. Thus, an economist might advise that, if certain changes in governmental or industrial policy were made, certain results would follow. Whether such results are desirable, at a particular time and under given circumstances, is a judgment he might wish to leave for the administrator or legislative group to make. Similarly, the psychologist, sociologist, or educationist may say he is confident that certain results can be achieved by certain means. He may himself feel that such changes are desirable or undesirable and may urge accordingly. But advice is not research. The advice of scientists in all fields may be highly valuable to those groups who have been specifically charged by our society with responsibility for the making of social decisions. with ascertaining and weighing the various gains and losses which would accrue to different groups in our society as a result of the projected change. But disseminating and applying expert knowledge are different things from building up that knowledge. Both processes are important, but conceptually they are to be distinguished. When we are thinking of one we are not necessarily thinking of the other.

**Social science can aid man in determining his course.** Now that man has achieved unprecedented power over life and death, and over many of the conditions of living, he faces the need for new levels of guidance in his use of these powers. With new power comes new responsibility. Knowing what to do is man's greatest need. In this area of great need research is still man's ally.[11]

There are some who differ with this view. Taking their cue from certain criteria which physical scientists have established concerning their own work, they assert that research can have nothing to do with goals. Differences in the content and social setting of various sciences, however, should make patent certain distinctions. The problem of clarifying and evaluating social

[11] Douglas E. Scates, "On Our Research the Answers Hinge." *Phi Delta Kappan* 30:120-23; December 1948.

goals is not indigenous in the domain of non-social sciences. Workers in those fields appropriately have formulated rules which minimize extraneous considerations, but workers in social fields must be cautious of utterly mechanical borrowing. Physical conceptions are not adequate, without proper modification, for human phenomena. The subject matter of social research is immersed in human values, and social scientists cannot with integrity disregard what is so prominent an element in their field of study.

Perhaps objections to the consideration of goals as being part of the undertaking of social science stem from a misconstruction of the part that research would play in such an attempt. It seems necessary to make two points. The first is that science itself does not and never will control man. Man controls himself, within the limits of the conditions which surround him. When science is spoken of as becoming man's master, it is a mere figure of speech; for it is man who decides what he will do with science, the ends for which he will use it—which is the point that brings us back to the crux of our problem. When we once recognize clearly this relationship of man to science, there will be no talk of social science ruling man, or dictating to him, or dominating his will. Science is simply a clear vision existing in the mind of man, and the clear vision of desirable ends which social science may afford is but another tool to enable man to exercise his own will more perfectly. Research pictures, throws into relief, brings into sharp focus, and in other ways helps man see clearly, and then leaves man to follow his own bidding.

Research findings can never replace judgment. They only narrow the range in which judgment must operate. For example, if we have many facts, we do not have to employ judgment in the estimating of these facts, for they are supplied to us and, if they are accurate, they are better than our estimates of them would be and hence they tend to make our judgments better. But they do not go all the way in determining the judgment itself; that is a function which only man can discharge. The argument does not, therefore, hinge on research "dictating" to man. Man dictates to himself. In so doing, it should not be surprising that he may at times rely on knowledge that he has proved.[12]

Our problems are so often semantic. Much of the confusion regarding the possibility of research dealing with values lies in the margin of misconception surrounding the words we use in thinking and talking. Language produces so many artificialities! We create so many things merely by naming them, when in fact they have no separate existence. When once we see that man's judgments depend in part on his knowledge, concepts, and under-

12 G. T. Buswell, "Science and Social Philosophy: The Scientific Point of View in Education." *School and Society* 69:1-4; January 1, 1949.

standing, then we cease wondering whether research can improve his judgments, for it is the essential nature of research to build up understanding. When, further, we recognize that science is something within man himself, a form of understanding, then we cease to raise the question as to whether man or science will make the final decision, for science and judgment both occur in the same mind.

Society, of course, has its forms of organization, its social machinery, and it is usual that the value judgments of one or a few persons, perhaps based on research findings, be accepted by others in the same political unit. Any legislation which requires this is not "science" enforcing itself on man, but it is rather the normal operation of our social processes, by which the decisions of certain persons are promulgated and applied to others in order that we may have an orderly, somewhat homogeneous, society. If, in a democracy, we do not believe that such promulgations are in accord with the greatest benefit to the group, we can change the persons who have administratively (or legislatively) decided what should be applied to the group. The issue here is not in the realm of science but in the area of politics.

The second misconception concerning the utilization of social research in the determination of goals lies in our lack of seeing clearly that goals form a hierarchy. There is not one goal but countless goals. Many of these are coördinate, but all of them enter into sequential patterns in which they become instrumental to some further, larger, or more fundamental goal which can be named but not fully defined. Consider the myriad specific objectives to be accomplished, if we and other peoples are to enjoy what we think of as a good life!

We do not need to delegate to social science the choice of the largest possible or most ultimate goal; to do so would indeed leave man little or no freedom of choice. But granted that our people might agree that we wished to pursue such a goal as "the good life," nebulous as that goal may be, research would aid greatly in helping to define that goal, structure it with countless details, enlarge and enrich it, thus giving us a much improved concept of our goal over and above what common thought would do. Then research could be called upon to tell us the steps which would effectively help us to move toward this goal. But meanwhile, utilizing all the insights and guides which philosophy can afford, researchers would be busy studying a more perfect form of the goal.

For the sake of a schematic illustration, we might say that, if goal $E$ is agreed upon by our society as being desirable, research might find that steps $A$, $B$, $C$, and $D$ are necessary in order to achieve $E$; these intermediate steps would then become intermediate goals—isolated, identified, and made clear through research. Research would, as indicated above, also aid in bringing about a much improved $E$ over what we started after. Research, however, does not stop there; it is ever in the lead. As society moves toward the realization of $E$, not only better forms of $E$, but even new kinds of goals, such as $F$ and $G$, will begin to emerge and research will be at work "filling them in." Perhaps even before society attains goal $C$ workers will be struggling with the definition of goals $F$ and $G$. Thus "the good life" beckons and guides, but remains always a little out of reach. We want ideals to be that way, and research aids in keeping them so. Research projects man's dreams ever farther ahead even while it brings their realization ever nearer. Thus man moves progressively toward the goal of the good life.

It should not be overlooked that a certain degree of human guidance is present in all science to the extent that the clear description of conditions and sequences brings to man's attention significant aspects and promising possibilities which he otherwise would not know. Such facts may in many ways enable man to make better decisions. In the infrahuman sciences, however, the concern with relative advantages of doing this or that is limited mainly to the choice between physical processes. Social issues are naturally incidental or peripheral to the main pursuit. The common social values of power to do and economy in doing are taken for granted and become the guiding framework within which much physical research (particularly of the applied sort) is done. Even basic research aims at power— the great resolving power of knowing and understanding. The analysis, description, comparison, essential mechanisms, antecedents, and likely consequences of fundamental human values are not the essential subject matter of the non-human sciences; they are, however, of major moment in the human sciences. They are by no means the whole of social science, but they are an integral portion of its domain. The focus of human research is on human living. Its concern is with the problems of life.

Accordingly, the *specific* attitude of the physical scientist, in not attempting to deal with human motives, drives, or purposes, cannot be invoked as an argument against doing so in the social field, because it does not fit the social field. The *larger* and more significant fact is that the physical scientists proceeded to develop a set of guiding principles which made their science good with respect to the phenomena with which it deals. Social scientists may invoke this larger pattern of wisdom and seek to be as competent in dealing with the fundamental elements in their field as physical scientists have become in theirs. Each science must adopt criteria that permit it to attack the problems with which it must deal. The adequate study of values (human valences, perhaps) constitutes the main challenge to the creative ingenuity of social scientists in developing new scientific criteria and new scientific procedures which are valid for their task. Social science cannot be a narrow copy of physical science without deserting its trust. In a unique field there must be a unique science.

**Social science and religion are complementary.** There is need for both. Man has found many of his criteria for living in his religion. Religion has a large role to play in society, and in any concept of the good life it would undoubtedly be depended on as an important institution both as a part of that life and as a means of bringing that life more nearly into being. However, if any great religion is to continue to be virile, the interpretations connected with that religion probably will be re-examined as society advances. A religion which seeks to be of help in a society having the scientific background of our time will afford interpretations that take into consideration the scientific concepts now so much a part of our lives. Research and religion both help society formulate its purposes by utilizing ideas that at any given time are held to be sound, and employing them to provide clearer interpretations. Thus religion comes into play alongside research in helping to make meaningful in the current mode of living the concepts of what is good and desirable.

In the general effort to create a better life for man on this earth there are a number of points at which social research may be called on to supplement religious thought. In the main these opportunities for research service to religion are much the same as those for the general service of research to society. Inasmuch as research activity is constantly contributing new ideas to the concepts with which society is at any time currently concerned, it necessarily contributes new elements to the detail of religious thinking. But for practical purposes research must go much further. Any application of the great fundamental ideals of a religion calls for much detailed knowledge of practical reality and society which religion does not of itself afford. The need for facts and research insights becomes ever greater as the units of society become ever larger and as the different segments of the world's population become more interdependent. We may, for example, accept the golden rule, but be unable to decide fully what it means in international relations where a particular policy might injure as many persons in certain nations as it would help in others. We need to know and consider many facts, and to have great understanding which only political, economic, psychological, sociological, and psychiatric research can provide, in order for us to know the extent to which any decision will aid in realizing an ideal rather than create unintended consequences so serious as to constitute a major wrong. Our acceptance of a great goal does not mean that we know automatically how to act in the pursuit of that goal, so as to make an improvement in the total welfare of the world. The well-meaning but ill-informed can wreak great havoc.

A second supplementary need arises in connection with the efficacy of specific religious practices, particularly in religious education. Do they achieve the results desired? As historical, comparative, and other forms of research open up new avenues of understanding concerning human beings, many unsuspected relationships may be found to hold. A tremendous amount of potential research lies in this area.

A third point of need for supplementation by research arises from the fact that there are in the world many different cultures and, for international purposes and world understanding, it is necessary to have some form of common denominator. Another nation (for example, another Christian nation in our own times) whose leaders do not accept the high principles which we claim may not be restrained by our religious and ethical standards. We need to know how to live with that other nation, how to live with all other nations, in such fashion that we will all move constantly toward that day when serious wars cannot be waged, and when no other forms of similar or equal suffering must be endured.

**International relations present endless problems for research.** For those who accept the avoidance of major wars as a great goal, the question becomes, What are the many intermediate goals that bring the great goal closer to realization? What are the forces which make for war? What are the satisfactions which people demand even at the price of war? What are the necessary and sufficient conditions for averting conflict? What are adequate means for effecting adjustments between peoples so that extreme tensions do not arise? So that the weaker do not always suffer? Only research —protracted, serious inquiry, data-gathering, experimentation, practical experience, and careful integration of the findings and insights from many fields of study—will bring us closer to this ultimate objective. Certainly education, psychology, sociology, and other social sciences have large roles in this great world arena. Each needs continued cultivation through research, in order that it may make its proper contribution.

It stands as a major blight on the total record of human accomplishment that we have not yet learned to avoid internecine warfare, and that we have to so large an extent failed to work out effective and satisfactory methods for adjusting human tensions. The only explanation, in a world in which research has everywhere accomplished marvels almost beyond imagination, is that research has virtually not entered this field. Our people have thought that research was not necessary. It is the common attitude that man and his wants and his problems can be resolved through self-interest and common sense, as they were when people were not so crowded, when social force had but small mass, and when activities in other areas of living were not executed with the speed and precision now possible. In a new world created by the findings of research, man himself must have new mental equipment in order to deal with the new world, and the means of obtaining this mental equipment are the same as those by which the modern form of living was developed, namely, research.

There is at this time the greatest urgency in all fields of human research. Man has become a multiple threat to himself. He needs judgment in proportion to his power. He has developed a modern world which, on the physical side, can function as a single society, but on the social side has no adequate scientific rationale by which human motives can be brought sufficiently into harmony, so as to make this single society a stable functional reality. With all the possibilities of a good life within reach, we yet lack that knowledge and understanding which will enable us to secure them. We look to human research for solutions of these problems.

As a matter of practical fact, during World War II and even earlier the United States began a reversal of its long-standing isolationist attitude and assumed a direct interest in political affairs in Europe and Asia. The signing of the Atlantic Pact in 1949 committed us legally to a many-sided coöperation with European nations and substituted an aggressive defense for the purely negative Monroe Doctrine more than a century and a quarter earlier in origin. Such a great change in attitude from that expressed by President Washington in his Farewell Address, and which prevailed as long as it could be maintained, has been brought about by research and the applications of research which have in effect shrunk the world to small size. Our interests are now necessarily widespread.

With those widespread interests, however, come the responsibilities for strength of many kinds. Naturally, we must be strong militarily; but this strength will lie not so much in numbers of men as in research leadership. Again, the strength of a nation lies in the physical and mental health of its people—in their ready energy, in their regular satisfactions and their anticipated satisfactions, and in their love for the underlying way of life that affords these satisfactions. Strength also comes from mental power and resourcefulness, from the education that has been widely diffused and intensively cultivated. And as a result of these and other favorable conditions, strength comes from the institutions, the habits, and the legal, political, economic, and other cultural systems which pervade the lives of the people. To afford world leadership we must be strong in many ways; in fact, in all the ways that strength may be called for by the practical turn of circumstances.

**Concluding statement.** The fundamental thesis of this chapter is that such strength as will be demanded for survival and for the good life can come only through research; not primarily research in the physical sciences

—granted that such research must be continued on a large scale and probably made more fundamental—but research on all of the many facets of living. The great complexity of our highly developed culture sets the range of the problems to be investigated. In the social realm we have made a beginning; whereas much has been done, there are aspects which lie virtually untouched, and nowhere in the social field do we have the basic underlying concepts that will do for social science what mass, distance, and time do for physical science. We yet lack a fundamental integrating thesis such as Newton's concepts of gravitation which synthesized observations on objects of a great range of magnitude. We have in the social sciences well explored beginnings; there are well-developed tools with which to work; but there is much to be done.

There is one further thought. Our educational system is busy studying its curriculum and improving its methods in an effort to keep the level of understanding of our people adequate to the rapidly changing effects of physical and biological science. But even so, the differential between the rate of physical-science progress and the rate of social-science progress, the scientific lag, may in itself be a weakening factor in our society. After prolonged study of the rate of cultural change along many lines, Hart comments:

> The *supremely* challenging fact is that . . . the apparently sudden increase in the potential power of aggressors is only a spectacularly dramatic expansion of technological developments . . . which have been slowly accelerating for hundreds of thousands of years, and which now have a speed of increase which threatens to disorganize civilization. . . . Baffling as are the problems of these opening years in the Atomic Age, the fact of technological acceleration means that the problems of the future will keep on compounding and expanding until they wreck our world, or until organized intelligence applies science effectively to mastering the social problems which technological acceleration creates. . . .
> Whenever science is systematically applied to promoting a given area of human purpose, man's achievements in that area leap forward spectacularly [p. 291].[13]

To meet this need for greatly increased social research, the main steps must be taken by various leaders of our society. Perhaps we naturally think first of those who exercise some control or influence over sources of financial support and of research. Certainly financial support is a major factor in any large program of research, but it is not as fundamental as the matter of gaining psychological support for the work. There must be a clear and strong recognition of the need and urgency of all social research. Many physical scientists in our country have already expressed themselves unequiv-

---

[13] Quoted from Hornell Hart, "Technological Acceleration and the Atomic Bomb." *American Sociological Review* 11:277-93; June 1946.

Also see William A. Van Til and Others, "Research on Human Relations and Programs of Action." *Review of Educational Research* 23:285-385; October 1953.

ocally on this point; for the protection of themselves and their families they want more social science. They speak the thoughts of many citizens.[14] It must be recognized, on the other hand, that many of the individual studies needed to build up psychological, educational, sociological, and other human research seem utterly trivial, senseless, and annoying to the common person when he hears of them. He may accordingly refuse to participate; he may try to get the study stopped; he may publish ridiculing notes in the newspapers or in magazines; and, if the research is supported by public funds, he may write his Congressman that public money is being wasted. These forms of resistance occur every day. Physical and biological scientists have been through all these and, in the early days, much more. Medical research still meets the antivivisectionists. The battle for research, even though it is to help our society, must be fought on the level of attitudes as well as on the financial and technical level. A major goal, therefore, of all those interested in the production of more social science must be the cultivation throughout our society of that degree of interest in, regard for, and expectancy of social research which is now generally the attitude toward physical and medical research. When this psychological stage is set, the rest will follow.

There are, however, many things which the individual can do as a student, as a professional worker, or as a citizen to aid in the furtherance of educational and other forms of social research. One may become interested in the problems and procedures of research in one of these fields and enter upon it vocationally. That is a high order of help; the field with all its opportunities and all its promise cannot advance without interested workers. But the majority of persons will not be interested to this extent; they wish merely to know about research as a part of their liberal education, or they may wish to be able to write a thesis, or perhaps to understand what they read in research magazines. All such interests are legitimate and helpful. As indicated in the preceding paragraph, it is of the utmost importance that a large number of persons in this country have some appreciation of the role of all research in our lives and especially of the unusual need for research in the social fields. Those who expect to teach will find continuous demands on them to know something of the research which is being done in their field of interest, to pass judgment on it, and perhaps to apply some of it. Administrators, legislators, and other citizens are called upon in similar fashion to express attitudes toward various aspects of social research

[14] The following statement epitomizes the view expressed by many writers: "It is trite, but frighteningly true, to say that the survival of this present civilization depends, not on the further development of natural science, but on the solution of certain serious intellectual problems in the social sciences." Kenneth E. Boulding, "Is Economics Necessary?" *Scientific Monthly* 68:235-40; April 1949.

which come to their attention, even if only in social conversation. Accordingly critical judgment, cultivated through careful study of the purposes, methods, and instruments of research, will have many opportunities to enter into the stream of thought that makes the mental life of a country hospitable, negligent, or intolerant toward research in the human field. Thus each person's opinion on research affects the future course of a people and their position in the world of nations.

## SELECTED REFERENCES

BARBER, Bernard. *Science and the Social Order.* Glencoe, Ill.: Free Press, 1952. xxiii + 288 p.

BERNAL, J. D. *The Social Function of Science.* New York: Macmillan Co., 1939. xviii + 482 p.

BERNARD, L. L., and BERNARD, Jessie. *Origins of American Sociology:* The Social Science Movement in the United States. New York: Thomas Y. Crowell Co., 1943. xiv + 866 p.

BOGARDUS, Emory S. *The Development of Social Thought.* Second Edition. New York: Longmans, Green and Co., 1947. x + 574 p.

BORING, E. G. *A History of Experimental Psychology.* Second Edition. New York: Appleton-Century-Crofts, 1950. xxi + 777 p.

BRONOWSKI, Jacob. *The Common Sense of Science.* Cambridge: Harvard University Press, 1953. 154 p.

BROWN, G. Burniston. *Science:* Its Method and Its Philosophy. New York: W. W. Norton and Co., 1951. 189 p.

BRUBACHER, John S. *A History of the Problems of Education.* New York: McGraw-Hill Book Co., 1947. 688 p.

BURCHARD, John E., Editor. *Mid-Century:* The Social Implications of Scientific Progress. Cambridge: Massachusetts Institute of Technology Press, 1950. xx + 549 p.

BUSH, Vannevar. *Endless Horizons.* Washington: American Council on Public Affairs, 1946. 182 p.

BUSH, Vannevar. *Science—The Endless Frontier.* Washington: Government Printing Office, 1945. 184 p.

CONANT, James B. *Science and Common Sense.* New Haven: Yale University Press, 1951. xii + 371 p.

CONANT, James B. *On Understanding Science:* An Historical Approach. New Haven: Yale University Press, 1947. xv + 145 p.

CROWTHER, J. G. *The Social Relations of Science.* New York: Macmillan Co., 1941. xxxiv + 665 p.

DENNIS, Wayne, and Others. *Current Trends in Psychological Theory.* Pittsburgh: University of Pittsburgh Press, 1952. 213 p.

DEWEY, John. *Problems of Men.* New York: Philosophical Library, 1946. 424 p.

DINGLE, Herbert, Editor. *A Century of Science:* 1851-1951. New York: Roy Publishing Co., 1951. ix + 338 p.

DUNSHEATH, Percy, Editor. *A Century of Technology:* 1851-1951. New York: Roy Publishing Co., 1951. ix + 346 p.

DURANT, Will. *The Story of Philosophy.* Revised Edition. New York: Simon and Schuster, 1933. 592 p.

DU VIGNEAUD, Vincent. *A Trail of Research.* Ithaca, N. Y.: Cornell University Press, 1952. xiii + 191 p.

FEIGL, Herbert, and BRODBECK, May, Editors. *Readings in the Philosophy of Science.* New York: Appleton-Century-Crofts, 1953. ix + 811 p.

FESTINGER, Leon, and KATZ, Daniel, Editors. *Research Methods in the Behavioral Sciences.* New York: Dryden Press, 1953. xi + 660 p.

FLUGEL, J. C. *A Hundred Years of Psychology.* Revised Edition. New York: Macmillan Co., 1951. 424 p.

GOOD, Carter V., BARR, A. S., and SCATES, Douglas E. *The Methodology of Educational Research.* New York: Appleton-Century-Crofts, 1936. Chapters 1, 15.

HOLLIS, E. V. *Toward Improving Ph.D. Programs.* Washington: American Council on Education, 1945. xii + 204 p.

IRVING, John A. *Science and Values:* Exploration in Philosophy and the Social Sciences. Toronto: Ryerson Press, 1952. xi + 148 p.

KANTOR, J. R. *The Logic of Modern Science.* Bloomington, Indiana: Principia Press, 1953. xvi + 359 p.

LANGFELD, Herbert S., and Others, Editors. *A History of Psychology in Autobiography,* Vol. 4. Worcester: Clark University Press, 1952. xii + 356 p.

LARRABEE, Harold A. *Reliable Knowledge.* Boston: Houghton Mifflin Co., 1945. vii + 685 p.

LEPLEY, Ray, Editor. *Value:* A Coöperative Inquiry. New York: Columbia University Press, 1949. 487 p.

LINTON, Ralph, Editor. *The Science of Man in the World Crisis.* New York: Columbia University Press, 1945. 532 p.

LUNDBERG, George A. *Can Science Save Us?* New York: Longmans, Green and Co., 1947. 122 p.

LYND, R. S. *Knowledge for What?* The Place of Social Science in American Culture. Princeton: Princeton University Press, 1939. 268 p.

MURPHY, Gardner. *An Historical Introduction to Modern Psychology.* Revised Edition. New York: Harcourt, Brace and Co., 1949. xiv + 466 p.

ODUM, H. W. *American Sociology:* The Story of Sociology in the United States through 1950. New York: Longmans, Green and Co., 1951. vi + 501 p.

PETERS, R. S. *Brett's History of Psychology.* Edited and Abridged. New York: Macmillan Co., 1953. 742 p.

PHI DELTA KAPPA COMMISSION ON RESEARCH. "Educational Research: A New View." *Phi Delta Kappan* 35:1-68; October 1953.

PLEDGE, Humphry T. *Science Since 1500.* New York: Philosophical Library, 1939. 357 p.

ROBACK, A. A. *History of American Psychology.* New York: Library Publishers, 1952. xiv + 426 p.

ROE, Anne. *The Making of a Scientist.* New York: Dodd, Mead and Co., 1953. ix + 244 p.

RUSSELL, Bertrand. *The Impact of Science on Society.* New York: Columbia University Press, 1951. 64 p.

SARTON, George. *A Guide to the History of Science.* Waltham, Mass.: Chronica Botanica Co., 1952. xvii + 316 p.

SARTON, George. *A History of Science:* Ancient Science through the Golden Age of Greece. Cambridge: Harvard University Press, 1952. xxvi + 646 p.

"The Scientist in American Society: Symposium." *Scientific Monthly* 78:129-41; March 1954.

SIBLEY, Elbridge. *Support for Independent Scholarship and Research.* New York: Social Science Research Council, 1951. xv + 116 p.

STORR, Richard J. *The Beginnings of Graduate Education in America.* Chicago: University of Chicago Press, 1953. x + 196 p.

TOULMIN, Stephen. *The Philosophy of Science:* An Introduction. New York: Longmans, Green and Co., 1953. xiii + 176 p.

TYLER, R. W., and Others. *Graduate Study in Education.* Fiftieth Yearbook, National Society for the Study of Education. Chicago: University of Chicago Press, 1951. xix + 369 p.

ULICH, Robert. *History of Educational Thought.* New York: American Book Co., 1945. xii + 412 p.

VAN TIL, William A., and Others. "Research on Human Relations and Programs of Action." *Review of Educational Research* 23:285-385; October 1953.

WILSON, Logan. *The Academic Man.* New York: Oxford University Press, 1942. viii + 248 p.

ZNANIECKI, Florian. *The Social Role of the Man of Knowledge.* New York: Columbia University Press, 1940. viii + 212 p.

# 2 Formulation and Development of the Problem; Research Programs and Needs

THIS CHAPTER DESCRIBES the common difficulties on the part of the beginning research worker (and of many experienced investigators) in recognizing problems, and outlines in some detail certain stimulating sources of problems. It evaluates and illustrates from the long history of science the major criteria for selection of the problem. The statement and definition of the problem are analyzed at length and illustrated by means of numerous examples. The functions, sources, and testing of hypotheses are described in relation to problem-solving. Brief comment is made on coördination of the numerous large projects and many thousands of individual studies into a more effective and better supported research program.

## RECOGNITION OF PROBLEMS

**Numerous problems in the social sciences.** It is not surprising that many graduate students and workers in the field, when searching for a thesis problem, conclude that most of the problems in education, psychology, sociology, and other social areas already have been investigated. To use education as an example, if a liberal interpretation of research is employed and unpublished studies are included, it is estimated that during the decade between 1940 and 1950 the grand total of studies (including earlier decades) in this field went well beyond 100,000.[1] The number of Doctors' dissertations in education per year just preceding World War II approached 400, with a frequency of 1077 reached in 1951-52. The number of Masters' and second professional degrees in education conferred in 1951-52 totaled 26,382 (many awarded without a thesis requirement). In 1951-52 the number of doctorates[2] granted in psychology was 636, and in sociology

[1] W. S. Monroe, Editor, *Encyclopedia of Educational Research*. Revised Edition. New York: Macmillan Co., 1950. p. ix.

[2] A. H. Trotier and Marian Harman, Editors, *Doctoral Dissertations Accepted by American Universities, 1951-1952*. New York: H. W. Wilson Co., 1952. p. xv. The number of doctorates in education cited in this source sometimes has been smaller than the total given in the annual compilation (discontinued during World War II) of theses in education issued by the United States Office of Education; for example, Ruth A. Gray, *Bibliography of Research Studies in Education, 1939-1940*. Office of Education Bulletin No. 5, 1941. Washington: Government Printing Office, 1941. xiv + 404 p.

R. C. Story, *Earned Degrees Conferred by Higher Educational Institutions, 1951-52*. Office of Education Circular 1952, No. 360. Washington: Government Printing Office, 1952.

(including anthropology) 212. The annual output of books in education, excluding courses of study and annual reports of state and of city school systems, just preceding World War II was 800, not to mention the thousands of studies and reports published in educational periodicals. (During the early 1950's these numbers undoubtedly have been exceeded.) Although the number of graduate theses, publications, and journals is smaller in psychology, in sociology, and in other social sciences than in education, graduate advisers in these areas also find perplexed students who wonder whether any part of their fields of concentration has been left untilled by earlier investigators.

This chapter will reassure beginning workers in the social-science fields that a host of problems remain for solution. The variables of time, place, community, administrative organization, learner, teacher, and curriculum in the social areas are such as to render most conclusions much more difficult to formulate than in the fields of physics, chemistry, mathematics, and astronomy. Most social problems are not settled for all time. Historical sources accumulate with each passing day or week, and earlier studies need bringing up to date or reinterpretation in the light of new evidence. The survey type of investigation, as a cross-section of current status, is soon out of date; in many school systems certain types of data are gathered annually. All too few experiments are repeated to verify the results of earlier research.

**Problem awareness.** The initial difficulty for many graduate students and beginners in research in selecting a thesis topic is inability to identify research problems that are clearly discernible to experienced investigators and thesis advisers. The ability and insight essential to recognition of problems suitable for research purposes differ from the background necessary for sensing of practical tasks or operations (sometimes routine) of the day or hour in school, home, and community. Many of these day-by-day difficulties or common problems are solved by practical persons in terms of judgment, without recourse to research approaches. Therefore, one of the challenges to the beginner in research is to reorient his thinking about these practical problems or issues, so as to secure the research perspective.

Too frequently "problem blindness" is accompanied by an expectation on the part of the student that he will be "assigned" a problem by some faculty member. The following quotation from Buckingham, with its good-natured sarcasm and clever wording, is not intended to give the student a "thesis complex" or to make him apologetic in seeking a conference with

xviii + 109 p. This source cites 1146 doctoral degrees in education for 1951-52, a larger number than represented in the annual list of dissertations. (The Wilson compilation does not include field studies or field projects.)

his graduate adviser. The professor has an obligation to help the student decide upon a problem, sometimes to aid in evaluating the merits of two or more possible thesis topics presented by the graduate candidate. Before seeking a thesis conference, it is desirable for the student to read the later chapters on research methods, in order to determine tentatively the approach most appropriate to his resources: research, professional, and practical. In other words, the sole purpose of this discussion and of Buckingham's sparkling anecdote is to be helpful and to caution the student to do a reasonable amount of preliminary thinking and reading concerning choice of a problem before seeking assistance from his graduate adviser. The student proceeds with the conference as follows: [3]

"I've got to write a Master's thesis," says he, "and I'd like to talk to you about a topic." The statement ends with a slight upward inflection as if, in spite of its grammatical form, a sort of question were implied. After an awkward pause Mr. Blank (the student) repeats that he would like to talk about a thesis topic. Whereupon the editor (and professor) suggests that he go ahead and do so.

It transpires, however, that the editor-professor has misconceived Mr. Blank's meaning. He has no topic to talk about. In fact, instead of coming with a topic, he has come to get one. He looks so expectant, too; purely, as one might say, in a receptive mood.

No, he has no problems to suggest. He gives one the impression of having just learned about this thesis business, and of being entirely open-minded on the subject. At least, one gathers that he has no bias toward any particular topic and certainly no preconceived notions.

A conversation ensues. The editor—playing for the nonce his professorial role —asks in what department Mr. Blank is majoring, what courses he has taken, what positions he has held, and for what type of educational service he is fitting himself. At one stage of the resulting exchange of ideas Mr. Blank brightens. With some modesty, yet with the undeniable air of a discoverer, he suggests that he might correlate intelligence and achievement in the high school. He could give some tests in the school with which he is connected; and his friend, the principal of the $X$ school, would probably let him give some tests there; and maybe he could get one or two more schools if he stopped to think about the matter. And, Oh yes! how many schools does the professor think would be needed to get results that you could depend on? On being told that intelligence and achievement—so far as either is now measurable—have already been correlated by hundreds of people, Mr. Blank helplessly withdraws within himself, a discouraged seeker after truth in a world where all the problems have been solved.

It would be both interesting and revealing to know how frequently inquiries of the following type (received by one of the authors) come to graduate professors and research specialists.

[3] Quoted from "The Editor Turns Professor." *Educational Research Bulletin* 6:252-53; September 14, 1927. Also see:

Vineta Colby, "The Nephew of William Hamilton Sutton (A Story)." *American Association of University Professors Bulletin* 37:372-87; Summer 1951. The life history of a doctoral dissertation, with a dash of humor and irony.

R. A. Davis, "Writing a Thesis in Education." *Peabody Journal of Education* 27:285-95; March 1950.

The president of the junior college where I teach suggested that I write to you concerning a personal problem. I have recently been appointed registrar of our junior college, and am working for the degree of Doctor of Education at a neighboring university in the field of junior college administration. I would be very grateful if you would suggest a practical problem that I could investigate which could be used as a subject for the thesis or document, as it is called, in partial fulfillment of the requirements for the above mentioned degree. I am anxious to do a worthwhile piece of work and, if possible, to associate it with my present position.

The reply given below might well have included the additional suggestion that the newly appointed registrar first analyze the needs of his office and institution, which the recipient of his letter had never seen, rather than to ask for an "assignment" at long range.

The best reply I can make to your letter is to suggest sources where problems in the junior-college field are analyzed. For many years the September number of the *Journal of Educational Research* (more recently the *Phi Delta Kappan*) included a research bibliography, the first topic of which deals with problems requiring further investigation. The January number of this journal (more recently the *Phi Delta Kappan*) listed the doctoral dissertations under way. Other references concerned with needed research in the junior-college field are enclosed for your consideration.

Even able scientists and inventors sometimes overlook problems and answers close at hand.[4] Moses G. Farmer was so upset that he could not sleep for a week, after reading the first description of Bell's telephone. He upbraided himself for failure to invent the telephone, saying the discovery had flaunted itself before him a dozen times within ten years, but he had been too blind to see it.

Chance is frequently considered as playing an important part in scientific discovery; however, as Pasteur has well said, "In the field of observation, chance favours only the prepared mind." The careful observer notices and interprets clues that have escaped the attention of less alert investigators. Several persons before Röntgen noticed the fogging of photographic plates that led Röntgen to the discovery of x-rays. Earlier investigators now recall having noticed the inhibition of certain colonies by molds before Fleming followed up this observation to discover penicillin. Fleming said that he was not actually doing research, but was just "playing"; this is another way of saying that the scientist frequently may be doing something interesting to satisfy his own intellectual curiosity. Such discoveries are not the result of mere chance, accident, or "play," but, rather, involve careful observation and broad background in noting and interpreting clues.

The foregoing illustrations suggest that many students, investigators, and

[4] T. A. Boyd, *Research*. New York: D. Appleton-Century Co., 1935. p. 274.
W. I. B. Beveridge, *The Art of Scientific Investigation*. New York: W. W. Norton and Co., 1950. p. 33-34, 148.

field workers may have a blind spot for difficulties in their own school systems, communities, and laboratories, or may even be so organized intellectually as not to see the world about them in the form of problems to be solved. This condition causes many such workers to look for thesis problems or field projects outside their communities, thus overlooking the challenge of local issues. There need be no prejudice against problems distant in time or space, even though it seems especially desirable for investigators in the social-science fields to devote a reasonable share of time and energy to the identification and solution of problems in their own communities. (Examples of local studies are cited later in this chapter.) In all fairness to graduate students, as suggested above, they are not alone in overlooking some of the important conditions, problems, and solutions close at hand. This quite human tendency to leave a prophet without honor in his own country and to let distance lend enchantment has been recognized and described frequently by poet and story-teller. In the following illustrations the quest went far afield, but the answer was found near home.[5]

In Hawthorne's story of "The Great Stone Face" the people, with the exception of Ernest, were all too ready to see in the returned wanderers— Gathergold, Old Blood-and-Thunder, Old Stony Phiz, and the poet—the likeness of the Great Stone Face. However, the truth was as the poet shouted, when Ernest spoke to the people from a natural pulpit at sunset, "Behold! Behold! Ernest is himself the likeness of the Great Stone Face," a resemblance that Ernest least of all granted or even suspected.

It was in Hawthorne's *The Great Carbuncle* that Matthew and Hannah, newly wed, sought the dazzling jewel in the company of the Seeker, the Cynic, Master Ichabod Pigsnort, Doctor Cacaphodel, the poet, and Lord de Vere, some of whom had even journeyed across the sea for the quest. After seeing the great red gem shining in the brow of the cliff above the enchanted lake, Matthew decided that, instead of its awful blaze, "The blessed sunshine and the quiet moonlight shall come through our window. We will kindle the cheerful glow of our hearth, at eventide, and be happy in its light."

Another striking illustration is Lowell's "The Vision of Sir Launfal." The young knight who scornfully tossed the leper a piece of gold as he left the castle gate to seek the Holy Grail, returning old and broken after a fruitless search, found in this same beggar and the wooden bowl the object of his quest.

> In many climes, without avail,
> Thou hast spent thy life for the Holy Grail;
> Behold, it is here,—this cup which thou
> Didst fill at the streamlet for me but now.

[5] Carter V. Good, "You'll Find Your Problems in Your Own Back Yard." *Journal of Educational Research* 32:42-43; September 1938.

## SOURCES OF PROBLEMS[6]

Among the fruitful sources of problems are the various phases of the graduate instructional program. Another approach is through the analysis of an area of knowledge or of existing needs. Additional sources are the extension of completed investigations or the "budding out" of studies in progress. The more detailed list of sources discussed in succeeding pages is as follows:

1. Specialization
2. Instructional program pursued
3. Program of reading
4. Analysis of an area of knowledge
5. Consideration of existing practices and needs
6. Repetition or extension of investigations
7. "Offshoots" of studies under way.

**Specialization.** The scholarship that should result from intensive specialization in one or more subdivisions of the chosen field of training will reveal both the accomplishments of completed research and the problems yet unsolved. In many instances this area of specialization quite appropriately coincides with the worker's vocational choice. The attendant activities may involve the graduate instructional program, reading, writing, teaching assignment, administrative duties, professional organizations, or independent investigation. Examples of types of specialization helpful as a background in the identification and solution of problems follow.

The German psychologist Ebbinghaus, after receiving his Doctor's degree at Bonn in 1873, was able to devote the next seven years to an independent life of study, with part of the time spent in France and England.[7] Many nationally known research workers of today wrote their Doctors' dissertations in areas of specialization still represented in their present activities. A few of these doctoral titles may be cited: a deceased investigator in factor analysis, "The Indexing of a Mental Characteristic"; an expert in eye-movement photography, "An Experimental Study of the Eye-Voice Span in Reading"; a widely known investigator of reading problems, "Studies of Elementary-School Reading through Standardized Tests"; and a now deceased research adviser and consulting expert to a large manufacturer of school seating equipment, "A Study of School Postures and Desk Dimensions." Certain students with at least a graduate year of specialization in the

[6] For supplementary analyses see:
T. H. Briggs, "An Uncultivated Field." *Teachers College Record* 38:637-47; May 1937.
Carter V. Good, "Sources of Problems for Research." *Elementary School Journal* 42:745-54; June 1942.
Carter V. Good, A. S. Barr, and Douglas E. Scates, *The Methodology of Educational Research.* New York: Appleton-Century-Crofts, 1936. p. 36-68, 777-855.
[7] Edwin G. Boring, *A History of Experimental Psychology.* New York: D. Appleton-Century Co., 1929. p. 379-80. Also see the 1950 edition.

field indicated below (plus advanced work in education) found this special training the chief factor in undertaking the abbreviated thesis topic named: history of education (the history of a municipal university), history (the history of a state department of education), psychology (individual and group competition as motivational factors in achievement in arithmetic), English (modern novels as material for a socialized curriculum), music (a survey of music education in the public schools of a state), health and physical education (guidance in a summer camp), and Latin (trends in the teaching of secondary-school Latin).

A caution against overspecialization is in order. Judd thought that psychology suffered from a lack of fundamental unity because of the tendency of most workers in this field to engage in narrow specialization by way of interests and research.[8] It should be remembered that Fechner, who played a leading role in the formal beginning of experimental psychology, was at different times in his career physiologist, physicist, philosopher, psychophysicist, and experimental estheticist.[9] Seldom has G. Stanley Hall been equaled in variety of training, interests, reading, and professional activities.

**Instructional program pursued.** Adequate graduate courses include numerous suggestions concerning needed research, through the medium of lectures, discussions, reports, and reading. Stimulating contacts between professors and students outside the classroom are unusually profitable in the selection and development of problems for investigation. Examples [10] of the influence of the professor on his students or of the senior scholar on younger workers are that of Weber on Helmholtz, Fechner, and Lotze; Saint-Simon on Comte, and Comte on Herbert Spencer; James Mill on John Stuart Mill, Bain, and Spencer; Bain on William James, and James on Dewey, Thorndike, and Woodworth; Wundt on Cattell, G. Stanley Hall, Judd, and Titchener; Cattell on Thorndike; Darwin on Galton, and Galton on Pearson; Dewey, Thorndike, and Judd on many educational, psychological, and social workers active during the middle of the twentieth century and later. It is an interesting intellectual exercise to trace a common thread of theory or meaning through the work of several generations of scientists, as in some of the illustrations just cited.

Critical papers prepared for a course or seminar frequently provide helpful leads to the graduate thesis. It is important to keep systematic notes

[8] Charles H. Judd, *A History of Psychology in Autobiography*, Vol. 2. Edited by Carl Murchison. Worcester: Clark University Press, 1932. p. 229-30.

[9] Edwin G. Boring, *op. cit.*, p. 274.

[10] Gardner Murphy, *An Historical Introduction to Modern Psychology*. New York: Harcourt, Brace and Co., 1932. xx + 471 p. Also see the 1949 edition.

Charles A. Ellwood, *A History of Social Philosophy*. New York: Prentice-Hall, 1938. xvi + 581 p.

Herbert S. Langfeld, Editor, *A History of Psychology in Autobiography*, Vol. 4. Worcester: Clark University Press, 1952. xii + 356 p.

concerning needed research; otherwise such problems may leave one's memory never to return. Soon after Clark Hull began graduate work at the University of Wisconsin, he began keeping a permanent notebook of original ideas concerning a variety of psychological subjects as they came to him. This note system was begun primarily as a compensation against the poor memory that persisted after Hull suffered an attack of typhoid fever. When reading a new book he would enter in his notebook the new ideas suggested by the reading, or occasionally reasons for disagreement with what the author said. Sometimes on returning from a seminar Hull would write out his views on the subject discussed. Near the end of his career this series of notebooks totaled twenty-seven volumes. To his surprise, Hull found that these notebooks were valuable not primarily as aids to his memory, but as stimuli to systematic thinking. Hull reports that he frequently tried to induce promising graduate students in his seminars to keep systematic notebooks on original ideas, and sometimes purchased notebooks for presentation to them, but had little success in securing the adoption of his own practice by way of note-taking.

A type of paper, divided into three assignments, that has proved useful in the graduate classes (especially courses on research methods) of one of the authors is as follows:

1. If you are working on a thesis or field project, that is the most appropriate subject for further development during the course. Otherwise select some topic for library study that holds a definite interest for you, which may develop later possibilities for a thesis or field project. State the problem, historical background, sources of data, investigational procedures, limitations, and significance for education (probably based in part on your canvass of related literature). With the consent of the professor in another course, a joint report may be prepared for the two courses.

2. Prepare as complete and up to date a bibliography as possible, within the limits of the past three years, and using the guides recommended, so as to cover all types of related literature, including Masters' and Doctors' theses. Use the official form for all bibliographical references.

3. Proceed as far as time will permit with the summary or synthesis of the related studies. Use the *Encyclopedia of Educational Research* (1941 and 1950 editions), *Review of Educational Research, Psychological Bulletin,* and occasional surveys of the literature in the *American Journal of Sociology* and the *American Sociological Review,* as examples of good summarizing technique. However, reviews in these guides are usually broader in scope and sometimes briefer in citation of individual studies than will be the case in the chapter of the thesis or project dealing with related literature. In other words, the journals in particular cover more ground and have less space for comment on each investigation. In writing your summary, note the research methods employed, the major conclusions reached, the unsolved problems, and applications. If you can find one or more local studies in your field of interest, treat such reports especially analytically and critically in terms of the principles developed in our course. A good summary follows a topical arrangement rather than the "running

or annotated bibliography" form of organization. In other words, the points of view, methods, and conclusions of *different authors on a given sub-topic* are compared and synthesized, with educational applications and interpretations pointed out. This summary should be accompanied by the statement of the problem and the bibliography, which were submitted as earlier assignments.

**Program of reading.** Both extensive reading over a range of topics for breadth of background and intensive reading on selected themes for analytical, evaluative purposes are desirable aspects of the graduate program, as well as potential sources of problems. In all scientific endeavor the identification and solution of problems depend in a large measure on the work of predecessors and coworkers. The freedom and ease with which the results of research have been published during recent decades, and the number of workers as well, are primarily responsible for the rapid advance in the sciences.

Examples of the interdependence of research workers are numerous.[11] Since Pasteur had a horror of useless suffering, he probably would not have conducted his experiments on dogs and other animals without the use of chloroform, the practical realization of which was made possible by five American experimenters—Long, Jackson, Wells, Morton, and Warren. Banting could not have developed insulin without a method of accurate blood-sugar analysis, a procedure rendered efficient by sixty years of persistent work in hundreds of laboratories. Marconi, in inventing the wireless telegraph, was indebted to many men, including Lord Kelvin, Clerk Maxwell, and Hertz. Studies of eye-movements in reading were made possible by the motion-picture camera and by improved incandescent lamps as a light source.

In spite of handicaps in securing the works of others, even such early scholars as Roger Bacon, Leonardo da Vinci, and Galileo reveal an impressive knowledge of the writings in their fields of interest.[12] The tendency to exaggerate Bacon's achievements is tempered when it is realized that the inspirations for his experiments may be found in Alhazen, Albertus Magnus, Grosseteste, Abélard, and others. The inventions and discoveries of Leonardo give an impression of extraordinary originality, but, when checked against the five thousand manuscript pages of his notebooks, his indebtedness to other workers and wide reading are revealed; seventy-two medieval and classical authors are quoted by him. Galileo's analysis of the trajectory of a projectile was evolved primarily from facts provided by shipwrights, builders, gunners, and other technicians, and from the work of predecessors.

[11] T. A. Boyd, *op. cit.,* p. 279-80.
[12] J. G. Crowther, *The Social Relations of Science.* New York: Macmillan Co., 1941. p. 209, 277-78, 316.
Also see Ernest A. Moody, "Laws of Motion in Medieval Physics." *Scientific Monthly* 72:18-23; January 1951.

To cite more recent examples of the emphasis placed on wide reading by research workers, Thomas A. Edison when a boy undertook the impossible task of reading everything in the Detroit Public Library. He later formulated and followed this fundamental rule of research: first, find out everything everybody else has done, and then begin where they left off.[13] Judd, in his psychological autobiography, describes how his own undergraduate training in America and graduate work in Germany included opportunities for unusually extensive reading, and in his parting advice to beginning students recommends that they select teachers with broad interests and read extensively.[14] Thorndike considered himself an investigator rather than a scholar, in the sense of devoting his time to books, but estimated in 1936 that he had spent well over twenty thousand hours in reading and studying scientific books and journals.[15] The voracious reading, unusual erudition, and range of information of William James explain his unusual success in bringing together the work of the Scottish, English, French, and German schools of psychology.[16]

On the other hand, there are striking instances [17] of scholars who have neglected a thorough canvass of earlier writings in their fields of specialization. Agassiz found the study of things themselves far more attractive than what was printed in books about things, saying that he usually contented himself with paging through the volumes of natural history for later use in identifying such objects as he had an opportunity to examine in nature. Descartes had little respect for tradition or the classics, and was impatient of interference by the great men of the past; in this instance, a type of intellectual radicalism probably enabled Descartes to do more original work than might otherwise have been possible. In the later years of his life, Comte practiced what he called "cerebral hygiene," a custom of refraining from reading the books of other social thinkers, which meant that his own thinking, both scientific and philosophical, was not always abreast of the times. The truth is that a synthetic thinker like Comte, with an encyclopedic mind, had borrowed ideas from many predecessors, even though he recognized only three such persons in founding a scientific social philosophy—Aristotle, Montesquieu, and Condorcet. Comte was never willing to acknowledge his great debt to Saint-Simon, just as Herbert Spencer never admitted his obligation to Comte. With few exceptions, Sumner paid no attention to

13 T. A. Boyd, *op. cit.*, p. 72.
14 Charles H. Judd, *op. cit.*, p. 212, 218, 234.
15 Edward L. Thorndike, *A History of Psychology in Autobiography*, Vol. 3. Edited by Carl Murchison. Worcester: Clark University Press, 1936. p. 268.
16 Gardner Murphy, *op. cit.*, p. 207-9.
17 Edwin G. Boring, *op. cit.*, p. 159.
T. A. Boyd, *op. cit.*, p. 77-78.
Charles A. Ellwood, *op. cit.*, p. 360-69, 441-42, 504-9.

the work of other writers in sociology, not even mentioning in bibliography or index the names of Comte, Ward, and Giddings. In his *Folkways,* Sumner does not list a single great contemporary in psychology, not even William James. However, Sumner did draw upon the ideas of Spencer, Darwin, Lippert, and Gumplowicz. These failures to acknowledge indebt-edness represent a sort of dishonesty that is deplored in scientific work of today, or they may even indicate psychiatric difficulties in the scientists' personalities.

Certain suggestions are made below to guide the graduate student in canvassing special types of educational, psychological, and sociological literature, with particular reference to locating unsolved problems. A detailed discussion of bibliographical and library guides is found in another chapter.

1.   Published studies in certain fields have been analyzed to determine the frequency with which problems in each major subdivision have been investigated, thereby indicating gaps or areas with relatively little emphasis by way of research.

2.   Authoritative statements, critiques, or summaries of the research accomplishments in a particular field frequently include evaluations of the results reported and the techniques employed, as well as suggestions for further investigation. (The *Encyclopedia of Educational Research* and *Review of Educational Research* are especially suggestive.)

3.   Discussions of current trends are suggestive in terms of problems for study; many movements, procedures, and innovations are initiated without careful appraisal either before or after adoption.

4.   Prophecies of future developments imply a program of research and implementation of the findings before realization of the predictions made.

5.   Lists of studies and theses under way may be helpful in suggesting similar studies involving different conditions, communities, or areas.

6.   Outlines of problems for investigation often prove stimulating, although such lists of needed research seldom go far toward development of problem or technique, and are not to be viewed as research or thesis "assignments."

Numerous references [18] illustrating the foregoing types of literature (useful in locating problems for investigation) are listed in the classified bibliography of this chapter.

In reviewing the literature of a particular area, it should prove helpful in identifying significant problems to ask the following searching questions: [19]

---

[18] Also see Carter V. Good, A. S. Barr, and Douglas E. Scates, *op. cit.,* p. 38-68, 88-103, 777-855.

[19] Quoted from Henry W. Holmes and Others, *Educational Research.* Washington: American Council on Education, 1939. p. 12-18.
Also see Carter Alexander and Arvid J. Burke, *How to Locate Educational Information*

1. In the field of your interest, what practical problems have to be met by those who do the actual work?
2. In current and recent research, what problems are under active attack?
3. What facts, principles, generalizations, or other findings have resulted from research in your field?
4. What practical implications for school work may be drawn from these results?
5. To what extent have the findings of research actually been applied in your field?
6. What problems remain to be subjected to research and what problems are now emerging?
7. What are the chief difficulties to be met in prosecuting the researches yet to be conducted in your field?
8. What are the interrelations between research in your field and research in adjacent fields?
9. What research techniques or procedures have been developed in your field?
10. What concepts have been operative, either explicitly or implicitly, in the research in your field?
11. What assumptions have been implicit or openly avowed in the research in your field?

A practical example of the application of these eleven questions, by Mark A. May, to the field of measurement of abilities, aptitudes, and achievement is available, with the following rearranged headings: [20]

1. Practical problems in the use of tests
2. Specific problems under attack
3. Research techniques developed
4. Results of previous studies
5. Concepts and theories
6. Basic assumptions
7. New problems in measurement research
8. Measurement research and education
9. Implications for education
10. Application of research to practical problems
11. Limitations and handicaps to research.

This section may well end with the caution that dependence on the ideas of others should not be permitted to stifle originality and initiative. For several centuries before the experimental contributions of Galileo, scientific progress was greatly retarded by too implicit reliance on tradition and the ideas of the past, particularly the works of Aristotle. (This concept is further illustrated in a subsequent part of this chapter, dealing with avoidance of duplication in selecting problems for study.)

---

*and Data.* Third Edition. New York: Bureau of Publications, Teachers College, Columbia University, 1950. p. 161-78.
[20] Henry W. Holmes and Others, *op. cit.,* p. 51-81.

**Analysis of an area of knowledge.** In analyzing a field of knowledge, the area under consideration should be reasonably limited in scope. For example, research areas in psychology, in order to serve effectively as sources of specific problems for investigation, should be considerably narrower than the customary fields of psychology (such as child psychology or abnormal psychology). More appropriate areas for analysis are physical growth, mental development, reading-readiness tests, or prenatal conditioning.

On the other hand, an area should be large enough to prove meaningful, in terms of permitting the development of integrating conceptual patterns or schemes. It is ordinarily more useful for practical purposes in discovering a research problem to know the status of research in such areas as audition, language development, or projective techniques than to have the same kind of appraisal or information concerning binaural beats, the phonetic range of the one-year-old, or the thematic apperception test.[21]

To subdivide a particular field into its constituent parts and to identify research problems in each subarea are tasks requiring insight and background, but are profitable procedures in discovering needed research. Much of the background for such an analysis comes through the instructional and reading programs discussed in earlier sections of this chapter. An example [22] from the area of educational diagnosis and adjustment illustrates the identification of problems in the various subdivisions of this field.

1.  What are the various categories into which cases for educational diagnosis fall? Progress has been made in recognizing the subdivisions of the physically handicapped, as well as the mentally handicapped and talented, but diagnostic groups in certain newer instructional areas and the various types of social maladjustment (owing to personality difficulties and behavior disorders) require further differentiation.

2.  At what point does a given child become a subject for diagnosis and developmental or remedial treatment in one of the diagnostic categories—the mentally or physically handicapped, those who are maladjusted socially, morally, or emotionally, those who perform below their level of learning capacity, and others whose latent talents are never given expression?

3.  What instruments and procedures are available in identifying cases for educational diagnosis?

4.  How many children and youth fall in each diagnostic group—for a given school system, for a state, for the nation?

5.  What factors are associated with the occurrence of defects and talents?

6.  What results are associated with the presence of handicaps and special abilities?

[21] Dael Wolfle and Others, "Standards for Appraising Psychological Research." *American Psychologist* 4:320-28; August 1949.

[22] Quoted from Carter V. Good, "Problems and Techniques of Educational Diagnosis and Adjustment." *School and Society* 48:261-67; August 27, 1938.

Also see Douglas E. Scates, "What Can Research Contribute to Our Understanding of the Physically Handicapped?" *Journal of Educational Research* 31:20-28; September 1937.

7. What are the contributions of case histories and genetic studies to the work of educational diagnosis?

8. What preventive measures are available and usable?

9. What treatment for developmental and remedial purposes can be provided?

10. What are the best types of curriculum materials and teaching techniques for the various groups of children requiring developmental or remedial instruction?

11. What are the after-school history, the vocational opportunities, and the adjustments necessary for the different diagnostic groups?

12. What are the problems of organization, administration, finance, law, buildings, equipment, special classes, special teachers, clinics, and supervision for the given school system or state?

13. What is the local history of the successes and failures of the past in dealing with problems of educational diagnosis?

**Consideration of existing practices and needs.**[23] An earlier section of this chapter points out that beginners in research often appear to be insensitive to problems close at hand. A systematic analysis of existing practices and needs in a particular field is a challenging intellectual exercise, whether the area examined is local, state, regional, or national. The gaps in knowledge identified through such a canvass should be viewed as challenges rather than accepted in laissez faire fashion as insuperable barriers to improvement. Included among such problems are those manifest in actual practice —how a left-handed child learns to write; those made evident by proposals for new types of practice—the unit plan of teaching; and problems brought out by new proposals in the philosophy of society and of education—the effect of school competition on social attitudes.

It sometimes is desirable and profitable for the student to reëxamine his thesis problem in the light of the needs of a new position or of a different professional assignment. The following examples illustrate changes in thesis topics made by students who had not gone far with the original problem. An assistant state superintendent of public instruction, entering upon personnel work in a state university, changed from an investigation of capital outlay for school buildings in the state to a study of the development of the personnel and guidance program in the higher institution to which he went. A doctoral candidate who became a state supervisor of trade and industrial education gave up a study of the junior colleges in his state in favor of a state-wide survey of the educational opportunities in the field he supervised. When another doctoral candidate with a year of graduate training in the history of education took up a position in a municipal university, he decided to write the history of the institution rather than a biography of

[23] T. H. Briggs, "An Uncultivated Field." *North Central Association Quarterly* 12:214-20; October 1937.
Henry W. Holmes and Others, *op. cit.,* p. 172-73.

William T. Harris. After appointment as safety-education specialist in the curriculum department of a city system, the worker's thesis topic changed from an analysis of the educational concepts in the writings of H. G. Wells to the development and evaluation of a program in safety education for the city in question. When an elementary-school principal in the same city was sent by his school board and superintendent to observe departmentalized practices in the schools of certain large cities, he gave up a history of his city school system in favor of an evaluation of the reorganized elementary school in selected cities.

The suggestion that many beginners in research may well study tangible problems representing existing practices and needs parallels the early history of research in education. It was natural and sensible that the scientific movement in education began with concrete inquiries into the achievement of pupils in spelling and arithmetic. Recent attempts to measure such intangible things as attitudes face difficulties that would have prevented similar investigations in the earlier days of the measurement movement. In general, it seems best to do the thing near at hand until the way opens to deal with problems farther off or more difficult with respect to approach. However, a common criticism of local studies and surveys is the same as that voiced about Le Play's concrete, inductive method of social investigation, an approach that did not grasp society as a whole and allowed facts of great importance to escape.[24] The more than thirty thousand local social surveys in the United States in large part have been devices to support local programs of social improvement or to provide graduate theses. As such, these studies have been useful, but few have made fundamental contributions to the social sciences.

**Repetition or extension of investigations.**[25] Earlier in this chapter it is pointed out that history is never complete, that surveys of status can be accurate only for the time and area represented, and that many experiments should be repeated for purposes of verification. The physicist and chemist defend duplication of experiments, under various conditions in different laboratories, for fear that some uncontrolled factor may have been present in the original experiment. Lord Rayleigh discovered the inert gases in the atmosphere after hundreds of determinations had failed to indicate their presence. Faraday was slow to accept the results of other investigators and made it a rule to repeat every experiment about which he wrote or lectured, a practice that led him to the great discovery of electromagnetic induction.

On the other hand, many observations or discoveries have not been fol-

24 Charles A. Ellwood, *op. cit.,* p. 416-17.
25 Henry W. Holmes and Others, *op. cit.,* p. 43-44.
T. A. Boyd, *op. cit.,* p. 75-76.
W. I. B. Beveridge, *op. cit.,* p. 36-37, 104.

lowed up to reach important conclusions or applications. Although Stein-haeuser discovered in 1840 that cod-liver oil cured rickets, this fact of major importance remained unverified for the next eighty years. Fleming described crude preparations of penicillin in 1929, but after a time discontinued this work without developing a therapeutic agent. It remained for Florey to develop penicillin as a therapeutic agent. Landsteiner identified the human blood groups in 1901, but not until anticoagulants were found and blood transfusion was developed during World War I did his discovery assume real importance. Mendel's discovery of the basic principles of genetics was published in a good scientific journal, but was ignored for thirty-five years.

**"Offshoots" of studies under way.** Sometimes a problem, method, or discovery that "buds out" of an investigation in progress proves more fruitful than the original line of research. For example, Thorndike describes three methods of work, with a preference for the last: (1) to observe and think about the facts that come our way; (2) to gather deliberately by observation or experiment any promising facts that can be readily secured; and (3) to put an important question and then strive in every way possible for facts to answer it. In following the third approach, the very doing of one part of the work may cause the investigator to think of another line of attack. Sometimes fruitful methods come to mind late in the course of an investigation. The idea of the delayed-reaction experiment, as a method of studying animal mentality, came to Thorndike after two years of work with animals. His idea that the difficulty of a task for intellect (or any other ability) can be measured only in the case of a task composed of enough elements to involve all of intellect (or of the ability) came after thirty years of study of intellect and after more than a year of special investigation of means of measuring difficulty for the intellect.[26]

Numerous other examples of problems or discoveries as offshoots of work under way are available, especially with application to the field of medicine.[27] When Pasteur was injecting into chickens the microbes that cause cholera, owing to a shortage of fresh chickens he happened to include two that had previously recovered from the disease. Instead of dying from the virulent dose of cholera germs, these two chickens were not affected in the least, which led Pasteur unexpectedly to the principle of immunization. Emil von Behring was testing out the theory that diphtheria might be cured by means of some chemical when he discovered that an antitoxin for diphtheria could be made from the blood of an animal that had recovered from the disease. When the French physicist Becquerel was experimenting with

---

[26] Edward L. Thorndike, *op. cit.*, p. 269.
[27] T. A. Boyd, *op. cit.*, p. 17, 87-90, 163, 169-70.

radium, he happened to carry a small quantity in his pocket and soon found that the effects of the radium destroyed the tissue of his skin, which led to the use of radium in the treatment of cancer.

The areas of invention and industry are replete with examples of research from which important offshoots have "budded out." William Perkin, in trying to convert aniline into quinine, made instead the first of the aniline dyes, purple mauve. Edison was working with a piece of lampblack mixed with tar (prepared for use in his telephone transmitter) when he hit upon the idea of using this material as a filament for the incandescent lamp; it worked, although this particular material did not prove good enough for commercial use. Irving Langmuir, when investigating the so-called "Edison effect," a blue glow that sometimes appears on the filaments of incandescent lamps (or may surround hot metal filaments through which electricity is flowing), made a scientific and practical discovery soon put to use in the low-voltage, high-power vacuum tube for long-range radio transmission. Willis R. Whitney, in an effort to utilize the mercury arc as a source of light, discovered new facts that made possible its application in an important unexpected field, that of the alternating current rectifier. His apt statement concerning the "budding out" of the problem is: "We found nature easy to follow and difficult to drive. We usually wanted what she gave for our seeking, but we could seldom get exactly what we thought we wanted at the time. We wanted light. She gave us rectifiers." [28]

## CRITERIA FOR SELECTION OF THE PROBLEM [29]

Factors to be considered in selection of a research or thesis problem are both external and personal. External criteria have to do with such matters as novelty and importance for the field, availability of data and method, and institutional or administrative coöperation. Personal criteria involve such considerations as interest, training, cost, and time. A more detailed list of criteria for selection of the problem (these will be discussed in the succeeding pages) follows:

1. Novelty and avoidance of unnecessary duplication
2. Importance for the field represented and implementation
3. Interest, intellectual curiosity, and drive
4. Training and personal qualifications
5. Availability of data and method
6. Special equipment and working conditions
7. Sponsorship and administrative coöperation
8. Costs and returns
9. Hazards, penalties, and handicaps
10. Time factor.

[28] *Ibid.,* p. 270.
[29] Carter V. Good, "Criteria for Selection of the Research Problem." *Peabody Journal of Education* 19:242-56; March 1942.

**Novelty and avoidance of unnecessary duplication.** Another chapter of this book outlines in detail the library guides for determining what work has been completed in a particular field. An earlier section of the present chapter describes as a source of problems the repetition of experiments or the extension of investigations; however, this means deliberate, planned repetition rather than accidental or blind duplication through ignorance of the area and literature represented.

The following inquiry received in 1939 by one of the authors and the reply are illuminating with respect to duplication of effort, owing to failure to canvass the available literature.

As an assistant during the past few years to a university professor and specialist in the field of educational jurisprudence, I have noted your contributions in the American *Yearbook of School Law*. Your compilation of doctorate abstracts in the 1939 *Yearbook* is not only enlightening, but also quite shocking in one particular part.

After writing my Master's thesis on "Teacher Tenure" at an eastern college, I have spent the last three years compiling data on "Tort-Liability of Teachers" for the Doctor of Philosophy degree at an eastern university. I had submitted the "brief" and it was approved.

However, I note in your 1939 compilation a completed thesis (1937) on the same topic. Three years of effort are frustrated because this thesis has been accepted before mine. I had attempted to find out if there had been any work done on this subject, but all these efforts proved fruitless.

The purpose of this letter is to respectfully inquire if, in your knowledge, there has been any thesis published or any work done in the field of "Corporal Punishment in the Public Schools of the United States." I would indeed appreciate any information that you could give me on this point.

It seems to me that it is unfair for students to be expected to know of the work which other students may be doing in other universities in the country. Is there any institution, to your knowledge, where a thesis topic could be filed so as to prevent a recurrence of this hardship?

In order to encourage initiative on the part of the student and the practice of canvassing systematically the appropriate guides, the reply by one of the authors was limited to a brief statement, with a list of library guides attached.

Beginning with 1931, the January number of the *Journal of Educational Research* included a list of doctoral dissertations under way in education [later taken over by the *Phi Delta Kappan*].

It is true that the student you mention completed his dissertation in 1937. However, his problem was listed as under way in the January, 1935, number of the *Journal of Educational Research*. I regret that a number of the graduate professors and graduate students either do not know of this annual service of the *Journal*, or neglect to make the canvass of studies under way before taking up a new doctoral problem.

With respect to your new problem, I suggest that you examine the January *Journal of Educational Research* [beginning with 1947 in the *Phi Delta Kappan*] for studies under way, and canvass the sources listed on the enclosed mimeographed pages, in order to determine what work has been completed.

A question of duplication arises in the case of two specialists in music education who wrote dissertations on the same national organization in music, one at a mid-western university and the other at a southern graduate school separated by a distance of only three hundred miles. The student who completed his study in 1948 could have found the earlier dissertation listed in the 1943 *Doctoral Dissertations Accepted by American Universities*. It is difficult to explain why the paths of the two men did not cross in the national office of the music organization, except that the earlier investigator based his study almost entirely on the publications (yearbooks, bulletins, and journal) of the association rather than on the sources in the national office. The 1948 investigator, when working through the records in the central office, heard no mention of the 1942 doctoral candidate. Both reports are voluminous, 600 pages for the 1942 dissertation and 500 pages for the 1948 study. It is possible and probable that the emphasis and interpretation differed sufficiently so that each study made a substantial contribution.

An almost unexplainable example of duplication is found in the thesis projects of two professors (and doctoral candidates) in different state universities of Ohio, both of whom were working on the certification of teachers in Ohio, one at a graduate school in the same state and the other at a university on the eastern seaboard. In 1935 the dissertation of one candidate was published at the eastern school, to the great surprise and chagrin of the other investigator, who then took up another problem. The latter candidate could have found the thesis of the successful doctoral investigator reported as under way in the January, 1933, number of the *Journal of Educational Research* (some lists in the *Phi Delta Kappan*) well before he (the disappointed graduate student) began work. This instance of duplication is all the more surprising in view of the fact that both men were in the same state, were engaged in similar occupational pursuits, and no doubt were using many of the same records of the state department of education and of other agencies or institutions interested in certification. (It should be noted here that in some instances independent studies of the same problem, made at different institutions, are permitted, probably with the hope of securing a worth-while contribution in each case.)

There are even instances of great scientists and able scholars who have been negligent and sometimes contemptuous of the literature and of earlier investigations in their fields of specialization,[30] as described in the examples

[30] T. A. Boyd, *op. cit.*, p. 74-75.
W. I. B. Beveridge, *op. cit.*, p. 2-3.

cited in an earlier part of this chapter. Certain scientists have considered it undesirable or even unwise to study closely the related literature dealing with a particular problem under way. They have believed that in reading the earlier investigations one's mind is conditioned to see the problem in the same way and thus may overlook a new or more fruitful approach. Charles Kettering thought that as a result of studying conventional textbooks we fall into a rut, escape from which may take as much effort as to solve the problem itself.

Through neglect of earlier research, Pasteur blundered in representing himself as the first to discover that microscopic animals could live without breathing; Leeuwenhoek two centuries earlier and Spallanzani a hundred years before Pasteur had found the same thing. Pasteur also rediscovered the fact that microbes cause meat to spoil without giving proper credit to Schwann, who was the first to make that observation.

Byron aptly expressed the dilemma of creative workers: "To be perfectly original one should think much and read little, and this is impossible, for one must have read before one has learnt to think." To solve this dilemma it is essential to read critically as a stimulus to thinking. Certainly it is a serious handicap to investigate a problem in ignorance of what is already known from related studies.

A challenging statement by George D. Stoddard, relating to the difficulties of accomplishing penetrating, large-scale research in child development, applies with equal force to many other educational, psychological, and social fields: [31]

1. Masters' theses and doctoral dissertations are fragmentary and opportunistic in nature. (The problem has to be small and clean-cut; carried on in the midst of a busy academic life; and brought to an early completion. There is a premium on safety.)
2. The journals themselves demand short articles. They are a bottle neck to the long-continued, monographic research. Long researches are expensive to publish and there are few channels open.
3. Most researchers are not scholars as well. There seems to be something of a dichotomy as between the two types. The worker can become master of an area and be a good teacher, writer, or lecturer on the subject. On the other hand, as a scientific, laboratory researcher he is likely to get engrossed in his own contributions. His ideas show originality and power, but they may ignore or override the work of other competent persons.
4. The time factor is important. Longitudinal studies, for example, by definition require a long interval of time. Except in rather elaborate research institutes, it has not appeared feasible to get one person to work on a project for five years or more, or to get a succession of workers to articulate their findings longitudinally.

[31] Quoted from Henry W. Holmes and Others, *Educational Research*. Washington: American Council on Education, 1939. p. 44-45.

5. In spite of our elaborate graduate arrangements in universities and research institutes, it would appear that few expert researchers are produced. The demonstration of high scientific aptitude and excellent training in a discipline, together with a thorough knowledge of allied fields; the freedom from too many other demands, as in teaching or administration; the courage to risk academic and professional standing through avoidance of the casual, opportunistic publication in favor of the substantial monograph—all these are scarce attributes.

The question of novelty or newness is not merely one of duplication of earlier investigations. It involves the recency of the data summarized, especially in the case of survey studies made during a period of great economic, educational, or social change. The city superintendent of schools (and doctoral candidate) who early in 1940 made an industrial survey of his community, a youth and employment survey of the high-school graduates, and a canvass of parents and high-school pupils concerning attitudes toward the curriculum found the data inadequate as a basis for curriculum reorganization late in 1941. In the intervening period great industrial changes as a result of the national defense program had taken place, with marked effects on employment, attitudes, and the school program.

The question of duplication arises when two graduate students propose a joint thesis, a type of coöperative effect seldom permitted, although many wives of candidates have well earned a share in the graduate degrees awarded their husbands. It is true that there are many commissions, surveys, and research agencies with large programs of investigation in which graduate studies are worked out as complementary parts of a research pattern. Also, in certain historical areas, different chronological periods are treated separately in graduate theses; for example, the constitutional and legal basis of education in Ohio, 1800-50, by one doctoral candidate; 1850-1900 by a second doctoral student; and 1900-30 in a Master's thesis. The problem of pupil transportation requires a series of studies for regions with different geographic, climatic, population, and road conditions, as in Wyoming, Ohio, and West Virginia, and transportation studies of many local school districts.

It frequently happens that two or more scholars, scientists, or inventors may be working simultaneously on the same problem, each without knowledge of the other, and may announce their findings at almost the same time. In such instances, history has viewed the discovery as a joint contribution: for example, James and Lange, a theory of the emotions; Darwin, Spencer, and Wallace, a theory of evolution; Lancaster and Bell, a system of monitorial instruction; Newton and Leibnitz, the calculus as a general method and a system of notation for it; the Wright brothers and Langley, heavier-than-air flying; Bell and Gray, the telephone; Faraday and Henry, the principles of electromagnetic induction; Mendelyeev and Meyer, similar classifications of the chemical elements; and Mayer, Mohr, Helmholtz, and

Golding, the generalization of the conservation of energy.[32] This background from the history of science, invention, and education may be useful in the evaluation of independent graduate theses dealing with the same problem.

**Importance for the field represented and implementation.** This criterion of importance, in choice of a problem, involves such matters as significance for the field involved, timeliness, and practical value in terms of application and implementation of the results. This topic already has received some attention in the earlier section of this chapter dealing with consideration of existing practices and needs as a source for locating research problems. Scientific work in education, psychology, and the social sciences in general has an especially urgent obligation to play a social role in rendering service to society and humanity,[33] as was emphasized in Chapter 1.

It is high time that the social responsibilities of scientists and of research workers be recognized and accepted. Emphasis on material production and on the instruments of war has led to partial neglect of problems of human welfare, health, domestic life, and education, with the biological and social sciences starved in deference to the more immediately profitable physical and chemical sciences. Wars and economic crises have shown that science can be used for destructive and wasteful purposes rather than for progressive improvement of the conditions of life. Since science and research are determining factors in the destiny of mankind, a social policy for science must be formulated to guarantee that such knowledge will be used for the welfare of society. The problems and projects of today (especially the research in atomic energy), together with the present world scene, present sober testimony that on the proper relation of science, technology, philosophy, education, and society depend the welfare and even the very existence of science, social institutions, and mankind.

Francis Bacon was aiming at the invention of a method that would solve not only particular scientific problems, but also provide for the adaptation of the results to the social process. The core of Bacon's work was not so much science as the social relations of science. He was critical of Galileo's

---

[32] Edwin G. Boring, *op. cit.,* p. 165, 502-3.
T. A. Boyd, *op. cit.,* p. 280.
J. G. Crowther, *op. cit.,* p. 450.
Charles A. Ellwood, *op. cit.,* p. 437-41.
Gardner Murphy, *op. cit.,* p. 121, 216-17.
[33] Carter V. Good, "Educational Progress During the Year, 1940." *School and Society* 53:330-37; March 15, 1941. For extended discussions of this problem see:
J. D. Bernal, *The Social Function of Science.* New York: Macmillan Co., 1939. xvi + 482 p.
J. G. Crowther, *op. cit.* xxxiv + 665 p.
Florian Znaniecki, *The Social Role of the Man of Knowledge.* New York: Columbia University Press, 1940. viii + 212 p.

method of abstracting problems entirely from their general and social context. Scientists, in the main, followed Galileo for three centuries, accumulating discoveries in areas of research artificially isolated from the general body of knowledge and social affairs.[34]

An illustration of failure to recognize a socially valuable problem is found in the report of two research students who went to investigate a racial conflict in a certain community. They returned with the statement that everything was harmonious between Orientals and Americans, a race riot having just been settled amicably, hence there was nothing to investigate. They overlooked an excellent opportunity to study an accommodation process, an adjustment between races.[35]

The element of timeliness is illustrated by studies of the tuitional value of motion pictures, an important problem about 1922. If similar studies were undertaken today for the simple purpose of ascertaining whether children secure value received for time spent in viewing an instructional film, the problem would be considered relatively unimportant, since an affirmative answer is already well known.[36]

The research worker is not expected, as a general rule, to implement the results of his studies, however desirable this consummation may be. He is not even compelled to point out the practical applications of his findings, although this step seems essential, especially in the social sciences. Actually the scientist in education cannot leave himself out of implementation; research in education is part of the process of education itself.[37] Even in the physical aspects of child development, traits cannot be measured as if they were independent entities growing without some central control on the part of the organism. In the field of reading, research advanced from study of relatively mechanical factors toward the purpose of the reader and the social uses of the process. Guidance investigations moved away from the notion of fitting a pattern of aptitudes into a pattern of demands to a consideration of the individual in relation to society. Research in educational finance must concern itself with forces of public opinion and common desire. Survey testing became of secondary importance as compared with functional use of measurement for segregation or classification, diagnosis, prediction or prognosis, evaluation, and standardization of desirable practices. "When it comes to education there is no avoiding the step from the study of the elements of a problem, objectively considered, to the study of what can be

[34] J. G. Crowther, op. cit., p. 351-52.
[35] Emory S. Bogardus, Introduction to Social Research. Los Angeles: Suttonhouse, 1936. p. 5.
[36] Douglas E. Scates and Charles F. Hoban, Jr., "Critical Questions for the Evaluation of Research." Journal of Educational Research 31:241-54; December 1937.
[37] Henry W. Holmes and Others, op. cit., p. 181-82.

done to acquaint the individual or the group with the situation. Educational research leads into education. How to implement research is a part of research itself." [38]

Even where applications of scientific discoveries are clearly indicated, there are almost countless examples of the thwarting of science in such fields as health, nutrition, medicine, housing, recreation, education, industry, and invention, owing to economic and social factors, tradition, competition, the profit motive, war, and prejudice.[39] Another chapter will consider in more detail the problems of reporting and of implementation of research.

**Interest, intellectual curiosity, and drive.** The history of science and the pages of this chapter and book are studded with the names of scholars led (and sometimes driven) to their discoveries by consuming intellectual curiosity. One of the personal motives for research most frequently mentioned by scientists themselves is pure curiosity, accompanied by genuine interest and a derived satisfaction or enjoyment. Only an insatiable curiosity and driving interest could have compelled Aristotle to undertake so varied a program of activities which identify him in the language of today as professor, philosopher, psychologist, logician, moralist, political thinker, biologist, founder of literary criticism, and author of books on all these subjects.[40] Herschel was a musician until the age of forty, but his curiosity and strong interests in astronomy and in the making of telescopes led to the spectacular discovery of the planet Uranus, origination of descriptive astronomy, and a lasting impetus to the construction of large telescopes. Galileo's interests cropped out in his freshman days at the University of Pisa, and he soon gave up premedical work in favor of mathematics and natural science. Although poor, he evidently was not interested in monetary rewards; a professor of medicine then received the equivalent of about $2000 a year, and a professor of mathematics only about $65.

The desire to understand fully, and to construct a completely coherent system of ideas that will explain phenomena, frequently is so strong that scientists and scholars go to extremes in concentration, sometimes withdrawal from human contacts, and even in reluctance to publish anything short of perfect solutions of problems.[41] Cavendish had his meals passed through a hole in the wall of his room, to avoid speaking to anyone and to reduce interruptions to a minimum. He failed to publish his invention of

[38] *Ibid.*, p. 182.
[39] J. G. Crowther, *op. cit.*, p. 576-91.
[40] Frederick Slocum, "Intellectual Curiosity." *School and Society* 48:157-63; August 6, 1938.
[41] J. G. Crowther, *op. cit.*, p. 511-16.
    James W. Thompson and Bernard J. Holm, *A History of Historical Writing*, Vol. 2. New York: Macmillan Co., 1942. p. 108, 180-81, 216, 507.
    Herbert S. Langfeld, *op. cit.*, p. 27-52, 323-39.

electrical condensers, which was rediscovered by Faraday. Newton asked that his first paper, the solution of a problem in annuities, be published without his name attached, for fear of increasing the number of his acquaintances. Darwin worked on the *Origin of Species* for more than twenty years, and might never have published it without pressure from Lyell.

Historians frequently have been prodigious workers with remarkable powers of concentration. Ranke continued incessantly busy at work until the age of ninety-one. With tremendous energy he drove his assistants to exhaustion. One assistant served Ranke from 9:30 A.M. to 2:00 P.M., and the other from 7 P.M. to 12 P.M., with no recreation and no holidays allowed except Christmas. His own library of twenty-five thousand volumes filled five large rooms, with the books piled two and three deep on shelves and floor. Ranke objected to any systematic arrangement of the books, saying that he would not be able to find what he wanted.

Theodore Mommsen was so completely absorbed in his work that every morning, after entering the train on his way to the University in Berlin, he always occupied the same seat, and immediately began to read. His fellow passengers never interrupted him. On arriving at the university station the conductor informed the professor, who would then hurry out to be on time for his morning lecture at eight o'clock. Johann Droysen, like Mommsen, was a prodigious worker and would spend as much as fifteen hours at his desk. Immanuel Kant devoted his entire life to ideas. At Königsberg he was born, lived, taught, and died, having never traveled, or married, or done "anything except think."

Striking differences in intellectual curiosity and scientific interests are noted in the work of Huxley, a great propagandist for science, and of Darwin, a great research worker. Huxley's diary of the voyage on the *Rattlesnake* is concerned with personal psychological problems and resistance to fits of depression, whereas Darwin's diary of the voyage on the *Beagle,* in spite of his poor health, is devoted to the collection of facts and the development of scientific ideas.

Edwin G. Boring, the psychologist, in his autobiography speaks of himself as a compulsive person, whose compulsions have driven him on inexorably to goals, with these drives operating for minutes or for years and satisfied only by achievement. He attributes his achievement to these irresistible compulsions and to his capacity for hard work on an eighty-hour week and a fifty-week year. Boring also speaks of a persistent sense of insecurity, established at the age of five and dominant through his fifties, as a factor in driving forward in his work and writing.

Edward C. Tolman, another psychologist, speaks of his drive as an attempt to be creative; in his earlier years, whenever he felt particularly inept on some social or academic occasion, he would go home talking to himself in some such words as: "Well, I'll show them, I will be better known in my field than they will be in theirs." Then he would return to his laboratory or study with increased motivation. This was a compulsive academic ambition or drive, a self-ideal of becoming truly successful in the academic world.

It follows that the graduate student's choice of area, problem, or method will depend to a large extent on his interests, and on such criteria as novelty, importance for the field represented, and training. He will be aided in crystallizing or identifying such interests by the earlier suggestions in this chapter concerning sources of problems, particularly the analysis of existing practices and needs.

**Training and personal qualifications.** In the earlier discussion of one's area of specialization as a fruitful source of problems are a number of illustrations of specialized types of training appropriate for undertaking the particular investigations cited. It should be recognized, however, that such fields as education, psychology, and sociology are greatly indebted to workers with specialized training in other disciplines, especially during the early stages when the foundations were being laid for a new science. To use psychology [42] as an example, contributors to the early development of psychology include Descartes, philosopher and physiologist; Leibnitz and Locke, philosophers and men of political affairs; Berkeley, philosopher, bishop, and educator; Hume, philosopher, historian, and politician; Hartley, learned physician; James Mill, historian and diplomatist; John Stuart Mill, philosopher, logician, and political economist; Charles Bell, Flourens, Johannes Müller, and E. H. Weber, physiologists; Lotze, metaphysician; Helmholtz, physiologist and physicist; Bain, really a psychologist but formally a logician; Fechner, physicist and philosopher; and Wundt, physician and physiologist who in 1875 accepted a chair of philosophy at Leipzig, although his experiments and work made it possible without reservation to call him the senior psychologist in the history of psychology. Many later psychologists have continued to pursue special training in medicine and physiology.

Stanley Hall came into psychology through circuitous channels in his thirties, with a diversified background of training and experience, including theological preparation, European study, college teaching, and physiology. The broad training and experience of Edward B. Titchener included

---

[42] Edwin G. Boring, *op. cit.*, p. 223-24, 310.
    A. A. Roback, *History of American Psychology.* New York: Library Publishers, 1952. p. 155-56, 188-89.
    Herbert S. Langfeld, *op. cit.*, viii + 356 p. Reviewed by Lewis M. Terman, *Psychological Bulletin* 50:477-81; November 1953.

music, collection of coins, classical languages, half a dozen modern languages, linguistics and philology, biology, physiology, and anthropology.

While most of the founders of modern psychology were migrants, usually from philosophy but sometimes from other disciplines, it is also interesting to note the number of modern psychologists who entered the field in roundabout ways. Edwin G. Boring, L. L. Thurstone, and Edward C. Tolman were engineering graduates, while Godfrey Thomson took his doctorate in physics, Agostini Gemelli in both medicine and biology, and Jean Piaget in the natural sciences. Certainly the impact or influence of these men on contemporary psychology has been great, but it is impossible to say whether less or more than if they had entered psychology by a more direct route. Some of these psychologists were able to apply their previous training in science to certain types of psychological problems more effectively than if they had not detoured, but in other cases the detours were costly in time. An unanswered question is whether undergraduate courses in the physical or biological sciences may provide a better foundation for the future psychologist than do the usual undergraduate courses in psychology. At the undergraduate level is training in the logic and techniques of the more exact sciences fully as important as the acquisition of psychological information?

Edward C. Tolman, in his autobiography, speaks of the variety of sources that influenced him in his psychological points of view, including his own students, his professors during graduate study, associates in the field of psychology, the Gestalt psychologists, a year's stay in Vienna (involving both the academic and psycho-analytical traditions of European psychology), war-time experiences that developed points of view relating to personality psychology, and contacts with a group of workers interested in sociology, anthropology, personality, and social psychology.

Walter Bingham's interest in music as a hobby provided background for his doctoral dissertation. As a youth he learned to sing and to play a number of instruments. Later, in selecting a topic for a doctoral dissertation, dealing with the nature of melody, it was only natural that the problem would involve both his interest in psychological experimentation and his non-vocational activities in music.

Graduate students may well interpret the preceding illustrations and the subsequent examples as a suggestion to avoid overspecialization or narrowness in their programs of training, although they can hardly hope to match the background of da Vinci or Tarde.[43] The versatility of Leonardo da Vinci should be interpreted in the light of his training as an apprentice in

43 J. G. Crowther, *op. cit.,* p. 253.
Charles A. Ellwood, *op. cit.,* p. 417-26.

the shop of Verrocchio, a distinguished painter, goldsmith, and craftsman who had some knowledge of sculpture, architecture, and engineering. Gabriel Tarde's contributions to sociology were derived primarily from his training for the law and his long period of service as a criminal judge in France. He saw how crime was so frequently the result of contagion and association, and decided that most of the characteristics or behaviors of human society are socially acquired and socially transmitted.

Many able historians have utilized a remarkable background of scholarship.[44] Barthold Niebuhr at the age of eighteen knew eighteen European languages, as well as Hebrew, Persian, and Arabic. With his phenomenal memory he went on to master philosophy, mathematics, physics, chemistry, natural history, history, Roman law, and practical politics and administration. Theodore Mommsen was a marvel of German scholarship with 1513 different titles among his published works; he wrote these thousands of pages in longhand. Mommsen was a scholar in at least six fields of knowledge: epigraphy, numismatics, history, law, archaeology, and early Italian philology. Adolf von Harnack has at least 1800 titles of books and articles to his credit, an output of high quality and a record of achievement that invite comparison with Mommsen. Connop Thirlwall possessed a remarkable background of scholarship, having learned Latin at three, Greek at four, and published a collection of sermons and poems at twelve years of age.

Ward, Sumner, and Giddings, pioneers in sociology, are outstanding examples of varied training, broad scholarship, and extensive reading in their areas of special interest.[45] Lester Frank Ward earned his living for forty years as a governmental worker while equipping himself through scientific study and the reading of great books in philosophy as background for his future work in sociology. During these years he did part-time study in evening classes in Washington, completing the Bachelor's and Master's degrees, in addition to a diploma in medicine and a law degree. He also studied botany, geology, and anthropology.

William Graham Sumner was able to use a dozen languages in studying cultural-anthropological problems. He had no financial assistance for research and little help, yet his files of notes compare favorably with the work of many later research workers supported by relatively large financial grants. Sumner compiled fifty-two drawers and boxes of notes averaging 3000 sheets each. His extensive reading included history, theology, metaphysics, and general literature. Franklin Henry Giddings read widely in European philosophy and sociology, and had six years of experience in

---

[44] James W. Thompson and Bernard J. Holm, *op. cit.*, p. 153, 489, 502, 567.
[45] Howard W. Odum, *American Sociology:* The Story of Sociology in the United States through 1950. New York: Longmans, Green and Co., 1951. p. 78-94.

journalism and six years of teaching in experimental situations at Bryn Mawr and Columbia; he also wrote excellent poetry.

On the other hand, able scientists have not always made a good showing in meeting formal examination requirements. Paul Ehrlich was passed through his final medical examinations by the grace of his examiners, who recognized his special talents, while Einstein failed at the entrance examinations to the Polytechnic School. It may be that the inventive and critical scholar is even at a disadvantage in accumulating factual information, as compared with the student who accepts without question and memorizes what he is told or what he reads.[46]

The worker's physical resources must be considered in relation to the contemplated field and problem. James Rowland Angell, near the end of his college course, considered the pursuit of medicine, but weak eyes compelled him to forego the arduous microscopic work that was and is an essential feature of the medical training program.[47] If medicine was the loser, psychology and university administration gained a competent worker.

Freedom from bias is an essential prerequisite for successful research in the social sciences. The chapter on the historical method discusses this important personal qualification in detail, with numerous illustrations. For the present, there is the case of the young college woman who undertook to write a hero-worshiping paper on the career of a fascist leader and in despair asked the instructor for an extension of time, because the evidence was "all on the wrong side of the question." [48]

The wise graduate student will consider carefully both the subject-matter content and the treatment of research methodology in his program of training (past, present, and future) in selection of the thesis problem. Through organized courses and seminars, supplemented by independent reading, the necessary background concerning content and research methods can be secured. For example, to write the history of a state department of education, the student should know at least the history of the particular state and of the nation, history of education in the state and in the United States, school administration, and the historical method. In this particular instance, the graduate investigator in question had substantial advanced work in all the fields mentioned. The student may well become acquainted with the different investigational procedures described in this book, through utilizing the available courses and seminars where certain of these methods

[46] W. I. B. Beveridge, *op. cit.*, p. 136-37.

[47] James Rowland Angell, *A History of Psychology in Autobiography*. Vol. 3, *op. cit.*, p. 5.

[48] Cecil B. Williams and Allan H. Stevenson, *A Research Manual*. New York: Harper and Bros., 1940. p. 30. Also see the 1951 edition.

For examples drawn from graduate theses in education see Carter V. Good, A. S. Barr, and Douglas E. Scates, *op. cit.*, p. 72-73.

are analyzed in detail, before definitely formulating his thesis problem. It has even been suggested that, if life were longer and time less fleeting, those engaged in educational research should know the entire range of research in psychology, biology, and sociology, as well as possess basic training in the humanities, history, philosophy, and science.[49]

The content of certain sections of this chapter and of the chapter on library technique, in fact the emphasis of the entire book on problem-solving, suggests that classroom instruction is only one source of training. John Stuart Mill never went to school except to his father. What he learned through personal accomplishment and exacting paternal instruction was further impressed on him by later becoming the tutor of his younger sisters and brothers.[50] It should be remembered, however, that Mill's native equipment was such as to enable him to begin study of Greek at the age of three years.

**Availability of data and method.** Closely related to the criterion of training and personal equipment is that of availability of satisfactory data and an appropriate method. The data under consideration must meet certain standards of accuracy, objectivity, and verifiability. The contemplated problem should be viewed in the light of the possible research approaches.

Earlier pages have already emphasized the desirability of becoming familiar with the purposes served by the several investigational procedures before making a definite choice of the research or thesis topic. One of the things that graduate students in education should try to avoid is the questionnaire complex, the tendency to turn to the questionnaire as an instrument before careful formulation of the problem and before thoughtful consideration of an appropriate method. Investigational methods serve varying purposes. The normative-survey type of research is not expected to yield rigorous data concerning causes. The experimental method is not pointed toward a description of prevailing conditions or practices.

Sometimes a theoretically desirable procedure breaks down under actual field conditions; for example, an experimental investigation of motion pictures in the school, involving eleven thousand children in more than three hundred classes, taught by nearly two hundred teachers.[51] It was impossible for the investigators to keep in close contact with all the centers; consequently conditions could not be kept uniform. In one school keen rivalry developed between the control and experimental teachers. In many schools visual aids other than those contemplated in the experiment were used.

[49] Henry W. Holmes and Others, *op. cit.,* p. 184-86.
[50] Edwin G. Boring, *op. cit.,* p. 217.
[51] Ben D. Wood and Frank N. Freeman, *Motion Pictures in the Classroom.* Boston: Houghton Mifflin Co., 1929. 392 p.
Douglas E. Scates and Charles F. Hoban, *op. cit.,* p. 244.

In other instances teachers were so unfamiliar with the instructional use of motion pictures that exaggerated conditions resulted.

It is pointed out in the chapter on the historical method that certain types of problems defy solution, in terms of available data and techniques, because of the vastness and complexity of the problem (for example, the causes of the fall of the Roman Empire) or because of the loss or suppression of evidence. Probably Channing's survey of the entire sweep of American history will be the last attempted by one author. A doctoral candidate gave up a study of the social and educational attitudes of one thousand school-board members in a particular state when the interview technique seemed the only feasible approach. In turning to another problem, a survey of secondary-school organization in one of the Spanish-speaking countries of South or Central America, he still had to consider the availability of data and method in terms of the language factor, necessary travel, and his knowledge of comparative education.

In certain instances the approach to a problem opens through a fortunate combination of circumstances, increased insight on the part of the investigator, or a change in occupational status or professional assignment.[52] Darwin's trip on the *Beagle* through the South Seas, 1831-36, gave him a magnificent opportunity to observe and collect plants and animals. A graduate student who called on a prominent citizen to investigate a local conflict received the reply that everything was quiet; a more experienced worker, who understood the sense of local pride possessed by the community "booster," found that bitter racial conflicts actually were in progress in the locality. As pointed out earlier, a school principal was able to study the departmentalized elementary school when his school board sent him on a field trip to observe the reorganization procedures employed in a selected group of cities. Specialists in music education and in trades and industries were enabled to make state-wide surveys of the opportunities in their respective fields on appointment to state supervisory positions.

**Special equipment and working conditions.** The chapters dealing with the several research methods include descriptions of the special sources, equipment, and working conditions commonly represented in the several types of investigation—historical, survey, experimental, case, and genetic. Consideration is given earlier in the present chapter to personal qualifications and to training in the use of special techniques and of physical or material equipment.

It should be emphasized that the quality of scientific work resides not in the ornateness of the laboratory equipment or the complexity of the

[52] Gardner Murphy, *op. cit.*, p. 119.
Emory S. Bogardus, *op. cit.*, p. 4-5.

measuring and recording instruments, but in the soundness of the thinking and the validity of the evidence for solution of the problem.[53] The major purpose of equipment is to refine the process of observation: to provide control of conditions and accuracy or permanence of recording. The most important instrument (element) in research is the mind of man.

As early as 1879, when Stanley Hall was in his thirties, he exposed the fallacy of theatrical methods and "brass-instrument" psychology. He insisted that curves, instruments, and flashing charts would not insure the accuracy of a doubtful generalization, and objected to the fad of reducing everything to mechanics and motion, a movement that was spreading in the 1870's.

Desirable as elaborate equipment and adequate financial support may be, there are many instances of problem-solving outside the laboratory or study. Helmholtz said that after he had been working on a problem for some time happy ideas for a solution came to him at some place other than his working table. Darwin was riding in his carriage when his theory of evolution came to him. Watt was walking on Sunday afternoon when he invented the condensing steam engine. Morse conceived the telegraph on a return trip from Europe. The aria of the beautiful quartet in the "Magic Flute" came to Mozart while playing billiards.

It sometimes has been claimed that an unexpected insight (or intuition), even in sleep, brings forth the solution to a problem. Scientific discoveries probably do not take place spontaneously, but what appear to be sudden insights may come from a mind with a rich background of experience or knowledge. Certain conditions are favorable to the emergence of solutions to problems; for example, freedom from competing problems or worries and periods of relaxation or sleep.

Improvised laboratories sometimes have produced remarkable results. Many men of genius, and others of lesser talents, have a drive and a power of concentration to accomplish their tasks in spite of the handicaps of working conditions, as illustrated earlier in this chapter.[54] The Curies conducted their long search for radium in a shed that had been a dissecting room. Bell experimented on his telephone in a Salem cellar and in a Boston attic. Pasteur discovered pasteurization in an old room that had been a cafe. Goodyear "stumbled across" vulcanization of rubber in a New England kitchen.

[53] T. A. Boyd, *op. cit.*, p. 55-62.
W. I. B. Beveridge, *op. cit.*, xii + 171 p.
A. A. Roback, *op. cit.*, p. 158.
[54] Edward L. Thorndike, *A History of Psychology in Autobiography*, Vol. 3, *op. cit.*, p. 267-68.
Edwin G. Boring, *op. cit.*, p. 159, 209-10.
A. A. Roback, *op. cit.*, p. 129.

Interesting examples may be cited in the field of psychology. William James contended that he began instruction in experimental psychology at Harvard either in 1874-75 or 1876 with equipment described by Stanley Hall as a "tiny room under the stairway of Agassiz Museum . . . with a metronome, a device for whirling a frog, a horopter chart, and one or two bits of apparatus."

E. L. Thorndike candidly mentions an extreme ineptitude and distaste on his part for using machinery and physical instruments. He regrets the absence in his training of a systematic course in the use of standard physiological and psychological apparatus and of extended training in mathematics, modestly suggesting that his work might have been better had he been "at home" with apparatus for exposing, timing, registering, and the like.

Two more recent illustrations [55] in psychology are taken from the autobiographies of Hull and Thurstone. Clark L. Hull conceived the idea of building a machine that would do nearly all of his correlation work automatically. Although Hull could not make mechanical drawings and his assistant could not read such drawings, they got along very well by making marks free-hand on bits of paper at the mechanic's work bench. Hull had an idea of how the wheels should go around to do certain things, and so did the mechanic; therefore, they easily understood each other.

L. L. Thurstone, another psychologist, has described certain favorable domestic conditions for his work, including relaxing summer vacation periods and the participation of his wife in research and writing. Thelma Thurstone has been a partner in the projects in psychometric research, including daily laboratory work, planning of projects, supervision of test construction, and interpretation of results.

Descartes once left Paris in disgust because his friends insisted upon disturbing him in his quarters. During the very productive period of twenty years before his death, he is said to have lived in thirteen places and in twenty-four houses, with his whereabouts unknown except to a few intimates who respected his seclusion and forwarded communications to him. Driven by financial pressure, James Mill composed several volumes of the *History of India* at one end of a table, while his son, John Stuart Mill, at the other end was the pupil of the father, among other things learning Greek and interrupting his father for the meaning of every new word.

There is a trend, especially in psychology, for research workers to use similar methods and tools, so as to permit comparisons between the results of different investigations. When research on maze learning began, each investigator designed his own maze; as to subjects one experimenter studied

[55] Herbert S. Langfeld, *op. cit.*, p. 143-62, 295-321.

the learning of frogs, another used white rats of the Wistar strain, and another bred his own rats, while a fourth investigator collected stray cats. At the present time, experimenters using mazes are in fairly general agreement on the multiple-unit maze as a standard. Even greater standardization exists in the sensory fields by way of electronic equipment, standard units of measurement, Munsell colors, and similar developments.[56]

**Sponsorship and administrative coöperation.** In graduate departments of instruction it is common practice for the thesis to be sponsored by a faculty adviser in whose area of specialization the problem lies. When a committee gives this advice, as is usually the case for the doctoral dissertation, the chairman is the major adviser. In selecting his problem, the candidate will do well to consider the availability of a particular professor for the duration of the graduate program. Leave of absence, a heavy teaching schedule, an already excessive number of advisees, concentration on writing or research, numerous speaking engagements, ill health, or personality difficulties on the part of a particular professor may render him relatively unavailable for additional assignments to the extent that the graduate student may wish to turn elsewhere for thesis guidance or at least to consider the hazards involved in securing the necessary conferences and advice. It is recognized that the beginning graduate student often lacks the factual background to act judiciously in choosing an adviser; however, students have a way of educating one another about the problems of a particular department or institution and about the characteristics and idiosyncrasies of individual professors.

In many instances the sponsorship of a department, institution, or school system is necessary to collect certain types of data or to use special sources. Permission from the responsible school officers usually must be secured to administer tests to children, to interview employees or to distribute questionnaires among them, to observe pupils and teachers at work, to rate school buildings or equipment, to introduce innovations in materials and methods, or to study problem pupils. Official permission ordinarily is necessary to use the minutes of a board of education or the records of a school unit—state, county, city, or smaller local system. As a general rule, a graduate student would be unwise to attempt a thesis problem where administrative coöperation is withheld. Occasionally an institution or school system is willing to sponsor officially a thesis that relates closely to the work of the sponsoring organization or promises to solve one of its pressing problems, although unfortunate experiences in public relations have rendered most universities and administrative officers wary about too frequent use of this practice.

[56] Dael Wolfle and Others, *op. cit*

**Costs and returns.** Graduate instruction and research are expensive. Fortunately for the student, only a part of the cost is passed on to him. Endowments, gifts, taxes, and grants from foundations make possible reduced tuition rates, as well as scholarships, fellowships, and assistantships. These same sources of revenue have provided financial assistance for certain types of theses and investigations, such as those involving large-scale testing programs, extended tabulations, intricate laboratory equipment, or expensive travel. In advance of final selection of the thesis problem, the candidate must consider carefully his own financial resources, in the light of such facilities and assistance as can be provided by the institution.

Graduate students are not alone in encountering financial difficulties in pursuit of their objectives. Thorndike says that he made it a rule early in his career to spend so little and earn so much as to be free from financial worry, and in so doing became a person of considerable means. It seems the rule rather than the exception for inventors, scholars, and scientists to meet pecuniary problems in connection with their investigations, writing, and research.[57]

Newton at one time in his life was so poverty-stricken that he had to ask relief from paying the weekly dues of a shilling to the Royal Society. Charles Goodyear, after discovering how to vulcanize rubber, died in debt to the extent of $200,000. John Fitch, discouraged and poverty-stricken after his series of experiments with the steamboat, took his own life. LeBlanc discovered how to make cheap alkali, but died in a French poor-house. Comte, after losing his position and suffering other reverses, found his income so reduced that he told John Stuart Mill of his difficulties. Mill, with the aid of Grote, the historian, raised about 20,000 francs as a gift for Comte, in order that he might continue study and publication of his books, but after five years Comte was again in financial straits. Herbert Spencer was an invalid most of his life, with a very uncertain income. He put more into his early books than he received from them, since he usually employed an amanuensis. Only within the last few years of his life did he receive any substantial revenue from his books, and even in those years the publication of *Descriptive Sociology* took from him a large part of his earnings (because this writing, eight large atlases, was largely the work of secretaries employed for the purpose).

Some scientists have had large personal resources, which they used in the pursuit of research.[58] Roger Bacon was a member of a wealthy family

[57] Edward L. Thorndike, *A History of Psychology in Autobiography.* Vol. 3, *op. cit.,* p. 270.
Charles A. Ellwood, *op. cit.,* p. 364, 439-40.
T. A. Boyd, *op. cit.,* p. 53-54.
A. A. Roback, *op. cit.,* p. 154-55, 189-90.
[58] J. G. Crowther, *op. cit.,* p. 208, 436.

and probably earned substantial fees while lecturing in Paris between 1236 and 1251. He spent £10,000, in modern money, on the purchase of books, experiments and instruments, journeys to meet scholars, and secretaries. Within a period of eighteen years, Lavoisier received an income of £60,000, much of which was spent on research. Charles Darwin was an English gentleman of wealth and leisure, which provided favorable conditions for his work.

Stanley Hall founded the first psychological journal in English (except *Mind*), the *American Journal of Psychology,* in 1887. It is not generally known that Hall found it necessary to sink $8000 (a fortune in those days) of his own money in this publication, in order to keep it going.

With very little help, Titchener carried on a voluminous correspondence with hundreds of colleagues and even with young men barely out of graduate school. His letters were carefully written and never mere routine. Much of his time and energy went into things extraneous to psychology proper, since he typed most of his letters and editorial comments, with added material in script.

The illustrations just cited suggest that the work of the scholar or scientist guarantees no fixed monetary return. Often the chief reward is the satisfaction of an intellectual interest in the solution of a problem. Pasteur declared, "I could never work for money, but I would always work for science," while Agassiz said, "I have no time to make money." [59] It is true that the work of both these scientists was supported by educational institutions. For the graduate student, who usually is interested in tangible returns on completion of his program of advanced study, there is reasonable expectation of one or more of the following developments: advancement on the salary schedule, promotion, enhanced reputation, or cultivation of an area of specialization. (In Chapter 1 is a more extended discussion of the satisfactions and rewards of research.)

**Hazards, penalties, and handicaps.** The illustrations of the preceding section indicate the pecuniary hazards that frequently attend the pursuit of scientific work. In the selection of certain types of problems, the worker may well consider other special hazards, penalties, or handicaps [60] of a personal, social, or professional character, not necessarily with the thought of avoiding or giving up a particular study but of making the choice with open eyes. For example, there are agencies that have sought to place restrictions on animal experimentation in psychology, medicine, and other fields, with the result that the American Psychological Association finds it desir-

59 T. A. Boyd, *op. cit.,* p. 283-91.
60 Gardner Murphy, *op. cit.,* p. 87.
A. A. Roback, *op. cit.,* p. 141-42, 185-86.
Herbert S. Langfeld, *op. cit.,* p. 143-62.

able to maintain a Committee on Precautions in Animal Experimentation, which has available a printed list of rules and precautions for such research. Pressure groups and institutional taboos have handicapped the investigation of problems of social hygiene and sex in the fields of sociology, psychology, and education. Opposition frequently is voiced against the reporting of results that run counter to the beliefs or programs of certain economic, social, patriotic, or religious groups.[61]

When Fechner was suffering from what today might be called a "nervous breakdown," he increased his difficulties by undertaking the study of positive after-images from bright stimuli, particularly the sun. This produced violent pain in his eyes and partial blindness, from which he did not recover for several years.

It may be that a nervous disorder endured by William James during his twenties was of some advantage in his intellectual development, since this condition gave him first-hand experience with and psychological insight into abnormal conditions, and took him abroad in search of a cure, with profitable visits to intellectual and artistic centers of Europe.

Edward B. Titchener was a man of majestic bearing whose tic (blinking) probably appeared to the young student as a strange flaw in a famous psychologist, but the personality of the great man was so natural and spontaneous that during the course of the seminar or lecture the tic was disregarded and forgotten.

Clark L. Hull, the psychologist, was handicapped by ill health. A severe attack of typhoid fever was almost fatal and left him with a generalized bad memory for names. Later an attack of poliomyelitis left one leg badly paralyzed and crippled. When he began studying the 1400 pages of James' *Principles of Psychology* his eyes were so weak that his mother read the material to him, although later his eyes improved to the extent that he was able to read normally.

Galileo was highly praised by some, ridiculed by others, and summoned before the Inquisition at the age of seventy-eight to recant his so-called heretical teachings. With health broken, he returned home to continue productive work. Totally blind at eighty, he continued work, dictating to some of his faithful disciples.

In the chapter on the historical method is an account of the physical

---

[61] H. K. Beale, *Are American Teachers Free?* New York: Charles Scribner's Sons, 1936. xxiv + 855 p.
William Gellerman, *The American Legion as Educator.* Contributions to Education, No. 743. New York: Teachers College, Columbia University, 1938. 280 p.
Bessie L. Pierce, *Citizens' Organizations and the Civic Training of Youth.* New York: Charles Scribner's Sons, 1933. xviii + 428 p.
Bruce Raup, *Education and Organized Interests in America.* New York: G. P. Putnam's Sons, 1936. 238 p.

handicaps encountered by the historians Parkman and Prescott, who for long periods were almost blind. At one time Parkman used a frame with parallel wires to guide his black crayon as he wrote.

Müller and Mill present a contrast between certain physical and mental hazards in a too intense life of research and scholarship.[62] Karl Otfried Müller, archaeologist and historian, worked too strenuously in the hot July days in the Greek climate, caught fever when digging at Delphi, and died a victim of his thirst for knowledge. When urged to take care of himself, Müller replied, "No siesta for me. My brain is as strong as iron: I need not cover my head for fear of sun-stroke. All this spring the weather has been cold and damp. Your sun of Attica is not half so terrible as he is described."

The type of stern and uncompromising education received by precocious John Stuart Mill from his father meant that he had no boyhood friends, no child's play, and little youthful reading. The son's curriculum included Greek at three years of age; Æsop's *Fables,* the *Anabasis,* all of Herodotus, some of Plato, and many other standard Greek works before eight; and Latin, geometry, and algebra at eight years. Later, there were several years of mental depression when Mill, brought up in an austere personal life to scorn all emotion, began to doubt the value of his political and social activities.

To be the butt of ridicule is frequently the price paid by pioneers. People laughed at Fulton's steamboat, Stephenson's locomotive, the Wright brothers' flying machine, the horseless carriage, the achievement tests of James M. Rice, and at the I.Q. Harvey needed unusual courage to announce the amount of blood he calculated that the heart pumped out, and feared injury to himself from the envy of others. He was ridiculed and abused, with the result that his practice suffered, and only after a struggle of some twenty years was the theory of the circulation of the blood generally accepted. In modern times Einstein suffered an organized campaign of persecution and ridicule in Germany. Röntgen's first announcement of his discovery of x-rays was greeted with ridicule. Certain scientists have demonstrated an aptitude for persuading the public to accept their discoveries, whereas other investigators have failed in interpretation and implementation because of lack of skill in human relations. Harvey had the good sense to dedicate his book to King Charles, drawing a parallel between the king and realm, and the heart and body. Although some scientists and scholars have failed in the area of human relations, the candidate for a graduate degree or a

[62] James W. Thompson and Bernard J. Holm, *op. cit.,* p. 497.
Edwin G. Boring, *op. cit.,* p. 217-18.

university position can hardly afford to do so, as long as no sacrifice of principle is involved.[63]

Even to specialize in the field of psychology at one time required considerable courage and hardihood on the part of the candidate; for example, Joseph Jastrow, who had received the world's first Ph.D. degree in psychology in 1886 from Johns Hopkins, at that time could find no post open to him. Later, in 1888, Jastrow was appointed to the staff at the University of Wisconsin and immediately made plans for organizing a psychological laboratory.

At times it has been hazardous for the graduate student or younger staff member to cross swords with a senior professor. Hugo Münsterberg disagreed with Wundt in setting up a problem in the Leipzig laboratory and was shifted to another (innocuous) problem which was accepted as a doctoral dissertation. Later Münsterberg used the rejected dissertation for another purpose, but lost the favor and friendship of Wundt and was thereby seriously handicapped in securing a position.

These are some of the penalties of "pioneering," although in the interest of accurate perspective for the modern student of the psychological and social sciences it should be said that ordinarily he will not encounter such difficulties. Many agencies and institutions have contributed toward smoothing the path of the research worker of today.

**Time factor.** Graduate students quite properly are interested in the length of time necessary to complete the program for an advanced degree. They are eager to begin or to continue their professional careers and usually have limited financial resources. As a general rule, the minimum amount of graduate work for the Master's degree is one year, and for the Doctor's degree, three years. The time required for completion of the thesis depends on the variables of the student, problem, department, adviser, and institution. Most students have their course work finished before the thesis is completed. Few good Doctors' dissertations are accepted with less than the equivalent of a full year of work, while a Master's thesis of similar quality may require half that time. By their very nature, historical, experimental, case, and longitudinal genetic studies frequently require more time than the several types of normative-survey work. Many students have found it profitable both intellectually and professionally to do at least part of their graduate work in full-time residence during the academic school year rather than to depend entirely on the part-time courses of the regular year or the summer-session program. In general, competent graduate students find

[63] W. I. B. Beveridge, *op. cit.,* p. 103-107.
A. A. Roback, *op. cit.,* p. 131-32, 193-94.

that they can complete the thesis or dissertation with a reasonable expenditure of time.

For many types of scientific investigation, relatively long periods of sustained attention are necessary, rather than an hour or two of spare time per day or week. As Cannon aptly says: [64]

> This time element is essential. The investigator may be made to dwell in a garret, he may be forced to live on crusts and wear dilapidated clothes, he may be deprived of social recognition, but if he has time, he can steadfastly devote himself to research. Take away his free time and he is utterly destroyed as a contributor to knowledge.

Lest the beginning graduate student and others become too impatient with the time requirements for careful training and research, a few examples may be cited from the lives and works of famous scholars and scientists.[65] Copernicus worked nearly forty years on his problem before he published his only book, on the heliocentric theory of the motions of the planets. Galileo's *Dialogues Concerning Two New Sciences* was published in 1638 when he was seventy-four years of age, after he had spent fifty years in collecting and developing the material. John Locke did not attain fame as a philosopher until the publication of his *Essay* in 1690 (begun in 1671), when he had reached the age of fifty-seven.

William James was relatively slow in his development and program of writing, and required considerable persuasion to complete a textbook in psychology, his famous *Principles of Psychology* (1890), after twelve years of hard work. Certain divergent or contradictory elements of his background and personality may have contributed to his comparatively slow development and to periods of indecision. These forces included his native endowment, environment, temperament, artistic bent, diversified schooling, a nervous ailment, studies in Germany, French contacts, wide reading, and perhaps his Celtic origin. The contribution of James as a great psychologist and philosopher, however, was enhanced by a personality of unusual magnetism, charm, spontaneity, and sincerity.

On the other hand, George Berkeley, Locke's immediate successor in British philosophy, published his two important contributions in successive years, 1709 and 1710, when he was about twenty-five. Berkeley's philo-

[64] W. I. B. Beveridge, *op. cit.*, p. 149-50.
Quoted from W. B. Cannon, *The Way of an Investigator.* New York: W. W. Norton and Co., 1945.
[65] Edwin G. Boring, *op. cit.*, p. 169-70, 179, 186-88, 495.
J. G. Crowther, *op. cit.*, p. 308, 513.
T. A. Boyd, *op. cit.*, p. 177-81.
James W. Thompson and Bernard J. Holm, *op. cit.*, p. 76-79, 429, 548.
Charles Oman, *On the Writing of History.* New York: E. P. Dutton and Co., 1939. p. 208-11.
A. A. Roback, *op. cit.*, p. 99-100, 138-53.

sophical successor, David Hume, also matured early, publishing his most important work at twenty-eight; later in life, court fame and society distracted him from greater philosophical accomplishment.

John Dewey was only twenty-six years of age when he produced his *Psychology*, which means that he was writing this book at the age of twenty-four or twenty-five. This textbook is regarded as a remarkable feat for a man in the middle twenties, and even seventy years later could be read with profit because of the prophetic vein in which it was written. He continued to write and produce through a long life of nearly ninety-three years, with a considerable part of his published work appearing after his retirement from Columbia University at the age of seventy.

Both time and money have been expended freely in science and invention. Darwin spent more than twenty years in preparation of the *Origin of Species*. Pasteur used five years to find his remedy for hydrophobia. Faraday needed ten years to "change magnetism into electricity." Fifteen years of research and $5,000,000 went into the discovery of synthetic indigo. Many years of work and $3,500,000,000 produced the atomic bomb.

Comprehensive historical writing is especially time-consuming. Edward Gibbon, before beginning his *Decline and Fall of the Roman Empire,* considered for several years the possibility of undertaking various historical projects. However, when he visited Rome in 1764 his decision was made with almost dramatic suddenness. Then for four years he was in a period of doubt as to formulation of the project. Thorold Rogers wrote his monumental work, *A History of Agriculture and Prices in England,* in seven volumes over a period of forty-two years, compiled from original and contemporaneous records. Ludwig von Pastor spent fifty years of hard labor on his fifteen-volume work, *History of the Popes.* In writing two volumes he visited eighty libraries and examined more than six hundred printed books, in addition to using hundreds of documents. Pastor was very nearsighted from constant poring over documents and subject to occasional breakdowns due to his strenuous application, but possessed tremendous powers of concentration.

Certain research workers and scholars have planned studies of such large scope as to prove impossible of accomplishment, even within a long lifetime. One view holds that it serves society better to complete a few worthwhile projects than to spend a lifetime preparing for a work of such large proportions that it is no more than started when the would-be author passes on. Lord Acton began early to read history and was granted a long life, with ample leisure and a private library of large dimensions, but died leaving behind him only one good book, some lectures, and a large number of scattered reviews and essays. He had in mind a great book that was never quite clear in scope to his friends who knew him best, but apparently required the accumulation of such a mass of detailed data that no one mind could have formulated it completely. In this instance, and in many other cases, the goal of an ideally complete and perfect book may have prevented the writing of several good books that might have been or could have been written by able scholars.

Money, equipment, and personnel resources will not necessarily shorten the period of development and maturation essential for successful research. When Charles F. Kettering was doing research for the National Cash Register Company, he estimated that a certain project would require a year for completion. When asked to double his force and reduce the time to six months, his reply was, "Do you think that by putting two hens on the nest a setting of eggs could be hatched out in less time than three weeks?" [66]

## STATEMENT OF THE PROBLEM

**Thesis topic compared with statement of the problem.** As a rule, the title of a thesis can do no more than name the topic or particular field represented. The necessary space in the introductory chapter, preferably in the first or early paragraphs, should be used to give an adequate statement of the problem. To use the question form in this introductory section, as compared with a declarative statement, has some advantages by way of sharpening and clarifying the problem to be attacked, although both forms are generally acceptable. Whatever the form of statement, the phrase "a study to show" should be avoided, so as to shun the appearance of initial bias, since the purpose of research is to seek an impartial answer to the question proposed rather than to prove something.

The more common errors in phrasing research or thesis topics are: (1) to list broad fields or areas of study instead of naming specific problems; (2) to narrow or localize the topic to the point where it may prove too small or too unimportant for thesis purposes; and (3) to employ wording of an unscientific, rhetorical, hortatory, emotional, or biased character, or to imply emphasis on undigested data or the "voice of experience."

**Broad areas of many problems.** Most graduate advisers have had the experience of hearing beginners in research propose as thesis topics broad fields in which many specific research problems lie. For the sake of emphasis, the phrasing of some of the following fields or areas is exaggerated beyond what even the most naive student would suggest as a thesis topic.

1. Historical and comparative education in medieval and modern times
2. The supervision of schools

[66] T. A. Boyd, *op. cit.*, p. 177.

3. The learning of school children
4. Adolescent and child psychology
5. Teaching of Latin and classical languages
6. School boards of the United States
7. School buildings, apparatus, equipment, and supplies
8. School textbooks, the curriculum, and courses of study
9. Character education
10. Personality development
11. Guidance and counseling
12. Vocational education
13. Student teaching
14. The three R's
15. Educational finance and school costs
16. Public education in the United States
17. Child and genetic psychology
18. The effect of various factors on learning
19. The effect of various factors on growth and achievement
20. Public relations, educational interpretation, and professional ethics.

**Restricting an overly broad topic.** As the result of preliminary work on a too extensive problem, the topic frequently is narrowed to something more workable. The following changes in the tentative dissertation topics of doctoral candidates represent a common occurrence in graduate work (and possibly an intermediate stage in formulating the title): from a history of music in general to the historical development of a single college of music; from a history of the work in higher education of a religious denomination to the history of a particular college in the group; from a decade of controversy to a decade of controversy in American higher institutions; from a study of the classification tests used in penal institutions to the evaluation of intelligence tests used for the classification of persons in a girls' industrial school; and from a study of pupil performance in long division to the verbal thought and overt behavior of children during learning of long division. Some of the revised titles seem rather broad and probably underwent further restriction.

The student who proposed as a thesis topic "The Teaching of English as Revealed in the Courses of Study of the Countries of the English-Speaking Nations of the World" took in a vast geographical and professional territory. The "teaching of English" is a field extending through all levels of instruction—elementary, secondary, and higher. It includes many problems of objectives, selection and organization of materials, teaching and learning procedures, and measurement of results. There are thousands of English courses of study in the United States alone, extending over several decades. The English-speaking countries encircle the globe. Such facts may explain in part why this student proceeded in the muddled fashion described later in the chapter.

**Broadening a too restricted or excessively localized topic.** Occasionally, as the result of experience and added insight, a provisional thesis topic proves too narrow or too localized to promise satisfactory results. The student who first explored the possibility of a biographical treatment of a well known supervisor of music in a large city broadened his study to cover the historical development of school music in the particular city system. Other illustrations of the broadening of thesis topics are from the history of a small, relatively new high school in a city system to the history of the local school system itself; from the administration of the student-government organizations in the secondary schools of a particular area to the organization and administration of the citizenship and extra-curricular programs in the same schools; from a study of La Fontaine's fables in French elementary and secondary education to consideration of the fable in its relation to contemporary French education; and a shift from eighteenth-century English romances to the English fiction of the same period as a source of information concerning the education of the time. In certain of these illustrations of actual changes made in titles, the revisions are in the direction of rather broad topics. Sometimes one part of a tentative topic is broadened while another part is narrowed; for example, from an investigation of the relation between the hearing span and reading rate and comprehension to a study of the visual and auditory determinants of the rate of reading.

**Unscientific, hortatory, argumentative, or raw-data topics.** The topics listed below involve excessive rhetoric, special pleading, debate tactics, emotional bias, unassimilated experiences, or other procedures of an unscientific character. For the sake of emphasis, the wording of some of the topics is exaggerated, although many of the titles will have a familiar sound to thesis advisers who have had extensive experience with beginners in graduate work.

1. An argument for free textbooks in a post-depression period
2. Reasons pro and con for the popular election of the city superintendent of schools
3. Talks to mothers' clubs on child and adolescent psychology
4. A position against homogeneous grouping, based on the concept that in a democracy the voice of the people should rule
5. A running stenographic record of one hundred lessons by skilled teachers, illustrating the socialized recitation
6. Dictaphone records of fifty well planned homeroom programs
7. The code of ethics adopted unanimously by the two hundred teachers of a small city system
8. Successful disciplinary devices used by a principal with forty years of experience
9. Talks on guidance to junior high school boys
10. Reasons and illustrations supporting the point of view that teachers are born and not made

11. Sound films of twenty well received assembly programs
12. The aspirations of the teachers of today for the schools of tomorrow
13. Specimens of creative work (poems, drawings, and handwork) from the activity school
14. Teaching as a great adventure and a life of service
15. An essay on equalization of educational opportunity, based on the concept that the wealth of the state should educate the future citizen, wherever the child and resources may be
16. Talks on social hygiene given by a dean of girls to adolescent girls
17. An impressive discourse on the need for return to fundamentals in education, by a charter member of the essentialist movement
18. An argument against pedagogical dictatorship, with a special plea for democracy in administration and supervision
19. A principal's experiences in public relations and educational interpretation
20. The activity concept, pupil activity versus teacher domination.

**Topics with reasonable restriction and objective approach.** Below are two lists of research projects that represent a reasonable restriction of the title and imply an objective approach, although further delimitation in title may seem desirable in certain instances. These problems have been worked out as doctoral dissertations in well known graduate schools and are psychological or sociological in character. Many of the illustrations of the several preceding pages are from the field of education.

### Illustrative Research Projects in Psychology

Emotional Factors Affecting the Pacifist
The Dream: Its Source, Formation, Meaning, and Therapeutic Value
A Comparison of Objective Criteria of Industrial Performance with Age
Prediction of the Adjustment and Academic Performance of College Students by a Modification of the Rorschach Method
Clothing and Appearance: Their Psychological Implications for Teen-Age Girls
Psychological Variables in the Behavior of Voters
The Effects of Practice on the Factorial Equations for Visual, Spatial, and Perceptual Tests
An Analysis of Different Methods Used in the Prediction of General University Achievement
Changes in Motor Performance as a Function of Conditions of Practice and Nature of Rests
Speech Development During the First Year of Life: A Quantitative Study
The Effects of Pacing and Distribution on Intercorrelations of Motor Abilities
A Comparative Study of Psychological Factors Involved in the Responses of Mentally Retarded and Normal Boys to Arithmetic Problems
Patterns of Performance on the Revised Stanford-Binet and Arthur Point Scales as Related to Success on the Metropolitan Achievement Test
Individual Differences in the Frequency and Affective Character of Childhood Memories
The Reliability of a Set of Problem Categories for Use in the Clinical Counseling of College Students
Screening the Neuro-Psychiatrically Unfit Selectee from the Armed Forces

Electroencephalographic Studies of Behavior Problem Children

An Evaluation of the Thematic Apperception Test for the Study of Certain Personality Factors by Comparison with Autobiography

Psychological Research and Services in an Army Air Forces Convalescent Hospital

Prediction of Success in Learning to Fly Light Aircraft

An Evaluation of Non-Directive Psychotherapy

A Comparison of Chronic Delinquents and First Offenders of Normal or Superior Intelligence

A Comparison of College Students Classified by a Psychological Clinic as Personality Maladjustment Cases and as Vocational Guidance Cases

A Historical Evaluation of Psychoanalysis

A Study of the Genesis and Dynamics of Psychopathic Personality.


### Illustrative Research Projects in Sociology

A Study of the Cultural Evolution of an Indiana Agricultural Community

Upland Southerner and Yankee in the Old Northwest: A Study in Cultural Adjustment

A Sociological Survey of Disease in Four Alleys in the National Capital

Differential Concepts of Parenthood

The All-Negro Society in Oklahoma

One Hundred Years of Public Services for Children in Minnesota

The Social Categories of Friendship

Changes in Race Accommodation in a Southern Community

The Attitudes of Rural and Urban High School Students toward the Values of Rural Living

Some Personal, Family, and Home Farm Factors Related to the Dissociation of Sons from Parental Farm Families

A Family-Centered Program of Rural Reconstruction in West China, with Special Emphasis on the Preschool Child

Efforts of Various Nations to Check the Decline in the Rate of Population Growth

European Migrations in the Interwar Period

Differential Fertility in Louisiana

Tradition and Change in the Status of Chinese Women

The Building Workers: A Study of an Industrial Subculture

Factors Associated with Negro Unemployment in Urban United States

The Relationship between Certain Factors in the Home Background and the Qualities of Leadership Shown by Children

A Sociographic Study of the Friendship Patterns on a College Campus

The Methodist Church and the Problem of War and Peace: An Analysis in Social Understanding

The Relative Roles Played by Clergymen and Physicians as Counselors Regarding Selected Types of the Emotional Problems of Young People

The Social Significance of the Educational Aspects of the Coöperative Movement

The Relationship between Attitude and Information Concerning the Japanese in America

The Adjustment of the Lutheran Church to Social Change in the Modern World

The Changing Role of the College Nisei During the Crisis Period: 1931-1943

Social Factors Affecting Participation in Rural Adult Educational Programs

The Oxford Group Movement: A Typological Analysis

The Anarchist Movement in the Nineteenth Century: A Social Psychological
  Study
The Rural-Urban Fringe—an Interstitial Area: A Study of the Transitional
  Area Surrounding the Urban Center of Madison, Wisconsin.

**Ways to state the problem.** Earlier in this chapter is a suggestion that
the question form of stating the problem has possible advantages by way
of sharpening the issue, although a declarative statement of the purpose
probably is more common and is quite acceptable. There are at least the
following variations in form for stating the problem, from which a choice
may be made in accordance with the preference of the investigator and the
requirements of the problem.[67]

1.  A question or questions
    *a.* A single question
    *b.* Several questions
    *c.* A single question followed by several sub-questions
2.  Declarative statement
    *a.* A single statement
    *b.* A single statement containing several phases
    *c.* A series of complete statements
    *d.* A general statement followed by subordinate statements
3.  Statement followed by restatement in the form of a question
4.  A statement followed by a series of theses.

A number of examples, illustrating the manner in which investigators
have stated their problems, follow. These statements are direct quotations
from the investigations cited in the footnotes.
A study of the interests of youth in the radio, motion picture, and
reading opens with a series of questions: [68]

Is it the medium itself or a major adolescent interest in adventure, humor, or
love which attracts the pupil?
Is one youth so fascinated by the radio and so aural-minded that he will listen
to anything that the loudspeaker offers but will avoid other media?
Do the social attractions of the motion picture theater and the continuous
movement on the screen so condition another pupil to the motion pictures that
he prefers the movies to all other entertainment and limits his leisure interests
to this activity?
Is it possible that the variety of newspaper reading, its appeal to all types of
reading ability, and its increasing use of the picture make such reading preferable
above all others to some adolescents?
Is it the unique form and the brilliant color of the funny book together with
the ease of reading picture stories that attract a youth, and make him peruse

[67] Quoted from Walter S. Monroe and Max D. Engelhart, *The Techniques of Educational
Research.* University of Illinois Bulletin, Vol. 25, No. 19. Bureau of Educational Research
Bulletin, No. 38. Urbana: University of Illinois, 1928. p. 14-20.
For an analysis of the characteristics of introductory statements in 1700 articles see J. R.
Shannon, "Art in Writing for Educational Periodicals: The Introduction." *Journal of Edu-
cational Research* 44:599-610; April 1951.
[68] Quoted from Alice P. Sterner, *Radio, Motion Picture, and Reading Interests.* Contribu-
tions to Education, No. 932. New York: Teachers College, Columbia University, 1947. p. 5-6.

with eagerness any material found in that medium, which in another form h? would reject?

Do other adolescents find that print has for them manifold advantages over all the other media, and thus feel that books are almost the only medium worthy of their attention?

Or is modern youth so adaptable and so accustomed to all these media that his use of any one is due merely to its accessibility and its capacity to satisfy certain interests?

Is it that he seeks wherever he can find them the themes that please him, employing any medium merely as a means for indulging such tastes?

This study [69] will analyze the functioning of sociality, the degree of acceptance with which an individual reacts to others of his own sex and age. It will also examine the consistency of sociality in boys ten to twelve years of age and investigate two dimensions of its functioning, extensity and intensity. Other questions for which answers will be sought are:

What is the relation between sociality and relations with peers?

How accurately do individuals rate themselves in sociality?

What is the relation between self-ratings and self-satisfaction?

How do negatively toned incidents, such as rebuffs or aggressive actions, affect the expression of sociality in situations involving interaction among individuals?

The purpose of this study [70] was to compare three methods of improving the reading speed and comprehension of college freshmen. The three methods are: (1) college work with no special exercises in reading; (2) college work with practice in special reading exercises; and (3) college work with practice in reading the same special exercises under conditions of controlled eye movements. The use of mechanical devices for controlling eye movements is widespread, but the effectiveness of reading under conditions of controlled eye movements, as compared with other means of improving reading, has not been definitely established. The present study attempts to provide information on this point.

The specific problems which were set up for Kitay's study were formulated as follows: [71]

1.  To determine the existence and nature of differences in the life histories and personal outlooks of those who favor and those who oppose the church.

2.  To discover factors associated with the development of favorable and unfavorable attitudes toward religion.

3.  To determine whether conservative or radical religious attitudes are associated with conservatism or radicalism on social issues and whether there is evidence to support the theory of a general conservatism and radicalism in social attitudes.

4.  To find out on what specific social and politico-economic issues religious radicals and conservatives differ most.

[69] Quoted from Ruth E. Hartley, *Sociality in Preadolescent Boys.* Contributions to Education, No. 918. New York: Teachers College, Columbia University, 1946. p. 3.

[70] Quoted from Frederick L. Westover, *Controlled Eye Movements Versus Practice Exercises in Reading.* Contributions to Education, No. 917. New York: Teachers College, Columbia University, 1946. p. 1.

[71] Quoted from Philip M. Kitay, *Radicalism and Conservatism toward Conventional Religion.* Contributions to Education, No. 919. New York: Teachers College, Columbia University, 1947. p. 1-2.

5. To ascertain the productiveness of personal documents, such as autobiography and essay, in an investigation of this nature.

The purpose of this study,[72] broadly stated, was to investigate the effectiveness of a method of teaching arithmetic in which children's immature procedures in dealing with number are accepted as normal and valuable steps toward their achievement of competent, mature behavior with reference to number. More narrowly, the objective of the investigation was to determine the effect upon the arithmetical development of children of their temporary use of certain immature procedures, when careful guidance is given by teachers. These procedures are designated as "intermediate," since they occur between the initial awareness of number and the achievement of mature modes of dealing with number relationships. The study was limited to the development of understanding in the four fundamental processes, on the part of the second-grade children.

*Preliminary problems.*—Two preliminary problems which were basic to the major purpose of the study may be stated as follows:

1. The discovery of the intermediate procedures that were being used by children at the beginning of the study.

2. The selection of those intermediate procedures which showed promise as aids to more mature understanding of number ideas by pupils.

*Sub-problems.*—In the evaluation of a teaching technique in which the immature or intermediate procedures of children are regarded as of central importance, a number of pertinent questions arise. Such questions, which may be regarded as sub-problems, include the following:

1. In what ways can experience be provided for all children on the selected intermediate procedures?

2. Is it possible for some children to bypass some intermediate procedures without jeopardizing understanding?

3. Do some children tend to move to more advanced procedures before understanding is present?

4. How can readiness for a more advanced intermediate procedure be determined?

5. Do children willingly discontinue the use of immature procedures?

6. Under what circumstances are less mature methods dropped and replaced by more mature methods?

7. What steps can be taken by the teacher to encourage children to discontinue the use of immature methods?

8. As children are taught intermediate procedures, to what extent is their later thinking characterized by increasingly higher levels of maturity in dealing with number situations?

9. What problems do teachers encounter as they attempt to guide children through succeeding maturity levels in dealing with number situations?

## DEFINITION OF THE PROBLEM [73]

**Ways to define the problem.** The relatively brief introductory statement of the problem should be followed by a more detailed definition and de-

[72] Quoted from Edwina Deans, "The Effect of Certain Immature Procedures on the Learning of Arithmetical Processes by Second-Grade Children." *Abstracts of Graduate Theses in Education, 1944-1953,* Vol. 5. Cincinnati: Teachers College, University of Cincinnati, 1954.

[73] Carter V. Good, "Definition of the Research Problem and Formulation of the Working Hypothesis." *Harvard Educational Review* 13: 77-87; January 1943.

limitation. Although a single study may not include all of the forms of definition listed below, these are the possibilities from which to choose.[74]

1. Analysis of the major problem or problems in terms of subordinate problems
2. Statement of the limits or scope of study
3. Orientation of the problem
    a. A historical account, remote or recent
    b. A survey of previous studies or related studies
    c. An analysis of previous studies or related subjects
    d. Preliminary survey
4. Description of the general nature of the problem
    a. Type
    b. Source
    c. Procedure
5. Statement of limitations of technique employed
6. Recognition of assumptions and implications
7. Importance, value, or significance of study to education
8. Definition of terms.

A "horrible example" that violates all the foregoing procedures for definition of the problem, as well as sound principles for selection and statement of a thesis topic, is reported here at some length. The communication was received by the Commissioner of Education for Alaska.[75]

I am preparing a thesis upon the subject: "The Teaching of English as Revealed in the Courses of Study of the Countries of the English-Speaking Nations of the World." I am writing you for such information and suggestions as you may be able and will kindly give me. I shall certainly appreciate whatever help you may give me along this line. Life is full of duties and we all have our own work to do; but I find that sometimes there are those who from education, training, experience and contacts in life, know off-hand what it would take a long time for others to learn from research and a long period of reading.

Do you know some interesting books on Alaska: her history, her economic problems, commerce, imports, exports, human relations, religion, etc., etc.—everything of interest without our taking so much time "to think clearly" at this time.

Of course, my subject is on Education and English; but these subjects require background which Alaska has.

I have to present my subject in an original way, giving a new slant or fresh ideas or a definite contribution to knowledge.

What is it then that Alaska has or does in a different way from other English-Speaking Countries or "outlying" parts of the United States? (May I state that we in "the States" consider you "an integral part" of the United States just as we do Hawaii. Of course you know these things. Are Alaska, American Samoa, Canal Zone, Guam, Hawaii, Philippine Islands, Puerto Rico, and Virgin Islands —all in the same class educationally as to organization? Alaska has one University and from a perusal of it, you seem to have everything.

---

[74] Quoted from Walter S. Monroe and Max D. Engelhart, *op. cit.,* p. 20-25.
[75] "How Would You Answer This One?" *Alaska School Bulletin* 22:12-13, 15; September 1939.

[Marginal note]: Could you give me the names of a few of the best books on the teaching of English used in Alaska? (All phases or just one branch of the work.)

I wonder if climate would be the determining factor in some cases. Hawaii has her "tropical influences" in her curriculum as does the Philippines, Puerto Rico. (I always think of Cuba and want to include her in the American School System, just as I want to include Canal Zone which is a protectorate. I am always at a loss to know what to do with Canal Zone. She only has about three cities, I believe.)

American Samoa, Guam and the Virgin Islands—(How about Wake Island?) As we think of these, what could we say of them educationally? Could we tell something interesting about them, giving their climate, area, capitals or principal cities and occupations and lead up to the need of a certain kind of education which they have or do not have and give the school census, the educational statistics including the number of teachers and the grades, classification and organization of the schools and the language existing in the islands or outlying parts and the efforts that are being made to instruct the children and the citizens or parents. What dialects have they in these "parts"?

[Note at top of page 2: Did your school children get a chance to see the King and Queen or hear them on the Radio?]

Of course we are interested in Alaska for your sake—and because of the "Gold Rush"—her nearness to Asia—Anthropology,—her fisheries—and I am interested in the Indians and the Esquimeaux and their carvings and also the Art of the Indians as manifested in their carvings on the totem poles, etc., etc.

I am especially interested in the railroad centers of Alaska—the cities visited by Harding and those cities made famous by the passing of Will Rogers. Keeping in mind my thesis, will you tell me something of interest about education in these cities? What Indian or Esquimeaux or other dialects have you in Alaska? I think the Americans speak the same as the Pacific Northwest or Van Couver if they are Canadians. May I hear from you? Thanks.

Very truly yours,

P.S. We are interested in Samoa because of Stevenson. I wonder if very much attention is paid to education in Samoa or Virgin Islands? I wonder what type of education is given there?

**Analysis of the problem into its constituent elements.** Some of the earlier illustrations of this chapter concerning the statement of the problem indicate the manner in which a major problem is subdivided into subordinate questions or problems. The definition of the problem is really the planning of the investigation, with an indication of the data and techniques needed to answer the questions raised. In a well organized report, the conclusions of the last chapter will make specific reference to the purposes stated in the introductory chapter.[76]

The initial formulation of the problem may not hold in all its phases throughout the course of the investigation. In the earlier discussion of this

[76] Max D. Engelhart, "The Defining of Educational Research Problems." *Official Report of 1940 Meeting.* Washington: American Educational Research Association, N.E.A., 1940. p. 22-24.

chapter on sources of problems, it is suggested that the "budding out" of a study may lead to a related issue of more importance than the original project. The necessity for redefinition of the problem under certain conditions, as a matter of intellectual honesty, is stressed by Thorndike, who says that often he has had to do corrective and supplementary experiments and to discard work because in its course a better way was found.[77]

**Limits or scope of the investigation.** Certain of the preceding illustrative statements of problems indicate at least in part the scope of the studies represented. Many of the foregoing examples of thesis topics that were either restricted or broadened in their development illustrate early stages in defining the limits of a particular study. More detailed accounts of the scope of selected investigations are included in a following section on "sources of data and method."

**Orientation and related literature.** The earlier discussions of a systematic program of reading as a source of problems, and of avoidance of unnecessary duplication in the selection of problems, suggest library procedures that should provide the setting for the investigation under consideration and an overview of the related studies. Detailed information concerning use of the appropriate library guides and illustrative reviews of the literature in particular areas are found in another chapter. Even though it may not be feasible in some reports of research to devote a section or chapter to earlier investigations in the same field, the worker himself is obligated to make a critical examination of such related studies. From this survey of the literature may come hypotheses, suggestive methods of research, and comparative data useful in the interpretation of results. In view of this usefulness of the related literature, it is surprising to note the number of published studies and unpublished theses in which the earlier investigations are by-passed or treated only superficially.

Without entering into the details of library technique at this time, selected examples of what constitutes related literature may be given. Studies related to the historical development of the elementary-school curriculum in a southern state include not only earlier curriculum investigations in the same state, but also curriculum studies in other states with similar conditions. Orientation for writing the history of a Negro college is provided by other historical studies of higher institutions for Negroes the country over and of any college in the particular state represented. The history of a municipal university finds its setting in investigations of the development of such institutions in the several states and in studies of higher institutions in general within the particular state. An analysis of the public vote

[77] Edward L. Thorndike, *A History of Psychology in Autobiography*, Vol. 3, *op. cit.*, p. 267.

of a city on issues of school finance is related to other studies of voters' attitudes, made in the fields of education, sociolgy, and political science, and to certain investigations in the area of school finance. An evaluation of modern novels as material for socialized curriculums should include consideration of investigations of the integrated English-social studies program, as well as other analyses of fiction with a social theme.

Ordinarily, textbooks and purely subjective discussions are omitted from the review of related studies, yet there are areas of investigation where well founded insights and shrewd hypotheses are important stimuli to research and as such have a place in the summary of pertinent literature. In fields where research has not yet provided definite and practical conclusions, it may be desirable to report briefly such suggestive literature as is based on careful observation or empirical tryout under close scrutiny.

Earlier in this chapter, the discussion of the part played by the instructional program in the stimulation of problem-solving includes a suggested exercise based on a review of the literature in a particular field. As a part of this exercise it is recommended that the studies analyzed be evaluated in terms of assumptions, sources, techniques, conclusions, applications, and unsolved problems. It is also urged that the related literature be summarized by topics rather than as a "running" bibliography, which means that the conclusions of authors dealing with a particular subtopic should be compared and synthesized.

The challenge to the reviewer of research is to strike a balance between tedious detail and wordiness on the one hand and superficial sketchiness on the other. It should be remembered that a summary of related studies, like the historical narrative, must move forward with reasonable directness and rapidity. The reader cannot expect inclusion of many details in the typical summary, and can go to the original study when necessary to secure additional information. One study is worth a paragraph, whereas another may be disposed of in a sentence. Similar studies on occasion may be grouped to good advantage, with a representative investigation discussed in some detail and the others mentioned as being similar.

Adequate evaluation of research requires background and insight not possessed by the majority of students during their first year of graduate work. As helpful orientation for evaluation, certain suggestions are in order.[78] In describing showy but unsound studies, attention may be directed to hidden weaknesses, assumptions that are not made explicit, crucial factors that are not controlled or measured, important points of procedure that are glossed over without proper reporting, and conclusions

---

[78] Adapted from instructions originally compiled for committee members who prepare issues of the *Review of Educational Research.*

that do not follow rigorously from the facts. In evaluation of studies one must be careful of personal biases. Opinion should not be ventured unless the reviewer has familiarized himself with the work of a given field. Ordinary adjectives expressing approval or praise are omitted; research is expected to be of high quality. Where a study is unquestionably of outstanding merit, some indication of this fact is in order, but more by way of emphasis than direct commendation. When making critical evaluations, the reviewer should avoid a generally denunciatory attitude, or a scathing tone. It should be borne in mind that the available research probably reflects the current level of progress in a given field and, although of slight ultimate value, it may be a necessary step in the direction of more penetrating work. Instead of employing derogatory adjectives, the reviewer should point out weaknesses and suggest possibilities for better work.

**Sources of data and method.** For adequate definition of the problem, sources of data and methods for securing evidence must be carefully selected and clearly outlined in the introductory section of the report. The availability of adequate data, of special equipment, and of a satisfactory technique has already received brief attention in the discussion of criteria for selection of the problem. Some of the preceding illustrations of certain phases of the definition of the problem include limited information relating to sources and techniques. Although the goal of the investigator is to secure the best data obtainable, through use of the most refined technique available, neither data nor method will be perfect. Therefore, as a matter of intellectual honesty and for accuracy of interpretation and reporting, any limitations in sources and procedure must be pointed out, frankly but not apologetically.

The details concerning sources and procedures appropriate to the several types of problems are given in the various chapters devoted to research methods—historical, survey, experimental, case, and genetic. For the present, brief illustrations of the manner in which the definition of the problem includes an account of sources of data and method will suffice.

The general procedure was historical, employing a wide variety of sources. College records include minutes of the board of trustees from the founding of the school in 1837, minutes of the faculty from 1904, catalogues, special bulletins of the college, and student publications. The correspondence of the college presidents (complete from 1904), the diary of an early member of the board of trustees (1845-1866), and the unpublished memoirs of a former faculty member were useful. Records of Muskingum County were helpful in tracing the financial history of the college and its property holdings. A number of studies of the policies of Muskingum College have been published since 1930. Zanesville and New Concord newspapers provided some information not available in college records. Some data were secured through interviews with persons long associated with the college and with the community in which it is located. Local and general historians, investigations of the development of other higher institutions, general works on educational history and theory, and monographs on special problems of higher education provided backgrounds for the present study.[79]

The problem of this study [80] can be stated as an attempt to adjust the social-studies programs of New England schools to the life and problems of New England. The different steps in the solving of this problem are (1) analyzing the works of American regionalists to discover the meanings of regionalism in the social sciences and in American life, in order to indicate the implications of regionalism for the social studies in American schools; (2) surveying and analyzing the works which have dealt with New England as an American region, in order to write a summary analysis of the life and problems of New England; (3) surveying the social-studies programs in New England schools, in order to determine to what extent New England schools are now informing youth about the economy, resources, problems, and recent social trends of New England; (4) formulating a statement of what the social-studies programs of New England schools ought to teach New England youth about the life and problems of New England; and (5) presenting plans for implementing the suggested program for the social studies, and a discussion of the materials available for teaching the regional life of New England, together with a statement of needed materials for educational purposes.

The design of the investigation [81] was to select from a college population of over 100 students, made available for study, the 25 individuals who were most favorable in their attitudes toward the church and the 25 individuals who were least favorable, and to compare them with respect to their life histories, personal data, and social attitudes. These individuals were to be selected on the basis of scores obtained on a scale measuring attitudes toward the church which was administered to the entire group. The whole population was to be utilized in studying the relationship between religious and political, economic, and other social attitudes. The term "attitude" is used throughout this study although verbalized statements of attitude or opinion are really referred to. Attitudes in the strictest sense refer to predispositions or sets toward responding in a given manner. Opinions, however, are a means of inferring attitudes.

The plan involved securing from 152 college students autobiographies and essays on their attitudes, replies to a personal data questionnaire concerning themselves and their parents, and scores on an attitude toward the church scale, a sociological attitude scale, and a politico-economic attitude scale. However, only the autobiographies, essays, and questionnaires of those students who were definitely favorable or unfavorable to the church were to be used in the final analysis. This procedure was adopted in order to limit the number of papers to be read and to make sure that there was a clear-cut separation into groups of differing attitudes.

As has been shown, there have been other studies of reading under conditions of controlled eye movements and reading under ordinary motivated practice, but none of them has met all the requirements for a completely satisfactory

[79] Quoted from John H. Bright, "Historical Development of Present-Day Problems of Muskingum College." *Abstracts of Graduate Theses in Education, 1944-1953,* Vol. 5. Cincinnati: Teachers College, University of Cincinnati, 1954.

[80] Quoted from Royce H. Knapp, *American Regionalism and Social Education.* Harvard Studies in Education, Vol. 30. Cambridge: Harvard University Press, 1947. p. 9-10.

[81] Quoted from Philip M. Kitay, *Radicalism and Conservatism Toward Conventional Religion.* Contributions to Education, No. 919. New York: Teachers College, Columbia University, 1947. p. 19.

comparative study.[82] These requirements are: (1) three equivalent groups—two experimental and one control; (2) adequate numbers in each group—thirty or more; (3) measures on alternate forms of the same battery of tests for all subjects before and after the period of training; (4) a follow-up study to see whether improvement persists and whether improvement in reading is followed by an improvement in academic marks earned; and (5) rigorous insistence that all known factors operating on the two experimental groups shall be the same except for the variable experimental method.

In order to meet the last requirement a special piece of apparatus for controlling eye movements was developed that would permit the use of the same exercises in the same size and style of type under the same illumination for the two experimental groups. A practical requirement, in this connection, was that the experimental set-up should permit the easy and cheap preparation of the exercises for each of the experimental groups. It was further required that the same procedures, instructions, measures, records, and encouragement be used by the same experimenter with the two experimental groups.

**Need for the study.** A straightforward statement of the value of the investigation and of possible application of the results is in order. The two extremes to guard against are an apologetic attitude, in contrast to a claim to discovery of an educational or social panacea. The earlier comments concerning the survey of related studies in a field and of existing practices and needs in a particular area (as sources of problems), as well as the preceding discussions of the factors of novelty and of importance for the field represented (as criteria for selection of the problem), should provide adequate background for a brief introductory statement of the need for the investigation.

**Terminology.** Technical terms and words or phrases with special meanings should be defined; for example, *articulation, integration, correlation, fusion, progressive education, activity method, action research, non-directive therapy*. The Pacific Coast Race Relations Survey had not gone far before it became evident that different research workers were using even such common terms as *race, community,* and *competition* in different ways, and hence were misunderstanding one another.[83] (Assistance in the formulation of definitions can be secured from available dictionaries of educational, psychological, and sociological terms.) [84]

[82] Quoted from Frederick L. Westover, *Controlled Eye Movements Versus Practice Exercises in Reading*. Contributions to Education, No. 917. New York: Teachers College, Columbia University, 1946. p. 18.

[83] Emory S. Bogardus, *op. cit.,* p. 11. Also see:
William J. Goode and Paul K. Hatt, *Methods in Social Research*. New York: McGraw-Hill Book Co., 1952. Chapter 5.

[84] Carter V. Good, Editor, *Dictionary of Education*. New York: McGraw-Hill Book Co., 1945. xl + 495 p.
Philip L. Harriman, *New Dictionary of Psychology*. New York: Philosophical Library, 1947. 364 p.
H. C. Warren, Editor, *A Dictionary of Psychology*. Boston: Houghton Mifflin Co., 1934. x + 372 p.
H. P. Fairchild, Editor, *Dictionary of Sociology*. New York: Philosophical Library, 1944. viii + 342 p.

**Initial assumptions.** Research, like geometry, begins with certain basic assumptions or postulates. In Euclidean geometry a straight line is the shortest distance between two points. In a measurement investigation the postulate may be that whatever is exists in some amount and can be measured. (It should be noted, however, that by means of available techniques and tools certain phenomena can be evaluated only by observing and describing characteristics or behavior, rather than by direct measurement.) In planning research studies and in developing school or community organization, the premise (in a democracy) is that coöperation rather than strife, and respect for the individual rather than rigid regimentation, are desirable. It was assumed for many years that intelligence tests measured innate capacity to learn, but in more recent years some evidence has accumulated to indicate that scores on such tests are affected by environmental and training factors. In an investigation of factors affecting problem-solving ability in arithmetic, the worker assumes a definite correspondence between ability and tested achievement. Most investigations of pupil transportation and of state equalization of school support involve the premise that larger school units are desirable.

To use a more detailed illustration, an analysis of regionalism in relation to the social-studies curriculum opens with five basic assumptions: [85]

The fundamental tenets which underly this study and influence its approach, its method, and its recommendations should be stated at the outset.

1. If schools are to prepare young people for competent adulthood in society, they must always operate within the economic, social, political, and moral ideals and values of society.

2. A fundamental part of the preparation of youth for social competence consists in giving youth the best possible understanding of society.

3. In most American schools the social studies carry the major responsibility for presenting the best possible understandings of society to youth.

4. Since society is in many respects in constant flux, and since new descriptions, interpretations, and analyses are continually being produced, the social studies programs of the schools must reflect these newer findings if they are to function effectively in bringing youth to socially competent adulthood.

5. There is continuous need for educators to analyze developments in the social sciences to the end that recent and vital findings are included within the social-studies programs of the schools.

To the extent that certain of these assumptions are open to question, in the same measure the results of the particular study are subject to challenge. In many investigations the initial assumptions lack the force of a postulate in geometry, resemble a not yet fully tested hypothesis, and are

[85] Quoted from Royce H. Knapp, *American Regionalism and Social Education.* Harvard Studies in Education, Vol. 30. Cambridge: Harvard University Press, 1947. p. 3-4.

Merle Curti and Others, "Propositions." *Theory and Practice in Historical Study:* A Report of the Committee on Historiography. Social Science Research Council Bulletin No. 54. New York: The Council, 1946. Chapter 5.

themselves subjects for further study. (See the next section of this chapter for examples of the working hypothesis.) Many assumptions are not susceptible to validation through known scientific procedures or may lie in the realm of values and philosophy; for example, the premise that respect for the individual rather than rigid regimentation is desirable as a way of life and of education. Much research has been discredited by subsequent investigations that avoided the assumptions on which the earlier studies were based. Since assumptions underlie each step in research, they should be stated not only in the definition of the problem and procedure, but also in connection with the conclusions, of which they are an integral part. In the first section of the chapter bibliography are listed a number of references that include illustrative statements of assumptions or postulates.

## THE WORKING HYPOTHESIS[86]

**Definition and function of the hypothesis.** A hypothesis is a shrewd guess or inference that is formulated and provisionally adopted to explain observed facts or conditions and to guide in further investigation. The man on the street says, in making a deduction that he cannot fully validate at the time, "I have a hunch that . . . ," or "My opinion is. . . ." In a similar situation, the scientist formulates a working hypothesis for testing against the data. Therefore, in a sense, the hypothesis takes the place in research that is held by opinion in everyday life. They differ in that while both hypothesis and opinion are preceded by consideration of the facts, only in the case of the former is it a rule to test by further comparison with the data.

It is difficult to draw a sharp line between hypothesis and theory. The essential difference is one of complexity and extent of testing against the facts. In its initial stages a theory usually is called a hypothesis, but in dealing with more types of data and their logical implications, if the elaborated hypothesis fits the facts, it becomes known as a theory. A law represents an order or relation of phenomena that is invariable under the given conditions and permits of no exception in its operation.

The function of the working hypothesis is guidance in the search for evidence, by way of limiting the area of investigation, sensitizing the worker

[86] Carter V. Good, "Definition of the Research Problem and Formulation of the Working Hypothesis," *op. cit.,* 77-87.

Morris R. Cohen and Ernest Nagel, *An Introduction to Logic and Scientific Method.* New York: Harcourt, Brace and Co., 1934. Chapter 11.

Harold A. Larrabee, *Reliable Knowledge.* Boston: Houghton Mifflin Co., 1945. Chapters 5-12.

William H. George, *The Scientist in Action:* A Scientific Study of His Methods. London: Williams and Norgate, 1936. p. 220-21, 266-67.

William J. Goode and Paul K. Hatt, *op. cit.,* Chapters 6, 7.

W. Edgar Vinacke, *The Psychology of Thinking.* New York: McGraw-Hill Book Co., 1952. xiii + 392 p.

to pertinent data and relationships, and providing a unifying concept.[87] It is true that random search may turn up a multitude of facts, but of such diversity and so unrelated as to add to the difficulties of thinking and problem-solving. In studying delinquency areas, Clifford R. Shaw did not observe at random all facts pertaining to delinquency, but limited himself to the elements suggested by his hypothesis, to the effect that significant differences existed in the rate of delinquency in different areas of the city of Chicago.[88] In experimentation the wording of the hypothesis will determine the particular line along which the experiment is to develop; once expressed, it becomes the groundwork upon which the experiment is built.[89] If the hypothesis is changed before the completion of the experiment, this means that a new experiment is begun.

**Examples of hypotheses.** It is frequently impossible to learn about the rejected hypotheses and false starts in scientific work, because some investigators are reluctant to reveal such information. Since the report usually is prepared at the completion of the study, the reader learns only those details of procedure that the author chooses to include. This situation renders especially welcome such reports as that by Brownell, which is a painstaking evaluation of a device employed in the teaching of fractions in arithmetic, with a detailed account of the various steps and leads followed in the attempt to solve the problem.[90]

In the field of educational finance, there is the hypothesis of the separability of finance and control.[91]

It holds that the allocation of responsibilities for finance and control among local, state, and federal agencies should each be determined by its own rationale rather than on the popular assumption that each flows from the other. Assumption of the validity of this idea underlies the general federal aid bills which have been supported by the National Education Association since the World War. In this period considerable evidence has been brought to the fore supporting it. Most of this evidence has been negative, in the sense of proving that control does not necessarily follow support and demonstrating that many instances where unpredicted controls have followed support, such control was in the bond in the sense that wide discretion was given central administrative authorities. The assumption of the validity of this hypothesis has been one of the motivating forces behind the development of objective measures of ability and need and objective formulas for the expression of the relationship of ability and need.

[87] John Dewey, *How We Think:* A Restatement of the Relation of Reflective Thinking to the Educative Process. Boston: D. C. Health and Co., 1933. p. 167-69.

Allen Johnson, *The Historian and Historical Evidence.* New York: Charles Scribner's Sons, 1926. p. 157-59.

[88] Pauline V. Young, *Scientific Social Surveys and Research.* New York: Prentice-Hall, 1939. p. 65. Also see the 1949 edition.

[89] M. A. Tinker and K. H. Baker, *Introduction to Methods in Experimental Psychology.* New York: D. Appleton-Century Co., 1938. p. 1. Also see the 1947 edition.

[90] William A. Brownell, "An Evaluation of an Arithmetic 'Crutch'." *Journal of Experimental Education* 2:5-34; September 1933.

[91] Quoted from Paul R. Mort, "Research in the Structural Aspects of Educational Finance." *Educational Research.* Washington: American Council on Education, 1939. p. 150.

As a formal approach, use of the "null" hypothesis has become more common in educational, psychological, and social research as the techniques developed by Fisher [92] have become more widely known. According to this procedure, one assumes that no significant difference or relationship exists and then seeks to ascertain the improbability of the null hypothesis.

Leverrier observed certain perturbations in the orbit of the planet Uranus, not explained by the actions of known bodies, and made the inductive inference that the cause was some as yet unobserved planet, whose position and pull he calculated mathematically. Other astronomers, by means of the telescope, found Neptune within one degree of the spot indicated by Leverrier.

Selected illustrations of hypotheses concerned with social problems may be cited.[93] LePlay, in the nineteenth century, was the leader in the attempt to find a concrete method for the investigation of social facts that would furnish a secure inductive basis for the scientific study of human society. His method was that of detailed study of the income, expenditures, and geographical location of individual families, as well as their religious, moral, and social condition. His followers expanded the method until it became virtually the social survey in the broad sense, although with the family remaining as the starting point, including the place, work, property, intellectual culture, and religion of the family, the city and state in which the family was located, contacts with foreign societies, and relations between geographical and social conditions.

As may be deduced from a number of the illustrations cited, the working hypothesis, when checked against the evidence, may emerge as a central theme for purposes of interpretation; for example, the development of three themes in a historical study of music education.[94]

1. Music in the schools has been an important factor in the cultural life of the city. Civic interest in school music has been usually high in Cincinnati.
2. The background of the people who came to live in Cincinnati has exerted a strong influence on the development of public-school music in the city. New Englanders introduced school music and the Germans helped build an outstanding program.
3. One of the educational results of the interaction of these two groups was a systematic method of instruction in music. This system brought considerable fame to the city in the nineteenth century and its success enabled it to resist

---

[92] R. A. Fisher, *The Design of Experiments.* Sixth Edition. Edinburgh, Scotland: Oliver and Boyd, 1951. xii + 244 p.
Max D. Engelhart, *op. cit.,* p. 23.
[93] Charles A. Ellwood, *op. cit.,* p. 411-17.
James W. Thompson and Bernard J. Holm, *A History of Historical Writing,* Vol. 1. New York: Macmillan Co., 1942. p. 103.
[94] Quoted from Charles L. Gary, "A History of Music Education in the Cincinnati Public Schools." *Abstracts of Graduate Theses in Education, 1944-1953,* Vol. 5. Cincinnati: Teachers College, University of Cincinnati, 1954.

the inroads of new educational thought in the twentieth century. The development of this system, its downfall, and the transformation to the present program of music education present a third theme.

Strabo (63 B.C.-24 A.D.) formulated the hypothesis or conjecture that, since the inhabited world was only one-third of the circumference of the globe, which he calculated at 25,200 geographical miles, there might be two or more continents besides those then known. The hypothesis of Columbus was that, since the world is round, he could reach Asia by sailing west. Margaret Mead, in *Growing Up in New Guinea,* started with the postulate that the only way to arrive at any conception of the original nature of the child is to study it as modified by different environmental conditions, observed in a controlled cultural setting.[95]

Other examples [96] may be cited briefly. Fifty hypotheses dealing with social change are grouped under the seven subdivisions of origins, sequence, direction, leadership, propaganda, matrix, and intellectuals. A series of hypotheses about governmental relationships deals with centralization in general, national-state relations, central-local relations, state-local relations, interstate relations, and central and local governments. The chapter on the historical method includes additional examples of the use of hypotheses found in historical research.

A variety of psychological hypotheses may be illustrated briefly.[97] In certain instances the term *theory* rather than *hypothesis* has been employed, but as pointed out above the difference is primarily one of complexity and stage of testing reached. Weber advanced the hypothesis that for each of the senses there is a constant fraction for "just noticeable differences." Hamilton's conception of redintegration, that each impression tends to bring back into consciousness the whole situation of which it has at one time been a part, was overworked, since his hypothesis neglects to explain

[95] Margaret Mead, *Growing Up in New Guinea:* A Comparative Study of Primitive Education. New York: W. Morrow and Co., 1930. 372 p.
Pauline V. Young, *op. cit.,* p. 65.
[96] Goodwin Watson, "Some Hypotheses Concerning Social Change." *Journal of Educational Sociology* 14:9-17; September 1940.
Charles S. Ascher, "Hypotheses Regarding Government Relationships." *Journal of Educational Sociology* 14:18-21; September 1940. Also see:
G. Lowell Field, "Hypotheses for a Theory of Political Power." *American Political Science Review* 45:716-23; September 1951.
Olaf F. Larson and Donald G. Hay, "Hypotheses for Sociological Research in the Field of Rural Health." *Rural Sociology* 16:225-37; September 1951.
Harold N. Lee, "Theoretic Knowledge and Hypothesis." *Psychological Review* 57:31-37; January 1950.
Edgar W. Vinacke, "The Basic Postulates of Psychology." *Scientific Monthly* 67:110-14; August 1948.
Harold Webster, "Dynamic Hypotheses in Psychology." *Psychological Review* 59:169-71; March 1952.
[97] Gardner Murphy, *op. cit.,* p. 83, 105-6, 110-11, 120-21, 124-25, 214-17, 230-31, 282-83, 397-98, 400-401.

the process of forgetting. The associationism of Bain went to an extreme in his explanation of the behavior of a mother in fondling her child, to the effect that warm and soft things are pleasant, hence maternal joy. In criticizing Bain's hypothesis, William James remarked that lonely parents might be supplied with pillows heated to the appropriate temperature. Darwin's working hypothesis was the survival of the fittest, with an organism considered "fit" if, in a given environment, it was well adapted to securing food and to warding off its enemies. Galton's hypothesis that criminality is due to biological and hereditary forces is an extreme instance of neglect of environmental factors. William James' explanation of the emotions in terms of the sequence of events is that we "see the bear, run, and are afraid." The hypothesis of Münsterberg that the more open the neural pathway, the more conscious the mental process attending it, overlooks reflex action and the operation of habitual behavior. The recapitulation concept of G. Stanley Hall, that the child passes through a series of stages similar to those in the life of the racial group, was based on faulty anthropology. Spencer explained play as an outlet for surplus energy, whereas Groos maintained the hypothesis that play is also a preparation for life activities, the exercise of instincts prior to their full development. Lashley has advanced the hypothesis that points in the cortex are "equipotential" in relation to learning. The glandular theory of personality has undergone further testing, after uncritical acceptance in many quarters.

**Sources of hypotheses.** Hypotheses originate from essentially the same background that serves to reveal problems; namely, the knowledge, insight, and imagination that come from a thorough instructional program, wide reading, familiarity with existing practices and needs in the area represented, and first-hand contact with pertinent data. This statement is profusely illustrated in the examples of hypotheses cited in the preceding section, although certain of such concepts eventually proved fallacious, as is true of some of the hypotheses of even the most learned scientists and scholars. Experimentation and measurement are not the main sources of hypotheses, but are means of testing them, although a hypothesis may be the result of a generalization that extends beyond the findings of an earlier investigation or may be an offshoot of a study under way. Analogy is another source of hypotheses, which requires careful use because of the tendency to overlook differences when dealing with similarities.

Dewey suggests that the philosophy of education is a source of the science of education in the degree to which it provides working hypotheses of comprehensive application, which means that hypotheses are intrinsically philosophical in nature, good or bad philosophy as the case may be.[98] He emphasizes that education is in urgent need of direction by large and fruitful hypotheses, a need which also prevails in psychology, sociology, and the social sciences in general.

**Testing of hypotheses.** The hypothesis should be evaluated in terms of agreement with and explanation of the observed facts, absence of conflict with satisfactorily proved generalizations, success for purposes of prediction, simplicity and clarity of statement, and logical consistency.[99] Certain of the examples of hypotheses cited in this chapter and in the chapter on the historical method illustrate the manner in which a particular hypothesis fails to stand up when tested against such criteria.

A single investigation ordinarily involves the formulation and testing of multiple hypotheses rather than one, although many scientists have been reluctant to reveal or have neglected to describe rejected hypotheses.[100] In simpler language, too many investigators have been overly cautious about making and reporting mistakes; scientists who are exceptionally cautious are not likely to make either errors or discoveries. As Whitehead has aptly expressed it, "Panic of error is the death of progress." Humphrey Davy said, "The most important of my discoveries have been suggested to me by my failures." Charles Darwin states in *Life and Letters* that, with the exception of the Coral Reefs, he could not recall a single first-formed hypothesis that had not after a time been given up or greatly modified.[101] In commenting on his work during 1891, including the solution of certain problems in mathematics and physics over which great mathematicians had puzzled in vain, Helmholtz wrote as follows: [102]

But any pride I might have felt in my conclusions was perceptibly lessened by the fact that I knew that the solution of these problems had almost always come to me as the gradual generalization of favourable examples, by a series of fortunate conjectures, after many errors. I am fain to compare myself with a wanderer on the mountains, who, not knowing the path, climbs slowly and painfully upwards, and often has to retrace his steps because he can go no farther—then, whether by taking thought or from luck, discovers a new track that leads him on a little, till at length when he reaches the summit he finds to his shame that there is a royal road, by which he might have ascended, had he only had the wits to find the right approach to it. In my works I naturally said nothing about my mistakes to the reader, but only described the made track by which he may now reach the same heights without difficulty.

[98] John Dewey, *The Sources of a Science of Education.* New York: Horace Liveright, 1929. p. 54-55.
[99] Morris R. Cohen and Ernest Nagel, *An Introduction to Logic and Scientific Method.* New York: Harcourt, Brace and Co., 1934. p. 207-15.
[100] William H. George, *op. cit.*, p. 227-31.
Allen Johnson, *op. cit.*, p. 165-67.
W. I. B. Beveridge, *op. cit.*, p. 58-59.
[101] Allen Johnson, *op. cit.*, p. 166-67.
[102] William H. George, *op. cit.*, p. 229-30.

A strikingly similar view has been expressed by a worker in medical research and physiology, whose pioneer studies have been especially influential in psychology: [103]

Investigators do not march straight to their goal with ease and directness. In their imagination they see a possible fact and they set forth to learn whether their foresight can be realized. Or they come upon something which is puzzling and challenging and which they wish to explain; then they try in various ways to relate it to other phenomena that would solve the riddle. Obstacles and difficulties are sure to be encountered. The search for understanding is an adventure or, more commonly, a series of adventures. If an attempt in one direction fails, the failure is not discouraging to an eager explorer. There are other possible approaches to the end in view and relentlessly, one after another, these are tried.

To add an illustration of the testing of a relatively old hypothesis, McAtee has sought to disprove Darwin's hypothesis, to the effect that bumblebees are indispensable as pollinators of red clover.[104]

Even if they were, dependent parts of Darwin's argument do not follow. He refers to destruction of bumblebee nests by field mice, and of the mice by cats, and concludes: "Hence it is quite credible that the presence of a feline animal in large numbers in a district might determine, through the intervention first of mice, and then of bees, the frequency of certain flowers in that district!" He might as well have started the chain with old maids, as some innovators have, and then gone on to include the success of agriculture and possibly the fate of the nation, as red clover is a leading forage crop and heartsease a prime weed. Domestic cats certainly do not as a rule regulate the population of field mice; they prefer an easier way than that of making a living. American studies show that at least half the food of prowling cats consists of garbage. The role of field mice in destroying bee nests was in turn overestimated.

These illustrations suggest, in agreement with Dewey, that seldom does a hypothesis prove valid in precisely the same form as first set forth, or an initial proposition about the state of facts remain unchanged with respect to content and significance throughout the course of an important scientific inquiry.[105]

Even a half century ago a noted geologist recognized the possible contribution of multiple hypotheses. Although the single working hypothesis serves an important purpose, as a means or procedure for the testing of facts and their relations, it is sometimes at the risk of becoming the controlling idea of the investigation. The very fact that a single hypothesis may lead research effectively along a given line may invite neglect of other equally promising lines of inquiry; for example, the hypothesis of natural

[103] Quoted from Walter B. Cannon, *The Way of an Investigator.* New York: W. W. Norton and Co., 1945. p. 22.

[104] W. L. McAtee, "The Cats-to-Clover Chain." *Scientific Monthly* 65:241-42; September 1947.

[105] John Dewey, *Logic: The Theory of Inquiry.* New York: Henry Holt and Co., 1938. p. 142.

selection just before the beginning of the twentieth century. The less mature student is more inclined to accept a single interpretation or theory than to recognize several concurrent factors in their proper relationships. Therefore, as a safeguard against narrowness in thinking and in research, the method of multiple working hypotheses has been urged, with an attempt to identify every rational explanation of the phenomena under consideration. The interaction of several hypotheses may amplify the recognized scope of each, may sharpen the discriminating edge of each, and may contribute to the methods of proof.[106]

Workers in fields of social research should avoid formalism and slavish imitation of the approaches of physical science in the development of hypotheses and theories. In the field of psychology four criteria have been presented by four psychologists writing as a team, relating to formulation of hypotheses and their organization into scientific theories. These criteria have limited value for social research, owing to their formal character, preoccupation with the concepts of physical science, and rejection of "value" terms. In Chapter 1 and elsewhere in this book, it is pointed out that many evaluative or "value-laden" studies in education are made each year; for example, surveys to determine the need for certain types of schools. It is granted that "value" terms must be capable of definition in working terms, *on the same basis* as all other terms in the statement of the problem and procedure. With this background, the four criteria are summarized as follows: [107]

1. To what extent have first-hand observations which lead to testable hypotheses been made? In relatively undeveloped sciences, such as psychology, education, and sociology, it is probably safer and more fruitful to keep the hypotheses closely related to actual observation of the types of behavior involved.

2. What is the stage of theory development? In the different areas of psychology there is great variation in the stages of theory development; for example, reasonably accurate tests have been devised to measure many types of intellectual or mental abilities, but there is a relatively small amount of theory behind these tests. In contrast, theory in the field of learning is more highly developed, but has had relatively slight impact on practical problems of training. The stage of development of theory in a research area may be any one of four types: non-existent; vague, such as the instinct theory or the Freudian theory; specific, such as the case of the doctrine of identical elements as an explanation of transfer of training;

[106] T. C. Chamberlin, "The Method of Multiple Working Hypotheses." *Scientific Monthly* 59:357-62; November 1944. First appeared in the *Journal of Geology* 5:837-48; 1897.
[107] Dael Wolfle and Others, *op. cit.*, p. 320-28.

or quantitative rational theory, as illustrated by visual theories and Hull's theoretical formulation of learning phenomena.

3.   Are the problems that have been formulated, as well as the theories, stated in scientific terms? Before one can determine whether the lecture method is more or less effective than the small discussion group in college teaching, it is necessary to define precisely the two instructional methods and the criteria to be used for comparing them. A problem must represent a replicable situation, value terms must be excluded, and variables must be defined.

4.   Do the formulated concepts, theories, and problems cover the area? The theoretical or conceptual organization of an area helps to answer this question; for example, identification of gaps in the known series of chemical elements as pointed out by Mendelyeev's construction of the periodic table. In the field of psychology, conceptual schemes for considering visual discrimination data have identified new types of discrimination problems for investigation.

There are no rigidly fixed stages at which the formulation and testing of the working hypothesis take place in reflective thinking and research, although the development of hypothesis or theory usually progresses through certain generally recognized steps.[108] Dewey's apt characterization of the mental sequence or steps in problem-solving and reflective thinking uses the term *shuttle-like*. His well known analysis of the steps following the selection of the problem topic is: (1) suggestions, in which the mind turns toward a possible solution; (2) intellectualization of the difficulty into a quite specific problem to be solved, a question to be answered; (3) use of one suggestion after another as a leading idea or working hypothesis to guide observation and collection of data; (4) mental elaboration of the idea or hypothesis through the process of reasoning; and (5) testing the hypothesis by appropriate action.[109]

## A COÖRDINATED RESEARCH PROGRAM: RESEARCH NEEDS[110]

It has been said of educators that they lack the vision and the courage to ask for the funds and resources urgently needed for educational research. It is pointed out that specialists in the military establishment, in governmental departments, and in atomic energy have demanded and se-

108 John Dewey, *How We Think, op. cit.,* p. 106-18.
A. C. Benjamin, *An Introduction to the Philosophy of Science.* New York: Macmillan Co., 1937. p. 214-30.
109 John Dewey, *How We Think, op. cit.,* p. 107-16.
110 Carter V. Good, "How Much for Educational Research?" *Phi Delta Kappan* 33: 140-41; November 1951.

cured funds that stagger the imagination. A quite appropriate question is to ask what educational research could do with similar funds, administered under some such organization as the National Science Foundation. To the extent desirable, how can the many thousands of thesis investigations and other individual research projects be coördinated effectively?

**Our human resources.** A positive comment can be made on the vision of national leaders in conserving our human resources in certain times of emergency or social crisis. There is even evidence to indicate that educational, civic, and governmental leaders in time of war have become particularly sensitive to the forces of education as a means of recouping physical and material losses. The Morrill Act for developing instruction and research in the agricultural and mechanical arts was passed during the dark days of the Civil War in 1862. The Smith-Hughes Act for vocational training in the high schools was enacted during World War I in 1917. The far-reaching legislation of the G.I. Bill was brought about during World War II.

**How much for research?** It is interesting and significant to note the way in which competent students of research have raised their sights in estimating the funds that are needed. During the depression days of the early 1930's, Thomas Briggs dreamed of what could be done for the cause of secondary education if there were some millions of dollars available.[111] With what seemed unusual courage for that dismal economic period, he took the position that he did not know what an improved program of education would cost (particularly secondary education) or where the money could be secured, but that educators should assume the attitude of a father whose child is ill. A father who seeks to restore his child to health cannot estimate exactly the funds needed, but spends what he needs and can for the welfare of his child.

It is possible to estimate approximately the funds that were used during the late 1940's for purposes of educational research,[112] including the chief agencies interested in educational research: the U. S. Office of Education, state departments of education, research departments in local school systems, university bureaus of research, national and state education associations, philanthropic foundations, and the American Council on Education. Public funds for one year of educational investigation through federal, state, and local agencies, and nongovernmental sources, probably totaled only a few million dollars. The annual budget for administrative expenses of the U. S. Office of Education has been less than $2,000,000, with the

---

[111] Thomas H. Briggs, "If There Were Millions." *Teachers College Record* 35:633-66; May 1934.

[112] M. M. Chambers, "Twenty Million Dollars Worth of Educational Research." *School and Society* 67:273-76; April 10, 1948.

major part allocated to non-research purposes. The annual budget for special projects of the American Council on Education has gone somewhat beyond $1,000,000, although sums in excess of that amount sometimes have been granted for single projects extending over a period of five or six years. The National Education Association has used for research only a fraction of its annual budget (at present in excess of $2,000,000). A sum of $100,000 to $200,000 per year has been considered generous for most university bureaus of educational research, and is far beyond the funds available for research divisions in state education departments, state education associations, and local school systems.

Scates has recommended that an annual budget of $9,000,000 might well provide for activities in educational research as follows: One to six large-scale projects at $75,000 to $500,000 each; fifty to one hundred research centers at $10,000 to $50,000 each; and three hundred individual workers at $1,000 to $15,000 each.[113] The coöperation of hundreds and even thousands of able workers in certain projects has made possible the completion of large undertakings at only nominal cost; for example, the *Dictionary of Education* [114] for $13,000 and the *Encyclopedia of Educational Research* [115] for a sum of similar proportions. These are indeed modest figures, when compared with the $3,500,000,000 as the estimated cost of the atomic bomb and the $14,000,000,000 used for more than eight million veterans under the G.I. Bill, before the end of 1951. (See the more general discussion of expenditures for research in Chapter 1.)

**Coördination of research.** Chambers has pointed out emphatically the absence of any central agency for planning and coördinating research projects, which might justifiably aggregate an expenditure of some $20,000,000 per year.[116] He suggests the need for a well organized printed budget of educational research that might cover five hundred pages. This national budget for educational studies could be revised annually, with the coöperation of many competent and interested persons and agencies. How many bureaus of research could outline specifically adequate plans for using an additional $100,000 for a year or $500,000 over a five-year period? How many graduate departments of education could produce definite plans for research use of $100,000 on the part of staff members and graduate students?

113 Douglas E. Scates, "The Nature and Need of Educational Research." *Science* 103:657-61; May 31, 1946.

Douglas E. Scates, "Needed: A New Pattern of Support for Educational Research." *Journal of Educational Research* 39:641-51; May 1946.

114 Carter V. Good, Editor, *Dictionary of Education.* New York: McGraw-Hill Book Co., 1945. xxxix + 495 p. Scheduled for revision in 1956.

115 Walter S. Monroe, Editor, *Encyclopedia of Educational Research.* Revised Edition. New York: Macmillan Co., 1950. xxvi + 1520 p.

116 M. M. Chambers, *op. cit.*

The potential coördinating agencies for a greatly expanded program of educational research include the U. S. Office of Education, the American Council on Education, the National Education Association, and the National Science Foundation, although at this time it is not clear just what part the latter organization will play in the several areas of the social sciences. The National Science Foundation, with the help of the U. S. Office of Education, is regarded as a major instrument for research teamwork between federal and state governments and endowed institutions.[117]

## CONCLUDING STATEMENT

The beginner in research frequently has a "problem blindness" for the numerous issues or difficulties that are readily apparent to the trained and experienced investigator. Helpful sources of problems are: (1) specialization, (2) instructional program pursued, (3) program of reading, (4) analysis of an area of knowledge, (5) consideration of existing practices and needs, (6) repetition or extension of investigations, and (7) "offshoots" of studies under way.

Essential criteria for consideration in selection of the problem are: (1) novelty and avoidance of unnecessary duplication, (2) importance for the field represented, (3) interest and intellectual curiosity, (4) training and personal qualifications, (5) availability of data and method, (6) special equipment and working conditions, (7) sponsorship and administrative coöperation, (8) costs and returns, (9) hazards and penalties, and (10) the time factor. In the selection of a thesis or research problem, overly broad topics, too restricted or excessively localized problems, and hortatory, argumentative, or raw-data topics should be avoided.

The statement of the problem may be in the form of a question or a direct statement. The phases of more detailed definition of the problem include: (1) analysis of the problem into its constituent elements, (2) limits or scope of the investigation, (3) orientation and related literature, (4) sources of data and method, (5) need for the study, (6) terminology, and (7) initial assumptions.

The working hypothesis provides guidance in the search for evidence. Hypotheses originate from essentially the same sources as do problems. An investigation of some complexity and importance usually involves the formulation and testing of a number of hypotheses before the correct solution is found.

[117] John E. Ivey, Jr., "The National Science Foundation: An Educational Challenge and Crisis." *School and Society* 72:81-83; August 5, 1950. Also see:
S. W. Van Court, "Program Design in Research: An Exploratory Study of Coöperatively Planned Doctoral Dissertations in Educational Psychology." Unpublished Doctor's thesis, New York University, 1951. 351 p.

The potential coördinating agencies for a greatly expanded program of educational research include several national organizations active in educational inquiry. Estimates of the funds needed annually should be raised to hundreds rather than tens of millions of dollars. The great variety of problems for study has been analyzed in the references of the extensive chapter bibliography that follows.

## SELECTED REFERENCES

### I. Phases of the Formulation of the Problem

ABELSON, H. H. *The Art of Educational Research:* Its Problems and Procedures. Yonkers-on-Hudson, N. Y.: World Book Co., 1933. Chapter 2.

ALMACK, J. C. *Research and Thesis Writing.* Boston: Houghton Mifflin Co., 1930. Chapter 2.

ALPERN, Morris L. "Ability to Test Hypotheses." *Science Education* 30:220-29; October 1946.

ASCHER, Charles S. "Hypotheses Regarding Government Relationships." *Journal of Educational Sociology* 14:18-21; September 1940.

BARR, Arvil S., DAVIS, Robert A., and JOHNSON, Palmer O. *Educational Research and Appraisal.* Philadelphia: J. B. Lippincott Co., 1953. p. 5-13, 308-13, 335-39.

BENJAMIN, A. C. *An Introduction to the Philosophy of Science.* New York: Macmillan Co., 1937. p. 214-30.

BIXLER, H. H. *Check-Lists for Educational Research.* New York: Teachers College, Columbia University, 1928. Chapter 2.

BLACKSTONE, Earl G. "How to Plan a Research Study." *National Business Education Quarterly* 16:8-14; March 1948.

BOGARDUS, E. S. *Introduction to Social Research.* Los Angeles: Suttonhouse, 1936. Chapter 1.

BOYD, T. A. *Research.* New York: D. Appleton-Century Co., 1935. xviii + 319 p.

BUNKER, John W. M. "Educational Problems of Graduate Student Theses Based on Sponsored Research." *Journal of Engineering Education* 38:385-89; January 1948.

CHAMBERLIN, T. C. "The Methods of Multiple Working Hypotheses." *Scientific Monthly* 59:357-62; November 1944.

COHEN, M. R., and NAGEL, Ernest. *An Introduction to Logic and Scientific Method.* New York: Harcourt, Brace and Co., 1934. p. 207-15.

COOMBS, Clyde H. "Some Hypotheses for the Analysis of Qualitative Variables." *Psychological Review* 55:167-74; May 1948.

DEWEY, John. *How We Think:* A Restatement of the Relation of Reflective Thinking to the Educative Process. Boston: D. C. Heath and Co., 1933. x + 301 p.

DEWEY, John. *Logic:* The Theory of Inquiry. New York: Henry Holt and Co., 1938. 546 p.

DEWEY, John. *The Sources of a Science of Education.* New York: Horace Liveright, 1929. 77 p.

ELMER, M. C. *Social Research.* New York: Prentice-Hall, 1939. Chapter 4.

FIELD, G. Lowell. "Hypotheses for a Theory of Political Power." *American Political Science Review* 45:716-23; September 1951.

FRY, C. L. *The Technique of Social Investigation*. New York: Harper and Bros., 1934. Chapter 1.

GEORGE, W. H. *The Scientist in Action:* A Scientific Study of His Methods. London: Williams and Norgate, 1936. 355 p.

GOOD, Carter V. "Criteria for Selection of the Research Problem." *Peabody Journal of Education* 19:242-56; March 1942.

GOOD, Carter V. *Criteria for Sound Research in Business Education*. Sixth Annual Delta Pi Epsilon Lecture. Cincinnati: South-Western Publishing Co., 1947. 27 p.

GOOD, Carter V. "Definition of the Research Problem and Formulation of the Working Hypothesis." *Harvard Educational Review* 13:77-87; January 1943.

GOOD, Carter V. "Problem Solving and Methods of Research in Business Education." *National Business Education Quarterly* 16:13-19, 54; October 1947.

GOOD, Carter V. "Sources of Problems for Research." *Elementary School Journal* 42:745-54; June 1942.

GOOD, Carter V., BARR, A. S., and SCATES, Douglas E. *The Methodology of Educational Research*. New York: Appleton-Century-Crofts, 1936. p. 31-103, 185-204, 777-855.

GOODE, William J., and HATT, Paul K. *Methods in Social Research*. New York: McGraw-Hill Book Co., 1952. Chapters 6, 7.

HARDING, T. Swann. "Human Problems in Scientific Research." *American Journal of Economics and Sociology* 8:77-84; October 1948.

HAYNES, B. R., and HUMPHREY, C. W. *Research Applied to Business Education*. New York: Gregg Publishing Co., 1939. Chapter 2.

HENDRICKSON, Gordon. "Some Assumptions Involved in Personality Measurement." *Journal of Experimental Education* 2:243-49; March 1934.

HOLMES, H. W., and Others. *Educational Research:* Its Nature, Essential Conditions, and Controlling Concepts. Washington: American Council on Education, 1939. viii + 186 p.

IHDE, Aaron J. "The Inevitability of Scientific Discovery." *Scientific Monthly* 67:427-29; December 1948.

JAHODA, Marie, DEUTSCH, Morton, and COOK, Stuart W. *Research Methods in Social Relations*. Part 1, Basic Processes. New York: Dryden Press, 1951. Chapter 2.

JOHNSON, Allen. *The Historian and Historical Evidence*. New York: Charles Scribner's Sons, 1926. Chapter 7.

LARRABEE, Harold A. *Reliable Knowledge*. Boston: Houghton Mifflin Co., 1945. vii + 685 p.

LARSON, Olaf F., and HAY, Donald G. "Hypotheses for Sociological Research in the Field of Rural Health." *Rural Sociology* 16:225-37; September 1951.

LEE, Harold N. "Theoretic Knowledge and Hypothesis." *Psychological Review* 57:31-37; January 1950.

LUNDBERG, George A. *Social Research*. Second Edition. New York: Longmans, Green and Co., 1942. xxi + 426 p.

MARQUIS, Donald G. "Research Planning at the Frontiers of Science." *American Psychologist* 3:430-38; October 1948.

MAY, Mark A. "Research in the Measurement of Abilities, Aptitudes, and Achievement." *Educational Research*. Washington: American Council on Education, 1939. p. 68-72.

MONROE, W. S., and ENGELHART, M. D. *The Scientific Study of Educational Problems*. New York: Macmillan Co., 1936. Chapter 2.

Monroe, W. S., and Engelhart, M. D. *The Techniques of Educational Research.* Bureau of Educational Research Bulletin, No. 38. Urbana: University of Illinois, 1928. Chapter 2.

Newbury, Edward. "Philosophic Assumptions in Operational Psychology." *Journal of Psychology* 35:371-78; April 1953.

Northrop, F. S. C. *The Logic of the Sciences and the Humanities.* New York: Macmillan Co., 1947. 402 p.

Odum, H. W., and Jocher, Katharine. *An Introduction to Social Research.* New York: Henry Holt and Co., 1929. Chapter 21.

Pfiffner, J. M. *Research Methods in Public Administration.* New York: Ronald Press, 1940. Chapter 5.

Reeder, W. G. *How to Write a Thesis.* Bloomington, Ill.: Public School Publishing Co., 1930. Chapter 2.

*Research Methods Applied to Health, Physical Education, and Recreation.* Revised Edition. Washington: American Association for Health, Physical Education, and Recreation, N.E.A., 1952. p. 42-83.

Rose, Arnold M. "Generalizations in the Social Sciences." *American Journal of Sociology* 59:49-58; July 1953.

Rose, Arnold M. "The Selection of Problems for Research." *American Journal of Sociology* 54:219-27; November 1948.

Scates, Douglas E. "Types of Assumptions in Educational Research." *Journal of Educational Psychology* 26:350-66; May 1935.

Schumpeter, Joseph A. "Science and Ideology." *American Economic Review* 39:345-59; March 1949.

Searles, Herbert L. *Logic and Scientific Methods.* New York: Ronald Press Co., 1948. xii + 326 p.

Shaw, Franklin J. "Some Postulates Concerning Psychotherapy." *Journal of Consulting Psychology* 12:426-31; November 1948.

Smith, H. L. *Educational Research, Principles and Practices.* Bloomington, Ind.: Educational Publications, 1944. p. 46-61, 81-99.

Smith, Mapheus. "Hypothesis vs. Problem in Scientific Investigation." *Philosophy of Science* 12:296-301; October 1945.

Spahr, W. E., and Swenson, R. J. *Methods and Status of Scientific Research.* New York: Harper and Bros., 1930. Chapter 7.

Stephens, J. M. *Educational Psychology:* The Study of Educational Growth. New York: Henry Holt and Co., 1951. Chapter 4.

Symonds, Percival M., and Stewart, R. A. D. "Educational Planning: Dissertation and Project Requirements." *Teachers College Record* 49:510-19; May 1948.

Tyler, Ralph W. "Assumptions Involved in Achievement-Test Construction." *Educational Research Bulletin* 12:29-36; February 8, 1933.

Vinacke, W. Edgar. "The Basic Postulates of Psychology." *Scientific Monthly* 67:110-14; August 1948.

Vinacke, W. Edgar. *The Psychology of Thinking.* New York: McGraw-Hill Book Co., 1952. 369 p.

Watson, Goodwin. "Some Hypotheses Concerning Social Change." *Journal of Educational Sociology* 14:9-17; September 1940.

Webster, Harold. "Dynamic Hypotheses in Psychology." *Psychological Review* 59:168-71; March 1952.

Welch, Livingston. "Observation and Hypothesis in Psychology." *Journal of Psychology* 25:89-98; January 1948.

Werkmeister, W. H. *The Philosophy of Science.* New York: Harper and Bros., 1940. 551 p.

WHEELER, R. H. "A Set of Postulates for Educational Theory: I, The Background." *Journal of Educational Research* 28:321-33; January 1935.

WHEELER, R. H. "Postulates for a Theory of Education: II, A Methodology for Educational Research." *Journal of Educational Research* 29:187-95; November 1935.

WHITNEY, F. L. *The Elements of Research.* Third Edition. New York: Prentice-Hall, 1950. p. 68-96, 446-59.

WILLIAMS, C. B., and STEVENSON, A. H. *A Research Manual.* Revised Edition. New York: Harper and Bros., 1951. p. 62-75.

WOLFLE, Dael, and Others. "Standards for Appraising Psychological Research." *American Psychologist* 4:320-28; August 1949.

YOUNG, Pauline V. *Scientific Social Surveys and Research.* Second Edition. New York: Prentice-Hall, 1949. Chapters 5, 6.

## II. Sources of Problems in the Literature

### A. Treatment of Topics in the Literature

ALLPORT, G. W. "The Psychologist's Frame of Reference." *Psychological Bulletin* 37:1-28; January 1940. Based in part on an analysis of psychological journals to discover trends by way of the problems treated.

ARSENIAN, Seth, and LAIRD, Frederick J. "Graduate Research in Guidance and Personnel Work During a Two-Year Period." *American Psychologist* 7:189-91; June 1952.

BECKER, Howard. "Distribution of Space in the *American Journal of Sociology,* 1895-1927." *American Journal of Sociology* 36:461-66; November 1930.

BECKER, Howard. "Space Apportioned Forty-eight Topics in the *American Journal of Sociology,* 1895-1930." *American Journal of Sociology* 38:71-78; July 1932.

BETTS, E. A., and BETTS, Thelma M. *An Index to Professional Literature on Reading and Related Topics.* New York: American Book Co., 1945. vii + 137 p.

BOWMAN, C. C. *The College Professor in America: An Analysis of Articles Published in the General Magazines, 1890-1938.* Philadelphia: The Author, 1938. 196 p.

BUTLER, Elizabeth A. "An Analysis of Published Criticisms and Suggestions Related to Teacher Training." *Journal of Educational Research* 43:146-49; October 1949.

CITRON, A. F., and Others. "Ten Years of Intercultural Education in Educational Magazines." *Harvard Educational Review* 15:129-33; March 1945.

DAVIS, R. A., and BALLARD, C. R. "The Development of Research in Learning." *Journal of Educational Psychology* 23:226-35; March 1932. Analysis of material on learning in sixty-five journals, 1890-1929.

DAVIS, R. A., and GOULD, S. E. "Changing Tendencies in General Psychology." *Psychological Review* 36:320-31; July 1929. An analysis of 110 textbooks in general psychology published over a thirty-nine-year period.

DUNCAN, H. G., and DUNCAN, Winnie L. "Research Interests in Sociology." *Sociology and Social Research* 19:442-46; May-June, 1935. Explores the interests of sociologists as recorded in the census of research projects published annually in the *American Journal of Sociology;* the data consist of 1973 projects between the years 1928-1934.

ELLIS, Albert. "What Kinds of Research Are American Psychologists Doing?" *American Psychologist* 4:490-94; November 1949.

FERNBERGER, S. W. "Publications, Politics, and Economics." *Psychological Bulletin* 35:84-90; February 1938. Based on an analysis of psychological titles appearing in different languages, as listed in the *Psychological Index*.

FRANKE, Paul R., and DAVIS, Robert A. "Changing Tendencies in Educational Research." *Journal of Educational Research* 23:133-45; February 1931. Analysis of periodical literature in education, 1890-1929.

GOOD, Carter V. "Fields and Types of Research in Education, 1918-31." *Journal of Educational Research* 24:33-43; June 1931. Covers topics treated in doctoral dissertations.

GOODENOUGH, Florence L. "Trends in Modern Psychology." *Psychological Bulletin* 31:81-97; February 1934. Based on the *Psychological Index* since 1894 and on *Psychological Abstracts, 1927-1932*.

HUNT, W. A., and LANDIS, Carney. "The Present Status of Abnormal Psychology." *Psychological Review* 42:78-90; January 1935.

JOHNS, R. L., and MORPHET, E. L., Editors. *Problems and Issues in Public School Finance:* An Analysis and Summary of Significant Research and Experience. New York: Bureau of Publications, Teachers College, Columbia University, 1952. xiv + 492 p.

LEARY, Bernice E. *A Survey of Courses of Study and Other Curriculum Materials Published Since 1934.* Office of Education Bulletin No. 31, 1937. Washington: Government Printing Office, 1938. vi + 185 p.

LOUTTIT, C. M. "Psychological Journals: A Minor Contribution to the History of Psychology." *Psychological Review* 38:455-60; September 1931. An analysis of the subject-, country-, and time-distribution represented in psychological journals.

MALLER, J. B. "Forty Years of Psychology." *Psychological Bulletin* 31:533-39; October 1934. An analysis of American and European publications in psychology, 1894-1933.

MCGUIRE, Carson, and SMITH, Sidney B. "Child Development in Periodical Literature." *Child Development* 19:112-24; March-June, 1948.

MCMILLIAN, Nathaniel B. *An Analysis of Regional Items in the Content of Southern State Education Association Journals, 1935-1949.* Bulletin of the Bureau of School Service, Vol. 23, No. 4. Lexington: University of Kentucky, June, 1951. 91 p.

OJEMANN, Ralph H., and Associates. "A Functional Analysis of Child Development Material in Current Newspapers and Magazines." *Child Development* 19:76-92; March-June, 1948.

SHANNON, J. R. "The Relative Frequency of Use of Types of Procedure and Sources of Data in Research in Education." *Journal of Educational Research* 41:41-46; September 1947.

SHANNON, J. R. "Teachers and Doers in Educational Research." *Journal of Educational Research* 43:142-45; October 1949.

SMITH, Lawrence J. "Research Workers in Selected School Subjects." *Journal of Educational Research* 45:255-73; December 1951.

SMOKE, K. L. "The Present Status of Social Psychology in America." *Psychological Review* 42:537-43; November 1935. Analysis of topics treated in the literature of this field.

STRANG, Ruth. "Trends in Educational Personnel Research." *Personnel Journal* 10:179-88; October 1931. Covers 571 articles on personnel, 1920-1930.

TYSON, Robert. "Content of Mental Hygiene Literature." *Journal of Clinical Psychology* 5:109-14; April 1949.

VAUGHN, James. "Psychology in the Laboratory." *Journal of General Psychology* 24:135-43; January 1941. Analysis of laboratory manuals.

VINCENT, Clark E. "Trends in Infant Care Ideas." *Child Development* 22:199-209; September 1951. Based chiefly on periodical literature.

### B. Surveys of Progress and Critiques of Research

ABBOTT, Edith. "Twenty-One Years of University Education for the Social Services." *Social Service Review* 15:671-705; December 1941.

ABEL, Theodore, BOCK, Kenneth E., and REED, Stephen W. "The Present Status of Social Theory." *American Sociological Review* 17:156-67; April 1952.

ABELSON, Harold H. "Role of Educational Research in a Democracy." *Journal of Educational Sociology* 21:454-61; April 1948.

ALLEN, Frederick H. "Developments in Child Psychiatry in the United States." *American Journal of Public Health* 38:1201-9; September 1948.

ALPER, B. S. "Forty Years of the Juvenile Court." *American Sociological Review* 6:230-40; April 1941.

ANDERSON, J. E. "The Contributions of Child Development to Psychology." *Journal of Consulting Psychology* 6:128-34; May-June 1942.

*Annual Report of the Federal Security Agency, Office of Education.* Washington: Government Printing Office. See the current number.

BALDRIDGE, Marie. "Three Decades of Language Study." *Childhood Education* 26:117-21; November 1949.

BARNES, H. E., and BECKER, Howard. *Social Thought from Lore to Science,* Volumes I, II. Boston: D. C. Heath and Co., 1938. xxiv, lxxxiv + 790 p.; viii, lxxxvii + 388 p.

BENNETT, Henry E. "Fifty Years of School Seating." *American School Board Journal* 100:41-43, 125; March 1940.

BERNAL, J. D. *The Social Function of Science.* New York: Macmillan Co., 1939. xviii + 482 p.

BERNARD, L. L., and BERNARD, Jessie S. "A Century of Progress in the Social Sciences." *Social Forces* 11:488-505; May 1933. The development of historical research, political science, political economy, professional economics and commerce, sociology, social-science organizations and publications, graduate social sciences, and the expansion of research.

BERNARD, L. L., and BERNARD, Jessie S. *Origins of American Sociology:* The Social Science Movement in the United States. New York: Thomas Y. Crowell Co., 1943. xvi + 866 p.

BONNER, Hubert. "Field Theory and Sociology." *Sociology and Social Research* 33:171-79; January-February 1949.

BORING, E. G. *A History of Experimental Psychology.* Second Edition. New York: Appleton-Century-Crofts, 1950. xxi + 777 p.

BOULDING, Kenneth E. "Is Economics Necessary?" *Scientific Monthly* 68:235-40; April 1949.

BROWER, Daniel. "The Problem of Quantification in Psychological Science." *Psychological Review* 56:325-33; November 1949.

BROWNELL, William A. "Criteria of Learning in Educational Research." *Journal of Educational Psychology* 39:170-82; March 1948.

BROWNELL, William A. "Learning Theory and Educational Practice." *Journal of Educational Research* 41:481-97; March 1948.

BRUNO, Frank J. "Twenty-Five Years of Schools of Social Work." *Social Service Review* 18:152-64; June 1944.

BUCKINGHAM, B. R. "The Accomplishments and the Promise of Educational Research in Increasing the Over-All Value of Education to the Nation." *Improving Educational Research.* Washington: American Educational Research Association, 1948. p. 89-93.

BUROS, Oscar K., Editor. *The Fourth Mental Measurements Yearbook.* Highland Park, N. J.: Gryphon Press, 1953. 1189 p.

BUROS, Oscar K., Editor. *The Third Mental Measurements Yearbook.* New Brunswick, N. J.: Rutgers University Press, 1949. x + 1047 p.

BUROS, Oscar K., Editor. *The Nineteen Forty Mental Measurements Yearbook.* Highland Park, N. J.: Mental Measurements Yearbook, 1941. xxvi + 674 p.

BUROS, Oscar K., Editor. *The Second Yearbook of Research and Statistical Methodology Books and Reviews.* Highland Park, N. J.: Gryphon Press, 1941. xxii + 383 p.

BUROS, Oscar K., Editor. *Statistical Methodology Reviews, 1941-1950.* New York: John Wiley and Sons, 1951. 458 p.

BUSWELL, G. T. "Outlook for Research in Arithmetic." *Elementary School Journal* 47:243-53; January 1947.

CAIN, J. Harvey. "A Decade of Progress in Accounting and Financial Reporting for Colleges and Universities." *Educational Record* 21:497-505; October 1940.

CAMPBELL, C. G. "Scientific Laboratory Furniture During the Past Fifty Years." *American School Board Journal* 100:44-45; March 1940.

CARMICHAEL, Leonard, Editor. *Manual of Child Psychology.* New York: John Wiley and Sons, 1946. viii + 1068 p.

CARTWRIGHT, Benjamin A. *Four Decades of Development of Psychology in State Teachers Colleges.* Contribution to Education, No. 235. Nashville, Tennessee: George Peabody College for Teachers, 1938. 167 p.

CARTWRIGHT, M. A. *Ten Years of Adult Education.* A Report on a Decade of Progress in the American Movement. New York: Macmillan Co., 1935. xiv + 220 p.

CASWELL, Hollis L. "Speeding Curriculum Change." *Teachers College Record* 48:304-11; February 1947.

CONANT, James B. *On Understanding Science:* An Historical Approach. New Haven: Yale University Press, 1947. xv + 145 p.

CONANT, James B. "The Role of Science in Our Unique Society." *Science* 107:77-83; January 23, 1948.

CONANT, James B. *Science and Common Sense.* New Haven: Yale University Press, 1951. xii + 371 p.

COOK, Walter W. "Accomplishments and the Promise of Educational Research in the Educative Process." *Improving Educational Research.* Washington: American Educational Research Association, 1948. p. 79-84.

COTTRELL, L. S., and GALLAGHER, Ruth. *Developments in Social Psychology, 1930-1940.* Beacon, N. Y.: Beacon House, 1941. 58 p.

CROWTHER, J. G. *The Social Relations of Science.* New York: Macmillan Co., 1941. xxxiv + 665 p.

DAHLKE, H. Otto, and MONAHAN, Thomas O. "Problems in the Application of Sociometry to Schools." *School Review* 57:223-34; April 1949.

DANIEL, Glyn E. *A Hundred Years of Archaeology.* New York: Macmillan Co., 1950. 343 p.

DAVIES, Daniel R. "Educational Administration at Mid-Century." *Teachers College Record* 54:125-30; December 1952.

DAVIS, R. C. "American Psychology, 1800-1885." *Psychological Review* 43:471-93; November 1936.

"A Decade of Progress in Special Education." *Journal of Exceptional Children* 10:195-216; May 1944.

DEFFENBAUGH, W. S. "Some Developments in City School Administration During the Past Fifty Years." *American School Board Journal* 100:39-41; March 1940.

DINGLE, Herbert, Editor. *A Century of Science:* 1851-1951. New York: Roy Publishing Co., 1951. ix + 338 p.

DOUGLASS, H. R. "Three Hundred Years of Method in the Secondary School." *Educational Administration and Supervision* 21:321-33; May 1935.

DOUGLASS, H. R. "Twenty-five Years of Research in Secondary Education." *Journal of Educational Research* 38:346-50; January 1945.

DUNSHEATH, Percy, Editor. *A Century of Technology:* 1851-1951. New York: Roy Publishing Co., 1951. ix + 346 p.

*Economic Research and the Development of Economic Science and Public Policy.* New York: National Bureau of Economic Research, 1947. 198 p.

ELIASSEN, R. H., and MARTIN, Robert L. "Teacher Recruitment and Selection During the Period 1944 Through 1947." *Journal of Educational Research* 41:641-63; May 1948.

ELINSON, Jack. "Attitude Research in the Army." *Journal of Applied Psychology* 33:1-5; February 1949.

ELLIS, Albert. "Critique of Systematic Theoretical Foundations in Clinical Psychology." *Journal of Clinical Psychology* 8:11-15; January 1952.

ELLWOOD, C. A. *A History of Social Philosophy.* New York: Prentice-Hall, 1938. xvi + 581 p.

ELMER, M. C. "Backgrounds for Present Sociological Research." *Sociology and Social Research* 34:13-20; September-October 1949.

ELVEHJEM, C. A. "Seven Decades of Nutrition Research." *Science* 109:354-58; April 8, 1949.

EUBANK, E. E. "Errors of Sociology." *Social Forces* 16:178-201; December 1937.

EVENDEN, E. S. "Twenty-five Years of Teacher Education." *Educational Record* 24:334-44; October 1943.

"The Field of Clinical Psychology: Past, Present, and Future." *Journal of Clinical Psychology* 1:1-20; January 1945.

"Fifty Years of Sociology." *American Journal of Sociology* 50:421-548; May 1945.

FINCH, James K. "A Century of Engineering Progress: 1852-1952." *Scientific Monthly* 75:99-108; August 1952.

FLANAGAN, John C. "Contributions of Research in the Armed Forces to Personnel Psychology." *Personnel Psychology* 1:53-62; Spring, 1948.

FLUGEL, J. C. *A Hundred Years of Psychology.* Revised Edition. New York: Macmillan Co., 1951. 424 p.

FOWLKES, John G. "A Program for Continued Progress in the Preparation for School Administration." *Nation's Schools* 47:38-40; April 1951.

FRENCH, W. M. "A Century of Teacher Training in New York." *Education* 56:215-23; December 1935.

GARRETT, Henry E. *Great Experiments in Psychology.* Third Edition. New York: Appleton-Century-Crofts, 1951. 400 p.

GASKILL, Evelyn R., and MUDD, Emily H. "A Decade of Group Counseling." *Social Casework* 31:194-201; May 1950.

GOLDSCHMIDT, Richard. "Fifty Years of Zoology." *Scientific Monthly* 71:359-69; December 1950.

GOLDSMITH, Maurice. "One Hundred Years of British Science." *Scientific Monthly* 74:170-79; March 1952.

GOOD, Carter V. "Twenty-five Years of the Literature of Research Methodology." *Journal of Educational Research* 38:375-76; January 1945.

GRACE, Alonzo G. "Educational Progress." *Phi Delta Kappan* 33:122-26; November 1951.

GRAY, Giles W. "Research in the History of Speech Education." *Quarterly Journal of Speech* 35:156-63; April 1949.

GRAY, William S. "Implications of Research for the Improvement of Reading." *Education* 70:539-47; May 1950.

GREGG, Alan. "A Critique of Medical Research." *Scientific Monthly* 58:365-72; May 1944.

GREGG, Alan. "The Profession of Psychology as Seen by a Doctor of Medicine." *American Psychologist* 3:397-401; September 1948.

GRIZZELL, E. D., and Others. *Educational Studies and Their Use:* An Exploratory Study of the Processes of Implementation in Secondary Education Series I, Vol. 4, No. 11. Washington: American Council on Education, January 1940. viii + 74 p.

GUILFORD, J. P. "Creativity." *American Psychologist* 5:444-54; September 1950.

GUILFORD, J. P., Editor. *Fields of Psychology.* Second Edition. New York: D. Van Nostrand Co., 1950. 779 p.

HALL, Oswald. "Sociological Research in the Field of Medicine: Progress and Prospects." *American Sociological Review* 16:639-44; October 1951.

HAMLIN, H. M. "Twenty Years of Federal Aid." *School Review* 45:257-65; April 1937.

HARPER, C. A. *A Century of Public Teacher Education.* Washington: American Association of Teachers Colleges, N.E.A., 1939. 175 p.

HARTMANN, George W. "How Can Research Help Determine What Should Be?" *Improving Educational Research.* Washington: American Educational Research Association, 1948. p. 148-53.

HENDRY, C. E. *Decade of Group Work.* New York: Association Press, 1948. 189 p.

HILL, John G. "Fifty Years of Social Action on the Housing Front." *Social Service Review* 22:160-79; June 1948.

HINRICHS, A. F. "Progress in Occupational Outlook Research." *Occupations* 24:325-29; March 1946.

HOLLINGSHEAD, August B. "Community Research: Development and Present Conditions." *American Sociological Review* 13:136-56; April 1948.

HOSELITZ, Bert F. "The Social Sciences in the Last Two Hundred Years." *Journal of General Education* 4:85-103; January 1950.

HOUSE, F. N. *The Development of Sociology.* New York: McGraw-Hill Book Co., 1936. viii + 456 p.

HULL, Gordon F., Jr. "Fifty Years of Physics: A Study in Contrasts." *Science* 104:238-44; September 13, 1946.

HUNT, Herold C. "Midpoint: A Challenge to Education." *North Central Association Quarterly* 25:163-67; October 1950.

JACOBSON, P. B. "Research Shows Twelve Changes in Fifty Years of Secondary Education." *Nation's Schools* 49:38-41; January 1952.

JASTROW, Joseph, and Others. *The Story of Human Error.* New York: D. Appleton-Century Co., 1936. xvii + 445 p.

JERSILD, Arthur T. "Child Psychology in the United States." *Teachers College Record* 50:114-27; November 1948.

JONES, G. P., and POOL, A. G. *A Hundred Years of Economic Development.* New York: Macmillan Co., 1940. 420 p.

JUDD, C. H. "A Century of Progress in Education." *Phi Delta Kappan* 16:40-54; August 1933.

JUDD, C. H., and Others. *A Century of Social Thought.* Durham, N. C.: Duke University Press, 1939. vii + 172 p.

KAEMPFFERT, W. *Science Today and Tomorrow.* New York: Viking, 1939. 275 p. Describes the impact of science on society.

KENDALL, Katherine A. "Social Work Education in Review." *Social Service Review* 24:296-309; September 1950.

KOOS, L. V. "Report on Research and the Junior College Journal." *Junior College Journal* 19:526-31; May 1949.

LANDIS, P. H. "The Development of Rural Sociology in the United States." *Sociology and Social Research* 22:329-35; March-April 1938.

LASTRUCCI, C. L. "The Status and Significance of Occupational Research." *American Sociological Review* 11:78-84; February 1946.

LEVY, Hyman. *Modern Science.* New York: Alfred A. Knopf, 1939. x + 736 p.

LINDESMITH, Alfred R., and STRAUSS, Anselm L. "A Critique of Culture-Personality Writings." *American Sociological Review* 15:587-600; October 1950.

LINTON, Ralph. "The Present Status of Anthropology." *Science* 87:241-48; March 18, 1938.

LIVELY, C. E., and Others. "Symposium on Objectives and Methods of Sociological Research in Health." *Rural Sociology* 14:199-219; September 1949.

LONDON, Ivan D. "A Historical Survey of Psychology in the Soviet Union." *Psychological Bulletin* 46:241-77; July 1949.

LOOMIS, Charles P., and PEPINSKY, Harold B. "Sociometry, 1937-1947: Theory and Methods." *Sociometry* 11:262-86; August 1948.

LUNDBERG, George A. *Can Science Save Us?* New York: Longmans, Green and Co., 1946. 122 p.

MACIVER, R. M. "Some Reflections on Sociology During a Crisis." *American Sociological Review* 6:1-8; February 1941.

McCOLLUM, E. V. "Fifty Years of Progress in Nutritional Research." *Scientific Monthly* 71:376-79; December 1950.

MEADOWS, Paul. "Theses on Social Movements." *Social Forces* 24:408-12; May 1946.

MEES, C. E. K. *The Path of Science.* New York: John Wiley and Sons, 1946. 250 p.

MILLER, S. M. "The Rise of Industrial Sociology." *Sociology and Social Research* 36:90-96; November-December, 1951.

MONROE, W. S. "Educational Measurement in 1920 and in 1945." *Journal of Educational Research* 38:334-40; January 1945.

MONROE, W. S. "How Has Educational Research Contributed to the Development of Teacher Education?" *Journal of Teacher Education* 2:60-63; March 1951.

MONROE, W. S. "Progress Toward a Science of Education." *Twenty-fourth Annual Conference on Educational Measurements.* Bulletin of the School of Education, Indiana University, Vol. 13, No. 4. Bloomington: The University, September 1937. p. 43-51.

MONROE, W. S., Editor. *Encyclopedia of Educational Research.* Revised Edition. New York: Macmillan Co., 1950. xxvi + 1520 p.

MOORE, Harold E. "The Place of Research in the Expanding Role of Education in City School Systems." *North Central Association Quarterly* 23:377-81; April 1949.

MORRISON, J. Cayce. "The Accomplishments and the Promise of Educational Research in the Organization and Operation of Schools." *Improving Educa-*

*tional Research.* Washington: American Educational Research Association, 1948. p. 75-79.

MURCHISON, Carl, Editor. *A Handbook of Child Psychology.* Second Edition, Revised. Worcester: Clark University Press, 1933. xii + 956 p.

MURCHISON, Carl, Editor. *A Handbook of General Experimental Psychology.* Worcester: Clark University Press, 1934. xii + 1126 p.

MURCHISON, Carl, Editor. *A Handbook of Social Psychology.* Worcester: Clark University Press, 1935. xii + 1190 p.

MURCHISON, Carl, Editor. *A History of Psychology in Autobiography,* Vols. 1, 2, 3. Worcester: Clark University Press, 1930, 1932, 1936. 516, 407, 328 p. Also see Vol. 4, edited by H. S. Langfeld.

MURPHY, Gardner. *An Historical Introduction to Modern Psychology.* Revised Edition. New York: Harcourt, Brace and Co., 1949. xiv + 466 p.

MURPHY, Gardner, and MURPHY, Lois B. *Experimental Social Psychology.* New York: Harper and Bros., 1931. xiv + 710 p.

MUSE, Paul F. "Nature of Child Growth and Development." *Teachers College Journal* 20:60-61; January 1949.

NATIONAL RESOURCES COMMITTEE. *Research:* A National Resource. Washington: Government Printing Office, 1938. 255 p.

NATIONAL RESOURCES COMMITTEE. *Technological Trends and National Policy.* House Document No. 360. Washington: Government Printing Office, June 1937. x + 388 p.

NELSON, Herman W. "School Heating and Ventilating During the Past Fifty Years." *American School Board Journal* 100:37-38, 125; March 1940.

NOFFSINGER, F. R. "A Century of Progress in Schoolhouse Construction." *American School Board Journal* 89:39-40; December 1934; 90:21-22; January 1935; 90:37-38; March 1935; 90:36; April 1935; 92:52; January 1936.

NOFFSINGER, F. R. "A Century of Progress in Schoolroom Lighting." *American School Board Journal* 96:41-42, 89; April 1938.

NOFFSINGER, F. R. "A Century of Progress in Schoolroom Planning." *American School Board Journal* 95:47-48, 39-40, 29-30; September, October, November, 1937.

NOFFSINGER, F. R. "A Century's Progress in School Heating and Ventilation." *American School Board Journal* 91:38-39, 37-38, 36; July, September, November, 1935.

NOFFSINGER, F. R. "A Century of Progress in School Water Supply." *American School Board Journal* 92:30; April 1936.

NYSTROM, A. J. "Fifty Years of School-Map Making in America." *American School Board Journal* 100:61, 106; March 1940.

ODUM, H. W. *American Sociology:* The Story of Sociology in the United States to 1950. New York: Longmans, Green and Co., 1951. 512 p.

ODUM, H. W. "The Errors of Sociology." *Social Forces* 15:327-42; March 1937.

OJEMANN, Ralph H. "Recognition of Motivational Forces in the Individual." *Improving Educational Research.* Washington: American Educational Research Association, 1948. p. 119-24.

*One Hundred Years of American Psychiatry.* New York: Columbia University Press, 1944. xxiv + 649 p.

OPPENHEIMER, Robert. "Encouragement of Science." *Science* 111:373-75; April 14, 1950.

PARSONS, Talcott. "The Prospects of Sociological Theory." *American Sociological Review* 15:3-16; February 1950.

PARSONS, Talcott, and BARBER, Bernard. "Sociology, 1941-46." *American Journal of Sociology* 53:245-57; January 1948.

PATERSON, D. G. "Applied Psychology Comes of Age." *Journal of Consulting Psychology* 4:1-9; January-February 1940.

PENNIMAN, T. K. *A Hundred Years of Anthropology.* Revised Edition. London: Duckworth and Co., 1952. 512 p.

PERKINS, Keith J. "The Opportunities and Responsibilities of Clinical Psychology in the Field of Community Services." *Journal of Clinical Psychology* 6:9-13; April 1950.

"Personnel Problems and Reconversion." *Teachers College Record* 47:1-42; October 1945.

POOLEY, Robert C. "Contributions of Research to the Teaching of English." *English Journal* 37:170-75; April 1948.

RANDALL, J. H. *The Making of the Modern Mind:* A Survey of the Intellectual Background of the Present Age. Revised. Boston: Houghton Mifflin Co., 1940. xiv + 696 p.

RATHS, Louis E. "Research in Educational Sociology." *Journal of Educational Sociology* 25:437-40; April 1952.

REDD, George N. "Limitations of Research on the Education of the Negro." *Journal of Educational Research* 42:321-31; January 1949.

REED, Glenn A. "Fifty Years of Conflict in the Graduate School." *Educational Record* 33:5-23; January 1952.

RELLER, T. L. "One Hundred Years of the City Superintendency: Next Steps." *American School Board Journal* 96:27-30; February 1938.

REMMERS, H. H. "The Expanding Role of Research." *North Central Association Quarterly* 23:369-76; April 1949.

REUTER, E. B. "Some Observations on the Status of Social Psychology." *American Journal of Sociology* 56:293-304; November 1940.

RICE, Arthur H. "For Teacher Organizations—A Century of Progress." *Nation's Schools* 49:102-106; June 1952.

ROGERS, C. R. "The Psychologist's Contributions to Parent, Child, and Community Problems." *Journal of Consulting Psychology* 6:8-18; January-February 1942.

RUGG, Harold. "After Three Decades of Scientific Method in Education." *Teachers College Record* 36:111-22; November 1934.

RUSSELL, W. F. "A Century of Teacher Education." *Teachers College Record* 41:481-92; March 1940.

SCATES, Douglas E. "Educational Research in the United States: Progress and Problems." *Educational Administration and Supervision* 34:385-411; November 1948.

SCATES, Douglas E. "The Parallel Roles of Physical and Social Science." *Scientific Monthly* 64:14-20; January 1947.

SCATES, Douglas E. "Recent Research and Currents in Education." *Phi Delta Kappan* 30:238-43; March 1949.

SCATES, Douglas E. "Research and Progress in Educational Administration." *Journal of Educational Research* 38:351-64; January 1945.

SCHMIDT, H. W. "Fifty Years in School-Building Design and Construction." *American School Board Journal* 100:31-35; March 1940.

SEAGOE, May V. "Improving Research on the Learning Process." *Improving Educational Research.* Washington: American Educational Research Association, 1948. p. 100-106.

SEDGWICK, W. T., and TYLER, H. W., revised by TYLER, H. W., and BIGELOW, R. P. *A Short History of Science.* New York: Macmillan Co., 1940. xxi + 512 p.

SEELIG, M. G. "Medical Progress in the Last Hundred Years." *Science* 86:275-79; September 24, 1937.

SELIGMAN, Edwin R. A., and JOHNSON, Alvin, Editors. *Encyclopedia of the Social Sciences.* New York: Macmillan Co., 1930-1934. Fifteen volumes.

SHAPIRO, Harry L. "The Responsibility of the Anthropologist." *Science* 109:323-26; April 1, 1949.

SHEPHERD, W. *Science Marches On.* New York: Harcourt, Brace and Co., 1939. 420 p.

SINGLETON, W. Ralph. "Some High Lights of the First Half Century of Genetics." *Scientific Monthly* 71:401-7; December 1950.

SMITH, B. Othanel. "Science of Education." *Encyclopedia of Educational Research.* Revised Edition. Edited by Walter S. Monroe. New York: Macmillan Co., 1950. p. 1145-52.

SOMBART, Werner. "Sociology: What It Is and What It Ought to Be: An Outline for a Noö-Sociology." *American Journal of Sociology* 55:178-93; September 1949.

SPEARMAN, C. *Psychology Down the Ages,* Volumes I, II. New York: Macmillan Co., 1938. xviii + 809 p.

Staff of the Horace Mann-Lincoln School of Teachers College. "Charting a Course for Educational Progress." *Teachers College Record* 48:35-60; October 1946.

STEVENSON, G. S., and Others. "Twenty-five Years of Child Guidance." *Mental Hygiene* 27:267-78; April 1943.

STORY, M. L. "Fifty Years of Secondary Education: A Midcentury Appraisal." *School Review* 59:153-56; March 1951.

STRANG, Ruth. "Major Limitations in Current Evaluation Studies." *Educational and Psychological Measurement* 10:531-36; Autumn 1950.

TAVES, Marvin J., and GROSS, Neal. "A Critique of Rural Sociology Research, 1950." *Rural Sociology* 17:109-118; June 1952.

TAYLOR, F. S. *The March of Mind:* A Short History of Science. New York: Macmillan Co., 1939. xiv + 320 p.

TILDSLEY, J. L. "Fifty Years of Secondary Education." *High Points* 20:5-17; April 1938.

TRAXLER, Arthur E. "Research in Reading in the United States." *Journal of Educational Research* 42:481-99; March 1949.

TYLER, Ralph W. "The Accomplishments and the Promise of Educational Research in Sharpening the Tools of Educational Science." *Improving Educational Research.* Washington: American Educational Research Association, 1948. p. 84-89.

ULICH, Robert. *On the Reform of Educational Research.* Occasional Pamphlets of the Graduate School of Education, Harvard University, No. 2. Cambridge: Harvard University, 1937. 26 p.

WALLIN, Paul. "An Appraisal of Some Methodological Aspects of the Kinsey Report." *American Sociological Review* 14:197-210; April 1949.

WATERFIELD, R. L. *A Hundred Years of Astronomy.* New York: Macmillan Co., 1938. 526 p.

WATSON, Goodwin. "Psychological Contributions to World Understanding." *American Psychologist* 4:65-68; March 1949.

WENDT, G. *Science for the World of Tomorrow.* New York: W. W. Norton and Co., 1939. 316 p.

WEST, R. L. "A Century of Public Teacher Education." *Educational Forum* 4:17-24; November 1939.

WILLIAMS, Cornelia D., and Others. "Basic Considerations in Planning Research in General Education." *General Education in Transition*. Edited by H. T. Morse. Minneapolis: University of Minnesota Press, 1951. p. 233-81.

WILLIS, Ivan L. "Education at the Mid-Century: An Appraisal of Its Present Status." *North Central Association Quarterly* 25:195-202; October 1950.

WIRTH, Louis, Editor. *Eleven Twenty-Six: A Decade of Social Science Research.* Chicago: University of Chicago Press, 1940. 498 p. Research at the University of Chicago.

WOOD, J. M. "Twenty Years' Progress," *Junior College Journal* 10:511-18; May 1940. Progress in the junior-college movement.

WOODWORTH, R. S. "The Adolescence of American Psychology." *Psychological Review* 50:10-32; January 1943.

WRIGHT, Helen R. "Social-Work Education Today—Some Questions." *Social Service Review* 24:74-83; March 1950.

YOUNGBLOOD, Bonney. "Rural Sociological Research in the State Agricultural Experiment Stations." *Rural Sociology* 14:111-15; June 1949.

ZANDER, Alvin. "Psychological Research in the Community Mental Health Service Field." *Journal of Clinical Psychology* 6:15-19; April 1950.

ZNANIECKI, Florian. "European and American Sociology after Two World Wars." *American Journal of Sociology* 56:217-21; November 1950.

ZNANIECKI, Florian. *The Social Role of the Man of Knowledge.* New York: Columbia University Press, 1940. viii + 212 p.

### C. Tendencies and Trends

BEACH, Frank A. "The Snark Was a Boojum (Status of Comparative Psychology)." *American Psychologist* 5:115-24; April 1950.

BERDIE, Ralph. "The Field of Applied Psychology." *Journal of Applied Psychology* 24:553-75; October 1940.

BERNARD, Luther L. "Sociological Trends in the South." *Social Forces* 27:12-19; October 1948.

BETTS, Emmett A. "The Improvement of Reading in Elementary Schools." *Educational Record* 29:141-61; January 1948.

BILLS, A. G. "Changing Views of Psychology as Science." *Psychological Review* 45:377-94; September 1938.

BLAESSER, W. W., and FROEHLICH, Clifford P. "Major Issues and Trends in the Graduate Training of College Personnel Workers." *Educational and Psychological Measurement* 10:588-95; Autumn 1950.

BORING, Edwin G. "Current Trends in Psychology." *Psychological Bulletin* 45:75-84; January 1948.

BRIGGS, Thomas H. "The Secondary School Curriculum: Yesterday, Today, and Tomorrow." *Teachers College Record* 52:399-448; April 1951.

BRIGHAM, R. I. "Trends in Negro Education: A Reader's View." *Journal of Negro Education* 15:43-54; Winter 1946.

BRUNER, Jerome S., and ALLPORT, Gordon W. "Fifty Years of Change in American Psychology." *Psychological Bulletin* 37:757-76; December 1940.

BRUNO, Frank J. *Trends in Social Work as Reflected in the Proceedings of the National Conference of Social Work, 1874-1946.* New York: Columbia University Press, 1948. xiii + 387 p.

BURROWS, Raymond. "Present-Day Trends in Music Education." *Teachers College Record* 52:213-25; January 1951.

COLE, W. E., and CROWE, H. P. *Recent Trends in Rural Planning.* New York: Prentice-Hall, 1937. xvi + 579 p.

COMBS, A. W., and Others. *Current Trends in Clinical Psychology.* New York: New York Academy of Sciences, 1948. p. 867-928.

COOK, Katherine M. *Review of Conditions and Developments in Education in Rural and Other Sparsely Settled Areas.* Office of Education Bulletin No. 2, 1937. Washington: Government Printing Office, 1937. iv + 70 p.

DARLEY, J. G., and BERDIE, Ralph. "The Fields of Applied Psychology." *Journal of Consulting Psychology* 4:41-52; March-April, 1940.

DAVIS, Robert A. "Trends in the Study of Classroom Learning." *Improving Educational Research.* Washington: American Educational Research Association, 1948. p. 112-19.

DENNIS, Wayne. "Historical Beginnings of Child Psychology." *Psychological Bulletin* 46:224-35; May 1949.

DENNIS, Wayne, and Others. *Current Trends in Industrial Psychology.* Pittsburgh: University of Pittsburgh Press, 1949. 198 p.

DENNIS, Wayne, and Others. *Current Trends in Psychology.* Pittsburgh: University of Pittsburgh Press, 1947. vii + 225 p.

DENNIS, Wayne, and Others. *Current Trends in Psychological Theory.* Pittsburgh: University of Pittsburgh Press, 1952.

DENNIS, Wayne, and Others. *Current Trends in Social Psychology.* Pittsburgh: University of Pittsburgh Press, 1948. vii + 299 p.

DEUTSCH, Abraham. "Trends in Testing." *High Points* 29:39-53; January 1947.

DRAKE, C. E. "Trends in the Field of Evaluating Secondary Education." *Educational Administration and Supervision* 26:241-56; April 1940.

EDWARDS, Newton. "Education and Postwar Socioeconomic Trends." *Elementary School Journal* 46:132-40; November 1945.

ERICKSEN, Stanford C. "Two Indices of Changing Interests in American Psychology." *American Psychologist* 4:83-84; March 1949.

EUBANK, E. E. "European and American Sociology: Some Comparisons." *Social Forces* 15:147-54; December 1936.

FORD, G. S. "Some Trends and Problems of the Social Sciences." *School and Society* 44:489-97; October 17, 1936.

GLICK, P. C. "Family Trends in the United States, 1890 to 1940." *American Sociological Review* 7:505-14; August 1942.

GOOD, Carter V. "Education After Two Years of War." *School and Society* 59:337-39; May 13, 1944.

GREENWOOD, Ernest. "Recent Trends in Social Work Research." *Sociology and Social Research* 35:250-59; March-April 1951.

GUILFORD, J. P., Editor. *Fields of Psychology.* Second Edition. New York: D. Van Nostrand Co., 1950. 779 p.

GUTHRIE, Edwin R. "The Status of Systematic Psychology." *American Psychologist* 5:97-101; April 1950.

HARMS, Ernest. "Child Guidance Yesterday, Today, and Tomorrow." *School and Society* 72:129-32; August 26, 1950.

HARRIS, Noel G. *Modern Trends in Psychological Medicine.* London: Paul B. Hoeber, 1948. xii + 450 p.

HOLY, T. C. "Modern Trends in Heating and Ventilation." *Harvard Educational Review* 7:369-77; May 1937.

JAMES, C. Evan. "Trends in Child Development Research." *Childhood Education* 29:73-76; October 1952.

JOHNSON, B. L. "Junior-College Trends." *School Review* 52:606-10; December 1944.

JUDD, C. H. "Facing the Future." *Educational Record* 19:125-40; April 1938. Analyzes trends in terms of administrative units of the school system, vocational education and general education, equality of educational opportunity, and scientific study of educational problems.

KANTOR, J. R. "Current Trends in Psychological Theory." *Psychological Bulletin* 38:29-65; January 1941.

KENT, R. A. "The Past and the Present." *Bulletin of the Association of American Colleges* 24:436-51; December 1938. Trends in the liberal arts college.

KOCH, Sigmund. "The Current Status of Motivational Psychology." *Psychological Review* 58:147-54; May 1951.

KOCH, Sigmund. "Theoretical Psychology, 1950: An Overview." *Psychological Review* 58:295-301; July 1951.

KUHLMANN, F. "Retrogressive Trends in Clinical Psychology." *Journal of Consulting Psychology* 5:97-104; May-June 1941.

LLOYD-JONES, Esther. "Personnel Work Today." *Journal of Higher Education* 13:81-86, 116; February 1942.

McDONALD, Ralph. "Next Steps in Meeting Our Expanding Opportunities." *College and University* 24:481-94; July 1949.

MILLER, J. Hillis. "Higher Education and the Problems of This Decade." *Educational Record* 32:335-49; October 1951.

MORT, Paul R. "New Developments in Educational Dynamics." *Teachers College Record* 48:425-28; April 1947.

MOWRER, E. R. "Recent Trends in Family Research." *American Sociological Review* 6:499-511; August 1941.

MUNRO, Thomas, and Others. *Art in American Life and Education.* Fortieth Yearbook of the National Society for the Study of Education. Bloomington, Ill.: Public School Publishing Co., 1941. xx + 819 p. Includes discussions of research in art, trends, and graduate work for the art teacher.

NETTLER, Gwynne. "Toward a Definition of the Sociologist." *American Sociological Review* 12:553-60; October 1947.

NEUMEYER, M. H. "War Time Trends in Recreation." *Sociology and Social Research* 28:359-75; May-June, 1944.

NIMKOFF, Meyer F. "Trends in Family Research." *American Journal of Sociology* 53:477-82; May 1948.

NOYES, Edward S. "Recent Trends in the Comprehensive Examination in English." *Educational Record* 21:107-19; January 1940.

ODUM, H. W. "The State of Sociology in the United States and Its Prospect in the South." *Social Forces* 17:8-14; October 1938.

OGBURN, W. F. "Social Trends." *American Journal of Sociology* 45:756-69; March 1940. Deals with research on social trends.

RICHARDS, Eugene S. "A Proposed Pattern for Sociology." *Sociology and Social Research* 32:705-10; January-February 1948.

ROCKWOOD, Lemo D. "Trends in Family Life Research." *Journal of Home Economics* 34:647-54; November 1942.

SHANE, Harold G. "Recent Developments in Elementary School Evaluation." *Journal of Educational Research* 44:491-506; March 1951.

SLETTO, Raymond F. "Next Steps in Social Measurement." *Sociometry* 10:354-61; November 1947.

SMITH, A. A. "Recent Trends in Rural Social Work." *Sociology and Social Research* 23:466-73; May-June 1939.

SMITH, Mapheus. "An Approach to a Systematic Social Psychology." *Sociology and Social Research* 32:507-12; September-October 1947.

STRAYER, George D. "Changing Concepts of Educational Administration." *Teachers College Record* 40:469-82; March 1939.

STURTEVANT, Sarah M., STRANG, Ruth, and McKIM, Margaret. *Trends in Student Personnel Work.* New York: Bureau of Publications, Teachers College, Columbia University, 1940. 110 p.

SYMONDS, P. M. "Trends in Educational Research." *Journal of Educational Research* 34:300-302; December 1940.

TAINTER, M. L. "An Industrial View of Research Trends." *Science* 103:95-99; January 25, 1946.

TAYLOR, Griffith, Editor. *Geography in the Twentieth Century:* A Study of Growth, Fields, Techniques, Aims, and Trends. New York: Philosophical Library, 1951. x + 630 p.

THAYER, V. T. "Current Trends in the Development of General Education." *Educational Record* 20:373-94; July 1939.

TIMASHEFF, N. S. "Definitions in the Social Sciences." *American Journal of Sociology* 53:201-209; November 1947.

TOLLEY, William P. "American Education and the Testing Movement." *Educational Record* 29:86-96; January 1948.

TRAXLER, Arthur E. "Emerging Trends in Guidance." *School Review* 58:14-23; January 1950.

"Trends in Postwar Adult Education." *Adult Education Journal* 5:1-55; January 1946.

TYLER, Ralph W. "Trends in the Preparation of Teachers." *School Review* 51:207-12; April 1943.

TYLER, Ralph W. "Trends in Teaching—How Research Is Affecting Our Understanding of the Learning Process." *School Review* 59:263-72; May 1951.

VINCENT, M. J. "Current Trends in Sociology." *Sociology and Social Research* 23:27-44; September-October 1938.

WHEAT, Harry G. "Changes and Trends in Arithmetic Since 1910." *Elementary School Journal* 47:134-44; November 1946.

WOOD, H. B. "Trends in Teacher Education." *Educational Administration and Supervision* 28:87-103; February 1942.

WOODWORTH, R. S. *Contemporary Schools of Psychology.* Revised Edition. New York: Ronald Press, 1948. ix + 279 p.

ZNANIECKI, Florian. "The Scientific Function of Sociology of Education." *Educational Theory* 1:69-78, 86; August 1951.

### D. Predictions and Prophecies

BENJAMIN, Harold. "American Education in the Twentieth Century—Second Half." *Third Yearbook,* American Association of Colleges for Teacher Education. Oneonta, N. Y.: The Association, 1950. p. 184-190.

BLAKESLEE, A. F. "Science Five Thousand Years Hence." *Science* 92:387-88; November 1, 1940.

BRIGGS, T. H. "A Vision of Secondary Education." *Teachers College Record* 34:1-17; October 1932.

BRUNNER, E. deS. "Sociology Tomorrow." *Rural Sociology* 11:95-102; June 1946.

CARTWRIGHT, M. A. "A Preview of Postwar Adult Education." *Educational Forum* 10:273-80; March 1946.

CHAPIN, F. S. "Looking Forward in the Social Sciences." *Sociology and Social Research* 29:431-41; July-August 1945.

Chicago, University of, Members of the Department of Education. "Education in the Year 2031." *School Review* 39:337-49; May 1931.

CONDON, E. U. "Science and Our Future." *Science* 103:415-17; April 5, 1946.

CYR, F. W. "The Future of Rural America." *Teachers College Record* 47:110-18; November 1945.

ELLWOOD, C. A. "The Prospects of Sociology." *Social Science* 15:302-4; July 1940.

ELSBREE, W. S. "Next Steps for the Teaching Profession." *Teachers College Record* 47:243-50; January 1946.

ENGELHARDT, N. L. "School Administration Then, Now, and Tomorrow." *American School Board Journal* 100:21-24; March 1940.

EURICH, Alvin C. "Mid-point: The Vision of the Future." *North Central Association Quarterly* 25:168-73; October 1950.

FORKNER, H. L. "Business Education—Its Present and Probable Future." *Teachers College Record* 44:493-500; April 1943.

FURNAS, C. C. *The Next Hundred Years:* The Unfinished Business of Science. New York: Reynal and Hitchcock, 1936. xiv + 434 p.

GUMMERE, R. M. "Twenty Years on; or, the Next Two Decades in Private Secondary Education." *School and Society* 54:129-34; August 30, 1941.

HINCKS, C. M. "The Next Quarter Century." *Mental Hygiene* 19:69-77; January 1935. Deals with the work and future of the National Commission for Mental Hygiene.

HUGHES, R. M. "Higher Education in 1980." *Journal of Higher Education* 9:77-83; February 1938. Predicts secondary and college enrollments.

HUGHES, W. H. "Research and Public Education in 1950." *Nation's Schools* 6:21-24; July 1930.

JOHNSON, C. S. "The Next Decade in Race Relations." *Journal of Negro Education* 13:441-46; Summer 1944.

JUDD, C. H. "The Future of American Education." *School Review* 50:621-28; November 1942.

KELLY, R. L. "The Next Fifty Years in the American Colleges of Liberal Arts." *Bulletin of the Association of American Colleges* 24:407-22; December 1938.

LUNDBERG, G. A. "The Future of the Social Sciences." *Scientific Monthly* 53:346-59; October 1941.

ODUM, H. W. "Sociology in the Contemporary World of Today and Tomorrow." *Social Forces* 21:390-96; May 1943.

OGBURN, W. F. "Future Trends in Education." *Elementary School Journal* 40:95-105; October 1939.

PEIK, W. E. "Looking Ahead in American Teacher Education." *Third Yearbook,* American Association of Colleges for Teacher Education. Oneonta, N. Y.: The Association, 1950. p. 9-21.

"The Position of the Negro in the American Social Order in 1950." *Journal of Negro Education* 8:551-616; July 1939.

RAPAPORT, David. "The Future of Research in Clinical Psychology and Psychiatry." *American Psychologist* 2:167-72; May 1947.

"Report of California Planning Conference on Leadership in Secondary Education: Secondary Education During the Next Half Century." *California Journal of Secondary Education* 27:330-64; October 1952.

SEASHORE, Carl E. "Whither Ahead of Science in Music." *Education* 67:152-56; November 1946.

SMITH, R. L. "Next Steps in Coöperative Education." *Journal of Educational Sociology* 16:521-28; April 1943.

SNEDDEN, David. "American Education in 1960." *Teachers College Record* 37:625-43; April 1936.

SNEDDEN, David. *American High Schools and Vocational Schools in 1960.* New York: Bureau of Publications, Teachers College, Columbia University, 1931. vi + 122 p.

SNEDDEN, David. "Some Anticipations: American Colleges and Universities in 1980." *Journal of Higher Education* 4:347-52; October 1933.

STRAYER, G. D. "Looking Forward in Education." *Teachers College Record* 43:489-96; March 1942.

TYLER, Ralph W. "Next Steps in Improving Secondary Education." *School Review* 60:523-31; December 1952.

VITELES, M. S. "Postlude: The Past and Future of Industrial Psychology." *Journal of Consulting Psychology* 8:182-86; May-June 1944.

*Vocational Education in the Years Ahead:* Report of a Committee to Study Postwar Problems in Vocational Education. Vocational Division Bulletin No. 234, Office of Education. General Series No. 7. Washington: Government Printing Office, 1945. xiv + 329 p.

WELLS, F. L. "Clinical Psychology in Retrospect and Prospect." *Journal of Psychology* 27:125-42; January 1949.

WILKINS, Roy. "Next Steps in Education for Racial Understanding." *Journal of Negro Education* 13:432-40; Summer 1944.

WOODY, Clifford. "Some Next Steps in Teacher Education." *Journal of Educational Research* 37:670-83; May 1944.

WRIGHTSTONE, J. W., and MEISTER, Morris, Editors. *Looking Ahead in Education.* Boston: Ginn and Co., 1945. xvi + 150 p.

ZOOK, George F. "The Past Twenty Years—The Next Twenty Years." *Junior College Journal* 10:617-23; May 1940. A view of the junior-college movement.

### E. Unsolved Problems and Needed Research

ADKINS, Dorothy C. "Needed Research on Examining Devices." *American Psychologist* 3:104-106; March 1948.

ALILUNAS, L. J. "Needed Research in Teacher Mental Hygiene." *Journal of Educational Research* 38:653-55; May 1945.

ALLPORT, F. H. "Some Research Suggestions on Morale." *Journal of Social Psychology* 14:257-61; August 1941.

American Council on Education. "Problems Facing American Education: A Symposium." *Educational Record* 23:511-66; July 1942.

ANDERSON, G. Lester. "Unsolved Problems in Teacher Education." *Third Yearbook,* American Association of Colleges for Teacher Education. Oneonta, N. Y.: The Association, 1950. p. 22-33.

BAKER, F. E. "Major Issues in the Education of Teachers." *Childhood Education* 14:389-93; May 1938.

BARNARD, John D. "Problems Related to the Teaching of Problem Solving That Need to Be Investigated." *Science Education* 34:180-84; April 1950.

BARTLETT, F. C., and Others. *The Study of Society:* Methods and Problems. London: Kegan Paul, Trench, Trubner and Co., 1939. xiv + 498 p.

BAUER, Harry C. "A New Field for Scientists." *Educational Record* 27:433-40; October 1946.

BENNE, Kenneth D. "An Approach to Issues Underlying Curriculum Development." *Journal of Educational Research* 41:561-76; April 1948.

BLOOM, B. S. "Some Major Problems in Educational Measurement." *Journal of Educational Research* 38:139-42; October 1944.

BLOOM, Leonard. "Concerning Ethnic Research." *American Sociological Review* 13:171-82; April 1948.

BLOOM, Leonard. "Militarization as a Research Field." *Sociology and Social Research* 28:194-99; January-February 1944.

BOARDMAN, Charles W. "Some Postwar Problems of the Secondary School." *North Central Association Quarterly* 20:203-10; January 1946.

BOGARDUS, E. S. "Ten Group Work Problems." *Sociology and Social Research* 22:273-80; January-February 1938.

BOUCHER, C. S. "Some Current Educational Problems and Some Possible Re-adjustments." *North Central Association Quarterly* 14:362-84; April 1940.

BOYCE, G. A., and BEATTY, W. W. "Six Issues in Secondary Mathematics." *Clearing House* 11:102-7; October 1936.

BRIGGS, T. H. "If There Were Millions." *Teachers College Record* 35:633-66; May 1934. Outlines a series of problems in secondary education that require study.

BRIGGS, T. H. "An Uncultivated Field." *North Central Association Quarterly* 12:214-20; October 1937.

BRIGGS, T. H., and Others. *Issues in Secondary Education:* A Report of the Committee on the Orientation of Secondary Education. Bulletin of the Department of Secondary-School Principals. Washington: The Department, N.E.A., January 1936. 372 p.

BROOKER, F. E. "Neglected Areas of Curriculum Implementation." *Educational Record* 20:241-55; April 1939. Urges utilization of motion pictures and the radio.

BROWN, K. I. "Four Basic Issues for Colleges of Liberal Arts in the Post-War Period." *North Central Association Quarterly* 19:177-83; October 1944.

BROWNELL, William A. "Frontiers in Educational Research in Arithmetic." *Journal of Educational Research* 40:373-80; January 1947.

BRYSON, Lyman, FINKELSTEIN, Louis, and MACIVER, R. M., Editors. *Perspectives on a Troubled Decade:* Science, Philosophy, and Religion, 1939-1949. New York: Harper and Bros., 1950. xvii + 901 p. Summarizes ten years of effort to interpret the major intellectual issues of our times.

BURGESS, Ernest W. "The Family and Sociological Research." *Social Forces* 26:1-6; October 1947.

BURTON, William H., and Others. "Needed Research on Textbooks," *Phi Delta Kappan* 33:297-300; January 1952.

BURTT, H. E., and Others. "Market Problems and Market Research." *Journal of Consulting Psychology* 5:145-93; August 1941.

BUSWELL, G. T. "Needed Research on Arithmetic." *The Teaching of Arithmetic.* Fiftieth Yearbook of the National Society for the Study of Education, Part II. Chicago: University of Chicago Press, 1951. p. 282-97.

CARMICHAEL, O. C. "Some Educational Frontiers." *School and Society* 68:193-96; September 25, 1948.

CARMICHAEL, O. C. "Some Issues in the Higher Learning." *Educational Record* 19:323-31; July 1938.

CARTWRIGHT, M. A. "Suggested Studies in Adult Education." *Teachers College Record* 43:618-24; May 1942.

CASWELL, H. L. "Research in the Curriculum." *Educational Leadership* 7:438-45; April 1950.

CASWELL, H. L. "Research Needed for Fundamental Curriculum Development." *Educational Administration and Supervision* 22:517-22; October 1936.

CHAMBERS, M. M. "Issues in Educational Law." *Practical Values of Educational Research.* Washington: American Educational Research Association, 1938. p. 65-69.

CHAMBERS, M. M. "Twenty Million Dollars Worth of Educational Research." *School and Society* 67:273-76; April 10, 1948.

CHAPIN, F. S., and QUEEN, S. A. *Research Memorandum on Social Work in the Depression.* New York: Social Science Research Council, 1937. xii + 134 p.

CHARNOW, John. *Topics for Research Concerning Public Assistance Programs.* Washington: Committee on Social Security, Social Science Research Council, 1941. 72 p.

CHARTERS, W. W. "Neglected Areas in Teacher Education." *Curriculum Journal* 8:197-200; May 1937.

CHEIN, Isidor, COOK, Stuart W., and HARDING, John. "The Field of Action Research." *American Psychologist* 3:43-50; February 1948.

CHITTENDEN, Gertrude E. "Breaking Ground in Family Life Research." *Journal of Home Economics* 41:364-66; September 1949.

CLAGUE, Ewan. "New Frontiers in Occupational Research." *Occupations* 27:535-37; May 1949.

CLARK, John R. "Issues in Teaching Arithmetic." *Teachers College Record* 52:205-12; January 1951.

CLOUD, A. J., and LEUENBERGER, H. W. "Problems of Junior College Education." *Junior College Journal* 9:4-7; October 1938.

COLVERT, C. C., and BRIGHT, H. F. "Research Problems Preferred by Junior College Administrators." *Junior College Journal* 20:350-54; February 1950.

Committee on Research and Publications. *Suggested Problems for Research Study in Vocational and Industrial Arts Education.* Revised Edition. Proceedings of the American Vocational Association. Washington: The Association, 1949. 22 p.

Committee on Studies in Social Aspects of the Depression. *Studies in the Social Aspects of the Depression.* New York: Social Science Research Council, 1937. Thirteen volumes, each outlining a research program in a particular social area, including education, consumer problems, crime, family, health, reading habits, minority peoples, mobility of population, recreation, relief policy and practice, religion, rural life, and social work.

COOPER, Shirley, and Others. "A Symposium on Needed Research in District Reorganization." *Phi Delta Kappan* 32:356-59; April 1951.

COREY, S. M. "Teachers as Investigators." *Progressive Education* 27:131-32; February 1950.

COTTRELL, Leonard S., Jr. "New Directions for Research on the American Family." *Social Casework* 34:54-60; February 1953.

COTTRELL, Leonard S., Jr. "The Present Status and Future Orientation of Research on the Family." *American Sociological Review* 13:123-36; April 1948.

COWEN, P. A., and COXE, W. W. "Issues Involved in Enlarging School Administrative Units." *American School Board Journal* 101:19-21; August 1940.

CRAIG, Gerald S. "Unfinished Business in Elementary Science." *Teachers College Record* 50:410-16; March 1949.

CRARY, Ryland W. "Challenging Areas in Developing Social Studies Curriculum." *Teachers College Record* 48:140-47; December 1946.

CUNNINGHAM, Ruth. "Unfinished Business in Curriculum Development." *Teachers College Record* 48:312-18; February 1947.

CUNNINGHAM, Ruth, and MIEL, Alice. "Frontiers in Educational Research in Elementary School Curriculum Development." *Journal of Educational Research* 40:365-72; January 1947.

CUNNINGHAM, Ruth, and Others. "Recommended: Group Research for Teachers." *Teachers College Record* 50:108-13; November 1948.

CURTI, Merle. "Immediate Problems of the Schools." *Teachers College Record* 43:431-41; March 1942.

CYR, F. W. "Needed Research on the Reorganization of School Districts in Rural Areas." *Teachers College Record* 38:293-315; January 1937. Deals with basic assumptions, social and economic factors, administrative structure, legal and historical research, and the reorganization process.

DASHIELL, J. F. "A Neglected Fourth Dimension to Psychological Research." *Psychological Review* 47:289-305; July 1940.

DAVIS, M. M. "Social Medicine as a Field for Social Research." *American Journal of Sociology* 54:274-79; September 1938.

DAVIS, Watson. "Possibilities of Future Technologic Development." *Science Education* 30:261-66; December 1946.

DAWSON, H. A. "Pressing Problems in Financing Public Education in the Southern States." *Peabody Journal of Education* 15:233-41; March 1938.

DAY, E. E. "Issues Confronting Higher and Professional Education." *Journal of Higher Education* 13:59-65; February 1942.

DIMOCK, H. S. "Some Issues for Religious Education Raised by Recent Character Research." *Religious Education* 33:87-92; April-June 1938.

DOBBS, H. A. C. *Operational Research and Action Research.* Washington: Institute of Ethnic Affairs, 1947. 21 p.

DONOVAN, H. L. "Problems of Research of the University." *Peabody Journal of Education* 22:65-71; September 1944.

DOUGLASS, Harl R. "Scientific Investigation of Instructional Problems." *Journal of Educational Research* 29:130-38; October 1935.

DRAPER, Edgar M. "Curriculum Research: Biggest Responsibility of Every Teacher." *Clearing House* 24:387-92; March 1950.

DUNLAP, Knight. "The Method and Problems of Social Psychology." *Psychological Review* 47:471-85; November 1940.

DURRELL, D. D. "Research Problems in Reading in the Elementary School." *Elementary English Review* 13:101-6, 111; March 1936.

EATON, W. H. "Research on Veterans' Adjustment." *American Journal of Sociology* 51:483-87; March 1946.

EDMONSON, J. B. "Some Debatable Issues in Health Education." *School and Society* 48:221-25; August 20, 1938.

"Educational Issues in Psychology: A Report of the February 1952 Conference of the APA Education and Training Board." *American Psychologist* 7:456-60; August 1952.

Educational Policies Commission. *Research Memorandum on Education in the Depression.* Social Science Research Council Bulletin No. 28, 1937. New York: The Council, 1937. xii + 173 p. Suggests problems for investigation and illustrative methods of attack.

EIKENBERRY, D. H., and Others. *National Committee on Research in Secondary Education:* Problems and Questions in Secondary Education Suggested for Investigation. Office of Education, Washington: C. A. Jessen, Secretary of Committee, 1937. iv + 57 p. A list of 997 problems for study.

ELLIS, A. C. "Problems in Adult Education Needing Study." *School and Society* 46:449-57; October 9, 1937.

ELLIS, A. C. "Research for Urban Universities." *Journal of Adult Education* 9:57-61; January 1937. Urges study of aims, subject matter, curriculum, method, guidance, and administration in adult education.

ENTERLINE, Herman G. "Summary of Needed Research in Business Education Administration and Supervision." *National Business Education Quarterly* 20:43-52; May 1952.

ESSEX, Don L., and Others. "School Plant and Equipment." *Review of Educational Research* 18:1-72; February 1948.

EVANS, Francis C., and Others. "Symposium on Viewpoints, Problems, and Methods of Research in Urban Areas." *Scientific Monthly* 73:37-50; July 1951.

FAULKNER, Ray. "A Research Program in Art Appreciation." *Journal of Educational Research* 33:36-43; September 1939.

FAUSOLD, Samuel. "Some Problems Which Challenge American Educators." *School and Society* 46:193-200; August 14, 1937.

FITZPATRICK, E. A. "Need for Catholic Studies in the History of Education." *Catholic School Journal* 51:148-49; April 1951.

FITZPATRICK, E. A. "Needed Research in Teaching Religion in the Elementary School." *Catholic School Journal* 38:157-59; June 1938. Suggests the need for better understanding of the will, feelings, emotions, appreciations, and attitudes.

FLEEGE, U. H. "Issues and Problems Facing Catholic Secondary Education." *Catholic Educational Review* 44:213-22; April 1946.

FOSTER, R. G. "Objective Methods of Sociological Research Generally Applicable to Child Development Studies." *Journal of Educational Sociology* 9:79-87; October 1935.

FOX, Robert S. "Needed Research in the Elementary School Curriculum." *University of Michigan School of Education Bulletin* 23:39-42; December 1951.

FREDERICK, O. I. "Research Technics and Problems Involved in Studying Areas of Human Activity." *Practical Values of Educational Research.* Washington: American Educational Research Association, 1938. p. 104-10.

FUNCHESS, Lloyd W. "Research Is Needed in Music Education." *Phi Delta Kappan* 30:349-50; April 1949.

GATES, Arthur I. "Frontiers in Educational Research in Reading." *Journal of Educational Research* 40:381-88; January 1947.

GATES, Arthur I. "Needed Research in Elementary School Reading." *Elementary English Review* 13:306-10, 318; December 1936.

GATES, Arthur I. "New Fields for Educational Psychologists." *Journal of Consulting Psychology* 5:111-16; May-June 1941.

GAUMNITZ, W. H. "The Importance of the Small School—Its Major Problems." *Phi Delta Kappan* 19:209-13; April 1937.

GEYER, D. L., HUGGETT, A. J., and MARSHALL, D. K. *Current Issues in Education.* Chicago: Werkman's Book House, 1942. 92 p.

GLOCK, Charles Y. "Some Implications of Organization for Social Research." *Social Forces* 30:129-34; December 1951.

GODDARD, R. W. "Basic Issues for Junior Colleges in the Post-War Period." *North Central Association Quarterly* 19:184-89; October 1944.

GOLDTHORPE, J. H. "Some Unsolved Problems in Federal Grants-in-Aid." *American School Board Journal* 103:13-15, 59; December 1941.

GOOD, Carter V. "Problems and Techniques of Educational Diagnosis and Adjustment." *School and Society* 48:261-67; August 27, 1938.

GOOD, Carter V. "You'll Find Your Problems in Your Own Back Yard." *Journal of Educational Research* 32:42-44; September 1938. Needed research in the area of educational diagnosis.

GOOD, Carter V., BARR, A. S., and SCATES, Douglas E. *The Methodology of Educational Research.* New York: Appleton-Century-Crofts, 1936. p. 777-855.

GOODYKOONTZ, Bess. "New Problems in Elementary Education." *Nation's Schools* 16:23-26; September 1935. Deals with need for reorganization, effectiveness of coöperation, need for restatement of functions, and curriculum expansion.

GRAY, A. L. "Needed Research in the School-Plant Field." *Review of Educational Research* 21:63-68; February 1951.

GRAY, H. A. "Needed Research in the Field of Audio-Visual Learning Aids." *Practical Values of Educational Research.* Washington: American Educational Research Association, 1938. p. 72-77.

GRAY, W. S. "Needed Research in Reading." *Elementary English* 29:100-108; February 1952.

GRAY, W. S., Editor. *Current Issues in Higher Education.* Chicago: University of Chicago Press, 1937. viii + 153 p.

GREENE, H. W. "Crucial Problems in the Higher Education of Negroes." *School and Society* 46:245-46; August 21, 1937.

GRUNDFEST, Harry. "The Scientists' Postwar Problems." *Scientific Monthly* 60:130-40; February 1945.

GUERTIN, Wilson H. "Mental Hygiene: New Frontier in Education." *Elementary School Journal* 49:93-97; October 1948.

HAGGERTY, W. J. "Current Issues in General Education." *School Review* 46:497-514; September 1938.

HAGOOD, Margaret J., and DUCOFF, L. J. "Some Measurement and Research Problems Arising from Sociological Aspects of a Full Employment Policy." *American Sociological Review* 11:560-67; October 1946.

HAITEMA, John S. "Administrative Research Necessary for Special Education." *Journal of Educational Research* 40:628-37; April 1947.

HALL, R. B. *Area Studies:* With Special Reference to Their Implications for Research in the Social Sciences. New York: Social Science Research Council, 1947. iii + 90 p.

HALLENBECK, Wilbur C. "New Needs in Adult Education." *Teachers College Record* 48:487-93; May 1947.

HAMILTON, C. Horace. "Some Current Problems in the Development of Rural Sociology." *Rural Sociology* 15:315-21; December 1950.

HARRIS, Chester W. "The Appraisal of a School—Problems for Study." *Journal of Educational Research* 41:172-82; November 1947.

HARVEY, Julien H. "Contemporary Problems in Accident Prevention and Safety Education." *Journal of Educational Sociology* 20:78-84; October 1946.

HASLETT, A. W. *Unsolved Problems of Science.* New York: Macmillan Co., 1935. xi + 317 p.

HAUSER, Philip M. "The Labor Force as a Field of Interest for the Sociologist." *American Sociological Review* 16:530-38; August 1951.

HAYES, Samuel P., Jr. "Some Psychological Problems of Economics." *Psychological Bulletin* 47:289-330; July 1950.

HAYWARD, B. W. "Major Problems of an Administrator in the Readjustment of the Educational Program." *Harvard Educational Review* 15:293-300; October 1945.

HEATON, Kenneth L. "Educational Planning." *Harvard Educational Review* 19:30-39; Winter 1949.

HENDRICKSON, Gordon. "Needed Research in Music Education." *Journal of Educational Research* 31:672-77; May 1938.

HENDRICKSON, Gordon. "Some Needed Research in Elementary Education." *Elementary School Journal* 51:127-35; November 1950.

HERRICK, V. E. "Present Problems Facing the Elementary School." *Elementary School Journal* 43:513-19; May 1943.

HERRICK, V. E. "Present Problems Facing the Elementary School: A Second Report." *Elementary School Journal* 44:575-82; June 1944.

HJELTE, George. "Research in Recreation." *Research Quarterly of the American Association for Health, Physical Education, and Recreation* 10:3-9; March 1939. Suggests needed studies.

HOCHWALD, Hilde L. "The Function of Social Work Research." *Social Casework* 34:29-33; January 1953.

HOFFER, C. R. "Youth as an Object of Sociological Study." *Sociology and Social Research* 20:417-21; May-June 1936.

HOLLINGSHEAD, A. B. "Behavior Systems as a Field for Research." *American Sociological Review* 4:816-22; December 1939.

HOLY, Thomas C. "Basic Research, Urgently Needed." *Nation's Schools* 41:28-30; February 1948.

HOLY, Thomas C. "Needed Research in the Field of School Buildings and Equipment," in "The School Plant." *Review of Educational Research* 5:406-11; October 1935.

HOLY, Thomas C. "Some Current Problems of School Finance and Revenue." *American School Board Journal* 105:15-17, 62; November 1942.

HOPPER, Rex D. "Sociological Research in a Time of Crisis." *Social Forces* 26:13-18; October 1947.

HORN, Francis H., Editor. *Current Issues in Higher Education, 1953.* Proceedings of the Eighth Annual National Conference on Higher Education, Chicago, Ill., March 5-7, 1953. Washington: Association for Higher Education, N.E.A., 1953. xii + 292 p.

HUNKINS, R. V. "Wanted: A Literature for Operative School Administration." *American School Board Journal* 119:23-24; September 1949.

HUNT, J. McV. "Toward an Integrated Program of Research on Psychotherapy." *Journal of Consulting Psychology* 16:237-46; August 1952.

"Imperative Needs of Youth of Secondary-School Age." *Bulletin of the National Association of Secondary School Principals* 31:3-144; March 1947.

Institute of Adult Education. *Suggested Studies in Adult Education.* New York: Teachers College, Columbia University, 1942. 26 p.

JENKINS, David H. "Research in Group Dynamics." *Social Education* 8:347-50, 355, 369; December 1948.

JENSEN, Kai. "Needed Research." *Child Development and the Curriculum.* Thirty-eighth Yearbook of the National Society for the Study of Education, Part I. Bloomington, Ill.: Public School Publishing Co., 1939. Chapter 21.

JESSEN, C. A. *Needed Research in Secondary Education.* Office of Education Bulletin No. 28, 1937. Washington: Government Printing Office, 1938. 69 p. Based in large part on the findings of the National Survey of Secondary Education.

JONES, Archie N., and EVANS, G. K. "Areas of Needed Research in Music Education." *Education* 72:23-27; September 1951.

JONES, H. E. "The Problems of Child Development." *Journal of Consulting Psychology* 6:123-27; May-June 1942.

JUDD, C. H. *Problems of Education in the United States.* Recent Social Trends Monographs. New York: McGraw-Hill Book Co., 1935. 214 p. Reveals important current trends and presents some of the problems that inevitably arise in a social system that is undergoing rapid evolution.

KATONA, Arthur. "Campus as a Research Area." *Journal of Higher Education* 19:93-96; February 1948.

KAZDAN, C. S. "Postwar Problems in Education." *Journal of Educational Sociology* 19:351-58; February 1946.

KILPATRICK, William H. "Crucial Issues in Current Educational Theory." *Educational Theory* 1:1-8; May 1951.

KIRK, Samuel A. "Needed Projects and Research in Special Education." *The Education of Exceptional Children.* Forty-ninth Yearbook, National Society for the Study of Education, Part II. Edited by Nelson B. Henry. Chicago: University of Chicago Press, 1950. Chapter 17, p. 320-34.

KNIGHT, E. W. "Some Current Educational Issues and Theories." *School and Society* 52:505-11; November 23, 1940.

KOOS, Earl L. "A Research Approach to Community Planning." *Journal of Educational Sociology* 20:218-22; December 1946.

KOOS, L. V. "Research Preferred for Junior Colleges." *Junior College Journal* 17:61-71; October 1946.

KORNITZER, Henrietta. "Problems for Research in the Education of Partially Seeing Children." *Journal of Educational Research* 40:592-97; April 1947.

KYKER, B. Frank. "Needed Research in Business Education." *National Business Education Quarterly* 16:21-25, 54; October 1947.

KYTE, George C. "Frontiers in Educational Research in the Supervision of Elementary Education." *Journal of Educational Research* 40:348-55; January 1947.

LA BRANT, Lou. "Needed Research in Language Expression." *Elementary English* 29:35-38; January 1952.

LEE, Edwin A. "Major Problems in Occupational Adjustment." *Educational Record* 21:57-70; January 1940.

LEHMAN, Ruth T. "Critical Issues in Home Economics." *Journal of Home Economics* 40:59-61; February 1948.

LEONARD, J. P. "Current Conflicts in the Curriculum." *Curriculum Journal* 11:298-302; November 1940.

LINDER, I. H. "Neglected Areas of School Administration." *American School Board Journal* 98:50-51; April 1939.

LINDER, I. H. "Twelve Basic Questions on Curriculum Construction." *American School Board Journal* 96:27-29; March 1938.

LIONBERGER, Herbert F. "The Diffusion of Farm and Home Information as an Area of Sociological Research." *Rural Sociology* 17:132-43; June 1952.

LOMAX, Paul S. "Current Problems in Business Education." *Journal of Business Education* 13:20-22, 24; November 1937.

LOMAX, Paul S. "Needed Research in Basic Business Education in the Secondary Schools." *United Business Education Association Forum* 5:11-13; March 1951.

LORGE, Irving D. "Research Needs." *Adult Education* 1:73-79; December 1950.

LOWENFELD, Berthold. "Research in the Education of the Blind." *Journal of Educational Research* 40:583-91; April 1947.

LUNDBERG, G. A. "What Are Sociological Problems?" *American Sociological Review* 6:357-69; June 1941.

MAASKE, Roben J., and Others. *Needed Research in Adult Education.* Washington: N.E.A., June 1949. 32 p.

MAASKE, Roben J., and Others. *Needed Research in Teacher Education.* Oneonta, N. Y.: A.A.C.T.E., 1954. 62 p.

MACKENZIE, Gordon N. "Frontiers in Educational Research in Secondary School Curriculum Building." *Journal of Educational Research* 40:356-64; January 1947.

MACLACHLAN, John. "Distinctive Cultures in the Southeast; Their Possibilities for Regional Research." *Social Forces* 18:210-15; December 1939.

MALLER, J. B. "Proposed Studies of the Social Aspects of Rehousing Families of Low Income." *Journal of Educational Sociology* 15:309-11; January 1942.

MATHEWS, C. O. "Issues in the Construction and Use of Educational Measurements." *Journal of Educational Research* 33:452-56; February 1940.

McCLOY, C. H. "Some Unexplored Areas for Research." *Research Quarterly of the American Association for Health, Physical Education, and Recreation* 10:3-10; December 1939. Stresses physical education.

McCLUSKY, F. D. "The Immediate Needs in Visual Education." *Educational Screen* 16:213-15, 217; September 1937.

McCONNELL, T. R. "Some Unresolved Problems of Secondary Education." *North Central Association Quarterly* 27:258-66; January 1953.

McGRATH, Earl J. "Need for Experimentation and Research." *General Education in Transition.* Edited by H. T. Morse. Minneapolis: University of Minnesota Press, 1951. p. 16-28.

MEAD, A. R., HINES, V. A., and McLENDON, Ida R. "Proposals for the Improvement of Educational Research." *Journal of Educational Research* 42:1-7; September 1948.

*Memorandum on University Research Programs in the Field of Labor.* Washington: Committee on Labor Market Research, Social Science Research Council, 1947. 42 p.

MERTON, Robert K. "Selected Problems of Field Work in the Planned Community." *American Sociological Review* 12:304-12; June 1947.

MOORE, Wilbert E. "Current Issues in Industrial Sociology." *American Sociological Review* 12:651-57; December 1947.

MORGAN, Agnes F. "New Frontiers in Nutrition Research." *Journal of Home Economics* 41:367-69; September 1949.

MORGAN, D. S. "Issues Concerning Vocational Education in the Secondary Schools." *North Central Association Quarterly* 15:25-30; July 1940.

MORPHET, Edgar L. "Issues in Public Education Support." *Phi Delta Kappan* 30:85-86, 90; November 1948.

MORRISON, J. C. "Research in Educational Reconstruction." *Elementary School Journal* 44:451-57; April 1944.

MORRISON, J. C. "Some Issues for Postwar Elementary Education." *Elementary School Journal* 45:15-22; September 1944.

MORRISON, J. C. "State Issues in Post War Education." *American School Board Journal* 109:9-12; July 1944.

MUSSELMAN, Vernon A. "Significant Research Needed in Business Teacher Education." *National Business Education Quarterly* 17:31-33; March 1949.

MYKLEBUST, Helmar R. "Research in the Education and Psychology of the Deaf and Hard of Hearing." *Journal of Educational Research* 40:598-607; April 1947.

National Commitee on Coördination in Secondary Education. *Suggested Studies in Secondary Education:* A List of Problems for Research. Washington: Civic Education Service, 1939. 101 p.

"Needed Research in Science Education." *Science Education* 31:199-247; October 1947. A series of papers.

"Needed Research in Teacher Education." *Phi Delta Kappan* 32:144-46; December 1950.

"Needed Research Studies in Junior High School Science Teaching: Preliminary Report of Junior-High School-Science Committee." *Science Education* 32:175-85; April 1948.

NEUMEYER, M. H. "The Field of Research in Recreation." *Research Quarterly
of the American Association for Health, Physical Education, and Recreation* 10:11-19; December 1939.

NORTON, John K. "Frontiers in Educational Research in General Administration." *Journal of Educational Research* 40:327-34; January 1947.

OJEMANN, Ralph H. "Research in Planned Learning Programs and the Science
of Behavior." *Journal of Educational Research* 42:96-104; October 1948.

OPPENHEIMER, J. J. "Some Problems in Personnel Research." *Journal of Higher
Education* 10:363-68; October 1939.

O'SHEA, Harriet E., and Others. "Needed Research on Gifted Children." *American Psychologist* 9:77-78; February 1954.

OTTO, Henry J. "Curriculum Issues in Elementary Education." *Educational
Leadership* 7:21-25; October 1949.

OTTO, Henry J. "Frontiers in Educational Research in Elementary School Organization and Administration." *Journal of Educational Research* 40:340-
47; January 1947.

PALMER, Gladys L. *Research Planning Memorandum on Labor Mobility.* Social
Science Research Council, Pamphlet 2. New York: The Council, 1947.
22 p.

POFFENBERGER, A. T. "Some Unsolved Problems in Human Adjustment."
*Science* 87:124-29; February 11, 1938.

POLLAK, Otto. *Social Adjustment in Old Age:* A Research Planning Report.
New York: Social Science Research Council, 1948. xi + 199 p.

POTTER, Thelma M. "Some Current Problems of Business Education." *Teachers
College Record* 45:478-82; April 1944.

"Problems of Educational Sociology as Seen by the Sociologist." *Journal of
Educational Sociology* 9:4-55; September 1935. A symposium, each article
having a bearing on either educational theory or practice and treating education as a process of social adjustment.

"Problems of Private Junior Colleges." *Junior College Journal* 10:534-50; May
1940.

"Problems of Public Junior Colleges." *Junior College Journal* 10:519-33; May
1940.

RAINEY, Homer P. "New Frontiers for Education." *Junior College Journal*
19:501-9; May 1949.

REDDICK, L. D. "The New Race-Relations Frontier." *Journal of Educational
Sociology* 19:129-45; November 1945.

REINER, William B. "Needed Research in Evaluation in Science Teaching."
*High Points* 34:13-19; November 1952.

REMMERS, H. H. "Psychology—Some Unfinished Business." *Psychological Bulletin* 41:713-24; December 1944.

*Research Frontiers in Human Relations.* Philadelphia: American Philosophical
Society, 1948. p. 325-410.

REUTER, E. B., MEAD, Margaret, and FOSTER, R. G. "Sociological Research in
Adolescence." *American Journal of Sociology* 42:81-94; July 1936. Needed
research on the adolescent world, culture and personality, and institutional
demands.

REYNOLDS, R. G. "Some Larger Tasks for Elementary Schools." *Teachers College Record* 39:363-74; February 1938.

RUSSELL, D. H. "Trends and Needs in the Study of Special Abilities and Disabilities." *Teachers College Record* 42:239-49; December 1940.

RUSSELL, John D. "Critical Issues in Higher Education." *North Central Association Quarterly* 22:149-61; October 1947.

RUSSELL, John D. "Issues in Higher Education for 1947." *Junior College Journal* 17:357-66; October 1946.

RUSSELL, W. F. "A Privileged People." *Teachers College Record* 47:77-88; November 1945.

SARASON, Seymour B. "The Psychologist's Behavior as an Area of Research." *Journal of Consulting Psychology* 15:278-80; August 1951.

SCATES, Douglas E. "Nature and Need of Educational Research." *Science* 103:657-61; May 31, 1946.

SCATES, Douglas E. "What Can Research Contribute to Our Understanding of the Physically Handicapped?" *Journal of Educational Research* 31:20-28; September 1937.

SCHWEBEL, Milton, and ASCH, M. J. "Research Possibilities in Nondirective Teaching." *Journal of Educational Psychology* 39:359-69; October 1948.

SHRYOCK, R. H. "The Need for Studies in the History of American Science." *Isis* 35:10-13; Winter 1944.

SILVERMAN, S. Richard. "Need for Research in the Education of the Deaf and Hard-of-Hearing." *Journal of Exceptional Children* 13:33-35; November 1946.

SMITH, D. E. *Challenging Problems in American Schools of Education.* New York: Teachers College, Columbia University, 1935. 47 p.

SMITH, Mapheus. "Suggestions for Sociological Research in Child Development." *Journal of Educational Sociology* 9:105-10; October 1935.

SMITH, Nila B. "Areas of Research Interest in the Language Arts." *Elementary English* 29:31-34; January 1952.

SMITH, Payson. "Unsolved Problems of Teacher Education." *Educational Forum* 4:5-16; November 1939.

SMITHEY, W. R., Editor. *Some New Problems in Secondary Education.* Secondary Education in Virginia, No. 26. Charlottesville: University of Virginia, 1940. 60 p.

"Some Issues and Problems Raised by the Conference on Education for the Gifted." *Teachers College Record* 42:432-60; February 1941.

SOUTHWORTH, W. H. "Research Needs in School Health." *American Journal of Public Health* 42:133-38; May 1952.

SPAULDING, F. T. "Some Special Problems in the Secondary Education of Negroes: A Critical Summary." *Journal of Negro Education* 10:24-33; January 1941.

SPENCE, Ralph B. "Community Development and Research." *Adult Education Bulletin* 12:132-40; June 1948.

STODDARD, G. D. *Frontiers in Education.* Stanford University, Calif.: Stanford University Press, 1945. vi + 42 p.

STRETCH, Lorena B. "Pressing Problems in Southern Public Education: In Instruction." *Peabody Journal of Education* 15:241-46; March 1938.

STUMPF, Florence, and COZENS, F. W. "Hidden Possibilities for Research in Physical Education and Recreation." *Research Quarterly of the American Association for Health, Physical Education, and Recreation* 18:104-8; May 1947.

SWEETSER, F. L. "A New Emphasis for Neighborhood Research." *American Sociological Review* 7:525-33; August 1942.

SYMONDS, Percival M. "The Lag in Clinical Research." *Journal of Educational Research* 38:371-74; January 1945.

TATE, Mildred B. "Family Life Research for the Home Economist." *Journal of Home Economics* 41:182-84; April 1949.

TAYLOR, Erwin K., and MOSIER, Charles I. "The Methods of Science Applied to the Problems of Personnel." *Personnel Psychology* 1:1-6; Spring, 1948.

TEAD, Ordway. "Major Issues in Today's Higher Education." *College and University* 24:465-80; July 1949.

TEAD, Ordway. "Significant Issues in American Education." *Southern Association Quarterly* 12:344-54; February 1948.

TEAD, Ordway. "Spiritual Problems of the Teacher." *Harvard Educational Review* 15:239-49; October 1945.

THOMPSON, Wayne N. "Contemporary Public Address as a Research Area." *Quarterly Journal of Speech* 33:274-83; October 1947.

THORNDIKE, R. L., Editor. *Research Problems and Techniques.* Army Air Forces Aviation Psychology Program, Research Report No. 3. Washington: Government Printing Office, 1947. viii + 163 p.

TONNE, Herbert A. "Blind Spots in Research in Business Education." *National Business Education Quarterly* 16:16-21; March 1948.

TRAXLER, Arthur E. "Some Comments on Educational Research at Midcentury." *Journal of Educational Research* 47:359-66; January 1954.

TROW, William C. "Frontiers in Educational Research in General Educational Psychology." *Journal of Educational Research* 40:321-26; January 1947.

UNRUH, Adolph. "Problems Confronting the Junior Colleges." *Junior College Journal* 18:191-95; December 1947.

WAGLEY, Charles. *Area Research and Training:* A Conference Report on the Study of World Areas. Social Science Research Council, Pamphlet 6. New York: The Council, 1948. v + 58 p.

WAPLES, Douglas, BERELSON, Bernard, and BRADSHAW, Franklyn R. *What Reading Does to People:* A Summary of Evidence on the Social Effects of Reading and a Statement of Problems for Research. Chicago: University of Chicago Press, 1940. xii + 222 p.

WATSON, R. I. "Measuring the Effectiveness of Psychotherapy: Problems for Investigation." *Journal of Clinical Psychology* 8:60-64; January 1952.

WEATHERFORD, Allen E. "Major Research Problems in Recreation." *Journal of the American Association for Health, Physical Education, and Recreation* 23:19-20; December 1952.

WEAVER, Robert C. "A Needed Program of Research in Race Relations and Associated Problems." *Journal of Negro Education* 16:130-35; Spring 1947.

WERNER, Heinz. "Process and Achievement—A Basic Problem of Education and Developmental Psychology." *Harvard Educational Review* 7:353-68; May 1937.

WESLEY, E. B. *Teaching the Social Studies.* Second Edition. Boston: D. C. Heath and Co., 1942. 652 p. Includes sections on methods of research, results of research, and needed investigations in the social studies fields.

WESLEY, E. B. "Want a Thesis Subject?" *Social Education* 4:235-41; April 1940. A list of problems in the social studies field.

WHELPTON, P. K. *Needed Population Research.* Lancaster, Pa.: Science Press Printing Co., 1938. 196 p. Covers both needed investigations and completed research.

WHITE, Robert. "Frontiers in Educational Research in Secondary School Administration and Organization." *Journal of Educational Research* 40:335-39; January 1947.

WILHELMS, Fred T. "Research in Consumer Education." *National Business Education Quarterly* 16:22-29; March 1948.

WILLEY, M. M. "Basic Issues for Higher Education in the Post-War Period." *North Central Association Quarterly* 19:171-76; October 1944.

WILLIAMS, Roger J. *The Human Frontier.* New York: Harcourt, Brace and Co., 1946. 314 p.

WIRTH, Louis. "Housing as a Field of Sociological Research." *American Sociological Review* 12:137-43; April 1947.

WITTY, Paul, and PARKER, Beryl. "The Whole of Childhood—Some Suggestions for Research." *Childhood Education* 16:408-13; May 1940.

WOLMAN, Benjamin. "Scientific Study of Educational Aims." *Teachers College Record* 50:471-81; April 1949.

WOODWORTH, R. S. *Psychological Issues.* New York: Henry Holt and Co., 1939. xxv + 421 p.

WORKS, George A., and Others. "Current Issues in Accrediting." *North Central Association Quarterly* 16:313-31; January 1942.

WRENN, C. Gilbert. "Basic Studies on the Supply and Demand of Research Talent." *American Psychologist* 4:159-64; June 1949.

WRIGHTSTONE, J. Wayne. "Frontiers in Educational Research in the Measurement of Aptitudes and Achievement." *Journal of Educational Research* 40:389-96; January 1947.

WRISTON, H. M. "Problems of Higher Education." *School and Society* 52:113-19; August 24, 1940.

ZACHRY, Caroline B. "Later Childhood—Some Questions for Research." *Progressive Education* 15:522-28; November 1938.

ZIRBES, Laura. "Gaps in Curriculum Research." *Educational Leadership* 7:187-92; December 1949.

ZIRBES, Laura. "Needed Research in Education." *Educational Leadership* 10:129-31; November 1952.

# 3 Survey of Related Literature and Library Technique

THE CHAPTER ON formulation of the problem has outlined in some detail the possible contribution of a careful survey of the literature related to the study under consideration. Included were these topics: (1) an organized program of reading as a source of problems, (2) novelty and avoidance of unnecessary duplication as a criterion for selection of the problem, and (3) a survey of related literature as an important part of the definition of the problem.

The body of the present chapter and the classified bibliography provide guidance for a systematic canvass of periodicals, books and monographs, and graduate theses related to the problem. Various types of library tools in education, psychology, social science, and other fields are described: guides and indexes to the literature; continuing or serial bibliographies; extensive individual bibliographies; major summaries of research; and biographical, institutional, and statistical directories or handbooks. Limitations of space permit the listing of only those frequently used guides most helpful to workers in education, psychology, and the social sciences. For additional information, excellent manuals are available.[1]

Advice concerning bibliographical form is given in the chapter on preparation of the research report. At this point, the student is reminded that only one reference should be placed on each card or sheet of paper and that full identifying information for each reference should be entered. The technique of note-taking is discussed in the chapters on the historical method and on the reporting of research.

[1] Carter Alexander and Arvid J. Burke, *How to Locate Educational Information and Data.* Third Edition. New York: Bureau of Publications, Teachers College, Columbia University, 1950, xix + 441 p.

I. G. Mudge, *Guide to Reference Books.* Sixth Edition. Chicago: American Library Association, 1936. xii + 504 p. Also see earlier editions and the informal supplements.

Constance M. Winchell, *Guide to Reference Books.* Seventh Edition. Chicago: American Library Association, 1951. xvii + 645 p.

Louis Shores, *Basic Reference Books:* An Introduction to the Evaluation, Study, and Use of Reference Materials with Special Emphasis on Some 300 Titles. Second Edition. Chicago: American Library Association, 1939. xiv + 472 p.

H. S. Hirshberg, *Subject Guide to Reference Books.* Chicago: American Library Association, 1942. xvi + 259 p.

Mary N. Barton, *Reference Books:* A Brief Guide for Students and Other Users of the Library. Second Edition. Baltimore: Enoch Pratt Free Library, 1951. 99 p.

## EDUCATIONAL GUIDES

**Comprehensive or general guides.** The heading of this paragraph refers to general guides that cover various types of published literature—periodicals, books and monographs, and printed graduate theses. Subsequent sections of this chapter are concerned with more specialized guides which usually deal with only one of the major types of literature: (1) articles in periodicals, (2) books and monographs, and (3) graduate theses in general.

Before proceeding to a systematic examination of the specialized library guides to the literature of a field, it is desirable to secure orientation concerning the particular problem by reading the type of overview treatment found in textbooks and reference works. This orientation should result in at least a partial list of subtopics for use in searching through the library guides.

The topic of "Instructional Methods in Education and Psychology Courses" may be used as an example of procedures appropriate in most instances for use of the guides in the 1940's, during the next decade, or later. It happens that a book, *The Background for College Teaching,* drew most of its references and illustrations from the fields of education and psychology.[2] As a general rule, the existence of such a volume must be discovered through use of certain of the guides described on succeeding pages. The topics treated in the book suggest appropriate headings for a more detailed bibliographical canvass. Assistance in the selection of headings is available in the form of two lists of educational subject headings.[3] (Also see the more recent headings in the *Education Index.*)

Examination of the *Encyclopedia of Educational Research* (1941 and 1950 editions) reveals an article on methods of teaching in higher institutions, with most of the references from education and psychology.[4] The major subheadings of the article (instructional, study, and testing procedures; motivation; and diagnosis of errors and remedial instruction) may be considered, along with the topics of the textbook mentioned above, in preparing a composite list of headings for the more detailed bibliographical survey. In approaching the guides described in this section of the chapter, this composite list of subtopics reads as follows: class size; ability grouping; student interests, incentives, and motivation; instructional procedures,

[2] Luella Cole, *The Background for College Teaching.* New York: Farrar and Rinehart, 1940. xxiv + 616 p.

[3] Clyde Pettus, *Subject Headings in Education:* A Systematic List for Use in a Dictionary Catalogue. New York: H. W. Wilson Co., 1938. 188 p.
L. Belle Voegelein, *List of Educational Subject Headings.* Columbus: Ohio State University Press, 1928. xiv + 338 p.

[4] Carter V. Good, "Colleges and Universities—Methods of Teaching," *Encyclopedia of Educational Research.* Edited by W. S. Monroe. New York: Macmillan Co., 1941. p. 242-48. Also see the 1950 edition, p. 273-79.

including lecture, recitation, project, problem, and independent-study techniques; study habits, involving study environment, attention in class, note-taking, reading, reviewing, and work attitudes; the inferior student, diagnosis of weaknesses, and remedial instruction; the superior student and provision for maximum development of his talents; examination and testing procedures; assignment of marks; and evaluation of the effectiveness of the college teacher.

The most important index for workers in education is the *Education Index,* which began publication in January, 1929. It aims to list all educational books in the United States (with the exception of elementary and high-school textbooks); all articles in a large number of the important educational journals; additional educational articles in certain non-educational periodicals; and many monographs, bulletins, reports, book reviews, courses of study, and state documents in the field of education. The various headings relating to the illustrative topic "Instructional Methods in Education and Psychology Courses" may be located in the *Education Index* by judicious determination of the essential key words of the subtopics enumerated above. Students who require more detailed guidance in the use of the *Education Index* may turn to another source.[5]

The *Review of Educational Research* began publication in January, 1931, and covers a variety of research materials, even a limited number of unpublished graduate theses. As a rule, it has included fifteen major subdivisions of education within a three-year cycle. Examination of the *Review* reveals a chapter in each of four numbers (plus scattered references in later issues) concerned with our illustrative topic, with the accompanying bibliographies providing numerous references.[6] A twelve-year index of the contents of the *Review* is a valuable tool; in 1947 the *Phi Delta Kappan* began publication of a brief summary of the contents of each number of the *Review.*[7]

[5] Carter Alexander and Arvid J. Burke, *op. cit.,* p. 108-25.

[6] Carter V. Good, "Education, Psychology, and Professional Training," in "Psychology and Methods in the High School and College." *Review of Educational Research* 4:513-19; December 1934.

I. H. Anderson, "Education and Psychology," in "Psychology and Methods in the High School and College." *Review of Educational Research* 8:19-24; February 1938.

S. M. Corey, "Methods of Teaching," in "General Aspects of Instruction." *Review of Educational Research* 12:299-304; June 1942.

G. C. Kyte, "Methods of Teaching," in "General Aspects of Instruction." *Review of Educational Research* 15:218-26; June 1945.

William E. Young and Others, "The Curriculum: Learning and Teaching." *Review of Educational Research* 18:217-92; June 1948.

William H. Bristow and Others, "The Curriculum: Learning and Teaching." *Review of Educational Research* 21:169-243; June 1951.

[7] Douglas E. Scates, "Twelve-Year Index." *Review of Educational Research,* Special Issue: i-vi, 1-65; December 1944.

A. N. Hieronymus, "Education for Work, Citizenship, Leisure." *Phi Delta Kappan* 33:133-34; November 1951. Based on the October, 1950, issue of the *Review of Educational Research.*

It is helpful to list below the issues of the *Review of Educational Research,* grouped by major areas, and to note the appearance of a particular topic at intervals of three years.

1.  History of Education and Comparative Education. VI:4 (October 1936); IX:4 (October 1939).
2.  Social Backgrounds of Education. VII:1 (February 1937); X:1 (February 1940); XIII:1 (February 1943); XVI:1 (February 1946); XIX:1 (February 1949); XXII:1 (February 1952).
3.  Organization and Administration of Education. I:3 (June 1931); IV:4 (October 1934); VII:4 (October 1937); X:4 (October 1940); XIII:4 (October 1943); XVI:4 (October 1946); XIX:4 (October 1949); XXII:4 (October 1952).
4.  Legal Basis of Education. III:5 (December 1933).
5.  Finance and Business Administration. II:2 (April 1932); V:2 (April 1935); VIII:2 (April 1938); XI:2 (April 1941); XIV:2 (April 1944); XVII:2 (April 1947); XX:2 (April 1950).
6.  School Plant and Equipment. II:5 (December 1932); V:4 (October 1935); VIII:4 (October 1938); VII:2 (April 1942); XV:1 (February 1945); XVIII:1 (February 1948); XXI:1 (February 1951).
7.  Teacher Personnel. I:2 (April 1931); IV:3 (June 1934); VII:3 (June 1937); X:3 (June 1940); XIII:3 (June 1943); XVI:3 (June 1946); XIX:3 (June 1949); XXII:3 (June 1952).
8.  Pupil Personnel, Guidance, and Counseling. III:3 (June 1933); VI:2 (April 1936); IX:2 (April 1939); XII:1 (February 1942); XV:2 (April 1945); XVIII:2 (April 1948); XXI:2 (April 1951); XXIV:2 (April 1954).
9.  Psychological Tests and Their Uses. II:3 (June 1932); II:4 (October 1932); V:3 (June 1935); VIII:3 (June 1938); XI:1 (February 1941); XIV:1 (February 1944); XVII:1 (February 1947); XX:1 (February 1950); XXIII:1 (February 1953).
10. Educational Tests and Their Uses. III:1 (February 1933); V:5 (December 1935); VIII:5 (December 1938). Future issues to be merged with topic 22 and topic 9.
11. Growth and Development. III:2 (April 1933); VI:1 (February 1936); IX:1 (February 1939); XI:5 (December 1941); XIV:5 (December 1944); XVII:5 (December 1947); XX:5 (December 1950); XXII:5 (December 1952).
12. Mental and Physical Health. VI:5 (December 1936); X:5 (December 1940); XIII:5 (December 1943); XVI:5 (December 1946); XIX:5 (December 1949).
13. The Curriculum. I:1 (January 1931); IV:2 (April 1934); VII:2 (April 1937). Future issues to be merged with topic 14.
14. The Educational Program: Learning, Teaching, and the Curriculum. (The first three cycles included Supervision, which subsequently appears in topic 3.) III:4 (October 1933); VI:3 (June 1936); IX:3 (June 1939); XII:3 (June 1942); XV:3 (June 1945); XVIII:3 (June 1948); XXI:3 (June 1951); XXIII:2 (April 1953); XXIV:1 (February 1954); XXIV:3 (June 1954); XXIV:4 (October 1954).
15. Special Methods and Psychology of Elementary School Subjects. I:4 (October 1931); I:5 (December 1931); V:1 (February 1935); VII:5

(December 1937). Research subsequently treated under topics 12, 17, 18, 19, 20.

16. Psychology and Methods in High School and College. I:5 (December 1931); II:1 (February 1932); IV:5 (December 1934); VIII:1 (February 1938). Research subsequently treated under topics 12, 17, 18, 19, 20.
17. Language Arts and Fine Arts. X:2 (April 1940); XIII:2 (April 1943). (Prior to 1943 Fine Arts appeared in XI:4 Part I.) XVI:2 (April 1946); XIX:2 (April 1949); XXII:2 (April 1952).
18. Fine and Applied Arts, Commercial Education, and Home and Family Living. XI:4 Part 1 (October 1941). (Fine Arts subsequently covered in topic 17.)
19. The Natural Sciences and Mathematics. XII:4 (October 1942); XV:4 (October 1945); XVIII:4 (October 1948); XXI:4 (October 1951).
20. The Social Studies. XI:4 Part 2 (October 1941).
21. Education of Exceptional Children and Minority Groups. XI:3 (June 1941); XIV:3 (June 1944); XXIII:5 (December 1953).
22. Methods of Research and Appraisal in Education. IV:1 (February 1934); IX:5 (December 1939); XII:5 (December 1942); XV:5 (December 1945); XVIII:5 (December 1948); XXI:5 (December 1951); XXIV:5 (December 1954).
23. Adult Education. XX:3 (June 1950); XXIII:3 (June 1953).
24. Education for Work, Citizenship, and Leisure. XX:4 (October 1950).
25. Research on Human Relations and Programs of Action. XXIII:4 (October 1953).

The cycle of twenty (more recently eighteen) lists of annotated references published each year in the *School Review* and *Elementary School Journal* began in 1933 and for a time cumulated annually under one cover.[8] Of the bibliographies listed below, those dealing with "Higher Education," "Educational Psychology," and "Teacher Education" are the most pertinent for our topic of "Instructional Methods in Education and Psychology Courses."

Another comprehensive guide is the Monroe and Shores catalogue of more than four thousand annotated bibliographies and summaries listed

### Monthly Selected References in the *School Review*

| | |
|---|---|
| Secondary-School Instruction: I, Curriculum, Methods of Teaching and Study and Supervision, and Measurement | January |
| Secondary-School Instruction: II, The Subject Fields | February |
| Secondary-School Instruction: III, The Subject Fields | March |
| The Extra-Curriculum | April |
| Educational Psychology | May |
| Guidance | September |
| Organization and Administration of Secondary Education | October |
| Statistics, the Theory of Test Construction, and Factor Analysis | November |
| Higher Education | December |

[8] For example, *Selected References in Education, 1938.* Supplementary Educational Monographs, No. 47. Chicago: Department of Education, University of Chicago, February 1939. x + 221 p.

**Monthly Selected References in the *Elementary School Journal***

Public-School Administration .......................... January
Preschool and Parental Education ..................... February
Kindergarten-Primary Education ..................... March
Exceptional Children ............................. April
Foreign Education ................................ May
Elementary-School Instruction: I, Curriculum, Methods of Teach-
    ing and Study, and Supervision ..................... September
Elementary-School Instruction: II, The Subject Fields ........ October
Elementary-School Instruction: III, The Subject Fields ....... November
Teacher Education ............................... December

under author and subject in one alphabet.[9] The location of several bibliographies through use of this volume may result in a total of hundreds of references on the particular topic under consideration. This listing of bibliographies and summaries in education, for the period since July, 1935, has been kept up to date by the *Education Index.*

The *Bibliographic Index* [10] lists current bibliographies in a wide range of subjects. The first number, published in 1938, contains 4400 references.

For a time, 1936-43, the journal *Education Abstracts* provided useful summaries of a variety of educational publications. The *Loyola Educational Digest* also suspended publication in 1943.

Attention has already been directed to the comprehensive character of the *Encyclopedia of Educational Research* as a critical evaluation, synthesis, and interpretation of reported studies in the field of education.[11] Another volume, the *Encyclopedia of Modern Education,* is not limited to research sources.[12] Two older encyclopedias in education may prove useful for the period preceding their dates of publication.[13] The *Dictionary of Education,*[14] as well as more specialized dictionaries in limited areas, is helpful as a means of orientation, although of course a dictionary defini-

[9] W. S. Monroe and Louis Shores, *Bibliographies and Summaries in Education to July, 1935.* New York: H. W. Wilson Co., 1936. xvi + 470 p.

[10] *Bibliographic Index:* A Cumulative Bibliography of Bibliographies. New York: H. W. Wilson Co., 1938—.

[11] *Encyclopedia of Educational Research.* Revised Edition. Edited by W. S. Monroe, under the auspices of the American Educational Research Association. New York: Macmillan Co., 1950. xxvii + 1520 p. For a full description of the encyclopedia see:
    W. W. Charters, "The New Encyclopedia of Educational Research." *Educational Research Bulletin* 20:99-105; April 16, 1941.
    Also see Robert B. Sutton, "Needed—A New Encyclopedia of Education." *Educational Record* 33:471-80; October 1952.

[12] Harry N. Rivlin and Herbert Schueler, Editors, *The Encyclopedia of Modern Education.* New York: Philosophical Library, 1943. xvi + 902 p.

[13] Paul Monroe, *Cyclopedia of Education.* New York: Macmillan Co., 1911-13. Five volumes.
    Foster Watson, *The Encyclopedia and Dictionary of Education.* London: Pitman, 1921. Four volumes.

[14] Carter V. Good, Editor, *Dictionary of Education.* New York: McGraw-Hill Book Co., 1945. xl + 495 p. Scheduled for revision in 1956.

tion of fifty words or less cannot deal with the literature and concepts in the manner possible in an encyclopedia.

**Guides to periodicals and serials.** The inclusive term of *serials* may be defined as "any publication issued serially or in successive parts more or less regularly." [15]

Reference was made above to the *Education Index,* established in 1929, as a comprehensive author and subject guide to educational literature, including the indexing of periodicals. [16] It cumulates in bound volumes at intervals of one year and three years respectively.

For the years prior to 1929 it is necessary to consult the *Readers' Guide to Periodical Literature* and the *International Index to Periodicals,* with the discontinued *Poole's Index to Periodical Literature* covering an earlier period. The *International Index* includes more than twice as many periodicals as the *Readers' Guide* and concentrates on scholarly American and foreign journals in comparison with the general periodicals indexed by the *Readers' Guide.* For the convenience of the user, the general periodical guides are listed counter-chronologically, since this is the order in which they are most likely to be examined:

> *International Index to Periodicals,* 1907—. New York: H. W. Wilson Co., 1916—.
> *Readers' Guide to Periodical Literature,* 1900—. New York: H. W. Wilson Co., 1905—.
> *Annual Library Index,* 1905-10. New York: Publishers' Weekly, 1906-11.
> *Annual Literary Index,* 1892-1904. New York: Publishers' Weekly, 1893-1905.
> *Poole's Index to Periodical Literature Supplements.* Boston: Houghton Mifflin Co., 1882-1906.
> *Poole's Index to Periodical Literature,* 1802-81. Revised Edition. Boston: Houghton Mifflin Co., 1891.

In a sense, the monthly *Book Review Digest* is a specialized periodical index, in that it provides excerpts from the reviews which appear in some eighty book-review periodicals. [17] It lists approximately four thousand books in the course of a year, and cumulates at intervals.

Workers in such special fields as agriculture, fine arts, industrial arts (including engineering, trade, and business), and law have been supplied with appropriate periodical indexes. [18]

---

[15] Louis Shores, *op. cit.,* p. 144.

[16] *Education Index:* A Cumulative Author and Subject Index to a Selected List of Educational Periodicals, Books, and Pamphlets. New York: H. W. Wilson Co., 1929—.

[17] *Book Review Digest,* 1905—. New York: H. W. Wilson Co., 1905—.

[18] *Agricultural Index:* Subject Index to a Selected List of Agricultural Periodicals and Bulletins, 1916—. New York: H. W. Wilson Co., 1916—.

*Art Index:* A Cumulative Author and Subject Index to a Selected List of Fine Arts Periodicals and Museum Bulletins, 1929—. New York: H. W. Wilson Co., 1929—.

*Industrial Arts Index:* Subject Index to a Selected List of Engineering, Trade, and Business Periodicals, Books, and Pamphlets, 1913—. New York: H. W. Wilson Co., 1913—.

*Index to Legal Periodicals and Law Library Journal.* New York: H. W. Wilson Co., 1914—.

Information concerning educational journals, as to editor, publisher, number of issues per year, address, and subscription price, may be found in the current yearbook of the Educational Press Association.[19] The *Education Index* includes a convenient check list of the journals indexed.

A number of comprehensive lists of serials are available. The Ayer list is a bibliography of newspapers and periodicals, but includes much additional information.[20] The Gregory union list of serials shows the extent to which more than 75,000 different serials are found in the more important libraries in the United States and Canada.[21] Ulrich's list of titles represents the periodicals published in the United States and in foreign countries that have proved most useful in American collections.[22]

For more detailed information concerning use of the guides to serials, the reader is referred to selected authoritative sources.[23] These references contain tabulations of the years covered by the various indexes to the literature.

**Guides to books and monographs.** The card catalogue of the local library, with its author and subject headings, indicates the books available on the shelves, although the resulting bibliography will be no better and no more complete than the library itself. To locate a number of book references on the same topic, it is preferable to use the subject heading first, and then turn to author headings if necessary.

The previously described *Education Index* is the most useful guide to books and monographs in education for the period since January, 1929.

For the period covering the 1926-46 references, *School and Society* has published (usually in March or April) a classified annual bibliography of educational books, monographs, yearbooks, and bulletins, with a selected list of sixty books marked with an asterisk. The titles of the sixty books of the year also have appeared in a spring number (usually April or May) of the *Journal of the National Education Association.*[24] The complete annual bibliography in *School and Society* during the several years preceding World War II numbered from eight hundred to nine hundred refer-

[19] Educational Press Association of America, *Yearbooks.* Washington: Educational Press Association, 1926—.

[20] *Directory of Newspapers and Periodicals.* Philadelphia: N. W. Ayer and Sons, 1880—.

[21] Winifred Gregory, Editor, *Union List of Serials in Libraries of the United States and Canada.* Second Edition. New York: H. W. Wilson Co., 1943. 3065 p. Also see supplements.

[22] Eileen C. Graves and Carolyn F. Ulrich, Editors, *Ulrich's Periodicals Directory:* A Classified Guide to a Selected List of Current Periodicals, Foreign and Domestic. Sixth Edition. New York: R. R. Bowker Co., 1951. 534 p.

[23] Carter Alexander and Arvid J. Burke, *op. cit.,* p. 85-107.

Louis Shores, *op. cit.,* p. 143-86.

Eleanor M. Witmer and Margaret C. Miller, "Guides to Educational Literature in Periodicals: Indexes, Abstracts, Bibliographies." *Teachers College Record* 33:719-30; May 1932.

[24] Julia L. Certain and Others, "Outstanding Educational Books of 1952." *NEA Journal* 42:302-03; May 1953.

ences. With the 1947 books the *Phi Delta Kappan* took over publication of the educational bibliography of the year.[25]

The *United States Catalogue* lists for the research worker and librarian virtually all books in print in this country on a particular subject.[26] If only author or title of a book is known, further identification is possible through the dictionary arrangement of authors, titles, and subjects in one alphabet. Each entry includes information concerning author, title, edition, date, pub-lisher, price, and paging. The *United States Catalogue* is kept up to date by the monthly *Cumulative Book Index,*[27] which cumulates at irregular in-tervals during the year, annually into a supplement, and after several years into a large supplement. In a sense, the *Publishers' Weekly*[28] supplements the monthly *Cumulative Book Index,* in that it describes and indexes new books in a convenient reference and buying list.

Selected bibliographies of books, such as the *A.L.A. Catalogue* and the supplements, are important in book selection and in reference work, with the probability that the volumes listed actually will be on the library shelves.[29] For volumes later than 1941, *The Booklist*[30] provides semi-monthly selections and evaluations of books that can be used as a supple-ment to the *A.L.A. Catalogue* supplements.

The previously mentioned *Book Review Digest* offers guidance in the evaluation of some four thousand books during the course of a year.[31]

Detailed information has been compiled concerning two hundred series of professional books, bulletins, and monographs in education published since 1900.[32]

**Guides to graduate theses.** Beginning with the titles of 1926-27, the comprehensive guide to Masters' and Doctors' theses in education was the annual *Bibliography of Research Studies in Education,*[33] published by

[25] Julia L. Certain and Others, "Educational Books of 1951." *Phi Delta Kappan* 33:389-403; April 1952.

[26] *United States Catalogue.* Fourth Edition. New York: H. W. Wilson Co., 1928. 3164 p. *United States Catalogue Supplements,* 1928—. New York: H. W. Wilson Co., 1933—.

[27] *Cumulative Book Index,* 1898—. New York: H. W. Wilson Co., 1898—. Monthly.

[28] *Publishers' Weekly.* New York: R. R. Bowker Co., 1872—.

[29] *A.L.A. Catalogue,* 1926. Edited by Isabella M. Cooper. Chicago: American Library Association, 1926. 1295 p.
*A.L.A. Catalogue Supplement,* 1926-1931. Edited by Marion Horton. Chicago: American Library Association, 1933. 330 p.
*A.L.A. Catalogue Supplement,* 1932-1936. Edited by Marion Horton. Chicago: American Library Association, 1938. 357 p.
*A.L.A. Catalogue Supplement,* 1937-1941. Chicago: American Library Association, 1943. 306 p.

[30] *The Booklist:* A Guide to New Books, 1905—. Chicago: American Library Association, 1905—.

[31] *Book Review Digest,* 1905—. New York: H. W. Wilson Co., 1905—.

[32] Daniel M. Bridges, "Professional Series in Education." Unpublished Master's thesis, Duke University, 1938.

[33] For example, Ruth A. Gray, *Bibliography of Research Studies in Education, 1939-1940.* Office of Education Bulletin No. 5, 1941. Washington: Government Printing Office, 1941. xiv + 404 p. As late as 1953, publication of this series had not been resumed.

the United States Office of Education (publication suspended during World War II). To return to our illustrative topic of "Instructional Methods in Education and Psychology Courses," the pertinent headings in this guide are: "psychology—educational," "curriculum studies—psychology," "higher education," "teacher training," and "college professors and instructors." The bulletins of the Office of Education to be consulted in canvassing graduate theses in education up to 1940 are listed below:

Bulletin No. 22, 1928, for 1926-27.    Bulletin No.   5, 1935, for 1933-34.
Bulletin No. 36, 1929, for 1927-28.    Bulletin No.   5, 1936, for 1934-35.
Bulletin No. 23, 1930, for 1928-29.    Bulletin No.   6, 1937, for 1935-36.
Bulletin No. 13, 1931, for 1929-30.    Bulletin No.   5, 1938, for 1936-37.
Bulletin No. 16, 1932, for 1930-31.    Bulletin No.   5, 1939, for 1937-38.
Bulletin No.   6, 1933, for 1931-32.    Bulletin No.   5, 1940, for 1938-39.
Bulletin No.   7, 1934, for 1932-33.    Bulletin No.   5, 1941, for 1939-40.

The Office of Education has on file in its library a· considerable number of theses which are available for lending. From time to time, lists of the recently acquired theses are published. Interlibrary loans of graduate theses usually can be arranged between institutions, with the student paying the cost of transportation.

During the period 1917-27 the Bureau of Educational Research, University of Illinois, compiled annual or biennial mimeographed lists of theses in education, although these bibliographies are not generally accessible. A printed volume [34] by the same agency includes the titles of Doctors' dissertations in education for the decade 1918-27.

Beginning with the titles of 1912, the Library of Congress printed an annual volume of published Doctors' dissertations in all fields.[35] The last number appeared in 1940 and covered 1938. Since this publication was usually two years late and omitted unpublished dissertations, another agency began a complete annual listing [36] with the titles of 1933-34.

Doctors' dissertations under way in education were listed annually in the January *Journal of Educational Research,* 1931-46, and subsequently have appeared in the *Phi Delta Kappan.*[37]

[34] W. S. Monroe and Others, *Ten Years of Educational Research,* 1918-1927. University of Illinois Bulletin, Vol. XXV, No. 51. Urbana, Ill.: University of Illinois, 1928. 368 p.

[35] U. S. Library of Congress, *A List of American Doctoral Dissertations in 1912—.* Washington: Government Printing Office, 1913—.

[36] *Doctoral Dissertations Accepted by American Universities,* 1933-34—. Compiled for the National Research Council and the American Council of Learned Societies by the Association of Research Libraries. New York: H. W. Wilson Co., 1934—. Edited by Donald B. Gilchrist, 1934-39; by Edward A. Henry, 1940-44; by Arnold H. Trotier, 1945—.

[37] Carter V. Good, "Doctors' Dissertations Under Way in Education, 1949-1950." *Phi Delta Kappan* 31:268-92; February 1950.

Rolfe L. Hunt, "Doctors' Dissertations Under Way in Education, 1950-51 and 1951-52." *Phi Delta Kappan* 32:263-93; February 1951 and 33:305-38; February 1952.

Many graduate institutions now publish abstract volumes or lists of their theses, usually representing all the graduate work of the particular university, but sometimes devoted to summaries or lists of the theses of a given department. A basic guide to such summaries and lists of theses [38] is available, while an older source also may prove helpful.

At times some higher institutions have not been too careful in the housing and cataloguing of dissertations and theses, particularly the older studies. John Dewey's doctoral dissertation (1884) at Johns Hopkins University, on the psychology of Kant, was never published and no copy is available, since the Johns Hopkins library did not preserve the manuscript.[39]

The annual *Bibliography of Research Studies in Education* of the Office of Education, as described above, includes the titles of institutional reports in the form of summaries and lists of theses, under the heading of "research, educational—reports." The *Education Index* offers similar guidance under the topics of "abstracts, educational," "degrees, academic," "degrees, Doctors'," "degrees, Masters'," and "dissertations, academic."

**Guides to special educational areas and problems.** In addition to the guides described above, special aids have been prepared to facilitate canvassing of the literature of a limited educational area. The classified chapter bibliography includes guides to such fields as school administration, school law, elementary education, secondary education, teacher education, testing, occupations, personnel work, curriculum, business education, physical and health education, reading, speech, rural education, Negro education, Boy Scouts, public documents, and publications of the United States Office of Education. Yearbooks dealing with mental measurements, statistical methods, school law, and comparative education enable the student and research worker to keep in touch with current developments in these fields. Dictionaries of statistical terms, measurement and guidance, occupational titles, social work, education, psychology, sociology, economics, and philosophy provide orientation for interpretation of the concepts represented.

**Continuing or serial bibliographies and summaries in limited areas of education.** Many of the previously described guides to the literature are in effect continuing bibliographies of comprehensive scope. For a number of specifically limited subdivisions of education there are also serial bibliographies or summaries of research. Most such references in the classified chapter bibliography are annual in their appearance and have continued

---

[38] Thomas R. Palfrey and Henry E. Coleman, *Guide to Bibliographies of Theses—United States and Canada.* Second Edition. Chicago: American Library Association, 1940. 54 p.

Clara E. Derring, "Lists and Abstracts of Masters' Theses and Doctors' Dissertations in Education." *Teachers College Record* 34:490-502; March 1933.

[39] A. A. Roback, *History of American Psychology.* New York: Library Publishers, 1952. p. 98.

over a number of years. In a few instances a particular series has been published at irregular intervals and by this time may even have been discontinued. As a rule, the bibliography or summary for a particular year refers the reader to the earlier numbers in the series. Among the topics represented in the chapter bibliography are educational books of the year, major educational projects and large-scale investigations, deliberative committee reports, methods of research, dissertations under way, teacher supply and demand, junior college, school buildings, arithmetic, reading, science teaching, modern language teaching, and Negro education.

**Extensive individual bibliographies and summaries in limited areas of education.** In contrast to the continuing or serial guides to the literature in limited subdivisions of education, described in the preceding section, many individual bibliographies and summaries on particular problems have been prepared. The illustrative references of this type in the chapter bibliography are limited to selected guides that have appeared since 1935. For 1930-45 a fall number of the *Journal of Educational Research* (and subsequently the *Phi Delta Kappan*) has included such bibliographies and summaries in an annual list of selected references on research methods.[40] As pointed out above, the *Education Index* and the *Bibliographic Index* are continuing the listing of bibliographies begun by the Monroe and Shores volume.[41] Another source [42] includes many of the major bibliographies and summaries published prior to 1936.

**Biographical, institutional, and statistical directories and handbooks in education.** A number of handbooks of information and directories include biographical facts concerning individuals, or statistical or personnel data for institutions. Among the overlapping illustrative references of this type in the chapter bibliography are those dealing with leaders in education, scholars, scientists, specialists in philosophy, college and university presidents, public and private schools, universities and colleges, graduate schools, junior colleges, school supplies and equipment, educational buildings and grounds, professional organizations, scientific societies, and registration statistics of higher education. The most widely used educational directory probably is that issued annually in four parts by the United States Office of Education: (1) state and county school officers, (2) city school officers, (3) colleges and universities, and (4) educational

---

[40] Carter V. Good, "Research Methods Bibliography: Selected Bibliography on the Methodology of Educational, Psychological, and Social Research, 1945-46, 1946-47, 1947-48, 1948-49, 1949-50, 1950-51." *Phi Delta Kappan* 28:210-15, January 1947; 29:146-52, November 1947; 30:19-26, September 1948; 31:38-46, September 1949; 32:11-15, 18-22; September 1950; 33:45-52, 61; September 1951.

[41] W. S. Monroe and Louis Shores, *op. cit.*

[42] Carter V. Good, A. S. Barr, and Douglas E. Scates, *The Methodology of Educational Research.* New York: Appleton-Century-Crofts, 1936. p. 168-84, 864-71.

associations and directories.[43] In the instances where the educational and learned associations issue publications, such journals, yearbooks, directories, or proceedings are named.

In addition to the specialized *Leaders in Education,* the general biographical directories—*Who's Who in America, Who's Who,* and the *International Who's Who*—include a number of educators, especially those in major administrative positions.

## PSYCHOLOGICAL GUIDES

**Comprehensive guides in psychology.** Many of the educational guides cover a considerable amount of psychological research. In fact, there are certain areas where it is difficult, if not impossible, to draw a sharp line between the two disciplines; for example, learning and conditioning, personality and character, vocational guidance, mental tests, or childhood and adolescence. Therefore, for selected topics the student of psychology may find pertinent information in the previously described educational guides, including the *Encyclopedia of Educational Research, Education Index,* and *Review of Educational Research.* There may be times when the investigator with his concentration of study in a particular field may find it desirable to use the guides for the several areas (education, psychology, and social science) discussed in this chapter.

The major comprehensive guide to the literature of psychology is the monthly journal *Psychological Abstracts,*[44] founded in 1927. An extra number published in December is the author and subject index for the year; it includes a list of current bibliographic sources. For the period from 1927-36, at the end of which the *Psychological Index* [45] (established in 1895) suspended publication, the two journals performed an overlapping service. As the titles of the publications indicate, one includes abstracts or brief summaries, whereas the other is merely an index or list of references. Prior to 1927 the *Psychological Index* is the only major comprehensive guide available for the psychological literature.

The major subject divisions under which the contents of *Psychological Abstracts* are classified follow:

General
Physiological Psychology
Receptive and Perceptual Processes

---

[43] United States Office of Education, *Educational Directory.* Washington: Government Printing Office, 1912—.

[44] *Psychological Abstracts.* Washington: American Psychological Association, 1927—. Published bimonthly beginning in 1954.

[45] *Psychological Index.* Princeton, N. J.: Psychological Review Co., 1895-1936.

Response Processes
Complex Processes and Organizations
Developmental Psychology
Social Psychology
Clinical Psychology, Guidance, Counseling
Behavior Deviations
Educational Psychology
Personnel Psychology
Industrial and Other Applications

The *Annual Review of Psychology* [46] provides periodic summaries of contemporary psychological literature, with two major purposes: to cover publications considered noteworthy, and to emphasize an interpretative and evaluative approach to the literature. The contents of Volume 4 are as follows:

Child Psychology
Learning
Vision
Hearing
Somesthesis and the Chemical Senses
Individual Differences
Personality
Social Psychology and Group Processes
Industrial Psychology
Comparative Psychology
Physiological Psychology
Abnormalities of Behavior
Clinical Methods: Psychodiagnostics
Clinical Methods: Psychotherapy
Counseling: Therapy and Diagnosis
Special Disabilities
Educational Psychology
Statistical Theory and Research Design
Theoretical Psychology

A published list of topics in psychology should prove useful in identifying appropriate headings for canvassing psychological materials,[47] although this guide should be supplemented by consulting current sources.

A handbook of the literature of psychology and a compilation of available bibliographies are valuable for the periods represented.[48]

In certain large areas of psychology extensive summaries and guides

[46] Calvin P. Stone, Editor, *Annual Review of Psychology*, Vols. 1, 2, 3, 4, 5. Stanford, Calif.: Annual Reviews, 1950, 1951, 1952, 1953, 1954. ix + 330, ix + 389, ix + 462, 500, 448 p.

[47] M. E. Haggerty, *Topics in Psychology*. Minneapolis: University of Minnesota Press, 1929. 86 p.

[48] C. M. Louttit, *A Handbook of Psychological Literature*. Bloomington, Ind.: Principia Press, 1932. 273 p.

C. M. Louttit, *Bibliography of Bibliographies on Psychology*, 1900-1927. Washington: National Research Council, 1928. 108 p.

have been provided: experimental psychology,[49] social psychology,[50] child psychology,[51] and applied psychology.[52] Bimonthly the *Psychological Bulletin* (American Psychological Association, 1904— ) publishes one or more critical surveys of the literature dealing with a specific problem in one of the areas covered by *Psychological Abstracts*.

Psychology is well equipped with dictionaries [53] which perform an orientation function in the interpretation of psychological terms, concepts, principles, and procedures.

**Psychological journals.** The periodical literature of psychology is indexed in the *Psychological Index* and in *Psychological Abstracts*. For selected topics, certain of the previously described guides to educational materials and to the general literature may prove useful.

**Books, monographs, and theses in psychology.** Published volumes in psychology are listed in the *Psychological Index* and in *Psychological Abstracts*. Additional guides to books, monographs, and theses in psychology are the same as the comprehensive sources described under the preceding section on education.

**Illustrative summaries and bibliographies in limited areas of psychology.** In addition to such surveys of the literature as are printed in the *Psychological Bulletin,* occasional summaries or bibliographies dealing with a limited subdivision of psychology appear as individual publications. Illustrative references dealing with a variety of problems may be found in the chapter bibliography.

[49] Carl Murchison, Editor, *A Handbook of General Experimental Psychology*. Worcester: Clark University Press, 1934. xii + 1126 p.
S. S. Stevens, Editor, *Handbook of Experimental Psychology*. New York: John Wiley and Sons, 1951. xi + 1436 p.
[50] Carl Murchison, Editor, *A Handbook of Social Psychology*. Worcester: Clark University Press, 1935. xii + 1190 p.
[51] Carl Murchison, Editor, *A Handbook of Child Psychology*. Second Edition, Revised. Worcester: Clark University Press, 1933. xii + 956 p.
Leonard Carmichael, Editor, *Manual of Child Psychology*. New York: John Wiley and Sons, 1946. 1068 p.
*Child Development Abstracts and Bibliography*. Washington: Society for Research in Child Development, National Research Council.
[52] Douglas H. Fryer and Edwin R. Henry, Editors, *Handbook of Applied Psychology*. New York: Rinehart and Co., 1950. 2 vols.
[53] J. M. Baldwin, *Dictionary of Philosophy and Psychology*. New York: Macmillan Co., 1901, revised 1928. Three volumes.
James Drever, *A Dictionary of Psychology*. Baltimore: Penguin Books, 1952. 315 p.
Horace B. English, *A Student's Dictionary of Psychological Terms*. Fourth Edition. New York: Harper and Bros., 1934. x + 131 p.
M. Erdelyi and F. Grossman, *Dictionary of Terms and Expressions of Industrial Psychology ("Psychotechnics") in German, English, French, and Hungarian*. New York: Pitman, 1939. viii + 98 p.
Philip L. Harriman, *New Dictionary of Psychology*. New York: Philosophical Library, 1947. 364 p.
Richard H. Hutchings, *A Psychiatric Word Book*. Seventh Edition. Utica, N. Y.: State Hospitals Press, 1943. 255 p.
H. C. Warren, *A Dictionary of Psychology*. Boston: Houghton Mifflin Co., 1934. x + 372 p.

**Biographical directories in psychology.** Two volumes of the *Psychological Register*,[54] a biographical and bibliographical directory of American and foreign psychologists, appeared in 1929 and 1932 respectively. The 1932 volume includes 2400 psychologists from forty countries. The projected first volume was intended to include psychologists who had died before the inauguration of the series, extending back as far as the Greek scholars.

For more recent information, the yearbook of the American Psychological Association may be consulted, although this annual publication includes only the name, training, position, field of instruction, and major research interests of each individual.

*American Men of Science* [55] and the *Biographical Directory of American Scholars* [56] contain the biographies of a number of the better known psychologists. Many of the previously listed educational and general directories include information concerning certain psychologists, especially those engaged in teaching educational psychology or serving in administrative positions. The historical surveys of developments in psychology, listed in the chapter on formulation of the problem, include biographical information concerning the psychologists of the past, while the four-volume *History of Psychology in Autobiography* [57] consists of extended résumés of the lives and works of selected psychologists, a number of whom are living at this writing.

## SOCIAL-SCIENCE GUIDES

**Comprehensive guides.** Certain of the general educational guides described earlier in this chapter contain considerable material of interest to workers in other areas of the social sciences. This statement is especially applicable to the *Encyclopedia of Educational Research,* the *Education Index,* the *Review of Educational Research,* and the *Bibliographic Index.*

The basic reference tool for the social sciences in general is the fifteen-volume *Encyclopedia of the Social Sciences*,[58] covering the fields of anthropology, economics, education, history, law, philosophy, political science,

[54] Carl Murchison, Editor, *Psychological Register.* Vols. 2, 3. Worcester: Clark University Press, 1929, 1932. x + 580 p., xiv + 1269 p.

[55] Jacques Cattell, Editor, *American Men of Science:* A Biographical Directory. Eighth Edition. Lancaster, Pa.: Science Press, 1949. vi + 2836 p.

Stephen S. Visher, *Scientists Starred, 1903-1943, in "American Men of Science."* Baltimore: Johns Hopkins Press, 1947. xxiii + 556 p.

[56] Jacques Cattell, Editor, *Biographical Directory of American Scholars.* Lancaster, Pa.: Science Press, 1952. 1072 p.

[57] Carl Murchison, Editor, *A History of Psychology in Autobiography.* Worcester: Clark University Press, 1930, 1932, 1936. 3 vols. xviii + 516, xx + 407, xx + 327 p.

Herbert S. Langfeld and Others, Editors, *A History of Psychology in Autobiography.* Vol. 4. Worcester: Clark University Press, 1952. xii + 356 p.

[58] Edwin R. A. Seligman and Alvin Johnson, Editors, *Encyclopedia of the Social Sciences.* New York: Macmillan Co., 1930-34. Fifteen volumes.

psychology, social work, sociology, and statistics. Its purpose is to provide a synopsis of progress in these areas and a repository of facts and principles. It includes biographical articles and bibliographies.

The *London Bibliography of the Social Sciences* [59] is a valuable compilation of some 600,000 entries, arranged alphabetically by subject with an author index, and based on the holdings of nine London libraries.

*Public Affairs Information Service* [60] is a comprehensive index of periodicals, books, pamphlets, and other materials, particularly those with emphasis on sociology, economics, and political science. It is published weekly, and cumulates five times a year and annually.

*Social Science Abstracts* promised to solve the indexing and abstracting problems of the social-science subjects, but could finance itself for only four years, 1929-32. The result is four volumes plus an index.

Other useful tools [61] in the social sciences are a compilation of research guides and references and a bibliography on methods of research. A historical treatment of sociology includes information concerning the presidents of the American Sociological Society, organizations, textbooks, and journals. [62]

**Periodical guides in the social sciences.** Reference was made above to the indexing of periodicals by the *Public Affairs Information Service* and to *Social Science Abstracts* (1929-32). Much social-science material is indexed in the general periodical guides identified in the earlier section on education.

The titles of journals dealing with the social-science fields may be located in the sources described in the preceding section on periodical guides in education. The index volume of *Social Science Abstracts* contains a long list of the journals represented. The yearbook of the Educational Press Association of America includes the titles of the social-science journals of most interest to workers in education. The annual educational directory, published by the United States Office of Education, lists alphabetically the educational, scholarly and scientific, and youth-serving associations of this country with an interest in education, accompanied by information concerning the journal and yearbook publications of each organization.

[59] *London Bibliography of the Social Sciences.* London: London School of Economics, 1931-1934. Four volumes and supplements.

[60] *Public Affairs Information Service.* New York: Public Affairs Information Service, 1915—.

[61] Louis Kaplan, *Research Materials in the Social Sciences.* Madison: University of Wisconsin Press, 1939. 36 p.

William J. Goode and Paul K. Hatt, *Methods in Social Research.* New York: McGraw Hill Book Co., 1952. Chapter 9.

Dorothy C. Culver, *Methodology of Social Science Research:* A Bibliography. Berkeley: University of California Press, 1936. x + 159 p.

[62] Howard W. Odum, *American Sociology:* The Story of Sociology in the United States through 1950. New York: Longmans, Green and Co., 1951. vi + 501 p.

Much of the pamphlet material indexed in the *Vertical File Service Catalogue* [63] is pertinent to the social-science fields.

**Guides to books, monographs, and theses in the social sciences.** The comprehensive guides to published books and to theses, as described in the section on education, may be used for canvassing materials in the social sciences. The *Encyclopedia of the Social Sciences,* the *London Bibliography of the Social Sciences,* and *Public Affairs Information Service* are described above. In addition, certain continuing or serial guides to theses in sociology, history, political science, and economics are published: Doctors' studies under way in sociology,[64] current research projects in sociology,[65] graduate degrees conferred in sociology,[66] doctoral dissertations in progress in history,[67] and dissertations under way and recently completed in political science and political economy.[68] These sources may be used to canvass studies completed or under way.

**Guides to special areas and problems of the social sciences.** Especially extensive guides have been prepared for certain subdivisions of the social sciences: bibliographies and guides in history,[69] dictionaries [70] of American biography and of American history, and a guide to materials in

[63] *Vertical File Service Catalogue:* An Annotated Subject Catalogue of Pamphlets, 1932. New York: H. W. Wilson Co., 1932—.

[64] "Doctoral Dissertations in Sociology, 1952." *American Journal of Sociology* 59:76-85; July 1953.

[65] "The 1949 Census of Current Research Projects." *American Sociological Review* 14:507-34; August 1949.

[66] "Higher Degrees in Sociology, 1952." *American Journal of Sociology* 59:61-75; July 1953.

[67] *List of Doctoral Dissertations in History Now in Progress at Universities in the United States.* Washington: American Historical Association, Library of Congress Annex, 1947. 39 p.

[68] "Doctoral Dissertations in Political Science." *American Political Science Review* 41:754-70, August 1947; 42:759-80, August 1948; 43:787-811, August 1949; 44:689-717, September 1950; 45:779-816, September 1951; 46:819-47, September 1952; 47:811-42; September 1953.

"Doctoral Dissertations in Political Economy in Progress in American Universities and Colleges." *American Economic Review* 37:772-92, September 1947; 38:750-76, September 1948; 39:1108-41, September 1949; 40:745-84, September 1950; 41:786-828, September 1951; 42:732-77, September 1952; 43:764-95; September 1953.

[69] H. P. Beers, *Bibliographies in American History.* New York: H. W. Wilson Co., 1938. 339 p.

William W. Brickman, *Guide to Research in Educational History.* New York: New York University Bookstore, 1949. Chapters 2-4.

George Sarton, *A Guide to the History of Science.* Waltham, Mass.: Chronica Botanica, 1952. xviii + 316 p.

Edith M. Couter and Melanie Gerstenfeld, *Historical Bibliographies:* A Systematic and Annotated Guide. Berkeley: University of California Press, 1935. 206 p.

G. M. Dutcher and Others, Editors, *A Guide to Historical Literature.* New York: Macmillan Co., 1931. xxx + 1222 p.

*International Bibliography of Historical Sciences,* 1926—. New York: H. W. Wilson Co., 1930—. Published annually.

[70] Allen Johnson and Dumas Malone, Editors, *Dictionary of American Biography.* New York: Charles Scribner's Sons, 1928-1937. Twenty volumes and index.

Also see *Biography Index:* A Cumulative Index to Biographical Material in Books and Magazines. New York: H. W. Wilson Co., 1946—.

James T. Adams and R. V. Coleman, Editors, *Dictionary of American History.* New York: Charles Scribner's Sons, 1940. Five volumes and index.

political science.[71] Dictionaries of terms in sociology,[72] social work,[73] and economics [74] are available.

The annual census [75] of social research conducted by the American Sociological Society uses such subheadings as social psychology, marriage and family, history and theory, community, industrial sociology, population, criminology and juvenile delinquency, public opinion, race and ethnic relations, social change, urban sociology and ecology, rural sociology, methods of research, educational sociology, sociology of religion, political sociology, social welfare, cultural sociology and anthropology, occupational sociology, social organization, and social pathology.

In the classified chapter bibliography are listed selected guides to library resources in certain regions, government documents, legal research, and social-science research at the University of Chicago. The chapter bibliography also includes selected summaries of certain topics in the social-science literature: sociology in general, educational sociology, rural sociology, social studies, social attitudes, personality traits, and human ecology.

**Social-science directories and yearbooks.** The social sciences are well equipped with directories and statistical and current events yearbooks. The annual educational directory published by the Office of Education includes useful information concerning educational and social directories and yearbooks, as well as a compilation of educational, civic, and learned associations in the United States with an interest in education. Extensive handbooks [76] list the scientific, learned, and technical organizations of the United States, Canada, and Great Britain. Two surveys [77] of organized

[71] Laverne Burchfield, *Student's Guide to Materials in Political Science.* New York: Henry Holt and Co., 1935. 426 p.

[72] Constantine M. Panunzio, *A Student's Dictionary of Sociological Terms.* Berkeley: University of California Press, 1937. 49 p.

H. P. Fairchild, Editor, *Dictionary of Sociology.* New York: Philosophical Library, 1944. viii + 342 p.

[73] E. F. Young and Others, *The New Social Worker's Dictionary.* Los Angeles: Social Work Technique, 1941. 160 p.

E. F. Young, *Dictionary of Social Welfare.* New York: Social Sciences Publishers, 1948. vi + 218 p.

[74] Byrne J. Horton, Julien Ripley, and M. B. Schnapper, *Dictionary of Modern Economics.* Washington: Public Affairs Press, 1948. ix + 365 p.

Harold S. Sloan and Arnold J. Zurcher, *A Dictionary of Economics.* New York: Barnes and Noble, 1949. viii + 268 p.

[75] "The 1949 Census of Current Research Projects." *American Sociological Review* 14:507-34; August 1949.

[76] National Research Council, *Handbook of Scientific and Technical Societies and Institutions of the United States and Canada.* Washington: The Council, 1948. 371 p.

R. S. Bates, *Scientific Societies in the United States.* New York: John Wiley and Sons, 1945. 246 p.

*Scientific and Learned Societies of Great Britain.* 57th edition. London, England: Allen and Unwin, 1951.

[77] W. P. Gee, *Social Science Research Organization in American Universities and Colleges.* New York: D. Appleton-Century Co., 1934. x + 276 p.

F. A. Ogg, *Research in the Humanistic and Social Sciences.* New York: Century Co., 1928. 454 p.

research in the social sciences are now out of date, but may prove useful for certain historical purposes.

There are directories of social work agencies,[78] political leaders and programs,[79] municipal officers and activities,[80] and workers in sociology.[81] Four of the widely used annual handbooks [82] of information are the *World Almanac, Statesman's Yearbook, American Yearbook,* and *Statistical Abstract of the United States.* Four of the better known encyclopedias publish annual supplements.[83]

The biographical directories listed earlier in this chapter include many of the leading workers in the various social-science fields. The *Encyclopedia of the Social Sciences, Dictionary of American Biography, Dictionary of American History,* and the surveys of social-science progress (listed in the chapter on formulation of the problem) contain pertinent biographical information concerning workers in the social sciences.

## TRENDS IN LIBRARY SERVICES

Trends in library reference services indicate that the next step is in the direction of coöperation, as reflected in the formation and expansion of regional union catalogues and bibliographic centers, and organization of coöperative storage libraries for infrequently used research materials.[84] It has even been suggested that one approach to successful housing and use of the tremendous volume of library materials may be through an "automatic electronic library," to which the customer could refer by remote

[78] *Social Work Yearbook:* A Description of Organized Activities in Social Work and in Related Fields. New York: Russell Sage Foundation, 1930—.
[79] *Political Handbook of the World:* Parliaments, Parties, and Press, 1927—. New York: Council on Foreign Relations, 1927—.
[80] *Municipal Yearbook.* Chicago: International City Managers' Association, 1934—.
*Municipal Index.* New York: American City Magazine Publishing Corporation, 1924—.
[81] *The 1953 Directory of Members of the American Sociological Society.* New York: American Sociological Society, New York University, 1953.
[82] *World Almanac and Book of Facts.* New York: New York World, 1868-1931; World-Telegram, 1932—.
*Statesman's Yearbook:* Statistical and Historical Annual of the States of the World. New York: Macmillan Co., 1864—.
*American Yearbook:* A Record of Events and Progress. New York: Thomas Nelson, 1937—. Earlier issues were published by different firms.
United States, Bureau of Foreign and Domestic Commerce, *Statistical Abstract of the United States,* 1878—. Washington: Government Printing Office, 1879—.
[83] *Americana Annual:* An Encyclopedia of Current Events, 1923—. Chicago: Americana Corporation, 1923—.
*Britannica Book of the Year:* A Record of the March of Events, 1937—. Chicago, Encyclopedia Britannica, 1938—.
*New International Yearbook:* A Compendium of the World's Progress for the Year. New York: Dodd, Mead, and Co., 1907-31; Funk and Wagnalls Co., 1932—.
*World Book Encyclopedia Annual:* A Review of the Events of the Year, 1931—. Chicago: Quarrie, 1932—.
[84] Julian Brandes, "Recent Trends in Library Reference Services." *School and Society* 70:193-95; September 24, 1949.

control, utilizing a recording of the document and a wire communication network to "play" the record by remote control over a loud speaker or automatic typewriter anywhere.[85]

An even broader concept of library services emphasizes the fact that international understanding is based on free interchange of the cultural records of nations as collected and preserved by libraries, educational institutions, and cultural organizations in general. International exchange of resources involves a number of possibilities and problems, such as (*a*) exchanges between institutions; (*b*) exchange of government publications; (*c*) national bibliography; (*d*) reproduction of research materials; (*e*) coördination of book acquisitions; (*f*) reconstruction of foreign libraries; (*g*) copyright, tariff, and postal regulations; (*h*) translations; (*i*) exhibits; and (*j*) interchange of personnel.[86]

With respect to the efforts of scholars and scientists, the chief aims of international scientific coöperation are exchange of information, attainment of objectives which scientists of a single institution or nation cannot accomplish alone, and development of an *esprit de corps* which may counteract the evils of human international politics. The means by which these aims may be approached include (*a*) various forms of coöperative research; (*b*) international conferences and congresses; (*c*) activities of international commissions and committees responsible for the solution of specific problems; (*d*) personal contacts, visits, and correspondence; (*e*) exchange of research materials, specimens, and literature; (*f*) exchange of professors, research workers, and students; and (*g*) various publications (for example, scientific journals, abstracting journals, textbooks and reference books, popular books and journals, directories, and bibliographies and indexes).[87]

## CONCLUDING STATEMENT

This chapter has outlined the major library tools for a systematic canvass of the literature in education, psychology, and the social sciences. In addition to the comprehensive or general guides, there are specialized instruments for canvassing periodical literature, books and monographs, and graduate theses, as well as for dealing with a variety of special problems.

Knowledge of library techniques and tools, and skill in the use of the guides to the literature, can make at least three contributions to problem-solving. (1) A carefully planned program of reading frequently is the

[85] Fred L. Walker, Jr., "Blueprint for Knowledge." *Scientific Monthly* 72:90-101; February 1951.

[86] Robert B. Downs, "International Exchanges." *Science* 105:417-21; April 25, 1947.

[87] Frans Verdoorn, "The Development of Scientific Publications and Their Importance in the Promotion of International Scientific Relations." *Science* 107:492-97; May 14, 1948.

source of significant problems. (2) A systematic canvass of the related literature is the means of determining whether the proposed study unnecessarily duplicates some earlier investigation. (3) The knowledge secured from such reading, in terms of sources, procedures, and results, represents essential orientation for definition of the problem, selection of method, and interpretation of findings.

## SELECTED REFERENCES

### I. General Discussions of Library Technique

ABELSON, H. H. *The Art of Educational Research:* Its Problems and Procedures. Yonkers-on-Hudson, N. Y.: World Book Co., 1933. Chapter 4.

ALEXANDER, Carter, and BURKE, Arvid J. *How to Locate Educational Information and Data.* Third Edition. New York: Bureau of Publications, Teachers College, Columbia University, 1950. xix + 441 p.

ALMACK, J. C. *Research and Thesis Writing.* Boston: Houghton Mifflin Co., 1930. Chapter 9.

BARTON, Mary N. *Reference Books:* A Brief Guide for Students and Other Users of the Library. Second Edition. Baltimore: Enoch Pratt Free Library, 1951. 99 p.

BERELSON, Bernard. "The Role of the Social Scientist in Library Research." *Rural Sociology* 14:244-49; September 1949.

BIXLER, H. H. *Check Lists for Educational Research.* New York: Teachers College, Columbia University, 1928. Chapter 2.

BOGARDUS, E. S. *Introduction to Social Research.* Los Angeles: Suttonhouse, 1936. Chapter 1.

BRADFORD, S. C. *Documentation.* Washington: Public Affairs Press, 1948. 146 p.

BRANDES, Julian. "Recent Trends in Library Reference Services." *School and Society* 70:193-95; September 24, 1949.

BRICE, Edward W., and COPELAND, Emily A. "Elements of Research and Library Instruction: An Attempt Toward Integration." *Journal of Educational Research* 45:293-98; December 1951.

BRICKMAN, William W. "Reference Aids in Educational Research." *School and Society* 71:324-31; May 27, 1950.

BRICKMAN, William W. "Reference Works in Education." *School and Society* 68:457-63; December 25, 1948.

BRITT, Steuart H. "The Psychologist and the American Documentation Institute." *American Psychologist* 4:180-81; June 1949.

BROWN, Zaidee. *Short Cuts to Information:* Time Savers for Teachers, Librarians, and All Who Must Find the Answers. New York: H. W. Wilson Co., 1943. p. 97-124.

BRYAN, R. C. *Keys to Professional Information for Teachers.* Kalamazoo: Western Michigan College of Education, 1945. iv + 44 p.

BUTLER, Pierce, Editor. *The Reference Function of the Library.* University of Chicago Studies in Library Science. Chicago: University of Chicago Press, 1943. x + 366 p.

CAMPBELL, Angus, and METZNER, Charles A. *Public Use of the Library and Other Sources of Information.* Ann Arbor: Institute for Social Research, University of Michigan, 1950. vii + 76 p.

CARNOVSKY, Leon. "Public Libraries." *Encyclopedia of Educational Research.* Revised Edition. Edited by Walter S. Monroe. New York: Macmillan Co., 1950. p. 690-701.

COLE, Dorothy E. "Graduate Theses Accepted by Library Schools in the United States from July, 1938 to June, 1945." *Library Quarterly* 17:43-57; January 1947.

CORDASCO, Francesco, and GATNER, Elliott S. M. *Handbook for Research and Report Writing.* New York: Barnes and Noble, 1951. vii + 142 p.

DAVIDSON, P. G., and KUHLMAN, A. F., Editors. *The Development of Library Resources and Graduate Work in the Coöperative University Centers of the South.* Nashville: Joint University Libraries, 1944. 81 p.

DOWNS, Robert B. *American Library Resources:* A Bibliographical Guide. Chicago: American Library Association, 1951. 428 p.

DOWNS, Robert B. "International Exchanges." *Science* 105:417-21; April 25, 1947.

ELMER, M. C. *Social Research.* New York: Prentice-Hall, 1939. Chapter 22.

EVANS, Luther H. "The Library of Congress as the National Library of Science." *Scientific Monthly* 66:405-12; May 1948.

FRY, C. L. *The Technique of Social Investigation.* New York: Harper and Bros., 1934. Chapter 2.

GOOD, Carter V. "Bibliographical and Documentary Techniques in Education, Psychology, and Social Science," in "Methods of Research and Appraisal in Education." *Review of Educational Research* 12:460-78; December 1942.

GOOD, Carter V. "Library Resources and Documentary Research," in "Methods of Research and Appraisal in Education." *Review of Educational Research* 18:373-81; December 1948.

GOOD, Carter V. "Library Resources and Documentary Research." *Review of Educational Research* 21:329-336; December 1951.

GOOD, Carter V. "Resources for Educational Research." *Phi Delta Kappan* 35:49-52; October 1953.

GOOD, Carter V., BARR, A. S., and SCATES, Douglas E. *The Methodology of Educational Research.* New York: Appleton-Century-Crofts, 1936. p. 104-84, 856-63.

HAYNES, B. R., and HUMPHREY, C. W. *Research Applied to Business Education.* New York: Gregg Publishing Co., 1939. Chapters 7, 8.

HILBISH, Florence M. A. *The Research Paper.* New York: Bookman Associates, 1952. 292 p.

HIRSHBERG, H. S. *Subject Guide to Reference Books.* Chicago: American Library Association, 1942. xvi + 259 p.

HIRSHBERG, H. S., and MELINAT, Carl H. *Subject Guide to United States Government Publications.* Chicago: American Library Association, 1947. vii + 228 p.

HOCKETT, H. C. *Introduction to Research in American History.* New York: Macmillan Co., 1931. Chapter 1. Also see the 1948 revision.

JOHNSON, Loaz W. "What Administrators Want and Will Use from Research Workers." *Growing Points in Educational Research.* Washington: American Educational Research Association, 1949. p. 7-12.

KERR, Chester. *A Report on American University Presses.* Washington: Association of American University Presses, 1949. 302 p.

LUNDBERG, George A. *Social Research.* Second Edition. New York: Longmans, Green and Co., 1942. p. 122-28.

MONROE, Walter S. "Literature of Education." *Encyclopedia of Educational Research.* Revised Edition. Edited by Walter S. Monroe. New York: Macmillan Co., 1950. p. 334-36.

MONROE, Walter S., and ENGELHART, M. D. *The Scientific Study of Educational Problems.* New York: Macmillan Co., 1936. Chapter 13.

ODUM, H. W., and JOCHER, Katharine. *An Introduction to Social Research.* New York: Henry Holt and Co., 1929. Chapter 21.

PFIFFNER, J. M. *Research Methods in Public Administration.* New York: Ronald Press Co., 1940. Chapter 10.

*Research Methods Applied to Health, Physical Education, and Recreation.* Revised Edition. Washington: American Association for Health, Physical Education, and Recreation, N.E.A., 1952. p. 84-124.

REEDER, W. G. *How to Write a Thesis.* Bloomington, Ill.: Public School Publishing Co., 1930. Chapter 3.

RICHEY, Herman G. "Library and Bibliographical Procedures," in "Methods of Research in Education." *Review of Educational Research* 9:453-55; December 1939.

RIDER, Fremont. *The Scholar and the Future of the Research Library.* New York: Hadham Press, 1944. 249 p.

RUSSELL, David H., and SHRODES, Caroline. "Contributions of Research in Bibliotherapy to the Language-Arts Program, II." *School Review* 58:411-20; October 1950.

RUSSELL, Harold G., SHOVE, Raymond H., and MOEN, Blanche E. *The Use of Books and Libraries.* Seventh Edition. Minneapolis: University of Minnesota Press, 1951. v + 91 p.

SCATES, Douglas E. "Library Resources and Documentary Research," in "Methods of Research and Appraisal in Education." *Review of Educational Research* 15:336-51; December 1945.

SHORES, Louis. *Basic Reference Books:* An Introduction to the Evaluation, Study, and Use of Reference Materials with Special Emphasis on Some 300 Titles. Second Edition. Chicago: American Library Association, 1939. xiv + 472 p.

SPAHR, W. E., and SWENSON, R. J. *Methods and Status of Scientific Research.* New York: Harper and Bros., 1930. Chapters 8, 9.

SMITH, H. L. *Educational Research:* Principles and Practices. Bloomington, Ind.: Educational Publications, 1944. Chapter 4.

THORPE, Marjorie H. *Where Can I Find—?* A Manual of Sources for Educational Research. Syracuse, N. Y.: The Author, 1941. 24 p.

VORMELKER, Rose L. *Special Library Resources.* New York: Special Libraries Association, 1941. 776 p.

WALKER, Fred L., Jr. "Blueprint for Knowledge." *Scientific Monthly* 72:90-101; February 1951.

WAPLES, Douglas, BERELSON, Bernard, and BRADSHAW, Franklyn R. *What Reading Does to People.* University of Chicago Studies in Library Science. Chicago: University of Chicago Press, 1940. xii + 222 p. A summary of evidence on the social effects of reading and a statement of problems of research.

WHITNEY, F. L. *The Elements of Research.* Third Edition. New York: Prentice-Hall, 1950. p. 97-108, 460-82.

WILKINS, W. D., and ANDERSON, W. H. "Usefulness of Periodicals in Education." *School and Society* 52:501-4; November 16, 1940.

WILKINS, W. D., and ANDERSON, W. H. "Who's Who Among the Magazines." *Phi Delta Kappan* 23:105-11; November 1940.

WILKINS, W. D., and GROSS, Lucy. "Usefulness of Educational Periodicals for Research." *School and Society* 79:9-11; January 9, 1954.

WILLIAMS, C. B., and STEVENSON, A. H. *A Research Manual for College Studies and Papers.* Revised Edition. New York: Harper and Bros., 1951. p. 16-61.

WILSON, L. R., and TAUBER, M. F. *The University Library.* Chicago: University of Chicago Press, 1945. x + 570 p.

WINCHELL, Constance M. *Guide to Reference Books.* Seventh Edition. Chicago: American Library Association, 1951. xvii + 645 p.

YOUNG, Pauline V. *Scientific Social Surveys and Research.* Second Edition. New York: Prentice-Hall, 1949. Chapter 7.

## II. Selected Guides to Special Areas and Problems

ALEXANDER, Carter, and BURKE, Arvid J. *How to Locate Educational Information and Data.* Third Edition. New York: Bureau of Publications, Teachers College, Columbia University, 1950. p. 154-60.

American Library Association, Committee on Public Documents. *Public Documents, State, Municipal, Federal, and Foreign.* Chicago: American Library Association, 1934. 233 p.

BAY, J. Christian. "Some Vital Books in Science: 1848-1947." *Science* 107:485-91; May 14, 1948.

BEALS, R. A., and BRODY, L. *The Literature of Adult Education.* New York: American Association for Adult Education, 1941. xviii + 493 p.

BETTS, E. A., and BETTS, Thelma M. *An Index to Professional Literature on Reading and Related Topics.* New York: American Book Co., 1945. viii + 137 p.

BLACKWELL, A. M. "A List of Researches in Educational Psychology and Teaching Method Presented for Higher Degrees of British Universities from 1918 to the Present Day." *British Journal of Educational Psychology* 14:99-105; June 1944.

BOYD, Anne M. *United States Government Publications.* Second Edition, Revised. New York: H. W. Wilson Co., 1941. 548 p. Also see 1949 edition.

BRICKMAN, William W. "A Bibliography of Recent Educational Bibliographies." *Educational Administration and Supervision* 27:481-512; October 1941.

BRICKMAN, William W. *Guide to Research in Educational History.* New York: New York University Bookstore, 1949. ix + 220 p.

BROWN, Stanley B., and LYDA, Mary L. "Doctoral Studies Completed in Education, 1949-50." *Phi Delta Kappan* 33:355-72; March 1952.

BURKE, A. J., and ALEXANDER, Carter. "Guide to the Literature on Public School Administration." *Elementary School Journal* 37:764-78; June 1937.

BUROS, Oscar K., Editor. *The Fourth Mental Measurements Yearbook.* Highland Park, N. J.: Gryphon Press, 1953. 1189 p.

BUROS, Oscar K., Editor. *The Third Mental Measurements Yearbook.* New Brunswick, N. J.: Rutgers University Press, 1949. xv + 1047 p.

BUROS, Oscar K., Editor. *The 1940 Mental Measurements Yearbook.* Highland Park, N. J.: Mental Measurements Yearbook, 1941. xxvi + 674 p.

BUROS, Oscar K., Editor. *The 1938 Mental Measurements Yearbook.* New Brunswick, N. J.: Rutgers University Press, 1938. xvi + 415 p.

BUROS, Oscar K. *Educational, Psychological, and Personality Tests of 1936:* Including a Bibliography and Book Review Digest of Measurement Books and Monographs of 1933-36. New Brunswick, N. J.: Rutgers University, 1937. 141 p.

BUROS, Oscar K. *Educational, Psychological, and Personality Tests of 1933, 1934, and 1935.* Studies in Education, No. 9. New Brunswick, N. J.: Rutgers University, July 1936. 83 p.

BUROS, Oscar K. *Educational, Psychological, and Personality Tests of 1933 and 1934.* Studies in Education, No. 7. New Brunswick, N. J.: Rutgers University, 1935. 44 p.

BUROS, Oscar K., Editor. *Statistical Methodology Reviews, 1941-1950.* New York: John Wiley and Sons, 1951. 458 p.

BUROS, Oscar K., Editor. *The Second Yearbook of Research and Statistical Methodology Books and Reviews.* Highland Park, N. J.: Gryphon Press, 1941. xxii + 383 p.

BUROS, Oscar K., Editor. *Research and Statistical Methodology Books and Reviews, 1933-1938.* Reprint. New Brunswick, N. J.: Rutgers University Press, 1938. 100 p.

CARR, W. G. "Deliberative Committee Reports of 1941." *School and Society* 55:199-206; February 21, 1942.

CHAMBERS, M. M. *The Colleges and the Courts, 1946-50.* New York: Columbia University Press, 1952. x + 202 p.

CHAMBERS, M. M., Editor. *Yearbook of School Law.* Washington: American Council on Education, 1933—.

CHERRY, Annie M., and Others. "Guide to the Literature on Rural Education." *Elementary School Journal* 36:748-59; June 1936.

CONRAD, Richard. "Systematic Analysis of Current Researches in the Sociology of Education." *American Sociological Review* 17:350-55; June 1952.

COOK, P. A. W. "A Guide to the Literature on Negro Education." *Teachers College Record* 34:671-77; May 1933.

COWLEY, W. H. *The Personnel Bibliographical Index.* Columbus: Ohio State University, 1932. vi + 434 p.

CURETON, T. K. "Doctorate Theses Reported by Graduate Departments of Health, Physical Education and Recreation, 1930-1946 Inclusively." *Research Quarterly* 20:21-59; March 1949.

CURETON, T. K. "Guide for Tracing Research in the Health, Physical Education, and Recreation Field." *Research Quarterly* 15:150-80; May 1944.

CURETON, T. K. *Masters Theses in Health, Physical Education and Recreation.* Washington: American Association for Health, Physical Education and Recreation, N.E.A., 1952. iii + 292 p.

CYR, F. W., and CUNIN, S. "A Guide to Research in School Law." *Journal of Educational Research* 30:509-21; March 1937.

DECH, A. O. "A Guide to the Literature of the Curriculum." *Teachers College Record* 35:407-14; February 1934.

DICKINSON, Asa D. *The Best Books of the Decade: 1936-1945.* New York: H. W. Wilson Co., 1948. 295 p.

DOWNS, R. B. *Guide for the Description and Evaluation of Research Materials.* Chicago: American Library Association, 1939. Mimeographed.

DOWNS, R. B. *Resources of New York City Libraries:* A Survey of Facilities for Advanced Study and Research. Chicago: American Library Association, 1942. xiii + 442 p.

DOWNS, R. B. *Resources of Southern Libraries.* Chicago: American Library Association, 1938. xii + 370 p.

DREVER, James. *A Dictionary of Psychology.* Baltimore: Penguin Books, 1952. 315 p.

FAIRCHILD, H. P., Editor. *Dictionary of Sociology.* New York: Philosophical Library, 1944. viii + 342 p.

FLACK, H. W. "Library Guide to Physical Education." *Peabody Journal of Education* 16:335-53; March 1939.

FRYER, Douglas H., and HENRY, Edwin R., Editors. *Handbook of Applied Psychology.* New York: Rinehart and Co., 1950. Two vols. xix + 380 + ix p., 381-842 p.

GARBER, Lee O. *The Yearbook of School Law 1952.* Philadelphia: The Author, School of Education, University of Pennsylvania, 1952. iv + 106 p.

GARBER, Lee O. *The Yearbook of School Law 1951.* Philadelphia: The author, School of Education, University of Pennsylvania, 1951. iii + 89 p.

GOOD, Carter V., Editor. *Dictionary of Education.* New York: McGraw-Hill Book Co., 1945. xl + 495 p. Scheduled for revision in 1956.

GOODE, William J., and HATT, Paul K. *Methods in Social Research.* New York: McGraw-Hill Book Co., 1952. Chapter 9.

GOODENOUGH, Florence L. "Bibliographies in Child Development: 1931-1943." *Psychological Bulletin* 41:615-33; November 1944.

GROPP, Regina. "A Guide to the Literature on Commercial Education." *Journal of Business Education* 10:19-20; June 1935.

GUY, Hollis P. "Research in Business Education Completed or Under Way, 1951-52." *National Business Education Quarterly* 20:1-23; March 1952.

HACKETT, R. C. "Educational Research in Progress." *Junior College Journal* 22:219-23; December 1951.

HARRIMAN, Philip L. *New Dictionary of Psychology.* New York: Philosophical Library, 1947. 364 p.

HICKS, F. C. *Materials and Methods of Legal Research with Bibliographical Manual.* Rochester, N. Y.: Lawyers Coöperative Publishing Co., 1933. 651 p.

HILL, D. S. *The Libraries of Washington.* Chicago: American Library Association, 1936. xvi + 296 p.

HOLBROOK, Franklin F. *Survey of Activities of American Agencies in Relation to Materials for Research in the Social Sciences and the Humanities.* Washington: American Council of Learned Societies, 1932. xiv + 184 p.

HOPPOCK, Robert. *Occupational Index,* and *Occupational Abstracts.* New York University: Occupational Index.

HORTON, Byrne J., RIPLEY, Julien, and SCHNAPPER, M. B. *Dictionary of Modern Economics.* Washington: Public Affairs Press, 1948. ix + 365 p.

HUGHES, E. H. *Business Education Index, 1941—:* An Author and Subject Index. . . . New York: Business Education World, 1942—.

JOHNSON, H. Webster, and MCFARLAND, Stuart W. *How to Use a Business Library with Sources of Business Information.* Cincinnati: South-Western Publishing Co., 1951. vi + 122 p.

Joint Committee of the Music Teachers National Association and the American Musicological Society, *Doctoral Dissertations in Musicology.* New York: Music Teachers National Association, 1952. 82 p.

KANDEL, I. L., Editor. *Educational Yearbook.* International Institute of Teachers College, Columbia University. New York: Bureau of Publications, Teachers College, Columbia University, 1924—. Deals with school systems of various countries and with major educational problems of the world.

KURTZ, A. K., and EDGERTON, H. A. *Dictionary of Statistical Terms and Symbols.* New York: John Wiley and Sons, 1939. xiv + 191 p.

LAMKE, T. A., and SILVEY, Herbert M., Editors. *Master's Theses in Education, 1951-1952.* Cedar Falls, Ia.: Research Publications, 1953. 168 p.

LANCASTER, J. H. "A Guide to the Literature on Education of Teachers." *Educational Administration and Supervision* 19:363-72; May 1933.

LATHAM, A. J. "Guides to Psychological Literature." *American Psychologist* 9:21-28; January 1954.

LEIGH, Marjorie C. "A Guide to the Literature of Teacher Training." *Peabody Journal of Education* 17:388-94; May 1940.

LYDA, Mary L., and BROWN, Stanley B. *Research Studies in Education:* A Subject Index of Doctoral Dissertations, Reports, and Field Studies, 1941-1951. Boulder, Col.: The Authors, 1953.

MANSKE, A. J., and ALEXANDER, Carter. "Guide to the Literature on Secondary Education." *School Review* 42:368-81; May 1934.

MARTZ, Velorus, and BALLINGER, Stanley E. "A Guide to the Source Materials Relating to Education in the Laws of the State of Indiana, 1816-1851, Part One: 1816-1838." *Bulletin of the School of Education, Indiana University* 29:1-96; July 1953.

MARTIN, Michael, and GELBER, Leonard. *The New Dictionary of American History.* New York: Philosophical Library, 1952. vi + 695 p.

McMILLLIAN, Nathaniel B. *An Analysis of Regional Items in the Content of Southern State Education Association Journals, 1935-1949.* Bulletin of the Bureau of School Service, Vol. 23, No. 4. Lexington: University of Kentucky, June, 1951. 91 p.

McSWAIN, E. T., and ALEXANDER, Carter. "Guide to the Literature on Elementary Education." *Elementary School Journal* 35:747-59; June 1935.

MENDENHALL, Paul, and ALEXANDER, Carter. "Guide to the Literature on the Boy Scouts of America." *School Review* 48:363-67; May 1940.

MENNINGER, Karl A., and DEVEREUX, George. *A Guide to Psychiatric Books with Suggested Basic Reading List.* New York: Grune and Stratton, 1950. vii + 148 p.

MONROE, Walter S., Editor. *Encyclopedia of Educational Research.* Revised Edition. New York: Macmillan Co., 1950. xxvi + 1520 p.

MONROE, Walter S., and Others. *Locating Educational Information in Published Sources.* University of Illinois Bulletin, Vol. 27, No. 45. Urbana: University of Illinois, 1930. 142 p.

ODUM, Howard W. *American Sociology:* The Story of Sociology in the United States to 1950. New York: Longmans, Green and Co., 1951. 512 p.

PORTER, Dorothy B. "Library Sources for the Study of Negro Life and History." *Journal of Negro Education* 5:232-44; April 1936.

REMMLEIN, Madaline K. *The Law of Local Public School Administration.* New York: McGraw-Hill Book Co., 1953. xi + 271 p.

REMMLEIN, Madaline K. "Tools and Procedures in School Law Research." *Growing Points in Educational Research.* Washington: American Educational Research Association, 1949. p. 166-75.

*Research Relating to Children:* An Inventory of Studies in Progress. (July 1, 1949—March 31, 1950.) Clearinghouse for Research in Child Life. Washington: Federal Security Agency, Social Security Administration, Children's Bureau, 1950. 374 p.

RONEY, W. H. "Important Works in Sociological Literature." *Sociology and Social Research* 23:137-43; November-December 1938. A list of important sociological works, as voted upon by twenty-three American sociologists.

RUNES, D. D., Editor. *The Dictionary of Philosophy*. New York: Philosophical Library, 1942. 343 p.

SANDERS, Chauncey. *An Introduction to Research in English Literary History*. New York: Macmillan Co., 1952. p. 61-93.

SARTON, George. *A Guide to the History of Science*. Waltham, Mass.: Chronica Botanica, 1952. xviii + 316 p.

SCATES, Douglas E. "Research Bureaus." *Encyclopedia of Educational Research*. Revised Edition. Edited by Walter S. Monroe. New York: Macmillan Co., 1950. p. 1031-34.

SCHMECKEBIER, L. F. *Government Publications and Their Use*. Washington: Brookings Institution, 1936. 446 p. Also see 1939 edition.

SCHOFIELD, William. "Research in Clinical Psychology: 1951." *Journal of Clinical Psychology* 8:255-61; July 1952.

SEARS, Jesse B. "School Surveys." *Encyclopedia of Educational Research*. Revised Edition. Edited by Walter S. Monroe. New York: Macmillan Co., 1950. p. 1126-33.

SEFTON, Allene. "A Guide to the Literature of Physical Education, Including Certain Aspects of Health Education and Recreation." *Research Quarterly of the American Physical Education Association* 6:3-47; December 1935.

SEGEL, David. *Educational Research Studies of National Scope or Significance*. Biennial Survey of Education in the United States, 1938-40, Vol. 1, Chapter 10. Washington: Government Printing Office, 1941. iv + 35 p.

SLOAN, Harold S., and ZURCHER, Arnold J. *A Dictionary of Economics*. New York: Barnes and Noble, 1949. viii + 268 p.

SMITHER, W. J. "Dissertations in the Hispanic Languages and Literatures, 1952." *Hispania* 36:164-69; May 1953.

SOUTH, E. B. *A Dictionary of Terms in Measurement and Guidance*. New York: Psychological Corporation, 1939. iv + 88 p.

SOUTH, E. B. *An Index of Periodical Literature on Testing*. New York: Psychological Corporation, 1937. xii + 286 p. Covers 1921-1936.

*A Survey of Surveys*. Nashville: Division of Surveys and Field Services, George Peabody College for Teachers, 1952. 52 p.

SUTTON, Robert B. "Needed—A New Encyclopedia of Education." *Educational Record* 33:471-80; October 1952.

TAUBER, Abraham. "A Guide to the Literature on Speech Education." *Quarterly Journal of Speech* 20:507-24; November 1934.

THOMPSON, Elizabeth H. *A. L. A. Glossary of Library Terms*. Chicago: American Library Association, 1943. viii + 159 p.

THORNTON, G. R. "The Need for an Encyclopedia of Psychological Information." *Journal of General Psychology* 30:237-54; April 1944.

United States Employment Service. *Dictionary of Occupational Titles:* Part I, Definitions of Titles. Job Analysis and Information Section, Division of Standards and Research, United States Employment Service. Washington: Government Printing Office, 1939. xxxii + 1288 p. Also see later supplements and editions.

United States Office of Education. *List of Publications of the Office of Education, 1910-1936*. Office of Education Bulletin No. 22, 1937. Washington: Government Printing Office, 1937. x + 158 p.

United States Office of Education. *Preliminary Bibliography of Current Periodicals, Quarterlies, Yearbooks, and Bulletins in Business Education, with*

*Annotations, Excerpts, Reviews, and Index.* Misc. 2221. Washington: Office of Education, June, 1939. vi + 33 p.

WALKER, George H., Jr. "Masters' Theses Under Way in Negro Colleges and Universities, 1951-52." *Negro Educational Review* 3:68-79; April 1952.

WARREN, H. C. *A Dictionary of Psychology.* Boston: Houghton Mifflin Co., 1934. x + 372 p.

WINN, R. B., Editor. *Encyclopedia of Child Guidance.* New York: Philosophical Library, 1943. xvi + 456 p.

WITMER, Eleanor M. "Educational Research: A Bibliography on Sources Useful in Determining Research Completed or Under Way." *Teachers College Record* 33:335-40; January 1932.

WITMER, Eleanor M. "Significant Education Books, 1947 and 1948." *Teachers College Record* 50:482-89; April 1949.

WITMER, Eleanor M., and FEAGLEY, Ethel M. *A Beginner's Guide to Bibliography with Examples Drawn from the Field of Education.* Revised. New York: Teachers College Library, Columbia University, 1935. 32 p.

WITMER, Eleanor M., and MILLER, Margaret C. "United States Office of Education Serial Publications." *Teachers College Record* 34:302-11; January 1933.

WOODWORTH, Robert S. *Contemporary Schools of Psychology.* Revised Edition. New York: Ronald Press Co., 1948. 279 p.

Works Progress Administration. *Index of Research Projects,* Vol. I. Washington: Works Progress Administration, 1938. vi + 291 p. Includes abstracts of studies in education under the W.P.A.

WYER, J. I. *United States Government Documents.* Chicago: American Library Association, 1933. 56 p.

YOUNG, E. F. *Dictionary of Social Welfare.* New York: Social Sciences Publishers, 1948. vi + 218 p.

### III. Illustrative Continuing or Serial Bibliographies and Summaries

BUSWELL, G. T., and JUDD, C. H. *Summary of Educational Investigations Relating to Arithmetic.* Supplementary Educational Monographs, No. 27. Chicago: Department of Education, University of Chicago, 1925. viii + 212 p. Also see supplements in the *Elementary School Journal.*

CARR, William G. "Deliberative Committee Reports of 1940." *School and Society* 53:164-71; February 8, 1941. Also see earlier reports.

CERTAIN, Julia L., and Others. "Educational Books of 1951." *Phi Delta Kappan* 33:389-403; April 1952.

CERTAIN, Julia L., and Others. "Outstanding Educational Books of 1952." *NEA Journal* 42:302-03; May 1953.

COLEMAN, Algernon. *An Analytical Bibliography of Modern Language Teaching.* Vol. III, 1937-1942. New York: King's Crown Press, 1949. xiii + 549 p.

COLEMAN, Algernon, Editor. *An Analytical Bibliography of Modern Language Teaching.* Vol. II, 1932-1937. Chicago: University of Chicago Press, 1938. xviii + 561 p.

CURTIS, F. D. *Third Digest of Investigations in the Teaching of Science.* Philadelphia: P. Blakiston's Son and Co., 1939. xviii + 420 p.

"Doctoral Dissertations in Sociology, 1952." *American Journal of Sociology* 59:76-85; July 1953.

Educational Policies Commission. *Deliberative Committee Reports, 1939.* Washington: The Commission, N.E.A., January 1940. 54 p. Also see earlier reports.

ELIASSEN, R. H., and ANDERSON, Earl W. "Investigations of Teacher Supply
and Demand Reported in 1952." *Educational Research Bulletin* 32:68-76,
83-84; March 11, 1953.

GOOD, Carter V. "Doctors' Dissertations Under Way in Education, 1949-1950."
*Phi Delta Kappan* 31:268-92; February 1950.

GOOD, Carter V. "Research Methods Bibliography: Selected Bibliography on
the Methodology of Educational, Psychological, and Social Research,
1950-51." *Phi Delta Kappan* 33:45-52, 61; September 1951.

GRAY, William S. *Summary of Investigations Relating to Reading.* Supplementary Educational Monographs, No. 28. Chicago: Department of Education, University of Chicago, 1925. viii + 276 p. Also see annual supplements in the *Elementary School Journal* and *Journal of Educational
Research.*

GRAY, William S. "Summary of Reading Investigations July 1, 1952 to June 30,
1953." *Journal of Educational Research* 47:401-39; February 1954.

"Higher Degrees in Sociology, 1952." *American Journal of Sociology* 59:61-75;
July 1953.

HILTON, M. E., and Others. *Guide to Guidance:* Selected Bibliography of 1949
Publications. . . . Vol. 12. Syracuse, N. Y.: Syracuse University Press,
1950. 58 p.

HUNT, Rolfe L. "Doctors' Dissertations Under Way in Education, 1951-1952."
*Phi Delta Kappan* 33:305-38; February 1952.

KNOX, Ellis O. "Negro as a Subject of University Research in 1951." *Journal
of Negro Education* 21:484-91; 1952.

MILLER, W. M. "American Doctoral Degrees Granted in the Field of Modern
Languages in 1951-1952." *Modern Language Journal* 37:152-58; March
1953.

SARTON, George. "Seventy-third Critical Bibliography of the History and
Philosophy of Science and of the History of Civilization (to November
1948)." *Isis* 40:124-88; May 1949.

SMITH, H. L., and MOORE, H. E. *Bibliography of School Buildings, Grounds,
and Equipment, Part V.* Bulletin of the School of Education, Indiana
University, Vol. 21, March, 1945. Bloomington: The University, 1945.
79 p.

STONE, Calvin P., and TAYLOR, Donald W. *Annual Review of Psychology.*
Vol. 3. Stanford, Calif.: Annual Reviews, 1952. ix + 462 p.

THARP, James B., Editor. *Annotated Bibliographies of Modern-Language Methodology for the Years 1946, 1947, and 1948.* Columbus: College of
Education, Ohio State University, 1952. x + 74 p.

TROTIER, Arnold H., and HARMAN, Marian, Editors. *Doctoral Dissertations
Accepted by American Universities, 1950-1951.* No. 18. New York: H. W.
Wilson Co., 1951. 266 p.

#### IV. Illustrative Individual Bibliographies and Summaries since 1935

BARR, A. S. "The Measurement and Prediction of Teaching Efficiency: A
Summary of Investigations." *Journal of Experimental Education* 16:1-81;
June 1948.

BEUST, Nora E. *Professional Library Education.* Office of Education Bulletin
No. 23, 1937. Washington: Government Printing Office, 1938. vi + 75 p.

BRADBURY, Dorothy E., and SKEELS, Esther L. *A Bibliography of Nursery
School Education, 1935-39.* Detroit: National Association for Nursery
Education, 1939. iv + 64 p.

BRECKENRIDGE, Marian E., and VINCENT, E. Lee. *Child Development:* Physical and Psychological Growth Through the School Years. Second Edition. Philadelphia: W. B. Saunders Co., 1949. viii + 622 p. Includes an especially complete bibliography.

BROWNELL, W. A., DOTY, R. A., and REIN, W. C. *Arithmetic in Grades I and II:* A Critical Summary of New and Previously Reported Research. Duke University Research Studies in Education, No. 6. Durham, N. C.: Duke University Press, 1941. xii + 175 p.

BURTON, W. H., and Others. *Children's Civic Information 1924-1935.* Southern California Education Monographs, No. VII. Los Angeles: University of Southern California Press, 1936. xxii + 308 p.

CABOT, P. S. de Q. *Juvenile Delinquency:* A Critical Annotated Bibliography. New York: H. W. Wilson Co., 1946. 166 p.

CALIVER, Ambrose, and GREENE, Ethel G. *Education of Negroes:* A Five-Year Bibliography, 1931-1935. Office of Education Bulletin No. 8, 1937. Washington: Government Printing Office, 1937. vi + 63 p.

CHAMBERS, M. M., and EXTON, Elaine. *Youth—Key to America's Future:* An Annotated Bibliography. Washington, D. C.: American Council on Education, 1949. vii + 117 p.

CHANDLER, A. R., and BARNHART, E. N. *A Bibliography of Psychological and Experimental Aesthetics,* 1864-1937. Berkeley: University of California Press, 1939. 190 p.

CONLEY, William H., and BERTALAN, Frank J. *Significant Literature of the Junior College, 1941-1948:* An Annotated Bibliography. Washington: American Association of Junior Colleges, 1949. 40 p.

COOPER, Isabella M. *Bibliography on Educational Broadcasting.* Chicago: University of Chicago Press, 1942. ix + 576 p.

"Coöperative Educational Experiments." *Educational Method* 20:267-334; March 1941. Describes the work of major research commissions and large-scale educational investigations.

DALE, Edgar, and Others. *Motion Pictures in Education:* A Summary of the Literature. New York: H. W. Wilson Co., 1937. 472 p.

DALE, Edgar, and VERNON, Norma. *Propaganda Analysis:* An Annotated Bibliography. Bureau of Educational Research, Series 1, Vol. I, No. 2. Columbus: Ohio State University, 1940. ii + 30 p.

DAY, Daniel. "Methods in Attitude Research." *American Sociological Review* 5:395-410; June 1940.

DOMAS, Simeon J., and TIEDEMAN, David V. "Teacher Competence: An Annotated Bibliography." *Journal of Experimental Education* 19:101-218; December 1950.

DUBATS, G. M., and Others. *Bibliography of Research Studies in Business Education, 1941-1948.* Indiana Business Studies, No. 32. Bloomington: Indiana University, 1949. 78 p.

DUNHAM, H. W. "Topical Summaries of Current Literature: Social Attitudes." *American Journal of Sociology* 46:344-75; November 1940.

EELLS, W. C. *Surveys of American Higher Education.* New York: Carnegie Foundation for the Advancement of Teaching, 1937. xii + 538 p. An analysis of such surveys, including extensive lists of surveys of higher institutions.

ELIASSEN, R. H., and MARTIN, R. L. "Pretraining Selection of Teachers During 1940-1943." *Journal of Educational Research* 38:666-77; May 1945.

FRAZIER, B. W. *Education of Teachers:* Selected Bibliography, October 1, 1935 to January 1, 1941. Office of Education Bulletin No. 2, 1941. Washington: Government Printing Office, 1941. vi + 60 p.

FRAZIER, B. W. *Education of Teachers:* Selected Bibliography, June 1, 1932, to October 1, 1935. Office of Education Pamphlet No. 66. Washington: Government Printing Office, 1936. vi + 42 p.

FREEMAN, M. H. *Bibliography of Research Studies in Business Education, 1920-1940.* New York: Business Education World, 1943. viii + 55 p.

GARRETT, Henry E. *Great Experiments in Psychology.* Third Edition. New York: Appleton-Century-Crofts, 1951. 400 p.

GILKINSON, Howard. *Outlines of Research in General Speech.* Minneapolis: Burgess Publishing Co., 1943. 80 p.

GLOSS, G. M. *Recreational Research.* Baton Rouge, Louisiana State University: The Author, 1940. 63 p.

GOHEEN, Howard W., and KAVRUCK, Samuel. *Selected References on Test Construction, Mental Test Theory, and Statistics, 1929-1949.* Washington: Government Printing Office, 1950. 209 p.

GOOD, Carter V. "Review of Selected Books on the Methodology of Educational, Psychological, and Social Research, 1940-1943." *Journal of Educational Research* 37:66-80; September 1943.

GOOD, Carter V. "Review of Selected Books on the Methodology of Educational, Psychological, and Social Research." *Journal of Educational Research* 38:226-33; November 1944.

GOOD, Carter V., and Others. "Summary of Studies Relating to Exceptional Children." *Journal of Exceptional Children,* Extra Issue: 1-60; January 1938.

HARRISON, M. Lucile. *Reading Readiness.* Boston: Houghton Mifflin Co., 1936. viii + 166 p. A summary of studies of reading readiness.

HILDRETH, Gertrude H. *Bibliography of Mental Tests and Rating Scales, 1945 Supplement.* New York: Psychological Corporation, 1946. 86 p.

HILGARD, Ernest R., and MARQUIS, Donald G. *Conditioning and Learning.* New York: D. Appleton-Century Co., 1940. 429 p.

HILL, Mozell C. "Negroes in the United States: A Critique of Periodical Literature." *Social Forces* 26:218-23; December 1947.

HOLMES, H. W., and Others. *Educational Research:* Its Nature, Essential Conditions, and Controlling Concepts. Washington: American Council on Education, 1939. viii + 186 p.

KAPLAN, Oscar J., Editor. *Encyclopedia of Vocational Guidance,* Vols. I and II. New York: Philosophical Library, 1948. xxi + 1422 p.

KIRCHER, Clara J. *Character Formation through Books:* A Bibliography. Washington: Catholic University of America, 1944. 80 p.

KIRK, Samuel A., and ERDMAN, Robert L. *Education of Mentally Handicapped Children:* Selected Annotated Bibliography. University of Illinois Bulletin, Vol. 46, No. 14. Urbana: University of Illinois, 1948. 47 p.

KNIGHT, Edgar W. *What College Presidents Say.* Chapel Hill: University of North Carolina Press, 1940. xvi + 377 p.

LARSON, William S. *Bibliography of Research Studies in Music Education, 1932-1948.* Revised Edition. Chicago: Music Educators National Conference, 1949. 117 p.

LAYTON, Elizabeth N. *Surveys of Higher Education in the United States, 1937-1949.* Circular No. 257. Washington: Office of Education, May, 1949. 24 p.

LAZARSFELD, Paul F., and STANTON, Frank N., Editors. *Communications Research, 1948-1949*. New York: Harper and Bros., 1949. xviii + 332 p.

LENDE, H. *Books about the Blind:* A Bibliographical Guide to Literature Relating to the Blind. New York: American Foundation for the Blind, 1940. 215 p.

MANN, George C. *Bibliography on Consumer Education*. New York: Harper and Bros., 1939. x + 286 p.

MARTENS, Elise H., and REYNOLDS, Florence E. *An Annotated Bibliography on the Education and Psychology of Exceptional Children*. Office of Education Pamphlet No. 71. Washington: Government Printing Office, 1937. iv + 42 p.

MAY, Mark A., and DOOB, Leonard. *Research on Competition and Cooperation*. Social Science Research Council Bulletin No. 25. New York: The Council, 1937. 200 p.

MCGRATH, Earl J. *Bibliography in General Education*. Washington: American Association of Junior Colleges, 1950. 32 p.

MENEFEE, Louise A., and CHAMBERS, M. M. *American Youth:* An Annotated Bibliography. Washington: American Youth Commission of the American Council on Education, 1938. xii + 492 p.

Michigan Department of Public Instruction. *What Does Research Say?* A Statement of the Implications of Educational Research for Teaching in Elementary School. Bulletin No. 308. Lansing, Michigan: State Department of Public Instruction, 1937. 146 p.

MITCHELL, A. Graeme. *Pediatric Bibliography*. Monographs of the Society for Research in Child Development, Vol. 6, No. 1. Washington: Society for Research in Child Development, National Research Council, 1941. vii + 119 p.

MONROE, Walter S. *Teaching-Learning Theory and Teacher Education 1890 to 1950*. Urbana: University of Illinois Press, 1952. vii + 426 p.

National Council for the Social Studies. *The Contribution of Research to the Teaching of the Social Studies*. Eighth Yearbook. Cambridge, Mass.: The Council, 1937. 239 p.

National Education Association. "Annotated Bibliography of the First Fifteen Yearbooks of the Department of Elementary School Principals." *National Elementary Principal* 17:1-77; November 1937.

National Education Association. *The Implications of Research for the Classroom Teacher*. Joint Yearbook of the American Educational Research Association and the Department of Classroom Teachers. Washington: National Education Association, 1939. 318 p.

PFAUTZ, Harold W. "The Current Literature on Social Stratification: Critique and Bibliography." *American Journal of Sociology* 58:391-418; January 1953.

PRESCOTT, D. A. *Emotion and the Educative Process:* A Report of the Committee on the Relation of Emotion to the Educative Process. Washington: American Council on Education, 1938. xviii + 324 p. Reviews the experimental work in this field.

"Publications from 1898 to 1940 by E. L. Thorndike." *Teachers College Record* 41:699-725; May 1940.

QUINN, James A. "Topical Summary of Current Literature on Human Ecology." *American Journal of Sociology* 46:191-226; September 1940.

REID, I. D. *Negro Youth, Their Social and Economic Backgrounds:* A Selected Bibliography of Unpublished Studies, 1900-1938. Washington:

American Youth Commission, American Council on Education, 1939. 71 p.

SCHAFF, W. L. *A Bibliography of Mathematical Education.* Forest Hills, N. Y.: Stevinus Press, 1941. 144 p.

SCHETTLER, Clarence. "Topical Summaries of Current Literature: Personality Traits." *American Journal of Sociology* 45:234-58; September 1939.

SHORES, J. Harlan. *A Critical Review of the Research on Elementary School Curriculum Organization, 1890-1949.* University of Illinois Bulletin, Vol. 47, No. 8. Urbana: University of Illinois, September 1949. 29 p.

SMITH, A. H., Editor. *A Bibliography of Canadian Education.* Bulletin No. 10 of the Department of Educational Research, University of Toronto. Toronto: University of Toronto, 1938. 302 p.

SMITH, H. L., and PAINTER, W. I. *Bibliography of Literature on Education in Countries Other Than the United States of America.* Bulletin of the School of Education, Indiana University, Vol. 13, No. 2. Bloomington: Indiana University, March, 1937. 341 p.

SMITH, H. L., and PAINTER, W. I. *Bibliography of Literature on Education in Countries Other Than the United States of America,* (January 1, 1919, to December 31, 1924). Bulletin of the School of Education, Vol. 14, No. 1. Bloomington: Indiana University, December, 1937. 139 p.

SMITH, H. L., and PAINTER, W. I. *Bibliography of Literature on the Teaching of English from January 1, 1930, to January 1, 1936.* Bulletin of the School of Education, Indiana University, Vol. 13, No. 1. Bloomington: Indiana University, December, 1936. 300 p.

SMITH, H. L., and O'DELL, E. A. *Bibliography of School Surveys and of References on School Surveys.* Bulletin of the School of Education, Indiana University, Vol. 14, No. 3. Bloomington: Indiana University, 1938. 144 p.

STOGDILL, Ralph M. "Personal Factors Associated with Leadership: A Survey of the Literature." *Journal of Psychology* 25:35-71; January 1948.

STRANG, Ruth. *Bibliography Relating to Reading on the High School and College Level.* New York: Teachers College, Columbia University, 1938. 194 p.

STUIT, Dewey B., Editor. *Personnel Research.* Princeton: Princeton University Press, 1947. 513 p.

*Summary of Research in Commercial Education.* Eighth Yearbook of the Commercial Education Association of the City of New York and Vicinity. New York: New York University Bookstore, 1938. 173 p.

THISTLETHWAITE, Donald. "A Critical Review of Latent Learning and Related Experiments." *Psychological Bulletin* 48:97-129; March 1951.

THOMAS, M. H. *A Bibliography of John Dewey, 1882-1939.* New York: Columbia University Press, 1939. 246 p.

THONSSEN, Lester W., and Others. *Bibliography of Speech Education, Supplement:* 1939-1948. New York: H. W. Wilson Co., 1950. 393 p.

TRAXLER, Arthur E. "Research in Reading in the United States." *Journal of Educational Research* 42:481-99; March 1949.

TRAXLER, Arthur E. *Ten Years of Research in Reading—Summary and Bibliography.* Educational Records Bulletin, No. 32. New York: Educational Records Bureau, 1941. vi + 195 p.

TRAXLER, Arthur E., and TOWNSEND, Agatha. *Another Five Years of Research in Reading—Summary and Bibliography.* Educational Records Bulletin, No. 46. New York: Educational Records Bureau, 1946. vi + 192 p.

VINACKE, W. Edgar. "The Investigation of Concept Formation." *Psychological Bulletin* 48:1-31; January 1951.

WILLIAMS, R. M. "Review of Current Research in Rural Sociology." *Rural Sociology* 11:103-14; June 1946.

WIRTH, Louis, Editor. *Eleven Twenty-Six:* A Decade of Social Science Research. Chicago: University of Chicago Press, 1940. 498 p. Lists social studies research at the University of Chicago.

WITMER, Eleanor M. "Significant Education Books, 1947 and 1948." *Teachers College Record* 50:482-9; April 1949.

### V. Selected Biographical and Institutional Handbooks and Surveys, and Statistical and Current Events Yearbooks

ADAMS, Arthur S. "President's Annual Report, A.C.E." *Educational Record* 35:25-60; January 1954. Also see later reports.

American Council on Education. *The History and Activities of the American Council on Education.* Washington: The Council. See the current edition.

*American School and University:* A Yearbook Devoted to the Design, Construction, Equipment, Utilization, and Maintenance of Educational Buildings and Grounds. New York: American School Publishing Corporation, 1928—.

ASHBY, Lyle W. "The National Education Association." *Phi Delta Kappan* 31:99-121; November 1949.

BATES, R. S. *Scientific Societies in the United States.* New York: John Wiley and Sons, 1945. 246 p.

BENNETT, Suzanne, and BORING, Edwin G. "Psychological Necrology (1928-1952)." *Psychological Bulletin* 51:75-81; January 1954.

BLANCHARD, B. E. "Some Characteristics Peculiar to Educators." *Journal of Educational Research* 46:515-23; March 1953.

BOGUE, Jesse P., Editor. *American Junior Colleges.* Third Edition. Washington: American Council on Education, 1952. x + 604 p.

CATTELL, Jaques, Editor. *American Men of Science:* A Biographical Directory. Eighth Edition. Lancaster, Pa.: Science Press, 1949. vi + 2836 p.

CATTELL, Jaques, Editor. *Directory of American Scholars:* A Biographical Directory. Lancaster, Pa.: Science Press, 1952. 1072 p.

CATTELL, Jaques, and ROSS, E. E., Editors. *Leaders in Education:* A Biographical Directory. Third Edition. Lancaster, Pa.: Science Press, 1948. 1208 p.

CHAMBERS, M. M., Editor. *Universities of the World Outside the U.S.A.* Washington: American Council on Education, 1950. xvii + 924 p.

FLEXNER, Abraham. *Funds and Foundations:* Their Policies Past and Present. New York: Harper and Bros., 1952. xiii + 146 p.

FOSHAY, Arthur W. "The Bureau of Educational Research Annual Report (Ohio State University)." *Educational Research Bulletin* 32:225-33; December 9, 1953. Also see later reports.

GOOD, Carter V., Editor. *A Guide to Colleges, Universities, and Professional Schools in the United States.* Washington: American Council on Education, 1945. xvi + 681 p.

*Handbook of Scientific and Technical Societies and Institutions of the United States and Canada.* Washington: National Research Council, 1948. 371 p.

HUGHES, Raymond M. *Study of American Graduate Schools Conferring the Doctorate, 1937-38 to 1941-42.* Ames, Ia.: The author, Iowa State College, 1946. 67 p.

IRWIN, Mary, Editor. *American Universities and Colleges*. Sixth Edition. Washington: American Council on Education, 1952. xi + 1105 p.

KNAPP, R. H., and GOODRICH, H. B. *Origins of American Scientists:* A Study Made under the Direction of a Committee of the Faculty of Wesleyan University. Chicago: University of Chicago Press, 1952. xiv + 450 p.

KNAPP, R. H., and GREENBAUM, Joseph J. *The Younger American Scholar: His Collegiate Origin*. Chicago: University of Chicago Press, 1953. xiii + 122 p.

*N.E.A. Handbook for Local, State, and National Associations, 1952-53*. Washington: National Education Association, 1952. 384 p. See the current edition.

*N.E.A. History:* The National Education Association, Its Development and Program. Washington: National Education Association. See the current edition.

NOBLE, William J., and HALEY, K. D. C. "Canadian Men of Science." *Science* 119:167-72; February 5, 1954.

PATTERSON, H. L., Compiler and Editor. *Patterson's American Educational Directory*. Chicago: American Education Co., 1904—.

PEATMAN, John G. "Policy and Plans of APA: How Scientific and How Professional Is the American Psychological Association?" *American Psychologist* 4:486-89; November 1949.

RUNES, D. D., Editor. *Who's Who in Philosophy*. New York: Philosophical Library, 1942. viii + 293 p.

*School Supply and Equipment Directory*. New York: School Management, 1934—.

SHANNON, J. R., and SHANNON, Esther J. "Who Really Is Who in American Education?" *School and Society* 70:131-33; August 27, 1949.

United States Office of Education. *Educational Directory*. Washington: Government Printing Office, 1912—.

WALTERS, Raymond. "Statistics of Attendance in American Universities and Colleges, 1953." *School and Society* 78:177-88; December 12, 1953. Also see later reports.

WHIPPLE, Guy M. *Commemorating a Quarter of a Century of Service of the National Society for the Study of Education*. Bloomington, Ill.: Public School Publishing Co., February, 1926. 44 p.

*Who's Who, 1848—*. London: Black; New York: Macmillan Co., 1848—.

*Who's Who in America, 1899-1900—*. Chicago: A. N. Marquis Co., 1900—.

*Who's Who in American Education*. New York: Robert C. Cook Co., 1928—.

# 4

# The Historical Method

THIS CHAPTER FIRST outlines the scope and use of history. Next the three major processes of the historical method are described at length: (1) collection of data, including consideration of such sources as documents and relics, of primary and secondary materials, and of note systems; (2) criticism of data, covering the processes of external and internal criticism; and (3) the writing of history (historiography), including problems of organization of materials, general philosophies and more specific schools of historical interpretation, and such detailed processes of historical writing as identification of the problem, inductive reasoning, use of hypotheses, causation, historical perspective, the principle of synthesis, and certain aspects of style. Finally, numerous illustrations of the application of the historical method to the fields of education, psychology, and sociology are given.

## DEFINITION AND SCOPE OF HISTORY

### Definition and Area of History

The origin of the word *history* means the search for knowledge and the truth, "a searching to find out." "History is any integrated narrative or description of past events or facts written in a spirit of critical inquiry for the whole truth." [1] A newspaper report of some current event, a debate in Congress, or a diplomatic exchange is not history, because it cannot be written as an inquiry into the *whole* truth. The campaign book of a political party reviewing the events of the four years preceding publication is not history, since it is not written as a *critical* inquiry into the truth. Even a careful historical novel, which holds many historical values, is not history, because it is not primarily an inquiry into past *truth* at all, but rather an artistic use of the imagination to entertain the reader.

History may be considered as embracing the whole field of the human past, as broad as life itself, although the data must be viewed with historical perspective as part of the process of social development rather than as isolated facts. Biography becomes history when the individual is considered

[1] Allan Nevins, *The Gateway to History*. Boston: D. C. Heath and Co., 1938. p. 22-23.

in relation to the society of his time, but is not history when limited to a single life in isolation. Antiquarian research does not become history merely because it preserves material for inspection in museum-like fashion.

The human past includes many fields of social experience that frequently have been of more importance than the history of politics or military exploits; for example, culture, ideas, institutions, law, religion, literature, art, travel, engineering, industry, technology, medicine, science, philosophy, economics, education, psychology, anthropology, and sociology.[2]

Although able historians, such as the presidents of the American Historical Association, have differed widely in their concepts of history as related to immediate usefulness in dealing with current problems, literary merit, relative importance of facts, philosophy and science, and the role of the individual, they are agreed on the richness of the content of history (including social, cultural, economic, and intellectual developments) and on a broad view of the past (extending far beyond study of politics, diplomatics, constitutions, and "drum and trumpet" war materials).

Specific illustrations of the application of the historical method and of the relationship of history to the fields of education, psychology, and sociology will be given later in this chapter.

### History as Science, Philosophy, Art

In their annual addresses most of the presidents of the American Historical Association have either ignored the subject of the science and philosophy of history, dealt with it only incidentally, or hurriedly passed it by.[3] Some of these historians, in emphasizing the interpretation and meaning of facts, have endorsed the search for tendencies, themes, patterns, and laws of history. A few of these specialists have discussed one or more philosophical or theoretical problems as applied to history; for example, discovery of laws, unity and continuity, possibility or impossibility of prediction, and oversimplification growing out of the search for clues or keys.

[2] Herman Ausubel, *Historians and Their Craft:* A Study of the Presidential Addresses of the American Historical Association, 1884-1945. New York: Columbia University Press, 1950. p. 300-358.

Harry E. Barnes, *A History of Historical Writing*. Norman: University of Oklahoma Press, 1937. Chapter 12.

Gilbert J. Garraghan, *A Guide to Historical Method*. Edited by Jean Delanglez. New York: Fordham University Press, 1946. p. 1-32.

Louis R. Gottschalk, *Understanding History:* A Primer of Historical Method. New York: Alfred A. Knopf, 1950, p. 26-37.

H. C. Hockett, *Introduction to Research in American History*. New York: Macmillan Co., 1931. p. xi. Also see the 1948 edition.

James T. Shotwell, *The History of History*. New York: Columbia University Press, 1939. Chapter 1.

J. M. Vincent, *Aids to Historical Research*. New York: D. Appleton-Century Co., 1934. Chapter 1.

[3] Herman Ausubel, *op. cit.,* p. 189-255.

Such European writers as Benedetto Croce, Oswald Spengler, and Arnold Toynbee apparently have had little influence on the ideas expressed in the addresses of the presidents of the American Historical Association.

Much futile argument has been waged over the question of whether history is science or art, when, in reality, it is both.[4] If the term *science* may be applied to fields in which the methods of inquiry are critical and objective, and the results are accepted as organized knowledge by a consensus of trained investigators, then history qualifies.[5] The research in history is science and the narration is art. The historical imagination and rhetoric of the master of style make a contribution to narration, although they need the sobering influence of the scientific historian with his critical evaluation of sources. History can be and should be scientific in method, within reasonable limits; historiography is more likely to be art, philosophy, or some special point of view. Detailed discussion of the problems of criticism of sources and of narration is reserved for later sections of this chapter.

History differs from the natural sciences in that it is based not upon experimentation, but upon reports of observations which cannot be repeated, although similar events may occur. It is this interest in the unique that makes it impossible for the historian to take advantage of experimentation; he cannot conjure up the figures of the past and cause them to reproduce the famous scenes of history.[6] Parenthetically, it should be pointed out here, and left for later discussion, that modern students of education, psychology, sociology, and history itself are not so much interested in the purely unique events of the past as in the synthesis of historical data to serve as a functional guide in analyzing current problems and conditions.

A quantitative emphasis may be found in current history, in part the influence of the economists, which adds another approach to a discipline once considered as narrative in character. As an illustration, an analysis

4 Louis R. Gottschalk, *op. cit.,* p. 8-13.
    J. J. Jusserand and Others, *The Writing of History.* New York: Charles Scribner's Sons, 1926. p. 3-4.
    Allan Nevins, *op. cit.,* p. 27-32, 349-51.
    J. T. Shotwell, *op. cit.,* p. 9-11.
5 F. M. Fling, *The Writing of History.* New Haven: Yale University Press, 1920. p. 20.
    Gilbert J. Garraghan, *op. cit.,* p. 40-43.
    William J. Goode and Paul K. Hatt, *Methods in Social Research.* New York: McGraw-Hill Book Co., 1952. Chapter 2.
    A. M. Schlesinger, "History." *Research in the Social Sciences.* Edited by Wilson Gee. New York: Macmillan Co., 1929. p. 229-30.
    Morris Zucker, *The Philosophy of American History:* The Historical Field Theory. New York: Arnold-Howard Publishing Co., 1945. Chapter 4.
6 F. M. Fling, *op. cit.,* p. 23-24.
    Allen Johnson, *The Historian and Historical Evidence.* New York: Charles Scribner's Sons, 1926. p. 45-47.

of expenditures for education during the first half of the last century is a quantitative approach that would reveal how much the southern states were spending per pupil as compared with the northern states. Quantitative history, utilizing statistical information,[7] may deal with numerical data such as the U. S. census for a given year or may base certain computations upon such data, as in calculating by decades the rate of increase of the population of the United States. Government statistics have been gathered through the centuries; for example, the census of the empire taken by the Romans and the custom receipts for London and other English ports under Edward III.

History and sociology are complementary.[8] Both fields are concerned with explaining the past, although the sociologist is interested chiefly in generalized descriptions of social behavior and in types of societal evolution, without the historian's preoccupation with time-and-place relationships and unique events. For that matter, there is room for both points of view in history itself: to preserve the historical uniqueness of events or personalities and to seek fundamental continuing forces or cyclical variations.

The preparation of an adequate written history has been basic to the development of social science,[9] although many specialists at present make a distinction between history and social science. History, however, is one of the social sciences, and there is much in common between history and such fields as economics, sociology, anthropology, and political science. This relationship has meant that history and the other social sciences have been closely associated in their development, and that there has been a reciprocal influence in their evolution.

In Germany the philosophy of history has received considerable emphasis, although in England the philosophy of the Hegelian type has never been particularly in favor. However, scholarly work in England has been done in a field related to sociology and history under the label of "the natural history of institutions." The development of sociology has been influenced by the work of historians and anthropologists who have studied the history of human institutions.

Schmidt points out that history has made progress in both content and methodology by utilizing the content and tools of ethnology and prehistory.

---

[7] Gilbert J. Garraghan, *op. cit.*, p. 151-52.
Bureau of the Census, with the coöperation of the Social Science Research Council, *Historical Statistics of the United States, 1789-1945:* A Supplement to the Statistical Abstract of the United States. Washington: United States Government Printing Office, 1949. viii + 351 p.
[8] A. M. Schlesinger, *op. cit.*, p. 222-23, 227-28.
F. M. Fling, *op. cit.*, p. 16-18.
[9] Floyd N. House, *The Development of Sociology.* New York: McGraw-Hill Book Co., 1936. Chapters 7, 8, and 13.

As to content, history now possesses an orderly approach to the centuries of human history not covered by written documents, including the movements of population over the entire surface of the inhabitable earth. As to techniques, history has benefited by methodological tools that have established spatial and temporal relationships between cultures, as well as cause-and-effect relationships.[10]

## VALUE AND USE OF HISTORY

If history is to be more than an almanac or chronicle of the unique events of the past, it has definite obligations to stress functional use of evidence, and possibilities for applying its data to current issues and problems. Nevins suggests that history enables communities to grasp their relationship with the past, and to chart on general lines their immediate forward course; by giving peoples a sense of continuity in all their efforts, and by chronicling events of enduring worth, it confers upon them a consciousness of unity and a feeling of the importance of human achievement. "Seated at the roaring loom of time, for six thousand years man has woven a seamless garment. But that garment is invisible and intangible save where the dyes of written history fall upon it, and forever preserve it as a possession of generations to come." [11]

One of the most prominent themes in the presidential messages of the American Historical Association is that of the immediate usefulness of history in dealing with contemporary problems.[12] Many of these annual addresses emphasize for the historian the importance of a social consciousness and of concern over large public issues. During World War I, the depression period, World War II, and the more recent post-war years, the historian could hardly escape his social responsibilities, since he was also a citizen with the press of current events about him. Whether interested in ancient, medieval, modern European, or American history, these specialists with rare exceptions have urged that history be used to throw light on the present, have searched the past for solutions to contemporary problems, and have seemed anxious to avoid the charge of antiquarianism. Many modern historians in both the United States and Europe have insisted that, like economists, political scientists, sociologists, and psychologists, they

---

10 Wilhelm Schmidt, *The Culture Historical Method of Ethnology:* The Scientific Approach to the Racial Question. New York: Fortuny's, 1939. p. 338-39.

11 Allan Nevins, *op. cit.,* p. 3, 5.

12 Herman Ausubel, *op. cit.,* p. 17-119. Also see:

Louis R. Gottschalk, *op. cit.,* p. 251-80.

Herman Ausubel, J. Bartlet Brebner, and Erling M. Hunt, Editors, *Some Modern Historians of Britain:* Essays in Honor of R. L. Schuyler. New York: Dryden Press, 1952. 385 p.

likewise have solutions to current problems and satisfy contemporary social needs.

## FUNCTIONAL HISTORY OF EDUCATION AND PSYCHOLOGY

Emphatic views have been expressed advocating development of a functional history of education and psychology.[13] Reisner maintains that sound thinking about the social process of education must depend upon a knowledge of the origins which influence its present state; that the serial approach makes easier the recognition and identification of significant causal factors in the complicated present situation; and that an understanding of the insights of educational thinkers of the past may protect us against too ready acceptance of half-truths, as well as reveal the comprehensive meaning of education which the future may make into a reality. To cite an example, a comparative study of the evolution of nationalism and democracy, as well as of the thinking of great leaders, may contribute to an understanding and evaluation of present-day educational and social problems in countries that vary greatly in their forms of government and systems of schools. Expressed in somewhat different terms, the history of education is the "sovereign solvent" of educational prejudices, aids in detecting pedagogical "fads and frills," and shows how the functions of social institutions shift with the passage of time. In fact, all human history may be viewed as a grand experiment on the part of mankind to test out the philosophies, plans, panaceas, or nostrums of persons more gifted in leadership, even though they are not always the most amply endowed with intelligent prevision.

Concrete illustrations of the types of questions that the history of education seeks to answer are: [14]

1. The question of evolution. How did progressive education arise and develop? We seek to establish trends.
2. The question of resemblance. How is education in Denmark like that of Italy, and how unlike? We institute comparisons.
3. The question of value. Why should the chief state school officer be chosen by a lay board rather than by popular election? We find causes and reasons.

Another example of the possible contribution of historical background concerns problems in the philosophy or principles of education—the rela-

[13] Edward H. Reisner, "The History of Education as a Source of Fundamental Assumptions in Education." *Educational Administration and Supervision* 14:378-84; September 1928.

E. W. Knight, *Education in the United States.* Boston: Ginn and Co., 1934. p. 38. Also see the 1951 edition.

Wilson Gee, *Social Science Research Organization in American Universities and Colleges.* New York: Appleton-Century-Crofts, 1934. p. 5.

[14] Quoted from H. G. Good, "The Possibilities of Historical Research." *Journal of Educational Research* 29:149-50; October 1935.

tive emphasis to be placed on education as a social process and as a process of individual adjustment and development. Should the school seek to cultivate the individual intelligence of the pupils or to promote a pattern of thinking in keeping with the social and political philosophy approved by the existing government? Should the social studies prepare the pupil for effective and critical participation in a changing civilization or inculcate attitudes of docility and acceptance of the status quo? [15]

Knight Dunlap points out the need for training specialists to do research and to give instruction in the history of psychology, indicating that few persons are qualified for this type of scholarship or service. He characterizes the history of psychology as application of the genetic method to psychology itself, involving (1) critical study of the evolution of hypotheses, postulates, techniques, and discoveries of psychology, and (2) utilization of historical approaches to the solution of certain special problems of psychology, as in the historical method of social psychology.[16]

Dunlap classifies the historical studies in psychology as follows:

1. Topical surveys, dealing with specific psychological concepts, such as Greek theories of cognition
2. Surveys of periods, and expositions of the views of particular men or groups, such as the history of Greek psychology
3. Source books, sometimes making available important materials in foreign languages
4. Biography, providing accounts of the lives of men who have made significant contributions to psychology
5. General histories of psychology, some devoted to the late modern period, and others purporting to cover the entire scope of psychological history.

The foregoing discussion of the value and use of history has been presented with full realization of the dangers incident to drawing "lessons" from history. To apply historical facts and conclusions to the study of current problems requires not only a knowledge of the content of history but also an understanding of the critical methods by which sources are tested as a basis for synthesis into history.[17] These processes of criticism and of historical writing will be treated later in this chapter. Then, too, there are many problems that must be attacked by other methods to secure satisfactory answers. History is not able to reveal to a school board how

[15] Edward H. Reisner, "The More Effective Use of Historical Background in the Study of Education." *The Use of Background in the Interpretation of Educational Issues.* Yearbook No. XXV of the National Society of College Teachers of Education. Chicago: University of Chicago Press, 1937. p. 196.
[16] Knight Dunlap, "The Historical Method in Psychology." *Journal of General Psychology* 24:49-62; January 1941.
[17] H. G. Good, "Historical Research in Education." *Educational Research Bulletin* 9:7-8; January 8, 1930.

other school systems are modifying their salary schedules in a period of economic stress, although it can show how such adjustments have been made in similar periods of financial pressure in the past. Also, there is no desire or intent on the part of the authors of this book to overemphasize the contribution of history to educational background, since a number of other fields, including psychology, sociology, comparative education, and philosophy, are important in the interpretation of educational issues.[18]

## HISTORICAL RESEARCH IN OTHER SOCIAL AND SCIENTIFIC AREAS

In emphasizing the contribution made by significant historical and comparative materials in such areas as philosophy or principles of education, elementary education, secondary education, higher education, educational administration, training of teachers, rural education, and adult education, attention should be directed to the application of historical sources and techniques to other important fields of science. It has even been suggested that the historical approach is universal in the professions—when the physician secures the case history from the patient, when the lawyer asks the client to tell the whole story from the beginning, or when the psychologist or psychiatrist delves into the past of the patient's mental malfunctioning or lack of adjustment. Many genetic, biographical, and case studies in psychology are essentially historical in approach. The nebular hypothesis and Darwin's theory of evolution are excellent examples of the historical approach; geology is the story of the earth's development; and historical anthropology is the key to the understanding of social origins and societal evolution.[19] The economist has provided information concerning the ways of the business cycle and leads for experimenting with the eradication of this social malady.[20]

Writers in the broad area of social research, especially in the field of sociology, have emphasized the contribution of the historical approach to the study of genetic development and evolution, reconstruction of the

---

[18] *The Use of Background in the Interpretation of Educational Issues.* Yearbook No. XXV of the National Society of College Teachers of Education. Chicago: University of Chicago Press, 1937. vi + 227 p.

B. H. Bode, "Where Does One Go for Fundamental Assumptions in Education?" *Educational Administration and Supervision* 14:361-70; September 1928.

F. N. Freeman, "Psychology as a Source of Fundamental Assumptions in Education." *Educational Administration and Supervision* 14:371-77; September 1928.

C. C. Peters, "Educational Sociology as a Source of Fundamental Assumptions in Education." *Educational Administration and Supervision* 14:385-92; September 1928.

[19] Edward H. Reisner, "The More Effective Use of Historical Background in the Study of Education," *op. cit.,* p. 186-87.

[20] Wilson Gee, *op. cit.,* p. 6.

cultures of early peoples, anthropology, and archaeology.[21] It is emphasized that all social data may be traced back to antecedents and that
cultural backgrounds are a part of every research picture in the social
sciences, with an understanding of the nature of culture traits in a social
situation frequently serving as the explanation of a conflict problem.[22]

Historical interpretation has a reciprocal relationship to such fields as
sociology, psychology, education, economics, political science, jurisprudence, ethics, geography, and anthropology,[23] as will be stressed later in
the section on the writing of history.

## COLLECTION OF DATA

### Delimitation of the Problem

The subject for research must be selected and the problem delimited
before proceeding with the collection of data. In an earlier chapter such
factors as novelty, interest, value, training, availability of data, cost, and
time requirements were emphasized as important in the selection of the
problem. At this time a brief supplementary statement may be made about
the choice and delimitation of the historical subject.[24]

Rather commonly the beginner in research chooses too broad a topic,
which in reality may include many problems large enough for separate
investigation. To treat in a graduate thesis a particular state in a given
presidential campaign holds out reasonable promise of thorough treatment,
as is not the case in attempting a history of political parties in the United
States. The history of a local school system or of a single high school is
more appropriate for most Master's candidates in education than is a
broader topic. Illustrations cited in an earlier chapter indicate the manner

[21] M. C. Elmer, *Social Research*. New York: Prentice-Hall, 1939. p. 72.
H. W. Odum and Katharine Jocher, *An Introduction to Social Research*. New York:
Henry Holt and Co., 1929. p. 211.
Pauline V. Young, *Scientific Social Surveys and Research*. New York: Prentice-Hall,
1939. p. 205-7. Also see the 1949 edition.
[22] E. S. Bogardus, *Introduction to Social Research*. Los Angeles: Suttonhouse, 1939.
p. 12-13.
[23] Harry E. Barnes, *op. cit.*, p. 360-66, 386-91.
[24] Carter Alexander and Arvid J. Burke, *How to Locate Educational Information and
Data*. Third Edition. New York: Bureau of Publications, Teachers College, Columbia Uni-
versity, 1950. p. 320-25.
William W. Brickman, *Guide to Research in Educational History*. New York: New York
University Bookstore, 1949. Chapter 1.
C. G. Crump, *History and Historical Research*. London: George Routledge and Sons,
1928. Chapter 2.
F. M. Fling, *op. cit.*, p. 33-37.
Louis R. Gottschalk, *op. cit.*, p. 62-70, 174-78.
H. C. Hockett, *Introduction to Research in American History*. New York: Macmillan
Co., 1932. p. 1-3. Also see the 1948 revision.
Allan Nevins, *Masters' Essays in History*. New York: Columbia University Press, 1933.
p. 4-5.

in which doctoral topics have been narrowed with time and deliberation. A candidate who began with "A Decade of Controversy" later delimited the subject to "A Decade of Controversy in American Institutions of Higher Learning." "A Study of Negro Land-Grant Colleges" became "The Functions of Prairie View State College in the Development of Public Education for Negroes in Texas."

Less commonly a doctoral problem is broadened as the study progresses; for example, from "A History of Findlay College" to "A History of Higher Educational Work in the Church of God"; and from "The Colonial School-masters of Maryland, Virginia, and North Carolina" to "Colonial School-masters, 1635-1775."

Since history does not exist in a vacuum, but draws its content from an area of subject matter, the worker who would trace the history of a particular problem in education, psychology, sociology, or in some other field must be well trained in the particular area. One who writes the history of mathematics must know mathematics as well as history. An examination of titles cited later in this chapter and in the chapter bibliography as examples of historical work in education, psychology, and sociology will demonstrate the twofold training required for successful historical writing in a given field; this point is especially well illustrated in the research and writing of specialists interested in historical sociology.[25] In certain instances, ability to use a foreign language is necessary.

An earlier chapter has dealt with the survey of the literature related to the particular research problem, including the library guides in the social areas. Later in the present chapter attention will be directed again to selected historical guides. The broad program of reading as background for selection of a problem in a field of interest may well proceed from the best general treatises to specialized volumes and printed collections of sources, then to calendars of documents, expert bibliographies, and reviews in historical, educational, psychological, sociological, or other journals, according to the type of problem represented.

### Historical Sources

In proceeding with a systematic discussion of the historical method, there are three major steps or processes to be considered: (1) collection of data, with consideration of documents and remains or relics, of primary and secondary sources, of bibliographical procedure, and of organization of materials; (2) criticism of the data collected, including the processes of external criticism and internal criticism; and (3) the presentation of the

[25] For example, Harry E. Barnes and Howard Becker, *Social Thought from Lore to Science*, Vols. I and II. Revised Edition. Washington: Harren Press, 1952. 790 + cx; viii + 1178 + cxxxv p.

facts in readable form, involving problems of organization, composition, exposition, and interpretation. The first of these problems is analyzed in the pages immediately following.

**Sources in history.** Existing classifications of historical sources differ in certain respects, although there is reasonable agreement in listing two broad divisions: (1) reports of events, called documents, consisting of impressions made on some human brain by past events and consciously recorded for the purpose of transmitting information, and (2) physical objects or written materials of historical value, known as remains or relics, produced without the conscious intention of imparting connected information. In remains or relics, one sees the actual objects that have been handed down from the past; through documentary sources one sees not the event of the past, but what the witness thought the act was. The importance of a working classification of sources will be emphasized later; for the present it is sufficient to suggest that sometimes man more nearly reveals the truth unconsciously through physical objects or remains left behind than through the documents which he deliberately records.

A division of sources originally developed for the field of history is expanded below, so as to apply to other social sciences, including sociology.[26]

1. Consciously transmitted information
   a. Written sources: chronicles, annals, biographies, memoirs, diaries, genealogies, certain classes of inscriptions
   b. Oral tradition: ballads, tales, anecdotes, saga
   c. Artistic productions: historical paintings, portraits, scenic or portrait sculpture, coin types, and figures on ancient coins
2. Relics, or unconscious testimony: human remains, clothing, food, dwellings, language, social institutions, products of the hand, utensils, arms, implements, machinery, industrial techniques, fine arts, products of the mind, business records, books, literature, manners, customs, burials, ceremonials
3. Inscriptions, monuments, public documents of certain classes: May have qualities belonging to either of the preceding classes; sometimes called

[26] L. L. Bernard, "The Sources and Methods of Cultural and Folk Sociology." *The Fields and Methods of Sociology, op. cit.,* p. 346-65.

F. M. Fling, *op. cit.,* p. 24-25, 42-47.

C. L. Fry, *The Technique of Social Investigation.* New York: Harper and Bros., 1934. p. 31-40.

Gilbert J. Garraghan, *op. cit.,* p. 103-23.

Louis R. Gottschalk, *op. cit.,* p. 41-61, 70-73, 86-117, 179-80.

J. O. Hertzler, "The Sources and Methods of Historical Sociology." *The Fields and Methods of Sociology.* Edited by L. L. Bernard. New York: Ray Long and Richard R. Smith, 1934. p. 260-73.

Wilhelm Schmidt, *op. cit.,* p. 89-90.

J. M. Vincent, *Historical Research.* New York: Henry Holt and Co., 1911. p. 18.

J. M. Vincent, *Aids to Historical Research.* New York: D. Appleton-Century Co., 1934. p. 21-26.

Thomas Woody, "Of History and Its Method." *Journal of Experimental Education* 15:175-201; March 1947.

Pauline V. Young, *op. cit.,* p. 215-19. Also see the 1949 edition.

"memorials." A gravestone containing only a name is a relic, but the addition of dates and information concerning the deeds and virtues of the deceased renders it a memorial with the characteristics of a document or consciously transmitted information.

Another classification of sources suggests that the originally few and simple categories have gradually become more complex and will continue to expand in the future.[27]

1. Physical remains: historic sites, roads, aqueducts, pyramids, fortifications, buildings ruined or whole, furniture, pottery, implements, weapons, and museum pieces of many kinds; usually more valuable for social and economic history than for political history, and more useful for descriptive than analytical elements of history
2. Orally transmitted material, such as folklore, legends, ballads, sagas, and traditions
3. More elementary and durable kinds of representative materials, not written in the ordinary sense, such as inscriptions baked upon clay, chiselled stones, stamped coins, woven tapestries, vases, and sculptures
4. Hand-written materials, including papyri, bricks bearing cuneiform writing, vellum or parchment manuscripts, and modern documents
5. Printed books and papers
6. Motion-picture film, microfilm, and recordings, including radio and television
7. Personal observation—by the writer or by people whom he interviews.

**Historical sources in education.** A workable, although incomplete, classification of sources in educational history includes the two major captions of documents and remains.[28]

*Documents*
1. Leg's'ative acts such as constitutions, laws, charters
2. Court decisions
3. Executive and other official records
   a. Proceedings of administrative officers and bodies
      (1) Minutes of boards of education
      (2) Reports and orders of principals, superintendents, presidents
      (3) Reports of committees, including recommendations for executive action
      (4) Systems of student records and salary lists
   b. Proceedings of deliberative bodies, such as the National Education Association and the North Central Association
   c. Reports of commissions; for example, the Educational Policies Commission
   d. Reports of school surveys and of official observers; for example, the report of Victor Cousin
   e. Courses of study
   f. Catalogues, prospectuses, advertisements

[27] Allan Nevins, *The Gateway to History, op. cit.,* Chapters 3 and 4.
Harry E. Barnes, *op. cit.,* p. 368-71.
[28] H. G. Good, "Historical Research in Education." *Educational Research Bulletin* 9:7-18, 39-47, 74-78; January 8, January 22, and February 5, 1930.

4. Newspapers and periodicals
    *a.* Articles
    *b.* News notices
    *c.* Advertisements
5. Personal materials
    *a.* Autobiographies, memoirs, reminiscences, and biographies
    *b.* Annals and histories written by actors in the events narrated
    *c.* Letters
    *d.* Legal instruments executed by individuals in a personal capacity, contracts, wills, and deeds
    *e.* Legal instruments conferring powers upon individuals; for example, certificates
    *f.* Lecture notes
6. Literary materials, as the novels of Charles Dickens or Edward Eggleston. (All literature has a potential use in the history of education. A great amount of such material is found in the publications of the Early English Text Society and similar bodies.)

*Remains*
1. School buildings and their furnishings
2. Photographs of buildings or furnishings, or of children, teachers, and parents engaged in educational activities
3. Forms of diplomas, attendance, and certificates, and record blanks
4. Various physical devices of the school for teaching, punishment, exercise, or health
5. Textbooks, manuscript exercise-books made by pupils, and pupils' maps and drawings
6. Under certain conditions all kinds of written materials, if the problem is to observe what people unconsciously reveal about themselves rather than to determine what they consciously or deliberately say about themselves.

Examination of this classification of sources and of the titles of studies in the history of education indicates that many types of materials have not been fully utilized, especially in the case of remains. It is true that collections of educational remains are not so numerous or so readily accessible as are documentary sources.

Under different conditions with varying purposes, the same source may be considered both a document and a remain.[29] In studying letters written before the time of Noah Webster, to determine variations in spelling, rather than the messages deliberately recorded, such sources would properly be classified as remains. On the other hand, if these same letters are analyzed to secure information concerning attitudes toward public education, they are considered as documents. Obviously a diploma in blank is a remain, but when filled in with the name of "John Jones" and with testimony concerning his character and scholastic attainments, it becomes a document. Textbooks and exercise-books are not deliberately or consciously recorded

[29] Carter V. Good, A. S. Barr, and Douglas E. Scates, *The Methodology of Educational Research*. New York: Appleton-Century-Crofts, 1936. p. 252.

descriptions of school practice and procedure during a given period, despite the light they throw on such problems, and therefore must be considered remains. However, the author's preface, which usually comments on curricular or teaching problems, is a documentary source.

The case of the textbook illustrates very well the value of distinguishing between documents and remains; in the preface, the author may deliberately lay claim to modern curriculum material and progressive teaching method, but the accompanying text, or the pupils' exercise books or examination papers, may serve as mute witnesses to the contrary. A school officer may write in his annual report of the humane methods of discipline employed, whereas the physical devices used for punishment may reveal the inaccuracy of the documentary source.

The annual report or written account by a person such as Horace Mann, or the oral testimony of an eyewitness who observed textbooks in use and even quoted sections from them, would be a document. In the instance of a document, the brain of one human being and the attempt of the observer to record his impression of what happened have come between the original event and the user of the source materials; for example, the opinion of a judge, minutes prepared by the secretary of a board of education, a superintendent's annual report, a school-survey report, a college catalogue, or a course of study.

**Social research sources.** Many of the sources previously listed in this chapter are valuable in the fields of sociology and social work, as well as psychology. The following list of documentary sources further illustrates the range and variety of materials available for social research, especially for facts about birth, death, marriage, divorce, whereabouts, property, immigration, and conduct.[30]

1. For establishing dates of birth: certificates of birth, baptismal certificates, immigration records, naturalization papers, insurance policies, Bible and other religious records, court records, hospital records, children's institution records, and the records of other social agencies
2. For proof and for date of death: the records of the board of health and of hospitals
3. For proof and for date of marriage: the records of marriage licenses and marriages (civil) and of marriage ceremonies (church)
4. Whereabouts of members of the immediate family, and of their friends and connections: records of birth, death, marriage, and property, as well as directories, voting lists, enlistment records, police precinct books, receipts of foreign drafts, and cemetery records
5. Property data: records of real estate, inheritance, insurance, bank deposits, pensions, and cemetery lots

[30] Mary E. Richmond, *Social Diagnosis.* New York: Russell Sage Foundation, 1917. p. 271-72.
M. C. Elmer, *Social Research.* New York: Prentice-Hall, 1939. p. 76-80.

6.  Records of arrest and of trial: data as regards conduct
7.  Back files of newspapers and their indices: dates of such incidents as an accident, arrest, award, death, or disappearance.

**Primary and secondary sources.**[31] Primary sources, the only solid bases of historical work, are the original documents or remains, the first witnesses to a fact. Reference to the preceding lists of documents and remains provides numerous illustrations of primary sources. The court stenographer's record and the newspaper reporter's account of a trial are primary sources (records of what the writers saw and heard), whereas an account of the trial (an editorial, for example) by one not present, even though based on a stenographic report, tends to lose its primary character. In other words, only one mind, that of the observer of the event, should come between the original happening and the user of the sources.

For tracing the historical development of school buildings and equipment, primary sources include pictures of buildings and equipment, legislation, state manuals specifying laboratory and library equipment, museum pieces of school furniture, diaries and letters describing the old schools, order blanks for requisitioning equipment or supplies, oral testimony of those who attended the old schools, architect's sketches and plans, and remains of buildings. Secondary sources on the same topic typically include such materials as histories of education, bibliographies, encyclopedias, and sections of books on school administration, which usually are several times removed from the original event.

The registration cards in a university registrar's office are a primary source for studying the age, sex, racial, or scholarship distribution of the students, as is the compilation of these records in the university catalogue, although a newspaper report based on such figures is a secondary source. The complete census reports of the federal government are primary sources, but census figures appearing in the *World Almanac* or the *Statistical Abstract of the United States* represent a secondary source. Even secondary sources of a statistical character are subject to error in the process of transcription, reprinting, selection, rearrangement, and manipulation. Therefore, it is far better to check the data, statistical or verbal, against the primary source rather than to depend on the secondary source.[32]

The classification of a source as primary or secondary depends in part on the problem and purpose; in one instance it may be primary and in another secondary. Ordinarily textbooks in the history of education are

[31] H. G. Good, "Historical Research in Education," *op. cit.*, p. 43-47, 74-76.
    William W. Brickman, *Guide to Research in Educational History*. New York: New York University Bookstore, 1949. Chapter 5.
[32] G. A. Lundberg, *Social Research*. New York: Longmans, Green and Co., 1929. p. 87-89. Also see the 1942 revised edition, p. 125-28.

secondary sources, usually many times removed from the original event, but for the worker who wishes to study the organization of materials and style of writing employed by authors in this field these books become primary.

It is necessary in some historical studies to begin with secondary sources and to work back to the primary sources when the latter are not known in the beginning. For example, in making up a list of old arithmetic text-books, it may be necessary to begin with encyclopedias, available articles and bibliographies on the subject, and histories of arithmetic, which are secondary sources, and from these work back to the arithmetic texts, the primary sources in this instance.[33]

In spite of insistence on the use of primary sources, members of gradu-ate departments of instruction are able to cite extreme instances of ap-parently immature or poorly trained graduate students who seem totally unable or unwilling to go beyond a few secondary sources on a given his-torical topic.[34] In a study of the educational history of a junior high school in a large city, the local newspapers and the reports of the school board were scarcely touched, the former being used only twice. In treating the development of art education in the same school system, a candidate for the Master's degree devoted 122 of a total of 188 citations to five secondary sources. Another student, in attempting to trace the educational develop-ment of a state school system over a given period of time, never seemed to get beyond a state history or two (secondary sources), except for the reminiscences of a minister and the notes of a federal officer. A historical investigation, in its preliminary form, of higher education in a particular state utilized almost entirely existing state histories, seemingly unaware of the materials to be found in college catalogues, reports of college presi-dents, and other official records; the bibliography included only three college catalogues, one volume of statistics, two handbooks, one letter, and one annual state report.

Along with reading the original sources, visitation of place of origin enhances the vitality of history, whether the problem deals with a person, a people, or a movement. Aristotle says that a Libyan, when asked to name the best manure, replied: "The land-owner's footprints." When asked about the best feed to fatten a horse, a Persian answered: "His master's eye." [35] Livy neglected factors of geography and topography. Had he visited Lake Trasimenus, only some thirty miles from his birthplace, he would have written differently about that famous battlefield.

---

[33] H. G. Good, "Historical Research in Education," *op. cit.*
[34] Carter V. Good, A. S. Barr, and Douglas E. Scates, *op. cit.,* p. 254-55.
[35] Thomas Woody, *op. cit.,* p. 175-201.

When economics and political science became differentiated from history during the latter part of the last century, they borrowed from historiography an interest in documentation and archives. Sociologists likewise are interested in documentary research, but maintain that non-official documents also are important, including personal letters, autobiographies, diaries, life histories, and similar records (described in the chapter on case and clinical techniques). Historiography in turn has introduced something of the comparative and generalizing methods of sociology, in an attempt to become helpful as an interpretation of present and future trends.[36]

Collections of private letters, in spite of certain limitations, are valuable sources of historical evidence that fall into three classes: [37]

1.  Collections published by the writer himself (for example, Pliny's letters) which may omit evidence that would place the author in an unfavorable light or which might injure a friend or supporter.
2.  Publication of letters by a relative or a literary executor (for example, Colonel Gurwood's publication of the Duke of Wellington's official correspondence) who may be in sympathy with the writer and may omit damaging passages or even entire letters.
3.  Collections published by an editor who has no personal relations with the writer and therefore feels free to release all evidence, whether favorable or unfavorable to the author of the letters.

Diaries may have the same advantages and disadvantages as letters for purposes of historical research, although an author who publishes his own diary may delete entries that reflect unfavorably on his life or insight. Also, as in the case of letters, many self-centered persons may describe themselves and their motives as they wish to appear rather than as they actually are. An exception to this category is Samuel Pepys, who probably wrote with complete candor and honesty in his diary, since he could hardly have expected anyone to decode his special type of shorthand.

Samuel Johnson said that no one was qualified to write the life of a man except one who had eaten and drunk and lived in close relationships with him; by this criterion James Boswell was almost ideally qualified to write the *Life of Johnson* as a classical example of biography written by an associate who knew his subject well. Boswell, however, omitted interesting details that recently have come to light, in following what he considered the dictates of good taste in biography. How helpful it would have been to Douglas Freeman, in following the Army of Northern Virginia through its campaigns, had he been able to talk with Robert E. Lee.[38]

36 Floyd N. House, *op. cit.,* Chapter 7.
37 Charles Oman, *On the Writing of History.* New York: E. P. Dutton and Co., 1939. p. 68-71.
38 Dumas Malone, "Biography and History." *The Interpretation of History.* Edited by Joseph R. Strayer. Princeton: Princeton University Press, 1943. p. 119-48. Also see the 1950 edition.

**Guides to historical materials.** An earlier chapter outlined the major library guides available for canvassing publications (such as books, periodicals, and theses) in the social research area, with special reference to education, psychology, and sociology. The guides to historical materials are cited in that earlier chapter and are also listed in the bibliography at the end of the present chapter.

**Note-taking and note systems.** In all probability the process of note-taking has been going forward as the compilation of the bibliography progresses; in fact, the expansion of the bibliography, analysis of content, and note-taking well may proceed simultaneously up to the end of the investigation. Samples of form for references and related principles of note-taking are given in the chapter on reporting of research. The footnotes and chapter bibliographies of this book also serve as illustrations of documentation and bibliographical style. Proper documentation in the writing of the narrative depends on the presence of full bibliographical information in the note system. The details of note-taking and note systems, owing to space limitations, must be left to other available treatises,[39] with room at this time for only a summary statement of the essential steps and procedures.[40]

To make good progress in answering historical questions the student should collect the material systematically. For this purpose he will need a well-arranged plan of note-taking. W. H. Prescott because of his blindness deliberately acquired the ability to hold in mind and to place into an orderly sequence the details of long chapters of his works; but most people are not geniuses. If they want to have access to large quantities of detailed information they must write it down. This means a system of notes. Great historians like McMaster, James Ford Rhodes, and Edward Gibbon are known to have taken the notes for their extensive writings in bound note-books. Of this practice one can only say that they succeeded by means of a system that is not the best.

A note-system should be flexible, that is, it should be possible to add to it at any point without disarranging the older material; and it should be possible to rearrange the notes at will. This requires that the notes be taken on separate sheets, slips, or cards. Each piece should as far as possible contain a complete item, but when the matter to be noted is too extensive it may be continued on successive pieces and these numbered in series. Not more than one item should

[39] Carter Alexander and Arvid J. Burke, *op. cit.,* p. 52-57, 179-93.
William W. Brickman, *op. cit.,* Chapter 6.
C. G. Crump, *op. cit.,* Chapter 4.
E. W. Dow, *Principles of a Note-System for Historical Studies.* New York: Century Co., 1924. vi + 124 p. plus detailed illustrations and reproductions of various types of notes.
Gilbert J. Garraghan, *op. cit.,* p. 124-30.
Louis R. Gottschalk, *op. cit.,* p. 19-21, 73-85.
H. C. Hockett, *op. cit.,* p. 10-23, 46-55.
Chauncey Sanders, *An Introduction to Research in English Literary History.* New York: Macmillan Co., 1952. p. 408-11.
W. E. Spahr and R. J. Swenson, *Methods and Status of Scientific Research.* New York: Harper and Bros., 1930. p. 145-48.
[40] Quoted from H. G. Good, "Historical Research in Education," *op. cit.,* p. 77-78.

ever be placed upon a single piece. Each piece should have a subject-heading at the top and a margin for indexing, etc., at the left. For most kinds of historical note-taking two sizes of paper are desirable. What the sizes shall be will be determined by convenience in using and convenience in filing. Probably the most useful sizes are the 3 x 5 or 4 x 6 cards for small items and the ordinary lettersize paper for larger passages.

About three different kinds of notes are regularly made by historical workers. The first is the bibliographical note which always contains the standard data, author, title, pages, place and date of publication, and other formal facts about a document. The second kind is the subject note which contains one item of information about a particular topic, with the source whence it was obtained. The great body of notes collected by any student will usually come under this head. One caution may be given here. Do not copy out long passages in readily accessible works but rather abbreviate and summarize. A third kind may be called the method notes. In collecting such material one constantly comes across suggestions or thinks of ideas which seem useful in interpreting the facts. Such suggestions or interpretative ideas do not fit into either subject or bibliographical entries, but they must be noted or they will be forgotten. Finally, when any extensive body of information is collected, an index and a more or less elaborate system of cross references become useful. Each card or sheet will indeed have, at the top, a title which gives in a word or two the particular contents of that piece. These titles themselves form a sort of index. But the cards are constantly being rearranged for special purpose. A separate index, modified from time to time, will help in the final organization and discussion of the materials.

George Bancroft, at work in the 1840's on his voluminous history, had on hand a number of quarto-size blankbooks, in which one or more pages were given to the successive days of the years. Data gathered by him in reading and research were duly entered in these books on the page or pages corresponding to the particular day and year to which they belonged. Even as late as the 1890's, the able American historian James Ford Rhodes made use only of blankbooks for his notes, the card system being at that time something of a novelty. A major limitation in using a blankbook for note-taking is that insertions cannot readily be made. Also the arrangement of the notes in either a logical or topical order is difficult to work out satisfactorily, even though an index to the contents of the notebook is provided.[41]

## CRITICISM OF DATA

The historian subjects his sources to external and internal criticism. External criticism is concerned with the genuineness of the document itself, whether it really is what it purports or seems to be and whether it reads true to the original. Internal criticism deals with the meaning and trustworthiness of *statements* that remain within the document after any spurious or interpolated matter has been removed from the text. In other words,

[41] Gilbert J. Garraghan, *op. cit.*, p. 125.

external criticism deals with data relating to form and appearance rather than meaning of contents, whereas internal criticism weighs the testimony of the document in relation to the truth. However, there is no sharp line of demarcation between these two phases of historical criticism; both progress simultaneously in many instances, with a great deal of overlapping. In fact, external criticism may employ internal evidence from the document (through a study of its contents), and internal criticism may use external evidence concerning authorship, or time and place of writing. These terms, *external* and *internal,* refer to the *purpose* or objective of criticism and not to *method* or procedure in dealing with sources, or whether one looks within or without the document to accomplish the desired purpose. Therefore, any differentiation between the two is in terms of the statements to be proved rather than the means employed to establish such proof.[42]

External criticism sometimes is called lower criticism, because it is a preliminary and preparatory step, providing the data to be used in the second phase known as internal or higher criticism. These terms, *lower criticism* and *higher criticism,* sometimes have been used in the literature of historiography, but more commonly in the areas of religion and theology than in historical research in general or in educational history. Since there has been considerable confusion and inconsistency in definition of these terms, it is probably the better part of wisdom to omit such terminology from discussions of the methodology of historical criticism.

### External Criticism [43]

**Problems of external criticism (authenticity).** In testing the genuineness of a document or remain, the problems of external criticism involve the questions of authorship and textual criticism to determine all the conditions that may have influenced the production of the document, such as time, place, purpose, and circumstances of composition, and what part of the document is true to the original. The questions that follow are illustrative of problems of external criticism, and are also useful in the process of internal criticism; that is, in determining the truth and value of the statements made in the document.[44]

1.  Who was the author, not merely what was his name but what were his personality, character, position, and so forth?
2.  What were his general qualifications as a reporter—alertness, character, bias?

[42] For a similar statement see Carter V. Good, A. S. Barr, and Douglas E. Scates, *op. cit.,* p. 257-58.
[43] Gilbert J. Garraghan, *op. cit.,* p. 168-231.
[44] Quoted from H. G. Good, "Historical Research in Education." *Educational Research Bulletin* 9:17-18; January 8, 1930.

3. What were his special qualifications and disqualifications as a reporter of the matters here treated?
   a. How was he interested in the events related?
   b. How was he situated for observation of the events?
   c. Had he the necessary general and technical knowledge for learning and reporting the events?
4. How soon after the events was the document written? For one purpose the century of composition may be sufficient; for another the very hour may be essential.
5. How was the document written, from memory, after consultation with others, after checking the facts, or by combining earlier trial drafts?
6. How is the document related to other documents?
   a. Is it an original source; wholly or in part?
   b. If the latter, what parts are original; what borrowed; whence? How credible are the borrowed materials?
   c. How and how accurately is the borrowing done?
   d. How is the borrowed material changed; how used?

It is true that the development of certain auxiliary sciences, and of printing and photography, has contributed greatly to the work of external criticism. Before the invention of printing, when manuscripts passed through the hands of many copyists in the course of the centuries, there were opportunities for inadvertent errors in the form of unintentional omissions or insertions, and even for deliberate changes in the text. Microphotography has now made it possible to reproduce and transmit entire books, bulky records, newspapers, and manuscripts for projection in some distant library, thus further reducing the probability of the type of error encountered in external criticism.

The problem of authenticity is relatively infrequent in education, psychology, sociology, and anthropology, as compared with numerous instances of forgery of historical documents, in whole or in part. Even though there may not be the same incentive to perpetrate frauds and forgeries in the modern literature of education, psychology, and sociology as in history, literature, art, relics, antiques, business documents, natural science, and exploration, still there are motives for deception and trickery: (1) the use of a well known name may increase the sale and prestige of a manuscript; (2) the reputation of prominent persons, who are too busy or who lack the necessary training to write effectively, may be increased through employment of "ghost" writers; and (3) pseudonyms may be used to mystify or to stimulate the curiosity of the public. Among the numerous types of invention or forgery that appear are: (1) proverbs, epigrams, or witty sayings of famous people, who somehow always seem to have had at tongue's end a brilliant phrase or retort at the right moment; (2) invented speeches placed in the mouths of famous personages by the older historians, after the fashion of novelists; (3) insertion of applause in the written record of Congressional addresses that never were delivered; (4) genealogies and family trees; (5) interpolations or insertions for deceptive purposes by copyists or others; and (6) business documents, works of art, relics, and antiques.

**Use of auxiliary sciences.** The following brief summary statement [45] will illustrate the way in which certain auxiliary sciences are employed by the historian in the work of external criticism, where the problems of genuineness are frequently varied and intricate, although it is granted that the typical student of a historical problem in education, psychology, or sociology virtually presupposes (sometimes wrongly) the genuineness of the materials employed, especially the printed sources. Even a partial list of the important auxiliary fields is imposing: anthropology, archaeology, astronomy, cartography, chronology, diplomatics, economics, education, exact sciences, genealogy, geography, geology, heraldry, historical method and philosophies, languages, law, literature, military affairs, natural history, numismatics, paleontology, paleography, philosophy, philately, politics, and psychology.

Epigraphy is the study of inscriptions and the art of deciphering them. Diplomatics is the science of charters and diplomas and includes a knowledge of the practices of chanceries and of the forms used in them. Paleography is the study of writing, which has a history all its own. The handwriting of a given scriptorium is usually quite characteristic. Besides, handwriting varies from age to age so that it alone is often quite competent to locate a manuscript in time. Philology in all its branches is of the greatest use in determining date and authenticity. To give some very elementary examples, the word *choose* was in the eighteenth century frequently spelled "chuse"; *clothes* was spelled "cloathes"; *entire,* "intire"; and so on. The young poet Chatterton, it seems, first wrote out his verses in the English of his own day; but wishing to represent them as a "historical find," he then proceeded to give them an antique air by substituting ancient words for modern ones. Not knowing the older language at first hand he resorted to Kersey's dictionary for these older words. Kersey, however, had made numerous mistakes, and when Chatterton ignorantly copied these, he betrayed both the source of his archaic vocabulary and the fact of his forgery.[46] Archaeology, anthropology, and prehistory in general have had the greatest

[45] Quoted from H. G. Good, "Historical Research in Education," *op. cit.,* p. 13-14. Also see:
Gilbert J. Garraghan, *op. cit.,* p. 81-99.
Edward M. Hulme, *History and Its Neighbors.* New York: Oxford University Press, 1942. p. 131-91.
C. V. Langlois and C. Seignobos, *Introduction to the Study of History.* New York: Henry Holt and Co., 1898. p. 42-59.
Chauncey Sanders, *op. cit.,* p. 1-60.
J. M. Vincent, *Aids to Historical Research, op. cit.,* Chapters 3-11.
J. M. Vincent, "History and Auxiliary Sciences." *A Guide to Historical Literature.* New York: Macmillan Co., 1931. p. 1-45.
J. M. Vincent, *Historical Research, op. cit.,* Chapters 4-8.
Thomas Woody, *op. cit.,* p. 175-201.
[46] R. L. Marshall, *The Historical Criticism of Documents.* London: Society for Promoting Christian Knowledge, 1920. p. 26.

influence upon the study of history; and the first of these might almost be called the science of remains. Chemistry and the paper-maker's art may be able to say, and have often said, that a given document, written on woodpulp, for example, and with a particular ink, cannot be older than the definite date when these materials were first manufactured. Coins and medals are often of great historical value. Indeed, there is no field or item of human knowledge that may not be called upon to give evidence for or against the genuineness of some particular document or remain.

The additional illustrations that follow suggest the range of the major problems of external criticism; the student who wishes other examples or illustrations of critical processes not here represented should turn to the sources cited in the footnotes of this section, especially to the references given at the end of this division, in which literally scores of illustrations may be found.

**Forgeries and hoaxes.** Forgery was practiced even in the days of the Egyptian pharaohs. They often claimed for themselves the deeds of their ancestors by erasing the name of the hero from a wall and by chiseling in their own names, or by reproducing on another slab or monument the record of another's achievements with their own names inserted in place of the real hero.[47]

A letter of Charles VI of France, under date of March 15, 1403, was found to be spurious or a forgery for several reasons: a style different from that in Charles' letters known to be genuine, a script different from that in use in the king's chancery, a signature unlike genuine signatures of the king, the method of entering the date, and misplacement of the notary's signature.[48]

A pamphlet, "Shall We Have Common Sense? Some Recent Lectures Written and Delivered by Geo. W. Sleeper," purportedly printed at Boston in 1849, anticipates in a general way Darwin's theory of natural selection and the germ theory of disease. It is deemed a forgery or a hoax for several reasons: (1) no other copy has been found; (2) although supposedly registered in the District Court of Massachusetts, no entry was found in the records; (3) the single existing copy was said to have been found in a bookshop, in either Cincinnati or Cleveland, which cannot be located; and (4) according to experts, no such type face as that used in the title page was in existence before 1870.[49]

In the history of education, the forged autobiography of Walafrid Strabo (409 *ca.*-449 A.D.), first published in a German source in 1856-57, has

[47] James W. Thompson and Bernard J. Holm, *A History of Historical Writing.* New York: Macmillan Co., 1942. p. 6.

[48] Gilbert J. Garraghan, *op. cit.,* p. 184-85.

[49] Allen Johnson, *The Historian and Historical Evidence.* New York: Charles Scribner's Sons, 1926. p. 73-74.

been frequently copied as authentic, although in reality it is a creation of the nineteenth century.[50]

A certain long-standard cyclopedia of American biography includes at least forty-seven sketches of men who never existed. The unknown author was paid by space and to increase his remuneration created characters out of thin air, including a scientist who supposedly won fame by combating the Asiatic cholera in South America in 1783, fifty-two years before it first appeared there.[51]

Certain letters attributed to Lincoln contain errors of which he could hardly have been guilty. In a letter dated May 9, 1834, is the phrase, "that North East quarter of Section 40." Since Lincoln was an experienced surveyor, he must have been fully aware that a Congressional township contained only thirty-six sections, and could not have made such a blunder. The same letter states that a family named Bixby was "leaving this week for Kansas," whereas the territory of Kansas was not organized and opened for settlement until 1854; this geographical term in all probability was not even in use as early as 1834. Other conclusive tests examined the paper, ink, pedigree of the letters, handwriting, style, views expressed, and historical inconsistencies. Since the handwriting bore no resemblance to Lincoln's, the defenders of the letters claimed that he had used two different hands. One of the spurious letters attributed to Ann Rutledge speaks of a Spencerian copy book not used until 1848, whereas Ann died in 1835.[52]

*The Journal of a Spy in Paris during the Reign of Terror* purports to have been written, day by day, in 1794 by Raoul Hesdin, and was published in London in 1895. The authenticity of the document is questioned for the following good reasons.[53] No clear account was given of its century-long resting place, of the finding of it, or of its discoverer. The editor on whose authority the document was published refused to reveal his own identity, or to submit the original manuscript to scrutiny. Raoul Hesdin, reputedly a pseudonym, could not be identified with any of the known spies of the time, and his activities could not be reconciled with the expected activities of a paid spy. The content of the Journal was admittedly "neither very new nor very important," which is the safest type of material for forgery. The style of the unknown editor's letters of defense was similar to that of the journal, while the document itself was very unlike the lan-

[50] H. G. Good, "Historical Research in Education," *op. cit.,* p. 16.
[51] Allan Nevins, *op. cit.,* p. 131-32.
[52] H. C. Hockett, *op. cit.,* p. 66.
P. M. Angle, "The Minor Collection: A Criticism." *Atlantic Monthly* 143:516-25; April 1929.
Allan Nevins, *op. cit.,* p. 124-25, 136-37.
[53] H. G. Good, "Historical Research in Education," *op. cit.,* p. 14-16.

guage of the eighteenth century when it purportedly was written. Most conclusive of all in establishing the forgery, the document, claimed to be a day-by-day record, antedates by days and even months some of the events recorded, in one instance referring under date of May 27 to a trial that did not take place until July 15 to 20.

**Inventions and distortions.** The Greek historian Thucydides labored to invent elaborate speeches which he put into the mouths of his leading characters. However, these orations were not intended merely for rhetorical effect, but contained the politics and diplomacy which set forth his philosophy of history. In the area where Thucydides labored most, namely (without the speaker's text) to invent orations for statesmen, the modern historian would give up the task.[54] Although such inventions seem incongruous and unreal today, many historians until comparatively recent times have used the same literary device.

In the later days of controversial republican politics in Rome, most statesmen and men of action left narratives to justify their conduct at the bar of history. Those who could not write such statements employed others to do so. "The dictator Sulla (138-78 B.C.) after his retirement from public life wrote an autobiography, which seems to have resembled the semi-fabulous narrative of an Oriental rather than that of a sober Roman; for it points to a series of miraculous occurrences coincident with his public work to show that the hand of the Goddess Tyche was visible throughout." [55] Caesar's *Commentaries,* while written primarily to justify himself before the Roman people, represents a marked contrast to the sort of nonsense found in Sulla's autobiography and in similar writings. Caesar's work contains not a word of open eulogy of the author and presents the narrative as if from an impersonal observer. However, this external illusion of impartiality and sense of self-restraint increase the impression of reality and make what was left out speak for the writer.[56]

Parson Weems's highly rhetorical *Life of George Washington* contains numerous inventions in the form of long dialogues, set speeches, anecdotes, and the immortal tale of George, the hatchet, and the cherry tree. Weems's only authority for the story was an "aged lady" who as a "distant relative" had sometimes visited the Washingtons. According to Weems's grandson, the story of the cherry tree probably was suggested by the fact that one of Weems's own children had cut down a "Pride of China" tree and frankly confessed his misdeed. However, despite Weems's inaccuracy as a historian and carelessness as a biographer, his warm enthusiasm and simplicity of

---

[54] J. T. Shotwell, *op. cit.,* p. 210.
[55] *Ibid.,* p. 284-85.
[56] *Ibid.,* p. 285-86.

writing in bringing to life the person of Washington produced a biography that is supposed to have reached between forty and seventy editions, and made the legend of the cherry tree a part of the national folklore.

Although so eminent a pioneer historian as Jared Sparks should not be compared with Parson Weems, he was capable of "dressing up" the everyday language of Washington to fit the character of almost superhuman traits created by a worshipful public. In correcting Washington's spelling, Sparks apparently felt that it would be improper for the spelling lapses of a great man to go before the public. Sparks is also accused of omitting from his published work correspondence or expressions that did not agree with his purpose of exalting some individual character or geographical section of the country, and perhaps even of manufacturing a source or narrative when needed.[57]

For purposes of research and scholarship, the text should be reproduced exactly as in the original, with no attempt to correct spelling, revise grammar, or substitute words, although editors at one time felt free to tamper with texts. There may be certain instances when editing is permissible, as in preparing non-critical editions for the general reader or for school purposes, provided the sense of the original is not thereby impaired.

In certain instances community pride or patriotic spirit has led to counterfeiting of local traditions. There are so many earthen fortifications attributed to the De Soto expedition that it is said 1000 able bodied men could not have constructed them in a century.

Late appearance of a tradition, especially after the death of the person involved, may give rise to doubt.[58] Since no mention of the Ann Rutledge-Lincoln episode appeared until thirty-one years after her death, it seems to be mainly legendary. Some twenty years after the death of Luther, persons hostile to his memory circulated the legend that he had committed suicide. Captain John Smith's first and second versions of his adventures in Virginia vary considerably. In the later version the two hundred hostile Indians became three hundred, and Pocahontas was described dramatically as having saved his life, whereas she was barely mentioned in the earlier book.

**Authorship and time.** The problem of external criticism is much less commonly one of forgery or invention than of authorship, time, and filiation of documents, that is, with their dependence upon each other, with inter-

[57] Allan Nevins, *op. cit.*, p. 134, 162-63.
Gilbert J. Garraghan, *op. cit.*, p. 228.
Michael Kraus, *A History of American History*. New York: Farrar and Rinehart, 1937. p. 210-12.
[58] Allan Nevins, *op. cit.*, p. 139-40.
Gilbert J. Garraghan, *op. cit.*, p. 265
Michael Kraus, *op. cit.*, p. 27.

polation and borrowing. The question of authorship frequently is involved in the cases of men in public office (presidents, governors, university officers, and school superintendents), who may employ advisers or assistants in the preparation of papers or addresses. If the language proves not to be that of the reputed author, there still remains the more important question of whether his ideas are presented accurately in the phrasing of another. For example, Washington's "Farewell Address" raises the problem of determining what contribution each of three men made to it, since Madison drafted a portion of it, embodying the President's suggestions, and Hamilton later extended and completed the draft, incorporating additional suggestions made by Washington.[59] A portion of this address presents a point of view on education, sometimes quoted in textbooks on the history of education, which is really that of Hamilton and does not express what Washington intended to say about education.[60] "Promote then, as an object of primary importance, institutions for the general diffusion of knowledge. In proportion as the structure of a government gives force to public opinion it is essential that public opinion should be enlightened."

When a document is known to have been written by some one of a small group of identified persons, a comparison of the tricks of style found in the document with the writings of each member of the group should determine the authorship. Such a question of authorship is involved in discovering which numbers of *The Federalist* were written respectively by Madison, Hamilton, and Jay.[61] Madison and Hamilton left conflicting lists of the essays which they claimed.

It is believed that the historian Bancroft wrote the message which Andrew Johnson sent to Congress in December, 1865, although the discovery was not made until some forty years later. This unusual service is considered in part responsible for Bancroft's appointment to the ministerial post in Berlin which he held from 1867 to 1874.[62]

To determine the time of production of a document, internal evidence often is used to give an answer. From mutilated textbooks in such fields as history and geography, it is sometimes possible to learn from the maps and events cited the approximate date of publication, utilizing the historical knowledge of when different states were admitted and towns founded.[63]

Woody describes a manuscript found in the University of Pennsylvania archives, without author, date, or place indicated, bearing the title of "Observations for the Explication of the foregoing Accounts." "There is no

[59] H. C. Hockett, *op. cit.*, p. 63-64.
[60] H. G. Good, "Historical Research in Education," *op. cit.*, p. 16.
[61] H. C. Hockett, *op. cit.*, p. 63.
Allan Nevins, *The Gateway to History*, *op. cit.*, p. 155-56.
[62] Michael Kraus, *op. cit.*, p. 235.
[63] H. C. Hockett, *op. cit.*, p 64-65.

external indication of its source, whether by gift or purchase; it is in relatively good condition, but apparently old; there is no sign of later alteration,
or intentional mutilation. The fact of its being among other original manuscripts related to the University suggests, but does not prove, its relevance
thereto." [64] Woody goes on to list a series of tentative observations or
hypotheses as to identification of the document in terms of authorship,
place, time, and purpose.

**Borrowings.** An example from the history of education illustrates the
point that the inclusion of material in a document does not guarantee that
it was written by the immediate author, since borrowed materials are used
in many ways with various degrees of freedom.[65]

"A Contemporary Account of Horace Mann's Reply to the Boston Teachers"
has this sentence: "Though he dislikes the use of the rod for children, he evidently has no objection to whipping schoolmasters, and in this case, he has
certainly plied the birch with remarkable dexterity and strength of arm." [66]
When B. A. Hinsdale came to write his account of this incident in our history, [67] he incorporated this sentence in it, changing only the tenses of the
verbs and giving the citation to the *North American Review.* Then Professor
Cubberley, treating this controversy between Mann and the Boston masters
wrote in a textbook, without quotation marks or citation, as follows: "Though
he objected to severe punishment for children, he apparently had no objection
to giving a sound drubbing to a body of schoolmasters." [68]

A student received a doctoral degree based in part on a thesis that ended
with a program designed to provide for a certain type of exceptional child.
After publication of the dissertation, a psychologist in another institution
discovered that the plan had been lifted almost in its entirety from a new
book in the same field, without any acknowledgment of the borrowing.
The sponsoring university promptly withdrew the monograph from circulation, although apparently there was no available machinery for recalling
the degree itself.

For more than a century John Marshall's *Life of George Washington,*
published in 1804, was thought to possess great original value as the product of a great mind and to constitute a classic in its defense of Federalism.
However, the work has been pronounced a mosaic of borrowings, copied
almost literally, and then carelessly pieced together. In one volume instances of unacknowledged copying were found on 268 of the 488 pages.
It is true that Marshall wrote during a period when authors copied freely

[64] Thomas Woody, *op. cit.,* p. 175-201.

[65] Quoted from H. G. Good, "Historical Research in Education," *op. cit.,* p. 16-17.

[66] "Mr. Mann and the Teachers of the Boston Schools." *North American Review* 60:224-
46; 1845.

[67] B. A. Hinsdale, *Horace Mann and the Common School Revival in the United States.*
New York: Charles Scribner's Sons, 1898. p. 193.

[68] E. P. Cubberley, *Public Education in the United States.* Boston: Houghton Mifflin Co.,
1919. p. 279.

from a variety of sources without acknowledgment of the borrowings.[69] To cite an example from a much earlier period, Livy borrowed liberally from Polybius, not always giving him credit.

**Other examples of external criticism.**[70] Space has been available for only a limited number of illustrations of the processes of external criticism. The reader may turn to other references for a variety of examples of (1) determination of circumstances attending production of the document by (*a*) internal analysis, (*b*) comparison with other documents, and (*c*) detection of spurious documents; and (2) determination of the original form of the document by textual criticism, which involves (*a*) discovery of the origin of corruptions (the only safe course being the process of collation or comparison of the copy to be used with the original), (*b*) conjectural emendation where no variant readings are available, and (*c*) comparison of variant readings.

## Internal Criticism [71]

**Principles and problems of internal criticism (credibility).** After questions of authorship, time, place, and genuineness have been answered and the actual language or text of the original document has been determined as nearly as possible, it remains for internal criticism to determine the accuracy and value of the statements made. The shift of emphasis is from the *document* as such to *statements* within the document. Proof of the genuineness of a document by external criticism does not guarantee that it tells the truth. Although much of internal criticism is textual criticism, it also involves such factors as the competence, good faith, position, and bias of the author. Internal criticism is positive in nature when it seeks to discover the literal meaning and the real meaning of the text. It is negative when every possible reason is sought for disbelieving the statements made, questioning critically the good faith and accuracy of the author. Although

---

[69] Allan Nevins, *op. cit.*, p. 153-55.

W. A. Foran, "John Marshall as a Historian." *American Historical Review* 43:51-64; October 1937.

Michael Kraus, *op. cit.*, p. 155-59.

[70] William W. Brickman, *op. cit.*, Chapter 5. Includes many pertinent examples of external criticism from the field of educational history.

F. M. Fling, *op. cit.*, Chapters 3-5.

Louis R. Gottschalk, *op. cit.*, p. 118-38.

H. C. Hockett, *op. cit.*, p. 60-79.

Allen Johnson, *op. cit.*, Chapter 3.

C. V. Langlois and C. Seignobos, *op. cit.*, p. 71-100.

Allan Nevins, *The Gateway to History*, *op. cit.*, Chapters 5, 6.

Chauncey Sanders, *op. cit.*, p. 95-124, 142-206.

W. E. Spahr and R. J. Swenson, *op. cit.*, Chapter 4.

J. M. Vincent, *Historical Research*, *op. cit.*, Chapters 3-10, 20.

J. M. Vincent, *Aids to Historical Research*, *op. cit.*, Chapters 2-10.

[71] Gilbert J. Garraghan, *op. cit.*, p. 232-317.

both positive and negative criticism are essential in historical research, the student should not go so far as to be cynical and hypercritical.[72]

In preparing a history of the American Psychological Association, Fernberger gives an interesting illustration of the fact that even the minutes prepared by a recording secretary cannot always be trusted as evidence of what actually happened at a particular meeting.[73] The published facts of the founding of the American Psychological Association indicate that seven psychologists (Hall, Fullerton, James, Jastrow, Ladd, Cattell, and Baldwin) met at Clark University on July 8, 1892, to discuss the advisability of forming an association. Since Cattell and Jastrow were still living when Fernberger prepared his history of the A.P.A., they were asked to probe their memories concerning this important event in psychological history. Both replied, however, that they were not able to be present at the meeting of July 8, 1892.

In internal criticism of sources, certain basic principles are essential: [74]

1. Do not read into earlier documents the conceptions of later times.

2. Do not judge an author ignorant of certain events, necessarily, because he fails to mention them (the argument *ex silentio*), or that they did not occur, for the same reason.

3. Underestimating a source is no less an error than overestimating it in the same degree, and there is no more virtue in placing an event too late than in dating it too early by the same number of years or centuries.

4. A single true source may establish the existence of an idea, but other direct, competent, independent witnesses are required to prove the reality of events or objective facts.

5. Identical errors prove the dependence of sources on each other, or a common source.

6. If witnesses contradict each other on a certain point, one or the other may be true, but both may be in error.

7. Direct, competent, independent witnesses who report the same central fact and also many peripheral matters in a casual way may be accepted for the points of their agreement.

8. Official testimony, oral or written, must be compared with unofficial testimony whenever possible, for neither one nor the other is alone sufficient.

9. A document may provide competent and dependable evidence on certain points, yet carry no weight in respect to others it mentions.

Specific problems of internal criticism, some of which are answered in part by the processes of external criticism, are as follows: [75]

[72] For a similar statement, see Carter V. Good, A. S. Barr, and Douglas E. Scates, *op. cit.*, p. 261-62.

[73] Samuel W. Fernberger, "The American Psychological Association, 1892-1942." *Psychological Review* 50:33-60; January 1943.
Wayne Dennis and Edwin G. Boring, "The Founding of the APA." *American Psychologist* 7:95-97; March 1952.

[74] Thomas Woody, *op. cit.*, p. 175-201.

[75] F. S. Chapin, *Field Work and Social Research*. New York: Century Co., 1920. p. 37-38.
G. A. Lundberg, *Social Research*. New York: Longmans, Green and Co., 1929. p. 89-90. Also see the 1942 revised edition, p. 127-28.

1. What did the author mean by this particular statement? What is its real meaning as distinguished from its mere literal meaning?
2. Was the statement made in good faith?
   a. Had the author interest in deceiving the reader?
   b. Was the author under pressure to tell an untruth?
   c. Was he influenced by sympathy or antipathy to tell an untruth?
   d. Did vanity influence him?
   e. Was he influenced by public opinion?
   f. Is there evidence of literary or dramatic motives to distort the truth?
3. Was the statement accurate? or more particularly:
   a. Was the author a poor observer because of mental defect or abnormality?
   b. Was the author badly situated in time and place to observe?
   c. Was he negligent or indifferent?
   d. Was the fact of such a nature that it could not be directly observed?
   e. Was the author a mere witness or a trained observer?
4. When it appears that the author was not the original observer it is necessary to determine the truth and accuracy of his sources of information.

**Literal meaning and real meaning of statements.** The positive aspects of internal criticism involve the attempt to discover the literal meaning and the real meaning of the document. The literal meaning and the real meaning are usually the same in modern documents except in the case of figures of speech, although such is not true of many of the older sources. To determine even the literal meaning of writers such as Chaucer, Spenser, and Shakespeare is no small task, because of the presence of unfamiliar or obsolete terms and reference to strange institutions and customs. The student of history must know the language of the author and of the time and locality in which he wrote. Some of the source materials of history are written in a foreign language which must be translated. Cotton Mather once apologized in strange terminology for detailing certain events, large in the lives of the colonists but which might seem trivial to the outside world, in these words: "If a war between us and a handful of Indians do appear no more than a Batrachomyomachie [battle of frogs and mice] to the world abroad, yet unto us at home it hath been considerable enough to make a history." [76]

Even in modern documents the real meaning may not be clear owing to allegory, symbolism, irony, satire, jests, hoaxes, allusions, implications, metaphors, hyperboles, and other rhetorical figures and literary artifices. Some political speeches and platforms are notorious examples of documents containing ambiguities, intended as a rule to catch votes. A literal-minded student said of the Whigs in a certain campaign that they did not frame a platform until the night before the election, basing his conclusion on the textbook statement to the effect that the Whigs framed no platform

[76] Michael Kraus, *op. cit.,* p. 21.

until the eve of election.[77] George Bancroft [78] employed a rhetorical style of writing that requires considerable tempering in assigning an appropriate shade of meaning; for example, "History has ever celebrated the heroes who have won laurels in scenes of carnage. Has it no place for the founders of states; the wise legislators, who struck the rock in the wilderness, so that the waters of liberty gushed forth in copious and perennial fountains?" At another time he said in writing of the hanging of the regicide Hugh Peter for opposition to monarchy, "The blood of Massachusetts was destined to flow freely on the field of battle for the same cause; the streams were first opened beneath the gallows."

**Competence of the observer.** Internal criticism directed toward questioning either the competence and accuracy or the truthfulness and honesty of the witness is known as "negative criticism," because it cannot determine the truth of statements. As a matter of fact, every possible reason for disbelieving is sought and every statement is questioned as long as any reasonable basis for doubt can be found. Tests of an author's competence include his status as a trained eyewitness or observer, presence of emotional stress as affecting observation, extent to which the position for observing was favorable, extent to which memory is used after a lapse of time, and use of original sources.[79]

Following a bomb explosion on Wall Street, New York City, nine self-styled eyewitnesses were questioned. Eight of them said that there were a number of vehicles in the block, and three testified positively that a red motor truck carried the bomb. Only one, a retired army officer, testified that the explosion occurred upon a small horse-drawn truck and that the only other vehicle in sight was a motor car across the street; he alone was correct. His acquaintance with explosives, training in correct observation, and experience under conditions of stress qualified him as an expert witness, the only accurate observer in the group of nine.

An illustration of a curious fallacy in observation was recorded by the Greek historian Herodotus, who overlooked the fact that the temperature of a stream probably remains relatively constant and that the change in atmospheric temperature through the day causes the water to seem cooler or warmer as the day progresses.[80]

[77] H. C. Hockett, *op. cit.,* p. 81-82.
[78] Michael Kraus, *op. cit.,* p. 223-25.
[79] H. C. Hockett, *op. cit.,* p. 82-90.
W. E. Spahr and R. J. Swenson, *op. cit.,* p. 113-22.
Allen Johnson, *op. cit.,* p. 24-25.
A psychologist has aptly observed that "the towering genius of the great scientist often lapses into childish babbling as he turns to problems in which his personal desires give structure to his thought." Gardner Murphy, "The Freeing of Intelligence." *Psychological Bulletin* 42:1-19; January 1945.
[80] Quoted from W. I. B. Beveridge, *The Art of Scientific Investigation.* New York: W. W. Norton and Co., 1950. p. 95.

The water of this stream is lukewarm at early dawn. At the time when the market fills it is much cooler; by noon it has grown quite cold; at this time therefore they water their gardens. As the afternoon advances, the coldness goes off, till, about sunset the water is once more lukewarm.

A significant contrast between James Madison and Major William Jackson is found in the conditions for reporting the debates in the Federal Convention of 1787. Madison as an educated, intelligent, experienced, careful eyewitness worked under almost ideal conditions for observation, note-taking, and writing out his complete notes. Jackson apparently owed his appointment as official secretary of the Convention to influence rather than fitness. His minutes were little more than brief disorderly notes. He had burned all loose scraps of paper in his possession before delivering the records of proceedings to Washington; this probably meant that certain important documents were thus destroyed, which were neither copied into the minutes nor otherwise preserved by him.[81]

A good example of careful observation of the scenes of historical events is found in the work of Francis Parkman, born in 1823, who wrote the narrative of the Anglo-French conflict for control of North America. In his vacations from classroom studies he took long walks through the woods, tracing the battle lines that still scarred the then peaceful forest, and took trips to the West to gather information concerning the Indians. However, Parkman displayed bias in appraising the Indian in these words: "Ambition, revenge, envy, jealousy, are his ruling passions. He will not learn the arts of civilization, and he and his forest must perish together." Certainly the white man was far from blameless in his conduct toward the Indian with respect to rum, women, treachery, and cruelty. In spite of this bias, it is through the careful observation, keen insight, and romantic imagination of this half-blind historian that we see the "heroism and villainy that stained with blood the green carpeted wilderness he loved as much as life itself." [82]

Memory is untrustworthy, especially after a long lapse of time and with the approach of old age.[83] Therefore, an entry in a diary or similar source, if recorded by a responsible person, probably is more accurate than recollection. John Quincy Adams in 1844 based on his notable diary his assertion that Andrew Jackson, a quarter of a century earlier, had approved the relinquishment of the claim of the United States to Texas; Jackson's denial was based only on memory. It is true that Adams often wrote late at night when fatigued mentally and physically, with resulting inaccuracies

---

[81] H. C. Hockett, *op. cit.*, p. 84-85.
[82] Michael Kraus, *op. cit.*, p. 273, 277, 290.
[83] H. C. Hockett, *op. cit.*, p. 87-88.
Allen Johnson, *op. cit.*, p. 89.

in his portraits of contemporaries, and that his own prejudices and regard for the opinions of posterity colored his accounts of daily happenings. In 1925 an aged politician stated in an interview that he had been unable to follow the leadership of William Jennings Bryan during the campaign of 1896, but the contemporary accounts of the politician's speeches advocated Bryan's election.

**Tests of truthfulness and honesty.** The potentially competent witness may actually know the truth, but for some reason may reveal it only in part or in a distorted form. A number of tests of truthfulness are available.[84] What is the personal or vested interest of the author? To what race, nation, party, region, sect, social level, economic group, or profession does the observer belong, which might introduce elements of bias or prejudice? To what extent is the statement a conventional form where set formulas rather than true sentiments are expressed? Is there evidence of vanity or boasting? Is the author writing to please some particular individual, group, or even the general public? Are exaggerations and embellishments in the form of literary artifices and rhetorical flourishes employed to produce desired effects?

Livy, in his patriotic ardor, does less than justice to the enemies of Rome. Matthew Paris, a leading medieval chronicler, is influenced by anti-papal prejudice. Macaulay is notoriously unfair to the anti-Whigs. From his ultra-democratic viewpoint, Grote could see no good in the Greek "tyrants." A recent reissue of his *History of Greece,* admittedly a work of value, omits the chapter on the "Tyrants" as a distortion of the facts. Froude's *History of England* is saturated with anti-Catholic feeling. Gardiner's *History of the Commonwealth* has not escaped the imputation of bias in favor of the Cromwellians. Bancroft's exaggerated nationalism often results in one-sided presentation of the facts. Parkman's stirring narratives of the French-English conflict in North America are out of focus as a result of his preoccupation with Anglo-Saxon "superiority." Mommsen's *History of Rome* has its patent prejudices, in regard to Cicero. Motley's *Rise of the Dutch Republic* is unfair to the Spanish actors in the drama. Rhodes' *History of the United States* betrays animus against certain political figures, against Douglas, for instance, while the accuracy of the picture he draws of slavery has been called into question. Osgood's *American Colonies* has been charged with prejudice against the Quakers. Von Holst, in his *Constitutional and Political History of the United States,* is against the South.[85]

Thomas Carlyle (1795-1881) was basically a moralist, who was sometimes inclined to suppress evidence in favor of artistic effect, although his writing contains great passages. Francois Guizot (1787-1874) was a politician, journalist, and historian, but always a moralist. He did not critically examine the evidence in order to reach a conclusion, but chose his mate-

---

[84] H. C. Hockett, *op. cit.,* p. 90-96.
W. E. Spahr and R. J. Swenson, *op. cit.,* p. 96-112.
[85] Quoted from Gilbert J. Garraghan, *A Guide to Historical Method.* Edited by Jean Delanglez. New York: Fordham University Press, 1946. p. 50.

rials to fit a preconceived thesis. Sainte-Beuve said, "Guizot's history is far too logical to be true." A serious fault of Francis Bacon (1561-1626) was that he altered arbitrarily both literary and documentary sources as his imagination and philosophical theory dictated, although he did not intend deliberately to deceive, but to clarify and interpret by incorporating his own opinions.[86]

Thomas Macaulay (1800-59) revealed a tremendous pride in England as his particular bias, with his central theme that of English superiority, which appealed to national patriotism. He was sometimes witty at the expense of historical truth: "The Puritans hated bear-baiting; not because they thought it cruel to the bear, but because it amused the spectators."

Jules Michelet (1798-1874) frequently became lost in the emotional stream of his narrative and actually felt a deep sympathy with his subjects, sometimes even becoming affected physically, as when he became ill from the strain of writing about the Reign of Terror. Although Michelet was capable of deep insight, his emotional reactions caused him to feel deeply the passions of his subjects of the French Revolution, with the result that he wrote as an enthusiastic patriot or an emotional poet.

Napoleon did not encourage critical historiography, although he did not object to historians so long as they devoted themselves to glorifying him. His preference was for historians to spend their time in exposing the weaknesses of the ancient French monarchy and the church. His prejudice was anti-Bourbon and anti-clerical.

Voltaire (1694-1778) made two major contributions to historiography by surveying history as a whole and by conceiving history as a record of all phases of human activity, although there were serious defects in his work—lack of philosophical and sociological insight, lack of a connecting link in his narrative and leaving to chance what he could not explain on obvious grounds, treatment of history as a school for statesmen, and a variety of prejudices.

The Greek writer Herodotus, regarded as the father of history, could not rid himself of a strong native prejudice against the Ionians, even though he wrote in their language. They are virtually the only people to whom he is almost consistently unfair. In his words,

[They] have built their cities in a region where the air and climate are the most beautiful in the whole world; for no other region is equally blessed with Ionia, neither above it nor below it, nor east nor west of it. . . . [Yet] of all its [Greek] tribes the Ionic was by far the feeblest and least esteemed, not possessing a single State of any mark excepting Athens.

[86] For numerous illustrations see Thompson and Holm, *op. cit.*, Vol. 1, p. 612; Vol. 2, p. 66-68, 228, 238-41, 263, 297-98, 302.

In the narrative he has a Scythian say that the Ionians "are the basest and most dastardly of all mankind . . . but the faithfullest of slaves." [87]

The minister historians of colonial New England wished posterity to learn, through the record of dangers met and overcome, lessons of pride and courage. The writing of such a record of achievement gave an opportunity to thank divine providence for guidance in these actions and to render an account to later generations. William Bradford in his writing was certain that only the intercession of divine providence kept Plymouth Colony alive, although he was also grateful for the aid of the natives Squanto and Samoset. John Winthrop describes, as "a thing worthy of observation," what happened to a volume made up of the Greek Testament, the psalms, and the common prayer, the latter of which the Puritans heartily disliked. The book, having been stored in a room with corn, was found with the common prayer "eaten with mice, every leaf of it, and not any of the two other touched, nor any other of his books, though there were above a thousand." [88] Cotton Mather's reputation as a colonial historian has suffered severely because of the superstitions he shared with others in his day. He says, "Molestations from evil spirits have so abounded in this country, that I question whether any one town has been free from sad examples of them." He showed more skepticism of the tales of the "red devils" or Indians than of the devilish spirits in the white man's society. [89]

John Smith's vanity and boastfulness are assigned by critics as the reason for doubting the story of his rescue by Pocahontas, since it was not until after she had become a celebrity, and after her death, that Smith published his account. Evidence of bias in his recording of events at Jamestown is found in his sharp censure of opponents and glowing accounts of his own achievements. He described himself as always a match for the Indians, except where great odds overcame him. Yet his works contain much reliable information, and he is regarded as a man of real courage. [90]

Horace Walpole's *Memoirs of George the Third* were written supposedly between 1766 and 1772, but "transcribed" by the author in 1775, and enlarged by the addition of new matter in 1784. The point of view in 1784, after the American Revolution, is in marked contrast to certain of his opinions expressed before 1775. [91]

The bias in the writing of Parson Weems concerns the glorification of Washington's name and assigning to a great but quite human character the

[87] J. T. Shotwell, *op. cit.*, p. 177-78.
[88] Michael Kraus, *op. cit.*, p. 22, 34, 43.
[89] *Ibid.*, p. 62, 67.
[90] Michael Kraus, *op. cit.*, p. 22-29.
[91] Allen Johnson, *op. cit.*, p. 85-87.

traits of almost superhuman nobility. Weems also preached the lessons of industry, temperance, and frugality, using an extremely oratorical style of writing. As a moralist and uplifter, he crusaded in his books not only for temperance reform but against gambling.[92]

An instance of marked bias is found in John Quincy Adams' *Memoirs,* where he accuses Thomas Jefferson of loose morals, of being a free thinker, irreligious and probably atheistic, of displaying utter selfishness in trying to gratify an inordinate ambition, of duplicity, of treachery to superiors and friends, and of deliberate falsehood. In evaluating this staggering indictment, made by a statesman famous for both astuteness and probity, possible elements of bias and prejudice in the makeup of Adams must be examined. At sixty-three, Adams' memory was not always accurate. Jefferson had defeated Adams' father for the presidency, which indirectly terminated J. Q. Adams' comfortable post as Minister to Prussia. During Jefferson's administration Adams was a political independent, distrusted by and frequently at odds with both parties. Finally, his New England background, religion, and attitude toward cards, horse racing, and mere amusement were such as to cause him to brand the Virginian as irreligious and immoral.[93]

The case of Jefferson emphasizes a major problem in the writing and editing of biography, namely, to deal judiciously with sensational stories about the private life of the subject. Most of the lurid (and untrue) stories about the personal life of Thomas Jefferson came from the sharp pen of an unscrupulous journalist who had turned against his benefactor. In editing the *Dictionary of American Biography* it was a constant problem to know what to do with the "dirt." One point of view was that derelictions in matters of public concern were more important for historical purposes than private immorality. Trivial stories concerning Samuel Adams or Patrick Henry should not overshadow the debt their country owes them. The quite human foibles of George Washington must not be permitted to obscure his greatness of character.[94]

To accomplish its major purposes, biography should provide orientation in history for its subject, must tell the truth about what the man did, must provide value-judgments in taking the measure of the subject, and provide authentic information. The importance of certain personal elements varies with the particular subject. Family details may prove less important for a soldier or a sailor than for a literary man who works at home. Personal appearance was more significant in the careers of Daniel Webster and

[92] Michael Kraus, *op. cit.,* p. 160-62.
[93] Allan Nevins, *The Gateway to History, op. cit.,* p. 194-96.
[94] Dumas Malone, *op. cit.,* p. 119-48. Revised 1950. Also see:
Chauncey Sanders, *op. cit.,* p. 125-41.

William Jennings Bryan than for Samuel Johnson, or a mathematician, or a scientist. Physical condition usually is important; for example, the physical collapse of Woodrow Wilson or of Franklin D. Roosevelt in relation to international affairs.

The ancient writers of history frequently combined actual events with legend and myth in such a manner that the critical historian must engage in the sport of hunting myths, in company with the student of folklore. When a member of Alexander's staff was reading to him an account of how Alexander slew his opponent's elephant with a single blow of his spear, this hero worship was too much for the young conqueror's sense of historical accuracy, for he snatched the book and threw it into the water with the comment that the author of such untruth also should be ducked.[95]

When a witness gives contradictory versions of the same episode or event, the circumstances under which the several versions are given may aid in determining which story is correct.[96] It is said that Napoleon had three different ways of commenting on the execution of the Duc d'Enghien. Speaking in private with a confidant he regretted it; in a circle of friends he mildly apologized for it; before strangers, he boldly defended it. His true feelings probably are expressed in the first statement.

The purpose for which correspondence was prepared may determine its reliability or accuracy. Official letters exchanged between governments frequently are open to misrepresentation. Sometimes a government's foreign representative transmits two sets of reports, one to be given to the public, and the other of a confidential nature addressed to the responsible heads of government.

In some instances, bias is not apparent on the surface of things. Both President James K. Polk and John C. Calhoun were staunch Democrats, Southerners reared in neighboring states, and slaveholders. Yet, writing in his diary of 1847, Polk accused Calhoun of utter selfishness, base intriguing, and an entire lack of patriotism and party spirit. Search reveals the source of such animosity and bias. Two years earlier, when Polk was urging hostilities against Mexico, Calhoun spoke and voted against war to the last. One year earlier, when Polk was reluctant to settle the Oregon boundary on the 49th parallel Calhoun strongly urged that compromise. In 1847, when Polk wished to annex a large part of present-day Mexico, Calhoun vigorously opposed unlimited annexation, and wished to carry the line no farther south than it now stands.[97]

George Bancroft, born in 1800, reveals an exaggerated patriotism in his

[95] James W. Thompson and Bernard J. Holm, *op. cit.*, Vol. 1, p. 42.
[96] Gilbert J. Garraghan, *op. cit.*, p. 252-312.
[97] Allan Nevins, *The Gateway to History, op. cit.*, p. 196-97.

writing.[98] He told the people what they wished to hear about the past: the conquest of a vast territory, victories in behalf of religious and political freedom, dramatic clashes of personalities in debate or war, and the conflict of ideas (usually presented in a manner reflecting the ideological controversies of the historian's own generation). He glorifies his native country in these words: "The United States constitute an essential portion of a great political system, embracing all the civilized nations of the earth. At a period when the force of moral opinion is rapidly increasing, they have the precedence in the practice and defence of the equal rights of man." Thus, the young republic was characterized as the leader among nations. One of his sweeping patriotic phrases reads: "Tyranny and injustice peopled America with men nurtured in suffering and adversity. The history of our colonization is the history of the crimes of Europe." Bancroft characterized the American Revolution as a crusade of virtuous and disinterested patriots in behalf of the liberties of civilization, and described the Constitution as the product of a group of unique mental giants, never before equaled, and not to be matched in the future.

Marked bias is shown in the treatment accorded the Civil War period by certain historical writers of the Nationalist School—Von Holst, Schouler, Burgess, and James Ford Rhodes. Although trained in the use of documents and in the weighing of evidence, they went beyond the statement of facts, despite professions of impartiality, to sentence the offending South on two counts, as the assailant of a new deity in the form of the national state and as the defender of a decadent civilization immoral with respect to slaveholding.[99]

As is to be expected, nationalistic historical writing is frequently subject to grave prejudice.[100] At one time national history in Germany received expression in exaggerated narratives recounting the glories of the German empire or the later achievements of the Hohenzollerns. Droysen (1804-84) in his eulogistic *History of Prussian Policy* not only exhibited extraordinary prejudice in favor of the "mission" of the Hohenzollern dynasty, but limited his work almost entirely to the superficial field of Prussian foreign politics. Even the great historian Leopold von Ranke (1795-1886) showed a pietistic bias in favor of a providential theory of history and undue enthusiasm for Luther, the Hohenzollerns, and Prussia. Both German nationalism and French nationalism were greatly accentuated after the war of 1870, with the exhibition of marked bias in the historical writing of the time, and in the school textbooks as well—histories, geographies, and readers.

98 Michael Kraus, *op. cit.,* p. 199, 223, 225.
Harry E. Barnes, *op. cit.,* p. 231-32.
99 Michael Kraus, *op. cit.,* p. 336-37.
100 Harry E. Barnes, *op. cit.,* p. 209-10, 217-18, 220, 245-46, 277-80.

A popular dogma in England during the nineteenth century stressed the political superiority of the Anglo-Saxon peoples, a variant of the Aryan and Nordic myths. J. A. Cramb detected as a governing principle in England's past wars "that higher power of heroism which transcends reason." A similar condition of fervid nationalism prevailed during the 1914-18 war period and for some time thereafter in the leading countries involved, with many historians in Germany, France, England, and the United States lending their efforts to a propagandistic type of writing. The writing and textbooks in the totalitarian states during the period of World War II and after reveal the extreme bias that results from censorship by an all-powerful state.

**Other examples of internal criticism.** The foregoing illustrations should render concrete some of the major problems of internal criticism in determining the literal meaning and real meaning of statements, in evaluating the competence and accuracy of the observer, and in assessing the truthfulness and honesty of the witness. Numerous other examples [101] of the application of such tests are available, including tests for anonymous statements, for determinable facts, and for discredited statements. Two especially extended illustrations deal with a problem [102] in American history and with the question, What arithmetic textbooks were published within the present limits of the United States in the eighteenth century? [103] Both current literature and the materials of the past in education, psychology, sociology, and other social and scientific fields, as well as the area of news reporting, reveal many instances for application of the principles developed in the preceding discussions of external and internal criticism.

## THE WRITING OF HISTORY[104]

Historical composition is a synthetic and constructive process that involves the mechanical problem of documentation, the logical problem of

[101] F. M. Fling, *op. cit.*, Chapter 6.
H. G. Good, *op. cit.*, p. 39-47, 74-76.
Louis R. Gottschalk, *op. cit.*, p. 139-71.
H. C. Hockett, *op. cit.*, p. 79-111.
Allen Johnson, *op. cit.*, Chapter 4.
William W. Brickman, *op. cit.*, Chapter 5. Includes numerous apt illustrations of internal criticism from the history of education.
C. V. Langlois and C. Seignobos, *op. cit.*, p. 141-208.
Allan Nevins, *op. cit.*, Chapter 7.
Chauncey Sanders, *op. cit.*, p. 207-52.
W. E. Spahr and R. J. Swenson, *op. cit.*, Chapters 5-6.
J. M. Vincent, *Aids to Historical Research, op. cit.*, Chapter 12.
J. M. Vincent, *Historical Research, op. cit.*, Chapters 11-21.
[102] H. C. Hockett, *op. cit.*, p. 105-11.
[103] H. G. Good, "Historical Research in Education," *op. cit.*, p. 41-47, 74-76.
[104] Gilbert J. Garraghan, *op. cit.*, p. 321-49.
Charles A. Beard and Sidney Hook, "Problems of Terminology in Historical Writing."

determining the relative importance and arrangement of the various topics, and the philosophical problem of interpretation. The writing of history usually presents more perplexing difficulties than either the collection or criticism of data.

## Documentation

Procedures and problems in documentation are discussed in another chapter and need not be repeated here. In the same chapter and in the footnotes and bibliographies of this book are numerous examples of form for documentation. Other unusually detailed illustrations of form for foot-notes and bibliographies, drawn from the field of history, are available.[105]

## Selection and Organization of Materials

General problems of classification and analysis of data have been out-lined in another chapter. Likewise, general principles for effective or-ganization and presentation of materials have been suggested elsewhere. Therefore, it is necessary at this time only to discuss briefly certain prob-lems of organization, especially important in the field of history.

**Chronological versus thematic organization.** The older type of historical writing usually followed a strictly chronological arrangement (an almanac of dates, facts, and events) with a long series of so-called chapters, each covering a relatively short time span, sometimes only a few months. One history, intended for use in the public schools, contained 244 chapters and 495 pages of discussion, an average of about two pages per chapter.[106] The arrangement was primarily in terms of presidential administrations.

The possibilities for topical or thematic grouping of materials have been recognized in the literature. A functional organization of materials in the history of education has sought to meet the criticism that older educational histories and courses represented a mass of comparatively unrelated facts, with little consideration of the social forces operating and a minimum of application to the activities and problems of schools and workers, past and present. An illustration may be cited that includes helpful suggestions for both the organization and teaching of historical materials, and at the same time presents examples of both meaningful chronological units and sig-

---

*Theory and Practice in Historical Study:* A Report of the Committee on Historiography. Social Science Research Council Bulletin No. 54. New York: The Council, 1946. Chapter 4.

William W. Brickman, *op. cit.,* Chapter 5. Includes many excellent illustrations of interpre-tation and synthesis in writing the history of education.

Carter V. Good, "Some Problems of Historical Criticism and Historical Writing." *Journal of Negro Education* 11:135-49; April 1942.

[105] H. C. Hockett, *op. cit.,* p. 116-30.

Gilbert J. Garraghan, *op. cit.,* p. 381-95.

[106] S. G. Goodrich, *A Pictorial History of the United States.* Philadelphia: E. H. Butler and Co., 1843, 1854, 1859, 1865, 1881, 1886. 528 p.

nificant topical units. Table I represents the organization of a course in history of education that retains the merits of a sequential study of significant chronological periods and in addition uses historical data to explain major types of educational activity and organization.[107] During the first

**TABLE I** [108]
**Two Methods for Organizing Content in History of Education**

| By Units Which Are Largely Chronological Periods | By the Major Types of Educational Structure and Teaching Activities Which the Historical Material Helps to Explain | | | | | | | | | | | |
|---|---|---|---|---|---|---|---|---|---|---|---|---|
| | 1 | 2 | 3 | 4 | 5 | 6 | 7 | 8 | 9 | 10 | 11 | 12 |
| | The Organization of Schools | The Control and Support of Education | The Training of Teachers | The Teacher's Relation to the School Curriculum | The Techniques of Instruction | Pupils' Activities in Learning | Motivation and Pupil Discipline | Tests and Provisions for Individual Differences | Physical Education and Health | Care of the School Physical Plant | The Teacher's Responsibility for Extracurricular Activities | The Home and Community Activities of Teachers |
| A. The Background of the Rennaissance about 1100-1300 | | | | | | | | | | | | |
| B. Classicism about 1300-1500 | | | | | | | | | | | | |
| C. The Reformation about 1500-1750 | | | | | | | | | | | | |
| D. Inductive thinking and realism about 1550-1750 | | | | | | | | | | | | |
| E. Social changes and the development of educational theory and practice about 1750-1900 | | | | | | | | | | | | |
| F. Education as an expression of national consciousness about 1750-1900 | | | | | | | | | | | | |
| G. Education in America about 1620-1900 | | | | | | | | | | | | |
| H. Modern conceptions and tendencies in education 1900-1929 | | | | | | | | | | | | |

part of the course the students worked through the chronological periods (at the left of the table) to understand the sequence and story of educational development, and later reorganized the materials according to topical units (at the right of the table) in the form of school organization and teaching activities. History can be written by following either plan of organization. An appropriate combination of the chronological and topical plans seems desirable; [109] for example, in presenting a major chronological period the chief influences and forces operating, and the major forms of educational organization and instructional activity, may advantageously be outlined.

Unfortunately, for purposes of a functional understanding of educational history, the selection and organization of materials for the general and systematic course commonly offered in the history of education have been

[107] R. W. Tyler, "A Course in History of Education." *Educational Research Bulletin* 9:57-65, 133-35; February 5 and March 5, 1930.
Also see John S. Brubacher, *A History of the Problems of Education.* New York: McGraw-Hill Book Co., 1947. 688 p.
[108] R. W. Tyler, "A Course in History of Education." *Educational Research Bulletin* 9:57-65, 133-35; February 5 and March 5, 1930.
[109] Allan Nevins, *The Gateway to History, op. cit.,* p. 355.

such as to answer too frequently in the negative the following questions: Has the organization observed the conditions of good story telling? Does it show point, purpose, and meaning? Does the selection of materials exhibit a unified and goal-seeking experience? Does the student recognize the significance of the meanings of the story for his better understanding of current educational problems? [110]

Brubacher avoids certain of the shortcomings of the older histories of education by using as a functional basis of his organization, not the great epochs of the past, but the major problems or areas of contemporary education: for example, chapters on the aim, method, and curriculum of education; on elementary, secondary, and higher education; and on political, psychological, and philosophical bases of education.[111]

A major difficulty for many writers has been the failure to select, organize, and present materials in such fashion as to promote an understanding of a significant motif, such as (1) the concept of the school as a special agency of the culture or an understanding of the function of the school through an appreciation of how society operates for the education of the immature individuals of the group, (2) culture-historical development or the evolution of culture and civilization, and of education as the servant and expression of that culture, or (3) philosophical-ethical experience or the implications of the evolution of philosophic and ethical outlooks for the organization of the materials and methods of education. Quite naturally, difficulties arise when there is a division of purposes by attempting to deal with more than one major motif in the same body of content, even though the materials themselves may represent the incidents germane to two or more narratives. This point of view suggests that there is no single basis for selection and organization of materials, or resulting single course known as the history of education, but rather many narratives, each with its own purpose and principle of selection of material, organized to serve specific professional objectives. Such a conception of history implies a multitude of problems to be attacked and narratives to be written, for which there are available reasonably adequate sources of information on selection, organization, grouping, and synthesis of materials.[112]

Many historians of the twentieth century consider overemphasis on facts a major obstacle or hindrance to well written history (and likewise to good history); they are convinced that some facts must be discarded for

---

[110] E. H. Reisner, "The More Effective Use of Historical Background in the Study of Education," *op. cit.*, p. 187-95, 205-6.

[111] John S. Brubacher, *op. cit.*, xiii + 688 p.

[112] C. G. Crump, *op. cit.*, Chapter 5.

F. M. Fling, *op. cit.*, Chapter 7.

C. V. Langlois and C. Seignobos, *op. cit.*, p. 211-51.

J. M. Vincent, *Historical Research, op. cit.*, p. 294-99.

the sake of clarity and conciseness, with the needs of the present an important criterion in the selection or omission of facts. Some of these specialists
agree with Macaulay's view of facts in isolation as the dross of history and
insist that the meaning or significance of facts is what really matters in
writing good history which will rank as literature.[113]

### Trends in Historiography:
### Philosophies and Schools of Historical Interpretation

History is rewritten because of the errors and inadequacies of existing
history, discovery of new sources, significant reinterpretation of old data.
and changing viewpoints toward the past, as illustrated in the next paragraph. When society changes its point of view from time to time, possibly
every decade or two, any new social theory or evidence formerly overlooked in historical writing should receive adequate attention in the reinterpretation of history. As pointed out later in this chapter, it is essential to
give appropriate emphasis to all causal factors or forces in a synthetic or
eclectic treatment of historical events, rather than to follow a particular
philosophy or school of thought that may exclude some part of the evidence.

To cite examples of new sources and reinterpretation, Charles W. Wal-
lace, after examining hundreds of thousands of papers in the London Public
Record Office, in 1910 discovered six previously unknown documents of
Shakespeare. William Barton and Louis Warren found new Lincoln materials as the result of laboring through thousands of old papers in Kentucky
County archives. Newly discovered evidence has played an important part
in the rewriting of the history of the American Revolution and of the
American Civil War. During the latter part of the past century social and
economic conditions began to receive the attention of historians, compared
with an almost exclusive former emphasis on political and military exploits.
Certain historical judgments or viewpoints that have undergone revision
include the following: [114]

Before the age of Columbus the earth was believed to be flat.
The Middle Ages were a "night of a thousand years," "a wedge of barbarism"
thrust in between the world's two great civilizations, ancient and modern.
There was no science in the Middle Ages.
English History is mainly Anglo-Saxon in its origins.
Spanish and Portuguese maritime adventure and commerce at the close
of the fifteenth century turned toward the West, because the overland route to
the Orient was closed by the Turks.

[113] Herman Ausubel, *op. cit.*, p. 148-88.
[114] Gilbert J. Garraghan, *op. cit.*, p. 413-23.
Also see Charles A. Beard, "Grounds for a Reconsideration of Historiography." *Theory and Practice in Historical Study, op. cit.*, Chapter 1.

The American Revolution was "a spontaneous uprising of the whole colonial population without faction or disagreement among them."

The Reconstruction policy of the sixties was wise and "patriotic."

**General philosophies of history.**[115] A distinction should be made between a general philosophy of history and a school of specific interpretation of historical materials. The general philosophies listed below are not only broader in scope than specific schools of historical interpretation, but also do not lend themselves to pragmatic tests of their workability, at least not for many centuries to come. The principal philosophies of history characterized below, with the exception of the first two, have originated within the past three centuries.

1. The Greek and Roman historians viewed Fate as controlling human destiny.

2. The Christian philosophy of history was based on the dominant ideas of divine concern for mankind and of changes in history as slowly tending toward the progress and universality of the true religion.

3. According to Voltaire's rationalistic theory, the events of history were attributable not to design but to chance or fortuity.

4. Hegel's doctrine was that every epoch in history was inspired and dominated by some specific idea.

5. The Darwinian theory of evolution, as applied to history, means that in social institutions, as well as in the animal kingdom, the rule of the survival of the fittest applies and that acquired characteristics of society are passed on to succeeding generations.

6. The Marxian philosophy applied to history is that the mode of production in economic life primarily determines the general character of the social, political, and cultural processes of life, which shift as the economic foundation changes.

7. Since the World War of 1914-18 a rhythm-philosophy explains history as a series of pulsations, the swing and counter-swing of the pendulum, a series of cycles of summer-fall-winter-spring seasons, with the present period representing a very bleak season in civilization and world affairs.

General agreement on any one of these general philosophies is neither possible nor desirable because of the restrictions it would place on historical scholarship, even though few works in history are directly touched by one of these broad theories. This means that as a rule both the reader and the writer of history will be more concerned with the special interpretations of history that follow.

[115] Allan Nevins, *op. cit.*, p. 240-50.
Harry E. Barnes, *op. cit.*, p. 42-43, 147-206, 330-35.

**Specific schools of historical interpretation.**[116] The more limited scope of a specific interpretation of historical materials permits a pragmatic test of the explanation: for example, in terms of the school of economic determinism, the effect of economic factors on the framing of the Constitution of the United States; whereas one cannot test the cycle and evolutionary philosophies of history for many centuries in the future, if at all. It is true that many of the best historical works have not represented any special interpretation or school of thought, but have been written according to the individual bent of the author.

There are at least seven definite schools of historical interpretation, each of which has made an important contribution to our knowledge of historical development, although they are not mutually exclusive, but in a large measure supplementary. Most of these theories have passed through a relatively long period of evolution, with certain variations developing from time to time.

1. The personal, biographical, or "great-man" theory is the best known and has been emphasized most by the conventional historians. It holds that the great personalities of history are the main causative factors in historical development, and that history is collective biography.

2. The spiritual or idealistic interpretation of history is found in the discovery of spiritual forces coöperating with geographic and economic factors to produce truly personal conditions, and in human activities finding expression in social relations for the more complete subjection of physical nature to human welfare.[117]

3. The scientific and technological theory views human progress as directly correlated with the advances in natural science and technology, emphasizing that the prevailing state of scientific knowledge and its technical interpretation will determine the existing modes of economic life and activities.

4. The economic school of historical interpretation contends that the prevailing type of economic institutions and processes in society will, in a large measure, determine the nature of the resulting social institutions and culture.

5. The geographical theory holds that the actions of man cannot be fully understood or adequately described when divorced from their physical setting.

6. Sociological interpretation of history draws from sociology (the science of the life and activities of men in groups) a knowledge of both

[116] Harry E. Barnes, op. cit., p. 357-60.
Allan Nevins, op. cit., p. 265-71.
[117] Shailer Matthews, The Spiritual Interpretation of History. Cambridge: Harvard University Press, 1916.

the causes and results of group life as the basis for a generalized view of the social process and of social causation.

7. The relatively recent synthetic, eclectic, pluralistic, or "collective psychological" theory is considered the most inclusive and most important type of historical interpretation, holding that no single category of causes is sufficient to explain all phases and periods of historical development, and that only the collective psychology of any period is strong enough to dominate the attendant historical development. Therefore, the new history is necessarily eclectic in approach and interpretation in contrast to the older, conventional history which overstresses political causation or holds that historical development is entirely arbitrary.

A few examples will illustrate specifically how certain schools of history interpret historical development.[118] According to the theological or spiritual philosophy of history, Thomas Carlyle wrote of the French Revolution as a gigantic object-lesson in the penalty that quackery, greed, and evil bring upon themselves and as an illustration of the working of a higher power to make crooked ways straight. One economic interpretation of history calls the Reformation an economic rebellion of the German nation, and another places the whole movement of the Reformation on an economic basis. Charles A. Beard rewrote, in terms of economic forces, the history of American colonization, American expansion, the Revolutionary and Civil Wars, and party conflicts. The geographical theory of Ellsworth Huntington holds that the stimulating effect of certain climates, together with rich natural resources and other factors, explains the rise of great civilizations in such favored lands as the western part of the European continent, the British Isles, and eastern North America.

Prominent American historians over a period of sixty years who have seen fit to discuss the personal factor in history have considered the following problems: the influence of the individual in relation to the science of history, the need to save particular historical figures from the adulation of zealots and the hostility of iconoclasts, the desirability of rescuing undeservedly forgotten historical persons, and the need to judge individuals in the light of their own setting and sometimes by other standards. During the 1930's and 1940's the subject of the individual in history entered only slightly into the addresses of the presidents of the American Historical Association, although certain of these specialists had in mind specific historical figures to whom they attributed varying degrees of causal influence. This omission may seem strange during a period when dictators and democratic leaders loomed so large in domestic and international affairs, and

118 Allan Nevins, *op. cit.,* p. 38-44, 265-71.

when the destiny of nations seemed to hinge on the decisions of sometimes one, or two, or three persons.[119]

A description of schools of historical interpretation suggests that almost inevitably the historian is influenced by some preconceived point of view. This human tendency with its accompanying limitations was illustrated by a number of examples earlier in this chapter under the heading of internal criticism. Yet the force of conviction may add values by way of color, narrative power, and portraiture to the work of great historians. For example, Macaulay wrote his history of England as a Whig, an earnest member of a party in whose rapid rise he played a part as member of Parliament and Cabinet Minister. Gibbon held the mistaken conviction that the Byzantine Empire was weak and miserable, and that the degeneracy, cruelty, and factionalism associated with it made the study of events at Constantinople of minor importance. Parkman's strong convictions were racial and religious—that English civilization was superior to French, and the Protestant religion more favorable to free institutions than the Catholic. Bancroft wrote under the influence of a passionate American nationalism and an equally strong devotion to equalitarian democracy. Nevertheless, the goal of the historian is that of unprejudiced truth. Detailed supplementary information is available concerning trends in the development of historical interpretation, schools of history, and illustrative writings.[120]

**Training for interpreting and writing the new history.** If an eclectic point of view, in the best sense, is followed in historical interpretation, many fields of knowledge may contribute to such interpretation and to

[119] Herman Ausubel, *op. cit.,* p. 256-99.
[120] Herman Ausubel, *op. cit.,* 373 p.
Herman Ausubel, J. Bartlet Brebner, and Erling M. Hunt, *op. cit.,* 385 p.
Harry E. Barnes, *op. cit.,* p. 26-402.
J. S. Bassett, "The Present State of History-Writing." *The Writing of History.* By J. J. Jusserand and Others. New York: Charles Scribner's Sons, 1926. p. 98-109.
Louis R. Gottschalk, *op. cit.,* p. 193-250.
F. N. House, *op. cit.,* Chapters 7, 8.
Michael Kraus, *op. cit.,* p. 21-572.
C. V. Langlois and C. Seignobos, *op. cit.,* p. 296-315.
Allan Nevins, *op. cit.,* Chapters 1, 2, 9.
A. M. Schlesinger, *op. cit.,* Chapter 7.
Bernadotte E. Schmitt, *Some Historians of Modern Europe.* Chicago: University of Chicago Press, 1942. ix + 533 p.
J. T. Shotwell, *op. cit.,* p. 14-35, 107-377.
F. J. Teggart, *Theory of History.* New Haven, Conn.: Yale University Press, 1925. xx + 231 p.
J. M. Vincent, *Aids to Historical Research, op. cit.,* Chapter 1.
J. M. Vincent, *Historical Research, op. cit.,* Chapter 1.
Caroline F. Ware, *The Cultural Approach to History.* New York: Columbia University Press, 1940. ix + 359 p.
Morris Zucker, *The Philosophy of American History:* The Historical Field Theory. New York: Arnold-Howard Publishing Co., 1945. xxii + 694 p.
*The Marcus W. Jernegan Essays in American Historiography.* Edited by W. T. Hutchinson. Chicago: University of Chicago Press, 1937. x + 417 p.

the training of the historian, as emphasized earlier in this chapter in the discussion of the auxiliary sciences. A vigorous analysis of the information and training necessary to write the new history includes background in archeology, anthropology, geography, psychology, sociology, economics, political science, jurisprudence, and ethics, although it must be admitted that few persons are thus equipped to write history.

The historian must master the fundamental facts and principles of anthropo-geography, as interpreted by the most up-to-date exponents of regional geography, whose viewpoint is that of cultural anthropologists. The student of the new history must be thoroughly acquainted with man and his behavior, normal and abnormal. He must have mastered the rudiments of physiological chemistry and endocrinology. No person unfamiliar with the glandular basis of human behavior can hope to interpret intelligently the conduct of men, past or present. Human behavior cannot be understood when sharply separated from that of other animals, particularly that of our fellow simians. Hence the necessity for full acquaintance with comparative psychology. Other divisions of psychology equally important in understanding the mainsprings of men are: behavioristic psychology, with its stress upon social conditioning, for purposes of interpreting a personality in relation to early life and social surroundings; psychoanalytical psychology, for the light shed upon the unconscious motivation of conduct and the intimate facts of personal history and daily life; and social psychology, for clarification of the effect of crowd-psychological situations upon man and of the multifarious interactions between group and individual. Anthropology must be cultivated, not only for its emphasis upon the evolutionary basis of man and his institutions, and for its clarification of the new time- perspective of human development, but even more for the elucidation of the laws and processes of cultural advance. No one can engage competently in the new history who is not familiar with sociology—the basic and elemental social science, introductory to all others—as well as with the special social sciences of economics, political science, jurisprudence, ethics, and the like.[121]

Other discussions of the contribution to historical interpretation made by certain fields of knowledge emphasize many of the areas mentioned in the preceding paragraph and in addition point out the value of such fields as language, literature, art and architecture, logic, and philosophy in the training of the historian. It is taken for granted that the author of good history must read widely in the rich historical offerings available.[122]

A partial summary of trends in historical writing and interpretation may be drawn from the presidential addresses of the American Historical Association:[123] historical background should serve to explain the present and its problems; history at its best should be good literature; facts are

[121] Summarized from Harry E. Barnes, *op. cit.*, Chapter 15; also see Chapter 14.
[122] J. S. Bassett, *op. cit.*, p. 115-26.
F. M. Fling, *op. cit.*, p. 27-32.
Allan Nevins, *op. cit.*, Chapters 10, 11. For an artistic characterization of the wide scope of historical materials available see Chapter 14.
A. M. Schlesinger, *op. cit.*, Chapter 7.
J. M. Vincent, *Historical Research, op. cit.*, Chapters 22, 23.
[123] Herman Ausubel, *op. cit.*, p. 13.

impotent when used alone; study of the science and philosophy of history frequently has proved of little value, but can be fruitful; individuals should be viewed not as independent agents but as products of their setting; and the content of history should be as rich as the past itself. In these same presidential addresses certain points of view rarely have been defended: that the past should be studied for its own sake and only incidentally for the present; that content rather than form is of major importance in historical writing; that the chief purpose of the historian is to discover new facts; that the science and philosophy of history should be emphasized; that the "great-man" approach to history is valid; and that history should be limited for all practical purposes to such subjects as politics and constitutions.

## Special Problems of Historical Writing and Interpretation

Certain other problems of historical writing have not yet been treated directly in this chapter, although most of them have been discussed in their general setting of research methodology in other chapters. These problems include the setting up of major questions to be answered, use of inductive reasoning, formulation and testing of hypotheses, causation, historical perspective, development of a guiding thesis or principle of synthesis, and framing of generalizations or conclusions.

**Identification of the problem.** The selection, definition, and delimitation of the problem to be attacked have been analyzed in a broader setting in another chapter. Also, the earlier discussion of this chapter on the selection and organization of materials deals in part with the formulation of the problem. Only when a perplexing question has been identified and correctly stated does profitable study of history begin.

Certain types of problems defy solution.[124] Some are too vast and complex; for example, the causes of the fall of the Roman Empire. Others are insoluble because of the loss or suppression of historical evidence. Analysis of the psychological motives or attitudes of an individual or of a people presents almost insuperable difficulties. The answer to whether Burr's conspiracy was against the United States or against Spain rests upon what was in Burr's mind in 1805-06. What was dominant in the minds of millions of people in the Lower South that led them to secede in 1861? What motivating influences caused the framers of the Constitution of the United States to make no mention of education, when schools are of such vital importance in a democracy? Other difficult problems concern questions of time, identity, character, motive, origins of ideas, place, and specific cause. To cite another example, was the eight-grade elementary school in the

[124] Allan Nevins, *op. cit.*, p. 207-8.

United States the result of European influence, a native development, or a joint product of these two factors?

The difficulties enumerated in the preceding paragraphs, and the content of this chapter, concerned with the wide scope and almost limitless number of historical problems, present strong reasons for the writing of coöperative history. It is thought that Channing's survey of American history in its entirety will prove to be the last attempted by an individual working alone. The trend is toward series of comprehensive histories written by groups of persons treating separate periods,[125] although in coöperative writing the problem of synthesis is difficult. A comprehensive history of education on a world-wide basis is virtually impossible of accomplishment by one person; even a complete history of education in the United States is a staggering challenge to an individual. As is to be expected, the doctoral dissertations dealing with historical themes, whether in history proper, education, psychology, or sociology, are usually delimited to deal with a problem of reasonable scope.

**Inductive reasoning and use of hypotheses.** After assembling and classifying all the pertinent facts that bear on the problem (discussed earlier in this chapter), the next step is to analyze the evidence according to the inductive method, which is of course the method open to the historian. Illustrations of the inductive process, inductive-deductive relationships, and hypotheses have been given in other chapters dealing with the characteristics of scientific method, delimitation of the problem, experimentation, and in part with generalizations. Therefore, only a few additional examples need be given here. In history, as in other fields of research, penetrating inductive inferences from known facts that offer only a partial explanation have been substantiated by fuller investigation.[126] (It is pointed out elsewhere in this book that superimposing a general explanatory concept upon the facts or testing a working hypothesis represents a deductive process; in fact, the inductive and deductive processes occur almost simultaneously in consciousness.)[127]

Channing asks why the Confederacy collapsed in April, 1865, with an unexpected speed and completeness. He formulated and tested by means of the evidence a number of hypotheses. Did the breakdown result from

[125] Michael Kraus, *op. cit.*, p. 319, 573-94.
M. C. Elmer, *op. cit.*, p. 84-85.
H. W. Odum and Katharine Jocher, *op. cit.*,
[126] Allan Nevins, *op. cit.*, p. 214-31.
Allen Johnson, *op. cit.*, Chapter 7.
John H. Randall and George Haines, "Controlling Assumptions in the Practice of American Historians." *Theory and Practice in Historical Study, op. cit.*, Chapter 2.
[127] John Dewey, *How We Think*. Boston: D. C. Heath and Co., 1910. p. 68-78. Revised Edition, 1933, p. 107-18, 167-68, 196-97.
Allen Johnson, *op. cit.*, p. 167-70.

the military defeat of the Confederacy? Was the collapse caused by a dearth of military supplies? Was the defeat due to the starving condition of the Confederate soldiers and people in April, 1865? Was the collapse due to the distintegration of Southern morale and the despair of the people? Channing accepts and offers evidence to substantiate the last hypothesis, although this conclusion is not satisfactory, since it evades the question, Why did morale collapse? [128]

Thomas Carlyle's theory or hypothesis of historical interpretation was that great men have been the major causal factors in important events; he overlooked the effect of stirring times or crises in producing the man of the moment or the hero. The "great-man" interpretation of historical events was played down by Cato (234-149 B.C.), who did not mention the Roman generals by name or use other proper names. Cato took the position that Rome's battles were won by the common soldiers and that it was unjust to give the glory to the generals.

The hypotheses explaining the fall of the Roman Empire range from that of Gibbon on the refusal of the Roman soldiers to wear armor, to moral corruption, overtaxation, overpopulation, disintegration of the Roman army through staffing with barbarian officers (John B. Bury), soil exhaustion and "climatic pulsations" (Ellsworth Huntington).

Walter P. Webb maintains that the opening up and economic exploitation of the Plains Region of the United States was conditioned by a new "technique of settlement," based on certain mechanical inventions, such as barbed wire, the six-shooter, and the water mill.[129]

Some dangers in the use of the hypothesis in historical writing are: (1) operation of bias or prejudice to supply a ready hypothesis that is not tested rigorously, as illustrated in certain of the examples of this chapter concerned with schools of interpretation and with bias; (2) oversimplification, as in the case of Channing's explanation of the sudden collapse of the Confederacy, when a combination of causal factors probably operated; and (3) rejection of the obvious hypothesis in favor of some bizarre explanation, as in attributing the authorship of Shakespeare's plays to Bacon or to some other person.[130]

**Causation.** Cause-and-effect relationships are included also in treating other research methods. The preceding discussion of hypotheses indicates that usually multiple causation is the explanation of any important historical event. The same conclusion was reached earlier in this chapter in the description of schools of historical interpretation, with emphasis on

[128] Allan Nevins, *op. cit.*, p. 217-20.
[129] Gilbert J. Garraghan, *op. cit.*, p. 157-60.
[130] Allan Nevins, *op. cit.*, p. 220-25.

the merits of the synthetic or eclectic point of view in determining cause-and-effect relationships.[131] Channing's explanation of the swift collapse of the Confederacy would have been stronger and sounder had he assigned to each causal factor its proportionate weight. When the historian decides that the British convoy system was easily the most important factor in defeating the German submarine in 1917, he can then give whatever credit is due to the depth charge and other antisubmarine devices, and to American aid in warships and merchant tonnage.[132]

Although monistic theories of historical change have been sharply criticized, one should avoid the skeptical view that, because no historical account can be complete, scientific history is impossible.[133] To cite an illustration, an economic explanation of history may leave a gap that psychology has to fill: [134]

An explosive part is played in historical events by unconscious defense mechanisms against bisexuality, father or mother fixation, sadism, masochism, exhibitionism, and other instincts. The content of radicalism may suddenly swing to the opposite extreme: leftists might change to radical conservatives and vice versa, because of a blind inner urge. Revolutions, the origin of religions, cannot be explained by economic (materialistic) reasoning alone. Not only the "how" of historical developments is created by exceptional men but also the "what".

Physical environment, including topography, climate, and potential wealth, has influenced history: the relation of the mountain ranges and valleys of ancient Greece to failure in achieving political unity, England as an island in relation to centuries of uninterrupted development, Belgium's low-lying terrain as a highway of armies in Europe, and location of most of the large cities of the United States on the sea or on other bodies of water.[135]

So-called negative facts may aid in the identification or interpretation of causes. Since Alexander the Great had no son capable of succeeding him, subsequent events were correspondingly affected. Lincoln's death on the eve of Reconstruction undoubtedly influenced that movement in the direction of a radical turn.

Early history frequently associated trivial causes or supernatural ex-

[131] For a critical analysis of the concept of causation see F. J. Teggart, op. cit., Chapter 4. Gilbert J. Garraghan, op. cit., p. 350-62.
Howard K. Beale, "What Historians Have Said About the Causes of the Civil War." Theory and Practice in Historical Study, op. cit., Chapter 3.
Louis R. Gottschalk, op. cit., p. 209-50.
[132] Allan Nevins, op. cit., p. 225-31.
[133] Morris R. Cohen, The Meaning of Human History. LaSalle, Ill.: Open Court Publishing Co., 1947. ix + 304 p.
[134] Fritz Wittels, "Economic and Psychological Historiography." American Journal of Sociology 51:527-32; May 1946.
[135] Gilbert J. Garraghan, op. cit., p. 354-55.

planations with important events and great social changes.[136] For example, it was maintained that the cackling of geese saved Rome; that Cleopatra at the height of her career ended her life by the bite of an asp, leaving Rome free to develop unhindered its colossal power; and that consequently the world was profoundly influenced by the cackling of fowls and the bite of a reptile. The cause assigned to the Trojan war was a quarrel over a beautiful woman, Helen of Troy. A dream of Darius, king of Persia, was made responsible for the rebuilding of Jerusalem.

It is related that, when the Norsemen had settled somewhere near the New England coast in 1003-04, as they traded with the natives a Norse bull ran out of the woods, bellowing loudly. This terrified the natives, who hastened away in their canoes, and later returned to battle the Norse. The newcomers, therefore, decided to return to their own country, so it has been amusingly suggested that the bellowing of a Norse bull delayed the settlement of America for five hundred years.

Use of the supernatural element in the form of the oracles, especially those of Delphi, helped Herodotus to ignore his chief defect, an absence of the sense of historical causation. Livy included the supernatural element, particularly in dealing with crises, when by miracle or portent the gods revealed themselves, with numerous omens and prodigies.

**Historical perspective.**[137] A special difficulty in using historical evidence and in interpretation is that of evaluating events and personages, distant in time or space, in terms of the contemporaneous standards and conditions then prevailing rather than in terms of our own time and culture. The cruelties of the Inquisition, when measured against the practices of the Middle Ages, are believed milder than those of the contemporaneous civil law, unjustified as such excesses seem in the light of twentieth-century standards. It is not possible accurately to write the history of Tibet by applying the psychology of the Western world, to evaluate Japanese music according to the conventions of European music, to judge Egyptian pictorial art in terms of classical modern art, to appreciate from the vantage point of a sleeper-plane the difficulties of Daniel Boone and others in blazing the Wilderness Trail, or from the deck of a modern liner to understand the fears of the sailors of Columbus. The so-called brutal policy of England toward Ireland in the time of William Pitt must be evaluated according to the conditions of 1798 when Britain with only twelve million people lay between a hostile France of twenty million population and a

---

[136] J. M. Vincent, *Historical Research, op. cit.,* p. 263-64.
Michael Kraus, *op. cit.,* p. 8-9.
J. T. Shotwell, *op. cit.,* p. 191-92, 295-96.
[137] Allan Nevins, *op. cit.,* p. 231-36.
Thompson and Holm, *op. cit.,* Vol. 1, p. 497.
Gilbert J. Garraghan, *op. cit.,* p. 362-67.

half-hostile Ireland of six million. Yet, in evaluating the events and figures of distant times and other lands in terms of their contemporaneous setting, a few fundamental moral standards should be held absolute and applied equally to all modern ages, especially to murder, robbery, and cruelty which are always crimes against humanity.

**Thesis or principle of synthesis.**[138] Although many histories are untouched by any special interpretation or school of historical writing, few histories of distinction lack a thesis or principle of synthesis. A central theme or principle of synthesis may prove helpful in the gathering of evidence and in interpretation, although it is unwise to force the data into a particular frame of reference. There is a considerable amount of historical research that brings events to light without weaving them into a highly synthesized narrative or interpreting them according to some basic theory or philosophy.

Treitschke's thesis, insistence upon the importance of national unity and a powerful central government, changed the attitude of millions of Germans toward their national unity. Henry Osborn Taylor took the unusual view that the true key to the medieval mind was in the Latin rather than in the vernacular writings of the period.

Macaulay, in his essay on Machiavelli (1469-1527), developed the thesis that the characteristics which have rendered the Italian thinker hateful belonged to the age rather than to the man. Macaulay rejected the hypotheses (1) that Machiavelli's private character was hypocritical and grasping, and so warped his judgment of right and wrong; (2) that his public conduct lacked integrity, and he therefore laid down the immoral doctrines in his writings to excuse his own official behavior. Macaulay found the true explanation of Machiavelli's unethical doctrines in the state of moral feeling and the desperate disorders of Italy at the time, necessitating a desperate remedy by way of consolidating the small Italian states under a powerful central ruler upheld by a national army. This means that Machiavelli has been unjustly criticized for stating with great clarity the seemingly indecent principles upon which men acted in his day and have followed since that time; *The Prince* was written to give an accurate picture of government, politics, and diplomacy in the Italy of 1500 rather than as a manual for princes.

Frederick J. Turner's thesis on the effect of the frontier upon American life and character has colored not only all historical thought in this country, but also literary, social, and political thought, even though valuable correctives have since been applied to this thesis.

---

138 Allan Nevins, *op. cit.*, p. 271-75, 352-53.
Michael Kraus, *op. cit.*, p. 453-54, 461-66, 510-13.

Bancroft and Parkman supported the thesis of a conflict between liberty-loving people and traditionalists. Charles A. Beard has advanced a thesis of economic determinism, showing in his interpretation of the United States Constitution a direct relationship between the holders of the government debt and their desire for a strong government which would pay it off, although he has since emphasized the interplay of the heritage, politics, culture, economics, and international filiations of any civilization as being important in historical interpretation and causation.

As a rule, a number of more detailed generalizations or conclusions, in keeping with the guiding thesis or principle of synthesis, are developed in each major section of the historical work.

**Literary aspects of historical writing.**[139] The major principles for effective presentation of data and for scientific writing have been summarized in another chapter. Earlier sections of the present chapter deal with problems of documentation and with selection and organization of historical materials. Therefore, only a brief summary statement of certain problems of style especially important in historical writing seems necessary at this time.

There is more than one way of writing effective history and, as may be expected, historians have no more agreed among themselves on the literary aspects of historical writing than on theories of interpretation. As a matter of fact, they sometimes have been contemptuously critical even of the work of great historians.[140] Carlyle said of Macaulay's *History of England from the Accession of James II* that it contained "a very great quantity of rhetorical wind and other ingredients, which are the reverse of sense," while Prescott labeled Carlyle's *French Revolution* "perfectly contemptible" and Hallam said of the same book, "I have tried to read it but I can't get on, the style is so abominable." In turn, Carlyle characterized Hallam's *Literature of Europe in the 15th, 16th, and 17th Centuries* as a mere "valley of dry bones." Yet, there are certain common elements in the writing of the masters of history.

1. *Mastery of Materials.* Effective modern historical writing shows evidence of scholarship, research, and mastery of materials, presented without ostentation. (The processes of critical scholarship in historical research have been discussed earlier in this chapter, especially under the topics of collection of data and criticism of data.) Thackeray said of Macaulay that he read twenty books to write a sentence, and traveled a hundred miles to make a line of description. The method of composition

---

[139] A treatment especially helpful in terms of principles and examples in the preparation of this section was Allan Nevins, *op. cit.,* Chapter 13.
   Gilbert J. Garraghan, *op. cit.,* p. 396-407.
[140] Allan Nevins, *op. cit.,* p. 23-25.

of such great historians as Macaulay, Parkman, and Prescott was to digest the materials thoroughly, and to fill their minds with the subject before beginning to write. This procedure was especially necessary for Parkman and Prescott, who for long periods were almost blind, and had to have materials repeatedly read aloud by assistants. Such an enforced slow rate of composition was compensated for by formulation of a well considered plan and thoroughly digested materials. At the time Parkman began *The Conspiracy of Pontiac* his eyesight was so affected that he used a frame with parallel wires to guide his black crayon, and for the first half year his rate of composition averaged only some six lines a day.[141]

Mastery of sources has always been a challenge and frequently a burden to the ablest historians of any period.[142] Pliny the Elder was a man of insatiable curiosity and an omnivorous reader who read when traveling, eating, and when in the bath. He constantly dictated to his slave secretaries, who always accompanied him. Richard Hakluyt found his labor of love, *The Principall Navigations, Voyages, Traffiques, and Discoveries of the English Nation,* printed in 1589, a great burden. For this great work he learned several languages, corresponded with eminent geographers, and traveled widely to interview returned ship captains. Frantisek Palacky (1798-1876) left in print and manuscript enough material to fill fifty ordinary volumes. When Palacky visited Rome and the Vatican in 1837 he is said to have read through 45,000 documents in ten weeks and copied 400 of them with his own hand. George Grote (1794-1871) began to collect materials for his history of Greece twenty-three years before publication of the first volume, with this colossal work of twelve volumes completed in 1856. Leopold Ranke (1795-1886) had an enormous respect for facts and accuracy, and found genuine history more attractive and interesting than romantic fiction, which probably explains how he could continue a vast output of study and writing until the age of ninety-one. In his last year he began to plan a new project, a philosophy of history, but died before he got to it.

Even well known historians have sometimes been careless in borrowing from sources or inaccurate in using sources.[143] Charles Firth raised a question as to how far Macaulay relied upon his own research in domestic and foreign archives, as compared with his indebtedness to the fifty volumes of notes and transcripts compiled by James Mackintosh and made available to Macaulay by the Mackintosh family.

James Froude (1818-94) was amazingly inaccurate and careless in

---

[141] Michael Kraus, *op. cit.,* p. 275.
[142] Thompson and Holm, *op. cit.,* Vol. 1, p. 83, 613; Vol. 2, p. 170, 492-93, 633.
[143] Thompson and Holm, *op. cit.,* Vol. 1, p. 76-77, 539-40; Vol. 2, p. 71, 253, 299, 306-7.

copying from his sources and in proofreading, although it should be remembered that he did the bulk of his work from almost illegible manuscript sources, written in five different languages. He wrote with prejudice, as a literary artist rather than a scientific historian.

The errors and faults of Baronius were not those of dishonesty, but lack of knowledge. One Benedictine scholar reported two thousand errors in Baronius, and a German scholar, Lucas Holstein, found eight thousand mistakes. Gibbon's judgment was that Baronius had "sunk to the lowest degree of credulity which was compatible with learning."

Alphonse Lamartine (1790-1869) was not consciously untruthful, but de Tocqueville said that he had never known a mind with "more contempt for the truth." Dumas paid Lamartine a dubious compliment when he said, "You have raised history to the level of the novel." Lamartine never gave proof for his statements, and one critic filled 113 pages with factual errors in Lamartine's history.

Livy (59 B.C.-17 A.D.) worked with such a large mass of data that he was sometimes overwhelmed and not able to synthesize or organize his material effectively, resulting in contradictions and chronological errors. Hume (1711-76) neglected historical sources and was averse to hard work; this laziness brought harsh criticism to him for failure to check the facts. His two chief prejudices were the Whigs and religion.

Failure to digest materials may be due to (1) a false vanity that seeks to impress by including such crude working materials as discarded data, rejected hypotheses, and long quotations and citations; (2) a timidity that causes the inclusion of unnecessary data and raw material as a protection against attack; and (3) lack of literary discernment, which causes some writers to think that a patchwork of quotations and citations or crude summaries of original material are almost as good history as a fused and digested narrative.[144] Guiding principles for use of quotations and citations are presented in another chapter.

2. *Working Outline.* Before note-taking has gone far, a preliminary outline is necessary to guide the selection and arrangement of notes; then, as the accumulated material is digested, the outline can be revised as radically as necessary. Even Macaulay, with his retentive memory and lucid mind, carefully outlined his best works in advance, and in one instance discarded a subject after finding it unmanageable on the basis of a preliminary sketch.

A difficulty in planning, previously discussed in this chapter, is that of reconciling the chronological order with the topical method of treatment. As pointed out, a combination of the two frequently proves desirable. For

[144] Allan Nevins, *op. cit.,* p. 347-49

example, in treating a temporal period of development in the history of a university, such as expansion during the 1920's, a sense of progression can be promoted by taking up in turn each major topic—enrollment trends, curriculum, school plant, finance, student life, and faculty personnel. It has already been suggested that any mechanical arrangement of materials or outline, according to the reigns of kings and emperors or the administrations of presidents, is unsatisfactory for purposes of functional organization and interpretation of history.

Although symmetry or balance in the plan or outline is a desirable goal, historical materials do not always arrange themselves in such smooth patterns. It is generally known among educational historians that in writing school history much more information is available concerning legislation, school board regulations, enrollments, buildings, programs of studies, and budgets than concerning the philosophical, psychological, sociological, economic, and cultural forces affecting the schools of the state, city, or county during a given period.

3. *Progression.* Good history has progression; that is, it moves forward, although it does not always show in mechanical fashion the original condition, the action, and the results. This movement of progression should employ a thesis or principle of synthesis as a theory of causation to explain cause-effect relationships. It will be recalled that the problems of synthesis and causation have been analyzed earlier in this chapter.

4. *Emphasis on Major Elements.* The major elements in any piece of effective writing, historical or otherwise, stand out in bold relief like the large cities, rivers, bodies of water, and mountain ranges on a map. A good working outline, a guiding thesis, and more detailed generalizations for the major sections of the work are essential to the accomplishment of this purpose and to the subordination of details. This frequently means that painstakingly gathered data must be discarded to promote condensation and precision, and to prevent too many details from crowding off the scene the main actors and events of the narrative.[145]

Herodotus, in writing the history of Greece, often departed on many side excursions, with careless art passing from story to story and land to land—Persia, Egypt, Babylon. He permitted his characters to talk in garrulous fashion, while he frequently seemed to stand by and chuckle. Antipater, the distinguished Roman jurist and teacher of oratory, introduced both speeches and anecdotes, and broke the narrative with all kinds of diversions so that the reader should not suffer ennui; instead of giving the figures of Scipio's expedition to Africa, he relates that birds fell from

[145] J. T. Shotwell, *op. cit.,* p. 179-84, 279-80.
Michael Kraus, *op. cit.,* p. 102-3.
James W. Thompson and Bernard J. Holm, *op. cit.,* Vol. 1, p. 53, 120, 615, 623.

heaven at the noise of the shouting soldiers. Love of digression from the narrative, on the part of Polybius, has made it possible to piece together the allusions to his own life and in this way to form a sketch of his life. Dio Cassius digressed in his writing to discuss the cause of solar eclipses.

John Foxe (1516-87) digressed in the *Book of Martyrs* to include popular sermons and his own reflections on what he recounted. John Knox (1505-72) is more reliable than Foxe, in spite of his evident bias and belief in miracles and omens. Knox avoided the popular appeal and digressions or artifices of style.

William Douglass, who settled in Boston in 1718 to practice medicine, also wrote history. In his closing chapter on Virginia, for some unknown reason, he injected a discussion of smallpox, and in writing of other colonies he sometimes included digressions on medicine.

5. *Art of Narration and Science of History.* While the purpose of history is not primarily to entertain or to please, there is no reason why good history should not possess literary excellence. It was pointed out early in this chapter that both the science of research and the literary art of narration are essential for effective historical work. The concept of history as an art, however, should not be pushed to the point of filling in missing details through sheer play of the imagination, merely for the sake of completeness and symmetry, as does the painter or poet; therefore, certain gaps or missing links may be a characteristic of authentic history.

6. *Dramatization, Rhetoric, and Style.* The preceding paragraphs dealing with literary aspects of historical composition, at least by implication, suggest that the narrative can be written simply and clearly, without excessive dramatization, exaggerated rhetorical flourishes, or undue appeal to the emotions. In other words, historical writing should possess the characteristics of a good story. Dramatization and rhetoric are frequently overdone when narrating the splendor of kings and the noise of battle in political and military history.

The emphasis of the presidents of the American Historical Association on the practical uses of history would suggest a corresponding interest in literary style as a vehicle to command the attention of the layman and general reader. However, over a period of sixty years few of these specialists discussed history as literature; as a general rule, they took it for granted that history should be well written or considered this subject only incidentally. In a few instances they discussed literary style in relation to the practical value of history and to securing readers, or gloried in history as literature for esthetic reasons, or took the position that the historian had more important things than style to worry about (and even viewed style as essentially irrelevant to sound historical scholarship). If some competent historians fall short of a good literary style, it should be remembered that some novelists, journalists, and literary critics also fail to reach this goal.[146]

Interesting contrasts are found in the style of individual Greek and Roman historians.[147] Herodotus possessed great skill as a storyteller, with simplicity, naturalness, and charm, as well as an easy and graceful style. In spite of the narrative and anecdotal qualities of his writing, his history possessed unity, power of synthesis, and critical judgment in advance of other writers of his time.

Thucydides mastered a terse, flexible style that enabled him to express his thought with effective brevity, with his phrases said to crack like a rifle shot. A phrase that combines high thought with grandeur of expression is probably the most quoted sentence from Thucydides: "The whole earth is the sepulchre of famous men."

Caesar wrote with such a quality of self-restraint, without open eulogy of the author, and in such simple, lucid phrases that over a long period of time his works have even stood the test of use in school at the secondary level. One should not be deceived, however, by Caesar's simplicity and clarity of style, or by his apparent truthfulness, since his *Commentaries on the Gallic War* are not merely military narratives, but a form of political propaganda intended to influence public opinion, to defend himself against his accusers, and to represent the conquest of Gaul as a war of necessity and patriotism (as commented on briefly earlier in this chapter).

Livy believed that history was a form of rhetorical exposition, which explains his rather flowery style. His gift for vivid and picturesque narration is summed up effectively in Byron's phrase, "Livy's pictured page."

Tacitus employed the orator's method of exposition. He recited events and interpreted movements by the device of direct discourse, putting his own words into the mouths of the interlocutors in the drama. This tedious literary device of the ancient historical writers was first introduced by Thucydides. Tacitus was a great writer and moralist whose dramatic technique and selection of material revealed his anti-Caesarian prejudice. His forcible and terse style is the antithesis of Cicero's balanced and flowing form of expression. Examples of the condensed and weighty thought of Tacitus are as follows:

"No hatred is so bitter as that of near relations."
"The more corrupt the state, the more numerous the laws."
"Everything which we now hold to be of the highest antiquity was once new."

Dio emphasized the literary and rhetorical aspects of historical writing common to antiquity, and sketched the characters of emperors and others

---

[146] Herman Ausubel, *op. cit.*, p. 120-47.
[147] Thompson and Holm, *op. cit.*, Vol. 1, p. 25-26, 32-33, 70-71, 76-77, 86-88, 118.

with a view to effect rather than exact truth. Dio collected a large number of anecdotes relating to well known characters, probably invented in part; for example, the famous statement attributed to Augustus: "I found Rome of clay; I leave it to you of marble."

There is usually a relationship between the period in which the historian lived and the literary style employed. Prescott, Motley, and Bancroft were American patriots, as well as literary artists, which quite naturally influenced their style; Bancroft was even given to bursts of oratory in his first editions. Bancroft's narratives dramatized the triumphs of democracy, the conquest of a vast territory, victories in behalf of religious and political freedom, and the clash of personalities in debate or war, which deeply touched an increasingly prideful people. Some of his rhetorical excursions and literary flourishes have been cited earlier in this chapter in discussing the process of criticism; yet on occasion he could write simply and impressively, as when speaking of the failure of Raleigh to plant a colony: "If America had no English town, it soon had English graves." [148] On the other hand, Bancroft's rhetoric is high flown and redundant in describing the effect of the battles of Lexington and Concord: "With one impulse, the colonies sprung to arms; with one spirit, they pledged themselves to each other 'to be ready for the extreme event.' With one heart, the continent cried: 'Liberty or Death.' " [149]

Bancroft's literary mantle was seized by Schouler,[150] who wore it rather ungracefully in writing that: "Proud in our annals was the year 1818, when the whole nation felt itself soaring upward in a new atmosphere, exhilarated and bold, like an eagle loosened from confinement." Schouler's comment on nullification is suggestive of the language of medieval chivalry: "These were glorious days for the Constitution's allied defenders; the one matchless in debate, the other terrible in action and clad in popular confidence like a coat of mail."

McMaster reminds us of Bancroft, when he said in 1898,[151]

Our national history should be presented to the student as the growth and development of a marvelous people. . . . We are a people animated by the highest and noblest ideals of humanity, of the rights of man, and no history of our country is rightly taught which does not set this forth. . . . There is no land where the people are so prosperous, so happy, so intelligent, so bent on doing what is just and right, as the people of the United States.

Von Holst, a professor in both Germany and the United States who wrote American history of the Nationalist school, found it difficult to write dis-

---

[148] Michael Kraus, *op. cit.*, p. 223.
[149] *The Marcus W. Jernegan Essays in American Historiography, op. cit.*, p. 21.
[150] *Ibid.*, p. 352, 353-54.
[151] *Ibid.*, p. 393-94.

passionately. In characterizing the annexation of Texas as an expansionist movement solely the result of Southern desires for more slave territory, he writes with forced imagery of the Congressional process of annexation: "The bridal dress in which Calhoun had led the beloved of the slavocracy to the Union was the torn and tattered constitution of the United States." [152]

Heinrich von Treitschke (1834-96), with his great oratory and rhetoric, preached the pride and power of a united Germany and the inferiority of non-Germans. His political ideas were those of an emotional patriot or a special pleader and agitator rather than a historian. As Treitschke put it, "My blood, alas, is too hot for an historian." [153]

Hildreth did not often permit himself the luxury of so flowery and eloquent a style as that used in describing the three principal figures of Federalist politics—Hamilton, Washington, and Jay: "We have a trio not to be matched, in fact, not to be approached in our history, if indeed, in any other. Of earth-born Titans, as terrible as great, now angels, and now toads and serpents, there are everywhere enough. Of the serene and benign sons of the celestial gods, how few at any time have walked the earth!" [154]

Notwithstanding all the suggestions of this chapter concerning historical writing and literary style, it must be admitted that certain topics lend themselves with great difficulty to a graceful and interesting style. For example, there are not many "purple patches" in the constitutional and legal basis of a state school system or in the laws and court decisions governing city school budgets, however important such studies may be for certain purposes. Yet, current newspaper "strips" dealing with legal problems may keep readers in real suspense for a number of installments of drawings before finally picturing the court decision.

The preceding paragraphs dealing with the literary aspects of historical writing by no means exhaust the subject but rather present in outline form the major problems involved. A variety of additional sources may be used for purposes of supplementing and expanding this summary of principles of historical composition and exposition.[155]

[152] *Ibid.,* p. 342.
[153] Thompson and Holm, *op. cit.,* Vol. 2, p. 220-23.
[154] *Marcus W. Jernegan Essays in American Historiography, op. cit.,* p. 35-36.
[155] J. S. Bassett, *op. cit.,* p. 109-14, 127-39.
C. G. Crump, *op. cit.,* Chapter 5.
F. M. Fling, *op. cit.,* Chapters 7, 8.
Louis R. Gottschalk, *op. cit.,* p. 13-19, 181-98.
H. C. Hockett, *op. cit.,* p. 134-41.
E. H. Reisner, "The More Effective Use of Historical Background in the Study of Education," *op. cit.,* p. 187-90.
J. M. Vincent, *Historical Research, op. cit.,* Chapters 24, 25.

## ILLUSTRATIONS OF THE HISTORICAL METHOD

It remains to cite selected examples of the application of the historical method, since study of actual historical investigations is fully as important as knowledge of the principles of historiography outlined in this chapter. Space permits only a few illustrations in the fields of education, psychology, sociology, and other sciences. An almost unlimited number of additional examples in these and other areas may be located by using the appropriate library guides (described in an earlier chapter) for canvassing books, periodicals, theses, and other types of literature. Also, selected guides to historical materials have been cited earlier in the present chapter and are listed in the chapter bibliography.

### History of Education

**General field of educational history.** Two admirable illustrations carry the reader through the various stages in attacking the problem of how progressive education [156] came to arise and develop, and through the essential steps in compiling a list of arithmetic textbooks [157] published within the present limits of the United States during the eighteenth century. These examples emphasize a description of the appropriate processes of historical research rather than of the detailed results secured. Such analyses should be particularly helpful to the graduate student in rendering concrete the steps and procedures of historical research, and were written primarily for that purpose.

A brief summary and bibliography of 975 titles [158] in historical and comparative education cover a wide range of problems and illustrate the types of studies available. The fields represented are history of American education during the colonial period, studies since the beginning of the national period, and state histories of education; history of education in Canada, England, France, Germany, Italy, and the Scandinavian countries; and comparative education. A characterization of trends in the history of education cites investigations with emphasis on school organization, administration, educational law, comparative education, and the relation of the school to society.[159] Another publication is an example of a type of his-

[156] H. G. Good, "The Possibilities of Historical Research," *op. cit.,* p. 148-53.
[157] H. G. Good, "Historical Research in Education." *Educational Research Bulletin* 9:41-47, 74-76; January 22 and February 5, 1930.
[158] Newton Edwards and Others, "History of Education and Comparative Education." *Review of Educational Research* 6:353-456; October 1936. Also see:
Edgar W. Knight, "History of Education." *Encyclopedia of Educational Research.* Revised Edition. Edited by Walter S. Monroe. New York: Macmillan Co., 1950. p. 551-56.
M. M. Chambers and Others, "History of Education and Comparative Education." *Review of Educational Research* 9:333-448; October 1939.
[159] H. G. Good, "Current Historiography in Education," in "Methods of Research in Education." *Review of Educational Research* 9:456-59, 593-94; December 1939.

torical writing, although its primary purpose is to interpret educational issues in the light of contemporary American philosophy, historical study of philosophy and psychology, legal and governmental basis of education, social trends, national backgrounds and comparative education, and historical sociology.[160] The guides to such educational materials as books, periodicals, and theses (already listed in an earlier chapter) will reveal any desired number of additional illustrations in the various subdivisions of educational history.

**Legal research in education.** A special type of historical research utilizes as sources: (1) statutory law (constitutional provisions and legislative or statutory enactments), and (2) case or common law (principles applied by the courts in deciding issues not covered by statutory law.) These sources are so specialized and extensive as to require access to a good law library if satisfactory work is to be done. Research in school law includes the same problem-solving processes of collecting data, criticism, and interpretation discussed in this chapter, with of course certain special applications.

Detailed outlines of the materials and methods of research in the legal aspects of education (classifications of law, sources of school law, and the indexes and other bibliographic aids) are readily available, and space will permit only a listing of selected references.[161] Attention should be directed particularly to a statement that summarizes selected special approaches and uses of legal research in education, notes changes and additions among the legal bibliographic aids, offers certain suggestions regarding the analysis and digesting of legal materials, and discusses needed research.[162]

An outstanding pioneer example of research in school law is Edwards' detailed analysis of the legal basis of school organization and administration, which is a comprehensive treatment for the topics of school and state,

---

[160] *The Use of Background in the Interpretation of Educational Issues.* Yearbook No. 25 of the National Society of College Teachers of Education. Chicago: University of Chicago Press, 1937. p. 86-210.

[161] Carter Alexander and Arvid J. Burke, *op. cit.,* p. 326-37.

W. L. Coffey, "How to Find the School Law." *Fourth Yearbook of School Law.* Edited by M. M. Chambers. Washington: American Council on Education, 1936. p. 117-54.

F. W. Cyr and S. Cunin, "A Guide to Research in School Law." *Journal of Educational Research* 30:509-21; March 1937.

Newton Edwards, "Methods and Materials of Legal Research." *Review of Educational Research* 4:85-91; February 1934.

Newton Edwards, "Where and How to Find the Law Relating to Public-School Administration." *Elementary School Journal* 27:14-24; September 1926.

Carter V. Good, A. S. Barr, and Douglas E. Scates, *op. cit.,* p. 270-79.

F. C. Hicks, *Materials and Methods of Legal Research with Bibliographical Manual.* Second Edition. Rochester, N. Y.: Lawyers Coöperative Publishing Co., 1933. xvi + 651 p.

Madaline K. Remmlein, "Tools and Procedures in School Law Research." *Growing Points in Educational Research.* Washington: American Educational Research Association, 1949. p. 166-75.

[162] M. M. Chambers, "Legal Research in Education," in "Methods of Research in Education." *Review of Educational Research* 9:460-65; December 1939.

district organization and control, school districts and municipalities, school officers, legal authority of boards of education, school-board procedure and records, contractual authority and liability of school boards, school money, school debt, acquisition and use of school property, contractor's bond, tort liability of school districts, personal liability of school officers, employment of teachers, dismissal of teachers, pensions and minimum wages, school attendance, rules and regulations of boards of education, and discipline and punishment of pupils.[163]

A valuable bibliographical and summary review of the literature in this field includes many pertinent examples of legal research in its 398 references covering the topics of federal and state relations to education; constitutional basis of public education; state administrative organization; district organization and control; administration of local school systems; school finance; school property; tort liability of school districts and personnel; legal status of teachers; legal status of pupils; textbooks and curriculum; and legal aspects of higher education.[164] The *Yearbook of School Law* (1933-42), in its ten résumés of the decisions of the higher courts affecting educational systems and institutions, has presented illustrations of legal research over a wide range of topics.[165] This series also has summarized Doctors' dissertations on school law and has listed the appropriate Masters' theses. Numerous studies and graduate theses of a legal character were listed over a period of years under the headings of "educational laws and legislation" or "educational legislation" in the bibliography of educational research issued by the Office of Education.[166]

Suggestive discussions of a more general type, without specific reference to legal problems in education, deal with jurisprudence as a field for re-

[163] Newton Edwards, *The Courts and the Public Schools.* Chicago: University of Chicago Press, 1933. xvi + 582 p. Also see:

Robert R. Hamilton and Paul R. Mort, *The Law and Public Education.* Chicago: Foundation Press, 1941. xxv + 579 p.

Madaline K. Remmlein, *School Law.* New York: McGraw-Hill Book Co., 1950. xxi + 376 p. A major contribution, with a chapter organization in terms of problems of teacher personnel and pupil personnel, an appendix dealing with the legal guides, editorial comments at the beginning of each chapter and other editorial notes, and illustrative extracts from the statutory and case materials.

H. R. Trusler, *Essentials of School Law.* Milwaukee: Bruce Publishing Co., 1927. xlvi + 478 p.

Frederick Weltzin, *The Legal Authority of the American Public School.* Grand Forks, N. D.: Mid-West Book Concern, 1931. 286 p.

[164] Newton Edwards and Others, "The Legal Basis of Education." *Review of Educational Research* 3:369-468; December 1933. Also see:

M. M. Chambers and Newton Edwards, "School Law." *Encyclopedia of Educational Research, op. cit.,* p. 1089-98.

[165] For example, *Tenth Yearbook of School Law.* Edited by M. M. Chambers. Washington: American Council on Education, 1942. viii + 200 p. Also see:

Lee O. Garber, *The Yearbook of School Law 1952.* Philadelphia, Pa.: The Author, School of Education, University of Pennsylvania, 1952. iv + 106 p.

[166] For example, Ruth A. Gray, *Bibliography of Research Studies in Education,* 1939-1940. Office of Education Bulletin No. 5, 1941. Washington: Government Printing Office, 1941. xiv + 404 p.

search,[167] the politico-juristic approach to problems in social science,[168] problems of judicial procedure in arriving at the facts of a case,[169] a case study of problems of method in international law,[170] and the use of the law library.[171]

**Bibliographical and summarizing studies.** As the literature of education has expanded, there has been a corresponding increase in the number of summaries of research in particular areas. When such work is well done, it meets the criteria for sound historical research, involving similar problems of compilation of bibliography and collection of data, criticism of evidence, and interpretation, synthesis, and exposition. The primary sources are the reports of the various investigations summarized.

A critical and well integrated summary of the studies of the twentieth century dealing with arithmetic probably requires a broader grasp of research methods, and greater skill in synthesis and interpretation, than the biography of an educational leader or the typical history of a high school. When the results of several hundred investigations in the field of arithmetic are brought together, it should be possible to identify generalizations, trends, and needed research in a manner not discernible so long as each study is viewed separately rather than in relation to similar investigations and to the entire pattern of research in arithmetic. Rarely is a major discovery made through a single piece of research, so as to result in sweeping changes in the complex processes of teaching or learning;[172] more commonly it is by a combination of findings from a number of studies that sound generalizations are formulated and applied to school procedure, as illustrated in the trend toward the teacher-demonstration method in laboratory work as compared with individual experimentation by the pupils.

It is true that many graduate departments of instruction have not encouraged students to attempt the summary type of thesis, possibly because of the tendency on the part of too many candidates to submit reports of the annotated or running-bibliography variety. A significant study or thesis in this field will classify, compare, synthesize, and interpret the points of view, procedures, and results of the various investigations analyzed, with a clear indication of the pertinent educational, psychological, sociological, or other implications.

When summaries attempt to cover too broad an area within a quite

---

[167] Roscoe Pound, "Jurisprudence." *Research in the Social Sciences, op. cit.,* Chapter 6.
[168] H. W. Odum and Katharine Jocher, *op. cit.,* Chapter 11.
[169] J. M. Vincent, *Aids to Historical Research, op. cit.,* p. 146-53.
[170] S. A. Rice, Editor, *Methods in Social Science.* Chicago: University of Chicago Press, 1931. p. 118-36.
[171] W. E. Spahr and R. J. Swenson, *op. cit.,* Chapter 9.
[172] B. R. Buckingham, "The Accumulation of Minute Advantages." *Journal of Educational Research* 16:136-38; September 1927.

limited space allotment, the result is little more than a running, annotated bibliography. However valuable any annual reviews of the literature in such broad fields as education [173] and sociology [174] may be as guides to current materials, they cannot hope to meet the standards of historical writing in terms of planning, progression, synthesis, interpretation, and generalization, when only a few pages of space must represent an overview of several hundred references. Such a bird's-eye view identifies the source materials for the history of educational or sociological literature, but falls decidedly short of the goal of history as an integrated narrative written in the spirit of critical inquiry. This difficulty no doubt was a major factor in the evolution of the titles of Knight's three annual reviews of educational literature in the United States, from "Literature of Education" to "Some Literature of Education" to "Books on Education." The *Review of Educational Research* has been working toward the solution of similar difficulties; in some instances an overview of a thousand studies has been given in a hundred pages of this journal. The summaries in the *Psychological Bulletin* have dealt with research in more narrowly delimited fields, with a relatively liberal space allotment, and, therefore, have succeeded somewhat better than the *Review of Educational Research* in the work of synthesis. No matter how valuable and complete a bibliography may be, it represents typically an early stage of historical research.[175]

Numerous illustrations of bibliographical and summarizing studies in a variety of fields, including education, psychology, and sociology, are cited in an earlier chapter dealing with the survey of related literature. It should be emphasized again that every graduate thesis or scientific study may well begin with the orientation provided by a careful review of the related research.

### History of Psychology

The principles and processes of historical research outlined in this chapter apply to the field of psychology, as to any area of historical problems and sources. One of the major approaches of psychology, the genetic method, is sometimes wrongly labeled as primarily historical in character. The genetic method, however, follows by observation a process of develop-

[173] E. W. Knight, "Literature of Education in the United States, 1935." *Social Studies* 27:103-19; February 1936.
E. W. Knight, "Some Literature of Education in the United States, 1936." *Social Studies* 27:530-45; December 1936.
E. W. Knight, "Books on Education, 1937." *Social Education* 2:35-43; January 1938.
[174] Louis Wirth and E. A. Shils, "The Literature of Sociology, 1934." *Social Studies* 26:459-75, 525-46; November, December 1935.
Louis Wirth and E. A. Shils, "The Literature of Sociology, 1935 and 1936." *Social Education* 1:449-511, 575-85; October, November 1937.
[175] W. S. Monroe and Louis Shores, *Bibliographies and Summaries in Education to July, 1935*. New York: H. W. Wilson Co., 1936. xvi + 470 p.

ment, such as the growth of a small child's vocabulary, noting the change as it takes place from day to day. This same developmental approach could be used in following the deterioration of mental functions in old age, the genesis of an abnormal fear, or the unfolding of genius, except that ordinarily such cases are not identified in time to make systematic observation possible at the earlier stages. The typical study of abnormality or genius usually begins after some marked phase of maladjustment or exhibition of talent has become apparent, and the movement of the investigation is backward toward reconstruction of the earlier stages. This particular type of developmental study, with a backward movement or historical approach, becomes in psychology or elsewhere the biographical or case-history or life-history method.[176] To cite an example, an attempt to estimate the I.Q.'s and to characterize other mental traits of three hundred geniuses [177] born between 1450 and 1849, based on data found in their biographies, is definitely historical, whereas the follow-up studies by observation of a thousand gifted children,[178] over a period of years through childhood to maturity, are genetic in approach.

The genetic and case methods are described in detail in other chapters, where the essential relationships and differences between historical, genetic, and case methods are pointed out at greater length. The rules of historical research apply to the writing of biography, which means that sound biography is good history. Sources of evidence especially valuable in child psychology for the historical approach, whether the result is narrative biography or life history of the case type, include a variety of materials (outlined in the chapter on the genetic approach) also adaptable to other research patterns.[179]

The decades of the 1930's, 1940's, and later witnessed unusual activity in writing the history of psychology and in summarizing its literature. The histories cover psychology in autobiography,[180] systems of psychology,[181]

[176] R. S. Woodworth, "Psychology." *Research in the Social Sciences, op. cit.*, p. 162-64.

[177] Catharine M. Cox, *Genetic Studies of Genius*. Vol. 2. Stanford, Calif.: Stanford University Press, 1926. xxiv + 842 p.

[178] L. M. Terman and Others, *Genetic Studies of Genius*. Vols. 1, 3. Stanford, Calif.: Stanford University Press, 1925, 1930. xvi + 648, xvi + 508 p.

L. M. Terman and Melita H. Oden, *The Gifted Child Grows Up:* Genetic Studies of Genius. Stanford, Calif.: Stanford University Press, 1947. xiv + 450 p.

[179] J. E. Anderson, "The Methods of Child Psychology." *A Handbook of Child Psychology*. Second Edition, Revised. Edited by Carl Murchison. Worcester: Clark University Press, 1933. p. 10-11.

J. E. Anderson, "Methods of Child Psychology." *Manual of Child Psychology*. Edited by Leonard Carmichael. New York: John Wiley and Sons, 1946. p. 13-14.

[180] Carl Murchison, Editor, *A History of Psychology in Autobiography*, Vols. 1, 2, 3. Worcester: Clark University Press, 1930, 1932, 1936. xviii + 516, xx + 407, xx + 327 p.

Herbert S. Langfeld and Others, Editors, *A History of Psychology in Autobiography*. Vol. 4. Worcester: Clark University Press, 1952.

[181] Edna Heidbreder, *Seven Psychologies*. New York: Appleton-Century-Crofts, 1933. x + 450 p.

experimental psychology,[182] and broader historical treatments.[183] Carefully synthesized summaries of psychological research, like similar reviews in education, represent a type of historical research. Especially comprehensive summaries deal with general experimental psychology,[184] child psychology,[185] social psychology,[186] experimental social psychology,[187] and the heredity-environment problem.[188] Reference may be made again to the summarizing type of work found in the *Psychological Bulletin,* in the *Annual Review of Psychology,* and in the *Review of Educational Research* (which also covers certain psychological topics). The library guides described in an earlier chapter and the bibliography of the present chapter may be used to locate a variety of psychological studies that are historical in character.

## Historical Sociology

Historical sociology is considered by educational workers as the core of a historical approach to study of the social background of education. A promising procedure is to trace the evolution of education and culture through four periods of development: [189] (1) primitive cultures in which education took place adequately without the aid of the school; (2) the stage at which writing appeared and the most important religious and ethical documents of the people were reduced to permanent written form, necessitating types of schools and of education appropriate to the particular culture—such as Chinese, Jewish, Greek, and Roman; (3) introduction of science and philosophy as the means of describing the operations of nature

[182] E. G. Boring, *A History of Experimental Psychology.* New York: Century Co., 1929. xviii + 699 p. Also see the 1950 revision.

[183] Gardner Murphy, *An Historical Introduction to Modern Psychology.* Revised Edition, New York: Harcourt, Brace and Co., 1949.

J. C. Flugel, *A Hundred Years of Psychology.* Second Edition. New York: Macmillan Co., 1951. 424 p.

C. E. Spearman, *Psychology Down the Ages,* Vols. 1, 2. London: Macmillan and Co., 1937. xii + 454, viii + 355 p.

R. E. Brennan, *History of Psychology.* New York: Macmillan Co., 1945. 277 p.

Wayne Dennis, Editor, *Readings in the History of Psychology.* New York: Appleton-Century-Crofts, 1948. 598 p.

A. A. Roback, *History of American Psychology.* New York: Library Publishers, 1952. xiv + 426 p.

[184] Carl Murchison, Editor, *A Handbook of General Experimental Psychology.* Worcester: Clark University Press, 1934. xii + 1126 p.

[185] Carl Murchison, Editor, *A Handbook of Child Psychology.* Worcester: Clark University Press, 1931. 712 p. Second Edition, Revised, 1933. xii + 956 p.

Leonard Carmichael, Editor, *Manual of Child Psychology, op. cit.,* viii + 1068 p.

[186] Carl Murchison, Editor, *A Handbook of Social Psychology.* Worcester: Clark University Press, 1935. xii + 1190 p.

[187] Gardner Murphy and Lois B. Murphy, *Experimental Social Psychology.* New York: Harper and Bros., 1931. xiv + 710 p.

[188] Gladys C. Schwesinger, *Heredity and Environment.* New York: Macmillan Co., 1933. xii + 484 p.

[189] E. H. Reisner, "The More Effective Use of Historical Background in the Study of Education," *op. cit.,* p. 197-202.

and of finding reason and justice in social institutions and codes, precipitating intellectual conflicts and the development of experiences that provided the materials of secondary and higher education; and (4) tremendous changes in social organization and education of the past century and a half as the result of developments in science, industry, technology, political democracy, and the national state. Sociologists themselves, when writing books on investigational methods, recognize the importance of the historical approach by including treatments of this method of research.[190]

The sources of data for historical sociology and for cultural and folk sociology have been enumerated in an earlier section of this chapter concerned with historical sources. Archaeology and anthropology are cognate sciences of major importance in the historical study of social problems. Archaeology is the science of the remains of previous cultures. Anthropology, the science of man, deals with communities and groups of mankind, in terms of bodily form, physiological and psychological functions, and behavior; it attempts to reconstruct the early history of mankind and to express in the form of laws ever recurring modes of historical events. Historical sociology is concerned with studying the history of society, the development of culture, and the evolution of social institutions.

Background from these social fields is essential to the eclectic, synthetic, or "collective psychological" school of history, which insists that history must include an explanation of the development of culture and civilization —ideas and intellectual history, traditions, esthetic achievement, science and technology, material culture, and economic, social, and political groupings and institutions. Numerous historical writings illustrate this broadened perspective and interest of the historian in tracing events from a social point of view.[191]

Selected examples of historical work from the fields of sociology and closely related social areas include comprehensive historical overviews of the development of sociology and social thought;[192] a century of anthro-

---

[190] L. L. Bernard and Others, *The Fields and Methods of Sociology*. New York: Ray Long and Richard R. Smith, 1934. Chapters 2, 8, Part 1; Chapters 2, 8, Part 2.
M. C. Elmer, *op. cit.*, Chapter 5.
Robert E. Park, "Sociology." *Research in the Social Sciences, op. cit.*, p. 33-38.
H. W. Odum and Katharine Jocher, *op. cit.*, Chapters 10, 14.
Pauline V. Young, *op. cit.*, Chapter 9.
[191] Harry E. Barnes, *op. cit.*, Chapters 12, 13.
Harry E. Barnes, *Historical Sociology:* Its Origins and Development. New York: Philosophical Library, 1948. x + 186 p.
[192] Harry E. Barnes and Howard Becker, *op. cit.*
Harry E. Barnes, Editor, *An Introduction to the History of Sociology*. Chicago: University of Chicago Press, 1948. xvi + 960 p.
L. L. Bernard and Jessie Bernard, *Origins of American Sociology:* The Social Science Movement in the United States. New York: Thomas Y. Crowell Co., 1943. xvi + 866 p.
Emory S. Bogardus, *The Development of Social Thought*. Second Edition. New York: Longmans, Green and Co., 1947. x + 574 p.

pology;[193] case analyses of studies concerned primarily with attempts to discover spatial distributions and temporal sequences, interpretations of change as a developmental stage, and interpretations of temporal sequences with consideration of special types of causation;[194] and a bibliographical note on American cultural history.[195]

Reference has already been made in this chapter to certain brief summaries of the literature of sociology[196] which may be regarded as a type of historical approach. Summaries have been issued at three-year intervals for educational sociology and related social areas.[197] Additional examples of historical work in sociology may be located through the bibliographical and library guides listed in an earlier chapter. As pointed out in discussing the history of psychology, the biographical, case-history, and life-history methods, which have historical aspects, are treated in the chapter on case and clinical approaches.

## CONCLUDING AND SUMMARY STATEMENT

History of education was a relatively frequent requirement in the early teacher-training programs of this country. In the early days of graduate work in education, the historical or philosophical thesis was popular. All too commonly both the course of instruction and thesis consisted of a mass of historical facts without functional application to social issues or to the activities and problems of educational workers. During the second and third decades of the twentieth century other courses and tools of research

---

C. A. Ellwood, *A History of Social Philosophy*. New York: Prentice-Hall, 1938. xvi + 581 p.

F. N. House, *op. cit.*, viii + 456 p.

Howard W. Odum, *American Sociology:* The Story of Sociology in the United States through 1950. New York: Longmans, Green and Co., 1951. vi + 501 p.

F. J. Teggart, *op. cit.*, Chapters 7-16.

[193] T. K. Penniman, *A Hundred Years of Anthropology*. Revised Edition. New York: Macmillan Co., 1952. 512 p.

[194] S. A. Rice, Editor, *Methods in Social Science*. Chicago: University of Chicago Press, 1931. xiv + 822 p.

[195] Michael Kraus, *op. cit.*, p. 481-91.

[196] Louis Wirth and E. A. Shils, *op. cit.*

[197] Charles C. Peters and Others, "Educational Sociology." *Review of Educational Research* 7:1-112; February 1937.

Edmund deS. Brunner and Others, "Social Background of Education." *Review of Educational Research* 10:1-72; February 1940.

Lloyd A. Cook and Others, "The War, Education, and Society." *Review of Educational Research* 13:1-62; February 1943.

Herman H. Remmers and Others, "Social Foundations of Education." *Review of Educational Research* 16:1-95; February 1946.

Newton Edwards and Others, "The Social Framework of Education." *Review of Educational Research* 19:1-90; February 1949.

N. L. Gage and Others, "The Social Framework of Education." *Review of Educational Research* 22:1-59; February 1952.

Edwin R. Carr, Edgar B. Wesley, and Wilbur F. Murra, "Social Studies." *Encyclopedia of Educational Research, op. cit.*, p. 1213-38.

(tests, surveys, and experiments) made heavy claims on the attention of students and investigators. There is evidence to indicate that a new type of history has regained some of the lost ground. Each school system and school, subject and activity, institution and culture, laboratory and library, scientist and leader represents a story of evolution and development. Little of this history has been written.

History is ideally an integrated narrative of past events, representing a critical search for the whole truth, with a field of inquiry as broad as the human past and life itself. Good history is both science and art; sound research is science and a masterful style of narration is art. The "seamless web" of history should be more than an almanac or chronicle of the unique events of the past; its data should be applicable to current issues and problems.

For collection of data, documents and remains are the chief primary sources, the first witnesses to a fact and therefore the only solid bases for historical research, although classifications of sources have been broadened within recent years. In the case of secondary sources, more than one mind has come between the historical event and the user of the sources. To make satisfactory progress in answering historical questions, it is necessary to collect material by means of a well arranged note system.

The sources are subjected to external and internal criticism. External criticism is concerned with the genuineness of the document as such, and deals with data of form and appearance rather than meaning of contents. Internal criticism determines the meaning and trustworthiness of statements within the document, that is, weighs the testimony of the document in relation to the truth. External criticism makes use of certain auxiliary sciences and a variety of procedures in dealing with forgeries and hoaxes, inventions and distortions, authorship and time, and borrowings. Internal criticism seeks to determine the literal meaning and the real meaning of statements, the competence of the observer, and the truthfulness and honesty of the observer or author.

Historical composition is a synthetic and constructive process that involves the mechanical problem of documentation, the logical problem of selection and arrangement of topics and subtopics, and the philosophical problem of interpretation. An appropriate combination of the chronological and topical plans for arrangement of topics and materials is recommended. Few works in history have been directly touched by one of the broad philosophies or theories of history, such as the evolutionary hypothesis or the rhythm philosophy (cycle theory). Specific schools of historical interpretation, such as economic determinism, permit a pragmatic test, through use of historical materials, and are of more general interest to writers and users of history, although many of the best historical works have been written according to the individual bent of the author rather than in keeping with some special interpretation or school of thought. The development of a newer type of history, which is eclectic in approach and interpretation, necessarily depends on the contributions of many sciences for gathering and interpreting evidence and for training the workers.

Historical writing and interpretation include a variety of special problems. Only when a perplexing question has been identified and correctly stated does profitable study of history begin. Inductive reasoning is the procedure open to the historian, in making penetrating inductive inferences from known facts that offer only a partial explanation. In turn, the superimposing of the general explanatory concept upon the facts or the testing of the working hypothesis represents a deductive process. As a rule, multiple causation is the explanation of any important historical event. The problem of historical perspective presents great difficulties, because of tendencies to evaluate events and personages distant in time or space according to the standards of our own time and culture. Few histories of distinction lack a thesis or principle of synthesis, such as the effect of the frontier on American life and character. The literary aspects of historical writing include mastery of materials, the working outline, the principle of progression, emphasis on major elements, and the art of narration and dramatization.

The numerous historical works available in a variety of social and scientific fields suggest that in the decades of the 1930's and 1940's, which began as a period of world-wide economic and social disturbance, followed by a World War and then by a "cold war," there may have been a turn to a newer type of history as an ally of the scientific movement, with the hope of solving thereby at least in part the staggering problems of human maladjustment.

## SELECTED REFERENCES

ADAMS, H. B. *Historical Scholarship in the United States, 1876-1901, as Revealed in His Correspondence.* Edited by W. S. Holt. Baltimore: Johns Hopkins Press, 1938. 314 p.

ADAMS, James T., and COLEMAN, R. V., Editors. *Dictionary of American History.* New York: Charles Scribner's Sons, 1940. 5 vols. and index.

ALMACK, J. C. *Research and Thesis Writing.* Boston: Houghton Mifflin Co., 1930. Chapter 7.

American Association for Health, Physical Education, and Recreation. *Research Methods Applied to Health, Physical Education, and Recreation.* Revised Edition. Washington: The Association, N.E.A., 1952. p. 125-35.

American Historical Association, Committee on the Planning of Research, A. M. Schlesinger, chairman. *Historical Scholarship in America.* New York: R. R. Smith and Ray Long, 1932. ix + 146 p.

American Psychiatric Association. *One Hundred Years of American Psychiatry.* New York: Columbia University Press, 1944. 649 p.

ARROWOOD, Charles F., and Others. *The Use of Background in the Interpretation of Educational Issues.* Twenty-fifth Yearbook, National Society of College Teachers of Education. Chicago: University of Chicago Press, 1937. vi + 227 p.

ASHLEY-MONTAGUE, Montague F., Editor. *Studies and Essays in the History of Science and Learning Offered in Homage to George Sarton on the Occasion of His Sixtieth Birthday, 31 August, 1944.* New York: Henry Schuman, 1947. xiv + 594 p.

AUSUBEL, Herman. *Historians and Their Craft:* A Study of the Presidential Addresses of the American Historical Association, 1884-1945. New York: Columbia University Press, 1950. 373 p.

AUSUBEL, Herman, BREBNER, J. Bartlet, and HUNT, Erling M., Editors. *Some Modern Historians of Britain:* Essays in Honor of R. L. Schuyler. New York: Dryden Press, 1952. 385 p.

BARNES, Harry E. *Historical Sociology:* Its Origins and Development. New York: Philosophical Library, 1948. x + 186 p.

BARNES, Harry E. *History and Social Intelligence.* New York: Alfred A. Knopf, 1926. xviii + 597 p.

BARNES, Harry E. *A History of Historical Writing.* Norman: University of Oklahoma Press, 1937. xiii + 434 p.

BARNES, Harry E. *An Introduction to the History of Sociology.* Chicago: University of Chicago Press, 1948. xvi + 960 p.

BARNES, Harry E. *The New History and the Social Studies.* New York: Century Co., 1925. xvii + 605 p.

BARNES, Harry E., and BECKER, Howard. *Social Thought from Lore to Science,* Vols. I and II. Revised Edition. Washington: Harren Press, 1952. 790 + cx; viii + 1178 + cxxxv p.

BARNES, Harry E., BECKER, Howard, and BECKER, Frances B. *Contemporary Social Theory.* New York: D. Appleton-Century Co., 1940. Chapter 15, "Historical Sociology," p. 491-542.

BARR, Arvil S., DAVIS, Robert A., and JOHNSON, Palmer O. *Educational Research and Appraisal.* Philadelphia: J. B. Lippincott Co., 1953. p. 215-22.

BAUER, R. H. "Bibliographical Guide to the Study of History; with Selected References for Historical Research." *Social Studies* 43:64-69; February 1952.

BAUER, R. H. "Study of History." *Social Studies* 39:150-58, 220-30, 267-72, 303-11; April-November, 1948.

BAUER, R. H. *Study of History:* With Helpful Suggestions for the Beginner. Philadelphia: McKinley Publishing Co., 1948. 36 p.

BEARD, C. A. "Currents in Historiography." *American Historical Review* 42: 460-84; April 1937.

BEARD, C. A. "That Noble Dream." *American Historical Review* 41:74-87; October 1935.

BEARD, C. A. "Written History as an Act of Faith." *American Historical Review* 39:219-29; January 1934.

BECKER, C. L. *Everyman His Own Historian.* New York: Appleton-Century-Crofts, 1935. 325 p.

BEERS, H. P. *Bibliographies in American History:* Guide to Materials for Research. New York: H. W. Wilson Co., 1938. 339 p.

BELLOT, H. Hale. *American History and American Historians.* Norman: University of Oklahoma Press, 1952. x + 336 p.

BERNAL, J. D. *Science in History*. London: C. A. Watts and Co., 1949.

BERNARD, L. L., and BERNARD, Jessie. *Origins of American Sociology:* The Social Science Movement in the United States. New York: Thomas Y. Crowell Co., 1943. Part 11, "The Historical Method and Social Science," p. 721-80.

BERNARD, L. L., and Others. *The Fields and Methods of Sociology*. New York: Long and Smith, 1934. Part 1, Chapters 2, 8; Part 2, Chapters 2, 8.

BLACK, J. B. *The Art of History*. London: Methuen and Co., 1926. viii + 188 p.

BLAIR, Glenn M. *Educational Psychology, Its Development and Present Status.* University of Illinois Bulletin, Vol. 46, No. 13. Urbana: University of Illinois, September 1948. 34 p.

BOGARDUS, Emory S. *The Development of Social Thought*. Second Edition. New York: Longmans, Green and Co., 1947. x + 574 p.

BOGARDUS, Emory S. *Introduction to Social Research*. Los Angeles: Sutton-house, 1936. xi + 237 p.

BORING, E. G. *A History of Experimental Psychology*. Second Edition. New York: Appleton-Century-Crofts, 1950. xxi + 777 p.

BORING, E. G. *Sensation and Perception in the History of Experimental Psychology*. New York: D. Appleton-Century Co., 1942. xv + 644 p.

BOWMAN, Francis J. *Handbook of Historians and History Writing*. Dubuque, Ia.: W. C. Brown Co., 1951. v + 110 p.

BRADFORD, S. C. *Documentation*. Washington: Public Affairs Press, 1948. 146 p.

BRENNAN, R. E. *History of Psychology*. New York: Macmillan Co., 1945. 277 p.

BRICKMAN, William W. *Guide to Research in Educational History*. New York: New York University Bookstore, 1949. ix + 220 p.

BRICKMAN, William W. "History of Education." *School and Society* 79:69-75; March 6, 1954.

BRUBACHER, John S. *A History of the Problems of Education*. New York: McGraw-Hill Book Co., 1947. 688 p.

BURCHFIELD, Laverne. *Student's Guide to Materials in Political Science*. New York: Henry Holt and Co., 1935. 426 p.

CASE, Lynn M. "The Military Historian Overseas." *American Association of University Professors Bulletin* 34:320-34; Summer 1948.

CATE, J. L., and ANDERSON, E. N. *Medieval and Historiographical Essays in Honor of James Westfall Thompson*. Chicago: University of Chicago Press, 1938. x + 499 p.

CHAMBERS, M. M., and Others. "History of Education and Comparative Education." *Review of Educational Research* 9:333-448; October 1939.

CHEYNEY, E. P. *Law in History and Other Essays*. New York: Alfred A. Knopf, 1927. vii + 173 p.

COATES, Wilson H. "Relativism and the Use of Hypothesis in History." *Journal of Modern History* 21:23-27; March 1949.

COBB, J. C. *The Application of Scientific Methods to Sociology*. Boston: Chapman and Grimes, 1934. 161 p.

COCHRAN, Thomas C. "The 'Presidential Synthesis' in American History." *American Historical Review* 53:748-59; July 1948.

COHEN, I. Bernard. "Sense of History in Science." *American Journal of Physics* 18:343-59; September 1950.

COHEN, Morris R. *The Meaning of Human History*. LaSalle, Ill.: Open Court Publishing Co., 1947. ix + 304 p.

COLLINGWOOD, Robin G. *Idea of History*. New York: Oxford University Press, 1946. xxvi + 339 p.

CONE, Carl B. "Major Factors in the Rhetoric of Historians." *Quarterly Journal of Speech* 33:437-50; December 1947.

COULTER, Edith M., and GERSTENFELD, Melanie. *Historical Bibliographies.* Berkeley: University of California Press, 1935. 206 p.

CROCE, Benedetto. *History as the Story of Liberty.* Toronto: George J. McLeod, 1941. 324 p.

CROCE, Benedetto. *Theory and History of Historiography.* New York: Peter Smith, 1933. 317 p.

CRUMP, C. G. *History and Historical Research.* London: George Routledge and Sons, 1928. ix + 178 p.

CULVER, Dorothy C. *Methodology of Social Science Research:* A Bibliography. Berkeley: University of California Press, 1936. x + 159 p.

CURTI, Merle E., Editor. *Theory and Practice in Historical Study:* A Report of the Committee on Historiography. Social Science Research Council Bulletin No. 54. New York: The Council, 1946. xi + 177 p.

DARGAN, Marion. "Biographical Approach in American History." *Journal of Higher Education* 20:137-39; March 1949.

DAVIDSON, P. G., and KUHLMAN, A. F., Editors. *The Development of Library Resources and Graduate Work in the Coöperative University Centers of the South.* Nashville, Tenn.: Joint University Libraries, 1944. 81 p.

DENNIS, Wayne, Editor. *Readings in the History of Psychology.* New York: Appleton-Century-Crofts, 1948. 598 p.

DENNIS, Wayne, and BORING, Edwin G. "The Founding of the APA." *American Psychologist* 7:95-97; March 1952.

DESTLER, Chester M. "Some Observations on Contemporary Historical Theory." *American Historical Review* 55:503-29; April 1950.

DORFMAN, Joseph. "The Jackson Wage-Earner Thesis." *American Historical Review* 54:296-306; January 1949.

DOW, E. W. *Principles of a Note-System for Historical Studies.* New York: Century Co., 1924. vi + 124 p.

DOWNS, R. B., Editor. *Resources of Southern Libraries:* A Survey of Facilities for Research. Chicago: American Library Association, 1938. viii + 370 p.

DUNLAP, Knight. "The Historical Method in Psychology." *Journal of General Psychology* 24:49-62; January 1941.

DUNNING, W. A. *Truth in History, and Other Essays.* New York: Columbia University Press, 1937. xxviii + 229 p.

DUTCHER, G. M. "Directions and Suggestions for the Writing of Essays or Theses in History." *Historical Outlook* 22:329-38; November 1931.

DUTCHER, G. M., ALLISON, W. H., FAY, S. B., SHEARER, A. H., and SHIPMAN, H. R., Editors. *A Guide to Historical Literature.* New York: Macmillan Co., 1931. xxx + 1222 p.

EDWARDS, Newton. *The Courts and the Public Schools.* Chicago: University of Chicago Press, 1933. xvi + 582 p.

EDWARDS, Newton, and RICHEY, Herman G. *The School in the American Social Order.* Boston: Houghton Mifflin Co., 1947. 880 p.

EDWARDS, Newton, and Others. "The Social Framework of Education." *Review of Educational Research* 19:1-90; February 1949.

EDWARDS, Newton, and Others. "History of Education and Comparative Education." *Review of Educational Research* 6:353-456; October 1936.

EDWARDS, Newton, and Others. "The Legal Basis of Education." *Review of Educational Research* 3:369-468; December 1933.

EINSTEIN, Lewis D. *Historical Change.* New York: Macmillan Co., 1946. vi + 132 p.

ELLIS, Elmer. "Profession of Historian." *Mississippi Valley Historical Review* 38:3-20; June 1951.

ELLWOOD, C. A. *A History of Social Philosophy*. New York: Prentice-Hall, 1938. 581 p.

ELLWOOD, C. A. *Methods in Sociology:* A Critical Study. Durham, N. C.: Duke University Press, 1933. xxxiv + 214 p.

ELMER, Manuel C. *Social Research*. New York: Prentice-Hall, 1939. xvi + 522 p.

EVANS, Luther H. "The Library of Congress as the National Library of Science." *Scientific Monthly* 66:405-12; May 1948.

FEDERN, Karl. *Materialist Conception of History*. New York: Macmillan Co., 1939. xiv + 263 p.

FERGUSON, Wallace K. *The Renaissance in Historical Thought:* Five Centuries of Interpretation. Boston: Houghton Mifflin Co., 1948. xiii + 429 p.

FERM, Vergilius. *A History of Philosophical Systems*. New York: Philosophical Library, 1950. xiv + 642 p.

FERNBERGER, Samuel W. "The American Psychological Association, 1892-1942." *Psychological Review* 50:33-60; January 1943.

FESTINGER, Leon, and KATZ, Daniel, Editors. *Research Methods in the Behavioral Sciences*. New York: Dryden Press, 1953. p. 300-326.

FIRTH, C. H. *Essays, Historical and Literary*. New York: Oxford University Press, 1938. viii + 247 p.

FLING, F. M. *The Writing of History:* An Introduction to Historical Method. New Haven: Yale University Press, 1923. 196 p.

FLUGEL, J. C. *A Hundred Years of Psychology*. Second Edition. London: Gerald Duckworth and Co., 1951. 424 p.

FORTESCUE, John. *The Writing of History*. London: Williams and Norgate, 1926. 74 p.

FRY, C. L. *The Technique of Social Investigation*. New York: Harper and Bros., 1934. 316 p.

FULLER, B. A. G. *A History of Philosophy*. Revised Edition. New York: Henry Holt and Co., 1947. viii + 560 p.

GARBER, Lee O. *The Yearbook of School Law 1951*. Philadelphia: The Author, School of Education, University of Pennsylvania, 1951. iii + 89 p.

GARRAGHAN, Gilbert J. *A Guide to Historical Method*. Edited by Jean Delanglez. New York: Declan X. McMullen Co., 1946. xv + 482 + 30 p.

GEE, W. P. *Social Science Research Methods*. New York: Appleton-Century-Crofts, 1950. p. 280-99.

GEE, W. P. *Social Science Research Organization in American Universities and Colleges*. New York: Appleton-Century-Crofts, 1934. x + 276 p.

GEE, W. P., and Others. *Research in the Social Sciences:* Its Fundamental Methods and Objectives. New York: Macmillan Co., 1929. x + 306 p.

GEORGE, H. B. *Historical Evidence*. Oxford: Clarendon Press, 1909. 224 p.

GIDDINGS, F. H. *The Scientific Study of Human Society*. Chapel Hill: University of North Carolina Press, 1924. vi + 247 p.

GILSON, Etienne H. *History of Philosophy and Philosophical Education*. Milwaukee: Marquette University Press, 1948. 49 p.

GOLDENWEISER, A. A. *History, Psychology and Culture*. New York: Alfred A. Knopf, 1933. xii + 475 p.

GOLDMAN, E. F., Editor. *Historiography and Urbanization:* Essays in American History in Honor of W. Stull Holt. Baltimore: Johns Hopkins Press, 1941. 220 p.

GOOD, Carter V. "Bibliographical and Documentary Techniques in Education, Psychology, and Social Science," in "Methods of Research and Appraisal in Education." *Review of Educational Research* 12:460-78; December 1942.

GOOD, Carter V. "Library Resources and Documentary Research," in "Methods of Research and Appraisal in Education." *Review of Educational Research* 18:373-81, December 1948; 21:329-36, December 1951.

GOOD, Carter V. "Some Problems of Historical Criticism and Historical Writing." *Journal of Negro Education* 11:135-49; April 1942.

GOOD, Carter V., BARR, A. S., and SCATES, Douglas E. *The Methodology of Educational Research.* New York: Appleton-Century-Crofts, 1936. Chapter 6.

GOOD, H. G. "Current Historiography in Education," in "Methods of Research in Education." *Review of Educational Research* 9:456-59, 593-94; December 1939.

GOOD, H. G. "Historical Research in Education." *Educational Research Bulletin* 9:7-18, 39-47, 74-78; January 8, January 22, and February 5, 1930.

GOOD, H. G. *A History of Western Education.* New York: Macmillan Co., 1947. 575 p.

GOOD, H. G. "The Possibilities of Historical Research." *Journal of Educational Research* 39:148-53; October 1935.

GOTTSCHALK, Louis. *Understanding History:* A Primer of Historical Method. New York: Knopf, 1950. 290 p.

GOTTSCHALK, Louis, KLUCKHOHN, Clyde, and ANGELL, Robert. *The Use of Personal Documents in History, Anthropology, and Sociology.* Social Science Research Council Bulletin No. 53. New York: The Council, 1945. xiv + 243 p.

GUTHRIE, E. F. "Historical Materialism and Its Sociological Critics." *Social Forces* 20:172-84; December 1941.

HAINES, George. "Global War and the Study of History." *Social Forces* 22: 142-49; December 1943.

HARSIN, P. *Writing of History.* Berkeley: University of California, 1935. 96 p.

HEATON, Herbert. "Recent Developments in Economic History." *American Historical Review* 47:727-46; July 1942.

HICKS, F. C. *Materials and Methods of Legal Research.* Second Edition. Rochester, New York: Lawyers Coöperative Publishing Co., 1933. xvi + 651 p.

HIGHAM, John. "The Rise of American Intellectual History." *American Historical Review* 56:453-71; April 1951.

HOCKETT, H. C. *Introduction to Research in American History.* Revised Edition. New York: Macmillan Co., 1948. xiv + 179 p.

HOLLINGWORTH, Harry L. *Leta Stetter Hollingworth:* A Biography. Lincoln: University of Nebraska Press, 1943. 228 p.

HORTON, John T. "Historismus for the Undergraduate." *Journal of General Education* 2:27-34; October 1947.

HORTON, P. B. "Does History Show Long-Time Trends?" *Scientific Monthly* 55:461-70; November 1942.

HOSELITZ, Bert F. "The Social Sciences in the Last Two Hundred Years." *Journal of General Education* 4:85-103; January 1950.

HOUSE, F. N. *The Development of Sociology.* New York: McGraw-Hill Book Co., 1936. viii + 456 p.

HOWE, Laurence L. "Historical Method and Legal Education." *American Association of University Professors Bulletin* 36:346-356; Summer 1950.

HULME, E. M. *History and Its Neighbors*. New York: Oxford University Press, 1942. 197 p.

HUTCHINSON, W. T., and Others. *Marcus W. Jernegan Essays in American Historiography*. Chicago: University of Chicago Press, 1937. x + 417 p.

*International Bibliography of Historical Sciences, 1926—*. New York: H. W. Wilson Co., 1930—. Published annually.

JASTROW, Joseph, and Others. *The Story of Human Error*. New York: D. Appleton-Century Co., 1936. xvii + 445 p.

JOHNSON, Allen. *The Historian and Historical Evidence*. New York: Charles Scribner's Sons, 1926. 180 p.

JOHNSON, Allen, and MALONE, Dumas, Editors. *Dictionary of American Biography*. New York: Charles Scribner's Sons, 1928-1937. Twenty volumes and index. Also see: *Biography Index:* A Cumulative Index to Biographical Material in Books and Magazines. New York: H. W. Wilson Co., 1946—.

JOHNSON, Edgar. *One Mighty Torrent:* The Drama of Biography. New York: Stackpole Sons, 1937. 595 p.

JONES, Gwilym P., and POOL, A. G. *A Hundred Years of Economic Development in Great Britain*. New York: Macmillan Co., 1940. 420 p.

JUSSERAND, J. J., and Others. *The Writing of History*. New York: Charles Scribner's Sons, 1926. vii + 143 p.

KAPLAN, Louis. *Research Materials in the Social Sciences*. Madison: University of Wisconsin Press, 1939. 36 p.

KAUFMANN, Felix. *Methodology of the Social Sciences*. New York: Oxford University Press, 1944. viii + 272 p.

KEESECKER, Ward W. *Know Your School Law*. Office of Education Bulletin No. 1, 1952. Washington: U. S. Government Printing Office, 1952. iv + 26 p.

KELLETT, E. E. *Aspects of History*. New York: Thomas Nelson and Sons, 1938. 160 p.

KENT, Sherman. *Writing History*. New York: F. S. Crofts and Co., 1941. xiv + 136 p.

KEOHANE, Robert E. "The Great Debate Over the Source Method." *Social Education* 13:212-18; May 1949.

KLIBANSKY, R., and PATON, H. J., Editors. *Philosophy and History:* Essays Presented to Ernst Cassirer. New York: Oxford Press, 1936. xii + 360 p.

KRAUS, Michael. *A History of American History*. New York: Farrar and Rinehart, 1937. x + 607 p.

LAISTNER, M. L. W. *The Greater Roman Historians*. Berkeley: University of California Press, 1947. viii + 196 p.

LANGFELD, Herbert S., and Others, Editors. *A History of Psychology in Autobiography*. Vol. 4. Worcester, Mass.: Clark University Press, 1952. xii + 356 p.

LANGLOIS, C. V., and SEIGNOBOS, C. *Introduction to the Study of History*. New York: Henry Holt and Co., 1898. xxvii + 350 p.

LARRABEE, Harold A. *Reliable Knowledge*. Boston: Houghton Mifflin Co., 1945. Chapters 14-16.

LINGELBACH, W. E. *Approaches to American Social History*. New York: D. Appleton-Century Co., 1937. viii + 101 p.

LOEWENBERG, Bert J. "Some Problems Raised by Historical Relativism." *Journal of Modern History* 21:17-23; March 1949.

*London Bibliography of the Social Sciences*. London: London School of Economics, 1931-1934. Four volumes and supplements.

Lowith, Karl. *Meaning in History:* The Theological Implications of the Philosophy of History. Chicago: University of Chicago Press, 1949. ix + 257 p.

Lundberg, G. A. *Social Research:* A Study in Methods of Gathering Data. Second Edition. New York: Longmans, Green and Co., 1942. xxi + 426 p.

MacDonald, A. F. *Elements of Political Science Research.* New York: Prentice-Hall, 1928. vi + 94 p.

MacIver, R. M. *Social Causation.* Boston: Ginn and Co., 1942. x + 414 p.

Macmurray, John. *Clue to History.* New York: Harper and Bros., 1939. xii + 243 p.

Madge, John. *The Tools of Social Science.* New York: Longmans, Green and Co., 1953. p. 80-116.

Mandelbaum, Maurice. *The Problem of Historical Knowledge.* New York: Liveright Publishing Corporation, 1938. x + 340 p.

Marshall, R. L. *The Historical Criticism of Documents.* New York: Macmillan Co., 1920.

Martz, Velorus, and Ballinger, Stanley E. "A Guide to the Source Materials Relating to Education in the Laws of the State of Indiana, 1816-1851, Part One: 1816-1838." *Bulletin of the School of Education, Indiana University* 29:1-96; July 1953.

Miller, Hugh. *An Historical Introduction to Modern Philosophy.* New York: Macmillan Co., 1947. x + 615 p.

Miller, Hugh. *History and Science.* Berkeley: University of California Press, 1939. x + 201 p.

Monroe, Walter S. *Teaching-Learning Theory and Teacher Education 1890 to 1950.* Urbana: University of Illinois Press, 1952. vii + 426 p.

Monroe, Walter S., and Engelhart, M. D. *The Scientific Study of Educational Problems.* New York: Macmillan Co., 1936. xvi + 504 p.

Morison, Samuel E. "Faith of a Historian." *American Historical Review* 56: 261-75; January 1951.

Moulton, F. R. "The AAAS and Organized American Science." *Science* 108: 573-77; November 26, 1948.

Mulhern, James. *A History of Education.* New York: Ronald Press, 1946. 647 p.

Murchison, Carl, Editor. *A History of Psychology in Autobiography.* Worcester: Clark University Press, 1930, 1932, 1936. 3 vols. xviii + 516, xx + 407, xx + 327 p.

Murphy, Gardner. *An Historical Introduction to Modern Psychology.* Revised Edition. New York: Harcourt, Brace and Co., 1949. xiv + 466 p.

Nagel, Ernest. "Some Issues in the Logic of Historical Analysis." *Scientific Monthly* 74:162-69; March 1952.

Needham, Joseph, and Pagel, Walter, Editors. *Background to Modern Science.* New York: Macmillan Co., 1938. xii + 243 p.

Neurath, Otto. *Foundations of the Social Sciences.* Chicago: University of Chicago Press, 1944. iii + 50 p.

Nevins, Allan. *Gateway to History.* Boston: D. C. Heath and Co., 1938. vii + 412 p.

Nichols, R. F. "Confusions in Historical Thinking." *Social Philosophy and Jurisprudence* 7:334-43; July 1941.

Nichols, R. F. "Postwar Reorientation of Historical Thinking." *American Historical Review* 54:78-89; October 1948.

ODUM, H. W. *American Sociology:* The Story of Sociology in the United States through 1950. New York: Longmans, Green and Co., 1951. vi + 501 p.

ODUM, H. W. "Folk Sociology as a Subject Field for the Historical Study of Total Human Society and the Empirical Study of Group Behavior." *Social Forces* 31:193-223; March 1953.

ODUM, H. W., and JOCHER, Katharine. *An Introduction to Social Research.* New York: Henry Holt and Co., 1929. xiv + 448 p.

OGG, F. A. *Research in the Humanistic and Social Sciences.* New York: Century Co., 1928. 454 p.

OMAN, C. W. C. *On the Writing of History.* New York: E. P. Dutton and Co., 1939. xii + 307 p.

ORTEGA Y GASSET, José. *Toward a Philosophy of History.* New York: W. W. Norton and Co., 1941. 273 p.

PENNIMAN, T. K. *A Hundred Years of Anthropology.* Revised Edition. London: Duckworth and Co., 1952. 512 p.

PERDEW, Philip W. "Analysis of Research in Educational History." *Phi Delta Kappan* 32:134-36; December 1950.

PERDEW, Philip W. "Criteria of Research in Educational History." *Journal of Educational Research* 44:217-23; November 1950.

PERDEW, Philip W. "History of Education and the Educational Professions." *Educational Forum* 12:311-23; March 1948.

PETERS, R. S. *Brett's History of Psychology.* Edited and Abridged. New York: Macmillan Co., 1953.

PIPER, Raymond F., and WARD, Paul W. *The Fields and Methods of Knowledge.* New York: Alfred A. Knopf, 1929. Chapter 6, "History," p. 117-33.

PLANCK, MAX. *Scientific Autobiography and Other Papers.* New York: Philosophical Library, 1949. 192 p.

"Plans for the Historiography of the United States in World War II." *American Historical Review* 49:243-52; January 1944.

PLEKHANOV, G. V. *In Defense of Materialism:* The Development of the Monist View of History. London: Lawrence and Wishart, 1948. 303 p.

PLEKHANOV, G. V. *Materialist Conception of History.* London: Lawrence and Wishart, 1941. 64 p.

POSTAN, M. M. *Historical Method in Social Science.* New York: Macmillan Co., 1939. 38 p.

QUALEY, Carlton C. "Recent Scholarship and Interpretation in American History." *Social Education* 15:217-22; May 1951.

READ, Conyers. "The Social Responsibilities of the Historian." *American Historical Review* 55:275-85; January 1950.

REIFF, Henry. "Historiography and Government Research." *Journal of Higher Education* 22:129-37; March 1951.

REISNER, E. H. "The History of Education as a Source of Fundamental Assumptions in Education." *Educational Administration and Supervision* 24:378-84; September 1928.

REMMLEIN, Madaline K. *The Law of Local Public School Administration.* New York: McGraw-Hill Book Co., 1953. xi + 271 p.

REMMLEIN, Madaline K. *School Law.* New York: McGraw-Hill Book Co., 1950. xxi + 376 p.

REMMLEIN, Madaline K. "Tools and Procedures in School Law Research." *Growing Points in Educational Research.* Washington: American Educational Research Association, 1949. p. 166-75.

RENIER, Gustaaf J. *History:* Its Purpose and Method. London: George Allen and Unwin, 1950. 271 p.

RICE, S. A., and Others. *Methods in Social Science.* Chicago: University of Chicago Press, 1931. xiv + 822 p.

RIDER, Fremont. *The Scholar and the Future of the Research Library.* New York: Hadham Press, 1944. 249 p.

ROBACK, A. A. *History of American Psychology.* New York: Library Publishers, 1952. xiv + 426 p.

ROBINSON, James H. *The New History:* Essays Illustrating the Modern Historical Outlook. New York: Macmillan Co., 1912. vii + 266 p.

ROBINSON, James H. "Newer Ways of Historians." *American Historical Review* 35:245-55; January 1930.

ROWSE, A. L. *The Use of History.* New York: Macmillan Co., 1948. ix + 247 p.

RUGG, Harold. *Foundations for American Education.* Yonkers-on-Hudson, N. Y.: World Book Co., 1947. 826 p.

RUSSELL, Bertrand. *A History of Western Philosophy.* New York: Simon and Schuster, 1945. xxiii + 895 p.

SALVEMINI, G. *Historian and Scientist:* An Essay on the Nature of History and the Social Sciences. Cambridge: Harvard University Press, 1939. x + 203 p.

SANDERS, Chauncey. *An Introduction to Research in English Literary History.* New York: Macmillan Co., 1952. vi + 423 p.

SARTON, George. *A Guide to the History of Science.* Waltham, Mass.: Chronica Botanica Co., 1952. xvii + 316 p.

SARTON, George. *A History of Science:* Ancient Science through the Golden Age of Greece. Cambridge: Harvard University Press, 1952. xxvi + 646 p.

SARTON, George. *The Life of Science.* New York: Henry Schuman, 1948. vii + 197 p.

SARTON, George. "Seventy-third Critical Bibliography of the History and Philosophy of Science and of the History of Civilization (to November 1948)." *Isis* 40:124-88; May 1949.

SCATES, Douglas E. "Library Resources and Documentary Research," in "Methods of Research and Appraisal in Education." *Review of Educational Research* 15:336-51; December 1945.

SCHMIDT, Wilhelm. *The Culture Historical Method of Ethnology:* The Scientific Approach to the Racial Question. New York: Fortuny's, 1939. xxx + 383 p.

SCHMITT, B. E., Editor. *Some Historians of Modern Europe:* Essays in Historiography by Former Students of the Department of History of the University of Chicago. Chicago: University of Chicago Press, 1942. ix + 533 p.

SCHRECKER, Paul. *Work and History:* An Essay on the Structure of Civilization. Princeton: Princeton University Press, 1948. xviii + 322 p.

SCHWARTZ, Emil. *Philosophy of History.* Boston: Christopher, 1940. 98 p.

SELIGMAN, Edwin R. A. *The Economic Interpretation of History.* New York: Columbia University Press, 1924. ix + 166 p.

SELIGMAN, Edwin R. A., and JOHNSON, Alvin, Editors. *Encyclopedia of the Social Sciences.* New York: Macmillan Co., 1930-1934. 15 vols.

SHANAS, Ethel. "The American Journal of Sociology through Fifty Years." *American Journal of Sociology* 50:522-33; May 1945.

SHANNON, David A. "Facts, Dates, and History." *Teachers College Record* 54:159-64; December 1952.

SHILS, Edward A., and FINCH, Henry A. *Max Weber on the Methodology of the Social Sciences.* Glencoe, Ill.: Free Press, 1949. xvii + 188 p.

SHOTWELL, J. T. *The History of History.* Vol. 1. New York: Columbia University Press, 1939. xiv + 407 p.

SMITH, Henry L. *Educational Research, Principles and Practices.* Bloomington, Ind.: Educational Publications, 1944. p. 110-22.

SPAHR, W. E., and SWENSON, R. J. *Methods and Status of Scientific Research.* New York: Harper and Bros., 1930. xxii + 534 p.

SPEARMAN, C. *Psychology Down the Ages.* Vols. 1, 2. London: Macmillan and Co., 1937. xii + 454, viii + 355 p.

SPIEGEL, Henry W., Editor. *The Development of Economic Thought.* New York: John Wiley and Sons, 1952. xii + 811 p.

SPIELMAN, William C. *Introduction to Sources of American History.* New York: Exposition Press, 1951. 175 p.

STAVISKY, Leonard P. "Forgotten Canons of Historical Writing: Reappraisal of Edward Gibbon." *Social Studies* 40:147-50; April 1949.

STEPHAN, Frederick F. "History of the Uses of Modern Sampling Procedures." *Journal of the American Statistical Association* 43:12-39; March 1948.

STRAUS, William L. "The Great Piltdown Hoax." *Science* 119:265-69; February 26, 1954.

STRAYER, Joseph R., Editor. *The Interpretation of History.* Second Edition. New York: Peter Smith, 1950. 186 p.

TAYLOR, A. M. "A Vitalistic Philosophy of History." *Journal of Social Philosophy* 11:137-80; January 1941.

TAYLOR, H. *History as a Science.* London: Methuen, 1933. vii + 138 p.

TAYLOR, H. O. *Historian's Creed.* Cambridge: Harvard University Press, 1939. 137 p.

TEGGART, F. J. *Theory and Process of History.* Berkeley: University of California, 1941. x + 323 p.

THILLY, Frank. *A History of Philosophy.* Revised by Ledger Wood. New York: Henry Holt and Co., 1951. xx + 658 p.

THOMPSON, James W., and HOLM, Bernard J. *A History of Historical Writing.* New York: Macmillan Co., 1942. xvi + 676, x + 674 p. 2 vols.

THURSFIELD, Richard E., Editor. *The Study and Teaching of American History.* Seventeenth Yearbook, National Council for the Social Studies. Washington: The Council, 1947. xviii + 442 p.

TOMARS, A. S. "Some Problems in the Sociologist's Use of Anthropology." *American Sociological Review* 8:625-34; December 1943.

TOYNBEE, Arnold J. *A Study of History.* 6 vols. London: Oxford University Press, 1934-39. Abridgement by D. C. Somervell, 1947.

ULICH, Robert. *History of Educational Thought.* New York: American Book Co., 1945. xii + 412 p.

VINCENT, J. M. *Aids to Historical Research.* New York: D. Appleton-Century Co., 1935. vii + 173 p.

VINCENT, J. M. *Historical Research:* An Outline of Theory and Practice. New York: Henry Holt and Co., 1911. 350 p.

VISHER, Stephen S. *Scientists Starred, 1903-1943 in "American Men of Science."* Baltimore: Johns Hopkins Press, 1947. London: Oxford University Press, 1947. xxiii + 556 p.

WARE, Caroline F., Editor. *Cultural Approach to History.* New York: Columbia University Press, 1940. x + 359 p.

WATSON, Robert I. "A Brief History of Clinical Psychology." *Psychological Bulletin* 50:321-46; September 1953.

WEBB, Sidney, and WEBB, Beatrice. *Methods of Social Study*. New York: Longmans, Green and Co., 1932. vii + 263 p.

WERKMEISTER, W. H. *A History of Philosophical Ideas in America*. New York: Ronald Press Co., 1949. xvi + 599 p.

WHEELER, H. F. B. *This Thing Called History*. London: Macdonald and Co., 1945. ix + 156 p.

WHITNEY, F. L. *The Elements of Research*. Third Edition. New York: Prentice-Hall, 1950. p. 192-209.

WILEY, Earl W. "State History and Rhetorical Research." *Quarterly Journal of Speech* 36:514-19; December 1950.

WILLIAMS, C. H. *Modern Historian*. New York: Thomas Nelson, 1938. 318 p.

WITTELS, Fritz. "Economic and Psychological Historiography." *American Journal of Sociology* 51:527-32; May 1946.

WOODY, Thomas. "Of History and Its Method." *Journal of Experimental Education* 15:175-201; March 1947.

WRIGHT, John K., and PLATT, Elizabeth T. *Aids to Geographical Research*. New York: Columbia University Press, 1947. xii + 331 p.

YOUNG, Louise M. *Thomas Carlyle and the Art of History*. Philadelphia: University of Pennsylvania Press, 1939. 219 p.

YOUNG, Pauline V. *Scientific Social Surveys and Research*. Second Edition. New York: Prentice-Hall, 1949. Chapter 8.

ZACHARIAS, H. C. E. *Protohistory*. St. Louis: B. Herder Book Co., 1947. vii + 391 p.

ZEUNER, Frederick E. *Dating the Past:* An Introduction to Geochronology. Second Edition. New York: Longmans, Green and Co., 1950. 474 p.

ZNANIECKI, Florian. *The Method of Sociology*. New York: Farrar and Rinehart, 1934. 338 p.

ZUCKER, Morris. *The Philosophy of American History*. Vol. 1, *The Historical Field Theory*. New York: Arnold-Howard Publishing Co., 1945. xxii + 694 p.

# 5

# The Descriptive Method:
## GENERAL DESCRIPTION

CHAPTER 5 IN its several parts presents at length the broader theoretical aspects of the descriptive method (sometimes characterized as a survey or normative approach to the study of conditions). Concepts and procedures of general description, analysis, and classification are discussed and illustrated in considerable detail. The scope of this book and space limitations do not permit a similar treatment of the types of descriptive investigation that may be labeled enumeration, measurement, and evaluation, except as illustrated briefly and incidentally in the discussion of data-gathering instruments and procedures in Chapter 6.

## INTRODUCTION

For constructive thinking about practical affairs, knowledge of the existing situation is essential. One may have standards which he wishes to maintain in his work; he must obtain facts concerning his tasks in order to know whether he is keeping close to those standards. One may have goals to which he aspires; to make plans for reaching these goals, he must find out what the present situation is, in order to know where to begin. A survey of present conditions is an essential guide to one's thinking, whether in evaluating the course he is now following, or in embarking on a new venture. For any purpose, the starting point is important.

In any dynamic situation, however, facts concerning the existing conditions are only one part of the picture. The second important part is the conditions desired. For example, in judging the work we do, we need not only information describing the work itself, but we must also have standards with which to compare the level of work. The goals which direct effort toward a new level are as important (basic) as the starting point or the present status of progress; one determines his whereabouts not only in terms of what he is near and how far he has come but also in terms of where he wishes to go. Hence, the norms and goals that one accepts must be clear and definite if they are to be sound guides. We must find ways of translating criteria into various practical working terms for assessing status if they are to be workable and effective. Further, we may wish to review and reanalyze our conceptions and statements of these criteria as we gain more experience with them and can judge them better. Criteria may need to be reëxamined also as other conditions change and place them in a new light.

When we know where we are at present and where we wish to be, a third kind of knowledge is needed. This is concerned with how to get where we wish to be. Such knowledge is gained mainly from studies that deal with causation. Descriptive studies, however, have an important part to play even in developing this kind of understanding. For example, one must always be concerned with structure and with properties, whether he is dealing with the materials and forces of physical and biological science or with the groups and dynamics of social science. Description tells us what we reckon with. Further, it is becoming clear that, through noting the coincidence of certain conditions and certain apparent consequences, survey studies furnish valuable clues as to cause-effect relationships. In both these ways descriptive studies help us in learning how to accomplish desired purposes.

In addition to these matters, we all have a general need for knowing what the world is like, simply in order to live in it, to try to understand it, to make adjustments to reality, to carry on our daily work. Much of the necessary knowledge for these purposes comes from direct experience. On the other hand, few persons can have enough direct experience with the wide variety of cultures and living conditions over the face of the world to have knowledge of the great diversity of ways in which mankind lives. Hence, detailed accounts by persons who can have such contacts are essential to afford us adequate background for appreciating what one or another group has, and for understanding the richness and variety of human cultures.

In order to meet the demands for knowledge along these various lines, a rather large variety of forms of descriptive study have been developed. Some of these are fairly simple, others are elaborate; certain ones are mainly on the level of common sense and general experience, whereas others are highly technical and involve theory.

## NATURE AND USES OF DESCRIPTIVE STUDIES

The preceding paragraphs have indicated in the large how descriptive studies serve mankind. It may be appropriate here to treat the subject in somewhat more detail. What are these descriptive studies like? For what are they used? In what way do they contribute to science?

It should be rather obvious that the administrator, who is charged with the responsibility for the work under his supervision, is constantly in need of information as to the conditions in his school or school system. Much of this information comes by word of mouth or by personal visitation and observations; but a moment's reflection will suggest that a great deal of the information needed cannot be obtained in this way. To take a simple example, the superintendent does not ordinarily have direct contact with the classrooms of his school system each day as a means of knowing the pupil attendance; so he sets up a reporting system that will enable him, by reading summary figures, to keep in touch with this factor and to take action when special attention seems to be needed. Further, on the basis of these figures he can make the required reports to the state department of education, can answer the requests of the United States Office of Education in its biennial surveys, and can contribute to other studies concerning attendance.

When the gathering of data has been set up into a system of reporting which is maintained constantly, we will not refer to such reporting as a study. If, however, the same data were gathered especially to meet a request, and if the results were utilized in certain frames of thought, then the preparing of the report forms, the reporting of the data, the summarizing, the analyzing, and interpretation would, all together, constitute a descriptive study. For example, the superintendent or the board of education might want to know about the size of the classes in the schools. Possibly the interest in this subject originated with the teachers, who communicated with the superintendent about the matter. Nobody is likely to take any action without having definite facts. How many classes are there of each different size? Is overcrowding something that can be handled by changes within one or two schools, or is it a general problem in all of the schools? Is the average class size above or below that for the state as a whole, or for similar communities in the state? Are the taxpayers of the district willing to spend more money to reduce the number of pupils per teacher? Is the problem one which requires additional school housing as a remedy? When these and other relevant facts are in hand, a decision for action can be made. The gathering of these varied facts which describe the status of the school system in these respects will constitute one or more studies.

Studies that describe various aspects of school work are of value to persons other than administrators. When the teacher gives a test to his class, he is, in effect, making a descriptive study of the status of the class, probably both of the individual pupils in the group and (through calculating an average) of the class as a whole. We would not ordinarily formalize the giving of a test by referring to it as a study, but when the task is done with unusual thoroughness (as by giving and comparing a number of tests), when the results are subjected to unusually careful analysis and are fitted into certain searching frames of thought so as to answer questions of special interest, we could refer to the undertaking as a study.

Descriptive studies are of large value in providing facts on which professional judgments may be based. For example, how can one think intelligently about the curriculum which is appropriate for the American high school if he does not know that most high schools are small? Consider how elementary-school teaching is benefited by our increasing knowledge of the nature of eight-year-old children (their habits, interests, abilities and capacities, reaction patterns, and language development). Secondary-school teaching, the curriculum, and guidance functions have been changed markedly by our increasing knowledge of the adolescent, his problems in maturing into adult status, and his general outlook for life. Or think of the movement known as life-adjustment education, which accepts as a major point of reference the adolescent's very natural query, "What's in it for me?" "What does studying this particular required subject mean for my future, in terms of values I hold, rather than in terms of what somebody else wants to push on me?" We operate our adult world primarily in terms of self-interest (of individuals and of groups); as we gain more understanding of the adolescent we are coming to see that he, like the rest of us, has strong self-interest. With such increasing insight, our practices change accordingly. We may not be conscious of the part descriptive research is playing in our everyday educational work, but the accumulating body of facts nevertheless affects educational practice with the force of a great tide.

Descriptive studies contribute to science because they afford penetrating insights into the nature of what one is dealing with, perhaps what he is trying to study in other ways. When we wish to develop more complex forms of scientific understanding, we will fit these descriptive facts into more complex frames of relationship. For example, by observing children of different ages we can differentiate our findings according to age and obtain some picture of the trend of development. By relating our descriptive observations to the presence or absence (or the strength) of certain other conditions, we can gain knowledge of causal relationships. Descriptive studies provide essential knowledge about the nature of objects and persons; and they contribute again at recurring intervals as our science grows from one cycle, or level of insight, to another.

There is another and very fundamental way in which descriptive studies make their contribution to science. They help fashion many of the tools with which we do research. Specifically, they play a large part in the development of instruments for the measurement of many things, instruments that are employed in all types of quantitative research. The development of data-gathering instruments, including schedules, check lists, score cards, and rating scales, will be treated at some length in the chapter which follows; we wish here merely to point out that they are instruments of description and that descriptive studies contribute to their development in two ways—first through creating directly a demand for them, and second through providing the normative, standardizing procedures by which the scales are evaluated and calibrated.

Perhaps this is the appropriate place to point out that certain studies of standards or values—not those representing a chain of philosophical reasoning, but those providing a more direct assessment—fall in the class of descriptive studies. These may be of several kinds. The simplest form is the furnishing of normative standards based on what is prevalent or what common practice does. These standards are simply averages or percentile points from a set of data representing current conditions. Test norms are of this sort; so are standards with regard to the average number of square feet of playground space needed per elementary-school child. Another form of standards is those which are set through describing schools believed to follow good practices. Certain score cards and rating scales are of this type. A third type of standards is to be found in those scales (such as a handwriting scale) which consist of specimens arranged in order according to the judgments of a group of persons. A fourth form of normative material represents the direct expressions of many people—what they want, what they like, what they prefer. Public-opinion polls and attitude surveys are of this type. When instruments have been developed along such lines as these, and the supporting body of representative data has been established, the two together may be employed to secure a far more accurate assessment of the appropriateness or desirability of some practice, condition, or specimen than general judgment by itself is likely to do.

## COMMENT ON TERMINOLOGY

What we are characterizing as descriptive investigations includes all of those studies that purport to present facts concerning the nature and status of anything—a group of persons, a number of objects, a set of conditions, a class of events, a system of thought, or any other kind of phenomena which one may wish to study. The investigations herein described are sometimes referred to as *status studies*. In other instances, *normative studies,* meaning those which establish standards through the study of what is prevalent, or the term *surveys,* is applied. Sometimes the label *normative-survey* is used to combine both of the foregoing ideas, with respect to data relating to standards and to status. The term *descriptive studies* is employed here as being somewhat more general and more encompassing than any of the others.

One sometimes hears the phrase, "the comparative method." While it is true that the great majority of descriptive studies do involve comparison, it is something like "putting the cart before the horse" to emphasize this aspect. Comparing is simply one of the things that normally is done with descriptive data after they have been gathered. Comparison is a continuation of the descriptive process; through comparison we find additional meaning in the status of any phenomenon. Comparison is, therefore, a means of rounding out the description.

Although almost all forms of research might be considered in a broad sense as descriptive studies, such extended application is likely to take the distinctive meaning from the term. It seems better to restrict the term to those studies which are concerned with general nature and standing (in the scale of human values) and with a particular time. It is of course possible to extend descriptive studies across an interval of time, by taking observations at different points of time and then forming trends, with curves, cycles, and wave patterns. One can regard such form of observation or analysis simply as comparisons of data that represent status at different times. The argument can be advanced that they provide *norms of change,* just as the data for any single point of time may constitute a norm for condition or status. Whether one wishes to include such investigations under the scope of descriptive studies or place them in a separate category, such as *sequential studies* or *developmental* (genetic) *studies,* is somewhat a matter of debate. This procedure or approach may be referred to occasionally in the present chapter, but will not be given extended treatment. These studies have a more or less distinctive set of interests, but do not involve peculiar problems of a technical nature beyond the making of status investigations (descriptive) in such a way as to yield comparable data at different times. (Attention may appropriately be directed to the chapter on genetic, growth, and developmental investigations.)

Descriptive studies are to be thought of as somewhat in contrast to what may be termed explanatory studies. The latter may describe how a change takes place, but they also try to explain it. Thus, while such investigations (dealing with dynamic relationships, and often termed causal studies) may be thought of as a kind of description, they are something more than description—just as in English composition, exposition is recognized as a form different from description. The purpose of the explanatory study is not simply to portray facts, but rather to relate a sequence of facts in a way that makes them intelligible and which accounts for a given result in terms of antecedent steps that one can recognize and understand. Thus explanation is frequently drawn on to account for some existing condition, either now or in the past. Historical studies fall in this class, and include general history, educational history in particular, genetic studies, and case studies. Outside our immediate field of interest, historical geology (which seeks to account for the present state of the physical world in terms of known geological principles), and dynamic astronomy (which seeks to explain the birth and subsequent history of stars), are good examples of the explanatory processes of physical science.

Explanatory studies, in combination with experimental studies, carry the burden of finding adequate causes, of assessing the effects of these causes, and of describing the mechanisms (the necessary structures and the chain of events) by or through which causes act. Although the purposes of such studies do contain elements of description, their principal aim is much broader; they seek to account for change. Hence, there need be no confusion with the more limited class with which we are dealing in the present chapter under the term *descriptive studies*.

## PLAN OF PRESENTATION

Because of the very large number and variety of descriptive studies, it seems appropriate to divide them into certain types and to treat each type separately. In doing so, there is no presumption that the classes here employed are fundamental; they are used simply to group together those forms which can be treated together and to aid the reader in locating discussions that may be of immediate interest to him. The investigations are divided on a somewhat mechanical basis, but have some logical basis of similarity.

The sections which follow will accordingly deal with various types of descriptive study under the headings of general description, analysis, and classification. General description will be treated in the pages immediately following. Analysis and classification will be discussed in the two succeeding parts of Chapter 5. In presenting each of these types an attempt will be made to analyze the underlying rationale (the purpose, the supporting logical structure, and the kinds of serviceability). Selected examples will be given to illustrate concepts and procedures. A discussion of the construction of instruments by which data may be gathered for the purposes of descriptive studies will be presented in the chapter that follows.

Other forms of description, represented in such processes as enumeration, measurement, and evaluation, are left for appropriate treatment in the many texts that deal with statistical methods, measurement, and appraisal. The omission of these topics here is not in any sense a suggestion of lack of importance but is rather a division of labor. The present treatment will emphasize those aspects of descriptive method which commonly do not find a place in the various texts on quantitative methods.

## GENERAL DESCRIPTION AS A FORM OF RESEARCH

In going through school a student has many occasions to write papers on one or another subject. As he advances, his writing becomes more mature; it is more specific, more accurate, has greater depth, and deals with subjects which older persons normally think about. The graduate student may inquire whether research is simply an extension of this maturing process. This question is particularly appropriate as one enters upon the present section of the chapter, where the material dealt with is not highly technical.

The answer is that while research should have the characteristics of mature thought and writing, these are not in themselves sufficient. Research is not just serious writing. Essays, logical expositions, arguments, and various other forms which present the personal thoughts and convictions of the writer do not ordinarily come within the class of research. Research requires data, observations which are factual. By this, we mean that the data should be accurate and devoid of immediate interpretations that are peculiar to the individual. They should be such that other skilled observers would agree to them. Having a set of carefully gathered relevant data as the basis for one's writing is one of the presumptions of research. Accordingly, research does not consist of pure essays; it is not statements which one makes because he is personally convinced that they are true; but rather it is statements based on facts which competent observers are likely to recognize as facts.

The purpose of research is to find new truth. This "truth" may have many different forms, such as increased quantity of knowledge, a new generalization or new "law," an increased insight into factors which are operating, the discovery of a new causal or modifying relationship, a more accurate formulation of the problem to be solved, and so on. The person who thinks of research as a matter of making an outline and then beginning to write must stop to consider that his plans almost always must include the gathering of data. (The exceptions occur when some other worker turns over his raw material for a second analysis.)

It may come as something of a shock to note how many times in life one talks as if he could make things true just by saying them, particularly by saying them with considerable emphasis and increasing self-conviction. In many of life's situations the force or conviction with which one speaks helps determine the effect on other persons of what one has to say. But force is utterly of no avail in helping truth to be born, and wanting ever so much for things to turn out a certain way does not in itself change the objective situation. Just writing, therefore, however skillfully done, does not in itself constitute research.

Most research is characterized by a variety of quantitative material and is fairly easy to recognize. In the present section, however, we are dealing with a type of study which is not to any marked extent quantitative, but is primarily a matter of verbal description. In this connection there are probably two questions that come to mind: What kind of data does one gather in non-quantitative studies? Why are some descriptions thought of as research and others not? These questions form the background for the discussion which follows immediately.

**The role of non-quantitative data.** There are occasions in research when one may justifiably rely on verbal, or fairly general, statements of fact. These occasions grow in part out of the nature of the material and in part out of the purposes for which one is doing research. One is likely to gather verbal (rather than precise quantitative) facts when he is recording fairly complex aspects of a situation, when he is interested mainly in indicating the general nature of conditions, and is content to point out the difference between one case and another in qualitative terms. Even though theoretically all differences of quality can be resolved into differences in the quantities of defined elements, the attempt to express complex conditions in quantitative form is often entirely beyond the limits of convenience, practicality, or need. Think how much easier it is to recognize one's dwelling place by the common points of visual familiarity than by a legal description of the plot on which it stands (the latter devolving heavily on quantities, but being almost unintelligible to most persons). Or, in referring to an automobile, does one not find it more convenient to name the make of the auto than to give almost innumerable figures in an attempt to express its every aspect quantitatively? Think for example of the great labor in describing quantitatively the curves of a single side! For purposes of refined technical consideration and comparison, the use of detailed quantities is demanded, but more general purposes may be served by non-quantitative description.

As a determiner of the kind of facts that are gathered, the attitude and interests of the research worker also will play some part. Many persons have a fondness for words, often with an accompanying dislike for figures, or vice versa. Such attitudes grow out of past experience with the two types of material, perhaps a series of successes or failures with one type, so that a person has a strong preference for a certain type of material, buttressed by feelings of "at homeness" and accustomed success. These attitudes are subject to change as one's experiences vary with the passage of time, but the predisposition of the worker may often determine his choice of problems or the nature of his attack on them. The method of general description should not, however, be chosen on negative grounds—because one feels that he does not know anything else. As one proceeds through his graduate work, he is expected to acquire some understanding of specialized techniques of research. If he chooses general description, it should be on a positive basis: because the problem he desires to work on can best be treated in this manner, or because his previous experience indicates that he can do especially well with this sort of attack.

One should not be too easily content. The foregoing treatment is not meant to suggest that ordinarily one can do "just as well" by employing words as by utilizing quantities. Usually both are called for. Figures add an element of definiteness which cannot be fully supplied by non-quantitative description. The progress of scientific knowledge (in both the social and the physical fields) is accompanied by an increased use of specific, quantified facts. It is common for scientific ideas to start as rough, uncertain notions, expressible in only the most general terms, and in a generation, or perhaps a century later, become a set of highly specific, quantified interrelationships expressible in terms of a formula. One can go just so far with verbal description; to go further, one must employ quantities. Number is part of progress.

Perhaps it is in order to note that even though many persons are inclined to choose verbal types of material because they are "afraid of" figures, quantitative studies frequently prove simpler and easier to handle. Research has rather exacting requirements for accurate, specific statements, limited to supportable facts. These requirements are in sharp contrast to the easy-going, vague, impressionistic, and irresponsible types of speaking and writing which make up most of our informal communication. When one comes face to face with the demands of research, he may conclude that his preference for verbal data was based on a mistaken concept of easiness. Penetrating, sharply discriminating thought and observation are called for in research, and often these are more easily obtained (or at least simulated) by the use of well defined, somewhat standardized concepts used in quantitative work than when left open to the general judgment and free interpretation of the individual.

**Examples of non-quantitative description.** In keeping with what has been said, for research that depends on verbal data one would look in areas where aspects of structure and variation are complex, and where the description and the differentiation are satisfactorily dealt with by words, rather than by measurement with uniform units. Studies in comparative education [1] furnish rather satisfactory examples. When one wishes to describe the educational conditions and practices in another country, he is likely to resort largely to verbal description. This is primarily because his interest is mainly on this level of generality. Some figures probably will find a place in these descriptions; that fact need not rule them out of the present class of general description, since any actual study is likely to cut across the different classes of research set up in a textbook. But, allowing for such quantitative material as the number of children enrolled, the amount of money spent, and so on, the bulk of the description for foreign (or even native) school systems will be verbal.[2] This does not mean merely that the bulk of the report is verbal; that is true of almost any research report. It means that the preponderance of the basic data (facts) will be verbal.

One who is unaccustomed to such work may inquire, "What do you mean by verbal data?" Let us suppose that one has gone to another country to study its school system. Perhaps he is in the office of the national minister of education. He is asking such questions as, "What is the underlying national philosophy with regard to education? What are the purposes which education is expected to serve? What subjects are emphasized in the curriculum? What is the essential psychology that guides the teaching of these subjects? How are school districts determined (if there are such)? What is the administrative organization within the nation, or within its subdivisions? How is the education of teachers provided?" and so on, until he has enough material to prepare his description. The answers to these questions, recorded at once in one's notebook and verified by further interviews, observations, review, and reading, constitute verbal data.

Within our own land also the opportunities for descriptive and comparative studies of this general type are virtually without limit. Suppose, for example, one wished to make a study of compulsory education in the forty-eight states. Whether he undertook to describe the administrative machinery which had been set up to enforce the laws, or to analyze the various provisions contained in the laws, or to outline the different social and educational philosophies underlying legislation, he would rely primarily

---

[1] A large number of examples, together with a description of the values of such studies, their special research requirements, and references to orienting literature are given in the article on "Comparative Education," R. H. Eckelberry in the *Encyclopedia of Educational Research*, 1950. The *Education Index* uses the heading "Education, Comparative." For articles describing education in foreign countries (without an emphasis on comparison), see the heading "Education," with subheads for particular countries in the geographical series of subheads.

[2] Texts with illustrations of this type of description will be found in the dozen or so bulletins published by the Division of Comparative Education of the United States Office of Education during the 1940's. These dealt mostly with Latin America, and also included Japan. An easy way to locate such a group of bulletins intact is to consult the Price List on educational publications issued by the Superintendent of Documents of the Government Printing Office, Washington 25, D. C.

on verbal (rather than numerical) forms of information as his basic data. The same thing is true if one were to make a study of the functions of the departments of education in the different states. One may, in fact, find an interesting example of such a report in a publication by the United States Office of Education.[3] In this report there are four tables of the usual sort for summarizing purposes, but there are thirty-three tables of the presence-or-absence sort. These tables contain check marks to indicate those functions which were performed in the department of a given state. Such tables are non-quantitative and may be regarded simply as a short-cut form of statement. The combination of these with an analytical and explanatory text represents a form of verbal description which is unusually systematic and highly specific. It is the next thing to a quantitative treatment, while not relinquishing the flexibility and the intimacy of general description.

Literature containing research reports in education, in psychology, or in sociology will furnish examples in many areas in which verbal description constitutes the basis of the studies. In psychology, for instance, it will be recalled that although Wilhelm Wundt initiated and emphasized laboratory work, he also pointed out that "folk psychology" or the general culture and values held by the people constituted an important second field of psychological study.[4] Obviously the latter would be primarily of the verbal sort. (It may be interesting to note that one of the major divisions of material in *Psychological Abstracts* is currently entitled "Social Psychology.") We would expect to find a large dependence on verbal data in such psychological studies as the following: A descriptive catalogue of play activities common among six-year-old children; acts of aggression found among boys on the school play ground; personal problems brought to a camp counselor by adolescent girls; the content of beginning courses in psychology as offered in American colleges; the psychological impact of bombing raids on a large city; description of certain elements of the nervous system as revealed through physiological studies; an analysis of similarities and differences in the psychoanalytic systems of Freud, Jung, and Adler.

Among sociological studies will be found a great many which rely on general descriptive approaches. Leading sociological magazines contain many research articles that fall in this class, even though there is a strong proportion of studies with data and relationships in quantitative form.[5]

---

[3] Fred F. Beach and Others, *The Functions of the State Departments of Education.* Office of Education Miscellaneous Publication No. 12. Washington: Government Printing Office, 1950. 70 p.

[4] Wilhelm Wundt, *Elements of Folk Psychology.* Translated by Edward Le Roy Schaud. London: G. Allen and Unwin; New York: Macmillan Co., 1916. 532 p.

[5] One may wish to consult the indexes which are available for two of the leading sociological magazines: *American Journal of Sociology,* Index for volumes 1—52, 1895-1947; and *American Sociological Review,* Index for volumes 1—15, 1936-1950.

Many of the understandings we would like to possess in connection with such fields as anthropology, the structure and functioning of society, and particularized aspects of culture represent forms of knowledge having a breadth and a complexity which must of necessity lean heavily on verbal description. This need for general description should be apparent in such subjects as the following:

1. Family and environmental backgrounds of twenty persons who became school superintendents in large cities
2. Contemporary changes in the pattern of economic functions of the family in the United States
3. The redirection of educational goals in small cities in the state of Washington
4. Factors contributing to racial tension in Detroit
5. Sociological aspects of adult-education programs in Los Angeles
6. Childhood determinants of later personality traits as observed among a certain tribe of Indians in Arizona
7. The sweat system in the garment trades of Chicago
8. Inferences regarding certain aspects of culture as deduced from designs on art objects
9. Contrasting marriage customs among three native tribes in Central America.

A monumental classic of the general descriptive type is *The Polish Peasant*.[6] This deals in large part with problems of adjusting to new social conditions. The basic source of the data was documents—letters written by Poles, autobiographies, correspondence published in newspapers, and records of various social agencies. Chosen by the Social Science Research Council as one of a series of studies for formal evaluation,[7] this study became the center of much interest with respect to its methodology and the methodology of sociological research in general.

The critical discussion of this investigation raised questions that are pertinent to all broad descriptive studies, including history, which almost necessarily posit either explicitly or implicitly a certain conceptual pattern that serves both for selecting the data from the original sources and for imbuing the data with an explanatory or integrating principle. This principle helps account for the observations and presumably could be used as a general basis for prediction in the future. Whether such conceptual frames could be verified by the data adduced, or whether other interpretative schemes would be more closely supported by the data, is a basic question. There is usually no sure answer. The problem, however, is not peculiar to social science; the physical sciences have faced such problems of inter-

[6] W. I. Thomas and Florian Znaniecki, *The Polish Peasant in Europe and America.* Originally published by Richard C. Badger, Boston, 1918-1920. 5 v. Out of print.
[7] Herbert Blumer, *An Appraisal of Thomas and Znaniecki's "The Polish Peasant in Europe and America."* Critiques of Research in the Social Sciences, I. New York: Social Science Research Council, 1939. 210 p.

pretation for a long time. Note, for example, the controversy over the basic nature of light, now nearly three centuries old. Two rival conceptions seem to be equally well supported by observations. And the nature of the nucleus of the atom is currently in great uncertainty.

It will be apparent that certain of these studies might also be classed under other headings, or dealt with elsewhere in the present text. For example, some of them would be regarded as history, and others as case study or investigations of growth and development. Some will necessarily verge on the analytical, since all description is to some extent analytical.

**Characteristics of non-quantitative research.** It was noted earlier in this chapter that not all descriptive writing is to be characterized as research, and it may be helpful at this point to be more explicit on where we would draw the dividing line. What is the difference between an ordinary descriptive paper and one which might be called a research report? What are the factors which one should watch, if he wishes his writing to be thought of as research?

It must be stated at once that non-quantitative research is the most difficult to identify and to differentiate from an ordinary essay or other personal treatments. Studies having some depth and seriousness of purpose are easily recognized as research when they are based on counting and measurement; that is, when they are supported by technical procedures. We have more trouble in differentiation when it comes to studies that lack these quantitative characteristics—which may seem to be nothing more than "looking and writing." We shall not attempt here to deal with the general question of the difference between all research and casual experience, but only with the differentiation so far as it affects descriptive writing.

It may be more interesting to derive the answers by considering actual examples of research. Let us turn first to a report which bears some of the more common aspects of research studies. For this purpose we may use a bulletin from the United States Office of Education dealing with vocational technical training.[8] This survey is concerned, first of all, with the extent of the work opportunities for persons having technical training of less than college grade. It lists the kinds of work (occupations) on this level to be found in each of twenty-two industries. It also describes present educational facilities available for giving the needed training. The data were gathered in the field in various states, through interview and by consulting documents—payroll lists, job descriptions, and training catalogues. Published reports and correspondence furnished other facts. The data are

---

[8] U. S. Office of Education, Consulting Committee on Vocational-Technical Training, *Vocational-Technical Training for Industrial Occupations.* Vocational Division Bulletin No. 228. Washington: Government Printing Office, 1944. 307 p.

almost entirely verbal; only one table is based on observations; four tables are taken from other sources as background material.

What are the characteristics of this study that would lead one to think of it as research rather than as a more casual or routine piece of work? An analysis of the report will reveal the following characteristics:

1.  New data were gathered. That is, the study does not depend on secondary sources (except in minor part). Although it is not essential that a study gather fresh data in order to be considered research, the fact that original observations are made is a major consideration. Such data are in themselves often something of a contribution, even before analysis.

2.  The concept of the trait being studied (vocational-technical training) is carefully defined. The first chapter of the report is given to this; sixteen characteristics are noted. (See also p. 138-39.) This step is a matter of clarity which any truly scientific investigation will take pains to include.

3.  The procedure followed in making the study is described at length. This comprises Chapter 2 of the report. Again, this is an important part of regular research.

4.  The study is related to its social background. Chapter 3 discusses trends in a number of factors which bear on the growing need for this kind of training. This discussion augments and supports the findings that are presented later.

5.  The data (in terms of kinds of work opportunities in each industry) are specific and definite, and are presented in systematic fashion.

6.  The data appear to have been competently gathered. Mature workers with training and experience in vocational education did the interviewing and consulted the records. The study was at all times under the close direction of career workers in this field.

7.  Auxiliary data which throw light on the conditions or which give added meaning to the facts are presented frequently.

8.  The data are summarized and interpreted. The meaning of the data for educational practice is given in a series of thirty-six conclusions and recommendations (Chapter 7).

9.  Needs for further research are described. This is not a necessary condition, but it adds to the research contribution.

10.  The report was reviewed by ten experts in vocational education, which gives the reader additional assurance that the conclusions are dependable.

To obtain some further light on our question, we may turn to a different report—one that does not exhibit many of the obvious and common characteristics of research, but which depends on certain inherent qualities for this classification. A study of certain personnel practices [9] will serve. This investigation is not a quantitative survey, not an experiment, not a series of case studies, but a general description. Why might this report be called a research report instead of just a statement of the opinions of the writer? There are no tables; the data are not given in detail; there are few specific statements of findings; the report contains much opinion mixed in with the text; it does not have the usual form of a research study. Its unequivocal classification as research is admittedly difficult; hence, if it is to be called research, we must look searchingly for distinguishing characteristics.

Although different persons will vary in their judgment, the report is classified here as research for these reasons:

1. New data were gathered. The author visited forty-six institutions and studied their personnel policies locally.

2. The sources were selected according to plan. The institutions were chosen with regard to their distribution among certain types or classes, and with consideration of geographical distribution.

3. The observations were made carefully and were verified. The author himself interviewed from four to seven persons "in positions of responsibility for staff problems" (p. viii) in each institution to check on the facts he was gathering, and to see whether certain policies were recognized by different staff members as being in effect at a given institution.

4. The observations were made systematically. A set of specific aspects of personnel practices were taken up at each institution visited.

5. The observations were not made mechanically (woodenly or routinely), as by a clerk. This is an important point and one where persons who do not understand research are likely to go astray in their thinking about it. It is true that certain uniformities of concept (definition) must be preserved; that is particularly true in the case of counting and measuring, where the assumption is implicit in these processes. But in a study of the present type, where the phenomena are complex and often subtle, it is particularly important that the data-gathering be done with insight, sensitivity, understanding, and judgment. Further, it is expected that this insight will be an expanding one as the study progresses, often necessitating callbacks or second contacts with earlier sources. If one is to present a picture that is true with regard to both the essential and the modifying conditions, he must be prepared to discriminate finely, to sense areas that need further follow-up, and to reject numerous facts which are interesting but not relevant to the point. Further, one must be continually formulating general notions and revising these as the data-gathering progresses. It should be

[9] Lloyd S. Woodburne, *Faculty Personnel Policies in Higher Education*. New York: Harper and Bros., 1950. 201 p.

clear that the background, sensitivity, judgment, and skill of the researcher are major considerations in this type of observation.

6. The findings are summarized in a series of statements that represent the essence of the multitude of data which were originally taken. Some summarization, and usually some comparison, are important aspects of research.

7. The work was done in the spirit of research. The report is not presented as being something more than it is—it is offered as a starting point for further thought (p. ix), not as the answer to all problems. While the study contains some opinion, this is made evident and is not masked. It is clear from the material that the report was not written with any desire to make the facts come out a certain way or to make the project sound like something more than an essentially factual document.

If we were to generalize the statements about these two studies, we should have something like the following to guide our thinking:

1. The research report usually has a distinctive form, with definite attention given to describing the methodology, the sources, the population, the trait being studied, and other appropriate methodological or technical details.

2. Presumably original observations are taken.

3. Each step in the work proceeds with meticulous care and with due consideration for the large plan and purpose of the work. The data are verified and evaluated.

4. The data are resolved, or organized into certain more general terms, and are sometimes related to a single, over-all thesis. Certainly the data will be summarized in some form or other, as systematic as possible. What is done with the data is a definite part of the contribution of the study.

5. The background, sensitivity, and general competence of the investigator, as well as the spirit with which he works, are vital elements.

Whether a study must have more or less than the qualities in this list, probably no definite rule can be stated. These qualities vary in degree; various types of research have their own criteria. One should aim, in doing his own research, not at the minimum requirements of research, but at a fairly full-bodied attack.

**Auxiliary forms of reporting.** General descriptive reports are encountered in a large variety of forms. Some of these are probably to be regarded as research and some are not. For the guiding of one's own research, such questions are not of large moment; but some attention to them should throw light on the nature of research and may help answer certain perplexing questions that arise in one's thinking.

One of the most persistently difficult questions to settle is, Does some one part of a complete study, undertaken and reported by itself, constitute research? For example, the Ministers of Education of eleven countries contributed reports on what happened to their schools and universities during World War II.[10] These reports are based on first-hand experience and observation. In and by themselves, they scarcely are to be regarded as research; they are descriptive and narrative reports. Yet they constitute source material which may well become the data for history writing, or for other interpretative, analytical, or generalizing processes based on these and other documents—and such integrative work itself probably would be called research.

Again, the volume of the Eight-Year Study which describes novel curriculum practices,[11] how they were derived, and what their values are, if read by itself entirely apart from any awareness of the experimental setting in which the work was going on, would scarcely be taken for research. It lacks too many of the elements earlier listed. Yet, as a part of the total five-volume report, it takes its place unquestionably as a part of a large research undertaking.

Some studies do not gather fresh data but are simply analysis or reanalysis of data which other workers gathered and reported. If these are sufficiently extensive or thorough, they will almost certainly be recognized as research, since we give high place to penetrating analysis and interpretation. At the other end of the research process, before the data-gathering step, there is a large amount of writing which defines problems, states hypotheses, points out significant elements that enter into a situation, and refines concepts— all of which are useful to the person who may undertake research in the area discussed. In thus calling attention to problems needing study, helping in the formulation of them, and perhaps raising the level of insight and understanding, this sort of writing contributes in a significant fashion to the progress and improvement of the stream of research. It is thus a part of research, but it is scarcely complete enough in itself, when viewed alone, to be called an individual piece of research.

In contrast to articles and other treatments which, individually, represent only portions of what would be a complete research study, there are analyses that are much broader than any single study, and represent research-based descriptions. These may be thought of as secondary presentations based on wide reading and interpretation of research; the general findings of one or more studies are employed somewhat loosely in a larger

---

[10] *Education Under Enemy Occupation in Belgium, China, Czechoslovakia, France, Greece, Luxembourg, Netherlands, Norway, Poland.* Office of Education Bulletin No. 3, 1945. Washington: Government Printing Office, 1945. 71 p.

[11] Harry H. Giles, S. P. McCutchen, and A. N. Zechiel, *Exploring the Curriculum.* Adventure in American Education, Vol. 2. New York: Harper and Bros., 1942. 362 p.

context. That is, the research is not presented directly but is used somewhat indirectly as the basis for the views of the secondary writer. Individual studies may or may not be cited in footnotes; sometimes they appear only in the bibliography. This is the form which many of the educational yearbooks take; for example, the yearbooks of the National Society for the Study of Education, of the American Association of School Administrators, and other similar series. Certain textbooks are so closely based on research that they might be considered as writing of this type.

This class of secondary research writing would include such series or treatises as those comprising the special issue of the *American Journal of Sociology* devoted to "The American Family" (Vol. 53, p. 417-519; May 1948) or those devoted to education as a phase of the cultural process (Vol. 48, p. 629-764; May 1943). Some of the original studies on which writing of this type is based may fall outside the area of general description. It is the secondary form of writing, which takes the general findings of the underlying studies as basic verbal material for a general treatise of an area, that interests us in the studies at this point.

We conclude that there are varied forms of descriptive writing which, in the large, contribute significantly to the amount and the quality of research, but which, looked at individually, fall short of certain essential features of research. By way of analogy, a tree needs its branches, but a branch should not be called a tree. Similarly, a house built of wood is something less than, and something more than, a tree. In scientific context, the names which we use are for convenience and accuracy of distinction; they do not imply discredit on any category. The fact that certain types of writing are not to be classed as research does not in any way imply a lessening of their value for the purpose for which they were written.

**Problems in descriptive writing.** General descriptive studies may be regarded as constituting approximately the same type of writing as history, except that they deal with the present time instead of relating a sequence of events throughout a period of time. Since the kinds of data gathered are of the same general character, the problems of carrying on the work would be much the same in the two fields. The principal problem is that of sources —locating productive sources, evaluating them through all possible means at the disposal of one who is technically trained in this work; obtaining enough background so as to be able to understand and interpret the sources correctly; then using them judiciously. The chapter on historical research deals with these problems at some length, and they will not be reviewed at this point.

For the beginner in this type of work it is likely that certain more general problems will loom large. For instance, there are the demands of good

English—good writing, particularly of the descriptive and expository types. Achieving a high standard in writing is something of a lifelong pursuit; it does not come easily. Closely related to expression or composition is ability in the use of logic—again a skill which ordinarily develops slowly. It is well for any writer to examine the logical structure of his paper after he has written it, preferably by preparing an abstract or outline and looking critically at it. Is the problem clearly stated? Are all essential terms adequately defined? Does the development follow a logical course? Does it "stick to the subject"? Do the conclusions relate to the purposes of the study stated in the early part? Are matters of opinion—the personal coloring and value-judgments of the writer—clearly indicated as such and separated from the relatively impersonal, logical interpretations? (These matters are discussed at length in the chapters on development of the problem and on reporting.)

In general, the beginning graduate student is warned against undergraduate attitudes. He is not working primarily to please a teacher, to see how little he can get by with, to expand his writing beyond the limits of substance, or to exemplify a studied indifference toward matters of form. The research report is not the proper medium through which to expound personal views and beliefs. Research represents formal writing; it need not be stuffy, but it presumes to be acceptable to serious readers. And its purpose is to make a contribution. One does not inquire to himself, I wonder if I can get by with this? but rather, Have I described what I set out to do with such fidelity and such penetration that I have contributed a clear new picture which amounts to new truth? To present this advice in positive or constructive terms: As one progresses in graduate study, he will sense that certain attitudes and minor goals which characterized so much of the undergraduate work no longer seem adequate. They do not meet the demands of graduate work. In reporting research, one is taking his place in the ranks of a profession where standards of quality prevail and where the criterion is not superficial display but fundamental worth.

Mature writers in the field of descriptive research become aware of other problems in keeping with their developing insights. There is, at all levels of work, the problem of making sharp distinctions—of making certain that cases belong in the classes to which they are assigned and that these classes have the qualities which they are assumed to have. But behind all such direct questions is the larger matter of the over-all framework of interpretation. What do the facts mean? The answer lies in part in the scheme of thought that is imposed on the data. There are many forms which will fit, depending on the background and inclination of the worker. All studies posit, either explicitly or implicitly, a certain conceptual pattern which functions both in selecting the data from the original sources and in imbuing the data with meaning. Whether the particular conceptual frame adopted by a particular worker can be verified by the data (which it helped select), or whether other interpretative schemes would be more closely supported by the data they would bring forth, is often a question that must await a larger body of evidence,[12] and perhaps a more mature science. When one works from any particular point of view, he must bear in mind that his ultimate goal is that of finding some integrating principle which is to some extent explanatory while being descriptive, which will serve to encompass the facts of other but similar groups of cases, and which will prove most useful both in the developing framework of scientific theory and in the world of practical application.

General description is characteristic of the early stage of work in an area where the significant factors have not been isolated, and where perhaps one would not have means for measuring them if they were identified. It is, therefore, a method of exploration; but, in addition, general description plays its part in all research reports, and there are still areas in which it is better fitted for the purpose (for the kind of description desired) than would be quantitative data.

**Analytical description.** The line between simple description and analysis is not a sharp one, and as a matter of fact it is not a very strong one, for analysis is a form of description. And, conversely, description of any kind is to some extent analytical, in that it deals with particular aspects and not with vague, amorphous generalities. Insofar as there is a distinction, however, it lies in the fact that there are aspects of graduated generality; some are over-all and some are detailed. In analysis, one describes something —an object, idea, event, or group—in rather detailed terms, and usually in terms of components which, when taken together, make up the whole.

Analysis is likely to be important in any science, for it is concerned with such questions as, What is the internal nature of this thing? What makes it have the characteristics and the properties it does? What happens when its parts are modified or affected one at a time? Such knowledge gives added power to predict and to control. In chemistry, for example, the ability to break up a given substance into elements, or the ability to describe the structure of the molecules, is of fundamental importance—not as a classroom exercise for students, but for the power it gives chemists to create new substances by utilizing their knowledge. In biology, including physiology, form and structure are likewise fundamental, forming one of the major divisions (morphology) of the field.

[12] An enlightening discussion of the difficulty inherent in supporting a general hypothesis is afforded in the debate over Blumer's critique of the Thomas-Znaniecki study. This discussion is included in the reference in an earlier footnote of this chapter.

In research in social fields, analysis is similarly of importance. As in other sciences, however, it quickly becomes technical. Much of the analysis is likely to be concerned either with the subdividing of a group of cases, or with breaking some concept, such as "ability," into elements. The division of Chapter 5 which follows will deal with analysis as one form of descriptive research.

# The Descriptive Method:
### ANALYSIS

## ANALYTICAL DESCRIPTION

**Introduction: Meaning of analysis.** Analysis moves in the direction of satisfying one of man's deep desires, namely, the desire to uncover what lies beneath the surface. What is there behind the outside which is so readily seen? Or what is the meaning, in terms of specifics, of some general idea that is so glibly referred to? What is the inside like? Does this exterior, or general character, which things exhibit at man's first approach wrap within itself a world as complex, as fascinating, and as instructive as the world of outward relationships? Does this barrier conceal the ultimate nature of what each thing really is—and why it behaves as it does? Is it the last curtain behind which man must look, in order to gain a rather full knowledge of the secrets which nature has so long kept locked up?

Before the vast reaches of the unknown we all, scientist and layman, stand in humility. Who has not, as a child, and again as an educated adult, wondered what the center of the earth was like? What thoughtful person has not contemplated in imagination the region of infinite fascination which is the bottom of the sea? Currently, explorations are being made to find some of these answers. The curiosity that has led to the knowledge which metallurgists have gained about the internal structure of metals, including alloys, though it might seem idle and purely theoretical, leading nowhere, has given each one of us daily benefits in the form of many metal products which we employ routinely. In the newspapers and magazines we read frequently about the fairyland which chemists have discovered, and in part created, within the molecule—that fabulous unit of structure of everything around us, too small to be comprehended by most of us, yet being manufactured synthetically in our industries to yield artificial rubber, plastics, nylon, and all the other synthetic fibers. This unit, discovered by intensive and persistent analysis, has become the key to manufacture of a whole world of substances which have certain properties that man has specified for them to have.

The physicist has gone even further. The molecule is still too big for his concerns. He selects the little units that make up the molecule—little worlds of his own interest. He analyzes them, describes them, exposes them to our mental view, and tells us that each one is like our solar system, with relatively great reaches of space in it. Then, as though he were working with the tools of a superhuman artisan, he proceeds to take apart the very center of this little billionth-of-an-inch world he knows about and, through his infinitely skillful manipulation, he brings into being the essence of new substances—new elements, things which probably the universe has never before known, creations of man's own handiwork.

The story which is already so far along in the physical sciences serves but to set the advanced pattern for similar work in the social field. It establishes beyond doubt the possibilities and benefits of analytical procedures, of trying to find answers that afford temporary respite to man's driving curiosity, which keeps on saying, "I wonder?" In wondering, man is in touch with worlds more marvelous than he had ever dreamed of. Who is there—teacher, psychologist, or layman—who does not often ask of himself, "What goes on in the human mind? Of what does a thought, a wish, a resolve consist?" What inner reactions and mechanisms generate and guide the forces that move us? What are the structures or the processes which are capable of producing both wavering irresolution and unyielding determination, animal-like unrestraint and deliberate, delicately adjusted choice? What are the source and nature of the cross-currents and eddies, and sometimes the turbulence, which we find in life? What are the means by which we learn, and thus keep alive man's hope of a better world in which to live?

All who teach covet a finer knowledge of the way in which the birth of an idea takes place. We know less of mental growth than of physical. Is learning to be viewed simply as a process? Or is it a matter of adding on one building block after another? Does an area of expanding comprehension represent just more blocks? Or a different kind of structural relation among them? Or something that cannot be thought of in terms of units at all? The same questions arise when we think of ability in cross section. We have learned something of its dimensions; possibly we know a little of its nature, but we still do not have clear answers to those questions of inner structure which escape purely dimensional approaches. What elements of thought join together to form the developing nucleus of a new insight? Why do some "ideas" have strength and virility so that they continue and grow, and perhaps guide a lifetime of effort, in contrast to other ideas which never quite form, or which partly crystallize only to vanish like a snowflake in the palm of one's hand?

We live in an open world of problems. It would make little difference if answers to all these questions were already known, for beyond them lie questions of even more fundamental significance. As the researcher penetrates more deeply, he is conscious that he is getting ever closer to the inner realities of nature, but there are always further steps to be taken. There are no permanent barriers to analytical exploration. In the physical world, the sons of today's physicists will be exploring units of matter so small that at present their existence is only vaguely suspected. In the biological world, a generation hence, we shall undoubtedly understand more of the inner workings of the individual cell which may, to carry out its manifold functions, manufacture as many as ten thousand different enzymes.[13] And in the psychological realm, who knows what another half-century will see in the way of advances in our knowledge of the essential nature of ability, of learning, and of forgetting?

One may be inclined to raise the question, How can this come about? Can man peer into his brain and watch the functioning of his mind? The answer is that new problems, springing from new conceptions, bring forth new methods of observation. There may be periods of delay, but throughout the history of science the demand for new instruments and methods of detection, identification, and measurement has always seen these instruments and procedures develop. Thus, though the technology of research may at times lag, in rough measure it keeps pace with the needs of advancing thought in a field of research. In fact, it seems probable that research progress waits more often on sound theory than on instrumentation; and any fear for the future of research should rest not so much with the question of how one will observe the phenomena he wishes to study, as with the question of how he will conceptualize them. That is, if research workers who have adequate insight, imagination, and the willingness to venture will propose penetrating theories having sufficient scope, clarity, and cogency, these concepts will captivate the interest and provide a compelling challenge to workers whose resources lie in the realm of devising means for bringing manifestations of phenomena within the range of man's observational senses. As new ideas are proposed for study, new means of refined observation will almost certainly follow.

Thus, in the field of analysis, as with other forms of research, the most brilliant achievements of today will but pave the way for even greater accomplishments in areas which present work will have brought within focus. Where barriers appear, new resources will be found; when the horizon looms close, new vistas will open, beckoning beyond. With vision continually freshened by new accomplishments and by new conceptualizations, man goes forever forward in his penetration of the unknown. Worlds

[13] David M. Bonner, "Genes as Determiners of Cellular Biochemistry." *Science* 108:735-39; December 31, 1948.

within worlds, as yet unperceived, provide the challenge for tomorrow's quest.

## THE ROLE OF ANALYSIS

Analysis is among the first of the methods which a researcher will call upon in his effort to reduce a field "to size"; that is, to extract a manageable chunk from the infinite complexity of the real world. The human mind, contemplating a problem area, is faced with the questions, What can I find to take hold of in this area? Where can I catch on? And after all, what is worth while? The latter question can never be answered with sureness; partly because we cannot foresee future values, and partly because we can never tell what the mind will turn up with. The ultimate value of what we do is a matter of speculation, a risk, a hope. The creative mind may find the basis for a large integrating idea by starting almost anywhere. That is the challenge, the sport of research. For research at its best is the game of mental kings—masters of controlled observation and kings of creative intellectual power. We would not want to take the risk out of research and make it a sure thing, for when that happens it becomes a lifeless routine. We all strive to find our proper place on the scale at some point between the two extremes of risk and routine, realizing that we live in an age when persons all around us are making lucky "strikes."

The first two questions, however, are usually partly solved for the worker by virtue of some previous experience in the field, or by recognition of some general principle whose potential ramifications need testing. One can, however, well appreciate the problem of the early workers in education, or psychology, or sociology, looking out upon the vast area of their field and wondering, At what point can I begin to bring order into this field? It should be apparent that the common goals of analysis, such as those set forth in this section, afford a reasonable beginning point. That is, what are the significant aspects that reveal something of a given set of phenomena in the field? What are the components of the phenomena? What is their quantitative characterization? Their form? Their integrated structure? What are the forces that play one upon the other; what is their interaction; in what course are they resolved? What changes take place, and how? Relatively mature answers to these questions will call upon the aid of all the methods known to research, but answers to these problems remain particularly the goals of the analytical approach.

In the introduction to these analytical processes it is perhaps appropriate to observe that research is not simply the application of a set of techniques. There is no magic to the "scientific method." The magic lies rather in the careful, painstaking, devoted attention of the researcher, in his constant, exacting watchfulness, in his alertness to perceive significant relationships, in his unswerving determination to preserve the integrity of his data and of his conclusions—and then, occasionally, his willingness to venture a new interpretation (a new explanatory, generalized principle). This may be put forth either as required by, and well supported by, his data, or set forth frankly as a venture, because it seems to be suggested by his data and may be found of value in other studies. Needless to say, the beginner in a particular area is not likely to have an intellectual grasp of the field sufficient to offer such integrations; but, on the other hand, for the beginner to enter the field of research with the belief that he must always confine his thinking to the limits of his observed facts would be a misleading orientation, fatal to subsequent creative contributions.

## THE SCOPE OF ANALYSIS

The idea may have suggested itself to the reader that analysis is closely tied up with the whole of research. Clearly, it is. In some form or other it enters into every step or every phase of research. It is so close to the heart of certain undertakings that it becomes difficult to say whether they are primarily a process of analysis or primarily something else which incorporates analysis. For that reason, it is a difficult subject to treat. It is as broad as research itself and it is inseparably interwoven with many other research processes.

Because of these conditions, certain delimitations become necessary, and a few statements should be made with regard to the treatment that follows. Obviously, it cannot be a complete treatment or it would encompass the remainder of the text. As one aid in keeping the discussion within compass, where analysis is an integral part of a somewhat more general process, which is given separate treatment later on, a presentation of the analytical aspect will not be dealt with at length in the present section, but will be left for the more complete treatment later. For example, classification clearly devolves upon analysis; either the general category requires logical analysis to see how it can profitably be split up into smaller categories, or the individual cases call for analysis, in order to reveal their idiosyncrasies and to ascertain what categories are appropriate for them. But such engaging steps will be reserved for treatment in the section on classification.

Similarly, the present discussion will deal with the analysis of individual cases, or other organized units, such as an intact group of cases, rather than with the analysis of aggregates in widely disparate settings. The grouping and classification of the latter represent a form of statistical analysis and will be left mainly to specialized textbooks. For example, dividing up (analyzing) a large number of scattered cases, such as the total number of persons in the United States, into subgroups—often on the basis of quantitative characteristics (as occurs in the usual frequency distribution), or other categories (as place of birth or occupation)—is not a form of analysis which deals with organized or intact groups of individuals. Accordingly, it will not be dealt with here. For some persons, this statistical analysis will be the sort that first comes to mind. While it is unquestionably a form of analysis, it is a form of relatively ultimate analysis which begins by making its own grouping, and it can properly be given brief attention in the section of this chapter that deals with classification.

Experimentation will be treated in a subsequent chapter, but it is appropriate to point out here that there is often a close relationship between experimentation and analysis. This relationship is two-directional. On the one hand, many experiments are undertaken purely for the sake of analysis. They aid in separating things which might seem to be alike. In fact, so much experimentation is of this character that it is not uncommon to see the two terms combined, as in *experimental analysis*. On the other hand, and in the other direction, thoughtful analysis is an almost necessary part of any experiment that is well conducted. Before undertaking the experiment, the researcher will carefully analyze his problem, the conditions which are likely to enter into the situation, and the logical design of his contemplated procedure. He will probably also plan in advance the subsequent analysis of his observed data. Because of this close connection, the reader will find that many statements in the present section apply equally to experimentation, and some of them will involve experimentation as the practical method of realizing the analytical goal. In other words, experimentation is often a means of implementing the analytical undertaking.

Other forms of analysis are apparent in the chapter dealing with historical methods, and a particular form of analysis is manifested later in connection with methods of case study. As has been said, some form of analysis appears in every form of research undertaking. It is our purpose here to focus attention on analysis as a process, so that it may be better understood and thus take its proper place in the whole scheme of the research enterprise.

## NATURE OF ANALYSIS

The inward direction represented by analysis has as its purpose discovering the nature of things. Of what are they composed? What is their structure? What are the substructures or the special organizations that occur here and there as units within the larger structure? How are all these individual parts and unit assemblies or organs integrated into an internal system? What are the forces that hold them together, and the strains that tend to tear the system apart? What makes the system work? How is it regulated? And, from the point of view of continuing research, what new questions are brought to light by analytical work which will serve as guides for further research?

Through such analysis, the researcher, like the explorer of a new land, is seeking to chart a new area. He may find parts or factors which were not previously known to exist; that is one of the rewards of the successful person. In any event, he is constantly on the alert to detect, identify, and delineate elements which hitherto were not understood. It is the purpose of research to deal with the new. It is the quest of all research to ascertain new knowledge, whether of hitherto unknown parts or a new understanding of known parts, so as to give man manipulative control over the behavior (or over the construction) of the whole.

The "whole" is a problem in classification. That is, what is a "whole"? The answer is that it is anything which, for his purpose, the researcher regards as a "whole." The "whole" will be any level of generality with which the researcher, bent on analysis, decides to start (a whole civilization, a continent, an institution, a group, an object or person, an organ, a cell, a period of time, an event, and so on), the point being that, for his interest, the whole selected furnishes a basis for proceeding downward to explore its internal nature. One may be surprised to find that very frequently the thing explored is simply an idea—a concept which exists in man's mind. In the examples which follow, this will arise again and again. Processes, likewise, often constitute the "whole" to be analyzed. In fact, from philosophical points of view, everything is simply a process, even solid matter itself. For somewhat more practical purposes, however, we find it profitable not to go to such an extreme, and we normally regard objects as objects. In the biological sciences, students will be familiar with the type of analysis represented by dissecting biological specimens; in chemistry, students are familiar with qualitative and quantitative analysis. In mathematics, a large part of the thought is given to analysis.

One important form of analysis, which usually involves experimentation to help find the answer, has as its goal the identification of the particular element or aspect (in some complex thing) which is most important in leading to a certain result. That is, in any complex mixture of factors (which is always present) what is it that is essential or dominant? What factor really is effective? In the phrase of mathematics, what is the necessary and sufficient condition? It must be recognized, although it has commonly been overlooked in the physical sciences, that any specification of conditions, and any identification of the most effective factor, assumes that countless other factors are held constant or at least operate within the normal range of what is regarded as usual, common, or normal. Taking this normal range of other factors for granted, we can center attention on finding the one which seems to be varying enough to be chiefly responsible for some result. Even though it is known that this quest is usually too simple in its conceptualization, because it is normal for a whole complex of factors to vary together, it is nevertheless, in many cases, profitable. Both in everyday experience and in formal science, there are many instances of this successful search for the thing that is dominant, distinctive, essential, or in some way outstandingly significant. Primitive man had found that certain plants, when eaten, had certain effects on the human body; he had gone so far as to separate these out from plants in general. This is an analytical process. Modern man, of course, has gone further and in many cases has identified the particular chemical element in these plants which is effective. Further, because of his knowledge of analytical chemistry, man has, in many cases, been able to produce these essential elements of plants synthetically in the laboratory, so that most modern medicines are simply chemicals.

As another common example of this same process, a news report some years ago noted that miners working in the heat of the South African diamond mines had learned that chewing on salt pork would help restore their energy when they were exhausted. This finding is simply one of those unanalytical discoveries made by mankind in the process of trying one procedure or another. Modern medical research, by means of protracted analytical study, has found that the body loses a large amount of salt (and certain other needed substances) from heavy perspiration in extreme heat. Accordingly, it is recognized that salt was the essential factor which made salt pork effective. This finding symbolizes the goal which is sought by much analytical research. In educational work, for example, we are basically interested in ascertaining what factors are significant in bringing about good learning, effective teaching, good administration, and so on. The answers, when developed, will represent triumphs of the analytical process.

As a matter of orientation, we point out that analysis is not necessarily concerned with the smallest possible unit which may be conceived. As a matter of fact, there is no such thing; as man has successively discovered new smaller units, his conception has kept pace and gone on to the next step. In the present treatment, the major emphasis will be on analysis toward what may be called proximate rather than ultimate units. These terms are borrowed from chemistry, but they are highly suggestive. We may draw upon a familiar example for illustration. For instance, if one is interested in purchasing coal (perhaps for heating school buildings) and wishes to compare different brands that are for sale, a proximate analysis is usually what he wants. It tells how much volatile matter, sulphur, ash, moisture, and so on are in a sample that has been analyzed. These are constituents which the consumer wishes to know about, because they are useful in his thinking and judging. In other words, they are terms or concepts with which he is reasonably familiar and which enter into his thinking. An ultimate analysis, on the other hand, would break the coal down into single chemical elements which would be of significance to a chemist, but would not mean much to most consumers. There is again an intermediate group of concepts, neither ultimate nor proximate in the common sense. For example, a'recent article in a popular magazine was headed, "Two Hundred Chemicals From a Lump of Coal." Some of these were undoubtedly elements, but probably most of them were more complex products, but of such a technical nature as to be of interest only to manufacturers dealing in highly technical processes. It should be clear that it is common, in practical analytical work, to stop at different levels, according to the interest or purpose of the one who is making the analysis or of those who are going to use the results.

In stating that the present treatment will, for the most part, emphasize something short of ultimate analysis, we mean two things. The first is that, for many purposes, it is appropriate, whether in education or in other fields, not to seek a breakdown into the most elementary unit possible. Although this seems obvious, it is sometimes necessary to refer to such an idea as a corrective for the notion sometimes put forth that one has not really done anything in the way of research until he has gone to some presumed ultimate. However, the biologist finds it useful for many of his purposes to think in terms of cells, which are not, in any sense, ultimates. The psychologist desires to know about the sense organs and the nervous system of the body but, for the most part, is not so much interested in single cells as the biologist. The teacher is primarily interested in the health, emotional adjustment, and learning of the child, not so much in the detailed structure of his nervous system or in its individual cells. The sociologist cares more about groups of persons and their institutions. Thus, the workers in each scientific field decide on the level of the phenomena in which they will center their chief interest.

There can be no general theoretical statement concerning the limiting depth for analysis in any particular field, except that one usually wishes to go at least one level below the phenomena in which he is most interested, to provide at least a minimum degree of explanation. He may wish to go further than that, in order to tie in his subject with the thinking in some other field of science. But if he goes several levels below his phenomena, he will find that the characteristics which are the central subject matter of his discipline have disappeared, and that he is in reality working in the domain of another field of science. He must decide for himself whether this is what he wishes to do.

The second and correlative meaning of an interest in limited depth of analysis is that one will direct his attention toward organized parts. For example, suppose one is interested in analyzing a textbook. Such an analysis can be carried out in terms of units which are on many different levels. He may, for example, analyze the content of the textbook in terms of what the different chapters deal with; or in terms of smaller topics, and he can go on down into paragraphs, sentences, words, and letters. (For some purposes, it is significant to count individual letters.) On the other hand, he may divide the material into text, tables, graphic material, exercises, bibliography, and so on. Different interests lead to the using of different kinds of units in analysis, and the unit employed for one purpose may be of little value for another purpose. A teacher will usually be interested, first of all, in the over-all organization, proportion or emphasis, and general quality of the treatment which is given individual subjects. Accordingly, the teacher's interest will not be satisfied by pushing the level of analysis down to certain units which no longer represent this interest. Thus one is likely to be concerned with organized parts, in contrast to unorganized units—such as the number of letters, the number of words, and so forth. It is true that, in reading, there is much interest in the number of new words, but this is in addition to a concern with context that is interesting to the pupil.

In summary, these points are made, lest one be disturbed by statements that certain types of analysis are not final. Analysis is never final. The history of science indicates that, with the passage of time and continued effort, new subordinate levels can always be found. For example, in our own century, physicists have found that what was thought about 1900 to be the ultimate unit is not ultimate in any sense. While the atom is now broken up into a dozen or so different particles, every year or two brings a discovery of some additional particle, and there can be little doubt but that, by the end of the century, these particles themselves will be seen not to be final. In fact, electrons are already being viewed as waves of energy instead of as solid particles. It is, therefore, not only reasonable but scientifically justifiable for one to seek that level of analysis which seems appropriate for his purposes within the range of his science—which reveals and explains the phenomena with which his science deals.

It is one of the positions in the present treatment that analysis properly deals with integrating elements as much as with parts. This is not ordinarily assumed. Most of the explicit discussion of analysis deals with what may be called parts; and, correspondingly, much of the criticism of the analytical method springs from this very fact. In our view, whether one looks for parts, or for relationships, or for forces, is simply a matter of what one decides to look for—all within the scope of the analytical process. One is clearly as legitimate a goal and a product of analytical attack as is another. For example, in speaking of sentences, it seems absurd to think that one might analyze a sentence into vocabulary but not into sentence structure. Or, that in analyzing personality, one would be confined to the identification of what may commonly be called "traits" of personality and could not pay attention to their interrelationships (the organization between them). Similarly, in investigation of the organization of a school system, or of any other institution, or of society in general, it is as necessary, for analytical purposes, that one be concerned with the pattern of structure, the arrangement of the different parts in the whole, and the various ways in which they function coöperatively or restrictively, as to deal with recognition of the "parts." In short, relationships between static elements (pattern, organization, and structure) or between the dynamic aspects of elements (forces and systems) are as much a subject of analysis as are the simpler parts on which these organized concepts may be constituted.

It will be profitable for research workers to keep clearly before themselves the idea that the analysis into parts is only a beginning and that the real goal of analysis is an explanation of the entire system (which embraces parts and relationships and forces that make the "whole" what it is, and determine its properties).

Like other forms of research, analysis proceeds on the basis of both observation and thought. That is, in addition to direct observation, much analysis is done on the level of logic. The "objective" emphasis in research dealing with human beings, which was necessary in shaping its original orientation, has often left researchers with a notion that thinking is something to be ashamed of. The very opposite is the truth, and it is emphasized throughout this entire text that thinking and good judgment are essential parts of sound research. The difficult thing is to learn to keep thought and observation in proper balance. Neither can be dispensed with, and neither by itself is adequate.

In seeking to achieve this proper balance, it is sometimes difficult not to come to despise one element or the other. It is so easy, for example, to show the many ways in which logic has misled mankind (both in philosophy and in science alike) that one may arrive at the sweeping conclusion that logic is no good. But it is equally easy to cite many instances in which direct observation, even with instruments, has misled mankind; and so one can, if he wishes, go to the extreme of saying observation is worthless. What we had better do is realize that, whether observing or thinking, it is *man* who is fallible; and research, involving both observation and thought, is the principal means by which man discovers and corrects his mistakes. (In this statement, as in many other places in the text, we wish to include the entire range of modern philosophy as part of the thought process of synthesis, interpretation, and evaluation.) Research thus becomes something more than a sideline endeavor; it becomes the principal hope of mankind; for, where he is wrong today, he will know better tomorrow.

Thought patterns, in analysis as elsewhere, must often be drawn from common experience. In fact, it may be argued that all scientific thinking is expressed in terms based on units of man's experience, else he could not understand it. (That may be why, for example, we have difficulty with concepts of extremes, such as infinite space, which may or may not have limits; or with the differential calculus, which reduces a difference to zero yet retains a trace of movement. We do not have direct experiences with such things and so have difficulty in thinking of them as realities.) Physical science took its start in everyday notions, and was both helped and hindered by them, because they are usually partly true but need a great deal of refining (by analysis and experiment). Similarly, social science had to start with what we think about human beings, and has likewise been helped and hindered by such beliefs. The insights of keen observers are a great help to research, whether it is physical or social; and the insights of the experienced researcher are to be regarded as a significant part of his research. They are not basically different from the thoughts of the non-researcher, but they presumably grow out of (research) conditions more favorable to penetrating analysis, and also out of a very different purpose or motivation —not just to get on with the work of the world, but to discover what the nature of the world is like, so that its work can be done more efficiently, with less burden and with greater benefit to man.

## STUDY OF GROUPS VERSUS STUDY OF SINGLE CASES

Analysis as a form of study is accompanied by many questions and many controversies. Some of these have been dealt with in the preceding paragraphs. But there are others. Some persons will argue that analysis destroys virtually everything in which they have an interest. This position will be touched on particularly in the subsequent section on components. Other persons argue that research must deal with many cases, not one or a few. Both approaches have their values. The choice between extensive and intensive study must be made, not on what somebody says is or isn't research, but on a careful consideration of the kind of knowledge one wishes to obtain.

Insights do not necessarily derive from studying groups. In fact, one may with some warrant assert that most insights arise from close observation and understanding of a single complex case. This point may be clarified by introducing a comment about the nature of generalizations (scientific principles and laws) themselves. Although the distinction seems not to be commonly recognized, it is nevertheless apparent that generalizations may be divided into two classes: namely, those which deal with properties or characteristics of single cases and those which relate to (apply to) properties or characteristics of groups (but not to individuals in the group). Many (perhaps most) generalizations of science do not relate to properties of groups as groups but to properties which are directly true of each single example, taken one at a time, from any designated class.

To illustrate this distinction, examples of two kinds will be introduced: first, examples of the individual-case laws; second, illustrations of the group-case laws; there are other instances of generalizations which can be derived so as to apply in either way. The reader who has a background in physical science will, perhaps, have the most questions to ask concerning this point; hence, a number of illustrations will be taken from his field, with examples from human science following.

For scientific generalizations pertaining to cases individually rather than to a class as a unit, we may turn to the section in physics dealing with classical machines and note that the principles of the lever apply individually to each lever of a given class. These principles do not deal with the characteristics and properties which might arise from an aggregation of levers, other than to assume that the result would be a summation or multiplication of the characteristics of an individual case. Nothing additional is recognized. Further, the variation in *actual* levers which might be constructed is ignored; the fact that a dozen beam scales might give that many different indications of weight is no concern of the scientist. The proper design and safeguarding of a beam scale, so that it will give a reasonably true weight under the varying conditions of use, are the concern of the engineer, inventor, designer, manufacturer, and the user. Thus, a multiplicity of factors that differentiate one practical case of a lever from another, and which might properly enter into any description of (actual) levers, are all missing from the generalization which is designed to apply to any idealized case. True, the principle applies to all of a group of levers in a given class, but it ignores any group properties which may be present and hence must be called an individual-case generalization.

Again in physics, one may at first think of the classical laws relating to force as dealing with groups, since mass may be conceived of as the summation of atoms, molecules, and the like. Yet it will be seen at once that gravity, inertia, momentum, and other forms or manifestations of force act upon or characterize each unit particle of mass (as fine as one may wish to divide it). The fact that an aggregate of these infinitesimal units may enter into a calculation simply means that they are conceptually all alike, and hence the mass of them, as a pure summation, may be treated by addition or multiplication. The basic laws of force are, nevertheless, generalizations based on (applicable to) the smallest physical particle one may wish to conceive. If they were generalizations based on groups, they would contain some recognition of the difference (other than an additive or multiplicative one) between an individual case and a group of cases.

In the fields of chemistry and physics, somewhat jointly, or concurrently, the analyses that have been made of the structures of the atom and the molecule are analyses of single units. The atoms of a given element are presumed to be (nearly) all identical; at least the same major pattern prevails, with somewhat minor variations for ionization, isotopes, and the like. The molecules of a given substance which, again with certain variations, have the same chemical constituents and the same analytic (graphic) patterns are represented conceptually by the same model (of an individual case). On the other hand, by way of contrast, the study of crystal structure, or in fact the entire study of the physics of solids, represents definitely a *group* study, since it deals with patterns of interrelationships and these cannot be described in terms of individual atoms or molecules.[14]

Similar examples may be found in the human sciences. In psychology and education, the principles of learning, of forgetting, of transfer of training, and so on, apply to individual persons. They are patterns of behavior which hold true in reasonably similar manner for all persons who may be classed as normal and of a certain maturity level. Much, or according to some psychologists, nearly all, of psychology is concerned with the behavior of individuals, and its generalizations are those which hold for individuals considered one at a time.

Let us now look at examples of group-derived generalizations which are designed to represent characteristics of groups and are, accordingly, to be applied to groups rather than to individual cases one at a time. It appears that there are several types of these, and that they can conveniently be discussed under four categories.

1.   One type of group generalization is that which is expressed in terms

---

[14] For a general, more or less popular account of recent research and contemporary concepts in the field of solids, see Gregory H. Wannier, "The Nature of Solids." *Scientific American* 187:39-48; December 1952.

of proportion of the cases in the group, often in the form of probability. Usually, when this type is used, we do not have enough information about individual cases to make predictions for them, but we can nevertheless predict for a *group* of future observations. A simple illustration is coin tossing, or dice tossing; we ordinarily do not have enough information about the many factors affecting each event to predict what it will be; yet, given objects which are fairly accurate replicas of our theoretical concepts, we can predict reasonably closely what proportion of cases (events) will turn out a certain way. As to the individual event, however, we can say nothing; probability is distinctly a group concept and applies only to groups. A person may, of course, take action based on his expectancy, perhaps based on calculated likelihood, but such expectancy or likelihood exerts no influence whatever on the subsequent event. The next event is as free as the first.

The same condition obtains in many areas of physics where proportions of molecules or atoms (as in Brownian movements or atom bombardments) can be predicted to do certain things, even though the particular particles which will "succeed" cannot be picked out in advance. In ever increasing measure physical science is becoming statistical. *Quality control* in manufacturing is a representative application of the principle being discussed; it is based on the recognition that products cannot be turned out precisely as intended, but that so long as a given proportion of the cases fall within assigned limits of variation, that is all we can expect. In the biological field, heredity furnishes a well known example; certain proportions of offspring inherit certain degrees of particular characteristics of parents, but individual predictions cannot be made. In the social field, the prime illustration is life insurance, based on demographic and actuarial data. Life tables indicate average expectancies for groups, and become the basis of sound business practices, even though nothing whatever is known about the future life span of any particular individual.

In all these illustrations, based on what is commonly called chance, there is a presumed lack of fixity in the relationships between one causal factor and another, so that even a knowledge of the many factors involved, and their average relative strength, would be inadequate for making predictions in the individual case. But, if it has been ascertained that these factors (or degrees of each) combine in certain characteristic patterns certain portions of the time, and it can be assumed that the same factors and the same kinds of relationship between them will persist, then proportional predictions can continue to be made.

2. A second type of group-derived generalization results from using the average as a representation of the group of cases and offering it as a

typical result. This practice differs from the preceding set of illustrations for, even though probability may be thought of as something "on the average," we are here assuming that we know all the individual values, but prefer to disregard them for some reason, such perhaps as the desire for simplicity of thought or presentation. This is a common procedure, since the mind cannot deal readily with a large variety of differing values. In much of the school testing with standardized tests, comparisons between averages are made. It will be clear that an average represents a group and reports nothing about an individual. It is in fact a statistical way of ignoring individuals; that is, ignoring the variations existing in a group. It is of course true that, if all the values in a series were the same, the average would have that value; but in the world of reality this does not occur, so that an average must be thought of as group derived and group descriptive, in contrast to representing an individual case.

In this connection it is worth noting that these comments apply not only to the mean and median (the common averages of scale position) but to most statistical results, because structurally they are averages also. That is, the common measures of variation, the usual forms of correlation, the regression lines, other fitted curves, estimated errors of measurement, and so on, are basically averages and hence are group functions, conveying no sure knowledge whatever about any individual case in the group.

3. As a third type of knowledge growing out of the study of groups, we have the full-frequency distribution—the most characteristic device, perhaps, of all statistical work. An average can be calculated without knowing the value of each case, if the total is given; or it can be calculated on an adding machine without tabulation of the individual cases and hence without knowledge of the frequency structure lying behind the average. Knowledge of the frequency distribution, however, affords an *analytical* picture of the group and reveals a number of important group characteristics. Perhaps these characteristics can be summed up under the two words *shape* and *spread*. These aspects are basic to many inferences. Frequency distributions carry the implication of probability, as discussed in the first type of group information.

Often the shape of a distribution (that is, the curve representing frequency values distributed along a specified trait) is the essential information sought. This is true both in practical and in theoretical fields of work. For example, if one is providing seats and tables for children in the first grade of a school, how many chairs of each height will normally be needed? A merchant near a high school wants to know how many gym suits of each size to order for his fall trade when school opens. A superintendent scans the distribution of class sizes in his school system to see that the departures from average are not too great. An unexpected spread or shape of distribution on any trait may be the starting point for an investigation, either for practical or theoretical purposes.

4. A fourth type of group information which may be generalized (that is, used as a basis for prediction or comparison in situations other than that in which gathered) grows out of the fact that a group itself generates new qualities, characteristics, properties, or aspects which are not present in an individual case. This is true even if all the cases should (theoretically) be exactly the same (as is assumed in much theoretical science). A simple illustration may serve to make the general point. For example, in a school classroom several chairs can be arranged in order, and probably in a variety of patterns. Now order and pattern of arrangement are characteristics generated by a group; when the group is reduced to a single case, they vanish. Order and arrangement clearly do not represent simple summations of the properties of individual cases; they represent properties of *relationships* within a group—properties which can arise only between two or more cases.

This is the point referred to earlier: the physical structure of a crystal cannot be studied by observing atoms and molecules individually; the varying patterns of relationship between these units are as important as the units themselves. Owing to the recency of research in this area, this point is one which only tardily has been given attention. Earlier, as has been the case in much psychology, attention was focused on the structure and properties of the individual unit; but it slowly became clear that while such concern yielded a good description of the unit, it failed to describe the properties of the substance which was composed of these units. Variation, structure, and dynamic interrelationships had to be brought into the picture.

The same is true of many of the phenomena dealt with in social psychology and sociology—coöperation, opposition, organization, specialization, leadership, communication, democracy, cohesion, imitation, morale, supervision, teaching, morals, the reciprocal sharing of emotions, and a great many other group properties or group activities and effects. These are interpersonal or even intergroup relationships, and must be studied as such. Were an individual all by himself in this world, these characteristics would have no existence. The *individual's part* in these group forms can, of course, be studied by itself (that is, the behavior of an individual in a group situation); and obviously the group properties or behavior will be affected by the kinds of individuals in it; but the study of individuals one by one would no more satisfactorily account for *group* properties than the study by physicists of individual atoms and molecules would account for electrical conductivity or other properties of metals. There are always elements of ordered variation, structured organization, and intricate interaction which lie in the domain between individuals and are not embraced by the study of intra-individual phenomena.

Most of the foregoing statements could be made about groups even when composed of units which are similar. When, however, the members of a group vary in significant ways, the distinctively group effects may become more pronounced. In chemistry, for example, it is commonplace for the products of interaction between two different substances (two different kinds of molecules) to have virtually none of the ordinary properties of the original units. Common table salt, for instance, could not be imagined as a tasty, edible, and (in small amounts) beneficial substance from the prior study of sodium (a corrosive metal having a startlingly violent reaction with water) and of chlorine (an irritating, suffocating gas of repugnant odor and of high toxicity). Whereas the capacity to produce this product lies in part in each of the original units, the *properties* of the resulting product do not. And, to be sure, even the *capacities* could not be studied except as seen in the interaction and in the product.

With reasonable heterogeneity there is greater complexity and, consequently, greater variety of emergent properties. The lives of two people dwelling together take on qualities different from those their lives would possess if living alone; the joint product is different from the sum of two single lives. When, especially, two persons of opposite sex come together to create a home, bring children into existence, nurture and educate them, and develop all the sentiments, interests, motivations, and value patterns which go with a maturing family, countless new elements have been brought into the situation, as compared with the summation of those elements which develop in completely separate lives. When the structure of society is seen in terms of a very large number of institutions, of which the family is but one, it should be evident that a great many properties or aspects come into being and add infinite complexity to the life of a nation. It should be just as evident that the study of those characteristics which emerge from groups must include the direct study of groups and group behavior and not simply individuals.

In order to sharpen and summarize the distinctions between useful ideas that may be obtained from studying individuals and from studying groups, we may note how different ways of deriving information on the same problem will change the nature of the conclusions (and generalizations) which are obtained. A researcher may, for example, be interested in certain principles of learning. He may study a number of cases (subjects) and conclude that there are certain general characteristics of learning which are true in every case. (These probably will have to be stated in relatively general or idealized form, in order to be true for all the cases observed.) He will then embody his findings in his conclusions. Since they are present in every case that came to his attention, they are definitely generalizations which apply to individuals. On the other hand, a researcher who wishes to study these same characteristics of learning from the standpoint of his interest in a group, in order to note average and deviation tendencies which might be expected in other *groups,* will arrange the measurements from the individual cases in order of magnitude, note the shape of the distribution, calculate appropriate averages, and probably calculate measures of variation. Such statistical results will be group results, for they present a picture of the group of cases considered as a whole, or in relation to each other, not in isolation.

It may be noted in passing that these statistical group characteristics, while providing a valuable supplement to the study of individual patterns, are likely to be more empirical, more specific, less theoretical, and less universal than the pattern stated in general form for an individual case. They are not given primarily to describing patterns found in the individual but to indicating *what proportion of the cases in a group* have a prescribed pattern falling within certain magnitude limits. We are speaking here of *statistically* grouped results of individual behavior. On the other hand, studies which observe directly distinctively group properties (for example, order or arrangement) should come up with descriptions having the same quality as the descriptive generalizations of any other individual unit.

The same type of comparison will be extended to one further example. It is quite possible for the statistical combining to cover up or obliterate the very thing that is observed in the individual case, and thus give results which, while correct for a group, have lost the distinctive character which made them of interest. This point is one of long standing in connection with physical growth rates. One way of studying growth with respect to height, for example, is to measure the same individual children from year to year and keep the results *for each child separate.* Growth curves for individuals may then be plotted and studied. Over the same age ranges they will probably show marked variety. Suppose, on the other hand, we decide to plot a curve which will represent the *average* height for each age. (After all, averages are supposed to be more reliable than individual measures!) The resulting curve will be useful in indicating what to expect from similar *groups,* but it will tell nothing whatever about the way individual children grow. The child who is growing very rapidly at age ten may be offset (in the average) by one who is growing slowly at that age. The average curve may, in fact, be highly misleading, if thought of as a norm for individual growth; for it might be that no child in the group from which it was derived had a growth curve anything like the shape of the average curve. If this proved to be so, our group results would have covered up the thing (the individual pattern over time) in which we would usually be most interested.

One does not want to jump immediately to the conclusion that group, or average, results are always or even generally bad. They are notably unsatisfactory where shape, or trend, or structure is involved (these aspects of patterned interrelationship), unless one groups together only those patterns which differ little and which may therefore be regarded as the "same" pattern. If one averages patterns which are so different that he thinks of them as being different, he gets strange results. This is true not only for growth curves but also for other things which are ordinarily classified according to common-sense concepts. For example, it is known that a few persons in a thousand have their hearts on the right side instead of the left. If one calculated the average distance of people's hearts to the left of the middle of their body, and included those on the right side (as negative values), he would probably get a kind of average he did not intend. Or, if one averaged the handedness tendencies of left-handed and right-handed persons, he would probably cover up anything he was interested in; he probably wants a frequency distribution. Perhaps, in handwriting, one wished to discover whether children made their a's and o's distinctively different. If he averaged the height of the connecting line which follows the o, he would have a result that blurred the picture of what he wanted. He probably wants to divide the children into about three groups: those who made their o's definitely different from their a's; those who dropped the line following an o just enough, so that their attention should be directed to their undesirable habits; and, third, those who dropped the line so low that their o's were practically indistinguishable from their a's and who needed remedial work. One could then count the children in each such category, but without any thought of averaging. One can, of course, create as many categories as he thinks he can distinguish with profit; and he may prefer strictly individual cases, but for any practical use he probably will group the cases according to the remedial treatment he thinks they merit; and for theoretical purposes (generalizing from this observed group to children in other similar groups) it becomes almost necessary to put the individual specimens into classes, in order to talk about them with reasonable simplicity. One may, however, even in research theory, desire to pick certain individual specimens as typical of a particular class, and display these or analyze them further, for the greater understanding which comes from the "whole picture" of an individual case.

In planning a study, or planning the analysis of the observations, we must not fall into the error of assuming that one type of attack is inherently *better* than another; each attack is best for the purpose it best serves. Patterns, or qualitatively different conditions, make a poor average; that is, the result is usually not anything we can interpret with clear meaning to ourselves or others. In all statistical work, it is important to consider whether the cases are all sufficiently similar to enter into a single summarizing statistic. The implementation of this point rests on judgment, and it is more often overlooked than not, but it is of basic, logical importance. It may be pointed out that it is the source of many errors, in physical as well as social science. For example, basic theoretical formulations in chemistry (and physics) were held up for many years, because scientists found that the atomic weight of the element chlorine was 35.5. This finding did not agree with theoretical expectation, and interfered with the acceptance of those theoretical formulations which did not agree with the observed value. It was not until 1919 that the British physicist Aston found that ordinary chlorine was a mixture of two kinds of chlorine (two isotopes), having atomic weights of 35 and 37. Using his new technique of mass spectrography, he found that in ordinary chlorine about one-fourth of the atoms had a weight of 37, and three-fourths had a weight of 35, giving rise to the (weighted) *average* value observed for the gas of 35.5.[15] With this distinction, the commoner type of pure chlorine fitted into its place in the theoretical scheme, and further, the discovery led the way to the analysis of all other gases, most of which (even though thought to be chemically pure) contained a certain per cent of their isotopes.

This example, even though from another field of science than our own, shows the need for careful *analysis* of the cases which are *thought* to be the same. The discovery was one of those triumphs of the careful analytical method—a container of ordinary chlorine was analyzed into two types of chlorine when, before that, two types were not known to exist. (Hitches or disagreements of this kind between theory and observation often lead to great forward steps when the cause of the difficulty is ascertained through analysis.)

For many purposes an average furnishes all the information that is needed. This is particularly true when interest centers primarily in a total, or aggregate, the structural composition of which does not change markedly or does not matter. For example, the purchasing agent of a school system can order supplies for his stock room on the basis that his school system allots, on the average, a certain number of sheets of drawing paper for

[15] George Gamow, *Atomic Energy in Cosmic and Human Life,* p. 14. New York: Macmillan Co., 1946. 161 p.

each fourth-grade pupil, and a certain number of fourth-grade children are expected in the following year. Such an average basis may not serve for distributing supplies to individual schools, since the use may vary considerably from school to school, depending on the ability and interest of the teachers, the needs of the children from different neighborhoods, and so on. Again, textbooks in the third grade have a certain average length of life. The purchasing agent knows, accordingly, that a certain proportion of them will have to be replaced each year, so long as that text is used, and he can order accordingly. Where averages are used as one step toward obtaining an aggregate, their use is likely to be satisfactory, except when some condition arises to change the shape of the frequency distribution, or alter its general level.

With this introduction, it seems appropriate to present an overview of the detailed objects and objectives of analysis, and then follow with pertinent illustrations and discussion.

## VARIETIES OF ANALYSIS

There are many varieties of analysis to meet the numerous questions which man's inquiring mind asks, and to deal with the many kinds of objects or phenomena that are of interest. We shall present here an outline which may be helpful in considering this broad area, and may also be used by a researcher to suggest problems in which he might find an interest in working. That is, he may see opportunities for applying one or more of these forms of analysis in some area where he already has a developed interest or where he senses some problem that is significant to him.

In considering what things one might analyze, it does not seem that there are any limitations other than those which apply to research in general. One may analyze anything that he is prepared to analyze. In fact, the range of things which can be analyzed may be somewhat greater than in some other forms of research, for analysis deals in part with certain purely mental phenomena, such as ideas or concepts. In these areas of mental activity it is exceedingly difficult to draw any definite line between research and non-research. For example, published articles of an analytical character might include a stimulating, perhaps provocative, analysis of a problem or problem area, a statement of unsolved problems, a review and critique of the current status of research in an area, a proposal of a new frame of thought for interpreting the research on a large problem, a statement of one or several general principles set forth as hypotheses to be tested by research, and other similar treatises. While any one of these might possibly be ruled out as being "not research," because it was only a portion of the full research process, the vital need for such logical, analytical, synthetic, orienting, and heuristic treatments must be recognized. If research is viewed as a process by which man repeatedly corrects his course, analytic and evaluative review is the process by which research studies its own forward movement. In the total research effort, such analyses and constructive proposals are of the greatest importance.

These comments suggest the breadth of the field open to analysis. In order to be a little more concrete, we will try to list some of the kinds of things which may be regarded as units or wholes, subject to descriptive and explanatory analysis. The following are offered:

1. Concepts; abstract ideas or notions in general. Perhaps along with this would go systems of thought; interpretative schemes.
2. Individual objects, persons, or events, including their characteristic properties or behavior and attitudes.
3. Groups—of objects, persons, or events, including their normal dynamic or behavioral aspects. Perhaps we should also have to include here the various unit delimitations of time, space, and magnitude—such as years, nations, and size groups—for these are regularly characterized in terms of groups and group characteristics.
4. Situations or "fields"—small, particularized situations, including all the ascertainable conditions or factors of significance which may interact or which may have a bearing on a given thing. (Category 3 plus other factors.)
5. Activities, processes, performances—including such as play, problem-solving, learning, teaching, growth. (In comparison with earlier categories, the emphasis here is more on sustained, ordered, special-purpose processes.)

A certain amount of overlapping in these categories will be apparent. The list can be modified as one may desire; it is intended to be suggestive rather than definitive.

In making analyses, the foregoing list may be thought of as what one looks *at;* we turn now to a list which may be thought of as what one looks *for.* That is, in viewing any of the objects, groups, or transactions which one may be studying, what is it he might take as his objective when he penetrates beyond the exterior, or goes from the general to the particular? Certainly one can think of a large number of things in answer to such a question. As a matter of convenience, however, we have set up categories which will help call attention to those objectives of analysis that are often of major interest. These are given in the list below; they represent the things one seeks to distinguish, to differentiate, isolate, identify, describe, and discriminate as parts or relationships which make up and characterize a unit whole.

1. General aspects
2. Components (parts, elements, members)
3. Form, organization, and structure

4. Dynamics: forces and systems
5. Progressive stages (unfoldment, growth, development, decline) (This subject is left to a later chapter on growth and development.)

Perhaps simple illustrations should be given to help make clear the meaning of these terms. Since mechanical things are simpler than living things, we might begin with some familiar object such as a clock. Its *general aspects* would be over-all characteristics, such as appearance, size, suitability, and the like. The *components* of an object can be analyzed on several different bases. For example, in terms of raw materials, one could name such products as wood, plastics, metals, glass. Or, in terms of parts, the components could be listed as wheels, levers, and so on. One might wish to quantify his list and determine *comparative amounts* of the whole or of the components: how much or how many of this, that, or the other thing. *Form* might be applied to the design of the entire clock, or to the design of any of its parts. *Structure* has many aspects. There is the static structure which maintains an object in a given state (for example, keeps it from collapsing). More engaging is the *dynamic* structure—the whole sequence of moving parts which receive the initial force and transform it successively until the desired result (in this case, accurate indication of elapsed time) is produced. Force would relate to the effect of gravity on a pendulum, the energy put into a spring, or perhaps the electric impulses from a current. We might go on and analyze gradual changes (past or contemporary) in the clock. *Progressive stages* would be represented in the successive steps in the original invention (it took modern man nearly a hundred and fifty years of continued effort to invent and develop a good clock), or in its manufacture, or its need for cleaning and repair, or perhaps a decision to discard. (These gradual changes are left for treatment in the chapters on historical method and on growth, genetics, and development.)

For simplicity, we chose the clock, but by the same token it fails to illustrate many things that are of the greatest interest to workers in the biological or human fields. We will not go through the entire list again, but would point out that the topic of *dynamics* will apply to many complex systems that are relatively self-directing and self-balancing, such as the human body, personality, and democratic society. The objective of analysis is to identify and determine the nature, course, and balancing operations of these interactions. The topic of *progressive stages* points particularly to the processes (and steps) of growth, accomplishment, change. The heading of *force* would relate to motivation, hungers, attraction, instincts, and the like.

A number of comments need to be made about the preceding lists. For one thing, any item in the second list may, in turn, become the *object of* analysis and its own nature studied intensively. It would then take its place in the first list. If this seems somewhat confusing, it is on the same order as the idea we probably all learned in elementary school, namely, that any part of speech could, on occasion, be used as a noun. To illustrate, form is subject to mathematical or statistical analysis and description; so are dynamic systems. In this way, all the items of the second list might be added to those of the first. As a matter of fact, "growth" and related ideas already appear in both lists (in slightly different form), because of their intense interest for the field of human study. Perhaps the simplest way to think of this coalition is to recognize that, after the first level of analysis, the thing differentiated (presumably something in the second list) will, in turn, become the object to be analyzed when the next more penetrating level of analysis is undertaken.

A second comment is that, as may have been apparent, it is exceedingly difficult to make up a list of things to look for in analysis, because of the many and divergent interests of the broad field of human research, or of educational research in particular. In somewhat technical terms, the list cannot be uni-dimensional, and some compromises must be made in order to weave the various basic lines of interest together. For example, a purely statistical approach, with a classificatory and intensity emphasis, has its own set of interests. (As stated earlier, these statistical conceptions are not given major attention in the present section, since we are more interested here in approaches that reveal some organization.) Again, phenomena which are primarily distributed over time are always somewhat unique in the interests that attend them. Any firm dividing line between the conceptual or mental, and the objective, is basically impossible to draw and would be a fiction if we should attempt it, for knowledge of the external world is immediately mental. (We have, however, reserved one category in the first list for certain cases which are avowedly abstract.) There is further the marked cleavage between the purely mechanical and the living; and there is growing recognition of a significant difference between closed systems and open systems, though the concepts are still not entirely filled in. We share with the reader a recognition of these incompatibilities, but we find the list of some service for purposes of organization.

One may be somewhat surprised that "causes" do not appear in the list. They are intended to be covered particularly in the head for "dynamics," and to a lesser extent in some of the other categories—perhaps all of them. The direct attempt to prove causal connections, however, is avowedly the province of experimentation and will be dealt with more fully later. Finally, we may record that such terms as *factors, explanations, sequences, consequences,* and *changes*—all attractive, and many times in and out of our working notes—were found somewhat too broad and too widely applicable to be finely discriminating.

The thoughtful reader may be inclined to feel that some of the objectives listed are not necessarily approached by means of what we commonly regard as analysis. We think this is correct. No doubt the objectives sought by analysis may often be approached rather directly *after* they have been revealed, described, and their properties made known by analytical and subsequent study; but the original detection, identification, and adequate conceptualization may have required the most ingenious and tedious forms of analytical effort. Observational procedure will be different when something is well known and when it is as yet unknown.

With these outlines as a framework for thought, we turn to illustrations of analytical study in the fields of education, psychology, and sociology. And, when it seems necessary for the purpose of making a point clear cut, or for suggesting additional attacks or goals which the human sciences might consider, an illustration will be drawn from other fields of science. No attempt, however, will be made to illustrate systematically the search for each kind of analytical objective in each of the kinds of units or wholes; rather, by calling attention to studies of most interest under each of the heads in the second list, it is assumed that the application of analytical methods to the various objects in the first list will be made clear.

## I.  GENERAL ASPECTS (IN ANALYSIS)

One need not think of analysis as something far distant from the ordinary processes of living. There are elements of analysis in his everyday thinking and speaking. In commenting on the doings of other persons, he is likely to pick out salient characteristics which he thinks are more significant than others. In deciding whether to do one thing or another, one will try to analyze the major factors in the choices and then weigh them. When he sits down to write a letter, of the myriad happenings he could write about, he tries to select those which will be of most interest to the other person. In all these processes, there are differentiation, comparison, selection—common elements in analysis.

In research, one will do these same things, only he will do them with more circumspection. He will carry his processes somewhat further. He will dwell on them longer, and more thoughtfully. One will consider his ideas from a broader, and perhaps less personal, background. He will examine them critically from more angles. He will employ instruments to aid his observation if he can. He will interweave careful observation, interpretation, and testing of ideas, which is the pattern basic to all research.

**Aspects vary with one's interests and interpretation.** Any group of cases contemplated for study will have an infinity of aspects from among which the researcher must select. The recogniton and selection of those aspects which the investigator believes will be of significance for his purposes are one of the first forms of analysis. Until one becomes acquainted with research, he may think that this step is somewhat automatic, and that it may be done without conscious attention. The matter is not, however, so simple, and one is expected to give considerable thought to it. As some background for this step, it may be well to consider something of the nature of aspects.

One may be inclined to think of any object as having but a limited number of aspects—perhaps a few presumably "objective" properties or characteristics which can be named over quickly. For example, if it is a physical object, one may think of weight, size, momentum, temperature; but as soon as one starts writing down a list, he will have difficulty in determining where to stop. As a matter of fact, there is no place to stop. Any phenomenon has as many aspects as there are ideas which can be applied to it, including not only our own perceptions of the object (such as color, attractiveness, general desirability) but also all instrumental or physical reactions to it (weight, temperature, hardness, chemical reactions). In reality, all the ways in which something can be fitted into a larger scheme or pattern of thought, and all the ways in which it can be conceived of as analyzed into parts or components, must be included in the list of potential aspects.

To illustrate this point, consider something familiar; and, to make the matter more simple, take a physical object, let us say, a house. The bare facts of its physical nature are likely to be seen in terms of such frames of reference as its style of architecture, its tendency to be in keeping with the character of the neighborhood, adaptation to its immediate plot of ground, homelikeness, appearance of largeness or smallness, suitability for one's own family, convenience of its internal arrangements, its need of decorating and repair, and so on. In turn, for evaluation, each of these aspects will be projected against some particular purpose or interest in the house, such as for occupancy, for investment, for historical preservation, for sentiment, for remodeling, for tearing down, and so on through every possible interest that human beings can have in a house. Thus aspects become complex, and vary according to the perspective of the viewer.

These are all aspects of the house, as perceived by a human being. They are something more than what can be recorded with a measuring tape, but that is because of the limited capacity of the measuring tape. These aspects arise from the projection of the physical facts against a cultivated background of perception. Such aspects avowedly do not have reality apart from the interaction of the house-in-its-setting and the mind of a human being. This is not to be an occasion for surprise. An aspect of anything is contributed to in part by the nature of the reactor (color is not an aspect for an insect which can see only grey). Such a condition is not anything peculiar to the social sciences; it is an everyday observation in the biological and physical sciences, as well as in our common experiences. Upon thought, it will be seen that the characteristics of any physical object (even in physical science) have no reality except in terms of interaction with something else.

It may be that such words as *reality* or *existence* prove troublesome to one's thinking in trying to understand such statements as the foregoing; if such be the case, such phrases as *significant reality, knowable property,* and *ascertainable existence* can be substituted. We are not striving here to press any epistemological point, but only to make the very practical observation that an aspect is always in part a response or reaction; an "object" does not have an (observable, or sensible) aspect except to some reactor (an instrument, a human being, a chemical reagent) capable of entering into a relation with that particular aspect and contributing a part of the observable reaction.

The point being made is fundamental for orientation in social science. In the social world, it is human reactions in which our primary interest lies. If we were restricted to mechanically determined aspects, on the basis of some presumed criterion of "objectivity," we would have little basis for developing a truly social science. Thus, for example, when we think of a single human being, we find that there are so many aspects (interpretative perceptions) of human beings which have been recognized by man that it requires a significant portion of all the words in the dictionary to name them.[16] Interestingly enough, this idea of properties as interaction has been commonplace in the physical sciences for some time; although we judge that a physical scientist is likely to be less ready to extend it to the social field. That is, he is used to the idea of interaction in his area, but he tends to think of the human being as an undesirable interactor—as a factor to be kept out of scientific data. In our field, the human being is the heart of our concern, and our chief data are the products of human interaction. In thinking, therefore, about physical-science methodology and in borrowing concepts (which we can often do to advantage), we must make this clear-cut distinction with respect to what is the center of interest. The physical scientist primarily studies things in interaction with other physical things; the social scientist primarily studies things (or persons) in interaction with

---

[16] Gordon W. Allport and H. S. Odbert, *Trait-Names:* A Psycho-Lexical Study. Psychological Monographs, Vol. 47, No. 211. Washington: American Psychological Association, 1936. 171 p.

human beings. And in both fields, the property or aspect studied is contributed to (exists or has reality) in part because of the reactive capacity of the responding agent (the observer).

One may object that this view makes aspects quite capricious, a matter of the individual observer. This is partly true, but is not true in the full sense in which it might at first seem. It is partly true in that, for example, a noise is not a noise (is not an aspect of some situation) for the person who was born deaf and cannot hear; color is not an aspect for the person who is blind and who never knew color; various concepts (such perhaps as "entropy," "elasticity of demand," "complementarity," and so on) are not aspects of a situation to the person who has never developed these sophisticated ideas, nor been aware of such tendencies; nor would they ever become aspects to a person who was very low in the intelligence range. Similarly we may say that, to the adult, the world has many aspects which it does not have for the child.

On the other hand, the recognition of an aspect is not so highly individual and personal as is the assessment of the degree of that aspect. That is, different persons might not agree in naming the color of some object, but they would agree that color (of some kind) was an aspect of the object. Different persons would probably agree that "beauty" is an aspect of art, although they might differ greatly in their judgments of how beautiful any particular object was. When one makes this distinction between the recognition of a general trait (aspect), and the assessment of the degree or value which an object might have on this trait, he will see that the perception of an aspect is not so individualistic a matter as might at first appear.

One may inquire, If aspects depend so much on the observer, how can one gather data which are "objective"? Perhaps he can't. We are today much less concerned with the older notion that pure objectivity is possible, or desirable, in the study of human affairs than we are with reliability, namely, the extent to which different observers agree. (Such a concept is usually limited to competent observers.) Someone may say that this is all the older "objectivity" meant, and, in truth, it was occasionally so defined; but, in general, it had additional connotations, such as that the observer could note happenings with the fidelity and detachment of a physical instrument. And even here, the concept probably attributed to physical instruments more powers than they have; the physical scientist knows that his instruments to some degree affect and distort the phenomena they are supposed to record. Never in the external world, but only in the realm of pure thought, do we find the perfection so often assumed.

We share with those who wish that matters might be otherwise. It is simpler to live in a world where things are what they seem. But when the physicist tells us, after long analytical study, that a solid object is in reality mostly space—that the constituents of the very atoms are dispersed like the planets of our solar system—we must realize that the sense of solidness is a simplified human concept. Perhaps in interaction with most other things the object would also prove to have some solidity; yet it might not prove "solid" to x-rays, gamma rays, or shorter wavelengths. Whether it is solid depends on what it is interacting with. Thus, as we have previously noted, a property (at least as sensed, or known) is an interaction. But we can also draw lessons from man's early history and from contemporary anthropology. Those who are not fully convinced by physical-science examples may still respect the progress of man's more common thinking. If one does not agree that the observer shares in creating the impression of what he perceives, then he must feel that what is perceived is in the object itself. He is back with primitive man. Books of mythology and folklore are replete with descriptions of how man has perceived good or evil intent in many facts of nature; and not only feared, but took active steps to appease, attack, and exterminate the spirits which he "saw" in cases of sickness, drought, typhoon, and other disasters.[17] In the thinking found among primitive persons, "the effect produced in the observer is projected and believed to be an inherent attitude of the object."[18] Wherein is our thinking different, in terms of its projective character, when we believe our perceptions are wholly "objective" in their origin?

**Aspects are selected in the light of one's purpose.** From the great range of possible aspects of any phenomena, the researcher has the problem of selecting those with which it seems appropriate for him to deal in his particular study. Such selection will be done in the light of his purposes. The objective is to select those aspects that will prove to be most important, either for immediate practical use, or for contributing to scientific theory. To select those aspects which are most likely to be immediately useful, one will have to project his thinking into the situations where his findings may be wanted, and consider the uses to which they might be put.

If one is seeking to contribute to theory, he will consider the selection of aspects in terms of that purpose; but his selection is likely to be attended with some uncertainty. Perhaps this selection will not be difficult for those persons who think that every study should deal with some sharply stated, very narrow question—usually represented in the form of an exactly worded hypothesis. There may be places for such a view of research. But certainly it is not the only one. In the main, research is a matter of follow-

17 James George Frazer, *The Golden Bough*. Third Edition. London: Macmillan and Co., 1911-15. 12 vols. Or the one-volume edition, p. 547, 562-63.
18 William A. White, "The Language of Schizophrenia." *Archives of Neurology and Psychiatry* 16:395-413; October 1926.

ing along, gaining new conceptions as one makes his observations, stumbling upon aspects which one didn't know existed, starting over again perhaps several times with new definitions and with a modified purpose. The great discoveries in physical science have not come from supposedly crucial experiments to test hypotheses, but rather from alert, sensitive exploration; exploration carried on with a purpose, certainly, but a purpose not so rigidly held as to interfere with new insights, with the full recognition of unanticipated discoveries.

As we have said, the researcher will seek to observe those aspects which will prove most significant for scientific theory. To state such a principle, however, is little more than to state a goal. One usually cannot tell—scientists may not know for fifty years afterward—what aspects are of great value. How can one know whether his findings will be trivial or revolutionary? The matter is supposed to be safeguarded by proposing hypotheses which are derived from some general theory that is being tested in various ways by a number of studies; the aspects relevant to the hypothesis would then presumably be of value. They should be; but the original theory may be untenable, or the questions not closely related to reality and, by keeping his attention fixed on the rigidly logical formulation of a narrow proposition, the researcher may miss entirely the main body of truth that his study brings to the surface, but which he is unprepared to see. The history of the older sciences is full of such instances; the matter is one of fairly common occurrence and is not just a theoretical possibility.[19]

There are unavoidably certain restrictive influences in the emphases of the various "schools of thought" in any field. They differ essentially in the aspects of any situation which they attend to. Thus, for example, in psychology and sociology the behaviorists emphasize a certain set of aspects which are readily observable, and regard many other aspects as "hypothetical constructs" or "intervening variables." Presumably the followers of different schools would assert that their differences lie deeper than this; but we would point out that the large mental superstructure of interpretation is based on, and built out of, the giving of attention to an arbitrarily selected set of aspects which they have chosen as being of interest for their theories. Attending to certain aspects more than to others is not a peculiarity of

[19] Almost any full historical account of the study of phlogiston will point out that the early and continuing evidence contrary to the theory was overlooked, because researchers faced their data with a frame of reference which focused attention on the wrong thing. In two books, which deal with central elements in research method, Conant brings out the point repeatedly that existing scientific ideas often block more correct ones from being formulated.
James B. Conant, *On Understanding Science.* New Haven: Yale University Press, 1947. See especially p. 83, 103.
James B. Conant, *Science and Common Sense.* New Haven: Yale University Press, 1951. See especially p. 171.

scientists; we all do it regularly in our everyday lives. One has to, in order to avoid complete confusion. But, for scientific purposes, it is worth understanding that the researchers who follow any particular school of thought have developed a certain frame of interpretation which in turn gives perceptual coloring to the restricted set of aspects chosen for attention and thus these observations unavoidably support the frame of thought that in part created them. The leading workers in each school undoubtedly feel that all this is desirable, and it must be granted that it does seem worth while to explore engaging points of view to see how much they may contribute by way of explaining and integrating occurrences. But there is always a question about the slanting of the findings and conclusions of researchers whose point of view is highly restricted by their devotion to a predisposing pattern of thought. Not that what they report is untrue, but with a more open mind they might have seen and reported very different things.

As a consequence of the inability to foretell the value of a particular bit of knowledge, some persons go to the extreme of saying that the only scientific procedure is to study everything possible about any object. They may even argue that, sooner or later, we need to know everything about it and hence it does not matter from what angle one starts. Other persons must eventually carry on the process until everything possible about a phenomenon has been explored. In some of the older sciences, where certain phenomena to be studied are known to be of basic importance, this conception has actually been carried through. For example, there was recently published a sheet with eighty-eight quantitative facts on it about different aspects of the element oxygen; and of course many other facts are known about oxygen which are not described in quantitative terms. But it would scarcely seem worth while to make such thorough study of something that was not established as being of basic importance. In the human sciences we have scarcely established elemental phenomena of such lasting significance as a chemical element.

The idea of studying at random is likely to be frowned on partly because researchers are not solely interested in knowing everything about everything; they also desire to develop useful, integrating generalizations. Such generalizations will probably come more slowly (or not at all) from an uninspired, blunderbus attack on phenomena than they will from a planned attack growing out of questions which seem to have some urgency. Whether of the immediate, practical kind or of the more fundamental, theoretical kind, a well formed set of questions will add purpose and definition to a research study.

While there is no method that will guarantee the best advance selection of aspects for study, there are helpful approaches. In addition to a carefully considered set of major questions to be answered, our recommendation is that the investigator keep his mind as open as possible, and give thoughtful and broad consideration to any evidence which might be significant. Close adherence to a fixed frame of reference may prove to be at the cost of a larger contribution to science. A researcher should have a major purpose in his work, certainly, and should select for systematic attention those aspects of the situation which would seem, after analytical evaluation, to have relevance to his main questions. At the same time, however, we should emphasize that the more fixed the view, the less receptive is the researcher to evidence which suggests a reformulation of the original conceptualization.

As one of the first steps in almost any research undertaking, selective analysis is a part of the successive delimitation which is so characteristic of research. No set of rules can be adequate for this essentially human process. After careful thought, aspects for study should be selected in the light of one's purposes and the scientific thinking of the time, with recognition of the possibility that certain of these tenets are wrong. One should conduct his entire study with an awareness that the major discoveries in research come to the worker who maintains a mind that is alert and ready to think, rather than to one who approaches his problems with a set of rigidly held concepts.

**Aspects chosen for study reflect themselves in one's plans for gathering data.** The foregoing discussion relates directly to the plans one makes for obtaining his observations. Since most research for the purpose of description or explanation is systematized, one will probably either select or prepare a data-gathering schedule of some kind. In either case the instrument is expected to represent the aspects which he has in mind to study. If he is preparing the instrument himself, the aspects selected will find expression in the different queries of a questionnaire, in the different items of a test, in the outline for an interview, in a check list or rating scale, or in whatever scheme he has for systematizing the gathering of data. This does not mean that there will be one item in his instrument for one aspect; there may be one or many; or one item may throw light on several aspects. The statement means merely that the plans with regard to aspects should find direct expression in one's plans for taking observations.

While a discussion of the preparation of data-gathering instruments will be given in a subsequent chapter, the matter is referred to briefly at the present point, in a preparatory way, in order to make the connection between the discussion of aspects and the subsequent work on the instrument or on other plans for the gathering of data. The two following topics will deal directly with certain considerations in the conversion of aspects into specific statements for data-gathering.

For the sake of orientation and, lest a certain degree of confusion arise, we make the statement here that the present treatment of "analysis" is quite apart from what is thought of in connection with the analysis of data (which is a later process in the research study and which is discussed in the several chapters on research methods). Not that the two processes are unrelated, for success in the analysis of the observed data depends on prior success in taking observations which prove sufficient for the derivation of meaningful results. Yet in the research undertaking the two processes, connected in causal sequence, are well separated in time. We are in the present section giving attention to the earlier process of analyzing the problem and structuring our conceptions of the data needed, in the hope that by proper care at this stage we may be spared undue disappointment later when the study is nearing its end.

In fact, although we may say this again elsewhere, we recommend that the investigator draw up summarizing tables, of the sort he will make at a later stage, and try filling them in with data which his schedules might obtain. He can in this way test whether his schedules will yield the requisite information, at least for those questions with which he started.

**The breadth of the aspects chosen may be adapted according to need.** While dealing with processes of analysis, we must not gain the impression that our goal is always to select the narrowest or most detailed aspect possible. When one splits too finely for his real purpose, he may have difficulty in synthesizing or reconstructing the highly specific facts into a whole-bodied answer to his questions. The discussion is not intended to prejudice the case one way or the other, for or against refined specifics or more general aspects, but simply to bring out that there is a relationship between purposes and the extent to which aspects should be narrowed.

For illustration, let us take an apparently simple object such as a textbook. We wonder whether anyone ever asked himself what the aspects of a textbook are—what different things about it can be studied. (Certainly there are far more than we will even suggest here; we will simply mention a few for illustrative purposes.) First, a textbook has certain gross physical characteristics—height, width, thickness, weight, number of pages, kind of cover, color, and so on. How should these be provided for if one is making up an observation schedule, a questionnaire, rating scale, or the like? There are two ways (at least) of handling such matters. One is to list all the detailed aspects the researcher can think of, and gather data on each one. The other way is to think of the purpose for which one would use the information and see whether he could frame a general question that might get at the heart of the matter better, and thus save gathering many facts, only to have to interpret them (if possible) later on. For example, if his purpose were to evaluate or/and select a textbook, he might simply ask the general question, Is the book of such size, shape, and weight that it is convenient for children to carry and to use in ways they are likely to?

It may be that one has purposes in mind that require detailed data, in which case general, purpose-reflecting questions may not be satisfactory, but their possibility should be considered. They involve judgments, to be sure; but certain judgments may be made more validly with the specimen before the worker, than when one has only a set of detached figures. We may consider certain illustrations of the issue.

A certain kind of type face will be used in printing the book. One is probably not so much concerned with the factual information that the type has such and such a name, and is of a given size, and has so much leading (space between the lines) as he is with whether the type is easily and quickly read by the reader for whom the book is designed. He will also be somewhat concerned with economy, and with the esthetic appearance of the page. The observing and recording of detailed facts on these aspects may answer his purpose, and again they may not. That is, since studies have shown that certain sizes, styles, and leading of type, and certain lengths of line are desirable for children of different ages,[20] one may find it satisfactory to record the specific facts about a book and later compare these recorded specifics with standards established by research. Or, the accepted standards may be copied onto the rating sheet as a guide to judgment, and the judgment made at the time of recording, so that one simply notes whether the text is satisfactory, exceptionally good, or questionable or unacceptable with respect to typography and page format.

There are both advantages and dangers in the more general and complex type of response, but it should presumably be employed whenever it satisfactorily meets the need. A host of detailed specifics may exhaust one's patience (especially that of the respondent to a questionnaire), may be a nuisance when it comes to analyzing the data, and may fail ultimately to fit together so as to give an answer to the basic question. On the other hand, the more general reaction-type question may fail to produce certain specific information needed, it does not permit the reader of the research report to exercise his own judgment and interpretation, and can lead to careless, sloppy answers. Certainly the factors which should be considered in rendering a general reaction should be specified on the data-gathering

---

[20] Considerable research on this problem has been done by Miles A. Tinker and Donald G. Paterson. One may find their studies by looking under their names in the *Education Index* over a number of years past.

schedule, even if one is doing the observing himself. Often one will find it advantageous to gather both detailed and general data.

There are, of course, far more subtle (and more important) aspects of a textbook than those so far mentioned. What of its content? Content itself has many aspects. Is it in general adapted to the level of development of the reader for whom it is intended? Is it psychologically sound? Does it appeal to and stimulate the interest of the reader? Is the factual content correct? Does the material fit well into the curriculum of a particular school? Does it promote the personal and social development of the reader? For what kinds or types of children will it be particularly helpful? In general, each of these aspects to be given consideration would be analyzed further into subaspects (perhaps components), so as to yield judgments which would support a more general conclusion. But in any case the recognition, the selection of, and the rendering of decisions on such aspects call for professional insight and judgment. In the face of such questions as those suggested, one may sense the utter folly of attempting to make analyses of educational materials, or other social utilities, with the thought that human reactions must be kept out of the data. In what way, for example, can a textbook be psychologically sound, or interesting, *apart from the reactions of human beings?* (Certain aspects of textbook analysis are presented in the next chapter.)

We leave this topic in an unfinished state, as indeed we have to leave nearly all topics, because there are aspects of it which seem better dealt with elsewhere. For example, research literature is full of many arguments over the very point here dealt with; some schools of thought are opposed to any kind of analysis (at least any kind which has the word *analysis* attached to it). To deal with these arguments would require more space than is available.

**Large aspects need to be made specific.** In any case, a trait (aspect) which is to be studied needs definiteness. One of the fundamental obligations of the researcher is to see that the aspects he expects to study are carefully defined. He will find that, whereas a very loose concept will usually do for everyday living (where it is sometimes regarded as an act of courtesy to pretend that one knows what the other person is talking about), quite the reverse is true in research. The reader of a research report wants (and is entitled) to know exactly what is meant in every important word. This requires that the investigator himself analyze his meaning carefully, and write down his meaning in some extensiveness. Otherwise, he will not be able to gather his data with any consistency and, accordingly, will not be able to make statements about them with much significance.

When one has selected an aspect for study (virtually always by naming it) he should, before he begins gathering any data, ask in penetrating fashion, What does the name of this aspect mean? What do I want it to mean, for my particular study? For, while he does not want to depart from widely accepted usage with regard to meanings, often (or usually) a term has so many meanings that any specific meaning is simply a choice. Thus, a particular name of an aspect may not mean at all the same thing in different studies. Experienced research workers know this, hence they demand a very clear statement of just what the term does mean in each individual study. And this includes as well the steps taken to carry out or implement this meaning. What was its meaning in terms of actual doing? Normally the actual questionnaire, test, or other instrument used will be shown in the report as an essential part of this explanation.

For purposes of illustration, let us take the fairly simple aspect, "size of a school system." It may be the major point of a study, or one of the auxiliary factors to be employed in analysis of the data; but in any case it needs definition. This definition will usually take the form of more detailed or specific aspects which will be included or excluded. In other words, what ideas make up this more general idea?

Perhaps one has never been prompted to raise a question as to what the aspect "size of a school system" really means. But if he is to deal with it in his study, he is face to face with the problem of defining it. He will find, first, that his definition will grow and change to some extent during the process of his work, as he comes across one case after another that raises questions his definition has not provided for. Second, his decisions written into his definition will at places have to be arbitrary, made for the purposes of his study, and sometimes without sure conviction that one decision is better than another, but with the realization that some decision must be made and that it must be recorded and reported, so that a later researcher can try a different decision, if he feels it might be advantageous.

Will one have the size of his school systems represented by the number of square miles in the district? By the number of pupils, number of teachers, number of school buildings, number of classrooms, aggregate area of the school grounds, amount of money spent per year, or by some other aspect of size? And if he decides, let us say, on number of pupils, he will find that even this concept has so many aspects (meanings, interpretations, facets) that it requires further specification in order to be definite. Will "number of pupils" be the number enrolled (usually meaning a cumulative, never decreasing number during the year); or will it be average daily membership (the number belonging); or average daily attendance; or an actual number at a given time rather than an average over a time period? In areas where there is a heavy seasonal migration, the differences between these figures may run from 100 per cent to 300 per cent. Then one has to consider the manifold activities of the school system —all aspects of its work. What about evening-school enrollments? Late afternoon classes, presumably for employed persons? Summer session-enrollments? Pupils taught in hospitals and homes by visiting teachers? Perhaps the school system operates correctional schools, which is somewhat unusual. Perhaps it operates a teachers college for the college education of teachers in preparation. What about the pupils sent by bus to some other school district for schooling? (Some school districts maintain no schools of their own. What is their size?) What about pupils transported into the system from another school district? And tuition-paying pupils who live outside the district but come in by choice?

Perhaps one's first inclination is to say he doesn't know the answers to these questions and doesn't care; it will not make any difference anyway. He can be certain that it does make a great deal of difference to the school systems concerned, and also to someone else who is making a similar study, or to someone who is reading over several studies and wants to understand why they came out with such different results. Any school superintendent and board of education will care a great deal, if the cost per pupil in their school system is shown to be exhorbitantly high, because somebody "didn't care" how he defined number of pupils, and happened to get very different concepts represented in the reports from different school systems. And apart from practical objections to his work, what good are his findings?

It is probable that, unless the researcher has had considerable experience in the field in which he makes his study, he will not be prepared to frame final definitions in advance. This is to be expected; a study usually reveals conditions that even one with considerable experience in the area had not previously noted. An investigator should not feel chagrined at his lack of knowledge; rather he should take it as normal in even apparently simple studies for him to have to revise his ideas as he proceeds. This revision of concepts should be seen as one of the major outcomes of a study, quite apart from, or in addition to, the more formal findings. Accordingly, the changes in conception may well be recorded among the summarizing statements at the end of a study. This will enable the next researcher to have the benefit of the earlier investigator's experience; and it should be a guide to those who formulate further problems for attack.

We have indicated at various points that one should do preliminary, exploratory work in the taking of observations. It is this matter of selecting and refining of aspects that we have in mind. Otherwise, one may have to begin over again several times, since any material change in his definitions of traits (aspects) will require that he discard the data he has already obtained or tabulated.

So far, we have been discussing the specification of a concept in terms of more specific aspects. The problem devolves primarily on definition; presumably there would be little question about the obtaining of proper figures once the concept is set. There are other situations, however, where the matter of judgment at the time of observation is prominent. Is a case this or that? In such circumstances, it has been found that splitting a general, judgmental aspect up into more detailed, specific aspects is likely to render the judgments of different observers more comparable. In other words, it tends to remove some of the observer variation (unreliability), resulting in what is often referred to as greater "objectivity."

Thus, in the preceding topic dealing with aspects of a textbook, it was mentioned that many of the general aspects would have to be made more specific (that is, stated in terms of smaller, more narrow aspects), in order for one to arrive at a dependable judgment, one which he could explain and defend and make perfectly clear to a reader of his report. To take another example, one may be called on to judge the quality of teaching. Such a complex process as teaching will be seen by different observers in very different ways, depending on what their backgrounds have led them to see in any given situation. On the other hand, if the general concept (aspect) "quality of teaching" has been carefully analyzed and split up into detailed acts, or other components, which depend less for their recognition and counting, or assessment, on the background and interpretation of the individual observer, there is likely to be far less difference in the observations of different persons.

Insofar as such fractionating does not omit vital elements which are relatively uncorrelated with those specifics chosen for observation, the process of substituting more specific, definite aspects for the larger ones seems desirable. It is probable, however, that in all cases something is lost; that is, some qualities of the essence of the general aspect are likely to be (unwittingly) surrendered in order to obtain some gain in reliability. Whether this amounts to a net gain in the validity of the observations is something to be pondered. The present emphasis in research is largely in the direction of greater reliability. Perhaps another generation will shift the emphasis to validity, but this is a much harder task. It can be accomplished only slowly.

There may be situations where the process of expressing general aspects in terms of more specific ones breaks down because of its weight; it simply becomes too cumbersome. There may be other cases where the analysis of the general aspect leaves much to be desired; the specifics simply do not add up to give a satisfactory picture of the larger idea. We should hesitate, in such circumstances, to counsel that one give up his proposed study, provided he can do something that is reasonably indicative. It may be that, by proceeding, he can motivate greater interest in the area, and possibly stimulate the energies of other researchers who will work out a method of achieving the needed reliability. In such ways does research progress.

It may now be apparent that this matter of dividing up large ideas (usually with the thought that they will later be put together again) is one which is generally typical of the whole research effort. It is, in fact, the basic idea behind data-gathering schedules, including questionnaires and all measuring or evaluative instruments. It is, therefore, one of the first steps. In the present section we are treating the idea in terms of its contribution to definiteness through the naming of specific aspects to be included or omitted. In the later section on "components" we will view the matter in terms of breaking up the general idea in a way so that the more specific or elemental aspects will add up to yield a picture of the larger one.

**Factor analysis is sometimes employed to avoid duplication in aspects.** Since the early 1930's factor analysis has had fairly wide use in the attempt to reduce the number of aspects which one need observe.[21] If two aspects correlate perfectly (that is, if a case which is highest in the group with respect to one aspect is also highest with respect to the other, and so on down the scale) then there is no need to take observations on both of them, since either aspect can be estimated dependably from the other. Thus the number of aspects to observe could be cut from two to one. Or, if four different aspects had a high average intercorrelation among themselves, perhaps the researcher could, by studying the aspects represented, determine what elements they had in common and thus deduce the nature of some new aspect which could be substituted for them. In this way (with appropriate rather lengthy calculations) one can obtain a smaller number of aspects to study in lieu of the original larger number.

The technique has had extensive use. We shall give here only a few illustrations that seem appropriate in the present setting; some additional illustrations and references will be given in the later section on analysis into components.

The staff of the Teacher Education Study (Los Angeles) employed factor analysis in the attempt to obtain significant aspects of teaching ability. That is, of the infinite number of aspects of teaching, what reasonable number of aspects will afford a satisfactory indication of the level of quality?

[21] Although Charles Spearman published the first paper in America in this field in 1904, the majority of publications have appeared after 1930.

As a beginning point for a series of studies in this area,[22] the literature in the field was reviewed and a collection of critical behaviors (or incidents) was made; that is, especially effective or ineffective classroom behaviors. Twenty-five of these basic traits (aspects or dimensions) were formed into a Classroom Observation Scale and a number of teachers were rated on each of these traits. The purpose of this rating was not, however, to yield an over-all rating of the teachers, but rather to provide a set of data which would yield correlations among the twenty-five aspects, so that they could be factor analyzed. Five factors were obtained from data on elementary-school teachers and six factors for high-school teachers. Our interest here is not in the specific factors found, but rather in the method. According to the formal reasoning of the procedure, teachers' classroom behavior can, to a considerable extent, be described, and differences between better and poorer teaching accounted for, in terms of five or six aspects or factors. Whether these "factors" can actually be observed in the classroom with satisfactory reliability is something which would require further test; if so, they would be useful for a large variety of studies. Judgment is involved at various steps in the process of deriving these aspects, notably in the original selection of aspects for the list, in  the rating of behavior on the list, and again in the identification and characterization of the factors (after the mathematical work is completed), and in lesser ways at other points. The procedure does, however, afford a means of telescoping or reducing the number of aspects originally employed to a much smaller number, without depending wholly on inspection and deliberation for this reduction.

It may be that the traits discussed in the preceding paragraph are actually something more than what we normally think of as aspects. Those who are enthusiastic in their claims for factor analysis would probably assume so. Perhaps further research will reveal the answer. It must be borne in mind, however, that these analyzed "factors" are correlated among themselves, and cannot therefore be thought of as pure elements.

In an ingenious application of the method to nations, Cattell [23] has attempted to discover a reasonably small number of aspects which would

22 A brief overview or résumé of the three principal studies in this group, together with three additional ones, is given in David G. Ryans and Edwin Wandt, "Investigations of Personal and Social Characteristics of Teachers." *Journal of Teacher Education* 3:228-31; September 1952. For more detailed reports of the separate studies, see the following:

Alfred C. Jensen, "Determining Critical Requirements for Teachers." *Journal of Experimental Education* 20:79-85; September 1951.

David G. Ryans, "A Study of Criterion Data (A Factor Analysis of Teacher Behaviors in the Elementary School)." *Educational and Psychological Measurement* 12:333-44; Autumn 1952.

David G. Ryans and Edwin Wandt, "A Factor Analysis of Observed Teacher Behaviors in the Secondary School: A Study of Criterion Data." *Educational and Psychological Measurement* 12:574-86; Winter 1952.

23 Raymond B Cattell, "The Dimensions of Culture Patterns by Factorization of National Characters." *Journal of Abnormal and Social Psychology* 44:443-69; October 1949.

describe (and differentiate) the culture of nations. He obtained data on seventy-two different aspects of seventy nations and derived twelve aspects ("dimensions") with which one can describe national cultures. It may, however, prove difficult to obtain data on these twelve aspects, since, in the main, they are highly complex and not covered by the usual published statistics of nations. Further, as a methodological note, it must be borne in mind that these resulting aspects describe the original seventy-two aspects, and not directly the cultures. Any aspects of culture that were not represented in the original data will not be found (except by accident) in the resulting "factors." In addition, a certain amount of fidelity is lost.

In the same fashion, Hofstaetter [24] made a study of the aspects which would differentiate the cultures of the forty-eight states in the United States. He started with data on sixteen aspects and derived three aspects that were uncorrelated with each other. Since eight of his original sixteen aspects were related to schools and education, it would not be surprising for him to come out with at least one factor related to education. He did.

In connection with the literature on factor analysis, a word or two as to terminology may be appropriate. For those who think primarily in terms of measurement, *dimension* is a favorite term. It indicates the statistical trait, or nature of the scale or continuum, along which a measurement is taken. *Aspect* is a somewhat broader, more inclusive term; for it refers as readily to qualitative or categorical concepts as to quantitative extensions. From two of the technical dictionaries we take the (partial) definitions: "Dimension. (*math.*) measurable extent of any kind." [25] "Ability, dimension of: ability as measured by a particular aspect of performance, such as speed, range, or power." [26] In the use made of the terms in the present discussion, *aspect* represents any observable (including measurable) trait or quality or characteristic. It appears, however, that one will occasionally find the term *dimension* used somewhat loosely, in about the same sense as *aspect*—to include qualitatively described variables.

**Observer interpretation of aspects may enter different studies at different points.** Throughout the discussion of aspects we have emphasized their interactional character—the fact that their nature, their detection, and their assessment depend in part on the reacting agent, whether an instrument or a human observer. The personal contribution of the human observer may vary from little to much. In such forms of observation as copying data from one record to another, scoring objective tests by a key,

24 Peter R. Hofstaetter, "A Factorial Study of Cultural Patterns in the U. S." *Journal of Psychology* 32:99-113; July 1951.
25 Howard C. Warren, Editor, *Dictionary of Psychology.* Boston: Houghton Mifflin Co., 1934. 372 p.
26 Carter V. Good, Editor, *Dictionary of Education.* New York: McGraw-Hill Book Co., 1945. 495 p.

and counting cases which are regularly obvious, the observer's contribution may be relatively routine. In other instances, such as grading an essay test, classifying objects or actions as falling in certain complex categories, or otherwise imputing to an object or event certain qualities which the observer believes it to have, his role may involve a considerable amount of judgment. And judgment is an aspect of his own personality.

The principal point to bring out here is the relation of this element of observer interpretation to research procedures. In what ways and at what points does it come into the process? And how does it affect what one does? Sometimes the element of human interpretation is introduced into the work at an early stage (at the time the data are first recorded), and sometimes at a later stage (after the initial records have been made). And then there are those studies that are relatively mechanical throughout, in which interpretative elements (other than purely formal ones) are not present in strong degree at any point. Let us examine these three situations, taking them up in reverse order.

The relatively mechanical study is the form which will be chosen by those persons who feel that rigorous formality is the essence of research method, and that the judgment and interpretation of the researcher must be kept to the minimum possible throughout the study, else he will not be doing research. The personal element contributed by the observer may be small in studies where cases are clear-cut and fall with little or no question (that is, without the exercise of judgment) into categories adopted for the study. This condition requires, for one thing, that the adopted categories be simple and obvious. Copying data from documentary sources (when the categories in the original source are clear and dependable), summarizing such initial records as questionnaires which had alternative responses provided on them, or scoring and tallying objective tests, are examples that may be regarded as falling in this general class. So also will be the readings or recordings of instruments in a psychological laboratory. The results of these procedures are usually quantitative and their classification may require no more than the ordinary technical understanding of class intervals in a frequency distribution. The subsequent interpretation may be of the wholly formal type, such as that normally involved in statistical work, and expressed commonly in some form of comparison of quantities.

Judgment will have been exercised at every step of the research—in the selection and formulation of the problem, the definition of cases to be included and excluded, the selection of the source field or conditions of observation, the selection of the aspects to be represented in the questionnaire, test, or other instrument, the precise wording of these, the choice of analytical procedures for deriving meaning from the data, and the selection of suitable bases for comparison. Although every step in research is *necessarily* shot through with judgment, and the resulting conclusions are the product of these successive decisions, the worker who follows the pattern above will be adhering to the code of many researchers who feel that any direct influence of the investigator on the data is a fundamental iniquity. Satisfying as formality may be to some personalities, and, on the other hand, intolerable as sloppiness in research is, it seems important to point out two things: (1) that, to purely formal methodology, many pressing problems in the human field are utterly inaccessible; and (2) that the conclusions of any study inescapably bear the impress of the researcher, even if only in their unembellished formality.

Lest misconstruction arise from the foregoing paragraph, we feel it desirable to add our conviction that rigor is always desirable where it is attainable without too great sacrifice; but, in the interests of coming to grips with central human problems and of a vigorous forward movement of research in the human field, we feel that, where the spirit of exploration and venture is withered by a subservience to formalism, the price is too high. Beginning students of research may well pay a great deal of attention to learning the expectations of more mature research workers, if they want their work accepted; but they should never conceive of the end goal of their learning as being a complete enshroudment in a mechanical formalism.

The second type of study, namely, that in which observer reaction is kept to a minimum during the initial stage of data-gathering but may be required later, is represented by studies in which it is possible to take relatively full records, such as a stenographic account, a sound recording, a photograph, or a moving picture. In such cases the element of interpretative judgment can be delayed until one begins to analyze these records. Thus, to bring out the aspects he desires, one may create analytical, interpretative categories after viewing or listening to these records, and he may then make tabulations of things which occur in the records, in contrast to doing these things in advance of gathering the initial data, as in the third type of study. Further, he may go over the records several times, or have others do this, in order to check his judgment as to the classification of things that occurred. Questionnaires of the free-response type (sometimes called "open-end" questions) will call for interpretation as soon as one begins classifying the responses. Likewise, essay tests which must be graded, or other specimens that call for judgment in their rating or other classification, are examples of material which involves observer reaction to a rather large degree. In fact, because observer variability may be great, the use of some of these materials, unless properly safeguarded, will be avoided in research where it is possible to do so.

In the preceding paragraph we have employed the term *observer* as being synonymous with *researcher,* or his assistants, meaning specifically the one who classifies the cases. We are not here referring to the "subject" in visual or perceptual experiments in psychology, nor to onlookers in social situations.

In the third type of study, judgment is exercised in making the initial record. It may be that the mechanical means of recording referred to in the second type of study are inconvenient, prohibitively cumbrous, expensive, unavailable, disturbing, or inadequate to the subtleties and complexities of the situation to be observed. One may, therefore, observe practices in a school classroom, or observe the behavior of children at play or in a nursery school, or analyze the procedures of a deliberative group, making direct tallies of events which are to be recorded. These tallies require that a set of categories appropriate to the situation and to one's purposes have been prepared in advance; and they also require (usually) very quick judgment on the part of the observer as to placement of an event according to the established categories—in addition to the judgment as to whether the item qualifies for inclusion at all. (It is true that these categories may be so simple as to place the work under the first type of study, but this is not typically the case.) In an interview, a large amount of judgment is called for in carrying on the conference and in recording what was brought out. If one employs a rating scale, the rating is basically a matter of judgment, even when the scale is supplemented by detailed directions and calls for many supporting facts. There are many other situations in which the original record is a judgment of some kind on the part of the researcher or his assistants. In most of the work of this third type, probably the initial record of the data will be made in classified form; that is, by tallying in categories. The record may, in addition, relate the data to particular individuals, and to other variables.

In all three types of study there will be a certain amount of interpretation after the data have been analyzed (that is, tabulated into appropriate categories, and perhaps statistical measures calculated, if the data are quantitative in any sense). Again, the amount of the researcher's judgment which comes into the report will depend on the criteria accepted by the investigator for his work. Interpretation can be wholly formal, even if technically advanced and ingenious; and presumably a great deal of formal interpretation is called for in most cases. But the worker who does not strive to present his report in the smallest possible compass can do a great deal to expand the significance of his findings. He will do this probably through amplifying the thought structure in which the problem is set, through suggesting ramifications of the significance of the findings into various areas of utility, and perhaps engaging to some extent in various forms of speculation. As one form of speculative, personal contribution, he may be able to supply some embracing, integrating idea that will give unity and synthesis, simplicity and power to his findings. All these things are well in keeping with our expectations of scientific research; they are mostly contributions of the researcher; they are further representations of the idea that what one sees in a problem (from the initial aspects of cases to the broader interpretations of what one has found) is a matter of the personality and training of the investigator.

Again, it seems proper to set some limits on the construction of these statements. One is not free to read into his data fanciful interpretations that are repugnant to scientific frames of reference. If he resorts to schemes of thought which scientists avoid he will find difficulty in having his work accepted by other scientists; and, if few or no scientific workers recognize his work as research, then probably it isn't. But the statements in the preceding paragraphs are directed against an extreme devotion to a goal which is, in any case, unattainable; and which, in the present stage of research in the human field, is almost certain to prove a great retarding influence. In fact, even in the oldest sciences, a high premium is still placed on creative guessing (within the frame of scientific interpretation) in the proposing of explanatory theories. It would be a mistake, in any field of scientific endeavor, to permit the notion that research is a drab, monotonous routine of self-repression while one looks at endless cases in an utterly machine-like fashion. While the opposite extreme of free self-expression is equally inappropriate, it must be realized that in all scientific endeavor there is a demand for the worker who can and will think creatively.

**Aspects may emerge as a product of study.** Up to this point we have been dealing with systematic studies, those which employ a definite schedule for taking and recording observations, and presumably use a fairly definite system of categories for the classification of the observations. The question may arise as to whether all aspects have to be planned and provided for in advance. Doesn't one ever plunge into an unknown area and discover new aspects? Isn't this often the very goal of his study?

The answer is emphatically Yes. Throughout the treatment of systematic work, we have tried to emphasize that at every point in his work the researcher should be alert to new insights, new views, new aspects which he did not have when he started. In other words, even though most research is of the systematic kind, one should never feel that drawing up his schedules closes the door to the recognition of unforeseen aspects. And many an investigator ends his study wishing he could begin all over again, for by the time his observation or his analysis has advanced he has become convinced that his study has proceeded along a line (attending to certain aspects) which is not nearly as important as the new views he has obtained, the new aspects that have emerged. If time prevents a new start, he can simply report his convictions, along with his findings, as a basis for a fresh start either by himself or some other researcher at a later time.

Of course, even those aspects which are listed in one's original schedules are tested during the study; that is, do they exist (operate) in significant degree, or are they ineffective, so far as the observations extend? Even such studies, therefore, represent a search for the generality or the effectiveness of certain aspects. In the analysis of data, one has further opportunity to observe (discover, perhaps even create) new perspectives, and hence new aspects, of his cases. Each level of analysis produces its level of aspects. In these senses, aspects are products of one's study. Some with which the researcher started drop out before he is through; others are created during the process of the work.

There are, however, other ways in which one may approach his work. He may be engaged in a non-quantitative study, in which the analyses of his observations are primarily logical, or judgmental. One does not usually start out with observation instruments, but structures his thought as he proceeds. This is typical in historical and legal research; and while these procedures have been dealt with in the chapter on historical method, we refer to some of them here for purposes of illustration. We could say that the sensing of themes or the characterization of periods is a product of the analysis of the observations, and hence is covered by the preceding paragraph. Yet dealings with nonstatistical material seem to call forth such different mental processes that, even when the steps being undertaken are basically comparable to those involving tallies and counts, separate statements seem to be called for.

As illustrations, therefore, of deriving aspects by direct study (involving, of course, judgment), we may mention those characterizations which are picked out as being representative, central, essential, or dominant. Anyone who is writing history is likely to give characterizing names to various eras or periods, as "the Napoleonic era," "the colonial period," but the process goes beyond such simple cases and involves the discerning of principal characteristics of a more complex type. For example, "Education in the Emerging Democratic State" [27] and "Education for the Emerging Industrial Age" [28] are two headings, referring to somewhat different periods,

[27] Title for Chapters 9 and 10 in Newton Edwards and Herman G. Richey, *The School in the American Social Order:* The Dynamics of American Education. Boston: Houghton Mifflin Co., 1947. 880 p.
[28] Title for Part V in George S. Counts, *Education and American Civilization.* New York: Teachers College, Columbia University, 1952. 496 p.

which represent the authors' analysis of those periods and the selection of these themes as being the dominant notes. They are thus something more than just topics to be written about, like "The War of 1812." The person doing historical research and historical writing is often admonished to seek such an analytical characterization of a period, preferably one which suggests the nature or direction of a change, or of the forces that were dominant.

Somewhat the same process is involved in the analysis of the essential issues in the contemporary scene, in a debate, or in a case at court. For example, what are the dominant or outstanding problems which characterize the financing of education? [29] Or what are the principal problems of life as faced by human beings? (We will return to this problem later on.) In the matter of deciding cases at law, lawyers and the court will examine with the greatest of care all relevant cases which are on record to see whether they match the present one in every particular. If logical analysis reveals that the preceding cases differ in any material aspect, they are not regarded as necessarily presumptive with regard to the present case.

Without here going into the whole matter of the analysis of documents, we may refer to further examples of this general type. In an effort to distill from the relevant literature the basic principles on a problem of administration, one researcher selected statements that seemed to represent the central ideas of many articles relating to the subject. These were then combined, on the basis of similarity, into a smaller number of somewhat more complex statements.[30] A compendium of elementary-school objectives was issued as representing frankly "editorial judgment and discretion" in summarizing the curriculum convictions of thirteen consultants and ten critics. "What emerged is something different from a summary . . . it is an interpretation." [31]

It may be argued in all these cases that the essential process is one of mental examination, identification, evaluation, and selection. When we pick out the principal issues, central elements, essential conditions, dominant factors, salient examples, critical incidents, or characteristic statements, we are selecting aspects on the basis of logical analysis and judgment. To say this is not to disparage the practice. The judgment of the informed scholar may well be better than a host of so-called objective

[29] National Conference of Professors of Educational Administration, *Problems and Issues in Public School Finance:* An Analysis and Summary of Significant Research and Experience. Edited by Roe L. Johns and Edgar L. Morphet. New York: Teachers College, Columbia University, 1952. 492 p.

[30] Donald Faulkner, "What Are the Functions of Internal Administration?" *Journal of Higher Education* 12:378-85; October 1941.

[31] Nolan C. Kearney, *Elementary School Objectives,* p. 50. Mid-Century Committee on Outcomes in Elementary Education. New York: Russell Sage Foundation, 1953. 189 p.

facts collected and analyzed without benefit of competent judgment. We think, in fact, we should prefer it.

It is presumed that the person who makes scholarly judgments has collected and examined carefully a very large number of facts and has exercised the cautions appropriate to the historical or other logical discipline. It is assumed, furthermore, that the scholar is under no obligations or compunctions other than to represent in his work the most informed, penetrating, and logical thinking of mankind in quest of understanding. The background competence and the freedom of the researcher to think with integrity are paramount in all research. When, under appropriate circumstances, the researcher makes judgments as to similarity and dissimilarity, likely consequences, relative importance, or representativeness, although these involve personal interpretation and decision, we cannot see that this judgment is of a different quality from those judgments which must be made at nearly every point in research. Both enter into the product. Where judgment is called for, let it be exercised, under the safeguards of scholarly pursuit. Research is the alternation of observation and interpretation. Each provides an essential element.

We should perhaps carry our thought one step further. There is likely often to be some misunderstanding of the quality of the research offering. The researcher who, with *quantitative* data before him, offers out of his well grounded conceptions a new explanatory hypothesis is presenting a product of his judgment, just as when the worker with *qualitative* data renders an interpretative judgment. In neither case is the product presumed to have the force of finality. Nor is the verdict surrounded with a sacredness beyond the high respect we feel compelled to pay those who have the competence to represent the rest of mankind in these areas of difficult and refined thinking where there is opportunity for but few to work. The point is that the conclusions of a research worker carry no enduring force beyond the element of truth they may contain. They are subject to the challenge of others who have disciplined minds, to the critical examination of all who are competent to review them, and to complete overthrow by those who find that similar results do not follow from the stated conditions, or that there are more significant ways of viewing the original situation. Save where social authority enters the domain of research and requires or prohibits, there is no *must* in research findings beyond the fact that they afford mankind a pattern of understanding and a means for achieving his ends. If he does not desire those ends, he need not accept the findings; or if other researchers can discover better means, the original offering may be disregarded. There is no compulsion to accept beyond the desire for the ends made possible by the research conclusions.

**Further comments relative to the nature of aspects.** Several points regarding the nature and significance of aspects have been placed here for those who wish to think further along these lines.

First we shall take up the question of the significance of aspects, their meaningfulness or lack of meaning. We sometimes come across the warning that aspects are superficial, presumably trivial, and have little or nothing to do with the essential character of whatever is being studied. Accordingly, a study based on the observation of aspects could have little hope of contributing anything of consequence.

While we wish to encourage research that may be called basic or fundamental, as well as research which deals with more immediately useful answers to questions, we think that perhaps the warning may be overdone. Perhaps the point is that some aspects have little significance when judged in terms of their practical or theoretical use, but this does not mean that aspects have nothing to do with the essential character of something. We would hold that every characteristic aspect is significant (practically and theoretically) at some level of differentiation. That is, all stable or characteristic aspects are in part the manifestation of some element of the nature of the object being studied, so that they are to be classed as important or trivial only in terms of their relation to the immediate purpose, and not on the basis of general, absolute standards.

If, for example, one is studying learning, he has a choice of some half dozen criteria or kinds of evidence of the level of learning reached, such as the amount which a person can reproduce from memory, number of errors made in the reproduction (or in choosing courses in a maze), length of time required for doing what has been learned, ease with which material can be relearned after it has been forgotten, extent of its "overlearning," cultivation of collateral or attendant skills that are needed to yield a high quality of performance, amount of generalization which takes place, and so on. Who can say which one of these is a "mere" aspect, and which an essential property, of what we ordinarily mean when we use the word *learning?*

Of course some aspects, elements, or properties are more uniquely characteristic (more distinguishing at the immediate level) than others. But *any* stable aspect or property of anything is significant in designating the large class to which the thing belongs, and thus its significance attaches (perhaps without our being aware of it) to the thing in question. Consider, for example, the aspect "size"; one may say that size is a perfectly general aspect, it applies to everything having physical existence, and, therefore, distinguishes nothing. This, however, is far from the case. Certainly our own response to objects depends a great deal on their size. So does the response of the rest of the world, animate or inanimate. Small particles defy (or overcome) the laws of gravity, because their size permits them to respond more to other forces; thus we have Brownian movements in gases, small particles floating endlessly in the air, and even needles floating on the surface of water. If bacteria were not small, could they enter our body cells and cause the manifold illnesses they do? Perhaps it is to statistics, if not to common sense, that we owe a debt for placing great emphasis on the magnitude, intensity, or quantitative aspects of anything and everything, since, apart from quantity, most of the things we believe are not true. That is, by changing or ignoring only a few quantities, we find that scientific laws, structures, essential natures, properties, and common-sense experiences can be so distorted as to lose their meaning. Size, proportion, and balance are of the essence of nature (human and physical) as we know it.

It may be profitable, however, to examine certain ways in which, seemingly or actually, aspects are superficial when compared with what we would like to know, if we had full understanding. For the sake of establishing continuity we shall number the points, and shall treat each briefly.

1. Certain aspects observed at a particular time may be something of an "accident," a fortuitous coming together of certain things rather than what is typical, reasonably enduring, or recurrent. Such conditions occur; we should agree that a temporary aspect of the relatively chance type may hold little interest; hence we have assumed or spoken of *characteristic* aspects. On the other hand, the rare occurrence is sometimes of the greatest interest to researchers, and chance is an object of widespread study. Both may enter into predictions regarding the future, whether or not they have to do with the essential nature of something. (They may, for example, reveal something of the essential nature of the system of which the thing being studied is but a part.) In the field of research, we must be cautious in naming things in which we are *not* interested, lest we find we have parted with some of our birthright.

2. An aspect may be a somewhat incidental effect (or at least so we think) when we should like to know the whole sequence in the cause-effect chain of relationships. This statement suggests the wistful spirit of research. However much we have, we want more. Certainly. We should not regard this as a criticism of studying aspects, but rather as an expression of man's insatiable desire to know, to understand. The discontent with "an aspect" may be extended in still another direction: one may wish a full syndrome, a descriptive picture of all the things which go together in a natural or usual manner; and, further, one may wish to project this picture backward through time so that he obtains also a natural history of the development.

All these desires are perfectly legitimate goals of research. They are all recognized and dealt with at other points in this text; we shall give explicit attention to them at those appropriate places; but meanwhile we may point out that we have been employing the term *aspects* in a very broad sense, and when cause-effect relationships and patterns of ecological complexes and natural histories have all been observed and analyzed and described, it will be found that they have all been observed and analyzed and described in terms of aspects. But, since some of these relationships are somewhat special, we shall give them special names and treat them in later sections under "analysis."

3. Is there a physical apparatus, or mechanism, or bodily organ, or other means whereby effects are produced? This interest is one of the main goals of research concerned with a full explanatory description. We shall treat it later. But, again, it will be detected and observed in terms of its aspects.

In this connection it seems desirable to point out that there are legitimately different concerns of different fields of study. Some persons feel that the study of human behavior is of no consequence, if they cannot find in the human nervous system, and other parts of the body, a full explanation not only of how, but of why, certain behavior occurred. As a long-time goal this is commendable, but we will not be inclined to belittle what knowledge we may obtain concerning human behavior while waiting for the fuller knowledge concerning the physiological correlates. The two fields may be cultivated by different sets of workers, each producing results of the greatest value.

4. Cannot aspects be split up into components? May not the observed aspect be the resultant of two contrary factors, so that only a small part of each is revealed in the resulting effect? This is always a possibility. It represents one of the research interests along the line of analysis. It constitutes the next major topic to be dealt with.

It is by pursuing any question in terms of various dimensions, or perspectives, according to man's developing curiosity that knowledge increases and understanding expands. But in whatever setting, as we are using the term, it is an aspect that is observed.

A second topic which we would take up in this summary for further treatment is a restatement and extension of the point made earlier, namely, that all qualities, characteristics, properties, or other conditions that an object (or person or event) is observed to have, involve something more than the object itself. They represent, in the degree to which they manifest themselves, an interaction between the object and some other thing.

There are certain very general facts of existence which we are, by our common logic, probably called upon to grant, even though we have no uncompromising means of sensing them. For example, we believe that the physical world has extension (occupies space); it must, therefore, have mass; it usually has some form of inner arrangement or structure (note, however, that the molecules of gases are not arranged in any structural order); and it has some degree of heat or energy. Though less obvious to us, it is also in motion, internally and externally. But aside from such fundamental conditions which are posited (and possibly including even these) the properties that anything has are interaction properties. Even though we assume that a chemical element has a certain internal structure which causes it to react in the ways it does, its actual reaction at any given time is in part a property of the thing it reacts with. When the second element or chemical is changed, the "properties" (the behavior) of the first element change.

But whatever the few fundamental and "strictly intra-individual" characteristics of any object which our logic may call upon us to grant, it is certain that the detection or expression of these characteristics is always a form of interaction with other things. In functional terms, the nature of anything may be thought of as the tendency (perhaps the probability) for it to react in certain ways when certain conditions occur. While philosophy accords a place to monadic properties, these can only be arrived at deductively, and the notion is probably used far too frequently and too loosely in all fields. For it is convenient and natural to do so. But when it is sometimes argued that in education or in other social fields one is under something of a handicap because he can never observe the real qualities (as intelligence, for example), but can observe only their manifestations, he is not thinking clearly; no researcher in any field of science observes or is able to record anything other than manifestations, namely, the interaction of one thing with another.[32] (The second thing may be a measuring instrument or it may not.) Thus, when one brings out that the personality of any person is in part a product of the situation, and is likely to show considerable variation when the situation changes, he is saying no more than what we must say of everything in the world, down to the single molecule or atom. The properties of an atom or molecule of any chemical element depend on what kind of other molecule it is next to (and of course also on other conditions), just as with human beings.[33] And under proper "situations" the

[32] For common-sense purposes, perhaps we should except space or distance, which may be sensed more by comparison (as with a ruler) than by interaction. But even here the human being (or a machine) that is observing or responding in other ways is interacting.

[33] This point should not be pressed so far that one seems to deny certain *general* tendencies, arrived at *inductively* and expressed as a proportion of many individual or specific interactions; for example, in the physical field, certain gases are referred to as reactive or inert according as they do or do not react readily and vigorously with a wide

atom will almost completely change its nature, permanently so (e.g., through nuclear fission and nuclear fusion). Can we wonder then that highly sensitive human beings may be subject to variability? And shall we complain that we cannot directly know essential properties, when scientists in all other fields are in precisely the same situation?

As something of an aside, it may be said that in every field of research some aspects (traits) are less readily accessible to the human senses than are others. Progress in such areas depends on the development of observation instruments, often in the form of measuring instruments, which are able to convert the manifestation of some aspect into such form that it becomes available to the human senses. We could ask for no better illustration than the common radio; out of the infinity of aspects of the space around us, the radio selects a certain aspect (an electromagnetic wavelength) which is quite insensible to us directly, and converts it to such form that it registers on our ears as sound. Most commonly, in scientific work, the instrument employed converts the original manifestation into the movement of a pointer over a scale, so that it is available to us through our sense of sight, which may thus observe small differences quite accurately. A common example is the speedometer on an automobile which registers the rate at which the wheels are turning, by converting generated electromagnetic forces into movements of a pointer over a dial. Many instruments having scales are found in psychological laboratories. All such devices are, in the large, doing the same thing that giving a test does, making some aspect in which we have interest accessible to our senses.

The third comment, with which this section will close, is a reminder that everything we observe (that is, sense in any way, directly or indirectly) may be regarded as an aspect. The term is perfectly general. This means that, logically, all of the classes of things treated in the sections which follow may be regarded as aspects. But, because we can classify them as particular kinds of aspects, it seems useful to treat them separately. The present section was denoted "general" both to emphasize that the aspects usually pertained to the whole, and to differentiate them from special classes of aspects such as those which follow.

---

variety of substances; likewise in the human field, a person may be called active, or lethargic, in accordance with the way he commonly reacts to the ordinary occasions of life. Such ideas represent generalizations rather than specifics or particulars. They are, however, perfectly legitimate conceptions. Thus the personality of an individual may have both its relatively specific interaction tendencies (dependent on a specific type of situation) and also those which we come to expect as usual, likely, prevailing under the common circumstances of life. *Both* are characteristic of the individual, the former being less general, less stimulated by most situational factors. In any event, the point of view emphasized in the text is helpful as a corrective for the enduring tendency to think dichotomously; for example, either a person *is* something ("has" a certain trait) or he isn't. We must recognize the need for making much more highly conditioned descriptions, if they are to be acceptably accurate.

## II.  COMPONENTS  (IN  ANALYSIS)

**Introduction.** Breaking up a whole into its components is one of the most fascinating forms of analysis. It is, in fact, the type which will somewhat unconsciously come to one's mind when he thinks of analysis. It is perhaps the first step in boring into something, in trying to peer beneath the surface, in seeking to find out what something is made of.

The present topic is the first of the specialized forms of analysis which is taken up. As a specialized form, it is not different from aspects in general; it is simply to be thought of as one subclass of aspects. Thus, all that has been said in the preceding section about aspects in general is applicable to the subject of discovering, identifying, or selecting those aspects which may be regarded as components.

By components we mean those elements or parts that add up, which can be combined to form the whole object. We should like to leave the matter there; but so many questions will arise in the mind of the thoughtful person that it seems necessary to add various modifying and interpretative comments to this simple statement. First, that which is known as an element or part may take so many forms that one must not limit his thinking to a physical model; analysis includes actions (such as learning, or behavior in general) and even thoughts: we might say, particularly thoughts, since it is our general concepts (class names, including almost any common noun) which pose most of the problems for the research worker. On the other hand, what is a whole is again a matter of where one starts his thinking or his observing; *anything* can be a whole, and when one is through breaking it up into finer parts, he still has wholes; they become the whole that is the starting point for the next more penetrating round of analyses. If, therefore, the terms *whole* and *unit* seem confused in their meaning, it seems unavoidable; we start with wholes or units and we end with wholes or units. The meaning will have to be understood from the context—supplied, we might say, as is the case in research work, by the organizing thoughts of the reader.

What is the difference between aspects in general and the special class which we designate "components"? First, aspects in general may be chosen at random; those selected for study do not have to fall in the same class or level of thought. For example, the general aspects of a school building chosen for attention might be such as its esthetic effects (style of architecture, adaptation to plot, color, as subaspects), its utility (functional adaptation to the many purposes for which it will be used), its cost (over-all, per square foot, per cubic foot), its safety provisions (degree of freedom from fire hazard, design, special provisions), its age, the kind of heating system it has, and so on. These various aspects named do not seem to lie on the same plane of generality, nor in the same logical class. Just what ones of the group named would be regarded as forming a homogeneous group would be a matter of judgment; there is no final way of determining; but we believe almost anyone would agree that those named are too diverse to be thought of as components which could be added together into one unit idea. As a contrasting example of those aspects of a school building which we should regard as components we would mention its rooms; or, more generally, its classrooms, its specialized rooms, its utility or service rooms, and any other categories needed to make up the general idea of space utilization in the building. Such subdivisions, being based on the one aspect "space," can be combined to make up the total space in the building. They are therefore components of this total whole.[34] In the same way one could select, according to his purpose and interest, any other set of aspects of the building which would make up some total that might be of interest; for example, the various kinds of building material used, the various functions it is designed to accommodate (adding up to its total utility), and so on.

The general aspects of a curriculum might be its breadth and richness, or its narrowness and poverty; its center of emphasis (is it strictly college preparatory, vocational, or life-centered?); its flexibility or rigidity; and so on. Its components, on the other hand, would probably be its subjects, or activities; and, if the idea of determining what these are, what is to be regarded as a unit area, at once seems to present difficulties, we would point out that they are the difficulties common to research. Lines have to be drawn; one will attempt to draw them where they can be identified, both in his study and in practice, and where they will be of significance for the development of conclusions. We will come back to this problem later in connection with the discussion of "classification." We might add also that it is desirable to draw lines (make categories for purposes of observation and classification) where they will not destroy or erase the spirit of what is going on—its purpose, its verve, its continuity. This is a difficult objective; it has led some workers to abandon the whole idea of analysis and analytical observation. We should say that, like any other research method, analysis should be employed for what it may reveal, and should not be utterly rejected out of disappointment because any one research attack will not portray everything man may wish to know.

As a third illustration, we might consider a statistical concept, an index number of the cost of living. General aspects of the index number might

[34] This total or whole is to be thought of as some general aspect of the object, and not the whole in all of its possible aspects.

be such as the stability or variability of its monthly values, its tendency to vary with certain other economic variables, its tendency (owing to the particular formula used or the selection of items to be priced) to be too high or too low as judged by other indications. Its components, on the other hand, would be the various groups of things included—housing, food, clothing, and so forth.

We have given these illustrations because they will help in considering further differentiations, and because they should help in affording a general introduction to the idea of analysis into components. As a second basis of differentiation, general aspects are likely to apply to the object (person, action, idea) as a whole; hence, if they are taken away, the thing virtually cannot exist. That is, a building can have a pleasing or other effect on those who view it; but one can scarcely remove this general aspect entirely (that is, its impression of some kind) and have a building. Likewise, one can scarcely subtract the general aspects of a curriculum or of an index number. Or, more simply, one can *change* the design of a chair, but he cannot entirely eradicate any design whatever from what he may construct in the way of a chair. On the other hand, a component can be subtracted or removed and leave an object which is simply less complete. Thus one might eliminate a room from the plans for a building, drop a subject from the curriculum, omit some group or commodity from an index number, or leave off some part of a chair (as its arms) and still have a result which was the original thing, only less full or complete.

In many instances, a general aspect may be broken up further into sub-aspects, and they will all apply whether the object is large or small, complete or somewhat incomplete; whereas components are likely to be the parts which make something large or small, complete or incomplete. This differentiation may become obscure, however, in the case of concepts; these mental images or abstract constructs are such airy things that there may at times be no tenable dividing line between general aspects and those special aspects which are components. The distinction is again difficult in the case of action. For purposes of organizing the discussion, we have made such lines as seemed reasonable without thought that they were in all cases fundamental or invariable.

One may sense the lack of a certain type of very common analysis, namely, dividing a group of cases into subclasses and counting the number of cases in each subgroup, commonly referred to in statistical work as a "breakdown." For the sake of orientation, we repeat the delimitation made at the beginning of the treatment of analysis, to the effect that such classification of unit cases will be left to the topic of "classification." We are here concerned with the analysis of *organized* wholes into parts, with the resulting parts (or subgroups) retaining a certain amount of distinctive organization of their own. When one distinctive part is removed, the total loses part of its functional characteristics. In the statistical shuffling of individual units, the organizational aspects are not of interest; units regarded as similar are lumped together into the same category, without thought of any original connections with other units and without the assumption of any connections among those lumped together. It is recognized again that this distinction between functional units and statistical units cannot in all cases be preserved strictly.

**Analysis of physical things into components is primarily the responsibility of other disciplines.** With regard to physical things, characteristically, education and other social disciplines have their major interest in things other than physical objects, and this attitude extends in some measure also to physiological organisms. That is, the human sciences are concerned primarily with interaction, or behavior (including in this term feelings and thoughts), and their interest in the physical background of these activities extends only so far as may be necessary. This is far from suggesting that the interest is nonexistent or negligible; schooling requires the usual physical facilities of our culture, and learning takes place in bodies that are highly complex and sensitive, and which need to be maintained in healthy, normal condition. But our need for full understanding does not center in the same areas as that of the physical scientist or biologist. We rely on the chemist to dissolve our building materials in a test tube and on the physiologist to divide the human body into various kinds of organs and cells. Accordingly, our concern with these areas might be said to be no more than secondary.

Further, we seldom care about components of physical or physiological units apart from other aspects of these components-in-their-setting, which we may refer to as *structure* and *function*. The example of considering a school building from the standpoint of component areas and uses of space has already been referred to, but obviously even this reference carried functional connotations. It is quite true that, logically, component parts or elements will be discovered before their function is ascertained with certainty; but, within the realm of the purely physical, those concerns seem to lie with other disciplines. Our discussion will, therefore, postpone any treatment of this subject until later sections which deal with structure and function as objectives of analysis.

Should the thought arise that people, being physiological organisms, are the unit of which society is composed and that their description and distribution represent a form of component analysis, we should agree; but the analysis of society is in no sense a physical or physiological analysis and would not come under the present head. (It is true that Herbert Spencer regarded society in the framework of a biological organism, but the analogy was fundamentally faulty and has been dropped.) The statistical distribution of persons with varying characteristics will be dealt with under the topic of "classification."

**Analysis is frequently useful to determine the component elements of concepts and activities.** It would seem that research is in large part dividing up and putting together again. As developed earlier, the very selection of aspects, and the definition of a problem for study, are steps in delimitation. Many of man's questions can be answered only by going further in analysis. There are of course some questions that can be answered only by dealing with units as wholes; yet the very recognition of any unit short of the entire (known and unknown) universe is of necessity a dividing up, and those who argue for the study of wholes are arguing for an arbitrary, even if sometimes defensible, position. If we do not make some selection, some dividing of the totality of conditions and activities in any situation, there seems little or nothing that the human mind can get hold of. And if we strive to ascertain the components of a general conceptual area (such as that represented by many of our common nouns) we are likely to know more about that area than if we insist that to divide nature is to destroy it. We recognize that where we draw lines, we circumscribe our thinking; we cut off the easy flow of ideas across those boundaries, whereas we know that in the world of reality there are no wholly segregated units, no closed systems. They exist only in the mind, yet they afford man's finite mind a system of concepts sufficiently limited and definite so that it can deal with them. To divide nature in any way is to destroy or ignore certain interconnections, as well as the properties and functions of those interconnections; yet it is what the mind *must* do every moment of its active state. To attend to any thing (any sensation or finite group of sensations, any perception, concept, or system of concepts and interrelations) is to *separate* that thing, for the time being, from the infinity of other things to which the mind might be attending. Man is confounded by undifferentiated, boundless infinity. Any branch of research and science basically devolves upon the capabilities of the human mind. It cannot supersede them. It must find its means of development and its ultimate limits within the framework set by these capabilities.

As examples of the need for dividing large concepts or areas of activity into components, we shall refer to three illustrations drawn from the areas of curriculum development, learning, and administration.

One approach to curriculum development is to select from American (and in part, international) life those activities (including thinking and feeling) which the individual is likely to be called on to perform; or perhaps we should say, those which he *should* perform, as judged by the aspirations and goals of our culture (including its religious, philosophical, and competitive elements), in interaction with its geographical factors and its world setting. From these activities will be eliminated such things as may be adequately cared for in other ways—that is, by the home, by normal environmental conditions, and by various social institutions. While in earlier years of this century such a list might be thought of as indicating the range of things that should be taught, at the present time detailed lists are more likely to be viewed as available material on which to draw, in choosing learning experiences which will help each individual child to achieve a satisfying and constructive life (as a child, as an adolescent, as an adult, and as a senescent). No *one* person can take on skills or full understandings without limit, and usually the limit is set by his interests. In order to achieve the maximum learning, it is necessary to view the curriculum, not primarily in terms of the vast amount that "should" be known, but rather in terms of the evolving capacities, interests, and needs of the developing person.

For purposes of the present discussion, however, we are primarily interested in the listing and classifying of the activities of our culture—bearing in mind that *activities* is used in a broad sense. The study of these (both the detailed activities and the classes of activities) is a study of components of American life. The classification of the detailed activities into groups or areas of living will of course vary when done by different persons. If a researcher is hopeful that he could find a unit of activity so small that there would be no difference in the way it could be classified, we would feel constrained to point out that there is nothing which exists which does not become a different thing when viewed in different perspectives. For example, if one is studying the use of arithmetic in life, the question of whether a certain instance is to be called (classified as) a use of decimals, or per cent, or ratio, or fractions, or multiplication, or approximation, or mental arithmetic, or two-step problem-solving, or arithmetic in carpentering, or something else, depends primarily on the categories being employed—what one is looking for and what mental concepts he is looking with. A particular instance of arithmetic use might be *all* of the classes named; hence, to avoid ambiguity, one would have to employ compound categories having all these dimensions. This becomes unmanageable in practice and breaks down. But, more to the point, if one were looking at this same act of using arithmetic with a different set of interests (a different set of categories), it might be seen as an act of reading, or thinking, or intelligence, or personality, or civic responsibility, or of something else. What something is depends on what one is prepared to see it as; for any one thing is an infinity of things, depending on the particular perspective into which it is fitted.

Accordingly, there is no *one* way of obtaining either detailed components or classes of components, in the sense that what one comes out with is *the* set of components. It is simply the components when a certain set of categories and definitions have been employed. For always, components, as with other aspects, are in part the result of the imposition of concepts; and concepts are contingent things, depending on interest, purpose, definition, setting, implementation. Hence, so long as one is free to establish categories which he believes to be appropriate, he will obtain a different set of components.

An illustration of categories which represent facets of American life is to be found in the four major heads employed by the Educational Policies Commission: [35] (1) self-realization; (2) human relationship; (3) economic efficiency; and (4) civic responsibility. These categories are not directly activities, but areas or purposes; they assist in classifying the more detailed components of desirable American life. As part of the work of the Eight-Year Study [36] a committee sponsored by the Progressive Education Association offered a similar set of categories: (1) personal living; (2) immediate personal-social relationships; (3) social-civic relationships; and (4) economic relationships.

A large number of such compilations have been made. Some years back Harap [37] reviewed thirty of them. Articles in the *Encyclopedia of Educational Research* [38] give a number of these lists, including the famous "Seven Cardinal Principles" of 1918 and going back to the five categories of Herbert Spencer in 1860. Bobbitt, who in the 1920's was working on exhaustive, detailed lists of activities, in 1941 was content to write on fifteen areas of living.[39] The Mid-Century Committee on Outcomes in Elementary Education [40] organized its statements of desirable outcomes under

[35] Educational Policies Commission, *The Purposes of Education in American Democracy.* Washington: National Education Association, 1938. 157 p.

[36] Harry H. Giles, S. P. McCutchen, and A. N. Zechiel, *op. cit.*

[37] Henry Harap and Others, *The Changing Curriculum.* New York: D. Appleton-Century Co., 1937. 351 p.

[38] William H. Bristow and O. I. Frederick, "Curriculum Development," p. 309; J. G. Umstattd, "Secondary Education: Curriculum," p. 1175-77; Guy M. Wilson, "Arithmetic," p. 45-46; and other individual school subjects. See also "General Education," p. 490. *Encyclopedia of Educational Research.* Revised Edition. New York: Macmillan Co., 1950.

[39] Franklin Bobbitt, *The Curriculum of Modern Education.* New York: McGraw-Hill Book Co., 1941. 419 p.

[40] Nolan C. Kearney, *op. cit.*

Mid-Century Committee on Outcomes in Elementary Education, *Supplement to Elementary School Objectives.* Princeton, N. J.: Educational Testing Service, 1953. 211 p. Contains the original, unassimilated suggestions of contributors.

nine heads. Within each of the nine categories are five subdivisions referring to four kinds of outcome ("behavioral change") and the limiting factors or conditions in the development of these. Each of these subdivisions is further divided according to three different levels of development as represented by the end of the third, sixth, and ninth grades. This makes, in effect, 108 categories of goals, plus the 27 on the limiting conditions set by nature and culture. Within this framework some two thousand specific outcomes are described—desirable and attainable presumably for the average child, but judged by many of those who took part in the work as actually falling closer to ideals (p. 37).

The division of life's activities into groups of varying kinds and scope is accomplished mainly by judgment. Sometimes this is the judgment of an individual, sometimes of a group; often, of an individual after extensive interaction with one or more groups; and always with some reference to the emphases and boundary lines of tradition and convention, for people thought in the past, even as they think today. There is not likely to be reason for disregarding entirely the contributions of persons who thought before our day.

We have some further interest in this work, however, beyond its practical utility in education and its illustration of the enormous benefits which may accrue from proper and reasonable division of a great complex into manageable component groups and then into more specific components. Our further interest is in noting the part that research plays in this dividing up, in this forming of categories, in this developing of an orderly, integrated plan. The judgments which can be rendered today with regard to curriculum goals are relatively mature judgments; they may, it would seem, safely be classed as "good." Has this level of understanding and maturity come about simply by deliberative thinking? Do people of the present day think longer than those of a former day? In what way, and why, should the thinking of one generation be better than the thinking of a previous generation?

The essential difference in the thinking of the present and of earlier times on curriculum matters is a vast body of research. The amount of this research is great. In the main, it may be said to fall in two general classes. One class is concerned with the analysis of our culture, the activities of our people. While we have been referring to this, the illustrations given were on the upper levels, where divisions were made by judgment. Beneath these judgments lie the detailed studies of what words people use in speaking, in writing, and what words children have trouble with in spelling; what phases of arithmetic people use in homes, in various vocations, and what parts prove troublesome to children to learn; what aspects of life our published literature deals with; what are the thoughts of writers of fiction, editorials, and analytical treatises, and so on.[41]

The second large class of research studies bearing on the curriculum includes all those which have to do with child development, growth rates, maturation, drives, interests, conditions of learning, and so on—studies relating to the biology, psychology, social psychology, sociology, and psychiatry of the child and adolescent.[42] These studies have provided a wealth of knowledge and insights as to what it is reasonable to expect of children, under what conditions they will learn and under those they will not, over what length of time a given concept should be developed (perhaps several years instead of half an hour), and what individual differences in rate of development and in interests really mean.

All of these studies have done much to shake the adults (who plan curriculums and set objectives) out of a tendency to see the curriculum purely through the eyes of an adult, and bring home to them the many realities involved in what the curriculum means to children, different individual children, as they face it day after day and it impinges on their own immediate urges and their developing interests. The studies of children and youth also help avoid the idealizing of childhood and the easy generalizations concerning what someone else "ought" to do. While it is perhaps inescapable that adults should reflect their hopes and wishes in their judgments (as acknowledged in the Mid-Century Committee report), we are today in much better position than ever before to answer Herbert Spencer's persistent question, asked in the middle of the last century, "What knowledge is of most worth?" Out of the newer understandings of young people—perhaps we should say out of the greater willingness to face facts when research makes them indubitably clear—we have such recognition of the realities of life as individual programs and values and differing purposes of young people which are reflected in the movement for Life-Adjustment

[41] This literature is too extended to refer to here in any direct form. Certain references to it will be given later in the treatment of documentary analyses in another chapter. One should consult the references in the *Encyclopedia of Educational Research,* given earlier; also, the heads, "Analysis of Social Needs" and the various cross references, in the *Twelve-Year Index to the Review of Educational Research* (1931-1942) or a later similar index. Many of the early references, and a fairly full discussion of them, will be found in:

Carter V. Good, A. S. Barr, and Douglas E. Scates, *The Methodology of Educational Research.* New York: Appleton-Century-Crofts, 1936. p. 346-52, 355-64.

[42] Obviously no summary of such diverse fields is available. Their contribution is to some degree given explicit recognition in the articles previously referred to in the *Encyclopedia of Educational Research.* The following two references bring a great many such studies to bear on the curriculum:

"The Curriculum: Learning and Teaching." *Review of Educational Research* 21:169-243; June 1951. Six chapters dealing with the contributions of research to as many aspects of curriculum development.

Robert J. Havighurst, *Human Development and Education.* New York: Longmans, Green and Co., 1953. 338 p.

Also see the numerous references in the later chapter on genetic, growth, and developmental studies.

Education,[43] as well as the sociological emphasis on the need for some commonness of educational content, reflected in various secondary-school and college programs that require "a common body of socially significant experience for all pupils." This is often expressed as one of the aims of the core curriculum [44] and of general education [45] on the college level.

To the direct results of analytical research, which are frequently revealing as well as orienting, must be added the work of the many curriculum groups who have tested out the findings of research by making use of them in curriculum modification plans, tempered with the practical judgments of those whose first-hand experience has been with children in school. No research study is ever to be thought of as reasonably complete until its conclusions and recommendations have been tested under working conditions of various kinds; and such tests, of course, provide the basis not only for improved practical judgments but also for further research concerning the questions raised.

We have pointed to curriculum work as representing not only the immediate topic of arriving at components (of life and of the curriculum) through judgment backed by research, but also showing how research finds its way into practice. Some persons decry the extent to which research does not immediately find its way into school practices. Remarks are likely to be heard about many research studies being made simply to gather dust on library shelves. No doubt they do, and no doubt many a study is lost so far as direct influence is concerned. We will not at this point enter into a discussion of the matter, other than to note that those who understand research would say many a study *should* be laid aside and most studies should *not* have direct influence on practices. Whether too many get ignored, we cannot say, but we know that research requires "seasoning"; the evidence in one study may be pondered, but it probably should await the evidence

---

[43] National Commission on Life Adjustment Education for Youth, *Vitalizing Secondary Education*. Report of the First Commission. Office of Education Bulletin No. 3, 1951. Washington: Government Printing Office, 1951. 106 p.

For numerous references, see *Education Index* heads: "National Commission on Life Adjustment Education," and "Life Adjustment Education Program," beginning with Vol. 7, July 1947.

This movement is described as one among a number of curriculum-revision activities in the chapter on "Curriculum Developments in Secondary Schools," in American Association of School Administrators, *American School Curriculum*. Thirty-first Yearbook. Washington: The Association, 1953. 551 p. A corresponding chapter deals with the elementary-school curriculum.

[44] See p. 64-68 of the Thirty-first Yearbook in preceding footnote.

[45] T. R. McConnell and Others, "General Education," *Encyclopedia of Educational Research, op. cit.*, p. 489-500.

National Society for the Study of Education, *General Education*. Fifty-first Yearbook, Part I. Chicago: University of Chicago Press, 1952. 377 p.

In the *Education Index*, see the head "Curriculum—Colleges and Universities," for articles on general education, beginning with Vol. 3, July 1935; in Vol. 6, July 1944, articles appeared also under "Curriculum—Junior Colleges"; and beginning with Vol. 7, July 1947, a separate head for "General Education" was introduced, containing six columns of references.

of a great many more studies to see whether the results discovered will also be found under varying conditions. Not one but hundreds of research studies are important. The worst enemies of research are those who would take its findings literally and immediately, without proper safeguards of repetition, and perhaps without the proper interpretative tempering of both practical and philosophical judgments. Throughout the long history of research, all fields will reveal a great number of research studies which led in the wrong direction. To use research results too soon is to lead certainly to the discrediting of research in the eyes of its users, and then in the eyes of its supporters.

**Job analysis and description portray positions in terms of their components.** A second large area of work which involves the ascertaining of component activities is found in job analysis. This has been a growing field during the past half-century as research workers, and practical administrators, have learned that it is possible to analyze some of the more complex, elusive things in human behavior and to set these forth specifically. Probably no one with a strong psychological background would grant that the job descriptions which are commonly made contain all the psychological factors it would be desirable for them to have, but it is also true that job description and classification have brought about definite improvements in personnel administration.

In government (federal, state, and local, as well as in the armed forces) and in large industries, the description of jobs is regarded as essential for a number of purposes: to insure some uniformity of classification for similar activities and responsibilities, to provide some basis for equitable pay in the large number of jobs that are similar, some rationale for personnel administration and for the development of a theoretical study of administration, some foundation for reasonable expectancies of promotion from various job levels, and to serve as a basis for establishing employment standards and for making personnel selection tests for job applicants.[46]

46 For a single-chapter discussion, see the first two references following; for more complete treatments, see the other references.

W. Brooke Graves, *Public Administration in a Democratic Society.* Boston: D. C. Heath and Co., 1950. 759 p. Chapter 8, "Position Classification and Compensation," p. 126-49. Includes a good list of references.

Dale Yoder, *Personnel Management and Industrial Relations.* New York: Prentice-Hall, 1942. 848 p. Chapter 5, "Job Analysis, Description, and Classification," p. 101-129.

Jay Lester Otis and Richard H. Leukart, *Job Evaluation, a Basis for Sound Wage Administration.* New York: Prentice-Hall, 1948. 473 p.

Civil Service Assembly, Committee on Position-Classification and Pay Plans in the Public Service. Ismar Baruch, Chairman. *Position-Classification in the Public Service.* Chicago: Civil Service Assembly, 1941. 404 p.

A bibliography of over seventy references is given in: Howard W. Goheen and Samuel Kavruck, *Selected References on Test Construction, Mental Test Theory, and Statistics: 1929-1949.* U. S. Civil Service Commission. Washington: Government Printing Office, 1950. 209 p. See Section II, "Job Analysis," references 33-105. Revisions of this publication are planned.

Professional workers in public-school systems and state colleges and universities, by virtue of having professional standards set for their qualification and certification, sometimes lose sight of the fact that they are, nevertheless, employed, paid, and promoted on systems of thought developed along the same lines as those involved in the classifying of positions in other large employing agencies. Many of the general principles developed out of the analysis, description, and classifying of positions in these public and large industrial agencies are worth knowing about.

There is a gradual effort to get away from the analysis and description of jobs simply in terms of the kinds of activities engaged in, and to include elements of quality, as well as various other requirements of the work. Certain qualitative aspects are to be found in the use of the "critical incidents" technique, recently developed by Flanagan.[47] Further efforts along the line of quality and the specifying of aptitudes, personality, and temperament traits which are required, are to be encouraged. The analysis of dynamic, long-time motivational elements in both the job and the person are also important, and difficult.

Job analysis is of basic interest to those who are concerned with building curriculums and teaching young people in preparation for vocations.[48] It is, in fact, but a specialized form of analyzing the activities involved in life at large.

For many purposes it is essential to have some broad grouping of jobs. This is important for educational purposes, because it is impossible to offer in any school system detailed training for the thousands of specialized jobs that exist. The same need is felt by vocational counselors, by large employers who may find it desirable to transfer workers, and by the armed forces which often have to shift persons to meet acute demands under emergency situations. Attempts to work out a basis for grouping which would be satisfactory have been under way for some time.[49] A large-scale

[47] John C. Flanagan, "Job Requirements." Wayne Dennis and Others, *Current Trends in Industrial Psychology,* p. 32-54. Pittsburgh: University of Pittsburgh Press, 1949. 198 p.
[48] See the discussion and fourteen references, p. 580-81, of "Industrial Education," by Arthur B. Mays, in the *Encyclopedia of Educational Research, op. cit.*
For current references, see the head "Job Analysis" in the *Education Index,* and in the December Index Numbers of *Psychological Abstracts.*
For the earlier studies, made enthusiastically in the 1920's, see the early issues of the *Review of Educational Research,* especially 1:387-88, and 4:189. See the head, "Occupational Analysis," in the *Twelve-Year Index to the Review of Educational Research* (or a later edition of the Index).
[49] Marion R. Trabue, "Functional Classification of Occupations." *Occupations* 15:127-31; November 1936.
Herbert A. Toops, "Some Concepts of Job Families and Their Importance in Placement." *Educational and Psychological Measurement* 5:195-216; Autumn 1945.
Carroll L. Shartle, "Developments in Occupational Classification." *Journal of Consulting Psychology* 10:81-84; March-April 1946.
Clyde H. Coombs and George A. Satter, "A Factorial Approach to Job Families." *Psychometrika* 14:33-42; March 1949.

study has been under way for several years, representing various governmental interests, known as the Functional Occupational Classification Research Project, under the immediate sponsorship of the Bureau of Employment Security, of the Department of Labor. Aspects which are tentatively considered in the grouping of jobs include work actions, specific knowledge, technical requirements, particular industry, physical demands, working conditions, worker aptitudes, interests, temperament traits, and the time required for specific training. To obtain job clusters from these aspects has required not only careful adaptation and study of measuring instruments (tests), but also the development of new statistical techniques concerned with matching, or measuring similarity.

In the field of education, many studies have been made of the contents of various kinds of jobs (jobs of individuals or jobs of organized units). These studies have been made in four different ways. One procedure has been to analyze the concept of the job in terms of large functions, based primarily on general experience and judgment. A second procedure has been to analyze documentary statements of duties. A third approach has been to ascertain the activities actually engaged in by persons on the job— the process most commonly thought of as job analysis. A fourth method has dealt with amounts of time devoted to various duties, perhaps based on actual records, perhaps on estimates. A few illustrations of each type of study will be given.

Inasmuch as public education in the United States is one of the activities or functions of government, there may be some interest in considering a full list of government functions in which education appears as one item.[50] Functions of state departments of education have been analyzed under four large heads: leadership, regulatory, operational, and service activities.[51] The general functions involved in supervisory activities, as set forth in various studies, have been collated.[52] (Here again we see how advance in one area of research depends on developments in other areas.)

In similar fashion, the job of the school superintendent has been analyzed into eight component functions: (1) planning and evaluation; (2) organization of the units and services of the school system; (3) personnel administration; (4) business, finance, and the school plant; (5) auxiliary services (health, food, transportation); (6) information and advice; (7) coördina-

[50] Marshall E. Dimock and Gladys O. Dimock, *Public Administration*. New York: Rinehart and Co., 1953. 531 p. See "A profile of what government does," p. 24-27.

[51] U. S. Office of Education and National Council of Chief State School Officers, *Functions of State Departments of Education*. Office of Education Miscellaneous Publication No. 12. Washington: Government Printing Office, 1950. 70 p.

[52] A. S. Barr, William H. Burton, and Leo J. Brueckner, *Supervision:* Democratic Leadership in the Improvement of Learning. Second Edition. New York: Appleton-Century-Crofts, 1947. Chapter 1, p. 3-41.

tion and direction of activities in the school system; and (8) instruction.[53] These divisions are the ones which have been recognized for some time in public and industrial administration.[54] We should note that the fifth and eighth functions are substantive areas, of less generality than the other six, and represent analysis along a different dimension. While one may wish to include these two for purposes of emphasis, they do not contribute to the homogeneity of the list.

The analysis of documentary sources, particularly studies of the laws covering the duties and responsibilities, as well as the powers and rights, of school personnel constitute a second type of approach to the analysis of the position or job. Although most persons do not come directly in contact with state laws, because these are interpreted for them through local rules and regulations, such laws are, nevertheless, the fundamental control, and they set the framework, and sometimes the details, of the work of a public-school employee. They may cover either broad functions or specific activities. Compilations of both the statutes and the leading court decisions have been made in numerous studies.[55] Since the literature is scattered and often in the form of unpublished theses, we give here only two direct references as examples.[56] The Research Division of the National Education Association issues an annual summary of court decisions affecting the superintendent and the teacher, under the title, *The School Teacher's Day in Court.*

Rules and regulations of boards of education constitute another source for the analysis of duties. One study, for example, dealt with statements concerning the duties of the school principal, as given in the rules of 150 different school boards.[57] Such rules usually cover duties of many classes of workers in school systems.

[53] American Association of School Administrators, *The American School Superintendency.* Thirtieth Yearbook. Washington: The Association, 1952. 663 p. Chapter 4, "The Organization of the Superintendency," p. 65-102.

[54] Planning, organizing, staffing, budgeting and finance, reporting, coördinating, directing. Luther Gulick, "Notes on the Theory of Organization," p. 13. *Papers on the Science of Administration.* Second Edition. Edited by Luther H. Gulick and L. Urwick. New York: Institute of Public Administration, 1947. 195 p.

[55] Theodore L. Reller, "Administration—City School," *Encyclopedia of Educational Research,* 1950. p. 11-14.

See the many references on powers and duties of school boards, superintendents, principals, teachers, and others in Harlan Updegraff, "Administration of Local School Systems," in "The Legal Basis of Education," Chapter V. *Review of Educational Research* 3:391-98; December 1933.

See also relevant sections of Newton Edwards, *The Courts and the Public Schools.* Chicago: University of Chicago Press, 1933. 591 p.

[56] National Education Association, Research Division, "Legal Status of the School Superintendent." *Research Bulletin* 29:87-130; October 1951. See section VI, "Powers and Duties."

"Legal Status of the Public-School Teacher," in same magazine, 25:27-70; April 1947.

[57] Summarized in Paul B. Jacobson and William C. Reavis, *Duties of School Principals.* New York: Prentice-Hall, 1941. p. 192-95.

The third type of analysis of the work involved in a particular kind of job is based on activities reported as actually performed. Studies of this type are essentially of the character, What do you do on your job? The outstanding example of such a study is still the one made some years ago under the direction of Charters and Waples,[58] dealing with the duties of teachers. Reports of specific activities were received from over six thousand experienced teachers who listed things they did on their jobs. In the aggregate, these items numbered around two hundred thousand; however, only about twelve thousand were studied intensively, since it was found that additional groups of reports did not add any new activities. Twenty-one previous studies of teacher activity were located and analyzed for possible additional items. The literature on what teachers *ought* to do, as expressed by various writers on the subject, was examined to see whether it would add anything to what teachers reported they were doing. Finally, the list was checked for completeness by 2300 teachers. The result was a list of 1001 activities in which teachers engage. If one wishes to know what specific activities are embraced by the category of "teaching," here is one answer, although well founded criticisms have been made of certain aspects of this study.

Various specialized teaching positions have been studied in terms of activity analysis; for example, the teacher of business subjects,[59] the physical education director,[60] and school personnel worker.[61] Other studies can be located in the *Education Index* under the head, "Job analysis."

Other studies present analyses of activities performed by school principals.[62] The first study cited is based on a questionnaire returned by 46 principals of small elementary schools in Kansas. The second investigation was based on a check list of activities which was responded to by 658 principals of elementary schools. The activities were then rated by 44 educators as to relative importance. While the activities should not be regarded as representing current practices at the present time, the study is cited as

[58] Werrett W. Charters and Douglas Waples, *The Commonwealth Teacher-Training Study.* Chicago: University of Chicago Press, 1929. 666 p.

[59] William R. Blackler and Others, "Analysis of the Job of the Teacher of Business Subjects in the Secondary Schools of California." *Balance Sheet* 33:343-45; April 1952.

[60] James H. Humphrey, "Job Analysis of Selected Public School Physical Education Directors." *Research Quarterly of the American Association for Health, Physical Education, and Recreation* 24:56-66; March 1953.

[61] Council of Guidance and Personnel Associations, "Job Analysis of Educational Personnel Workers." *Occupations* 30: supplement 1-22; October 1951. (See also the study reported in Jacobson and Reavis, *op. cit.,* p. 137-53.)

[62] Don F. Geyer, "A Study of the Administrative and Supervisory Duties of the Teaching Principal in the Small Elementary School." *Bulletin of Information,* Vol. 22, No. 7. Emporia, Kan.: Kansas State Teachers College of Emporia, July 1942. 39 p.

William P. Dyer, *Activities of the Elementary School Principal for the Improvement of Instruction.* Contributions to Education, No. 274. New York: Teachers College, Columbia University, 1927. 102 p.

an example of a certain type of procedure. The National Survey of Secondary Education (1932) produced an extensive list of supervisory activities on the high-school level.[63] Activities of school clerks have been analyzed in considerable detail.[64]

For many purposes one will desire something more than a list of different kinds of activities; he will want some additional element as to importance or relative weight. Thus, Charters and Waples had their list of teacher activities rated by competent judges for four different aspects—frequency with which a teacher performed an activity; importance of the activity; difficulty of learning the activity; and the practicality of learning it in the training school before beginning to teach.[65] Dyer likewise had his list of principal's activities rated by judgment as to relative importance.

Formulas which seek to indicate the teaching load of teachers, particularly in high school and college, are another means of indicating differing weights of activities, or unit assignments. One of the oldest and best known formulas for this purpose is that of Douglass.[66] An example of its use is to be found in a survey of seven Ohio counties.[67] Although no such formula is completely satisfactory, it may be helpful for both administrative and research purposes. In constructing such a formula, one is limited in part by the fact that an elaborate, detailed formula will prove too tedious in use; and also by the fact that, while such a formula might presumably represent estimated time required for various duties, there are also other factors, sometimes of a psychological (emotional) sort, which affect the difficulty or hardship of work.

These studies on relative weight or significance of various elements in making up the total load of a job are closely related to studies of the amount of time involved. We, therefore, come to the fourth type of analysis referred to, which is probably the most interesting and also the most difficult. When carefully made, such studies involve the keeping of records; these are tedious, and probably not at all in line with the habits (or major interests) of professional workers. Nevertheless, a number of such studies have been made.

The school principal seems to have been the worker most extensively studied in terms of time spent on various duties. Jacobson and Reavis report

[63] Reproduced in rearranged form (rank order) in Paul B. Jacobson and William C. Reavis, *op. cit.*, p. 508-12.

[64] Reproduced in George C. Kyte, *The Principal at Work*. Revised Edition. Boston: Ginn and Co., 1952. p. 477-81.

[65] Charters and Waples, *op. cit.*, p. 24-30, 102-136.

[66] Harl R. Douglass, *Organization and Administration of Secondary Schools*. Boston: Ginn and Co., 1945. p. 115. Or see Jacobson and Reavis, *op. cit.*, p. 500.

[67] Kenneth J. Crim, "Teaching-Loads of Ohio High-School Teachers." *Educational Research Bulletin* 28:141-48; September 14, 1949. A further analysis appeared in the same journal, 28:205-212; November 9, 1949.

data from three studies.[68] A national study was reported in the Twenty-seventh Yearbook of the elementary school principals.[69] A study based on a time record kept by twenty-five principals for one day a week over a period of time in the New York metropolitan area, and other studies analyzing actual time records, appear in the *National Elementary Principal* for October 1953, Vol. 33.

A national study of the time spent by teachers, both elementary and high-school, was published in 1951 by the Research Division of the National Education Association.[70] This study follows up an earlier one made ten years previously. Replies were received from 2200 teachers, representing a proportional sample of urban and rural, elementary and high school, male and female teachers, and geographic areas. The study asked teachers to report on a questionnaire the number of hours given per week to various kinds of duties. The results show an average total of forty-eight hours per week for both elementary and secondary-school teachers; and, in addition, they show how this time is divided up into various components, according to functions or activities.

As a master's thesis, one teacher obtained the coöperation of thirty-four teachers in keeping detailed records of time spent on both professional work and personal activities over a period of five sample weeks during the year.[71] Such a study runs the danger of unrepresentative sampling, but adds to one's confidence in the specific amounts of time, especially since the total recorded had to add up to twenty-four hours for each day.

The time spent by college faculties has been studied in various surveys of higher institutions. Some years ago the faculties of the four higher educational institutions in Indiana reported an average of between fifty and fifty-five hours per week.[72] A summary review of surveys of higher education from 1908 to 1934 lists seventy-one surveys dealing with teaching load, and thirty-two surveys dealing with total faculty load.[73]

From time studies one can answer such questions as, What makes up a principal's day? or What does a teacher do with his time? Whereas the

[68] *Op. cit.*, p. 5-8, 11-12, 25.

[69] National Education Association, Department of Elementary School Principals, *Elementary-School Principalship, Today and Tomorrow*. Twenty-seventh Yearbook, 1948. Chapter VI, "How the Principal Uses His Time," and Chapter IX, "Community Relationships of Principals." *Note:* these yearbooks are regularly published as the first number each fall of a magazine; the reference for this yearbook is, therefore: *National Elementary Principal* 28:5-412; September 1948.

[70] National Education Association, Research Division, "Teaching Assignments and Time Schedules." *Research Bulletin* 29:10-20; February 1951.

[71] Adele Facinoli, *Out-of-School Time and Activities of Thirty-four Teachers*. Durham, N. C.: Duke University, 1944. Master of Arts thesis. 133 p. (Typewritten)

[72] *Report of a Survey of the State Institutions of Higher Learning in Indiana*. Floyd W. Reeves, Director. Indianapolis: Board of Public Printing, 1926. p. 98.

[73] Carnegie Foundation for the Advancement of Teaching, *Surveys of American Higher Education*. Prepared by Walter C. Eells. New York: The Foundation, 1937. See p. 474-75.

lists of functions and activities obtained by certain procedures give a picture of the variety of tasks which make up the totality of a job, the studies that include time enable one to know the centers of emphasis and the proportional breakdown of the total. The psychological factors (the pleasures and satisfactions, and the problems and anxieties) are not included in simple studies of activities and time. They are, however, known to be important components of a job's characteristics, when analyzed along a different dimension. They can be, and have been, approached directly by studies designed to deal with them. They were made a special part of a 1949 study of teaching load.[74] A check list for evaluating "background factors" has been prepared.[75] As part of a study of "Living and Working Conditions of Teachers," forty-four elements entering into "load pressures" were rated by 578 teachers.[76] The kinds of problems which arise and call for solution in one's work have been the object of many studies.

**More than one type of components is involved in a complete analysis.** Job analysis divides up a large activity (the job) into more specific, component activities. Sometimes this dividing is done in large terms, thought of as functions, and sometimes it is done in terms of small tasks or detailed acts. The latter are somewhat easier for the human mind to get hold of, to recognize, to use as a basis for differentiation; they have somewhat more concrete meaning than do the larger, more general conceptions.

On the other hand, it is becoming clear that an analysis into simple acts leaves a great deal out; it may in fact omit the distinguishing characteristics of a job, such for example as "responsibility." The many personal characteristics which fit a worker to do certain tasks are not well described in terms of detailed acts; like the beauty of a piece of art, they lose character when broken into bits. Such personal qualities as dependability, intelligence, resourcefulness, responsibility, coöperativeness, tact, judgment, and the like are not the sort of thing one describes when he says that a job consists of doing a certain kind of work for about a third of the time, doing something else for about half the time, and so on. The manner in which work is done does not in itself add up to a certain number of tasks completed; rather, it adds up to a certain qualitative result—the general "how" of the work, the quality of the product, the residual or future feelings of other persons.

Our position here is that job analysis, like other forms of analysis, may

[74] National Education Association, Research Division, "Evaluation of Factors Relating to Teaching Load." *Research Bulletin* 29:20-28; February 1951.
[75] National Education Association, Department of Classroom Teachers, *Factors Making or Marring Good Teaching.* Washington: The Department, 1950. 17 p.
[76] George G. Croskery, "The Canadian Teachers' Federation." *Phi Delta Kappan* 31:378-83; April 1950.

result in, or utilize, at least two kinds of components—one, a specific task or unit of work; the other, a qualitative aspect (really a complex of aspects) which transcends the mechanical work unit and includes other factors. This conclusion is not new; Charters recognized it on empirical grounds and regularly included a study of personal characteristics which were desired of the worker, along with an analysis of kinds of duties.[77] There are some persons who would object to including personal elements in a job analysis and description. That simply depends on where one wishes to draw the line; they can be included or they can be left out. For different purposes one can draw the lines of his analysis closely or loosely. But a job is often analyzed for the purpose of ascertaining what it requires of the worker and, if qualitative standards are not included, they are out simply because they have been left out. Actually, they are aspects (components) of the job when one chooses to look at them.

We are dealing here with a point that we should like to make general. It is one of the problems in analysis which is often disturbing and sometimes leads to the depreciating of analysis. It is sometimes claimed, or charged, that analysis leaves something out. Of course it does; we have repeatedly called attention to this fact, but so does any research process. We analyze for the purpose of simplifying, because natural complexity, taken entire, is too much for us. Nature viewed as an amorphous whole is meaningless. But setting limits for attention is not in itself peculiar to research; we do it every moment of our lives when we direct attention here rather than there; we are selecting. Again, our physical bodies select from the environment around them what they need, and try to avoid what is injurious to them; they do not respond indifferently to every chemical or physical or biological element around them. Even chemical elements react in given ways only to *certain* other elements; no element reacts in the same way to everything. Selectivity seems to be an order of nature. It is not to be wondered at that man has found it an ally in his careful observing and thinking of the internal nature of things.

Perhaps the key to the occasional disappointment with analysis lies in what we have previously mentioned, namely, that analysis into components does not yield *the* components but only *a* set of components of anything, and that these components, when aggregated, may add up to only *one* general aspect of the whole. (Clearly, there is likely to be more than one

---

[77] See for example a well known early study: W. W. Charters and Isadore B. Whitley, *Report on Analysis of Secretarial Duties and Traits.* New York: National Junior Personnel Service, 1924. 186 p. Also, published separately: *Summary of Report* on Analysis of Secretarial Duties and Traits, 1924. 62 p.
Charters and Waples, *op. cit.,* p. 14-19; 51-76; 223-44.

aspect represented, because of correlation, but for purposes of simplicity we shall speak of *one* aspect.) In other words, if a job is analyzed in terms of activities which can be expressed on a time scale, we will get, when we combine them, an analytical description of the job according to time and activity. If we analyze the job from the standpoint of desired quality of performance (as one complex of general aspects of the job), we should obtain components of the qualitative aspects, and these should in turn add up to the qualitative requirements, but not necessarily to any *other* kind of total. These examples deal with only two general types. In the earlier section on general aspects we pointed out that anything can have an infinity of aspects, depending on what can be done with it, and on the frame of thought from which it is viewed. Theoretically, then, the perception of anything can be analyzed into conceptualized components in an infinity of ways. Practically, each perceptual aspect can be subdivided as many times as there are subdividing conditions or degrees which can be observed or inferred. But the components obtained from any one perceptual view will not ordinarily add up to a total which has meaning in terms of a different point of view. This is a point commonly overlooked in criticisms of analysis as a useful research process.

The analysis along one line leaves out the elements which analysis along another line would preserve. If one has need for more than one set of components, more than one *kind* of components, he must analyze more than once, from different points of view. Apparently, disappointment over the results of analysis comes from not understanding what to expect from it; from expecting, or desiring, too much from it. Analysis into units of any kind will cut across all of the organizing, relational, integrating aspects which, in the whole, permit these units to add up to the whole with all of its characteristics; when these interrelating aspects have been removed, the sum of the resulting units will not equal the whole, but only that general aspect of the whole which was employed as the basis of subdivision when deriving the units. To arrive at *other* aspects of the whole through a process of putting together the analyzed parts, one will have to start with the product of *other* lines of analysis.

One may think that it ought to be possible to get units so small that they would fit into any kind of integration, leading to any desired whole. Seeking the answer in this direction, however, is self-defeating; the smaller the unit, the more that is omitted from it—and the more that has to be added back to it of the other aspects or elements which make the whole different from a mere sum of these units, and which give to the whole its distinctive properties. To some persons, this is the goal of science, namely, to obtain units so small and so essentially elemental that only their occurrence or nonoccurrence matters.[78] The history of physical science, however, shows this to be a somewhat illusory goal. The more physics advances, the more elemental units it finds. It not only finds more kinds of atoms, but more kinds of units within the atom, and further disintegration of aspects. During nearly all of the nineteenth century, scientists thought of the atom as composed of a single substance. With the turn of the century, physicists recognized two kinds of elementary material, and as recently as twenty years ago they spoke of the universe as being built out of two kinds of building blocks, positive and negative elements of the atom. During the past two decades, however, a dozen kinds of particles have been discovered in the atom.[79] The pace is increasing. Who knows but what the next generation, or the next century, will find even these units broken down still further? In research, no element stays elementary for long.[80]

Furthermore, these diverse elemental particles of the atom do not have mere presence or absence, and do not enter into all kinds of integration without having other features added. For example, they are arranged in different ways in the atom. They have energy and action and a positive or negative charge. Out of their kinds, number, organization, action, and charge, the various properties of different kinds of atoms and molecules are built up. But note that these properties are in no sense built up from simply the presence or absence of a given kind of particle. It is only when one's analytical perspective is stripped down to looking at a certain aspect that the elemental particles have only that aspect; when man opens up his view, he sees that the particles have various aspects.

We are here dealing, in effect, with the minimum level to which analysis can go; that is, with the minimum number of elements or aspects which a very simple object can have. From this we can get an idea of the aspects it is necessary to add back in as one reconstructs a whole from separated

[78] Certain things can be ascertained from such all-or-none units, but many of the things one wishes to know cannot. For example, we can count people, as elemental social units, but such counting tells us nothing about how social life is organized—its institutions, customs, ideals, etc.

[79] "Atom's Newest Particles." *Life Magazine*, May 15, 1950, p. 69-72.

[80] Of course one finally gets down to the point where things have lost so many of their characteristics they are no longer what one expects to find. Advancing quantum mechanics calls for a new view of the nature of elementary particles which gives them a possible transitoriness. The ultimate constituents of matter may have a discontinuous existence rather than a continuous one. "An atom lacks the most primitive property we associate with a piece of matter in ordinary life." Elementary particles are, nevertheless, assumed to occur: "We do observe single particles." But their occurrence seems to be a matter of statistical probability rather than definite identity. We need not "give up speaking and thinking in terms of what is really going on in the physical world." "There is, indeed, no reason to ban it [the common terminology] provided we are aware that, on sober experimental grounds, the sameness of a particle [from moment to moment] is not an absolute concept." Erwin Schrödinger, "What Is an Elementary Particle?" *Endeavour* 9:109-116; July 1950.

Similar views are expressed in Henry Margenau, "Conceptual Foundations of the Quantum Theory." *Science* 113:95-101; January 26, 1951.

units—from units which are perhaps only classified and counted. We are not certain what the minimum level of analysis ultimately will prove to be; we can only speak in terms of the current stage of the most advanced form of analytical science today, namely, physics. Whether this level has the minimal properties which will someday be discovered, we do not know. But at present, taking the simplest unit that has been analyzed, namely, the hydrogen atom, we can scarcely avoid noting the aspects we have already mentioned: (1) there are *two* particles, not just one; (2) the particles are of different kinds and each has a number of different properties; (3) their electrical charges form an interrelated pattern: they are opposites; (4) the particles have a certain organizational relationship; (5) one particle (perhaps each) is in active motion with respect to the other, and this motion itself has a number of characteristics. Out of such aspects as these (and there may be more) [81] the various properties of the gas hydrogen emerge.

What of the other elements? They have more *kinds* of particles, more variation in numbers, more complex organization, a great binding energy in the nucleus, and more variation in the composition of different atoms of the same element. In these more complex atoms, certain aspects emerge which are present, but go unnoticed, in the simple hydrogen atom; for example, when there are two particles, there are two things; but attention should also be directed toward the fact that there is *one of each;* in other words, the aspect of *relative* number. And, when one thinks of the presumed orbit of the outer particle (electron), he must recognize that the aspects of diameter and pattern are present.

Since we have been considering the simplest thing which man knows of (and has analyzed into components), we presume that anything which exists as a distinctive kind, any organized entity, any functioning unit, will have at least these aspects. Certainly they are present in the cells of living things and they are present in sociological groups. When, therefore, one wishes a minimally complete analysis—one which will enable him to add the analyzed components back together again in such a way that they will account for the whole and its characteristics—he will have to make a number of different analyses of the whole, one with respect to each of the general aspects in the minimum list.

We regard the foregoing discussion as somewhat schematic; that is, it is only an outline, a suggestion. It is far too simple. For, when one begins to analyze anything of the size and complexity so that it is sensible to mankind in his everyday experiences, he will find many aspects in addition to those named; and he will discover that they are applied over and over again, in successive levels of a very intricate hierarchy of orders. But the discus-

[81] The two known isotopes of hydrogen introduce additional characteristics.

sion may be helpful to those persons who wonder why "the whole is more than the sum of its parts"—when "parts" have been analyzed out along only one or a few lines. The whole is never more than its parts when all aspects of the whole are included among its "parts."

**Concepts often call for analysis and division in preparation for their study.** There are many points at which it seems desirable to repeat the statement that what passes as common knowledge on the street is often not well understood by the scientist. The point is that much of what is "known" fails to meet the exacting standards of research. Consider, for example, the concept of *learning*. Anyone thinks he knows what learning is. But when he sets about to study it, he finds it difficult to establish just what the concept means, or should mean, for there are a number of other phenomena which seem to occur under the same circumstances as learning does. One may be surprised to read that "Psychologists have not to date agreed upon a definition of learning." [82] The major problem is to distinguish between learning, maturation, and fatigue—for "all three are inferences from performance changes, and the performance may reflect the operation of one or all three in combination." A number of variables enter into the conditions, the process, and the product. What variables one is able to separate out, what factors remain reflected in his data, and what aspects of learning itself are actually taken as representing learning of a given type, are all matters which depend upon the way one sets up his experiment, and measures and interprets his data.

When one is thinking of learning on a broad scale, such as the growth and development of concepts, as in the field of arithmetic, the complexities of the study are apparent and the need for careful separation of many factors is accentuated. Whether the detailed components which can be conceptually identified in the general concept can, in actual practice, be identified and then controlled or separated, is always something of a question—until by unusual skill and resourcefulness someone has unquestionably succeeded in doing it.

Whatever is said of learning holds also for forgetting. It is commonly thought that forgetting is simply a matter of the passage of time. Yet forgetting does not seem to vary so much with the amount of elapsed time as with several other factors. Shall one then say that these other factors are components of the trait of "forgetting"? Or are they simply to be regarded

[82] Arthur W. Melton, "Learning." *Encyclopedia of Educational Research, op. cit.,* p. 668-90.

For more extensive review and summary treatments one may consult *Annual Review of Psychology,* Chapter on "Learning." Published annually, beginning with 1950, by Annual Reviews, Stanford, Calif.

S. S. Stevens, Editor, *Handbook of Experimental Psychology.* New York: John Wiley and Sons, 1951. Chapters 15-18, 20.

as contributing factors? The answer to such a question is not easy. Often such questions cannot be answered except by arbitrary definition, for in any case the notion of "forgetting" is an imposed concept—a way of viewing certain forms of mental activity, or at least certain changes in mental activity—and hence it can be defined as researchers agree to define it, including or excluding such elements as they wish. As another example, the question of what the concept of "thinking" should include, as contrasted to factors which are conceived simply as affecting the process, is possibly even more difficult.[83]

The relation of a whole to its parts is of particular interest whenever groups of people are involved as an object (unit) for study. The point here is that, as human beings, we are used to beginning our thinking with ourselves. The idea of a group of any kind seems to us as a sort of imposed idea. We think that we (individually) are the real units, and that the group is a sort of accidental, transitory, and artificial entity with no definable limits. A number of writers have taken this view. Actually, of course, the view is a biased one, prejudiced by the human being's natural (and legitimate) concern with and for himself. A moment's thought will reveal that we, individually, are the transitory unit in a society which has a much longer existence than any one of us. Our social institutions are designed to have a certain stability from one generation to the next. If one turns his attention to the more ephemeral groups, such as a temporary committee, it is still a matter of point of emphasis whether the committee, or the segment of experience of any individual in that committee, is to be regarded as the more transient and fleeting.

Because, however, of man's tendency to think of himself as the natural unit, and of groups as somewhat synthetic, the usual process of starting with a whole and analyzing it is likely to be reversed, and the form of thought is often of the nature, What makes individuals into a group?[84] If one should study this question, he would probably find that the concept of social integration had a number of different aspects, and that it was probably profitable to study it in terms of each of these aspects. Thus, one researcher recently divided the general concept into four separate kinds of integration[85] and described each. He noted that it seemed better to

[83] See, for example, Wilhelm Reitz, "Higher Mental Processes," *Encyclopedia of Educational Research, op. cit.,* p. 540-51.
[84] We are here using the term *group* to mean any kind of collection or aggregate, and not with the technical niceties and distinctions employed in rigorous sociological usage. For delineations of the latter, one may consult:
George A. Lundberg, *Foundations of Sociology.* New York: Macmillan Co., 1939. Chap. 9, "Types of Groups."
Earle E. Eubank, *Concepts of Sociology.* Boston: D. C. Heath and Co., 1932. Chapter 8.
[85] Werner S. Landecker, "Types of Integration and Their Measurement." *American Journal of Sociology* 56:332-40; January 1951.

begin research with these components of the general concept, and then build up what generalizations seemed appropriate, than to study the undivided, general notion of integration.

We have here presented several examples, out of an endless number which exist, of the need for and the utility of examining a concept carefully to see what its proper constituents are (or what one wishes to define it as containing), and hence what its limits are and what factors or elements should be eliminated, in order that one's data will reflect the concept he wishes to study and not a number of factors which he wishes not to include. Often the division of an idea (concept) into kinds, and the study of each one separately, will lead to more penetrating observation than will the attack on a more general formulation.

This idea has many more applications which come under the heading of measurement, or preparation for measurement, and these will be mentioned now.

**For purposes of constructing measuring instruments it is often necessary to ascertain the component elements of the concept to be represented**. Measurement of almost any kind may seem like a perfectly obvious thing—one simply employs the proper measuring instrument for whatever one wishes to measure. But in so doing, one should recognize that there may have been many years of effort in the production of that instrument: first, in the refining of the concept of the trait (aspect) to be measured; and second, in the preparation, testing, and calibration of the instrument itself. In both of these processes, the subdivision of the original concept is likely to be called for.

For example, if one is preparing a test in arithmetical computation, he will consider what should go into the test—what he wants represented in the concept "arithmetical computation." If it deals with the four fundamental processes, in what proportion will these four components be represented? When this question is answered, the analysis can proceed downward almost endlessly, dealing with what different number combinations should be involved, what situations or settings, and so on. All of these types of arithmetic ability are components of the general concept, whether one is conscious of them or not. Dealing with them consciously permits one to choose his coverage rather than just "trusting to luck."

Tests of arithmetic in the upper grades are likely to recognize computational ability and problem-solving ability as two general components of the concept of arithmetic ability. If one were preparing a test for reading ability, he would find that this ability has many components ranging from essential skills in moving the eyes, through the various elements of the perceptual process and acquaintance with language, to the background experiences which permit one to obtain meaning from language. And behind the more direct and obvious elements that make reading possible are the emotional and motivational factors (so often taken for granted and overlooked) which may exercise the major control over whether one learns to read at all, or whether one finds reading sufficiently interesting and rewarding to keep his attention on what his eyes are passing over. If one could ascertain the necessary and sufficient conditions for (the factors entering into) reading at various levels of maturity, he would have a long list. Having such a list, he could select more intelligently those which he wished his test to cover.

The need for analysis of this kind can perhaps best be seen by considering some trait (aspect, or ability) that is not already well represented in tests with which one may be familiar. For example, if one were preparing a test to get at meaning or understanding in a particular school subject, he would have to think carefully about what aspects of the subject would constitute understanding as contrasted with simple knowledge.[86] (This would involve an analysis both of the subject and of the concept of understanding.) Or, suppose one were to prepare a check list for democratic practices in his school; he would have to do some careful analysis of what the concept "democratic practices" meant to him. As another example, there has recently developed some interest in the measuring of listening ability. This does not refer to hearing tests (comparable to visual tests in the case of reading) but rather to an ability which might be regarded as a parallel to reading ability. Clearly, the first step in preparing a measuring procedure for listening ability would be to define the ability, and the kind of definition that would be of most help would be one which specified the principal elements in the ability. In this instance a group of eleven persons were requested to report, according to their judgment, what skills listening ability should include.[87] Five specific skills were suggested.

The process which has just been refered to is fairly common. The initial analysis of ideas, concepts, or categorical notions in general is likely to be carried through on a judgmental basis. Sometimes the procedure is almost blind trial-and-error. Those who are familiar with the history of intelligence testing will recall the many trials which Binet made early in the century, experimenting first with one trait (ability) and then another,

---

[86] National Society for the Study of Education, *The Measurement of Understanding*. Forty-fifth Yearbook, Part I. William A. Brownell, Chairman. Chicago: University of Chicago Press, 1946. 338 p.

[87] James I. Brown, "Measurement of Listening Ability." *School and Society* 71:69-71; February 4, 1950. See also his "Construction of a Diagnostic Test of Listening Comprehension." *Journal of Experimental Education* 18:139-46; December 1949.

For later articles on this subject, see the heads "Listening" and "Comprehension Tests" in the *Education Index*.

hoping to find one that would differentiate between persons in the way his judgment indicated it should. (This is not a procedure to be scoffed at; the major measurements of physical science had their beginnings in precisely this fashion, and units of time and of space were still in a relatively crude stage until the Renaissance.) Binet finally came to a composite of various kinds of activity as the most satisfactory, and we are, in the main, still employing a composite. This is logical, since we expect intelligence tests to measure a rather general, average form of ability. It is true that there are sometimes practical uses in indicating two subclasses of this general ability, one referring to verbal facility and the other to quantitative ability; but it is also true that if we split up the measurement of intelligence into a great many separate facets or elements and deal with each separately, rather than taking them together to form a composite or average, we are departing from the usual concept and purpose of intelligence measurement. Something would be gained in specificity and something would be given up in the way of generality.

A division of the general idea (the trait to be measured) is especially necessary in the construction of various kinds of indexes (sometimes spoken of as formulas), such as indexes of the cost of living, an index of teaching load, index of the capacity of a school building, index of readability, and so on. In such indexes, the aspects which are to be included are definitely represented by some term or specific part of the formula, so that what is not provided for (consciously) does not get into the result, except in that it may be correlated with some aspect which is covered. Hence the analysis of the total idea into components is deliberate. This does not imply that all of the possible components (resulting from a particular line of analysis) are included; they may simply be sampled. For example, in calculating any of the various common economic indexes for the country, no one thinks of including every single item that is sold or produced, but classes of items are sampled.

There are series of aspects which can be viewed either as a set of general aspects, or as components of a total concept, depending on the way one wishes to think of them for a given purpose. For example, Reavis named six aspects of a school building and its site which must be considered in any appraisal.[88] These involve (1) safety, (2) adaptation to educational program, (3) operation and maintenance costs, (4) flexibility for changing programs, (5) long-term view of location, and (6) internal and external artistic effect. To think of these as components rather than as

[88] William C. Reavis, "The School Survey as a Basis for School-Plant Planning," Chapter 6, p. 67-79. *Administrative Planning for School Programs and Plants.* Edited by Dan H. Cooper. Sixteenth Annual Conference for Administrative Officers, 1947. Vol. X. Chicago: University of Chicago Press, 1947. 160 p.

a set of separate aspects, one merely has to develop a concept which will combine them, such as the idea, "goodness of the school" or "satisfactoriness of the school." Reavis did not combine them into an instrument for appraisal, but a check list or rating scale of the usual type would represent such a combination. We mention this illustration to show the structure of such instruments. One may wish to consider the major categories on other check lists for school buildings,[89] thinking of them as components of a whole. All such instruments should be inspected from this point of view: to what extent will the ratings in the various categories, when taken together, give a satisfactorily complete picture of general goodness or satisfactoriness?

It seems reasonable to say that, in general, the construction of rating lists of this type has not been given adequately systematic consideration. A double analysis is called for. First, one must decide on those general aspects of a school building (or other object, situation, or trait) which he wishes to include in his rating, resulting in a set more or less like the list of six proposed by Reavis. One may decide to include as few or as many of these general aspects in his rating scale as he wishes; but, if he decides on only a few, the title to the scale should indicate its restricted nature. These general aspects should then be kept separate in the scale, so as to yield separate totals; these totals might all be the same (perhaps 1000 points each) or they might be different, with the thought that the different totals would constitute something of a weighting, in case the scores on the various aspects should be added together. Then the second analysis begins. Each of the general aspects included is analyzed into those component elements or subaspects which, when taken together (totaled or averaged), will give a satisfactory indication of the state of the building (or/and site) with respect to that particular general aspect. It is possible that a reverse order of analysis could be used; that is, the building could be broken down into parts or forms of service (functions), and then the qualities of each of these considered in systematic fashion. This procedure furnishes an excellent analytical check when the building is being planned. It seems likely, however, that totals in terms of general aspects will serve more purposes. In any case, a profile of separate totals would be more revealing than a single, over-all total or average.

Any check list, rating scale, score card, or the like which attempts to cover both types of analysis in one single list of aspects is something like an achievement test made up to cover all the school subjects in the curriculum and yield a single total score. This extreme is not likely to be

---

[89] There are many such instruments. Holy and Herrick give a bibliography of lists and standards, p. 1115, *Encyclopedia of Educational Research, op. cit.* For continuing references, see *Education Index,* "School Buildings—Rating."

attempted. Yet it seems doubtful that the two types of analysis have been followed as systematically as they deserve to be.

Interestingly enough, under certain circumstances it is possible to begin the process at the other end. That is, differentiating items can be collected and then grouped into classes (representing general aspects) afterwards. This is the case with the critical-incidents technique recently developed by Flanagan (the American Institute for Research) and referred to in connection with job analysis. More was not said about it at that point because it is basically not a job-analysis technique; it is essentially a qualitative or appraisal technique, and the analysis is something of an accessory element. In constructing a rating instrument of this type, one collects instances of behavior on the part of an employee which his supervisor regards as distinctively poor or good; in effect, types of specific acts that tend to make that employee above or below average. These are then classified according to categories which are created for the purpose. The number of instances that fall in one or another of the categories is not necessarily an indication of the importance of that category for the job, but it is an index of the importance of that category in terms of number of acts likely to be observed which make a supervisor feel an employee is superior or inferior.

In connection with the double analysis into components which was called for in rating lists, it is interesting to examine an appraisal instrument embodying critical incidents. These incidents are not in themselves an analysis of the job into component activities; neither are they an analysis of the traits required of the worker. The analysis of the job comes from the categories which are set up to classify the incidents. If these categories are made with a view to the essential activities of the work to be done (and they are likely to be), then the resulting instrument will be systematic in this respect. It is of course possible that the number of instances in some category might be vanishingly small; but, practically, that would probably be remedied by seeking more. As for the second type of analysis, namely, that of worker traits (abilities, habits of work), the incidents are not to be considered as attempting this. Rather they seek to index these traits, to indicate something of the desirable or undesirable degree of them. They are in the nature of test items; that is, the incidents (or test items) indicate the tendency of a certain character or ability to be present and manifest itself; but they do not (ordinarily) analyze the trait—that is, they do not split it up into its component, longitudinal elements. They explore qualitative aspects, but not systematically. They are, therefore, comparable with test items. They represent something like a building score card constructed by asking teachers and principals (and perhaps pupils and parents) what they had found particularly good about a certain building and what they had found especially bad about it. We do not know that this has ever been tried; it probably would call attention to aspects very different from those found by systematic analysis; it might result in an interesting type of instrument.

Sometimes an analytical list is prepared, not especially for purposes of rating, but to assist administrators and deliberative groups in considering systematically the various aspects entering into a determination of what to do. One such list [90] divides up the services of a city school system into twenty different types. These are components of the total service which a school system might render. A second level of analysis provides a list of twenty-nine organizational and functional aspects of each form of service. These aspects indicate specific features which need to be considered in instituting a new service or in maintaining one that is already operating. A third list of twenty-one items represents subaspects, or more detailed considerations which would enter into a judgment on the desirability of instituting a service, or on the status of one that was in operation. The list is, therefore, systematic with respect to three levels of analysis, and presents aspects on three levels of generality. It thus recognizes the hierarchical nature of the aspects which persons in practical work, charged with the responsibility for exercising judgment, must consider.

In the present section, a number of different illustrations have been given of the way in which the concept of a trait to be measured needs to be broken up into elements. The intent has not been to imply that all of the elements must be included. Once one has the general idea analyzed, there are several things he can do. Perhaps a list of purposes in this kind of analysis would be helpful. The following may be listed:

1. To arrive at a clearer notion of the essence of the trait. What is its essential nature? Some aspects seem less important than others; possibly some are more or less accidental accompaniments. (For example, speed of handwriting is not ordinarily thought of as an important element of speed in arithmetic ability, and educators would probably like to eliminate it.) Analysis should help in centering attention on what is important, what is near the core of the idea.

2. To insure that no essential or highly characteristic aspect is omitted from the measurement; in general, to make sure that one has the desired coverage of the various aspects of the trait. This may be accomplished through sampling, as in an index number and in carefully planned objective tests. The idea of coverage may be applied both to areas of the subject and

[90] Douglas E. Scates, "Check-List for Studying School Services." *American School Board Journal* 92:17-19; June 1936.

to types of ability (in arithmetic, these may be the same; in geography, the two are likely to be widely different).

3. One may wish to break up the trait into parts, after discovering its complexity, making separate parts of a test (or separate tests), with separate scores, for the major divisions or kinds of the trait (for example, a test battery covering several subjects).

4. One may wish to eliminate from his measuring instrument certain aspects which, without careful analysis, might have seemed to belong in the concept of the trait. (For example, spelling ability is seldom included in intelligence tests; it is not regarded as being so central or critical for the purpose as are certain quantitative abilities; yet, some sixty years ago, spelling was popularly taken as a major indication of good education and keen intelligence.)

5. To avoid undue overlapping in the aspects or elements measured, since this is uneconomical of testing time. This goal probably cannot be achieved well by simple mental analysis; it can be done better through correlating measurements of the several aspects. But it could scarcely be done at all without this analysis of the concept and the corresponding subdivision of the measuring instrument. The use of a number of full tests for each likely or conceivable part of the trait, as is done in factor analysis, is better.

6. To determine appropriate weights for the several elements which make up the general trait. One may not be certain of his judgment as to what these relative weights should be; but, without some analysis and thought, he can exercise no judgment whatever, and a very minor (not essential) aspect might accidentally receive more weight than an aspect regarded as central. (In a course in geography, the ability to draw maps might accidentally occupy a disproportionate part in a test, if constructed without analytical attention to the nature and components of the goal; or, in an index on cost of living, watercress might be weighted the same as potatoes.)

7. To afford an analytical knowledge and understanding of the measuring instrument, so that when revision seems called for, in order to improve one or another of its functions, the process can be undertaken intelligently and effectively.

**Factor analysis is a technique which may be of aid in deciding upon components of a trait.** In the preceding section it was assumed that the analysis of the general concept of what was to be measured would be studied and refined primarily by mental processes. These would include not only discussion and judgment in determining what elements were desired in the general idea, but also the later trying out of the instrument to see whether the results seemed to be what were wanted. Again, we should emphasize that this general approach is not one of weakness, and is not one which the social sciences are peculiarly dependent on. It is the method that has been employed in the approach to all basic phenomena in all fields of science, and it is in fact *still* being used in physical science for the refining of the concept of such fundamental things as "force." In other words, with some three hundred years of increasingly refined study, the physical sciences are still improving (by pure reasoning) the concepts of the nature of some of their elemental measurements.[91]

This is really not an occasion for surprise, since each important new discovery in any field of study is likely to throw some light (and some new questions) on previously existing concepts. The main characteristic of science is not its inexorable rightness, but its continuous self-examination and improvement. We refer to the matter here as a point of orientation (historical and comparative perspective) and also as a guide to expectation; we must not assume that the concepts of what we want our measuring instruments to measure are ever finally settled. Nor should we be surprised that these concepts are undergoing constant criticism and challenge. That is of the nature of science.

It is possible, however, to derive a certain amount of aid from the technique known as factor analysis, in determining components of a trait [92] to be measured. This is a statistical method which consists essentially of (1) giving a rather large number of tests which are presumed to measure some aspect of the general trait and which will represent a wide range of elements that might enter into the general trait; (2) calculating intercorrelations among these tests to find those which tend to measure (or be saturated with) the same element or factors; (3) deducing (mentally) what this trait (factor) is that a particular subgroup of correlated tests are measuring in common, and giving it a name; (4) repeating this process, by technical statistical means, until a satisfactory number of factors have been distilled out. Ideally, these factors will be reasonably few in number (maybe half a dozen) and will, together, account for a large portion of what was measured by the original set of tests. This, then, is the goal of factor analysis, namely, to produce a rather small number of traits (factors, or component elements) which will come reasonably close to covering the

[91] Joseph   H. Keenan, "Definitions and Principles of Dynamics." *Scientific Monthly* 67:406-14;  December 1948.

[92] The word *trait* is used in a very general sense, as is common in statistical work. In this usage it is practically synonymous with dimension, factor, variable, ability, or general aspect. Only in discussions of personality will the word be used to imply a personality trait.

same field (the general trait in all its aspects) as the larger number of varied tests.[93] Some of the limitations of the method will be considered later; let us first look at some examples of its application.

Thurstone, employing one type of factor analysis, has broken up general mental ability (intelligence) into the following nine (sometimes only seven) specific components, or factors: spatial ability, perceptual speed, numerical ability, verbal-relations ability, word fluency, memory, induction, deduction, and problem-solving.[94] These factors are not uncorrelated, as it was originally hoped they would be, and therefore overlap each other to some extent. Speed is an element in several of them. Other studies and other methods or conceptions of factor analysis lead to somewhat different results.[95] These components are not to be thought of as final; they can always be broken down further or abstracted differently. They are probably something of an improvement over the "faculties" of an earlier day which were handed down philosophically without the aid of tests and analytical statistics.[96] While some of the former "faculties" are confirmed in Thurstone's list (for example, memory and reasoning), the "faculties" included such a heterogeneous assortment that they could scarcely be regarded as coördinate (for example, from the generality of self-preservation and imagination, to the specific content of language and number, and such personality characteristics as caution and impulsiveness).[97] The faculties were (like many of the modern "factors") thought to be basic and separate elements of all mental activity.

Other areas of personal behavior have been analyzed by the methods of

[93] This subject has a large bibliography, including several comprehensive texts and a number of more compact descriptions. For a useful bibliography see the article on "Factor Analysis" by Karl J. Holzinger in the *Encyclopedia of Educational Research, op. cit.*

For continuing references, see the annual bibliographies in the November issue of the *School Review* prepared by Frances Swineford (and formerly Karl J. Holzinger). (These began in June 1939 and continued in June issues through 1948, then appeared in May 1949, and subsequently in November.)

See also the *Annual Review of Psychology* issued in the spring of each year beginning with 1950—chapter on "Statistical Theory and Research Design," or consult the head "Factor Analysis" in the Index. This head is also carried in the *Education Index* and in the December Index Number of *Psychological Abstracts.*

[94] See *Encyclopedia of Educational Research, op. cit.,* p. 432, 544, 603. Reported originally in L. L. Thurstone, *Primary Mental Abilities.* Psychometric Monograph No. 1. Chicago: University of Chicago Press, 1938. 121 p.

[95] See, for example, "Analytical Structure of General Intelligence," p. 603, in *Encyclopedia of Educational Research, op. cit.* To this reference should be added the studies employing the bi-factor approach (general, group, and specific factors); see studies by Frances Swineford, *Education Index,* Vols. 5 and 7.

[96] Edwin G. Boring, *A History of Experimental Psychology.* Second Edition. New York: Appleton-Century-Crofts, 1950. p. 203, 205, 216.

See "Faculty." *A Cyclopedia of Education,* Vol. II, p. 569-70. Edited by Paul Monroe. New York: Macmillan Co., 1911.

[97] Frank N. Freeman, *Mental Tests.* Revised Edition. Boston: Houghton Mifflin Co., 1939. p. 434-35.

factor analysis into component elements. For example, Thurstone has divided temperament into factors.[98] He states that "temperament" refers to "those non-intellective traits of personality which are relatively stable, . . . and which are not often markedly changed in social experience" (p. 11-12). This, he notes, is narrower "than the much larger domain that is called personality." Many additional studies could be cited which differentiate various personality traits by means of factor analysis, but we are not here dealing with the entire realm of personality.

**Comments on factor analysis as a technique for deriving components of a general concept.** The interpretation of the results of factor analysis is by no means simple and there is at present wide disagreement concerning what it is that a factor-analysis study has really produced. Any technical discussion would be out of place here, but it seems reasonable to state a number of general characteristics and conditions of the method which may be helpful to researchers who are considering its use, or the interpretation of its products.

In the common case, factor analysis is based on test results and begins with the correlation of these results. The final factors are accordingly subject to the limitations which these conditions impose.

1. These limitations are of a substantial order; for example, the results will not (cannot) differentiate and identify any "factor" which is not covered by the original battery of tests. That is, whatever elements may lie outside the set of tests used will lie outside any "factors" which are found. It is theoretically possible (though unlikely) that the most central element of the general trait would be missed, through inclusion, in the original battery, of tests which deal entirely with "fringe" elements and no central element. What is more likely is that elements of moderate importance will be omitted; this is almost certain to happen in a field that has not previously been well explored and mapped by a large number of individual, independent studies which, in the aggregate, have employed a large variety of tests—a larger variety and a larger number than are likely to be employed in any single factor-analysis study.

2. No factor will show up as a distinct group factor except when the original tests employed differ sufficiently among themselves with respect to that factor to reveal it. That is, those factors which are common to all the tests (and there are likely to be a great many of them) will appear in the form of some composite general factor, if the method of factor analysis employed is such as to recognize a general factor, and if the persons (or other cases) tested differ sufficiently with respect to this factor to make it

98 L. L. Thurstone, "The Dimensions of Temperament." *Psychometrika* 16:11-20; March 1951.

affect the intercorrelations of the scores on the different tests. This leads to the next statement.

3.  Certain factors (elements) of ability may be essential parts of the larger general ability and yet not show up as "factors" at all, not even as an unidentified portion of a general factor, if the group of persons tested do not differ sufficiently with respect to this factor to make it stand out. For example, if all the persons in any study were the same, or nearly the same, in numerical ability, this form of ability would not show up as one of the "factors" of intelligence. It is only when the cases in the group differ enough with respect to any particular element of ability (and when tests are used which will properly reflect this variation) that the element or factor can show up in the results. Hence, this condition is additional to that in the second statement, and elements will not appear even in the general factor, unless the group of cases (persons, usually) vary sufficiently in this respect. (This is the simple, well known condition for correlation; the coefficient will be negligibly small, if one of a pair of traits has negligible variation.) Factor analysis rests on variation, not structure.

Practically, this third limitation may not be important, so long as one wishes to utilize the results of factor analysis with groups similar to the one studied. But theoretically it is of considerable importance, for it means that there is an unknown list of factors entering into common ability, or almost any other general concept, which are likely not to be revealed, no matter how important they may be structurally. For example, the ordinary pencil-and-paper group intelligence test demands such abilities as knowledge of the English language up to a minimum point, hearing, seeing, reading, writing (or marking), understanding and following directions, and such broader but fundamental abilities in getting along in our society as the willingness to follow directions, the disposition to work at a high speed simply because told to, the ability to get to the designated testing place at the appointed time, keeping one's mind from blanking out due to fear and excitement at being tested, restraining one's emotions when meeting frustrating tasks in the test, being orderly and not disturbing others, and various other forms of coöperative, socially oriented behavior. No list of such essential elements could be made exhaustive. Yet, because we have brought young people up in our culture with sufficient uniformity of behavior (at least among those who remain in school), a host of elements which are foundational to, and which would affect, mental ability as measured by tests just do not show up as "factors" at all. Practically, we do not have to care, except when we are testing persons who do not know common English or who are exceptional in some other way; but, theoretically, we are forced to be very careful about the statements we make concerning any particular list of component elements of a general ability. We simply ignore the great majority of essential elements.

4. There is nothing in the factor-analysis technique which will define the limits of a general concept; the limits must be set by judgment, supported by deliberation, discussion, and tryout. For example, should the concept of intelligence include spatial relationships, the ability to judge distances, compare shapes, detect differences in pattern, sense relationships in patterns, predict the results of mental manipulation of given patterns, and so on? In the Thurstone factors, this is included. Should the concept of intelligence include mechanical ability? Or should that be reserved for special tests of mechanical aptitude? Does motor ability or motor speed (the ability to move accurately and rapidly) belong in the concept of intelligence? Both mechanical and motor factors were included (and distinguished) in studies of mental ability by Spearman and Holzinger, and others. Should freedom from emotional blocking (negativism, contrariness, stubbornness, inhibition, lack of effort, inability to adjust, to make decisions) be included in intelligence? In one's practical, everyday use of his intelligence, such factors may be of more significance than the amount of abstract intelligence. Most psychologists, however, have preferred to keep these separate. Spearman early urged recognition and inclusion of such broad factors as perseveration, oscillation, and will. All questions of this type, whether with relation to intelligence, learning, or any other broad concept, must be decided aside from the technical processes of factor analysis.

5. The factorial composition of a general concept can be changed by changing the tests used. This follows from earlier statements, but merits separate attention. At the present point we wish to note that the way a general concept is divided up (the set of factors which appear) is a product of the kinds of tests employed. Tests that devolve upon very complex abilities are likely to yield factors of greater complexity than are tests which individually call for simpler and more homogeneous forms of ability. The former have less definition, less resolving power. And, as was commented in an earlier section, the factor analysis of a set of sixteen traits, eight of which dealt with some aspect or form of education, was almost certain to produce a factor which represented education. Presumably the mature worker in an area where considerable sophistication has been built up will select his original tests, or other series of data, in such a way as to give balance to the likely elements in the area; but these things are matters of judgment and the advanced state of work in an area, and lie entirely outside the routine use of the factor-analysis technique. Until a large amount

of exploration has been done, the researcher can only guess at the elements which are to be revealed; and in any case he is likely to be limited in the means (the tests or other data, the cases, competent assistants, time, and money) at his disposal.

6. Different elements in a general concept may be measured very unevenly and possibly on different levels of complexity, due to varying degrees of difficulty in their measurement. For example, imagination, creativeness, social understanding, and the like are judged to be important personal attributes, and they may even be important elements of intelligence, but they are not likely to be revealed as "factors" because of the difficulty of measuring them. If tests exist for them, such tests are likely to be so complicated or special as to be omitted. Further along this same line, it is not at all certain that the factors derived from tests are actually coördinate—are of the same level of simplicity. As indicated in the preceding statement, the complexity of the resulting factor is partly dependent on the complexity of the abilities called for in a group of tests. It might be that such abilities as imagination, judgment, caution in drawing inferences, and the like are logically more complex than such a factor as speed (which may be primarily energy), or routine number work; and that, even if tests were included, there might result a considerable range in the complexity of the revealed "factors."

7. It is to be doubted that the compositional structure of a general trait (for example, intelligence) is uniform throughout its range, or over the various conditions to which the concept is commonly applied. Those persons who have a very high degree of intelligence and those who have a very low degree must have different factors present. The child of five who has a mental age of ten on tests, and the adolescent of twenty who has a mental age of ten on tests, are not to be described in the same terms, regardless of their similar test results. Qualitatively their abilities are different, and any attempt to describe both of them in terms of the same set of "factors" is bound to result in inadequate or inappropriate description for at least one of them—save when a researcher prepares a composite list of factors appropriate to the two cases and then gives zero weight (or loading) to a number of factors in describing the quality of intelligence in each case. Further along this line is the question as to whether intelligence on the adult level is the same thing as intelligence on the child and adolescent level, whether it is properly conceived in the same general terms. If not, then the factorial composition would necessarily change as different elemental tests, appropriate to the different concepts, were developed and employed. As to the effects of culture, and the nature of intelligence in various cul-

tures, the field is open to almost endless debate. How can "factors" (component elements) be determined once and for all, if the boundary of the general concept is indefinite or variable?

8. "Factors" resulting from factor analysis must not be thought of as finally simple. It is apparent in much of the literature that writers have thought of them as ultimates. Some psychologists have been convinced they were inherited. The frequency with which the "factors" are referred to as "scientific," "primary," "unitary," and "real" seems to suggest distinctive characteristics which in fact are not exclusive. The elements which result may be "unitary" in the sense that anything to which one gives attention may be regarded as unitary; that is, the entire universe is one unit. In general, what is unitary is almost wholly a matter of purpose and of conception: anything to which a unitary concept can be applied thereby becomes a unit for purposes of further thinking. It is entirely inconceivable that the "unitary traits" derived by ordinary factor-analysis methods cannot be broken down further when one desires to do so. This is not to say that they must be broken down, for they may be reasonably useful in their present form. But it is clearly quite possible to break up spatial perception and manipulation, or any other "factor," into various kinds; and, even though the resulting kinds may show some correlation, so do most of the present "factors." The whole question is not one of possibility but of purpose and utility.

It must be borne in mind that when anything is broken up beyond a certain point, it loses some of its common distinguishing characteristics. Thus, when reading ability is broken down into constituent abilities such as eyesight, coördination of the eye muscles, and so on, many of the aspects which we think of as reading have been lost. Physicists are at present having the same experience with the atom: the particles into which it is being broken clearly do not have the properties of the atom itself, and may not even have continuity of existence. The line between matter and pulses of energy may have been reached at this level. One must always be prepared for reaching (and perhaps continuing beyond) the point in analysis where the thing he is breaking down loses identity.

Against this background of thought, when one says that "any general factor must be regarded as a composite," is it not appropriate to inquire whether the same must not be said about "unitary factors"? Can anyone think of anything that is not a composite?—and at the same time unitary? Is something not called "unitary" or elemental when it is approached from a more general starting point, and called complex or composite when it is approached from the starting point of the more detailed? Man's thoughts always represent a certain perspective, a point of view; yet man seems to believe that his thoughts spring from the objective world. When man thinks, he creates—and next he accepts his creation!

9. The form of the factors which are produced by factor analysis depends on the statistical technique which is chosen; that is, on a priori assumptions or conceptions. Whether one obtains only group factors (those appearing in several tests), or a general factor (one running through all the tests), or specific factors (those unique to each particular task, or test), whether he obtains correlated (oblique) or independent (orthogonal) factors, or whether he obtains mathematical axes which satisfy mathematical criteria but are difficult to identify with any kind of conceivable elemental ability, are all matters that are determined (arbitrarily) in advance of his work by his choice of a method. For the different methods, though translatable from one to the other,[99] produce results which have different characteristics—results that fit different preconceptions of the way ability, or other general concepts, are made up. Sometimes a worker is brought up under one school of thought and does not realize that his training has already made these choices for him. But when one states that he does or does not find a general factor, it means merely that he elected to follow a method which did or did not reveal the common factor. What is probably true is that there are a fair number of *general* "factors" (tendencies or elements which have been interacting with segments of one's culture over a period of years so as to produce certain general abilities, habits, drives, and so on) which run through one's responses to virtually all paper-and-pencil tests; and below these are probably a very large number of identifiable *group* "factors" (abilities, habits, drives, and so on, having somewhat the same history as the general ones, only being narrower in their range of applications), these factors varying greatly in strength and in breadth or coverage and in correlation among themselves. In other words, these group factors are in reality on an indefinitely large number of different levels, between the general factors and the specific. What may be called a *specific* factor may be a matter of debate; probably these could be made to show up, if there were any reason for doing so. That is, virtually any specific factor can be made into a group factor by adding to the original set of tests more tests that have some of this factor in them. But it is conceivable, for example, that all the pupils from a certain city school system might be generally good in arithmetic, but might have a specific weakness in

99 "... solutions which are unique for a given plan of analysis may be obtained. Once any two solutions are obtained, however, it is possible to convert one to the other by suitable rotation of the references axes. Thus all solutions are comparable in the sense that it is possible to pass from one to another." Karl J. Holzinger, "Factor Analyis." *Encyclopedia of Educational Research, op. cit.,* p. 430. This subject is treated at length in:

Karl J. Holzinger and H. H. Harman, *Factor Analysis.* Chicago: University of Chicago Press, 1941. 417 p.

handling zero's, or a specific strength in dealing with per cents. If there were any purpose in doing so, separate tests could be constructed which would reveal these relatively specific variations as "factors" when a study was made of these and other pupils.

In research, many findings are forced by one's assumptions. Factor analysis provides an unusually clear illustration of the warning we so often state, that one finds what one looks for. One's conceptions carve out from the totality of nature (virtually create) those aspects which one is prepared to receive.[100] It requires the greatest of strength to hold with proper caution results which one obtains from direct observation or from technical processes.

10. The determination of the nature of a factor, after the mechanical part of the calculation has been completed, is, as everyone familiar with the procedure knows, a matter of some difficulty. To ascertain from an examination of the group of tests which are, to varying degrees, saturated with a particular but as yet unidentified "factor" calls for insight, imagination, and judgment. If one holds onto the full, complex description of this factor as represented by the data before him, he has done nothing to simplify the picture. If, on the other hand, he disregards many of the complex elements of this "factor" which is about to be born, and follows the usual custom of giving it a simple name, he is likely (almost certain) to be throwing a great deal of reality away.

It is at this point that factor analysis has one of its big opportunities. (Its other major opportunity is in the original conceptualization of the problem and the selection of tests or other indicia to represent this conceptualization.) Such situations are likely to encounter corresponding weaknesses in human nature. For, with the opportunity to sense something new (something that is hitherto unknown to man's experience as a separate and specific thing), there is a strong tendency to think in terms of the commonplace. "We might have expected that factor analysis would reveal factors that would be inaccessible to ordinary observation . . . but we do not seem to reach new conceptions from our exploration of abilities by factor analysis." [101]

We would scarcely wish to take sides with those persons who have a proclivity for inventing new terms and new concepts in wholesale manner,

[100] "The concepts held by the research worker are as a pair of colored glasses through which he looks out upon the world; they tincture all that he sees. . . . One does not sense facts in a mental vacuum but in an ordered and active mind. . . . Facts are but one element in the perceptual process; the active concepts of the observer furnish other elements." Douglas E. Scates, "The Conceptual Background of Research." T. R. McConnell, Douglas E. Scates, and Frank N. Freeman, *The Conceptual Structure of Educational Research,* p. 22-37. Supplementary Educational Monographs, No. 55. Chicago: Department of Education, University of Chicago Press, 1942. 47 p.

[101] Frank N. Freeman, *op. cit.,* p. 439.

to the confusion of all who read and try to follow their reports. But it is a fact that, in the processes of careful analysis, the physical and biological sciences have found it necessary at appropriate times to recognize sub-stances (or units) which were hitherto unknown to man, unrevealed through any previous experience or analysis. And it is undoubtedly true that most research workers need to be encouraged into creativity.

11.  In order to avoid lengthening the list of statements, we shall make a number of relatively technical points briefly in one group.

*a.* Purely as a metric matter, the factors produced by factor analysis usually come far short of providing the full measurement afforded by any one test or by the entire set of tests. It is fairly common for the obtained factors to account for something like 50 to 66 per cent of the variation in the test results. Presumably the remainder of the variation could be made up by other kinds of factors which might come from adding other kinds of tests to the original set. This might, of course, call for kinds of tests which we do not yet have the requisite skill or knowledge to produce. The shortcomings of practical limitations need be no permanent bar to theory; but when writers make the tacit assumption that "factors" are invariably better than the original tests, or even that specially designed tests to meas-ure these "factors" can be substituted for the original tests, the point is not one of theory but of practical conditions. One needs to examine the studies on which the "factors" are based and ascertain how much is lost when the factors are used. It is not customary to make this fact prominent in reports.

*b.* The weighting of the several factors for making up either a single test score or an over-all composite measure (such as intelligence) is of course an average set of weights, growing out of the group. They may not fit any individual. Further, these weights may vary considerably with differ-ent ages, different forms of schooling, different cultural experiences, etc. These are areas for extended study.

*c.* It is assumed that the different "factors" combine in additive, linear fashion. The mathematics is adapted to this assumption and forces results which are in conformity. It is not known to what extent some factors might contribute a multiplicative element to certain aspects of one's abilities, or contribute in some other way besides merely *adding* to other factors. The matter cannot be ascertained from factor-analysis results, because, being products of a certain mathematical treatment, they can be put back into the system and will reproduce the original measurements. There is, there-fore, no check to be found within the system itself.

*d.* The correlation coefficients from which factor analysis customarily takes its start must meet the conditions known to be required for the usual interpretation of correlation coefficients. These conditions (beyond a few formal, mathematical ones) are not often given in textbooks; in fact, they are more numerous than is commonly assumed and must (at present) depend on rather wide reading in the field and considerable experience.

*e.* The results of factor analysis can scarcely be said to yield pictures of organization or of patterns, although these terms are not infrequently used in connection with factor studies. The factor analysis will yield something of a profile—a series of "factors" or elements with their relative weights for reproducing test scores or for describing individual cases, but there the description stops. Nothing is revealed concerning structure in the sense of organization or patterns. If one wishes information as to the form of organization of any two or more traits which may exist in an individual case, this knowledge will have to be obtained by other means.

*f.* Factor analysis is not primarily a means of prediction; it normally operates without any outside criterion. Its results, therefore, do not usually have the benefit of checking and adjusting in terms of some single measure (or composite criterion) outside the set of tests with which work began. Its processes are carried on chiefly in terms of mathematical rules and internal criteria, with judgment and insight entering at critical points. These produce results in accordance with specified assumptions, rigorous logic, and researcher interpretation, but do not guarantee the over-all satisfactoriness of the outcome.

From what has been said, it will be clear that factor studies do not come out with *the* components of a general concept, but rather with *a* set of components which reflect various contingencies of research procedures at various points in the undertaking. Much of the literature accords "factors" a degree of respect—we might almost say "reverence"—which is far out of keeping with a technique that has the obvious limitations we have noted. The "factors" are, in fact, often regarded by factor enthusiasts as having such a degree of finality, rigidity, and determinativeness as to render them the same as the "faculties" of the former faculty psychology.[102] The procedure is sometimes referred to as "objective." The mathematical calculations can be said to be; and without question the mathematical scheme of

[102] "It is hard to see that it makes any difference whether memory, language, mathematical facility, spatial ability, imagination, etc., are called faculties or primary abilities." Frank N. Freeman, 1939, *op. cit.,* p. 441; see also p. 437.

"The Scottish School (1764 *et seq.*) furnished faculties, which came to public notice and scientific disapproval under the phrenologists (1810), and now have reappeared in functional America as abilities, aptitudes and the traits which factor analysis yields." Edwin G. Boring, *op. cit.,* p. 738.

"For [certain] writers ... factors acquire a static reality which appears to me to be closely related to Aristotle's essences. For [other] writers ... factors are but convenient categories permitting the simplification of test results to make predictions about people with maximal efficiency, a very different interpretation." Joseph McV. Hunt, "Psychological Services in the Tactics of Psychological Science." *American Psychologist* 7:608-22; November 1952. (Quotation from p. 612, footnote 11.)

thought has its beauties. But the "objective" portion of the work is preceded and is followed by critical steps of judgment which are as far reaching as the mechanical steps. A factor study is neither purely mathematical nor purely judgmental, but is a mixture of the two processes with no automatic protection from the shortcomings of either.

In this respect it is like other research methods, and there would be no occasion for making the foregoing statement if it were not that so much of the literature about factor analysis as a method sets it forth as having revolutionary qualities and boundless promise, and so much of the literature reporting factor studies presents "factors" in the guise of basic, fixed elements of human nature, regardless of tests, groups, age, or culture; they are entities, they have "existence"; they are somehow more "real" than test scores, even though they are products of test scores (or other series of basic data). We do not desire to do the method injustice; we think those who have painted factor studies as something in a different class from other statistical techniques have already done the injustice. Factor analysis has values, and we shall present various studies illustrating some of its values; but its values share the limitations of any statistical approach. This means that they afford only a formal analysis of given data. What infinite number of factors the original data represent, what special conditions caused them to take on the specific values they did, whether they satisfy the assumed conditions for the analysis to proceed, what the results of the formal analysis can be interpreted to mean—these are matters for insight, understanding, and inference.[103]

Factor analysis as a method is likely to be rejected by those who are opposed to any kind of avowed analysis. These persons will normally include those who follow the gestalt school of psychology and also those students of personality who emphasize unique, individual patterns. Prominent among the latter is Gordon W. Allport.[104] On the other hand, test makers may find a great many values in factor analysis, such as aiding in determining certain of the constituent elements in the scores of certain

[103] One can find a number of articles giving cautions about the use of factor-analysis techniques. We cite here only two fairly recent ones.

J. P. Guilford, "When Not To Factor Analyze." *Psychological Bulletin* 49:26-37; January 1952. Guilford is a strong supporter of factor analysis and assumes the shortcomings lie with the researcher. He gives important cautions, although many of them devolve upon mature sophistication in the specific area of work, and upon hindsight. His comments seem to us clear admissions that the technique is not appropriate for routine use, because one cannot know in advance how to avoid the pitfalls he mentions. His oft-repeated phrase, "experimental variables," can probably be read "tests" or "test scores" with added concreteness.

Quinn McNemar, "The Factors in Factoring Behavior." *Psychometrika* 16:353-59; December 1951. Written in good-humored, but pointed satire.

[104] Gordon W. Allport, *Personality*. New York: Henry Holt and Co., 1937. Chapter 9, "The Search for Elements," particularly p. 242-48.

tests.[105] It is clear that certain of the characteristics of "factors" are determined by desire and utility in test construction. Thus, the nature of the "factors" is shaped by the demand for "psychological interpretation," which in effect means concepts of behavior that can be sensed or/and measured, for which tests can be constructed. Aside from this demand, the more mathematical methods (principal axis or principal component) would avoid some of the technical difficulties and hazards, and might yield greater predictability (invariance) of results.

As against the somewhat prejudicing demands of practical utility, the general purpose of factor analysis may be stated in some mathematical elegance: "to manipulate a set of data in such a way as to identify a relatively small number of latent variables which can account for the covariances of a larger number of variables." [106] This, of course, is something different from identifying and naming some "factor" which is involved in a number of complex and widely different tests (or other series of data) and which cannot be subsumed under any concept anyone can think of, either now or in the indefinite future. But practical demands are strong and the factor must be conceptualized and named; further, a test (or other observation scheme) must be constructed for measuring it in relatively pure form. So long as the results of factor analysis are held in tentative form, as somewhat crude stepping stones along a continuing path of progress, the method takes its place alongside all other methods of research. But when presumptions are made concerning special characteristics or qualities of such formal analyses, and the results are presented as partaking of the immutable, one has to take recourse in reviewing the fallible steps in the proceeding. When factor analysis is set in the following perspective, as offering results for further study and for testing by many other kinds of research, then the procedure is entitled to scientific respectability and confidence. For, in all research, we believe not in the single study but in the long course of scientific investigation.

Factors resulting from factor analysis are intended to suggest variables or patterns of variables which can be studied in non-factorial, experimental investigations. Thus directly, by summarizing and identifying sources of variance, and indirectly, by suggesting areas that can be studied more intensively by other psycho-physical methods, factor analysis contributes to achieving the basic goal of any science, viz.: the accumulation of data and determination of principles which enable us to make accurate predictions in a particular discipline.[107]

[105] Educational Testing Service, *Conference on Factorial Studies of Aptitude and Personality Measures*. Princeton, N. J.: Educational Testing Service, April 1952. 33 p. (Mimeographed.)

[106] Quoted from "Some Goals of Factor Analysis." *Conference on Factorial Studies of Aptitude and Personality Measures*, p. 26. Statement prepared by John B. Carroll, Raymond B. Cattell, and Edmund E. Dudek.

[107] *Ibid.*

Lest, however, one fall into the prevailing current error of assuming that certain "factors" are "established" and, therefore, are universally and necessarily component aspects of human behavior (or of any other series of measurements), we make one final comment. It was pointed out in an earlier section that any whole could be viewed from as many different points of view as one cared to. Again, dividing some trait (or object) into components could be carried on along whatever lines (dimensions, in measurement terminology) one cared to. Those "factors" which are "established" represent *one* such line of cleavage. They appear and reappear because they are looked for, and because test instruments are employed which yield them. An entirely different set of tests and a different frame of conceptual interest would reveal other factors—and not a single one of the "established factors" might appear. Not only can human behavior (or any other complex concept) be divided in an indefinitely large number of ways, in terms of different degrees of complexity or breadth of the resulting category, but on any given level of complexity (if we knew exactly what that meant in terms of working procedures) the whole could be divided in an infinity of ways, just as a geographical area can be divided by drawing a number of lines one place or another. And one resulting area is no more unitary or homogeneous than that produced by another method of subdivision, except when looked at from certain points of view, for certain purposes. Those factors which test makers are so ready to acknowledge as basic, near-universal, and so on, are simply those that fit conveniently into current test thinking. They are no more natural, basic, fundamental, inherent, primary, or finally unitary than any other set of component aspects which might be obtained from the same human behavior. Like any other research results, they are in significant degree artifacts of a particular point of view and its accompanying procedures, justified because of utility rather than because of ultimate rightness.

**Given amounts of space and time may be divided into component segments in terms of observed characteristics.** It is commonplace for us to think of subdividing areas and time intervals by employing immediately the ordinary measuring units of these traits. While it is true that any object or event is subject to description and subdivision into small units (as of area) through measurement, in the case of space and in time many persons will perhaps at first think that measuring units are the only way of dividing them. The direct use of such units, however, leads to analyses of the statistical type in which similar but non-contiguous (scattered) cases are grouped and counted. The further description and illustration of such work are left to texts dealing with statistical method.

On the other hand, one may apply to the analysis of space and time the same kind of unit we have illustrated thus far, namely, categories representing different *kinds*. The subdividing or differentiating of the given area or time interval will then proceed (as in other cases) on the basis of noting differing *kinds of conditions*. For a nearly-too-simple example, the United States may be thought of as divided (analyzed) into forty-eight states and the District of Columbia. These categories or cases are distinguished by the observable *condition* of having separate and somewhat different political systems. To be sure, each state does occupy space, but units of distance are employed to describe it, not to produce it. A division of the United States according to units of distance alone would, by contrast, produce such categories or cases as townships (in the geographical sense) and sections. Again, with reference to time, we commonly think of the (approximately) twenty-four-hour day as divided into two components, daytime and nighttime. A person may define daytime in various ways, but in any case it is a *condition*—either that the sun is up, or that one can see by natural light. Defining such categories does not ordinarily start out with units on the scale (of time or distance), but rather with a description of the condition, or series of conditions, which we have recognized and differentiated. When this has been done, measuring units are commonly employed to give additional forms of description, such as the limits, and hence the location and extent, of the condition specified. In establishing the category (or case), therefore, the conditions are primary, and the measurements of space or time are secondary.

Starting with the entire world, it is commonplace to think of the surface as divided into two kinds of components, land and water. One may wonder if the inhabited portions of the world could not be divided into component cultural areas. The task is sometimes attempted,[108] although not without serious problems. The example cited employed topography, climate, races, languages, religion, and industries as factors in the work. Any such dividing will necessarily represent compromises among the various factors on which the divisions are based, and there is always a tendency (perhaps justified) to let simple contiguity assume large weight. Similar processes have been used to divide the world (or smaller areas) into sections of one kind or another, such, for example, as types of climate, types of vegetation, and so on. World maps, as in atlases, often portray such features.[109]

---

[108] Richard J. Russell and Fred B. Kniffen, *Culture Worlds.* New York: Macmillan Co., 1951. 620 p.

[109] For example, see *Goode's School Atlas:* Physical, Political, and Economic, by J. Paul Goode. Revised by Edward B. Espenshade, Jr. New York: Rand, McNally and Co., 1950. 270 p. This atlas makes extensive use of such maps; in fact, when the physical maps showing altitude are counted, virtually all of the maps portray areas divided into component parts on the basis of topographical or cultural conditions over and beyond simple political boundaries.

Analyzing the United States into regions is a matter that has received a relatively large amount of attention.[110] It is usually done on the basis of examining the cultural activities of the people living in various parts of the country, giving special attention to selected quantitative indicators of economic activity, then deciding where to draw the dividing lines on the basis of judgment. Not infrequently, special stipulations are imposed (such as that no single state shall be regarded as a region in itself), and sometimes particular factors are given large weight for special purposes. Regions are employed extensively in the description of the various areas,[111] in the gathering and reporting of basic data,[112] and in making analytical comparisons between the different parts of the United States.[113]

A somewhat different approach is employed by anthropologists, who do not have a wealth of statistical data for past periods or uncivilized peoples. They rely on various other evidences of culture—such as technology, beliefs, social organization, customs, religion, art, and music—where such evidences can be obtained.[114] The work is fascinating for those who are interested in human history and in the differentiation and comparison of various cultures, especially those antedating the coming of the white man on this continent [115] and hemisphere.[116]

Factor analysis may be employed for the purpose of aiding in the determination of regions (or other areas) where it is desired to have each region rather homogeneous; that is, where the purpose is to draw dividing lines so as to produce maximum homogeneity within each region and maximum

[110] Howard W. Odum and Katharine Jocher, Editors, *In Search of the Regional Balance of America*. Sesquicentennial Publication. Chapel Hill: University of North Carolina Press, 1945. 162 p. Published also in *Social Forces* 23:245-404; March 1945. (Entire issue.)
Merrill Jensen, Editor, *Regionalism in America*. Madison: University of Wisconsin Press, 1951. 442 p.
[111] Of rather general interest are weather differences. From among many geographical studies by Visher we cite the following: Stephen S. Visher, "Precipitation Regions in the United States." *Scientific Monthly* 58:386-92; May 1944.
[112] For example, the U. S. Bureau of the Census issues most of its tables for the United States organized in terms of four regions (the Northeast, North Central, South, and West) and nine divisions (each embracing from three to nine states). The Research Division of the National Education Association sometimes employs these Divisions and Regions in summarizing educational data.
[113] For a systematic comparison of regions with respect to population and economy, over a twenty-year period (1929-1949), see U. S. Department of Commerce, Office of Business Economics, *Regional Trends in the United States Economy*. Washington: Government Printing Office, 1951. 121 p. This publication employs seven regions, somewhat different from the nine Divisions of the Bureau of the Census. These follow the six regions proposed by Odum, with his Northeast region divided into New England and Middle East groupings.
See Howard W. Odum, *Southern Regions of the United States*. For the Southern Regional Committee of the Social Science Research Council. Chapel Hill: University of North Carolina Press, 1936. 664 p.
[114] Alfred L. Kroeber, "Culture Area." *Encyclopaedia of the Social Sciences*. New York: Macmillan Co., 1931. Vol. IV, p. 646-47.
[115] Alfred L. Kroeber, *Cultural and Natural Areas of Native North America*. Berkeley: University of California Press, 1939. 242 p.
[116] Alfred L. Kroeber, *Anthropology*. Revised Edition. New York: Harcourt, Brace and Co., 1948. Chapter 18, "American Prehistory and Ethnology," p. 772-839.

heterogeneity between regions. Such a goal is common as an ideal, and factor analysis will help in approximating it. One such study [117] is outstanding. It is not given further discussion here, since it will be dealt with more fully later in connection with the drawing of limits for classes. One will note, however, upon careful reading of the report that judgment (and some relatively arbitrary decisions) are called for in this work, as is the case in all factor studies. For example, in the present study, many states had to be assigned to one region or another on the basis of judgment, and without clear-cut evidence to support the decision one way or another, after the statistical methods had revealed highly conflicting characteristics. Such experiences are unavoidable.

In connection with studying cities, it is common to draw maps which divide the city into various component areas on the basis of differing cultural or other conditions. While this is perhaps most typical of sociological [118] interests, it is an essential in any long-time planning for the location of school sites.

The U. S. Bureau of the Census has developed a number of different kinds of unit areas for reporting (and analyzing) census data. Some were employed for the first time in 1950. For the most part, these units are designed to represent areas which are reasonably homogeneous with respect to economic and demographic characteristics. Such units were laid out after a long period of research and careful study of definitions. For example, one of the new units in the 1950 census is the State Economic Area, which subdivides states along county lines to form component areas that are economically homogeneous. Further discussion of these units, with references, will be given in connection with the forming of categories for classification. Perhaps it will be evident that such units may be viewed either as components of a larger area, or as categories for gathering and reporting data. Spatial and temporal delimitations (areas and time intervals) form especially interesting categories.

Illustrations of dividing a time period into components are not so abundant, since we do not often think of time as being limited; that is, the scale goes on indefinitely. We can, however, suggest a number of examples. The time analyses of occupations, of jobs, or of employed groups, discussed earlier in connection with job analysis, become examples if we think of them as representing, not primarily the total amount of time spent, but

[117] Margaret J. Hagood, "Statistical Methods for Delineation of Regions Applied to Data on Agriculture and Population." *Social Forces* 21:287-97; March 1943. This study is also reported in Margaret J. Hagood and Daniel O. Price, *Statistics for Sociologists*. Revised Edition. New York: Henry Holt and Co., 1952. p. 541-46.

[118] For an example, see Eshreff Shevky and Marilyn Williams, *The Social Areas of Los Angeles:* Analysis and Typology. Berkeley and Los Angeles: University of California Press, 1949. 172 p.

rather how the time is divided up—what types of activity (in terms of time required) make up the total.

One may think of the year as divided into several seasons. If he thinks in terms of the calendar (the dates of the spring and fall equinoxes and the summer and winter solstices), he is thinking primarily in terms of four approximately equal divisions of the time scale. Of course these dates do mark a certain position of the sun and hence represent a condition, but this is a somewhat strained, technical matter. A clearer illustration of dividing the year into seasons on the basis of observed conditions can be found in the work of Visher,[119] who studied temperature, rainfall, and other climatological data for different parts of the United States and decided that not every part of the country had four seasons.

Further illustrations of this sort of component will be taken up later and discussed in connection with the subject of "classification"; for it turns out that time units and spatial units can be viewed also as categories set up to classify material, and not simply to divide a total concept or scale range into components. In fact, we presume that is their most common or familiar form. Hence, we will not offer further discussion at this point.

In keeping with the general intent, in our treatment of analysis, of not getting into the area of statistical classification and consequent numerical analysis, we have tried to emphasize examples of components which could be thought of as intact units, groups, or concepts rather than simply as categorical groupings of scattered statistical units. The distinction can be illustrated readily in terms of spatial (areal) units. A map which shows lines dividing a particular state into economic regions presents these regions in intact form; their shape and all their spatial interrelationships with other areal units are maintained. By contrast, a composite bar diagram which showed the per cent of the land area of that state devoted to each type of major economic activity would represent a statistical analysis with nothing intact but the abstract concepts (the categories). Some of our examples are of this latter type; for example, the proportion of time given to different activities on a job; but that is because the original form of intact description of what an individual person does first, then next, and so on, is so idiographic and perhaps inconsequential that it loses interest for any general purpose. We give this note, however, to help keep the distinction clear, and to point out that the chief interest in this treatment of components is in ascertaining *kinds* rather than amounts. The ascertaining of amounts is a quantitative aspect, which is a problem of enumeration, measurement, and evaluation.

[119] Stephen S. Visher, "When American Seasons Begin." *Scientific Monthly* 59:363-69; November 1944.

**There are many different levels of components; each level may be of interest.** In leaving this subject of analysis into components—which, in the minds of many, will undoubtedly be thought of as comprising the whole subject of analysis—it seems important to emphasize explicitly that there is no one level of component which represents analysis any more than some other level. One may select the level of greatest interest to his work. Although we are well aware of this by common sense, we sometimes get tricked into false positions when thinking abstractly—thinking in terms of mere words, forgetting much of the reality that should be associated with them.

Normally, one will not push his analysis many levels at one time. That is, starting at whatever point he regards as a whole, he probably will not attempt to cover a number of different levels in any one study, since the different levels have different interests and serve different purposes, and usually require very different types of approach. For example, if we may think of human physiology, the analysis into systems (such as the circulatory, the respiratory, and so on) represents a certain level. This would undoubtedly call not only for a description of the system, but for some description of the organs composing the system and of their functions. But a careful examination of the tissues composing these organs, taken individually, would be a further level of penetrating analysis. It would call for some description in terms of kinds of cells; yet the intensive detailed study of the structure of cells themselves would be a level in itself. Thus the process continues.

One will be tempted at once to say, "Well, it appears that you do not ever understand anything until you have analyzed down through all the levels." Perhaps so. But there are difficulties in this view. The difficulties lie along two directions of thought. First, it is a mere academic idea, or abstract intellectual extension, to talk of analyzing "down through all levels." What does it mean? Man has as yet found no stopping point. The postulate of research is that no barrier is final. Areas of interest, "things," lose their composition and qualities when pushed below certain limits, so that one no longer is quite sure what he is pursuing; we have illustrated this in connection with the atom, reading ability, and so on. The limit recedes, the original goal disintegrates. The notion of *complete* analysis is an empty notion, born perhaps of a wish, or perhaps of unexamined extrapolation from restricted experience.

An equal difficulty lies in another direction; for when one has analyzed minutely, he has very little which will tell him about the whole. We have repeatedly mentioned that the more finely one analyzes, in the sense of subdividing, the more he leaves out. It is interrelationships, as surely as the firmer substances, which make reality. In fact, Korzybski states emphatically that structure (relationship) is the only thing we can know about the world,[120] and the writings of modern physicists tend to reduce even the firmer substances to action. With some truth we can say that the further one analyzes, the less he knows; for the *principal* knowledge of a thing is on the level of the thing itself, and while man's curiosity, and man's needs, make analytical knowledge imperative, a knowledge of subdivisions alone cannot in itself be complete.

We seem to face something of a paradox—the necessity of analysis and the inadequacy of analysis. Yet it is not particularly different from the paradox of science itself. We are familiar with the idea that every new finding changes to some degree the meaning of all previous knowledge. We are prepared to grant that present knowledge is not final. We wonder in what calendar year it will be? Do we not expect research to continue as long as man has the will? Does it not seem proper to bring into question the compatibility of such beliefs as these with our former notion of "understanding" or of "knowledge"? Perhaps we have been thinking in terms of absolute understanding, in a world where absolutes have no place. It is easy to make this mistake. We complicate our problems when we take for granted what is impossible.

It may be desirable to illustrate some of these points. We have previously referred to the analysis of a textbook. If its contents are analyzed into topics, one has considerable organization, and meaning, left in the unit of analysis. If its contents are analyzed down into single letters (how many *a*'s, how many *b*'s, and so on), the analysis has proceeded to a level where all relationships have been stripped from these letters and consequently the results are of limited utility. Letter frequency counts may be of value to one who is designing a typewriter keyboard, or building a printer's font of type, or working in simple cryptanalysis, but certainly separate letters give little hint as to most of the things we care to know about the book. Word counts, when the categories are astutely made, have more values, but the thing to keep in mind is that analysis is possible and useful on a great variety of levels, according to one's purpose. Analysis can stop far short of the smallest conceivable unit and still be analysis.

The same question of relative completeness of fragmentation occurs when some living organism is analyzed into chemical elements. To get from the various kinds of chemical elements back to a living, functioning

---

[120] "Since Einstein and the newer quantum mechanics, it has become increasingly evident that the only content of 'knowing' is of a *structural* character" (p. 60). "The only possible link between the objective world and the linguistic world is found in *structure, and structure alone*" (p. 61). Alfred Korzybski, *Science and Sanity*. Third Edition. Lakeville, Conn.: Institute of General Semantics, 1948. 806 p. (See all of Chapter 4, "On Structure.")

organism requires that so many things be added back into the given materials—things which were lost in the process of reduction—that for social scientists this sort of analysis does not have great usefulness or appeal. Admittedly it is essential for certain forms of knowledge, but it lies predominantly outside the field of our interests. We can see more use in analyses which are not pushed beyond fundamental kinds of food needed in nutrition, or the kinds of tissues and organs which make up the human body. Since our interests center in the functioning whole (for example, a person), we desire to be able to see a relationship between the unit of analyzed knowledge and this whole.

We have from time to time referred to statistical analysis. In its elementary form, namely, the counting of cases, categories are commonly used which are relatively simple; that is, they cut through any semblance of organization as completely as does the dividing of living organisms into chemical elements. For example, if the population of the United States is analyzed into groups according to age, or height, amount of education, place of birth, and so on, as is usual in statistical classification, organizational relationships which make up society are disregarded throughout the procedure. The persons are observed wherever they may be found (within the specified limits of the study) and are counted quite without respect to any form of organization between them, and at the end they are presented in completely artificial groups, with no organizational aspects possible. When all the people have been counted and classified there is nothing in the resulting distribution that suggests a society. We have simply so many people, pigeonholed. To form a society we would have to get them out of their pigeonholes and into organized life.

There is no implication here that statistical knowledge is not important. We think it fundamental; without hesitation and with no reservations, we regard it as absolutely essential for the operation of a modern civilization of any size. But for the purposes of human science we must view it for what it is. And we here view it as a form of analysis that has stripped the utmost of organizational relationships from around the cases, and therefore a form which would require the greatest amount of organizational elements to be added back into the data before we would have anything like a lifelike society—before the parts would add up to anything resembling the whole.

It is of course possible to obtain a certain amount of organizational information when counting. For example, the federal census reports both the number of families (organized groups) and the aggregate number of persons living in families. In like fashion, one can gather information on the number of members in various organizations. One can set the categorical pattern as complex as he wishes and gather information on those cases which fit his pattern. But obviously what one is ascertaining is simply the number of cases and not the pattern; he established the pattern before he began counting. He is, therefore, simply quantifying the specified pattern.

At least this is all that the formalities of research call for; but we have tried to point out that good research is not attained by complying with formalities. The researcher who cares will constantly be studying the adequacy and sensitivity of his categories. He will do this while taking observations and while contemplating, or making, analyses of his data. He may modify his categories and start over again. It may be that the modification of his categories, representing new conceptions, will be his major contribution. Thus, Einstein contributed to a revolution in modern thinking by shifting from categories of space and time to the single category, space-time. In the social sciences, we are still looking for fundamental categories.

One further comment on statistical work seems in order. It may be suggested by some that correlation reflects and reveals organization. The statement is often made. We would say that, for a group of cases, correlation reflects any average tendency toward concomitance (sameness of relative value), but gives no hint of organization. It has nothing whatever to say about what connects any pair of values—what ties them together. We would prefer to reserve the word *organization* for something where the connection can be known.

**Concluding comment: Analysis into components results in units which fit together in various ways.** In this section on components of a whole attention has been given to different kinds of elements or units—things we could draw a mental boundary around or, as it were, wrap up in a conceptual envelope. It may have been noted that these components seem to be of several different kinds. Some of the elements, for example, may be thought of as something like strands—they run longitudinally through the length of a concept or trait, from one range of the scale to another. This is particularly so when the concept itself seems to have length, to exist principally in terms of extent along some dimension. Such components seem to be elements of the quality of the trait itself, and may be spoken of as *qualitative* elements.

There are other situations in which the components may be thought of as cross-sectional (perhaps something like railroad ties, or the space between them) at right angles to the direction of thought. For example, the several levels or degrees of some trait which seem to be qualitatively different; the sequence of phases that seem to account for development; the series of events that make up a story. Each of these may represent the entire quality of the concept at that particular point where it is viewed, yet not presume to represent all of the qualities that may appear at different points along some line of changing values. When, in our thinking, these segments have been stripped of their qualitative differences—that is, all except changes which may be regarded as more and more of some specific thing —we call the differences *quantitative*. When, however, attention is paid to the fuller realities, with their many forms of varying qualities, we would speak of these successive stages simply as *sequential* or *ordered* components.

Again, there are those concepts, or concept segments, which do not seem to fall in any particular direction; they are not associated with longitudinal or cross-sectional ideas; they represent entities without any dimensional connotations. Divisions into classes or kinds, where the original concept is not related prominently to a scale, would seem to be of this sort. As examples, one might think of those portions or aspects of our culture which are separated out for representation in the school curriculum. Probably we could regard such classes as *topological;* that is, areas which, when represented on paper, need have no fixed shape or definite size. They do, however, have some form of order; that is, they have relationships. Everything does.

Often the relationships among the component parts or elements are definite and prominent. We can see this most readily among physical or physiological objects—the parts of a machine, the cells in the organs of the body, the particles of an atom, the pieces in mosaic art, the streets of a city, the way children are seated in a classroom, the order of books in a library. In some cases the order in these parts follows from an organization in our concepts (for example, the library, the alphabet, and so on). It appears that we are not finished with components when we have identified them. We may often be concerned with the patterns which relate them and thereby contribute to the properties of the whole. The next section will deal with these matters—with forms and relationships.

## III. FORM, ORGANIZATION, AND STRUCTURE (IN ANALYSIS)

Form, in its various manifestations and interrelationships, has been singled out for explicit attention in this section because it is of major interest and importance. In any full analysis, over-all form or general design, and internal organization, composition, or structure, must be given a large share of attention. These aspects are often (though not always) dealt with primarily in terms of their manifold interrelationships. In fact, in those analytical areas where physical science is advanced, relationships of one kind or another occupy such a large portion of attention that the thinking is done mainly in terms of mathematical equations, because these afford an admirable means for expressing many forms of relationship. In some schemes of thought, relationships are viewed as virtually the only important aspect to be dealt with. For example, the English scientist Eddington states: "The relativity theory of physics reduces everything to relations; that is to say, it is structure, not material, which counts. The structure cannot be built up without material; but the nature of the material is of no importance." [121] Social scientists do not have to go to this degree of abstraction in facing most of the problems confronting them; but it should be recognized that in both the social and the physical (and physiological) worlds, relationships constitute a fundamental, important, and fascinating aspect for study.

There are many kinds of relationships in organized wholes of one sort or another. Many of those which have to do with form or organization exist, or can readily be represented, in spatial terms. Others inhere in the sequence of condition or stages viewed along a time continuum, as in a story or trend. Many relationships are of interest primarily because of their causal significance; they represent the flow or control of energy. Sometimes concurrent events are viewed merely as concomitants—relationless, for one's purposes. Certain logical relations are of a classificatory nature and deal with the genus-species form of hierarchial generality, or with simple sameness-difference aspects—the degree of belongingness to a certain class. Some relationships involve authority; some establish goals. They vary from the simple (as in numerical differences) to the complex and intricate. Clearly, as is the case with other aspects, the particular relationships sensed will depend in large part upon the nature of one's interest in viewing an object or situation.

Such a suggestive list makes obvious the need for sharp delimitation. We are concerned here only with those relationships which grow out of form and organization, and of these, the emphasis will be on logical, non-quantitative relations. Many quantitative relations represent special subjects or disciplines to be dealt with in separate books—statistics (including frequency curves, trend curves, growth curves, learning curves, wave patterns, profiles, graphs, maps, and so on); geometry; algebra; and other forms of mathematics. The same holds for logic, symbolic logic, and communication theory. Classification (with its many relationships) constitutes a later section. Thus, the list of exclusions helps bring to light the all-prevailing character of relationships, and the very limited set of them which can be illustrated in the present section.

---

[121] Arthur S. Eddington, *Space, Time, and Gravitation:* An Outline of the General Relativity Theory, p. 197. Cambridge, Eng.: University Press, 1920. 218 p.

It might seem natural to divide the treatment of relationships into static forms and dynamic forms. This is the classical division in mechanics, where the branch dealing with statics is concerned with holding things in equilibrium (as a dam, a bridge, or a building), and the branch dealing with dynamics is concerned with the directing of force so as to cause movement or change (as in a pump, a printing press, an automobile). As a matter of fact, something of this sort will be done; but it will be done only roughly and approximately. There are certainly such things as social structure; they exist in our laws, our practices, our expectancies. Societies and institutions attain a certain degree of stability in their form and status, and maintain their structure for some time. The present section is devoted to some of these more stable aspects and to the controlling conceptions behind them. The more dynamic aspects of relationships will be dealt with in the following section.

At the same time it must be recognized that human beings and their constructions are enmeshed in continuous action programs. Deliberative bodies meet continually to change laws and rules. Societies and institutions rise to meet challenges or fall in the scale of competition. Even relatively static school buildings are to be viewed in terms of varied human uses and are planned for flexibility so as to adapt to change. As human beings, we may strive for equilibrium in many spheres, but the striving is an ongoing process; in the active arena of human living we neither achieve nor maintain equilibrium by holding tight. It appears that the striving rather than the equilibrium is the real thing. To live is to act; and to live in a changing world is to change. To be is to do. Against this background of continuous activity and adaptation we shall scarcely expect to draw a tight boundary around the concept of "statics." Any such line would be arbitrary and intrusive. The present topic represents an emphasis rather than a delimitation.

Analysis may consist of discriminating among general aspects, or of discerning parts in the whole, as in the two preceding sections. But analysis may consist also of identifying the relationships among aspects or parts, as dealt with here. One of the major purposes of analysis is seeing the whole in terms of its parts—not primarily in order to understand the parts but primarily in order to understand the whole. Why does it function as it does? Where do its properties come from? The study of relationships as an essential and fundamental object of interest provides certain of the integrations and the integrating elements which make the difference between a simple collection of parts and a whole. It is the interrelationships which have much to do with the distinctive qualities of any object or concept. In the wrecked automobile, the parts have been moved. The interrelationships have been changed. It will not run.

In the preceding section, on analyzing a whole into its components, it was mentioned that some attention should be given to the recombinability of the resulting parts. The present section, through directing attention to the detection and identification of the combinatorial or integrative aspects which pervade the whole, contributes to that end. The area being dealt with finds reflection in a number of words—such as *form, shape, pattern, design, organization, structure,* and so on, in which the idea of relationship is an essential element. The area is, however, somewhat broader than "relationships" as a single class concept; it also seems to have more dimensions (elements) than are carried by the terms *integration* or *integrative aspects,* though it lies in this direction. The terms in the section heading are meant to be suggestive rather than definitive. In the area as treated several ideas have been combined, partly in order to avoid making tedious distinctions, and partly because of language difficulties: all of the appropriate words have so many overlapping senses that it would be unduly confusing to employ them in entirely separate sections as representing discrete ideas. The integrating element lies in the emphasis on relationships.

As a matter of general orientation, however, it should be pointed out that concern with relationships is not the sole end of research. Research has many tasks, and no single interest is paramount. While, therefore, the present section emphasizes the integrative aspects which hold the parts of a whole together in effective design, it is not meant to imply that these aspects are exclusively or preëmptively the goal toward which all research yearns. The broad goal of research is not so circumscribed. As between relationships and parts, both are necessary to a fuller understanding of the other and both must be studied. If one chooses, it is entirely reasonable to study parts for the sake of understanding those parts. It is recognized that one will understand any particular part more fully by studying both its internal structure and its external relationships; but no single study is required to essay the full scope of research. Accordingly, neither the study of parts nor the study of relationships alone is to be regarded as a final end. Of course no specific research interest is presumed as final or complete. The hope in research is not in narrowness but in breadth; and not in finality but in continuance. The world of possibilities is endless. Space goes outward and time goes onward; and the mind of man is forever occupied with analysis and synthesis. Research, as the handmaiden of man's active mind, serves nothing less than the totality of man's interests.

The worth of research is that, as a form of human activity, it is challenging and rewarding; it justifies social support, because it constantly enriches and broadens life through increasing understanding and enabling man to do more things he wishes to do. Research studies make their contribution whether dealing with a fragment or an overriding law of the universe. In calling attention, therefore, to relationships and the possibility of making them the direct object of study, we do not mean to imply that they displace interest in other forms of analysis.

Before proceeding to the immediate illustrations of the subject, there are three questions which are deserving of consideration. These questions have to do with the meaning of form and relationships; that is, how are these aspects set in human experience and to what extent do they represent analyses of the object, as compared with representing the background of man's mind? What service can they accomplish in the analytical process?

**Can form and relationships be elementary?** The question is sometimes raised as to whether form and its attendant relationships can be sensed directly. Is form, or any configuration, something which the human mind must put together (fabricate) after noting particulars? Is a relationship something which must be derived deliberately from a study of data?

In the middle of the twentieth century, after Gestalt psychology [122] has established its basic protest over the elementism of the Wundtian tradition, it may seem odd to refer to any such question about form. Psychologists have generally accepted the fact that one can see certain "wholes" or patterns as such, and that one does not have to put them together inductively. The process seems to be one of recognition rather than of derivation. With familiar objects or patterns, the recognition comes first, the details later, if at all. Of course, as always, the term *whole* is ambiguous and equivocal. We assume that, out of the continuous ocean of stimuli that surround us, those "wholes" which emerge for prior attention are the ones which, in familiar backgrounds and combinations, the human organism has found it useful to recognize. In any case, we are relieved from the necessity of assuming that no degree of generality can be sensed directly, but must be built up piecemeal.

The case for relationships, however, is not so clear. These are presumed to be analytical, and hence derived. Boring points out that "Relations have always made trouble in psychology. They seem to come quite immediately into experience and yet not in the same sense that sensations come; thus it was never clear to the elementists whether they could speak of relational elements or not." [123] This passage refers primarily to pre-Gestalt psychologists; but the question reappears at times. Korzybski places relations among

[122] The emphasis of Gestalt psychology, introduced into America in the 1920's, on the priority of configurations over their elements is well known. See Edwin G. Boring, *op. cit.,* Chapter 23, "Gestalt Psychology," p. 587-619.

Carl Murchison, Editor, *Psychologies of 1930.* Worcester: Clark University Press, 1930. Part V, "Configurational Psychologies," p. 141-204. Chapters by Köhler, Koffka, and Sander.

[123] Boring, *op. cit.,* p. 368.

his "unspeakables"—things which cannot be spoken of directly, because one can speak only of his reactions to them.[124] Hence, they become a second-order of abstraction, a sort of introspection. Without presuming that we always catch Korzybski's fine shadings, we are, nevertheless, not inclined to place simple relationships in any different class from other perceptions that one would normally speak of as "facts." Would we deny that we can sense motion, rate, slope, distance, direction, time, and so on? Except as relationships, however, we undoubtedly cannot; but motion against a background, rate as judged by experience, angles resulting from different degrees of slope, distance in relation to ourselves or from one point to another, direction projected against other directions as reference axes, and time in relation to activity—as relationships, they become sensible. It may even be that we have no perceptions apart from relationships; for relationships are involved in all differentiations and integrations.

It is of course possible for the Gestalt argument to be turned against relations. Presumably a relationship in a figure or form is one of the analytical aspects of the whole; as a detail, it should, therefore, according to the general argument, be sensed after the whole. The case for wholes is a case against detailed relationships. We think this will often be true; yet we would argue that the entire matter rests with the viewer's interest. It is a question growing out of the shifting "whole." What for one purpose becomes the immediately emergent "whole" that is recognized against a background, for another purpose itself becomes the background against which the detail is looked for and immediately seen.

An illustration may suffice. Assume the simplest kind of relationship, a direct difference. The heights of two children may be measured, the heights compared, and the difference obtained. Obviously the relationship was derived. One might argue that this is characteristic; all relations are observed in the same way. But suppose he cannot really see the full height of either child; perhaps they are standing behind a desk, and all he can see is the *difference* in heights. Does this follow the presumed pattern of first seeing the two heights separately, which he cannot do? Or, we might ask, is the difference between two heights, observed directly, anything different from observing the height of a single individual? Isn't one's height itself a difference (a relationship) between two points? Perhaps we may inquire again, is it not likely that relationships are an inherent part of all perception?

Man's analytical powers often mislead him. Because any perception of relationship can conceivably be split up further (as anything can), one is sometimes tempted to think that the relationship *must,* therefore, be built

124 Alfred Korzybski, *op. cit.,* Chapter 12, "On Order," p. 151-87; see in particular p. 155.

up; hence, only the details are real. It would be as logical to argue that, because any "whole" figure can be derived through contrasting and abstracting it from a background, therefore one must start with the background, and the general background is the initial real thing. We would avoid both extremes and think in terms of purpose, interest, and attention. No doubt one sees both background (the general situation encompassed by his view) and many specific aspects simultaneously; each helps him identify and recognize the other. His interest will determine where his attention will dwell—what he will see most clearly or most dominantly.

While there is no question but that man can build one level of abstraction upon another and thus utilize relationships which are far removed from the level of direct sensory experience, it seems perfectly clear that there are many relationships which he can perceive directly. Simple relationships may be observed like other sense data.[125] They are equally real and equally available to man. With regard to the simple kinds we would hold with the physicist who, knowing the difference between the world as revealed by physical analysis and as perceived by human beings, closed his chapter on scientific observation with the statement: "In this sense the observation of relationships comes *before* the observation of parts or of individual facts. The basic facts used in science . . . are not first seen in isolation. . . . A change or difference, as such, may be directly perceived."[126]

**Do form and relationships exist only in man's mind?** Are they simply a human construct? Simply a way of looking at things? Do they actually have existence outside of man's thinking? In common language, Can they be real? Is form or relationship something "out there," or is it simply "here" in my mind?

The question is a somewhat different reflection of the one just dealt with. If a configuration could not be sensed directly, then it might not exist outside of man's thinking. If it can be sensed directly, it may have external existence.

The question as to form would seem to be easily disposed of. One would not question the existence of simple geometrical forms—the triangle, the rectangle, the circle—any more than he would question the existence of

125 Consider, for example, the peculiar difficulty in comparing the experience of two time intervals. One might easily argue that the subject (the person) makes separate mental estimates of the two durations and then compares his estimates. Perhaps so; but one psychologist, summarizing experiments and literature on the subject, states without hesitation: "The errors are in the outcome of the *comparison:* there is *no separate estimate* of either the standard or the variable." (Italics ours.) Herbert Woodrow, "Time Perception." *Handbook of Experimental Psychology, op. cit.,* Chapter 32, p. 1224-36.

126 William H. George, *The Scientist in Action,* p. 144. London: William and Norgate, 1936; New York: Emerson Books, 1938. See Chapter 8, "Are Facts First Seen in Isolation?" p. 133-44.

anything. Would one's watch run without wheels? Form is one of the basic elements by which things are recognized. Some trouble will arise when the question is generalized to include all degrees of complexity, for quickly the particular form which is perceived becomes a matter of what elements are emphasized in a complex pattern. The common optical illusions are a case in point. But the familiar object is recognized because it has form.

As to relationships, we would completely turn the original question around. Is there anything which does not have an infinity of relationships? Eddington's statement on the point has already been quoted. Korzybski notes that "The structure of the actual world is such that it is *impossible* entirely to isolate an object." [127] Whitehead states, "Nothing is in isolation. . . . No factor which enters into consciousness is by itself or even can exist in isolation." [128] Dewey and Bentley emphasize relatedness in an extreme (full) degree in their view of transactionalism.[129] It seems almost as though we might be doing the right thing by trusting our common sense.

Perhaps the most convincing proof of relationships is to be found entirely outside man. Certainly biological nature and purely physical nature react to differences as much as man does. This is merely to assert some form of causation, interaction, or transaction in the animate and in the inanimate worlds. Examples are legion. Why would a river flow, if it were not responding to a (sometimes very slight) difference between a horizontal plane and the slope of its bed? Many physical and physiological processes operate on astonishingly small margins; take away the slight "difference" and something goes wrong; frequently the process stops entirely. Do we not employ observational instruments to supplement our own senses, because physical things (instruments) can be found or contrived which will respond to more differences than our own senses will? In other words, not only spatial and temporal relations exist in external nature but also dynamic relations. Have we forgotten that Newton conceived the principle by which every molecule of the entire universe is dynamically related to every other molecule in the universe? It is not just in man's mind that the apple falls to the ground!

There are, however, structures and relationships in man's mind which play their part. They facilitate, to some extent stereotype, perception. They may be of higher orders; that is, abstractions or configurations built out of sensed relations. It is possible for them to have little connection with

---

[127] Alfred Korzybski, *op. cit.*, p. 57; see also p. 99, 130, and elsewhere.
[128] Alfred N. Whitehead, *The Aims of Education*. New York: Macmillan Co., 1929. Quotations from the Mentor Books edition, No. M41, p. 124, 133.
[129] John Dewey and Arthur F. Bentley, *Knowing and the Known*. Boston: Beacon Press, 1949. Chapter 4, "Interaction and Transaction," p. 103-18; Chapter 5, "Transactions as Known and Named," p. 119-43.

any phase of reality outside the mind that thinks them. But the basic materials of thought and interpretation are simply earlier experiences with the world of outer realities—experiences from which man builds up his assumptive world, his anticipation of expected relationships.[130] If man meets the "message" of his sensory organs with a predisposing, interpretative framework, is it not because his experiences with the external world give justification?

We are dealing in an area where it is easy to go too far in either direction; thinking about the relative contributions of the external world [131] and of man's perceptive mind must be kept within a limited range. So long as one's reactions are basically responses to the outer world, the world of physical reality contributes its part to those reactions. On the other hand, as soon after life begins as the developing nervous system will permit, ramified, interrelated, memory-directed interpretative tendencies affect the incoming impulses and contribute something to them. Any relationship, therefore, which is perceived is partly read into the situation; but, assuming the perception is accurate, the relationship is also partly in the situation. The question is no different from the one dealt with all along in connection with aspects and components, and observation in general. They are all joint products. Human beings read relationships into the external world in the same nervous system—we might almost say in the same way—in which they read color into light waves, sound into air vibrations, and solidity into substances which are as sparse as the space of the heavens. Naturally, man will draw from his accumulated experience with the inner and outer worlds to add certain elements to the external facts in the process of sensing them.

The question which may be lurking in one's mind probably turns not so much on simple spatial and temporal relationships, which he would undoubtedly grant, but more on the matter of highly developed methods of analyzing and portraying form and relationships, and perhaps on the elaboration of meaning and significance. As for the former, one may think of various branches of mathematics—geometry and analytic geometry in particular, and perhaps the calculus. These deal with form and its relationships, but obviously they are highly developed, after many man-centuries of

[130] "Man builds up his assumptive or form world largely in an unconscious and non-intellectual way, in the process of adjustment and development as he goes about the business of life, that is, as he tries to act effectively to achieve his purposes." Hadley Cantril and Others, "Psychology and Scientific Research, I: The Nature of Scientific Inquiry." *Science* 110:461-64; November 4, 1949. Quotation from p. 461.
See also Hadley Cantril, *The "Why" of Man's Experience*. New York: Macmillan Co., 1950. Chapters 4, 5.
[131] By *external* we mean outside the reactive centers of the human body—as the brain and many lower centers. The uncountably numerous sensations arising from within the body are clearly to be classed as external.

creative and critical thought. These must be viewed as highly sophisticated patterns of mental relationships. If one should ask, Are these relationships in nature? the answer is that, so far as the conclusions are good, the net relationships between the given data and the conclusions must exist— though the elaborate course of formal reasoning by which man reaches the conclusion is one of his own inventions. Man creates many interrelationships himself. He does this, for one thing, by introducing reference points, norms, and axes. He utilizes the results as a base for his further thinking. Relationships are part of man's mental tools.

In the area of elaborate meaning and significance, however, man may get even farther away from relationships which may be thought of as existing externally. For illustration, let us take the very simple case of two dots. In the physical world, when viewed from a particular point, these can have position—position relative to each other and relative to the observer. But that is about all. We could introduce other factors, such as brightness, color, motion, temporal variation, background factors, and so on; but, if we keep these out, position, including distance between the points and from the observer, seems to exhaust the physical relationships which are immediately observable. Man's interpretative background, however, can imbue two dots with an infinity of relationships, both to each other, and to the observer and his world. For one thing, the direct relationship between the dots need not be thought of in terms of a straight line; one may conceive of them being connected by any manner of line he may wish to imagine, no matter how extensive and involved. Or he may imagine an extended pattern, and think of the two dots as occupying various positions in his conjectured pattern, such, for example, as being at the center and on the perimeter of a polygon, at the foot of an ellipse, any place in an informal figure, or (with great license) suggesting outlines after the manner in which constellations of stars are imagined to suggest figures in the heavens. (Several constellations consist of only two stars.)

But the foregoing are only spatial aspects. Man can endow the dots with special meanings. For example, it is conventional to use them as a colon, or for "is to" in a proportion, as a diaeresis, or umlaut, or phonetic symbol, or perhaps for valence electrons of an atom. In music, they mean "repeat." On dice and dominoes, they indicate the numeral two, perhaps with additional connotations in the game being played. In the International Morse code, two "dots" mean *I* or *O,* according to the time interval (or space) separating them; in the Braille alphabet for the blind, two dots (according to relative position) mean five different letters and four numbers. On tabulating machine cards, two dots (holes) can cover the entire alphabet. On the cards or tapes fed to certain modern digital computing machines, two dots could be used to represent one of two digits of a binary system in which all numbers can be expressed. In a direct code, they could stand for *yes* or *no* or for any assigned meaning, no matter how complex. Students of American history (or literature) may recall the traditional lantern signal to Paul Revere.[132] And those who are familiar with astronomy will know something of the various double stars—the fascinating story of discovery, research, and interpretation in connection with these two points of light.[133]

It may be that we have been a little unfair in our comparison; we have introduced additional facts and concepts. But that is just what man does. He has this host of additional facts and meanings in his mind and he connects them with simple configurations whenever it seems appropriate. When one considers the possible connections between two dots and man's ready interpretative schemes, he gains some idea of the difference between what may be referred to as "simple, objective facts" on the one hand, and meaning on the other.

This illustration has been given at some length, because it is important with respect to the roles that observation and interpretation play in research. While "two dots" may not be thought to have a close connection with research in human fields, the illustration was made almost as simple as possible, so as to make the point clear. It is almost impossible to draw the line between what may be thought of as "objective" facts, and interpreted facts. Even with two points, we had to admit a third (reference) point for the viewer, which introduces the effect of the viewer and his viewpoint on what is seen. The conclusions should make us somewhat cautious. We will not claim too much for our observations. We will be careful about calling them "objective" in any 100 per cent sense, for we realize that our particular frame of reference—our instruments, our categories, our purposes—have colored them, detracting, adding, and altering. This is being widely conceded in physical science; we must be equally aware of it in human science.

The impression should not be gained that there is something wrong about interpretation, and that the goal is to avoid it. We are scarcely ready to say that it is too bad we are human beings. The power of interpretation is peculiarly a human power, and its use is essential to producing a science that is a human product; that is, a science which can be used by human beings. We do not know what a strictly "objective" science would be, but certainly it would not be a human one. Our own interpretation would be, first, that we should stop talking about "objectivity" except to imply observation and

132 "One, if by land, and two, if by sea," in Henry Wadsworth Longfellow's "Paul Revere's Ride."
133 William C. Dampier, *A History of Science*. Third Edition. Cambridge, Eng.: University Press. New York: Macmillan Co., 1942. p. 430-31.

interpretation that have been examined carefully and critically, but which are, in no complete sense, "objective" and never can be. Second, that we employ interpretation frankly and avowedly, making as clear as we can the reference points in our thinking—that is, the views, perspectives, values by which we read meaning into the data. Third, that we regard all our findings as representing current work rather than as finalities. They are the products of a certain point of view, a certain procedure, when applied; new points of view, new procedures, or even new data obtained under apparently similar conditions may give different results. We will, therefore, welcome such additional studies as contributing to a growing body of evidence —*never* any more final than was the view of the atom in 1900, but representing simply the current evidence and interpretation. And, finally, if one feels disillusioned and disappointed about research that it does not produce the "last" word with every study, we suggest that one view it as representing the best thought and observation that man has been able to achieve at a given time. Notwithstanding the normal human discontent with anything short of the absolute, can man reasonably expect more than research offers? Does not research represent man at work with the best tools at his command, actively seeking ways to solve his problems?

**Are form and relationships sufficiently elementary to serve as units in analysis?** This is the third of the three questions to be considered. We have dealt with the question of whether form and relationship could be observed rather directly, or whether they had to be derived by successive steps; and with the question of the extent to which form and relationships might be construed as existing outside of man's thoughts, as compared with the elaborate patterns of interpretation by which man reads meaning and utility into his observations. The third question has to do with the unitary or elementary nature of observed form and relationships, not from the standpoint of their perception or external existence, but from the standpoint of their utility, their satisfactoriness as elements to be used in analysis.

Perhaps it should be said at once that no unit of analysis is to be regarded as final; accordingly, we shall regard both form and relationships of any given degree of complexity as being subject to further analysis. But into what? That is the essential question. Can they be resolved into something else that is simpler, easier to understand and manipulate mentally? Or do they simply break down into further elements of form and relationship? That is, are they qualitatively elementary?

A part of the answer can be given directly. We regard relationships as analytical aspects of form. That is, form *can* be broken into relationships of various appropriate types. And relationships themselves can be expressed in a great variety of ways—numerically, geometrically, and in other expressions of logic and mathematics. Hence, in progressive analytical sequence we can pass from form to relationship to various ways of expressing the relationship.

But this is not the whole story. The full answer to the question involves to some extent the matter of how much we are willing to give up. At the outset of this section dealing with organization we pointed out that it related to certain forms of integration, of tying together; it is, in fact, primarily of interest as supplementing the products which can be obtained simply by dividing something into components. That is, while form and relationships may themselves be components of more general patterns, they nevertheless are presumed to retain some of the elements which, in any complex whole, exist over and beyond the separate components into which the whole is likely to be broken. How far, then, do we want to go in surrendering what form and relationships themselves may directly contribute to understanding?

This is not a question to be answered in any absolute sense, but rather as a matter of judgment after consideration. We have spoken before of the disintegration of a trait when it is broken down beyond a certain point. Thus intelligence can be subdivided until it is merely irritability of protoplasm, which is not intelligence. Reading can be subdivided until it becomes the discrimination of two different shades, which can be taught to a chick. And a straight line can be broken conceptually into a series of more or less discrete dots. For certain purposes, there may be sound reasons for carrying analysis to such lengths; but it should be kept in mind that, when the essential qualities of the original have been left far behind, as when living organisms are broken down into chemical elements, one may have results about which he cannot draw conclusions that are useful for his purposes. He is a long way from the original. When one pursues the analysis of something beyond the direct concerns of his field, it is likely that he has entered the domain of another discipline which deals primarily with other levels of organization. This may at times be profitable, but one should do it after consideration and with awareness of his course.

It is possible to analyze form down to the level where one is no longer dealing with form. A triangle can become three separate, unrelated lines; these no longer constitute form in the usual sense. So long as one holds to the direct consideration of form, form of some kind is to be regarded as elementary. That is, the elementary attribute of form is still form. One cannot go beyond form without losing it; it vanishes when disintegrated, and ceases to be the direct content of perception and thought. It is possible, if one so desires, to substitute some analytical means for expressing form, through various relationships. It is also possible, from such relationships, often to get back to the original form, but the essential content of form is missing so long as one deals only with relationships.

If this be so, one may be curious as to what he can do with form. He may be prompted to inquire, When a person has observed form, what has he observed? How can be talk about it? What can he do with it? The questions are quite real. How can one identify form? Describe it without vagueness? Utilize it in a scheme of thought? The answers are not as simple and ready, perhaps, as answers about what one would do with a measurement. Yet, a part of the answer is to be found by turning the situation around. If the person who habitually deals in quantities finds a complex three-dimensional form something of a handicap or a nuisance, may the person who is concerned with artistic painting not feel that a measurement is something of less value than a model? Do not appropriateness and utility have some relation to the background and pattern of one's thinking?

It is possible, however, to be more definite. The goal of analysis is to yield something useful, either directly in itself, or in explaining the whole. In analyzing form, one will desire simpler forms that are familiar, which can be identified in communication, and can be manipulated in schemes of thought and action. The common, conventional forms furnish one definite answer. We refer to such as geometrical forms, domino patterns, and so on. One has general ideas about a triangle, for example. He can expand those ideas through familiarity and study of triangles. Certain triangle forms have definite names. Triangles can be employed in analyzing many more complex figures—not to mention themselves. They can be used constructively in formal art designs, in engineering, geodetic surveying, navigation, and astronomy. They furnish an illustration of a simple form meeting needs of many kinds.

What about curves and complex figures? In part, the answer is the same, but in part it is more difficult. Circles, ellipses, and other conic sections are available; but they are not so generally understood. They quickly become technical. The mathematical curves represented by polynomials and by other forms of equation are available for a great many cases, but again are not widely familiar. There is also the differential and integral calculus, which represents an extremely analytic approach to form, and yet is able to reproduce that form. Thus, mathematics has a large stock of answers for the person who wishes to identify, name, communicate, reproduce, and in other ways utilize form. As mentioned at the outset, advanced areas of physics may deal entirely in mathematics. Outside of the geometrical forms, however, these mathematical means are not directly form, but are relationships.

As for complex forms, there is no good answer. Painting, sculpture, and so on remain arts.[134] One can describe in words as well as possible; he can measure certain features, if that is desirable; one can photograph or draw; but it is virtually impossible or impracticable to reduce complex forms to simple units. What are the principles of good composition in art work? Our answer must rest on this level. Analysis is not the principal tool.

With these arguments given, we shall call attention to certain applications of analysis under the heads of "form," "organization," and "structure."

### Form

The word *form* has a large variety of meanings, as can be ascertained by looking at Webster's unabridged dictionary. It is readily thought of in connection with physical manifestations, but is not limited to them. In music, for example, it has a technical sense quite removed from physical objects, and in logic it relates to the structure of an argument.[135] We may also speak of mathematical form and grammatical form, without reference to anything physical. The idea of form runs through all sciences. In biology, form (morphology) is one of the large divisions of the field. If we were writing in the field of physics, we should deal with wave form. In education and other social fields, form is often of major interest.

Up to the present point we have been using the word *form* in a fairly general sense. For the sake of organizing the treatment, however, we shall restrict the meaning in the present topic, leaving the more complex forms of organization for the following topic. The sense in which we shall use the term here is primarily that of a figure, an outline, shape, or configuration. We shall, however, include some reference to motion, as in handwriting, dancing, and sports.

Perhaps handwriting affords the most widespread interest as a subject in which the analysis of form, both of movement and of the finished product, is of basic importance. In over-all form, handwriting has undergone a number of changes within the memory of older persons. In the last quarter of the last century certain European doctors concluded that writing slanted letters was injurious to health, because of the bodily position assumed by pupils, so the writing style was changed over to vertical letters. Awkward-

---

[134] It is possible to show mathematical relationships underlying certain complex forms in nature and in design. Such analyses are engaging and may be helpful, but they leave the details of form still to be accounted for. See, for example, D'Arcy W. Thompson, *On Growth and Form*. Revised Edition. New York: Macmillan Co., 1942. 1,116 p. See also Matila C. Ghyka, *Geometry of Art and Life*. London and New York: Sheed and Ward, 1946. 174 p. Jay Hambidge, *Practical Applications of Dynamic Symmetry*. New Haven: Yale University Press, 1932. 109 p.

[135] For example, "The validity of deductive reasoning depends only on the logical form of reasoning." [Note the statement is about "validity," not about the truth of a conclusion. In logic, the two are distinct.] Max Black, *Critical Thinking:* An Introduction to Logic and Scientific Method. Second Edition. New York: Prentice-Hall, 1952. p. 47.

ness was ignored. With time, however, the slanting style crept back into practice, only to be superseded a generation later by manuscript writing in the first and second grades.[136]

If one wished to analyze handwriting, for what could he look? Early studies were concerned with the form of movement. While certain educators were advocating movement of the arm only (writing from the shoulder), Judd analyzed the movements of adult writers by putting tracers at various parts of the arm and found that mature writers used three motions—of the fingers, the hand, and the arm. This was one of the early examples of the psychological analysis of a school subject in a laboratory,[137] reflecting the European influence in psychology which Judd brought back with him from Wundt's laboratory. Again, Judd surrounded the pencil or penholder with a sliding sleeve, so that one could not exert pressure, and found that the writing went to pieces. It was thus learned that one of the important cues in the guiding of one's handwriting is the kinesthetic sensation of pressure variation from one part of the stroke to another—notably, for example, at the ends of the longer strokes. It has been learned also that the speed of movement changes considerably in different parts of letters and that correctly formed letters require these adjustments of speed. Thus, various subtle elements entering into the proper form of movement, and hence the proper formation of letters, were isolated and identified.

Analysis of the form of the completed handwriting itself is generally accomplished by inspection. The over-all form of the writing is usually judged by a handwriting scale adapted to survey purposes, such as the one by Thorndike or Ayres. For analytical purposes (including diagnosis), there is an analytical scale by Freeman, as well as certain score cards. Types of errors made by school children have been observed and counted. It has been shown that directing the attention of children to their errors and helping them to analyze their letter formation are helpful.

What particular features of handwriting make it most legible? This question becomes of more interest when one has gone through the various aspects of handwriting which have been listed in the numerous analytical studies, and has learned what aspects might be competitors in such a question. Using paragraphs which represented various types of faults in writing, Quant studied the eye movements of readers and reached the con-

---

[136] A brief historical account, together with a summary of research findings and a leading bibliography, will be found in Paul V. West and Frank N. Freeman, "Handwriting." *Encyclopedia of Educational Research, op. cit.,* p. 524-29.

For a fuller historical résumé, together with the type of treatment of such subjects prior to research, see Frank N. Freeman, "Writing, Psychology of." *A Cyclopedia of Education, op. cit.,* Vol. 5, p. 822-27.

[137] Charles H. Judd, *Genetic Psychology for Teachers.* New York: D. Appleton-Century and Co., 1911. 329 p.

clusion which most persons probably would have guessed, namely, individual letter formation.[138] What else is there to handwriting? One may observe the writing of his friends, or his students, and see what aspects he can discern for himself; or, he may wish to read some of the literature.

Using the well developed motion-picture techniques of the experimental laboratory at the University of Chicago, Boraas submitted several forms of handwriting to detailed time and form analysis.[139] He studied the speed of pen movement in making various parts of the letter, the changes in speed from one portion of a stroke to another portion, and the resulting quality of writing; also, whether the writing produced under certain conditions of speed, and variations in speed, was stable or deteriorated under continuous fast writing. From such an analysis one can conclude: (1) what kinds of letter forms (for a given letter) can be made most rapidly and legibly, and will deteriorate least under pressure; (2) what the importance of change in speed in different portions of a stroke is; (3) where the errors (deformations) usually occur in a letter, and what factors seem to account for them.

From such analyses as these it is quite possible that new forms of writing will evolve. That is, with a knowledge of what kinds of letter strokes are made most rapidly, and stand up better under stress, those persons who set the form of writing for pupils to copy are likely, sooner or later, to make modifications in their copy in the light of speed and stability of letter formation, instead of just drawing letters which have an esthetic appeal but which (judging from the writing of our associates, if not our own) nobody pays any serious attention to. When we note the tremendous changes which have occurred in the teaching of reading during the past half century, under the influence of analytical research, we should not be surprised at the prospect of changes in other subjects when adequate and proper research attention is directed to them.

Closely related to the analysis of handwriting for the purpose of better instruction, and possibly better models to copy after, is analysis for purposes of revealing certain personality tendencies. This work is commonly known as graphology, but is sometimes called graphodiagnostics, and may be regarded as falling in the area of diagnosis or psychodiagnosis. The work is looked upon with skepticism, though often not with complete denial. One writer, acquainted with European practices, states that graphology in Europe "overshadows any other kind of psychodiagnostics, such as the Rorschach, paper-and-pencil testing, or questionnaire inquiry," but concedes that it has encountered "great resistance in the United States."

[138] Leslie Quant, "Factors Affecting the Legibility of Handwriting." *Journal of Experimental Education* 14:297-316; June 1946.
[139] Harold Boraas, "Photographic Analysis of Certain Letter Forms with Respect to Speed Changes and Stability." *Journal of Experimental Education* 20:87-96; September 1951.

It is not hard to understand why it has encountered resistance in the United States. The psychologists and educationists in this country are becoming research minded, and graphology has in the main been sponsored by persons who were little interested in research. In fact, they have felt that research was not readily applicable to their field. With recollection, however, of the absurdities of phrenology, the unsupported claims of palmistry, the long history of quackery in reading fates and character from the stars, from numbers, cards, tea grounds, handwriting, and almost anything around which mystery and esoterics could be thrown, with the attitude of those sponsoring graphology that their subject was immune to research, with inviting opportunities to do research in measurement and experimentation, the research workers of America have mainly given attention to other things.

It may be, however, that the claims for the use of handwriting can themselves be analyzed, classified, made definite and then subjected to research for verification or rejection. Since the surprising viability of the Rorschach test, even in America, researchers are somewhat more willing to give time to investigating possibilities and claims for expressive and projective methods. Wolff, a psychologist with European background, has worked extensively in the field, and has included in his recent work a number of research studies and a bibliography.[140] He recognizes that graphology can be established only "if basic graphological elements can be correlated with basic mental and emotional patterns."[141] He regards graphology not as a projective means: "As a direct expression of inner motions in outer motions, handwriting is a graphogram, more similar to an electroencephalogram than to a Rorschach inkblot." One other reference is here cited to emphasize the clinical aspects or uses of graphology.[142]

The present discussion of analysis in the study of handwriting is intended to show the role that analysis of form can play, and the ways in which it contributes to significant research and to practical understanding. We are not here dealing with experimentation as a research method and consequently the experimental outlines of the studies referred to have not been discussed; they can be looked up in the original sources. The illustrations here given help make clear the way in which analysis, as primarily a thoughtful process, prepares the way for good experimentation, or for other forms of data-gathering which throw light on the analytical ideas that one develops. It is not intended to imply, however, that mental analysis comes first and then stops; rather, as in all forms of research, there is (or should

[140] Werner Wolff, *Diagrams of the Unconscious:* Handwriting and Personality in Measurement, Experiment, and Analysis. New York: Grune and Stratton, 1948. 423 p.
[141] In a book review, *Psychological Bulletin* 50:163-64; March 1953.
[142] Ulrich Sonnemann, *Handwriting Analysis as a Psychodiagnostic Tool.* New York: Grune and Stratton, 1950. 280 p.

be) a continual interaction between thought and observation. It is the purpose here to emphasize the role of analysis, and through doing so to suggest its possibilities for use in future studies.

We have treated handwriting somewhat fully as an example of the analysis of form. We will deal with other applications briefly. Those who are interested in art will find virtually unlimited examples, although many of them belong more clearly under the heading of "pattern" or "structure," as we are using the terms, and so we will reserve treatment until later. Our present emphasis is primarily on outline.

Form appears in connection with body growth, body posture, and body build. The literature in these areas is voluminous;[143] for specific treatments a few individual references will be given. During growth, the proportions of the various parts of the body change greatly. These varying proportions have been measured, photographed, and diagrammed.[144] We regard ratio (proportion) of parts as definitely a form of analysis; and in this instance it is employed to analyze shape or form, and to make comparisons as that form changes over time. Logically, the analysis could be extended to include the study of growth curves, but the plotting and analysis of curves are judged to fall beyond the limits of the present treatment.

Body posture has been given special attention by groups interested in physical education, and various methods for measuring and analyzing it have been developed.[145]

The matter of body build, constitution, or somatotype has been a subject of high interest and controversy for several decades. There is first of all the problem of successfully typing the form and build of the human body—

[143] Kai Jensen, "Physical Growth." *Review of Educational Research* 22:391-420; December 1952. See also previous issues of the *Review* on "Growth and Development," as the December issues of Vols. 20, 17, 14, and 11, and the February issues of Vols. 9 and 6.

Nancy Bayley, "Child Development"—Introduction, and Sections I and V, *Encyclopedia of Educational Research, op. cit.*

"Growth and Development." A section (Chapters 7-11), *Handbook of Experimental Psychology, op. cit.*, 1436 p.

See issues of *Human Biology* for further studies.

Also see the later chapter on genetic, growth, and developmental studies.

[144] Howard V. Meredith and Virginia B. Knott. "Changes in Body Proportions during Infancy and the Preschool Years: III, The Skelic Index." *Child Development* 9:49-62; March 1938.

Nancy Bayley and Read D. Tuddenham, "Adolescent Changes in Body Build." National Society for the Study of Education, *Adolescence*. Forty-third Yearbook, Part I. Chicago: University of Chicago Press, 1944. Chap. 3, p. 33-55.

H. A. Harris and Others, *The Measurement of Man*. Minneapolis: University of Minnesota Press, 1930. 215 p.

[145] Thomas K. Cureton, Jr., "Bodily Posture as an Indicator of Fitness." Supplement to the *Research Quarterly* 12:348-67; May 1941. 93 references in bibliography. Published by the American Association for Health, Physical Education, and Recreation.

Margaret S. Poley, Ellen D. Kelly, and Howard V. Meredith, "Problems Relating to Antero-Posterior Standing Posture." American Association for Health, Physical Education, and Recreation, *Research Methods Applied to Health, Physical Education, and Recreation*. Washington: The Association, 1952. p. 166-72.

with its countless aspects (multidimensionality) and its indefinitely small gradations, on one aspect or another, from case to case. The history and scope of the efforts are given by Shock.[146] The problem is further complicated by the fact that there has been an interest from the first in relating the body types to personality types.[147] The task would be much simpler, if either body or personality types had been successfully established previously.

The most noteworthy effort in this country to construct a set of categories, and an index, of body build is that of Sheldon and colleagues,[148] who went further and prepared also a "Scale of Temperament" with which they correlated the physical ratings. Although the factors entering into these physiological indexes are presumed by some to be hereditary, they are apparently affected by nutrition.[149] It may be that the classification is of greater utility for purposes of physical education and competition in sports than for other purposes.[150] The stability and values of the somatotypes are continuing to be studied.[151]

We shall close this topic by referring briefly to form in bodily action. A steady educational interest is maintained in this area by those who are concerned with physical education, sports, and related subjects.[152] Occasionally form is employed in experimental studies to test the effects of

[146] Nathan W. Shock, "Child Development—VI. Constitution Types." *Encyclopedia of Educational Research, op. cit.* p. 156-63. Bibliography of seventy references; for further bibliography see the subsequent reference to Thomas K. Cureton.

[147] A compact account with emphasis on both personality and body build is given in Kimball Young, *Personality and Problems of Adjustment.* Second Edition. New York: Appleton-Century-Crofts, 1952. p. 232-40.

A fuller account, with historical background is given in Anne Anastasi and John P. Foley, Jr., *Differential Psychology.* Revised Edition. New York: Macmillan Co., 1949. Chapter 13, "The Quest for Constitutional Types," p. 421-56. Bibliography of forty-nine references.

[148] William H. Sheldon, S. S. Stevens, and W. B. Tucker, *The Varieties of Human Physique.* New York: Harper and Bros., 1940. 347 p.

William H. Sheldon, "Constitutional Factors in Personality." Joseph McV. Hunt, *Personality and the Behavior Disorders.* New York: Ronald Press Co., 1944. Vol. I, Chapter 17.

[149] Gabriel Lasker, "The Effects of Partial Starvation on Somatotype: An Analysis of Material from the Minnesota Starvation Experiment." *American Journal of Physical Anthropology* 5:323-41; September 1947.

[150] "Studies Related to Body Build." American Association for Health, Physical Education, and Recreation, *Research Methods Applied to Health, Physical Education, and Recreation.* Revised Edition. Washington: The Association, 1952. p. 159-62.

Thomas K. Cureton, Jr., "Body Build as a Framework of Reference for Interpreting Physical Fitness and Athletic Performance." Supplement to the *Research Quarterly* 12:301-330; May 1941. 100 references in bibliography. Published by the American Association for Health, Physical Education, and Recreation.

[151] "Somatotypes—Body Build—Constitution." *Review of Educational Research* 22:405-406; December 1952.

For current references, see in the *Education Index* the head, "Constitution (Physiology)—Types."

[152] Alfred W. Hubbard and Others, "Research Methods in the Mechanics of Sports and Physical Education Activities." American Association for Health, Physical Education, and Recreation, *Research Methods Applied to Health, Physical Education, and Recreation, op. cit.,* Chapter 10, p. 219-53. Bibliography of 138 references. See also Chapters 8 and 9.

different ways of performing in track, swimming, gymnastics, golf, and other sports.[153]

Analysis of form may also serve historical purposes. For example, certain native Indian dances have been analyzed from the standpoint of musical form and dance form in order to trace their origin, and the origin of the tribe. The elements in the present culture of the tribe can be related to elements in earlier known cultures through careful analysis of such forms.[154]

## Pattern and Organization

This is the second topic dealing with integrative or organizational aspects. While all three topics or divisions of this unit on "Form, Organization, and Structure" are concerned with the way parts are related to each other, the interest shifts somewhat from one to the other. The preceding topic was devoted to the kind of form which could be looked at in outline, or from the outside. The present topic deals with patterns in which the detailed, inner organization is of primary interest. That is, the interrelationships are of large importance in themselves, and not just as a means of analyzing form. While this idea has been used as a basis for dividing the discussion, there is no implication that the dividing line is sharp or in all cases clear cut.

There is perhaps the more difficult division between interest in the somewhat static aspects and in the more active, dynamic aspects of an object or action. In human science, virtually everything which is discussed has its role to play in some ongoing scheme, some set of purposes. Inasmuch, however, as it is impossible to treat everything together, some separation seems necessary and, accordingly, those interests which are primarily concerned with such aspects as interaction and force and goals will be dealt with in a later section. This is in accordance with the plan laid down earlier.

Because the number of subjects which could be included in this topic is very extensive, we shall have to be selective and refer only briefly to each one, being content to outline the rich possibilities of analytical study in this area and leaving the fuller description of how the processes are carried on in each study to the reading of the original report itself. We shall take up the illustrations under two heads, "spatial" and "operational."

Designing a school building is a subject of wide educational and civic interest. While the artistic and architectural features may be left to the architect, the educational provisions of the building and the layout of the floor plans are matters of vital concern to the professional educator. Conse-

[153] For example, see Alexander Waite, *Effects of Varied Instructions on the Learning of a Certain Motor Skill*. Durham, N. C.: Duke University, 1940. Doctor's thesis. 131 p.
[154] Gertrude P. Kurath, "The Tutelo Harvest Rites: A Musical and Choreographic Analysis." *Scientific Monthly* 76:153-62; March 1953.

quently a fairly large amount of educational literature is devoted to these problems. The general scheme of thought that has come to be approved is to analyze (that is, think through, evaluate, and specify in detail) the educational program which is appropriate to the community; next, consider the long-time building program in the light of likely population developments; and then determine the educational provisions which a new building (or new addition) should include. These analytical steps were given recognition in a yearbook of the American Association of School Administrators.[155]

The design of individual classrooms, both for general and for special purposes, is undergoing continual change in the light of a broadening interpretation of education. Whereas once all elementary school rooms were the same—contained a standard number of fixed seats and some sort of cloak room, with blackboard and windows filling the free wall space— there has through the years been an increasing recognition that educational activities consist of something more than sitting in a seat and studying, standing in the aisle and reciting, and passing to the blackboard and writing. A careful analysis of child nature, of the varied types of learning which help him mature, and of the physical facilities which will permit and foster these experiences, has led to the designing of classrooms that are adapted to the modern conception of education.[156] At least one junior high school has provided a conference room (10 by 14 feet) adjacent to each classroom to accommodate group or committee work.[157]

Special attention has been given to the layout of the office suite for the principal.[158] Further references will not be given, since many floor plans are published in current issues of the *American School Board Journal* and the *Nation's Schools*.[159] Our interest in the subject here is that individual school rooms require careful designing and that school-building layouts call for analysis of the interrelationships between different rooms and other space units. In other words, the floor plans must provide not only enough class-

---

[155] American Association of School Administrators, *American School Buildings*. Twenty-seventh Yearbook. Washington: The Association, 1949. 525 p.

[156] Both general and special classrooms, on the elementary and secondary school level, are discussed in James D. MacConnell, "Space and Facility Requirements." *Review of Educational Research* 21:17-27; February 1951. Forty-eight references in bibliography.

This is the seventh issue which the *Review* has devoted to school plant and equipment, beginning in December 1932 and appearing at approximately three-year intervals.

[157] Clarence Hines, "Pacific Northwest: For Long Rainy Season Try Trilateral Lighting." *Nation's Schools* 41:34-36; February 1948. One may wish to see other articles adjacent to this one covering "Schoolhouse Planning for Three Climates."

[158] This material has been gathered together in the two following publications:

George C. Kyte, *The Principal at Work*. Revised Edition. Boston: Ginn and Co., 1952. "Plans for the School Office," p. 181-89.

Paul B. Jacobson and William C. Reavis, *Duties of School Principals*. New York: Prentice-Hall, 1942. "Office Facilities," p. 180-89.

[159] For current references, see "School Buildings—Designs and Plans."

rooms and other facilities but must do so in such a way as to provide a proper organization of these different units. The securing of this organization is a matter for careful analysis on the part of the educators and the architect, in the light of the educational and community functions which the building is to render. An *unorganized* analysis of the space can be given simply as a table of amounts or per cents—such as the amount or per cent of floor space given to classrooms, special activity rooms, gymnasiums and playrooms, kindergartens, auditoriums, and other rooms. The organized picture can be given only in terms of floor plans.

School districts form another spatial unit which, when looked at from the standpoint of a state as a whole, represents a certain pattern or organization. A considerable amount of research has been given to them.[160] One reason for this interest is that, about two decades ago, one-hundred thousand schools were operating in the United States with seventeen or fewer pupils in average daily attendance. In Illinois in 1945 there were eight thousand school districts which had nothing but one-room schools.[161] Small schools cannot give the pupils the educational opportunities that larger enrollments make possible, and the administration is generally inefficient.

The problem is essentially one of how to divide up space; that is, how to organize the area of a state for efficient educational purposes. For anyone who has read the literature, however, it is surprising how complicated the matter of redrawing a few lines can become. The school district is connected with long tradition, people's ideas of democracy and local control of education, and often other feelings. To aid in the work, an analysis has been made of the many factors entering into the desirable size and conditions of a school district, and standards have been set up.[162] There are still fewer than ten teachers employed in nearly three-fourths of all the school districts of the nation.[163] The great variety of research attacks upon this problem again afford an illustration of what can be done in the way of studying what, at the outset, might seem to be a simple problem—so simple

[160] The subject is well reviewed up to 1950 in Shirley Cooper and Howard A. Dawson, "School-District Organization." *Encyclopedia of Educational Research, op. cit.,* p. 1,083-89. One will want to consult a number of the basic references cited in the bibliography.

M. L. Cushman, "District Organization." *Review of Educational Research* 22:356-65; October 1952.

Shirley Cooper and Others, "Needed Research in District Organization." *Phi Delta Kappan* 32:356-59; April 1951.

[161] H. H. Hamlin and M. R. Sumption, *New Community Unit School Districts: Practices and Problems.* University of Illinois Bulletin, Vol. 48, No. 45. Urbana: University of Illinois, February 1951. 32 p.

[162] For a summary and review of criteria see Roe L. Johns and Edgar L. Morphet, "Relation of School District Reorganization to Finance and Business Administration." *Review of Educational Research* 20:115-23; April 1950. See also article cited in the *Encyclopedia of Educational Research,* by Cooper and Dawson.

[163] Council of State Governments, *The Forty-eight State School Systems.* Chicago: The Council, 1949. 245 p.

that one might say, I wonder what there is about this problem to study?

A somewhat similar problem, although of far less complexity, concerns the attendance districts of individual schools within a city, or in any larger school administrative unit. The problem is simpler, because the districts are still under the same administration, regardless of where the dividing lines are drawn. The problem is usually faced in reverse, namely, where should future schools be located in order to cover the city (or other comparable school district) adequately, without undue overlapping of potential attendance areas and without unduly large or small schools? This problem is faced in school-building surveys and in school-building programs. The existing coverage is usually indicated by drawing circles around the schools, the radius depending on the age of the children attending (that is, elementary vs. junior vs. senior schools).[164] This procedure was established during the 1920's by Engelhardt and associates, who made many school-building surveys.[165] Sometimes, however, squares are better than circles.[166]

Sometimes a location for a school is to be picked so as to satisfy certain special conditions. For example, when there is but a single school to be located in a newly formed district, or perhaps a single special school of some kind in a city, it is natural that the location should be selected so as to make the distance pupils have to travel as short as possible. The matter is not entirely simple, and some statistical function has to be calculated, such for example as making the aggregate travel distance for all pupils a minimum, or possibly making the travel distances of individual pupils as nearly equal as possible. (The two criteria are not the same.) Theoretical work has been done on the problem,[167] and also the theory applied and modified in the light of actual travel arteries existing in a city.[168]

The arranging of rooms and service features in a school building, the designing of bus routes to be efficient, and the locating of single schools, so as to make travel distances to them moderate, all involve certain principles of topology. Topology is a branch of geometry which deals with rela-

[164] This is a common technique and will be found in many surveys. For example, see T. C. Holy and John H. Herrick, *A Survey of the School-Building Needs of Cincinnati, Ohio.* Bureau of Educational Research Monographs, No. 29. Columbus: Ohio State University, 1945. 184 p. See Figures 9, 11, 13.

[165] N. L. Engelhardt, *School-Building Programs in American Cities.* New York: Teachers College, Columbia University, 1928. 560 p.

N. L. Engelhardt and Fred Engelhardt, *Planning School-Building Programs.* New York: Teachers College, Columbia University, 1930. See Chapters 7, 8.

[166] Paul Gossard, "Aids for the Scientific Study of Distances Pupils Travel." *American School Board Journal* 112:42-44; June 1946.

T. V. Goodrich and M. C. Lefler, "An Improvement in School Survey Maps." *American School Board Journal* 74:67, 148; March 1927.

[167] Douglas E. Scates, "Locating the Median of the Population in the United States." *Metron* 11:49-65; June 30, 1933. Originally published in International Congress for Studies on Population, *Proceedings.* Rome, Italy, 1934. Vol. 10, p. 167-83.

[168] Douglas E. Scates and Lucile M. Van Nortwick, "The Influence of Restrictive Routes upon the Center of Minimum Aggregate Travel." *Metron* 13:77-91; February 28, 1937.

tionships independent of any quantitative aspect. It is a peculiar sort of thing, in that it departs so strikingly from many aspects of reality, as we commonly think of them; yet its freedom from specific quantities enables it to serve well when one wants to think solely about the relationship aspect of anything—that is, positional (or adjacency) relationships. It is of particular value for planning routes around or through various areas, because the conclusions are general, and will hold for all applications regardless of the specific dimensions of shape and size.[169] Lewin found topological space a convenient way to represent graphically the Gestalt psychologists' belief in psychological isomorphism,[170] perhaps because of the parallelism in essential indefiniteness. In a later work he emphasized the path aspect of topology and called his development the geometry of hodological space.[171] (*Hodos* is the Greek word for "path.") While he was primarily concerned with behavior and motivation, his development of concepts relates to routes in topological space,[172] and one who is interested only in those aspects can read desired portions. In any case, one who cares to go behind the immediate practical job and develop general principles which may be helpful in solving problems of routing, position, and location will find topology available.

From matters involving the location and arrangement of schools in a district, we may turn to the city (or other inclusive area). We have previously referred to the analysis (differentiation, identification, description) of various areas in a city as constituting components of the entire city. It is possible also to view such areas in terms of their over-all pattern—what the city looks like when so divided. *Where* in the city do certain types of area tend to develop? Is there any generality to such patterns? What is the rationale behind them?

Sociologists have made extensive studies of the distribution of various

---

[169] Some of the basic ideas were written up popularly and engagingly in Albert W. Tucker and Herbert S. Bailey, Jr., "Topology." *Scientific American* 182:18-24; January 1950. The phase of topology dealing with networks is often met in recreational tracing problems, but it has attracted the attention of the best mathematicians. See, for example, Euler's memorandum in *Scientific American* 189:66-70; July 1953.

For a standard treatment see Solomon Lefschetz, *Introduction to Topology*. Princeton Mathematical Series, No. 11. Princeton: Princeton University Press, 1949. 218 p.

Waclaw Sierpinski, *Introduction to General Topology*. Translated by C. Cecilia Krieger. Toronto: University of Toronto Press, 1934. 238 p.

[170] Kurt Lewin, *Principles of Topological Psychology*. New York: McGraw-Hill Book Co., 1936. 231 p.

[171] Kurt Lewin, *Conceptual Representation and the Measurement of Psychological Forces*. Contributions to Psychological Theory, No. 4. Durham, N. C.: Duke University Press, 1938. 247 p.

[172] Why Lewin thought that the established topology was unsuited to his purposes is not clear. He says in several places (p. 2, 21, 23, and elsewhere) that he had to develop a new geometry which would yield direction and distance; what he developed (hodological space) yields non-metrical direction and "distance" in strictly topological fashion.

types of areas in cities and have developed a number of theories concerning them.[173] These studies may grow directly out of surveys of individual cities;[174] as such, they will be treated in a later chapter dealing with the technique of surveying. We are here viewing the subareas as a matter of spatial pattern or organization of city life, having a direct bearing on education through the curriculum and the location of schools. Sometimes the pattern is studied historically, and may be related to a single factor.[175] Much of the work is reported in treatises on human ecology.[176] While this subject is not restricted to cities, it has been most fully developed for them, and Hawley takes the view that the community is the basic unit of ecological organization. The subject of human ecology as a well defined area of research is said to have been started by Robert E. Park about 1915;[177] Park has recently published a volume summarizing his systematic views.[178]

Sometimes the pattern of land use and the various cultural features of a city are studied primarily with a view to improvement, to better use of land areas.[179] A large undertaking known as the Urban Redevelopment Study, begun in 1948, has eventuated in two large volumes.[180] The purpose of the investigation was to see whether methods could be found for ridding cities of "physical blight" (poor housing and generally run-down areas) and for developing city conditions of high desirability. Various factors entering into urban patterns are dealt with.

With these illustrations, we turn from the analytical description of spatial patterns to a group of subjects which we call operational. These have to do with establishing working relations between persons, organizing work to be done, and studying the details of processes. The integrating elements in the organization are largely conceptual; that is, working relations depend to a large degree on concepts of what is to be done, what each individual's

[173] For a very short introductory reference, see Paul K. Hatt and Albert J. Reiss, Jr., Editors, *Reader in Urban Sociology*. Glencoe, Ill.: Free Press, 1951. "Internal Structure of Cities," p. 227-32.

[174] Eshref Shevky and Marilyn Williams, *op. cit.*

[175] William F. Ogburn, "Inventions of Local Transportation and the Patterns of Cities." *Social Forces* 24:373-79; May 1946.

[176] James A. Quinn, *Human Ecology*. New York: Prentice-Hall, 1950. 561 p.

Amos H. Hawley, *Human Ecology: A Theory of Community Structures*. New York: Ronald Press Co., 1950. 456 p.

For a historical sketch and appraisal, see Louis Wirth, "Human Ecology." *American Journal of Sociology* 50:483-88; May 1945. Reprinted in Alfred M. Lee, *Readings in Sociology*. New York: Barnes and Noble, 1951. p. 139-48.

[177] Louis Wirth, in preceding footnote. Also, book review by Burgess in *American Journal of Sociology* 58:439; January 1953.

[178] Robert E. Park, *Human Communities*. Glencoe, Ill.: Free Press, 1952. 278 p. See especially Part II, Chapters 12-19.

[179] S. E. Sanders and A. J. Rabuck, *New City Patterns: The Analysis of and a Technique for Urban Reintegration*. New York: Reinhold Publishing Corp., 1946. 202 p.

[180] Coleman Woodbury, Editor, *The Future of Cities* and *Urban Redevelopment, Problems and Practices*. Chicago: University of Chicago Press, 1953. 764 p., 525 p.

responsibility is, and what the interests are on both sides of an employer-employee relationship. The purpose of such analysis of objectives and functions, with the resulting pattern of organization, is of course action (that is, accomplishment, results). As has been previously remarked, such organizations are, therefore, dynamic in purpose and in effectualization; it is only in their conceptual form, and perhaps when these concepts are drawn on paper, that the static aspects of the organization are prominent.

Theoretically, one should first divide the work into functions and then consider organizing a staff to cover these functions. Practically, most organizations simply grow and it is only when an agency or operation is surveyed that the functions and the staff organization are systematically considered. Texts on public administration often give a large amount of attention to organization.[181] It will be borne in mind that public schools are a form of public administration, and educational administrators may often obtain basic principles from the more general treatises. A set of papers analyzing administrative organization in terms of basic aspects was written some years ago and has recently been reprinted because of its enduring value.[182] Pfiffner treats methods of making an analysis of organization in a particular city.[183] (Further material along this line will be found in the next chapter on methods of making surveys.)

In the field of educational administration, many studies and texts deal with problems of organization of work. W. W. Charters, Jr., in treating "The School as a Social System," [184] drew upon studies of the general theory of organization. The *Review of Educational Research* has devoted a chapter to educational organization rather regularly at three-year intervals back to June 1931.[185] The functions and duties of school superintendents have been referred to in connection with job analysis; the organization of their work is treated at length in their Thirtieth Yearbook.[186] Many organization charts are shown. The National Education Association studied the current status of the unit and multiple-executive types of administrative

181 Marshall E. Dimock and Glady O. Dimock, *op. cit.* See especially Chapter 5, "Organization," p. 103-42.

Herbert A. Simon, Donald W. Smithburg, and Victor A. Thompson, *Public Administration.* 582 p. Deals extensively with organization; for example, Chapters 4 and 5 on "Building Blocks of Organization"; Chapters 6 and 7 on "Dividing the Work"; Chapters 9, 10, and 11 on "Securing Teamwork."

182 Luther H. Gulick and L. Urwick, *op. cit.*

183 John M. Pfiffner, *Research Methods in Public Administration.* New York: Ronald Press Co., 1940. 447 p. See especially Chapter 14.

184 W. W. Charters, Jr., "The School as a Social System." *Review of Educational Research* 22:41-50; February 1952. See especially p. 47 on "Theories of Organization," with various citations.

185 Harlan L. Hagman and Alfred Schwarts, "Theory and Structure of Local School Administration." *Review of Educational Research* 22:277-84; October 1952. See especially p. 279-80.

186 American Association of School Administrators, *The American School Superintendency, op. cit.,* Chapter 4, "The Organization of the Superintendency," p. 65-102.

organization in city school systems.[187] On the level of the principalship, various analyses of work organization and staff organization are summarized or referred to in texts and reviews on the subject—for the elementary-school principal [188] and for the secondary-school principal.[189] We should like to make a distinction between the organization of the work of the principal and the organization of the education on his level, namely, how individual schools are organized, how the curriculum is organized, and so on, but the original treatises do not always do so and hence the references given cover both areas. For those who are especially interested in the use of diagrams to help analyze and portray the organization of work functions, processes, and staff, pictographs are less formal and more engaging than simple line diagrams.[190]

There seems to be some tendency to look at administrative organization and operation less in terms of its technological aspects (that is, all the technical details of what to do and how to do it, which filled the literature of two or three decades ago) and more in terms of its social aspects—leadership, securing teamwork, and so on.[191] Perhaps the emerging emphasis is due to the large amount of attention which has been given to group dynamics, group discussion, leadership, and democracy in administration. Perhaps it is due to an increasing knowledge of social psychology in general. It may be the flowering of the basic element of democracy which places a high value on the individual, in addition to the work he is expected to do.[192] In any case, it furnishes an illustration of how a complex activity can be analyzed in various terms, such as activities, techniques, functions, or principles of social psychology. It bears out what we repeat so often, that the

[187] National Education Association, Research Division and American Association of School Administrators, *Status of Unit and Multiple-Executive Plans in 331 City School Systems in Cities 30,000 and Over in Population.* Educational Research Service Circular No. 6, 1951. Washington: The Association, 1951. 23 p.
[188] William C. Reavis and Others, *Administering the Elementary School:* A Coöperative Educational Enterprise. New York: Prentice-Hall, 1953. 631 p. See especially Chapter 8.
George C. Kyte, *op. cit.,* Chapters 1, 7, 8, 9.
Henry J. Otto, "Elementary Education—III, Organization and Administration." *Encyclopedia of Educational Research, op. cit.,* p. 367-83.
[189] Harl R. Douglass, *Organization and Administration of the Secondary School.* Revised Edition. Boston: Ginn and Co., 1945. 660 p.
Arwood S. Northby, "Secondary Education—III, Organization." Also, Charles W. Boardman, "Internal Organization." *Encyclopedia of Educational Research, op. cit.,* p. 1,165-73, p. 1,194-95. One will find other references by consulting the index, p. 17.
[190] Rudolf Modley and Dyno Lowenstein, *Pictographs and Graphs:* How to Make and Use Them. New York: Harper and Bros., 1952. 186 p. See especially Chapter 8, "Other Ways to Use the 'Little Man,' " p. 100-123.
[191] Francis G. Cornell and Darrell J. Inabnit, "Administrative Organization as Social Structure." *Progressive Education* 30:29-35; November 1952.
See also W. C. Reavis and Others, in preceding footnote. See also the text by Simon, Smithburg, and Thompson, cited earlier.
[192] "Educational administration is the selection, assignment, stimulation, guidance, and evaluation of human effort toward the development of human qualities." John Guy Fowlkes, "A Program for Continued Progress in the Preparation for School Administration." *Nation's Schools* 47:38-40; April 1951.

researcher sees what he looks for. The general background of his thinking, his vision, penetration, and insights are all as important as, or perhaps far more important than, the formal steps with which he approaches his study. The formalities must sooner or later be complied with, but without the ability and readiness to see in a subject those aspects which, when studied, will carry thinking forward, research may for years be prosecuted without gaining new ground.

The organization of research staffs is of interest to those who are directing a research group, or to those who are thinking of setting up a large-scale research undertaking. The matter is being given increasing attention in the literature, in part because of the large sums of money which the federal government is giving to research in the physical, biological, and psychological sciences, with the consequent variety of large-scale operations. There is also an inherent problem in the organizing of research staffs and the "administering" of research, including all aspects of planning for research, in that so many of the great forward steps in science have been matters of discovery and not of plan; and, in fact, the more one plans in terms of current knowledge and current interpretations, the more likely he is to preclude progress along some new line. As has been said about the discovery of penicillin, the more sophisticated one was about science the less likely he would have been to allot any funds for work in this area, because all previous research along that line had proved unproductive. Similarly, an individual director of a research group probably would not have planned work in that direction; it would have suggested that he did not know the field, for research had repeatedly shown it to be sterile.

Much of the real progress in research (whether physical, biological, or social) must depend on those individuals who have an idea that is contrary to many of the currently accepted "facts" and scientific theories, or must wait upon accidental discovery—with someone having the freedom (and the time and money and encouragement) to follow up on the discovery and explore it. Both of these important elements, namely, holding and working on ideas which are contrary to current scientific thinking, and having the freedom to explore leads when they unexpectedly develop and were not (could not be) planned for, are in danger of being precluded by careful organizing and planning. It is a fundamental problem; the more one applies ordinary principles of good organization, administration, and planning to the research enterprise, the more likely he is to defeat his large purposes. That is, he will accomplish, perhaps in mechanical fashion, the set "mission" on which he started; and this objective is likely to be worded so carefully that, if he simply "carries on," he cannot be criticized. But, in meeting the canons of "good administration" in thus carrying on, the director and his staff are accepting, and working by, a set of criteria which are ill adapted to the fostering of individual initiative, creativity, alertness to discovery, and exploration of the novel.

Among regularly established research laboratories in some of the large industries, young scientists who are looking forward to a career in scientific research may be forced to agree in advance that all of their productive ideas become the property of the company, and that patents and writing during their period of employment are restricted to what the company, with its definite commercial interests, may approve. Such a policy may have been found by experience to be necessary, or it may be dictated by the non-research administrators of the company; but it is scarcely calculated to stimulate the greatest productivity of the individual researcher. It is likely to (and often does) breed considerable jealousy and suspicion between members of a research staff, so that a worker does not even trust his supervisor; he fears that the supervisor (someplace along the hierarchical line) will himself take credit for the idea and seek a promotion.

Thus, the individual who is interested in analyzing the factors which do or should operate in a research organization will find that there are a number of personal, psychological elements present in rather strong degree which are not ordinarily present in such degree in more routine work. The problem is one which is mainly yet to be solved. It is, of course, part of the general problem of all administration and organization of giving adequate recognition to the individual without sacrificing the general goal of the group. It is part of the age-old problem of government, of organizing society in such a way that the individual gains maximum satisfaction and at the same time his society can maintain itself in a competitive world. The presumption of our civilization has been that the society will be strongest when the individual has greatest freedom; that is, up to a certain point. Going in either direction, that is, in the direction of control or in the direction of uncoördination, beyond certain limits freedom disappears and is not generally available. Fear and dependency and futility take its place. The problem in research organization is to find these limits, both qualitative and quantitative, within which the individual researcher will contribute most to the common goal.

The literature on this problem has, naturally, been developed in those areas where the largest amounts of money for research are being spent, but the problem and the principles are general. A number of Institutes have been held on the Administration of Scientific Research and Development, sponsored jointly by the American University (of Washington, D. C.), the

National Research Council (of the National Academy of Sciences), and the American Association for the Advancement of Science.[193] The matter has been treated from the viewpoint of one versed in public administration [194] and from the viewpoint of business administration.[195] The industrial research worker has contributed out of his experience.[196] Various organizations of scientists have been interested in it.[197] Probably the most important literature on the subject, however, is that which is being produced currently by research scientists and research administrators who are meeting, and analyzing, new experiences in group research.[198] Many of these reports appear in *Science,* one of the publications of the American Association for the Advancement of Science, in which education, psychology, anthropology, and various other social sciences have representation.

So far we have been referring to the analysis of functions or tasks, and of the working relationships between persons in connection with carrying out major objectives. Our view has been centered to some extent on aspects that may be thought of as somewhat static. In contrast to these aspects which are more or less simultaneous, one can look at the organization of work in terms of a temporal sequence or pattern. We have already mentioned flow charts, or routing schemes. These are important in many analyses of work processes. Along with these charts go such other concepts as operations, systems and systems research, and so on. We shall not go into these here other than to refer to *operations analysis.* This is a field which had rapid growth in military operations during World War II, being initiated primarily by the British. The work is concerned with analysis of any process or activity, so as to evaluate its success or effectiveness, and to work out procedures which would lead to improved efficiency. Usually

[193] George P. Bush and Lowell H. Hattery, Editors, *Teamwork in Research.* Washington: American University Press, 1953. 191 p. See especially Part I, "Organization for Teamwork."

George P. Bush and Lowell H. Hattery, Editors, *Scientific Research:* Its Administration and Organization. Washington: American University Press, 1950. 190 p. See especially Part I, "Research Organization."

[194] John M. Pfiffner, *op. cit.,* Chapter 3, "Staff Relationships."

See also Ahlberg and Honey, in footnote below.

[195] Robert N. Anthony, *Management Controls in Industrial Research Organizations.* Boston: Harvard University, Division of Research, Graduate School of Business Administration, 1952. 537 p.

[196] C. E. Kenneth Mees and J. A. Leermakers, *The Organization of Industrial Scientific Research.* New York: McGraw-Hill Book Co., 1950. 383 p.

C. E. Kenneth Mees, *The Path of Science.* New York: John Wiley and Sons, 1946. 250 p. See Chapter 8, "Production of Scientific Knowledge."

David B. Hertz, Editor, *Research Operations in Industry.* New York: Columbia University Press, 1953. 472 p.

[197] American Philosophical Society, *Symposium on the Organization, Direction and Support of Research. Proceedings,* Vol. 87, No. 4, p. 291-364. January 1944.

[198] Charles V. Kidd, "Research Planning and Research Policy: Scientists and Administrators." *Science* 118:147-52; August 7, 1953.

Clark D. Ahlberg and John C. Honey, *Some Administrative Problems in Governmental Research.* Syracuse: Maxwell Graduate School of Citizenship and Public Affairs, of Syracuse University, 1951. 146 p.

scientists from a variety of fields worked together on a problem, often near the front lines of fighting, in order to diagnose difficulties and suggest improvements. The idea has since been employed in business and industrial activities and there would seem to be wide opportunity for its application. We give references which will outline the scope of the activity, in chronological order.[199] This subject is closely related to quality control, which is a statistical subject, and will not be discussed here.

In this same connection, namely, the pattern of events or values distributed over time, we should logically go on to the consideration of trends, growth, learning, and so on, but to do so would lead us too far afield. The study of trends is a statistical matter, and the study of growth will be taken up in a later chapter.

Of considerable interest to teachers and administrators is the matter of combinations of high-school subjects assigned to an individual teacher. Actual practices have been studied a number of times, revealing the large variety of teaching patterns which exist.[200] Research on this matter can be followed by consulting current issues of the *Education Index,* under the head "Teaching Combinations."

### Structure

This is the third topic in the unit on "form, organization, and structure." The first topic dealt with those patterns or configurations which could be looked at more or less in outline. The second topic shifted the interest to internal interrelationships. The third topic continues the emphasis on interrelationships, but also emphasizes the detailed form of the parts which enter into these interrelationships. That is, while organization may be thought of as existing between any kind of units, the concept of structure focuses con-

[199] H. A. C. Dobbs, *Operational Research and Action Research.* Washington: Institute of Ethnic Affairs, 1947. 21 p.

Lincoln R. Thiesmeyer and John Burchard, *Combat Scientists.* Boston: Little, Brown and Co., 1947. 412 p.

Charles Kittel, "The Nature and Development of Operations Research." *Science* 105:150-53; February 7, 1947.

William J. Horvath, "Operations Research—A Scientific Basis for Executive Decisions." *American Statistician* 2:6-8, 18, 19; October 1948.

J. G. Crowther and R. Whiddington, *Science at War.* New York: Philosophical Library, 1948. 185 p.

Horace C. Levinson and Arthur A. Brown, "Operations Research." *Scientific American* 184:15-17; March 1951.

[200] Stephen A. Romine, "Subject Combinations and Teaching Loads in Secondary Schools." *School Review* 57:551-58; December 1949.

Gene K. Lockard, "A Comparative Study of the College Preparation, Teaching Combinations, and Salaries of Kansas High School Administrators and Teachers (1946)." Studies in Education, Number 31. *Bulletin of Information,* Vol. 26, Number 11. Emporia: Kansas State Teachers College of Emporia, November 1946. 38 p.

Edward F. Potthoff, *The Combinations of Subjects of Specialization for High School Teachers of Foreign Languages.* Studies in Higher Education, Number 3. University of Illinois Bulletin, Vol. 40, No. 19. Urbana: University of Illinois, December 1942. 39 p.

siderable attention on the individual units, as well as on their arrangement. That is, structure is both building blocks and pattern or organization.

The term *structure* is not always used as we are employing it here. For example, one will encounter usages that treat structure as being purely interrelationships [201]—the concept for which we have used the term *organization*.

One may think of structure as something which exists in three dimensions and many illustrations of this sort will be referred to. On the other hand, structure refers also to conceptual schemes of thought, which perhaps have not spatial existence, although we often represent them in spatial terms; and structure will refer as well to two-dimensional examples. The present topic will not, therefore, be restricted to physical things.

For example, one may speak of the *organization* of society, referring to those relationships for the control or other administration of a group of persons more or less for a definite purpose. He would speak of the *structure* of society with regard to the detailed forms of social organization when viewed from the standpoint of the way these smaller patterns are themselves interrelated to form a composite whole.

The areas dealt with under the present heading will probably be recognized as more complex than those which have been taken up under the preceding two heads. That is, the three topics of form, organization, and structure are presumed to be in order of increasing complexity. Perhaps, for that reason, knowledge in these areas is likely to build up slowly over a long period of time. For example, in spite of the fact that medicine was a definite practice before the time of Christ, among the ancient Greeks, man is still a long way from having complete understanding of the human body. Knowledge is gained by many different kinds of acquaintance with the particular body of subject matter, after many different aspects have been studied, with many different concepts being formed and rejected or displaced.

For those who think that knowledge comes in ready-made packages, we must point out that in analytical work the observer's conceptions are of the greatest importance, since most of the things studied are not automatically divided up, but are subdivided primarily in terms of the conceptions with which one views them. These conceptions grow out of some utility, as well as some aptness or appropriateness. And, as with all observations, the concepts formed at any given time may not be correct, or they

[201] We cite the following statement as representing a definition of structure that is different from the way in which we are using the term in the present section:

"By a *structure* is meant a *totality of relations* conceived as a whole, and independently of the elements between which the relations hold." André M. Weitzenhoffer, "Mathematical Structures and Psychological Measurements." *Psychometrika* 16:387-406; December 1951. Quotation from p. 390.

may not be useful, and so may be discarded later. If we may illustrate again by the human body, we would simply note that the body is not made up of separate parts, even though we are given to thinking of it in that fashion. The parts are in reality all interconnected and it is only for our purposes that we find it convenient to recognize conceptual dividing lines where in many cases no line or sharp differentiation of any kind exists. For example, we commonly speak of a neck, although it is impossible to say exactly where a neck begins or ends. Anthropologists and others who make scientific measurements of different portions of the body encounter the greatest difficulty in doing so and, as in much of research, they have to introduce somewhat arbitrary definitions in order to make any measurements that are comparable from one worker to another. This interconnectedness among all aspects of the world is something which is coming to be recognized more and more in modern science and modern philosophy, in contrast to the older view that things distinguished conceptually (that is, by thinking of them as something different) were in reality very different in their essence. This does not mean that, in modern thinking, everything is the same thing; rather, the psychological nature of our thinking is being recognized, as well as the actual, common-sense awareness that many things which we name cannot be definitely delimited and have many interconnections with other things.

Hence, our idea of parts is often an imposed idea. What we call parts may actually have much greater similarity among them than difference.

The values in understanding the structure of an object, a group, or a process are much the same as the values provided by any type of scientific study. Perhaps this is an understatement, for, in our view, understanding is one of the highest goals of scientific research, and the analytical study of structure leads to a very high degree of understanding. Perhaps our understanding will never be complete; the fact that man still has not learned what makes the difference between a living cell and inorganic matter does not mean that one should despair. It is no argument that analytical knowledge is not worth while. One should simply stop to recognize the tremendous advance that has been made in physical, biological, and social understanding through the analytical approach to structure. The fact that there is more to be learned makes this form of research like all other forms of research, a never ending undertaking. The more one learns through research, the more he sees that he still wants to know.

Somewhat more specifically, a knowledge of structure gives mankind a more intimate acquaintance with the nature of the thing he is studying and how it operates. He can then predict more accurately what will happen, he can understand the needs of the object or of the activity, he can understand individual differences or variations among objects that are classed as being the same, and he can make diagnoses and remediation or other repairs, and perhaps direct fundamental changes in the thing or the process by virtue of his acquired understanding. It is because of these varied and important outcomes of a thorough understanding that we regard a knowledge of structure as giving a very high order of scientific insight. As compared with this, statistical knowledge, though valuable for many purposes, seems relatively superficial. It is; it has long been acknowledged to be, but this is far from saying that it is of small value.

For purposes of discussion the examples will be taken up under the following five heads: (1) physical structure; (2) physiological structure; (3) social structure; (4) language and conceptual structure; and (5) esthetic structure.

1. **Physical structure.** We see so many examples of physical structure around us everyday that it may seem unnecessary to discuss the area. It is, however, through analysis in the physical field that man has attained his greatest scientific achievements and worked out his greatest practical accomplishments. We refer primarily to chemistry and physics, although one may think, at the other end, of the magnitude scale of astronomy and the entire universe.

In the field of chemistry it is common knowledge that the same amounts of the same elements may be put together in different ways and result in substances which have very different properties. This fact has been known since about the middle of the last century. In 1910 it was known, for example, that one particular formula applied to seventy-one different substances having different properties, these variations arising simply from the different structural arrangement of the atoms in each molecule.[202] It is a common saying that a diamond is the same substance as charcoal; the difference is accounted for by the difference in structure; that is, the way the atoms are arranged. (The diamond has a hexagonal structure like the six carbon atoms in the famous benzene ring.) While it is common to represent the different patterns in structural chemistry by diagrams on paper, it is not assumed that these diagrams picture the structure in any real sense, because the structure in this case is three-dimensional.

The impressive accomplishments in the field of modern theoretical and industrial chemistry should go far to allay the misgivings of those who feel that the processes of analysis ruin rather than reveal nature. It is true that synthesis is a different process from analysis and does not follow automatically from the latter. It has great difficulties of its own in providing for

[202] William H. George, *The Scientist in Action*. London: William and Norgate. New York: Emerson Books, 1938. p. 118-22.

the reconstruction, step by step, of what an extended disintegration has torn down. To achieve a satisfactory reintegration is one of the crowning achievements of a mature science. It is obvious that our current standard of living owes much to the synthetic capacity of twentieth-century chemistry, such, for example, as in nylon and a host of other fabrics, plastics, synthetic rubber, and a great variety of medicines which duplicate the properties of natural agents.

It is generally agreed that atomic theory, as developed in physics and chemistry during the last hundred years, has proved by far the most fruitful theoretical approach ever undertaken. The essence of this approach is the abstraction of increasingly elementary constructs and situations from the complex macroscopic universe of common sense and the increasingly vigorous definition and description of these abstractions. I refer here ... to such abstractions as atoms, electrons, and quanta, which are purely theoretical constructs endowed with such attributes as to enable us to deduce logically from them the events we observe. It is by the use of such constructs that physical scientists have achieved their most notable triumphs. ... It is precisely this atomic and analytic approach which has made possible ... the most comprehensive and magnificent syntheses ever achieved by the human mind.[203]

Of course it is easier to tear down an organic structure than to build it up from simple materials.

> Humpty Dumpty sat on a wall,
> Humpty Dumpty had a great fall.
> All the King's horses,
> And all the King's men,
> Couldn't put Humpty Dumpty together again.

The Humpty-Dumpty problem will always remain a challenge. It is easier to analyze an egg microscopically and chemically than it is to reconstruct the complex protoplasm structurally and chemically, starting from elements. Similarly, in education and psychoanalysis, it is an easier process to diagnose difficulties and identify conditioning elements than it is to reconstruct a personality or develop an adequate set of new motivations. It is easier to inform a city that it is blighted by slum areas and is suffering from interclass hostility than it is to remove these handicaps. Yet the abilities needed to accomplish these reconstructions are among the end goals sought by research in the social fields. They are goals to which many kinds of research will contribute. The present treatment is concerned with the detection and identification of component parts or elements and their structural relationships, a necessary preliminary to any scientific diagnosis and subsequent redirection of growth.

The science of physics has been almost completely revolutionized during

[203] Quoted from George A. Lundberg, "The Proximate Future of American Sociology." *American Journal of Sociology* 50:502-13; May 1945. Quotation from p. 504-505.

the first half of the twentieth century. Abilities which at the beginning of the century were mere dreams are now accomplished facts. Students in our schools during the first decade of this century were taught that elements were immutable. Physicists now change one element into another by altering the basic structure (and composition) of the atom. One may think of this development as representing a perfection of experimental apparatus and, while this is true, it is well to keep in mind that the apparatus would be useless if there had not been a corresponding conceptual development. That is, theory (which amounts to a sort of shrewd or sophisticated guessing) must be developed along with, and to some extent in advance of, experimentation or the experimentation will not lead forward. The great accomplishments in the analysis of the structure of the atom,[204] and particularly of its nucleus, are to be thought of therefore as consisting of propaedeutic thinking, as well as very expert experimentation.

It is common knowledge that this ability to change the structure of the atom, with the tremendous force that is usually released by such a change, has led to the atomic bomb and the hydrogen bomb. These dramatic developments, with the respect and persistent fear that they engender, should not eclipse the more constructive powers which this knowledge has given to mankind. Nor should we lose sight of the great understanding about many processes in the universe which has come with the new knowledge of atomic fission and atomic fusion; whereas formerly the heat generated in the sun and in other stars was a mystery and all attempts to explain them were unsatisfactory.

Further, we may remind ourselves of the great progress being made in medical research through the use of manufactured isotopes—chemical elements that have all the properties of the regular chemical, but which can be given some special property (such as radioactivity), so that this element can be traced in physiological processes.

Thus, while we recognize the validity of many of the arguments which philosophers have leveled against analysis during the past several hundred years, we have before us such striking and altogether impressive examples of incalculable benefits arising from analytical processes in the physical sciences that we believe the emphasis in the discussion must perforce shift from the limitations of analysis over to the side of great admiration and wonder. Not that the limitations have disappeared, but rather that, through great effort, man's constructive genius has successfully applied the results of analysis to produce wholly unanticipated products, powers, and comprehension.

As one further illustration from the field of physical science, we refer

204 Erwin Schrödinger, "What Is Matter?" *Scientific American* 189:52-57; September 1953.

to crystals.[205] This is a fascinating field which, with minor exceptions, is a development of the twentieth century.[206] Bragg explains interestingly how different theories were developed and how certain ones of them were wrong and had to be discarded in the light of evidence; also how the whole attack on this field came about somewhat accidentally, as a sideline to work for an entirely different purpose.

The study of crystals has opened the door to the understanding of the solid state of virtually all matter, because nearly everything that is solid is composed of crystals. All metals are crystals and so also are all rocks, wood, textiles, muscles, and even nerves. As a matter of fact, glass is about the only well known substance that does not show a crystalline structure under the microscope. As a result of the study, "new minerals are being discovered which were previously unsuspected constituents of specimens, and minerals to which different names had been assigned are being shown to be of similar nature." [207] Also, physicists are beginning to understand how electricity is conducted, both by metals and by semi-conductors.[208] The same thing may be said for heat.

The practical person may be inclined to say, What's the use of studying the nature of solid things? All we care about is knowing how to use them. The answer is the same here as with other fields of science. The new knowledge gives rise to new understandings, and man can put his new understandings to work. For example, it is said at the present time that the entire field of metallurgy is still an empirical science which can simply measure and test materials, but cannot as yet make predictions about various qualities of new alloys that may be compounded. The theoretical understanding of solids will make possible such predictions and it also paves the way for the design of entirely new metal alloys—just in the same way that the analytical knowledge afforded by structural chemistry has permitted the making of all sorts of new chemical products. Already we have the example of one remarkable application of this new knowledge in the transistor—a crystal which replaces the electronic tube in radios and other devices.

With these illustrations, we will leave the analysis of structure in physical science and turn to the study of structure in biology and physiology.

2. **Physiological structure.** The very large amount of attention given

[205] Philippe Le Corbeiller, "Crystals and the Future of Physics." *Scientific American* 188:50-56; January 1953.

[206] Lawrence Bragg, "Recent Advances in the Study of the Crystalline State." *Science* 108:455-63; October 29, 1948.

[207] *Ibid.*, p. 459.

[208] Gregory H. Wannier, "The Nature of Solids." *The Scientific American* 187:39-48; December 1952.

A very readable, lucid account of the development of ideas with regard to crystals is given in Max Von Laue, *History of Physics.* Translated by Ralph Oesper. New York: Academic Press, 1950. 150 p. See Chapter 12, "Physics of Crystals," p. 116-24.

to structure (often spoken of as form) in biological fields is well known. As a matter of fact, sciences which are given to description, in part through analysis, are sometimes criticized by those sciences that are more mathematical. It would seem, however, that the lines along which any particular science develops are in large part determined by mankind's interest in certain aspects. Biology gives considerable attention to structure, because we are all interested in it. The scientific purposes and accomplishments which can result from this study of structure depend upon further theoretical work that may be developed; but the necessity of the basic understanding of structure should be clear from the examples in physics and chemistry already given.

In all cases, a knowledge of structure contributes greatly to an understanding of the nature of an object, and how its processes are carried on, whether or not the scientific interest is carried on to the purely quantitative side.

As an illustration of structure in great detail, we refer to certain models of protozoa which have been produced in glass at the American Museum of Natural History (in New York). These have been illustrated and described in a popularly written, fascinating article.[209] Certainly one's understanding of the nature and activities of these small animals is greatly increased by the knowledge that these models give. Further, when the characteristics of these models are related to known activities or properties of the animal, one is better prepared to account for the observed properties.

While it is generally accepted that the relating of form or structure and function, or properties, is a basic goal of both the physical and the biological sciences, one should not conclude that this goal has been achieved.[210] It was mentioned, for example, that in the case of metallurgy physical scientists still do not have a basic mastery of the relationships, although they have opened the door. In biology, the functions of the larger organs and parts of the organism are commonly understood in a general way, but are still not at all clear on the microscopic level. There is, however, a firm belief on the part of many biologists that structure is the most significant property of living matter, from the basic cell to the entire organism.[211]

Our particular interest lies in the human being. There are of course the technical medical texts; we cite one which is less technical than usual.[212]

209 Roy W. Miner, "Universe Through a Microscope; The Protozoa." *Natural History* 50:252-61; December 1942.

210 Max A. Lauffer, "Form and Function: A Problem in Biophysics." *Scientific Monthly* 75:79-83; August 1952. See also publication No. 12 of the Department of Biophysics, University of Pittsburgh.

211 American Society of Plant Physiologists, *Symposium on the Structure of Protoplasm.* Edited by William Seifriz. Ames: Iowa State College Press, 1942. 283 p.

212 Fritz Kahn, *Man in Structure and Function.* Translated from the German by George Rosen. New York: Alfred A. Knopf, 1943. 2 vols.

Researchers in psychology have long been interested in how the body functions with respect to its picking up sensations (from the outside, or from within itself), interpreting those sensations, and acting upon the interpretation. These subjects are dealt with at considerable length in appropriate sources.[213] The methods of studying these structures are sometimes implicit in the reports cited, but can be obtained more fully in the original references. Another source is cited, however, because it deals expressly with methods of research which yield analytic description of these operating physiological structures.[214]

Some persons are not at all interested in these studies of physiological structure, perhaps because their sole interest centers in a more social form of psychology, and they may be inclined to ask, Why does anybody study these things? The answer is that it is part of man's understanding of himself. Such knowledge does a great number of things. For one thing, it discloses many superstitious beliefs, or other forms of fanciful thinking, about the nature of man and how he functions. Sometimes the scientific structure of thinking is not as appealing to the individual as were his folk notions about the human being, but they nevertheless yield many practical results which afford mankind more power over himself and others than did the less scientific beliefs. For one thing, an awareness of the sensory processes gives us a completely different view of man's relations with the world, and thus of his knowledge and his science, from what we might otherwise entertain. The understanding of man's perception shows how much he contributes to the process of observation and science through his own sensory and perceptual processes. (It will later be pointed out that the particular culture of an individual, in turn, shapes his concepts and the lines of thinking in which he is likely to engage, so that even the kind of science he develops is conditioned not only by psychological sensations but also by sociological influences. This emphasis comes within the scope of the area known as the sociology of knowledge.)

A second way in which such knowledge is important is through enabling man to take care of defects in his sensory equipment and also in other organs of his body. One may be inclined to think that this field belongs entirely to the medical profession, but the psychologists have much to contribute, and the educators need to know a great deal in order to counsel their students. Thus, the fact that certain people are color-blind, more or

[213] S. S. Stevens, *Handbook of Experimental Psychology, op. cit.* See Chapters 2-6 on "Physiological Mechanisms"; Chapters 7, 11, 20; Section on "Sensory Processes," Chapters 22-32.

See appropriate chapters in the *Annual Review of Psychology,* issued each spring by Annual Reviews, Stanford, California.

[214] Tom G. Andrews, Editor, *Methods of Psychology.* New York: John Wiley and Sons, 1948. See appropriate chapters such as 5-11, 15, 16.

less so, is a matter of considerable psychological and sociological interest, entirely apart from any concern of the medical profession. The effect of various sensory (or other) deficiencies on the behavior of the individual and on his feelings or emotions is obviously a matter of direct concern to the psychologist and the educator.

Our present ability to supply persons with glasses that will correct deficient eyesight probably goes back to the time when the astronomer and mathematician Kepler "in 1604 decided that the crystalline body in the eye is not the percipient organ but a lens which focuses an image of the external world upon the retina." [215] We are now doing the same thing with hearing aids, as our knowledge of sound, sound transmission, and sensation improves; the same holds for prosthetics in general.

We refer particularly to one example, because it illustrates the part that concepts play, and the difficulty of arriving at sound concepts even regarding things which can be seen. According to a recent study, ideas of the structure of the liver which have been held for a hundred years are now found to be incompatible with the observations.[216] While the earliest account of the structure of the liver was given in 1849, and while the correct view of it (given in the cited paper) was presented by another researcher in 1866, his work was ridiculed by physiologists who were more prominent, and because of their prominence their view was accepted and the correct view dropped out of existence and was lost for nearly one hundred years. The error in the field of chemistry, in believing in phlogiston for virtually one hundred years, is often cited; again, when evidence to the contrary was in existence at the beginning. Apparently we have in the recent paper a similar illustration in the field of human physiology. These examples show the importance of the conceptual schemes which one entertains, whether in experimentation or in physiological analysis, in determining what one actually sees. He is almost certain to see what he believes. If this seems incredible, over so long a period as a hundred years, one must still recognize that good researchers were at work in these fields. The illustrations represent a limitation on the observational powers (perception) of mankind.

It is perhaps in the nervous system, including the various parts of the brain, that psychologists and educators have particular interest. Understanding in this area has proceeded rather slowly, largely because of the great intricacy of the system and because of what we might call its subtle aspects. It has been said of textbooks in psychology and educational psy-

215 Edwin G. Boring, op. cit., p. 677.
216 Hans Elias, "The Liver Cord Concept after One Hundred Years." Science 110:470-72; November 4, 1949.

chology which appeared during the first two or three decades of the present century that they began by outlining the nervous system, as something of a duty, and then proceeded to deal with various psychological subjects, with no reference whatever to the nervous system. If so, we can, at the vantage point of two or three decades later, see some reason for the hiatus or lack of integration between the two parts; although a tremendous amount has been learned during recent decades, we still do not have a sufficient understanding of the nervous system to answer many basic questions.

On the other hand, it should be emphasized that the structure, and the accompanying functioning, of the entire nervous system have been analyzed to the point where a great many things are known. One of the general results is that we now realize our ignorance of a great many things which previously we thought we knew. Another general result is that the nervous system (we use the term to include the brain) is far more complex than was realized a few decades back, and almost more complex than can at present be imagined.

From this recent knowledge of structure we get certain understandings about the large number of integrating centers throughout the body. The older notion of an afferent nerve carrying a stimulus from the outside to the brain, the connection in the brain, and the efferent nerves carrying the impulse to the effectors (muscles, glands, etc.) is at present so sketchy and grossly inadequate that it would scarcely be presented to students other than as something from the past. It seems reasonably clear at the present time that sensory stimuli ramify greatly as they are carried along any nervous tract and are not disposed of by one center but are felt to some degree by a large number of centers. Even a vague understanding of the complexity and diversity of the paths which a nervous current is likely to take, and of the large number of parts or portions of the body which are likely to be affected by such current, affords the background for a much better understanding of human behavior. All of us, in our everyday thinking and reacting to other persons, tend to conceive of their behavior in entirely too simple fashion. We incline to think of the other person as logical and deliberate in what he does, says, thinks, and feels. This is the common tradition on which we have been brought up. Nothing, however, could be farther from the facts, and if the great amount of research in analyzing the human nervous system did nothing else than make us aware of the utter absurdity of these common views and interpretations of other people, it would already have justified itself.

With some understanding of these different centers of connection and control, one is in a position to realize what is meant by such terms as *sub-*

*conscious* or *unconscious,* to understand why it is that a person does not roll out of bed in his sleep, how various anesthetics can be effective and still leave many of the bodily functions fully cared for, and so on. One ceases to think of behavior as behavior (including emotional reactions) as being narrowly logical. The difference between being able to do something, and being able to talk about what one does, or tell on paper why and how he does it, can better be understood. Many activities, at one time wholly conscious (directed perhaps by careful attention and perhaps trains of evaluative thought and selection) may eventually lose the conscious component and be taken over by centers, so that they are carried on, as we say, "without thought." Walking, for example, is one of these; so is typewriting for many persons, or driving an automobile.

In other words, if one seeks justification for *understanding* as one of the goals for analytical research, the very large number of applications which an understanding of the nervous system yields should prove an excellent illustration. Without question a great deal more will be known about human behavior when more is understood about the nervous system.

It is difficult to cite appropriate references, because those which are simple are entirely inadequate and those which are complex are too technical and difficult. A recent work of some proportions has been produced by a neurophysiologist as a basis for the understanding of behavior.[217] Extensive and complex as this treatise may be, it is nevertheless discussed in one book review as being too simple—to the extent of saying that "many important factors have been slighted in favor of the hypothalamic-cortical system," when various other centers or systems are important in understanding general behavior, emotion, and the "autonomic" activities.[218]

Readable descriptions are presented generally in the sources given in earlier footnote references (Stevens, Andrews, *Annual Review of Psychology*). For one who wishes merely to secure a general idea by glancing over a few pages, we suggest some of the material in the appendix of Warren's *Dictionary of Psychology*.[219] Since the integration (an extremely high state of organization) is the compelling aspect of the nervous system, we cite two references which dwell on this.[220]

[217] Ernst Gellhor, *Physiological Foundations of Neurology and Psychiatry*. Minneapolis: University of Minnesota Press, 1953. 556 p.

[218] Reviewed by Robert G. Grenell in *Science* 118:146; July 31, 1953.

[219] Howard C. Warren, Editor, *Dictionary of Psychology*. Boston: Houghton Mifflin Company, 1934. 372 p. See Table 10, "Human Reflexes Frequently Treated in Psychological Literature," p. 311-14, and Table 18, "Topography of the Human Central Nervous System," p. 325-39.

[220] Charles S. Sherrington, *Integrative Action of the Nervous System*. New Edition. New Haven: Yale University Press, 1948. 433 p. This is basically an old work; it was originally published in 1906, in London and New York.

Charles J. Herrick, "A Biological Survey of Integrative Levels." *Philosophy for the Future*. Edited by Ray W. Gellars and Others. New York: Macmillan Co., 1949. p. 222-42.

Not all parts of the nervous system are of equal phylogenetic age. . . . The thalamus . . . is older than the cerebral cortex. . . . The higher correlation centres in the cerebral hemispheres can act only through the agency of the lower centres, the brain-stem, and the thalamus. In other words, the cerebral cortex, the functioning of which is connected chiefly with the higher associations, is of such structure that no nervous impulse can enter it without first passing through the lower centres of the ventral parts of the brain and brain-stem.[221]

This quotation gives the neurological basis for the intimate connection between the emotions and the more purely logical processes. Whereas, in everyday life, one may be prone to think of the emotions as being something separate and distinct from thought, an analysis of the structure of the nervous system reveals that the emotional system has the *first* opportunity to respond, so that thoughtful controls of reaction necessarily occur *after* the complex emotional reactions have gotten started. This does not mean that the person cannot exercise some voluntary control over his emotions, but it indicates some of the difficulty in doing so and places the emphasis on the long training (probably a form of conditioning) of the emotional system itself to react less strongly. Of course, any simple statement relating to the nervous system is bound to be a gross oversimplification, but at least the foregoing statement gives a general outline of the problem. That is, for persons who are emotionally disturbed or unstable, the emphasis is to be placed more on the reëducating of the emotional reaction system and less on voluntary control, which is just the opposite of common thinking that places virtually everything in the behavior of the individual on the level of deliberate, volitional activity. The facts of conditioned learning and of the nervous system indicate the gross error in our common assumptions.

In these various illustrations, and in the literature dealing with the nervous system, one will note the close interrelationship between analysis and experiment. This has been commented on previously and will be noted again in the chapter on experimentation. A certain amount of analysis is necessary in advance of experimentation, if the latter is to be profitable; and, conversely, experimentation is almost a necessary part of analysis which goes beyond physical structure and assesses functions. Studies of the nervous system afford perhaps the fullest operation of this close coöperative relationship between the two lines of research approach.

There is one aspect of handedness that is interesting in the present setting. Statistical evidence indicates that handedness can be linked with certain ridge patterns in the palms of the hands. These ridge patterns are known to be established in the first four months of fetal development. This association of handedness with the ridge patterns indicates, therefore, that

[221] Quoted from Alfred Korzybski, *Science and Sanity*. Third Edition. Lakeville, Conn.: Institute of General Semantics, 1948. p. 157.

the tendency to be right-handed or left-handed, or ambidextrous, is one which is established before birth. This relationship can be explained in regular genetic terms by assuming a pair of genes which lack dominance, one being the gene for right-handedness and the other for left-handedness. Individuals with both genes for right-handedness will be strongly right-handed, and those with both genes for left-handedness will be definitely left-handed. Others, with one gene for the right hand and one for the left, would be naturally ambidextrous, and might be educated for writing with one hand or the other depending on how they are taught. This hypothesis would be in keeping with the known facts that some persons, when transferred from writing with the left hand to the right, begin to stammer, although in many cases, perhaps most of them, the forced change is accomplished with no ill effects. These differences in experience could be attributed to those individuals who might have two left-handed genes and those who might have a gene for each hand.[222]

The illustration just cited is interesting in that it shows the complex nature of research, and how the evidence from a great many different lines of attack is needed in order to explain certain observations. Thus, pattern or organization in the ridges on the palm of the hand becomes the key to indicate that a tendency to handedness (or to ambidexterity) has an anatomical basis, and is not solely a matter of training (that is, in those cases which are definitely predisposed toward one hand or the other). This evidence is purely statistical, which means that it is not final, but becomes indicative when known mechanisms can account for the statistical results. The mechanisms of inheritance, worked out by countless experiments and statistical analyses in the field of genetics, can readily account for the statistical findings. Furthermore, the theory (or the hypothesis) which has been advanced to link these different fields of study together also fits in with experience and experiment in changing persons from one hand to the other, with the findings from identical twins, and with the phenomenon of mirror writing and the extent to which it occurs in identical twins and in the population at large. The theory is not put forth as being final, but it is based on at least five separate statistical studies, and seems to account well for the many different lines of evidence that exist.

We mention this area also with the thought that it provides a salutary corrective to the thinking of so many persons who feel that, to answer a question, one should make an investigation. We would assume that such an attitude would be natural for the layman, but unfortunately it finds expression fairly often by research persons themselves. Perhaps simple ques-

[222] David C. Rife, "Heredity and Handedness." *Scientific Monthly* 73:188-91; September 1951.

tions of fact can sometimes be answered by a study, but any question which relates to explanation is likely to require a large number of studies, often or usually extending into various fields of science, and its proper answer may have to wait for many years until some related field of science has itself developed to the point where understandings are available that will afford the necessary explanatory relationships. Thus, in the area being discussed, the theory advanced would have no support, if genetics as a science had not been developed; and again, it would not have gotten a start, if it had not been for considerable prior study of the ridges on fingertips and on the palms of the hands. And again, the connection between these and inheritance would be unknown and perhaps unsuspected, if there had not been a large amount of study of prenatal life. The contrast between the requisite developments in these different fields, and their interrelationship by a theory, on the one hand, and the idea on the other hand of making a *single* study to answer a question or to tell one what to do in the practical case, should be clear.

3. **Social structure.** Within any society, there will be found many forms of behavior, expectancy, codified rules or laws, and other expressions of systematic habits and attitudes which both express and give structure to the society. The task of describing these at length belongs to the fields of anthropology, sociology, social psychology, and other specialized disciplines such as law, politics, public administration, business administration, and so on. Our purpose in taking the subject up here is to point out that, in describing social groups analytically, there are certain elements of structure which should be looked for, and also to cite certain examples of work that illustrate how these elements of structure can be ascertained and which also suggest the framework of thought with which one can begin his analysis in the area of his choice.

We shall begin with the small group. The term *sociometry* is now a common one and the idea has developed a fairly large literature. The sociometric approach is concerned primarily with dynamic aspects rather than formal ones. That is, the researcher is seeking not the formal or legal structure of a group or a community but rather those attractions, desires, likings, affinities, or preferences which make it more desirable or satisfying for one person to be with, or to work with, another particular individual. The study is concerned primarily with what we might call social valence, the tendency of two persons to seek each other out, in preference to others, for certain activities. These mutual or reciprocated choices do not always occur, but the approach studies the extent to which they do occur; it deals with forms of interrelationship based on attraction of a psychological, informal character. The chief means for studying these relationships is the sociogram, which is a graphic presentation of preferences based usually upon a questionnnaire.[223]

The sociogram, or the choices in tabular form, can be analyzed mathematically, and various devices for doing this have been presented.[224]

The method has been used a great deal by educators in studying children and their personality growth and the conditions which favor development.[225] Inasmuch as the work lies largely or entirely in the field of social psychology, sociologists have employed the technique in a number of studies.[226] Sociometry is obviously of value in the selection of leaders, and in the study of leadership.[227] The technique has also proved of interest in the psychological field; [228] it was used during the last war in the selection of certain persons for key services.[229]

[223] A sample, useful manual on the preparation of sociograms is the following: Teachers College, Columbia University, Horace Mann-Lincoln Institute of School Experimentation, *How to Construct a Sociogram.* New York: Teachers College, 1947. 37 p.

[224] A rather complete bibliography on quantitative analysis of sociograms is given in Merele M. Ohlsen, "Helping Teachers Interpret Sociometric-Test Data." *Journal of Teacher Education* 2:99-104; June 1951.
To this list should be added the following two references:
Leslie D. Zeleny, "Measurement of Sociation." *American Sociological Review* 6:173-88; April 1941.
W. W. Charters, Jr., "The School as a Social System." *Review of Educational Research* 22:46; February 1952.

[225] Ruth Cunningham and Associates, *Understanding Group Behavior of Boys and Girls.* New York: Bureau of Publications, Teachers College, Columbia University, 1951. 446 p. See especially Chapter 5, "Group Structure," p. 154-204.
Helen H. Jennings, "Sociometric Grouping in Relation to Child Development." Association for Supervision and Curriculum Development, *Fostering Mental Health in Our Schools.* 1950 Yearbook. Washington: National Education Association, 1950. 320 p. Chapter 13, p. 203-225.
Hilda Taba and Deborah Elkins, *With Focus on Human Relations.* Work in Progress Series. Intergroup Education in Coöperating Schools. Washington: American Council on Education, 1950. 227 p.
Helen H. Jennings, *Leadership and Isolation:* A Study of Personality in Interpersonal Relations. Second Edition. New York: Longmans, Green and Co., 1950. 349 p.
Joseph Justman and J. Wayne Wrightstone, "A Comparison of Three Methods of Measuring Pupil Status in the Classroom." *Educational and Psychological Measurement* 11:362-67; Autumn 1951.
Lloyd A. Cook, "An Experimental Sociographic Study of a Stratified Tenth Grade Class." *American Sociological Review* 10:250-61; April 1945.

[226] F. Stuart Chapin, *Experimental Designs in Sociological Research.* New York: Harper and Brothers, 1947. p. 148-51.
Theodore Caplow and Robert Forman, "Neighborhood Interaction in a Homogeneous Community." *American Sociological Review* 15:357-66; June 1950.
George A. Lundberg and Margaret Lawsing, "The Sociography of Some Community Relations." *American Sociological Review* 2:318-35; June 1937. Reprinted in Logan Wilson and William L. Kolb, *Sociological Analysis.* New York: Harcourt, Brace and Co., 1949. p. 271-86.
F. Stuart Chapin, "Sociometric Stars as Isolates." *American Journal of Sociology* 56: 263-67; November 1950.

[227] Leslie D. Zeleny, "Leadership." *Encyclopedia of Educational Research.* Revised Edition. New York: Macmillan Co., 1950. p. 662-68; see especially p. 664-65.

[228] Tom G. Andrews, *op. cit.,* p. 371-74, 658-59, 688-89.
*Annual Review of Psychology,* vol. 4: p. 19-21 (1953); vol. 3: p. 15 (1952).

[229] OSS Assessment Staff, *Assessment of Men:* Selection of Personnel for the Office of Strategic Services. New York: Rinehart and Company, 1948. 541 p. See p. 181-87, 298-99, 304-305, 329-30; see also certain other references in this text for difficulties encountered in foreign countries.

Moreno, who began his work in Vienna, Austria, early in this century, is the pioneer and founder of this field of work and the inventor of most or all of the special terms employed. He first used the word *sociometry* in 1915, invented the sociogram in 1923, and introduced these terms into America in 1932. His principal publication, *Who Shall Survive?*, was first published in 1934, revised in 1946, and has now appeared in a greatly enlarged edition.[230] A number of his papers, together with certain office memoranda, recently have been grouped together and published.[231]

Sociometric analysis of the valence structure of a group may be undertaken for purposes of description, for diagnosis and improvement of the working relationships within the group, for studying shifts in the organization or structure over a period of time, for studying the factors related to preferences, and so on. The term is found in the *Education Index,* in the *Review of Educational Research,* and in psychological and sociological indexes, so that one can easily maintain contact with current references. It should be pointed out that the matter of interrelationships between different members of a group is a large subject and is in part connected with dominance and aggression. As such, it can be observed in the animal kingdom as well as among people.[232]

There are, of course, many other lines of study with regard to small groups, but they deal in the main with action rather than with what we think of as structure. Fortunately, a comprehensive treatise has been published that deals with many aspects of groups, including organization, cohesiveness, pressures, standards, goals, structure, and leadership. A series of forty-one papers, each with its own bibliography, deal with the concepts involved in studying that particular aspect of the group organization or dynamics, and with the techniques of proceeding in the study.[233] "Structural Properties of Groups" constitutes Part Five of the book. (Also see the discussion of group-behavior analysis or small-group study in the next chapter.)

Family structure may be considered next, as one of the institutionalized groups of society. Parsons has analyzed the structure of the American

[230] Jacob L. Moreno, *Who Shall Survive?* Foundations of Sociometry, Psychodrama, and Group Psychotherapy. Second, Revised Edition. Beacon, N. Y.: Beacon House, 1953. 890 p. Contains extensive bibliography covering 1914-1952.

[231] Jacob L. Moreno, *Sociometry, Experimental Method and the Science of Society.* Beacon, N. Y.: Beacon House, 1951. 220 p.
Zerka Toeman, "Projects in Tests and Measurements from the Works of J. L. Moreno and the Files of the Sociometric Institute." *Sociatry* 2:407-19; December-March, 1948.

[232] Warder C. Allee, "Social Dominance and Subordination Among Vertebrates." Robert Redfield, Editor, *Levels of Integration in Biological and Social Systems.* Biological Symposia, vol. 8. Lancaster, Pa.: Jaques Cattell Press, 1942. p. 139-62.
A shortened version of this chapter is also published as "Group Organization Among Vertebrates." *Science* 95:289-93; March 20, 1942.

[233] Dorwin Cartwright and Alvin Zander, Editors, *Group Dynamics:* Research and Theory. Evanston, Ill.: Row, Peterson and Co., 1953. 642 p.

family and presents eight different types.[234] The structure of families in different societies is presented in the chapters written by Adams in a simply written book.[235] Chapin discusses structural patterns as one of three of the principal aspects by which families should be studied.[236] Jansen has dealt with solidarity and presented scales for measuring eight different types of interaction within the family which he regards as constituting solidarity.[237] Hill has used both statistical means and the case-study method to analyze the effect on family living of breaking the structure temporarily, as for war service.[238] A history of the different ways in which the family has been studied during a fifty-year period, including different forms of the family and their functions, has been presented briefly as a review.[239]

The family, like any other group, has its psychological structure. While this will relate to the interaction of each member of the family with every other one, the parent-child relationship is of particular importance and interest to educators. While the literature on the relation of parents and children and its effect on the children's personalities is extensive, we cite here only two references which have summarized studies, from the psychological point of view by Symonds [240] and from the sociological point of view by Bossard.[241] Further literature on psychological structure was recently summarized in the *Review of Educational Research.*[242]

Primary groups and institutions in general are often treated in the literature of sociology and of social psychology. Homans presents a conceptual analysis of the small group [243] and Shils has written a comprehensive summary of research on primary groups and of the theory or the conceptions which lie behind this research.[244] "The institutional structure" is the theme

[234] Talcott Parsons, "The Social Structure of the Family." Ruth N. Anshen, *The Family.* New York: Harper and Bros., 1949. p. 173-201.

[235] Stuart A. Queen and John B. Adams, *The Family in Various Cultures.* Philadelphia: J. B. Lippincott Co., 1952. 280 p.

[236] Francis S. Chapin, *Contemporary American Institutions.* New York: Harper and Bros., 1935. See p. 92. These tables are reproduced in George A. Lundberg, *Foundations of Sociology.* New York: Macmillan Co., 1939. p. 417.

[237] Luther T. Jansen. "Measuring Family Solidarity." *American Sociological Review* 17: 727-33; December 1952.

[238] Reuben Hill, *Families under Stress.* New York: Harper and Bros., 1949. 443 p.

[239] Mirra Komarovsky and Willard Waller, "Studies of the Family." *American Journal of Sociology* 50:443-51; May 1945.
Meyer F. Nimkoff, "Trends in Family Research." *American Journal of Sociology* 53:477-82; May 1948.

[240] Percival M. Symonds, *Dynamics of Parent-Child Relationships.* New York: Columbia University, 1949. 197 p.

[241] James H. S. Bossard, *Sociology of Child Development.* New York: Harper and Bros., 1948. 790 p.

[242] Lester A. Kirkendall and Ben Ard, "The Family, Education, and Child Adjustment." *Review of Educational Research* 22:51-58; February 1952.

[243] G. C. Homans, *The Human Group.* New York: Harcourt, Brace and Co., 1950. 484 p.

[244] Edward A. Shils, *The Study of the Primary Group.* Chicago: Department of Sociology, University of Chicago, September 1950. 31 p. (Mimeo).
George A. Lundberg, *Foundations of Sociology.* New York: Macmillan Co., 1939. Chapter 9, "Types of Groups," p. 339-74.

of a section in a book of readings,[245] in which the changing structure of the family is presented by Burgess.[246] Lundberg gives a frame of reference for the study of the institutions of a society.[247]

We pass on to the structure of society itself. Of course the groups and institutions which have already been discussed are an essential part of this picture. Any society will of course have a great many different structures according to the many different aspects from which one may wish to view that society and its culture. That is, there will be legal, political, economic, and many other structures that lie beyond the limits of our discussion. Parsons has presented a conceptual scheme for the analysis of society in terms of its structure, revealing the functional effects of different types of structure.[248] Murdock emphasizes types of family structure and kin groups in pointing out that major segments of man's social behavior exhibit scientific regularities.[249] Other writers have also proposed schemes for studying social structure [250] and some have done this primarily in terms of cultural patterns and values.

No discussion of the structure of society would be complete without reference to social class, or stratification. This has been the subject of outstanding investigations, primarily during the past decade; the problem, however, is as old as mankind itself and has an extensive literature. Fortunately, the literature has recently been reviewed extensively in a number of sources, so that it need not be repeated here. The *American Journal of Sociology* devoted its entire January 1953 issue to the subject, including a bibliography of 333 items published from 1945 through 1952.[251] This is, however, much more than a bibliography; Pfautz devotes sixteen pages to an analysis of current work in the field, showing historical trends, dealing with the development of concepts and theory, the methodology of describing and measuring social class, studies of existing conditions, and critical litera-

[245] Paul K. Hatt and Albert J. Reiss, Jr., *op. cit.*, Section 7, "The Institutional Structure and Processes."

[246] Ernest W. Burgess, "The Family in a Changing Society." Hatt and Reiss, above, p. 431-38. Reprinted from *American Journal of Sociology* 54:118-25; September 1948.

[247] George A. Lundberg, *op. cit.*, Chapter 10, "Characteristics of Populations: Institutional Aspects," p. 375-420.

[248] Talcott Parsons, *The Social System.* Glencoe, Ill.: Free Press, 1951. 575 p.

[249] George P. Murdock, *Social Structure.* New York: Macmillan Co., 1949. 387 p.

[250] Marion J. Levy, Jr., *The Structure of Society.* Princeton: Princeton University Press, 1952. 544 p.

Margaret Mead, "Research in Contemporary Cultures." Harold Guetzkow, Editor, *Groups, Leadership, and Men:* Research in Human Relations. Pittsburgh: Carnegie Press, 1951. p. 106-18. Reports current research being sponsored by the Office of Naval Research.

Clyde Kluckhohn, *Mirror for Man.* New York: McGraw-Hill Book Co., 1949. 313 p. Certain chapters review recent work on culture patterns.

Ruth Benedict, *Patterns of Culture.* Boston: Houghton Mifflin Co., 1934. 290 p. Published also as a Mentor Book, M2, by the New American Library, New York. A classic pioneer example of culture-pattern analysis.

[251] Harold W. Pfautz, "The Current Literature on Social Stratification: Critique and Bibliography." *American Journal of Sociology* 58:391-418; January 1953.

ture. The article is in itself an important review and contribution to research in this area. A reader in social stratification reprints fifty-eight carefully selected articles which cover a wide range of aspects.[252] The subject also constitutes a section in another reader.[253]

Educational implications of the class structure of society have been reviewed from the point of view of researchers [254] and of school administrators and teachers.[255] While we will leave the individual studies to the bibliographies already cited, we mention one that was made by a Bureau of Educational Research, particularly with implications for education.[256]

As background references one may wish to read the statement of principles by Davis and Moore,[257] and a discussion of the place accorded social class by American sociologists.[258] An encyclopedic article gives an overview of the ideas involved.[259] We refer again to the fact that differences in dominance or social prestige and privilege run through the animal kingdom (at least the vertebrates) as well as human society.[260]

For those who are interested in this field, the possibilities are large. One may be interested in employing the concepts and one or another of the available indexes for making surveys in a school community; such information may be helpful in understanding the backgrounds of pupils. One may be challenged to devise new indexes or measuring instruments. Or one may be interested in more general research on the historical antecedents of a given situation which is found, or in study of the relationships between various associated factors, either regarded as causes or as results or merely concomitants.

4. **Conceptual and language structure.** The matter of conceptual growth and development has been referred to before. It would be of extreme value for many purposes to have knowledge of the structural organization of concepts at different levels of maturity, and of the properties

[252] Reinhard Bendix and Seymour M. Lipset, Editors, *Class, Status and Power:* A Reader in Social Stratification. Glencoe, Ill.: Free Press, 1953. 723 p.

[253] Paul K. Hatt and Albert J. Reiss, Jr., *op. cit.,* Section 6, "The Status Structure and Processes," p. 344-428.

[254] Herman G. Richey and Nicholas Pastore, "The Larger Social Context of Education." *Review of Educational Research* 22:17-20; February 1952. See also related discussion and references on pages 25-30.

[255] American Association of School Administrators, *The American School Superintendency, op. cit.,* "Class Structure and the Schools," p. 25-28. Reviews major studies.

[256] Celia B. Stendler, *Children of Brasstown.* Bureau of Research and Service, College of Education. University of Illinois Bulletin, Vol. 46, No. 59. Urbana: University of Illinois, 1949. 103 p.

[257] Kingley Davis and Wilbert E. Moore, "Some Principles of Stratification." *American Sociological Review* 10:242-49; April 1945.

[258] Milton M. Gordon, "Social Class in American Sociology." *American Journal of Sociology* 55:262-68; November 1949.

[259] Paul Mombert, "Class." *Encyclopaedia of the Social Sciences,* Vol. 3, p. 531-36. New York: Macmillan Co., 1930.

[260] Warder C. Allee, *op. cit.*

of different structures. For example, what form of structure leads to better understanding, a sense of grasp, a more satisfying meaning, than some other structure? What structures will lead to the most facile learning; that is, to what forms of organization can new material be added most rapidly, with resulting good assimilation? How often must structures be examined, and remediation be undertaken, before further development is profitable? What forms of conceptual organization lead to the greatest retention? To what extent are components of confidence, familiarity, and perhaps expressive skills necessary in order for a conceptual area to be functionally of the largest value to the person? What forms of organization, together with emotional components of certain sorts, will best withstand attack of various kinds, such as sarcasm, scorn, ridicule, questioning, logical refutation, propaganda, or repeated failure?

This whole area is one of the weak spots in educational psychology, and in psychology in general. This does not mean that nothing has been done in the area, but rather that far less has been done than the subject warrants, considering its fundamental educational importance. Those studies which have been made have dealt primarily with single lines of development—rather narrow aspects, such as are likely to be measured by our standardized tests. This is readily understandable because of the large place which measurement of the ordinary kind occupies in our thinking and practices. Also, there is a strong attitude on the part of specialists in measurement that a good test is necessarily one which measures a narrow aspect. What is necessary for the study of conceptual development is just the opposite of these ideas. We need an approach that will reflect the pattern or organization of a concept, in a large number of dimensions, and not along any one. If it has not been stated specifically up to this point, it should at least be clear by now that organization is one of the things which measurement does not cover. This is recognized in physical science and in biological sciences; it seems often to be overlooked in educational and psychological studies. Relatively narrow or single dimensions (aspects) can be handled by measurement, but the pattern or organization or structure of these aspects, including their integration or interrelationships within the individual, is a property that requires something more than measurement. We need more adequate methods for the description of complexes. It may be that the continued preference of many college professors, as well as many high-school teachers, for the essay type of test is due to the fact that it reveals these elements of complex structure in the thinking of the individual in a more obvious and satisfying way than objective or short-answer tests normally do. It seems strange that, with a basic and widespread interest in these aspects, there has been so little research interest in this field: How well-rounded is a conceptual area? Is it extended adequately in all directions? This area has been well reviewed in the *Encyclopedia of Educational Research.*[261]

Studies of concept development and understanding probably have been pursued further in arithmetic than in other areas,[262] perhaps in keeping with the growing recognition of the need for making arithmetic meaningful and logical rather than memoriter. Similarly, social-studies concepts have been the subject of some investigation,[263] and drawings [264] and language [265] have been utilized as expressions or evidence of conceptual status and growth. Investigations of vocabulary relate to this field, but are usually not made in sufficient detail to be helpful for the present purpose. Studies of conceptual development are reviewed annually in the *Annual Review of Psychology.*[266]

It is of some interest to examine the structure of language in general, as contrasted to the individual's growth in command of language structure. In an easy-to-read discussion of different structures and changes in them with time, Whatmough describes four structural types which may be called: (1) isolated or highly positional (Chinese); (2) agglutinating, which develops meaning by adding syllables (Turkish); (3) inflections (English, Latin, and many others); (4) polysynthetic, in which the entire sentence, rather than a single word, is the unit of structure (Eskimo).[267] Having a knowledge of such structures, and their changes over time, one can understand what is currently happening to our language and other languages, and predict future trends. One can also (as has been done) indicate certain past conditions or states in advance of their actual discovery. Boas classifies language on the basis of three aspects—vocabulary, phonetics, and structure.[268]

[261] Margaret W. Curti, "Child Development—X, Concepts." *Encyclopedia of Educational Research, op. cit.,* p. 175-78. Thirty-eight references in the bibliography; see also p. 541-42.

[262] Guy M. Wilson, "Arithmetic." *Encyclopedia of Educational Research, op. cit.,* p. 48.

[263] Edwin R. Carr, Edgar B. Wesley, and Wilbur F. Murra, "Social Studies." *Encyclopedia of Educational Research, op cit.,* p. 1225-27.

[264] Florence L. Goodenough, "Child Development—IX, Drawing." *Encyclopedia of Educational Research, op. cit.,* p. 173-74.

[265] Dorothea McCarthy, "Child Development—VIII, Language." *Encyclopedia of Educational Research, op. cit.,* p. 167-70.

See also "Language-development" and "Language-research approaches" in the *Twelve-year Index to the Review of Educational Research,* or in a later edition of the Index.

[266] Usually located in the chapter on "child psychology"; see in particular Vincent Nowlis and Helen H. Nowlis, "Concepts." *Annual Review of Psychology.* Vol. 3. Stanford, Calif.: Annual Reviews, 1952. p. 2-3.

[267] Joshua Whatmough, "Natural Selection in Language." *Scientific American* 186:82-86, April 1952.

[268] Franz Boas, *Race, Language and Culture.* New York: Macmillan Co., 1940. "Language," p. 199-239.

Boas deals mainly with American languages, including Indian. Many studies are reviewed, and different aspects of speech and language are presented by Miller.[269]

One can of course examine the structure of meaning as connected with words and language. This is the field of semantics and has been explored rather fully by many writers up to the present time.[270]

There are many other aspects to the study of language, including logic itself,[271] but it would carry us far afield to refer to them in detail here.

5. **Esthetic structure.** Obviously structure (sometimes called form) is a major part of art. The extent to which structure can be analyzed into elementary components may be a question, but there is no question concerning the basic significance of the over-all effect of the total structure.[272] There are certain general principles which can be analyzed with regard to form, and these are commonly presented in books dealing with art in the design or style of furniture; one can pick out certain specific elements of any design, and attend to them. That is, the different periods of furniture design can be characterized by analytical description. The Fortieth Yearbook of the National Society for the Study of Education, just cited, has chapters on Flower Arrangement, Landscape Design, Public Architecture, City Planning, Handicrafts, Clothing, Dancing, and other forms or activities. These chapters, however, are devoted primarily to the functioning of such activities in American life of today rather than to an analysis of structural principles. Dancing has been subjected to analysis in terms of rhythmic patterns,[273] and of course poetry has, since medieval times, been organized or structured according to certain meters that form units of rhythm. Music, with its measure, has followed the same pattern. The structure of sounds that are produced by different musical instruments has been the subject of study for a half-century or more by physicists, and more recently the human voice has been subjected to minute analysis, particu-

[269] George A. Miller, "Speech and Language." *Handbook of Experimental Psychology, op. cit.,* Chapter 21, p. 789-810.

[270] Samuel I. Hayakawa, *Language in Thought and Action.* New York: Harcourt Brace and Co., 1949. 307 p.
Alfred Korzybski, *op. cit.*
For a reference to various other sources, and some discussion of their relative values, see the presentation in George A. Lundberg, *Foundations of Sociology, op. cit.,* p. 43-44.

[271] Max Black, *Critical Thinking:* An Introduction to Logic and Scientific Thinking. Second Edition. New York: Prentice-Hall, 1952. Part 2, "Language," p. 161-246.
The structure of logic is of course also involved, and this has been developed most in connection with deductive logic; see, in the same source, Part 1, "Deductive Logic," p. 3-158.

[272] Thomas Munro, "The Analysis of Form in Art." National Society for the Study of Education, *Art in American Life and Education.* Fortieth Yearbook. Chicago: University of Chicago Press, 1941. Chapter 24, p. 349-68.

[273] Betty L. Thompson, *Fundamentals of Rhythm and Dance.* New York: A. S. Barnes and Co., 1933. 230 p.

larly by researchers in the Bell Telephone Laboratories.[274] With such equipment it is possible to make remarkably detailed analyses of speech sounds and thus learn how infants begin to talk,[275] as well as helping persons to learn to speak better through watching visual patterns of their speech.[276] While the visual representation of the structure of speech sounds may not, in itself, be a matter of art, we would probably agree that good speech is pleasing and, therefore, has esthetic qualities. The sound spectograph is simply a means of analyzing and identifying the structural qualities which make for pleasantness or unpleasantness.

It would thus appear that, while certain forms of fine art present difficulties to attempts at structural analysis, there are still many esthetic forms which have been subjected to analysis. Even a physicist has been prompted to write, in a more or less engagingly lay fashion, of the pattern element in literature and music, as well as in his own field.[277]

## IV. DYNAMICS: FORCES AND SYSTEMS (IN ANALYSIS)

In the discussion of analysis, namely, things or aspects to be looked for in the analytical process, and concepts to guide one in his work in seeking an adequate description by analytical methods, we have thus far treated the three large topics: general aspects, components, and what we might call integrating aspects (form, organization, and structure). In the present topic we shall turn to the more active or dynamic aspects and center attention on them as objects of our analytical inquiry.

It was pointed out in the last topic that it was not entirely possible to make a distinction between form and function, between organization and activity, but that any such attempt to do so was primarily a matter of convenience. When, therefore, we deal in the present topic with dynamic aspects and with the systems or mechanisms through which forces are channeled, we are not denying the structures that were previously treated, but are simply building on them. That is, we are assuming whatever physical structure may be necessary and are here dealing with what might be regarded as the structure of dynamics. The discussion, however, will not be

274 The basic references, together with other material on the physics of speech, are given in J.C.R. Lieklider and George A. Miller, "The Perception of Speech." *Handbook of Experimental Psychology, op. cit.,* Chapter 26, p. 1,040-74.

275 Arthur W. Lynip, "The Use of Magnetic Devices in the Collection and Analysis of the Preverbal Utterances of an Infant." *Genetic Psychology Monographs* 44:221-62; 1951. This study is reviewed, along with others, in the *Annual Review of Psychology*, Vol. 4, p. 11-12, 1953.

276 See "Hearing Speech and Speech-like Sounds." *Annual Review of Psychology*, Vol 4, p. 103-107, 1953.

277 William H. George, *op. cit.,* Chapter 7, "Pattern," p. 115-32.

entirely limited to what this phrase may connote; we would say rather that the present topic deals with structure in action. We may at times have to dip back into a discussion of the structure itself, in order to relate it to the dynamic aspects.

The discussion of dynamics is necessarily closely related to causes and causation. This is unavoidable. We shall not, however, here go into the theoretical side of causation, leaving that to the later chapter on experimentation, where one is necessarily involved with causation as a concept and as a theory. We are here concerned rather with the content of the notion of causation, namely, specific causes or forces or other conditions which operate to bring about certain results.

The present treatment will be divided into three rather large topics, as follows:

1. Force
2. Dynamic systems
3. External (extra-personal) factors.

Dynamics are simply one special class of general aspects, treated earlier in a perfectly general way. They are, however, a class of aspects having peculiar interest, and they are, therefore, given special attention here. As in the preceding sections, our interest is in noting areas which are in need of further study, and in considering aspects that may profitably be looked for when an analytical study is undertaken. It is worth while to sense the significance and importance of these aspects through seeing where they fit into the general scheme of thought. The treatment here is, therefore, primarily aimed at the conceptual side; that is, at building up a conceptual framework from which to view the various phenomena or objects that one may wish to study. This is done in part through calling attention to studies which have already been made in these different areas. By reading the discussions and reports referred to, one will be able to obtain further details with which to structure his thought, and will become more intimately acquainted with procedures that have been tested in specific areas.

In this topic we are getting to the central questions with regard to "What makes things go?" These are usually questions of great interest.

## 1.  Force

It should be obvious that all the energy we have for living comes from the food we eat. Being human, and being intensely preoccupied with our decision-making and evaluating processes, in other words choices, we are prone to overlook the source of the energy with which we carry on our intellectual and emotional lives. Perhaps a great many persons would actually assume that they created energy, as when they exert great effort. Such ideas may be no handicap in lay thinking, but teachers and others who have the welfare of children to consider, as well as their own, must be aware of the ultimate dependence of energy upon proper nutrition. Further, the practical availability of energy for learning and for desirable social interaction (for living) depends not only on food but upon the health of the physiological system which utilizes that energy and makes it available for the human activity. Professional persons also must be prepared to go a step further and recognize that mental health is of just as great importance as physical health, perhaps much more so, because of its great power not only over learning and emotional processes but over physiological health as well. One will not long find a sick mind in a well body, because the various physiological processes of the body are subject to the mind and the emotions in the same way that the muscles are. It seems strange that this fact is so hard to realize; that is, everyone knows that his mind (using common terminology) controls his gross bodily movements, has some influence on his emotional feelings, but he seems to differentiate other bodily activities to such an extent that he is surprised to learn that his general condition of bodily health is itself to a large extent the product of the stimulation of his nervous system—more specifically, the result of the content of his thinking and its emotional colorings.

Perhaps, after all, it is not so surprising that the layman, or the social scientist, is somewhat unprepared for the newer scientific views of mental and bodily health, when the movement is relatively new even among the medical profession. It was in 1935 that Dunbar published a summary of some two thousand references dealing with the mind-body relationships. More recent bibliographies contain many more references.[278] The American Society for Psychosomatic Problems was organized in 1943, and the magazine *Psychosomatic Medicine* was started just a few years before. This area has been briefly treated for educators in the *Review of Educational Research;*[279] this article gives an orienting overview and a bibliography of sixty references, which will enable any interested person to secure a start in this field.

[278] Helen F. Dunbar, *Emotions and Bodily Changes:* Survey of Literature on Psychosomatic Relations, 1910-1945. Third Edition. New York: Columbia University Press, 1946. 605 p. (First Edition, 1935. 595 p.)

Association for Research in Nervous and Mental Diseases, *Life Stress and Bodily Disease.* Baltimore: Williams and Wilkins, 1950. 1,135 p. Includes bibliography.

Stanley Cobb, *Emotions and Clinical Medicine.* New York: W. W. Norton and Co., 1950. 243 p. Bibliography on p. 225-34.

Franz Alexander, *Psychosomatic Medicine.* New York: W. W. Norton and Co., 1950. 300 p. Bibliography on p. 272-88.

[279] Reynold A. Jensen, "Relationships Between Physical and Mental Health." *Review of Educational Research* 19:371-78; December 1949.

Thus far, we have been discussing the general subject of the energy available to the human being for general purposes of study and living, and the importance of having this energy available for effective use through conditions of good mental and physical health. Those persons interested in physical education and allied subjects have this same general interest, but they are also concerned with the use of energy in physical activities. For this area, a number of special interests exist and many special research techniques have been developed. The specialized treatises in this field are adequate and we will not review them here.[280]

We turn now from physical or physiological force to the more psychological side, the stimuli which lie behind physical expression. In simple terms, the fundamental question is, What makes people do things? Perhaps a more fundamental question is, Why do they do anything at all? On the other hand, we may be curious as to why we do some things so intently, determinedly, and sometimes violently.

This has been the subject of psychological study for many years. A number of different writers have presented classified schemes of urges, drives, and other named things which they thought accounted for human activity. An excellent history of this whole field of interest is given by Boring.[281] We have all heard about witchcraft, even in modern times; for example, in 1692 in our own colonies. We may not have realized, however, that the attitude which led men to see witches wherever they chose was a remnant from the Middle Ages of a feeling toward persons having motivational and nervous disorders which we today should probably classify under the terms neuroses or psychoses. In the Middle Ages every man was supposed to have perfectly clear and unrestricted freedom of the will, except when under the influence of magic or demons. With such a conception of the causation of mental disturbances and disorders, sound research was impossible. Without a reasonably appropriate set of concepts, analytical research will not produce dependable knowledge. All forms of research yield answers in terms of the concepts in which the researcher conceives his problem.[282]

Boring traces the interest in motivation (in the dynamics of human be-

[280] American Association for Health, Physical Education, and Recreation, *Research Methods Applied to Health, Physical Education, and Recreation, op. cit.,* 535 p. See especially Chapter 10, "Research Methods in the Mechanics of Sports and Physical Education Activities."
American Association for Health, Physical Education, and Recreation, *Physical Fitness:* Supplement to the *Research Quarterly,* Vol. 12, No. 2, p. 298-493; May 1941.
[281] Edwin G. Boring. *A History of Experimental Psychology.* Second Edition. New York: Appleton-Century-Crofts, Inc., 1950. Chapter 26, "Dynamic Psychology," p. 692-734.
[282] Thomas R. McConnell, Douglas E. Scates, and Frank N. Freeman, *The Conceptual Structure of Educational Research.* Supplementary Educational Monographs, No. 55. Chicago: University of Chicago Press, 1942. 47 p.

havior) through the early French period of concern with hysteria and hypnotism, through the eighteenth-century emphasis on hedonism (the desire to enjoy pleasure and avoid pain) in England, through the psycho-analytic movement beginning with Freud in Vienna, Austria, in the last half of the nineteenth century, and on up to the present time. It will be remembered that William James emphasized instincts, and Edward L. Thorndike prepared long lists of them. William McDougall emphasized purposes, but began his system with instincts, relating a basic emotion to each instinct.

This kind of dynamic psychology was popular because it was so simple and direct. It fell later into scientific disrepute, when psychologists discovered that anyone can make up his own list of instincts and that there is no way to prove that one list is more certainly correct than another. McDougall seemed to have borrowed too much from the faculty psychology of his Scottish ancestors who confused description with explanation. If you write well, they would have said, you have a faculty for writing. If you fight much, McDougall implied, you have an instinct for fighting.[283]

One will grasp something of the difficulty of formulating appropriate concepts in this area by considering the many different terms that have been employed; for example, sensory stimulation, reflexes, conditioned responses, instincts, basic drives, secondary drives, emotions, urges, ergs, deprivations, needs, appetites, rhythms, attitudes, valences, desire to dominate, desires, wants, interests, curiosity, aversions, anxieties, feelings of inferiority, obsessions, compulsions, imitation, rivalry, will power, determination, level of aspiration, hopes, incentives, rewards, goals, purposes, encouragement, and motivation. The list could be extended. It is clear that the "thing" which moves human beings to do something has many different aspects. It should also be fairly clear that we are not here talking about any one "thing," but a very complex human organism in a complex of stimuli. To view the matter of personal psychological force in any very simple fashion is to take a position which will demand answers that are very unfaithful to the realities of the situation.

While the detailed study of the adequacy of different factors or mechanisms as causes would properly be dealt with by experimental methods, experimentation is not fruitful unless it has been preceded by, and is accompanied by, a considerable amount of analysis, both logical and observational. The selection and conceptualizing of aspects which are of value in the larger frame of thought, and the integrating of the findings of analysis into a coherent system, are all parts of the descriptive process. Description feeds and, in turn, is fed by experimentation.

283 Quoted from Boring, *op. cit.,* p. 718.

A brief yet well outlined treatment of the entire subject of motivation is presented by Young.[284] This treatment points out that activity has at least three aspects—that of energy, purpose or direction, and the contribution of past experience. Much of the psychological experimentation on motivation has been connected with learning; reviews from this point of view have been presented by Miller and by Mowrer.[285] The subject is also dealt with in the *Annual Review of Psychology,* perhaps in a chapter on learning or on physiological psychology. There are a number of textbooks on the subject. The three references given here contain substantial bibliographies of the leading works.

In discussing motivation, it is often convenient to divide the consideration of factors into two classes—those stimuli which originate within the organism, such as tissue hunger and thoughts, and those stimulating conditions that exist in the environment. The former are denoted "motives" and the latter as "incentives." The distinction, like most dichotomies, is difficult to maintain, for an organism (including persons) does not in general react directly to the environment, but rather to its sensory and perceptual picture of the environment. Thus the incentives, if they are to be effective, must be internalized; must be perceived as desirable, and they then become inner stimuli and these fall in the class of motives. It is probably convenient to speak of incentives as an external class of conditions, and it is customary in psychology to do so; but as a matter of simple convenience we should not be constrained from saying that one may be *motivated* by incentives. One should recognize that, strictly, the matter is somewhat more complex, since it is one's inner response to the incentive (accepting or ignoring or rejecting) that will determine his motivational state; but so long as this is borne in mind, the more direct statement will suffice for most occasions. Incentives may be regarded as indirect motivators, and as probably relating more often to secondary (learned) drives than to the reduction (satisfaction) of basic needs. Some of the objection to the use of incentives in school work undoubtedly stems from a recognition that they are likely to satisfy the more superficial needs at the expense of attention and effort directed toward meeting basic needs, some of which play havoc with learning and with adjustment and wholesome growth when they are not properly met.

The second category which we would make might be called ideational, or abstract ideational, to emphasize that it does not grow immediately out

[284] Paul T. Young, "Motivation." *Encyclopedia of Educational Research, op. cit.,* p. 755-61.

[285] Neal E. Miller, "Learnable Drives and Rewards." *Handbook of Experimental Psychology, op. cit.,* Chapter 13, p. 435-72; see also Chapters 12, 14.

Orval H. Mowrer, "Motivation." *Annual Review of Psychology.* Vol. 3. Stanford, Calif.: Annual Reviews, 1952. p. 419-38.

of the situation. In this category we would put well established ideas, of goals, purposes, values; and perhaps we should also have to include well established habits of activity which might be touched off not by any specific stimulus, but simply by one's habit of doing certain things under very general circumstances, such as eating lunch whether one be hungry or not; dressing in conventional ways without thought as to why, and so on. This category would thus cover the well established routines of behavior and those which were on the more or less well established ideational level. These first two categories, in general usage and in educational usage, probably would be regarded as "motives," although routine habitual activities might simply be regarded as habits. Relating these first two categories to motivation agrees with the dictionary definition, one of which states: "That within the individual, rather than without, which incites him to action; any idea, need, emotion, or organic state that prompts to an action." [286]

It is possible that the strong behaviorist would regard tissue hunger and ideas as being the same sort of thing, but we can concede that only in a very strained sense. We would add further that we doubt that the term *motivation* is properly applied except when the cortex, involving matters of choice, is involved. That is, we scarcely regard it as appropriate to use *motivation* in connection with the eye-wink, or the knee-jerk, or the normal heartbeat.

Stimulating factors which are initiated in the environment would include at least two classes. Inasmuch as we are thinking of reactions that involve the nervous system, we will exclude from the discussion such gross physical responses as any physical object would have to its environment, such as responding to gravity, to temperature, and so on. Even these, however, cause some problem in classification, because they sometimes affect the nervous system. It is important, however, to point out that, aside from these responses of any physical object, the organism as a whole never reacts directly to its environment, but always to its sensory or perceptual stimulations originating in the environment. Again, we emphasize that this distinction is important, because it is very easy to think (erroneously) that the forces are in the environment rather than in the individual. Physical forces are undoubtedly in the environment, but psychological forces (by which we mean energy released in an organism) are in the organism itself, and go out of the response to sensations and perceptions. The importance of this distinction perhaps becomes clear in connection with perception.

In the environmentally initiated factors, we must recognize two classes; the first class would be strong negative stimuli, such as loud noises, extreme

286 *Webster's New Collegiate Dictionary*. Springfield, Mass.: G. and C. Merriam Co., 1949. p. 550.

heat or cold, loss of support, or sudden changes in direction of movement (although of course the sense organs for these latter sensations are from internal organs). These sensations may lead to the startle response or to withdrawing, and to emotions. But again, we would question that the term *motivation* is to be applied to these sensations until after the initial response, that is, until the response becomes to some extent deliberate. These could be recognized as a separate class of stimuli, but they are not particularly different from hunger, thirst, and so on, in that they are stresses directly on sensory systems and need not involve the higher brain centers, although of course eventually they do, in the same fashion that hunger does. Awareness is an attribute of what we may call consciousness, but awareness is not in the least necessary for many activities which the human body is prepared to perform. Perhaps these immediate sensations should be left under the simple head of stimuli.

The second set of environmentally initiated conditions may be referred to as perceptual. It is here that we find the greatest need for differentiation between what is in the environment and what is in the individual, because the stimulus in the environment may be very mild, yet exert a tremendous release of energy by the individual, as when he interprets his view of the environment as being threatening or alarming, even though it may not be. Again, a second individual with the same pattern of sensations might interpret the environment in an utterly different way and release no more than routine energy.

At this point we are prepared to ask how one is to distinguish between incentive and motivation. If persons in the environment set up a promise of reward, and the individual does not perceive the reward as being of any interest to him, is his response to be regarded as initiated by the environment or by his own internal interpretative scheme? On the other hand, if he is stimulated by the proffered incentive, are we to give a different answer? That is, the fact that an incentive is appealing is due to something within the person himself—presumably his goals, or standards, or ideas, or values; and, since it is these ideational or habitual responses which determine the reaction to the incentive, and since clearly these reactions are from within the organism itself, we cannot but feel that the term *incentive* is misleading. That is, the incentive has no appeal except for what is already internal to the organism. We cannot help seeing that the person is motivated by the incentive.

In summary, the force that a person exerts may be muscular, in the sense of physical work; but we are more interested in psychological force, which represents the impact of the individual's total behavior upon other persons, both individually and as groups. This impact may be in the form of new ideas which are accepted or rejected by others, it may take the form of persuasion or exhortation, and it has various other qualities suggested by the words forcefulness, positiveness, weakness, indecisive, and so on. All of these forms of expression must originate in energy received from chemicals taken into the body, in the form of food, medicine, and drink. The release of energy (really a translation) within the body may be accomplished directly by chemical means, and in part by neural means (thoughts, reflex actions, etc.), although even neural impulses may conceivably be chemical, if one wishes so to classify them. The emotions, which represent a complex, rather widely ramified reaction of the organism, with consequent awareness of certain physiological states giving rise to feelings, contribute their part to the release and expression of energy, perhaps through chemical means (stimulation of the glands) and through the nervous system also. Emotions may either intensify action or inhibit action, but, even in inhibiting, they represent an intensified reaction within the system. They are, therefore, a part of the general mechanism of expressing personal force.

The concept of psychological force is no more nebulous than is the concept of force in the physical world. In physical science, the concept has been built up solely in terms of effects produced. We can do the same thing in the psychological or human fields. Thus, presumably, the effective force of a leader (one who can put forth acceptable propositions and stimulate or guide the line of activity of a group) is greater than is the psychological force of another person who cannot do these things. Both, however, may expend the same amount of energy within their own bodies. The problem of psychological force is, therefore, a matter of the effectiveness with which energy released within the human body can be utilized by the person for transmitting stimulation to other persons.

Our reference to personal effectiveness, in connection with psychological force, is made from the point of view of calling attention to one facet, or one particular kind, of this personal force. Our interest here is simply in exploring concepts in the interest of a better description or definition. This is not the place to take up the different ways in which an individual may be more effective: that is, how the teacher can best teach (with the given personality which the teacher has at the time and with a particular set of pupil personalities before him); the way in which supervisors can best supervise, whether when dealing with professional persons, as in education, or when dealing with more routine workers; the ways in which a leader can be most effective, and so on. These are all areas in which personal effectiveness, as one kind of personal force, can be increased. They lie outside the scope of the present topic.

We are not here implying that it is desirable for a person to be as forceful as possible. We are simply attempting to "rough in" the general concept. Further, we would not omit various qualitative factors in force, such as acceptability versus irritating and disturbing qualities of one's manner of expression. Psychological force is to be viewed as having qualitative aspects of pleasantness and engagingness just as much as it has aspects of strength, or the degree to which it cannot, with effort, be resisted.

If in educational thinking more attention were paid to this concept of psychological force (effectiveness), we should have less emphasis on, and perhaps less contentment with, learning of the type that is primarily absorptive and which does not lead toward thoughtful interactions with other persons. Fortunately, this latter emphasis has come into education very strongly during the present half-century, in part under the influence of John Dewey and the various groups which have followed up his initial leadership, and also through considerable emphasis generally on group dynamics and the importance of personal interaction. We have not as yet adequate means for measuring psychological force, but explorations are going forward. When this subject has received adequate research attention, it will occupy as fundamental a place in thinking, research, and educational practice as physical force does in the physical sciences. Up to the present time, personal effectiveness has received very widespread recognition in our society by all of us thinking on the lay level. It has received very little research attention. One form of study is connected with leadership. Another type of investigation grows out of the large interest in small-group participation and relates to the effectiveness of an individual as a member of a small group having some objective. Again, the ratings of persons who work on teams, or other forms of organization, have a bearing on the subject, but in general the field is still wide open.

One way of thinking of personal psychological force is to look at it in terms of its energizing and driving value for the individual in connection with the accomplishment of some purpose. Does it stimulate him to the requisite hard work? Does it stimulate some determination, an undeviating adherence to a certain position or a chosen course without being deterred readily and easily? In other words, the amount of psychological force operating within an individual, with respect to a specific or a large purpose, may be judged by its inertia value, just as it is in physical science.

In summary, then, we would say that psychological force is one of the aspects which is worthy of research attention in any analysis of the behavior of human beings. It is, in fact, a matter of the greatest interest. It may not have been studied so much because of the difficulty of doing so, but any research field will remain difficult so long as it is unattacked.

This discussion has called attention to a number of aspects of force which are of importance for study. First there is the initial development of physiological energy—the transformation of the energy stored in food into energy available for muscular activity, for thinking and feeling, and for carrying on the ordinary bodily processes, including the essential warmth of the body's interior. It takes energy to learn, properly directed energy. A second aspect for study is the class of things which incite one to action, feeling, or thought. There is as yet no systematic list that has been widely accepted. Perhaps one will have to grow. The third phase of the subject is concerned with the expression of personal effort, either in physical work or in thinking toward a given goal. A fourth aspect of personal psychological force is to be thought of in terms of one's social effectiveness—the extent to which he can, under different circumstances, and as appropriate, fit into a situation in an acquiescent role, doing what is reasonably called for, or assume a role of leadership, or in other ways persuade, stimulate, and alter the thinking of other persons.

The problem is this: in analyzing the totality of life, with its various activities, can we abstract from the complex of situations those dynamic pushes and pulls which are useful in gauging the strength of tendencies to do, or not to do? This is a rather abstract goal, for it is general and is not connected with individual situations. Physical science, however, has found that the concept of force is useful in many ways. It is, in fact, one of the most important aspects of interrelations in physical science.

It is sometimes argued that force is not a cause; it is simply a concept abstracted from certain results or consequences. The matter seems to us to be basically semantic rather than actual. The whole question of what a cause is now is so much under debate among scientists in all fields that we question whether the distinction referred to is important. The matter is made more difficult when we recognize that engineers recognize static or stationary force, as well as that force which changes the rate of movement. For many purposes it is convenient to think of force as a causal influence; the fact that the force has antecedents simply makes it the same as all other causes; they too have antecedents.

Lewin was very much interested, at least in the earlier part of his work, in forces. His monograph on the measurement of psychological forces [287] has an attractive title, but the content is more elaborate, complex, and abstract than most readers will care for. With some exaggeration, we can, nevertheless, give the general flavor of the work by saying that a half-

---

[287] Kurt Lewin, *The Conceptual Representation and the Measurement of Psychological Forces*. Contributions to Psychological Theory, Vol. 1, No. 4. Serial No. 4. Durham, N. C.: Duke University Press, 1938. 247 p.

dozen new concepts are invented for each page of text. While we are constantly emphasizing the complexity of psychological life, and especially of the structure and function of the nervous system, we must concede that a certain amount of simplicity is helpful in constructing and understanding a thought model. It may be that certain of Lewin's ideas could be abstracted from the mass of material and made of general service. Other writing by Lewin dealing with forces may be found by consulting this subject in the index to a collection of his earlier papers.[288]

One way of measuring, or assessing in a general way, the strength of force is to determine the strength of the need. We shall take a number of illustrative statements from Symonds' writing.[289]

Of psychologies there are many varieties—behavioristic, gestalt, structural, and others, but all aim in their own way at a better understanding of the mind of man. Dynamic psychology studies the whole individual and how he adjusts to the situations—both outer and inner—that he confronts. Whereas behavioristic psychology concerns itself particularly with observable behavior and gestalt psychology with the way an individual perceives his world, dynamic psychology is concerned with the ways in which an individual satisfies his inner drives from the physical and social world in which he lives (Preface, p. ix).

No behavior has a single cause and there is room for explanations on a number of levels. However, ... most behavior has unconscious as well as conscious determinants and is unconsciously directed more often than most persons are willing to admit.

This book ... does not deal with the influence of physical and organic factors on human adjustment but limits itself to those factors which help to determine the formation of personality and character which are here called *dynamic,* that is, those which grow out of the psychological needs of the individual and the psychological motives by which an individual attempts to gain satisfaction and status and to avoid pain and the lowering of self-esteem. ... The dynamic processes herein described apply equally to the normal and the abnormal (Preface, p. xiii).

The recognition of needs of these types lies outside the scope of what some writers (mainly, the laboratory experimentalists) are prepared to give attention to or even admit. For most of us, however, these motivations which carry some emotional feeling tone are very real and are deserving of study. A treatment of drives [290] contains a discussion of many types of motivation that will not be found in the writings of other workers

---

[288] Kurt Lewin, *A Dynamic Theory of Personality:* Selected Papers. Translated by Donald K. Adams and Karl E. Zener. New York: McGraw-Hill Book Co., 1935. 286 p.

[289] Quoted from Percival M. Symonds, *The Dynamics of Human Adjustment.* New York: Appleton-Century-Crofts, 1946. 666 p. This volume contains a bibliography of 883 annotated references at the back; a somewhat reduced form of the same textual material was published three years later:
Percival M. Symonds, *Dynamic Psychology.* New York: Appleton-Century-Crofts, 1949. 413 p.

[290] Percival M. Symonds, *op. cit.,* Chapter 2, "Drives," p. 12-49 of the 1946 volume. The same chapter also appears in the 1949 edition.

who avoid psychoanalytic views. The laboratory experimentalist may not be so much interested in specific emotional reactions, because he is not so certain that he can handle them in his laboratory. But the clinically-interested psychologist is free to point out the fact that "hate in the form of aggression and hostility . . . directed out toward other persons is only too well known. The management of these fundamental tendencies to hate constitutes one of the major problems of civilized life." [291]

Maslow has suggested that needs arrange themselves in a hierarchy going from the most elemental and physiological to those which represent the higher development of the individual. He would place needs on five levels: the first level would comprise the basic physiological needs of hunger, sex, and so on. The second level would comprise the needs of safety, that is, of avoiding external dangers that might result in harm to the individual from the outside. In the third level there is the need for love—that is, to be given love, warmth and affection by another person. On the fourth level is the need for esteem—that is, self-respect, self-esteem, and also the respect and esteem of others. Finally, there is the need for self-realization, of being able to accomplish and achieve—to paint a picture, to secure a position, to occupy a place in one's group. Maslow suggests that these represent a hierarchy of five levels. Gratification of needs on the first or more basic levels frees a person for the higher social needs; for instance, if a person's physical needs and his needs for safety and love are taken care of, he can turn his attention and devote his energies to the more distinctly ego needs and efforts toward self-realization on the higher levels. On the other hand, if these more basic needs are not met, they claim priority, and activities on the higher levels must be temporarily postponed.

Those persons in whom a need has been satisfied are best equipped to deal with deprivations of that need in the future. It is the individual who has grown up in a secure and happy home, not deprived of his basic needs, who is best able to stand such privations in later life, while the individual who has suffered insecurities in childhood is the one who is first to succumb to difficulties and deprivations in later life. This principle was verified over and over during the war: the emotionally secure individual was the one able to stand the greatest shock of war conditions.

The healthy man is one whose basic needs have been met so that he is principally motivated by his needs to develop and actualize his highest potentialities. The maladjusted and neurotic person, on the other hand, is one who is dominated by his more basic needs. Since his previous insecurities have never made him feel entirely safe with regard to gratification of his more basic needs, he is never quite free to turn his attention to activities of self-realization and achievement.[292]

Whether or not the classification of these needs or drives that move a person to specific and general action is scientifically correct is not a matter

[291] Percival M. Symonds, *op. cit.,* 1946, p. 42.
[292] Quoted from Percival M. Symonds, *op. cit.,* 1946, p. 42-43; similarly, in the 1949 edition, p. 35-37. Symonds gives the following references to Maslow's original works:
Abraham H. Maslow, "Preface to Motivation Theory." *Psychosomatic Medicine* 5:85-92; 1943.
Abraham H. Maslow, "A Theory of Human Motivation." *Psychological Review* 50:370-96; 1943.

of major importance. The principal aspect of the classification is its utility in suggesting that the individual's attention will be taken up with the satisfaction of certain needs before others.

Perhaps all of us have wondered about anxiety. At times, it seems to be a normal part of life and, at other times, it seems to get out of hand. The proposal is now being advanced that there are two kinds of anxiety which may respectively be called normal and neurotic.[293] These differ from fear. Fear is regarded by May as a normal reaction to danger—a somewhat "impersonal" type of emotion, "whereas anxiety involves the very essence of one's psychic existence." One's concept of one's self is, when normal and wholesome, a systematized, organized, well integrated picture of

many competing trends and demands within the total personality, and it is when this unified whole is threatened that the individual experiences anxiety. Fear may be . . . a non-ego-involving event. Anxiety, on the other hand, always affects, as May repeatedly says, the very core of personality. . . . Normal anxiety is associated with conflicts wherein all the elements are fully conscious or easily capable of becoming so. Neurotic anxiety, on the other hand, occurs [when a conflict] has been resolved, not by the normal process of compromise, synthesis, integration, but by the expedient of repression. Now, when subsequently there is a threatened "return of the repressed," the individual may experience acute anxiety but be unable to identify fully its source or meaning. When this happens the anxiety is said to be "neurotic." [294]

The view by May is different from the one presented years ago by Freud, and is again somewhat different from any views which May summarizes in his book. Whether or not it will ever be possible to test these different views experimentally is something that may be wondered. The experiment is not the answer to all our needs. It may be that the decision between many competing theories will have to rest with clinical experience. Certainly, we have passed the time when views are to be accepted on the basis of the facility and plausibility with which any writer can state them. It is possible that a number of different views might be equally correct, but that one would be more serviceable than another.[295] Some resolution of the differences in view may grow out of the increasing knowledge in many different areas of personality study. Meanwhile, the advancing of various views as

[293] Rollo May, *The Meaning of Anxiety*. New York: Ronald Press Co., 1950. 376 p.
[294] Quoted from O. Hobart Mowrer, "Motivation." *Annual Review of Psychology,* Vol. 3, p. 436. Stanford, Calif.: Annual Reviews, 1952.
    A reviewer of May's work quotes: "the fears of man, especially the diffuse, free-floating anticipation of some catastrophe or personal threat, with the resultant feelings of uncertainty, dread, and the helplessness of psychic impotence, play a major role in the lives of many persons." George F. J. Lehner, *Scientific Monthly* 71:130; August 1950.
[295] It is to be recalled that, in physical science, there have been two competing views with regard to the nature of light for nearly 300 years. In this century, they were both proved to be correct. It is possible to have a variety of views that fit a given set of facts equally well. Each one may be useful for certain purposes.

to anxiety and neuroses by different writers sets the stage in a descriptive or explanatory fashion for more intensive analytical research by various means.

It is interesting to note that some research workers can get along without many of the concepts to which we have been referring. These are persons who have avowedly followed the behaviorist type of thinking and, while perhaps not denying that a person has feelings, they believe that science must be based on observable behavior and not on reports of individuals as to feelings and not on a set of concepts that represent inferred or postulated factors, which may be unnecessarily complex. Thus, values, purpose, motive, and so on are dispensed with, and attention is given solely to observed aspects of the situation and the observed behavior. "When the interaction of the observable components of a situation has been described scientifically, purpose and motive have also been described and all scientific 'purposes' have been served." [296]

Perhaps the present writers are more humanists than scientists, compared with such a criterion, for we must admit to some preference for the concepts which are more common in our culture; we like the words (and ideas) involved: purpose, motive, teleology, values, feelings, emotions, and so on. They seem close to the heart of human living. We regard it as a distinct loss rather than a net gain to discard them. The researcher may close his eyes to them and see only what is left, but we suspect that such an investigator is approaching human science through the eyes of the physicist. We have a continuing belief that such conceptions miss much of the reality of life. Machines can be made which "think," but we have yet to hear of a machine that feels. The conceptual schemes of the physicist will encompass the former, but a set of concepts peculiarly adapted to the realm of human living is necessary in order to accommodate the latter.

We turn attention from the individual to large groups. We may as well go directly to society itself and speak of the force of societal groups. These would include nations, persons of various races, of different religious convictions, and even political parties.

In this connection we need but mention intergroup tensions, which at times have led to riots, as well as other forms of persecution and international tensions that sometimes go beyond the bounds of discussion and ordinary expression and lead to wars.

If we are to have any large improvement in the social conditions of mankind, it is essential to learn something about these large forces which exert themselves in societal groups. One will undoubtedly have an initial question as to whether there is such a thing as social (or societal) force. Is not force simply in the insistence or in the attitude of the individual?

[296] George A. Lundberg, *Foundations of Sociology, op. cit.*, p. 222.

The answer is the same as it is for many other organized wholes; group forces are the sum of the psychological forces of the individual person plus an interaction effect which grows out of the fact that there is a group. Something is always added to a group, which is over and beyond the mere existence of a number of cases when taken separately. While writers for generations have argued the point one way and another, there is too much evidence within everyday observation and experience, as well as in the studies of the simpler life of animals, including insects, and even the one-celled animals, for us to avoid the conviction that there are properties in the group which cannot be present in the single case. Thus, one may learn to have a certain antagonism toward groups, because they have been characterized in a certain way, when he would feel no antagonism toward the individuals of that group by virtue of his personal experience with them. On the contrary, an interest in and a feeling of liking for groups can be cultivated in a person who has no experience whatever with individual members of the group.

In many cases, the attitude of an individual is formed for him by the presence of one or more "strong" personalities in his social community who have access to the opinion-molding channels of our society. The study of the forces of any societal group is, therefore, in part a study of the personalities and attitudes of those individuals whom the society chooses for its leaders, or who are in positions of leadership. Outstanding in this respect is the book by Adorno and others, *The Authoritarian Personality,* which seeks to analyze personality structure in terms of attitudes and rigidity.[297] How can the paradox of the person who is "jealous of his independence and inclined to submit blindly to power and to authority" be explained? This book, with its various constituent studies, is but one of a series of Studies In Prejudice, sponsored by the American Jewish Committee. To assume that man is a rational being is to overlook a large part of his nature. Thus, in one of these studies, there is a large body of evidence connecting prejudice with "phenomena beneath the realm of the conscious and the rational." [298]

While these studies have dealt primarily with the forces within the individual, they portray the nature of many persons who become social leaders in certain types of society or in certain social groups. The methods of work of such persons when they become leaders are dealt with in another study in this same series.[299] This book reports a study of the techniques of

[297] Theodor W. Adorno and Others, *The Authoritarian Personality.* New York: Harper and Bros., 1950. 990 p.

[298] Nathan W. Ackerman and Marie Jahoda, *Anti-Semitism and Emotional Disorder.* New York: Harper and Bros., 1950. 135 p.

[299] Leo Lowenthal and Norbert Guterman, *Prophets of Deceit.* New York: Harper and Bros., 1949. 164 p.

the American agitators of our own time and, through analyzing some of their speeches and writings, reveals the means by which they translate uncertain feelings among people into the beliefs and the action patterns that they desire to stimulate. Along this same general line of social issues are a volume on prejudice,[300] and a study on the motivation of radicals, which points out that the political radical who characteristically urges reforms, and hence starts social forces, is likely to be represented by a certain type of personality.[301]

Every school administrator and, to a lesser extent, the teachers are aware of pressures on the schools. In fact, many groups exist in America for the express purpose of getting things done in our society that they want done. Sometimes, they want changes brought about in the public schools and sometimes they desire to prevent changes. An analysis of the nature of these groups and their activities has been made from time to time, and we cite one recent study [302] and also a report which analyzes the nature of the problem and discusses underlying factors in the current waves of attacks on civil liberties and on democratic education.[303] The American Association of School Administrators has recently published a yearbook dealing with public relations as one positive form of dealing with pressures, which are well known in all forms of public administration.[304]

In the light of the considerable amount of conflict that persists in modern society, Bernard has suggested the establishment of an Institute of Conflict Analysis, in order to develop theories and practical procedures for dealing with such problems.[305]

Human groups can be studied from many different aspects. One may be concerned with the forces that tend to hold them together and which lead to effective activity or block effective activity along given lines. Three sections are given to these topics in a recent book, namely, group cohesiveness, group pressures on the individual, and group locomotion toward goals.[306] It is sound to recognize forces that hold groups together, and

---

[300] Gordon W. Allport, *Prejudice:* A Problem in Causation. Supplement Series to the *Journal of Social Issues,* No. 4, November 1950, p. 4-25.
[301] Thelma H. McCormack, "The Motivation of Radicals." *American Journal of Sociology* 56:17-24; July 1950.
[302] Association for Supervision and Curriculum Development, *Forces Affecting American Education.* Washington: The Association, 1953. 208 p.
[303] Ernest O. Melby and Morton Puner, Editors, *Freedom and Public Education.* New York: Frederick A. Praeger, 1953. 314 p.
[304] American Association of School Administrators, *Public Relations for American's Schools.* Twenty-eighth Yearbook. Washington: The Association, 1950. 327 p.
[305] Jessie Bernard, "Where Is the Modern Sociology of Conflict?" *American Journal of Sociology* 56:11-16; July 1950. See also her *American Community Behavior,* 1949.
[306] Dorwin Cartwright and Alvin Zander, Editors, *Group Dynamics:* Research and Theory. Evanston, Ill.: Row, Peterson and Co., 1953. Parts 2, 3, 4. Some of these same studies were originally published in the reference below. Also see footnote 243.
Harold Guetzkow, Editor, *Groups, Leadership and Men:* Research in Human Relations. Pittsburgh: Carnegie Press, 1951. 293 p.

forces that tend to tear them apart, just the same as the physical scientists have found forces within the atom that tend to hold it together and those that tend to tear it apart. To those references that have been given, we may add a check list by Brown for indicating the cohesiveness of a group which has been working together, as judged by those who participated in it.[307] Another writer has dealt with family solidarity which, again, represents the interplay between centripetal and centrifugal forces.[308]

**International relations.** The great forces which develop between large groups of people, such as nations, may lead on the one hand to greater security, and on the other hand to tension and war. At the present time, wars have become a catastrophe of tremendous proportions and all persons who are concerned with the welfare of society give thought to this problem. Analyses made to date indicate that our earlier thinking was entirely too simplified. Before World War II, many intelligent persons seemed to feel that we could have peace simply by wanting it. Possibly so; but further structural analysis of the forces which cause tensions between nations would indicate that the desire would have to be very strong, very widespread, and would require appropriate channels for its implementation. Furthermore, there would undoubtedly have to be other channels established for draining off some of the forces that develop. In other words, when one wishes to avoid a lightning bolt, he may set up a lightning rod which helps relieve the vast potential between the earth and a cloud overhead, so that the potential is dissipated and does not build up into the form of a great lightning stroke. This knowledge, however, did not come without many years of careful descriptive, analytical, and experimental study of lightning and the forces which produce it. We must expect to give equal attention to the great forces that develop between large groups of people, if we are to be as successful in avoiding the full destructive forms of conflict.

Goodwin Watson has pointed out the differences between our earlier, less sophisticated thinking and a fuller analysis, saying, "It is a little unrealistic to announce that prejudice is unnecessary without examining the forces which are likely to continue to create and perpetuate bias." [309] The problem has been analyzed by eight social scientists at the request of UNESCO, under the editorship of Hadley Cantril.[310] A second study sponsored by UNESCO represents a critical survey of the contributions of

[307] William H. Brown, "Potential Coöperation In Groups." *Phi Delta Kappan* 33:418-19, 435; May 1952.

[308] Luther T. Jansen, "Measuring Family Solidarity." *American Sociological Review* 17:727-33; December 1952.

[309] Goodwin Watson, "Psychological Contributions to World Understanding." *American Psychologist* 4:65-68; February 1949.

[310] Hadley Cantril, Editor, *Tensions that Cause Wars:* Common Statement and Individual Papers by a Group of Social Scientists Brought Together by UNESCO. Urbana: University of Illinois Press, 1950. 303 p.

anthropology, sociology, and clinical and social psychology to the problem of international relations.[311] The investigation does not cover political science, and the entire set of studies reviewed may present an inadequate picture in that "It completely neglects the structure of the international community and the distribution of power among national states as a situational factor conducive to war." [312] Another study sponsored by UNESCO was made under the direction of Gardner Murphy in India, and emphasizes factors that contribute directly to the breakdown of normal social structure.[313] We cite other significant studies in this area without further comment.[314]

## 2. Dynamic Systems

The preceding section has dealt with force. The present section will be devoted to systems through which force operates. The third large section of the treatment of dynamics will present factors that influence these systems from the outside. In the preceding section attention was called to the relatively automatic responses, inclinations, urges, and desires which stimulate the individual to thought, communication, and larger overt action; and, in groups, the tendencies for tensions to form with relation to other groups, the forces that tend to hold groups together and those which tend toward disintegration, the tendencies toward magnification or moderation of individual psychological forces through group processes, and the expression of group forces through organized channels.

Out of the totality of existence, from the welter of objects and events in this universe, the forces that activate, which move things, represent one of the most important aspects for analytical attention. Correspondingly, the system through which these forces operate—the collection of forces which exist at any particular place and the various objects or other condi-

[311] Otto Klineberg, *Tensions Affecting International Understanding.* Social Science Research Council Bulletin 62. New York: The Council, 1950. 238 p.

[312] Review by Barrington Moore, Jr., in *American Sociological Review* 15:686-87; October 1950.

[313] Gardner Murphy, *In the Minds of Men.* New York: Basic Books, 1953. 320 p.

[314] Alfred H. Stanton and E. Stewart Perry, *Personality and Political Crisis.* Glencoe, Ill.: Free Press, 1951. 260 p.

Pitirim A. Sorokin, *Fluctuation of Social Relationships, War, and Revolution.* Social and Cultural Dynamics, Vol. 3. New York: American Book Co., 1937. 630 p.

Gardner Murphy, Editor, *Human Nature and Enduring Peace.* Third Yearbook of the Society for the Psychological Study of Social Issues. Boston: Houghton Mifflin Co., 1945. 475 p.

Gunnar Myrdal, *Psychological Impediments to Effective International Cooperation.* Journal of Social Issues, Supplement Series No. 6. New York: Association Press, 1952. 31 p.

E. F. M. Durbin and John Bowlby, *Personal Aggressiveness and War.* London: Kegan Paul, Trench, Trubner and Co., 1939. 154 p. Also published by Columbia University Press.

Hornell Hart, *Social Science and the Atomic Crisis.* Supplement Series No. 2 to the *Journal of Social Issues,* April 1949. p. 1-30. See also the critique and rejoinder in *Psychological Bulletin* 47:509-16; November 1950.

tions that receive those forces, which translate them in different directions or into different kinds of energy, which perhaps provide a sequence of cause-effect relationships, perhaps with reciprocal action and balance, or design or purpose—these are systems necessarily of equal interest with the forces. For, without such systems, the forces would run rampant in utterly chaotic or anarchistic fashion.

Any machine may be regarded as representing a system of the type we are talking about. However, the concept is somewhat broader than a machine. The human body is a dynamic system; we regard personality also as a dynamic system. So is a family, a community, or any somewhat stabilized and regularized aggregate of conditions and forces. We assume that, in whatever set or system we are thinking of, conditions have to some extent regularized themselves, otherwise it is difficult to discuss the set as a system. Probably, however, the concept would be extended to cover storms, in the field of weather, and revolutions in the field of human organization. Researchers are finding regular patterns even in these unusual events. For the most part, however, without excluding anything that can be brought under surveillance, we are referring to systems of causation which have certain elements of perceptible stability.

For some time it has been common in the physical sciences to speak of a "closed system." That is, for purposes of convenience, a certain set of conditions and forces would be assumed to operate without any influence from factors outside the area of thought. Obviously, however, this concept is a gross artificiality, for "closed systems" cannot be made to exist outside the realm of human thinking. The distinction between closed systems and open systems, therefore, is simply a matter of what factors one cares to give attention to. The discussion of the human being, or of a human group, as an open system, does not mean that either of them is especially different from anything else in the physical or biological sciences, but rather emphasizes that in human affairs the absurdity of thinking in terms of closed systems is rather obvious. The fallacy has led to a great deal of trouble in the world, because much of our thinking about nations has tended in the direction of regarding each one as a closed system. It might be that some small community of persons could isolate themselves relatively from the rest of the world, such as persons who live on an island without communication with other persons, or those who live in mountain regions and have little contact with others. As a matter of fact, we know that such things do occur; but in the fuller sense, over and beyond the human contacts, there is always a dependence on some heat from the sun and some moisture from the atmosphere, as well as air to breathe and so on. It appears, therefore, that we can have varying degrees of open and closed systems, and that the terms should not be thought of as implying absolute concepts, but rather as indicating an emphasis on one or another type of condition (interchange beyond the limits of the system being considered), and in large part a matter of where one cares to place his emphasis, and what factors he cares to admit to his thinking. It is, of course, much easier to think about closed systems, for then, one can ignore all the factors from the outside.

The discerning of the interrelationships, and in many cases the chain of cause-effect sequences, is itself an object which is very challenging as a goal for analytical work. It has, in fact, become the object of a great deal of attention by current theorists and research workers. The production of electronic machines in recent years has further stimulated interest in the operations of the nervous system and of the other physiological processes of the human body, and has thrown considerable light on how these might work. It has contributed a number of concepts regarding structure and corresponding function which, although regarded by many persons as still too simple (and accordingly, inadequate), nevertheless, provides some analogies with which understanding of human processes is increased and further theory can be built. A number of references which describe (as well as is known at the present time) the structure and functioning of the nervous system, including the human brain, were given earlier in the section on structure. It is appropriate to list a few more at this point which emphasize certain properties of the nervous system. Perhaps the most striking of these special aspects is the one dealing with purpose, or teleology. Physical scientists rejected teleology (that is, explaining things in terms of some ultimate purpose) so severely that it has been a pattern in scientific thinking ever since the Renaissance to avoid any reference to purpose. Certain researchers who work in the human sciences have accepted from physical science this same pattern of thinking. It can be shown, however, that a machine can be designed, using electronic tubes, which can have purpose— not only a single purpose for which the designer constructs the machine, but purpose growing out of past experience.[315]

It is obvious that human beings have purpose and it would be absurd to deny this. On the other hand, it must be recognized that there are scientific

315 Filmer S. C. Northrop, "The Neurological and Behavioristic Psychological Basis of the Ordering of Society by Means of Ideas." *Science* 107:411-17; April 1948. Also published in much longer form as "Ideological Man in His Relation to Scientifically Known Natural Man." *Ideological Differences and World Order*. Edited by Filmer S. C. Northrop. Studies in the Philosophy of Science of the World's Cultures. New Haven: Yale University Press, 1949. Chapter 19, p. 407-28. In the latter reference, Northrop states that "The need for separating moral man from scientifically conceived and verified natural man no longer exists" (p. 426).

Arturo Rosenblueth, Norbert Wiener, and Julian Bigelow, "Behavior, Purpose and Teleology." *Philosophy of Science* 10:18-24; January 1943.

Walter Pitts and Warren S. McCulloch, "How We Know Universals; The Perception of Auditory and Visual Forms." *Bulletin of Mathematical Biophysics* 9:127-47; September 1947.

traditions of great weight, and that these influence scientific theory and research. The individual scientist is no more free to throw over the traditions that govern his field of work than is an individual to disregard the culture of the group in which he lives. The scientist would no longer be regarded as a scientist. When, therefore, scientific thought takes some forward step and happens to come out with conclusions which everybody holds in his nonscientific thinking, it may seem highly humorous to the nonscientific world, but it may, nevertheless, represent a considerable step forward in science. There is no question but that scientific tradition contains many ideas and practices which serve as retarding and diverting influences, in just the same way that the culture of any society contains many notions, beliefs, or convictions which keep the people in that group from living as rich and satisfying a life as they could otherwise attain. It is always important to remember that science is the product of human beings and, therefore, science suffers from many of the same tendencies and frailties of human beings that affect any section of their culture.

It may be said further that purpose is primarily a human conception. It is a way we have of looking at things. It is a convenient way of looking at them, because it is so natural and seemingly real to us. The concept, when used as a description or explanation, therefore, has considerable meaning to us. For that reason, the concept is useful; it describes or implies in a single word what might otherwise require many sentences to suggest, and then fail somewhat in giving the appropriate touch to the picture. Probably there is nothing to be gained by reading the idea of purpose into the physical world. Whether the term is serviceable, or has a tendency to be misleading, in biology is something which must await further trial and experience. Many botanists regard it as undesirable to say that the roots of a plant seek water, or that leaves turn toward the light. Whether such expressions are unacceptable because of scientific tradition, or because they say too much, or because they emphasize aspects which are less significant than others, is a question for the botanist. In the human field, however, and to some extent in the animal kingdom, the concept of purpose is not only natural but it seems almost necessary, if we are to explain many of the phenomena that occur with regard either to individual life or to organized group life.

One aspect of most living systems (individual organisms or groups) is that they are, within limits, self-regulating. This is a property of considerable interest in itself and is again an objective of analysis which is of high value. For example, there are many conditions in the human body that are maintained at a rather constant state. This was recognized one hundred years ago with regard to the amount of blood sugar, but was greatly expanded within the present century by Walter B. Cannon and given the term *homeo-stasis*. This subject is engagingly and comprehensively described in a readily available source.[316] A departure from the normal state (for example, hunger) is the source of biogenic drives,[317] and is also related to, perhaps both as cause and as a consequence of, emotion.[318] Recent research has dealt with the effect of the endocrine glands on homeostasis: what conditions of the body are no longer properly regulated when some of the glands, or their parts, are removed.[319]

**Personality.** The behavior of the human being, which we ordinarily call personality, is one of the most engaging examples of an organized dynamic system. The study of personality is, in fact, for many persons the core and the principal justification for the whole field of psychology. Just what is to be regarded as included by the term *personality* will vary somewhat with the writer. Most of us think of it as involving, to a large extent, the affective state (emotional colorings) of an individual and, although this is probably a common implication, some workers include any form of behavior and emphasize only that the scientific interest in personality is to be able to predict whatever behavior occurs.[320] Any scientific interest, stated in terms of pure predictions, may seem barren when compared with needs for understanding in a real situation. Although it has become somewhat of a fad for very scientific persons to think that the only objective of science is prediction, we should regard understanding as a considerably higher order of knowledge and the more worthy goal of science.

As a matter of fact, the thing most needed in connection with the study of personality is not simply a collection of readily observable aspects, nor their statistical prediction, but rather some understanding of the structure of personality. By that we mean those particular sets of meaning or interpretations (perceptions) which have become habitual attachments to otherwise routine stimuli, and become dominant factors in one's behavior. In this area of work, the psychoanalysts have done by far the greatest amount of work, have produced the most theory, and have the greatest influence on clinical practice.[321] Other schemes of interpretation have been proposed

[316] Edward D. Dempsey, "Homeostasis." *Handbook of Experimental Psychology, op. cit.,* Chapter 6, p. 209-35.

[317] *Op. cit.,* p. 355-57.

[318] *Op. cit.,* p. 504-07.

[319] Frank B. Strange, "Self-regulatory Behavior after Extirpation of Certain Endocrine Glands: A Review." *Scientific Monthly* 76:344-48; June 1953.

[320] "Personality is that which permits prediction of what a person will do in a given situation." Raymond B. Cattell, *Personality:* A Systematic Theoretical and Factual Study. New York: McGraw-Hill Book Co., 1950. 689 p. Also given in his "Concepts and Methods in the Measurement of Group Syntality." *Psychological Review* 55:48-63; January 1948.

[321] For a presentation of psychoanalytical frames of reference and interpretative schemes, as written by a psychologist, see Percival M. Symonds, *The Dynamics of Human Adjustment, op. cit.,* 666 p. See also his somewhat reduced and slightly simplified book: *Dynamic Psychology, op. cit.,* 413 p.

and are increasingly being brought to the front. It is not possible here to cite the large number of treatises which have appeared in book form in recent years, but we make reference herewith to a number of the leading texts.[322]

One of the great difficulties in studying personality is the development of concepts with which to work. Not that our language is not already full of thousands of terms which represent some aspect of personal behavior, but that many of these are slightly different variations of the same thing, and many of them are superficial aspects of something which is more constant and underlying. The long-time search is to discover, through analytical thinking and observation and experiment, those aspects of personality which would provide a thoughtful scheme of the greatest possible simplicity. That is, we seek the most fundamental concepts, those which will explain the largest portion of behavior with the fewest ideas. This is, in general, the goal of research in all fields. Allport, some years ago, referred to "the search for elements" of personality,[323] pointing out that certain physical scientists did not hold the study of personality in respect, because the researchers had not yet been able to produce elementary processes. Allport emphasized that attention should be directed toward dynamic structures. Some of the difficulties of keeping conceptual schemes and well supported observation in proper balance were emphasized by MacKinnon.[324] The great difficulty is that personality can be analyzed into whatever units or aspects one chooses to look at. He can make an element out of anything that he cares to carve out of the totality of human behavior. It was mentioned that the aspects selected should explain as much as possible. They should also fit well into a scheme of thinking, both practical and scientific, so that they can have some observational unity as well as conceptional unity,

[322] For a brief overview with references to research and various treatises, see Willard C. Olson, "Personality," *Encyclopedia of Educational Research, op. cit.,* p. 806-17.

Kimball Young, *Personality and Problems of Adjustment.* Second Edition. New York: Appleton-Century-Crofts, 1952. 716 p.

Gardner Murphy, *Personality:* A Biosocial Approach to Origins and Structures. New York: Harper and Bros., 1947. 999 p.

Gordon W. Allport, *Nature of Personality:* Selected Papers. Cambridge, Mass.: Addison-Wesley Press, 1950. 220 p. A reprinting of eleven of his articles which represent clarifications of the theory presented in his *Personality,* published in 1937 by Henry Holt and Co.

Raymond B. Cattell, *op. cit.* Also see *An Introduction to Personality Study.* London: Hutchinson's University Library, 1950. New York:Longmans, Green and Co., 1950. 235 p.

John Dollard and Neal E. Miller, *Personality and Psychotherapy.* New York: McGraw-Hill Book Co., 1950. 488 p.

Kurt Lewin, *Dynamic Theory of Personality, op. cit.*

Paul Horst and Others, *The Prediction of Personal Adjustment.* Bulletin 48, prepared for the Committee on Social Adjustment under the Direction of the Sub-Committee on Prediction of Social Adjustment. New York: Social Science Research Council, 1941. 455 p.

For continuing material see appropriate topics in the *Education Index, Psychological Abstracts,* and Index of *Annual Review of Psychology.*

[323] Gordon W. Allport, *Personality.* New York: Henry Holt and Co., 1937. 588 p.

[324] Donald W. MacKinnon, "Fact and Fancy in Personality Research." *American Psychologist* 8:138-46; April 1953.

and presumably have some life cycle of their own—a causation, a history, and perhaps modification. In other words, to be satisfactory, a unit must be observable and capable of serving as a unit in all the ways that we usually care to think about a unit. It is out of such units that we can mold a proper conceptual structure of personality which will permit us to understand human behavior with much more insight than we have been accustomed to show.

Cantril has presented a frame of reference that seems to fit the essentially human characteristics of human life.[325] The scheme of thought embraces the discerning of values or ends in terms of experience—both the experience of the individual and the lessons that can be transmitted by the long-time experience of the society in which one lives.

> Since man's purposive behavior is concerned with much more than the mere satisfaction of his bodily needs, it should help to understand man if a distinction is made between those actions determined entirely by the physiological processes which start them (the need for food and sex and various emotions reflexly related) and those activities which involve intellectual capacities and value judgments where the processes of weighing and integrating numerous factors are included and are accompanied by value overtones. There is generally a sense of "wanting to do" something in both instances, but the resulting quality of the experience we have in pursuing these two types of activity is radically different.[326]

We believe it is possible to hold such conceptions as Cantril outlines without in any sense being unscientific. One point of view may be as scientific as another, even though it is entirely different. Interpretative schemes are often wholly a matter of choice, one or another of them fitting the data as well as the other. We are not quite content with those points of view which regard all action as springing from the desire to escape something. For example, it may be in strictly Freudian tradition to hold the following: [327]

> To say that a man seeks pleasure is not an exact statement. A more precise statement is that man seeks to escape from pain or discomfort, and to achieve a state of equilibrium which is satisfying in the sense that pain or discomfort is absent. Fundamentally, the forces that motivate an organism are the discomforts.
> Fundamentally, all behavior looks toward the reduction of painful stimuli.

Such a view is optional; it is not one which is required by facts as research has produced them. That negativistic view omits the "emergent value attributes" of Cantril, which, in the experience of most human beings,

---

[325] Hadley Cantril, see footnote 326.

[326] Quoted from Hadley Cantril, *The "Why" of Man's Experience*. New York: Macmillan Co., 1950. p. 61.

[327] Quoted from Percival M. Symonds, *Dynamic Psychology*, p. 16, 25. New York: Appleton-Century-Crofts, 1949. 413 p.

are very real. We scarcely see the profit in denying them. And, although the words *purpose* and *teleology* do not appear in the subject index of Stevens' *Handbook of Experimental Psychology,* we would prefer, as a basis for a science of human beings, something in keeping with the following statement: [328]

> I believe we can have a science which leaves of man a human being—perhaps not as we have always thought him, but at least as we have always known him. For science is a matter of concepts as much as of objects, and a properly conceived social science will be sensitive to those qualities which we recognize as human. A science which is good is necessarily a science which fits.

In keeping with this notion that an individual has purposes and is striving to achieve certain goals and discharge certain functions in his social situation, there have been developed a number of descriptions of the key problems which are faced typically at different ages. A number of these descriptions have dealt with the problems peculiar to adolescence.[329] Such problems are obviously of basic concern to the curriculum maker and analyses are frequently a part of the curriculum literature.[330] From this point of view, one may see, as an advertising brochure points out, "not problem kids—just kids with problems." Should I stay in school? How can I discover my real interest? What kind of job can I do best? How can I get along better with my parents? As stated for one of the purposes of general education, "in terms of life's problems as man faces them," how can the curriculum be most serviceable?

More recently Havighurst has dealt with the various roles which the middle-aged person must play, in his home, community, and own scheme of aspirations.[331] Similarly, with the growing number of persons in our

[328] Quoted from Douglas E. Scates, "On Our Research the Answers Hinge." *Phi Delta Kappan* 30:120-23; December 1948.

[329] Robert J. Havighurst, *Human Development and Education.* New York: Longmans, Green and Co., 1953. 338 p. An enlarged revision of his *Developmental Tasks and Education,* originally published in 1948, University of Chicago Press, 86 p.

National Society for the Study of Education, *Adolescence, op. cit.* See Section 3, "The Adolescent and the Social Order;" Section 4, "Educational Implications," and especially Chapter 17, "Preparing Youth to Be Adults."

Stephen M. Corey, "Developmental Tasks of Youth." John Dewey Society, *American High School: Its Responsibility and Opportunity.* Eighth Yearbook. New York: Harper and Bros., 1946. 264 p. See p. 70-99.

For a short review of a number of studies in this area, see David Segel, *Frustration in Adolescent Youth.* Office of Education Bulletin No. 1, 1951. Washington: Government Printing Office, 1951. 65 p. See especially Sections 5, 6.

[330] J. G. Umstattd, "Secondary Education—IV, Curriculum." *Encyclopedia of Educational Research, op. cit.* See the various studies referred to on page 1176.

Orie I. Frederick and Lucille J. Farquear, "Problems of Life, I and II." *School Review* 46:337-45, 415-22; May, June 1938.

[331] Robert J. Havighurst, "Social Roles of the Middle-Aged Persons; A Method of Identifying the Needs of Adults." *The Human Development Bulletin,* Proceedings of the Fourth Annual Symposium, Sixth Issue, Spring, 1953, p. 40-46. Chicago: University of Chicago, Committee on Human Development, 1953. Also published in mimeographed form in *Notes and Essays In Education for Adults,* No. 4. Distributed by the Center for the Study of Liberal Education for Adults, Chicago, March 1953.

population over fifty years of age, attention is increasingly being given to the analysis of problems of persons who are looking forward to retirement or who actually have retired from activities. Accordingly, one conference has analyzed the "big six" needs of older persons as they attempt to play appropriate roles in our society.[332]

Thus far we have been dealing with personality as an organized system of forces within the individual, particularly as these are related to urges, drives, motivations,[333] purposes, goals, standards, criteria, values, and the carrying out of certain accepted or expected roles in life. While many re-searchers would leave such terms and concepts out of the picture, on the basis that scientific points of view do not find them compatible, Northrop and other workers in the references cited point out that purpose and social responsibility are not at all incompatible with scientific views and can, to some extent, even be built into machines. Therefore, purpose may, in the words of these writers, properly be looked at not only as a way of describing things, but as being in itself the cause of action.

It is inappropriate, however, to leave the discussion of personality, as an organized system of forces within the individual, without making specific reference to the emotions. The emotions are commonly thought of as pre-dominantly a matter of feeling on the part of the individual, yet it is recognized that there is a certain amount of consistency in the behavior of the individual when he is feeling a certain emotional tone. The concept of emotion is undoubtedly a tremendously oversimplified concept, insofar as the commonly held notion of an emotion may be regarded as embracing the whole of the physiological state and its manifestations. For instance, there is no one organ in the body for expressing emotion or for giving rise to the peculiar feeling when that emotion is being experienced. Emotions represent an extremely diffuse physiological reaction, involving in most (or all) cases, depending perhaps upon the strength of the emotion, a considerable part of the nervous system, the endocrine glands, and many of the bodily processes, all of which together give rise to certain bodily sensations that are registered in the brain as a certain feeling.

As we know from common experience, emotions have to do with the dynamic system. They point the organism toward or away from something, and tend to keep its attention engaged for long periods of time with the reaction to the object or situation. They normally magnify reactions, some-

[332] Federal Security Agency, Sponsor, *Man and His Years*. An Account of The First National Conference On Aging. Raleigh, N. C.: Health Publications Institute, 1951. 311 p. See the Section, "Basic Human Needs," p. 227-28.

[333] Ten terms relating to motivation are described and differentiated by Symonds, *op. cit.*, 1946, p. 48-9. Also one may consult a dictionary such as Howard C. Warren, *Dictionary of Psychology, op. cit.* One will expect to find variations in meaning from time to time and from one writer to another.

times to fantastic proportions, through the energy which they release in the system. Because of this quality, emotions are closely related to motivation. They seem to be only partly under the control of the cerebrum, being tripped off by perceptions which reach and stimulate the lower brain centers before reaching and stimulating the higher centers. Emotions often have the property of blocking attention or thought upon other things, so that one's normal values are likely to fade into relative insignificance when one's emotions are impelling his response in another direction. Thus, a person who is caught in a strong emotion usually does not care anything about the consequences of his behavior, even if such things pass before his mind. In fact, moderately strong or very strong emotions seem to give one the sense that the whole of life is wrapped up in that particular feeling.

Because of the tremendous complexity in general reaction of a person or an animal in emotion, the physiological correlates of emotion have been extremely difficult to trace, and the full description of the mechanism by which emotions express themselves and are felt by the individual have been very difficult to determine as regards their complete analysis and description.[334] Because the emotions tend to sustain themselves for a period of time (although seldom longer than a day or two), and because they are not readily amenable to rational control, they give rise to what may be called autonomous personality traits. Often the emotional reactions seem to have no logical cause; but that is simply because the perceptual system of one person is different from that of another. The interpretative reaction, which constitutes perception, is something that grows in the individual, beginning with his very earliest experiences as an infant. It may not be unreasonable to say that the individual's perceptual system regarding those things favorable and unfavorable to his well-being and complacency results from a process of conditioning. To change over the pattern of reaction from that which has been habituated calls for something beyond the "will power" or determination of the individual, although the latter may be helpful. Apparently, there is some process of deconditioning which is required. This is the field of psychotherapy, of which psychoanalysis is one branch, the latter being particularly centered in the tradition of Freud.

Emotions are of very large concern to educators, both because a moderated set of emotions is desirable among the citizenry, and also because

---

[334] Donald B. Lindsley, "Emotion." *Handbook of Experimental Psychology, op. cit.*, Chapter 14. This chapter contains a bibliography of 288 references, which may be considered as an adequate index to the literature up to 1950. Emotions are dealt with in connection with various other subjects reviewed annually in the *Annual Review of Psychology;* see the subject index.

A less technical but stimulating and suggestive report from the standpoint of experimentation is given in Henry E. Garrett, *Great Experiments in Psychology*. Third Edition. New York: Appleton-Century-Crofts, 1951. See Chapter 8, "Cannon and Experimental Studies of the Emotions," p. 148-70. Twenty-eight references in bibliography.

emotional disturbances will completely thwart attempts at teaching and learning.[335] With greater understanding of emotions and their origin and dynamic structure, there has been a marked change in the philosophy of teachers, from the older idea of repression, based on the notion that children were bad, over to the idea of coöperating with the child to gain certain satisfactions for his needs, with a continued effort to develop habits of expression in the child which are socially and personally wholesome.[336] It is, of course, recognized that some children have well established patterns of hate and other forms of retaliatory or malevolent feelings and aggressive actions.[337] Such children usually require clinical diagnosis and treatment.

Again we call attention to the nature of research. Those who think that research is merely a matter of counting and measuring cases, perhaps classifying selected observations, or that science consists ideally of bivariate concomitance (correlation) would do well to ponder the problems in the fields to which we have just been referring. Growth in understanding in such fields has come about in large part through simple observation, with the development of deeper insights through getting "hunches," which result in paying more attention to certain aspects of behavior and of preceding conditions, so as to learn whether one apparently has any relationship to another. Gradually, one will build something of a conceptual model of the mechanism or the dynamic structure of such broad systems as emotions or entire personality. Along the way, there is room for a considerable amount of definite experimentation, but no amount of formal experimentation is likely to suffice. A large amount of first-hand contact with the field in which the reactions occur is almost essential, apart from lucky guesses

[335] The subject of emotions has been treated particularly from the educational point of view in several articles in the *Encyclopedia of Educational Research, op. cit.* See p. 187-90, 507, 1163-64.

Lois B. Murphy and Henry A. Ladd, *Emotional Factors in Learning.* New York: Columbia University Press, 1944. 404 p.

[336] Alice M. Miel and Others, *Coöperative Procedures in Learning.* Horace Mann-Lincoln Institute of School Experimentation Publication. New York: Teachers College, Columbia University, 1952. 512 p.

[337] Fritz Redl and David Wineman, *Children Who Hate:* The Disorganization and Breakdown of Behavior Controls. Glencoe, Ill.: Free Press, 1951. 253 p.

Bruno Bettelheim, *Love Is Not Enough:* The Treatment of Emotionally Disturbed Children. Glencoe, Ill.: Free Press, 1950. 386 p.

Fritz Redl and David Wineman, *Controls From Within:* Techniques for the Treatment of the Aggressive Child. Glencoe, Ill.: Free Press, 1952. 332 p.

Martin L. Reymert, Editor, *Feelings and Emotions.* Mooseheart Symposium. New York: McGraw-Hill Book Co., 1950. 603 p. Contains 47 papers by representatives of various disciplines. See also in the *Education Index* the head, "Mooseheart Laboratory for Child Research," for earlier and later publications on children's emotions.

The Child Research Clinic of the Woods Schools, Langhorne, Pa., has published one or more reports each year since 1934 dealing with exceptional children, with an emphasis on the emotionally unstable child. These are listed in the *Education Index* variously under the heads: Conference on Education and the Exceptional Child, Institute on Education and the Exceptional Child, and Woods Schools.

which may lead immediately to a fruitful experiment. It must be recalled that Freud, who has been the father and a continued stimulus to a great deal of the work in this field, was not in any sense a formal experimenter and, in the views of many researchers today, would be regarded as utterly unscientific. This view may be correct. It is undoubtedly correct when research and experimentation are conceived in highly formal terms. It might be pointed out to persons who, with some pride and perhaps disdain, regard themselves as scientific, that it is perhaps amazing that one nonscientist could have influenced the main current of thought in a large and vital area of psychology for well over half a century. Such an example may well throw into relief the relative contributions of insightful conceptualization and of strictly formal methods.

While the authors of the present text are basically committed to research, they have sought at every point to emphasize that good research is more than formalities, and that conceptualization is an equal partner with observation. The background for fruitful conceptualization lies in intimate personal acquaintance with the field of study and in staying close to the situation in which observations are taken, throughout the period of study. We do not believe that research can be conducted except in a formal fashion by those who work out their complete plan in advance and perhaps direct the data-gathering from a distance.

**Self-regulation.** What is the mechanism, or structure, or means by which any dynamic system may be self-regulating, adaptive, and teleological (purposeful)? Since, in recent years, self-directing machines have more and more been developed, thinking along this line has a heavy emphasis on such concepts as feedback, servo-mechanisms, or in general terms, cybernetics. We will later discuss dynamic systems that do not depend upon mechanisms which serve this purpose, but for the present we may give attention to such mechanisms. Perhaps the name most commonly associated with this field is that of Wiener, a professor of mathematics at the Massachusetts Institute of Technology.[338] *The Scientific American* devoted an entire issue to the subject,[339] the New York Academy of Sciences held a conference on the subject,[340] and at least four conferences have been held to date by the Josiah Macy, Jr. Foundation.[341]

[338] Norbert Wiener, *Cybernetics.* New York: John Wiley and Sons, 1948. 194 p.
Norbert Wiener, "Cybernetics." *Scientific American* 179:14-19; November 1948.
Norbert Wiener, *The Human Use of Human Beings.* Boston: Houghton Mifflin Co., 1950. 241 p.
[339] *Scientific American* 187:41-160; September 1952. See the bibliography on p. 192, 194 for twenty-five additional references.
[340] Lawrence K. Frank and Others, *Teleological Mechanisms.* Annals of the New York Academy of Sciences 50:187-278; October 1948. Published separately.
[341] Josiah Macy, Jr. Foundation, Packanack Lake, N. J., Transactions of the Sixth Conference on Cybernetics, 1950, 209 p. Seventh Conference (1950), 1951, 251 p. Eighth Conference (1951), 1952, 240 p. Ninth Conference (1952), 1953, 204 p.

It must not be thought that the idea of feedback, or other forms of information for the control of behavior, is limited in any way to mechanical objects. The concept is just as important, perhaps far more so, in educational, psychological, and sociological fields. It is implied all the time in educational work when pupils are given information as to how well they are doing. Instructional tests and other exercises afford important information both for the pupil and for the teacher in orienting further effort. In the case of our own bodies, reference has already been made to homeostasis, namely, the tendency to maintain an internal bodily environment that is reasonably stable with respect to temperature, acidity, carbon dioxide, blood pressure, and many other aspects. When some one of these aspects gets beyond the range of what is normal, stimuli are set up in certain physiological mechanisms which tend to bring the state of body back to the normal range. In a larger sense, our "distance senses" such as sight, hearing, and smell, as well as the cutaneous senses, convey to us "information" that serves to guide our actions. For example, a number of experiments have been conducted on hearing one's own speech. Apparently, we listen attentively and much more carefully than we realize when we are talking and our speech is guided accordingly. If the speech, however, is recorded and played back for us to hear, with just the least delay (a fraction of a second) the speaker will change his manner of talking, may stammer, and may even undergo a minor personality breakdown.[342] Thus, there is continuous feedback in practically all of our activities, whether on the conscious level or not. The effect of feedback (giving information as to success) has been studied under controlled conditions.[343] Two writers on communication, with some attention to cybernetics, emphasized very heavily the role of self-correction in human beings—"the ability of an entity to predict events and also with the entity's ability to modify its action when these predictions are shown to be in error." [344]

The ability to move different parts of the body, and be aware of where each one is without watching it, is due to proprioceptive feedback from kinesthetic stimuli.[345] Some form of feedback controls certain reflexes, as well as voluntary actions. The neural mechanism, that is, the circuits in the nervous system and in the cerebellum have been described by Ruch.[346]

[342] *Annual Review of Psychology,* Vol. 3, 1952, p. 435, and Vol. 4, 1953, p. 105-106.

[343] *Annual Review of Psychology,* Vol. 4, 1953, p. 199.

[344] Jurgen Ruesch and G. Bateson, *Communication:* The Social Matrix of Psychiatry. New York: W. W. Norton and Co., 1951. 314 p.

[345] *Handbook of Experimental Psychology, op. cit.,* p. 1206, 1319, 1323-24, 1327-8. See also p. 154, 175, 198-206.

[346] Theodore C. Ruch, "Motor Systems." *Handbook of Experimental Psychology, op. cit.,* p. 198-206.

The general role of purposive behavior and concepts of teleology in the history of science were set forth at the Conference on Teleological Mechanisms held by the New York Academy of Sciences in October, 1946. Frank points out that these ideas were ruled out of science, beginning with the time of Galileo, and resulted in a highly analytical science which produced a number of useful results without them. More recently, however, it has been recognized that these are not only legitimate concepts but are essential for describing certain larger patterns of behavior. In Frank's own words: [347]

The concepts of purposive behavior and teleology have long been associated with a mysterious, self-perfecting or goal-seeking capacity or final cause, directive in all events, usually of a superhuman or supernatural origin. . . . To move forward to the study of events, scientific thinking had to reject these beliefs in purpose and these concepts of teleological operations for a strictly mechanistic and deterministic view of nature. . . .

The unchallenged success of these concepts and methods in physics and astronomy and, later, in chemistry, gave biology and psychology their major orientation. . . . However within recent years, there has been a growing perplexity in biology and psychology. As they have pursued this analytic method and disclosed ever more subtle and elusive factors and mechanisms, it seemed to carry them further and further away from the organisms and the personalities they were trying to understand. . . . Thus, we are witnessing today a search for new approaches.

The concept of teleological mechanisms, however it may be expressed in different terms, may be viewed as an attempt to escape from these older mechanistic formulations that now appear inadequate, and to provide new and more fruitful conceptions and more effective methodologies for studying self-regulating processes, self-orientating systems and organisms, and self-directing personalities. But these new concepts carry no psychic or vitalistic assumptions, nor do they imply that any mysterious, supernatural powers or psychic forces or final causes are operating the system or guiding the organism-personality. The idea of purposive behavior is not a regressive movement to an earlier stage in the history of ideas, but a forward movement toward a more effective conception of the problems we face today. We are moving toward a conception of a "natural teleology" as Woodbridge suggested in 1911.

Thus, the terms *feedback, servomechanisms, circular systems,* and *circular processes* may be viewed as different but equivalent expressions of much the same basic conception. The idea of self-regulation, with goal-seeking behavior, becomes applicable in the laboratory, in the clinic, especially for the study of personality, as well as in the field for study of social orders and cultures. . . . It is somewhat ironic that, in order to bring into biology and psychology the concept of purposive behavior and teleological mechanisms, we have leaned so heavily upon the models of man-made machines and artificial systems, such as computing machines, guided missiles, and other complicated electronic devices. . . . But this is a recurrent process in the history of ideas.

[347] Quoted from Lawrence K. Frank, "Foreword," *Teleological Mechanisms.* Annals of the New York Academy of Sciences, Vol. 50, October 1948. Quotation from p. 189-91. Most of this quoted material appears also in the quarterly magazine, *Human Biology* 23: 346-47; December 1951.

Some of the ideas and differentiations in this area of thinking should perhaps be made clear. The terminology of Rosenblueth, Wiener, and Bigelow has become relatively standard and we, therefore, follow them: [348]

Behavior
> Passive
> Active
>> Random
>> Purposeful
>>> Non-teleological
>>> Teleological (negative feedback)
>>>> Non-predictive
>>>> Predictive
>>>>> Successive stages predicted

The passive type of activity is described as that in which the input equals the output; that is, as much energy is put into the object as comes out and, therefore, the object is not a source of energy. This, of course, is quite the opposite of what happens in the nervous system and muscles in the human body or in many animals. The amount of energy necessary to excite a nerve is a very small fraction of the amount of energy which a motor nerve will put out at the other end. It was said earlier that the human body is a great magnifier, and that the strength of an attraction or purpose may have little or no relationship to the strength of the stimulus from outside the nervous system. It is particularly important to keep this fact in mind when understanding personality, and when thinking of "field theory" in connection with personal behavior. It is, in fact, characteristic of feedback systems that the amount of energy for guiding, controlling, or "triggering" them is very small in comparison with the amount of energy expressed in the response of the machine or the organism. A familiar example is the radio tube; for simplicity, it might be said that a radio tube magnifies the incoming signal something like one hundred times. That is, the behavior of the tube (its output) is controlled by incoming signals which are commonly one one-hundredth as strong. In the human being, it is not difficult to imagine reactions with perhaps millions of times the energy involved in the original stimulus. For, just as an infinitesimally small amount of wave energy in the air is multiplied successively in the radio, so in the human being any stimulus received by the nervous system may be multiplied successively by the nervous system itself and may, in addition, be magnified further through chemical conditions which are changed in the body (such as the well known increase in blood sugar during anger).

[348] Arturo Rosenblueth, Norbert Wiener, and Julian Bigelow, *op. cit.* This set of concepts has also been represented in the publications by Northrop, as cited previously, and again in *Human Biology* 23:355; December 1951.

With regard to purpose, some mechanisms are built to do a specific thing in a specific direction; a gun is sometimes described as not "purposeful," because it can be aimed in any direction and, accordingly, does not lead to a single consequence. On the other hand, mechanisms that have governors or other control mechanisms built in, or even those which repeatedly do a specific job (as a machine in a manufacturing industry), may be "purposeful," although manufacturing machines ordinarily do not put out more energy than is directly put into them. In the case of an organism, purposeful activity involves the selection of an objective. "When we perform a voluntary action, what we select voluntarily is a specific purpose, not a specific movement. Thus, if we decide to take a glass containing water and carry it to our mouth, we do not command a certain set of muscles to contract . . . ; we merely trip the purpose and the reaction follows automatically." [349] This follows as a consequence of the hierarchical nature of the nervous system, in which the selection is carried on primarily in the cerebrum and the details of executing the "idea" are largely carried on by the so-called lower centers. Such thinking, however, is schematic, because functions are not so fully localized as the foregoing statement would imply, and there is great ramification of nervous impulses throughout large portions of the nervous system, always with cross-connections and large amounts of almost instantaneous feedback. There is, however, a certain amount of differentiation or emphasis.

With regard to the concept of teleological activity, there are those mechanisms which can be constructed to guide themselves toward a certain goal by receiving signals from the goal and then making the corrections in terms of the difference between their present position (or behavior) and the objective. Machines can be built that are purposeful but which are not called teleological, because they do not continue to receive feedback information on the goal, or possibly because the feedback is technically known as positive and may, therefore, increase the error. In organisms, there is normally a large amount of feedback, as has been indicated earlier; however, it is possible that in some cases there is not such action. This is true in some diseases with the human being; and it has been suggested that a snake, after it starts to strike, does not guide its motion by further stimulus from the object.

Predicted behavior is that which can foresee future positions of an object and be guided not by present position of the object but by where it is likely to be at a certain time. Machines can be built with this characteristic. It is also one of the normal characteristics of higher organisms; for example, a cat can guide its behavior in terms of where a mouse is likely to be a mo-

[349] Rosenblueth, Wiener, and Bigelow, *op. cit.* Quoted also in Northrop, *op. cit.*

ment later. With this factor of prediction introduced, we get into really the higher powers of the human being, for there can be many levels of this prediction. We not only estimate trends, but we usually make some attempt to estimate the consequences of taking certain actions. One's thinking may go on in this direction for several successive levels. Thus, with machine analogies on most of the levels, it becomes clear that we can have behavior which expresses a great deal more energy than is in the signal (the stimulus), and which is not only purposeful in the large, but teleological in the sense of being continuously guided toward an accepted objective, even when the objective itself is moving or changing. One's thinking, further, may estimate consequences of action, and may guide one's behavior in keeping with these likely results.

One thing more should be added: as one approaches his original objective, or as he studies it further, his objective may change. With human beings and with society this is a continuing phenomenon. Both large and small goals change as we approach them, gain more familiarity with them, examine them further, and as competing goals come to our attention. We change our minds. In the large, we slowly modify our social philosophy. Under the impact of the human mind, with its tremendous powers for considering new aspects and incorporating them into a total resolution, values change.

**Unstructured dynamic systems.** Up to this point, we have been describing systems (whether machines or biological organisms) which might be regarded as rather highly organized or structured. Thus, while seeking to maintain either a stable state or seeking to reach a certain objective, their internal operation was regulated by definite structures. This held true whether one considered the closed feedback systems of most teleological machines or the more open, more complex systems of living organisms.

This type of thinking, however, does not cover all the systems of dynamic operation that exist. One of the clearest examples of systems which may maintain a relative equilibrium, but do not have any machine-like or organic parts for maintaining this equilibrium, is the ecological community. Examples have been most fully studied in the animal world. That is, the number of one kind of animal in the total animal population is to some extent dependent upon the number of certain other kinds of animals. It is known that such ratios fluctuate, but they fluctuate around a long-time average, so that the system may be said to maintain reasonable stability. Although such systems are classed by some as teleological systems,[350] there are no specific structural or mechanical parts, as of a machine,

---

[350] G. Evelyn Hutchinson, "Circular Causal Systems in Ecology." Lawrence K. Frank and Others, *Teleological Mechanisms, op. cit.* Bibliography of forty-three references.

which can be found that control these ratios among the different members of the animal community.

It also appears that homeostasis, namely, the tendency toward internal equilibrium in the human body, can be divided up into three different kinds, some of which are controlled by feedback (cybernetics) mechanisms, and others cannot be so controlled. For example, the regulation of metabolism, of growth, and of some other processes is not controlled by any single structural part of the body, but rather by complex interrelationships of many parts and many functions. A number of other processes or states of the body are contributed to jointly by special structural parts or mechanisms and again, by complex interaction, including chemical changes.[351]

The general theory relating to these relatively unorganized or unstructured systems of control may be referred to under several names, such as "open-system theory," or "dynamic interaction," or "general-system theory." The chief sponsor of this way of viewing behavior (of the individual or of groups) is Bertalanffy.[352] It is believed that there are principles of general-system theory which apply to all sciences—physical sciences, biological sciences, and human.[353] The theory was developed particularly to apply to open systems and to those which were self-regulating through dynamic interaction or in part, through structured mechanisms, but mainly without a particular structure or machine that takes care of the regulating. The means of regulation are, in many cases, not as yet understood. In certain ecological populations, food is the major factor; but so are other chemical conditions and certain cycles of relationships between different members. These are traced by Hutchinson in the earlier reference.

Attention has been called to psychological effects in the control of balance among the population. It has been found, for example, that in a population of rats those dominated by other (often larger, more aggressive) rats develop timidity and possibly neuroses and are inhibited about going out in search of food. These inhibited rats may produce as many young as the socially dominant rats, but the young do not live, for only a tenth of their offspring survive.

These observations give no direct evidence as to the cause of the differential survival rate of the young of these two groups of females. However, the histories

[351] Bertalanffy, as cited below, p. 356-57.
[352] Ludwig von Bertalanffy, "Towards a Physical Theory of Organic Teleology: Feedback and Dynamics." *Human Biology* 23:346-61; December 1951. 16 references in bibliography.
Ludwig von Bertalanffy, "The Theory of Open Systems in Physics and Biology." *Science* 111:23-29; January 13, 1950. 37 references in bibliography.
[353] Ludwig von Bertalanffy and Others, "General System Theory; a New Approach to Unity of Science." Symposium Held at Thirty-seventh Annual Meeting of the American Philosophical Association, Eastern Division, Toronto, December 1950. *Human Biology* 23: 302-61; December 1951. Six papers.

of the mothers indicate that there is a physiological and psychological disturbance in socially inhibited individuals which might have a deleterious effect on the progeny.... At any rate, social conditioning may be a potent factor in population control among mammals.[354]

While the chain of consequences in any unorganized dynamic system may be difficult to ascertain, studies which are being carried on indicate the extreme importance of factors that generally might be regarded as too slight for further attention.

The concept of unorganized or only partially organized systems of causal sequence is important not only in the study of any group being studied as a group, whether human beings or animals, or plants (the theory extends also into physics and chemistry), but it is extremely important in giving a perspective on the concept of causation. The idea of causation will be developed further in the chapter on experimentation, but it is appropriate to note here that any notion of causation of the simple mechanical type, such as when one end of the lever is pressed down, the other end rises, is a wholly inadequate notion for open systems generally and especially for those referred to as unorganized or unstructured. In complex situations it is usually more profitable to study multiple interaction than it is to think of isolating any two aspects and studying their correlation. The point is that the correlation soon becomes absurd when thought of in the practical situation, either because it is swallowed up in larger forces or because it predicts values which never would or could occur, since in the real situation the two factors do not exist in isolation, and other changes come in to block the simple linear relationship, or in fact any relationship between a particular pair of aspects. It is true that some of these correlations are useful, and perhaps one can never tell until they have been attempted; but the important thing is to keep clearly in mind the conception of complex interaction systems and to realize that the correlation which might be found between any two aspects is but an abstracted portion of changes in many aspects that probably have a reciprocating influence on those which have been selected. Further, to fail to keep in mind the realities and the strength of the background from which one has abstracted certain characteristics for study is well known to lead often to serious errors.[355]

Even though we have been using the terms *unorganized* and *unstructured*,

---

[354] Quoted from John B. Calhoon, "A Method for Self-Control of Population Growth among Mammals Living in the Wild." *Science* 109:333-35; April 1, 1949. Rodent Ecology Project, Johns Hopkins University, conducted under a grant from the International Health Division of the Rockefeller Foundation.

[355] Sidney Hook, "Determinism." *Encyclopaedia of the Social Sciences.* New York: Macmillan Co., 1931. Vol. 5, p. 113-14.

Arthur F. Bentley, "Kennetic Inquiry." *Science* 112:775-83; December 29, 1950.

it is probable that no system remains unorganized or unstructured for long, and that no system is completely of this character, even at what may be thought of as the beginning. What we have been thinking of is systems in which there is no specific apparatus, no single assembly of parts that constitutes a unit, that exercises the control—that is in itself a rather complete link between some stimulus and whatever change occurs. Further, whereas Bertalanffy makes his chief distinction between open and closed systems, we have organized the discussion around the organized or structured dynamic systems and those which are unorganized or unstructured. In the former, a closed system might be a machine set up to manufacture a product; an open system would be a person. In the unstructured or partially structured dynamic systems, the closed example would be the theory of gasses or the theory of thermodynamics, and the open system would be an ecological community which maintains a balance. In making these distinctions, however, it must be recognized that there are no sharp lines and that many cases occur on the borderline, or perhaps in both categories. This cannot be helped. Nature is not as simple as we find it convenient to make our thinking.

It may be debatable whether society (that is, the society in any nation) should be thought of under organized or unorganized systems.[356] It partakes of both. It is organized in many ways both through social machinery (as administrative officers, legislative activities, and the courts), through practices and laws, and many forms of institutions. On the other hand, many activities are carried on in society which have strong interactional effects, but which are not organized especially to produce a particular effect or to control a certain aspect of the society. Thus, there are friendships and countless casual activities. Those who are primarily interested in sociology, or in the practical activities of government, or in the affairs of a community will find appropriate literature available. Perhaps here, since the operation of various types of systems has been illustrated already, we shall be content with referring to the question of the extent to which a social group, having some autonomy, is like an individual biological organism. This is an old question in sociology, often associated with the name of Herbert Spencer, but actually introduced both before and after his time, with many proponents and opponents.[357]

[356] Florian Znaniecki, *Cultural Sciences*. Urbana: University of Illinois Press, 1952. 438 p. See Chapters 1-6, 11-13.

[357] Harry E. Barnes and Howard Becker, *Social Thought from Lore to Science*. Second Edition. Vol. 1. History and Interpretation of Man's Ideas about Life with His Fellows. Washington: Harren Press, 1952. See p. 677-92.

Floyd N. House, *The Development of Sociology*. New York: McGraw-Hill Book Co., 1936. Chapter 11, "The Organic Analogy," p. 120-31.

Pitirim A. Sorokin, *Contemporary Sociological Theories*. New York: Harper and Bros., 1928. p. 200-213.

While the analogy has been useful in suggesting many concepts and terms for the study of society and, in turn, for the study of organisms, and while it has helped to throw light on the nature of society through revealing differences between social groups and biological organisms, it has caused considerable conceptual difficulties. Perhaps the differences in the concepts that are applicable will be cleared up by a consideration of the operation of those dynamic systems which are highly structured and those which are more loosely structured. Biological organisms belong in the former group, and probably social groups belong more to the latter category.

It may be pointed out in leaving this subject that chance, one of the aspects which modern statistical theory deals with to a large extent, would come in the category of unorganized (but often closed) systems. That is, we call the system unorganized, because the relationship of one event to another event is not connected in any relatively fixed way, but great freedom is possible between one event or result and the next. If this concept could be extended to open systems, while influences are introduced more or less freely from the outside, and where the system is, in short, in active interrelationship with its environment, the theory would be much more realistic, but would probably be so complicated as to be unuseful. This is an area needing conceptual development.

The concepts of classical science are inadequate for study of dynamic systems which are to a large degree self-regulating through the operation of interacting, mutually adjusting factors. This is true both for the relatively structured systems (as parts of the human body and the nervous system) and for the more loosely organized or unstructured systems (as certain functions of the human body, of the mind, and in animal and human societies). The central difficulty does not lie simply in the unusual complexity (that is, numerous factors), but primarily in the fact that many or all of the individual components of the system are, within limits, themselves self-regulating and self-adjusting, in addition to being reciprocally interactive. Hence the end product may be achieved by various alternative means—by different degrees of action on the part of any one element—and the principal predictable regularity may not lie in the individual interrelationships but rather in the final state, or end product. This end product is often a matter of maintaining certain limits to the range of fluctuation of some particular aspect of the total system. In so doing, certain relationships, even though well established in the laboratory, may not even come into play because other parts may (for some subtle or chance reason) react to accomplish the same general end—though with differing internal effects. Such phenomena are commonplace in the field of medicine; they are just as common, though often unidentified, in the field we call personality, or perhaps human (and animal) behavior in general.

In the face of such complexes of complexes, we will draw upon our simpler notions of cause and effect for as much aid as they may afford, but never with the belief that they are adequate. Our analyses must find new conceptual models with which to approach our major problems. We are, however, in no sense alone in this need. Weaver [357a] notes the great swing in scientific conceptualization from the two-variable problem, which was characteristic in physical science up to about 1900, to the disorganized complexity of chance and probability theory. Thus the methodology went from one extreme to the other, leaving untouched a great intervening group of problems. Weaver refers to these as being problems of *organized complexity*. They involve a number of factors "which are interrelated into an organic whole." "These new problems," says Weaver, "require science to make a third great advance" (p. 7). The matter is of particular interest for the field of analysis: chance and probability are entirely unanalytical; the present problem is posed by a recognition of the need for an *analytical* attack on complex dynamic systems. Thus science (physical, biological, social) is searching for new conceptions with which to approach the problems it is now essaying to attack.

Much of the discussion in this section has been for the purpose of suggesting a new framework for viewing many phenomena with which we must deal. Conceptual models are important because the frame of thought with which one approaches analytical work determines the aspects he will observe and the form into which he will fit them when stating his conclusions. Concepts are both the eyes with which one sees and the beliefs with which one speaks.

The various essentially human aspects which have been described can legitimately be looked for. We maintain this in the face of the large amount of literature to the contrary. We recognize purpose not only as a descriptive frame of interpretation but actually as a cause in the behavior of all more or less intelligent organisms. Self-regulation is too obvious and common a physiological property to be questioned. Intelligence of the kind which the cerebrum permits makes possible not only choice but guidance by the expected consequences of choice. Accordingly, values arise and become causes. Those who make their own way must choose their own way. The researcher who closes his eyes to these aspects is himself choosing a perspective that is needlessly narrow. Analysis is not necessarily restricted to

[357a] Warren Weaver, "Science and Complexity." Warren Weaver, Editor, *The Scientists Speak,* Chapter 1. New York: Boni and Gaer, 1947. 369 p. See in particular p. 1-10.

the mechanical and the simple, except for those who elect to look only for such things.

### 3. Extra-personal Factors

The general outline and sequence of the treatment of dynamic aspects has been to deal first, with force; second, with systems through which the force operates and expresses itself (or we might say systems that utilize the force and make it effective); third, factors which influence these systems. We are here dealing with this third area. It is the area of factors outside the individual which help determine his behavior; it might be referred to as external dynamics. We use the term *extra-personal* in the sense of "extra-individual," not meaning to imply that the factors are not of human-nature origin. Many of them are.

Any description of how something has come to be the way it is involves a certain amount of history. History-writing and research are discussed in another chapter. Everything has its history, even the earth on which we live. The history of the individual person is dealt with in other chapters on case-study and genetic approaches. We shall here deal with the subject, not in the idiographic sense (that is, not in the sense of describing or accounting for a particular individual or a segment of societal activity), but rather in terms of general conditions which operate. The detection of these factors, in the large, is a part of analysis. The treatment will be divided into three topics:

1. Factors molding the individual's system of values, patterns of reaction, and habits of activity
2. Factors contributing to the behavior of the individual at a particular time
3. Factors which guide the development of knowledge in a society, including research.

These various factors are to be considered as influencing factors, and never as completely determinative in any final sense. They may at times, nevertheless, exercise such force that they play the role of a completely determinative factor.

**Basic conditioning factors.** Workers in different fields emphasize different sets of factors which they believe make a major contribution toward determining the personality, activity, and general behavior of human beings. For example, biologists will emphasize the genetic (inherited) contribution to the individual, pointing out that many limits are set on what the individual eventually becomes, according to the genes in the chromosomes which carry forward his inheritance from his parents.[358] These factors are

---

[358] Laurence H. Snyder, "The Genetic Approach to Human Individuality." *Scientific Monthly* 68:165-71; March 1949.

commonly recognized in psychological and educational literature.[359] Sometimes treatments are prepared by geneticists with emphasis on psychological aspects.[360] Many persons will recall the large amount of study given
to the question of the relative effects of "nature and nurture"—the extent
to which a person's intelligence was set by his physiological inheritance,
as compared with the extent to which a given level of intelligence was produced by the stimulation of his environment. Two sets of yearbooks were
produced on this subject a little more than a decade apart.[361]

The second large class of factors often looked to as an explanation, not
so much in individual personality as of the kind of thing one does in earning
a living, may be referred to as ecological. By this, we refer to the physical
environment, including soil, topography, climate, and associated factors.
We have earlier (in connection with the analysis of spatial components)
given a number of references to major sociological treatises, which will
not be repeated here. It might be pointed out that the term *ecology* is used
in two somewhat different senses. The sociologist is likely to employ it as
representing the spatial distribution of populations and perhaps their movements. The references given previously will cover this aspect. On the other
hand, the term, as used in biology, emphasizes some causal effect of
physical environment on the activities of the individual, and also the return
effect of the individual or group on the environment. This subject has not
been a major concern of sociologists, since they are primarily interested
in the social groups and social interactions. The geographer [362] and, to a
lesser extent, the historian [363] are interested in the interaction of man and
his physical environment. While it is obvious that the climate, soil, and
topography determine to a large extent the kind of economic activity that
men can engage in, sociologists have generally been critical of the attempts
of the geographer to account for the large portion of the culture of a
given society in these terms. The sociologists point out that ideas, customs,

[359] Mrs. Calvin S. Hall, "The Genetics of Behavior." *Handbook of Experimental Psychology, op. cit.,* Chapter 9, p. 304-29. Bibliography of fifty-two references.
[360] Paul R. David and L. H. Snyder, "Genetic Variability and Human Behavior. *Social
Psychology at the Cross-Roads.* Edited by John H. Rohrar and M. Sherif. New York: Harper and Bros., 1951. p. 53-82.
Laurence H. Snyder, *Principles of Heredity.* Fourth Edition. Boston: D. C. Heath, 1951.
515 p. See especially the last three chapters dealing with genetics in man and certain
psychological effects.
[361] National Society for the Study of Education, *Intelligence: Its Nature and Nurture.*
Thirty-ninth Yearbook, Parts 1, 2. Chicago: University of Chicago Press, 1940. Two vols.
National Society for the Study of Education, *Nature and Nurture:* Their Influence upon
Intelligence. Twenty-seventh Yearbook, Part 1. Chicago: University of Chicago Press, 1928.
Part 2 deals with the influence of nature and nurture on achievement.
Frank S. Freeman, "Nature and Nurture." *Encyclopedia of Educational Research, op.
cit.,* p. 772-77. Bibliography of twenty-eight references.
[362] Ellsworth Huntington, *Main Springs of Civilization.* New York: John Wiley and
Sons, 1945. 660 p.
[363] James C. Malin, "Ecology and History." *Scientific Monthly* 70:295-98; May 1950.

forms of social control, and many other psychological and sociological factors are exceptionally strong. The argument may be likened to that between heredity and environment in producing intelligence. Various writers, however, emphasize that in very warm and humid climates, man cannot be very active. Other writers emphasize the effect of sun spots (solar cycles) on the tendency of mankind to be active generally.[364]

It is in a third class of factors, namely, the cultural, that we find the greatest amount of work being done by psychologists, sociologists, and anthropologists. This is also the area of greatest interest to educators. For good reason the subject is best understood with reference to the period of infancy and childhood. There has been a growing acceptance of the idea that certain basic elements of the individual's personality are laid down during the early years of life and that these are changed only with especially fortuitous experiences, or with considerable effort—usually, requiring persistent help from someone outside the person himself.

Whether Freud, the father of psychoanalysis, was the first one to emphasize this point, we do not know. Certainly, it has been picked up and utilized extensively as a basis for study during recent years. Lundberg approaches the matter in terms of societal integration and, following Cooley, points out that "The primary group is the cradle and creator of human nature."[365] A number of studies have been summarized in text treatments.[366] In order to bring together the points of view of sociology, biology, anthropology, and psychology in a single volume, a number of writers have coöperated.[367] Along the sociological line we cite two other studies,[368] and a textbook summary.[369] We may note certain literature in the fields of psychiatry and psychology.[370]

[364] Charles G. Abbot, *Smithsonian Miscellaneous Collections*, Vol. 122, No. 4. "Solar Variations: A Leading Weather Element," August 4, 1953. 35 p.

[365] George A. Lundberg, *Foundations of Sociology*. New York: Macmillan Co., 1939. Chapter 8, "Societal Integration and Status," p. 290-333. The outstanding treatises of an earlier date by Cooley, Bernard, Markey, Piaget, and Mead are given in the first few notes at the end of the chapter.

[366] James H. S. Bossard, *The Sociology of Child Development*. New York: Harper and Bros., 1948. 790 p.

Ralph Linton, *The Cultural Background of Personality*. New York: Appleton-Century-Crofts, 1935. 157 p.

[367] Clyde Kluckhohn, Henry A. Murray, and David M. Schneider, Editors, *Personality: In Nature, Society, and Culture*. Revised Edition. New York: Alfred A. Knopf, 1953. 741 p.

[368] Margaret Mead, "Columbia University Research in Contemporary Cultures." *Groups, Leadership, and Men: Research in Human Relations*. Edited by Harold Guetzkow. Pittsburgh: Carnegie Press, 1951. p. 106-108.

Ruth Benedict, "Child Rearing in Certain European Countries." *American Journal of Orthopsychiatry* 19:342-50; April 1949.

[369] Kimball Young, *op. cit.*, Chapters 12, 13.

[370] William V. Silverberg, *Childhood Experience and Personal Destiny*. New York: Springer Publishing Co., 1952. 289 p.

Woods Schools Child Research Clinic, *Sociological Foundations of the Psychiatric Disorders of Childhood*. Proceedings of the Twelfth Institute on Education and the Exceptional Child. Langhorne, Pa.: Woods Schools, 1945. 122 p.

A fourth aspect sometimes mentioned as a contributing factor to the thinking of mankind, and to the ideas which he evolves, is the field of semantics. That is, what are the symbols and the language concepts with which he thinks? We have previously given references on this subject, so that we will here present only two leading works.[371]

**Current influences: Choice.** The foregoing discussion of extra-personal factors that contribute to the individual's behavior has dealt with those which presumably operate over a long period of time, that is, affect his behavior for the whole of life or for a large portion of it. They contribute to the basic patterns. We turn now to a second group of extra-personal factors which are primarily operative at a given time and may not have lasting effects.

It has remained for fairly recent research in human behavior to break away from the conception of the individual as a purely logical person, with his ultimate or long-time welfare always in the focus of his attention, to the recognition of the many factors that affect one's decision at a given time and which may, therefore, confuse choice and actually obscure a well-proportioned sense of values.

This interest has taken various forms. It may in part be due to, or may be one of the contributing factors in, the gradual recognition that the studies of human behavior, both in the case of the individual and in the case of groups, will need to include a large number of factors, rather than concern themselves in the traditional way with one factor regarded as the cause and another factor regarded as the effect. W. I. Thomas emphasized the "situational approach," in which an attempt was made to describe the total situation in which a person was when making a decision.[372] Naturally, this would contain some subjective factors. Obviously such an approach recognizes multiple causation, a concept that has been emphasized at several points in the present text.

Another emphasis on the manifold factors in the immediate situation is represented by what has come to be called "field theory," a concept taken over from physical science, in which, contrary to the older and simpler notions of classical machines, are recognized various factors (particularly forces) in the environment, both of the experiment and of the experimenter. We may quote briefly to give some idea of this notion:

---

See the *Annual Review of Psychology,* chapter on "Child Psychology." An especially cogent review was given in Volume 2, 1951, p. 10-20.

[371] Charles W. Morris, *Signs, Language, and Behavior.* New York: Prentice-Hall, 1946. 365 p.

Alfred M. Korzybski, *Science and Sanity, op. cit.* 806 p.

[372] William I. Thomas and Dorothy S. Thomas, *The Child in America.* New York: Alfred A. Knopf, 1928.

In principle, a field exists . . . only in empty space. Matter—considered as atoms—is the only seed of electric charges; between the material particles there is empty space, the seat of the electromagnetic field, which is created by the position and velocity of the point charges which are located on the material particles . . . the particle-charges create the field, which, on the other hand, exerts forces upon the charges of the particles.[373]

These concepts evolved in the latter part of the last century, when James Clerk Maxwell was developing equations for electric waves. The idea represented a shift in emphasis and in perspective with regard to the situs of forces. Formerly, forces were thought of as something which acted at a distance; now, they could be thought of as acting within the infinitesimally small spaces within solid matter.

Whether the term, *field theory,* as introduced into psychological literature is the same concept that was introduced into physics before the turn of the century seems questionable. The term seems rather a loose borrowing to suggest attention to a localized area. As defined by its promoter in psychology and education, namely, Kurt Lewin, field theory represented all that was currently good in scientific method and, in addition, had the distinctive properties of describing "the field which influences an individual . . . not in 'objective physicalistic' terms, but in the way in which it exists for that person at that time." In other words, what does the situation look like, or mean, to the individual? Field theory advocated starting "with a characterization of the situation as a whole," after which the "various aspects and parts of the situation undergo a more and more specified and detailed analysis." In that way, one would avoid overlooking anything. A peculiarity of the approach was that it had little interest in the past. "Past events do not exist now and therefore cannot have effect now." The theory did not rule out the past entirely, but neglected it.[374] In the same volume, Hartmann gives a more applied description.[375] The views are peculiarly "gestaltish" with the conviction that "the so-called *inherent* properties of an object are said to be ultimately traceable to forces impinging upon it from the surrounding field." This is difficult either to understand or to accept. Some of the examples given (for example, homeostasis) would fall in our classification under general-system theory (the unstructured dynamic systems) treated earlier. The two might be regarded as the same; in part, they are when many of the claims of field theory are shorn off. Brown

[373] Quoted from Albert Einstein, "Autobiographical Notes." *Albert Einstein; Philosopher-Scientist.* Edited by Paul A. Schilpp. The Library of Living Philosophers, Vol. 7. Evanston, Ill.: Library of Living Philosophers, 1949. p. 35.
[374] Kurt Lewin, "Field Theory and Learning." National Society for the Study of Education, *The Psychology of Learning.* Forty-first Yearbook, Part II. Chicago: University of Chicago Press, 1942. Chapter 6, p. 215-32.
[375] George W. Hartmann, "The Field Theory of Learning and Its Educational Consequences," Chapter 5, p. 165-214, in the work cited above.

gave another early treatment.[376] A collection of Lewin's papers has been published posthumously.[377]

From our view, the best treatment of field theory is given by Murphy in context, that is, as one concept in a series of views.[378] The views presented, however, are somewhat different from the original elaboration of the concept. Apart from theory, and of direct interest to teachers, probably the best treatment is to be found in an earlier collection of Lewin's papers.[379] Suggestive as this treatment is, in our view there is a fundamental error in the direction of the arrows in the diagrams; that is, the vectors. This is not a trivial matter. Neither is it a matter of difficulty of translation from the German. The writer makes it clear in too many places that he thinks of the force as being in the environment. For ordinary thinking, it may not matter. For an understanding of the forces that really operate in the field situation, the matter is crucial. In a psychological sense, the forces which impel one toward or away from some object are not in the object or in the environment at all, but reside solely in the individual's nervous system. All that the environment supplies is probably (normally) a weak signal, such as a light wave (sight), or a sound wave (hearing), or something of the sort. This simple stimulus, when interpreted by the person's perceptual patterns, may lead to a complete ignoring of the sensation (which is virtually what happens to most of the countless stimuli impinging upon us all the time), or it may lead to a moderate response, or to a violent response, but the energy (the force) is in the individual himself. The only psychological force which the environment supplies is a sort of trigger force. In fact, it is less than that, for the real triggering may be said to reside in the perceptual part of the nervous system of the individual. It is in this process of perception that the individual recognizes some things as desirable and other things as dangerous, and most things as simply guiding him as he goes about his purposes.

We recognize that it is difficult to produce phrases which are not awkward when one is to deal with this situation precisely. One might have to

[376] Junius F. Brown, *Psychology and the Social Order.* New York: McGraw-Hill Book Co., 1936. Chapter 15. "The Field Theory of Personality Genesis," p. 278-304; Appendix A, "The Mathematical and Methodological Background of Psychological Field Theory," p. 469-86; Appendix B, "The Topological and Non-Matricized Dynamical Variants in Social Field Structure," p. 487-501.

[377] *Field Theory in Social Science:* Selected Theoretical Papers. Edited by Dorwin Cartwright. New York: Harper and Bros., 1951. 346 p. For a critical review from the standpoint of a sociologist, see *American Journal of Sociology* 57:86-87; July 1951.

[378] Gardner Murphy, *Personality, op. cit.* See especially Chapter 39, "Field Theory," p. 880-902, and adjacent chapters.

[379] Kurt Lewin, *A Dynamic Theory of Personality, op. cit.* See Chapter 3, "Environmental Forces in Child Behavior and Development," p. 66-113. This chapter was previously printed in Carl Murchison, *Handbook of Child Psychology.* Worcester: Clark University Press, 1931. Chapter 14. Perhaps of equal interest to the educator will be Chapter 4 in the same work, "The Psychological Situations of Reward and Punishment," p. 114-70.

say, "I have a feeling of attraction toward the object," rather than to say, "I feel attracted to it." Such exactness, however, reminds us of other similar things which we do not like. One would scarcely desire to change the whole American idiom. The objection does not lie in the language so much as in clear understanding. For many purposes, it is essential to realize that the great release of energy in the case of strong emotions is not a "field characteristic," but is an entirely *personal* characteristic. The *field* supplies only a signal.

The complexity of causation, in contrast to simple bivariate analysis, was being recognized by situationism and by field theory, and also by workers who were dealing with other problems. For example, Dorothy Swaine Thomas, in speaking of her study of Swedish population movements, reported the same recognition of multiple causation and multiple interaction that was described in connection with the unstructured dynamic system; when thought of as representing a population in a group, it will provide some suggestion of the forces (the trigger forces or, at least, stimuli) which impinge on the individual.[380] This view has been described and presented, with a few additional elements, by the philosophers, Dewey and Bentley, under the name *transactionalism*.[381] We will not here go into a discussion of these views, but refer to them primarily for what they offer in the way of a conceptual system for thinking about (describing analytically) a complex of conditions and events.

We will close this section on current influences on the individual when he is making choices, or behaving in other ways, by noting that multiple causation applies alike to the individual and to a society. "History is a part of nature where multiple causation rules and where single effective causes are the over-simplifications, devised to bring the incomprehensible complexity of reality within the narrow compass of man's understanding." [382] The same thing should be said not only with reference to

[380] Dorothy Swaine Thomas, "Experiences in Interdisciplinary Research." *American Sociological Review* 17:663-69; December 1952.

The report of her original study was given in Dorothy Swaine Thomas, *Social and Economic Aspects of Swedish Population Movements* 1750-1933. New York: Macmillan Co., 1941. "In the light of all the available evidence, it became apparent that neither the demographic determinism of most economists (in which population is viewed as the independent variable and economic development as the dependent), nor the economic determinism which had characterized my approach to *Social Aspects of the Business Cycle*, were adequate explanations of observed interrelationships; that there was a continuous chain of interdependence among demographic variables, none of which, in the long run, 'can be considered a completely independent variable,' but each of which might in the short run 'show an immediate effect (i.e., become a dependent variable) or act as an immediate cause (i.e., become an independent variable)' and that the economic structure and way of life of the people continually modify and are modified by the chain of demographic events." Quoted from the preceding 1952 reference.

[381] Arthur F. Bentley, *op. cit.*

John Dewey and A. F. Bentley, *Knowing And the Known*. Boston: Beacon Press, 1949. 334 p.

[382] Edward G. Boring, *op. cit.*, p. 744.

human action, but with reference to most of the events which we observe. When countless factors are not required in the description, it is only because they are expected to fall within normal range.

**Sociology of knowledge.** As a final topic in connection with extra-personal factors, the sociology of knowledge represents a systematic attempt to study the effect of the culture of one's society upon his thinking and his creativeness. For example, it has been noted with some surprise that certain nations which have been very much advanced in some lines were very retarded in others. The question arises as to why. Why was it, for example, that the Romans with their advanced thinking in connection with law and social order and warfare, including many engineering feats of significance, were not able to contrive such a relatively simple thing as a steam engine? Or, why could not the Incas, with their well developed civilization before the European conquest of the Western hemisphere, hit upon such a simple thing as a plow? One can go through the histories of civilizations in this manner and compare achievements in one direction which, in difficulty and ingenuity, far exceed the difficulty of developing some other product that was neglected by (or impossible to) that civilization.

Much the same question can be asked about the development of knowledge, particularly what is referred to as modern scientific research, in the civilizations of Europe.[383] Many beginnings were made in the classical period which were abandoned and lost. There are obviously strong forces in a society which encourage thinkers and experimenters to proceed in certain directions, and discourage them from carrying on investigations in other directions. Apparently, it is the prevailing social philosophy, the great goals accepted by a society, which make it seem profitable for the individual to advance his thinking and develop artifacts of certain types. Just as definitely, there are attitudes in any society that make it difficult, and at least unprofitable, for a person to pursue studies in other directions. Society thinks that it simply does not want such products; there is no use even in knowing the answers to certain questions. Very often, in the social field, it would be disadvantageous for certain groups, if social science were developed.

It is seldom recognized that these forces are at work at the present time in our own society and that they greatly affect the kind of research which is being done in every field of endeavor. The individual is scarcely aware of this influence, because it enters into his thinking in a subtle

---

[383] Douglas E. Scates, "The Conceptual Background of Research." *Structure of Educational Research, op. cit.,* p. 22-37.
Edwin G. Boring, *op. cit.,* Chapter I, "The Rise of Modern Science," p. 3-24.

way.[384] Many persons, including law-makers and other leaders of social thought, are quick to say that certain areas simply do not fall within the proper limits of social science. It must be recognized that basic changes in conception, which often are required in order to accord with facts, are difficult; but in the long history of society the adaptations to the findings of physical science have paid off in many ways and we would expect adjustments to the findings of social science to profit society in a much higher way.

The one who pioneered in developing this field, known as the sociology of knowledge, was Mannheim.[385] A later work offers contrasting views to those of Mannheim and Sorokin.[386] The subject is still in a formative stage.

The historian also has his interpretations, based primarily upon a temporal comparison in contrast to the sociologist's or anthropologist's comparison from one location to another.[387] The ideas of the genius have causes; and "causes have their causes."

Much of the knowledge derived in connection with the general field of dynamics may be regarded as explanatory knowledge, and some of it has been refined through processes of experimentation. But most of it has been evolved directly through the process of analytical description, involving successively refined concepts through developing ideas and testing them to see whether they fit the data well and are useful. The general purpose of this treatment has been to aid in conceptualizing the problems for study. That is, what does one look for? While no answer can be thought of as final without representing a barrier to further improvement and research, it is important to recognize what has been done up to the present time by way of formulating individual concepts and the conceptual scheme in the various fields. One then has an idea of what is currently acceptable, and, if he presents a view that is entirely different, he will understand the defense which will be called for in supporting his own set of explanatory or integrating, descriptive ideas.

### Functional Irregularities

One of the things to look for in any analysis is those cases which seem not to follow the general group of similar cases, or not to fall in line with

[384] Jessie Bernard, "Can Science Transcend Culture?" *Scientific Monthly* 71:268-73; October 1950.

[385] Karl Mannheim, *Ideology and Utopia:* An Introduction to the Sociology of Knowledge. Translated from the German by Louis Wirth and Edward Shils. New York: Harcourt, Brace and Co., 1936. 318 p.

[386] Jacques Jerome Pierre Maquet, *The Sociology of Knowledge.* A Critical Analysis of the Systems of Karl Mannheim and Pitirim A. Sorokin. Translated by John F. Locke. Boston: The Beacon Press, 1951. 318 p.

[387] Edward G. Boring, *op. cit.,* p. 3-5, 742-45. See also in his index "Dynamics of History," "Great-Man Theory," and "Zeitgeist."

what is generally expected. Modern statistical analyses have shown that everything varies. Hence, when we talk about "falling in line" with what is expected, we must allow a considerable latitude in expectancy (at least in practical situations), because it is only in theory, only in the mind, that things turn out precisely according to some law or some specific expectancy. In any real situation, each case varies somewhat from another.

It would not do, therefore, to look for every case that is different from another case, because all of them are different, if we only look closely enough. The present topic, accordingly, does not deal with all the possible differences, but rather with those cases which depart so far from the general run of cases that they seem worthy of attention. In practical work, something usually has to be done about them, and in scientific work it is often the exceptional case that reveals some flaw in the conceptual generalization. That is, there is a reason for the case not following expectation. Possibly the reason is that the expectation was wrong and needs to be modified, perhaps through including additional factors in the thought scheme, so that the thinking will come closer to what actually happens.

We have previously referred to operations research or operations analysis, as it is variously called, as a means of studying procedures to determine whether they are as effective as they might be. That is usually a somewhat more constructive approach than one starts out with. In industrial work, the process known as quality control is normally the starting point. If data reveal that too many of the cases being produced depart undesirably from an acceptable range, then constructive studies are undertaken and may involve what is referred to as operations research.

In educational work the functional irregularities are familiar to all. They have been the object of special study by a large number of researchers. These studies have brought out the wide variety of factors which have a bearing on one's physical condition, behavior, inner states (emotions, aspirations, conflicts), achievements, decisions, and so on.

We will cite here the literature that seems to offer most in the way of summaries of research which afford examples of analysis into various forms of unusualness. It may be interesting, at the outset, to note that an encyclopedia has been prepared, dealing with terms in all phases of living which apply to conditions regarded as abnormal—usually, on the lower side.[388] Clearly, our interest on the research side does not center on the practical aspects of what teachers and administrators and clinicians may do so much as on ways in which studies can be designed to analyze and describe and explain the phenomena of this class. Obviously, the general

---

[388] Edward Podolsky, Editor, *Encyclopedia of Aberrations.* New York: Philosophical Library, 1952. 550 p.

class of "irregularities" or of conditions regarded as irregular or non-normal or unusual is a large and heterogeneous group. The unity in the class results from the fact that we are here viewing it as a particular aspect of conditions to be looked for as a special form of analysis.

Perhaps it should be pointed out that the unusual is not always the result of a set of causes linked together in a fixed pattern, but may be the result of a somewhat chance succession of factors which have tended to operate in the same general direction. We can take fairly simple examples from a machine. A manufacturing machine that has been designed to produce a certain product, within a specified limit of variation, unavoidably has a certain amount of looseness in its connection—in its gears, pulleys, levers, and so on. Ordinarily, this play in most parts will tend in various directions, so that in the end the looseness or play in particular parts will tend to offset other parts. Occasionally, however, it will happen that a particular item is produced by this machine at a time when the play has, by chance, all tended in the same direction. In other words, it has been additive and cumulative rather than offsetting. In that case, the product will be far from what is expected. In such a case, a very unusual product does not indicate that the machine is in need of repair or adjustment; it simply means that the particular item was the product of a chance or fortuitous combination of all of the looseness in the machine. Such things will occur; they are unavoidable. Modern statistical theory deals with them and they have to be allowed for. These chance combinations have to be given special consideration in the design of the modern, high-speed computing machines, both in the mechanical parts and in the electronic parts. The accumulation of undesirable looseness in electronics gives rise to what is termed "noise." This is one of the basic determining factors in the design of the high-speed computers; when the problem to be solved by the machine becomes highly complex, the digital type of computer has the advantage over the analogue type.[389]

A bad product does not, therefore, always indicate a defective machine. On the other hand, in the field of human activity, where our interest centers on each person as an individual, we seek to arrange conditions, so as to avoid the chance succession of unfavorable events for any one person. To do this, it is not sufficient simply to set up a good operating system; a well built machine guarantees a satisfactory system of operations in its sphere, but occasionally turns out a bad product. The main hope, therefore, is not to be looked for in this area. The hope lies rather in a system

[389] Louis N. Ridenour, "The Role of the Computer." *Scientific American* 187:116-30; September 1952.

of continual watchfulness and frequent checks and alertness to the early evidences of deviations, and the opportunity that exists (together with understanding) for applying adequate diagnostic and remedial procedures. Accordingly, in human affairs, we will not place so much trust in the system as in the continued attention given to the individual.

In our discussion we are centering attention primarily on the negative side, namely, on those deviants who seem to fall below what is expected. This seems to be the natural center of attention—to help those persons who are particularly in need of help. Many writers have argued that society would benefit just as much from an equal amount of special attention to those persons who are "more fortunate," who have received a succession of factors, all (or most) of which have tended to help them be above the normal range—above the great stream of mankind. There is no doubt but that educators and others could profit from special knowledge of what can be done to help such persons be even more effective. Certain research in this area will be cited later in the chapter on genetic studies; in the main, existing research lies in the other direction.

The field of the physically handicapped has been dealt with extensively. Some of the difficulties are structural and organic, and, therefore, fall outside the limits of the present topic. There are, however, a number of physical difficulties which might be regarded as functional, primarily in the area of health. The teacher and administrator should have sufficient knowledge of what constitutes a normal range of behavior for the child, so as to know when to refer children to the school nurse, or a doctor.[390]

With regard to the diagnosis of behavior problems and disturbed emotions, it is desirable for the teacher [391] and school administrator to have sufficient knowledge to help set conditions daily in constructive directions. Much of the research, however, will be of chief interest to the clinical worker.[392]

We may turn to the subject of diagnosis of achievement, or learning in

[390] A summary of the research in this area will be found in the *Encyclopedia of Educational Research, op. cit.*, under the heads, "Health, Education," "Pupil Personnel Work—VII"; "Student Personnel Work—XII."

[391] This literature is summarized each year in the *Annual Review of Psychology* under such chapter heads as "Abnormalities of Behavior"; "Clinical Methods: Psychodiagnostics"; "Counseling: Diagnosis"; and, beginning with 1954, "The Theory and Techniques of Assessment." Also see O. H. Mowrer, *Psychotherapy,* 1953.

[392] The research literature for educators is summarized by Norman Fenton, "Problem Children and Delinquents," *Encyclopedia of Educational Research, op. cit.*, p. 868-74. Bibliography of thirty-seven references.

An earlier summary was provided by Willard C. Olson, "Diagnosis and Treatment of Behavior Disorders of Children." National Society for the Study of Education, *Educational Diagnosis.* Thirty-fourth Yearbook. Chicago: University of Chicago Press, 1935. Chapter 18, p. 363-97. This treatment deals with the interpretation of what research has revealed, in terms of the educator, and deals also with recommended treatment.

school situations. These studies are summarized by Brueckner.[393] As indicated in this review, the factors that affect learning and proper growth in general are many and varied. The curriculum, teaching methods, physical conditions in the school, and other school factors are only one group out of a large group which bear upon the behavior and learning ability of the pupil. Modern research has called attention to these many factors in contrast to the earlier interest in narrow and specific difficulties. It may be that a specific lack of some item of knowledge may prove a handicap which can possibly grow and expand, but the factors that need major attention are usually more general. The National Society for the Study of Education devoted an entire yearbook to the subject of diagnosis.[394] This treatment, while based on research, is pointed toward interpretation and usefulness of the research knowledge. It covers not only general principles of diagnosis and some principles of remedial instruction, but also deals with a number of individual subject fields and also special types of personal and behavior disorders. Chapter 24 is unusual in that it deals with creativeness. Diagnosis from the standpoint of the administrator is dealt with in Chapter 25 of this yearbook, and has also been presented in a text especially for administrators.[395]

It does not seem appropriate here to go into individual fields of study, but because reading is so pervasive in school work, and because the principles of diagnosis have been well worked out in this area and may be of general interest, we cite several selected references in this field.[396] For further discussion and illustrations the reader is referred to the later chapter on case and clinical studies.

One area of wide interest is that of student "mortality" in relation to the school. Why do students drop out? It is, of course, easy to say that "they cannot make the grade." That may be the usual attitude of persons who are without the benefit of research background. In some cases, it is true that

---

[393] Leo J. Brueckner, "Diagnosis in Teaching." *Encyclopedia of Educational Research, op. cit.*, p. 314-21. Bibliography of forty-five references. See also, for college teaching, p. 276. Diagnosis in the various subject-matter areas is handled in individual articles in the Encyclopedia as a section under the name of the particular field of study.

[394] National Society for the Study of Education, *Educational Diagnosis, op. cit.*

[395] Paul B. Jacobson and William C. Reavis, *Duties of School Principals*. New York: Prentice-Hall, 1942. 812 p. See especially Chapter 17, "Educational Diagnosis and Remedial Treatment," p. 538-64.

[396] Arthur E. Traxler, "Current Organization and Procedures in Remedial Teaching." *Journal of Experimental Education* 20:305-12; March 1952.

Albert J. Harris, *How to Increase Reading Ability*. Second Edition. New York: Longmans, Green and Co., 1947. 582 p.

An early outline of detailed factors in reading disability was given in the *Review of Educational Research* 1:335-36; December 1931.

A manual which represents the application of research knowledge about reading difficulties is: Board of Education, City of New York, Bureau of Educational Research, *The Retarded Reader in the Junior High School:* A Guide for Supervisors and Teachers. Publication No. 31. Brooklyn, September 1952. 126 p.

students do not have the mental ability to continue. Such facts raise at least some question as to the level of intellectual ability at which each school should aim. This is partly a matter of social philosophy. How selective, on purely intellectual grounds, does our society want its school system to be? Certainly, this is not an answer for which educators themselves should assume the responsibility of deciding. As a matter of fact, acting on traditional concepts, faculties normally do decide upon such matters; but it is a wholesome corrective for their thinking to realize that beyond their own judgments lie the needs of their civilization and the rights of the people in their society to determine basic policies.

There is increasing evidence that students drop out of high school for a variety of reasons, perhaps the main one being a general, more or less diffuse recognition of the fact that the school and their interest do not seem to lie in the same direction, or perhaps that they are not being successful in meeting the requirements of the school. The two are usually related. To cite appropriate literature here would be to repeat references which have already been given; but we refer to one reference again because of its cogency and because it refers to many other studies.[397] Studies of dropouts in colleges are usually conducted in terms of rather obvious (and often superficial) factors. It is true that, as the individual gets older, there are more reasons for him to join in the normal course of living; and, as he advances higher in the educational scheme, there are more demands for basic intelligence, as well as a good educational background. The balance between these factors and the desire for an education—often with an awareness of its uncertain financial benefits—is probably more likely to be a basic factor than in the case of younger persons at lower levels of the school system. It is doubtful, however, that the most useful information concerning the adaptation of college to its actual or potential clientele will be obtained by research which stays on this level. As has been said throughout the discussion, analysis can be conducted on any level desired; and each level may have its values in terms of the knowledge produced. In the field of more basic human motivations, however, it seems evident that study of some of the larger, more general, more persistent factors is essential for a relatively complete understanding.

There is also a wider view. The role of the irregular or unexpected in the total scheme of mankind's thinking and behavior should be recognized. It was John Dewey who pointed out several decades ago that man's thinking began with something unexpected.[398] The same idea has been

[397] David Segel, *op. cit.*

[398] John Dewey, *How We Think*. Boston: D. C. Heath and Co., 1910. A new edition, with extensive rewriting, was published in 1933. 301 p.

outlined by Burtt.[399] The point is emphasized again by Cantril and others in dealing with the nature of research.[400] It is, therefore, the hitches, inconsistencies, incongruities, and nonsequiturs—those things that do not accord with what we have learned to expect—which are the start not only of man's general problem-solving processes, but similarly of his research undertakings. And, as stated previously, the exceptional case in one's data —the case which does not follow the general tendency very closely—may be the starting point for an entirely new level of research in that area. Thus, the analysis of functional irregularities is not simply to be viewed as a matter of "trouble shooting"; it is at the basis of a large part of man's mental activity and of his research undertaking.

[399] Arthur Burtt, *Right Thinking*. New York: Harper and Bros., 1946. Chapter 2, "Analysis of a Typical Case of Reasoning," p. 17-30.

[400] Hadley Cantril and Others, "Psychology and Scientific Research." *Science* 110:461-64, 491-97, 517-22; November 4, 11, 18, 1949.

# 5

# The Descriptive Method:
## CLASSIFICATION

## CLASSIFICATION IN DESCRIPTIVE RESEARCH

CLASSIFICATION, which in essence is seeing similarities and differences among experiences, is a basic process in research and in fact in all mental life. There seems to be a deep-seated tendency in the human mind to classify things—to group them according to kind, to draw delimiting lines around each kind, and to seek a fuller understanding of what each particular kind means. Grouping makes for economy of thought; it provides a conceptual unity for further study; it brings new properties into focus; it leads to an ordering of experience.

"In a real chaos life, or at least a rational life, would be impossible. So from earliest times the human mind sought out the elements of order in the world, and the first step in this direction consisted in the noting of similarities between things." [401] Classifying is so basically a part of man's mental life that class words have come to occupy a large portion of his vocabulary. After studying many languages, an eminent philologist exclaimed, "Man is a classifying animal." [402] Without classification, thinking is seriously handicapped.

The recognizing of classes or groups is a form of generalization and represents a certain advance in thinking. In man's earliest days he probably had no class ideas but only specifics. We conclude this because certain primitive languages today have no words for classes but only for individual things; that is, they have no word for "tree," which is a class of objects (embracing all varieties of trees and all individual trees), but have a particular name for each individual tree, each shrub, and everything else to which one wishes to refer—just as we use names for individual persons.[403] What a handicap to thinking! Without generalizing words and ideas—those which apply to a group or class of phenomena—thinking is

[401] Abraham Wolf, *Essentials of Scientific Method*, p. 28. Second Edition. London: George Allen and Unwin; New York: Macmillan Co., 1928. 174 p.
[402] Otto Jespersen, *Language:* Its Nature, Development, and Origin, p. 388. London: George Allen and Unwin; New York: Henry Holt and Co., 1922. 448 p.
[403] Jespersen and other philologists cite many examples; for instance, "In Baiairi (Central Brazil) each parrot has its special name, and the general idea 'parrot' is totally unknown." Jespersen, *op. cit.,* p. 429.

tied down to individual, isolated cases and what we are familiar with today as thinking could not take place at all.

**Classification underlies all science.** Classification is foundational to such activities as systematic observation, counting, measuring, and evaluating, for without definite classes these processes could have no immediate meaning. In some form or other classification is present in every step of research, beginning with the very formulation of the problem.

> The method of classification is the first method employed in every science. Long before there is that deeper insight into facts, which is required for the more advanced methods of science, the method of classification can be, and has to be, employed. Many sciences, indeed, remain for a long time in a merely classificatory stage. . . . This is especially true of botany, zoology, and ethnology, and was at one time almost equally true of chemistry, mineralogy, and some other sciences.[404]

The term *classification* is employed both in the sense of forming categories and in the sense of putting individual cases into (identifying with) the classes which have been formed. In corresponding fashion, the term *class* means both the category (the concept), and also the aggregate of individual cases that belong in that category (for example, a class of pupils in school). These dual meanings accord with everyday usage of the terms, as indicated in the dictionary. The terms, therefore, apply to the whole process of putting together things that one thinks belong together—the process of isolating and associating those things which, for either practical or theoretical purposes, it is found advantageous *to regard in the same way*.

Those who are wont to think of science in terms of the highly abstract mathematical phases of physics are likely to overlook the fundamental role of classification. They sometimes think that classification is unimportant and that only quantitative relations and other forms of generalization ("laws") are the realities of science. This is grossly in error. Generalizations grow out of specific classes of things and are true only for specific classes of things; and these classes, although often taken for granted, are just as essential a part of generalizations as are the quantitative and relational parts of the statements. The delimiting and describing of the particular kinds of things about which generalizations are made are, therefore, necessary steps in the making and refining of these generalizations.

**Classification calls for class concepts.** To appreciate the fundamental role of classification, one must view it in its full scope. Perhaps one's first tendency will be to think of classification as primarily the placing of cases into existing, well understood categories. Research workers would be fortu-

---

[404] Quoted from Abraham Wolf, *Essentials of Scientific Method,* p. 30. Second Edition. London: George Allen and Unwin; New York: Macmillan Co., 1928. 174 p.

nate, if that were the extent of their difficulties in this a.
fact, cases are placed into categories as a part of most res
where this can be done routinely and with little trouble,
itself constitute a major contribution; it is simply a step in
the data collected.

Prior to any such classification of cases, however, there mu
idea as to what the classes are like. It should be pointed out th
person takes many things for granted which the mature scientis ..nows
are not understood. If one has been in the habit of assuming that mankind
has already provided categories that are available for mapping out the
whole world of experience, and all that is left is to count cases which fall
in these categories, he has not sensed the full mission of research. Virtually
all concepts of science are continually undergoing change, and it is the
province of research to adapt, refine, and even create new concepts to
embrace classes of phenomena. Indeed, the most fundamental contribution
of research may be said to lie in the birth of a concept of something new
to man's thought. Only after such a concept has been envisaged, however
crudely at first, can man proceed to study his idea, and the cases it presumably embraces, and thus bring the phenomena eventually into a state
of rather complete description. Classification is thus one of the steps in producing a well-ordered systematic description.

Much of the history of physical science has consisted of inventing and
refining class concepts. By way of illustration, one may consider the long
course of evolution of the class concept "chemical elements." Some six
hundred years before the time of Christ certain Greek philosophers put
forth the idea that there were such things. This in itself was obviously a
hypothesis—a "hunch" that possibly there was a class of things which
were elemental and which, in different combinations, made up the universe.
This was a new class idea; from our present point of great familiarity with
the elements it is difficult to realize how great a contribution the mere idea
was. Of course it had to go through a long course of refinement and readjustment, as all scientific ideas do, and it is still being modified. The suggestion from one Greek school (that of Pythagoras, whose name is familiar
to students of geometry) was that the elements were four in number—
earth, air, water, and fire. In the Greek classical days, and in fact well
along through the days of alchemy toward the Renaissance, much emphasis
was given to properties, and it was at one time believed that the four elements were in turn built up of combinations of the qualities hot and cold,
wet and dry.[405] At a later time, the elements were thought to consist of three

[405] William C. Dampier, *History of Science*, p. 18. Third Edition. Cambridge, Eng.: University Press; New York: Macmillan Co., 1942. 574 p.

salt, sulphur, and mercury.[406] Perhaps one can see the tortuous course that the category "chemical element" had to go through before it reached its modern version. How could one say what an element was when the class concept was so crude? It is precisely through this process of the long inter- action of ideas and observations, and the adjustment of ideas till they fit the observed facts and at the same time have a useful purpose, that scien- tists (physical or social) refine their concepts and derive categories which are genuinely serviceable.[407]

In the younger sciences, this process of building the elementary class concepts must necessarily occupy a large portion of the total effort. In education, where the whole history of scientific work lies almost within the present century, it is proper that much attention be given to the rec- ognition and identification of significant classes of persons, things, events, and forces. In part, this means giving attention to the reliability and validity of our measuring instruments; that is, what do they really reflect? We speak of "intelligence"—a concept of recent origin which has proved of considerable utility for certain purposes; how much refining does the concept still need to make it of further value? Can the same instrument be employed to classify children, adults, and the senescent with regard to intelligence? To what extent is "intelligence" qualitatively different at dif- ferent levels of maturity? We will know better some years hence. With over 2500 years of experience behind it, the concept of chemical elements during our own lifetime has undergone revolutionary changes. The process of refining categorical concepts continues, even in the mature sciences.

**Classification is partly imposed.** It is perhaps commonplace to think that objects which are well known fall naturally into groups, on the basis of characteristics which are rather evident, and that these groups are essen- tially inherent and inflexible. Such beliefs characterized the thinking of the classical scholars, whose desire to find absolutes, such as rigid categories with no borderline cases, led them to warp their conclusions into the desired mold, in spite of abundant evidence to the contrary. There is always the tendency to let one's thinking fall into the easy pattern of the dichotomy— to see things as "all or none," as "white or black." This tendency toward absolutes was so strong that, for Plato to speak of "the good" was pre- sumably to indicate as definite a category as to speak of persons who are between 5 feet 11 inches and 6 feet in height. There are still occasional evidences of the persistence of these notions of rigidity for even loose

---

406 *Ibid.*, p. 80, 154.
407 The history of any science, viewed in terms of the slow emergence and refinement of concepts, is fascinating to the thoughtful person. The *idea* side is especially emphasized in Humphry T. Pledge, *Science Since 1500*. London: His Majesty's Stationery Office, 1939. New York: Philosophical Library. 357 p.

verbal categories, and of the fixity of typical characteristics.[408] The very elaborateness of such classification schemes as those in botany and zoölogy may suggest a certain amount of finality and possibly (as with Aristotle), even an element of determinism.

Modern scholarship does not support these notions. Perhaps scientists of the present century have learned not to let their preconceptions close their eyes to exceptional cases which actually occur. For example, in biology there are probably no more sports ("spontaneous" deviations from type) today than before, but biologists have stopped ignoring them. The statistician, with his insistence on counting cases in various categories (instead of only two categories), has made it impossible in most instances to think in the old terms of discrete categories.[409] Everything varies, and any "class" of objects in nature will be found to have so many variations, both quantitative and qualitative, that genuine difficulties arise as to what belongs in the class. We can set up neat systems of thought, but nature is not so neatly ordered.

Difficulties occur in both simple and complex classification schemes. In a classification scheme that exists on only a single level of ordination (that is, the categories are not further subdivided by subclasses, nor integrated into larger supergroups), actual cases are likely to be found which cut across any dividing lines that may be drawn—that is, if one searches widely and does not close his eyes to actual variations. Such cases may combine in all possible proportions the characters of two or more classes which may be set up, so that, theoretically, an infinity of categories would be necessary to accommodate the cases. In practical situations we may not care about making special provision for many of these borderline or overlapping cases. That is, for convenience, we may make and use fairly simple categories, such as for sex; but as a matter of principle we must recognize that exceptions occur.

Actuality is rarely as simple as our thoughts about it. In a questionnaire study, for example, it would seem a perfectly simple thing to count the number of questionnaires returned and the number not returned. But in such a dichotomy where will one count those returned by the post office

[408] See, for example, the advocacy of "analytic induction," with its assumptions of rigid categories, "essential" characters, and no exceptions, in the references discussed by W. S. Robinson, "The Logical Structure of Analytic Induction." *American Sociological Review* 16:812-18; December 1951.

[409] George Boas, "From Truth to Probability." *Harper's Monthly Magazine* 154:516-22; March 1927.

B. R. Buckingham, "Thinking Statistically." *Educational Research Bulletin* (Ohio State University) 6:142-43; March 30, 1927.

Richard von Mises, *Probability, Statistics, and Truth.* Translated from the second German edition by J. Neyman, D. Sholl, and E. Rabinowitsch. London: William Hodge and Co.; New York: Macmillan Co., 1939. 323 p.

for lack of current address? What about those returned which are only partly filled in? Such incompleteness may range by degrees from a minor omission all the way to a return that is wholly blank. How would one count (within the frame of two classes) a questionnaire that was complete, but which gave evidence that placed the reply under suspicion? Or a questionnaire filled in by someone who was not supposed to receive it? Or one which was partly or wholly illegible? And so on. The category "number returned" may be restricted to "number of usable returns"; practically, this may be an improvement, but it will be evident that the limits of such a category are matters of judgment and, therefore, arbitrary. Such a simple set of categories may be sufficiently accurate for most purposes, but they are to some degree forced and cannot, therefore, be thought of as absolute.

Problems of the foregoing type are accentuated when categories are to be formed by dividing up a scale of magnitudes. For example, at what specific height is a person tall? At what point on the intelligence scale does a person become "bright"? At what moment does adolescence end? If limits are fixed for such categories (they would have to be defined rather definitely if used in research), it is clear that such limits would be wholly man-made whether arrived at by agreement, tradition, statistical calculation, or other means. The point is, again, that natural qualities of cases cannot be depended on for the setting of limits to categories.

It might be assumed that the problem could readily be met by making the classification scheme more complex—by providing for a hierarchy of subclasses on whatever number of levels may be called for. Such a scheme, however, only adds new problems to the old. Instead of having only the problem of where to draw limits, one now has the problem of subclasses which violate the major definitions for higher levels, usually by combining several critical qualities. If one seeks to solve the difficulty by moving the disturbing class to a higher level, he may find that other groups will not "go along"—that new problems of the same type are created. These problems are not merely matters of immature thinking; they may be logically insoluble in terms of any reasonably systematic schemes. Consider, for example, the problem (or the impossibility) of differentiating in consistent terms between plants and animals. Of course the "man on the street" can tell the difference; his knowledge does not extend to the complicating cases. But certain groups of living things exist that have (or lack) one or more of the properties accepted as essential plant properties and also one or more of the properties accepted as essential animal properties. Thus, the genus of life known as Euglena is claimed by professional botanists as being in the plant kingdom, and by professional zoölogists as being in the animal kingdom. In this instance there does not seem to be any uncompromised basis for a decision one way or the other, since either decision would violate more general decisions already made.

It may be somewhat surprising to realize that there is no way to tell where the genus Euglena actually (inherently) belongs—but there is no such thing as essential objective categories. What is a plant and what is an animal is something that man determines. That is, he decides what qualities he desires to apply the term *plant* to, and what qualities he desires to apply the term *animal* to. (Apparently man's thinking at this point is too simple. It becomes obvious that not all living things can correctly be accommodated by the choice, "plant or animal"; however, under the influence of tradition based on hundreds of thousands of years of rather superficial experience with living things, man continues to try to make the convenient dichotomy do.) The important point is that these categories grow out of man's reactions to nature and reflect his (crude or refined) observations. Apart from man's thinking, there are no plants or animals; the corresponding objects exist, but not in these categories. As Charles H. Judd used to say in his lectures, "There are no vertebrates in nature. There are animals having backbones, but it is man who created the class (the idea) 'Vertebrata.' " Any classification represents the investment of observations with an idea.

These statements are not meant to imply that one is free to make class concepts in any fashion he may choose. It is assumed that the researcher's concepts will be formed in the light of his disciplined perception, will be tested by further observation, and be evaluated by all the critical faculties at the disposal of scientific workers. Physical and biological scientists have invented a large number of concepts which they have had to discard, because subsequent research failed to support them. It is, however, important to realize the extent to which classes are mental; they do not exist in nature apart from man's mind; they represent man's views of the world. *Nature provides the objects, man provides the classes.*

**Classes are created for utility.** With the foregoing background, it is possible to view classes in terms of their essential purpose, which is to serve some interest of man. The person whose thinking is swayed by a mechanical conception of objectivity will likely say, Man didn't make things similar; they exist that way. Quite true, but one cannot avoid the immediate question, Similar with respect to what? Any set of things which are similar are similar only in certain respects; in certain other respects they are different, and it may be that in all other respects they are different. One must not become so obsessed with the particular character or characters in which he is interested that he loses sight of the fact that these are, objectively, of no more importance than any other characters—than the multitude of characters on which the things are different. It is only when certain characters become the object of one's interest that these particular traits become important—important for him, and possibly for other persons. But why do these qualities become of interest to him? Particular characters are selected for attention in the belief or the hope that they will serve some purpose—to order the data, to describe the cases, and so on. In other words, classification is simply *selective association,* and for this selection to have any value, it must, sooner or later, serve a purpose.

It should be clear from everyday experience that anything can be classified in a myriad different ways, according to the aspect (the basis of classification) that is selected. Consider in how many different ways we classify human beings. For humanitarian purposes we seek to emphasize the unity of all mankind, and for democratic purposes we affirm the equality of individuals. But for many specialized purposes we find it serviceable to divide mankind into various classes. For example, we have laws which categorize the human race on the basis of citizenship, place of residence (as for school attendance), age (for school attendance, voting, employment, and so on), sex, family membership, amount of education (for example, for licensing to practice medicine), previous acts (as criminals), amount of income (for tax purposes), and so on almost indefinitely. In our ordinary social relations there are numerous less formal classes which we make: persons who are familiar or strange; who are thought of as friendly, or otherwise; who are employed by the same firm as we; whom we accept as social peers, and so on. While all these classes may have some factual basis, they are not all to be thought of as being perfectly obvious or natural; most of them are not at all "natural," but are the result of ideas connected with modern civilization. The classes are formed because they have service value.

Therefore, when one determines the basis of the classification he expects to use and sets the limits for each category, he determines what cases will be regarded as similar; that is, what cases will form a class. If one argues that these cases not only *will be regarded* as similar but that they actually *are* similar, the answer is that he is quite correct, for in some sense or other everything is similar to every other thing. But such generality is meaningless and unprofitable. It is only when the similarity, or association, is selective, and selective with regard to some purpose, that the similarity is of any importance. Further, it should be noted that any certain number of persons who might be placed together into a group by one of the bases referred to in the preceding paragraph might, on some other basis, be scattered into several different groups. *Cases form a class only when looked at in a certain way.* The way one decides to look at objects or events is a matter of choice, a choice to be made in the light of the purposes to be served.

One who is a student of biology or chemistry may wish to raise an objection that, in such sciences, the point being made is not true. The classification schemes are based on inherent qualities, the schemes are settled, and the place of any specimen is fixed. So it may seem. In order to make learning simple for the undergraduate, such impressions are often allowed to form. Biological schemes are likely to be based primarily on form and structure (morphology). Such a basis may seem inherent, in that it is observable, but it is no more inherent than size or weight or thousands of other characters; it has simply been found to be more significant for man's scientific thinking. Hence, the conventional scheme is widely accepted in scientific circles. But it must be seen as serviceable only for those purposes for which it actually has value; there are countless purposes for which it does not. For example, the common scientific classification scheme is of little or no value for indicating what plants have medicinal properties, or what ones are edible and what others are poisonous. It is not geared to the gardener's interest in differentiating wanted plants from weeds, in indicating what plants are hardy in northern winters, which ones will have yellow flowers, and so on. Not that these purposes are not real and significant—in horticultural catalogues these classes are likely to be employed —but for scientific purposes these bases of classification do not seem to have as great intellectual utility as do others. The formal scheme is just as definitely based on utility as is any classification any place; in this instance, it happens to be scientific utility. But such a statement is an indication of a goal rather than a sure quality.

The scientific classification schemes are not so fully settled as they are often made to appear. National and international bodies of scientists meet annually to consider revisions. Leading biologists question the propriety of many categories—either their limits or their placement. The advantage or desirability of placing a subcategory under one category rather than under another may not yet be convincingly demonstrated. The logic of organization depends basically on what trait it is decided to emphasize more than others. To assume that any classification scheme in science is fixed finally is to assume that the particular science is no longer in an active state of growth. It is embarrassing to all concerned to recall that students of physics and chemistry a generation ago were taught that the periodic table of elements was fixed, and that it could be shown theoretically no further elements beyond ninety-two were possible. Not only have additional elements extended the table, but so many varieties of elements have been discovered or manufactured that physical scientists have great difficulty in deciding what the concept of an element really is, or what it is desirable for it to be. As new insights afford new understanding, and as advancing knowledge sets new demands, class concepts must be adjusted to fit the new facts and serve the altered needs.

**Practical consequences of these perspectives.** These understandings of the nature of classes and of classification have important bearings on one's conception of the nature and the processes of research, and also on what the research worker will attempt to do. Three general consequences may be mentioned.

1. One's goals and criteria in making categories will be different from those he would hold to, if he thought nature formed her own inexorable classes. He will recognize that utility is a large element in his decision as to what a good category, or system of categories, is. In other words, purpose is a major criterion in one's choice of a basis for classification and in his setting of limits to categories; one is not seeking to describe nature solely in terms of objective aspects—for, to the extent that it could be done at all, it could be done in an infinity of ways. *There is nothing in nature to tell how to classify it*—until man has made up his classification scheme.

2. The nature of so-called "objective" science is more clearly seen. The term is commonly used; it has value when properly understood. It is not, however, at any time to be interpreted as meaning wholly objective, or objective to the exclusion of man's reactions and judgment. "Objective science" implies that ideas should be kept in accord with facts rather than be permitted to grow out of one's personal inclinations; and, in the field of human values, it implies that one will examine other values than those which he himself holds. But the term does damage to one's understanding of research and science if it is interpreted to mean that science has developed or exists independent of man's observation and thoughtful interpretation. Objectivity is necessarily a relative term.

3. Inasmuch as systems of classification must ultimately be evaluated in terms of utility (taking for granted that they are kept in accord with dependable observations), one will maintain an interest in criticizing these systems and in seeking to improve upon them rather than accept existing or proposed schemes with the thought that they represent the objective facts of nature and are, therefore, basic and immutable. There is no system of classification in any field which should be regarded as fixed and not subject to refinement, reorganization, and extension in the light of advancing knowledge. The door of science is continually open.

**Classification is potentially extensive.** While it is common to think of classification in terms of going from one level to the next—that is, from the starting point to the first superordinate or subordinate level—a moment's reflection will reveal that the process ordinarily may be continued further in the same direction, or may proceed in the opposite direction.

Anything one may take as a starting point is both a member of a still more general class and, in turn, something which can be subdivided. There are limits to present knowledge, to be sure, but the history of science makes it clear that present limits are temporary. Each new telescope opens up vast vistas containing myriads of new nebulae, and each new type of microscope brings into vision minutiae which formerly could only be postulated. Scientific progress moves constantly in the direction of detecting differences and making finer classes, while at the same time integrating thoughts into ever larger generalizations. Apparently there is nothing which cannot, sooner or later, be broken down further; or, in the other direction, included in some more comprehensive concept. It seems reasonable, therefore, to think of classification as extending over an infinite chain of steps—from one level of ordination to another without prospect of halt.

It is appropriate here to refer to the significant stanza written by the mathematician, Jacques Bernoulli, in 1713, in his *Ars Conjectandi,* and translated by Helen M. Walker; [410] it was reproduced in Chapter 1.

From among the great number of conceptual levels in any field that exist, or which are possible, one choses a particular level on which to begin his thinking and his observation. An object on this level (or perhaps on a more detailed level) is then viewed as a case. (The word *object* is here used to mean any phenomenon, or in fact any single class of phenomena.) One may proceed, in the upward direction, to associate the case with other cases he thinks are similar and thus form an embracing class of cases; or, in the downward direction, he may wish to view his case as a complex whole, to be broken into components. The point is that a case is whatever one decides to regard in that way—whatever it is reasonable for his purpose to employ as a case—whether this "case" be a single object, or a class of objects, or anything else. Wherever such terms as *case, class,* or *whole* are used, therefore, they are to be viewed as relative and not as absolute—for in an infinite series of levels, no level can be absolute. The terms are primarily terms of convenience, and take meaning from the context of one's thought or work. It is important that they not be interpreted in a limited way, as implying some particular level; otherwise the thoughtful person may spend the rest of his life trying unsuccessfully to find the level of generality on which "a case" occurs. Cases occur on all levels; in research, anything is a case when it is so treated.

To make these statements more concrete, it may be well to consider an illustration. If one is interested in studying public school buildings, these become his principal cases. To form a larger conceptual category, one might go to "public buildings (in general)." For a level above this, one

410 Helen M. Walker, *Mathematics Teacher* 36:87; February 1943.

could take the subject, "all buildings," or perhaps "architecture." And, still more generally, "the works constructed by man." In the other direction, school buildings as a class could be subdivided (classified) according to educational level, size, cost, material of which constructed, climatic conditions it was designed to meet, internal plan or arrangement, per cent of space devoted to instructional use, age, present condition of repair, and all the other aspects one could think of. Conceptual subdivisions of individual buildings, if one were so interested, would include various kinds of rooms or various uses of space; and one could make these his cases, if that were his purpose. Or, on a level still more subordinate, one's attention might be directed to furniture and equipment, or to material for floors.

A full recognition of the existence of an indefinitely large series of levels for attention (and for conceptual integration) in any field of study is of importance in several ways. In the first place, it will serve to avoid absurd disputes over what is a case, a whole, where one must start, and the like. A thing is a case or a whole, if one finds it useful to treat it that way, even though the "thing" may itself be a whole class of items. In the second place, it will aid one in seeing that a single step in either direction from his starting level is not necessarily a final one; it is only a beginning. In the third place, it will help one see why it is important to delimit carefully and rather fully the statement of one's research problem and the class of cases (the population) on which he is going to make his observations. Extensions of thought along qualitative, geographical, and temporal lines are always potentially present in the mind of a person (for example, the reader or user of a research report), and if the writer does not properly describe, in all important ways, the level of generality of his observations, the reader (and sometimes the researcher himself) cannot tell what, in the infinite hierarchy of possibilities, he is talking about.

There is another, and perhaps more fundamental, outcome of this perspective. An understanding of the many levels from which cases may be drawn enables one, with equal legitimacy, to choose whatever level of generality he may desire as the basis for selecting phenomena and drawing generalizations concerning them. Thus, the psychologist and the biologist emphasize the individual. The biologist, however, tends to subdivide and study structure, often giving considerable attention to the individual cell. The psychologist tends to think of the individual person (or animal), in his physical and social setting, as the proper level of integration for attention. The sociologist emphasizes societies and their cultures—functioning groups of human beings. The educator is perforce concerned with all these settings and perspectives, since he deals with the human being in all his relations to life. The point is that each of these interests is legitimate, because each has ultimate utility; and, if they are all of value in serving man's needs, the scientist who works on one level of integration or generality has little ground for questioning the appropriateness of another researcher choosing some other level of integration as the field from which to draw phenomena for his observation and his basis of generalization. Science will be made wherever there are researchers to make it and wherever there is value to be found in doing so.

## HOW CLASSIFICATION IS USED IN RESEARCH

The foregoing discussion of the general nature and role of classification provides a background for the more concrete consideration, in the present section, of ways in which classification is employed in research; and for the later discussion of various procedures in forming and delimiting categories. For one who is interested solely in practical applications, the present and subsequent sections may afford what guidance he needs. The more general discussion in the preceding section, however, will aid in a more complete understanding of the illustrations and in the avoidance of various misconceptions concerning the subject.

It was previously remarked that classification is present in all steps in research. It is involved in the formulation of one's problem, in the delimitation of the traits or aspects to be studied, in defining the population from which observations will be taken, in determining what will constitute a case, in planning sampling procedures, and so on. All these steps involve class concepts and usually call for a significant refinement of the ideas, with particular emphasis on their limits. The construction of questionnaires, tests, and other data-gathering schedules calls for clearly analyzed categories. When data have been obtained, putting cases together into groups on the basis of perceived similarities constitutes perhaps the most commonly thought of form of classification. In statistical (counting) studies, data are usually subdivided both qualitatively and quantitatively, so as to present a more detailed picture than that afforded by the total (or average) for the entire group; or perhaps so as to show the variation associated with other factors. Building up generalizations inductively represents classifying; the generalization is but a statement of the category concept that embraces the class of cases (possibly relationships) to which it applies. The integration of findings from various studies, and even the final step of dividing up all human knowledge into various domains, are high-level forms of classification.

In thinking of this subject, one will not, therefore, confine his attention simply to the aspect of forming groups. It will be seen that classification has many aspects and plays many roles. In some studies, it is inconspicuous; no series of categories may appear. The general descriptive studies discussed at the beginning of this chapter may be of this character, although even in such cases delimitations will be present and conclusions will be drawn; and the report itself will be divided into chapters. At the other extreme are studies in which the formation of categories is the end goal or the chief contribution of the work.

In the organizing of this present section on uses, many problems arose, as is usual when complex categories are to be formed. Since the subject of classification has a number of aspects and since actual research studies are infinitely varied, the forming of categories to organize a discussion of these two subjects in combination is met with a number of possibilities which is indefinitely large. No *single* basis for classification seemed desirable; hence a mixed basis was settled on, namely, one which would combine selected aspects of classification with certain research processes. The object was to present salient applications that would be illustrative of the several phases of classification, while at the same time showing their significant roles in research.

Accordingly, the following seven categories of use were chosen and the discussion will be organized under these heads. They are stated in the form of purposes or goals of the research worker as he faces various problems in the prosecution of his study.

1. To provide codified data
2. To form useful classes according to kind
3. To afford logical order and system
4. To develop the meaning of class concepts
5. To create cases through delimitation
6. To standardize observations which describe
7. To select and categorize scale indicators.

These topics follow something of a psychological order rather than a logical or chronological one. That is, they are arranged roughly in terms of the increasing complexity of the research study, and partly in terms of the increasing difficulty of the concepts involved in the classification process. The first topic, and to some extent the second, deal primarily with simpler studies and are concerned with grouping (that is, placing observed cases in existing categories). There is, in such instances, no direct contribution (nothing new) in the categories which are employed. In the third and fourth topics, and to some extent in the second, the concern is with logical considerations, primarily meaning and order. The last three topics deal with delimitation and definition; they are related primarily to measurement and causal studies, and the categories are more technical and complex. The reader who wishes to take up the topics in the order in which they are likely to occur in a complex study will, accordingly, begin his reading with the last three topics, for they deal with the preparatory steps—the planning phase of a more difficult type of data-gathering. The first four topics relate to data which are already in hand, and deal with the analysis (categorization) of such data. They therefore apply to the (usually) later phases of a study. They are here treated first because (*a*) many studies are not so complex as to require conscious attention to the last three topics—often one's data come readily; and (*b*) the later topics are more difficult for the inexperienced person to grasp.

It will be borne in mind throughout any discussion of classification that it is, in any and all of its aspects, essentially a form of description. At its base, classification is a matter of clarifying, refining, and organizing what it is one thinks he means when he employs a class name. The psychological aspects of classification are the principal ones and afford the great opportunities for making contributions in descriptive (and even in explanatory) research. It should not come as a surprise that the basic portion of description consists in getting clear ideas of what it is one is trying to describe, but it probably is a lifelong surprise to every research worker to realize anew in each research he undertakes how difficult (and challenging) is the process of developing penetrating insights into the real nature and character of the things he is studying. Research is, in essence, the process of turning a glibly named something into a highly structured concept. Classification, also, is just that.

The discussion of classification as a separate subject is not intended to indicate a sharp differentiation from the types of description which have preceded, nor from those that relate to quantitative work. Class names are employed in general description and, contrariwise, some general description will find a place in building clear notions of concepts used directly as categories. Differentiating a whole into components (analysis), is avowedly a form of classification. Category formation is necessarily involved in all counting and all measuring. The point is that, although as a matter of emphasis and convenience classification is discussed as a separate subject, it is to be thought of as closely related to, and actually as an integral part of, all other forms of description.

**Providing codified data.** Probably the simplest use of classification involves readily available, commonly used categories as a basis for dividing up cases into classes which are likely to be of direct interest for one or another purpose. For example, there come to mind the many categories employed in a school census, or in the United States censuses. For a variety of purposes, one would want such data divided (classified) according to sex, age, place of residence, nationality, and the like. Heads such as these are selected and used, because there is direct interest in the subdivisions (breakdowns) they provide. Possibly captions of this nature are so commonplace that one has never stopped to think of them as categories, but they are so in the same sense as any other categories employed in research. The principal difference is that in these cases the need for such classes has been recognized in everyday living, so that the class concepts have already been formed and the use of their names as class terms has become common and relatively routine.

Categories for the purpose of providing codified data may be of any variety which suits the data and the need. They may be purely mechanical (as all last names beginning with the same letter); qualitative without special order (as sex, color of hair, religious preference); qualitative with some relation to a scale (as tall, medium, or short; overweight, normal, or underweight; literate or illiterate); quantitative (as weight, score on a test, number of brothers and sisters); quantitative time units used as measures (age, years of experience, length of time required for travel to school); quantitative time units used as cases (*particular* calendar years, months, days of the week); quantitative spatial units used as measures (height, distance from school in miles, number of acres in school grounds); geographical units used as cases (*particular* states, counties, cities); and other varieties as one may care to name them, including innumerable compounds of two or more traits.

Simple categories are the type usually called for in reports regularly made in almost all forms of organized social endeavor; for example, the attendance reports that teachers have to make; the reports which the superintendent has to forward to the state department of education, and the statistical reports for the biennial survey of education conducted (since 1918) by the U. S. Office of Education. Questionnaire studies are likely to yield many such data; so are interviews, and opinion or attitude surveys (although here the use or interpretation of the results is shifting over to a somewhat different purpose). Data of this type are characteristic also of many studies of the group status or survey type. Such studies [411] usually describe a designated group of persons, or an institution, or area by gathering data which can be classified into categories that are relatively simple and easily understood. (These studies are numerous; it would be out of

[411] Examples are numerous; for specific illustrations one may consult:

Gene K. Lockard, *Comparative Study of the College Preparation, Teaching Combinations and Salaries of Kansas High School Administrators and Teachers, 1946.* Kansas State Teachers College of Emporia Bulletin of Information, Vol. 26, No. 11. Studies in Education, No. 31. Emporia, Kansas, 1946. 38 p.

National Education Association, Research Division, "Status and Practices of Boards of Education." *National Education Association Research Bulletin* 24:47-83; April 1946.

place here to give extensive examples, since they are presented in detail in the next chapter; our interest in them here is simply that they often employ the type of classification under discussion.)

Perhaps one is ready to raise the question, Aren't all data of this type? What is peculiar or special about the class being discussed here? For an answer, we must consider the entire outline of the treatment. In the uses which are dealt with under the heads that follow, the purposes for making classes are somewhat different and hence the data in them are likely to fall into a somewhat different pattern of thought. The distinction is, however, primarily one of degree and may not be clear cut. In the section immediately following, the emphasis is more on the classes or categories than on the number of cases falling in each one. The intent of the present section is not to invent a separate type of use of classification, but only to provide a place in our outline for giving recognition to the type that is commonest of all; while the type has practically no distinguishing features other than its simplicity, it would scarcely seem appropriate to ignore entirely what one will come upon most often in his reading of research reports. Hence we define the present type as being too simple, too uncomplicated, perhaps too untechnical to fall into any of the classes that follow.

The presently discussed use of classification assumes an interest in the data that fall in the categories. Hence it is the basis of enumerative studies. The purpose of such data is normally to describe, to give a quantitative picture of the group or area in terms of the number of cases in the different categories. Thus, although certain other purposes are accomplished at the same time, such as certain ones to be discussed in later sections, those results are incidental and are not here a large consideration.

Codified data are often general-purpose data; that is, they are often gathered, not for a specific purpose, but to serve a number of unknown uses which may arise later on. They are basic data for a variety of potential uses. Census data are clearly of this type. So are many of the descriptive data gathered in studies of the group status or survey type, referred to earlier. They are gathered in part with the thought that they may be of value to administrators, to subsequent students making comparative and trend studies, and for reference use by deliberative bodies. Such potential later use of descriptive data is in itself adequate justification for many data which are gathered—although it is frequently overlooked, and perhaps deprecated, by those persons who hold to the rather narrow view that everything done in research must be for the purpose of answering a previously formulated question. Unfortunately, the most significant questions may not occur to one until he is well along in gathering or analyzing his data; and for reference purposes (as trend or historical studies) the need for the data may arise fifty or one hundred years after a study has been completed. While it would not be desirable to gain an impression that research is a matter of gathering as many facts as possible in helter-skelter fashion, it would be equally undesirable to hold to the line that no fact should be gathered in descriptive studies which did not serve an immediate and crucial purpose in a given study. In studies concerned with the broad description of a group of persons or a geographical area or a given institution, the majority of the aspects studied will not, individually, be crucial; but taken together each may add important light to the complex description of a composite situation.

Those critics whose sole conception of research is that it deals with cause-effect relationships, or who insist that a study cannot be research unless it is attempting to defend some general thesis, sometimes ask, What is the use of knowing all that? What does it show? The answer is that the gathering of basic data which presumably have some important reference value is to be defended on exactly the same ground as the working out of some new laboratory procedure for forming a chemical compound (which may constitute the doctoral problem of a chemistry student). Both undertakings have made new knowledge available, which it is hoped will some day be of use in an important sequence of thought. Whether either one is likely to be of value depends on the good judgment of the person selecting or approving the study and upon the course of subsequent historical events.

One comes here, as in many other places, face to face with the question of what constitutes research. The gathering of data solely for general purposes, as in a census, will probably not in itself constitute what should be called research. In general, routine work is outside the scope of research. The special production or adaptation of a data-gathering schedule to a particular situation or purpose, however, is in itself an act of research and, for studies on the master's thesis level, many problems are acceptable, even though they are fairly mechanical—the thought being that they are, after all, primarily beginning experiences in research.

It will be apparent that any classification of data must be provided for in the original data-gathering. In very simple studies, where perhaps only one trait is being observed, or perhaps two or three traits with no connections to be made between them, the cases can be tallied at once in the appropriate category while the observation is being recorded. Ordinarily, however, one will record a number of aspects (traits) for each case observed, and all these, for a given individual, should be on the same record. In some instances, the actual categories will be on the prepared record form —such perhaps as boy and girl, or male and female; in other instances perhaps only the trait will be named on the record form, as "age," and the actual age will be recorded, probably to be put into statistical categories later on. Thus the categorizing process may take place at slightly different times, as a matter of convenience. The point made here is that such classification must at least be thought about and prepared for in advance of the data-gathering in a way which seems appropriate. And in every study, careful definitions will have to be formulated at the outset.

To summarize, this section recognizes probably the commonest type of classification, namely, the use of already existing concepts and perhaps common group names as bases for subdividing observations into classes in which there is direct interest, particularly statistical interest. It is assumed that these categories present no special problems in their formulation and that they are not required to have certain properties or serve special purposes such as those later to be described. The grouping, therefore, should be almost automatic.

While it is true that occasionally the categories described in this section may be employed as cases (particularly in demographic studies) that particular use is recognized and described in sections which follow.

**Forming useful classes according to kind.** This second topic in the series is intended to deal principally with the grouping of cases in hand as specimens ready for further observation, or with cases which have been recorded rather fully so that the descriptions are available for study and judgment—in contrast to items recorded simply in codified (perhaps quantitative) form. The present topic is not, strictly, a unitary head; it really consists of perhaps a half dozen different but related purposes, which lie so close together that it was not thought desirable to enter them all in the main outline. In fact, they overlap to such an extent that, when one groups his data for one purpose, the others (under the present head) are often automatically accomplished also. The parts of the discussion, therefore, must rest with possible differences in interest rather than with objective differences in the classes or the results of classification. With the understanding that any illustration introduced may serve to illustrate several, rather than only one, of the purposes discussed under the present head, the several interests will be taken up serially.

Perhaps the first interest—certainly the most natural one—is to group cases because it is mentally satisfying to do so, and perhaps annoying not to do so. As has been pointed out earlier, it seems to be a natural tendency of mankind to note similarities, observe common properties, and attend to the distinctions between differing groups. Since both the research producer and the research consumer share in these natural inclinations, one need not apologize for mentioning or employing this as a reason for grouping, although any grouping will almost unavoidably have other values also.

By way of example, if one made a study of the reasons high-school students give for leaving school before graduation, he would just "naturally" classify these reasons and report frequencies for these classes, rather than report separately each statement made by a student.[412] In so doing, he probably would begin by putting together those statements which seemed to him to mean almost exactly the same thing; and he probably would end by grouping these original combinations into somewhat larger, more inclusive categories. In fact, he might build up a hierarchy (several levels of ordination) among the reasons, for no purpose other than that it seemed more satisfying to him, and presumably more acceptable or significant to the reader, to have the findings in that form.

A comparative note, inserted somewhat parenthetically, may be helpful at this point. The suggestion in the preceding paragraph relates to classifying the responses (the reasons given). It is also possible to classify the respondents (the pupils). These two acts must be kept in mind as separate and distinct. Either series, the respondents or the responses, may be classified by itself, without categories being made for the other. If, however, categories are made for both series, each series will have its own set, appropriate to its own items. The pupils, for example, might be grouped according to any trait that seemed significant, such as age, intelligence, occupation of parents, etc. Now, if the responses also are grouped, say into six categories of reasons, a cross-tabulation or two-way table will result, perhaps with the classes of pupils down the side and the classes of reasons across the top. In other words, for *each* category of pupils, there would be the six kinds of reasons. (This is a common form of presentation; the results of opinion polls, for example, are characteristically presented in this way.) The classifying of the respondents may be done solely because of interest in description, or for the purpose of tracing possible causal connections between certain characteristics of the different groups of respondents and the kinds of responses they most often make. In either event, the *categories* of responses will be treated as *cases* in the analysis, almost the same as the categories of respondents are; they will be listed, assigned

---

412 This assumes that the nongraduates made replies in their own words rather than to check a list of statements already codified. For examples, one may consult:

Elizabeth S. Johnson and C. E. Legg, "Why Young People Leave School." *Bulletin of the National Association of Secondary School Principals* 32:14-24; November 1948.

U. S. Office of Education, "Why Do Boys and Girls Drop Out of School and What Can We Do About It?" Work Conference on Life Adjustment Education. Circular No. 269. Washington: The Office, 1950. 72 p. Reported also in *School Life* 32:136-37; June 1950.

For current and other references on this subject see the head, "Elimination from School," in the *Education Index*.

As an aside it may be said that many persons have long believed students left school for reasons much deeper and more subtle than the relatively superficial factors students are able to name. With our increasing knowledge of personality structure and motivation we may soon understand much better.

frequencies, and compared in terms of their character and frequency. The two series, therefore, even though different, are handled in the same manner.[413]

A second interest served by grouping observed cases according to kind may be spoken of as economy. Grouping reduces the number of items to be looked at and thought about, since the number of groups is obviously smaller than the number of ungrouped cases. The net result is a considerable reduction in the mental burden. To some extent, this interest is served by all grouping (classification), but there are occasions when it becomes a principal objective. For example, in one study,[414] 2800 trait actions of teachers were collected from respondents. These were stated in various ways, but were grouped with little difficulty under eighty-three trait names. This number seemed too large for convenient use; accordingly, many of these qualitative categories were combined, by means of pooled judgments of several persons, until there were only twenty-five categories (or enlarged traits). This number had been selected in advance as one which, on the basis of experience, had been found acceptable for practical use.

This reduction of a large number of cases to a smaller number of groups having somewhat broadened characteristics is a regular procedure in statistical work where one routinely tallies cases into qualitative or quantitative categories. Thus the specific quantitative value of each original observation is given up for the broader range of the class interval, in order to obtain a smaller number of group cases (class intervals) with which to work and think. (The cases tallied in any one interval, because of similarity of magnitude, may of course differ on many aspects other than this magnitude. This condition, however, is true in all forms of grouping.) In statistical work it is also routine to carry the reduction a step further and treat the entire observed group as a single case. This is done, for example, when one calculates a single value, as a total or an average, to stand for

---

[413] The discerning reader whose thinking is well advanced will see that there is more than what is stated in this paragraph, but our purpose is to keep the statement simple. More strictly, one never actually classifies respondents and responses, but classifies respondents (the person is the integrating unit here) according to two (or more) of their characteristics, the responses being, for purposes of classification, a characteristic (even though transient) just the same as sex, age, attitude, or place of residence may be a characteristic (with varying degrees of stability). Further, one will sense a certain priority in some characteristics, as compared with others; we may *mechanically* treat categories of age and categories of responses in the same manner, but we never quite treat them as the same logically, or meaningfully. Age, whether causal or not, is at least more primary; and the responses, whether consequents or not, are at least secondary, more definitely contingent. The terms *independent* and *dependent* variables, used often in mathematics, statistics, and physical science, are suggestive here, although they are unduly mechanical and must almost always be taken as merely schematic, since their implied absoluteness goes far beyond the realities of nearly all biological and social situations. This problem is treated in the chapter on experimentation.

[414] Werrett W. Charters and Douglas Waples, *The Commonwealth Teacher-Training Study*, p. 16-18. Chicago: University of Chicago Press, 1929. 666 p.

the group. The average (or any other statistic) is a summary characteristic and is employed to represent the group (as a single group case) in comparisons with other groups (also conceived as group cases), or with some established value, as a norm.[415] Thus, in statistical work, one of the first objectives is to reduce the large number of individual values to a moderate number of group cases (classes) and then to a single group case, for comparison with other similar groups. In the process, the specific values observed are sacrificed, but one's ability to think about the entire group, or a set of groups, is increased enormously.

A third interest in grouping observed cases is to reveal common properties. Of course this is likely to be a counterpart of reducing the number of cases (at least in qualitative classifications), but at the present point we are thinking of situations where the identification and isolation of these properties are the objective. One may seek descriptive characteristics that are more general (more pervasive of the group) than those which apply only to a single case, but will be less general than the entire population observed. For example, in one school district some five hundred conferences were held by teachers with parents regarding report cards.[416] These conferences were then analyzed with respect to points around which certain degrees of tension developed. Three types of attitude were identified which accounted for most of the tensions: (1) parents did not understand, or did not agree with, the goals of the school; (2) parents and teachers sought to protect vested interests; (3) parents or teachers lacked a basic understanding of children, and tended to reject, overprotect, or clash with the children. With these three major areas or classes of difficulty brought out, one is in a better position to take steps to remedy them than he would be, if he tried to deal with each individual disagreement. Another illustration of interest in common properties is found in the attempt to group the very large number of specialized jobs existing in our highly technical society, into larger "families" of jobs,[417] so that the basic elements of training called for by these larger groups might be provided, whereas it would be impossible to train for all of the specialties.

Somewhat similar is a method employed to derive certain principles of administration. One person [418] searched the pertinent literature, grouped

[415] External comparisons in such terms are likely to be legitimate, even though subject to supplementation by more detailed comparisons. Certain internal uses of a statistic also are legitimate, such as employing the mean and standard deviation to establish a scale of standard measures against which to compare individual values. One should, however, be cautious of such common internal interpretations as that the mean typifies each case in the group, or that everyone ought to be average to be normal.

[416] Louis Kaplan, "Tensions in Parent-Teacher Relationships." *Elementary School Journal* 51:190-95; December 1950.

[417] See a number of references given earlier under Analysis.

[418] Donald Faulkner, "What Are the Functions of Internal Administration?" *Journal of Higher Education* 12:378-85; October 1941.

together those statements which seemed to deal with the same thing, and then formulated statements to incorporate the essential elements of sameness for those which he had put into a group.

A fourth interest in forming classes which will embrace a number of individual (or smaller group) cases is to shift the level of attention; that is, to enable one to view a more general, more inclusive class; although, if one's thinking begins with the entire population in a given field, then the shift would be downward toward a more particular, more exclusive class (sometimes referred to as a subgroup). It is of course true that all classification does this very thing, but under certain circumstances this becomes the principal purpose of the integration. Perhaps the point can be illustrated most clearly by considering the different degrees of generality, or inclusiveness, in the primary concern of different persons in school systems. For the teacher, the main focus of attention is the pupil and the class; for the principal, it is the over-all condition of the school; and for the city superintendent, the welfare of the system. Similarly, those who are responsible for state, regional, and national policies must consider facts, problems, and actions appropriate to these levels.

While this illustration is basically geographical, it is assumed also that problems with different characteristics or qualities emerge on the various levels. With respect to enrollment, for example, the teacher is primarily concerned with the size of the class. The principal and superintendent are concerned about the overcrowding of the entire school and the planning, locating, and building of additional schools to avoid future overcrowding. National agencies, such as the National Education Association, the U. S. Office of Education, and others, need national totals on enrollment, on the trend in births, on the condition of school buildings, and so on, in order to inform the people of the whole nation about basic trends, present status, and impending needs. Thus, the enrollment data are grouped into successively more general categories (and totals) to enable each administrator to think about the situation as it affects his level of responsibility; in other words, to permit attention to be given to figures on the particular hierarchical level appropriate to the interest of each person.

This shifting of attention from cases on one level of generality or inclusiveness to another level, either upward or downward, is a regular and common thing, both in the practical affairs of the world and in research. It is particularly prevalent in statistical work, and one will often find cases on two or more levels of generality within a single table. While the idea may be seen easily from the geographical and statistical cumulations illustrated, it holds as well for all forms of hierarchical classification. Thus, in research studies the worker is expected to give both the relevant details of what he observes and their placement in some larger classifications. He should seek also to indicate a larger frame of thought which will place his entire work in a more comprehensive context, either in the practical world of affairs or in the development of theory and scientific generalizations. This latter step enables other scientists to view his study as but one case in a larger class, the class serving to integrate his work and that of many other persons into more useful generalizations.

A fifth interest in forming classes of cases is to give further structure to the field of thought. A set of classes introduces (at least) another level of concepts between the individual case and the whole field. It thus serves at once to divide up the field into (conceptually) structural areas, while at the same time it aids in keeping different kinds of individual cases from getting mixed together. If we may assume that the kinds which are established are relatively stable under varying circumstances, are readily identifiable, are reasonably homogeneous within each category and relatively distinct as between categories, and have properties which show significant differences, then these different kinds afford units for thought (and no doubt, for further study) that should aid materially in exploring and understanding the nature of the total field. As a matter of fact, this fifth interest is rather general and probably represents something of a summary of the other interests which have been mentioned.

By way of illustration we may refer to a study by Watson,[419] which had as one of its purposes the classifying of orchestral music according to mood (that is, happy, dignified, sad, and so on). Watson first noticed that pieces of music seemed to have five different types of meaning to individuals; he selected only one of these (namely, abstract meaning, or mood) for study. He found that groups of persons could rather consistently distinguish fifteen different kinds of music in terms of these abstract meanings. His categories were found to be stable across a fairly wide age range. While his study is complex and has enough different aspects so that it ilustrates many of the topics dealt with in this section, and in other sections as well, it indicates how the whole broad field of orchestral music can be broken down into a moderate number of "kinds" in terms of abstract meaning, or mood. Such categories are, therefore, available for both practical and research uses.[420] In any case, they aid in "mapping" the field of

[419] K. Brantley Watson, *The Nature and Measurement of Musical Meanings*. Psychological Monographs, No. 244, Vol. 54, No. 2. Washington: American Psychological Association, 1942. 43 p.
[420] If employed in further research, then these categories take on the same purpose as those described in the second type of use, namely, delimiting cases for study. In the study cited, however, they were investigated primarily to ascertain that they were different, identifiable, and stable categories. They are, therefore, one of the principal products of the study.

music for thinking, and give one the feeling that he has a better mental grasp of the field.

Further types of interest in grouping or classifying will not be taken up, although it might be well to mention that the purposes discussed later are served in part by the present group of interests. It may also be pointed out that the production of a set of useful categories is a necessary first step in the type of research use or purpose which is next presented. If this present type of classifying is not done as a separate, preliminary step, then it would have to be done as one of the early steps in providing a set of categories which give to a field some logical *order,* as well as subdivision.

It may be well to close this section by recalling a point made earlier. The present discussion has dealt with the production of useful kinds. One should not let his thinking slip into the attitude that the kinds he has produced are the only kinds, are basically correct kinds, or are uniquely natural. Always there are alternative bases for grouping which are just as natural, inherent, and real as any others that grow out of objective characteristics. In the study by Baldwin and associates referred to later the purpose was avowedly to *test* the proposed categories of parental behavior to see whether they were correlated with discernible, differential behaviors in the children. In the series of studies on teacher behavior and pupil behavior, by Anderson and associates, the same attitude of successive adaptation of categories was held to. In the investigation by Watson, it was recognized at the start that there were at least five different kinds of kinds —five different bases on which the selections of music might be classified; hence, the derived set of classes is presented as positively *not* the only way orchestral music can be classified. While in all of the studies cited, categories were being sought, there was no implication that the search was for something inherently fixed and obvious, but rather it was for something significant—significant perhaps because it aids in structuring one's field of thought, perhaps because it is found to have causal or consequential relation to other categories of things; in other words, categories which would prove useful. There is no other criterion for classification which is of any fundamental importance.

**Affording logical order and system.** This is one of the most important purposes of classification. The illustrations may be seen on every hand. Streets are laid out in a city, not only to provide arteries of transportation, but also to provide some system for the group of inhabitants, some means of identifying locations, some geographical structure to the large accumulation of dwellings, factories, and other buildings or public works, some means of grasping and dealing with the whole. Another simple illustration is the grouping of names in a telephone directory according to first letter, then making subgroups on second letter, and so on. So familiar is this process that one may not think of it as grouping at all; but let him start his thinking with the several million names in one of our largest cities in scrambled order. How would a person ever find a desired name? Alphabetical order is not inherent, nor more natural than other bases of grouping; it is simply conventional. It would be just as natural, in a purely objective (non-psychological) sense, to group on the basis of the final letter of a name, the length (number of letters in the name), the number of syllables, or some other aspect—for objectively, one aspect is just as real as another. By convention, we have agreed on certain principles and certain orders, but not all; telephone directories of different cities differ on many points of grouping and ordering.

Classification for the purpose of affording order is found to underlie all work done on a large scale. In a school system, or other large institution, there are different levels of generality of responsibility; these can usually be laid out on a chart. The school grades represent an ordered grouping; so does the curriculum, as well as chapters in a text. The subject-matter files in an office represent a categorical organization, as do also the budget categories and the accounting code. In a large system, these latter are usually worked out with some elaborateness; they are treated in considerable detail in texts on budgeting and accounting.

In the case of documentary material (as books), a very large amount of work has been done to provide system. Without this, library work would be impossible.[421] Students come to be familiar with either or both of the two principal systems of library classification in the United States, that worked out by Melvil Dewey and published in 1876,[422] commonly referred to as the "Dewey Decimal" system, and the Library of Congress system,[423] which was worked out because developments in certain fields had badly crowded the older Dewey scheme. In addition to the basic

[421] For a description of several library classification schemes see W. Howard Phillips, *A Primer of Book Classification*. London: Association of Assistant Librarians, 1949. 185 p.

[422] Melvil Dewey, *Decimal Classification and Relativ Index*. Fifteenth Edition, Revised. Lake Placid Club, Essex County, N. Y.: Forest Press, 1951. 927 p.

Smaller libraries will be interested in the *Abridged Dewey Decimal Classification and Relativ Index*. Seventh Edition, Revised. New York: H. W. Wilson Co., 1953. 315 p.

[423] The classification scheme consists of 23 volumes, issued by the Library of Congress and published by the Government Printing Office, Washington. First adopted in 1911 on a tentative basis and put in force in 1915. Revised from time to time.

For a brief, practical presentation, see: U. S. Library of Congress, *Subject Headings, A Practical Guide*. Prepared by Nella Jane Martin. Washington: Government Printing Office, 1951. 140 p.

A third system of classification, not so widely used, but noted for its underlying philosophy and clear delineations, is the Bliss Classification. Henry Evelyn Bliss, *A Bibliographic Classification*. New York: H. W. Wilson Co., 1940-1953. 4 vols. (Vols. 1 and 2 revised in 195? and issued as one vol.)

schemes, many special rules [424] are necessary to cover a large number of detailed questions which arise. Various libraries have issued their own rule publications.

One should not think of these classification schemes primarily as numerical systems; the numbers are merely the means of providing a certain conventional order for the locating of the documents, but they are not the basis of the system. The system consists primarily of the categories, the classes and subclasses into which the vast field of published material has been divided. The forming of such classes is a major undertaking, since a person must make almost countless decisions as to what concept shall be subordinate to another, and what shall be the general classes. One who has become familiar with the normal library classes now in existence can scarcely understand the difficulty of the earlier problems in devising classes.

These classification schemes are not static, and are supplemented from time to time by workers in special fields. Of particular interest to educators are those special lists which have been developed in their field.[425] The first extensive list of subject headings was that of Voegelein,[426] prepared in the Bureau of Educational Research of Ohio State University for a committee of the National Education Association. This list influenced the *Loyola Educational Index,* published later that same year, and the *Education Index,* which began in 1929. A later list by Pettus [427] was arranged in classified rather than dictionary (alphabetical) form, and contains definitions of the various heads and subheads. Such a list would be useful for educational divisions of libraries and also for personal collections of books. Many of the same classification problems had to be solved in devising a special index for research materials in education,[428] since previously existing lists omitted most of the technical heads. *Psychological Abstracts,* the new *Sociological Abstracts,* and the recent indexes to two sociological journals [429] are further examples of classification (grouping) systems for

[424] For example, see U. S. Library of Congress, *Rules for Descriptive Cataloging in the Library of Congress.* Washington: Government Printing Office, 1949. 141 p.

For an important early example, see Charles A. Cutter, *Rules for a Dictionary Catalog.* Fourth Edition, Rewritten. U. S. Bureau of Education Special Report on Public Libraries, Part 2. Washington: Government Printing Office, 1904. 173 p. First edition, 1876.

[425] Library aids in finding material in the fields of education, psychology, and social sciences have been treated systematically in Chapter 3. In the present discussion we mention only certain illustrations of systematic grouping.

[426] L. Belle Voegelein, *List of Educational Subject Headings.* Columbus: Ohio State University Press, 1928. 337 p.

[427] Clyde Pettus, *Subject Headings in Education.* New York: H. W. Wilson Co., 1938. 188 p.

[428] Douglas E. Scates, *Twelve-Year Index to the Review of Educational Research, Volumes 1-12 (1931-1942).* Special Issue of the *Review,* December 1944. 65 p. (A Twenty-four Year Index is now being prepared.)

[429] *American Journal of Sociology, Index to Volumes I-LII, 1895-1947.* Chicago: University of Chicago Press, 1948. 281 p.

*Index to the American Sociological Review, Volumes I-XV, 1936-1950.* New York: American Sociological Society, New York University, 1951. 184 p.

the purpose of giving system and order to documentary materials. Cross-referencing makes strong demands on careful classification; a special classification outline has been prepared at Yale University for those who are doing cross-cultural studies; [430] this consists of eighty-eight major categories, with subdivisions in each category, descriptions, and cross-references.

It is important to take some note of well developed systems in other sciences; much can be learned from them. In the biological sciences, one of the large areas of interest is known as taxonomy (classification). The basis of the scheme now generally accepted was worked out in the 1700's by the Swedish taxonomist Linnaeus.[431] The complexity of the task may be appreciated when it is realized that there are probably a million different species of animals and plants to be accommodated. Students who are not acquainted with the plan should spend enough time with it to note the beauty and power of a hierarchical set of categories on some six to eight levels. Such a classification scheme not only permits the grouping of plants and animals but standardizes their names over the world, and makes possible unlimited studies of interrelationships, theories of origin or descent, and generalizations concerning form and function. Thus, with proper classification, hypotheses are suggested and principles observed which, with large numbers of unsorted specimens, would be wholly impossible.

In the fields of chemistry and physics, one of the triumphs of classification is the periodic table in which the elements (or the atoms) are arranged systematically according to atomic number and fall into groups having similar characteristics. The grouping, on the basis of similar properties, was begun early in the 1800's,[432] before many basic ideas in chemistry were established, when atomic numbers were unknown, and atomic weights were only crudely measured and uncertain. But with such weights as were available, the elements then known could be arranged in rank order and it was noted that every so often, with a certain approximate rhythm, elements occurred which seemed to be similar. There were many mistakes made in the various conceptual schemes proposed for the grouping, but about 1870 the Russian chemist Mendelyeev proposed a scheme which was approximately correct.[433] With the knowledge of the structure or "archi-

[430] George P. Murdock and Others, *Outline of Cultural Materials*. Third Edition. Behavior Science Outlines, Vol. 1. New Haven, Conn.: Human Relations Area Files, 1950. 162 p.

[431] While long treatises on taxonomy are available, references are made here only to brief descriptions in historical notes.

Lorande L. Woodruff, *Development of the Sciences*, p. 230-33. New Haven: Yale University Press, 1923. 327 p.

Abraham Wolf, *History of Science, Technology, and Philosophy in the Eighteenth Century*, p. 426-34, 460-61. New York: Macmillan Co., 1939. 814 p.

[432] Humphry T. Pledge, *op. cit.*

[433] With increasing knowledge the table has undergone many refinements and certain revisions and extensions. Half a century ago when the Curies discovered radium (1898),

tecture" of the atom which has been gained in the twentieth century, new understandings are afforded as to the "why" of the periodicity, and as to the reason for certain earlier exceptions to the rule.

Of what interest is this periodic table to us? First, it should be helpful to derive certain ideas concerning its formation, and also ideas as to the values a systematic scheme of classification may have. It is serviceable to look for object lessons in sciences which are more mature than our own fields of endeavor. The first point may be to note that the table could not be formulated at all until "the time was ripe"—that is, until a great deal of descriptive knowledge was available. Before the table, there had to evolve slowly the concept of an element—the notion that such things existed. A working body of elements then had to be discovered, isolated, and gradually described. Growing out of many observations of interrelationships between the known elements, the concept of atomic weight was slowly taking form, but was uncertain and many contradictions were found in experiments. These atomic weights then had to be ascertained and added to the descriptions. With this knowledge, still in rough form, it was possible to classify the elements on something more than superficial similarity; they could now be classified on their gross characteristics and also on the atomic weights simultaneously, permitting some interesting speculations. Perhaps a second point should be made that, with much of the foregoing knowledge in hand, it took many workers (at least eight or ten different schemes were published; we do not know how many persons thought on the problem), and a lapse of about forty-five years before a reasonably good scheme emerged. Historically, this lapse of time may seem short; it is approximately equal to the *total period* in which educational and mental measurements have been available with which to make systematic observations in our own fields. Third, after a fairly good form of table was presented, the crude ideas have been further refined over the past eighty years, as new knowledge and new theories came forth. Again we may take hope; many of our concepts are now in about the same rough state as Mendelyeev's table in 1870. With some eighty years of work in the future, many relationships among *human* facts which are but roughly seen at the present will become clear, refined, and definite. Physical science, as we now have it, came from patience and unremitting effort maintained over long periods of time. Granted the same interval, social science will show comparable or even greater gains.

There are other equally valuable ideas to gain from this physical-science

---

only 74 of the elements were known. It is interesting to compare forms of the table, even as late as 1940, with forms of 1947 and later. Recent publications in chemistry and physics may be consulted.

experience. As our fourth point, we would note that a new trait (atomic number) was substituted for the earlier idea (atomic weight) as a basis for the quantitative classification of the elements. When this was done, certain inconsistencies disappeared from the table. This substitution (and many other similar instances from the history of physical science) makes clear that researchers must ever be on the alert for improved basic concepts and be ready to substitute a new point of view or a new factor for an old one. An idea held onto too long, no matter how venerable and how widely accepted, may prove a block to progress. Writers of the history of physical and biological sciences frequently call attention to such instances, especially where new evidence suggesting a different view was already available. (Scientists are not stubborn; one just cannot tell at a given time which view is better; but one can be alert, and keep an open mind, always seeking a better view.)

Fifth in our series of points on the formation of the classification table is that advances had to be made along many lines, each in turn waiting a little on the other, and each helping the other. Each idea which is evolved helps to reinforce or correct related ideas. It is utterly impossible to go very far in any one line of pioneering research without waiting for help from other lines that have a bearing on it, even though in the early stages the potential relationship may not be seen. Thus, atomic numbers could not have been substituted in the table until other work produced them; the table helped prove their superiority. It is this mutual checking between several lines of advance which affords the test of new theory and provides the only sound basis for the acceptance or rejection of new ideas. Certainly the thinking of a large body of scientists (whether physical or social) is not to be changed by a single study, even though the study might point out new conclusions that are correct; the thinking will be changed by the accumulation of evidence from many studies which, taken together, make it more reasonable to accept an interpretation than to ignore or reject it. Without this advance on a broad front, nobody knows what a correct observation or interpretation is. Certainly the great majority of new ideas put forth prove to be wrong, or at least sterile.

What are the values of a significant classification scheme? As has been suggested, it may be valuable even in its crude form, since related knowledge is likely also to be in a crude state, so that the two advance together. Thus we may say: (1) the classification scheme was one aspect of the broad advance along a variety of lines; it interacted with others to aid progress in understanding. It helped put other ideas to the test. It could, in turn, have been employed as a base for several advances in theory, although it was not—perhaps because physical scientists have not formed the habit of looking to classification as a basis for fundamental theory formulation. They have been taught instead to keep their attention on new observations. There is danger of loss in such preoccupation. (2) The table had gaps in it; Mendelyeev believed that additional elements would be discovered. In this he was correct, even though some of the elements had to be manufactured. The very incompleteness of the rough table was, therefore, a stimulus, and a partial guide, to further search. It focused attention on what was missing.[434] (3) The very success of the table in providing a systematic scheme of thought also kept prominent the intriguing question, Why? Why did elements which differed in atomic weight by values of about sixteen usually form families? And why did some of them not do so? Here was a constant challenge, springing from the order which the table revealed, and from the exceptions. The lesson is that many (all?) phenomena are more complex than they may seem and that many factors, rather than any one, are likely to be necessary for an explanation and a full basis of regularity. Recent knowledge in this field explains the irregularities by introducing new factors, thus giving rise to subseries which are special. In other words, no one basis is adequate for the full classification of the elements. This conclusion is not strictly at variance with the dictum of formal logic, that classification should be done on a single basis ("principle" it is often called), but actual logic is just not as simple as formal logic is made to seem. The point is that many levels are involved in any extensive classification, and different bases are invoked for the various levels. There may be more levels (special factors) called for in certain ranges of the cases than in others; nature was not made to fit textbook simplicity. (4) As a final point, the table is still useful, even with present rather full knowledge as to the structure of atoms. It is useful in guiding systematic thought, systematic with respect to the atomic numbers, the structure of the atoms, and their properties. This systematic sweep applies to more than a single family (group) of elements; it pervades the whole table. Thus, generalizations of varying scope become evident. Also, the general assumptions regarding cause and effect in science are sustained. When enough is known, it is seen that there are causal conditions for the differences in form or characteristics which can be noted.

To the philosophers falls the task of providing a scheme for classifying all the branches of knowledge (the sciences and other forms of systematic

[434] A table with similar effect was prepared by Brownell, to point up areas of research in arithmetic which were as yet uncultivated. He remarked that the blanks in his table were perhaps the most significant part of it. William A Brownell, "Techniques of Research Employed in Arithmetic." National Society for the Study of Education, *Report of the Committee on Arithmetic*, p. 415-43. Twenty-ninth Yearbook. Chicago: University of Chicago Press, 1930. Parts 1, 2. 749 p.

thought), and a number of persons at different times have worked out such schemes.[435]

**Developing meaning in class concepts.** It is so routine to employ class concepts in our thinking and conversation that we seldom stop to think how many of these ideas are only imperfectly understood. We may realize that we personally have but a superficial acquaintance with many general or class terms employed, but we usually feel confident that somebody understands them well. It frequently turns out, however, that the experts in a field are less sure of the nature and meaning of a concept (or category) than are the less well informed. As a matter of fact, it is the specific role of much descriptive research to begin work at this point—to take apparently simple ideas and explore their nature. A famous physicist (Albert A. Michelson) used to say in informal talks that his life had largely been devoted to the study of matters which seemed so simple to most people that they never bothered to inquire about them! His remark characterizes the history of science. It is the genius of the productive researcher to see questions where most persons routinely accept—and then to formulate these questions in terms which lead to penetrating research and to observations that can be integrated into a significant generalization.

A large amount of effort is constantly going into the description of even our commonest concepts. Consider for example the term *The United States of America*. Probably most of us would say that we knew its meaning well. Yes, we know its meaning by definition, perhaps as taught to us; and in part by our personal experiences. But such meanings are rather hollow and limited, as compared with meanings which can be arrived at by extensive, systematic fact-finding which will build up the concept and fill it with the concreteness of summarized details. For example, our government takes censuses (of population, business, agriculture, manufactures, etc.) every few years—for the specific purpose of ascertaining, with respect to the traits studied, the current meaning of the term *United States of America*. Undoubtedly, persons who are used to thinking that reality exists on the abstract level, and who have come to be content with such ideas, may object that a thing is what it is defined to be. We must counter by saying that, within the limits set by a definition, a thing is *what it is*. And what something is certainly is a matter to be determined. What it is, furthermore, is often a matter of its current status. What the United States is today is scarcely what it was in 1790; and what it is on any one day is not exactly the same as what it was the day before.

[435] Raymond F. Piper and Paul W. Ward, *The Fields and Methods of Knowledge,* p. 289-95. New York: F. S. Crofts and Co., 1929. 398 p.

Abram C. Benjamin, *An Introduction to the Philosophy of Science.* Chapter 18, "The Classification of the Sciences," p. 399-417. New York: Macmillan Co., 1937. 469 p.

This brief introduction is designed to make several points: (1) a fairly large proportion of the ideas we employ in common thinking are not thoroughly understood, even by experts in the areas concerned; (2) meanings arrived at by a "surface" approach, such as by definition, deal primarily with the shell of an idea; (3) extensive inductive approaches provide the basic data with which to fill in the general idea and develop understandings that have "flesh and blood" in place of formality and emptiness; (4) inasmuch as all the physical and animate world is undergoing change, either rapid or slow, a concept once filled in will tend to get out of touch with the external world, if it is not revised from time to time in the light of evidence.

These points are made in order to bring out the place of research which has for its goal the inductive description of a concept, or category. Such research is really very widespread and common. It is familiar to all of us, though perhaps we have not thought of it in this light. We are treating this type of research as one form of classification, because it seems to be such; it is a matter of identifying cases with a category which embraces them (probably accompanied or followed by analysis). It is thus one phase or form of classification. Possibly it will occur before some of the other types or stages of classification are developed. More likely, various forms of classification will proceed together, or alternately.

One further remark perhaps should be made for the sake of those persons whose training has been formal. In formal logic, description is a matter of placing a case in its proper class and then giving the differentiae —the particular ways in which this case (which of course may itself be a class, or general concept) differs from other coördinate cases in the same superordinate class. On the formal level these steps are satisfactory; as a matter of fact, in a purely abstract sense, they are quite adequate. What they overlook, however, is that our knowledge of the embracing class is likely to be woefully inadequate, and so is our knowledge of the specific differences, so that we have not fully described or defined something by naming its class and giving subclass differences. Such a scheme or pattern of thought may be good for exercises in formal thinking; but the research worker knows that people do not begin to know what they think they do, and so he dedicates his energies to finding out through careful observation—and through much critical thinking about what he observes.

It is not to be inferred that inductive description is necessarily statistical. Perhaps that is the easiest or simplest kind, because it strips each case down to two elements, the class into which it is put, and a frequency—the frequency being all that remains of the case after it is classified. But more often (perhaps always, in direct experience) ideas are built up by incorporating observations as fully as may be germane. The present topic will deal with so-called "qualitative" material.

It may be interesting to take an illustration of the qualitative type which is closely related to the example already used. Consider, for instance, the meaning of the word *democracy*. Perhaps, in school, pupils are taught definitions of the term. The teacher probably feels it his duty as a matter of self-respect to act as though he knew what the word means—and perhaps his textbook told him, so he is properly prepared. But in reality nobody knows what the word means. It means different things to different persons. "Ah, yes," someone will say, "but there are authorities. Certainly the authorities will know!" The person who finds himself thinking in this pattern has not yet caught the full meaning of research; or perhaps he is looking for definiteness in an area which is reserved for continuous redetermination in the "market place" of contemporary thinking. Certainly "experts" can tell almost any of us more things than we know about the meaning of "democracy"; but where or how did the experts come by their knowledge? Probably the most important means is by building up the concept inductively through a study of the history of the different meanings the idea has had.[436] Another means would be to study the different concepts of democracy held currently by different persons and different nations.

Both of these approaches are examples of the type of research here being discussed. The person who attempts to make such a study, however, will meet basic problems. When he finds that certain peoples had, or now have, certain social philosophies or beliefs, on what basis does he say that these beliefs are or are not forms of democracy? It is clear that some over-all criterion must be set up, else the study cannot be made at all. Presumably such a criterion must be evolved out of an analysis of the current concept (as held in different forms), out of the study of many writers who have dealt with this problem in the past, and out of some acquaintance with history and evolving forms of thought. But even so, many decisions must be made which involve personal judgment, so that the result will be in part personal.

Not all research of the inductive type will lean as heavily on personal judgment; but it must be pointed out that all research, save the most mechanical and routine, will to some degree involve personal judgment. For this reason, it becomes of the greatest importance to have research workers free to follow their scholarly quests in as broad a way as possible,

---

[436] For a compact review of many meanings at different times, see Harold J. Laski, "Democracy." *Encyclopaedia of the Social Sciences*, Vol. 5. New York: Macmillan Co., 1931. p. 76-85.

seeking all knowledge and all views where these can be found, without dictation or influencing pressures from those who employ them. For it is only through freedom of inquiry that one can attain the breadth which frees him from a narrow perspective. It is the scholar's obligation to seek facts and ideas from as broad a field as possible, to weigh the evidence carefully, and to come to conclusions that are as free as possible from the bias of any single point of view. These ideals of scholarly inquiry are more easily stated than achieved.

Ideas change. This should be neither surprising nor shocking, for as long as man has observed and thought, ideas have changed. We should not, therefore, expect the concept "democracy" to be a static thing—something which could be defined authoritatively once and for all. If it has been changing for several thousand years, if it has undergone radical changes since the time of Washington and Jefferson, does one expect it to stop changing all at once—for the convenience of the present and future generations? Research workers are basically prepared for change. They do their work primarily for the purpose of changing ideas. Concepts, like those of democracy, must undergo adaptive modifications as the conditions of living change and call for new interpretations and new judgments. Democracy is an idea which represents a hope, a faith that man can find forms of group living which, under given circumstances, will raise human life to as high a plane as possible. To arrive at a final, static definition of the concept would be to make it worthless—and any such result of research, could it be achieved, would constitute a net loss to mankind. Hence, research does not necessarily seek to produce fixed truth, but rather truth that has the substance of reality; and objective reality is a changing thing.

The title of a study in school law [437] names a concept which the author has proceeded to describe inductively. The way to ascertain what the category "discretionary powers of school boards" means is to find out what powers of this class exist. That process requires examining court decisions where discretionary powers have been at issue. When enough (reasonably recent) cases have been examined, so that no new light is found to be thrown on the concept by the study of an additional group of cases, the concept (the inclusive category which embraces these cases) may be said to be described. Some persons may prefer the term *defined*.

As in the historical or comparative study of the concept "democracy," and in fact all other inductive studies, we see here the need for some over-all delimiting concept which will serve to indicate to the researcher what cases (specimens, if one prefers the term) are to be counted as belonging

---

[437] John D. Messick, *Discretionary Powers of School Boards*. Durham, N. C.: Duke University Press, 1949. 147 p.

to the general class so that, when included, they constitute a valid part of the description. In the historical study, it was suggested that this delimitation, this guiding judgment, must come from careful, extensive, analytical, and perhaps philosophical study. In the legal study, one has the aid of a definition which is commonly recognized at law. Here, as discussed earlier, one finds that he has, to begin with, a valid legal definition of what a discretionary power is, but that he doesn't really know much from knowing the definition. The definition is merely an outline, the nature of the category as looked at from without; a sort of bounding line which delimits this category from the rest of thought. But the real knowledge of what goes into the outline, what makes up the substance of the category "discretionary powers," what one can expect of the concept when it is applied to the everyday world of human action—such is obtained by inductive research.

The study merits one more observation that applies generally to studies of this type. They almost never end in a simple amorphous form, where the specifics are merely listed in unordered fashion. Rather, the researcher finds it useful to group his specifics into intermediate categories; they are more convenient to work with in this form, and more easily assimilated and understood by the reader. In the historical study of "democracy," chapters might be formed to represent different time periods. In the study of "discretionary powers," chapters were formed around such practical subjects as school districts, purchase and sale of real property, management of schools, and so on. These chapters represent categories intermediate between the individual cases and the general concept; and each one of them is given meaning of its own, as is the general over-all category, through the individual cases placed in it.

In closing this discussion of inductive description of a general idea, it seems appropriate to mention one of its limitations. The inductive method is weak, in that it does not readily lead to the revelation and description of substructures—structural unities within the total. It is (usually) confined to the class of specifics with which it starts; true, these are often grouped into intermediate categories, but such are conveniences rather than natural, functioning organizations. For example, in building up a partial concept of the United States inductively by starting with individual people, one would not normally obtain a description of the various forms of organization (social institutions) by which a large group of people are able to live coöperatively. These essential structures would be missing from the picture. Or, if one wishes to think biologically, and start with the usual biological unit, the cell, a count of the number of different kinds of cells constituting a particular organism would fail to give an adequate picture of the various functioning systems or organs in the specimen. Again, the detailed activities of a job, for example, teaching, do not give a clear picture of the larger conceptual frames into which these fit under the influence of the guiding purposes of the teacher.

When, therefore, one begins induction with specifics which are themselves the units that enter into intermediate forms of structure, he will not obtain a knowledge of these intermediate organizations, unless they are made definite objectives of the study; and even then, it is doubtful that the inductive approach is the one a researcher would select. To start with units which have been stripped of their external organization, that is, their relationships to one another, and from them attempt to discern structure is to face head-on the old problem:

> All the King's horses and all the King's men
> Couldn't put Humpty Dumpty together again.

Fortunately one is not restricted to this type of approach. While inductive study has great power, it is not to be viewed as the only pattern of thought, or the only frame in which data may be gathered, for the purpose of obtaining closer acquaintance with the nature of a whole. Other methods are also concerned with determining the nature of a whole, through approaching the problem in the opposite direction—through starting with a conceptual unit and fractionating it in one way or another. In that process (such as through dissecting a biological specimen), it is normally easier to detect, isolate, and describe substructures (functioning systems within the whole, but larger than a small unit, such as a cell) than it is through starting with isolated small units. The two methods, induction and analytical differentiation, complement each other. They are not to be thought of as rivals; neither one can ever wholly do the work of the other. Each affords a check on the other; together they provide much dependable knowledge.

**Transition note.** As explained at the beginning of this series of purposes in classification, the four uses which have thus far been treated are those which have to do with the classification of data, and in most cases could be carried out after the observations have been obtained. As such, the categories affect rather directly the research product, since they are immediately a part of it, and they therefore contribute a large portion of the utility (or the inutility) of the results. By way of contrast, the three uses which are now to be presented represent types of category formation which normally need to be taken care of early in the planning of a study, presumably before the main body of observations are taken. Often, however, they will call either for extensive and carefully analyzed experience in the particular area of study, or for some preliminary data-gathering as a basis for trying out and adjusting the basic categories. In fact, it is likely that the formation of such categories will depend upon a succession of studies in which the categories are revised repeatedly in the light of findings from the preceding studies. Categories of the types to be discussed are basic to knowledge.

**Creating cases through delimitation.** Obviously any particular research deals with only a very small part of the totality of aspects of the entire universe. To delimit a study adequately so that the reader (as well as the researcher himself) may know what it deals with and what it does not— that is, to make clear the vast multiplicity of objects, conditions, events, aspects, forces, and interrelationships that are not (intentionally) included in the study and which, hopefully, are not reflected in undue degree in the conclusions—is a matter of some difficulty. It is usually done in steps— by a process of successive differentiation. The careful statement of one's research problem is expected to narrow the field of thought materially. The description of the population (the class of cases) that will be observed is likely to be the second major step in the delimiting process. Often the physical source-field from within which the observations (or cases) will be taken and any special conditions which are presumed to affect the cases are stated as further delimitations.

If we assume that the problem has been carefully stated [438] and that the general class from which cases are to be drawn has been named and (if necessary) at least partially described, the immediate concern is with ways in which this general class can be further differentiated within itself, so as to make the study significant. In other words, what subclasses or groupings within the general population should be formed in order to point up the study? What unit categories of quantitative variables may be employed to make the analysis useful?

Suppose, for example, one wished to study the effect parents have on the behavior, and on the more or less enduring aspects of the personality, of their children. An idea in such general form is satisfactory as an indication of purpose, but it is too large and too unstructured for immediate attack. To pursue it directly would mean starting out haphazardly to look for all effects of all parents. Without further delimitations and internal structuring of ideas, one would not know what to look for (and record) as "causes" or "effects," and he would naturally draw all sorts of erroneous conclusions about relationships, because his observations would not be systematic with regard to anything. [439]

---

[438] Selecting and stating problems for research were taken up more fully in an earlier chapter. The present discussion is for the purpose of showing how classification is employed to carry the successive differentiation forward.

[439] The impression should not be gained that there is no place for such general observation. In the early stages of work in any area it is virtually the only thing which can be done. See, for example, Fritz Redl and David Wineman, cited in footnote 337, p. 13-14, 22-26.

To give such a study significance, one would have to plan to divide parents into kinds on the basis of some variable (some differentiating factor or factors) which his knowledge in this area would suggest was possibly worth studying. Further, if knowledge in the area were sufficiently well advanced to make it desirable, one would also divide children (in terms of their behaviors and personalities) into categories. Usually this step will take the more restricted form of selecting aspects for observation, and of providing some rough quantification of these aspects (such, perhaps, as "much," "little," "negligible or not found"). In early work in an area, there are strong dangers in delimiting one's observations of consequences or effects too narrowly, lest one rule out the most important potential findings, or inadvertently curtail the large variation in the effects. In an area where the major explorations have been accomplished, however, it becomes desirable to categorize both the antecedent conditions (causes) and the consequences, possibly employing a quantitative scale in both instances. Having two systematic sets of categories (kinds of parental behaviors and kinds or degrees of children's behaviors), one would be in position to study the relationships between these sets of categories.

In order to see the way in which classification operates in delimiting cases for study, it should be recalled that cases occur on more than one level of generality or compositeness and that even a class of objects may, for research purposes, be used as a case. That is, a school class, a city, or an entire nation may be "a case," just as an individual person may.[440] Further, in different steps of a study, it is common to pass from cases on one level to cases on another. Thus, with regard to the study being discussed, in the observation stage of the work the cases will be the individual families, but when it comes to the analysis stage, it is the *categories* representing different kinds of parental behaviors that will be employed as cases. That is, the *kinds* of parents are the unit concepts which one describes, compares,

---

Researchers in education, psychology, sociology, and in the physical sciences as well, have spent many years just observing carefully, while insights were forming and ideas to be tested (hypotheses) were taking shape. The role of such general observation, however, is to provide background for the formulating of profitable questions for study; it is not directly and primarily for the answering of questions.

Further, in research of high quality (conducted in a non-mechanical fashion), the competent researcher will, during the conduct of the study, carry on a certain amount of observation that is more general than what his highly specified schedule calls for, in order: (*a*) to detect as early as possible whether the study as formulated is missing the point and should be modified, started anew, or abandoned; (*b*) to obtain enlightening special cases, exceptions, and notes on additional factors that should be mentioned in the interpretation of the findings; and (*c*) to gain further insights which provide the basis for subsequent, more penetrating or more successful studies. The good researcher, while adhering to his observation schedule, thinks and looks beyond it.

[440] One may wish to refer back to the section emphasizing classification as potentially extensive, where it was pointed out that, in research, anything becomes a case when it is so treated. Every concept has certain elements of divisibility as well as unity.

studies the effects of, and draws conclusions about; in the general logic of the study, these are, therefore, the principal cases. The number (in statistics, the frequency) of families which are observed in each category serves merely to give relative statistical weight to that category. These categories may be referred to as group cases or as composite cases to indicate that they are secondary cases more general than the original cases observed; but on their own level, apart from their relationship to the units of observation, these categories are simply cases, treated like any other cases. The important role of classification in forming these secondary cases, which often constitute the heart of the analysis, may thus be seen.

A number of interesting studies have been made which illustrate the foregoing points. For example, in one study [441] the parents in ninety-three families were classified into seven systematic categories. The homes in each category were studied with regard to effects common to that group and, in addition, for a typical home in each category, a detailed description was given of the parental (mother's) behavior and of the personalities of the children. For example, in a home of the aggressively rejectant type (that is, the parents showed major concern for their own comfort and convenience at the expense of the child's wishes, welfare, and development; they were determined to dominate, and controlled autocratically, often in unpredictable fashion and with harsh, deprecating comments), it was found over a period of time that the child became increasingly withdrawn, shy, and stubbornly resistant in situations calling for response (p. 24). In a home in which the rejection took the form of indifference and aloofness, instead of aggression, the child was desperately hungry for attention and affection, and constantly sought symbols of status within some group (p. 22). In homes that were without evidence of rejection, but which were autocratic and emotionally somewhat unstable, the children tended either to be rebellious and somewhat independent, or to be compliant but unhappy, timid, nervous, anxious, and with an undertone of bitterness and resentment (p. 28-29). At the more wholesome, constructive end of the series of parental categories were the democratic parents who were themselves emotionally mature, restrained, consistent; who exhibited warmth of affection without neurotic identification or indulgence; who respected the individuality of the child and let him enter genuinely into decisions.

[441] Alfred L. Baldwin, Joan Kalhorn, and Fay H. Breese, *Patterns of Parent Behavior*. Psychological Monographs, Vol. 58, No. 3; Whole Number 268. Washington: American Psychological Association, 1945. 75 p.

The following is a later study at this same research center: Alfred L. Baldwin, "Socialization and the Parent-Child Relationship." *Child Development* 19:127-36; September 1948. In this study, the effects of three variables were studied: democracy, control, and activity. Exploration to ascertain the most important (most explanatory) factors to look for will undoubtedly continue for some years; there is no thought that the factors reported on in either of these studies are final.

"Such a combination of factors produces a nearly ideal home" (p. 53), as judged by the effects on the children. One will, of course, not expect to find perfect parents or children; but, in homes classed in this category, the children, over a three-year period, increased in intelligence more than twice as fast as the normal rate (p. 64), and they excelled in such qualities as patience, planfulness, originality, creativity, and curiosity. (May they become research workers!)

Without systematic classification of the homes, these basic observations might simply have found their way into files along with countless other case studies of families that are excellent individual descriptions, which sharpen insights and aid in identification, but which lead to no general research conclusions. Through creating a set of categories that were systematic with respect to certain important factors, the general population of homes (of any and all kinds) was broken down into group cases (specific kinds) and the dynamic characteristics of these kinds could then be studied, compared, and differential conclusions drawn. Thus, by categorizing, one delimits group cases which make effective research possible.

In another study [442] with somewhat similar purpose, the selection began with the children. Three groups of children were selected who represented schizophrenic, neurotic, and normal children. The question was then asked, What kinds of parents do these different kinds of children have? Four categories of parents were recognized in the study. It was found that, among the schizophrenic children, the parents of the same sex as the child were characterized by demanding, antagonistic behavior. Among the children classed as neurotic, both parents showed this type of behavior. The parents of the normal children showed a predominance of encouraging behavior. This type of study and the one by Baldwin and others are complementary. In the present study, the relationship sought is between the two sets of categories (kinds of children and kinds of parents), and these categories are accordingly the cases in terms of which the analysis is made and the conclusions are drawn.

Social psychologists and anthropologists have usually structured their studies of parent-child relationships [443] by taking different cultures (often

[442] James E. McKeown, "The Behavior of Parents of Schizophrenic, Neurotic, and Normal Children." *American Journal of Sociology* 56:175-79; September 1950.

[443] Ruth Benedict, "Child Rearing in Certain European Countries." *American Journal of Orthopsychiatry* 19:342-50; April 1949.

Margaret Mead, "Research on Primitive Children." *Manual of Child Psychology,* p. 667-706. Edited by Leonard Carmichael. New York: Wiley and Sons, 1946. 1,068 p.

Harold Orlansky, "Infant Care and Personality." *Psychological Bulletin* 46:1-48; January 1949. A critical review of certain phases of infant care as personality determinants.

Clyde Kluckhohn and H. A. Murray, *Personality in Nature, Society, and Culture.* New York: Alfred A. Knopf, 1948. 561 p.

Douglas G. Haring, *Personal Character and Cultural Milieu.* Syracuse, N. Y.: Syracuse University Press, 1948. 670 p.

in different parts of the world) as representing different categories of parental behavior. Through building up a body of literature which describes relevant aspects of these cultures and also describes (presumably resulting) behaviors of the children, these workers make possible on a broad scale the same kinds of comparisons (though at present less systematic) as those in the foregoing studies.

Thus far we have been discussing the creation of cases in terms of kind, by the process of delimiting *qualitative* (complex) variation. There are times when one finds it to his purpose to create cases by delimiting *quantitative* variation. That is, he takes particular segments of some quantitative variable and treats each such segment as a case (perhaps better thought of as a group case, a category case, or secondary case because such more elemental or primary cases as objects, events, or people are usually employed as the "cases" for enumerative purposes). One then studies other variables (aspects of the case) to describe it. For example, one may study various aspects of groups of children who are classed as bright, normal, and so on (representing segments of the intelligence scale); or he may wish to study characteristics of (that is, describe) children who are tall, medium, or short, or overweight, normal weight, and so on (representing segments of height or weight); or study characteristics of children or their families when the family income (or perhaps the socio-economic status) is within certain limits; and so on. When one studies a trend, the time intervals (on the baseline of his graph) are his principal cases; the observed trend line is the description (even though it may represent number of persons, as in population growth). In all these instances the researcher starts with segments of a quantitative variable and treats these segments (or units or ranges) as his principal cases. This means that these quantitative units become idiographic (that is, take on individuality and are of interest in themselves), their identity is maintained throughout, and they are described in terms of various aspects which may be relevant to the study.

Simple and rather obvious illustrations of creating cases by the delimitation of quantitative variables are common in connection with space and time. We are so used to the conventional units in these instances, however, that we do not easily recognize them as delimited categories. Whenever a state, city, school district, or any other geographic unit is to be described (perhaps quantitatively through counting or measuring some attendant character), and probably to be compared with other units of the same kind, these spatial categories become the cases for one's study. For example, in a table which lists the states together with their population, or some other descriptive material, each state is used as a case. All such spatial units, however, are simply categories formed by drawing boundary lines at selected places. In the same way, the infinite extent of time is divided up into convenient units by drawing lines at selected intervals and, when these units become the center of attention in one's study, they become his cases. For example, if one wishes to study the variations in school attendance over a period of time, he will use for his group (or category) cases such temporal units as the school day, week, month, semester, or year. Each such unit is then *described* by the attendance noted for it (as expressed in terms of a smaller or primary case, the individual pupil).

It is of course true that the common temporal and spatial categories were originally formed for other than research purposes, but so were most of the other categories commonly employed in research. Further, one may find occasions when he needs to create new unit cases of time or space for special studies. In recent years the United States Bureau of the Census has created several new geographical units expressly for the purpose of making possible certain descriptive and comparative studies.[444]

In the uses of time and space that have been referred to here, it is important to maintain two distinctions. In the first place, one will not think of any temporal or geographical category as a composite *of the people,* or other individual objects, which may be counted within its limits. These are merely descriptive characteristics of the case at the particular time and place. The essence of these categories is purely time or space; and, if one wishes to think of them as composite cases, he will think of them as consisting of subdivisions of the essential traits they represent. Thus, a state may be thought of as composed of successively smaller subdivisions of space (for example, counties, school districts), and a year may be subdivided into months, weeks, days, and so on. Logically these units may become indefinitely small.

The second distinction to be made is between the two different uses of quantitative variables—that is, their use as cases, just described, and their possibly more common use for purposes of measurement (description). It will be recalled that in the last part of the discussion in the section on analysis, space and time were referred to in the measurement (descriptive) role. Some particular condition or degree of condition was taken as the principal case and space and time units were employed primarily to describe it; that is, to measure the extent of the existence or occurrence of each case (as,

---

[444] These include the census tract, introduced in 1910; the metropolitan district, introduced in 1940; and three new areas introduced in the 1950 census: the standard metropolitan area, the urbanized area, and the state economic area. Descriptions of these units are readily available in the publications of the Bureau of the Census and may be obtained directly from the Bureau on request.

Certain cities have revised the boundaries of districts of various kinds, in order to make them coextensive with the census tract boundaries, so that sociological data can be directly related and research studies made.

*so many* square miles, with no interest in their particular geographic location; or *so many* days, with no interest in their particular location in chronological time). Both uses of quantitative traits are sound and wholly legitimate, the choice depending on whether one's principal interest is in describing the particular cases created by delimitating quantitative ranges, or in describing the extent of certain specified conditions. In the first instance the quantitative variable is used idiographically; in the second instance, descriptively.

In practice, the two uses may not be so clear cut and alternative. For example, a county or state might be viewed either as a spatially delimited case or as a politically delimited case. Arguments can be advanced for both ways of looking at it, for actually it is idiographic with respect to both the quantitative and qualitative traits. Again, it must be borne in mind that any case can be counted; hence, any spatially delimited unit, used initially as a case, may in turn lose its identity and take on a measurement role if it is counted simply as one unit in a series of units employed to indicate size or degree of some larger category. For example, if a state be taken as a case for study, and subsequently counted as *one* to make up a total of forty-eight states, it becomes a descriptive element in characterizing the United States. It is *use,* not any kind of essential nature, that determines whether a unit is a case or a measure. Finally, we must recognize that there are many situations in which we employ the same quantitative trait in both capacities (that is, idiographic and descriptive) at the same time. If we study the length of the school day in different school systems, we are using both as a case (the school day, which is the thing being described and compared) and as a measure (the number of hours). Similarly, if we describe a school district in terms of its length or area, we are employing conventionally delimited space (the district) as the case, and units of distance or of area (space again) as the measure. In everyday life we use these fundamental traits in both ways without stopping to consider the distinction; but, in order to think clearly about their uses in research, it is desirable to recognize the two different ways in which these (or other) quantitative variables may be employed.

**Standardizing the observations which describe.** The preceding section has dealt with the creating and the defining (in general terms) of fairly large and complex categories which one may find appropriate to employ as the principal category cases in his study. (As indicated previously, that step is not appropriate to all studies; sometimes the interest is directly in things which can be observed. For such studies the present section can be read as referring to these direct observations, rather than as discussing observations to index the larger, more general concepts.) Having once chosen his categories to represent the larger, more general aspects which he feels are valuable, the researcher's next interest is in finding ways to describe them in terms of things which can be observed. The problem is one of selecting more detailed, specific things (as events, objects, persons, conditions) which can be observed readily and reliably, and which will serve to represent the larger ideas. Thus the larger ideas (category cases) are converted into smaller ideas which can be looked for in the data-gathering processes and which will indicate the presence or absence, or help build up the quality, of the larger idea.

The problem of finding these specifics involves all the ordinary problems connected with classification. The researcher must be thinking in both directions—in the direction of analyzing the general concept (category case) to see what it means in observable terms, and in the direction of building up, to see what observable specifics will, when taken together, add up to a satisfactory indication of each general idea. On the negative side, this step is partly a matter of delimitation: of the great multitude of specifics which might be observed, what ones will be ignored entirely because they do not fall within any of the categories that are regarded as germane to the study? On the positive side, this step is a matter of selecting those specifics which are judged worth observing because they will help describe the larger categories; and it is a matter of assigning each specific to the larger category for which it is judged best. This latter process may not be easy; it may require considerable trial and experimentation. Further, these specifics must be of such character that they can be judged immediately in the observation processes and (probably) tabulated at once into the larger categories. This step of laying out the specifics is, then, likely to be something more than a matter of building the observation schedule or instrument: one's plans must often go beyond the categories which are written on his schedule and decide on the appropriate classification of specifics too numerous and too detailed to appear on his schedule. Yet these specifics, often complex and often subtle, must have definite, instantly identifiable allocation to one's larger categories if his investigation is to have that consistency absolutely essential to a study that has meaning and value as research.

Perhaps the clearest need for a careful selection of specifics—of what will be included and what will be ignored, and where each kind of item will be recorded—occurs when one is dealing with events, as in behavior. Here we have an ongoing succession of events, of endless variety; some will be noted, many will not be. Most of them will not be recorded as simple, mechanical actions, because such cannot be interpreted afterwards; they will be recorded with a certain amount of interpretation at the time. It is true that the goal of observation is, theoretically at least, to record with such "objectivity" that no two observers would disagree on any action; but however enticing this aim may seem in the abstract, it is not entirely achievable. It is true that judgment must be narrowed greatly, if the results of observation are to be scientifically usable; but there is a point beyond which it is unprofitable to go, beyond which it is loss to go. Each event (action) that is observed, therefore, must be interpreted at least enough to classify it (place it) into some category that is set up in advance on the observation record. To the extent that this degree of interpretation renders the reports of different observers too dissimilar, then further study must be made of the categories, or further training of the observers must be considered, until an acceptable degree of agreement is attained.

As an illustration of the use of categories to standardize direct observation, we may take the study by Blum [445] of the behavior of doctors and of mothers in connection with visits to modern well-baby clinics. These clinics presumably espouse an educational point of view and the pediatricians are concerned with psychological as well as physiological aspects of the child's development. They seek to make a contribution to the emotional well-being of both the child and the mother. What do they actually do? How do they do it? To what extent do they probably succeed in these larger goals?

Blum studied eighty-one mothers in their visits to nineteen different pediatricians, who worked in five different clinics in New York City hospitals. To develop the categories for recording, Blum made preliminary visits to a number of clinics and took as complete notes as possible. From these, it was decided to eliminate certain routine items of no real significance; to eliminate mother-baby and pediatrician-baby conversation and record only remarks between doctor and mother (this was a matter of practicality; one could not record everything); and various categories of behavior were worked out, given brief names for recording, and in turn grouped into larger groups for purposes of systematic presentation. For example, to classify the concerns which mothers expressed, a list of fifty-five different items was needed; these were grouped into eight major groups, and in turn constituted but one of three sets of items to be observed.

Several points may be noted in connection with this study. In the first place, the categories, which established the range of the events to be noted, could not have been made in advance of the study by sitting down and writing them out. They required preliminary observation of the events and were adapted to the particular study and its purposes. (A person who had worked for some time in these clinics might conceivably have prepared the

445 Lucille H. Blum, "Some Psychological and Educational Aspects of Pediatric Practice: A Study of Well-Baby Clinics." *Genetic Psychology Monographs* 41:3-97; February 1950.

categories out of his intimate knowledge; but even so they would call for adjustment and reworking in the light of actual recording possibilities and in the light of the particular purposes of a given study.) In the second place, the categories were tried out with different observers to test their reliability. In the third place, they were revised (principally in the sense of being added to) as the need arose. Fourth, full verbatim statements were reported to illustrate (for the reader) what each of the categories meant. Fifth, the categories generally called for some judgment on the part of the observer; that is, to classify remarks under categories of reassuring, commending, explanatory, and negative behaviors called for a certain degree of judgment at the time, involving not only content but also manner and an awareness of what came before and after. Such judgment, insofar as it can be kept reasonably consistent and in keeping with common interpretations of the categories, is to be regarded as highly desirable or essential; without it, only the most mechanical of studies can be made.

One may have a slight curiosity as to what constitutes a case in this study. The answer is that it depends on one's interest—which may shift momentarily from one aspect or grouping to another. For different purposes of thought, one might say that the cases for observation (and in part for analysis) were the five clinics, the nineteen doctors, the eighty-one mothers, and the individual events (behaviors) recorded moment by moment. For purposes of analysis alone, the larger groupings of behaviors become group cases; thus, in the analytical tables it is found that the mothers expressed a total of fifty concerns over physical disorders of their babies, and this category, "concerns over physical disorders," can be entered into tables in various ways to show comparison and correlation with other such categories. But it can also be broken down into three subcategories, or into ten unitary categories, and in certain tables each of these is employed as a case. Thus, what is used as a case in a study depends in part on what is observed and recorded, and in part on what unit groups are employed in the analysis. When, for example, all of the data for a given clinic are thrown together, and compared with similar data for other clinics, then the clinic itself becomes the case for that portion of the analysis. If the matter seems complicated, this discussion should at least prevent one from giving a simple, dogmatic answer, or from looking for such an answer when it does not exist.

It may be worth considering what service these categories render in such a study. Perhaps the best way to do this is to consider what would happen without them. The observer would try writing down everything that occurred. Obviously he couldn't. He might use a recording machine to catch everything that was said, but what would he do with it? Without classification he might come out with such general conclusions as, "I like the first doctor's voice better than the second," "the third doctor seems more pleasant than the fourth," and so on. Our everyday living may be on that impressionistic order; science is more precise. To make analyses that will have some specificity and reliability, and which will permit of quantitative comparisons between one "case" and another (whatever the analysis at that point is employing as a case), one would have to employ categories; for classification is a necessary basis for quantification.

We find in this study considerably more freedom in what is employed as a case for purposes of analysis than in the preceding section, in the study by Baldwin and others, in part because it is a directly descriptive study, whereas the one by Baldwin was of the causal-comparative sort and was interested in a restricted number of relationships; and also in part because the data in the Blum study were gathered from such units as permit distribution and aggregation in hierarchical fashion.

Nothing that has been said in this section should preclude the constant alertness of the observer for discovering larger aspects, or at least other aspects, than those which his categories are designed to cover, when the additional aspects seem to be of significance in the area of his study. It is presumed that the categories employed will be based on sufficient experience and trial to afford reasonably satisfactory classifications; but it is also known as a matter of the history of research studies that many of them end with the conviction on the part of the researcher that he would have found far more useful conclusions, if he had used other categories (had looked for other aspects). Presumably he will state these matured insights as part of his conclusions so that succeeding research workers will have the benefit of them.

For example, at Stephens College a study was made of the effect of different sizes of class.[446] In the conventional approach, measurements of amounts of learning, as indicated by test performance, would probably be employed. The study presently referred to, however, noted rather general characteristics: that in an optimum sized group practically the whole class participated, and each student was held responsible by the group for his expressed ideas which he defended or revised, and the thinking of the group seemed to be cumulative and have progress. In classes that were too large, there was a sense of anonymity and irresponsibility; individual comments tended to be lost in the large number made, and little organization and progress were present in the discussion. On the other hand, it was concluded that classes may easily be too small as well as too large; in the too-

---

[446] Reported informally in the *Stephens College News Reporter* for May 1949, Vol. 8, by Vera Z. Washburne.

small group, the situation was intimate, remarks tended to be personal, and the discussion tended toward argument. There seemed to be too much personal offense; even remarks by the instructor were too often taken as personal criticism. Both the teacher and the group became distracted by single personalities.

Such a report is an excellent and refreshing illustration of a study that did not get caught in a formal, mechanical routine—out of which none of the foregoing comments would have come. On the other hand, it is evident that the kind of effects noted would require an observer of considerable maturity and insight; these aspects probably would not have been thought of by a less mature or insightful person, and probably could not be judged accurately, even if thought of. Again, such a study must be regarded as preliminary rather than as a finished investigation. The problem at this point becomes one of finding aspects of class discussion that are narrower than these rather general, judgmental observations, and which can, therefore, be observed more objectively and reliably. When that is done, the occurrences of the detailed aspects can be counted, and the extent to which the more general characteristics (as mentioned in the exploratory study) are true for classes of different sizes can be studied. In other words, finding specific, relatively objective indicators of the general ideas permits quantification and rather definite conclusions.

As the reader will probably have concluded, it is not necessary to think of every aspect as a category; but in practice they often are, because one's thinking occurs on so many different levels—the larger ideas must be broken up into smaller aspects, in order to gather data on them (as suggested in the earlier section on analysis). In any case, it is the province of the present section to deal with those instances where aspects do enter into a categorical system, and to show how classification is an aid to one in gathering his data.

**Selecting and categorizing scale indicators.** This topic continues the preceding one but with emphasis on measurement. In the study by Blum cited in the preceding section, it was possible for the researcher to conclude that the manner of a particular pediatrician was positive and reassuring (rather than negative, disturbing, and offensive) by counting the number of instances of detailed behavior classed under these different categories. If one were studying the effect of size of class on certain desirable aspects of discussion, it would be possible to say that a certain size was or was not conducive to these aspects, if one could count fairly detailed (fairly objective) aspects of the discussion which, when taken together, would indicate a certain degree of the characteristic in question.

These possibilities were not the main features of the studies referred to, but there are instances where such a process constitutes one's principal purpose. That is, he seeks a *quantitative expression* of the degree to which various broad characteristics occur, and in order to obtain this he purposely sets about to build an observation schedule that will yield a quantitative index. The result is a form of *measuring by means of counting*— measuring the relative intensity or pervasiveness of a broad character by counting the more detailed, more easily observable aspects which, taken together, are regarded as constituting the broader trait. (This is somewhat of an overstatement for the purpose of simplicity; the details do not have to make up the broad trait in its entirety; for purposes of measurement, their total merely has to correlate with it.)

In the present section, therefore, we are right at the heart of making a certain kind of scale, the kind which measures by counting indicative occurrences. This type of work was first mentioned in the earlier section on analysis where it was pointed out that, to index a general character (such as listening ability), it was desirable to analyze the trait (the ability) into components. The present section is a continuation of that process, carried to the level of still smaller, observable details. With respect to the topic immediately preceding, the present discussion is concerned more with the indexing (indicating) of quantitative categories than with the description of qualitative categories. (We do not wish to imply that there is any absolute difference between these two terms, but they are convenient labels to suggest somewhat different interests or centers of attention. By qualitative we mean to suggest complex differences more easily named than measured.)

The applications of this idea in educational studies are varied and widespread. They occur in score cards, readability formulas, determination of teaching load or of janitorial load, indexes of social class, and in fact most or all written tests of achievement, aptitude, and general ability. One of the more recently developed fields, content analysis, employs this process to a very large extent, as discussed in the next chapter. It seems probably better to leave the discussion of these practical applications to the next chapter, and to deal here only with the illustration of the categorical process which underlies all of the applications. When one understands this basic logical pattern, he can more easily see the many forms of application as belonging basically to the same family.

What we are here interested in is the selection of fairly detailed aspects that have a quantitative significance. This simply means that they are believed (on the basis of logic, judgment, or statistical evidence) to indicate a certain "thing"; that is, a certain state or tendency along a trait that is conceived of as having degrees. An illustration of this type of work is furnished by a study of the effect on pupils of certain methods of teachers in controlling (giving directions to) their pupils.[447] After considerable observation of children, the thesis was developed that behavior could profitably be divided along a continuum representing the degree to which it was dominative (at one end of the scale), or integrative, at the other end. These terms are described at length in the original publications (especially 1937 and 1939), but "dominative," as defined by the authors, seems to be close to authoritarian, dictatorial, aggressive, ascendant, rigid; such behavior represents an individual imposing set goals, fixed standards, or personal ideas or desires on another; expending energy against another; not trying to avoid or reduce conflict. It includes commands, directives, warnings, threats, refusals, disapproval, blame, punishment. "Integrative," as defined, seems to be close to democratic, coöperative, flexible; such behavior represents an individual seeking to find common purposes with another, expending energy in consonance with another, seeking to obviate or reduce conflict. It includes invitation, encouragement, explanation, free discussion, help, approval (of self-initiated activity). In later forms, approval and acceptance of *required* work were considered dominative; so also was giving permission, since it represents a decision by the teacher and presupposes that permission has to be granted, that the child is not free to act otherwise. Whereas dominative behavior is often frustrating and leads to resistance and contentiousness, or to coerced submission accompanied by a certain element of fear, integrative behavior is (defined as) positive in effect, tending to make the other person feel comfortable and unafraid. "There is no greater psychological security than for one to be accepted as he is." Integrative behavior does not make another person feel that his status is threatened or his wishes disregarded.

These details of description are given here, not for the purpose of approving or criticizing them, but simply to indicate something of the nature of the problem—the kinds of things one must consider and decide—in trying to divide behavioral interactions into two general categories, whatever they may be. It should be understood that there is no absolute criterion as to the rightness of these decisions; they are made on the basis of experience, logic, and judgment, and (in research) are modified in the light of trial and consideration of their effectiveness in differentiating between types of behavior which produce different effects on another person.

[447] This large study is reported in a series of three monographs by Harold H. Anderson and varying associates. The common title for the three is *Studies of Teachers' Classroom Personalities*, I, II, III. Applied Psychology Monographs, Nos. 6, 8, 11. 1945 and 1946. Available from the American Psychological Association, Washington, D. C. The categories are described in the second of the three monographs, which bears the subtitle, *Effects of Teachers' Dominative and Integrative Contacts on Children's Classroom Behavior*. Anderson's published studies in this area go back to 1937. For a brief presentation of the series and of related work, one may consult Douglas E. Scates, "Teaching as a Contribution to Personal Integration." *Journal of Teacher Education* 2:223-26; September 1951.

It should be added, as a purely logical matter, that in setting up such a scale, one does not necessarily assume that the best behavior would lie at or toward one end of the scale; it might lie at or near the middle. The characteristics one thinks of for each end of the scale, therefore, are not necessarily the most ideal, nor the most reprehensible, but merely the most extreme conditions along the scale which is being described. This is important in connection with evaluation, namely, that the scale of evaluation (goodness or desirability) is a very different thing from the scale set up to measure some other trait (as dominative-integrative behavior). The researcher must exercise care lest his thinking about values be warped by hearing value-laden words such as *integrative, democratic, progressive,* and the like. These are "tricks of the trade" in argument; in research, one will withhold his judgment as to value until the results are in.

As a matter of interest, a few of the conclusions (based on findings) may be cited. Among children: "Domination incites domination." "Integrative behavior in a child induces integrative behavior in the companion." "A secure child makes for security in a companion." [448] When the study was shifted from children in their relations to other children, to teachers in their relation to pupils, the same general results were found. For example, in the case of two teachers in the second grade:

> Fourteen statistically signficant differences between the children in the two rooms were found. . . . The children with the more integrative teacher . . . showed significantly lower frequencies of looking up at seat work, playing with foreign objects, and both conforming and non-conforming behavior. The children with the more integrative teacher were significantly higher in frequencies in several categories representing spontaneity and initiative and social contributions.[449]

It should not be inferred that the more integrative teacher in this comparison never "told" the class or individual pupils what to do; that might be the assumption from what has been said so far. The more integrative teacher *was dominative* nearly four times per minute, partly to the group as a whole but mostly to individual pupils. Her remarks which were counted as integrative, however, were somewhat more numerous—approximately 23 per cent. Whether this proportion is to be regarded as good, excellent, or nearly ideal is not known at this time. It was, however, sufficiently different from the ratio for another teacher—whose dominative comments were eight per minute and whose integrative statements were only about one-fifth as many—to bring out the fourteen differences re-

[448] Harold H. Anderson, *Domination and Social Integration in the Behavior of Kindergarten Children and Teachers,* p. 294-95, 383. Genetic Psychology Monographs 21:287-385; August 1939. Provincetown, Mass.: Journal Press, 1939.

[449] Quoted from Harold H. Anderson and Joseph E. Brewer, *Studies of Teachers' Classroom Personalities, II,* p. 124. 1946.

ferred to. Comparable data for teachers in general are not available; hence the percentile rank of these two teachers is not known. Results are tedious to obtain; the present figures were based on sixty hours of observation in each class.

These results have been given to show the end-product of the work; that is, what kind of data one is working toward, and what he can do with them. For our immediate purpose, however, interest centers not so much in the findings as in the method of preparing for the observations. It has been mentioned that the studies were in process over a period of several years, during which various data-gathering schedules were tried out, modified, and the ideas represented by the categories were refined. Two aspects of the process are clear: (1) the individual comments of the teacher had to be classified eventually as falling either in the dominative or integrative classes, but to classify every conceivable thing a teacher might say, without further guide, would be virtually impossible. Hence, (2) a framework of intermediate categories was constructed, and these were used in turn in both directions—to help decide what specific items of teacher comment would be included under each, and to help determine whether the intermediate category supported the dominative or integrative concept. Thus, through many intercomparisons and judgments, a list was built up which, for teachers, consisted of five situational types and twenty-six more specific categories. The latter were illustrated copiously with quoted comments of teachers, and were used for the recording of observations. They require fifteen pages to present. Similarly, a set of twenty-nine categories for recording pupil behavior was built up.

By these means, it was possible to come out with conclusions that different teachers varied by measured amounts in the extent to which they employed integrative versus dominative means of direction and stimulation of pupils, and that these differences in teacher behavior were associated with differences in pupil behavior. (The judgment of what differences in pupil behavior are desirable is another step and lies outside the immediate problem, so far as research is concerned. The practical person would probably make the judgment at once and assume only one conclusion was possible; the philosopher would relate the differences to a larger pattern of values that have been generally accepted or rejected by our society; the research person would seek ways of analyzing the differences further, so that they could be more explicitly viewed, or of following them through the later lives of the children to see what they tend to lead to—in either case seeking more enlightened bases of judgment.) In this connection, it must always be remembered that one must think quantitatively rather than in terms of absolutes; the question is not, Do we want people to be democratic? but *How* democratic do we want them to be? We never want extremes, however easy it is to talk that way. (One may recall the earlier discussion of the way in which classification is partly imposed, where it was pointed out that the notion of absolute categories belongs to the philosophers of earlier times.)

The point for the present section is that, basic to studies of the type discussed, is the classification of the detailed elements, the status indicators. Every statement of the teacher, in the present study, is regarded as falling in one or another of the two major categories, as "pulling" the totality of the teacher's behavior in one direction or another on the scale one is thinking of. Each statement is thus a status determiner; it adds its weight to the preponderance of one or the other main classes of statements in the aggregate of statements observed for a teacher, and thus it helps indicate the *degree* to which the teacher belongs in one or the other category—the point on the scale, from one end to the other, where this teacher falls.

Exactly the same procedure has been seized upon to index (measure) the character of documents or other communications. Statements (possibly words, phrases, sentences, or larger units) which tend to throw the weight of the contents in one direction or another are identified, classified, and then counted accordingly. By building up a set of carefully described categories that help place these individual units in one or another of the more general classes, the tendency (perhaps the leaning, coloring, bias, prejudice, or propaganda intent) of the communication can be ascertained. The crux of the procedure is the detection and proper classification of those unit elements that will reveal the trait in which one is interested, just as the crux of measuring integrative versus dominative tendencies of children or teachers rests on the initial proper classifying of the detailed elements. In either instance, detailed categories are gradually built up and described so that from this point on the work is reasonably objective. A fuller treatment of content analysis is reserved for the next chapter.

Operationally, the crux of the matter is the classification of the indicators, as stated; psychologically, the crux of such a study is the development of a concept of some trait that seems significant and which will probably prove worth studying. And, further, the determination of which category a particular indicator will fall in, and whether it should be included in the count at all, are psychological matters calling for careful, deliberate, technical judgment.

This procedure of ascertaining where, on the scale representing some fairly general concept, a particular specimen (a document, a teacher's behavior, and so forth) belongs is available whenever the general concept can be thought of as consisting of an aggregate of many elements, the preponderance of one or another class of these elements indicating a certain direction on the scale. In such a situation, "interaction" between the elements is not contemplated; that is, for purposes of quantitative indication, each element is thought of as a self-contained unit, and not as one which, in combination with others, produces new effects (or possibly more intense effects) over the simple sum of the units. In such thinking, the unit elements do not themselves actually constitute a scale, since all of them *may* be conceived of as of equal strength and color (in one or the other of the two major categories), but they constitute weights, or elements of pull, in one direction or the other. If *all* the elements counted for a given situation fell in one of the major categories, the situation would be more saturated, or pure, with respect to the quality (degree) represented by that category than if there were some elements from the opposite category (at the other end of the scale) to dilute, modify, or subtract from the purity of its character. This is the basic form of logic underlying the use of this technique for measurement purposes.

This procedure lay *behind* the large categories employed in the study of parent behavior by Baldwin and associates, as cited in an earlier section, where a home-rating scale had previously been used to select certain detailed elements which were later built into the three principal traits—democracy, acceptance, and indulgence. The process described in the present section is probably commoner than is recognized. For example, the making of objective tests is an illustration; each item is a specific designed to help indicate the general level of accomplishment. We will not go further into test-making here; our present purpose is to show ways in which classification, as a process, is of fundamental service in the conduct of research.

## CONCLUDING STATEMENT

Chapter 5 has presented a detailed analysis of the theory of descriptive methods (together with numerous examples), in relation to research studies identified as general description, analysis, and classification. The purpose and scope of this text have not permitted similar treatment of types of descriptive studies known as enumeration, measurement, and evaluation, except as summarized briefly in Chapter 6.

Because of the variety and complexity of the research concepts presented in Chapter 5, and because of the wide range of literature cited, no chapter bibliography has been attempted. In the footnotes of Chapters 5 and 6 are hundreds of illustrative investigations and references. At the end of Chapter 6 is a summary of major developments in the application of descriptive-survey techniques to a variety of areas and problems.

# 6

## Organized Forms of Descriptive-Survey and Normative Research:

### ILLUSTRATIVE SURVEYS AND PROCEDURES IN DATA-GATHERING[1]

## GENERAL NATURE OF DESCRIPTIVE, SURVEY, NORMATIVE, AND STATUS STUDIES

**Introduction.** The preceding sections of Chapter 5 on the descriptive method have discussed the general nature and theory of this approach to problem-solving, including general description, analysis, and classification. Chapter 6 in its several parts will describe descriptive-survey-status-trend studies in the educational, psychological, and social areas, including social, community, and school surveys, in terms of both illustrations and techniques. These investigational procedures and techniques embrace general principles of gathering data and of using published sources of statistics; sampling; questionnaire inquiries; interview studies; observational investigations, together with instruments of recording (sometimes mechanical means of recording); group-behavior analysis or small-group study (based on the concepts of group dynamics); content analysis of documentary and verbal materials, including textbook analysis; survey-appraisal procedures, utilizing rating scales, score cards, and check lists; and index numbers.

The discussions and illustrations of organized forms of descriptive research and of data-collecting techniques are presented in the same chapter, with full recognition of the fact that strict logic and the preferences of some readers might dictate a separate chapter for the data-gathering instruments commonly used in descriptive-survey and normative investigations (and also employed frequently in experimental, case, and genetic studies). It seems economy of time and effort, however, on the part of both authors and readers to present in one subdivision or section both the organized forms of inquiry and the problems of instrument-making for such a topic as the

---

[1] For a related discussion of descriptive-survey techniques and for illustrations covering an earlier period see Carter V. Good, A. S. Barr, and Douglas E. Scates, *The Methodology of Educational Research.* New York: Appleton-Century-Crofts, 1936. p. 286-481.

Also see the treatment of descriptive studies in Chapter 5 for a related discussion of terminology, nature and uses of descriptive investigations, and descriptive-survey studies as research.

questionnaire. Therefore, in this chapter the reader should not be too much concerned about the logic of coördinate topical headings in dealing with large forms of organized descriptive research, such as the social survey or school survey, in comparison with data-gathering techniques, such as the questionnaire or interview (frequently used as instruments in a large or complex descriptive study such as the social, community, or school survey).

Although many types of mental measurements and tests of achievement, intelligence, aptitude, and personality are used in survey testing, and as data-gathering instruments in experimental, case, and genetic investigations, this group of tools will not be treated here, because of the availability of numerous specialized books and courses on measurements in the fields of education and psychology. For an overview of this important area of research techniques, the Mental Measurements Yearbooks,[2] edited by Buros, and the comprehensive treatise edited by Lindquist, will prove valuable.

Descriptive-survey procedures have been used in many areas of investigation other than the educational, psychological, and social sciences. These approaches to problem-solving are appropriate wherever the objects of any class vary among themselves and one is interested in knowing the extent to which different conditions obtain among these objects. For example, ecology is a large division of biological science, as well as of geology and the social sciences.

The literature includes a number of terms characterizing the investigational procedures presented in this chapter: descriptive, survey, normative, status, and trend. As mentioned earlier, *description* includes induction, analysis, classification, enumeration, measurement, and evaluation. The word *survey* indicates the gathering of data regarding current conditions. The term *normative* is sometimes used because surveys are frequently made to ascertain the normal or typical condition (or practice), or to compare local test results with a state or national norm. The term *norm* also has another meaning in certain contexts—determining upon an authoritative standard, ideal, or model; deciding what ought to be, what is "right" or desirable or good.

**Cross-section surveys or status studies in relation to historical perspective.** Human beings are interested in various types of knowledge and in using a number of problem-solving techniques for securing answers to their questions. Many studies have sought to discover laws that describe relationships, but a much larger number of investigations have had other purposes. An earlier chapter on the historical method has presented the

[2] Oscar K. Buros, Editor, *The Fourth Mental Measurements Yearbook*. Highland Park, N. J.: Gryphon Press, 1953. 1189 p.
E. F. Lindquist, Editor, *Educational Measurement*. Washington: American Council on Education, 1951. 819 p.

techniques used by workers to discover what facts once were true in the world, or what events took place in some particular part of the world, before the present generation came to be. The historian has sought to provide an integrated narrative of past events, written in the spirit of critical inquiry to find the truth and report it. By appropriate methods in dealing with sources, in criticism of evidence, and in the writing and interpretation of history, the historical worker has been enabled to piece together bits of evidence so as to prepare a description of conditions at an earlier time, or to form a story of the succession of events; and, by careful interpretation based on the data and his own scholarly background, he has often been able to identify (supply) an explanatory thesis which would give additional meaning to the facts, and thus not only tell a story, but afford an explanation of how one condition led to another.

The present chapter is concerned primarily with history in the making. An interest in educational, psychological, and social problems has led curious persons to make and record the pictures of conditions as they are developing, instead of waiting until the events are long past and scholars and historians must dig these facts out of forgotten and sometimes musty records. This statement does not mean that historians are neglecting the history of the present, but certainly they will find it much easier to gather the facts of the present and of recent years by reason of the existence of many types of survey studies, to be discussed and illustrated in this chapter. Scientists and scholars have recognized that society is taking a more serious interest in the control of its affairs, as illustrated by the present concern of the general public over appropriate uses of the discoveries in the area of atomic energy. People have seen that lessons could be learned from studying past conditions and events, and now demand more detailed and accurate facts about current activities while the information can still be used as a guide in formulating policies and in working out plans for the immediate future.

Much of the significance and importance of descriptive-survey studies lies in the possibility of investigating the status of conditions at any given time and of repeating the survey at a later date, thus providing descriptions or cross sections at different periods of time, in order that comparisons may be made, the direction of change noted and evaluated, and future growth or development predicted. Such guidance is of relatively great importance in our complex and rapidly changing modern society. The historian is able to use these cross sections of current conditions at any given time as perspective in writing an integrated narrative of past events. Therefore, the descriptive-survey approach, which at first may appear superficial, in that it gathers data only for the present, without the perspective of a long historical sweep, may ultimately make possible sound historical writing through a series of cross-section pictures of conditions at different times in history. To cite a few illustrations, the annual school census, and the United States census at intervals of ten years, make possible the writing of the history of school enrollment and the history of the growth of population in the United States. The annual reports of the school superintendent of a city and of a university president, or the annual catalogue, contribute greatly to the writing of the history of a city school system or of a higher institution. The annual statistics of state departments of education and the biennial surveys of the United States Office of Education have been valuable in many types of historical studies and in making estimates of future trends.

**Trends as the dynamic aspects of status.** Descriptive-survey-status research is directed toward ascertaining the prevailing conditions (the facts that prevail in a group of cases chosen for study), and this method is essentially a technique of quantitative description of the general characteristics of the group. This approach to problem-solving seeks to answer questions as to the real facts relating to existing conditions. To use as an example the problem of illiteracy in the United States, pertinent questions revealed through a survey study would be somewhat as follows. What is the magnitude of the problem? Is it of urgent or shocking proportions? Where is the problem of illiteracy in the United States centered, as to regions, states, or in terms of other subgroups? What are the factors that enter into or cause illiteracy? With such facts as bases, men are in a better position to decide on appropriate courses of action in dealing with this condition.

Many survey-status studies emphasize present conditions with an implication of the idea that things will change. This vital interest in trends as the dynamics of status is in keeping with the general dynamic emphasis or outlook of present thought on research methodology. Although the status-survey study may be made as a matter of ascertaining facts, it is usually (and normally) made against a background of interests, purposes, and established values, so that the facts at once are seized upon by these mental backgrounds and employed in larger schemes of thinking or in application to specific problem situations.

During the past twenty to twenty-five years there has been a greatly increased interest in survey investigations in the educational, psychological, and social areas, including the participation of the federal government. Some of these status studies of groups have been repeated at intervals and the results compared to show trends in the educational, psychological, and social fields. However, a true growth study of the genetic or developmental type (to be discussed in a later chapter) follows an individual through, or a group of individuals, or a trend (growth) as in the number of teachers (growth of the teaching profession), securing growth trends or identifying developmental stages for the individual or the group. Whereas status studies may cover many traits or characteristics of the group, trends do not easily carry forward all these elements of the picture. In other words, trend studies differ, in common usage of the term, from broad description in that they follow one defined (somewhat narrow) trait through time. To cite an example, a study of the proportion of youth in high school, according to occupation of father, was made in 1922 by Counts; a similar investigation in 1932 by the National Survey of Secondary Education and later studies in the same area were made by other investigators, thus permitting interesting comparisons and interpretations of trends.[3]

A descriptive-survey study may be thought of in its relation to continuous (regular periodical) reports in any country or industry. A survey is simply one of these reports, a cross-section at a given time, but it is usually of particular importance or presents special information; it may be the beginning of such reports or, if they are going as a series, may be extensive in character. Acting as the initiating agency the survey has a unique opportunity to do two things: (1) to establish the value of facts or to show their value, so that regular reports may then later be called for; (2) to center attention on the most important things to be reported; it is a great challenge to ascertain the central elements or the dominant and fundamental factors that will indicate the general conditions.

**Relation of descriptive-survey studies to practical problems and needs.**
Do the data from descriptive-survey studies solve problems? The answer is that problems of a practical nature are not solved directly by data of any kind, since the solving of problems is a distinctly psychological process. Solutions to perplexing questions of a practical nature do not lie in data; they result from thinking, with the help of the increased insight that grows out of a study of data or evidence. It is essential to know the psychological side of research, and sometimes the social aspects by way of application or implementation of evidence, to distinguish between facts and inferences. The value of descriptive-survey data, as a basis for inferences that may aid in solving practical problems, probably will be more highly regarded by the school administrator in helping with his pressing difficulties than are

[3] George S. Counts, *The Selective Character of American Secondary Education*. Supplementary Educational Monographs, No. 19. Chicago: University of Chicago Press, 1922. 162 p.

Grayson N. Kefauver, Victor H. Noll, and C. Elwood Drake, *The Secondary-School Population*, Chapter I, "Changes in the Secondary-School Population," p. 1-26. Office of Education Bulletin No. 17, 1932; National Survey of Secondary Education Monograph No. 4. Washington: Government Printing Office, 1933. 58 p.

American Association of School Administrators, *The Expanding Role of Education*. Twenty-sixth Yearbook. Washington: The Association, N.E.A., 1948. 484 p.

the principles and laws growing out of experimentation in the laboratory. The administrator regards the data from the field, by way of descriptive-survey studies, as representing field conditions; this evidence is practical, because it has grown out of a real or actual survey situation, and is likely to answer the question of the school man in the field in terminology probably cast in his own language.

Therefore, the results of descriptive-survey investigations will have particular interest and importance for the school administrator, who would naturally like to know how other school systems are being run, in order that he may make comparisons with his own local schools. From this comparison he may find encouragement in noting that certain of his procedures and standards appear superior to the practices in other schools, or he may discover excellent practices in other systems that he can adapt to his own schools. Even if he does not find helpful suggestions concerning the solution of his problems, he may derive some comfort from learning that administrators and supervisors in many school systems are struggling with problems similar to his own.

Important psychological and social factors are involved in applying the results of research to field situations, particularly in a school system in a democracy controlled by a board elected by the public. Radical changes or major adaptations in school organization, curriculum, or instructional method are not ordinarily acceptable, if put into effect within a short period of time. This means that a theoretical, scientific principle discovered through carefully controlled experimentation would not ordinarily be acceptable, if the change were made within a relatively short period of time as a departure from current practice. This statement is no reflection on the insight or outlook of school administrators and school-board members, but is a recognition of the fact that many educational, psychological, and social factors must be taken into consideration before making sharp departures from existing plans of school organization, forms of curriculum development, or instructional procedure. Engineers and management in industry face similar problems in deciding when to introduce new developments or when to place a new model on the market. Sometimes directors in business and industry are more influenced by survey evidence (the present practices and plans of competitors) than by the new ideas or inventions of their own engineers. These illustrations suggest that the management of a large educational or business enterprise necessitates the consideration of many factors, of which technical research or evidence is only one item of importance. This extensive practical use of descriptive-survey data explains the predominant emphasis on survey studies as usually found in local, state, and national bureaus of research, particularly in research organizations in city school systems, state departments of education, teachers' organizations, the United States Office of Education, and in other national agencies.

The Research Division of the N.E.A., to cite an illustration, has depended chiefly on the survey method to gather evidence for the following series of bulletins published over the 1950-53 period.

Pupil Patrols in Elementary and Secondary Schools
Fiscal Authority of City Schoolboards
Personnel and Relationships in School Health, Physical Education, and Recreation .
Public-School Retirement at the Half Century
Teaching Load in 1950
Salaries and Salary Schedules of City-School Employees, 1950-51
Legal Status of the School Superintendent
Schools and the 1950 Census
Teacher Personnel Practices, 1950-51: Appointment and Termination of Service
Teacher Personnel Procedures, 1950-51: Employment Conditions in Service
The Effects of Mobilization and the Defense Effort on the Public Schools
Public-School Revenues, 1949-50
Rural Teachers in 1951-52
Salaries and Salary Schedules of Urban School Employees, 1952-53.

Critics of the descriptive-survey method sometimes say that it is not notably forward-looking; however, in reply it may be said that the survey or normative method can be of definite service in this direction. It may reveal practices or conditions or instructional procedures that are well above the average, representing advanced thinking in school organization or policy; for example, a survey of the practices and procedures of excellent teachers may serve as a goal for average teachers that will not be achieved for many years in the future. The survey method also helps to focus attention on practical needs that might otherwise remain unobserved for some time; many school systems do not realize fully the unsatisfactory conditions of some of their school buildings until a survey has revealed these poor facilities for housing the children of the city. It has already been said in this chapter that survey evidence may direct attention to current trends and permit responsible persons of insight to evaluate and direct these new tendencies in the process of taking shape. Therefore, while the survey approach to problem-solving is not essentially forward-looking in and of itself, it may indeed perform an important function in providing pertinent evidence for persons who are forward-looking.

**Relation of survey studies to other techniques.** At a number of points the descriptive-survey method contributes to other techniques of investigation. Reference already has been made to the value of cross-section surveys and trend studies at regular time intervals for use as basic data in doing historical research; for example, tracing population trends.

It is granted that the survey method is not suited to the testing of various principles under laboratory conditions; however, it does provide evidence of the results of certain tests under practical field conditions. Thus, the survey technique may serve as a valuable check upon laws that have been discovered in isolation from the normal complex of social forces found in the school setting or in other field situations. For certain laws of distribution, field study may yield direct evidence that cannot be obtained from any other source. During more recent years the sociologists, and to a lesser extent investigators in psychology and education, have regarded various areas of habitation as essentially natural laboratories for their purposes, and have developed appropriate techniques for the analysis of particular phenomena.

The descriptive-survey or normative approach has not characteristically delved deeply into interrelationships or causal factors. The typical survey has stopped with the disclosure of facts and a suggestion of relatively prominent possible connections between these facts and apparent causes, although more recently both educational and social surveys have shown an increased interest in the causes of the phenomena described. To cite an example, survey and case studies may serve complementary and supplementary purposes. "Especially necessary for the understanding of opinions are an understanding of the group identifications and loyalties of individuals, and the purposes that stem from these loyalties. This is one of the most compelling reasons to supplement survey data with more complete case studies." [4] Fuller details of causal relationships are presented in the chapters dealing with the historical, experimental, case, and genetic methods of investigation. In the chapter on the experimental method is a brief presentation of causal-comparative studies, which are relatively common and of major importance. Surveys provide the background of ideas and data from which many, more refined laboratory or controlled studies of causal relations are made.

In addition to complementary or supplementary relationships to other methods of research, the survey approach fits appropriately into the total research scheme or the series of stages in exploring a large field of investigation. The descriptive-survey method may serve as the reconnaissance stage of research in entering a new area, or it may represent a specific interest in current conditions within a field that has long since been thor-

4 Albert H. Hastorf and Hadley Cantril, "Some Psychological Errors in Polling—A Few Guides for Opinion Interpretation." *Journal of Educational Psychology* 40:57-60; January 1949.

oughly explored and developed by research. In a new area of investigation the early attacks often involve a sort of general "getting acquainted" with the field. How far does it extend? What are the phenomena like? What are the classes or kinds into which the phenomena can be placed? How many cases are there of each class? Later, as the investigator gains increased familiarity with the characteristics of the field under study, he will attack the more detailed aspects of the area and make more refined studies. This comment on the contribution of descriptive-survey studies, by way of exploration in a new field, does not mean that this role represents the complete sphere of service for survey techniques. At other places in this chapter are illustrations of a variety of contributions of descriptive-survey methods to problem-solving.

**Descriptive-survey studies as research.** The foregoing comments do not mean that the descriptive-survey method is either a superior or an inferior approach to problem-solving. While some scholars and scientists have held the survey method in rather low esteem, the important consideration is whether a particular approach to problem-solving answers significant questions. There is really no one best type of research in general; a particular investigational technique may be best for a given purpose, and the descriptive-survey method has its own major field of special usefulness. The challenge is to produce survey studies of high quality. Some descriptive-survey investigations have been so trivial, so poorly conceived or so narrowly carried out, or so lacking in penetrating analysis and careful interpretation that they fail to rise above the level of clerical routine and actually can make no claim upon the label of research. On the other hand, some of the survey studies cited as illustrations in this chapter involve great ingenuity, skill, and insight in planning and carrying forward the particular project, so that they not only have served well the immediate purpose by way of providing answers to questions, but also furnish excellent illustrations of techniques and set new standards for research in the areas represented.

It seems essential to ask whether all survey uses of such instruments as questionnaires, interviews, observation schedules, rating scales, score cards, check lists, and tests may be regarded as research. A brief answer is that there is an important difference between research and the routine use of a particular technique for collecting data. Research embodies considerable care in the formulation of the problem, and in the determination of the best procedures for attacking the problem, and always involves an element of novelty or newness. This comment does not imply that research is necessarily the best way to find an answer to a particular problem; immediate needs may be met or answers to pressing questions may often be found more expeditiously by a routine study than by an elaborate research investigation. Some of the illustrations used in this chapter to show the characteristics of the various descriptive-survey procedures, particularly techniques for collecting data, may not be regarded as research in the full sense, but they serve particularly well to reveal the characteristics of the techniques under discussion. When such data-collecting techniques find their place as a step or phase in a larger pattern of problem-solving, they become an important and legitimate part of research, as when standard tests are used to equate groups in experimentation.

To characterize more fully the research aspects of survey studies, even though survey investigations are commonly made to guide administrators, they can be research in the fullest sense of the word, if expertly and insightfully made. By "expertness" is meant awareness and knowledge of factors in research procedure which influence results, resourcefulness in adapting methods to needs and in knowing what procedures are available, and high ethical standards in insisting that the best or most appropriate method be used and followed strictly. "Insightful" relates to the field of work, knowing the factors and mechanisms, having shrewd hypotheses, inventing plausible ideas to be tested, and drawing generalizations that are not absurd. Such survey studies may be basic research, if they contribute to important (theoretical) generalizations.

In more explicit terms, descriptive-survey studies are research when they create or ascertain: (1) new categories that are revealing, or more useful than those already in use, or of more far-reaching significance; (2) concepts that afford a more basic grasp of the factors which enter into results or which represent results more certainly; (3) methods of detecting and identifying a factor, and perhaps measuring it (quantifying it), valuable for analysis and description; (4) certain relationships (occasionally correlation or causal) that obtain, either for practical or scientific interest or value; and (5) the structure of relationships—of the mechanism relating them, why and how certain factors cause certain results. Certain of these characteristics or outcomes go beyond the results usually secured through survey studies, but repeated investigations of cause and effect relationships (as in ecology) can produce such outcomes, or can set the stage; possibly experimental work must follow up to get at mechanisms. In view of the current interest in group dynamics and in the development of action research (or operational research) as methods of finding answers to important questions, a debate over defining relatively technical research in contrast to certain more functional or practical forms of problem-solving would seem academic in this book, with its variety of investigational procedures and illustrative studies.

**Types of descriptive-survey research.** Since there are many kinds of facts which the investigator may wish to gather and different kinds of sources for these facts, there are also many procedures or techniques that have been developed to meet the needs of these varying purposes and conditions. For example, when the investigator desires facts from people about themselves, he may interview them; or ask them to fill out a questionnaire, or to take a test or examination, or to produce some piece of work, often in verbal or written form, evidencing their skill or interest.

In presenting and discussing the various types of descriptive-survey or normative research, four general purposes will be kept in mind: (1) to show the different educational, psychological, and social areas that may be studied by the survey method; (2) to provide numerous illustrations of the data-gathering techniques applicable to these fields; (3) to identify the characteristics of the different types of descriptive-survey procedures, particularly as to the instruments for collecting data; and (4) to cite typical studies that will acquaint the student with the actual research in each field and provide suggestions or clues for further work on the part of the investigator.

It is recognized that these purposes cannot be fully realized within the limits of a single volume, when entire books have been devoted to a particular technique or procedure for collecting data; for example, the questionnaire, interview, observation, testing, and the more complex school survey and social survey. Therefore, this book will provide the reader with an overview of the particular field or technique of investigation and introduce in the footnotes enough references to the appropriate available literature on the subject, so that the student may become reasonably familiar with each type of survey attack. Those readers who expect to use a particular type of survey technique or to construct an instrument for purposes of data-gathering may meet their specific needs by a more intensive study of the wealth of literature listed in the footnotes and bibliographies of this chapter. It is economy of time and effort, in recognizing the complementary and supplementary uses of different research approaches, to remember that the various types of data-gathering instruments so freely used in the descriptive-survey method are also employed in studies that depend chiefly on other research procedures (a point emphasized earlier in this chapter). For example, in experimentation various measuring-testing and appraisal instruments (especially in group experimentation in the class room), as well as questionnaires, rating scales, and direct observations, are used freely. Case and genetic studies may employ a wide variety of data-gathering instruments, with the interview especially important in case and clinical studies. Therefore, the discussions and illustrations of data-gathering instruments will be of interest, not only to investigators who are contemplating use of the descriptive-survey method, but also to persons who plan to employ other types of research, whether experimental, case-clinical, or growth-developmental in approach.

## THE SOCIAL-SURVEY MOVEMENT[5]

It seems appropriate to open the discussion of the various organized forms of descriptive-survey research and of data-gathering techniques with a more complex type of investigation, such as the social, community, or school-survey study, which frequently employs a variety of procedures and instruments for collecting data; for example, questionnaires, interviews, observations, and score cards. Later sections of this chapter will present simpler or less elaborate types of descriptive-survey studies and the appropriate data-gathering techniques.

The social survey is a coöperative undertaking that applies research techniques to the study and diagnosis of a current social problem, situation, or population, within definite geographical limits and bearings, usually with a concern for formulation of a constructive program of social reform and amelioration. The intellectual processes are in part similar to the methodology of other research approaches, whether historical, experimental, case, or genetic; namely, determining the purpose and defining the problem (including geographical and chronological limits), analysis of the problem in the form of a schedule for collecting data, examination of documentary sources, the necessary field work to gather the data called for by the sched-

---

[5] Because of the variety and complexity of the procedures and instruments discussed in this chapter, the illustrative references and studies are listed in each section, and no chapter bibliography has been provided.

Mark Abrams, *Social Surveys and Social Action*. London: William Heinemann, 1951. 153 p.

F. C. Bartlett and Others, Editors, *The Study of Society:* Methods and Problems. London: Kegan Paul, Trench, Trubner and Co., 1939. p. 424-35.

Manuel C. Elmer, *Social Research*. New York: Prentice-Hall, 1939. p. 187-223.

Leon Festinger and Daniel Katz, Editors, *Research Methods in the Behavioral Sciences*. New York: Dryden Press, 1953. p. 15-97.

Wilson Gee, *Social Science Research Methods*. New York: Appleton-Century-Crofts, 1950. p. 300-329.

Marie Jahoda and Others, *Research Methods in Social Relations:* With Especial Reference to Prejudice. Part One: Basic Processes. New York: Dryden Press, 1951. p. 47-58.

D. Caradog Jones, *Social Surveys*. London: Hutchinson's University Library, 1949. 232 p.

George A. Lundberg, *Social Research:* A Study in Methods of Gathering Data. Second Edition. New York: Longmans, Green and Co., 1942. p. 349-96.

John Madge, *The Tools of Social Science*. New York: Longmans, Green and Co., 1953. 332 p.

Mildred Parten, *Surveys, Polls, and Samples:* Practical Procedures. New York: Harper and Bros., 1950. p. 1-23.

Pauline V. Young, *Scientific Social Surveys and Research*. Second Edition. New York: Prentice-Hall, 1949. xxviii + 621 p. This comprehensive volume is especially valuable for concepts, techniques, and examples of social and community surveys.

ules, and analysis, interpretation, and (sometimes) application of the results.

**Pioneer studies.** The early social surveys covered a wide range of subjects that were frequently general studies of entire communities, ranging in size and form from the local neighborhood or parish, city ward, town, and city, up to counties and states. Later there was a tendency to use the social survey to appraise one major aspect or phase of community life, such as health and sanitation, public education, housing, recreation, employment and industrial relations, child welfare, dependency and charitable effort, and delinquency and correction.

One of the earliest known attempts to gather systematically a specific body of facts was made by John Howard (1726-1790), an English philanthropist and prison reformer, who secured facts and figures directly from prisons and prisoners. Howard's emphasis on field observation, and enumeration and detailed recording of facts, influenced greatly the later investigators who studied prison conditions and social problems.

Frederic Le Play (1806-1882), a French social reformer and economist, introduced a new form of social study through his monographs on family standards of living, in which he used social-survey methods. In these monographs Le Play was especially interested in the study of family budgets, and combined effectively the case-study method and statistical procedures.

The English statistician and reformer Charles Booth (1840-1916) was interested chiefly in the conditions of poverty found in the East Side of London. Comprehensive study of modern community life originated with the work of Booth when he started in 1886 his great investigation, *Life and Labour of the People in London.*[6] The first volume appeared in 1892 and the seventeenth of the series in 1897, with a revision in 1902. Booth wished to show one-half of London how the other half lived and to help social reformers find remedies for the existing evils. In dealing with the factors affecting life and labor, Booth studied income, hours and conditions of work, housing, standards of living, number of children, size of household in relation to size and type of dwelling, type and frequency of sickness, leisure activities, club and union membership, and many other elements.

Near the beginning of the twentieth century, during a period of serious economic readjustment, B. S. Rowntree made a detailed investigation of working-class conditions in the provincial town of York, England. Rowntree sought to obtain greater precision than Booth had achieved in East Side London and to discover how the conditions of labor in a small town

---

[6] Charles Booth, *Life and Labour of the People in London.* London: Macmillan and Co., 1892-1903. 17 vols.

compared with those in a large city. Covering a much smaller area, Rowntree could explore his problem in greater detail, going from house to house and moving from block to block. In 1936, approximately a generation later, Rowntree repeated the investigation in York, in order to cover changes in the living conditions of the workers during a period of far-reaching social reform. Rowntree's complete investigation of every household in York enabled him to compare his results with the conclusions that would have been obtained by sampling methods.

**Later developments in England.** During 1912-1914 Arthur Bowley and A. R. Burnett-Hurst directed a comparative study of five middle-sized industrial towns in England, reported in 1915 in *Livelihood and Poverty.*[7] These investigators introduced the principle of random sampling into community studies; instead of covering every household in a given area, they visited at random one household in every twenty. Bowley made a follow-up investigation by restudying the same community ten years later.

A new survey of London life and labor [8] was made under the general directorship of Sir Hubert L. Smith, and published in nine volumes, 1930-1935. The new survey was made to discover the changes in the socioeconomic life of a new generation of London laborers, for comparison with Booth's earlier survey. The more recent investigation describes the habits of laboring people after the advent of the automobile, telephone, wireless, and cinema, all of which had vastly changed the life and labor of the people in the great city of London. The new survey made extensive use of the reports and services of school-attendance officers, the method of random sampling, direct field investigation, and machine tabulation.

**Beginnings in America.** In the United States, as noted in England, the social-survey movement found its beginnings in realistic, if not scientifically conducted, studies of social conditions. Jacob Riis wrote a vivid first-hand account of tenement conditions in New York City,[9] under the title of *How the Other Half Lives* (1890). He dramatized his descriptions of the filth, lack of sanitation, and oppressive surroundings of youth and age in America's wealthiest and largest city. This early period was characterized by the work and writing of the "muckrakers."

Jane Addams of Chicago's Hull House and Robert Woods of Boston's East End House initiated local community studies made by professionally trained workers and social economists; for example, the *Hull House Maps*

[7] Arthur L. Bowley and A. R. Burnett-Hurst, *Livelihood and Poverty*. London: King and Son, 1915.
[8] Hubert L. Smith, *The New Survey of London Life and Labour*. London: King and Son, 1930-35. 9 vols.
[9] Jacob Riis, *How the Other Half Lives:* Studies Among the Tenements of New York. New York: Charles Scribner's Sons, 1890.

*and Papers:* A Presentation of Nationalities and Wages in a Congested District of Chicago (1895), picturing the social and economic life of Chicago's ghetto. Lincoln Steffens wrote a series of muck-raking articles under the title of *The Shame of the Cities* (1904), which pictured the deplorable conditions of city corruption. Upton Sinclair's novel, *The Jungle* (1906), described graphically the working and living conditions of the meat-packing laborers.

**Later developments in the United States.** The Pittsburgh social survey was begun in 1909 by Paul Kellogg [10] as general director and a group of social economists and professional social workers. The survey sought to throw light on the forces that affect the lives of steel workers, to discover the underlying factors in the city's growth as they affect the wage earners, to secure an inventory of an urban industrial community, and to determine how far human or social engineering has kept pace with mechanical developments in a steel district. Publication of the results of this study was completed in 1914 in six volumes.

In 1914 Shelby Harrison began a social survey of Springfield, Illinois, in order to study social conditions in a relatively small American city. He published a summary of his findings in 1920 under the title of *Social Conditions in an American City*.[11] The nine major lines of inquiry included the work of the public schools; care of mental defectives, the insane, and alcoholics; recreational needs and facilities; housing legislation and trends; public health and sanitation; public and private charities; industrial conditions and relations; delinquency and the correctional system; and the administration of city and county offices, other than those included in the foregoing categories.

**Trends in the social-survey movement.** The publication of the Pittsburgh survey in 1914 stimulated many American communities to adopt the social survey as a practical and realistic method of investigating the complex and changing characteristics of American life. The rapid growth of the survey movement is indicated by the bibliography (up to 1928) by Eaton and Harrison, *Bibliography of Social Surveys*,[12] including a total of 2775 titles or projects. Some of these developments in the survey movement have been regional surveys, and other studies have been intensive investigations of crime, race relations, unemployment, and a variety of community problems and social services.

---

[10] Paul U. Kellogg, Editor, *The Pittsburgh Survey*. New York: Russell Sage Foundation, 1909-14. 6 vols.

[11] Shelby M. Harrison, *Social Conditions in an American City:* A Summary of the Findings of the Springfield Survey. New York: Russell Sage Foundation, 1920.

[12] Allen Eaton and Shelby M. Harrison, *A Bibliography of Social Surveys*. New York: Russell Sage Foundation, 1930.

The war and post-war years of the 1940's witnessed some relaxation in the social-survey movement. During this time relatively few surveys were undertaken by individual investigators; there was an increase in the number of research departments or agencies created within councils of social agencies and welfare federations for the purpose of conducting social surveys and similar investigations; federal and state governments became interested in making systematic social studies of conditions and problems in local communities. A further decrease in the number of social surveys made by individual investigators probably is indicated by the large masses of census data and other government reports on a variety of problems, including social security, economic conditions, employment and unemployment, wages, income, health, housing, child-welfare services, crime and delinquency, and a variety of other social problems.

Beginning with the first Pittsburgh survey, the problems of methodology began to receive increasing attention, particularly in surveys of communities. A second social survey of Pittsburgh (not a sequel to the famous first survey published in six volumes in 1914) utilized a wide range of research methods under the title of *A Social Study of Pittsburgh*,[13] published in 1938 in one volume of approximately a thousand pages, under the general directorship and authorship of Philip Klein and a group of able collaborators. The methods of research included statistical studies; ecological studies of Pittsburgh and its satellite districts as "natural" areas; case study of agencies, families, and districts as units; group and personal interviews; and schedules and questionnaires in the investigation of health, wages, and other problems. This modern tendency to use a variety of research methods for complementary and supplementary purposes is found frequently in such complex studies as social, community, and school surveys.

Sociologists have influenced modern trends in the social-survey movement through their emphasis on the total cultural pattern of community life rather than pathological factors alone; cultural studies of immigrant communities; the sociological concept of natural areas of significant culture traits, or population elements, with varying institutional activities, modes of life, and tradition; tabulation of census data by census tracts; study of trends in the growth of the city; and marked attention to social causation.

Young [14] has provided many examples of research techniques for social surveys in chapters dealing with human ecology, culture groups, social institutions, and community life in urban and rural natural areas. In the references listed at the beginning of this discussion of the social-survey

---

[13] Philip Klein and Others, *A Social Study of Pittsburgh*: Community Problems and Social Services of Allegheny County. New York: Columbia University Press, 1938.
[14] Pauline V. Young, *op. cit.*, p. 491-533.

movement, especially Young's *Scientific Social Surveys and Research,* in the illustrations of case studies of communities early in the chapter on case and clinical studies, and in Chapter 5 in the section on analysis, are many additional examples of recent social surveys. The studies reviewed by Abrams [15] and Jones [16] are chiefly surveys made in England. The examples given in Parten's volume include many opinion polls concerning vital social problems.

## COMMUNITY SURVEYS AND STUDIES [17]

**Purpose and definition.** There is no sharp line of demarcation between social surveys and community surveys or studies. A community survey may be made to provide a basis for planning future developments, for guiding trends, and for making early arrangements for probable future developments, such as wide streets or adequate water mains. Such purposes perhaps differ from the usual school survey, in that the recommendations of

[15] Mark Abrams, *op. cit.*

[16] D. Caradog Jones, *op. cit.*

[17] Ralph L. Beals, "The Village in an Industrial World." *Scientific Monthly* 77:65-75; August 1953.

Lloyd A. Cook and Elaine F. Cook, *A Sociological Approach to Education.* New York: McGraw-Hill Book Co., 1950. 514 p.

Leon Festinger and Daniel Katz, *op. cit.,* p. 15-97.

Bess Goodykoontz, "Selected Studies Relating to Community Schools," *The Community School,* p. 64-82. Edited by Nelson B. Henry. Fifty-second Yearbook of the National Society for the Study of Education, Part 2. Chicago: University of Chicago Press, 1953.

Wilbur C. Hallenbeck, *American Urban Communities.* New York: Harper and Bros., 1951. 617 p.

August B. Hollingshead, *Elmtown's Youth:* Impact of Social Classes on Adolescents. New York: John Wiley and Sons, 1949.

Marie Jahoda and Others, *op. cit.,* p. 611-41.

George C. Kyte, "Survey and Analysis of Community Conditions," *The Principal at Work.* Revised Edition. Boston: Ginn and Co., 1952. p. 37-58.

Truman M. Pierce, *Controllable Community Characteristics Related to the Quality of Education.* Metropolitan School Study Council, Research Studies, No. 1. New York: Teachers College, Columbia University, 1947. 88 p.

Stuart A. Queen and David B. Carpenter, *The American City.* New York: McGraw-Hill Book Co., 1953. 383 p.

Irwin T. Sanders, *Making Good Communities Better:* A Handbook for Civic-minded Men and Women. Lexington: University of Kentucky Press, 1950. 174 p.

Carl C. Taylor, "Techniques of Community Study and Analysis as Applied to Modern Civilized Societies." *The Science of Man in the World Crisis,* p. 416-41. Edited by Ralph Linton. New York: Columbia University Press, 1945. 532 p.

William A. Van Til and Others, "Research on Human Relations and Programs of Action." *Review of Educational Research* 23:285-385; October 1953. Chapters 3, 5, 8 deal with community surveys and programs of action.

W. Lloyd Warner and Others, *Democracy in Jonesville.* New York: Harper and Bros., 1949.

Coleman Woodbury, Editor, *Urban Redevelopment:* Problems and Practices. Chicago: University of Chicago Press, 1953. xvi + 525 p.

Coleman Woodbury, Editor, *The Future of Cities and Urban Redevelopment.* Chicago: University of Chicago Press, 1953. xix + 764 p.

Pauline V. Young, *op. cit.,* p. 491-533.

the community survey may be more general and in some cases not so critical as the findings of the school survey.

The term *community* has been used in several ways, sometimes referring to small and stable communities such as a peasant village or an immigrant area, and at other times designating a large and complex urban area such as Harlem or a ghetto community. In the literature of social research both large cities and small towns or villages have been labeled as communities. At times a small temporary unit has been referred to as a community; for example, a trailer camp (in other words, a community on wheels). Young defines the local community as characterized by a territorial area, common interests, common patterns of social and economic relations, a common bond of solidarity from the conditions of its abode, a constellation of social institutions, and subject to some degree of group control.[18] The terms or concepts of "natural area" and community are frequently used interchangeably in the literature of social research.

**Scope of the community survey.** Young regards a study of community life in urban and rural natural areas as including the historical setting, social influence of physical configuration, social isolation, social contacts, economic centers, demographic characteristics, and population mobility.[19] The major social problems to be investigated, which may include social disorganization, are poverty and dependency, unemployment, child labor, health, and crime and delinquency. The community survey should cover the constellation of social institutions represented: the local government, and the various organizations (economic and industrial, labor, health, religious, social welfare, delinquency control, police and criminal, educational, and recreational).

**Study of urban areas.** The following summary statement indicates that there is considerable agreement among various disciplines regarding the study of urban areas: [20]

1. An urban area is something more than a formal political phenomenon, e.g., a municipality. Such areas have objective characteristics that may be studied by the use of scientific method.
2. Urban areas are highly complex.
3. The varied aspects of an urban area necessarily include (*a*) population, (*b*) physical environment, (*c*) cultural-social environment.
4. All three aspects are closely integrated so that each of them can be carefully understood only in relation to the others; and an urban area per se can be fully understood only in terms of the integration of all three.

[18] Pauline V. Young, *op. cit.,* p. 492-93.
[19] *Ibid.,* p. 491-533.
[20] Quoted from James A. Quinn, "Concluding Comments, Symposium on Viewpoints, Problems, and Methods of Research in Urban Areas." *Scientific Monthly* 73:37-50; July 1951.

5. An urban area cannot be adequately understood apart from a broader network of relations within which it plays a specialized part.

6. Urban areas of varying size and inclusiveness may be studied—for example, the city as a whole, subareas within the city, the city-hinterland region.

7. Both static and dynamic aspects of urban areas need to be studied, e.g., structure, function, process, change.

8. Urban areas may be studied through use of different kinds (or levels) of analysis.

9. In order to obtain full knowledge of an urban area a variety of scientific disciplines must coöperate.

10. Each discipline presumably makes distinctive contributions of its own—viewpoint, kinds of problems studied, hypotheses, concepts, methods, techniques, principles of interpretation, or collection of facts.

11. The distinctive contributions of each discipline presumably are useful to one or more other disciplines.

12. Problems of urban planning and control depend on integrated knowledge derived from several coöperating disciplines.

**Community schools.** Goodykoontz has brought together accounts of many studies relating to community schools.[21] Most of these surveys are descriptive in character, with only a few analytical studies, and still fewer reports of experimental programs. However, these descriptive accounts of community schools have answered a number of pertinent questions: How can schools learn the community's needs and resources so as to serve it effectively? How have schools and communities worked together to improve the school program and the community? In what ways are community-school programs effective? Is the community school one answer to the need for life-adjustment programs?

**Self-surveys.** A form of action research is found in certain fact-finding projects called self-surveys, in which citizens of a community gather evidence about some social problem for the purpose of bringing about subsequent action to alleviate the problem or difficulty. To use an illustration in the area of intergroup relations, the community self-survey may lead to changes in the community based on the following assumptions: [22]

1. Individuals who participate in such an undertaking tend to become ego-involved in it and to feel a sense of personal responsibility to do something about the findings.

2. Group membership may support individual behavior in such a way as to give people the necessary courage to take action believed socially desirable.

3. In any self-survey centered on problems over which there are misunderstandings or apparent conflicts in the community, the experience of working together on a common problem may help change the attitudes, particularly in the area of intergroup relations.

21 Bess Goodykoontz, *op. cit.,* p. 64-82.
22 Marie Jahoda and Others, *op. cit.,* p. 611-41.

Many other examples of community surveys and studies may be located in the references at the beginning of this section, in the references of the preceding section on the social-survey movement, and in the illustrations of case studies of communities in the chapter on case and clinical studies.

## THE SCHOOL-SURVEY MOVEMENT[23]

**Early Surveys.**[24] As the social surveys in the early years of the twentieth century made progress in studying problems of municipal organization, housing, recreation, and other aspects of community life, it was only natural that procedures would develop for study of the schools. The school-survey movement had its real beginning in 1910 and in the years immediately following. Before 1910, studies of school systems were made either by public officials in carrying forward their regular duties or by investigators interested in some particular phase or problem of education. After 1910 a number of school systems imported experts from outside the system, in order to secure advice regarded as superior to the recommendations of local school officers.

In 1910 the superintendent of schools in Indianapolis was invited to spend a week in inspecting the schools of Boise, Idaho. The resulting report dealt with the problems of school buildings, teachers, the course of study, organization of the system, and the attitude of the community, and was published in the local Idaho newspaper. In 1911 Paul Hanus of

[23] A. S. Barr, Robert A. Davis, and Palmer O. Johnson, *Educational Research and Appraisal.* Philadelphia: J. B. Lippincott Co., 1953. p. 124-57.

Harold H. Church and Others, *The Local School Facilities Survey.* Bulletin of the School of Education, Indiana University, Vol. 29, Nos. 1 and 2. Bloomington: Division of Research and Field Services, Indiana University, 1953. vii + 96 p.

Walter D. Cocking, "The School Survey and Its Social Implications." *Educational Research Bulletin* 30:169-78, 196; October 9, 1951.

Carter V. Good, A. S. Barr, and Douglas E. Scates, *op. cit.,* p. 454-76. Reviews much of the literature before the middle 1930's.

Calvin Grieder, "School Surveys." *Review of Educational Research* 19:322-33; October 1949.

Charles H. Judd, "Contributions of School Surveys." *The Scientific Movement in Education,* p. 9-20. Thirty-seventh Yearbook of the National Society for the Study of Education, Part 2. Bloomington, Ill.: Public School Publishing Co., 1938. Especially interesting as historical background for the school-survey movement.

*Research Methods Applied to Health, Physical Education, and Recreation.* Revised Edition. Washington: American Association for Health, Physical Education, and Recreation, N.E.A., 1952. p. 315-28.

Jesse B. Sears, "School Surveys." *Encyclopedia of Educational Research.* Revised Edition. Edited by Walter S. Monroe. New York: Macmillan Co., 1950. p. 1126-33.

Henry L. Smith, *Educational Research, Principles and Practices.* Bloomington, Ind.: Educational Publications, 1944. p. 191-204.

George D. Strayer, Jr., *Planning for School Surveys.* Bulletin of the School of Education, Indiana University, Vol. 24, No. 2. Bloomington: Division of Research and Field Services, Indiana University, 1948. 36 p.

*A Survey of Surveys.* Nashville: Division of Surveys and Field Services, George Peabody College for Teachers, 1952. 56 p.

[24] Charles H. Judd, *op. cit.*

Harvard University inspected the schools of Montclair, New Jersey, and E. C. Moore of Yale University personally surveyed the schools of East Orange, New Jersey.

One of the questions debated in 1914 in the Thirteenth Yearbook of the National Society for the Study of Education was whether outside experts should be brought into a school system to determine its efficiency, and a number of strong statements in this yearbook maintained that a survey should be made by members of the local staff. However, it soon came to be general practice to bring in visiting experts for school surveys. It was thought that visiting specialists could render a more objective and impartial judgment concerning the efficiency of the schools under investigation.

Some of the early surveys grew out of controversial situations; for example, the 1911 investigation of the school system of Baltimore, Maryland, was for the purpose of settling a disturbance that had arisen as the result of the efforts of an able superintendent to raise the educational standards.

The relatively complex survey of the New York City schools is an outstanding example of the early years of the survey movement. For some years before 1911 the Board of Estimate and Apportionment of New York City had been critical of the Board of Education, because of the financial management of the school system and the drain on the treasury of the municipality. The New York survey, in progress from 1911 to 1913, covered various problems of the school system, including an independent survey of the physical and financial conditons of the schools by a staff of engineers and accountants. The cost of the investigation went beyond $95,000, with the results published in three large volumes. The New York report attracted nation-wide attention and gave considerable prestige to the survey movement, with the result that many large and small communities throughout the country initiated surveys of their own school systems.

The Cleveland survey of 1915-16, under the direction of Leonard P. Ayres, is regarded as a high point in the survey movement. The special features included major emphasis on vocational education, use of reading tests on a large scale for the first time in making a school survey, and a plan of publicity and interpretation to make the people of the city acquainted with the results of the study.

**Early trends.** After 1915 there was a tendency to make more specialized studies of limited aspects of education, since the large number of recommendations coming from comprehensive surveys had proved disconcerting and even confusing in some instances. There was a second tendency to have local bureaus of testing and research conduct the survey rather than to bring in outside experts; it was thought desirable and helpful to add to the administrative staff of the school system one or more specialists trained in methods of testing and measurement.

It soon became apparent that the number of surveys requested exceeded the supply of competent available surveyors. Staff members of university departments of education found it difficult and even impossible to meet the requests for school surveys. A considerable part of the survey load came to be carried by the United States Office of Education, the education division of the Russell Sage Foundation, and certain bureaus of municipal and governmental research. The Office of Education was particularly active in making state surveys, and during the late 1920's and early 1930's sponsored a series of national surveys covering land-grant colleges, secondary education, teacher education, and school finance. During the past quarter of a century the research and survey divisions of universities have made a large number of school surveys, including the work of Teachers College of Columbia University and George Peabody College for Teachers, as well as a number of the state universities.

**Types of school surveys.** Modern school surveys, according to purpose and type, may be classified into three types. The comprehensive survey, during recent years, has been used rather sparingly, since emergency conditions too often have forced school planners into a building program to care for the increased pupil population, without adequate time available for a complete study. The comprehensive survey usually covers:

1. Aims, outcomes, pupil achievement, curriculum, method, and instructional aids
2. Administrative problems and procedures of the schools
3. Financial policies and procedures
4. Operation and maintenance of the physical plant
5. Pupil transportation
6. Staff and personnel
7. School plant and related factors.

The educational survey covers the instructional program of the school and the related activities, policies, and procedures with a bearing on the effectiveness of the educational program. The educational and building surveys together make up a comprehensive survey.

Since the building survey is the most common type, and because of the urgent need today for such surveys in many population centers, it seems helpful to outline the essential steps and procedures of the plant survey. Also, for purposes of illustration, it is less complex to describe the survey of school facilities than to summarize the steps and procedures of the comprehensive survey. The following summarizing statements are developed at length in a manual [25] explaining the building survey, prepared to answer the questions of many school authorities who are greatly concerned about the large increase in the birth rate, the back log of needed school buildings accumulated since the close of World War I, and the great demand or competition for the tax dollar.

The survey of local school facilities usually investigates the community and the setting of the schools, an estimate of future school enrollment, school-plant planning, the pupil-transportation system, and the available financial resources to meet the needs of school buildings.

There are three possible methods of making a building survey. The survey of school facilities by outside consultants or experts is expensive, but is usually effective and objective, and is particularly advantageous in smaller communities.

A self-survey by the members of the local staff has the merit of contributing to the professional growth of the personnel, and of bringing about acceptance of the survey recommendations because of participation by local staff members, although there is the danger that the more technical procedures of the survey of building facilties may not be sufficiently understood by local school officers to produce a completely satisfactory investigation.

A coöperative building survey by members of the local staff and by a team of specialists has distinct advantages and should be used more frequently in the future, since it combines the merits of both the "expert" survey and self-survey. The coöperative investigation costs less than the building survey conducted wholly by experts, safeguards survey procedures and conclusions, and through the methods of coöperation promotes desirable field contacts between visiting specialists and local staff members. Expert professional assistance may be secured in a number of states from the state department of education or the state university, and in general from the independent survey expert or agency.

**Implementation and outcomes of school surveys.** A published appraisal [26] of the investigations made by the Division of Surveys and Field Services, George Peabody College for Teachers, is especially helpful in securing an overview of the procedures and practical results of survey studies. Over the past quarter of a century this agency has provided a wide variety of educational services, especially throughout the southern states, and since 1945 the Division has been particularly active in conducting school surveys. The purpose of the stock-taking reported in the *Survey*

25 Harold H. Church and Others, *op. cit.*
26 *A Survey of Surveys, op. cit.*

*of Surveys* was to analyze the procedures as background for improving the quality of the field service, and to study the local activities following a survey by way of implementing the recommendations, as a basis for identifying suggestions and procedures helpful to school administrators and community leaders. The evaluation, based on fifteen comprehensive school surveys conducted by George Peabody College, with the data gathered by interviews and conferences, and through documentary evidence, may be summarized briefly as follows:

1. The formal request for a local survey usually came from the board of education, upon the recommendation of the superintendent, although frequently the initiative came from such groups as a citizens' committee, an education association, or a chamber of commerce.

2. As a general rule the Division of Surveys and Field Services had complete charge of plans and procedures for making the investigation.

3. Comprehensive reports and illustrated digests were prepared by the survey staff and printed, with oral reports always made to the boards of education or survey commissions and to other interested groups invited to attend the meetings.

4. As a rule the survey reports were enthusiastically received by the public and by the press, with community groups and citizens' committees actively supporting the recommendations.

5. The superintendent of schools, more than any other individual or group, was responsible for implementing the survey recommendations, with new superintendents particularly appreciative of the guidance of the report in winning public support for school policies.

6. Members of state survey commissions played an important part in formulating survey recommendations, and assumed the responsibility for drafting bills embodying the recommendations for presentation to the legislature. It proved difficult to implement changes that depended on action by the legislative bodies of the city, county, or state, and especially when constitutional changes were necessary. Political strategy in bringing about legislative action on survey recommendations varied, with the unity of the forces supporting public education an important factor in success.

7. When survey proposals involved as a major consideration the consolidation of schools, there was always opposition in the small communities, which sometimes led to compromise or even failure in implementing the survey recommendations.

8. Almost one-half of the survey recommendations were adopted. More immediate results were brought about in city schools than in county or state systems. Differences in favor of the city over the county systems were especially significant in the areas of administration, business management, and physical plant.

9. The superintendents of county and city school systems reacted favorably to recommendations for reorganization of their administrative and supervisory staffs, not only adding new members but also organizing them into a few clearly defined divisions or departments under the leadership of assistant superintendents.

10. Improvement of instruction followed slowly after a survey, although the majority of the school systems reported the adoption of many significant recommendations.

11. The quick adoption of survey recommendations for schoolhousing re-flected the critical shortage of buildings following the war years; bond issues for new school buildings were generally approved in the counties and cities.

12. Recommendations for the improvement of pupil transportation were readily adopted, with state and county systems carrying out most of the concrete proposals for a complete system of school-bus operation.

13. Proposed programs for financing the schools were frequently delayed by a variety of restrictions, although state systems made some progress in financing public education.

14. Gains in revenue receipts were only moderate in county systems, whereas the compactness and well developed channels of communication in city schools secured relatively prompt action in increasing school funds. Recommendations concerning the business affairs of the schools were well received in both cities and counties.

15. The administrative officers in four school systems thought that the survey staff should have continuing follow-up contacts by way of consultative services in the system investigated, and suggested that survey specialists should spend more time in the classroom, as background for more accurate evaluation of the quality of teaching.

**Trends, next steps, and critique of survey studies.** School surveys have been sponsored by a variety of groups and organizations, including local boards of education, civic clubs, citizens' committees, chambers of commerce, the United States Office of Education, regional accrediting associations, national professional organizations, state legislatures, state departments of education, and private philanthropic foundations.

For nearly twenty years there has been an increasing trend toward including committees of lay citizens in the planning and carrying forward of studies of our schools; the survey is a valuable instrument for interpreting the schools and the educational program to the public.

New emphasis has been given during recent years to opinion polls concerning the school, probably in part the result of techniques developed in the evaluative procedures of the Coöperative Study of Secondary School Standards and in the public-opinion polls.

The survey specialist still plays an important part, but a role quite different from that of the earlier days of the "expert" survey. Today the advice of the specialist is sought on procedures for setting up and conducting the survey, interpreting the findings, formulating recommendations, stimulation of the local staff in finding good answers to important questions, and coöperation with the local school administrator or superintendent in his role of leadership.

It is a far cry from the survey of one week of inspection, made by a visitor for the purpose of evaluating a school system, to the modern comprehensive survey, which requires a relatively large staff of workers. Seldom does an individual investigator, working alone, attempt even the specialized building survey, except in a small school system and usually with the coöperation of the local staff. However, many graduate students have worked out worth-while and functional types of theses and dissertations through participation in comprehensive, educational, or school-plant surveys.

Surveys made at periodic or irregular intervals have given way in many school systems to the continuing study or survey, sometimes called an evaluation or an inventory. The coöperative planning survey at intervals of approximately ten years, with financial and personnel provisions between surveys for securing the assistance of specialists as consultants, will enable educational planning to go forward continuously to serve as an antidote to lethargy, a precaution against inbreeding of ideas, and a method of sound administrative planning of proven worth.

It is now recognized that many of the educational advances of the past fifty years can be attributed directly to the school survey, although immediate results have not always come from such investigations. However, the survey has been the initial stage in hundreds of school systems in charting a forward course of action that has challenged the attention of the people and later resulted in constructive action.

It is believed that the school surveys of the future will be a better instrument for educational progress. Surveys of the past have been used for two decidedly different purposes: as a formalized technique of administrative planning for determining the next steps in a school system, and to appraise the efficiency of a system and of the personnel. It has been suggested that a single survey should not seek the achievement of both purposes, since an attempt to combine the evaluation of school personnel with direct assistance to the school staff in planning, in a single operation or study, is incompatible with working *with* persons for their improvement. The direction and scope of the survey movement have moved toward a positive emphasis, away from a negative purpose or a search for malpractices; in other words, the search for and encouragement of desirable educational practices may well tend to crowd out or play down malpractices in the schools.

There is no longer an implicit assumption that the school survey is a highly objective, technical, impersonal procedure; a study of survey reports points out that their conclusions are 80 per cent subjective.[27] Much of the evidence in surveys is based on comparisons of the status quo in

[27] Dan H. Cooper, "Contributions of School Surveys to Educational Administration." *Educational Administration: A Survey of Progress, Problems, and Needs*, p. 46-59. Edited by William C. Reavis. Proceedings of the Fifteenth Annual Conference for Administrative Officers of Public and Private Schools, 1946. Vol. 9. Chicago: University of Chicago Press, 1946. 216 p.

one school system with current conditions in another system. The score cards and check lists used extensively in surveys involve a considerable element of subjectivity or personal reaction. However, there is real strength in a survey, as the result of its ability to focus personal opinions and reactions on the important problems of a school district.

School surveys differ from more exact and specific status studies, in that survey conclusions depend largely on committee deliberations or interpretations, with rather broad recommendations based largely on opinion (the impact of opinion on facts). Therefore, the school-survey recommendation represents a quite different situation, as compared with the engineer in charge of a survey of status in industry, who is able to say definitely what should be done, because in business or industry the goal is specific and well defined, to make a profit.

The Florida survey [28] may be used as an illustration of the type of recommendation commonly found in survey studies, particularly in state surveys. A major recommendation is that, in order to place the financing of schools on a sound and equitable basis, Florida should expand and modify its present plan of state aid into a comprehensive program of state and local school support which provides adequately for all items of school expenditure. This is a committee recommendation, and not an immediately factual statement. The recommendation comes from or is based on facts, plus an adopted pattern or frame of reference on the part of the committee; for example, the adoption of the general goal of a good school system, acceptance of the particular social philosophy that a good school system is desired for all, and that a particular plan of equalization is best, in contrast to leaving the matter entirely to local effort, or expecting federal aid to do all the equalizing, or in lieu of some other scheme. This is a rather typical kind of recommendation, as found in school surveys, and is legitimate when its nature is clear. The recommendation is made in the light of an analysis of facts, so that a part of its nature is factual, but another part is an adopted scheme of values.

The problem of objectivity has perplexed survey experts and other investigators of administrative problems in higher education. Too great devotion to the scientific method and a too narrow conception of research may center our attention on things that can be enumerated or counted (students, courses, faculty members, books, average teaching loads, unit expenditures, laboratory and classroom space per student, and duties of the academic dean) to the general neglect of careful observation by skilled and

[28] Florida Citizens Committee on Education, *Education and Florida's Future*, p. 63. Tallahassee, Fla., January, 1947. 92 p.

experienced observers and of logical analysis, as techniques for study of many important aspects of administrative organization and procedure in higher education.[29]

Most of the surveys of higher educational institutions and systems give major attention to the organization chart, the lines of authority, and the duties of the several groups and individuals in the administrative hierarchy. While these are important matters in a well administered institution, they do not guarantee the achievement of the major purposes of education; the structure of administrative organization occupies a central position to the almost complete neglect of the administrative process viewed as leadership in planning, coördination, and appropriate delegation of responsibilities.

One of the major difficulties in surveys of higher institutions arises from generalization from a few to a large number of colleges and universities in terms of adminstrative theory and practice. Such generalizations are dangerous and subject to error, in view of the individuality of institutions and of their differences in purposes, student and faculty personnel, and human and material resources. Perhaps the beginning of an answer to this problem is being found in a program of coördinated institutional studies that will recognize individuality and variation from school to school in reaching specific solutions to administrative problems of organization and procedure. While this type of research is useful in the study of administrative structure, it probably will yield significant returns in increased knowledge of the processes of leadership and stimulation of personnel.

To a considerable extent the stages of implementation of survey recommendations depend on the processes of group interaction or group dynamics. Certain related techniques of group-behavior analysis are analyzed in another section of this chapter. The processes of action research or operational research, as described in the chapter on reporting and implementation of findings, have a relationship to survey procedures, especially to the interpretation of results by way of application of specific recommendations to concrete school situations.

A relatively recent technique enables a newly appointed superintendent to ascertain how near ready his school district is to make changes or to be progressive, what improvements he can try, and how fast he can move. The investigation basic to this technique sought answers to the following questions:[30]

[29] Norman Burns, "Higher Education." *Review of Educational Research* 22:375-85; October 1952.
[30] Quoted from Truman M. Pierce, *Controllable Community Characteristics Related to the Quality of Education*. Metropolitan School Study Council, Research Studies, No. 1. New York: Bureau of Publications, Teachers College, Columbia University, 1947. xi + 90 p.

1. To what extent may the variability in adaptability among school systems be ascribed to variations among the communities in which the school systems are located?

2. What are some elements, or influences, which may be employed to exercise control over the direction of change in factors related to adaptability, in order that the community setting of the school system may be improved?

The question of whether a survey is good research may still disturb some investigators and students, even after reading the earlier parts of this chapter. The answer depends largely on whether we wish to restrict the label of research study to methods that contribute to generalized knowledge. If so, then a school survey is a practical study, and it is a contribution to knowledge only in so far as it provides clearer understanding of aims and procedures, forces definition of goals in education, reveals marked weaknesses in measuring instruments, identifies methods of using such instruments or of interpreting their use, or reveals that certain assumed causes are not of themselves sufficient causes. It seems worth while to distinguish between these two general types of study: (1) those investigations that deal with unique things, and which describe or explain them (for example, most historical studies, much research in geology, case reports, and school surveys), and (2) those studies which generalize, because they restrict themselves to aspects that may be removed from many elements of the unique situation and applied to many other situations which readily fit into the necessary conditions. However, in the social sciences the line between the two types of investigation is not so clear and distinct as often has been assumed, or as is frequently the case in the physical sciences, since many factors must be taken into account in the social fields. For example, history is not simply an explanation of unique events; it provides certain "lessons" and repetitive cause-effect formulas that may be applied again when the same or similar conditions obtain in sufficient proportion or dominance. This is a major reason for saying that we study history in order to secure an understanding of the operations in society. Likewise, from studying school systems we can learn much about the operation of schools, and also about the improvement of evaluative techniques.

## ILLUSTRATIVE DESCRIPTIVE-SURVEY AND NORMATIVE STUDIES

At this time it seems helpful to present a variety of illustrations of descriptive-survey and normative studies, in addition to the more complex social, community, and school-survey investigations cited earlier in this chapter, and in addition to the subsequent examples of descriptive-survey inquiries described briefly in the discussions of data-gathering techniques and procedures (questionnaire, interview, observation, group-behavior analysis, content analysis, and survey-appraisal). A wide range of survey problems is represented in the list of research bulletins published by the Research Division of the N.E.A., as listed early in this chapter.

No wholly satisfactory logical or functional scheme for classifying the illustrations of descriptive-survey studies is available. Most of the examples to be given under the topics listed in the preceding paragraph are classified in terms of research approach or data-collecting technique. At times in the research literature survey investigations [31] are classified according to geographical area (local, state, regional, and national). The descriptive-survey studies cited in this section of the chapter are grouped primarily according to purpose; for example, to follow up youth out of school, to describe the membership of a professional organization, to describe the characteristics of a group of institutions, to poll the opinion of a group of parents, to identify trends, and to engage in survey testing.

Another way of classifying survey reports is according to level of instruction (secondary or higher) or by type of preparation offered (junior college, teacher education, engineering, medicine, law, social work, and so on).[32]

**Descriptive and deliberative surveys and inquiries relating to institutions and agencies.** Over a period of years the Educational Policies Commission of the National Education Association and the American Association of School Administrators have published a long series of influential reports dealing with various aspects of public education.

The reports of the American Youth Commission of the American Council on Education are chiefly of the survey type, together with the interpretation resulting from the deliberations of the Commission.[33]

The National Survey of the Education of Teachers [34] and the Commission on Teacher Education [35] of the American Council on Education present an interesting contrast in procedure. The National Survey represents the most extensive fact-finding effort in teacher education. The Commission on Teacher Education was not charged with the task of undertaking

[31] Calvin Grieder, *op. cit.*

[32] W. C. Eells, *Surveys of American Higher Education.* New York: Carnegie Foundation for the Advancement of Teaching, 1937. 538 p.
  Elizabeth N. Layton, *Surveys of Higher Education in the United States, 1937-1949.* Circular No. 257, May, 1949. Washington: Office of Education, 1949. 24 p.

[33] Homer P. Rainey and Others, *How Fare American Youth?* Prepared for the American Youth Commission. New York: Appleton-Century-Crofts, 1937. 186 p.

[34] *National Survey of the Education of Teachers.* Office of Education Bulletin No. 10, 1933. Washington: Office of Education, 1933. 6 vols.

[35] Commission on Teacher Education, *Teachers for Our Times.* Washington: American Council on Education, 1944. 178 p.

research, experimentation, or discovering new knowledge concerning teacher education. Its major purpose was that of implementation or of promoting action. Therefore, the Commission drew heavily on the guiding concepts of competent leaders in teacher education, the experiences of forward-looking institutions for the preparation of teachers, empirically tested curriculum procedures and practices, and profitable experiences and activities of staff members in developing the curriculum.

The President's Commission on Higher Education, consisting of twenty-eight civic and educational leaders, was appointed in 1946, charged "with an examination of the functions of higher education in our democracy and of the means by which they can best be performed." The recommendations included increasing the number of community colleges, vesting in the state department of education whatever jurisdiction the state exercises over all education from the nursery school through the university, enactment of legislation forbidding discrimination in education against minority groups, federal scholarships for selected students beyond high school, and federal aid to the states for educational expenditures by publicly controlled institutions of higher education.[36]

To cite an illustration of another national commission and a different point of view with respect to the financial support of higher education, the Commission on Financing Higher Education[37] expressed the belief that higher education needs a larger measure of support, with the expectation that additional funds will be made available, either through private contributions or through government support. The Commission preferred private giving, plus contributions from business and industry, as compared with federal support of higher education, based on the belief that the strength of our higher education derives from diversity and competition among institutions. It was feared that such democratic values might suffer under a program of federal support.

The President's Materials Policy Commission[38] was instructed to study the materials problem of the United States and its relation to the free and friendly nations of the world. The reports are in five volumes, with the following titles: Foundations for Growth and Security, The Outlook for Key Commodities, The Outlook for Energy Sources, The Promise of Technology, and Selected Reports to the Commission.

[36] President's Commission on Higher Education. *Higher Education for American Democracy*. Washington: Government Printing Office, 1947. 6 vols.

[37] John D. Millett, *Financing Higher Education in the United States*. Staff Report of the Commission on Financing Higher Education. New York: Columbia University Press, 1952. 503 p.

[38] The President's Materials Policy Commission, *Resources for Freedom*. Volume I, Foundations for Growth and Security. Washington: Government Printing Office, 1952. viii + 184 p. A summary report for Volume I totals 82 pages.

A detailed survey of the organization, administration, and financing of public elementary and secondary education was made to highlight factors that tend to increase or decrease the economy and effectiveness of operation. The areas of investigation included educational load and attainment, as well as ability and effort to support education, characteristics of state and local agencies for organization and administration of schools, teaching personnel, physical facilities, and financial practices.[39]

An examination of the various state programs for financing the schools urged that the responsible officers consider carefully the effect of all state-aid legislation and appropriations upon the district structure as they modify current finance programs.[40]

A nation-wide study of district reorganization emphasized the weaknesses of the small-district system, the need for reorganization, and appropriate criteria to implement the process of reorganization.[41] The report was based on reorganization data from seven states, with a briefer treatment of ten other states.

The Coöperative Study of Secondary-School Standards [42] was characterized by the following procedures:

1. It was conducted coöperatively by the six regional associations, with the advice and assistance of many other groups and agencies.
2. The data for the evaluative criteria were based on the wealth of studies and literature on various aspects of secondary education.
3. The theoretical measure of the secondary school as an institution was validated by experimental try-out in two hundred representative secondary schools.
4. The resulting instruments serve a diagnostic purpose with respect to the strength and weaknesses of the school as an institution.
5. A technique was developed for evaluating a secondary school in terms of its philosophy and objectives.
6. The evaluative instruments and procedures emphasized growth on the part of the school rather than standardization of institutional characteristics and functions.
7. The evaluative procedures on the part of committees of specialists provide opportunities for in-service growth, professional understanding, and coöperation among educational workers.
8. The recommendations provide for revision of the evaluative criteria at regular intervals.

[39] Francis S. Chase and Edgar L. Morphet, Directors, *The Forty-eight State School Systems*. Chicago: Council of State Governments, 1949. 245 p.
[40] Edgar L. Morphet and Erick L. Lindman, *Public School Finance Programs of the Forty-eight States*. Circular No. 274. Washington: Office of Education, 1950. 110 p.
[41] National Commission on School District Reorganization. Howard A. Dawson and Floyd W. Reeves, Co-chairmen. *Your School District*. Washington: Department of Rural Education, National Education Association, 1948. 286 p.
[42] Coöperative Study of Secondary-School Standards, *Evaluation of Secondary Schools—General Report*. Washington: The Study, 1939. 526 p.
Coöperative Study of Secondary-School Standards, *Evaluative Criteria, 1950 Edition*. Washington: The Study, 1950. 305 p.

The National Association of Secondary-School Principals surveyed one thousand high schools, in order to ascertain their efforts in curriculum development to meet the imperative needs of youth.[43]

A comprehensive tabular guide [44] to American higher institutions was followed up eight years later by a survey [45] of the information thought especially important in admitting to higher institutions the veterans of the Korean campaign.

Three descriptive handbooks in the field of higher education are arranged in paragraph rather than tabular form, covering junior colleges,[46] colleges and universities in the United States,[47] and higher institutions outside the United States.[48]

A large part of a yearbook of the National Society for the Study of Education is substantially a descriptive, non-statistical survey of graduate work in education in the United States.[49]

**Membership analysis or surveys of organizations and groups.** The various studies and rosters of the nation's manpower, not only for the armed forces but also for all the essential activities of civilian and military life, are to be regarded as surveys, in many instances subjected to statistical analysis. The data very commonly are secured through personal questionnaires, with the chief features of the resulting report involving enumeration, classification, and identification.

One large-group description or survey deals with the opinions and attitudes of the American soldier,[50] under the following titles:

The American Soldier: Adjustment During Army Life, 1949
The American Soldier: Combat and Its Aftermath, 1949
Experiments in Mass Communication, 1949
Measurement and Prediction, 1950.

---

[43] Paul E. Elicker, Editor, "The Curriculum Study." *Bulletin of the National Association of Secondary-School Principals* 31:3-146; March 1947.

[44] Carter V. Good, Editor, *A Guide to Colleges, Universities, and Professional Schools in the United States.* Washington: American Council on Education, 1945. xv + 681 p.

[45] Commission on Accreditation of Service Experiences, *Accreditation Policies of Institutions of Higher Education for the Evaluation of Educational Experiences of Military Personnel.* Bulletin No. 9, June, 1953. Washington: American Council on Education, 1953. ix + 73 p.

[46] Jesse P. Bogue, Editor, *American Junior Colleges.* Third Edition. Washington: American Council on Education, 1952. x + 604 p.

[47] Mary Irwin, Editor, *American Universities and Colleges.* Sixth Edition. Washington: American Council on Education, 1952. xi + 1105 p.

[48] M. M. Chambers, Editor, *Universities of the World Outside the U.S.A.* Washington: American Council on Education, 1950. xvii + 924 p.

[49] Ralph W. Tyler and Others, *Graduate Study in Education.* Fiftieth Yearbook of the National Society for the Study of Education, Part I. Chicago: University of Chicago Press, 1951. xix + 369 p.

[50] S. A. Stouffer and Others, *Studies in Social Psychology in World War II.* Princeton: Princeton University Press, 1949-50. 4 vols.

A descriptive, evaluative report on the educational lessons from war-time training has been made by the Commission on Implications of Armed Services Educational Programs. In addition to the general report or summary volume,[51] the following titles have been published:

Utilizing Human Talent
Audio-Visual Aids in the Armed Services: Implications for American Education
Language and Area Studies in the Armed Services: Their Future Significance
Area Studies in American Universities
War-Time College Training Programs of the Armed Services
The Armed Services and Adult Education
What Comes of Training Women for War
Curriculum Implications of Armed Services Educational Programs
Opinions on Gains for American Education from War-Time Armed Services Training.

A number of other descriptive studies of the membership of institutions, organizations, and professional groups may be cited briefly:

An annual survey of statistics of attendance in higher institutions.[52]
The status of the members of the governing boards of thirty universities, and a critique of status and analytical studies of school-board personnel.[53]
The origins of American scientists.[54]
The overlapping membership in the American Statistical Association, the American Economic Association, the Econometric Society, and the Institute of Mathematical Statistics.[55]
Characteristics of the membership of the American Statistical Association.[56]
An occupational analysis of the membership of the American Sociological Society.[57]
Characteristics of members of the A.P.A. Division of Counseling and Guidance.[58]

[51] Alonzo G. Grace and Others, *Educational Lessons from War-Time Training:* The General Report. Commission on Implications of Armed Services Educational Programs. Washington: American Council on Education, 1948. xix + 264 p.
[52] Raymond Walters, "Statistics of Attendance in American Universities and Colleges, 1953." *School and Society* 78:177-88; December 12, 1953. Also see later reports.
[53] Hubert P. Beck, *Men Who Control Our Universities.* New York: King's Crown Press, 1947. 229 p.
W. W. Charters, Jr., "Research on School Board Personnel: Critique and Prospectus." *Journal of Educational Research* 47:321-35; January 1954.
[54] R. H. Knapp and H. B. Goodrich, *Origins of American Scientists:* A study made under the direction of a committee of the faculty of Wesleyan University. Chicago: University of Chicago Press, 1952. xiv + 450 p.
[55] Dickson H. Leavens, "Overlapping Membership of Societies." *American Statistician* 3:4-5; June-July, 1949.
[56] Abner Hurwitz and Floyd C. Mann, "The Membership of the American Statistical Association—An Analysis." *Journal of the American Statistical Association* 41:155-70; June 1946.
[57] Wellman J. Warner and Marjorie B. Davis, *The Roles of the Sociologist:* An Analysis of the Membership of the Society with Special Reference to Non-Teaching Occupations. New York: American Sociological Society, New York University, 1951. 15 p.
[58] Irwin A. Berg and Others, "Age, Income, and Professional Characteristics of Members of the A.P.A.'s Division of Counseling and Guidance." *American Psychologist* 7:125-27; April 1952.

An especially detailed survey of the membership of the American Educational Research Association.[59]

An annual survey of teacher supply and demand in the United States.[60]

The distribution and fraternity status of the membership of Phi Delta Kappa.[61]

In the chapter on the descriptive method certain illustrative studies in the form of job analyses of the duties and activities of elementary-school principals, superintendents, and teachers are similar in approach to status studies of particular groups.

**Follow-up studies.** A number of illustrative follow-up investigations at the secondary, college, and graduate-school level may be listed briefly:

A survey of college graduates in America, based on a sample of 17,053 persons (of whom nearly 56 per cent responded) derived from 1037 higher institutions. The inquiry included: effect of college education on earning power and marital pattern, the question of home versus career for the ex-coed, political opinions of college graduates, college education as a means of social mobility, and opinions concerning the assets and liabilities of higher education. The report is based on a 13-page questionnaire.[62]

A report based on the Harvard class of 1926 (450 graduates or 61 per cent of the class); the graduates gave information concerning: their social and political views, attitudes toward religion, careers, hobbies and extra-curricular activities, incomes and related financial matters, evaluation of Harvard and a Harvard education, marital histories and home life, and the opinions of the wives concerning Harvard.[63]

A career study of the graduates of the four municipal colleges in New York City (City College, Hunter College, Brooklyn College, and Queens College) based on a questionnaire inquiry.[64]

A survey of the professions and vocations followed by 232 men from eleven graduating classes of St. John's College at Annapolis.[65]

Follow-up studies of graduates of American University and Syracuse University.[66]

[59] Douglas E. Scates, "Analysis of a Professional Organization: The American Educational Research Association in 1948." *Growing Points in Educational Research.* 1949 Official Report of the American Educational Research Association. Washington: The Association, 1949. p. 111-42.

[60] Ray C. Maul, *Teacher Supply and Demand in the United States.* Report of the 1952 National Teacher Supply and Demand Study. Washington: National Commission on Teacher Education and Professional Standards, N.E.A., 1952. 40 p. Subsequent reports are published annually in the March issue of the *Journal of Teacher Education.*

[61] "Membership Statistics." *Phi Delta Kappan* 35:144-48; December 1953. Also see later reports.

[62] Ernest Havemann and Patricia S. West, *They Went to College:* The College Graduate in America Today. New York: Harcourt, Brace and Co., 1952. x + 277 p.

[63] Cornelius DuBois and Others, *Harvard 1926:* The Life and Opinions of a College Class. Cambridge: Harvard University Press, 1951. 98 p.

[64] Leonard J. West, *College and the Years After:* A Career Study of Municipal College Graduates. New York: Board of Higher Education, The College of the City of New York, 1952. 129 p.

[65] Richard D. Weigle, "Record of St. John's Graduates, 1937-1952." *School and Society* 76:5-9; July 5, 1952.

[66] C. R. Pace, "Follow-up Studies of College Graduates." *Growing Points in Educational Research.* Washington: American Educational Research Association, 1949. p. 285-90.

A survey of the status of holders of the Ph.D. degree, including the 1940 placement of 20,783 persons who earned the degree during the decade, 1931-40.[67]

A summary of a number of investigations of youth out of school, between the ages of 16 and 24, including a number of follow-up studies.[68]

A summary of a series of investigations made to discover the extent to which the needs of youth have been met, including a number of follow-up studies of high-school youth.[69]

A follow-up study of gifted children, which is also a case study, in that extensive data have been gathered for each individual; therefore, this investigation leads to generalizations concerning individuals, rather than generalizations about groups based on mass study comparing the status of groups.[70]

**Evaluative surveys of trends and status.** Reference may be made to the major keys to the literature of educational research for numerous illustrations of evaluative surveys of trends and status.[71] Many of these studies employ some form of testing or measurement as a data-collecting instrument.

## GENERAL PROCEDURES AND PROBLEMS OF GATHERING DESCRIPTIVE-SURVEY DATA

Before presenting illustrations of studies that utilize the data-collecting techniques (questionnaire, interview, observation, etc.) frequently employed in survey investigations, it is appropriate to outline a number of

[67] Ernest V. Hollis, *Toward Improving Ph.D. Programs.* Washington: American Council on Education, 1945. 216 p.

[68] M. M. Chambers, "Youth Out of School, 16-24." *Encyclopedia of Educational Research.* Revised Edition. Edited by Walter S. Monroe. New York: MacMillan Co., 1950. p. 1513-20.

[69] J. D. Hull and Howard Cummings, "Discovering the Extent to Which Youth Needs Are Being Met." *Adapting the Secondary-School Program to the Needs of Youth.* Fifty-second Yearbook of the National Society for the Study of Education, Part I. Chicago: University of Chicago Press, 1953. p. 62-80.

[70] L. M. Terman and Others, *The Gifted Child Grows Up.* Stanford University, Calif.: Stanford University Press, 1947. 448 p.

[71] David Segel, "Survey and Trend Studies." *Review of Educational Research* 12:492-500; December 1942.

Alvin C. Eurich and Others, "Evaluative Studies." *Review of Educational Research* 12:521-33; December 1942.

Irving Lorge and Harry Ordan, "Trend, Survey, and Evaluation Studies." *Review of Educational Research* 15:360-76; December 1945.

J. W. Wrightstone and Others, "Evaluation, Trend, and Survey Studies." *Review of Educational Research* 18:396-409; December 1948.

C. R. Pace and Arthur D. Browne, "Trend and Survey Studies." *Review of Educational Research* 21:337-49; December 1951.

M. R. Sumption, "School and Community Relationships." *Review of Educational Research* 22:317-28; October 1952.

Harold G. Shane and Edward T. McSwain, "Evaluation of the Educational Program." *Review of Educational Research* 23:171-80; April 1953.

J. W. Wrightstone, "Evaluation." *Encyclopedia of Educational Research, op. cit.,* p. 403-407.

Carter V. Good, A. S. Barr, and Douglas E. Scates, *op. cit.,* p. 297-324. Covers many of the survey-testing studies for the period before the middle 1930's.

general principles and problems of gathering descriptive-survey data. These selected topics include adequate planning and coöperation in gathering data, basic enumerative and descriptive records, report forms for research studies, report statistics and data, standards for statistical reporting, documentary sources or available published sources of data (in the next section), and sampling in relation to survey inquiries (in a later section of this chapter).

**Coöperation in gathering statistical data.** Gathering good statistics, whether in government or in any social area, is essentially a venture in coöperation. Some types of statistics are chiefly the result of coöperation between business and government, beginning at the point where a decision is made as to what statistics are needed and how they can be collected with a minimum burden of effort on the part of those who provide the statistics. Valuable assistance is available through established committees of leaders in business (appointed by government agencies), and through statistical committees of certain trade associations, which coöperate with the government.[72]

The United States Office of Education early learned the lesson of coöperation in its elaborate statistical studies. From the initial stage of preparing inquiry forms, through the construction of tables and the writing of the explanatory text, to the preparation of a mailing list for the published report, statistical publications of the Office of Education are coöperative projects of the statistical division and of the appropriate agency or person responsible for the special field of study. To use library statistics as an example, the report is a joint product of the statistical division and of certain specialists in library work. In short, the statistical division is responsible for collecting, tabulating, and organizing statistical data, while the specialists in library work decide what data are worth collecting, and assist in editing returns, formulating table headings, and writing the explanatory text or discussion.[73]

**Planning for data-gathering.** The major problem in research (and statistics) is that of securing the data (cases) that represent what the in-

[72] Philip M. Hauser and William R. Leonard, Editors, *Government Statistics for Business Use*. New York: John Wiley and Sons, 1946. 432 p. Revised, 1953.

F. C. Mills and C. D. Long, *Statistical Agencies of the Federal Government*. A Report to the Commission on Organization of the Executive Branch of the Government. New York: National Bureau of Economic Research, 1949. 201 p.

U. S. Bureau of the Budget, Office of Statistical Standards, *Statistical Services of the United States Government*. Revised Edition. Washington: The Bureau, 1952. 78 p.

[73] Charles H. Judd, *Research in the United States Office of Education*. Staff Study No. 19. Prepared for the Advisory Committee on Education. Washington: Government Printing Office, 1939. p. 86.

*Proposals Relating to the Statistical Function of the U. S. Office of Education*. A Report of the National Conference on the Office of Education Statistical Program. Office of Education Bulletin No. 2, 1946. Washington: Government Printing Office, 1946. viii + 21 p.

vestigator takes them to represent. Accurate measurement of cases and analysis are merely technical (simpler) problems.

There are many practical studies in which the problem is entirely one of properly gathering the data and arranging them with no more mathematical analysis than is involved in counting. Probably even in more scientific work this phase of gathering data is of much greater significance than is usually accorded it.

Purpose affects the form in which the investigator gathers data. In studying the salaries of staff members in a group of municipal colleges, only the mean may be desired. Therefore, order does not count and salaries need not be arranged in order of magnitude. In fact, salaries need not even be recorded; they can simply be punched into an adding machine, except that checking would be difficult. For calculating the median salary, the rank order is needed. Although the amount of detail to obtain in gathering data depends on what the investigator wishes to do with the figures, the experienced statistician probably will insist on the complete distribution, since with it he can see its shape, and calculate the mean and median.

A research director has remarked that the top administrator should say to the statistician, "These are the questions we want answered," rather than, "These are the data we want." Theoretically and ideally he was correct, but to answer either question successfully someone has to think, hard and repeatedly. Ideas must be successively refined, as one learns of new factors that affect the categories, the sources, and the processing. Both the school executive and the statistician should coöperate and make a contribution, since both have backgrounds of experience and training.

**Basic enumerative and descriptive records.** Data are gathered principally through three sources, all of which present problems, have their own peculiar and necessary safeguards, and depend on essential working practices:

1. Routine records and regular reports.
2. Documentary sources, meaning published data; these sources include the larger summaries or compilations of routine records and regular reports.
3. Data gathered especially for the purpose of the study or for answering the particular question.

There is a great need for better teacher-personnel records. Part of the difficulty has been the nature of the data concerning personnel problems. Seldom has a school system made any attempt to keep records for the purpose of determining the needs of teachers. The Board of Education keeps records chiefly for its own administrative purposes. It is important in planning future data-gathering that consideration be given to the need for better teacher-personnel records.

The user of figures or statistics fits them into a purpose or a scheme of his own: to prove or disprove something, to show a trend, to obtain ratios, to show differences, or to discover which is larger. The producer of enumerative statistics must understand these various uses to which his figures will be put by other persons; he must gather figures that will be as valid as possible for the various uses, which often means that he must collect several sets of statistics, because purpose affects counting. The producer of enumerative statistics must describe or label his data as well as possible, so that when used they will be used intelligently, and the user will not misinterpret the meaning of the figures.

**Report forms for gathering data.** There is the ever recurring problem of not having records entirely in the form desired. Questions are seldom framed to fit the available data, and vice versa. Questionnaires should be geared into regular reports so far as possible; for example, the investigator should study the regular, official report blanks of the state or of the nation and try to ask for the same items. A state department of labor or education might reasonably expect requests for statistics on even multiples of ten years (or smaller multiples). It is not expected that the available data will fit all questions, but certainly official requests and local needs can be met; for example, the questions most frequently asked by the local school board or superintendent. Basic records should be available which can be analyzed in many ways, to meet special needs when the occasion demands, even if not regularly summarized that way. For certain temporary or current conditions, it may be easier to gather special data than to try to have regular forms provide for all possible contingencies.

The investigator cannot hope to prepare an adequate and thoroughly satisfactory report blank or questionnaire the first time. Perhaps he should strive in this direction, but he is not likely to reach the goal. A satisfactory instrument requires some trial and improvement. The investigator must determine answers to the following questions and revise his form or schedule accordingly:

1. How do the data summarize? Will the responses permit the analyses that are desired? Do they yield the totals that are found useful for practical (or theoretical) application? Do the questions fit into the common concepts used in ordinary thinking in the operation of the enterprise?
2. How many responses are faulty—missing, inconsistent, ambiguous?
3. Are situations or conditions revealed or suggested which were not provided for?
4. Is there reluctance to answer honestly?

The regular courses for statistical training in colleges and universities have given little background for practical work in preparing record forms for securing routine data in the area of report statistics or aggregative statistics. The formal program of statistical training should give at least a reasonable concept of the practical nature of these jobs as an important part (probably the largest part) of statistical activity.

**Aggregative or report statistics.** As to the definitive characteristics of report statistics or aggregative statistics, they are a record (somewhat routine) for a given period of time; they are definitely idiographic; they often present highly incisive data on operations-information found useful in guiding the enterprise. The statistical worker in this area has constant opportunity to make reports more incisive, critical, and valuable. Report statistics seem to be definitely time-and-place data; they deal with on-going, continuing operations, and with reports of this continuing process.

There are always the danger and difficulty of having data too refined, with technical distinctions and refinements that the user may not understand, or may not even know about. Therefore, he may misunderstand or misinterpret the statistics. (This is the opposite difficulty from that of not having data sufficiently refined for the need.) To cite an example, most persons have in mind the two classifications of rural and urban, but the U. S. Bureau of the Census makes a finer classification (rural non-farm, and rural farm). One has to stop and think what he wants, when such a distinction is made; for example, a particular state is one-fourth urban, one-fourth rural non-farm, and one-half rural farm. Therefore, one can say that this state is three-fourths rural, or one-half rural, depending on what he means, and what he wishes to convey to the reader or listener.

In preparing report blanks for statistics, it is desirable to check with administrators, in order to determine whether the categories are acceptable and usable for the purposes for which figures are often needed. Also the statistician or investigator may need to check his totals when they are in hand, to determine whether they agree with the totals which the administrators have in mind or expect. This is a phase of reconciliation.

Report statistics are subject to error; for example, there is the interesting example of the state whose commissioner of education said during the summer that a huge number of new teachers would be needed for the coming year, since he had received reports of many vacancies from the school superintendents during the preceding spring. However, many of these vacancies meant that teachers were transferring to other school systems within the state; the report of a vacancy was true for a particular locality, but could not be cumulated to show the total number of vacancies for the entire state. Theoretically, every teacher in the state might move to a new position within the state, and actually no new teachers be needed. This illustration suggests the need for a special definition of "vacancy" before it is reported.

There are other examples of all-too-frequent defects or errors in reported data and in documentary sources. The deficiencies in both census and vital statistics from many nations in the Americas have been so great that the usual techniques of demographic analysis have been generally inapplicable, although recent censuses are partially closing the gap in existing quantitative data. Past statistical deficiencies, however, remain as unalterable facts, with many of the existing censuses mere estimates for segments of the population, vital statistics largely matters of inference, and the means of exact measurement of the past course of population movements now irretrievably lost.

The number of doctorates listed in the Wilson Company publication *Doctoral Dissertations Accepted by American Universities* is smaller than the total degrees awarded, since this annual volume omits those doctorates not based on research dissertations, which sometimes means exclusion of certain J.D. and Ed. D. degrees. As a rule, doctoral studies labeled as field projects or field studies probably have not been listed in the *Doctoral Dissertations Accepted by American Universities*. Statistics based on this publication must take into consideration the specific delimitations involved in preparation of the volume. Some dissertations are reported late and some institutions do not report at all. It is pertinent to cite a source giving very carefully derived figures on the number of doctoral degrees, 1873-1950, in all fields in the United States.[74]

Careful research agencies are especially thorough in checking and reviewing the reports received; for example, a well-known State Education Department has made it a practice under the terminology of "auditing" to check meticulously and review each report received from the schools throughout the state. Although this procedure is not quite the same technically as a field audit, wherein accounts are checked against vouchers and other primary instruments, it is much more than an editing or a casual review of reports. The workers at the capitol not only determine that all aspects of a report balance, but they check to see whether items are properly reported and whether they are consistent with other sources of data at hand in the State Education Department. To cite examples, all school superintendents of the state should have available in their offices accurate information concerning the amount of the contributions for teacher retirement, the amount of state aid for education in the district, enrollment statistics for school children, and bonded indebtedness for the school district. However, in a surprising number of instances there are errors in the

---

[74] Douglas E. Scates, Bernard C. Murdoch, and Alice V. Yeomans, *The Production of Doctorates in the Sciences: 1936-1948*, p. 14-33, 194. Washington: American Council on Education, 1951. 228 p. (Mimeographed.)

reports sent from the local school districts to the State Education Department. Therefore, the staff members as a precautionary measure check all such items against the records in the Department.

**Personnel and standards for statistical reporting and interpretation.** As early as 1921, Leonard P. Ayres pointed out that most of the business statisticians at that time in American industries had come up through the clerical or accounting forces and had been given the title of statistician because they proved somewhat more able than their fellow workers to compile rapidly the information demanded from time to time by the executive officers. Ayres emphasized that two conditions were necessary to carry forward the work of the business statistician along productive, scientific lines.[75]

1. To regard his office as one of interpretation and presentation, rather than of compiling primary records, to sort out the essential facts from the great mass of merely incidental data, and to interpret their significance
2. To present personally the results to those officers who base actions and policies upon the data, and to participate actively in the discussion of the data and the formulation of the policies.

It has been maintained that the statistical program of the federal government is well organized, perhaps better than the program in any other scientific field, with the key to improvement not in major reorganization, but in maintaining and expanding a relatively small group of highly trained personnel, and in making their skills more useful, particularly by strengthening central professional leadership and encouraging inter-agency loans of especially skilled statisticians.[76]

As early as 1947 the Division of Statistical Standards of the Bureau of the Budget of the United States had in effect the following constructive standards (in the form of a mimeographed statement) for reporting and publication of statistical data:

1. Every release or publication of statistical data, whether recurring or single-time, should clearly indicate the nature of the data and make reference to any detailed technical descriptions available.
2. For periodic reports of all but simple data and for one-time reports where applicable, there should be available a reasonably detailed statement containing the information essential to a competent technical appraisal of the data.
3. When published statistics are derived from a sample survey, there should be available a detailed description of the sampling plan.

[75] Leonard P. Ayres, "The Nature and Status of Business Research." An address delivered at the eighty-third annual meeting of the American Statistical Association at Pittsburgh, Pennsylvania, December, 1921. Cleveland: Cleveland Trust Co., 1921. 11 p.
[76] John W. Tukey, "Memorandum on Statistics in the Federal Government." *American Statistician* 3:6; February 1949.
Clem C. Linnenberg, "The Development of Federal Statistical Co-ordination, 1908-1949." *American Statistician* 3:6-10; April-May 1949.

Sampling plan and type of solicitation

Size of sample and proportion of coverage

Percentage of response and treatment of non-response

Weighting procedures and method of estimating the universe from the sample

Where possible, estimates of the sampling error and other measurements of the accuracy of the data

4. There should be within the agency established procedures and sets of instructions governing the processing of the data, and provision for periodic reëxamination of the procedures and instructions.

5. Before publication, the final compilation should be reviewed within the agency by persons familiar with the data and with related data in the same field, for the purpose of disclosing errors or inadequacies in the procedures followed and of discovering any likely source of misinterpretation.

6. Every press release which presents statistical data should be checked with qualified technicians within the agency for final review before release to make sure that the data are properly used and interpreted.

7. Any published description of data compiled by another agency should be checked by the agency which compiled the data.

8. In the preparation of analytical or interpretative reports, any special uses of data compiled by another agency should be reviewed with that agency to ensure that the use is based on proper undertsanding of the data.

9. In economic analyses, there should be a clear distinction between the actual data and inferences and interpretations made from the data, the sources of data used in the analyses should be indicated, and adjustments of the data identified and described to the extent practicable.

10. Forecasts and projections should be clearly labeled as such and distinguished from historical series, and where feasible the conditions and assumptions explained.

11. Analytical or interpretative reports should contain an explanation of any differences in assumptions or methods which give rise to apparent contradictions or discrepancies with reports issued by other agencies.

## USING DOCUMENTARY SOURCES AND PUBLISHED DATA

Use of documents and published sources for other than descriptive-survey purposes has been discussed in the chapter on library technique and the related literature and in the chapter on the historical method, and will be considered for yet another purpose later in the present chapter under the topic of quantitative documentary analysis. Many of the library guides to the published sources are listed in these earlier chapters. For many worthwhile studies the student may use available sources; for example, census data; it is not always necessary to gather original or "raw" data.

**Relation of history and statistics.** There is a point at which history and statistics meet. On the one hand, more statistics might well be used in historical writing; on the other hand, the historical method, or a better working knowledge of historical techniques, would be helpful in gathering statistical data. The experienced person in this field knows well the problems, but the beginner does not. Even the experienced investigator sometimes encounters frustration in gathering statistical data from documentary sources, because the task at first seems simpler than it actually proves to be.

It would be well if statisticians were trained to look at sources as critically as historians do; but usually statisticians assume that the records are accurate (at least within some vague notion of sampling error), that the figures mean what they appear to, and that they are consistent from year to year. The workers take these characteristics for granted, and then show annoyance when they discover that their faith is misplaced. It would be much more realistic to approach each source with proper doubt and hesitation (misgivings), rather than to turn hurriedly to a certain page, copy off the figure that seems on the surface to be what is wanted, and give no further thought to the matter.

**Major types of documentary sources.** There are three major types of documentary sources of data useful for survey studies. The extent to which the investigator will use these various sources depends upon his purposes. In general, it is the task of the statistician to take the raw material and make it into a meaningful set of statements. As a rule, the more background one can bring to this task, the richer the resources available by way of statistical techniques to serve his purpose, and the greater the array of basic data, the better his work can be.

1. Basic data are illustrated by the Census Report. They are unanalyzed, the basic totals are aggregates (specific figures for different times, places, and traits). They may occasionally contain some analyzed materials such as ratios and averages, but these are not the characteristic or predominant type of data.

2. Analyzed and compared data are at least partially analyzed, using routine techniques of statistical analysis applied in fairly simple form. They lack the more extended and refined analyses that are made in the special studies represented by the third group, and they also lack the large insight or background of interpretation which is characteristic of the third group. These analyzed data are represented generally in the *Statistical Atlas of the United States* published after two censuses.

In this second type of work, in dealing with various forms of analyzed and compared data, the user has to be cautious lest the analyzer has made selections that prejudice the case in some particular direction. Often comparison (particularly trend comparisons) will be carried back to a year that makes a desired showing for the present year. Other elements of selection will enter in, unknowingly, so that the analyzed data are not immediately usable, or dependable, or fair for all purposes. The investigator will generally be watchful of the purposes which may have actuated the analyzer, but, even if no special purposes have motivated him, the analyzed data may still be unsuitable for the purpose of the user.

3. Special treatments are in the nature of monographs or doctoral dissertations representing extended and special studies of a particular aspect of a

general field. They bring to bear upon the work, in addition to special techniques of statistical analysis, a considerable background of understanding and insight into factors that operate upon the conditions, usually also with considerable information which is not purely statistical or quantitative.

**Insight in questioning data.** One difficulty comes from trying to impose a new pattern on data, or of trying to impose a pattern that will not fit, one that is too simple, or one that assumes the facts are different from what they are. Or the pattern may call for facts that do not exist, at least not in the categories as the investigator desires to set them up.

Sooner or later one's concept of what he wants will be modified by, or adjusted to, what he finds can be obtained. The research worker must be prepared for such necessary changes, but is not expected to "give in" until he has exhausted every resource in getting at what he thought or believed desirable.

In research an anticipated step frequently turns out to be much more complicated and difficult than expected. If one learns to expect this in careful investigation, a feeling or sense of frustration will be avoided and one may say, "This is the way of research." It is imperative to pursue every new source that turns up, since each one may throw a new light on what is desired, either on a new concept of what is desired, or on the data at hand. The early results serve as a starting point for next steps, and these are sometimes in an oblique direction to clear up some minor point. The concept of interpretation grows with accumulating evidence, as illustrated by many of the descriptive studies reported in Chapters 5 and 6.

Insights from data develop slowly, and workers tire or become easily discouraged. The investigator starts out seeking data, and ends up seeking insight; at least he should begin by seeking adequate understanding of the data presented (or recorded). Progress in this sort of work is a matter of clearing up various uncertainties: first, of creating uncertainties through asking shrewd questions about the data, their source, accuracy, method of gathering and preparation, and scope, and then of answering such questions. If every worker at each stage or level had done his work well, research would be much easier than it is.

There are more specific, critical questions that may be leveled at data, by which to test the evidence and to know that one can or should search further. As in historical work, one of the first and continuing (persistent) problems is that of determining what the investigator wants. He must map out the field in general to determine whether every scrap of evidence is of relatively great importance, or whether there is so much evidence that he can choose only the most convenient source, or (and) whether there are competing and conflicting lines of evidence.

Are there inconsistencies within the same source materials, as in a series of annual reports for a city school system (discovered by looking at different reports)?

Are there differences between the source used and other sources?

Are the descriptions of method and scope entirely satisfactory?

Are there clear evidences of data that have been omitted (noted elsewhere in the same source or in other sources)?

Did the worker have the facilities and the resources to do a good job?

**Illustrations of using and evaluating data.** It is helpful to cite a number of illustrations. In an investigation of the number of Ph.D. degrees awarded, many of the sources were found to be originally the same (data gathered by the National Research Council and published through various channels) for the field of science. For all fields as a total, the results boiled down to two main lines or series, one fractional, plus scattered sources of independent data used as checks.

A procedure by way of checking evidence is to gather data more than once from the same source. The investigator himself may have done this, fully or partially, or may have had assistants do the checking. In gathering data concerning the number of doctors' degrees from the sources of a particular agency, several persons did rechecking of older figures, while the director of the investigation was working on later figures in the same source. In doing so he was developing improved concepts, learning what the terms and phrases of the agency meant, finding the pitfalls of the sources and where certain figures were buried, discovering how incomplete some of the sources were, and getting an idea as to what historical changes were taking place in the conceptions, refinements, and appearance of new kinds or sources of data concerning doctoral degrees (as from teachers colleges).

There is widespread the dubious notion that one should use published figures as they are, that it is not the responsibility of the user of the data to bear the onus of going behind the published report. To question published figures has been regarded by many persons as hazardous; one does not know enough to do so and, so long as one uses published data, who can quarrel with them? To cite an example, a city superintendent assumed the attitude that the pupil-enrollment statistics printed in the minutes of the board of education were "official" figures, even though an error was reported at a later date. Certainly a note of explanation would seem essential as a record in the school-board minutes and for purposes of citing the statistics of pupil enrollment for the particular year, since the label of "official" does not make the figures correct or provide for the education of fifty children not included in the printed statistical tabulation.

Additional examples of use of available documentary sources for investigational purposes may be mentioned briefly:

A roster of younger American scholars, based on four sources (university fellowship and scholarship awardees, recipients of governmental fellowships, holders of private foundation fellowships, and recipients of Ph.D.'s).[77]

A study of the origins of American scientists, with basic data assembled from two editions of *American Men of Science,* involving the sifting of 18,000 scientists from a total of 43,500 names in the two volumes.[78]

An analysis of certain biographical information concerning educators, as found in the 1949-50 edition of *Who's Who in American Education.*[79]

A study of the tenure of school administrators in Indiana, based on the official directories of the Indiana State Department of Public Instruction for a period of twenty years, with the exception of 1943-44 and 1945-46.[80]

It is important to understand the attitudes of persons engaged in recording data, in order to understand the validity or reliability of the data and to interpret them properly, since these attitudes have much to do with the figures recorded. For example, we do not have good trend figures on cancer, because it was formerly regarded as something of a disgrace, and still is so regarded in many rural communities. Physicians sometimes have recorded death as due to some other cause; therefore, comparison of the incidence of cancer in rural and in urban areas is not wholly valid. In many communities in the past, birth registrations were not regarded as highly important. Recorded figures of the past, more than for the present, were colored by political and social purposes. As data gatherers in the future become more technical and professional, these conditions of bias will not prevail to such a large extent; they will become increasingly interested in the truth rather than in coloring truth for an immediate ulterior purpose.

**Checking and copying from documentary sources.** We must recognize, as a distinct step, that after data have been gathered, the material must be examined, checked, evaluated, and edited. Much of the work of specialists engaged in research and statistical activities consists in doing this sort of thing: checking one source against another, finding many sources of data, evaluating each in terms of the other and in terms of how the material was gathered, and looking at the data for internal evidence of quality, care, completeness, consistency, and clarity. In many instances it may be necessary to write to the person who published the data, to inquire why the data are different from other sources, what definitions were used, the scope of the category or population, or the method employed.

As a result of checking of data by the readers of journals (or by the authors themselves) a number of "corrections" are published in later issues

[77] Robert H. Knapp and Joseph J. Greenbaum, *The Younger American Scholar: His Collegiate Origin.* Chicago: University of Chicago Press, 1953. xiii + 122 p.

[78] Robert H. Knapp and H. B. Goodrich, *op. cit.*

[79] B. E. Blanchard, "Some Characteristics Peculiar to Educators." *Journal of Educational Research* 46:515-23; March 1953.

[80] Raleigh W. Holmstedt, *The Tenure of Indiana School Administrators.* Bulletin of the School of Education, Vol. 29, No. 3. Bloomington: Indiana University, May 1953. 35 p.

of the particular journals. The novice who hurries through the professional literature may not see these corrections, but the scholar or specialist in the particular field is likely to note the corrections in a later issue of the journal and in some instances may have discovered the error.

The beginner in graduate work frequently needs to be cautioned against copying materials, for papers and theses, which he himself does not understand. Too often he thinks that, because the material was published, it is essentially excellent, or dependable, or significant. If the writer of a manuscript gets no meaning from the material he has reproduced, it is not likely that the reader will. If data are complicated, or subject to question or doubt, it is important to record (copy) essential supporting details, so that decisions made in the library can be reviewed later. This may save many, although not all, repeat trips to the library.

**Selected sources of current statistical data.** There are so many varied sources of current statistics that one cannot mention any large number of specific items; however, the more general ones are listed below.[81] The first

---

[81] Robert C. Angell and Ronald Freedman, "Use of Documents, Records, Census Materials, and Indices." *Research Methods in the Behavioral Sciences.* Edited by Leon Festinger and Daniel Katz. New York: Dryden Press, 1953. Chapter 7.

Marie Jahoda and Others, *op cit.,* p. 229-50.

George A. Lundberg, "Social Bookkeeping." *Social Research, op. cit.,* p. 397-413. Emphasizes demographic data and vital statistics, including the data-gathering agencies.

U. S. Bureau of the Budget, Office of Statistical Standards, *Statistical Services of the United States Government.* Revised Edition. Washington: The Bureau, 1952. 78 p. A description of the governmental collecting agencies and of the series of data represented.

U. S. Bureau of the Census, *Statistical Abstract of the United States,* 1953. Washington: Government Printing Office, 1953. 1041 p. The standard, authentic, and convenient annual source book for several thousand series of data, over varying periods of years, but usually going back to 1900 or before. The 1952 edition contains for the first time a section on "Comparative International Statistics." Sections deal with education, population, vital statistics, and thirty-three other topics.

U. S. Bureau of the Census, *Historical Statistics of the United States, 1789-1945.* A supplement to the Statistical Abstract of the United States. Washington: Government Printing Office, 1949. 363 p. Includes a historical background for current issues of the Statistical Abstract; contains three thousand statistical series; corrections are issued in annual volumes of the Statistical Abstract, as noted; the series are brought up to date, year by year, beginning with the 1949 Statistical Abstract.

U. S. Bureau of the Census, *County and City Data Book, 1952.* Washington: Government Printing Office, 1953. 608 p. A specialized supplement to the Statistical Abstract, issued at intervals, giving 101 items for each state, county, and city of 25,000 or more; before 1949 the data for cities and counties were published separately; an issue is planned to appear three times each decade.

Census publications of the Bureau of the Census on the census are almost endless; data for the 1950 census were published in a separate volume for each state, and one volume for the U. S. summary; data for each state are divided into three sections.

Inter-American Statistical Institute, *Statistical Activities of the American Nations, 1940.* Edited by Elizabeth Phelps, for the Temporary Organizing Committee. Washington: Inter-American Statistical Institute, 1941. 842 p. Covers the statistical services in twenty-two nations.

Maurice G. Kendall, Editor, *Sources and Nature of the Statistics of the United Kingdom.* Vol. 1. Published for the Royal Statistical Society. London: Oliver and Boyd, 1952. 352 p.

United Nations, Department of Economic Affairs, Statistical Office, *Statistical Yearbook, 1952.* New York: International Documents Service, Columbia University Press, 1952. 554 p.

J. F. Dewhurst and Associates, *America's Needs and Resources.* New York: Twentieth

four references are descriptions or discussions of sources rather than sources of statistics. The reader is reminded again that the chapter on library technique and the survey of related literature includes many of the library guides to sources of data.

Each state department of education is required to make an annual or biennial report. A useful manual deals with such reports in terms of: origins and changing concepts, legal basis, planning and development, editing, and printing and distribution.[82]

## SAMPLING IN DESCRIPTIVE-SURVEY STUDIES[83]

The purpose of this section is to present a simple, non-mathematical overview of the problems and procedures of sample theory. For the details of statistical techniques appropriate for sampling, the reader is referred

---

Century Fund, 1947. 812 p. Deals with the problems of using older data, and the changing factors that enter in, together with a frank discussion of the effect of errors.

*The Biennial Surveys,* published by the United States Office of Education, are especially important for statistics in the field of education.

As to sources within states, each state publishes large quantities of statistics. The investigator may examine the reports of the appropriate state-government agency, especially the state department of education; these data often are broken down by county and by city. In a number of states the state teachers' association has a research department or similar office that gathers significant data concerning the schools.

[82] Robert F. Will, *The State Department of Education Report.* Washington: Office of Education, 1953. vii + 58 p. Also see:

Paul L. Reason, Emery M. Foster, and Robert F. Will, *The Common Core of State Educational Information.* State Educational Records and Reports Series, Handbook 1. Washington: Government Printing Office, 1953. The basic guide for state systems of educational records and reports and a major tool for comparability of educational information; contains the list of items of educational information (with their definitions) which each state department of education should have available, plus a glossary of terms.

[83] Russell L. Ackoff, *The Design of Social Research.* Chicago: University of Chicago Press, 1953. Chapter 4.

A. S. Barr, Robert A. Davis, and Palmer O. Johnson, *op. cit.,* p. 158-87.

Z. W. Birnbaum and Monroe G. Sirken, "Bias Due to Non-Availability in Sampling Surveys." *Journal of the American Statistical Association* 45:98-111; March 1950.

William G. Cochran, *Sampling Techniques.* New York: John Wiley and Sons, 1953. xiv + 330 p. A fundamental presentation of sampling theory as it has been developed for use in sample surveys, plus systematic accounts of techniques that have proved useful in modern sample surveys.

Stephen R. Deane, "Sampling Control in Adult Education Research—A Case Study." *Adult Education* 14:84-88, 95; February 1950.

W. E. Deming, "On Errors in Surveys." *American Sociological Review* 9:359-69; August 1944.

W. E. Deming, "Some Criteria for Judging the Quality of Surveys." *Journal of Marketing* 12:145-57; October 1947.

W. E. Deming, *Some Theory of Sampling.* New York: John Wiley and Sons, 1950. xvii + 602 p.

Manuel C. Elmer, *op. cit.,* 1939. p. 323-44.

Leon Festinger and Daniel Katz, *op. cit.,* p. 15-55, 173-239.

W. J. Goode and E. K. Hatt, *Methods in Social Research.* New York: McGraw-Hill Book Co., 1952. p. 209-31.

Roe Goodman and Leslie Kish, "Controlled Selection—A Technique in Probability Sampling." *Journal of the American Statistical Association* 45:350-72; September 1950.

Morris H. Hansen, William N. Hurwitz, and William G. Madow, *Sample Survey Methods*

to the accompanying list of references, especially to the full-length text-book treatments.

**Sampling and statistical inference.** The questions asked by investigators, particularly in descriptive-survey research, usually concern groups. Statistical methods may be classified in two categories,[84] according to the nature of the groups under study:

1. When the group consists only of those individuals observed; for example, when the population about which the questions are asked is identical with the "sample" observed in collecting the data. This is usually true of the data in a

*and Theory.* Vol. I, Methods and Applications; Vol. II, Theory. New York: John Wiley and Sons, 1953. xxii + 638 p., 332 p.

E. E. Houseman, *Problems of Establishing a Consumer Panel in the New York Metropolitan Area.* Marketing Research Report No. 8, United States Department of Agriculture, Bureau of Agricultural Economics. Washington: Government Printing Office, 1952. 41 p.

Marie Jahoda and Others, *op. cit.*, p. 643-80.

Raymond J. Jessen and Others, "Observations on the 1946 Elections in Greece." *American Sociological Review* 14:11-16; February 1949.

Raymond J. Jessen and Others, "On a Population Sample for Greece." *Journal of the American Statistical Association* 42:357-84; September 1947.

A. J. King and R. J. Jessen, "The Master Sample of Agriculture: Development and Use, and Design." *Journal of the American Statistical Association* 40:38-56; March 1945.

Leslie Kish, "A Two-Stage Sample of a City." *American Sociological Review* 17:761-69; December 1952.

Harold D. Lasswell, Nathan Leites, and Associates, *Language of Politics.* New York: George W. Stewart Co., 1949. 398 p.

George A. Lundberg, *op. cit.*, p. 134-58.

Philip J. McCarthy, *Sampling:* Elementary Principles. Bulletin No. 15, April 1951, New York State School of Industrial and Labor Relations, Cornell University. Ithaca, N. Y.: Cornell University, 1951. 32 p.

Philip J. McCarthy and Frederick F. Stephan, "Area Sampling." *American Statistician* 5:20-21; February 1951

Lillian H. Madow, "On the Use of the County as the Primary Sampling Unit for State Estimates." *Journal of the American Statistical Association* 45:30-47; March 1950.

Eli S. Marks, "Selective Sampling in Psychological Research." *Psychological Bulletin* 44: 267-75; May 1947.

Eli S. Marks, "Some Sampling Problems in Educational Research." *Journal of Educational Psychology* 42:85-96; February 1951.

Quinn McNemar, "Sampling in Psychological Research." *Psychological Bulletin* 37:331-65; June 1940.

Mildred Parten, *op. cit.*

Alfred Politz and Willard Simmons, "An Attempt to Get the 'Not At Home' into the Sample without Callbacks." *Journal of the American Statistical Association* 44:9-31; March 1949.

J. G. Smith and A. J. Duncan, *Sampling Statistics and Applications:* Fundamentals of the Theory of Statistics. New York: McGraw-Hill Book Co., 1945. v + 498 p.

Frederick F. Stephan, "History of the Uses of Modern Sampling Procedures." *Journal of the American Statistical Association* 43:12-39; March 1948.

Frederick F. Stephan, "Sampling in Studies of Opinions, Attitudes and Consumer Wants." *American Philosophical Society Proceedings* 92:387-98; November 1948.

S. S. Stevens, "Probability," *Handbook of Experimental Psychology.* New York: John Wiley and Sons, 1951. p. 44-47.

Helen M. Walker and Joseph Lev, "Statistical Inference," *Encyclopedia of Educational Research, op. cit.*, p. 1271-90.

Frank Yates, *Sampling Methods for Censuses and Surveys.* London: Charles Griffin and Co., 1949. 318 p.

Pauline V. Young, *op. cit.*, p. 329-41.

Statistical Office of the United Nations, "The Preparation of Sampling Survey Reports." *American Statistician* 4:6-10, 12; June-July 1950.

[84] Helen M. Walker and Joseph Lev, *op. cit.*

school superintendent's annual report covering pupil enrollment by grades, pupil-teacher ratio, average salary of teachers, expenditures per pupil, comparisons of achievement-test scores with test norms, and similar questions.

2. When the individuals observed form a sample from a larger group or population (the principal object of inquiry). Statistical procedure (inference) is employed to utilize the information secured from the sample in answering questions about the larger population.

Since the population in most survey investigations is too extensive for complete enumeration, some portion or sample is studied, and the process of reaching conclusions about the problem population from the sample is known as statistical inference.

**Illustrations of early sampling.** Stephan has written a history of modern sampling [85] that is especially pertinent to the present discussion, because of its emphasis on the use of sampling in large-scale surveys rather than in the laboratory or in small-scale experimental studies. The history of sampling stems from many roots and has applications that branch out into many fields of science, commerce, manufacturing, agriculture, education, and government administration.

Illustrations of early sampling procedures may be summarized briefly. As early as 1754 estimates of the population of England were made from the number of houses on the tax list, plus a crude estimate of cottages not taxed, with the total of dwellings multiplied by a rather arbitrary factor of six persons per dwelling; other estimates were based on the reported number of baptisms, marriages, and burials. About 1765 and 1778, carefully prepared estimates for France were based on enumeration of population in certain districts and on the count of births, deaths, and marriages, as reported for the whole country; the districts from which the ratio of inhabitants to births was determined constituted a sample, a procedure not unlike certain later sampling techniques.

Laplace used vital statistics from thirty departments of France in preparing estimates of the total population from 1799 to 1802, with a major forward step in sampling by way of attempting to measure the precision of his estimate.

In discussing social surveys, reference has been made earlier in this chapter to the work of Bowley of London, who first designed the plan for securing a random sample of households (a plan that has met the rather strict requirements of research).

Stephan presents interesting examples [86] from the beginnings of four general lines of statistical work in which efficient sampling methods were needed: agriculture crop estimates; economic statistics of prices, wages,

85 Frederick F. Stephan, *op. cit.*
86 *Ibid.*

employment, and so on; statistical phases of social surveys and health studies; and public-opinion polling.

Earlier attempts at public-opinion polls during the present century were outdone in size by the *Literary Digest,* which started polling in 1916, and in 1920 mailed out eleven million ballots to persons listed in telephone directories and in other sources. In 1922 the *Literary Digest* conducted a poll on prohibition.

**Values of sampling.** The advantages of using relatively small samples, rather than a complete enumeration of the population in a survey, include saving in time and expense, possible use of the available funds for a more complete and analytical study, and the administrative feasibility of a sampling plan as compared with the complex organization required for canvass of the total population.

**Difficulties in sampling.** The possible disadvantages or difficulties of sampling are as follows: [87]

1. If the sampling plan is not correctly designed and followed, the results may be incorrect or misleading. (In this connection, see the three closing paragraphs of this section on sampling.)
2. If the characteristic to be observed occurs only rarely in the population (for example, people over ninety years of age), special problems arise in securing statistically reliable information.
3. Sample data involve more cautions in preparing detailed subclassifications, because of a smaller number of cases.
4. Sampling requires expert advice, an area in which there is a shortage of competent specialists.
5. There are characteristic limitations for each type of sampling.
6. Complicated sampling plans may prove as laborious as a complete enumeration of the population.

**Planning a sampling survey.**[88] The major problems in planning a sampling survey include:

1. Statement of the purposes of the survey
2. Definition of the population or universe
3. Selection of the sampling unit and the unit of tabulation
4. Location and selection of the source list
5. Deciding on the type of sampling to be used
6. Determining the size of the sample or the sample ratio
7. Testing of the sample in a pilot or exploratory survey
8. Interpretation of the data in the light of the reliability of the sample.

**Modern examples of sampling.** A number of modern illustrations of sampling are helpful. Kish assumes that the purpose of the particular survey and the available resources have led to the following complex design

[87] Mildred Parten, *op. cit.,* 109-12.
[88] Mildred Parten, *op. cit.,* p. 116-22.
A. S. Barr, R. A. Davis, and P. O. Johnson, *op. cit.,* p. 167-83.

for a sample of dwelling units in which interviews are to be taken: the purpose is to give every dwelling unit in the city a designated, equal probability of being selected into the sample. The dwelling units are to be chosen in two stages: first, a sample of blocks is to be selected with a given interval, and then within the selected blocks the sample of dwelling units is to be chosen with a designated interval. The steps in the selection procedure are as follows: [89]

1. Outlining the entire area (city)
2. Dividing the entire area into blocks
3. Numbering the blocks
4. Stratifying the blocks
5. Controlling the size of the sub-sample
6. Calculating the sampling intervals
7. Selecting the sample blocks
8. Listing the dwelling units
9. Selecting the sample dwellings
10. Identifying the dwelling units at the sample addresses.

The *Literary Digest* poll [90] of the 1936 presidential election is a remarkable example of results from a biased sample. While the sample was large (ten million ballots and 2,350,176 replies), the mailing lists were taken primarily from telephone directories and automobile registration lists, tending to overweight the proportion of cases in the upper socio-economic groups (with a resulting error of 20 per cent in the forecast). Since the ballots went by mail, it is probable that more persons in the higher income brackets returned their ballots. In 1936 many groups with relatively small incomes voted for Roosevelt; they were very inadequately represented in a sample based on telephone directories and automobile registration lists. *Fortune* secured returns from only 4500 persons (by interviews), chosen according to careful sampling procedures, with an error of only 1 per cent.

The Roper and Gallup polls failed to predict the presidential election in 1948. Although public-opinion polling had improved greatly during the preceding decade or more, the problems of representative sampling and of dealing with late changes in public opinion were such that a shrewd political observer and national leader outguessed the scientific pollsters and research specialists.

Adequacy of sampling appears at two levels as an important problem in investigations in the area of language usage. One aspect of the problem involves establishment of the fact that the nature of the language material itself is truly representative of the situations where the skills likely would

[89] Leslie Kish, *op. cit.,* p. 761-69.

[90] Daniel Katz and Hadley Cantril, "Public Opinion Polls." *Sociometry* 1:155-78; July-October 1937.

Pauline V. Young, *op. cit.,* p. 238-39, 331.

appear, particularly in study of vocabulary and word meanings. Available evidence indicates that the type of vocabulary used by an individual is conditioned largely by the subject discussed, which means that extension of the range of the subject matter analyzed will, in most cases, result in a corresponding extension of the vocabulary used.

The second aspect of the problem of sampling in investigating language usage involves the extent of the material necessary, in order to obtain statistically reliable results. The statistical technique of cumulative sampling has been used effectively to deal with this problem. Through this procedure it is possible to determine the effect of adding 10,000 or 20,000 words to the given base. Studies in capitalization and punctuation indicate that from 60,000 to 90,000 words of written material are necessary before the results cease to be affected significantly by additional data; in an investigation of vocabulary and word meaning a comparison of two samplings of 100,000 running words indicated few significant discrepancies.[91]

**Methods of selecting the sample.** *Restricted random sampling* involves certain restrictions intended to improve the accuracy of the sample. In *systematic sampling* every *nth* name from a list, or area from a map, etc., may be used. *Unrestricted random sampling* means that each individual or element in the population or universe has an equal chance of inclusion in the sample.

The procedures [92] commonly used to select random samples of human populations include: drawing by lot numbered slips of paper from a container, capsules from a gold-fish bowl, or balls from an urn; using tables of random numbers; and using a roulette wheel. Some of the lists frequently employed are as follows: changes in marital status, juvenile offenses, distribution of welfare and social services, registration of automobile owners, telephone directories, utility subscriptions, customers and consumers, voting registrations, post-office lists, school and other censuses, members of organizations and graduates of schools, city directories, tax lists, and pay rolls. Systematic lists give random samples only if one selects from them *at random* (as with random numbers), and not at regular intervals.

In *stratified random sampling* the population is first subdivided into two or more strata (classes), and then from each stratum is taken a predetermined number of observations (sample) at random. To cite a simple illustration, if a sample of men and women telephone subscribers is desired, the investigator may first divide the list of subscribers into two parts,

[91] Harry A. Greene, "English—Language, Grammar, and Composition." *Encyclopedia of Educational Research, op. cit.,* p. 384.
[92] William J. Goode and Paul K. Hatt, *op. cit.,* p. 215-16.
Mildred Parten, *op. cit.,* p. 224.
A. S. Barr, R. A. Davis, and P. O. Johnson, *op. cit.,* p. 163-64.

one consisting of men and the other women. Next, to obtain a 10 per cent stratified sample, the investigator draws a 10 per cent sample from each list (men and women).

*Purposive selection* is based on the principle of selecting individuals for the sample according to a criterion or criteria known as controls. Statisticians are generally unfavorable to this method, since the samples frequently are not equivalent to balanced random samples; this procedure has been largely replaced by principles of stratification, balancing, and similar procedures. Illustrative studies that have used the procedure of purposive selection have involved a sample of districts representative of Italy as a whole; townships in Iowa with the same averages as the entire state for a number of characteristics; "barometer" states or districts whose votes in elections have coincided with national figures; and use of "typical" industrial counties, manufacturing areas, and wheat-farming districts to develop national figures for various economic characteristics.

Other variations of sampling procedures, including cluster, area, sequential, and double or mixed techniques, are covered fully in the references listed at the beginning of this section. A number of other technical problems of sampling, including the details of appropriate statistical procedures, are discussed at length in these same references; for example, optimum size of the sample, factors affecting the sample size, requisite precision of prediction, evaluation of the data and sample, and types of validation criteria.

**Limitations of sampling.** It should be pointed out to graduate students that in many (probably most) of our educational studies we do not sample, that is, not in any systematic sense. We simply take selected intact groups, which are selected by unknown factors; therefore, we must be careful in generalizing from data derived from such groups. It was common in earlier studies to speak of "unselected groups," which meant merely that they were not consciously selected with regard to some particular factor; they may, however, have been highly selected on one or more factors of which the investigator was unaware.

On the other hand, some specialists with considerable statistical sophistication in education, psychology, and other social fields do not completely accept the purely statistical point of view in trusting a random sample, as do mathematical statisticians, who simply say the probability is such and such that the results will vary only a certain amount. It must be remembered that this statement contains the word *probability*. The tails of the normal curve go out to infinity in both directions; in other words, the rare and unusual bias or distortion in a perfect random sample does occur, and the investigator never knows when it occurs. Even by the most perfect of sampling procedures, the research worker cannot be certain that he actually has any better representative sample than when he takes an intact group (such as a particular class of pupils in a given school) with all of its unknown selective factors; that is, the amount of selection which enters into a given sample by the best of procedures is still unknown. What the mathematicians can say is that, if the investigator continues taking such samples, the process will be self-correcting as the result of using technically approved methods, but they cannot speak with finality about a single sample. While the use of approved procedures in sampling may give the investigator a feeling of confidence in a single sample, this is purely a psychological matter rather than an actuality.

Many of the processes of sampling call for a complete listing of the names of the individual persons or other units of sampling; without such a list it is impossible to secure a random sample. It is possible, however, to obtain other kinds of sample, particularly a quota sample, which may be quite satisfactory for a particular purpose. The requirement of a complete listing of all of the cases to be observed or omitted makes it impossible to apply many of the ideas and formulas produced by the statisticians, simply because the investigator does not have a complete list; for example, to sample the schools in the United States would require a complete roster, by name or other designation, of all the schools in the country; such a list probably is not available.

# Organized Forms of Descriptive-Survey and Normative Research:

## QUESTIONNAIRE AND INTERVIEW TECHNIQUES

## QUESTIONNAIRE INQUIRIES AND TECHNIQUES[93]

### Introduction

It is axiomatic that problems and methods of research must be mutually adapted to each other. Wundt and the experimental psychologists were dissatisfied with the inadequate experimental methods in use during the latter part of the past century. G. Stanley Hall and his followers were con-

[93] Albert B. Blankenship, *How to Conduct Consumer and Opinion Research:* The Sampling Survey in Operation. New York: Harper and Bros., 1946. xi + 314 p.

John A. Clausen, "Controlling Bias in Mail Questionnaires." *Journal of the American Statistical Association* 42:497-511; December 1947.

Lee J. Cronbach, "Pattern Tabulation: Statistical Method for Analysis of Limited Patterns of Scores, with Particular Reference to the Rorschach Test." *Educational and Psychological Measurement* 9:149-71; 1949.

Albert Ellis, "The Validity of Personality Questionnaires." *Psychological Bulletin* 43: 385-440; September 1946.

Albert Ellis, *Comparison of the Use of Direct and Indirect Phrasing in Personality Questionnaires.* Psychological Monographs, Vol. 61, No. 3, Whole No. 284. Washington: American Psychological Association, 1947. 41 p.

Manuel C. Elmer, *Social Research.* New York: Prentice-Hall, 1939. p. 412-23.

R. P. Fischer, "Signed Versus Unsigned Personal Questionnaires." *Journal of Applied Psychology* 30:220-25; June 1946.

Raymond Franzen and P. F. Lazarsfeld, "Main Questionnaire as a Research Problem." *Journal of Psychology* 20:293-320; October 1945.

J. B. Gerberich, "Study of the Consistency of Informant Responses to Questions in a Questionnaire." *Journal of Educational Psychology* 38:299-306; May 1947.

J. B. Gerberich and J. M. Mason, "Signed Versus Unsigned Questionnaire." *Journal of Educational Research* 42:122-26; October 1948.

Carter V. Good, A. S. Barr, and Douglas E. Scates, *The Methodology of Educational Research.* New York: Appleton-Century-Crofts, 1936. p. 324-43. Covers much of the questionnaire literature published before the middle 1930's.

William J. Goode and Paul K. Hatt, *Methods in Social Research.* New York: McGraw-Hill Book Co., 1952. p. 132-83.

Frank W. Hubbard, "Questionnaires." *Review of Educational Research* 9:502-507, 608-609; December 1939.

Frank W. Hubbard, "Questionnaires, Interviews, Personality Schedules." *Review of Educational Research* 12:534-41; December 1942.

Marie Jahoda and Others, *Research Methods in Social Relations:* With Especial Reference to Prejudice. New York: Dryden Press, 1951. p. 151-208, 423-62.

Leonard V. Koos, *The Questionnaire in Education.* New York: Macmillan Co., 1928. vii + 178 p.

Leonard V. Koos, "The Specific Techniques of Investigation: Observation, Questionnaire, and Rating." *The Scientific Movement in Education.* Thirty-seventh Yearbook of the National Society for the Study of Education, Part 2. Bloomington, Ill.: Public School Publishing Co., 1938. p. 375-90.

George A. Lundberg, *Social Research:* A Study in Methods of Gathering Data. Revised Edition. New York: Longmans, Green and Co., 1942. p. 159-252.

vinced that the problems and methods of the experimentalists, including the results of laboratory investigations, failed to answer many of the questions about childhood and youth. Therefore, the questionnaire came into wide use (and often abuse), and more recently has appeared also in the form of the history blank, clinical syllabus, and personality inventory. In these instruments and in similar data-gathering schedules the spirit and influence of Stanley Hall still live today.

Perhaps the first thing for the young or inexperienced worker to get in mind regarding the questionnaire technique of gathering data is that it is not a quick, easy, and facile method of investigation. It is relatively slow, requires a large investment of time on the part of the investigator, and often gives results that are highly disappointing, because of their incompleteness, indefiniteness, and the generally hostile attitude of recipients toward the flood of appeals made for coöperation in answering questionnaires. These statements do not mean that questionnaires or similar special reports have no place, or that such investigations are invariably poor; these comments do mean that experience reveals the technique to be far different, in terms of difficulty, from the notion held by many beginners in research and in graduate study.

The terms *questionnaire* and *schedule* are considered roughly equivalent for purposes of the present discussion, although in some investigations a technical distinction is made. The questionnaire usually has been defined as a form distributed through the mail or filled out by the respondent under the supervision of the investigator or interviewer. The schedule commonly has been regarded as a form filled out by the investigator or completed in his presence.[94]

W. P. Mauldin and E. S. Marks, "Problems of Response in Enumerative Surveys." *American Sociological Review* 15:649-57; October 1950.

John E. Nixon, "The Mechanics of Questionnaire Construction." *Journal of Educational Research* 47:481-87; March 1954.

Ralph D. Norman, "A Review of Some Problems Related to the Main Questionnaire Technique." *Educational and Psychological Measurement* 8:235-47; Summer 1948.

Mildred Parten, *Surveys, Polls, and Samples:* Practical Procedures. New York: Harper and Bros., 1950. p. 157-218, 383-484.

Stanley L. Payne, *The Art of Asking Questions.* Princeton: Princeton University Press, 1951. xiv + 249 p.

William M. Phillips, Jr., "Weaknesses of the Mail Questionnaire." *Sociology and Social Research* 35:260-67; March-April 1951.

"The Questionnaire." *Research Bulletin of the N.E.A.* 8:1-51; January 1930.

Alexander C. Sherriffs, "Intuition Questionnaire: New Projective Test." *Journal of Abnormal and Social Psychology* 43:326-37; July 1948.

Ruth Strang, *Counseling Technics in College and Secondary School.* Revised Edition. New York: Harper and Bros., 1949. p. 93-97.

Herbert A. Toops, "Questionnaires." *Encyclopedia of Educational Research.* Revised Edition. New York: Macmillan Co., 1950. p. 948-51.

Pauline V. Young, *Scientific Social Surveys and Research.* Revised Edition. New York: Prentice-Hall, 1949. p. 220-42.

Hans Zeisel, *Say It With Figures.* New York: Harper and Bros., 1947. p. 4-65.

[94] Mildred Parten, *op. cit.,* p. 157.

More space is given in this chapter to the questionnaire than to the individual discussions of other data-gathering techniques, because of frequent use of questionnaire procedures on the campus and in the field, especially by graduate students, and because of the need for a full and critical analysis of this descriptive-survey instrument. Also, many of the concepts and techniques of questionnaire procedure are applicable to interviewing and to developing certain other instruments for collecting data; therefore, cross-references to the present discussion of the questionnaire will save time and effort in later parts of this chapter.

## Uses and Applications of the Questionnaire

The use of a schedule or questionnaire in descriptive-survey studies extends the investigator's powers of observation by serving to remind the respondent of each item, to help insure response to the same item from all cases, and to keep the investigator from collecting only the unique, exceptional, or unusual facts particularly interesting to him. The questionnaire or schedule tends to standardize and objectify the observations of different enumerators, by singling out particular aspects of the situation (regarded as significant to the purpose of the study), and by specifying in advance the units and terminology for describing the observations. The survey blank is a device for isolating one element at a time and thus intensifying the observation of it.

A questionnaire is a form prepared and distributed to secure responses to certain questions; as a general rule, these questions are factual, intended to obtain information about conditions or practices of which the respondent is presumed to have knowledge. The questionnaire has been used increasingly, however, to inquire into the opinions and attitudes of a group. In reality there is no sharp dividing line between a questionnaire and a test, although they differ significantly in their common forms.

The questionnaire is a major instrument for data-gathering in descriptive-survey studies, and is used to secure information from varied and widely scattered sources. It is probably outranked in frequency of use only by the survey test. If all the practical field studies in education, including the operation and management of schools, are considered, testing and questionnaire investigations combined probably would account for more than half of the total investigations in education. This statement does not debate the question of whether all of these practical field studies may be classified as research; whether of research character or not, tests and questionnaires rank high in frequency of use.

The questionnaire is particularly useful when one cannot readily see personally all of the people from whom he desires responses or where there is no particular reason to see the respondent personally. This technique may be used to gather data from any range of territory, sometimes international or national.

A favorite type of questionnaire investigation is concerned with status, including the personal and professional characteristics of school officers and teachers (high-school principal, junior-high-school principal, city superintendent of schools, business manager, and teachers in rural schools). Within local school systems, particularly in cities, the questionnaire technique is commonly employed to secure information from the teaching staff about such problems as training, length of service, and duties.

Another common use of the questionnaire technique concerns the current practices in school systems. The Research Division of the N.E.A. has made extensive use of this data-collecting instrument in preparing its research bulletins. In the area of teacher personnel, descriptive-survey studies have depended largely on the questionnaire, covering current practices in the selection and placement of teachers, teaching load, size of class, number of classes, number of subjects, combinations of subjects taught, and the status of groups of teachers with respect to tenure, health, legal regulations, and supply and demand.

Many financial questions have been investigated through the questionnaire approach. Financial problems are always present, whether in a depression period with very limited resources or in a post-war period of expansion with an increasingly large number of children to be educated, buildings to construct, and teachers to supply. Among the questions investigated are the tax rate levied in the local district, amount of extra levies, amount of bonded indebtedness, current indebtedness, average expenditure per pupil, average teacher's salary, and reduction or increase in expenditures.

## Psychology of the Respondent [95]

The essentially coöperative nature of the questionnaire is a characteristic too frequently overlooked by beginners in research and even by more experienced investigators. Graduate students and many others are so close to their own studies that they may lose perspective concerning what reasonably may be asked of another person, usually a complete stranger. It is reasonably certain that the questionnaire goes to people who are already busy and, although they would like to be helpful, they commonly have large obligations and duties for which their positions are responsible. The

[95] Douglas E. Scates and Alice Yeomans Scates, "Developing a Depth Questionnaire to Explore Motivation and Likelihood of Action." *Educational and Psychological Measurement* 12:620-31; Winter 1952.

practical implications are that a questionnaire study should not be undertaken unless the problem is of genuine importance, not only to the investigator, but to the particular field of knowledge; the questionnaire should be so devised that it will involve a minimum of the respondent's time.

The investigator should not center attention on what he himself desires, but primarily on the respondent's psychology—his interest, motivation, and willingness and honesty in answering. What would the investigator do if he were in the respondent's place? How can one secure the respondent's attention, sympathy, interest, and coöperation? The need is not so much for ideal rapport as for coöperation and a desire on the part of the respondent to contribute to good results in the study.

The questionnaire maker must keep in mind the psychology of the potential respondent, because the recipient of the questionnaire is not personally interested in either the investigator or his project. If the recipient of the blank helps by way of a response, he probably is using time that he needs for his own work and is doing so in a spirit of generosity or helpfulness. The investigator should think first and last about the psychology of the recipient, and only secondarily about his own desires in constructing the questionnaire. Perhaps it is better to say, think first about the purpose of the investigation, then second (and long) or finally about the psychology of the potential respondent. To say things in ways the questionnaire maker understands is of lesser importance. What will the busy recipient of the blank, in a hurry and only mildly interested, think the investigator means when he reads the question at a high rate of speed? The investigator is not likely to produce a good questionnaire that will secure long, patient, and thoughtful answers, unless he can select a special clientele.

In many cases the respondent has mixed motives, as illustrated by a study of a proposed mutual-benefit system for sick leave, presumably sponsored by a state teachers' association. Mixed motives might prevail in answering this question: "Would you join a teachers' mutual-benefit system for sick leave"? The respondent might say "yes," after every other means of sponsorship had failed, but he might say "no" in a political effort to get the state legislature to provide for a mutual-benefit system. The respondents who reply "no" may be individualists who are in good health, "not socially minded or insurance minded," and who do not wish to carry the burden of weaker persons.

One reason why respondents do not give better answers is that they seldom see the investigator's side; they are not present at the end of the study, and they may never see the results used; neither do they immediately face the question in the presence of their administrators. An effective technique is to offer the individual respondent a well phrased summary, in order to motivate interest in questionnaire studies; the summary is not so important as motivation when one is filling out a questionnaire as a member of a business organization or of a school group, unless the respondent is identified, as when completing a personal questionnaire.

## Choice of Questionnaire in Comparison with Other Techniques

Is the questionnaire the most effective method for securing the desired data? A young high-school principal wished to determine the extent of teacher turnover in two counties of Indiana. Should he use the questionnaire or some other data-gathering technique? He found that the evidence with respect to teacher turnover was readily available in the office records of the county superintendents.

A graduate student wished to investigate the job opportunities available in the printing and tailoring trades of a large city for members of different racial and minority groups. Would the employers place themselves on record concerning such problems, in the form of a written statement? The young investigator found that the interview technique proved difficult but reasonably successful in attempting to secure this type of information. A questionnaire approach probably would have failed.

Another graduate student was interested in the policy of city newspapers with respect to publication of school news. Would the editors have answered a questionnaire? The young man and his wife combined a summer trip with a schedule of interviewing the editors in a selected group of cities, in preference to attempting a questionnaire approach. (By way of coöperation in the project, the wife calculated the column inches of space given to school news in selected issues of the newspaper, while her husband was interviewing the editor.)

A dynamic young teacher, who was highly regarded by the adolescent boys of a junior high school in an underprivileged area of a large city, wished to know what these boys did with their leisure time outside school hours. Would they have given truthful answers to a questionnaire inquiry? The teacher, who had won the confidence and admiration of the boys through his knowledge of Indian lore and his skill in Indian dancing, was able to secure information that he considered reliable, through skillful interviewing techniques—results that he probably could not have obtained through a questionnaire.

Could the highly personal information of the Kinsey reports concerning the sex behavior of the human male and of the human female have been obtained through questionnaires? Apparently the investigators answered in the negative, since elaborate interviewing was the technique employed.

A pointed letter to a graduate student emphasizes that the information requested in his questionnaire is already available through documentary sources: [96]

First of all, you are asking in the questionnaire certain questions you could easily answer for yourself by consulting *Who's Who in America* or the university catalogues.

More serious is the objection which I have to the rest of your questions; you are asking me for my opinions on very complex questions, and you formulate your questions in a way that indicates you expect a dogmatic answer. To do real justice to these questions, which concern the objectives and methods of . . . sociology, I would have to write you an essay, or several papers. It is hard to imagine that you really expect me to do this for you; if you do not, then why ask me these questions? Furthermore, it so happens that I have expressed my ideas on these matters in several publications; I admit that my opinions are in some cases not stated explicitly but by implication. Now there is an old and well established way of getting information about other scholars' opinions and theories; that is, by reading and by critical interpretation. There is no substitute for this. My advice to you is to forget about the questionnaire and to study the literature.

## Does the Recipient Have the Information, and Is He Free and Willing to Respond?

Is there good reason to believe that the persons receiving the questionnaire are in a position to give the information desired? If the recipients have the information or knowledge, are they free to respond? If free to answer, are the recipients willing to do so? Should a form of questionnaire with the name detachable or without a signature be used, to encourage frank and truthful responses?

The investigator must be careful to avoid asking people questions on subjects they do not know about, or about which they have no strong conviction, for some answer is likely to result. Later, when the investigator sits down to tabulate the answers, he will not know which ones are good and which are completely worthless, since they are mixed together.

A school principal complained bitterly about five or six questionnaires received from a graduate student. He said that the questionnaires were so extensive as to require three to four weeks of time for careful completion. The request came in the form of a mimeographed letter, without return envelopes or return postage. The principal said that he seldom secured any benefit from participation in questionnaire surveys, because he rarely received a summary of the findings.

If the respondent has the information readily available, is he free, and willing, to give a truthful reaction? A state department of education early in April made a canvass of the school administrators in the state, asking

---

[96] Quoted from Rudolf Heberle, "On the Use of Questionnaires in Research: Open Letter to a Graduate Student." *American Sociological Review* 16:549; August 1951.

whether they planned to return to their positions in September. Were the administrators willing to place themselves on record so early in the spring as having tentative plans for taking a new position at the beginning of the next school year? In other words, did they feel safe in declaring their positions vacant, when a contract for a new position had not yet been signed, even though preliminary negotiations were under way?

A questionnaire study followed up the graduates of a particular college curriculum during the depression period of the first half of the 1930's, inquiring about the effectiveness of the university curriculum in preparing the graduates for a livelihood. A return of approximately 50 per cent was secured, the replies indicating fair satisfaction with the curriculum in relation to employment. Is it probable that the 50 per cent with good news and reasonably satisfactory conditions of employment replied, whereas the other half may have been discouraged, with only bad news to report, and therefore did not answer?

A teacher of eighth-grade science had introduced a wide range of supplementary reading materials and visual aids, going far beyond the textbook form of presentation. He sent a questionnaire to the parents, asking for their evaluation of the extensive reading materials and procedures. Were the parents well enough acquainted with the teaching methods to give a helpful evaluation? If some parents had unfavorable reactions, did they feel free to identify themselves, in view of the relationship of their children to the teacher?

### Stages and Administrative Aspects of Questionnaire Surveys

Many of the statistical surveys made by the U. S. Bureau of the Budget are based on the questionnaire as a data-gathering instrument. The requirements, stages, and administrative aspects of such surveys include provision for the following items: [97]

1. Purpose of the survey
2. Relation to other surveys or programs
3. Development of the survey plan
   a. Respondents
   b. Extent of coverage
   c. Frequency and timing
   d. Method of collection
   e. Consideration of nonsampling errors
   f. Standard definitions and classifications
   g. Processing and interpretation of the data
   h. Allowance for pretests and follow-ups
   i. Comparison with data from other sources

[97] *Standards for Statistical Surveys.* Exhibit A, Circular No. A-46. Washington: Executive Office of the President, Bureau of the Budget, March 28, 1952. 10 p.

    *j.* Proposed calendar
    *k.* Cost estimates
  4. Questionnaire and accompanying instructions
  5. Pretests
  6. Follow-ups
  7. Development of the sampling plan for partial coverage surveys
  8. Supervision of field enumeration
  9. Manuals and other instructions for the conduct of the survey
 10. Progress and cost reporting
 11. Preparation and publication of the final report.

A particular organization interested in opinion research, after going into a firm or business concern to make a survey, is likely to do the following things:

1. Send a letter to each employee (probably to his home) some time in advance of a questionnaire, to explain the purpose of the survey and some of the questions, and to suggest that further explanation will be provided if desired.

2. Guarantee questionnaire returns, largely by assembling the workers in a room, asking them to fill out the questionnaire before leaving, without identification.

3. Send each employee a booklet after the study is made, including the results of the survey, with a statement from the management commenting on the results (offering an explanation, furnishing relative information, or setting forth a proposed plan). The purposes of this booklet are numerous, chiefly to make the employee feel that he is an important part of the company; to give him a feeling of integration, by way of adding to his belief in the importance of himself and his work; to keep him informed so that he can behave intelligently with regard to his employment; and to make him feel that such surveys are worth while, and thus increase his coöperativeness when the next study is undertaken.

The graduate student especially should give consideration to the administrative aspects of his proposed study, both in choosing a problem and in planning the attack—the cost, space, time span, and similar problems. A number of questions are especially pertinent to questionnaire studies. Will the project require sponsorship? Is it a problem that can be finished in the allotted time? Will it require endless clerical time? Tabulating machine work, or intricate calculating machine work that cannot be arranged for? A great deal of table or desk space—more than is available? Cost for stationery, mimeographing, paper, postage, and related expenses? The graduate student is forced to keep his work within attainable time limits, even though some flexibility is possible; he cannot stretch out indefinitely his days in the graduate school.

## Larger Forms of the Questionnaire

Questionnaires sometimes take the form of a check list, which is simply a set of categories for the respondent to check; for example, the duties of principals and superintendents, to be checked in terms of frequency of performance; a list of undesirable acts of pupil behavior, to be checked by the teachers for frequency; a list of the duties of secretaries, to be checked for frequency of performance; elaborate lists of the duties of teachers, distributed to ascertain the frequency of each activity.

The check list form of questionnaire is particularly dependent upon completeness of the original list, so as to provide a convenient, suggestive list on which the respondents may check their answers. The recipient comes to depend upon the list for suggestiveness and for a classification of his responses, with the result that he is not so likely to write in additional items. In fact, items which the respondent might have recorded, had there been no categories in the list, may be omitted when he checks a list, either because the respondent considers the given list inclusive of all desired items, or because he assumes an attitude of dependence on the list.

Some types of questionnaires (for example, the depth questionnaire) go beyond statistical data and factual material into the area of attitudes, and hidden motivations. If opinion is recognized as such and the results are carefully interpreted, this is a legitimate field of investigation for the questionnaire, by way of securing a cross section of thought or attitude. In this form the questionnaire may approach the test form so closely that one cannot draw a definite line between them and may not know whether to call the instrument a test or a questionnaire; it may be both. Opinions and attitudes are facts, in so far as the responses are typical of the individuals, but they are facts of opinion. They represent the leanings or attitudes of a person, whether right or wrong. These facts of opinion are different from opinions about facts (which are frequently untrustworthy). The depth questionnaire, like the depth interview, seeks to ascertain the motivation behind attitudes, interests, preferences, and decisions.

The closed form of questionnaire, employing check responses or similar answers, is commonly used to secure categorized data. This form is time-saving for both questionnaire and interviewing techniques, exercises a directive influence in securing responses, and greatly facilitates the processes of tabulating and summarizing.

Free-response questions, or "open-end" (open-form) questions, may provide a more adequate picture of how the respondent feels about a topic, what it means to him, and the background of his answer (especially in the exploratory stages of an investigation, with a limited number of cases). The free-response technique, however, presents great difficulties in terms of time and expense for tabulating and summarizing, whether used in questionnaire or interview studies. Focused or depth interviews (and questionnaires) make extensive use of the open-end question.

To compare questionnaires and reports, both are normally means of securing information from people at a distance. There is usually better motivation for reports, however, since they are typically required by some person with authority, and there may be penalties for failure to complete the report, for omitting some item of information, or for failure to make a particular deadline. Reports are usually made at periodical intervals, which means that the procedures for securing the desired information are likely to be well established and routine, or preparation can be made in advance to meet the problem of filling out the report at a given time. Reports usually deal largely with figures, without the variety of responses frequently requested in questionnaires. The problem of sampling and interpretation in the case of reports is relatively simple, since the returns are likely to be from the entire group. Reports frequently may be used to supplement, or to take the place of, certain types of questionnaires. However, reports are relatively slow in being assembled and summarized; therefore, the versatility of the questionnaire and the freshness of its returns render it an indispensable instrument for securing current information through descriptive-survey studies.

As discussed in the section on use of documentary records as sources of data, there is the ever recurring problem of not having records entirely in the form desired. In constructing a questionnaire, it is desirable to formulate the questions in keeping with the items of official requests or regular reports so far as possible. It is likely that recorded data in such agencies as state departments of education will be adapted to these official requests or reports.

## Questionnaire Construction

Is there a good reason, from the point of view of busy persons who receive the questionnaire, for taking the trouble to give the answers requested? This question will be answered in the affirmative, if certain procedures in questionnaire construction are followed carefully. Has every trivial question been scrupulously weeded out? Sometimes the number of questions can be reduced by one-half. Are the responses simple, possibly involving only check marks after a variety of suggested answers? Do the questions avoid unnecessary specifications or details? Is the information available in documentary sources, which would make a particular question or part of the questionnaire unnecessary? Do the questions apply to the situation of the respondent? The query frequently does not fit the conditions obtaining where it is sent, particularly when questionnaires are prepared for cities of a certain general size and are sent to cities of a markedly different size. Is the purpose clear, with definite limitations, so that the questionnaire maker does not ask for everything in "shotgun" fashion? Is the question crystal clear, not only to the questionnaire maker but to the receiver? Are the items so phrased that the responses can be summarized in some appropriate form? This does not necessarily mean that all the responses must be quantitative, or yes-no, or check marks, but that the problem of summarizing should be considered when the questionnaire is being prepared. If questions of opinions are asked, is the investigator certain that opinion is what he desires and that it is worth securing from the respondent? Is precoding of the questionnaire desirable, for punching the results on tabulating machine cards for summarization?

**Criteria for constructing questionnaires.** A suggestive summary of criteria for questionnaires covers nine major recommendations,[98] with particular reference to ascertaining the educational needs of employed adults:

1. It must be short enough so that the employee will not reject it completely in too many cases and so that it will not take too much time which might be a serious drain on the work of the employees.

2. It must be of sufficient interest and have enough face appeal so that the employee will be inclined to respond to it—and to complete it. This may or may not mean that long writing should be avoided; on matters of some real interest to the employee, he may enjoy writing at some length. This has been found to be true in the case of many who responded to the depth essay questionnaire at two Naval installations.

3. The questionnaire should obtain some depth to the response in order to avoid superficial replies. It is desired rather to arouse the background of the person and to get him to give real consideration to the many factors which enter into a decision. Only in such a way will his response have some stability, in contrast to a purely momentary or ephemeral feeling. This means that the proper mind set must be obtained and that enough time must be required to allow evaluation of factors which properly condition a decision. In this connection, the questionnaire must seek to avoid insincere expressions as well as a tendency to encourage "going along with" the suggestion in the questionnaire and checking more blanks than those which really apply to the individual.

4. This ideal questionnaire must not be too suggestive or, on the other hand, too unstimulating. This is particularly true with reference to choices. One does not wish to "put words in the mouth" of the employee or, by using enticing phrases or names of courses, get him to check a lot of them which he does not want. Conversely, as referred to in the preceding paragraph, one does not want him to fail to check certain courses because, just at the moment, they do not occur to him. (This is one of the problems to be evaluated in the present report; that is, more specifically, what the effect is of using a course check list in contrast to asking the employee to make his own suggestions.)

5. The questionnaire should elicit responses which are definite but not mechanically forced. That is, a response which is too vague or ambiguous or uncrystallized is not desirable—unless it accurately represents the state of mind of the individual. If it does, then forcing his decision into a "yes" or "no" type

[98] Quoted from Douglas E. Scates and Alice V. Yeomans, *The Effect of Questionnaire Form on Course Requests of Employed Adults.* Washington: American Council on Education, 1950. p. 2-4.

of category is itself undesirable. The questionnaire should accordingly encourage definiteness without forcing it where it does not exist in the mind of the respondent.

6. Questions must be asked in such a way that the responses will not be embarrassing to the individual. It must always be made as respectable as possible to answer "no" or to give a neutral response. Otherwise the responses will show a strong tendency to be socially acceptable. While this may be technically a form of insincerity, it is such a subtle yet powerful force that the individual is not usually aware it is operating. Since most individuals are brought up to feel that they desire to be acceptable to society, it does not occur to them that they are misrepresenting themselves when they give responses which they believe are normally desirable in the scale of values connected with their culture and with their immediate group.

7. Questions must also be asked in such a manner as to allay suspicion on the part of the employee concerning hidden purposes in the questionnaire. Interviewing has revealed many questions which arise in the minds of employees and which may seriously affect the responses. These involve such thoughts as: (1) Why do "they" (the administration) want to know these things? (2) What significance will there be in the fact that I do or don't have a certain educational background? (3) What meaning will be attached to this response? (4) Will I injure my status by giving a certain answer? While such considerations can be easily dealt with by judicious preparation of the group of employees before questionnaires are distributed, the instrument itself should be of such structure as to alleviate suspicion.

8. The questionnaire must not be too narrow, restrictive, or limited in its scope or philosophy. Questionnaires are almost always made from a certain point of view or frame of reference, but they should always hold the door open for obtaining other points of view or other emphases. There should be certain questions (or possibly opportunities in most of the responses) for obtaining suggestions as to other ways of accomplishing the goal or of looking at the whole matter. Such responses may be of more value than all of the codified responses received within the limits of the initial plan.

9. The responses to the questionnaire must be valid, and the entire body of data taken as a whole must answer the basic question for which the questionnaire was designed. Validity is, in the main, a technical term, including all of the practical aspects which have been named up to this point and possibly some others in addition. Validity will, for example, require some attention to the circumstances under which a questionnaire is administered. If the employee is being asked to indicate the likelihood of his participation in it, he will not be able to give as valid responses as he would if the proposed program were fairly definite and he could say "yes" or "no." There are, further, many emotional elements connected with any human activity, and an employee who feels that his response is being forced, or that he is being asked unjustly to make decisions, may either fail to coöperate or may react in a routine and superficial manner.

**Directions for answering questions.** There is no such thing as an ideal questionnaire; if it is perfect from one aspect, it is probably too much of something or other when viewed from another angle. If perfect and complete from the sender's view, it runs the risk of being overwhelming and forbidding from the receiver's end. If highly precise, it may be too exacting to be understood by the receiver. If fully explained, the receiver may not take the time to read a lengthy explanation; and, if the directions are not complete, he may condemn the maker of the questionnaire as a careless, ignorant, or stupid person. Therefore, there would be no profit in having the theoretically best questionnaire in the world, if persons do not respond to it; the questionnaire must be attractive, as well as theoretically "perfect."

A major problem of the questionnaire technique is to make certain that the questions are answered truthfully. In many instances the respondent does not know the answer, or he does not think in such refined, sharp terms; or he is apprehensive (afraid) to tell the truth; he may feel that the question is of a personal nature. In the early research on character and personality tests, many of the investigators did not seem to understand the conditions under which youth would reveal intimate information about themselves.

In designing the record blank and the directions, the investigator has to work back and forth shuttle-like to get the record blank to fit the directions, the directions to fit the blank, and both to carry out the purposes satisfactorily. In other words, no part of the questionnaire pattern [99] can be prepared wholly independently, but each is adjusted as work proceeds, in the light of developments of another part of the whole. When the interview is used in conjunction with the questionnaire, this is still another facet of the research pattern.

The investigator should not expect that a reader with a strong mind set will pay attention to (be guided by) each word in the directions. Because the purpose is carefully defined by a single word buried here and there is no guarantee that the reader will see that word and be guided by it. The respondent is likely to go through the questionnaire with a rush, marking crude answers here and there. The intent of the questions should be crystal clear.

**Varied purposes of questions.** In questionnaire construction, not every question is for the sake of obtaining information. Some are for such purposes as the following:

1. Getting the respondent's mind on the subject or area; that is, warming up, as one may do in writing an essay response. In dealing with questions about a radio program, there is little value in asking the respondent to evaluate a pro-

[99] Douglas E. Scates and Alice V. Yeomans, *op. cit.*

Douglas E. Scates and Alice V. Yeomans, *Developing a Depth Essay Questionnaire to Assess the Market for Further Education Among Employed Scientists and Engineers.* Washington: American Council on Education, 1950. 128 p.

Douglas E. Scates and Alice Yeomans Scates, "Developing a Depth Questionnaire to Explore Motivation and Likelihood of Action." *Educational and Psychological Measurement* 12:620-31; Winter 1952.

Douglas E. Scates and Alice V. Yeomans, *Developing an Objective Item Questionnaire to Assess the Market for Further Education Among Employed Adults.* Washington: American Council on Education, 1950. 48 p.

gram he may have heard in the morning until he gets it clearly in mind; therefore, one may ask, "What did you do this morning?" Then the respondent may recite one thing after another.

2. Some questions are included because the respondent expects them; he might feel that something is missing, be uneasy, or have disrespect for the questionnaire without such items.

3. Some questions are for the purpose of catharsis; after release of possible tensions, the respondent may think better or more rationally, with less idiosyncrasy.

To cite another example,[100] in a study of the extent and structure of the market for continuing education on the part of a group of scientists and engineers, the investigators desired to ascertain an individual's likelihood of taking college-credit courses after work hours if offered conveniently. The director of the project sought to justify inclusion of the in-service courses in the questionnaire because of larger purposes and interests (to sharpen the choices and the thinking of the respondents, and to give everyone something to respond to on the questionnaire).

**Questions and categories.** The items referred to in the questions should be definite in the mind of the respondent with respect to all or many of the most important ways in which they can vary; for example, in the teaching profession, matters of rank and level of position, within any type of teaching work. When a number of categories are offered in which to check, it is important to see that they represent real choices to the respondent—not academically conceived categories, possibly framed in language foreign or strange to the respondent; the choices must be phrased as the respondent would think of them. As such, the categories must be reasonably complete, moderately detailed, in the main non-overlapping (not necessarily completely so); as a rule, coördinate (not necessarily completely so). Although considerable detail may be interesting to the investigator, and more suggestive to the respondent, it requires great care in interpretation.

By way of concrete illustration, a graduate student sent out a questionnaire that had too tight a set of classes or categories. His failure to give the blank a preliminary tryout probably resulted in this shortcoming. His analysis of teacher turnover in a county school system included a classification of approximately eight reasons for leaving a teaching position. When he came to summarize the results, it required two pages of responses (thirty-one reasons) that had been written in by the respondents, which could not be accommodated in his classified list of eight reasons. Although he might not have been able to foresee thirty-one additional reasons for leaving a position, through a tryout of the questionnaire he certainly would

[100] *Ibid.*

have discovered certain large categories to cover the items written in the questionnaire blank, with perhaps a miscellaneous heading for items left over.

**Questions in relation to responses.** In questionnaire construction the investigator should consider whether the questions can be interpreted if the respondent does not answer fully. What is the logic of non-response? How many of the questions can be answered by "depends," "no," and other single words? What can be done if there are a great many such responses? Can the investigator interpret them logically, for the purposes of the study?

The questionnaire maker should avoid asking questions which a person will mostly answer with "yes," just to avoid unpleasantness or censure, or because he thinks that "yes" is the expected answer. This is a human tendency that is partially offset through skillful questionnaire construction. One technique is to include the opposite question, giving opportunity to respond that way, with a number of such pairs provided, and also an opportunity for comment and examples.

In general, questions should not be asked in either more or less specific terms than the respondent's thinking is likely to be. Therefore, the investigator must use judgment, and understand the nature of the group of respondents. One graduate student had a tendency to ask questions with legal specificity and exactness, which did not increase the precision of results, because the results cannot be any more precise than the attitude of the respondent or the knowledge he possesses.

In the chapter on formulation of the problem is a letter written by a student to the Commissioner of Education in Alaska. Obviously this is the kind of request that will secure no response, mainly because it is not focused. It reflects a wandering mind; asks for "everything." It would be interesting for a graduate student to go through this letter and select a few central items which might reasonably be investigated, in the light of the topic, and to formulate a few sentences, or questions, that would "go to the heart" of the matter, possibly in the form of a brief questionnaire.

In many cases the respondent will not make clear distinctions in filling out the questionnaire; hence, the investigator often asks two or more questions, in order to make the distinction (or limits) of a single question clear; for example:

Profession_____Occupational Specialty, or Specialization within Profession
_____Number of Courses_____Semester Hours_____

In considering the items in the preceding lines, it should be remembered that people have a tendency to magnify or to make the most favorable response. The investigator should allow for this tendency, at the same time hopefully attempting to secure accurate information concerning college training, through making the distinction clear by two questions.

In a college faculty a questionnaire was circulated to ascertain the desires of the staff members with respect to the handling of certain problems of organization and administration. A dichotomous questionnaire of six pages was submitted; on each item the staff member was to make a choice between two alternatives. This means that he voted on a great many things for which he had no strong conviction, and to which he had given no particular thought. Once he had voted, his response was considered meaningful, and was counted along with the reactions of staff members who had strong convictions. Therefore, the results were non-interpretable, because they were meaningless. This type of situation can be avoided by using a third alternative for each item, such as, "no definite feeling or conviction," or by giving general directions to the effect that the respondents should answer only the items on which they have a definite feeling. It is just as important to ascertain that a faculty member has *no* crystalized reaction to a particular proposal as it is to know that he has a definite conviction on another matter. Chance reactions should not be mixed up with firm convictions, or the results will be misleading.

**Ambiguous questions and responses.** The following question is an impossible one, in terms of an accurate answer, since it does not specify what base is desired in responding: "How does your present monthly salary rate for teachers compare (in per cent) with your pre-depression rate?"

A city newspaper printed a questionnaire concerning what its subscribers read. The reader was asked to check whether he read various items regularly, occasionally, or never. No instructions were given as to how to mark the questionnaire for a family. If any one member of the family read some item regularly, should that be checked? Or should the questionnaire be checked only for the head of the family? Or should each member of the family return his own questionnaire? While the latter plan might be desirable, the newspaper might desire a frequency tabulation based on subscriptions. The plan of having only one person, such as the head of the family, check his interests has the limitation of not representing completely the preferences of other members of the family, who may have something to say about whether the subscription to the particular newspaper is maintained. The newspaper should have made its desires clear.

In a group of municipal teachers colleges in a large city (referred to as the "home city" in this discussion), the administrators wished to know the localities where the graduates of the current academic year would be willing to accept positions. One of the items of a questionnaire was as follows:

> Upon completion of your course of study, where would you consider accepting a school position? (If you presently hold a school position, answer the question in relation to your next school position.)
> 1. The home city only (public or private schools)
> 2. Outside the home city but within daily commuting distance
> 3. 40-100 miles (non-commuting)
> 4. 100-200 miles
> 5. 200-500 miles
> 6. No limitation as to distance.

Some students checked only the first choice; several students checked several choices, or all the possibilities they would consider. How should the results be interpreted? How tabulated? Such questions should be avoided, since they leave the respondent uncertain, and secure various kinds of responses.

In interpreting these questionnaire returns, it is apparent that some students were of the opinion they should indicate their first choice only, whereas others thought they should indicate each locality in which they would consider accepting a teaching position. Consequently, some students indicated only one locality, while others indicated more than one. In tabulating the replies to this question, the students were classified according to a single locality. When more than one locality was indicated, the student was classified as being interested in accepting a teaching position in that locality checked which is most distant from the home city. To present the problem of interpretation in more detail, if a student circled Item 3 and only this number, should it be interpreted as meaning that he would be interested in accepting a teaching position only if it were in a community located 40-100 miles from the home city? Or, should it be interpreted to mean that the student would also be interested in accepting a teaching position in private or public schools in the home city or in a school located outside the home city but within daily commuting distance? From experience in counseling students and registrants for teacher placement, it seems within reason that the second interpretation be made.

**Placement of detailed lists.** In questionnaire construction, a device for making questionnaires seem not so long and, therefore, rendering them more likely to be filled out, is to place detailed material (such as a list of subjects) on a sheet or two at the end of the schedule, and simply refer to the list by a notation near the beginning of the blank or form; for example, "If you would like to engage in further study . . . please list on p. 3 the courses you desire." This device permits the questionnaire to go on two pages, plus a third page containing a list of courses. If not abused, this technique probably makes the respondent feel that he is moving through the questionnaire rapidly, since he thinks the list of questions is fairly short. At least the questionnaire seems to be reasonably brief. This procedure is especially useful in handling lists that do not apply to every respondent.

### Tryout or Pretesting

It is essential that the criticisms of qualified persons be secured before the final form of the questionnaire is prepared and mailed out. It is desirable to try out a few copies of the schedule and to examine the returns before the instrument is used on a large scale. Questionnaires and related instruments for gathering data (tests, classification schemes, check lists, rating scales, score cards, and other similar schedules) need validation in terms of practical use, in addition to whatever theoretical and statistical precautions may have been taken in the initial preparation of the data-gathering instruments. Experienced workers have learned that an individual is not likely to think of all the ways in which a group may respond, and that one cannot anticipate adequately the interpretations of others or the varying complexities of the situations that will arise.

A preliminary form of the questionnaire, prepared and tested before mailing in quantity, probably will lead to revision of certain items. The results of this tryout should be analyzed in a preliminary way to determine whether the data warrant conclusions significant for the purpose of the study. Rough tables should be drawn up to see whether the responses can be tabulated satisfactorily and whether the data of the tables provide significant answers to the major questions of the investigation. This preliminary step may lead to deletion of useless questions or to adding items that are needed to round out the study properly.

An engineer, who was giving advice concerning the construction of a questionnaire for scientists and engineers, suggested that the schedule should be tried out, because it might have weaknesses that would show up only under test (a phrasing to which he was accustomed in his own work). Another consultant on the same project recommended that a special study be made of those cases who do not respond in an initial tryout of the questionnaire, then attempt to make the blank so engaging or so well adapted to these non-respondents that they would not fail to answer the main questionnaire.

With particular reference to the questionnaire, the manual of the Bureau of the Budget emphasizes that it is desirable to test the feasibility of the survey plan in advance, with pretests designed and conducted to obtain answers to a limited number of explicit questions relating to such topics as the following:

Relative effectiveness and costs of alternative questionnaires, instructions, and operating procedures

Acceptability and intelligibility of the questions from the respondent's point of view

Possible misunderstandings of questions and procedure on the part of the interviewers

Clarity and applicability of definitions and classifications

Completeness of questions for correct coding and interpretation

Defects in the forms, maps, lists, instructions, etc.

Estimates of strata means and variances

Response rates.

## Evidence of Questionnaire Validity

If one asks, "How can the validity of a questionnaire be judged?" the answer must be determined by the possibilities that lie in a given situation. In some cases, where answers are definite and specific, it may be possible to check them against evidence already on record. This has been done in a number of studies of questionnaire validity. In the broader sense, however, validity must be judged in the light of various types of evidence: [101]

1. Is the question *on* the subject? Is the question saturated with the elements of the subject? Does it, when taken together with other questions, cover the many facets or aspects of the subject? Does it effectively exclude irrelevant factors from the response—those which are not desired? Does the question (or the response) contribute something which is unique—so that the individual item is not duplicating other items? The evidence on this point is partly a matter of analysis of the formulation of the question, as judged and tried out by various persons, and it is also partly a matter of study and analysis of the returns.

2. Is the question perfectly clear and unambiguous? Are its implications clearly understood? Is the general frame of reference from which it is asked, and from which the answers should be given, clear? This aspect is a major one in reliability (which is an aspect of validity). It can be checked on through trying out the instrument in advance and following each trial by interviews to get at the structure of thought lying behind the responses which were given.

3. Does the question get at something stable, something relatively deep seated, well considered, non-superficial, and not ephemeral, but something which is typical of the individual or of the situation? This is a second large aspect of reliability. The evidence for it can come in part from preliminary evaluation and tryout, but it must in the main come from research and study extending over a long period. The answer will depend partly on the entire questionnaire and its administration.

4. Does the question pull? That is, will it be responded to by a large enough proportion of employees to permit it to have validity? Does it seem to be engaging enough to get responses with some depth and reality to them? The criterion is particularly important in the negative sense; if persons do not respond the item cannot be valid.

[101] Quoted from Douglas E. Scates and Alice V. Yeomans, *The Effect of Questionnaire Form on Course Requests of Employed Adults, op. cit.,* p. 4-7.

5.  Do the responses show a reasonable range of variation? Sometimes this range will not be as large as expected, sometimes it will be larger, but certainly if there is no range of response where there should be, the question cannot be valid. In judging this aspect one will have to rely upon his general knowledge of the population, and this may be supplemented by other evidence with which a particular item should be correlated. However, if there is no variation, there cannot be any correlation.

6.  Is the information obtained consistent? Does it agree with what is known? Does it agree with expectancy—or if not, does its departure from what is expected seem to be valid? Does it fit in with the general pattern of information which is obtained, or does it seem to controvert other information? Does it form part of a pattern which is reasonable and logical? Or does it constitute the basis for further research—a special study designed to ascertain the explanation for inconsistency? Does a particular trait exhibit the correlation with certain other traits, on which evidence is obtained, which corresponding studies of similar groups or similar situations have led one to expect? In other words, here is the problem of determining not only if the responses show the proper variation but also if this variation correlates with other traits to the expected degree. This problem must be dealt with partly as a matter of analysis and partly as a matter of background and judgment growing out of experience with this type of work.

7.  Is the item sufficiently inclusive? That is, are the full scope and intent of the question so clearly indicated that the respondent will not omit parts of the response through lack of certainty as to what the question desired? For example, in a question on the educational history of the individual, he may wonder whether certain courses taken during service in the Armed Forces should be included, whether night school and correspondence courses are desired, etc. In asking an employee what courses he wants, is he permitted to respond that he wants certain courses only in review and refresher form? Is it pertinent for him to indicate that he thinks the courses should be given within work hours rather than out-of-hours? Is it possible for him to contribute an alternative idea to the effect that the desired result might be better obtained by a different means? (While the aspect was mentioned elsewhere in the list, it is to be thought of as part of the matter of comprehensiveness or inclusiveness or scope of an item.) The form of question should indicate clearly that such elements are to be included or excluded. The amount of credit or the length of a course (as one semester or one year or two years, meeting one hour a week or three hours a week or five hours a week) should be specifically asked for if this is important for the analysis of the data. Whether such elements are sufficiently present in the questionnaire item is something which can be evaluated in part from the early tryout and follow-up interviews before the instrument is regularly used. It will in part come from the experience of the questionnaire maker. And it will come finally from working with the responses—in how many cases is a certain aspect omitted when it is desired? Of course it is not possible sometimes to tell when certain things are completely omitted, but there are situations in which certain aspects of the response are obviously missing.

8.  Is there a possibility of using an external criterion to evaluate the questionnaire? In some cases it can be obtained. In the present study it was hoped to validate all of the instruments by ascertaining what persons actually enrolled in courses that were offered and what persons who had requested courses did not enroll when those desired courses were really given. Actually, such an external criterion did not become available in time for use in the study and is something which should constitute the basis of a continuing study over a period of years.

## Follow-up

Since a high percentage of returns, above 95 per cent, is now known to be important, if results (especially aggregates) are to be accurate, means of securing the returns become of increased importance. An analysis of the membership of a professional organization [102] involved the following ingenious procedures by way of following up the original questionnaire:

A card or letter calling attention to the questionnaire, one to two weeks after sending the blank.

Possibly a second reminder, probably only a post card.

A second mailing of the entire questionnaire, with a new cover page or accompanying letter, without waiting too long for this second mailing; persons may have misplaced the first questionnaire or it may have become buried on a desk.

Possibly a personal letter at this point, individually written and signed, as a special appeal for coöperation, with a return stamped envelope.

A short form of the questionnaire was mailed, asking for just a few questions or items of information (perhaps sent by airmail or special delivery), phrased so as to cover the items most essential to the study.

A second mailing of the short questionnaire was sent to a relatively small number by special delivery, with an encouraging personal letter. (It may be necessary to scratch off the list at intervals any persons unduly irritated or those who have good reason for not responding; however, these names must be included in the count in calculating percentages.)

Supplementary material went to all those who had returned the abbreviated questionnaire, including a few more essential items of information, and informing them that this is the last round.

Other special means and techniques included mailing of a questionnaire to the member, partially filled out in advance with answers deemed likely for him, together with a personal letter, suggesting that the information would not be used without his approval and asking that he go the rest of the way to complete the questionnaire; forwarding of liberal postage, transportation, or communication expenses; long distance telephone; and telegraph.

These painstaking and laborious devices secured a return of 99 per cent from a membership list of 600.

One device, developed to prevent delinquency in filing or completing questionnaires, was employed by a government agency interested in collecting periodic reports on a certain type of business. In its early surveys, the agency encountered considerable difficulty, because some of the firms failed to respond by the deadline date of the survey. A check of these delinquent organizations usually revealed that the person responsible for filling out the survey had not received it, often because of improper referral within the firm. This failure usually was not discovered until attention was called

---

[102] Douglas E. Scates, "Analysis of a Professional Organization: The American Educational Research Association in 1948." *Growing Points in Educational Research,* 111-42. 1949 Official Report of The American Educational Research Association. Washington: A.E.R.A., 1949.

to it by a broadside of telegrams after the passing of the deadline date. Under such circumstances, the government agency could make only estimates for the missing firms; such estimates are poor substitutes for survey responses from the firms themselves. A corrective device was developed in the form of a specially printed return post card, to be mailed back by the business immediately upon receipt of the survey material. The post card acknowledged receipt of the survey with note of the due date, and the name, title, and telephone number of the person responsible for completing the blank. Ten days after mailing of the survey blank, the return post cards were checked against the mailing list. Any firm which had not filed its return post card was then mailed a second set of survey material by registered mail, and asked again to acknowledge receipt by mailing the return post card. This device helps to reduce delinquency on the part of the respondent; it warns the collecting agency well in advance where non-response may be likely, and provides the name of the officer responsible for the report (tending to eliminate one of the causes of delinquency, namely, misrouting of the questionnaire).[103]

## Percentage of Returns and Bias

It is not satisfactory simply to mail out a certain number (no matter how large) of questionnaires and then take any proportion that happens to come back. Such data (if short of an acceptable per cent of returns) have never been dependable, and now are definitely known to be poor. The investigator should feel the necessity of devising carefully the whole program of work, starting with the framing of the original questionnaire, so as to secure a high per cent of returns. He does not naively make out a questionnaire, shrug his shoulders, and send it out, with the expectation that the post office will complete the job for him. The questionnaire maker says to himself, "I must secure from 90 per cent to 100 per cent returns (depending on the seriousness of the study) and I must work out an entire plan for accomplishing this objective."

Questionnaire workers are no longer content with fragmentary returns. They are studying methods of securing a larger percentage of returns through better questions, follow-up, and sponsorship; checking results to see whether typical; and studying non-response by more elaborate methods. Questionnaire users at one time assumed that non-respondents were the same as respondents; now they assume otherwise, unless there is evidence to the contrary. It should be said that questionnaire returns generally have

[103] *Statistical Reporter*, April 1952. Washington: Director for Statistical Standards, Bureau of the Budget, Executive Office of the President, 1952. p. 72-73.

fallen short of the goals described in the preceding statements. (In the per cents quoted below it is questionable to use decimal figures, when the sampling error probably is large.)

The mean percentages of questionnaire returns from a large number of different investigations were as follows: 170 masters' theses at Indiana State Teachers College, 71.74 per cent; 204 doctoral dissertations at Teachers College, Columbia University, 70.65 per cent; and 59 research studies reported in the *Journal of Educational Research,* 80.71 per cent.[104]

An example of doubtful sampling procedure is found in a questionnaire study of school clubs (as part of the program of extra-curricular activities in the high schools of a particular state). Of a total of 800 forms distributed, only 442 usable returns, 55 per cent, were received. The statement of the reporter is that the returns provide a geographic representation of the high schools of the state, but that the schools with higher enrollment are more liberally represented among the respondents. The final statement by way of the interpretation appears to be questionable or doubtful, to the effect that the schools responding are fairly representative of the conditions for school clubs existing within the state as a whole and are not more favorable than the actual status within the high schools of the state.

As another example of incomplete questionnaire returns, a staff member of a speech department in a college ventured the opinion that she had good returns from a questionnaire, 52 per cent, particularly since the blank was quite detailed and five pages in length. "Goodness" in this sense is entirely irrelevant, since it does not improve in the least the representativeness of the returns. This investigator should say, in writing up the report, that the results may be completely negated by the cases not represented, since they are approximately equal to the number of respondents. The proper procedure would have been to follow up the 48 per cent who had not replied.

To cite another illustration of bias in mail questionnaires, during World War II a blank was mailed to a selected list of farmers, for the purpose of evaluating the need for farm laborers. Most of the large operators returned the questionnaire listing their shortages, but most of the small farmers were too busy doing their own work to bother about replying. The result was a fantastic estimate of three or four laborers needed on the average farm. While the investigating agency had not been particularly wise in constructing and distributing the questionnaire, it did have enough ex-

[104] J. R. Shannon, "Percentages of Returns of Questionnaires in Reputable Educational Research." *Journal of Educational Research* 42:138-41; October 1948.

perience and insight to recognize the absurdity of the returns and suppressed the report.[105]

## Editing Returns

An investigator may need to check returns:

1. To see whether different parts of the questionnaire response are consistent.
2. To correct clear errors, as when a response is contrary to well known facts.
3. To bring the used or the intended summarizing categories into line with comments written on the questionnaire.

Some persons respond ambiguously to two categories when only one can be used, or they may respond to one with a question mark. There is the instance of the respondent who checked everything (incompatibles), revealing that a check mark was his way of showing he had read or checked off every item on the blank. (This was ascertained by talking with him personally.)

As an earlier step which precedes editing, in questionnaire construction the investigator should avoid non-exclusive categories that are compound in varying degrees, perhaps in hierarchical fashion. One probably should avoid detailed compound categories in so far as possible, particularly when unusual or technical. When the captions or categories are not mutually exclusive, the problem of editing of returns is difficult, involving more than the work of a clerk adding up columns and the count on a comptometer. It requires time to read the written notes and to interpret, then to rearrange the figures on the original record and to make a clear record of what was done and why, so that it will not be puzzling later. In some cases judgment will be necessary to detect errors in the returns, and in other instances the details or the totals will simply be in the wrong columns and must be caught and moved to the correct position. Careful checking usually calls for much more than mechanical and routine clerical operations. For this reason some persons argue the desirability of hand work, as compared with machine tabulation. The requirements of thorough checking also indicate the desirability of providing for written notes on the questionnaire and of encouraging the respondents to explain or comment, in addition to giving the figure requested in the categories.

Editing of questionnaire returns frequently requires that the blanks be reëxamined in the light of the analyzed data. In an analysis of the membership of a professional organization, when the 600 returns had been tabulated, two very general categories were found relatively high: "administrators not

---

[105] George W. Snedecor, "On the Design of Sampling Investigations." *American Statistician* 2:6-9,13; December 1948.

otherwise described," 26 cases; "none of the foregoing descriptions fits me," 18 cases. Such general descriptions tell one little or nothing, and may make a reader have an uneasy feeling about the study, as though it is sloppy and meaningless. In this instance the director of the project and his assistant went back through the pack of 600 cards, looking carefully at the full returns for these 44 cases, and on the basis of positions, titles, and institutions reported, they reclassified most of the forty-four cases into more specific and meaningful categories.[106] It may be that such general categories are necessary on a categorical blank, but respondents too easily drop into them; such classifications require less thought, less discrimination, on the part of the respondent.

In this same membership survey, the investigator needed to determine whether, for practical purposes of tabulation, Teachers College and Columbia University were the same. Many more persons reported having degrees from Columbia University than specified Teachers College, which is absurd in relation to the membership of an educational organization. Therefore, the investigator decided that, for purposes of the tabulation, the two categories had better be combined, *with a footnote explaining what had been done.*

Investigators, particularly graduate students, should keep their questionnaire returns until the end of the project or until the thesis is completed, probably until the graduate thesis has been accepted by the faculty. Questions frequently arise that have not been anticipated. Even in the investigator's own analysis, he may later need additional light on some questions or a further breakdown. For the same reason he should mark clearly how each questionnaire is counted, on items that are ambiguously or doubtfully marked by the respondent, because he probably will go through the questionnaires more times than anticipated. If ambiguous replies are not marked clearly as to handling, the answers in rechecking will not be consistent; for example, whether widows are counted as single or married, or how to classify a divorced person who has not remarried.

## Tabulating and Summarizing Returns

There is always the question of whether there is much gain in writing down the cautions one should observe in good office work with figures, whether in accounting operations or in research studies, since the person not imbued with the spirit of carefulness simply will turn away from such cautions. This wisdom has to be learned either through hard experience by the person who is held accountable for dependable results, or through

[106] Douglas E. Scates, "Analysis of a Professional Organization: The American Educational Research Association of 1948," *op. cit.*

apprenticeship with someone whom the novice respects, and from whom he is willing to learn attitudes of care and watchfulness.

In the physical handling of questionnaire returns for purposes of tabulating, there are three methods, with the choice dependent on the circumstances:

1. Sometimes the questionnaire can be used directly, without copying off the material before tabulation. This is likely to be true when the questionnaire is a single page, which permits the questionnaire to be handled much like a data card (with data transferred from questionnaires or other sources).

2. In an initial list table the responses for each questionnaire (or other case) may be put on a single line, which permits a preliminary overview of the results, by way of showing (perhaps better than data cards will) what the range is likely to be.

3. Data cards have their chief advantage for purposes of cross classification or tabulation, because they can be sorted once for a trait, and then sorted again on one or more secondary traits. Data cards also can be checked readily when tabulations are made. There is the physical advantage of allowing a sub-group of cards to be removed from the main pack for use at some other place.

Tabulation of simple, objective responses is relatively easy, but there are many cases where the response must be interpreted, built up from scattered evidence, or estimated. In some studies the questionnaire data are checked, or validated, or supplemented by going directly to a number of places (such as cities and counties) and checking on conditions and facts, then using such direct information for comparison with the questionnaire returns.

The problems of tabulating and summarizing questionnaire returns are numerous and varied, as illustrated by a membership analysis of a professional research organization.[107] For example, should all returned questionnaires be included in the tabulation, even if the blanks are marked "no longer member," "retired," "inapplicable?" Should only "usable" returns be counted? What degree of completeness is required before a questionnaire is considered usable? Should returns by telephone be counted? If the investigator knows one of the non-respondents well enough to fill in the questionnaire, should it be counted? If the information for a non-respondent is available in various records and can be pieced together by the investigator, should this non-respondent be included? Should a questionnaire received too late for inclusion in the tabulation be counted in the over-all statement of the percentage returned? What disposal should be made of a return in such bad handwriting that it cannot be read? If the investigator completes the questionnaire for a non-respondent, then telephones him the answers for a verbal approval, or mails the blank for

107 *Ibid.,* p. 111-42.

approval, should this "return" be counted statistically? When a secretary writes that the non-responding member of the organization is temporarily in a foreign country and cannot be reached in time to be included in the report? If the member's wife writes that her husband is in the hospital with a long illness and cannot reply? If the post office returns the questionnaire unopened, with the notation, "address unknown"? If the member is deceased, but died after the date set for the description of the group? If the reply is "resigned," but the resignation was after the date set for the survey?

A perplexing difficulty in handling and summarizing questionnaire returns is that they come in at different times. Probably the investigator never delays the beginning of the processing work (editing, checking for consistency and completeness, and related matters) until all the straggling returns have come in and all the follow-up is completed. There is no good reason for so delaying the summarizing process, since the returns should be edited and re-submitted at once if in error. These procedures necessitate complete records: notes clipped to each pile of returns labeling what has been done, what has not been done or what is to be done next, or what must be done before a particular pile of questionnaire returns is combined with some other pile.

If the investigator employs tabulating machines to summarize questionnaire returns, he should be prepared to check back many times against original data. Many cases will arise where he will have to (or wish to) identify the individuals at one or the other extreme of a distribution—he will read the machine cards, copy off the serial numbers, look up on the original returns where the data are written out in full. He may discover mistakes where suspected or may secure additional information for use in further analyses. He may wish to list by name (in the text of the report) the individual cases in the extremes (or other critical area) of a distribution (especially if the report is distributed only to persons who know such cases by name), as a matter of assuring the reader that such cases can exist and are authentic.

In one questionnaire inquiry a number of returns were counted which were blank, except for the name of the respondent. These should not have been counted, since they represent returns only in the physical sense and not at all in the research sense. By including such blank reports, one can spuriously run the percentage of returns high. These blank questionnaires should not appear in any of the tables. However, there still remains for decision the difficult question, How complete must a questionnaire be to justify inclusion in the tabulation of results?

It is important in questionnaire summarizing to make a marked distinction between zero as a frequency and "no information." Failure to make this differentiation in summarizing schedules is more likely to be serious than in most situations, because the condition arises so frequently in questionnaire work. For example, in an activity index of professional educators,[108] certain members have frequencies of zero; and a number of persons did not supply this information (or enough information for the investigator to compute it). It would not be satisfactory to average the "no information" group in with the others in calculating a mean; contrariwise it would be wrong to leave out the zero's because they were actual, correct values.

One graduate student, working on his thesis problem, had the first tabulation of his questionnaire returns summarized in a very rough way on five pieces of letter-size paper pasted end to end. Beginning workers frequently form large tabulation sheets in this way, possibly even starting with sheets about 17 x 22 inches. This procedure is not necessary, since the tabulation can be broken up into convenient units, even for the first rough work.

### Interpreting Questionnaire Returns

The questionnaire technique presents both opportunities and difficulties in interpretation of returns. It has been pointed out elsewhere in this book that descriptive-survey studies should prove valuable in broadening perspective and in calling attention to desirable ways of dealing with problems or issues, through noting emergent and novel or unique practices. Such examples are not likely to be sensed by the worker who depends upon a mechanical or clerical tabulation of questionnaire returns concerning practices and conditions.

Interpretation of results which are in the form of frequencies is often inadequate and difficult. If 60 per cent, or even 75 per cent, of a group of administrators replying to a questionnaire indicate that they solve a problem in a certain way, or perform a particular duty once each week or monthly, what should the conclusion be? Is this a desirable means of solving the particular problem? Is it necessarily more effective than another method that comes to light in the survey, of which the majority have not yet thought or heard? How can the investigator determine whether the particular duty is important? Can cruciality be inferred from frequency? Or can the importance of an event or a duty for a given individual be inferred from the prevalence of the event or duty for the majority of the group? It is widely known that a spirit of complacency frequently results when a descriptive survey reveals that conditions in one's school system or classroom are about the same as found in the majority of the

[108] *Ibid.*

schools canvassed. Although a particular principal or teacher may feel comfortable, with such facts in his possession, professional workers of insight know that progress comes only through the practices and procedures of persons who diverge from the mode.

A significant factor affecting the quality of questionnaire research is the extent to which questions of interpretation of responses are decided on the basis of slight, flimsy evidence; that is, guessing what a response means when one cannot read the handwriting or when the information given is fragmentary. Such items should be made the subject for checking, running back to more dependable sources of information. However, when a clerk lays a questionnaire before the director of the project and asks, "How would you interpret this?" the temptation is strong to give an answer based on general evidence. One needs to be mindful of the motto, "In research our business is not to guess; it is to find out."

An attempt to classify persons with respect to their latest formal or systematic academic education presented a number of problem cases that were difficult to classify in the categories set up. In one case seventy-six credits of undergraduate study in mechanical engineering had been completed, with no college degree. The pertinent questions concern his highest level of education and when it was attained. A reference to the answer on another page of the questionnaire showed that he was still taking courses and hoping to secure a degree. Therefore, his seventy-six credits were interpreted as three years of college work and the current year was recorded as his latest year of college study. In another case the four years of undergraduate study were completed in 1922, with an A.B. degree in mathematics; graduate courses for teacher credit were pursued in 1927 and 1931 in summer sessions, totaling eleven credits; one course was taken in a graduate school of agriculture in 1945-46, with four credits; and a quality-control course during the working day in 1950; highest degree reported, A.B. In this case the highest level of training was regarded as a bachelor's degree plus further training, and his latest year of active effort was recorded as 1946, since his work in 1950 did not seem to be at the level of college credit. To decide such matters, careful definitions had to be drawn up for the meaning to be attached to "formal or systematic academic education," so that cases could be handled uniformly and so that a definite, precise meaning could be conveyed to the reader of the research report.

Problem cases illustrate the ever present need for interpretation (putting together many lines of evidence in different parts of the questionnaire), the value of certain questions that permit lengthy answers (with the thought that certain information may be given, of value in throwing light on other questions), and in a few cases estimating certain answers in the light of general information when an estimate seems better than no evidence whatever. It should be borne in mind, however, that such estimates should constitute a very small portion of the total.

One investigator said that, in tallying the results of his questionnaires, if a business firm could not do a particular thing because the situation made it impossible, he nevertheless "gave the company credit" for the item and entered a "yes" response, because he knew the particular organization would have done so if possible; therefore, the answer he tallied "would not count against them." That is, if there was no college near the particular business organization, the investigator gave the company credit for coöperating with a college, provided the organization had a good training program, because he decided that the business or industry undoubtedly would have coöperated if possible. This procedure represents a degree of interpretation of responses which is wholly unjustified.

### The Literature on Questionnaire Inquiries

The literature on the questionnaire technique and numerous examples of questionnaire investigations are liberally represented in the references at the beginning of this section, and especially in such library tools as the *Encyclopedia of Educational Research, Review of Educational Research,* and *Education Index.* In other parts of this book, including the references at the beginning of this section, may be found supplementary materials pertinent to certain details of the questionnaire technique: classification, categories, enumeration, gathering data from documentary sources and records, analysis, coding, tabulation (hand and machine), and evaluation.

Two especially detailed treatments of the questionnaire and schedule may be characterized briefly. With engaging humor and a light touch, Payne has presented many-sided insights for framing questions, as secured from extensive experience in polling investigations. He includes many recommendations and examples in discussing definition of the issue or purpose of the study, major types of questions (free-answer, dichotomous, multiple-choice, and others), treatment of respondents, selection and use of appropriate words and language, and readability. The recommendations are summarized in a list of one hundred items at the end of the book.[109] Parten has provided an especially thorough and helpful treatment, with many illustrations and numerous references to the literature, covering the construction of schedules and questionnaires, procedures for the mail questionnaire, sources of bias, editing the schedule data, and coding and tabulating the data.[110]

[109] Stanley L. Payne, *op. cit.*
[110] Mildred Parten, *op. cit.*, Chapters 6, 11-15.

## INTERVIEW TECHNIQUES AND STUDIES[111]

The treatment of the interview in this section is considerably briefer than the preceding section dealing with the questionnaire, since many of the concepts and techniques presented in discussing questionnaire procedure are applicable to interviewing. Skillful interviewing, however, is

[111] Arthur L. Assum and Sidney J. Levy, "Analysis of a Non-Directive Case With Follow-Up Interview." *Journal of Abnormal and Social Psychology* 43:78-89; January 1948.

F. C. Bartlett and Others, *The Study of Society:* Methods and Problems. London: Kegan Paul, Trench, Trubner and Co., 1939. p. 317-27.

W. V. Bingham and B. V. Moore, *How to Interview*. Third Revised Edition. New York: Harper and Bros., 1941. 263 p.

A. B. Blankenship, Editor, *How to Conduct Consumer and Opinion Research:* The Sampling Survey in Operation. New York: Harper and Bros., 1946. xi + 314 p.

Margaret Blenkner and Others, "A Study of Interrelated Factors in the Initial Interview with New Clients." *Social Case Work* 32:23-30; January 1951.

R. F. Berdie, "Psychological Processes in the Interview." *Journal of Social Psychology* 18:3-31; August 1943.

David P. Boder, *I Did Not Interview the Dead*. Urbana: University of Illinois Press, 1949. xx + 220 p.

Emory S. Bogardus, *Introduction to Social Research*. Los Angeles: Suttonhouse, 1936. p. 104-50.

Earl F. Carnes and Francis P. Robinson, "The Role of Client Talk in the Counseling Interview." *Educational and Psychological Measurement* 8:635-44; Winter 1948.

B. J. Covner, "Studies of Phonographic Recordings of Verbal Material: Written Reports of Interviews." *Journal of Applied Psychology* 28:89-98; April 1944.

Stanley E. Davis and Francis P. Robinson, "A Study of the Use of Certain Techniques for Reducing Resistance during the Counseling Interview." *Educational and Psychological Measurement* 9:297-306; Autumn 1949.

Stephen R. Deane, "The Interview as a Tool of Adult Education Research." *Adult Education Bulletin* 14:150-57; June 1950.

Ernest Dichter, "Psychology in Market Research." *Harvard Business Review* 25:432-43; Summer 1947. On depth interviewing.

John T. Dickson and Others, "The Contribution of Social Workers to the Interviewing Skills of Psychologists." *Journal of Social Case Work* 30:318-24; October 1949.

Albert Ellis, "Questionnaire Versus Interview Methods in the Study of Human Love Relationships." *American Sociological Review* 12:541-53; October 1947; 13:61-65; February 1948.

M. C. Elmer, *op. cit.*, p. 345-58.

Horace B. English and Victor Raimy, *Studying the Individual School Child:* A Manual of Guidance. New York: Henry Holt and Co., 1941. p. 24-30.

Clifford E. Erickson, *The Counseling Interview*. New York: Prentice-Hall, 1950. 174 p.

Anne Fenlason, *Essentials in Interviewing:* For the Interviewer Offering Professional Services. New York: Harper and Bros., 1952. xi + 352 p.

Norman Fenton, *The Counselor's Approach to the Home*. Stanford University, Calif.: Stanford University Press, 1943. 32 p.

Norman Fenton, *The Counselor's Interview With the Student*. Stanford University, Calif.: Stanford University Press, 1943. 36 p.

Leon Festinger and Daniel Katz, Editors, *Research Methods in the Behavioral Sciences*. New York: Dryden Press, 1953. p. 327-80.

John F. Fraser, *A Handbook of Employment Interviewing*. Revised Edition. London: MacDonald and Evans, 1951. 214 p.

Annette Garrett, *Interviewing:* Its Principles and Methods. New York: Family Welfare Association of America, 1942. 123 p.

Carter V. Good, A. S. Barr, and Douglas E. Scates, *op. cit.*, p. 377-90. Covers a considerable amount of the literature on interviewing before the middle 1930's.

William J. Goode and Paul K. Hatt, *op. cit.*, p. 184-208.

Carl I. Hovland and Others, *Experiments on Mass Communication*. Studies in Social Psychology in World War II, Volume 3. Princeton, New Jersey: Princeton University Press, 1949. 345 p.

*The Interview in Counseling:* An Outline of Interviewing Procedure for Use of Com-

not to be regarded as an oral questionnaire. It will be noted that, in many texts dealing with questionnaire and interviewing procedures, the two data-gathering techniques are presented in one chapter, with an interlocking or

munity Advisory Centers. Washington: Retraining and Reemployment Administration, U. S. Department of Labor, 1946. vi + 25 p.

National Opinion Research Center, *Interviewing for NORC.* Denver: University of Denver, 1945. 154 p.

Marie Jahoda and Others, *op. cit.,* p. 151-208, 423-92.

Elizabeth Keating and Others, "Validity of Work Histories Obtained by Interview." *Journal of Applied Psychology* 34:6-11; February 1950.

Leonard S. Kogan, "The Electrical Recording of Social Case Work Interviews." *Social Case Work* 31:371-78; November 1950.

Stanley G. Law, *Therapy Through Interview.* New York: McGraw-Hill Book Co., 1948. xiii + 313 p.

J. H. Lorie and Harry V. Roberts, *Basic Methods of Marketing Research.* New York: McGraw-Hill Book Co., 1951.

Robert A. Love, "The Use of Motivation Research to Determine Interest in Adult College-Level Training." *Educational Record* 34:210-18; July 1953.

George A. Lundberg, *op. cit.,* p. 349-96.

John Madge, *The Tools of Social Science.* New York: Longmans, Green and Co., 1953. p. 144-253.

Robert K. Merton, Marjorie Fiske, and Patricia Kendall, *The Focused Interview.* New York: Bureau of Applied Social Research, Columbia University, 1952. xxv + 202 p.

Sidney H. Newman and Others, "The Reliability of the Interview Method in An Officer Candidate Evaluation Program." *American Psychologist* 1:103-109; April 1946.

R. C. Oldfield, *The Psychology of the Interview.* London: Methuen and Co., 1941. xv + 144 p.

Mildred Parten, *op. cit.,* p. 331-82.

Stanley L. Payne, *op. cit.*

John M. Pfiffner, *Research Methods in Public Administration.* New York: Ronald Press Co., 1940. Ch. 9.

Victor C. Raimy, "Self Reference in Counseling Interviews." *Journal of Consulting Psychology* 12:153-63; May 1949.

Francis P. Robinson, "The Unit in Interview Analysis." *Educational and Psychological Measurement* 9:709-16; Winter 1949.

Gertrude Sackheim, "Suggestions on Recording Techniques." *Journal of Social Case Work* 30:20-25; January 1949.

Douglas E. Scates, "The Silent Side of Teaching: Key to Its Understanding." *Journal of Teacher Education* 4:316-19; December 1953. On depth studies.

Julius Seeman, "A Study of Preliminary Interview Methods in Vocational Counseling." *Journal of Consulting Psychology* 12:321-30; September-October 1948.

Theresa R. Shapiro, "What Scientists Look For in Their Jobs." *Scientific Monthly* 26: 335-40; June 1953.

James D. Thompson and N. J. Demerath, "Some Experiences With the Group Interview." *Social Forces* 31:148-54; December 1952.

Ruth Strang, *op. cit.,* p. 100-148.

Ruth Strang, "The Interview." *Review of Educational Research* 9:498-501, 607-608; December 1939.

Alice L. Voiland, Martha L. Gundelach, and Mildred Corner, *Developing Insight in Initial Interviews.* New York: Family Service Association of America, 1947. 54 p.

Ralph Wagner, "The Employment Interview: A Critical Summary." *Personnel Psychology* 2:17-46; Spring 1949.

Ralph Wagner, "A Group Situation Compared with Individual Interviews for Securing Personnel Information." *Personnel Psychology* 1:93-108; Spring 1948.

Robert I. Watson, *The Clinical Method in Psychology.* New York: Harper and Bros., 1951. p. 83-100.

James D. Weinland and Margaret V. Gross, *Personnel Interviewing.* New York: Ronald Press, 1952. vii + 416 p.

Helen L. Witmer, Editor, *Psychiatric Interviews With Children.* New York: Commonwealth Fund, 1946. viii + 444 p.

Pauline V. Young, *Interviewing in Social Work.* New York: McGraw-Hill Book Co., 1935. 416 p.

Pauline V. Young, *Scientific Social Surveys and Research, op. cit.,* p. 243-64.

shuttle-like discussion of appropriate concepts and techniques. Many of the references listed at the beginning of the section on the questionnaire, including discussions of the art of questioning, provide essential background for an understanding of interviewing.

### Nature and Value of the Interview

When the interview is used for research purposes, the investigator is gathering data directly from others in face-to-face contacts, in contrast to certain other data-gathering procedures, such as the questionnaire. Certain types of information can be secured only by direct contacts with people; for example, intimate facts of personal history,[112] of personal habits and characteristics, of family life, and opinions and beliefs. While certain of this information can be obtained through use of a questionnaire, check list, or test distributed to groups of respondents, there are unique characteristics of the interview that render it much more than an "oral questionnaire." The special values of the interview, in comparison with the questionnaire, are these:

1. The interviewees may provide personal and confidential information which they would not ordinarily place in writing on paper; they may wish to see the investigator who is securing the information and to receive guarantees as to how the facts will be used; they may need the stimulation of personal contacts in order to be "drawn out"; and some interviewees may be too ignorant to read and write.

2. The interview enables the investigator to follow up leads and to take advantage of small clues; in dealing with complex topics and questions, the development or trend of the conversation is likely to proceed in any direction, and no instrument prepared in advance can fully meet the situation.

3. The interview permits the investigator to form an impression of the person who is giving the information, to arrive at some judgment of the truth of the answers, and to "read between the lines" things that may not have been said in words.

4. The interview provides an opportunity for the interviewer to give information and to develop certain attitudes on the part of the respondent, a procedure that is not possible in using a questionnaire or a test. This opportunity for "give and take" is especially important in the "treatment" or "therapeutic" interview, used extensively in case work. In this way the interview permits an exchange of ideas and information; it is not necessarily a one-way street.

---

[112] A. C. Kinsey and Others, *Sexual Behavior in the Human Male*. Philadelphia: W. B. Saunders Co., 1948. xvi + 804 p.

W. A. Wallis, "Statistics of the Kinsey Report." *Journal of the American Statistical Association* 44:463-84; December 1949.

Paul Wallin, "An Appraisal of Some Methodological Aspects of the Kinsey Report." *American Sociological Review* 14:197-210; April 1949.

A. C. Kinsey and Others, *Sexual Behavior in the Human Female*. Philadelphia: W. B. Saunders Co., 1953. xxx + 842 p.

## Applications of the Interview Technique

The interview is used in many practical situations for purposes other than research. In an employment interview, information is usually gathered concerning the applicant's training and experience, although such facts could readily be obtained by use of application blanks. The principal purpose of the face-to-face contact is to give the employer an opportunity to observe the reactions of the interviewee, to secure some basis for judging the quality of the individual's mental responses, and to note the social aspects of his behavior. Employment interviews, as a rule, are for practical purposes rather than systematic investigation.

Interviews are used extensively in education and in personnel work, including the teacher in his contacts with pupils and parents, visiting teachers, attendance officers, vocational counselors, deans, and school principals. Although these uses of the interview may be largely routine in the majority of such cases, and should not be considered as research, it may prove significant to note the practical applications of research techniques. There are conditions under which such practical applications of interviewing and of other techniques may become research, if the investigator will integrate his experiences into careful observations growing out of his regular work, so as to afford verified insights that increase one's understanding of the field represented.

The interview is an essential technique in social case study and in psychiatric work, and also in many diagnostic and therapeutic areas of education, psychology, and sociology, as illustrated extensively in the chapter on clinical and case studies.

The interview is a major tool for gathering evidence in the field, including censuses and similar enumerations, social and economic status of families, standards of living, family budgets, and family purchases and buying preferences.

Interviewing is helpful in certain types of analysis and appraisal. Many persons who are notably successful in their professional or occupational activities have certain methods of work, are guided by given standards, and react in particular ways, with the result that their performance is more successful than that of the average person. This information is important as a basis for training others. By skillful interviewing (and observation) the investigator can note the essential differences between successful and unsuccessful workers. The interview has been used to discover the traits and duties of good citizenship, secretarial duties and traits, and the characteristics or traits most essential for success in teaching. Data secured for such purposes through the interview technique involve four important limitations relating to the respondent: his experience, his judgment, his accessibility and willingness to divulge the information, and his ability to express himself clearly.

Bingham and Moore have provided an extensive discussion of interviewing techniques, as applied to a variety of fields: student counseling, occupational adjustment, applying for a position, employment offices, civil-service agencies, employer-employee relationships, public-opinion polls, commercial surveys and market studies, social case work, mental clinics, journalism, and law. The volume includes fifty-five rules or recommendations for interviewing, in relation to preliminary preparation, the interviewing process itself, and fact-finding purposes and procedures.[113]

Much of the consumer and opinion research utilizes questionnaire and interview techniques; for example, surveys reported to business and industry (market and consumer studies, industrial surveys, advertising, public relations, radio broadcasting, editorial problems and preferences of readers, and attitudes of employees); surveys reported to government (studies relating to the Office of War Information, census work, consumer requirements, and attitudes in the field of agriculture); and surveys reported to the public, relating to public opinion, including the various polls.[114]

The citizens of an Indiana city were interviewed to determine the characteristics they preferred in the local school-board members. The conversations took place at lunch counters, card games, billiard tables, barber shops, dentists' offices, ball games, and on buses and street cars. "The interviews were conducted so subtly that the one thousand subjects never suspected that they were being interviewed. The interviewer engaged his subject in off-hand or social conversation, but all the while knew what he was after, and recorded his data immediately afterward." [115]

The interview is valuable as a supplement to experimentation. To cite an illustration, studies of attitude, in the usual experimental form, may reveal no average change in the attitude of groups, but the interview may provide significant explanations: [116]

The controlled experiment will not tell us why there is no change. Its results show only the net effect of the propaganda on this attitude and not the more intricate dynamics of response which led to this net effect.... Failure of the

[113] Walter V. Bingham and Bruce V. Moore, *op. cit.*
[114] A. B. Blankenship, *op. cit.*
[115] John R. Shannon, "What One Thousand Terre Haute Citizens Look For in Voting for School Board Members." *American School Board Journal* 114:29-30; February 1947.
[116] Quoted from Paul F. Lazarsfeld and Robert K. Merton, "Studies in Radio and Film Propaganda." *Transactions of the New York Academy of Sciences, Series II,* 6:58-79; November 1943.

film may be due to the fact that two themes, each of which was effective, produced responses which cancelled each other out. The interview material thus enables us to provide a psychological explanation of responses which may not be registered in the experimental results. . . . This type of case not only illustrates a type of boomerang-response, but also shows how the focused interview enables us to supplement and enrich the value of the traditional controlled experiment.

## Types of Interviews

In the psychological and sociological literature of interviewing [117] may be found several classifications of interviewing techniques of data-gathering. (As pointed out earlier in this section, interviewing is used in many practical situations for purposes other than research.)

1. According to function (diagnostic, treatment, research)
2. Number of persons participating (individual, group)
3. Length of contact (short contact, prolonged contact)
4. According to the roles assumed by the interviewer and interviewee, in relation to the socio-psychological process of interaction

    Non-directive (uncontrolled, unguided, unstructured). [Non-directive or client-centered interviewing [118] as a technique or medium of counseling and therapy has been presented briefly, together with appropriate references, in the chapter on case and clinical studies.]

    Focused [as discussed in another part of this section.]

    Repeated, in order to trace the development of a social or socio-psychological process, as in following the progressive reactions of a voter in making up his mind in a presidential campaign.

An extensive treatment of counseling techniques in secondary schools and colleges outlines the following kinds of interviews: [119]

1. Intake interview, as the initial stage in clinic and guidance centers
2. Brief-talk contacts, as in schools and recreation centers
3. Single-hour interviews, a common type in schools and colleges, as compared with the much less frequent long series of interviews
4. Clinical psychological interviews, emphasizing psychotherapeutic counseling and utilizing case-history data and active participation by the counselor in the re-education of the client
5. Psychiatric interviews, similar to psychological counseling, but varying with the personality and philosophical orientation of the individual worker and with the setting in which used
6. Psychoanalytic interviews
7. The interview form of test, as illustrated by the Stanford-Binet Intelligence Test and sometimes in the form of a disguised intelligence test
8. Group interviews, as in selecting applicants for admission to college, trainees for special courses, or candidates for positions, or student opinion on particular topics
9. Research interviews (not a major type in the field of counseling).

[117] Pauline V. Young, *Scientific Social Surveys and Research, op. cit.,* p. 247-49.

[118] Carl R. Rogers, *Client-Centered Therapy.* Boston: Houghton Mifflin Co., 1951. xii + 560 p.

[119] Ruth Strang, *op. cit.,* p. 107-112.

## The Focused or Depth Interview

The focused (or depth) interview is described as significantly different from other types of research interviews that might appear superficially similar.[120]

1. The persons interviewed are known to have been involved in a particular concrete situation, such as viewing a film or hearing a radio program.
2. The hypothetically significant elements, patterns, and total structure of the particular situation have been previously analyzed (content analysis) by the investigator, and he has arrived at a set of significant hypotheses concerning the meaning and effects of determinate aspects of the situation.
3. On the basis of this analysis, the investigator has developed an interview guide, outlining the major areas of inquiry and the hypotheses which locate the pertinence of the data to be obtained in the interview.
4. The interview itself is focused on the subjective experiences of the persons exposed to the pre-analyzed situation; these reported responses enable the investigator to test the validity of his hypotheses and to ascertain unanticipated responses to the situation, thus giving rise to fresh hypotheses.

The depth of reports of an interview varies, since not everything reported is on the same psychological level, but may be thought of as varying along a continuum. At the lower end of the scale are mere descriptive accounts of reaction that permit little more than a tabulation of "positive" or "negative" responses, and at the upper end are reports setting forth varied psychological dimensions of the experience (symbolisms, anxieties, fears, sentiments, and cognitive ideas). The major problem of the interviewer is "to diagnose the level of depth on which his subjects are operating at any given moment and to shift that level toward whichever end of the 'depth-continuum' he finds appropriate to the given case." [120]

Depth psychology or depth interviewing seeks to get at the structure of motivation, that is, the dynamic structure of the individual. What makes him do certain things? Why do adults take courses of instruction? What do they seek? What factors motivate them to study on their own time? Are these flimsy hopes, in the case of persons who do not stay with the courses? Do other persons see the courses through to the end, because the process of instruction, including the associations, is pleasurable, or a variation and relief from one's occupation? Are the motivating factors different for varying courses related to an occupation, a recreation, or hobby, or a humanistic or cultural purpose?

Such studies of depth require insight and care. Superficial reasons will not give any depth. Reasons (or motivations) are complex and rich, with

[120] Robert K. Merton and Patricia L. Kendall, "The Focused Interview." *American Journal of Sociology* 51:541-57; May 1946.
Robert K. Merton and Others, *op. cit.* Also a later version in 1954.

varied structure, and with different components and weights for these elements. The investigator needs the depth interview first, then other types of interviews or skillful questionnaires. Persons usually do not know their real reasons; they have not explored their motivations fully; they are not experts in self-analysis, and probably do not know the proper terms to use in describing the elements in their motivation. Even if the subjects should know their real motives, they are likely to be embarrassed at telling the truth, at laying bare their own motives, hopes, and frustrations. They are habituated to giving socially approved reasons and excuses; they may have been taught not to complain, even when their reason may be a legitimate complaint; they may feel reluctant to disclose family needs for financial aid. Many persons are generally confused as to life goals, purposes, and directions for themselves; for example, leaving school may grow out of this confusion, out of a lack of purpose adequate to keep the individual in school, and not because of any more specific reasons. Therefore, the investigator should not force the individual to name a reason, if the cause is lack of a specific reason.

The following item from a depth essay questionnaire, under the heading of, "What would further education do for you?" is similar to the probing that would be done in a depth interview: [121]

It is probably true that most of us have some long-range plans or ideals concerning our work. Perhaps we wish to do our present job better; maybe we want a promotion to higher levels along the line of work we are now engaged in; or our ultimate goal may be to work toward some objective not connected with our present job. Some employees perform their job duties well and get along with satisfaction to everyone without taking any more education after they start work; others want to take courses off and on in the hope that these will help them to realize their plans. In the light of such considerations, will you comment on your own attitude toward the desirability of further courses (on-the-job or out-of-hours) in connection with your vocational desires and plans. [It may be noted that this particular question was found to have little validity; virtually all people think they would like more education. The item was retained, however, simply as an introduction, to "warm up" thinking in this particular area.]

Depth analysis or depth interviewing is of major importance in discovering the sources of one's willingness to make radical changes in his behavior, particularly as illustrated in public-opinion studies: "We must reach down into the deep matrix of American attitudes, probing those

---

[121] Quoted from Douglas E. Scates and Alice V. Yeomans, *Developing a Depth Essay Questionnaire to Assess the Market for Further Education Among Employed Scientists and Engineers, op. cit.*

Also see Douglas E. Scates and Alice Yeomans Scates, "Developing a Depth Questionnaire to Explore Motivation and Likelihood of Action." *Educational and Psychological Measurement* 12:620-31; Winter 1952. Includes thirteen references on depth interviewing.

half-conscious emotionally loaded dispositions from which the day-by-day verbally expressed attitudes on specific issues proceed." [122]

Lewin points out that, prior to the mid 1940's, fact finding in the area of intergroup relations was largely dominated by surveys, which were open to criticism because of rather superficial methods of poll taking and lack of the deeper searching of the interview type (intended to provide some insight into the motivations behind the sentiments expressed).[123]

In investigating public opinion, a questionnaire and depth analysis (or depth interview) were used effectively for supplementary purposes.[124] The questionnaire was more than a simple attitude scale, since it included questions concerning family and social background, group membership, sentiments and values, personality, and projective items. The depth interview and certain other clinical techniques, applied to selected individuals, provided a depth of insight and a picture of dynamic interrelationships that questionnaires alone could never give. Case studies of individuals provided fresh hypotheses concerning the personality traits, attitudes, social background, and group membership of the prejudiced and unprejudiced person.

### Preparation for the Interview

Interviewing is an art that requires careful study of the pertinent literature, appropriate training, and guided experience for satisfactory performance. While the extensive literature on interviewing technique is helpful, it cannot take the place of actual practice and guidance in acquiring the necessary skills of interviewing.

In discussing the questionnaire and other schedules in the preceding section, major emphasis was given to the importance of careful planning of questions. The preparation of questions for the interview is an equally painstaking task. While the interview should be pleasant and to some extent informal, it is not just a pleasant meeting or a haphazard series of questions and answers. It is necessary that a thread of questions provide for the interviewer the answers he is seeking, without gaps and doubtful interpretations. As a rule, the interviewer has a set of carefully prepared questions, to be introduced into the conversation at appropriate points, although he may vary these queries to adapt to individual circumstances. He can amplify the questions by following up leads as the opportunity may present itself. To avoid a meaningless or miscellaneous array of material after the

[122] Gardner Murphy, "Psychological Prerequisites for a Sound Foreign Policy." *Journal of Social Issues* 2:15-26; November 1946.

[123] Kurt Lewin, "Action Research and Minority Problems." *Journal of Social Issues* 2: 34-46; November 1946.

[124] Donald W. MacKinnon, "The Use of Clinical Methods in Social Psychology." *Journal of Social Issues* 2:34-46; November 1946.

interviewer has gathered his facts, careful planning must be done in advance of the interview, outlining the information necessary as a basis for conclusions that will satisfy the principal purpose of the investigation. This characterization of interviewing procedure applies particularly to data-gathering studies, with recognition of the fact that nondirective or client-centered counseling or therapy employs a contrasting type of interviewing technique.

The interview is both a challenge and an opportunity for the use of tact. Data of a factual or objective nature usually can be secured by direct questions, but information or attitudes of a personal or confidential nature may have to be obtained indirectly. The interviewee may recoil from the thought of revealing certain types of information or attitudes too openly or directly, and frequently does not know the significance of certain details that may have been omitted. It should be noted that children usually lack sufficiently mature concepts to give a complete account of experiences, ideas, or attitudes. If the interviewer is to sample thoroughly the knowledge, attitudes, and beliefs of the respondent, through skillfully drawing out responses representing various elements in the person's thinking and experience, appropriate tact and technique are the necessary tools.

As background for understanding and working effectively with people, interviewing draws heavily on knowledge provided by the social sciences, particularly concepts dealing with the makeup of the individual and his reaction to environment.[125] The interviewer must understand the respondent as a person, and at the same time must understand himself as a person, dealing with an individual (the interviewee) who differs from the interviewer in many significant ways.

## Further Details of Interview Technique

The present discussion of the interview emphasizes the basic psychological and social principles of interviewing, rather than the details of technique enumerated below. These particulars are treated at length in the references listed at the beginning of this section. Many of the concepts, procedures, and references presented in the section on the questionnaire apply to the preparation of questions and schedules for successful interviewing. The individual who wishes to do successful interviewing will need appropriate training and reading covering at least some of the following topics:

1. Preparation for the interview, and try-out procedures
2. Methods of beginning the interview (indirect social approach, spontaneous

125 Anne F. Fenlason, *op. cit.*

reaction to controlled stimuli, distribution of forms prior to the interview, direct frank approach)

3. Factors in the success or failure of the interview (number and length of interviews, rapport and sensitivity to the interviewee, physical setting, interviewer's reputation and knowledge of problems under consideration)

4. Reliability of the information obtained (subject's desire to make a good impression, kind of information sought, relationship between the interviewer and interviewee)

5. Recording the interview. In the literature of education, psychology, and sociology may be found many extensive extracts from records of interviews,[126] especially the reports of case studies. Many of the references in the chapter on case and clinical techniques include illustrative interviews as a vital part of data-gathering, diagnosis, and therapy in case study and case work.

[126] Stanley G. Law, *op. cit.*
Helen L. Witmer, *op. cit.*
Pauline V. Young, *Interviewing in Social Work, op. cit.*
Anne F. Fenlason, *op. cit.*

# Organized Forms of Descriptive-Survey and Normative Research:

## OBSERVATIONAL, SMALL-GROUP, CONTENT-ANALYSIS, AND APPRAISAL TECHNIQUES

---

## OBSERVATIONAL STUDIES AND TECHNIQUES[127]

The questionnaire, as presented earlier in this chapter, seeks to secure from the respondent answers to questions through a paper-and-pencil instrument. The interview, just discussed in the preceding section, explores

[127] Russell L. Ackoff, *The Design of Social Research*. Chicago: University of Chicago Press, 1953. Chapter 9.

Dorothy C. Adkins, "Principles Underlying Observational Techniques of Evaluation." *Educational and Psychological Measurement* 11:29-51; Spring 1951.

Robert F. Bales, *Interaction Process Analysis*. Cambridge, Mass.: Addison-Wesley Press, 1950. 203 p.

Roger G. Barker and Herbert F. Wright, *One Boy's Day:* A Specimen Record of Behavior. New York: Harper and Bros., 1951. x + 435 p.

A. S. Barr, Robert A. Davis, and Palmer O. Johnson, *Educational Research and Appraisal*. Chicago: J. B. Lippincott Co., 1953. p. 56-62.

Emory S. Bogardus, *Introduction to Social Research*. Los Angeles: Suttonhouse, 1936. p. 65-73.

Francis G. Cornell and Others, *An Exploratory Measurement of Individualities of Schools and Classrooms*. University of Illinois Bulletin, Vol. 50, No. 75. Urbana: University of Illinois, June 1953. 71 p.

Marie C. Duncan, "Recording Descriptive Data and Observer Reliability." *Pedagogical Seminary and Journal of Genetic Psychology* 78:159-64; June 1951.

M. C. Elmer, *Social Research*. New York: Prentice-Hall, 1939. p. 359-69.

Horace B. English and Victor Raimy, *Studying the Individual School Child*. New York: Henry Holt and Co., 1941. viii + 131 p.

Leon Festinger and Daniel Katz, Editors, *Research Methods in the Behavioral Sciences*. New York: Dryden Press, 1953. p. 243-99, 381-417.

Wilson Gee, *Social Science Research Methods*. New York: Appleton-Century-Crofts, 1950. p. 198-204.

Ruth Glassow and Others, "Photographical and Cinematographical Research Methods." *Research Methods Appliel to Health, Physical Education, and Recreation*. Revised Edition. Washington: American Association for Health, Physical Education, and Recreation, 1952. p. 204-18.

Carter V. Good, A. S. Barr, and Douglas E. Scates, *The Methodology of Educational Research*. New York: Appleton-Century-Crofts, 1936. p. 390-409. Covers much of the literature before the middle 1930's.

William J. Goode and Paul K. Hatt, *Methods in Social Research*. New York: McGraw-Hill Book Co., 1952. p. 119-31.

Ernest Greenwood, *Experimental Sociology:* A Study in Method. New York: King's Crown Press, 1945. p. 34-43.

W. A. Brownell and Others, *The Measurement of Understanding*. Forty-fifth Yearbook of the National Society for the Study of Education, Part I. Chicago: University of Chicago Press, 1946. xi + 338 p.

Marie Jahoda and Others, *Research Methods in Social Relations*. New York: Dryden Press, 1951. p. 129-50, 493-513.

what people think and do by what they express in conversation with the interviewer. Analysis of documentary material for quantitative purposes, to be treated in a later section of this chapter, is concerned with what people think and do, as revealed by what they put on paper. Observation seeks to ascertain the overt behavior of persons (and what it may reveal) by watching them as they express themselves in a variety of situations, selected to typify the conditions of normal living or to represent some special set of factors.

Observation is the most direct means of studying subjects, when the interviewer is interested in their overt behavior. In an interview people may tell what they think they do, but their reports often are different from their actual behavior, since human beings are not generally accurate observers of themselves. Furthermore, many of us do not wish to give accurate descriptions of ourselves, even if we could do so. The interview itself is a form of expression, and the investigator may be interested in studying the behavior of others when they are being interviewed, as certain aspects of personality may be revealed, in addition to noting what they say.

Arthur T. Jersild, "Direct Observation as a Research Method." *Review of Educational Research* 9:472-82, 597-99; December 1939.

Ethel Kawin, "Records and Reports; Observations, Tests, and Measurements." *Early Childhood Education*. Forty-sixth Yearbook of the National Society for the Study of Education, Part II. Chicago: University of Chicago Press, 1947. p. 281-314.

Helen L. Koch, "Methods of Studying the Behavior and Development of Young Children." *Methods of Psychology*. Edited by T. G. Andrews. New York: John Wiley and Sons, 1948. p. 624-63.

Harold A. Larrabee, *Reliable Knowledge*. Boston: Houghton Mifflin Co., 1945. Chapter 4.

George A. Lundberg, *Social Research*. Revised Edition. New York: Longmans, Green and Co., 1942. p. 159-81.

John Madge, *The Tools of Social Science*. New York: Longmans, Green and Co., 1953. p. 117-43.

Harold E. Mitzel and William Rabinowitz, *Reliability of Teachers' Verbal Behavior: A Study of Withall's Technique for Assessing Social-Emotional Climate in the Classroom*. Publication 15. New York: College of the City of New York, June 1953. v + 30 p.

Mildred Parten, *Surveys, Polls, and Samples*. New York: Harper and Bros., 1950. p. 82-85.

Saul B. Sells, "Observational Methods of Research." *Review of Educational Research* 15: 394-407; December 1945.

Saul B. Sells, "Observational Methods of Research." *Review of Educational Research* 18:424-47; December 1948.

Saul B. Sells and Robert W. Ellis, "Observational Procedures Used in Research." *Review of Educational Research* 21:432-49; December 1951.

Ruth Strang, *Counseling Technics in College and Secondary School*. Revised Edition. New York: Harper and Bros., 1949. p. 36-62.

Lovisa C. Wagoner and J. M. Castellanos, *Observation of Young Children: Their Behavior and Their Teaching*. Revised Edition. Oakland, Calif.: L. C. Wagoner, Mills College, 1951. xii + 142 p.

Edwin Wandt and Leonard M. Ostreicher, *Variability in Observed Classroom Behaviors of Junior High School Teachers and Classes*. Publication 16. New York: College of the City of New York, June 1953. iv + 31 p.

Robert I. Watson, *The Clinical Method in Psychology*. New York: Harper and Bros., 1951. p. 64-82.

Robert I. Watson, "Diagnosis as an Aspect of the Clinical Method: A Review," *Readings in the Clinical Method in Psychology*. New York: Harper and Bros., 1949. p. 405-27.

Pauline V. Young, *Scientific Social Surveys and Research*. Second Edition. New York: Prentice-Hall, 1949. p. 199-219.

**Factors stimulating observation as a research approach.** As long as man has had eyes to see, he has been free to observe in a great variety of situations. However, direct observation as a systematic research procedure in the fields of education, psychology, and sociology belongs primarily to the present century, with the chief advances in educational studies taking place during the past thirty years. Many research workers and scientists have had physical misgivings about the possibility of anything "objective" coming from the method of direct observation. Without debating this question, the fact remains that there are many aspects of behavior which can be studied satisfactorily in no other way. This book has emphasized the point of view that the first requirement of a research technique is its adaptation to the kind of data and to the observational conditions with which it must be used.

Factors that have given impetus to direct observation as a research method include the following: establishment of centers for research in child development; the demands of the newer or progressive education; a desire to probe aspects of behavior not accessible to the conventional paper-and-pencil test, interview, or laboratory technique; a wish to obviate certain of the judgmental errors likely to enter into the customary rating procedures; and emphasis on the need for studying children in natural or social situations, and for observing the functioning child (including his social and emotional behavior), rather than to rely exclusively on cross-sectional measurements of mental and physical growth.[128]

**Characteristics of observation for research purposes.** Characteristics that distinguish observation for systematic investigational purposes may be differentiated from ordinary "looking around" as follows (with illustrations drawn from procedures for observing children):

1. The observation is specific, not just looking around for general impressions, with carefully defined things to look for.

2. Observation of behavior for research purposes is systematic, not a chance "dropping in" on a situation at any time when one happens to be passing by. The length of the observation periods, the interval between them, and the number have been carefully planned, in the light of other factors relating to the daily program of the school the children attend, visiting hours, periods when children may be tired, and control of the situation if special factors are to be observed.

3. The observation is quantitative, usually with a tally of the number of instances a particular type of behavior has occurred; sometimes total duration of the particular conduct during the period of observation, or the distance traveled by a child, or some other countable or measurable characteristic; sometimes a diagram is made showing spatial relationships.

[128] Arthur T. Jersild and Margaret F. Meigs, "Direct Observation as a Research Method." *Review of Educational Research* 9:472-82, 597-99; December 1939.

4. A record is made of the observation immediately, or as promptly as possible, not entrusting the results to memory.

5. The observation is expert, that is, done by an investigator who is especially trained for such work. While many graduate students will not meet the conditions of this criterion, the difference between the observational skill of an investigator who is trained and a person who is not trained, both in the use of the technique and in the field to which the procedure is applied, is sufficient in itself to make the difference between valid and invalid results.

6. The results of systematic observation of behavior can be checked and often verified, by comparing the results of different observers or by repeating the study. Such checks, however, do not guarantee the validity of direct observation, which depends essentially upon the definitions of the acts that are to be regarded as falling within the category under study. In many cases validity must rest ultimately upon the consistency with which the findings of different research approaches point to the same general conclusion. The reliability of observation of behavior can be determined, however, and has often been found to be satisfactory. (Reference may be made to the section on classification in Chapter 5 for a discussion of categories.)

**Non-participant and participant observation.**[129] The investigator may play any one of several roles in observation of social situations—a visiting stranger, an attentive listener, an eager learner, or a participant-observer. Observation may be of a non-participant type, as when observing and recording conditions in a classroom, in a superintendent's or principal's office, in slums, factories, retail stores, banks, strikes, ceremonies and rituals, police station, court, or mayor's office.

Participation or role playing is not necessarily complete; it is possible to take part in many of the activities of the group, so as to be accepted as a member, and at the same time to carry on the role of observer and interviewer. To cite an illustration of quasi-participation, in a study of "corner boys" in an Italian slum, the investigator entered as the local historian under the auspices of a key member of a gang.[130]

In using participant observation, the investigator commonly lives with or shares in the life and activity of the group under study, as in observing the life and behavior of hoboes [131] or musicians.[132] The investigator may have disguised himself in such a manner as to be accepted as a member of the group, although he may not carry out exactly the same activities as the other members of the group, in order to be accepted as a participant observer. If the members of the group have accepted the observer as a

[129] William J. Goode and Paul K. Hatt, *op. cit.*, p. 120-24.
Marie Jahoda and Others, *op. cit.*, p. 134-48, 493-513.
Pauline V. Young, *op. cit.*, p. 201-10.
[130] William F. Whyte, *Streetcorner Society*. Chicago: University of Chicago Press, 1943.
William F. Whyte, "Observational Field-Work Methods." *Research Methods in Social Relations, op. cit.*, p. 493-513.
[131] Nels Anderson, *The Hobo*. Chicago: University of Chicago Press, 1923.
[132] Howard S. Becker, "The Professional Dance Musician and His Audience." *American Journal of Sociology* 57:136-44; 1951.

participant, their behavior and responses are least likely to be affected by the presence of the investigator.

**Uses and applications of observation.** Direct observation has been employed in a large number of studies of infants and young children, to record various activities and characteristics. It was only natural that, as interest in child study increased, the attention of investigators would center on a variety of aspects of child growth and development, and that an appropriate method of measuring the status of these characteristics would be needed. Interest in improved instructional procedures and in supervision, together with attempts to appraise and evaluate outcomes, has stimulated extensive use of observational methods.

In many of the earlier observational studies there was a tendency to gather all-inclusive data, omnibus accounts of everything a child did or said over long periods of minute observation. The voluminous data that resulted were unique for the particular child under observation, and sometimes led to improved insights on the part of the observer, but contributed little to the development of scientific generalizations or to techniques of observation.

As observational procedures have become more refined, there has been a tendency to restrict the data to a limited (although possibly very complex) characteristic of behavior that could be identified readily by a trained observer. The results of such observations have tended to become measurements of a single trait and can be studied as such. While the older case-history types of data were valuable for clinical use with an individual child, they were not readily amenable to statistical treatment, and each set of case material contained much of the peculiar ability, attitude, or even prejudice of the worker who gathered it. By limiting the scope of the data to be gathered and by careful definition of the characteristic to be observed, more recent observational investigations have eliminated much of the personal variation in the observer. The reliability of careful observational studies compares favorably with the reliability of paper-and-pencil tests.

Many of the studies in the series made under the auspices of the Child Development Institute of Teachers College, Columbia University, have used certain techniques of observation designed to overcome the difficulties of the older techniques (particularly the diaries and case studies). When the investigator was observing behavior in general (as in case studies) he noted and recorded different elements at different times, and the records tended to become a mixture of fact and interpretation, because the particular traits had not been well defined in concrete terms. To overcome these difficulties, in more recent observational studies the specific reactions of the child were emphasized and noted, with a given characteristic determined on the basis of its judged significance in the total behavior patterns of individuals. (Some of these later observational investigations proved too narrow, with acts recorded merely as acts which could not later be interpreted.)

Illustrations of direct recording of behavior through use of observational techniques include the following: interpersonal smiling responses in the pre-school years over a two-year interval, including 150 recorded observations; the spontaneous remarks of twelve nursery-school children during a period of four weeks; the behavior and changes over a period of seven weeks induced in a seven-year-old girl who moved suddenly from a small city apartment to an elegant country estate; recorded speech sounds for "only" infants and for those with older siblings; and one thousand and one recorded remarks overheard in conversations among the population of Manhattan.[133]

Direct observation of behavior is an important means of appraising or evaluating the work of progressive schools and of teachers interested in educational outcomes beyond the customary academic attainments. Many of the larger aims of education fall outside the range of the usual academic abilities, including such social characteristics of the individual as coöperation and adaptability, the self-reliant traits of appropriate independence and self-confidence, the dynamic traits of initiative and spontaneity, good judgment in choosing companions, and other elements of a well rounded individual and personality. Such characteristics cannot be appraised satisfactorily by the older forms of paper-and-pencil testing. It is necessary to look for (to observe) definite acts that are regarded as evidence of the progress toward the desired objectives. The frequency with which these significant acts or forms of behavior have occurred may be regarded as an index of the extent to which certain habits and attitudes have become established. Groups which demonstrate these significant acts with greater or less frequency show more or less evidence of having grown in the desired direction.

A different form of observation is represented by the anecdotal technique, which consists of writing down at intervals the revealing sayings or doings of children. Over an extended period of time, such records provide a significant picture of a child's development. This type of observation and recording involves situations that are as natural as possible in the classroom or school environment, free from the limiting conditions imposed by a prepared record form or a specially controlled situation. Therefore, the anecdotal technique depends largely on the selective ability

[133] Saul B. Sells and Robert W. Ellis, *op. cit.*

of the teacher and, when well kept, provides records of importance for guidance of children. (Anecdotal records are discussed at some length in the chapter on case and clinical studies.) Other uses of observation in relation to appraisal of educational practices (particularly use of check-lists, rating scales, and score cards) will be discussed in a later section of this chapter.

During recent years systematic observation of behavior has become a useful method for study of small groups; in many such studies observation has provided all or part of the data.[134] The observer has assumed various roles. In laboratory studies of groups, he has sat aside from the group, or behind a one-way screen, to record behavior. In field studies of groups in their natural settings, the observer has described the behavior of con-ference leaders, responses of children in a variety of clubs, and the struc-ture of play groups in a summer camp. In the investigation of groups an observer is usually necessary, because the members of the group, as a rule, cannot describe accurately their own behavior. (Small-group study or group-behavior analysis will be discussed in the next section of this chapter.)

The extended uses and adaptations of direct observation as a research technique include teaching method, classroom, summer camp, home, dis-cussion group, playground, museum, behavior of adults, and mental hygiene.

**Observation compared with experimental and laboratory studies.** Direct observation makes a contribution not common in controlled experi-mentation. The specific goal may be to note the particular stimuli in a complex social setting to which individual children react, and to study the consistency of this reaction in an individual, as well as the variability in such reactions between different members of the group. This point of view regards as artificial (unnatural) many experimental situations, especially in laboratories. It should be kept in mind, however, that the conditions represented in many observational investigations may approach and actu-ally satisfy the requirements for a carefully controlled experiment. (Con-trolled experimental studies will be discussed in another chapter of this book.) The basic conditions and factors of observation may be controlled by selecting the room, equipment, children, stimuli, and observers. The remaining requirement in controlled experimentation is to study and measure the effects produced by changing or manipulating a certain factor or variable. Observational studies that have approached controlled experi-mentation in technique have been made in the Iowa Child Welfare Re-

---

[134] Alvin Zander, "Systematic Observation of Small Face-to-Face Groups," *Research Methods in Social Relations, op. cit.,* p. 515-38.

search Station at the University of Iowa in the areas of nutrition, physical growth, child psychology, pre-school education, character education, and the relative influence of nature versus nurture in intellectual development. Pioneer work in adapting the observational technique has been done in the Institute of Child Welfare, University of Minnesota, particularly in devising and validating the "time-sampling" technique. Observational studies of the growth and development of infants and young children have characterized the work of the Clinic for Child Development at Yale University, depending primarily on photography as a recording technique. Many of these developmental investigations are summarized or characterized in the chapter on growth and genetic investigations.

A serious result of magnifying the merits of controlled experimentation is a tendency to neglect other techniques simpler in structure—in particular, direct observation of behavior. It would be of major importance to have full, running, authentic accounts of what happens from day to day in teaching a group of children some complex skill, or generalization, or attitude. Close observation and intelligent questions could reveal errors and their origins, rapid improvement and the reasons, instructional shortcomings and methods of correction, plateau periods in learning and corrective measures, and levels of progress from time to time or stage to stage.[135]

In studying problems of major importance through recording relatively simple forms of behavior, laboratory observation is only extending the method used in direct observation, namely, use of some characteristic of behavior as an indication of psychological response tendencies that underlie the overt activity. While laboratory studies, as a rule, are concerned with behavior in non-social situations, mechanically recorded observation may be used to study behavior in situations where the predominating stimuli are social, provided the means of recording portray sufficiently large or complex aspects of behavior to retain elements vital for one's purpose. Direct or indirect observation of social behavior, or the less restricted forms of laboratory observation, may be directed toward descriptive-survey, experimental, genetic, or case-study purposes; it is the larger frame of the study, rather than the data-gathering technique employed, that determines its research methodology or logical character.

**Special forms of recording.** In addition to note-taking during direct observation, there are special forms of recording that provide a more complete record of what takes place; for example, shorthand records of conversations, still or motion pictures, sound records, and other devices.

[135] William A. Brownell, "A Critique of Research on Learning and on Instruction in the School." *Graduate Study in Education.* Fiftieth Yearbook of the National Society for the Study of Education, Part I. Chicago: University of Chicago Press, 1951. p. 62-65.

Stenographic notes as observational records have provided evidence of the relative amounts of verbal participation by teacher and by pupils, extent to which participation is concentrated or scattered in the class, type of English used, and topical emphasis. On the other hand, stenographic records cannot reflect, except in a minor way, the dynamic aspects of the teacher's personality, enthusiasm of the group, shifting of overt attention, and tempo of the intellectual exchange, in addition to many other non-verbal elements in the classroom situation. Stenographic records of themselves do not afford a satisfactory basis for judging the work of a teacher beyond certain restricted aspects.

Stenographic records have been used to some extent in recording and analyzing oral English, but their administration is difficult, costly, and not entirely accurate. Some investigators in the area of oral English have utilized electric recording devices, which have made possible normative studies of language usage of different groups of children and their errors, genetic studies of the development of language patterns, and experimental investigations of the effects of different procedures.

Motion pictures have been used extensively in the study of physical activities and sports,[136] especially in observing the movement of the players of a football team. Such pictures have the advantage of presenting the action in slow motion, and of repeating the film for another look, so that the movement of an individual player or a football play can be analyzed. Motion pictures have been used with increasing frequency in studying gymnasium performance, and the sports of basketball, baseball, and track.

The recording of certain aspects of behavior by mechanical means tends to make the observation objective. The observer may look at the same record repeatedly and thus improve his judgment or appraisal of what actually happened, in contrast to the possibility of an immediate judgment based on a single impression of something that ceased to exist after an instant. Furthermore, other workers may also study the record and, if all agree that the behavior represents a certain type of activity, the observational method may be regarded as highly objective.

An important question with respect to mechanical methods of recording, in relation to descriptive-survey research, is whether they cover at one time enough different elements of behavior, of the individual and of the group, so that all the different types of significant factors are recorded. It has been pointed out in this section that the distinctive contribution of direct observation is in its capacity for dealing with complex phenomena, especially in typical social situations. There is danger of vitiating this

---

136 Ruth Glassow and Others, *op. cit.*, p. 204-18. See also certain chapters on laboratory and experimental research, p. 182-203, 254-300.

opportunity through making the characteristic one observes so narrow and simple that it loses the significance it should have for contributing to the understanding of behavior in actual social situations. It is true that this result may occur with or without the use of mechanical means of recording, but any objective or mechanical form of recording should not, in and of itself, impose further restrictions upon the nature of the characteristic under observation that can be avoided.

Mechanical recording is used extensively in laboratory studies and represents an indirect type of observation. (Controlled experimentation in the laboratory is discussed in a later chapter dealing with the techniques of experimentation.) Laboratory studies usually are confined to a type of behavior not immediately social in its stimulation or expression. Because of these facts and of the additional fact that the characteristic under study is usually made very simple, laboratory investigations are frequently considered as producing relatively artificial results, not typical of the normal social or classroom situations in school. While it is true that laboratory investigations, in the narrow sense, are not capable of measuring directly the complex types of response which constitute the domain of direct observation, experimentation may produce results of large significance for education, psychology, and the other social fields. This comes about primarily through discovery of some response which, though fairly simple in itself, is indicative of a variation in a much more complex response. To cite an example, although eye-movements in reading are relatively simple in themselves, they may be considered as an indication of the direction of one's attention. A great deal can be learned about the difficulties experienced by a person in reading, through the technique of eye-photography, by noting how many pauses are made in reading a line of type, where the pauses are made, what their duration is, and under what circumstances he makes regressive movements. In analyzing the eye-movements of a subject looking at a picture, the investigator may learn how people explore pictures, what features they note, as compared with what the artist looks at in the picture. Such laboratory studies may be of the descriptive-survey type, if made for the purpose of establishing status or prevailing habits, or they may be experiments, if for the purpose of studying variation in performance that follows changes in some factor, such as different sizes of type, different lengths of line, different kinds of reading material, or pictures in different colors.

A partial summary of the mechanical aids available for recording includes motion and still pictures, sound recording, a one-way vision screen or mirror, an experimental or isolation cabinet for infants, a photographic dome (with a one-way vision screen and tracks for movement of the camera), an electric-eye "ticker" to count the number of autos passing a given spot, a counting apparatus at the gate or door to keep a current record of attendance, an observer with a "ticker" device in his hand to count the number of persons passing a particular spot, a mechanical recording device attached to the radio in the home to indicate to headquarters that the radio is in use (or to record a vote on questions presented over the radio, or to register the extent to which the radio set is used), a record of the number of telephone calls placed per month, an applause meter, and an odometer on an auto.

As another example, an investigator of the procedures of good and poor problem solvers (engaged in solving verbal problems in arithmetic) employed a tape recorder as an aid to later interviewing by the investigator.[137] He sought to isolate and describe characteristics in problem-solving in arithmetic that showed evidence of thoughtful and meaningful understanding, as contrasted with adherence to purely mechanical manipulation, sheer guesswork, and trial and error.

An exploratory investigation of the errors made by violinists and clarinetists, at four levels of performing ability, on a specially prepared sight-reading test, employed a wire recorder to record the individual performance of each subject. Then the recordings were played back as many times as necessary to permit the investigator to diagnose the errors.[138]

A record of what a seven-year-old boy did in the situations confronting him in his home, school, and neighborhood from the time he awoke one morning until he went to sleep that night represents a minute-by-minute chronology, showing him interacting with parents, teachers, adults, and other children.[139] Eight trained observers took turns in gathering the data throughout the day. Each observational period was approximately thirty minutes in length, with brief notes made during the period and the observations dictated into a sound recorder immediately after the end of the period.

**Administrative aspects of observational studies.** The administrative aspects of planning for observation include factors that affect the success of the study: securing an appropriate group of subjects to observe, deciding and arranging any special conditions for the group, determining the length of each observation period, the interval between periods, and the number of periods. While these are in part matters of adjusting to local

[137] Clyde G. Corle, "The Characteristics of the Procedures of Good and Poor Problem Solvers in Sixth-Grade Arithmetic." Unpublished doctoral dissertation, Teachers College, University of Cincinnati, 1953.

[138] A. G. Thomson, "An Analysis of Difficulties in Sight Reading Music for Violin and Clarinet." Unpublished doctoral dissertation, Teachers College, University of Cincinnati, 1953.

[139] Roger G. Barker and Herbert F. Wright, *op. cit.*

conditions, the investigator must consider the general principles of sampling, especially as relating to different numbers of children and different numbers of periods. While the length of period of observation should be related to the type of activity under study, periods of a minute or two are suitable for some situations and periods of an hour or more are better for other activities or aspects of behavior. A few seconds of a motion-picture film may record a particular behavior under consideration, while an hour or more may be needed to observe the acts of aggression or coöperation of a group of children in a nursery school.

The physical position of the observer and the possible effect on the subject must be considered in planning systematic observation of behavior. It is obvious that the observer must maintain a physical position that will enable him to see or hear the aspects of behavior under study. In some settings, especially laboratory schools and nursery schools, one-way vision screens, or windows, or mirrors commonly are available for use by observers. Children in such situations, however, have been frequently observed and soon become accustomed to the presence of a visitor. With an increase in coöperative, democratic methods of instruction during recent years, it has been found that children in most school settings soon become habituated to the presence of visitors and observers.

**Units of behavior and scope of observation.** In defining the activities to be observed, the purpose is to include those activities truly representative of the general category under study, and to define them so carefully that questions regarding what to include do not arise. The validity of the results will depend in large part on how well the investigator chooses and defines activities that will contain the essential elements in which he is really interested. There may be some danger in the tendency to restrict the trait being observed to as narrow or simple an element of behavior as possible; if carried too far, this delimitation often defeats the peculiar advantage of the observation technique (in being able to deal with significant units of normal behavior). (For a discussion of categories, see the section on classification in Chapter 5.)

Every clinical worker uses the method of observation, although he may make no deliberate attempt to describe his techniques completely. On the other hand, some clinical specialists may have placed overemphasis on a number of favorite expressions, in the form of clinical "clichés," to describe the behavior of patients. While individual testing instruments are useful for clinical purposes, in providing observational findings and quantitative scores, the clinician should watch what the subject does, as a supplement to his concentration on whether the test is performed correctly.[140] A major

140 Robert I. Watson, *op. cit.,* p. 416-17.

difficulty in clinical work, when regarded as science, is not that it deals with phenomena at such a complex level, but rather that it utilizes such unreliable methods for identifying factors and determining their status (force, or degree). (Clinical studies will be treated more fully in the chapter dealing with case and clinical approaches.)

A tally may be used to record the frequency of a particular defined unit of behavior taking place during the entire time devoted to observation; for example, the number of different times a child recites during the total period of the observation or the total number of acts of coöperation or aggression. When the observation period is broken up into time units of five, ten, or thirty seconds, or possibly a minute or two, a tally may be entered in each time unit during which a child demonstrates the particular phase of behavior or activity; for example, when he laughs, is physically inactive, or engages in some act of coöperation or aggression. This form of tabulation sometimes is more meaningful than to know the gross count for the entire period of observation, such as an hour or more in a nursery-school setting; for example, acts of aggression or evidences of boredom may be present at certain times during the day because of fatigue or too long a period of time devoted to a particular type of activity; a tally of responses or units of behavior according to definite time units within the total observation period would permit analytical study of such variations. For certain purposes it may be important to note not only the frequency of different responses but also their extent or duration; for example, to distinguish between a lengthy answer from a pupil and a brief "yes" or "no" reply. In observing behavior, relative frequencies may be as important as absolute frequencies; for example, one child may engage in thirty instances of coöperation and ten acts of aggression, while another child may exhibit sixty instances of coöperation and only ten acts of aggression. The second child would seem to be relatively more coöperative.

In determining the scope of the observation, as applied to an individual child or to a group, certain decisions must be made. In observing one or two children, or "problem" cases, it is possible to record virtually every aspect of behavior.[141] On the other hand, in observing systematically the responses of a group of twenty or thirty children, probably only one, or two, or three major aspects of behavior can be observed and recorded successfully. Such group data would indicate trends or gross comparisons between different classes or groups with respect to certain performances, but might not yield reliable data for individual children. Under proper restrictions, however, observation of an entire group of children or pupils may throw helpful light on individual subjects, while an observation cen-

[141] Roger G. Barker and Herbert F. Wright, *op. cit.*

tering on one child in a group setting may provide some information useful in understanding other children in the group.

**Arranging for the record.** Not all the definitions or specifications will appear on the record form; they must be well understood in advance. The form of recording should be so arranged as to make note-taking easy and rapid, with the possibility of saving considerable time through appropriate use of symbols, abbreviations, and sometimes shorthand. In the earlier section of this chapter, dealing with the questionnaire, a number of suggestions have been made that are applicable to preparation of the record blank for observation, including the problems of analyzing and copying the data from the original record. If the record is to be made by a stenographer, a motion-picture operator, or by some other special means, in any case the investigators should make preliminary or exploratory observations in advance, as described in the section on classification in Chapter 5.

**Training for observation and reliability.** In training oneself or others to observe, it is important to remember that perception improves with practice; one learns to see characteristics of behavior by thoughtful practice in seeing them. It is not so much the physical side of seeing that is most important, but the psychological side, and this requires the building up of a recognition readiness before skilled seeing can take place. In view of the fact that it may require several months of looking through a microscope before one can see things that are in plain sight to the trained person, the investigator should expect to undergo training of several months in the observation of behavior characteristics before he begins to gather data for a careful study. The worker who expects to employ direct observation of behavior as a research tool should not underestimate the preparation essential to success in the use of this technique. At one time the observational method was popular, because it was thought to require no preparation and no apparatus; one simply watched the child, and the amount the observer was able to select, observe, and record accurately was dictated by his special genius, but that day is now far behind us.

As to the extensiveness of training for observing of the introspective type, "it is said that no observer who had performed less than 10,000 of these introspectively controlled reactions was suitable to provide data for published research from Wundt's laboratory. Some Americans, like Cattell, had the idea that the minds of untrained observers might also be of interest to psychology, and later a bitter little quarrel on this matter developed." [142]

---

[142] Edwin G. Boring, "A History of Introspection." *Psychological Bulletin* 50:169-89; May 1953.

Current literature emphasizes the inseparability of personality and learning, and recommends wider use of methods of observation in studying the personalities of pupils, particularly in matters relating to self-confidence, motivation, creativeness, and reaction to praise and censure:

> It seems probable that teachers as a group understand children far better than parents as a group. Still, the typical teacher does not appear to gain much in this respect through years of teaching. If this is true, educational psychology must assume much of the blame. We have not, in teacher-training courses, given teachers the basic training in mental-hygiene concepts and practices, nor in the dynamics of personality, required to enable them to make useful observations. One does not make significant observations merely because there is something that is observable. Much of what goes into observation comes out of one's own head.[143]

The chief advance of scientific observation over ordinary observation is the establishment of the reliability of the observations.[144] In determining the observer's reliability, the common procedure has been to compare, item by item, the records secured when two or more independent observers simultaneously record the same behavior. In some instances the observer can be checked against mechanical recordings of the behavior under study. It is simpler to evaluate the reliability of the observer when a predetermined list of categories is used than when a "running account" is employed.

As a general rule, reliability is likely to improve with an increase in the size of the sampling, although there are limits in taking advantage of this tendency, since some aspects of behavior by their very nature are not constant; for example, when children are making initial adjustments in a new situation. Since the behavior of individuals may vary significantly in different situations and settings, it is desirable to observe reactions in as diversified settings and circumstances as possible, so as to constitute a representative sampling of the child's daily life. An adequate understanding of the child's behavior cannot be secured solely through observation in the classroom; he may respond very differently in the hallway of the school building, on the playground, on the way home, or in his own home, particularly when he thinks the teachers or his parents are not observing him. In summary, if one's purpose is to observe a broad sample of behavior under the varying conditions of life, he will of course not confine his observations to any one environmental condition or setting (physical or social).

[143] Quoted from J. B. Stroud, "Educational Psychology." *Annual Review of Psycholgy,* Vol. 2. Stanford, Calif.: Annual Reviews, 1951. p. 290-91.

[144] As noted by Frank N. Freeman, "Foreword." In Harold H. Anderson and Joseph E. Brewer, *Studies of Teachers' Classroom Personalities,* II: Effects of Teachers' Dominative and Integrative Contacts on Children's Classroom Behavior. Applied Psychology Monographs, No. 8. Stanford University, Calif.: Stanford University Press, 1946.

**Observation and interpretation.** "The simplest observation in physics or psychology has in it the essence of a judgment or an interpretation." [145] According to Boring, even Helmholtz knew that

the observation depends upon the past experience of the observer, his unconscious inferences and the resulting modification of the sensory core. . . . There is the influence of a "laboratory atmosphere" upon observational results, which means that investigators are likely to observe what they are trained to observe, and there is also the contrary fact that good observers have to be trained.[146]

The uncertainty of direct observation is well illustrated by "flying saucers," owing to indefinite concepts, exaggeration, error, imagination, and absence of essential facts.[147]

The basic method in psychology is the same as that employed by common sense, viz., *observation* of datum, coupled with *interpretation* of its significance. The only difference is that psychology ordinarily follows the lead of the older sciences and makes use of ingenious and controlled techniques for securing observation normally not available to the layman; and in interpretation psychology is hedged in with various rules of evidence and logic which do not bind the layman or artist.[148]

It seems then that if the eye is used to observe it may be necessary not only to look *at* the detail to be observed, but also to look *for* it. We do not always find with our sense organs unless we also seek. . . . The demonstrator of experiments at a university exhibition of popular science has still more examples of this evidence that a part of observation consists in both looking at and looking for the object. . . . Perhaps we unconsciously add something derived from previous experience.[149]

In many of his statements, George as a physical scientist, and writing in the middle 1930's, has come close to psychological insights at times; he has sensed that the physical sciences are not as simple and direct as some persons think. While he describes the difficulties, he always turns back to a physical scientist's interpretations (a yen for perfect objectivity), although it is quite clear to George that this is virtually impossible. He does not quite realize the nature of perception, that all sensations are colored, interpreted before they reach man's cerebrum, again during cerebration, and again on the way out.

[145] Edwin G. Boring, "Psychology for Eclectics." *Psychologies of 1930*. Edited by Carl Murchison. Worcester: Clark University Press, 1930. p. 118.

[146] Quoted from Edwin G. Boring, *A History of Experimental Psychology*. Second Edition. New York: Appleton-Century-Crofts, 1950. p. 313.

[147] C. C. Wylie, "Those Flying Saucers." *Science* 118:124-26; July 31, 1953.

Donald H. Menzel, *Flying Saucers*. Cambridge: Harvard University Press, 1953. 319 p.

[148] Quoted from Gordon W. Allport, *Personality, a Psychological Interpretation*. New York: Henry Holt and Co., 1937. p. 369-70.

[149] Quoted from William H. George, *The Scientist in Action*. London: Williams and Norgate, 1936. p. 84-85.

Operational logic shows that "human consciousness is an inferred construct, a concept as inferential as any of the other psychologists' realities, and that literally immediate observation, the introspection that cannot lie, does not exist. All observation is a process that takes some time and is subject to error in the course of its occurrence." [150]

A person makes a judgment, not from a specific observation of a particular item, but from the impact of a whole system of thought upon that particular fact, not by itself, but as an item in a background situation, and also as one of many facts that belong to a certain class. Observation is thus conditioned heavily by expectancy. Observation is predominantly the functioning of a pattern that has been established in the mind, this pattern being aroused by something in the objective situation which suggests that it is the appropriate mental pattern to fit the situation. This tendency of a whole system of thought to condition one's perception explains why workers are so blind to many things that later become obvious as they focus attention specifically upon them (impartially upon them); it explains why mankind has gone for centuries at a time, not seeing the error of a certain type of philosophy or scientific generalization, tenet, belief, law, or principle. It explains why what we are now doing will seem so blind and childlike, when viewed by workers in the distant future who have shaken off some of our biased preconceptions, and who have achieved more perfect patterns of thought that permit them to observe more accurately the things we are now seeing through glasses clouded with ill-adapted response patterns. What one sees is principally a readiness to respond that is touched off by the objective situation. It is predominantly a readiness pattern that affects one, or registers on consciousness. We do not see as we think we do; we do not see simply and directly. Our seeing has become overgrown or encumbered with response patterns—complex, mature, crystallized, and inflexible. Observation also is conditioned by a tendency to act, which may be direct, and may even short-circuit conscious attention. Our action patterns may behave like our perception patterns, and may be very direct, so direct that consciousness or awareness may be negligible or fleeting.

Research is constantly examining its observations critically, to see whether the concepts behind them are sound and whether the observation process itself (including instruments) can be improved.

[150] Edwin G. Boring, "A History of Introspection," *op. cit.*

## SMALL-GROUP STUDY OR GROUP-BEHAVIOR ANALYSIS[151]

The preceding section on systematic observation of behavior already has directed the reader's attention to the importance of observation in study of small groups or in group-behavior analysis. The concepts and techniques of observation outlined in the preceding section apply, for the most part, to the present discussion of small-group studies, including: aspects of behavior observed and recorded, non-participant and participant observation, instruments for observation, forms of recording, categories or units of behavior, time units for tallying responses, length of the period for observation, scope of the observation, training and reliability of the observer, and observation in relation to interpretation.[152]

[151] American Philosophical Society, "Research Frontiers in Human Relations," *Proceedings,* Vol. 92, No. 5, November 1948. Philadelphia: The Society, 1948. p. 325-410.

Leland P. Bradford, Dorwin Cartwright, and Others, "The Dynamics of Work Groups." *Adult Leadership* 2:8-27; December 1953.

Leland P. Bradford and Jack R. Gibbs, "Developments in Group Behavior in Adult Education." *Review of Educational Research* 23:233-47; June 1953.

Jerome S. Bruner, "Social Psychology and Group Processes." *Annual Review of Psychology,* Vol. 1. Edited by Calvin P. Stone and Donald W. Taylor. Stanford, Calif.: Annual Reviews, 1950. p. 119-50.

Dorwin Cartwright and Alvin Zander, *Group Dynamics:* Research and Theory. Evanston, Ill.: Row, Peterson and Co., 1953. 642 p.

Leon Festinger, Stanley Schachter, and Kurt Back, *Social Pressures in Informal Groups.* New York: Harper and Bros., 1950. 240 p.

N. L. Gage, "Explorations in the Understanding of Others." *Educational and Psychological Measurement* 13:14-26; Spring 1953.

John W. Green and Selz C. Mayo, "A Framework for Research in the Actions of Community Groups." *Social Forces* 31:320-27; May 1953.

Harold Guetzkow, Editor, *Groups, Leadership, and Men:* Research in Human Relations. Pittsburgh: Carnegie Press, 1951. 293 p.

George C. Homans, *The Human Group.* New York: Harcourt, Brace and Co., 1950. 484 p.

Ronald Lippitt, *Training in Community Relations.* New York: Harper and Bros., 1949. 286 p.

John H. Rohrer and Muzafer Sherif, *Social Psychology at the Crossroads.* New York: Harper and Bros., 1951. 437 p.

Mary E. Roseborough, "Experimental Studies of Small Groups." *Psychological Bulletin* 50:275-303; July 1953.

Muzafer Sherif and M. O. Wilson, *Group Relations at the Crossroads.* New York: Harper and Bros., 1953. viii + 379 p.

S. R. Slavson, *Analytic Group Psychotherapy.* New York: Columbia University Press, 1950.

Herbert A. Thelen, "Educational Dynamics, Theory and Research." *Journal of Social Issues* 6:1-96; 1950.

George A. Theodorson, "Elements in the Progressive Development of Small Groups." *Social Forces* 31:311-20; May 1953.

William A. Van Til and Others, "Research on Human Relations and Programs of Action." *Review of Educational Research* 23:285-385; October 1953. Chapters 1, 2, 7.

Irving R. Weschler and Paula Brown, Editors, *Evaluating Research and Development.* Los Angeles: Human Relations Research Group, Institute of Industrial Relations, 1953. 104 p.

Alvin Zander, "Systematic Observation of Small Face-to-Face Groups," *Research Methods in Social Relations.* Edited by Marie Jahoda and Others. New York: Dryden Press, 1951. p. 515-38.

[152] Alvin Zander, *op. cit.,* p. 515-38.

**Characteristics of small-group study.** A broad illustration of small-group study or group-behavior analysis may be helpful. The nature of the phenomena observed may be the qualities of certain acts; the individual-member behavior may be considered as the quality of certain reactions (friendly, hostile, constructive, regressive, dishonest, or intolerant); the group behavior recorded by the observer may be the nature of the climate of group interaction (friendly, hostile, work-centered, and so on).

An understanding of the various approaches to study of groups involves at least three major problems or questions: the proper relation between data-gathering and theory building, the basic variables of group dynamics that determine the properties of groups, and the proper objects of study and techniques of observation. Cartwright and Zander have sought answers to some of these questions in a full-length treatment of research and theory in group dynamics covering: typical premises and methods used in research on groups, formation of groups and the development of group cohesiveness, nature of group pressures and the operation of group standards, group goals and the problems inherent in the movement of a group toward its objectives, structure of groups, and research on leadership.[153]

**The research literature of small-group study.** A pertinent review and summary of the research literature on group behavior for the period of the early 1950's includes ninety-four references. The topics covered are trends in small-group research, development in methodology, leader style and group atmosphere, communication in small groups, interpersonal perceptions, the decision-making process, emotional factors in group interaction, group size and the large meeting, and leadership and human-relations training.[154]

A summary and interpretation of 169 experimental studies of small groups covers the following topics: contrasts and comparisons between the behavior of groups and individuals, manipulation of social-structure variables important to group functioning (authority relationships), effect of cultural variables (sharing of values and goals in a group), manipulation of situational conditions (such as group task, size of group, communication networks), and personality variables affecting group behavior.[155]

Certain concepts, techniques, and illustrative references in other parts of this book have significant applications to small-group study or group-behavior analysis: the questionnaire, interview, and observation sections of the present chapter, the section on classification in the preceding chapter, and the chapters on experimentation and case study.

[153] Dorwin Cartwright and Alvin Zander, *op. cit.*
[154] Leland P. Bradford and Jack R. Gibb, *op. cit.*
[155] Mary E. Roseborough, *op. cit.*

## QUANTITATIVE (CONTENT) ANALYSIS OF
## DOCUMENTARY MATERIALS[156]

Quantitative analysis of documentary materials, like historical research, deals with records that already exist. Documentary analysis, however, is definitely quantitative; it was not concerned in the earlier studies with the general import or message of the existing documents, but with certain characteristics that can be identified and counted. Important parts of this type of investigation, in fact, possibly the most crucial parts, are to determine what characteristics to count, and to define them. The fact that the investigator works directly from documents does not mean that he avoids all problems of collecting and selecting data. It is true that in certain types of investigations he may need only the library as a source for bringing together a collection of books, but in other cases it may be necessary to collect the documentary specimens from a distance, or from a variety of settings and sources. In any case, problems of selection are involved, with respect to the specimens that are collected and the aspects to be noted.

**Earlier approaches to textbook analysis.** Textbook analysis is one of the simpler examples of quantitative study of documentary materials. This type of approach has been used frequently in graduate theses, particularly by masters' candidates. A student may choose any set of objective characteristics that he considers significant in a group of textbooks and note the extent to which they occur; for example, he may count frequencies as follows: sentences of different lengths, words that appear to be difficult,

[156] Bernard Berelson, *Content Analysis in Communication Research.* Glencoe, Ill.: Free Press, 1952. 220 p.

Bernard Berelson and M. Janowitz, *Reader in Public Opinion and Communication.* Glencoe, Ill.: Free Press, 1953. xi + 611 p.

Edgar Dale, "Quantitative Analysis of Documentary Materials." *Review of Educational Research* 9:466-71, 595-96; December 1939.

Edgar Dale and Others, *Mass Media and Education.* Fifty-third Yearbook of the National Society for the Study of Education, Part 2. Chicago: University of Chicago Press, 1954. x + 290 p.

Leonard W. Doob, *Public Opinion and Propaganda.* New York: Henry Holt and Co., 1948. vii + 600 p.

Leon Festinger and Daniel Katz, *op. cit.,* p. 419-70.

Carter V. Good, A. S. Barr, and Douglas E. Scates, *op. cit.,* p. 343-73. Covers a considerable amount of the literature before the middle 1930's.

William J. Goode and Paul K. Hatt, *op. cit.,* p. 325-30.

Marie Jahoda and Others, *op. cit.,* p. 235-44, 539-60.

Harold D. Lasswell, Nathan Leites, and Others, *Language of Politics.* New York: Stewart Co., 1949. vii + 398 p.

Henry J. Otto and Donald McDonald, "Learning Materials." *Review of Educational Research* 21:220-26; June 1951.

Marvin Spiegelman, Carl Terwilliger, and Franklin Fearing, "The Reliability of Agreement in Content Analysis" and "The Content of Comics: Goals and Means to Goals of Comic Strip Characters." *Journal of Social Psychology* 37:175-87, 189-203; May 1953.

T. D. Weldon, *The Vocabulary of Politics.* Baltimore: Penguin Books, 1953. 199 p.

Ralph K. White, *Value-Analysis:* The Nature and Use of the Method. New York: Society for the Psychological Study of Social Issues, Columbia University, 1951. 87 p.

pictures, tables, exercises at the ends of chapters, different topics represented, and lines or pages devoted to each topic. Other types of textbook analysis may deal somewhat more broadly with the kind of content (perhaps in relation to the objectives of the school subject represented), grade placement or general difficulty of the material, and vocabulary load or burden. While some forms of textbook analysis have been regarded as highly mechanical, several types of investigation have proved useful in textbook writing and in instructional procedures; for example, standard word lists have been used extensively by authors and teachers in determining the vocabulary appropriate at a particular age or grade level.

Documentary analyses of textbooks as a form of status study are evaluative when criteria have been set up, and validated; in that case the evaluation becomes no longer subjective, but objective and a form of measurement. There is always the danger that the criteria may be to some extent warped, incomplete, biased, dominating, or misleading. Hence, there are dangers and difficulties of interpretation.

**Earlier analyses of larger bodies of literature.** Certain larger bodies of literature (usually more extensive than a collection of fifteen or twenty textbooks) have been subjected to quantitative analysis. Among the earlier investigations in this field are the following illustrations: techniques of research employed in arithmetic investigations, classified with respect to problem and type of technique used; frequency study of investigations in arithmetic and reading, showing the historical trend and the number of investigations per author; major fields of human concern, as represented in the topics covered in periodical literature; column-inches of spaces devoted to various topics in newspapers over a period of time; number of columns devoted to each topic in an encyclopedia set of many volumes; classification of the topics apparently referred to by the 10,000 most frequently used English words; topics treated over a period of years in a weekly news magazine; duties and traits of a good citizen, as revealed by newspaper editorials and magazine articles on citizenship; civic and social shortcomings emphasized in the editorials of newspapers and magazines; social problems of the labor group, as identified in widely read books and labor periodicals; characteristics of human behavior approved and disapproved in a series of essays; approved social behavior, as identified by a canvass of certain books and magazine articles; shortcomings in the written English of adults, as revealed in letters writen for newspaper publication; and mathematics used in popular science, as found in certain magazines and books.

Many of these quantitative analyses of textbooks and larger bodies of literature were used to a considerable extent in curriculum development during the 1920's and 1930's, and later. The underlying theory is that, since not everything known can be taught in school, the knowledge regarded as most useful socially should be selected and taught; these basic elements, according to the primary assumption of documentary analysis, can be discovered through appropriate interpretation of frequency analyses of social activities and interests.

**Earlier analyses of assembled specimens (counts of words, errors, and items in reports).** While books, magazines, and newspapers are important for purposes of documentary analysis, equally significant investigations are based on materials from sources other than the library. An important source consists of materials written for other purposes and merely collected as specimens for purposes of analysis. Examples may be drawn from three types of assembled specimens—vocabulary studies, error studies, and investigations of record and report systems.

Vocabulary analysis has identified the most common words and the most readily understood words. Thorndike did pioneer work in this area with his list of 10,000 common words, and later lists of 20,000 and 30,000 common words.[157] Other examples of vocabulary analysis include frequency lists of the most common words in certain foreign languages; a common basic vocabulary for children of a particular age, both in reading and writing, to serve as valuable information in the preparation of readers and language textbooks; words regarded as technical or peculiar to a particular school subject in such fields as mathematics, geography, and history; frequency with which words are used in different situations, such as reading, writing letters, and speaking, to serve as the basis for the spelling curriculum and spelling textbooks; and the actual difficulty of words.

These various examples of vocabulary analysis have typically involved the gathering of children's compositions, social letters, and other specimens of child or adult usage of words in normal situations. Many of these investigations have secured supplementary information like counts of the words in published sources. Word lists represent only one type of illustration of the technique of counting frequencies of occurrence in informal usage; studies of informal usage of arithmetic and of other subjects also have been made, in addition to analyses of the more formal usage occurring in printed sources.

---

[157] E. L. Thorndike, *Teachers' Word Book*. New York: Columbia University, 1921. 134 p.

E. L. Thorndike, *Teachers' Word Book*, of the 20,000 Words Found Most Frequently and Widely in General Reading for Children and Young People. Revised Edition. New York: Teachers College, Columbia University, 1932. 182 p.

E. L. Thorndike and Irving Lorge, *Teachers' Word Book of 30,000 Words*. New York: Teachers College, Columbia University, 1944. 274 p. Also see:

Henry D. Rinsland, *Basic Vocabulary of Elementary School Children*. New York: Macmillan Co., 1945. 636 p.

As an example of documentary analysis, a teacher or a supervisor wishes to select supplementary reading books. He makes a word study to determine which supplementary books have a given number of new words not in the basic readers, and the extent to which the supplementary books repeat the words in the basic readers. The teacher or supervisor is now faced with a question of value judgment. How much repetition is desired? How many new words? The answer involves the emphasis, purpose, and philosophy of teaching reading.

Another group of quantitative studies concerned with informal usage has dealt with frequency of errors in usage rather than frequency of use. While the techniques in vocabulary analysis and in error studies are similar, the latter have depended more completely upon informal materials. Many of these investigations have been concerned with language in its various phases, since errors in this area (including reading and the mechanics of writing) normally constitute the bulk of the mistakes made in informal written materials. The earlier studies of errors emphasize the usage aspects of: spelling, arithmetic, geography, modern foreign languages, capitalization, punctuation, grammar, sentence structure, speech, and even the errors made by teachers. Later developments of a case and clinical nature encouraged diagnosis and remedial work in areas other than usage, as pointed out in the chapter on case and clinical studies, including science, health, behavior, vocations, music, art, leisure-time activities, and creativeness.

School records and reports represent another type of assembled specimens for purposes of quantitative analysis. A common procedure has been to collect a group of record forms or reports from a specified number of school systems for the purpose of noting certain characteristics of the forms and then counting the number of school systems with this characteristic (frequently an item on a blank). A more elaborate analysis of records and reports included such items as the following, in terms of frequency for each item: appearance on the pupil-record forms for a group of cities; as needed by superintendents or others to prepare the required reports made to the state department of education; as needed to make various studies listed in the literature as desirable; and as actually used by teachers and principals. Other analyses of records include the following examples: mechanical makeup of superintendents' reports, effectiveness of superintendents' reports in giving information and in the public-relations program, records of city school systems, records of county school systems, records of state school systems, cumulative record cards of pupils, report cards or other forms for parents, teachers' class registers, records of department heads in high schools, office records, principals' monthly and annual reports to the superintendent, superintendents' monthly reports to the school board, financial reports, and the records and reports of business managers.

**Interpretation of studies of frequency.** Interpretation of frequency analysis of documentary materials is similar in many respects to the interpretation of questionnaire returns, as discussed in another section of this chapter. There are similar problems in interpreting the practical significance of frequencies, particularly in curriculum development. While frequency may be an element of importance, it is only one element, and its significance must be evaluated by analyzing carefully its logical and functional contribution to the total picture. The concept of frequency involves two different aspects. If the investigator secures responses indicating the number of people who do a certain thing or the number of times the behavior occurs throughout the group, the frequency may be interpreted in the form of a proportion of the group, or as a per cent. In another sense, frequency may refer to a time concept. How often does a particular individual perform a given act or engage in a certain form of behavior or response? An important question concerning many of the earlier frequency studies voiced the fear that such investigation overstressed the commonplace or the average, and did not provide suitable goals for taking the next steps on the road to progress. Another criticism of the earlier studies was that many of them were concerned with details, whereas large numbers of teachers and educators wished to place stress on integrating principles and orienting ideas.

Interpretation of error studies in such areas as English usage and arithmetic may make them appear to have more intrinsic value than other frequency investigations, since they deal directly with deficiencies or shortcomings, and have been made for the express purpose of revealing weaknesses. A criticism of the earlier studies of errors is that they do not reveal why the child made the particular errors and, therefore, do not provide much help in teaching him. In most instances an error is a response habit that probably has a long history, growing out of a complex background of information and associations which at some time and place have become tangled. Error studies involve an implication that whatever children do not know they should learn. There is little value in revealing what a child cannot do, unless we also know what he should be able to do; we are interested in discovering what a child's habits or responses should be for each age and grade. Most of the earlier investigations of errors gave little attention to the psychology of learning and almost no help to the teacher on working the instructional materials into the child's experiences. By their very objectivity, the findings of error studies may tend to distort the true picture of the child's needs. Such investigations direct attention to certain very narrow aspects of the child's shortcomings and fail to reveal the condition of many other kinds of deficiency that probably exist in the pupil's abilities or habits (which may be of far greater import). A perspective that begins with and emphasizes errors, rather than with a more complete picture of the accomplishment desired, seldom reaches the more subtle, less conspicuous, but exceedingly important aspects of ability, such as interest, pleasure in doing or using, emotional adjustment, purpose, and other large integrating and dynamic patterns of performance and behavior. As in many other types of investigation, when interpreting frequency studies, the simpler and the more objective the facts, the more circumspect one has to be in drawing practical conclusions from them.

**Theory and technique of content analysis.** Simple statistical studies of an analytical type, based on documentary materials, probably should be differentiated from content analysis as such. The simple statistical investigations utilize categories already existing, or easily made, with no particularly subtle challenge; the categories do not have to emerge as to quality, only as to quantity. On the other hand, content analysis is highly subtle in its obligation to recognize, identify, and detect the presence of essential or significant factors represented in the categories, for the purpose of placement in larger categories. To put it another way, there is a gradual gradation, not a dichotomy, between mechanical, simple, statistical studies (such as the census) and pure content analysis; for example, membership analysis of a group is relatively simple.

Content analysis is measurement through proportion. Like other indexes based on counting, it employs a population or case unit (as percentile rank does); it is, therefore, measurement on a population or case scale—the simplest, most basic kind. Content analysis measures pervasiveness, and that is sometimes an index of the intensity of the force.

Content analysis, as employed in the early 1950's and later, has little relation to the earlier textbook analysis of the 1920's and the 1930's. While the newer type of content analysis is still largely counting, it is with a set of categories far more significant than anything contemplated in the older type of textbook analysis. The difference is somewhat like that between a casual interview (perhaps for employment purposes) and depth interviewing. The difference may be further illustrated by comparing a current review of the content or themes of motion pictures (a sharp challenge by way of determining appropriate categories) with the kind of analysis made in the earlier studies of motion pictures in the late 1920's and 1930's. When compared with this newer type of content analysis, earlier textbook analysis appears relatively superficial, undirected, and mechanical.

As early as the beginning years of the 1940's significant questions were being asked with respect to a new type of content analysis. How can content analysis be used to analyze propaganda in films, radio, and print in such a way as to determine what is likely to produce given effects? How can a procedure known as response-analysis actually determine the responses elicited by propaganda? Does propaganda have any necessary relation to truth or falsity? Since content can be adequately appraised only through systematic procedures, the investigational techniques vary from one extreme of counting the frequency of certain key symbols to the other extreme of determining the structure of the propaganda-as-a-whole or of an entire propaganda campaign.[158]

Doob has advanced the thesis that public opinion and propaganda are closely related, because both involve phases of human behavior. His technique of content analysis is based on the selection of themes and more or less quantifying them, with illustrations drawn from politics, business, and war.[159]

Berelson surveyed several hundred titles in the area of content analysis, to determine their contributions to this technique, in terms of definitions, assumptions, history, general rationale; uses in the social sciences and to a minor extent the humanities; "qualitative" content analysis in comparison with more objective and quantitative techniques; categories, sampling, and reliability. The content of communication includes that body of meanings through symbols (verbal, musical, pictorial, plastic, and gestural) which makes up the communication itself. Content analysis has been used to investigate such diverse topics as the following: the slogans of May Day propaganda in the USSR, dominant images in Shakespeare's plays, values in American plays as compared with German plays of the same period, treatment of minority ethnic groups in short stories published in popular magazines, comparison of newspapers and radio and their treatment of a sensational murder case, manner in which motion pictures reflect popular feelings and desires, similarities and differences in the political symbols that come to the attention of people in the major power states, and intelligence data secured from analysis of enemy propaganda.[160]

White has described a method by which any kind of verbal data (propaganda and public-opinion materials, autobiographies, clinical interviews, letters, conversational records, and other devices of personality study) can

[158] Paul F. Lazarsfeld and Robert K. Merton, "Studies in Radio and Film Propaganda." *Transactions of the New York Academy of Sciences,* Series II, 6:58-79; November 1943.
[159] Leonard W. Doob, *op. cit.*
[160] Bernard Berelson, *Content Analysis in Communication Research, op. cit.*

be described quantitatively and objectively, but with due consideration of the emotional dynamics.[161] He lists certain psychological factors on which data can be obtained—hostility, self-approval, social perception (stereotypes), self-picture and ego-ideal, areas of frustration, and ability to take another's viewpoint.

The central theme of the volume edited by Lasswell and Leites is that political power can be better understood to the extent that language is better understood.[162] The authors have assumed that the language of politics can be studied in a helpful manner by quantitative methods. Their treatment includes the technical problems of both quantification and applications (chiefly to the language of Communism since 1918). They suggest that specialists on problems of government, diplomatic history, and law will be more interested in the applications, while social psychologists and statisticians may wish to examine in detail the treatment of problems of reliability, validity, and sampling.

The purpose of an elaborate series of monographs is to make clear, through the technique of content analysis, the major trends of social change throughout the world within the past six decades; to estimate their direction, intensity, and tempo; and to seek explanations of their significance, with these changes described in relation to the goal values of shared power, respect, well-being, and safety.[163] A basic assumption of the investigators is that, through quantitative techniques of content analysis, major trends of our times can be indexed by changes in the composition and vocabulary of the wielders of power. It is hoped to do for certain branches of history what already has been done in the study of changes in population, production, consumption, and price. The three monographs on symbols cover roughly a sixty-year period of a sample of editorials in the "prestige papers" of the United States, Great Britain, France, Germany, and Russia. The aim of the series of studies is to make available a body of trend data concerning what is variously called ideology, public opinion, public atten-

161 Ralph K. White, *op. cit.*

162 Harold D. Lasswell, Nathan Leites, and Others, *op. cit.*

163 *Revolution and the Development of International Relations.* Hoover Institute Studies. Stanford University, Calif.: Stanford University Press.

Series A: *General Studies*, No. 1. *The World Revolution of Our Time:* A Framework for Basic Policy Research. By Harold D. Lasswell. 1951. 66 p.

Series B: *Elites*

No. 1. *The Comparative Study of Elites:* An Introduction and Bibliography. By Harold D. Lasswell and Others. 1952. 72 p.

No. 2 *The Politburo.* By George K. Schueller. 1951. 79 p.

No. 3 *The Nazi Elite.* By Daniel Lerner. 1951. 112 p.

Series C: *Symbols*

No. 1. *The Comparative Study of Symbols:* An Introduction. By Harold D. Lasswell and Others. 1952. 87 p.

No. 2 *The Prestige Papers:* A Survey of Their Editorials. By Ithiel Pool. 1952. 146 p.

No. 3 *Symbols of Internationalism.* By Ithiel Pool. 1951. 73 p.

No. 4 *Symbols of Democracy.* By Ithiel Pool. 1952. 80 p.

tion, public attitudes, cultural perspectives, political myths, class attitudes, class analysis, elite analysis, and social affiliations.

The vehicles through which national images may be conveyed include such media of mass communication as newspapers, magazines, books, radio broadcasts, films, dramas, lyrics of popular songs, and now television programs. There is good reason to believe that the mass media of the different nations play an important part in maintaining and aggravating internal tensions, by reason of the manner in which they picture national actions and characteristics. Therefore, the problem is a matter of interest and concern both to social science and to international relations.[164]

A psychological study of the movies, based on more than two hundred American, British, and French films, consists of four parts: the typical movie patterns of love and romance, family relationships, violence and crime, and, broadly, the relationship between the protagonists and those characters who observe and judge the protagonists. The authors have combined three classes of statements by way of interpretations: manifest recurrent themes, psychological interpretations of the emotional significance of such themes, and the relation of movie themes to cultural patterns in American life.[165] The significance of this type of analysis of the movies is far greater than the studies of movie content twenty years earlier.

It has been pointed out that, while emphasis on quantitative analysis of communication content has advanced the interests of research in this area, concern with quantification may have become so dominant that it often overshadows interest in the peculiar character of communication data. Current definitions of content analysis in the area of communication content tend to overemphasize the procedure of analysis, as compared with the character of the data available in the recorded communications.[166]

**Other illustrations of textbook and content analysis.** In the interest of variety and brevity, selected examples of textbook and content analysis in education, psychology, and sociology (with annotations) are listed below:

An analysis and classification of 334 different writings by 233 authors, published in forty-two magazines, and grouped into the following categories: schools, colleges, teachers, education for veterans, federal aid, schools of other peoples, adult education, UNESCO, and miscellaneous.[167]

[164] Donald V. McGranahan, "Content Analysis of the Mass Media of Communication," *Research Methods in Social Relations, op. cit.,* p. 539-60.

[165] Martha Wolfenstein and Nathen Leites, *Movies:* A Psychological Study. Glencoe, Ill.: Free Press, 1950. 316 p.

[166] Marie Jahoda and Others, *op. cit.,* p. 235-44.

[167] William Van Til and Evelyn Luecking, *What Popular Magazines Say About Education,* 1946-1948. University of Illinois Bulletin, Vol. 47, No. 9. Urbana: University of Illinois, September 1949. 51 p.

An analysis of journals published by state education associations, for the purpose of locating materials contributing to regional improvement in terms of criteria relating to: a point of view of regionalism instead of traditional sectionalism, awareness of the South as a region, abundant natural resources of the region, ample human resources of the region, the region's deficiency of technological skill, the region's deficiency of capital wealth, the region's deficiency of institutional services, waste of the region's resources, a plan or program for alleviating a problem or relieving a deficiency, and progress in the direction of regional improvement.[168]

*The Encyclopedia of Educational Research*—hundreds of examples of content analysis and frequency counts of usage and errors concerned with vocabulary, difficulty of reading materials, difficulty of test items, and job and activity analysis.[169]

A dictionary of approximately 16,000 educational terms,[170] based on vocabulary studies of the indexes of a large number of educational texts and journals, glossaries and dictionaries, a vocabulary analysis of 50 per cent of the space in the *Encyclopedia of Educational Research,* and a vocabulary analysis of the topical headings in the *Encyclopedia of Modern Education.*

An analysis of the acts of the Indiana General Assembly relating to formal education, classified under the following subject headings: township schools, county seminaries, Indiana College (Indiana University), private educational institutions, school lands, school funds, school officials, fines and license fees, school taxes, education of special groups, and libraries.[171]

An attempt to determine the principles of higher internal administration through analysis of the literature of higher education; portions of the literature were briefed for expressed or implied statements of principles of internal administration; original statements of principles were translated, in terms of standard dictionary definitions, and then condensed into general statements; the process of briefing the literature and condensation of these statements was continued until several hundred statements, as briefed consecutively from the literature, had failed to furnish any essentially new statements of principles of higher educational administration.[172]

[168] Nathaniel B. McMillian, *An Analysis of Regional Items in the Content of Southern State Education Association Journals, 1935-49.* Bulletin of the Bureau of School Service, Vol. 23, No. 4. Lexington: University of Kentucky, June 1951. 91 p.

[169] Walter S. Monroe, Editor, *op. cit.*

[170] Carter V. Good, Editor, *Dictionary of Education.* New York: McGraw-Hill Book Co., 1945. xxxix + 495 p. Revision scheduled for 1956.

[171] Velorus Martz and Stanley E. Ballinger, *A Guide to the Source Materials Relating to Education in the Laws of the State of Indiana, 1816-1851, Part I: 1816-1838.* Bulletin of the School of Education, Vol. 29, No. 4. Bloomington: Indiana University, July 1953. 96 p.

[172] Donald Faulkner, "Generalizations Through Condensation: A Research Technique." *Educational Research Bulletin* 19:492-93; November 20, 1940.

A comparison of the contents of eight textbooks on research methods, with the subject headings of selecting problems, procedures of research, treatment of data, reporting research, and miscellaneous.[173]

An investigation of the history of textbooks in arithmetic over a period of 150 years, giving spatial analyses at different periods, covering makeup, content, method, and written problems.[174]

A bibliography and topical index of 8278 references on reading and related topics.[175]

Identification of the elements of scientific method through documentary study of forty-three professional books and magazine articles containing analyses of scientific method in more or less usable form and detail; organization of these elements into an outline of twelve main items and forty-two sub-topics; after evaluation of this outline by twenty-two university professors of various branches of science, it was condensed and reorganized into ten major and seventeen minor elements, which were translated into language suitable for junior high school pupils, and checked in accordance with criteria approved by three specialists in the teaching of science.[176]

A review of studies concerned with analysis of textbooks in educational psychology, for the purpose of determining the percentage of space devoted to topics; one investigator used fifteen topics, another twenty-six, and Coladarci seven, who says that his seven areas are operationally defined.[177]

An analysis of the entries in *Psychological Abstracts* for the years, 1937-1946 inclusive, indicating the changing interests in American psychology.[178]

A comparison of the amount of professional writing done by men and by women psychologists, based on entries in *Psychological Abstracts* for 1939 (chosen as the most recent "normal" year before World War II changed professional habits).[179]

[173] J. R. Shannon and Marian A. Kittle, "An Analysis of Eight Textbooks in How to Do Research in Education." *Journal of Educational Research* 37:31-36; September 1943.

[174] Henry L. Smith and Others, *One Hundred Fifty Years of Arithmetic Textbooks.* Bulletin of the School of Education, Vol. 21, No. 1. Bloomington: Indiana University, January 1945. 149 p.

[175] Emmett A. Betts and Thelma M. Betts, *An Index to Professional Literature on Reading and Related Topics.* New York: American Book Co., 1945. vii + 137 p.

[176] Oreon Keeslar, "The Elements of Scientific Method." *Science Education* 29:273-78; December 1949.

Francis D. Curtis, "Milestones of Research in the Teaching of Science." *Journal of Educational Research* 44:161-78; November 1950.

[177] Arthur P. Coladarci, *Pre-Professional Experiences in Educational Psychology.* Bulletin of the School of Education, Vol. 27, No. 5. Bloomington: Indiana University, 1951. 30 p.

[178] Stanford C. Ericksen, "Two Indices of Changing Interests in American Psychology." *American Psychologist* 4:83-84; March 1949.

[179] Fannie A. Handrick, "Women in American Psychology: Publications." *American Psychologist* 3:541-42; December 1948.

Also see Wayne Dennis, "Bibliographies of Eminent Psychologists." *American Psychologist* 9:35-36; January 1954.

An investigation of the number of papers on different subjects, as listed on programs of the American Psychological Association over a period of fifty years, 1892-1942.[180]

A study of psychological reporting in *Time* magazine for the period from January, 1937 through June, 1947 (the education, medicine, and science sections of each of the 546 issues appearing during the period under study), with the resulting 271 articles on psychology classified according to the fourteen major subdivisions used in *Psychological Abstracts*.[181]

A content-analysis study of the symbolic content of the radio serial and how its symbols stimulate women both as members of society and as individuals with private worlds and private fantasies.[182]

An analysis of television programs, classified under seventeen headings: news, weather, public issues, public events, institutional, information, religion, drama, dance, music, fine arts, variety, personalities, quizz-stunts-contest, sports, homemaking, and children's programs.[183]

A review of articles in the *American Journal of Sociology* for a period of fifty years, giving the per cent of space devoted to different topics in each five-year period, with the findings interrelated with other factors in interpreting changes in point of view and emphasis in sociology.[184]

An attempt to develop a practicable method of measuring, as accurately as feasible, the degrees of verifiability attained in sociological articles and books; based upon the classification of articles in sociological journals, and of randomly selected sentences from those articles; only signed articles, providing five or more pairs of sample sentences, were used in the basic process.[185]

Textbook analyses in sociology: [186] a content analysis of twelve widely used textbooks in beginning sociology, concerned with the treatment of race; and a survey of thirty-three introductory texts in sociology, twenty-eight social-problems texts, and twenty-two family texts published over the

[180] Samuel Fernberger, "The American Psychological Association: 1892-1942." *Psychological Review* 50:33-60; January 1943.

[181] R. R. Blake, "Some Quantitative Aspects of *Time* Magazine's Presentation of Psychology." *American Psychologist* 3:124-26, 132; April 1948.

[182] W. L. Warner and W. E. Henry, "The Radio Daytime Serial: A Symbolic Analysis." *Genetic Psychology Monographs* 37:3-71; February 1948.

[183] Dallas W. Smythe, "An Analysis of Television Programs." *Scientific American* 184: 15-17; June 1951.

[184] Ethel Shanas, "The American Journal of Sociology Through Fifty Years." *American Journal of Sociology* 50:522-33; May 1945.

Also see Wayne McMillen, "The First Twenty-Six Years of the Social Service Review." *Social Service Review* 27:1-14; March 1953.

[185] Hornell Hart, "Measuring Degrees of Verification in Sociological Writing." *American Sociological Review* 12:103-13; February 1947.

[186] Chester L. Hunt, "The Treatment of 'Race' in Beginning Sociology Textbooks." *Sociology and Social Research* 35:277-84; March-April 1951.

A. H. Hobbs, *The Claims of Sociology: A Critique of Textbooks*. Harrisburg, Pa.: Stackpole Co., 1951. iv + 185 p.

period 1926-45, in terms of treatment of personality, marriage and the family, social controls, social disorganization, and social change.

A summary of textbook analyses, made in terms of the themes of comparative studies of wars, war and peace, civic attitudes, treatment of the Far East, place of Latin America, Canada and the United States, and minority groups.[187]

An analysis of 266 textbooks in the light of their handling of materials pertaining to intergroup relations.[188]

A content analysis of humor, based on three anthologies of jokes concerning three American ethnic groups; 300 Negro jokes, 160 Jewish, and 274 Irish, a total of 734 jokes; divided into six categories—dialect, theme, proper names, sex composition, occupations, and intergroup or intragroup composition.[189]

An analysis of approximately two thousand responses revealing attitudes of students and adults in terms of excellent and poor citizenship; a process of analyzing free responses to critical-incidents questions on citizenship, classified under nineteen categories.[190]

A study of 5188 terms, having 4294 different bases or stems, necessary to understanding and interpreting the business and economic news available through the mass media.[191]

## SURVEY-APPRAISAL PROCEDURES AND INDEX NUMBERS[192]

**Appraisal in relation to subjectivity.** Appraisal procedures differ in terms of whether direct judgment or some more objective form of evalua-

---

[187] I. James Quillen, *Textbook Improvement and International Understanding.* Prepared for the Committee on International Education and Cultural Relations of the American Council on Education and the United States National Commission for UNESCO. Washington: American Council on Education, 1948. vii + 78 p.

[188] J. L. Hanley, *Intergroup Relations in Teaching Materials:* A Survey and Appraisal. Washington: American Council on Education, 1949. 231 p.

Maxwell S. Stewart, *Prejudice in Textbooks.* National Conference of Christians and Jews. Public Affairs Pamphlet No. 160. New York: Public Affairs Committee, 1950. 31 p.

[189] Milton L. Barron, "A Content Analysis of Intergroup Humor." *American Sociological Review* 15:88-94; February 1953.

[190] Citizenship Education Project, *Content Analysis Manual:* Classification System for Analysis of Responses to Four Questions on Citizenship. Publication No. 9. New York: Teachers College, Columbia University, 1950. 52 p.

*Improving Citizenship Education:* A Two-Year Progress Report of the Citizenship Education Project. Publication No. 29. New York: Teachers College, Columbia University, 1952. 44 p.

[191] Dean R. Malsbary, "A Study of the Terms That People Need to Understand in Order to Comprehend and Interpret the Business and Economic News Available Through the Mass Media." *Studies in Education,* 1952. Iowa City, Iowa: State University of Iowa, January 1953. p. 199-204.

[192] A. S. Barr, Robert A. Davis, and Palmer O. Johnson, *op. cit.,* p. 51-157.

F. C. Bartlett and Others, Editors, *The Study of Society.* London: Kegan Paul, Trench, Trubner, and Co., 1939. p. 211-29.

tion is employed, although judgment is involved in both cases in the preparation of the instruments or selection and treatment of the factors represented. Direct judgment produces a type of data different from the evidence gathered by most of the descriptive-survey techniques discussed in this chapter, although questionnaires that call for the evaluation of

---

Emory S. Bogardus, *op. cit.*, p. 90-103.

Leo J. Brueckner, "Rating Scales, Score-Cards, and Check Lists." *Review of Educational Research* 9:524-27, 617-19; December 1939.

Oscar K. Buros, Editor, *The Fourth Mental Measurements Yearbook.* Highland Park, N. J.: Gryphon Press, 1953. 1189 p.

Dorwin Cartwright and Alvin Zander, *op. cit.*

Francis G. Cornell and Others, *op. cit.*

Francis G. Cornell and Others, *The Index of Local Economic Ability in State School Finance Programs:* A Review of the Theory and Practice in the Use of Measures of Local Taxpaying Ability Based upon Economic Indexes. Washington: National Educational Association, October 1953. 63 p.

E. W. Dolch and J. A. Clement, "Textbooks." *Encyclopedia of Educational Research.* Revised Edition. Edited by Walter S. Monroe. New York: Macmillan Co., 1950. p. 1478-81.

M. C. Elmer, *op. cit.*, p. 271-322.

Leon Festinger and Daniel Katz, *op. cit.*, p. 471-535.

Warren G. Findley and Douglas E. Scates, "Obtaining Evidence of Understanding." *The Measurement of Understanding.* Forty-fifth Yearbook of the National Society for the Study of Education, Part 1. Chicago: University of Chicago Press, 1946. p. 44-70.

C. G. F. Franzén and Others, *Use of "Evaluative Criteria" in the Indiana Secondary Schools.* Bulletin of the School of Education, Indiana University, Vol. 30, No. 1. Bloomington: Indiana University, January 1954. 82 p.

Carter V. Good, A. S. Barr, and Douglas E. Scates, *op. cit.*, p. 409-76. Covers many of the studies before the middle 1930's.

William J. Goode and Paul K. Hatt, *op. cit.*, p. 232-95.

Marie Jahoda and Others, *op. cit.*, p. 91-127, 185-208, 569-75, 681-711.

George A. Lundberg, *op. cit.*, p. 211-348.

Walter S. Monroe, "Index Numbers." *Encyclopedia of Educational Research, op. cit.*, p. 564.

Mildred Parten, *op. cit.*, p. 190-99.

Douglas E. Scates, "Index Numbers and Related Composites." *Review of Educational Research* 9:532-42, 622-25; December 1939.

Douglas E. Scates and Virginia Fauntleroy, "The Effect of Weights on Certain Index Numbers." *Journal of Experimental Education* 6:282-306; March 1938.

Saul B. Sells, "Observational Methods of Research." *Review of Educational Research* 15:390-99; December 1945.

Saul B. Sells, "Observational Methods of Research," *op. cit.*, December 1948, p. 428-34.

Saul B. Sells and Robert W. Ellis, "Observational Procedures Used in Research," *op. cit.*, p. 437-41.

Ruth Strang, *op. cit.*, p. 63-79.

Arthur E. Traxler, "Current Construction and Evaluation of Personality and Character Tests." *Review of Educational Research* 11:57-79; February 1941.

Arthur E. Traxler, "Current Construction and Evaluation of Personality and Character Tests." *Review of Educational Research* 14:55-66; February 1944.

Albert Ellis and J. R. Gerberich, "Interests and Attitudes." *Review of Educational Research* 17:64-77; February 1947.

Arthur E. Traxler and Robert Jacobs, "Construction and Educational Significance of Structured Inventories in Personality Measurement." *Review of Educational Research* 20: 38-50; February 1950.

David V. Tiedeman and Kenneth M. Wilson, "Development and Applications of Nonprojective Tests of Personality and Interest." *Review of Educational Research* 23:56-69; February 1953.

F. L. Whitney, *The Elements of Research.* Third Edition. New York: Prentice-Hall, 1950. p. 138-52.

J. W. Wrightstone, "Rating Methods." *Encyclopedia of Educational Research, op. cit.*, p. 961-65.

Pauline V. Young, *op. cit.*, p. 348-82, 443-54.

certain items, particularly when a choice from among several scaled opportunities is involved, yield the same type of data as the procedure of direct
judgment.

Appraisal is a form of classification or scaling according to subjective
values. If an instrument is used that makes the procedure relatively objective, the tool must have been calibrated in terms of human judgment when
it was constructed. In the techniques that are more directly subjective, the
value assigned to any specimen being rated depends more or less on the
individual doing the rating, and it may vary with the same individual from
time to time. Direct rating is probably the least satisfactory of the data-
gathering devices from the scientific or research point of view, although
for many practical problems it is the most important of the techniques for
gathering evidence. This is another illustration of the fact that for studying
many of our psychological and social problems the more formal methods
of objective science are not wholly adequate. In justifying the use of direct
judgment, it should be remembered that social scientists encounter many
problems that differ fundamentally from those of physical scientists, and
must utilize procedures appropriate to social areas. Selection of research
approaches in education, psychology, and sociology should not be primarily in terms of concepts useful in the physical sciences, but in terms
of adaptability to the particular field represented. In the behavioral
and human sciences, investigators should not avoid certain problems and
procedures merely because the work cannot be done perfectly, but should
use the available tools as a starting point for a long road of discovery
and constant improvement, both in techniques and in findings. All measurement involves some inexactness; astronomers long ago noted this fact
and labeled such individual differences in observation as the personal
equation or observational error.

Appraisal leans more heavily upon the human element than do the
more objective methods of investigation, since appraisal is undertaken for
the specific purpose of including the human element. It is not an attempt
to measure objective characteristics, but rather to determine the effect of
these characteristics upon human beings. It is concerned primarily with
human values and secondarily with the physical attributes to which these
values are attached (somewhat ephemerally). Therefore, our efforts to
improve the techniques of appraisal will not be directed toward eliminating
those changes in value that are truly characteristic of human preference,
for to do so would inject spurious elements in what we desire to keep
natural. We should strive only to free the expression of value from sporadic
elements, in order that we may secure a judgment of the essential characteristics of specimens that is true or typical for the individual judge at a

given time, with an expectation of reasonable variation from time to time, or place to place, or between one judge and another. Human beings have a large number of wants, desires, opinions, attitudes, preferences, and choices, however changeable these may be; appraisal is in effect the procedure by which we ascertain and make overt these characteristically variable reactions of a psychological or social character. For certain purposes an index of human values may be more important than any number of physical measurements (perhaps made with great accuracy and reliability).

Types of direct judgment or rating will be presented in the order of their increasing complexity or refinement of technique. As a rule, such techniques are a part of some larger pattern of research, frequently a descriptive-survey type of investigation.

**Rating of specimens or items.** Apart from simple estimation of the worth of any object, the most direct form of evaluation or appraisal is the comparison of various specimens that can be brought together, studied, and ranked in order. Although this form of appraisal is most likely to occur in the construction of a schedule or scale that is later to be used in rating, it is sometimes used directly. An investigator may secure the coöperation of a number of persons known as "judges" or a "jury," who rank or rate in some way the objects under consideration. The expression "jury technique" characterizes the pooled judgments of a number of persons, sometimes dozens or hundreds. One of the commonest forms of this technique is the rating of items in a list, as in determining the importance of items for school records or in rating the traits considered important for successful work as a teacher.

**Ranking of human beings.** Another type of direct comparison is to rank a group of human beings (the pupils in a class or the individuals of any other group in terms of one or more characteristics). Ranking does not necessarily involve the assignment of a particular numerical value to each individual, but only judging that one individual is higher or lower than another person in the group, with respect to the particular characteristic under study.

**Comparison with scaled specimens.** Another type of direct comparison is in the form of scaled specimens, such as a handwriting scale or a composition scale. The investigator compares the specimen to be rated with those that make up the scale, in order to determine whether his particular specimen is better or poorer than a certain sample in the scale. When he finds the approximate position that his specimen will occupy on the scale, he assigns the appropriate scale value to it, a procedure that requires less judgment than rating without the scale. This approach is common where readily handled products are to be rated, and was one of the early developments in the measurement movement, in the form of handwriting and composition scales. The use of such scaled specimens is an attempt to make individual judgment representative of average or group opinion, and in some cases it enables the individual to know the opinion of experts. By affording an objective representation of values, the scaled specimens aid in preventing undue variation in judgment from time to time, and tend to reduce the idiosyncrasies of individual judgment, in order that a more typical, truer evaluation may be secured.

**Check lists.** Schedules are sometimes prepared which consist essentially of a list of items with a place to check or mark "yes" or "no," for the purpose of calling attention to various aspects of an object or situation, to make certain that nothing of importance is overlooked. A check list may be used to direct attention to certain large aspects of a situation or setting, or to check against the completeness of details, according to the nature of the instrument used. Certain types of check lists are useful as an aid to recording, as in observing behavior, and have been discussed in more detail in an earlier section of this chapter. One form of check list may be used as a sort of scale, yielding a score. To note whether a characteristic is present or absent, and to count the number of favorable or unfavorable items checked, may provide a total for comparison with other similar totals, to indicate whether the thing evaluated is generally satisfactory. To determine the presence or absence of a given characteristic may require little or no judgment, or it may involve the exercise of considerable judgment. Areas of education in which check lists have been used include school buildings, school property, building plans, possible economies, purchase of school supplies, appraisal of the superintendent's report, organization of secondary schools, appraisal of secondary schools, evaluation of higher institutions, provisions and practices of state school systems, classroom instructional activities, supervision of instruction, and the characteristics of a successful teacher.

**Rating scales.** The rating scale is probably the most commonly used instrument for making appraisals, and is found in a large variety of forms and uses. The rating scale typically directs attention to different parts or aspects of the thing to be evaluated, but does not have as many items or categories as the check list or score card. The scale for assigning values to each of these aspects may take any one of a number of different forms—a series of numbers, a graduated line, qualitative terms such as excellent-strong-average-weak-poor, a series of named attributes peculiar to each scale, or a series of carefully worded descriptions of states representing different degrees of each aspect to be rated. In certain instances a special scale is eliminated, and the objects are rated on each characteristic in terms of per cent. Carefully codified criteria or standards probably should be regarded as a sort of rating scale; the essence is there but not the form. Examples may be found in the criteria for appraisal of the school plant, playgrounds, secondary schools, colleges and universities, and the sets of standards that accompany building score cards. A simple form of rating scale is commonly employed when judging contests of various kinds, such as debates and competitions in music; for example, the judges may be asked to assign a certain percentage of the weight to content, and another fraction to the form of presentation. Rating scales have been used extensively in evaluating teachers and in assessing personality and character. The problems of constructing rating scales are primarily the difficulty of securing satisfactory categories, and of providing criteria by which the satisfactoriness of the scale may be carefully determined. The investigator must have categories that possess approximately the same significance for all who will use the rating scale, and the categories must fit together into a satisfactory pattern, so that, when taken together, they will provide an adequate picture.

**Score cards.** Score cards as a group represent the most elaborate form of rating instrument for utilizing judgments directly. While there is no sharp dividing line between rating scales and score cards, and many investigators use the two terms interchangeably, certain differentiations can be made. The typical score card provides for more aspects or characteristics of the object to be appraised and has a definite number of "points" to be assigned to each item. A rating scale usually has fewer characteristics and uses a variety of different means of scaling, some of which are quite indefinite. A rating scale may have descriptions of various degrees of each trait or characteristic, whereas a score card may have general standards for criteria, printed separately and at some length, describing only a satisfactory or ideal level. The score card differs from the check list primarily in calling for an evaluation of each aspect rather than noting merely its presence or absence. Applications of the score-card technique are numerous: school buildings (probably the best known), selection of school-building sites, architectural service and building plans, school-building utilization, school-housing program, structural and housekeeping sanitation, janitorial services, school seating, school budget, school records and reports, guidance, organization of junior high schools, publicity material, parent-teacher association, elementary-school practices, evaluation of secondary schools, accrediting of higher institutions, homes of pupils, community conditions, and selection of textbooks (a frequent application of the score-card technique).

**Basic theory and interpretation of appraisal instruments.** Appraisal instruments are based on two fundamental assumptions. First, it is assumed that better judgment can be obtained concerning the significant aspects of an object or situation by centering attention on one aspect at a time. A question arises concerning the isolation of elements that are the crucial ones. It is possible that in evaluating complex situations the makers of observation and appraisal schedules may have omitted certain crucial intangibles. This problem has been discussed at greater length in the earlier section on observational techniques.

The second fundamental assumption involved in all instruments that yield a general total or composite rating is that general value can be approximated by a summation of the values of parts. If we grant that all of the really significant aspects have been included in the rating, there is still a question as to whether any mathematical function (such as a weighted sum) of the separate ratings will yield a relative value that corresponds well with one's reaction to the object or situation as a whole. The question is one of atomistic versus organismic conceptions of analysis, and involves the challenge raised by Gestalt psychology as to whether something is not lost when a complex whole is divided into parts (at least some element of pattern may be lost). The question of losing elements of organization or pattern through dividing things may be answered, at least in part, by including in the schedule elements of varying generality, some very detailed and some rather broad, so that a hierarchy of levels is represented. This subject was discussed at length in the section on analysis in the preceding chapter.

From the practical point of view, these questions are not too urgent. Improvements in practice or in objects such as school buildings are usually made in terms of details, which is in keeping with the nature and use of appraisal instruments. The evaluative instruments are not likely to be applied at any one time to objects or practices that vary in major respects; that is, a score card for buildings would not be applied to an experimental or laboratory building on a university campus constructed to represent an entirely new or special philosophy of education, and would not likely be applied to a structure built in keeping with some new theory of building construction that sought to make an epochal advance. Appraisal instruments are not adapted to the evaluation of fundamentally different things or situations, such as the buildings mentioned in the preceding sentence compared with typical schools, unless the instruments were especially constructed for that purpose.

It is probable that administrative actions are usually tempered by general opinion and common sense, which may tend to overcome certain shortcomings in the instrument of appraisal. These comments refer to use of appraisal instruments in practical rather than ideal situations. An ideal instrument probably would be so cumbersome and expensive in terms of effort and time that its use could hardly be justified. Possibly a combination of ratings on appraisal instruments and general judgment will be found more desirable for practical purposes than the research worker's dream of a perfect instrument. Appraisal schedules, as descriptive-survey instruments, reflect general tendencies, tempered by the superior and by the inferior, but they represent in the main the things to which we are accustomed. Major differences in objects or practices that involve questions of sharply changing philosophies and points of view must be evaluated by other means, principally by giving our best attention directly to the consideration of requirements and consequences, and this involves the difficult question of human values.

**Appraisal of institutions.** The selection of aspects of educational institutions for indicating the quality of service raises an important question of whether to rate the objective phases of an institution, including some of its administrative provisions and practices, or whether to evaluate the educational attainments of its pupils. The appraisal of educational outcomes on the part of the pupils is obviously the more functional approach, since measurement in this instance deals with the very purpose for which the school exists. It should be remembered, however, that few educational institutions exist solely for the development of the knowledge and skills measured by available achievement tests, which cover only a limited number of the objectives of our schools. It is not fair to credit or charge the school entirely with the responsibility for the current level of attainment of its pupils, since many social and psychological factors affect achievement.

It is not wholly satisfactory to use measures of the more objective elements of an institution as the sole basis for determining its worth, since many devices, services, and provisions are established with the hope that they will contribute to the desired development of the pupils, but without actual objective or statistical proof of the effectiveness of the particular service; for example, the library, laboratory equipment, guidance and counseling, supervisory services, and psychological and clinical resources. Therefore, it is clear that the conditioning factors provided by an institution are not in themselves a sufficient guarantee of their own effectiveness. In the evaluation of a school, it would seem desirable to include all the elements that seem significant in terms of a good educational influence, probably tests of various types for appraising the attainments of pupils; check lists, rating scales, and score cards for evaluating the service provisions of the institution; and probably other types of evidence, such as the after-school success of the graduates and the judgment of competent experts. Many of the national and regional accrediting organizations have developed check lists and schedules for use in evaluating the effectiveness of educational institutions at both secondary and collegiate levels.

**Index numbers and objectivity.** In their desire to make complex comparisons as objective as possible, educational and social workers have turned frequently to the use of index numbers. This device represents a particular form of analyzing quantitative data that can be gathered by one means or another, usually from available reports. As a rule, index numbers do not depend for their basic figures on judgment, i.e., after the characteristics to be reflected in the index number and their weightings have been determined the rest of the procedure is usually objective. An index number is essentially an average, in that it combines in one figure the average of a number of different factors (variable elements). It is an average of ratios, each of the factors being expressed as a per cent of its value at some other time (or perhaps at some other place). The technique is applicable whenever it is desired to represent in a single figure the average status of a number of factors, each expressed as a variation from a particular set of values that has been accepted as a base. The selection of a base year or base locality, with its attendant value for each factor, though not entirely without effect on the comparisons, is not a crucial problem and may be done arbitrarily to suit convenience.

**Uses of index numbers.** Index numbers have been applied to a number of phases of education (mostly administrative) and to many social and economic areas. The best known application of index numbers in education has been in the form of attempts to rate the educational activities of the various state school systems, a development in which Ayres pioneered.[193] Items commonly found in index numbers used for evaluating school systems include: "per cent of school population attending school daily," "average number of days schools were kept open," "average expenditure per child in average attendance," "expenditure per teacher employed, for salaries," and so on.

Index numbers have been applied to a large number and variety of areas, including city and county school systems, changes in prices of commodities, cost of school supplies, price (interest rate) for school bonds, cost of school buildings, cost of equipping new buildings, increasing cost of operating school buildings, cost of building materials, rates of union

[193] L. P. Ayres, *A Comparative Study of the Public School Systems in the Forty-eight States.* New York: Russell Sage Foundation, 1912. 33 p.
L. P. Ayres, *An Index Number for State School Systems.* New York: Russell Sage Foundation, 1920. 70 p.

labor, cost of living (food, clothing, housing, fuel and light, house furnishings, and miscellaneous), wholesale prices, retail prices, business activity, and employment and payrolls. Educational applications of index numbers have included the use of the United States cost-of-living index numbers to account in part for the increasing costs of education; comparison between the increase in expenditures for education and the increases in various indexes of industrial production and business activity; and use of index numbers for the cost of living to show variations in purchasing power of teachers' salaries, or to reflect variations in costs from year to year or from place to place (especially for teachers).

**Theory and interpretation of index numbers.** The objective character of the data utilized in the index number, and of the resulting series of figures, should not obscure the fact that the components of the index number may not, individually or in the aggregate, provide an adequate representation of the character that the investigator is seeking to index. The data must represent the concept (the problem) which one is studying, and they must represent the conditions in the field. The investigator must first select factors (items) for his index number that will represent as faithfully and completely as possible the general characteristic which he desires to study. Selection of items to represent complex, specialized concepts, such as cost of living, general business conditions, or the efficiency of school systems, requires thoughtful analysis of the particular concept.

Proper weighting is a second important problem. In the field of price indexes, the investigator may weight by the quantity sold, and there is little difficulty, but in indexes for more complex characteristics, such as business activity or the efficiency of school systems, the problem of weighting is important and sometimes difficult. The problem of weighting is still present, even though each item has the same value. There is a misconception that, when the investigator uses data as they are collected, the data are not weighted. They have, however, a natural weighting that is just as real (and may be just as wrong for certain purposes) as any artificial weighting that might be assigned. On the other hand, workers frequently reduce all of the factors to equal weighting, usually with the thought that they have thereby relieved themselves of all responsibility for judgment and made their work perfectly objective, but equal weighting may be less justifiable than natural weighting or some other arbitrary weighting. In many instances of weighting, the problem is primarily one of judgment.

For the data to be truly representative of the field conditions, the measures must be uniformly and carefully defined; for example, such an apparently simple thing as "one day of attendance" varies a great deal in its concept from one school system to another. The field must be properly sampled, that is, items or sources that are closely representative of other items or sources in the field must be gathered. In the case of the forty-eight states, all can be included, and the only sampling involved is in the initial selection of items to represent the concept, and perhaps in the further definitions of these factors in field terms. In the case of prices, one cannot gather data on all of the prices of any single commodity in every city and village in the United States, so he resorts to sampling the field and collects data from a certain number of the cities which he believes will also represent other cities.

In summary, the typical index number has certain rather definite characteristics, although in practice we find variations that depart from this typical pattern by all possible degrees; each one of the characteristics individually is lacking in some one or another type of value which is called an "index" or "index number," and usually several of the characters are lacking. The fairly definite characteristics of a typical index number are: "(a) a summation or average (b) of many elements, (c) these being a sample of a larger universe of elements, (d) each of the elements receiving a weight (e) which varies from observation to observation, (f) the values at any observation being expressed as a per cent of the value for some observation point selected as the base, (g) with various types of formula rectification for bias." [194]

**The literature of appraisal techniques.** Ratings and scales have been developed for many educational, sociometric, and psychometric areas of appraisal, including teachers, courses of instruction and school-subject fields, evaluation of outcomes, home environment, social distance, socio-economic status, attitudes, opinions, morale, social and personal behavior, personality and character, temperament, interests, jobs, evaluation and selection of personnel, employee service and efficiency, and many other fields. The details of construction and use of educational, psychometric, and sociometric instruments (tests, scales and scaling, score cards, and check lists) are treated at length in the references of this section. In the chapter on the case method are many additional references dealing with the case and clinical aspects of psychometric and sociometric techniques.

## CONCLUDING STATEMENT

The scope and variety of the organized forms of descriptive investigations and of the accompanying data-gathering techniques are too complex to permit an adequate summary statement within any reasonable space limits. For the same reason, a chapter bibliography has not been attempted;

[194] Douglas E. Scates, "Index Numbers and Related Composites," *op. cit.*, p. 532-33.

an extensive list of references accompanies each section of this chapter.

Certain developments of the 1940's and early 1950's have provided new or greatly improved tools or standards of practice for descriptive studies and have engendered a new respect for these approaches to understanding. Among these challenging techniques or theoretical concepts are:

The concept of trends as the dynamic aspects of status

Community surveys and studies, particularly in relation to the community school and its functions

Self-surveys and action research

Coöperative procedures in implementing the results of school and social surveys

Adaptability of school systems as related to factors in the communities served

Improved concepts and techniques of sampling

The depth questionnaire, and depth and focused interviews

New standards of follow-up in relation to percentage of questionnaire returns

Participant observation of behavior

Improved mechanical aids for recording

Small-group study or group-behavior analysis, as based on the concepts of group dynamics

New theory and technique for content analysis of documentary materials

Development and use of a wide range of educational, psychometric, and sociometric instruments of appraisal, including tests, scales, score cards, check lists, and indexes.

# 7

# The Experimental Method [1]

OF THE RESEARCH procedures discussed in this book, the experimental method is the problem-solving approach that attempts to follow most closely some of the canons of research in the physical and biological sciences. Experimentation, whether conducted in the laboratory, classroom, or other field situation, was formerly or is historically an attempt to control all essential factors except a single variable, which is manipulated or changed with a view to determining and measuring the effect of its operation.

The major topics presented in this chapter include historical backgrounds, causation, nature of the experiment and the concept of the single variable, experimentation in relation to other research procedures, laboratory techniques, group methods of experimentation, experimental design, the extensive research literature, evaluation of the experimental method, and the classroom teacher in relation to experimentation.

## HISTORICAL BACKGROUND

Workers with an interest in historical background [2] have told an interesting and challenging story of the development of experimentation in psychology, education, and related social fields. The background for experimental psychology is found in philosophical psychology in the work

[1] Carter V. Good, A. S. Barr, and Douglas E. Scates, *The Methodology of Educational Research*. New York: Appleton-Century-Crofts, 1936. p. 482-548. Covers much of the experimental literature prior to the middle 1930's.

[2] Edwin G. Boring, *A History of Experimental Psychology*. Second Edition. New York: Appleton-Century-Crofts, 1950. xxi + 777 p.

R. E. Brennan, *History of Psychology*. New York: Macmillan Co., 1945. 277 p.

Wayne Dennis, Editor, *Readings in the History of Psychology*. New York: Appleton-Century-Crofts, 1948. 598 p.

J. C. Flugel, *A Hundred Years of Psychology*. Second Edition. New York: Macmillan Co., 1951. 424 p.

Henry E. Garrett, *Great Experiments in Psychology*. Third Edition. New York: Appleton-Century-Crofts, 1951. 400 p.

Herbert S. Langfeld and Others, Editors, *A History of Psychology in Autobiography*, Vol. 4. Worcester: Clark University Press, 1952. xii + 356 p.

Gardner Murphy, *Historical Introduction to Modern Psychology*. Revised Edition. New York: Harcourt, Brace and Co., 1949. xiv + 466 p.

A. A. Roback, *History of American Psychology*. New York: Library Publishers, 1952. xiv + 426 p.

C. E. Spearman, *Psychology Down the Ages*, Vols. 1, 2. London: Macmillan and Co., 1937. xii + 454, viii + 355 p.

of Aristotle, Descartes, Leibnitz, Locke, Berkeley, Hume, Hartley, James Mill, John Stuart Mill, Bain, Herbart, and Lotze. The actual beginning or founding of experimental psychology is represented by the work of Weber, Fechner, Helmholtz, Wundt, Brentano, Stumpf, and G. E. Müller, with later contributions by Ebbinghaus, Külpe, Mach, Avenarius, Titchener, Lipps, Galton, James, Hall, Ladd, Scripture, J. M. Baldwin, Jastrow, Sanford, Münsterberg, Royce, Cattell, Thorndike, Terman, Judd, Woodworth, Dewey, and other specialists interested in the experimental method as applied to the problems of psychology, education, and certain related social areas.

G. Stanley Hall is given credit for "founding" the first psychological laboratory in America at Johns Hopkins University in 1883, although William James claims that he began instruction in experimental psychology at Harvard either in 1874-75 or 1876. The equipment used by James was described by Hall as a "tiny room under the stairway of Agassiz museum . . . with a metronome, a device for whirling a frog, a horopter chart, and one or two bits of apparatus." [3]

Hall founded the first psychological journals in America in which the early experimental studies appeared—the *American Journal of Psychology* in 1887 and the *Pedagogical Seminary* in 1891. He also played a leading part in establishing the American Psychological Association and served as its first president in 1892.

Although controlled experimentation is relatively recent in origin, as applied to study of psychological, educational, and social problems, there were significant attempts centuries ago to find answers to instructional problems by means of trial and observation of results: [4] Vittorino da Feltre (1378-1446) and Wolfgang von Ratke (1571-1635) in devising methods of teaching; Basedow's (1723-90) application of the theories of Comenius and Rousseau; Pestalozzi's (1746-1827) schools at Stanz, Burgdorf, and Yverdun; and Herbart's (1776-1841) practice school in connection with his pedagogical seminar. Much more recently certain pioneer experimental schools in the United States attempted to evaluate instructional theory and principles through tryout under actual working conditions: the Oswego Primary Teachers Training School established by Edward A. Sheldon in 1861, Francis W. Parker's experimental school inaugurated in Chicago in 1883, and the Laboratory School of the University of Chicago founded by John Dewey in 1896.

Application of controlled experimentation to the problems of education,

[3] A. A. Roback, *op. cit.*, p. 129.
[4] W. S. Monroe and M. D. Engelhart, *Experimental Research in Education*. University of Illinois Bulletin, Vol. 27, No. 32. Bureau of Educational Research Bulletin, No. 48. Urbana: University of Illinois, 1930. Chapter 1.

psychology, and sociology was advanced greatly through the invention of measures of intelligence and achievement, statistical techniques for analysis of data, and laboratory instruments for observation and recording. Among the early contributions were the measures of pupil ability for use in providing groups equivalent in terms of intelligence, devised by Cattell, Binet, Terman, and Otis; instruments for appraising pupil achievement, invented by Stone, Thorndike, Courtis, Hillegas, Buckingham, and Ayres; and the statistical tools so important in experimental work, developed by Galton, Pearson, and more recently R. A. Fisher and others. These instruments have been applied widely in the behavioral sciences.

## VARYING PHILOSOPHIES OF CAUSATION

Inasmuch as experimentation is concerned with dynamic or causal relationships, it is helpful to note that different schools hold widely divergent views or concepts of the causal process. The simple—and undoubtedly common (also narrow)—notion is that there is a sort of "one-to-one" correspondence between a particular cause and a particular effect. Thus, when one end of a lever is pushed down, the other end goes up—a predictable amount. We find this point of view emphasized particularly by those who have had a moderate amount of training in engineering and the physical sciences. Thus, Thurstone in his early statistics book [5] stated that the essence of all science was the relationship between two variables. Anything more complex than that, either in condition or in result, would, according to his view, necessarily result in an undesirable degree of "sloppiness" of logic and would mean that the experimenter would be unable to make any precise statement. Thurstone has occasionally reiterated this position in his later writings.

The same position is staunchly advanced by Courtis in his statement: "One of the early steps essential to a mature science in my field is the objective definition of elementary concepts; a second is the observance of the Law of the Single Variable in all experimentation." [6]

Perhaps an even stronger statement of his convictions was given by Courtis in a paper read before the American Educational Research Association in February, 1951:

I am a measurement man *of the old school.* I believe the methods of classical science are the only ones that lead to that type of prediction and control essential for the improvement of education. For me, the law of the single variable—

[5] L. L. Thurstone, *Fundamentals of Statistics.* New York: Macmillan Co., 1925. 237 p.
[6] Quoted from Stuart A. Courtis, "New Concepts in Education." *Journal of Educational Research* 45:571-84; April 1952.

that an effect can with certainty be ascribed to a given factor as cause, only when all other factors have been held constant—is absolute.[7]

Somewhat the same position is hinted at by Lundberg, a sociologist, in his insistence, in many of his writings, that science necessarily "consists exclusively of a body of related and verifiable statements of the 'if . . . then' type," and that scientific methods arrive *only* at " 'if . . . then' statements." Lundberg's position, however, gives recognition to the fact that "most of the generalizations of physics are (the result of) a rigorously restricted laboratory 'culture.' "[8] In other words, all of the conditions present in a laboratory affect the findings, even though physical scientists regularly fail to state them as a part of their observed generalizations.

There is, however, much evidence that a narrow, mechanical construction of causation is not held by many workers at the present time. It is, in fact, likely to be regarded as a view that characterizes past efforts in physical science. Thus, Weaver points out that:[9]

. . . The seventeenth, eighteenth, and nineteenth centuries formed the period in which physical science learned how to analyze two-variable problems. Thus during that three hundred years, science developed the experimental and analytical techniques for handling problems in which one quantity—say, a gas pressure—depends primarily upon a second quantity—say, the volume of the gas. . . . These two-variable problems are essentially simple in structure, and precisely for the reason that the theories or the experiments related to them need deal with only two quantities, changes in one of which cause changes in the other.

Weaver goes on to say that this simple kind of thought structure and of experimental design was necessary for progress in the early stages of physical science, and led to reasonably satisfactory theory and to many useful products, such as the telephone, phonograph, automobile, airplane, moving picture, radio, diesel engine, hydroelectric power plant, and so on.

"Subsequent to 1900—and actually earlier, if we remember heroic pioneers such as Josiah Willard Gibbs—the physical sciences developed an attack on nature of an essentially and dramatically new kind."[10] Departing from the simple two-variable problems, the scientists (with the aid of mathematicians) began to attack problems involving an indefinitely large number of factors, possibly millions of them. Such approaches eventuated in statements of probability. With this type of approach, when com-

[7] Stuart A. Courtis, "Basic Factors Determining Individual Differences in Test Scores." Mimeographed paper read before the American Educational Research Association, Atlantic City, February 20, 1951.
[8] George A. Lundberg, "Alleged Obstacles to Social Science." *Scientific Monthly* 70: 299-305; May 1950.
[9] Quoted from Warren Weaver, Editor, *The Scientists Speak*. New York: Boni and Gaer, 1947. 369 p. Quotation from Chapter 1, "Science and Complexity," p. 1, 2.
[10] *Ibid.,* p. 3.

bined with developments in statistical methods of analysis, it was found possible to make useful statements of *average* tendencies, or average consequences, connected with expected ranges of variation. Life insurance, although established early in the 1800's, is an example of this approach to prediction. The amount of telephone equipment needed in central exchanges to handle the volume of calls at any time is calculated on the basis of probability of the aggregate number of calls at any one time. Furthermore: [11]

> The motions of the atoms which form all matter, as well as the motions of the stars which form the universe, all come under the range of these new techniques. The fundamental laws of heredity . . . the laws of thermodynamics . . . the whole structure of modern physics . . . rest on these statistical concepts. Indeed, the whole question of evidence, and the way in which knowledge can be inferred from evidence, is now recognized to depend on these same statistical ideas; so that probability notions are essential to any theory of knowledge itself.

This great jump, however, from the two-variable relationship to the infinitely complex relationships accommodated by the concept of probability, leaves a large in-between area yet to be dealt with. Weaver speaks of this as the area of "organized complexity." Methods of dealing successfully with this area still await their full development.

Research in the life sciences has, apparently, from the beginning recognized the necessity for dealing with highly complex phenomena. Even in the nineteenth century, according to Weaver, it was recognized that the "significant problems of living organisms are seldom those in which one can rigidly maintain constant all but two variables. Living things are more likely to present situations in which a half-dozen, or even several dozen, quantities are all varying simultaneously, and in subtly inter-connected ways." [12] Hence, these sciences were, until more recently, given mainly to such processes as collection, description, and classification, together with "observation of concurrent and apparently correlated effects."

It is not our purpose here to go into a history of progress in the life sciences since 1900; we are discussing merely conceptions of causation and the adaptation of research methods, including experimentation, to the changing conceptions. It is clear, as a matter of history, that a great deal has been accomplished in the life sciences by means of direct experimentation, often with the simple two-variable type of attack. On the other hand, it is well known that a great many problems have as yet defied such attacks. It is also known that these are often problems which involve highly complex but patterned relationships. These problems in particular are

[11] *Ibid.*, p. 5.
[12] *Ibid.*, p. 2.

the ones for which Weaver feels that new research methods, differing both from the ordinary experiment and from the recourse to probability, must yet be developed. Such methods would presumably enable the worker to deal with a high order of interrelatedness among a reasonably large number of factors. It is possible that, with appropriate developments in each, a combination of statistical methods and experimentation will be found available to deal with the complex problems of the human and behavioral sciences.

It must always be borne in mind, however, that, in the thinking of some who are qualified to judge, the usual concepts of causation are grossly oversimplified. Max Born, a German theoretical physicist, proposes to retain the word *cause,* but only in an unusual sense. He regards prediction in detail, synonymous with absolute determinism, as a view which terminated with the nineteenth century. He holds that we cannot predict individual events, but we can only state their probabilities of occurrence. There is causality, but not determinism. Chance takes the place of the older sense of causation, and indeterminacy is the rule.[13]

The contrast between the seventeenth-, eighteenth-, and nineteenth-century conception of scientific law as relatively simple and mechanical, and the more recent complex and relatively uncertain interpretations of the conception of scientific law, is traced in an article by Lafleur.[14]

The importance of including in any formulation the great variety of factors that may be present in a situation, and which may be affecting, even though subtly, the behavior of an individual was emphasized by Kurt Lewin in his well known "field theory." [15]

The physicist Niels Bohr does not, perhaps, go quite as far as Born in insisting on indeterminacy and probability, but emphasizes the complementarity of observer and observed. That is, of course, the point on which Heisenberg developed his much-discussed principle of indeterminacy, put forth in 1927,[16] and concurred in by Bohr.

Bohr does not seek to overthrow completely the older conceptions. He says, "the complementary mode of description does indeed not involve any arbitrary renunciation of customary demands of explanation," but it seeks a more careful form of thought and expression. He feels that the notion of complementarity is valuable in fields of biology, sociology, and

13 Max Born, *Natural Philosophy of Cause and Chance.* London: Oxford University Press, 1949. 215 p.

14 Laurence J. Lafleur, "On the Nature of Scientific Law." *Scientific Monthly* 74:247-52; May 1952.

15 Kurt Lewin, *Field Theory in Social Science:* Selected Theoretical Papers. New York: Harper and Bros., 1951. 346 p.

16 William C. Dampier, *A History of Science.* Third Edition. p. 413. London: Cambridge University Press, 1942. 574 p.

psychology. "It must never be forgotten that we ourselves are both actors and spectators in the drama of existence." [17]

The lead in formulating a full philosophic framework for the modern, somewhat relativistic point-of-view concerning causation has been taken by Dewey and Bentley under the name of "transactional observation." [18] This point of view is explained at some length, with apt quotations, in a series of three articles by Cantril and associates.[19] While the concept is difficult to put in simple, direct terms, some of its characteristics may be gleaned from the following passages: [20]

"Observation of this general (transactional) type sees man-in-action not as something radically set over against an environing world, nor yet as merely action 'in' a world, but as action *of* and *by* the world in which the man belongs as an integral constituent." Dewey and Bentley contrast their position with *self-action* in which "things" are viewed as acting under their own powers, and with the common view of *interaction,* which is the view of classical mechanics, "where thing is balanced against thing in causal interconnection." In transactional observation, "systems of description and naming are employed to deal with aspects and phases of action, without final attribution to 'elements' or other presumptively detachable or independent 'entities,' 'essences,' or 'realities,' and without isolation of presumptively detachable 'relations' from such detachable 'elements.' " [21]

Cantril and associates note, however, that the transactional view does not necessarily exclude attention to self-action (such as "seen in the behavior of the simplest bodily cell, in the uniqueness of individual behavior") or to interaction. In fact, they suggest that "interactional assumptions appear to be essential first steps in providing an intellectual grasp of the form for the flow of transactional processes." The transactional view is regarded as being more general, more inclusive, and presumably as being adapted to dealing with certain relationships that escape the other views. The basic idea is traced by Dewey and Bentley back to the preface of James Clerk Maxwell's *Matter and Motion,* of 1877; but the implications of the idea were not widely recognized in physical science until the present century, and their employment in life sciences is still confined to a few writers.

The position of Dewey and Bentley was somewhat anticipated, although

[17] Niels Bohr, "On the Notions of Causality and Complementarity." *Science* 111:51-54; January 20, 1950.

[18] John Dewey and A. F. Bentley, *Knowing and the Known.* Boston: Beacon Press, 1949. 334 p.

[19] Hadley Cantril and Others, "Psychology and Scientific Research." *Science* 110:461-64, 491-97, 517-22; November 4, 11, 18, 1949.

[20] *Ibid.,* p. 464. (Quotation from Dewey and Bentley.)

[21] *Ibid.,* p. 464. (Quotation from Dewey and Bentley.)

not in the use of the term, by the philosopher Sidney Hook writing on "Determinism" for the *Encyclopaedia of the Social Sciences* (1931). His statement is especially significant: [22]

But culture is not only a structurally interrelated whole. It is a developing whole. Consequently, the results of morphological analysis only set the proper tasks of social theory. These are: What elements or combination of elements constitute the dynamic factors (independent variables) in social change? What is their comparative strength? What the resultant rate of change? Due to the enormous complexity of the elements involved, the difficulty of experimental control and the absence of a theory of measurement no body of detailed objective results has emerged comparable in any way to the achievements of other sciences. But perhaps the chief obstacle to the development of a scientific theory of social change has been the use of a crude, monistic theory of causation. Some single factor has been isolated and all other cultural changes simply explained in terms of its changes. This has often led to a disregard of the facts of reciprocity and interaction between social factors, to an attempt to call the reality of cultural effects into question (social epiphenomenalism; for example, the effective role of ideals in history is sometimes denied because they are causally conditioned by some material factor) and to a quest for remote ultimate causes of events instead of their proximate causes.

The substitution of a functional conception of causation for a simple monistic theory of cause and effect is a safeguard from errors of this kind. (In studying religion and cultural change) the relationship is expressed in terms of function, dependent and independent variables. If religion is selected as the independent variable, then we try to discover the definite ways in which other aspects of culture, for instance, the legal, vary with changes in religious conceptions. . . . But there is no logical compulsion to take religion as the independent variable. We could have taken art or politics or economics as independent variables and traced the functional dependence of law upon them. . . . Or we could have reversed the original function, taken law as the independent variable and shown how religion varies with its changes. . . . Strictly speaking, neither the one nor the other member of the functional equation can be called cause or effect. . . . We might take the functional relationship between any two variables, say religion and law, and try to show that the change in the function which relates the two is itself a function of some third variable, say economics.

This review of the varying conceptions of the nature of causal relations has seemed desirable as a setting for the interpretation of experimental design and procedure, since the utility of controlled experimentation must be judged in terms of its conformity with the notions of causation. In discussing the designs and forms ordinarily presented in treatments of experimental procedure, it will be kept in mind that there is some question as to the efficacy of these forms for providing answers in keeping with the more mature conceptions regarding the multifactored interrelatedness of phenomena.

[22] Sidney Hook, "Determinism." *Encyclopaedia of the Social Sciences,* Vol. 5, p. 110-14. New York: Macmillan Co., 1931.

## THE NATURE OF AN EXPERIMENT

Perhaps most research workers assume that they know what an experiment is; yet, when a large variety of studies is presented, questions begin to emerge concerning just where one wishes to draw the boundary line. It is common for certain physical-science writers to make the term *experiment* synonymous with scientific method, and the phrase *experimental science* is often used as though it were all of natural science. Such usages, despite the vigor with which they may be defended, can be regarded as nothing short of carelessness or mistaken judgment. The more careful writers take considerable pains to point out that scientific method embraces a great variety of activities. Vannevar Bush said, "I am decidedly not one of those who speak of the scientific method as a firm and clearly defined concept." [23] Conant suggests the preparation of a whole series of case histories, in order to illustrate the many aspects of scientific procedure.[24] Clearly, the experiment may be an important form of scientific work, but it is not the whole of the scientific approach.

The experiment is expected to reveal causal relations. In other words, it deals with dynamics, with forces, with interaction; it is not intended to give simply a descriptive picture of status or a chronicle of normal growth or change. It is anticipated, therefore, that this purpose will be preserved by whatever form of experiment is set up.

In the broad sense of the term, to experiment means simply to try—to try something in order to see what happens. This procedure in the somewhat informal, uncontrolled type of trial or experimentation is of little interest to the more formal writers, who seem to feel that you cannot "prove" a thing by doing it. Even so, the informal approach has considerable favor among a number of persons who feel that the formal requirements cannot be met, or that they interfere with the development of insights, or that they are so difficult as to be restricted to the most mature research workers.[25] Even here, however, the experimenter is the one who is manipulating at least some of the conditions.

Beveridge includes a great deal in a few words when he says: [26] "An experiment usually consists in making an event occur under known conditions where as many extraneous influences as possible are eliminated and

[23] Address at the George Westinghouse Educational Foundation Forum in Pittsburgh, Pa., May 16-18, 1946. *Science* 103:664; May 31, 1946.

[24] James B. Conant, *On Understanding Science.* New Haven: Yale University Press, 1947. 145 p.

[25] W. A. Brownell, "Critique of Research on Learning and on Instruction in the School." National Society for the Study of Education, *Graduate Study in Education,* p. 52-66. Fiftieth Yearbook, Part 1. Chicago: University of Chicago Press, 1951. 369 p.

[26] William I. B. Beveridge, *The Art of Scientific Investigation,* p. 13. New York: W. W. Norton and Co., 1950. 171 p.

close observation is possible so that relationships between phenomena can be revealed." It would seem that, if these essentials could be maintained, the precise form of the experiment would not matter. The problem, of course, is to "know" the conditions under which an event occurs, and to be able to observe the whole transaction sufficiently closely so that one can be reasonably sure causation is present. Rather than establishing a particular form of experiment, this definition would seem to set up criteria by which various forms could be judged.

Chapin describes experimentation as "observation under controlled conditions." [27] For him, however, control is often achieved as much through selection of cases as through manipulation of factors.

Questions may be raised as to the requirement of certain other elements in an experiment. To what extent must it be planned, in advance, rather than merely observed as something unfolding of its own accord? Wilson says: [28] "An experiment is a question framed on the basis of what is known and addressed to nature to elicit further knowledge. It thus transcends mere observation or collection of materials; it is consciously directed, purposeful observation." This view, it will be noted, does not specify that the experiment itself must be planned in advance, but only that the observation should have purpose; it thus implies something other than passivity and routine recording on the part of the researcher. John Dewey makes somewhat the same demands, namely, that in contrast to experience gained through trial-and-error, unguided by any conscious insight, an experiment represents directed observation guided by the purpose of the study and by an understanding of the conditions.[29]

Greenwood, after his extensive canvass of the literature, formulated the following definition: [30] "An experiment is the proof of an hypothesis which seeks to hook up two factors into a causal relationship through the study of contrasting situations which have been controlled on all factors except the one of interest, the latter being either the hypothetical cause or the hypothetical effect." (A fuller explanation of the concepts included in this definition is given in the chapter that ends with the quotation and in which "causal relationship" especially is treated at length. It will be noted that the definition is not in terms of manipulation of factors, but in terms of control. That is, it does not assume that the experimenter necessarily

[27] F. Stuart Chapin, *Experimental Designs in Sociological Research*, p. 1. New York: Harper and Bros., 1947. 206 p.

[28] E. B. Wilson, *Introduction to Scientific Research*. New York: McGraw-Hill Book Co., 1952. 375 p.

[29] John Dewey, *The Quest for Certainty*, p. 78-81, 84. New York: Minton, Balch and Co., 1929. 318 p.

[30] Ernest Greenwood, *Experimental Sociology*. p. 28. New York: King's Crown Press, 1945. 163 p.

arranges the conditions and it, therefore, includes natural, *ex post facto,* or retroactive experiments when control can be established by satisfactory means. The various means available for controlling "all the factors except the one of interest" occupy Chapters VI, VII, and VIII of Greenwood's treatment.)

In considering this definition formulated by Greenwood, it may be pointed out that the introductory phrasing seems a bit inept; probably *test* should be substituted for *proof* in the early part of the definition. Other parts of the statement are not entirely clear, but the general import can be deduced.

## THE CONCEPT OF THE SINGLE VARIABLE

An example from the simplest form of group experimentation may be helpful. In the classroom, the child's achievement is the result of several educative factors. In the simplest type of group experimentation the investigator attempts to appraise the effect of some one educative or "experimental" factor on a single group of pupils. The experiment begins with a measurement of the initial status or attainment of the children in the particular trait or ability to be influenced, such as speed in silent reading or accuracy in addition in arithmetic. The group is then subjected to the experimental factor, such as a particular type of drill material in reading or arithmetic. Finally a test of speed in silent reading or accuracy in addition is applied to determine the gain in achievement resulting from the application of the experimental factor. (The difficulties of one-group experimentation will be analyzed later in this chapter.)

Expressed in different terms, the hypothesis for the experiment, when determined and stated appropriately, involves an independent variable and at least one dependent variable.[31] To cite an example of a specific hypothesis, a blow delivered to the patellar tendon of the bended knee will cause the leg to straighten. The independent (experimental) variable is the blow delivered to the patellar tendon of the bended knee, and the dependent variable (result) is the straightening of the leg as the result of the blow. Therefore, the independent variable is defined as that factor manipulated by the experimenter, while the dependent variable is the factor that varies or changes as the result of manipulating the independent variable. In some instances an independent variable has an effect on several dependent variables; for example, the hypothesis may be that, when

[31] John C. Townsend, *Introduction to Experimental Method:* For Psychology and the Social Sciences. New York: McGraw-Hill Book Co., 1953. p. 52-57.
T. G. Andrews, Editor, *Methods of Psychology.* New York: John Wiley and Sons, 1948. p. 7-8.

a person becomes startled as the result of a loud noise, his arterial pulse rate increases, he perspires, and the pupils of his eyes dilate. The independent (experimental) variable is the loud noise producing the condition of being startled, and the dependent variable (result) is in the form of an increase in arterial pulse rate, perspiration, and the increased diameter of the pupils of the subject's eyes, as the result of the loud noise.

In the language of logic, controlled experimentation is an example of a canon or principle known as the method of difference; that is, to observe the effect of a variable applied to one situation or group, but not applied to a similar situation or equivalent group. It is of no more than historical interest to note Mill's phrasing of this concept: [32]

If an instance in which the phenomenon under investigation occurs, and an instance in which it does not occur, have every circumstance in common save one, that one occurring only in the former, the circumstance in which alone the two instances differ is the effect, or the cause, or an indispensable part of the cause, of the phenomenon.

Mill's canon, however, represents an ideal assumption that certainly is never even approximately fulfilled in a concrete situation such as a classroom or field setting; nor any place when working with human beings in the educational, psychological, and sociological areas where many uncontrollable variable factors are usually present. Even in the physical sciences, it is now known that a great deal of previously unsuspected variability exists. Therefore, it must be frankly recognized that the so-called law of the single variable is a theory rather than an accomplished fact in experimental studies of educational, psychological, and sociological problems. This chapter will present numerous illustrations of difficulties in controlling variables, and examples of questionable generalizations based on the assumption of only a single operating variable.

It is only natural that experimentation has been considered the classical method of science and frequently has been urged as the appropriate methodology for any system of investigation. It is a distinct advantage, with conditions artificially controlled, to present stimuli and to secure reactions without awaiting the occurrence of events in their natural environment over a relatively long period of time, as is necessary in history. It has already been pointed out, however, that experimentation has distinct limitations in the fields of education, psychology, and sociology, where it is

[32] Quoted from John Stuart Mill, *A System of Logic*. New York: Longmans, Green and Co., 1872. Book 3, Chapter 8.

For a penetrating criticism of Mill's canons see Morris R. Cohen and Ernest Nagel, *An Introduction to Logic and Scientific Method*. New York: Harcourt, Brace and Co., 1934. Chapter 13.

difficult and often impossible to control variable factors. Furthermore, there are many situations in which the investigator is more interested in a careful analysis of the interrelationships of various factors, as they operate normally under conditions that are reasonably typical, than in using a procedure which may do violence to a natural situation by attempting to hold all factors constant except the experimental variable.

## EXPERIMENTATION IN RELATION TO OTHER PROCEDURES

Beginning graduate students and others are sometimes confused in attempting to differentiate controlled experimentation from uncontrolled observation, or from testing-measurement techniques. Uncontrolled observation and recording of the normal behavior of children, with no attempt to influence or condition the type of response, are descriptive-survey (normative-survey) or genetic rather than experimental in character; for example, a frequency count of the words used orally by 1000 six-year-old children in their homes and schools. Uncontrolled observation shades into experimental procedure, however, when external conditions surrounding the child are controlled by eliminating the presence of the observer (through use of a one-way vision screen or mirror), selection and conditioning of the child's companions, use of an infant cabinet or clinical crib, or even by maintaining environmental conditions constant (such as teacher, children, and classroom). If these essential environmental factors are kept constant, except the passage of time, and the accompanying growth or maturation of the child is observed at intervals and recorded in the form of a growth or learning curve, such investigations are frequently labeled as experimental in character. Many such studies, however, are genetic in nature, with emphasis on analysis of causal factors which operate to produce change by way of growth or development, and will be given extended discussion in the chapter concerned with genetic, growth, and developmental investigations.

Use of recording equipment, such as provides silent or sound films, or eye-movement photographs, for purposes of observation only, may be considered descriptive-survey or normative-survey in character rather than experimental. In some laboratory studies this type of observation is a first step before manipulation of an experimental factor or variable; for example, in a laboratory eye-movement study of the way people look at pictures the variables may be presence and absence of color in pictures, silhouette and outline forms, partly finished and complete pictures, or various types of directions in looking at pictures.[33] In summary, these forms of observation may be employed either for the purpose of a descriptive survey or for the purpose of describing the status of cases before and after varying the experimental factor.

If measurement of intelligence or achievement is only for the purpose of determining the capacity or accomplishment of the child in relation to other pupils or to a norm, the procedure is normative-survey or descriptive-survey rather than experimental. The testing done at the beginning of an experiment to equate groups of children and at the end of the investigation to measure results may be labeled as of survey character, when considered alone. But such testing is a part of the larger purpose or pattern of the experiment and appropriately may be regarded as an essential part of the experimental methodology. As another illustration in the area of measurement, if an intelligence test is administered year after year to a particular group of children who have lived under normal and uniform (controlled) conditions, with maturation as the single variable operating, the resulting curve of mental growth may be considered a product of an experimental procedure. Investigation of the accompanying age norms and of the factors producing such growth or development takes on the characteristics of the genetic method.

Viewed broadly, it is possible to think of the administering of any standard test as an experimental procedure, since certain factors by way of test directions and classroom conditions presumably are controlled for the purpose of observing the performance of the child. The experimental factor may be thought of as the instruction undergone by the pupil between the testing periods, with the effect of this instructional variable measured by the test. Therefore, students and investigators who define the experimental method more broadly than is represented in this chapter do no actual violence to the principles of controlled observation and manipulation of an experimental factor by considering many observational, repeated survey-testing, and growth studies as types of experimentation.

## LABORATORY EXPERIMENTATION

Group experimentation in education is ordinarily conducted in classrooms for the purpose of evaluating instructional methods or learning procedures. This type of classroom investigation is closer to reality and to the continual flux of many factors than is the experimental analysis of learning and its underlying abilities as studied in the laboratory, although laboratory

---

[33] G. T. Buswell, *How People Look at Pictures:* A Study of the Psychology of Perception in Art. Chicago: University of Chicago Press, 1935. p. 10-16.

conditions may be carefully controlled, suitable apparatus and recording provided, and subjects studied individually.

Although the laboratory attack on educational problems is not new, dating back to the laboratory established by Wundt in Leipzig in 1879, it has received much less attention in schools for teacher education than have other approaches to understanding in education. While laboratory research is intensive, exacting, and time-consuming, and of necessity limited to a small number of cases or subjects, it does make possible a type of minute analysis of variables that can be provided by no other research method. In short, as the outcome of certain types of investigation, laboratory experimentation provides the chief basis for theorizing, may cross the boundaries of related disciplines, is interested in patterns of behavior and mechanisms of learning, and assumes that there are universal principles and uniform sequences in human nature. The investigator who uses large numbers of subjects in group studies (for example, group testing and measurement) may well utilize the analytical skills and insights of the laboratory specialist, while the laboratory worker in turn may recognize and attack to the advantage of education and psychology some of the more practical and urgent problems of instruction and learning that confront the teacher.

While the accuracy of observation has been greatly increased by standard tests, mechanical aids such as those employed in the psychology laboratory, repeated observations, and statistical techniques, it should be remembered that significant pioneer work has been done without elaborate equipment for experimentation. Numerous illustrations were given in the chapter on formulation of the problem to emphasize that the intellectual curiosity and ingenuity of the investigator are more important than ornate laboratory equipment or complex measuring and recording instruments. The major purpose of equipment and instruments is to aid in the process of observation through control of conditions or through better recording. It has been said that the most important instrument in research is the mind of man. Stanley Hall was particularly annoyed by the theatrical methods of what he called "brass-instrument" psychology, a technique that was spreading in the 1870's. Particularly in psychological experiments, there is a recommendation to use similar methods and tools, so as to permit comparison between the findings of different studies; for example, the multiple-unit maze, electronic equipment, standard units of measurement, and Munsell colors.[34]

In laboratory experiments certain techniques for controlling variable

[34] Dael Wolfle and Others, "Standards for Appraising Psychological Research." *American Psychologist* 4:320-28; August 1949.

factors [35] include using a light-proof and sound-deadened room to shut out the influence of light and noise. Certain conditions may be held constant, for example, temperature or humidity. Sometimes a variable in the form of a distracting noise, such as a buzzer in the hall of a school at the end of the class period, may be screened out through producing another sound in the laboratory loud enough (and constant) to eliminate the buzzer sound. The counterbalancing method is discussed and illustrated elsewhere in this chapter.

A helpful list of seventy-two pieces of laboratory equipment, together with brief descriptions and selected photographs, includes a tabular statement of the major uses of each piece of apparatus.[36]

## GROUP TECHNIQUES OF EXPERIMENTATION

While the equipment and conditions of the laboratory make possible experimentation with individual subjects, most educational, psychological, and social experiments in the classroom and in the field must be conducted with groups rather than with individuals. A working classification of group methods of experimentation is: one-group technique, equivalent or parallel-group technique, and rotation-group technique.

**One-group technique.** In a one-group experiment one thing, individual, or group has had introduced, varied, or subtracted some experimental factor or factors, with the resulting change or changes noted or measured; for example, a group of pupils might take in succession equivalent forms of a standard reading test, to determine whether there is any change in their scores on the different forms as the result of practice effect. In all experiments involving an interval of time during which significant change in the cases (subjects) would normally take place, it is desirable and necessary to know the normal or expected performance of the group, to serve as a basis for comparison with the results produced by manipulation of the experimental factor or variable. For example, if a first grade is instructed by an experimental method of teaching reading for a school year of nine months, the results at the end of the year can be interpreted only in comparison with the normal or expected performance for a group of similar intelligence and home background while following the customary or usual teaching procedure. It must be recognized, however, that any attempt to estimate the performance of a first grade in terms of an instructional procedure never actually undergone is hazardous.

[35] John C. Townsend, *op. cit.*, p. 64-67.
Benton J. Underwood, *Experimental Psychology*. New York: Appleton-Century-Crofts, 1949. p. 30-33.
[36] John C. Townsend, *op. cit.*, p. 107-28.

Although the one-group technique is the simplest of the experimental procedures for classroom use, it presents certain difficulties. With the factors of pupils, teacher, and school setting held constant, it might seem at first thought that the only variable present is the experimental factor or procedure; however, with the passage of time marked changes may take place in the group or in the teacher. If different forms of a standard test in reading are administered to a first grade at intervals of one month or even one week, results may vary for the following reasons: (1) gains may be greater between earlier forms of the test, since the typical learning curve indicates more rapid acceleration in the earlier stages of learning a particular skill; (2) practice effect may be a factor in increasing the scores on later forms of the test; (3) a change in attitude (greater confidence) or an improved method of attack may produce higher scores on a later form of the test; and (4) increased maturation with age, even though only a few weeks more, probably will affect achievement on the later forms of the test. This hypothetical example of reading in the first grade has been selected so as to make especially conspicuous the limitations of the one-group technique.

One of Chapin's illustrations of "ex post facto" or retroactive experimental design (actually a form of one-group technique) deals with poor housing and juvenile delinquency.[37] The earlier records of 317 families before they became residents of a public-housing project were traced for purposes of comparison with the period of living in the housing project, in order to compare the incidence of juvenile delinquency.

**Parallel-group technique.** The parallel-group procedure is an attempt to overcome the difficulties of the one-group technique, in that two or more groups, as nearly equivalent as possible, are employed at the same time. Under conditions controlled as carefully as possible, only a single factor or variable is manipulated or changed; the experimental factor is varied for one group (the experimental group), while the parallel group serves as the control for comparative purposes, undergoing customary (usual) or non-experimental conditions. If the investigator desires to vary more than one phase of the experimental factor, more than two equivalent or parallel groups are needed. For example, the experimenter may desire one group to take a standard test under conditions of encouragement, while an equivalent group takes another form of the test under conditions of discouragement; a non-experimental or control group would need to take a form of the standard test, using the regular directions accompanying the test.

Chapin reports a "cross-sectional" experimental design (parallel-group

37 F. S. Chapin, *op. cit.*

technique) that sought to analyze the relationship between the duration of Boy Scout tenure in the Minneapolis area and subsequent participation in community activities and in community adjustments on the part of these Boy Scouts four years after leaving the organization.[38] The control group had dropped out of scouting with an average tenure of 1.3 years, while the experimental group had completed an average of 4 years of tenure in scout work. The members of the two groups were paired in terms of a number of factors, and interviewed and scored for participation in community activities and in community adjustments.

One of Chapin's examples of what he calls the "before" and "after" experiment (actually a form of parallel-group technique) involves a program of rural hygiene in Syria. Three Arab villages were selected as controls, although only one survived the test as an adequate control. An attempt was made to control such variables as geographic, demographic, historical, economic, religious, domestic, educational, recreational, and sanitary factors. For two years the experimental village received systematic instruction in hygiene through visits from a traveling clinic, while the control villages received no such instruction and by geographic location presumably were isolated from any influence emanating from the clinic. At the end of the investigation the villages were measured on the same hygiene scale and their scores compared.

The investigator sometimes does not actually manipulate directly an experimental factor (after groups have been equated), but chooses the subjects from conditions of the present or past so as to involve reasonably controlled conditions and an experimental factor (a retroactive or an ex post facto procedure). To cite an illustration, the experimentor may pair certain pupils (who have already attended for a period of years segregated schools for a particular racial group) with other pupils who have attended non-segregated schools. The problem under study is to determine the effect of this variable (the type of school attended) on the achievement and attitudes of the children, who are paired in terms of a variety of measures. It is obvious that the experimental factor (the type of school attended) had been operating over a period of years, long before the investigator decided to form equated groups so as to measure the effect of the variable on the pupils.

**Rotation-group technique.** The rotation method is sometimes used when parallel groups are not available or there is doubt concerning the equivalence of the groups owing to such factors as initiative, industry, or study habits, which are always difficult if not impossible to control. This technique involves an exchange for the groups at intervals, in terms of the

[38] F. S. Chapin, *op. cit.*

procedures followed. The rotation technique is likely to be more valid when parallel or equivalent groups are available. To cite an example, one first grade might begin instruction in reading, using the customary "whole" method, while a parallel first grade would follow the "alphabet" method of learning reading. Then, at intervals of one month the two groups would exchange methods. This example has been so selected as to emphasize a major limitation of the rotation method, carry-over effect from one instructional procedure to another, making it difficult or even impossible to determine whether the achievement in reading at the end of a particular month is due to the "whole" method, the "alphabet" method, or to a fusing or blend of the two instructional methods in reading. In other words, once a group of children has undergone instruction in succession by two methods of teaching reading, the pupils thereafter probably will follow a combination of the two teaching techniques. As in the case of one-group technique, the time factor in relation to maturation also presents difficulties, since the variations of instructional procedure are applied and rotated at intervals of time during which all the pupils are growing older.

An illustration of an intricate pattern of rotating procedure, intended to equalize practice effect and other similar variable factors, involves a counter-balanced order of giving eleven sets of instructions in a ball-tossing experiment. In the pattern below the subjects (cases) are numbered from one to eleven and the instructions from A to K. It will be noted that "K" is the diagonal of the square and appears in each serial position in moving from the first to the eleventh subject. There are other sequences.

| Subject | Instructions |
|---------|--------------|
| 1 | A B C D E F G H I J K |
| 2 | B C D E F G H I J K A |
| 3 | C D E F G H I J K A B |
| 4 | D E F G H I J K A B C |
| 5 | E F G H I J K A B C D |
| 6 | F G H I J K A B C D E |
| 7 | G H I J K A B C D E F |
| 8 | H I J K A B C D E F G |
| 9 | I J K A B C D E F G H |
| 10 | J K A B C D E F G H I |
| 11 | K A B C D E F G H I J |

**Equating of groups.** In human experimentation the most difficult problems involve the equating of groups, control of variable factors, and assessing (measuring) of outcomes. Many gross errors have been made in attempting to equate groups, and in reaching conclusions based on comparisons between unequal groups. In educational experimentation the characteristics that require consideration include intelligence, age, achievement in the particular field of experimentation, study habits, personality traits, physical conditions, sex, and possibly race. The factors relating to the teachers include instructional techniques, classroom-management procedures, interest or zeal for the experimental factor, personality traits, physical condition, sex, and age. The more general school factors involve the instructional materials, time devoted to learning activity, characteristics of the particular class as a group, size of class and school, school organization and supervision, and the school plant. The extraschool factors that may affect an experiment include participation in extracurricular activities, the pupil's home life, and the community interest in and attitude toward the school. The approximate equating of groups of pupils may be less difficult than it appears, since many of the factors are positively correlated. It should be noted that in some instances the very factors listed in this paragraph will not be equated but will be part or all of the conditioning (independent or experimental) variable. A treatment of averages, spread or dispersion, and shape of the frequency distribution is beyond the scope and purpose of this chapter; the reader is referred to the available texts on statistical method.

**Pairing of subjects.** Pairing of pupils or subjects in the parallel groups is a refined technique that is more reliable (accurate) than depending solely on a comparison of the averages and variabilities of the groups considered as a whole. Probably the most accurate pairing procedure is to use identical twins, known as co-twin control,[39] as has been done in a number of psychological studies, although there are not enough identical twins available in a particular school community to make this procedure feasible for group experimentation. (If infants normally came in pairs, the shortage of teachers and building space would be even greater than it is.) Averages may cover up differences that are clearly apparent when the more analytical method of pairing is used for matching subjects with their

[39] Arnold Gesell, "The Method of Co-Twin Control." *Science* 95:446-48; May 1, 1942.
Arnold Gesell and Helen Thompson, *Twins T and C from Infancy to Adolescence:* A Biogenetic Study of Individual Differences by the Method of Co-Twin Control. Genetic Psychology Monographs, Vol. 24. Provincetown, Mass.: Journal Press, 1941. p. 3-121.
Dorothy Burlingham, *Twins:* A Study of Three Pairs of Identical Twins. New York: International Universities Press, 1953. x + 92 p. + 30 developmental charts.

mates, to form not only equivalent groups but equivalent subjects. To cite an exaggerated and implausible example, each man on one football team of eleven persons may weigh exactly 200 pounds and be just 6 feet in height. On another team one man may weigh exactly 200 pounds, with a height of 6 feet; with five men 7 feet tall and weighing 300 pounds; and five men 5 feet tall and weighing 100 pounds each. The two hypothetical teams are equal in height and weight, according to averages, but what coach would hazard a guess as to the performance of the team of giants and "pony" backfield men?

Usually there are pupils in both groups who cannot be matched or paired closely, and for the purposes of the experiment their scores or results may be disregarded, comparing only the performances of the paired individuals. While such a plan makes possible the use of classes without shifting pupils from their original sections, it does not remove the influence of an unusually bright pupil or a far below average learner. The bright pupil who cannot be paired with a mate in the other group may be a stimulus to the learning of his classmates, whereas the dull pupil who cannot be paired successfully may slow up the progress of the entire group where he is a member. For these reasons it would seem desirable to transfer such extreme cases to other sections, if administratively feasible for the school program and organization.

To cite an example of factors that probably would be considered in pairing pupils for an experiment in class size in high-school English composition, the essential items would include I.Q., chronological age, reading performance, grammar, composition, and spelling.

As an illustration of a large-scale experimental study in a social area, five hundred persistently delinquent boys ranging in age from eleven to seventeen years were matched against five hundred "truly" non-delinquent boys in terms of age, ethnic (racial) derivation, general intelligence, and residence in unprivileged urban neighborhoods.[40] The comparison of the delinquents and non-delinquents included family, school, and neighborhood life; physique and health; constituents of general intelligence; and traits of temperament, personality, and character structure.

An illustration of the pairing in the Glueck study,[41] selected from a total of five hundred matched pairs of boys, is as follows:

[40] Sheldon Glueck and Eleanor Glueck, *Delinquents in the Making:* Paths to Prevention. New York: Harper and Bros., 1952. viii + 214 p.

[41] Sheldon Glueck and Eleanor Glueck, *Unraveling Juvenile Delinquency.* New York: Commonwealth Fund, 1950. xv + 399 p.

Sheldon Glueck and Eleanor Glueck, *Delinquents in the Making:* Paths to Prevention, *op. cit.* A briefer, less technical version of *Unraveling Juvenile Delinquency.*

| Illustrative Pairs | National Origin | Chronological Age | Intelligence Quotient |
|---|---|---|---|
| ( Delinquent | Irish | 14-3 | 117 |
| ( Non-Delinquent | Irish | 13-4 | 120 |
| ( Delinquent | English | 13-6 | 53 |
| ( Non-Delinquent | Scotch | 13-10 | 58 |
| ( Delinquent | Rumanian | 15-6 | 97 |
| ( Non-Delinquent | Syrian | 14-10 | 99 |
| ( Delinquent | Czech. | 16-3 | 115 |
| ( Non-Delinquent | Polish | 16-3 | 115 |
| ( Delinquent | Portuguese | 13-4 | 80 |
| ( Non-Delinquent | Spanish | 12-6 | 84 |
| ( Delinquent | English Canadian | 12-5 | 97 |
| ( Non-Delinquent | English | 12-7 | 96 |

In the light of the background of this chapter and of the references cited, the reader will recognize the magnitude of the problems of experimental technique and statistical analysis in the Glueck experiment, with its complex sociological, psychological, and educational variables. There are special statistical formulas for use in evaluating the results of an experiment when cases have been individually paired in the fashion described. With the new statistical techniques which have become available and more or less well known in the last twenty years, the need for matching and pairing is less exacting than before, since there are ways of handling cases or groups which differ initially by moderate amounts. The student who does not wish to use these statistical methods, however, must depend on the older methods.

## CAUSAL-COMPARATIVE STUDIES IN RELATION TO EXPERIMENTATION

Certain studies made for causal-comparative purposes approach experimentation in purpose and procedure. Description for the purpose of attempting to establish likely causes (causal comparison) is different from description of two or more groups for the purpose of simple comparison. Therefore, the investigator will do different things with respect to the checking on the comparability of the cases, since data which are comparable for one purpose will not necessarily be comparable for another.

By way of illustration, to ascertain the characteristics of students who go into teacher preparation, as compared with students who specialize in other areas, the investigator might give tests and questionnaires to freshmen and later compare the returns for students who have gone into teaching with the results from the non-teaching students. This is selective comparison, something like "retroactive" experimentation, and is useful in the social fields, where often we cannot experiment readily.

In comparing the two groups, the experimenter would not equate, as a rule, except as indicated below. He would use the averages and distributions of the entire groups for each trait shown in the tests and questionnaires, and then compare the two groups in terms of averages, possibly the spread, and forms of overlapping.

If one group should happen to be older than the other by, let us say, two years on the average, then the investigator probably would want to know whether they study harder because they are older. Do they evidence more emotional maturity because they are older? This question might justify equating on the factor of age (by drawing representative samples in other respects but of equal age) and then comparing; because the investigator could argue that, even though the observed results were true for the two groups, they were temporary results (true only for the time being) and that when the other group grew two years older they would show the same characteristic. This assumption would need to be checked carefully against the evidence.

This procedure is really causal-comparative, but has a causal factor related to time, hence not a relatively permanent characteristic (a more or less accidental one). To assign causes will require matching or equating. Let us assume that one group of students is in noticeably better health than the other, and that they have higher incomes on the average, or in almost all cases. It may be suspected that the better health is the result of more medical attention and guidance, and more variation and leisure in their programs. The procedure would be to match certain individuals (representing a satisfactory sample of the two groups on other major traits), holding the incomes of the two groups constant (between the groups), then compare the results. This procedure is not for the purpose of ascertaining descriptively what the two groups are like in immediate characteristics, but to discover whether income is a conditioning factor in relation to what is observed—a causal-comparative approach or procedure.

The close relationship between experimentation and analysis is emphasized in Chapter 5, on the descriptive method, in the section dealing with analysis. A descriptive-survey investigation often reveals wide differences which are then made the subject of causal-comparative study to identify significant conditioning factors, and then later these factors are subjected to more intensive analysis, refinement, and verification through experimentation. This is a common sequence in research approaches. For example, the discovery that fluorine retards tooth decay (dental caries) was followed by extensive laboratory experimentation and then by practical tests "in the field," among children at large in selected cities and schools.

## ILLUSTRATIVE CLASSIFICATIONS OF EXPERIMENTAL DESIGN

**Logic.** Since Mill's five canons of logic are not serviceable in modern experimental design, they are listed here only by name as the methods of difference, agreement, joint difference and agreement, concomitant variation, and residue.[42]

**Sociology.** Greenwood in 1945 provided an extensive, critical analysis of the experimental literature in the area of sociology, including a number of examples from psychology. His examination of the theory and logic of experimental design is organized under five headings: the pure experiment, the uncontrolled experiment, the ex post facto experiment, the trial-and-error experiment, and the controlled observational study.[43]

Chapin's treatment of experimental design in sociology is complementary to Greenwood's analysis, by way of summarizing concrete studies to illustrate experimentation. Chapin's source book of examples of experimental design presents three major types, as applied to study of problems in the natural community situation: (1) a cross-sectional design, with controlled observations for a single date; (2) a projected design of "before" and "after" study, with an attempt to measure the effects at some future date of the social forces set in motion by some method of treatment or program, thus tracing the flow of social events; and (3) an ex post facto design, with some present effect traced backward to factors or forces operating at a prior date, using such records as are available, since no new measures of the past can be made in the present.[44]

**Psychology.** Psychologists have developed certain detailed procedures [45] for experimentation, some of which go beyond the purpose and scope of the present chapter. The so-called methods listed below refer to minor

[42] John Stuart Mill, *op. cit.*
John C. Townsend, *op. cit.*, p. 89-106.
[43] Ernest Greenwood, *op. cit.*
[44] F. Stuart Chapin, *Experimental Designs in Sociological Research, op. cit.* Also see:
F. Stuart Chapin, "Experimental Design in Sociology: Limitations and Abuses." With rejoinders by J. E. Hulett, Jr., and Stuart A. Queen, *Social Forces* 29:25-32; October 1950.
Margaret J. Hagood, A review of Chapin's book. *Journal of the American Statistical Association* 44:312-13; June 1949.
[45] John C. Townsend, *op. cit.*, p. 68-88.
T. G. Andrews, *op. cit.*
S. S. Stevens, Editor, *Handbook of Experimental Psychology.* New York: John Wiley and Sons, 1951. xi + 1436 p.
Benton J. Underwood, *op. cit.*

variations in technique and represent a common use of the term but not in the sense of major, fundamental methods of research.

Methods of expression and impression
Psychophysical methods
Methods of limits (or serial exploration, just noticeable difference, least notice-
able difference, or minimal change)
Method of average error (or reproduction, or equation)
Constant methods (or right and wrong cases, constant stimuli, or constant
stimulus differences)
Method of single stimuli (or absolute judgment)
Method of paired comparison
Method of rank order
Method of equal appearing intervals (or mean gradation)
Factorial and functional approaches
Savings method.

In summarizing studies [46] of transfer of training, Sandiford described the following methods of experimentation.

1. Individual method. A single person is studied under different conditions.

2. Single-group method. A group is studied under two or more different conditions, but no controls are set up.

3. Two-group, or equivalent-group, method. Two comparable groups are employed as experimental and control groups, the latter serving to indicate changes due to normal growth, or learning, during the period, without the experimental factor.

4. Two-pair-group, double-equivalent-group method. This is an elaboration of the preceding type. Of four equivalent groups, two are experimental and two are controls. Pre- and post-tests are given to all four groups, but the post-test is given first (and the pretest given last) to one experimental and one control group—the purpose being to equate or allow for differences in the difficulty of the pre- and post-tests.

5. Three-group method. This is an extension of the two-group method, which permits one group to receive an intermediate (lesser) form of the experimental factor. For example, the first is used as a control group, the second receives only practice in the experimental factor, and the third receives training in how to perform, as well as practice in doing so.

**Statistics of experimental design.** In the light of the newer statistical approaches which have come largely from the biological field, a classification of experimental forms would take on a very different character. The simplest disposal of this technical statistical problem for present pur-

[46] Peter Sandiford, "Transfer of Training." *Encyclopedia of Educational Research.* New York: Macmillan Co., 1941. p. 1306-13.

poses is to list significant chapter headings from a major book in this field.[47]

> Completely Randomized, Randomized Block, and Latin Square Designs.
> Factorial Experiments.
> Confounding.
> Factorial Experiments with Main Effects Confounded: Split-Plot Designs.
> Factorial Experiments Confounded in Quasi-Latin Squares.
> Balanced and Partially Balanced Incomplete Block Designs.
> Lattice and Cubic Lattice Designs.
> Balanced Incomplete Blocks.
> Lattice Squares.
> Incomplete Latin Squares (Youden Squares).

A treatment of the contributions of Fisher and of others to the design of experiments is beyond the purpose and scope of the present non-mathematical overview of the experimental method. The statistically and technically equipped reader is referred to the literature devoted to the design and analysis of experiments,[48] usually written by professors of statistics. Likewise, a discussion of the statistical concepts of average, variability, reliability of measures, significance of differences, and significance of relationships is beyond the purpose and scope of this chapter. Many textbooks and a number of graduate courses are devoted to the details of these concepts.

[47] William G. Cochran and Gertrude M. Cox, *Experimental Designs.* New York: John Wiley and Sons, 1950. ix + 454 p. Also see:

Oscar Kempthorne, *The Design and Analysis of Experiments.* New York: John Wiley and Sons, 1952. xix + 631 p.

E. F. Lindquist, *Design and Analysis of Experiments in Psychology and Education.* Boston: Houghton Mifflin Co., 1953. xix + 393 p.

[48] William G. Cochran and Gertrude M. Cox, *op. cit.*

Allen L. Edwards, *Experimental Design in Psychological Research.* New York: Rinehart and Co., 1950. xiv + 445 p.

R. A. Fisher, *The Design of Experiments.* Sixth Edition. New York: Hafner, 1951. xv + 244 p.

Oscar Kempthorne, *op. cit.*

E. F. Lindquist, *op. cit.*

D. A. Grant, "Statistical Theory and Research Design." *Annual Review of Psychology.* Stanford, Calif.: Annual Reviews, 1950. p. 277-96.

L. S. Kogan, "Variance Designs in Psychological Research." *Psychological Bulletin* 50:1-40; January 1953.

Helen M. Walker, "Statistical Inference." *Encyclopedia of Educational Research.* Revised Edition. New York: Macmillan Co., 1950. p. 1271-90.

Dee W. Norton and Everet F. Lindquist, "Applications of Experimental Design and Analysis." *Review of Educational Research* 21:350-67; December 1951.

Joseph Lev, "Research Methods and Designs." *Review of Educational Research* 18:410-23; December 1948.

C. C. Peters and Others, "Research Methods and Designs." *Review of Educational Research* 15:377-93; December 1945.

Paul Blommers and E. F. Lindquist, "Experimental and Statistical Studies: Applications of Newer Statistical Techniques." *Review of Educational Research* 12:501-20: December 1942.

## THE LITERATURE OF EXPERIMENTATION

Examples of psychological experiments characterized as "great" include Binet's scale for measuring general intelligence, the Army Alpha test and the development of group tests for measuring general intelligence, Galton's work in the measurement of individual differences, experimental investigation of personality, Pavlov's investigations of the conditioned reflex, studies by Franz and Lashley of the role of the brain in learning, Thorndike's experiments in problem-solving by animals and his "laws" of learning, Köhler's studies of perception and learning in relation to Gestalt psychology, experiments by Thorndike and Woodworth on the transfer of training, studies of memory and forgetting by Ebbinghaus, Watson and the behavior of the human infant, Cannon and the emotions, Helmholtz and visual and auditory perception, Cattell and the measurement of reaction time, and Weber and Fechner in the development of psychophysics.[49]

Many examples of experimental studies in psychology and in certain social areas may be located in the handbooks or manuals that cover the literature,[50] in *Psychological Abstracts* and the *Psychological Bulletin,* and in the *American Journal of Sociology* and the *American Sociological Review.*

Illustrations of experimental studies in education and in educational psychology numbering many hundreds may be found in the *Encyclopedia of Educational Research* and in the *Review of Educational Research.*[51]

[49] Henry E. Garrett, *op. cit.*
[50] Edwin G. Boring, *op. cit.*
Leonard Carmichael, Editor, *Manual of Child Psychology.* New York: John Wiley and Sons, 1946. viii + 1068 p. Revised, 1954. 1295 p.
L. W. Crafts and Others, *Recent Experiments in Psychology.* Second Edition. New York: McGraw-Hill Book Co., 1950. xvii + 503 p.
Henry E. Garrett, *op. cit.*
Carl Murchison, Editor, *A Handbook of Child Psychology.* Worcester: Clark University Press, 1931. 712 p. Second Edition, Revised, 1933. xii + 956 p.
Carl Murchison, Editor, *A Handbook of General Experimental Psychology.* Worcester: Clark University Press, 1934. xii + 1126 p.
Carl Murchison, Editor, *A Handbook of Social Psychology.* Worcester: Clark University Press, 1935. xii + 1190 p.
Gardner Murphy, *op. cit.*
Gardner Murphy and Others, *Experimental Social Psychology:* An Interpretation of Research upon the Socialization of the Individual. Revised Edition. New York: Harper and Bros., 1937. xi + 1121 p.
S. S. Stevens, *op. cit.*
[51] O. H. Mowrer, "Learning Theory." *Review of Educational Research* 22:475-95; December 1952.
Boyd McCandless and Sidney Rosenblum, "Psychological Theory As a Determiner of Experimental Pattern in Child Study." *Review of Educational Research* 22:496-525; December 1952.

## EVALUATION OF THE EXPERIMENTAL METHOD

The experiment, which since Galileo's time has been very important in modern physical science and which has been employed with great benefit in agricultural and biological fields generally, is regarded with mixed attitudes and receives varying evaluations in the social field. Early in the present century it was looked upon with much hope, and when measurement instruments had been established in a number of educational areas, by about 1920, the experiment was thought by many to hold the answer to nearly all questions. McCall, in his 1923 book, said somewhat enthusiastically: "Everywhere there are evidences of an increasing tendency to evaluate educational procedures experimentally." [52]

In 1937, however, Monroe wrote: [53]

> The number of controlled experiments reported in educational periodicals, bulletins, and monographs is large. . . . The direct contributions from controlled experimentation have been disappointing. . . . In its general outline the procedure of the controlled experiment is simple and easily understood. . . . But when the controlled experiments relative to a problem are critically examined, it is usually apparent that the question studied has not been answered conclusively.

He also quotes Douglass to the effect that "the controlled experiment has not fulfilled the expectations of its proponents a decade ago." [54]

Gee quotes a number of social scientists with regard to the possibility of, and the value of, experimentation in the social fields, commenting that "a wide disparity exists in the views of various authorities as to whether or not the experimental method is applicable in the social sciences." [55] He finds that a number of them not only say it is inapplicable but that it is impossible. Greenwood [56] cites certain writers to the same effect, noting that John Stuart Mill devoted a whole chapter to proving that experimentation was not possible in the social field. [57]

The main point of difficulty seems to be the idea of "the single variable," since it can readily be realized that social situations are entirely too complex to permit of holding all factors constant save one. The attempt is

[52] W. A. McCall, *How to Experiment in Education*. New York: Macmillan Co., 1923. 282 p.

[53] Walter S. Monroe, "General Methods: Classroom Experimentation." National Society for the Study of Education, *The Scientific Movement in Education*, Chapter 26, p. 319-27. Thirty-Seventh Yearbook, Part II. Chicago: University of Chicago Press, 1938. The same statements are made in his article on "Experiment" in the *Encyclopedia of Educational Research*, 1941 and 1950.

[54] Harl R. Douglass, "Scientific Investigation of Instructional Problems." *Journal of Educational Research* 29:135; October 1935.

[55] Wilson Gee, *Social Science Research Methods*. "Social Sciences and the Experimental Method," p. 346-52. New York: Appleton-Century-Crofts, 1950. 390 p.

[56] Ernest Greenwood, *op. cit.*, p. 86.

[57] John Stuart Mill, *op. cit.*, p. 573-78.

patently absurd. Peters and Van Voorhis, while feeling obligated to retain formal loyalty to the idea of "the law of the single variable," nevertheless, point out that we actually do not want this. That is, if we are studying the possible benefits of homogeneous grouping of pupils in classes, we expect the teaching methods and materials to be adapted to the new opportunities. To insist on holding them constant is absurd—it defeats the purpose of the change. Hence, they urge a "practical Gestalt" of all the appropriate changes and adaptations, although they still feel obligated somehow or other to speak of this assemblage as a "single variable." [58]

Greenwood points out that the great mass of variables, which admittedly cannot be controlled, can be handled satisfactorily through the statistical procedure of randomization.[59] Fisher introduced this technique [60] and it has been widely used. A number of statisticians, however, are coming to doubt that randomization is as satisfactory as it was formerly thought to be. Cochran and Cox go further and point out that, even where we can obtain evaluations of the effects of single factors, we probably want to know the joint effects of several factors varying simultaneously.[61]

When factors are not independent, the simple effects of a factor vary according to the particular combination of the other factors with which these are produced. In this case the single-factor approach is likely to provide only a number of disconnected pieces of information that cannot easily be put together.

It thus appears that, because of the availability of recent statistical developments, it is no longer necessary to talk as though we held every factor constant save one; and, further, it is quite respectable to do what we have always wanted to do, namely, study the effects of various combinations of factors, each in varying degrees. The "law of the single variable," therefore, appears to have been dropped as a requirement, not only by the philosophers (Dewey and Bentley's transactionalism), but also by the statisticians.

Studies in education that employ some of the newer statistical designs are cited by Helen Walker in her brief summary of what may reasonably be inferred from the results of statistical procedures.[62]

Often, too much is expected of the experiment. Note, for example, Monroe's statement that it did not seem to settle things "conclusively."

[58] Charles C. Peters and Walter R. Van Voorhis, *Statistical Procedures and Their Mathematical Bases,* p. 447. New York: McGraw-Hill Book Co., 1940. 516 p.
[59] Ernest Greenwood, *op. cit.,* p. 86-91.
[60] R. A. Fisher, *op. cit.*
[61] Cochran and Cox, *op. cit.,* p. 125.
[62] Helen M. Walker, "Statistical Inference." *Encyclopedia of Educational Research.* Revised Edition, p. 1271-90; see especially p. 1286-88 and bibliography. New York: Macmillan Co., 1950. 1520 p. Also see her 1953 book, *Statistical Inference.*

Statisticians would point out that in any case it can give only probable results. Cantril and associates point out that it is the business of an experiment not to end all, but to lead on to other experiments: [63]

> It should be emphasized that if an hypothesis is to be regarded as adequate it must be more than a statement or description of current data and more than a prediction that data will reproduce themselves. An hypothesis must be tested both in terms of its ability to predict immediate events and its promise of leading to further, more adequate hypotheses. For in scientific procedure there is a never ending process of hypothesizing, a constant flow of one hypothesis from another, with each hypothesis trying to go beyond established formulations in its inclusiveness.

Cohen and Nagel comment: "It is a common belief that a *single crucial experiment* may often decide between two rival theories. . . . Unfortunately, matters are not so simple." [64] They point out that experimentation in physics has not been able to decide between the two rival theories of light (corpuscular and wave). Conant states that "to suppose, with some who write about the 'scientific method,' that a scientific theory stands or falls on the issue of one experiment is to misunderstand science indeed." [65] He deals at length with the tenacity of false ideas, even after repeated experiments have cast doubt on them. He points out further that one may not understand what his experiment has proved, until some years of further experimentation and thought make clear to the experimenter the nature of his results.

Bancroft, a chemist, wrote at length on the erroneous conclusions to which experimentation in all sciences has led.[66] Various other writers have pointed out substantially the same thing. It becomes obvious that the only safeguard against error in conclusion from an experiment is not an impeccable technique, but rather: (1) great familiarity with the phenomena being studied, in order to know what many of the factors and conditions are, so that one can perhaps avoid absurd interpretations; (2) constant observation of all the details of condition and change that occur during the experiment, in order to detect extraneous factors; and (3) continued, unrelenting further experimentation—not just to verify the observations, but to obtain further insights into the nature of the phenomena, so that one can develop further understanding and theories sufficient to reject or substantiate (deductively) the conclusions already arrived at, through their inclusion in a larger, more embracing concept.

[63] Cantril and Others, *op. cit.*, p. 491.
[64] Morris R. Cohen and Ernest Nagel, *An Introduction to Logic and Scientific Method*, p. 219. New York: Harcourt, Brace and Co., 1934. 467 p.
[65] James B. Conant, *op. cit.*
[66] Wilder D. Bancroft, "The Misleading Experiment." *Rice Institute Pamphlet* 15:224-85; October 1928.

In short, it must not be thought that the experiment is an appropriate method for establishing rudimentary knowledge in any field. It is, rather, a tool for developing advanced states of knowledge. The experiment does not provide theories, it tests them. If the theories are inept, the experiment will give results which can scarcely help being misinterpreted. Murphy and associates rightly point out that "it takes many methods to make a science," and that the place of the experiment in social psychology is *after* knowledge has been advanced through several long processes of observation and speculation.[67] (For a related discussion, see the earlier section of this chapter on causal-comparative studies.)

Experiment in these cases is the crowning touch, the technical perfection of the analysis. It must be emphasized, however, that the experimental method in all these cases *comes late*. It comes after the problem has been defined and its salient characteristics so well formulated that we know what can be controlled and measured.

## EXPERIMENTATION AND THE CLASSROOM TEACHER

What does the classroom teacher need to know about the experimental method in relation to educational, psychological, and sociological research?

It may be clear from the foregoing discussion that the experiment is probably the most difficult, the most demanding, the most technically exacting procedure of all those to be found in research methodology. Hence, although we would agree that the regular classroom teacher should undoubtedly have some knowledge of formal experimental methods, it would seem the least likely of all methods in which the teacher should be encouraged to embark alone. Rather, the ideas concerning experimentation that are to be imparted to the teacher should be those which will have some more immediate meaning and benefit for him on the level at which he is likely to come into contact with experimental procedure.

(To cite an example, a person is not encouraged to diagnose his own diseases or to attempt repair of his own teeth. He is, however, encouraged to learn about the mechanics of his own body, in order that he may provide intelligent care for it and may coöperate, when need be, with the professional doctor or dentist. In the same way, the classroom teacher may be encouraged to obtain a sufficient understanding of the formal experimental method to permit him to understand and to coöperate intelligently when the opportunity is presented.)

[67] Quoted from Gardner Murphy, Lois B. Murphy, and Theodore M. Newcomb, *Experimental Social Psychology*. Revised Edition. "The Place of Experiment in Social Psychology," p. 10-15. New York: Harper and Bros., 1937. 1121 p.

More explicitly, the following areas are suggested as those which may well serve to map out a knowledge of experimental method sufficient to answer the needs of the classroom teacher:

1. The teacher should become familiar with a number of examples of experimental study which have yielded results of some significance for classroom teaching. This acquaintance with selected research reports would build up something of an appreciation for the experimental method, and for educational and psychological research in general. Examples can be found in various references already cited.

2. There should be imparted to the teacher certain rudimentary ideas about the nature of the experiment, what is involved, perhaps what the simple types are. Possibly he may some day be in a position to plan a simple study of his own, or he may see the opportunity or feel the need for some experimentation and be able to suggest it to his coworkers.

3. At some time the teacher may be called upon to participate in an experiment being conducted by a research worker. At such a time it would be helpful, if he knew something of the scientific spirit of inquiry as a background for his participation. Teachers are almost invariably inclined to try to "help along" with a study, so that the results come out the way they "should"—the way the teachers themselves or the researchers want them to come out. Then, too, the teachers naturally do whatever they think will be most helpful for each individual pupil, rather than abiding by the strict experimental procedure. They make many exceptions and departures from the prescribed rules set forth for the experiment. If they could be imbued with the spirit of experimentation and were able to shift their ideals temporarily from trying to help the pupils or to obtain certain results over to trying to be objective, impartial, and somewhat scientific— trying "to find out" rather than letting their compulsions guide them— then formal experimentation which involves classroom teachers could and would be more dependable.

4. Even so, the teacher should be encouraged toward an attitude that would permit him to welcome experimentation and in which he would retain the spirit of experimentation in the sense of being willing and eager to try something new in order to see how it works. This is a part of the scientific, exploratory spirit—a part of the adventure of teaching.

## CONCLUDING STATEMENT—THE OUTLOOK

During the 1920's and 1930's, workers in education and in educational psychology were overly optimistic in their expectations that most of the major problems of teaching and learning would be solved through the experimental method; in particular, the goals set for group experimentation were too high for realization. During the latter part of the 1930's, the 1940's, and especially in the early 1950's research workers in education, psychology, and other social fields have come increasingly to recognize that a balanced program of research methodology is necessary for solving problems. As a result, we now have the wide variety of relatively recent research studies cited as illustrations in the various chapters of this book (including the historical, descriptive-survey, experimental, case-clinical, and genetic-developmental investigations).

While the numerous problems of control, measurement, and interpretation in experimental research render accurate generalization difficult, we should remember the stimulating effect of such investigation on the experimenter and on both teachers and pupils, somewhat like a change in weather or in scenery. This stimulating influence as a valuable by-product of experimentation, along with a substantial body of dependable information, amply justifies more extensive participation in carefully planned and conducted experimental studies.

## SELECTED REFERENCES

ACKOFF, Russell L. *The Design of Social Research.* Chicago: University of Chicago Press, 1953. xi + 420 p.

American Association for Health, Physical Education, and Recreation. *Research Methods Applied to Health, Physical Education, and Recreation.* Revised Edition. Washington: The Association, N.E.A., 1952. p. 182-203, 254-314.

ANDREWS, T. C., Editor. *Methods of Psychology.* New York: John Wiley and Sons, 1948. xiv + 716 p.

BARR, A. S.; DAVIS, R. A.; and JOHNSON, P. O. *Educational Research and Appraisal.* Chicago: J. B. Lippincott Co., 1953. p. 224-56.

BARTLEY, S. Howard. *Beginning Experimental Psychology.* New York: McGraw-Hill Book Co., 1950. viii + 483 p.

BERG, Irwin A. "The Use of Human Subjects in Psychological Research." *American Psychologist* 9:108-11; March 1954.

BINGHAM, Walter V. "Psychology as a Science, as a Technology and as a Profession." *American Psychologist* 8:115-18; March 1953.

BLOMMERS, Paul, and LINDQUIST, E. F. "Experimental and Statistical Studies: Applications of Newer Statistical Techniques." *Review of Educational Research* 12:501-20; December 1942.

BOGARDUS, Emory S. "Experimental Research in Sociology." *Sociology and Social Research* 33:33-40; September-October 1948.

BORING, Edwin G. *A History of Experimental Psychology.* Second Edition. New York: Appleton-Century-Crofts, 1950. xxi + 777 p.

BRUNSWIK, Egon. *Systematic and Representative Design of Psychological Experiments.* Berkeley: University of California Press, 1947. 60 p.

BUGELSKI, B. R. *A First Course in Experimental Psychology.* New York: Henry Holt and Co., 1951. xxiii + 421 p.

BURLINGHAM, Dorothy. *Twins:* A Study of Three Pairs of Identical Twins. New York: International Universities Press, 1953. x + 92 p. + 30 developmental charts.

BUROS, Oscar K., Editor. *The Fourth Mental Measurements Yearbook.* Highland Park, N. J.: Gryphon Press, 1953. 1189 p.

CANTER, Ralph R., Jr. "The Use of Extended Control-Group Designs in Human Relations Studies." *Psychological Bulletin* 48:340-47; July 1951.

CARMICHAEL, Leonard, Editor. *Manual of Child Psychology.* New York: John Wiley and Sons, 1946. viii + 1068 p. Revised, 1954. 1295 p.

CHAPIN, F. Stuart. *Experimental Designs in Sociological Research.* New York: Harper and Bros., 1947. x + 206 p.

COCHRAN, William G., and COX, Gertrude M. *Experimental Designs.* New York: John Wiley and Sons, 1950. ix + 454 p.

CORNELL, Francis G., and MONROE, Walter S. "Experiment." *Encyclopedia of Educational Research.* Revised Edition. New York: Macmillan Co., 1950. p. 414-16.

CRAFTS, L. W., and Others. *Recent Experiments in Psychology.* Second Edition. New York: McGraw-Hill Book Co., 1950. xvii + 503 p.

DEIGNAN, Stella L., and MILLER, Esther. "The Support of Research in Medical and Allied Fields for the Period 1946 through 1951." *Science* 115:321-43; March 28, 1952.

DENNIS, Wayne, Editor. *Readings in Child Psychology.* New York: Prentice-Hall, 1951. xi + 624 p.

EDWARDS, Allen L. *Experimental Design in Psychological Research.* New York: Rinehart and Co., 1950. xiv + 445 p.

EDWARDS, Allen L., and CRONBACH, L. J. "Experimental Design for Research in Psychotherapy." *Journal of Clinical Psychology* 8:51-56; January 1952.

ELMER, M. C. *Social Research.* New York: Prentice-Hall, 1939. p. 235-70.

FESTINGER, Leon, and KATZ, Daniel, Editors. *Research Methods in the Behavioral Sciences.* New York: Dryden Press, 1953. p. 98-172.

FISHER, R. A. *The Design of Experiments.* Sixth Edition. New York: Hafner, 1951. xv + 244 p.

GARRETT, Henry E. *Great Experiments in Psychology.* Third Edition. New York: Appleton-Century-Crofts, 1951. 400 p.

GEE, Wilson. *Social Science Research Methods.* New York: Appleton-Century-Crofts, 1950. p. 330-60.

GEORGE, W. C. "The Responsibility of Scientists in This Era." *School and Society* 76:369-74; December 13, 1952.

GESELL, Arnold. "The Method of Co-Twin Control." *Science* 95:446-48; May 1, 1942.

GESELL, Arnold, and THOMPSON, Helen. *Twins T and C from Infancy to Adolescence:* A Biogenetic Study of Individual Differences by the Method of Co-Twin Control. Genetic Psychology Monographs, Vol. 24. Provincetown, Mass.: Journal Press, 1941. p. 3-121.

GLUECK, Sheldon, and GLUECK, Eleanor. *Delinquents in the Making:* Paths to Prevention. New York: Harper and Bros., 1952. viii + 214 p. A briefer, less technical version of *Unraveling Juvenile Delinquency.*

GOLDSMITH, Maurice. "One Hundred Years of British Science." *Scientific Monthly* 74:170-79; March 1952.

GOOD, Carter V.; BARR, A. S.; and SCATES, Douglas E. *The Methodology of Educational Research.* New York: Appleton-Century-Crofts, 1936. p. 482-548.

GOODE, William J., and HATT, Paul K. *Methods in Social Research*. New York: McGraw-Hill Book Co., 1952. p. 74-102.

GRANT, D. A. "The Latin Square Principle in the Design and Analysis of Psychological Experiments." *Psychological Bulletin* 45:427-42; September 1948.

GREENWOOD, Ernest. *Experimental Sociology:* A Study in Method. New York: King's Crown Press, 1945. xiii + 163 p.

HALL, Oswald. "Sociological Research in the Field of Medicine: Progress and Prospects." *American Sociological Review* 16:639-44; October 1951.

HOTELLING, Harold. "The Impact of R. A. Fisher on Statistics." *Journal of the American Statistical Association* 46:35-46; March 1951.

HUMPHREY, George. *Thinking:* An Introduction to Its Experimental Psychology. New York: Wiley Book Co., 1951. xi + 331 p.

HUNT, J. McV. "Psychological Services in the Tactics of Psychological Science." *American Psychologist* 7:608-22; November 1952.

HUNT, William A. "Clinical Psychology—Science or Superstition," *American Psychologist* 6:683-87; December 1951.

JAHODA, Marie, and Others. *Research Methods in the Study of Social Relations:* With Special Emphasis on Prejudice. New York: Dryden Press, 1951. p. 27-89.

KEMPTHORNE, Oscar. *The Design and Analysis of Experiments*. New York: John Wiley and Sons, 1952. xix + 631 p.

KIDD, C. V. "Research Planning and Research Policy: Scientists and Administrators." *Science* 118:147-52; August 7, 1953.

KOCH, Sigmund. "The Current Status of Motivational Psychology." *Psychological Review* 58:147-54; May 1951.

LACEY, Oliver L. *Statistical Methods in Experimentation:* An Introduction. New York: Macmillan Co., 1953. xi + 249 p.

LAFLEUR, Laurence J. "On the Nature of Scientific Law." *Scientific Monthly* 74:247-52; May 1952.

LANGFELD, Herbert S., and Others, Editors. *A History of Psychology in Autobiography*, Vol. 4. Worcester: Clark University Press, 1952. xii + 356 p.

LANIER, Lyle H., and Others. "Contract Research as a Problem in the Sociology of Science [and in Psychology]." *American Psychologist* 7:707-21; December 1952.

LAZARUS, Richard S.; DEESE, James; and OSLER, Sonia F. "The Effects of Psychological Stress Upon Performance." *Psychological Bulletin* 49:293-317; July 1952.

LEV, Joseph. "Research Methods and Designs." *Review of Educational Research* 18:410-23; December 1948.

LINDQUIST, E. F. *Design and Analysis of Experiments in Psychology and Education*. Boston: Houghton Mifflin Co., 1953. xix + 393 p.

LINDSAY, R. B. "The Survival of Physical Science." *Scientific Monthly* 74:139-44; March 1952.

LUCHINS, Abraham S. "Towards an Experimental Clinical Psychology." *Journal of Personality* 20:440-56; June 1952.

LUNDBERG, George A. "Science, Scientists, and Values." *Social Forces* 30:373-79; May 1952.

LUNDBERG, George A. *Social Research*. Revised Edition. New York: Longmans, Green and Co., 1942. p. 54-79.

MADGE, John. *The Tools of Social Science*. New York: Longmans, Green and Co., 1953. p. 254-89.

MANN, H. B. *Analysis and Design of Experiments*. New York: Dover Publications, 1949. x + 198 p.

MCGRATH, Earl J. "Need for Experimentation and Research," *General Education in Transition*. Edited by H. T. Morse. Minneapolis: University of Minnesota Press, 1951. p. 16-28.

MECH, Edmund V., and Others. *An Experimental Analysis of Patterns of Differential Verbal Reinforcement in Classroom Situations*. Bulletin of the School of Education, Indiana University, Vol. 29, No. 5. Bloomington: Division of Research and Field Services, Indiana University, September 1953. 26 p.

MORENO, J. L. *Sociometry, Experimental Method and the Science of Society*. New York: Beacon House, 1951. xiv + 220 p.

MUNN, Norman L. *A Laboratory Manual in General Experimental Psychology*. Revised Edition. Boston: Houghton Mifflin Co., 1948. xii + 224 p.

MURPHY, Gardner. *Historical Introduction to Modern Psychology*. Revised Edition. New York: Harcourt, Brace and Co., 1949. xiv + 466 p.

MURPHY, Gardner, and Others. *Experimental Social Psychology:* An Interpretation of Research Upon the Socialization of the Individual. Revised Edition. New York: Harper and Bros., 1937. xi + 1121 p.

NORTON, Dee W., and Lindquist, Everet F. "Applications of Experimental Design and Analysis." *Review of Educational Research* 21:350-67; December 1951.

OSGOOD, Charles E. *Method and Theory in Experimental Psychology*. New York: Oxford University Press, 1953. vi + 800 p.

OSGOOD, Charles E. "The Nature and Measurement of Meaning." *Psychological Bulletin* 49:197-237; May 1952.

PETERS, Charles C.; TOWNSEND, Agatha; and TRAXLER, Arthur E. "Research Methods and Designs." *Review of Educational Research* 15:377-93; December 1945.

PHILLIPS, Melba. "Dangers Confronting American Science." *Science* 116:439-43; October 24, 1952.

RAIMY, Victor C., Editor. *Training in Clinical Psychology*. New York: Prentice-Hall, 1950. xix + 253 p.

"Research Design in Clinical Psychology; Symposium." *Journal of Clinical Psychology* 8:3-98; January 1952.

RICHTER, C. P. "Free Research Versus Design Research." *Science* 118:91-93; July 24, 1953.

ROSEBOROUGH, Mary E. "Experimental Studies of Small Groups." *Psychological Bulletin* 50:275-303; July 1953.

SCHEELE, Leonard A., and SEBRELL, W. H. "Medical Research and Medical Education." *Science* 114:517-21; November 16, 1951.

SHAFFER, G. Wilson, and LAZARUS, Richard S. *Fundamental Concepts in Clinical Psychology*. New York: McGraw-Hill Book Co., 1952. 540 p.

SMITH, Eugene R., and TYLER, Ralph W. *Appraising and Recording Student Progress*. Adventure in American Education, Vol. 3. New York: Harper and Bros., 1942. xxiii + 550 p.

STEVENS, S. S., Editor. *Handbook of Experimental Psychology*. New York: John Wiley and Sons, 1951. xi + 1436 p.

STOKE, Stuart M., and Others. "Growth, Development, and Learning." *Review of Educational Research* 22:387-525; December 1952.

TAEUSCH, Carl E. "The Unlisted Freedom: Science." *Scientific Monthly* 75:12-18; July 1952.

TINKER, Miles A. *Introduction to Methods in Experimental Psychology.* Second Edition. New York: Appleton-Century-Crofts, 1947. vii + 232 p.

TOWNSEND, John C. *Introduction to Experimental Method:* For Psychology and the Social Sciences. New York: McGraw-Hill Book Co., 1953. ix + 220 p.

UNDERWOOD, Benton J. *Experimental Psychology:* An Introduction. New York: Appleton-Century-Crofts, 1949. vii + 638 p.

VALENTINE, Willard L., and WICKENS, Delos D. *Experimental Foundations of General Psychology.* Third Edition. New York: Rinehart and Co., 1949. xxi + 472 p.

VINACKE, W. E. *The Psychology of Thinking.* New York: McGraw-Hill Book Co., 1952. xiii + 392 p.

VISSCHER, Maurice B., Editor. *Methods in Medical Research,* Vol. 4. Chicago: Year Book Publishers, 1951. xiv + 306 p.

WALKER, Helen M. *Statistical Inference.* New York: Henry Holt and Co., 1953. xi + 510 p.

WATSON, Robert I. *The Clinical Method in Psychology.* New York: Harper and Bros., 1951. xii + 779 p.

WATSON, Robert I. "Research Design and Methodology in Evaluating the Results of Psychotherapy." *Journal of Clinical Psychology* 8:29-33; January 1952.

WEINLAND, Clarence E. "Creative Thought in Scientific Research." *Scientific Monthly* 75:350-54; December 1952.

WILSON, E. Bright. *Introduction to Scientific Research.* Chapters 4, 6, 8. New York: McGraw-Hill Book Co., 1952. 375 p.

YOUDEN, W. J. "The Fisherian Revolution in Methods of Experimentation." *Journal of the American Statistical Association* 46:47-50; March 1951.

YOUNG, Pauline V. *Scientific Social Surveys and Research.* Second Edition. New York: Prentice-Hall, 1949. p. 207-19.

ZNANIECKI, Florian. "The Scientific Function of Sociology of Education." *Educational Theory* 1:69-78, 86; August 1951.

# 8

# Case and Clinical Studies

THIS CHAPTER IS concerned with the characteristics, procedures, and sequence of the complementary processes of case study and case work. The five major phases of the case-study and case-work cycle are analyzed in detail to constitute the larger part of the chapter: (1) status of the situation or unit of attention; (2) collection of data, examination, and history; (3) diagnosis and identification of causal factors; (4) adjustment, treatment, and therapy; and (5) follow-up of the adjustment program. Consideration is given to records and problems of recording in case procedure. Other topics deal with the desirability of professional, institutional, and community coöperation in case and clinical studies, and with training for case study and case work.

## CHARACTERISTICS, APPLICATIONS, AND SEQUENCE

**Definition of case study.** The essential procedure of the case-study method is to take account of all pertinent aspects of one thing or situation, employing as the unit for study an individual, an institution, a community, or any group considered as a unit. The case consists of the data relating to some phase of the life history of the unit or relating to the entire life process, whether the unit is an individual, a family, a social group, an institution, or a community. The complex situation and combination of factors involved in the given behavior are examined to determine the existing status and to identify the causal factors operating.

The foregoing definition of case study may be rendered concrete by citing the titles of selected works that illustrate the application of this investigational procedure to individuals,[1] social institutions or agencies,[2] and communities or culture groups.[3]

[1] Clifford W. Beers, *A Mind That Found Itself:* An Autobiography. New York: Doubleday, Doran and Co., 1908. iv + 434 + xxi p. Second Edition, 1935.
W. E. Blatz, *The Five Sisters.* New York: William Morrow and Co., 1938. 209 p.
David P. Boder, *I Did Not Interview the Dead.* Urbana: University of Illinois Press, 1949. xx + 220 p.
W. T. Brannon, *"Yellow Kid" Weil:* The Autobiography of America's Master Swindler. Chicago: Ziff-Davis Publishing Co., 1948. 297 p.
John Custance, *Wisdom, Madness and Folly:* The Philosophy of a Lunatic. New York: Pellegrini and Cudahy, 1951. 254 p. Mostly written in a mental hospital by a patient.

726

Lucy Freeman, *Fight Against Fears.* New York: Crown Publishers, 1951. 332 p. A personal account of a woman's psychoanalysis, written in the layman's language.

Arnold Gesell and Others, *Biographies of Child Development:* The Mental Growth Careers of Eighty-four Infants and Children. New York: Paul B. Hoeber, 1939. xviii + 328 p.

Emil A. Gutheil, Editor, *The Autobiography of Wilhelm Stekel:* The Life Story of a Pioneer Psychoanalyst. New York: Liveright Publishing Corporation, 1950. ix + 293 p.

Joseph P. Harris, "The Senatorial Rejection of Leland Olds: A Case Study." *American Political Science Review* 45:674-92; September 1951.

Florence Hollis, *Women in Marital Conflict:* A Casework Study. New York: Family Service Association of America, 1949. 236 p.

Harold E. Jones and Others, *Development in Adolescence:* Approaches to the Study of the Individual. New York: D. Appleton-Century Co., 1943. xviii + 166 p.

Abram Kardiner and Lionel Ovesey, *The Mark of Oppression:* A Psychosocial Study of the American Negro. New York: W. W. Norton and Co., 1951. xviii + 396 p. Case histories of twenty-five American Negroes.

Sir Arthur Keith, *An Autobiography.* New York: Philosophical Library, 1950. vi + 721 p. An eminent pioneer among anthropologists tells of his life and work.

Jack Kerkhoff, *How Thin the Veil:* A Newspaperman's Story of His Own Mental Crack-up and Recovery. New York: Greenberg, Publisher, 1952. 311 p.

R. M. Lindner, *Rebel Without a Cause:* The Hypnoanalysis of a Criminal Psychopath. New York: Grune and Stratton, 1944. 310 p.

John B. Martin, Reporter, *My Life in Crime:* The Autobiography of a Professional Criminal. New York: Harper and Bros., 1952. 279 p.

Lucy S. Mitchell, *Two Lives:* The Story of Wesley Clair Mitchell and Myself. New York: Simon and Schuster, 1953. A personal and professional autobiography.

Marie I. Rasey, *It Takes Time:* An Autobiography of the Teaching Profession. New York: Harper and Bros., 1953. x + 204 p. Case history of an evolving philosophy and psychology of teaching.

*Red Dust:* Autobiographies of Chinese Communists. As Told to Nym Wales. Stanford University, Calif.: Stanford University Press, 1952. 238 p.

Anne Roe, *A Psychological Study of Eminent Biologists.* Washington: American Psychological Association, 1953. Reports data from the life histories and from three psychological tests of twenty eminent research biologists.

Clifford R. Shaw and M. E. Moore, *The Natural History of a Delinquent Career.* Chicago: University of Chicago Press, 1931. 280 p.

Elsie M. Smithies, *Case Studies of Normal Adolescent Girls.* New York: D. Appleton-Century Co., 1933. x + 284 p.

Frank E. Spaulding, *One School Administrator's Philosophy:* Its Development. New York: Exposition Press, 1952. 352 p.

Robert W. White, *Lives in Progress:* A Study of the Natural Growth of Personality. New York: William Sloane Associates, 1952. Presents, interprets, and compares the lives (case studies) of three normal people.

Norbert Wiener, *Ex-Prodigy:* My Childhood and Youth. New York: Simon and Schuster, 1953. xii + 309 p.

*Woman at Work:* The Autobiography of Mary Anderson as Told to Mary N. Winslow. Minneapolis: University of Minnesota Press, 1951. 266 p.

[2] Kenneth R. Andrews, Editor, *Human Relations and Administration. The Case Method of Teaching:* An Interim Statement. Cambridge: Harvard University Press, 1953. xvi + 271 p. Business organizations and the military services have found the case method a helpful technique in teaching.

R. F. Barton, *The Kalingas:* The Institutions and Custom Law. Chicago: University of Chicago Press, 1949. xii + 275 p.

H. M. Bond, "Education as a Social Process: A Case Study of a Higher Institution as an Incident in the Process of Acculturation." *American Journal of Sociology* 48:701-9; May 1943. In making this case study of a college for Negroes in Georgia, the faculty and students were subjects for study of the processes of acculturation.

Elizabeth S. Dixon and Grace A. Browning, *Social Case Records:* Family Welfare. Chicago: University of Chicago Press, 1938. x + 312 p.

Stuart A. Queen and John B. Adams, *The Family in Various Cultures:* A Survey of Eleven Family Systems in Eleven Cultural and Historical Settings throughout the World. Chicago: J. B. Lippincott, 1952. vii + 280 p.

Dore Schary, *Case History of a Movie.* New York: Random House, 1950. xix + 242 p.

Harold Stein, "Preparation of Case Studies: The Problem of Abundance." *American Political Science Review* 45:479-87; June 1951. Indicates the wide range of material available.

Harold Stein, Editor, *Public Administration and Policy Development:* A Case Book. New York: Harcourt, Brace and Co., 1952. 860 p. Applied to the area of public adminis-

728    METHODS OF RESEARCH

tration including the executive branches of the federal, state, and local governments; for example, a case study of the Office of Education Library.

Melvin M. Tumin, *Caste in a Peasant Society:* A Case Study in the Dynamics of Caste. Princeton: Princeton University Press, 1952. 300 p.

Edward Westermarck, *Short History of Marriage.* New York: Macmillan Co., 1926. xiii + 327 p.

Helen L. Witmer, "Case Studies of Two State Hospital Clinics." *Psychiatric Clinics for Children.* New York: Commonwealth Fund, 1940. p. 132-55.

Helen L. Witmer, *Social Work:* An Analysis of a Social Institution. New York: Farrar and Rinehart, 1942. xvi + 540 p.

Lin Yueh-Hwa, *The Golden Wing.* New York: Oxford University Press, 1948. xv + 234 p. An intensive study of two families in Fukien Province in China designed to show the forces molding family life and determining its fate.

³ Leland G. Allbaugh, *Crete:* A Case Study of an Underdeveloped Area. Princeton: Princeton University Press, 1953. 592 p.

Ralph L. Beals, "The Village in an Industrial World." *Scientific Monthly* 77:65-75; August 1953.

Lowell J. Carr and James E. Stermer, *Willow Run:* A Study of Industrialization and Cultural Inadequacy. New York: Harper and Bros., 1952. xxii + 406 p.

John B. Dollard, *Caste and Class in a Southern Town.* New Haven, Conn.: Yale University Press, 1937. 502 p. Second Edition, 1949.

Robert J. Havighurst and H. Gerthon Morgan, *The Social History of a War-Boom Community.* New York: Longmans, Green and Co., 1951. xix + 356 p.

August B. Hollingshead, *Elmtown's Youth:* The Impact of Social Classes on Adolescents. New York: John Wiley and Sons, 1949. xi + 480 p.

William C. Kvaraceus, "What the Elmtowners Think of the Elmtown Study." *School Review* 60:352-57; September 1952.

Francis J. Horner, *Case History of Japan.* New York: Sheed and Ward, 1948. xviii + 260 p. Complexity of Japanese character in the light of early Japanese history.

Francis L. K. Hsu, *Under the Ancestors' Shadow.* New York: Columbia University Press, 1948. xiv + 317 p. An anthropological study of a community in the Yunnan Province of China, showing the pervasive influence of ancestor worship on family life and social structure.

Elliott Jaques, *The Changing Culture of a Factory.* New York: Dryden Press, 1952 xxi + 341 p. Three-year case study of the psychological and social forces affecting the group life, morale, and productivity of a London industrial community; includes description, diagnosis, and treatment.

Alice Joseph, Rosamond B. Spicer, and Jane Chesky, *The Desert People:* A Study of the Papago Indians of Southern Arizona. Chicago: University of Chicago Press, 1949. xvii + 287 p.

Oscar Lewis, *Life in a Mexican Village:* Tepoztlan Restudied. Urbana: University of Illinois Press, 1951. xxvii + 512 p.

Robert S. Lynd and Helen M. Lynd, *Middletown:* A Study in Contemporary Culture. New York: Harcourt, Brace and Co., 1929. x + 550 p.

Robert S. Lynd and Helen M. Lynd, *Middletown in Transition:* A Study in Cultural Conflicts. New York: Harcourt, Brace and Co., 1937. xviii + 604 p.

Margaret Mead, *Coming of Age in Samoa.* New York: William Morrow and Co., 1928. xv + 297 p.

Margaret Mead, *Growing Up in New Guinea.* New York: William Morrow and Co., 1930. x + 372 p.

Donald Pierson, *Cruz das Almas:* A Brazilian Village. Washington: Government Printing Office, 1951. viii + 226 p.

Buell Quain, *Fijian Village.* Chicago: University of Chicago Press, 1948. xvii + 459 p. An anthropologist's account of Fijian institutions, ethics, and personalities.

Robert Redfield, *A Village That Chose Progress:* Chan Kom Revisited. Chicago: University of Chicago Press, 1950. xiv + 187 p.

Harriet O. Ronken and Paul R. Lawrence, *Administering Changes:* A Case Study of Human Relations in a Factory. Boston: Harvard University, 1952. xvii +324 p.

Irwin T. Sanders, *Balkan Village.* Lexington: University of Kentucky Press, 1949. xvi + 291 p.

Laura Thompson, *Culture in Crisis:* A Study of the Hopi Indians. New York: Harper and Bros., 1950. xxiv + 221 p.

Charles R. Walker, *Steeltown:* An Industrial Case History of the Conflict between Progress and Security. New York: Harper and Bros., 1950. xv + 284 p.

W. Lloyd Warner and Associates, *Democracy in Jonesville:* A Study in Quality and Inequality. New York: Harper and Bros., 1949. 313 p.

Two additional examples of community studies may be helpful if described in more detail. Later in this chapter and in the bibliography numerous illustrations of other types of case studies will be cited. (Also see the discussion and examples of community surveys in Chapter 6.)

In tracing the natural history of a social problem in a community, the case approach appears to be substantially the procedure employed.[4] For example, in following through the residence trailer problem in Detroit the sequence of steps included the awakening of the people in the locality to an awareness or consciousness of the problem, determination of policy and of means for effecting a solution, and the administering of a program of reform. However, a parallel study followed the same conceptual scheme in California cities, with the conclusion that the conceptual framework of a natural history of social problems was inapplicable to the rise and regulation of California trailer camps.

In the case history of a guidance program for a community, two loosely organized committees were named with two purposes: to finance a testing program for all graduating seniors in a county of North Dakota and to find ways of making a community guidance project a permanent activity. The case history of the community presented the geographical and social background, the development of the guidance project, financing the program, relations with the youth of the community, technical supervision and methods in the counseling project, broadening the guidance service, the counseling system of the city school, state-wide promotion of guidance activities, war-time services, and legislative support of the guidance project.[5]

The varied fields in which case study has been used to advantage include law and handling of juvenile offenders, medicine, psychiatry, psychology, education, guidance, cultural anthropology, sociology, social work, economics, political science, and journalism.

Some writers have made a distinction between the terms *case study, case work,* and *case method.*[6] As defined above, case study means intensive investigation of the particular unit represented. Case work refers especially to the developmental, adjustment, remedial, or corrective procedures that appropriately follow diagnosis of the causes of maladjustment or of favorable development. For example, social case work consists of the processes

[4] R. C. Fuller and R. R. Myers, "The Natural History of a Social Problem." *American Sociological Review* 6:320-29; June 1941.

Edwin M. Lemert, "Is There a Natural History of Social Problems?" *American Sociological Review* 16:217-23; April 1951.

[5] John G. Darley, *Testing and Counseling in the High-School Guidance Program.* Chicago: Science Research Associates, 1943. p. 186-212.

[6] Howard W. Odum and Katharine Jocher, *An Introduction to Social Research.* New York: Henry Holt and Co., 1929. p. 232-33.

Percival M. Symonds, *Diagnosing Personality and Conduct.* New York: Appleton-Century-Crofts, 1931. p. 555.

and procedures necessary in rendering service, financial assistance, or personal advice to individuals by representatives of social agencies, with due consideration of established policies and individual need. Case study and case work, even though they may not be done by the same person or agency, are complementary processes; therefore, this chapter includes consideration of the adjustment and follow-up techniques of case work. The expression, case method, frequently has been employed to describe a plan of organizing and presenting instructional materials in law, medicine, social work, and even in education, psychology, and sociology. As a rule, the case materials used are the product of case-study investigation.

**Contribution of case study.** The objectives of case study are no longer limited to consideration of situations or conditions of maladjustment, such as a behavior problem in school, a broken home, or an underprivileged community. Case study of normal or well adjusted children, of effectively functioning institutions, and of well organized communities aids in understanding the normal situation or well adjusted condition and places deviation from normal in proper perspective.

The unique contribution of case study to general knowledge has been outlined by Olson under six headings.[7]

1. Tabulation of cases under significant categories as a means of communicating to professional workers the nature of the problems involved; for example, classification of the cases referred to a bureau of juvenile research in terms of source of reference, age, sex, race, problem, intelligence, school grade, economic status, and interrelations between certain factors.
2. Evaluation of programs by studying the subsequent history of the persons affected; for example, to follow up habit-clinic children who manifested delinquency problems before the age of ten years, through securing judgments on improvement from parent, teacher, hospital, and agency.
3. Study of social and institutional group patterns existing in families, classes, schools, and communities.
4. Provision of case materials for instructional purposes in professional courses.
5. Illustration and validation of statistical results, as in supplementing statistical findings on twin resemblance by detailed case histories.
6. Formulation of generalizations on the basis of the body of knowledge that results through accumulation of published reports of cases of particular types, as in medicine and in certain social, psychological, and educational areas.

**Relation of case study to other research procedures.** Case study as an investigational procedure frequently employs supplementary or complementary techniques. To trace successfully the life history of an individual or the developmental processes of an institution or a community depends on judicious use of the sources and principles of historical research. Case

[7] Willard C. Olson, "The Case Method," Chapter 6 in "Methods of Research in Education." *Review of Educational Research* 9:449-646; December 1939.

study frequently utilizes such data-gathering instruments as tests, questionnaires, check lists, score cards, and rating scales. Direct observation is essential in most instances. The interview may serve as a device for observation of symptoms, collection of data, diagnosis, treatment, and follow-up. Certain of the developmental case studies are also genetic in character, as when tracing the growth of individual children, although ordinarily the movement of the case study is backward and that of the genetic method is forward. Statistical techniques are employed when cases are classified and summarized to reveal frequencies, types, trends, uniformities, or patterns of behavior. This statement of the relationships between case study and other problem-solving approaches emphasizes once more the complementary and supplementary uses of research techniques.

**Unity and sequence.** Earlier in this chapter case study was characterized as intensive investigation of the unit under consideration, and case work as the adjustment or developmental procedure employed. These complementary processes are analyzed as a sequence of steps in succeeding pages, although they may not be carried out by the same person or agency. Also, it should be pointed out that, while continuity in study, diagnosis, and treatment is a logical sequence, with the steps differentiated intellectually, in an actual life situation these steps may weave in and out shuttle-like.[8] While interviewing a person to collect information, certain treatment may take place, and later, when employing adjustment procedures, additional evidence may be secured. During the 1940's and 1950's the development of concepts of non-directive or client-centered therapy tended to minimize (in the work of client-centered therapists) the diagnostic process as a basis for therapy, a point of view that will be analyzed later in this chapter.

**Characteristics and skills of satisfactory case study and case work.** In addition to continuity, as emphasized above and as described in a subsequent paragraph, the essential characteristics of a satisfactory case study include completeness of data, validity of data, confidential recording, and scientific synthesis.[9]

1. Continuity: this chapter stresses the steps in case study and case work as a cycle of complementary processes; from another point of view, there is a desirable continuity of information provided by two successive psychological

---

[8] Gordon Hamilton, *Theory and Practice of Social Case Work.* New York: Columbia University Press, 1940. p. 34-60. Also see the 1951 edition.

Carl R. Rogers, *Client-Centered Therapy:* Its Current Practice, Implications, and Theory. Boston: Houghton Mifflin Co., 1951. xii + 560 p.

Carter V. Good, "The Sequence of Steps in Case Study and Case Work." *Educational Research Bulletin* 21:161-71; September 16, 1942.

[9] Francis N. Maxfield, "The Case Study." *Educational Research Bulletin* 9:117-22; March 5, 1930.

examinations at an interval of a year, and by an elementary-school record in relation to performance in high school.

2. Completeness of data, in so far as possible: the potential range of information includes symptoms, examination results (psycho-physical, health, educational, and mentality), and history (health, school, family, and social).

3. Validity of data: a doubtful birth date may be verified through the Bureau of Vital Statistics, and an employment record by reference to employers.

4. Confidential recording: [10] educational workers have something to learn from medicine with respect to the confidential nature of professional records; the difficulties of individual teachers or pupils in relation to discipline, failure, achievement, or mentality should be regarded as professional problems to be treated in a confidential manner. A subsequent section of this chapter deals at greater length with the ethics of case recording.

5. Scientific synthesis: this is an interpretation of the evidence that is more than a mere enumeration of the data secured; it embraces diagnosis in identifying causal factors, and prognosis in looking toward treatment or developmental procedures.

The social skills [11] of case work, with particular reference to adjustment procedures, include:

Social insight—a complex concept of great importance in meeting administrative, supervisory, teaching, and organizational problems in welfare agencies and social services

Empathy—social understanding of how other people feel

Sociality—positive behavior of deftness and spontaneity in friendly relations with others

Communication—the process by which we transmit experience or share a common experience

Coöperation—acting or working jointly with others

Participation—social interaction within a group directed to some end, or sharing a common experience

Organization—the process of systematically uniting in a group the persons who participate and coöperate in working toward a common end

Social counseling—assisting the client to formulate and analyze his problem, explore resources, determine a course of action, and secure needed services

Guidance for creative achievement—to liberate the powers of individuals for their own happiness and for contributions of social value.

**The cycle of case study and case work.** Analyzed in specific terms, the complementary steps in the cycle of case study and case work are as follows:

1. Recognition and determination of the status of the phenomenon to be investigated; for example, reading disability.

2. Collection of data relating to the factors or circumstances associated with the given phenomenon; factors associated with learning difficulty or

---

[10] This confidential relationship has been aptly analyzed and illustrated in:
Gordon Hamilton, *op. cit.,* p. 341-43. Also see the 1951 edition.
Margaret C. Bristol, *Handbook on Social Case Recording.* Chicago: University of Chicago Press, 1936. Chapter 15.
[11] Josephine Strode and Pauline R. Strode, *Social Skills in Case Work.* New York: Harper and Bros., 1942. x + 195 p.

reading disability may be physical, intellectual, pedagogical, emotional, social, or environmental.

3. Diagnosis or identification of causal factors as a basis for remedial or developmental treatment; defective vision may be the cause of difficulty in reading.

4. Application of remedial or adjustment measures; correctly fitted glasses may remove the cause of the poor performance in reading.

5. Subsequent follow-up to determine the effectiveness of the corrective or developmental measures applied.

Fenton uses five similar steps to analyze in detail problems of diagnosis and plans of treatment in children's cases, as the basis for individual guidance.[12]

## STEP 1: STATUS OF THE SITUATION OR UNIT OF ATTENTION

The identification of the need-situation, aspect of behavior, or phase of the life process as the unit for study is the first step in case study; for example, reading disability, habitual truancy, exceptional talent in music, superior mentality, or a breadwinner out of a job. Typically, the case has centered on the situation as the unit of attention rather than on the individual or client as such, although the development of non-directive or client-centered therapy has introduced a new emphasis.[13]

As clearer insights and more refined techniques become a part of the equipment of investigators who use the case-study method and other research procedures, more penetrating discrimination is exercised in identifying cases for corrective or developmental attention. For example, it was only natural that the rather obvious maladjustments of the physically handicapped (hard of hearing, deaf, partially seeing, blind, speech defective, crippled, and delicate) received attention before cases of low mentality, special talents, and deficiencies in the school subjects were studied. Even more recent is the recognition of types of social maladjustment, involving personality difficulties and behavior disorders. With increased knowledge, diagnostic areas of some years' standing become subdivided to provide for study of cases that require remedial or developmental opportunities. Adjustment problems and cases have been identified in such newer instructional and learning fields as health, speech, vocations, music, arts, leisure time, creativeness, and behavior. The "delicate" group of children

---

[12] Norman Fenton, *Mental Hygiene in School Practice*. Stanford University, Calif.: Stanford University Press, 1943. p. 167-262.

[13] Ada E. Sheffield, *Social Insight in Case Situations*. New York: D. Appleton-Century Co., 1937. p. 74-97. Stresses the need-situation as the unit of attention.

Carl R. Rogers, *op. cit.*

may be subdivided into anemic, cardiac, undernourished, and epileptic cases. To define the scope of these categories is not easy: the extent of deficiency necessary in vision, hearing, speech, or heart before a child is classified as subnormal; the level of general intelligence or of talent in music or art required to label a child as exceptional; the point at which the learner becomes a subject for remedial or developmental treatment in the school subjects; and the line of demarcation between normal persons and those with social, emotional, personality, or behavior disorders.[14] This work of definition is necessary before the various types of cases for corrective or developmental attention can even be counted within a classroom, building, school system, state, or nation.

Before proceeding with the search for the causal factors operating, it is desirable to know the extent or degree of the deficiency, maladjustment, or ability in question. In many instances direct observation can be verified or supplemented by use of data-gathering and recording procedures and instruments, as in the case of achievement in a school subject, special aptitude, general intelligence, and personality. As a matter of fact, virtually the entire range of investigational procedures and instruments is available for use in determining the status of the unit of attention, including records, tests, questionnaires, check lists, score cards, rating scales, interviews, and clinical and laboratory techniques.

An illustration may be cited to emphasize the need for use of all available symptoms, measures, and information in determining the exact status of the case, as in distinction between the corrective case and the remedial case. Morrison maintained that the corrective case is susceptible of treatment within the pedagogical resources of the regular program in which the pupil is enrolled, while the remedial case involves a degree of formality in handling and requires prolonged investigation and treatment.[15] In the absence of adequate evidence concerning the status of the case, teachers follow a quite human tendency to classify all obstinate corrective cases as remedial in character. Necessary procedures in identifying the genuinely remedial case include gathering of information concerning chronological age and years in school, backwardness in the several school subjects, instances of misconduct, and statements of teachers and others. All statements must be verified, and opinions touching matters of fact should be rejected. Opinions to the effect that a pupil is a poor reader, is weak in arithmetical problem-solving, or is dull mentally are of little value in identifying the status of a remedial case until the appropriate measuring

14 Carter V. Good, "Problems and Techniques of Educational Diagnosis and Adjustment." *School and Society* 48:261-67; August 27, 1938.

15 Henry C. Morrison, *The Practice of Teaching in the Secondary School*. Revised Edition. Chicago: University of Chicago Press, 1931. p. 640-47.

instruments have been employed to ascertain the facts in an accurate, objective manner.

This first step in case study is not entirely separate from the next step; therefore, certain of the examinations outlined below may be of assistance in determining the exact status of the phenomenon under observation.

## STEP 2: COLLECTION OF DATA, EXAMINATION, AND HISTORY

As suggested in the preceding paragraph, the second step in case study is a continuation of the data-gathering begun in the first stage of the investigation, but with emphasis on the search for facts that may serve later as a basis for diagnosis or identification of the causal factors operating. In addition to the procedures and instruments listed under the first step of case study, the life history, biography, autobiography, letters, and diaries frequently prove valuable sources of information.

**Examination and history outlines.** The range of data useful in studying the circumstances associated with the particular situation or unit is well illustrated in an abbreviated outline for use in pedagogical case study.[16]

I. EXAMINATION

   A. Psycho-physical
      1. Vision
      2. Hearing
      3. Coördination (neuro-muscular)
      4. Speech
   B. Health
      1. Height-weight ratio
      2. Nutrition
      3. Teeth
      4. General physical condition
   C. Educational
      1. Reading
      2. Arithmetic and number
      3. The handwriting adaptation and handwriting rate
      4. The primary composition adaptation
      5. Apperceptive mass
      6. Capacity of sustained application in study
      7. Lesson-learning attitude
   D. Mentality
      1. A general intelligence test of the comprehensive language type
      2. A non-language mental test

II. HEALTH HISTORY

---

16 *Ibid.*, p. 647-61.

III. SCHOOL HISTORY

    A. Promotions

    B. Character of learning exhibited or, in common parlance, "kind of work done"

    C. Has he moved about from school to school and especially from city to city or from country to city?

    D. Quality of the schools attended and especially teaching methods and administrative methods used

    E. Relations with individual teachers

IV. FAMILY HISTORY AND HOME CONDITIONS

    A. Ancestry, parents, and siblings

    B. Economic status and history

    C. Cultural resources of the home

    D. Relations within the home

    E. Attitude of parents toward society

    F. Adjustment of parents to American standards

    G. Control

        1. The most difficult of all is, of course, the well-to-do family that is entirely able to control its children but will not.

        2. Next in order of difficulty, perhaps, is the vicious home or that of sheer futile congenital incompetency.

        3. Finally, the dependent or semidependent home, in which children get beyond control, not by reason of parental neglect or incompetence, but because the parent, usually the mother, must be the breadwinner as well as the homemaker.

V. SOCIAL HISTORY AND CONTACTS

    A. What has been his church and Sunday-school history?

    B. Does the pupil play normally with boys and girls of his own age, and has he always done so?

    C. Has there been a summer-camp experience?

    D. What, if any, are his gang affiliations, wholesome or otherwise?

    E. Is there an abnormal sex history?

    F. Is there a court record, either actual or implied?

    G. Has the pupil engaged in "bumming" expeditions and if so what were the circumstances?

A few additional outlines for examination and history-taking may be mentioned.[17] An outline somewhat similar to that summarized above has been used over a period of years by a secondary-school adviser of girls and has provided the basic data for a series of case studies of adolescent girls. An institute for juvenile research stresses: the social history, medical study, psychological examination, recreation study, and psychiatric inter-

[17] Elsie M. Smithies, *Case Studies of Normal Adolescent Girls*. New York: D. Appleton-Century Co., 1933. p. 18-22.

    Paul L. Schroeder and Others, *Child Guidance Procedures*. New York: D. Appleton-Century Co., 1937. p. 40-147.

    C. M. Louttit, *Clinical Psychology*. New York: Harper and Bros., 1936. p. 34-44. Also see the 1947 revised edition.

    Cecil V. Millard, *Case Inventory for the Study of Child Development*. Minneapolis: Burgess Publishing Co., 1950. 29 p.

view. The examination blank used by a psychological clinic includes sections concerned with developmental history, parents and family, home, child's behavior, test performance, physical examination, delinquency, and speech defects. Other variations of forms suitable for examination and history-taking in educational, psychological, and social work are cited later in this chapter in the discussion of problems of recording.

**Personal documents.** As sources of data, such documents as the life history, biography, autobiography, diaries and journals, letters, records of dreams, and expressive interviews are valuable. Kluckhohn emphasizes the contributions of personal documents to anthropology, and suggests that the gains to the study of culture and personality could be great through collecting from a single culture retrospective autobiographies, contemporaneous life histories, and episodic and topical documents, utilizing a number of observers of both sexes from a representative sample of the society.[18]

Angell has analyzed a variety of studies [19] based on personal documents and identifies their contributions to the methodology of sociology in six categories:

1. Personal documents are collected with a view to the particular purposes of the study in hand, and the data therefore bear specifically upon the questions to be answered by the study.

2. Other types of data, particularly ecological and statistical, are combined with the data from personal documents both to give a more inclusive picture and to test the reliability of the documentary material.

3. There is increasing precision in conceptual analysis both before and after obtaining the personal documents.

4. Thorough-going attempts are made to use case studies for the prediction of human behavior, as in the effects of the impact of the depression upon family organization.

5. Hypotheses are so stated and methods sufficiently outlined in certain of these studies so that they can be checked by further investigation.

6. Logical and psychological procedures have been developed that should make more objective the use of the personal document and rid this method of much of the odium of inexactness associated with it.

Angell also has identified three circumstances that have handicapped the use of the personal document for at least two decades.

1. Much energy has been devoted to what may be called historical, rather than analytical, studies.

2. The sociologist's tools and techniques of analysis have not been

[18] Louis Gottschalk, Clyde Kluckhohn, and Robert Angell, *The Use of Personal Documents in History, Anthropology, and Sociology.* Social Science Research Council Bulletin No. 53. New York: The Council, 1945. p. 161-62.
[19] *Ibid.,* p. 221-22, 228-32.

sharp enough to deal penetratingly with the wealth of materials accumulated.

3. Comparatively few investigators have been using the personal-document method, with only limited opportunities for interstimulation among such research workers.

**The life history.** The life history differs from the usual autobiography in its emphasis on the natural history of the individual, his reactions to early social stimuli that have led to development of attitudes and values, evolution of a philosophy of life, personal experiences, anecdotes, mental and social conflicts, crises, adjustments, accommodations, and release of tensions; in other words, "a deliberate attempt to define the growth of a person in a cultural milieu and to make theoretical sense of it." [20] In terms of such a definition, the life-history view of social facts represents longitudinal rather than cross-sectional observation of culture. The life history does not stress judgments of merit, and ordinarily is not secured from famous persons, but from those who have encountered mental and social crises or conflict situations. It has the characteristics of an intimate personal document or confession that records through introspection inward stresses and attitudes rather than external events. In the preparation of the life history, the individual may tell his own story in autobiographic fashion, or an interviewer may elicit and record the narrative.

A definitive analysis of criteria considered indispensable for judging life-history technique has been outlined and illustrated at length by Dollard.[21]

1. The subject must be viewed as a specimen in a cultural series.
2. The organic motors of action ascribed must be socially relevant.
3. The peculiar role of the family group in transmitting the culture must be recognized.
4. The specific method of elaboration of organic materials into social behavior must be shown.
5. The continuous related character of experience from childhood through adulthood must be stressed.
6. The social situation must be carefully and continuously specified as a factor.
7. The life-history material itself must be organized and conceptualized.

Among the life histories to which Dollard applies his criteria are a number of well known studies.[22]

[20] John Dollard, *Criteria for the Life History*. New Haven: Yale University Press, 1935. p. 3. Reprinted in 1949 by Peter Smith.
[21] Quoted from John Dollard, *Criteria for the Life History*. New Haven: Yale University Press, 1935. p. 8.
[22] Paul Radin, Editor, *Crashing Thunder:* The Autobiography of an American Indian. New York: D. Appleton-Century Co., 1926. 202 p.

To cite an especially appropriate example, a series of life histories empha-sizes as a central theme the subject's life in Germany before and after January 30, 1933. In making a detailed psychological analysis of these life histories, the following schedule of information was employed for purposes of guidance and uniformity: development of attitudes toward National Socialism; frustrations in various spheres of activity; sources of frustration; reactions to suffering and cruelty; changes in mental activity with respect to fantasy, planning, and valuation; conformity behavior; feelings of insecurity and their alleviation; fluctuations in the level of aspiration; identifications with groups; aggressive behavior; regressive re-actions; defeat and despair responses; suicide attempts and fantasies; expression of wit and humor; plans and achievement of emigration; and post-emigration adjustment.[23]

As a quite different example, the life history of a forest tribe in Maine covers the habitat of the social group, the life activities (shelter, food, clothing, transportation, and implements and utensils), arts and decorative designs, and social life and family relationships.[24]

Gesell has attempted to reconstruct the developmental life history of Kamala, the human child and wolf girl, who presumably was reared by a mother wolf over a period of some seven years.[25]

**Autobiography, biography, and diaries.** Autobiography as historical narration is usually a relatively formal document, written with one eye on the judgment of the public, as is frequently true of the diaries of distin-guished persons who have anticipated publication. Autobiography and biog-raphy are written in retrospect, while entries in a diary are recorded concurrently as experiences and events take place. As an instrument of case study, autobiography gives a connected, genetic view of the develop-ment of the individual; may reveal the typical life history of members of a tribe, race, or community; is valuable in studying reticent or resistant persons; can be secured in groups at a minimum expenditure of effort on the part of the investigator; reveals interests and attitudes; and possesses therapeutic values for the subject in release of tensions and in increased

Clifford R. Shaw, Editor, *The Jack Roller:* A Delinquent Boy's Own Story. Chicago: University of Chicago Press, 1930. xv + 205 p.

W. I. Thomas and Florian Znaniecki, "Life-Record of an Immigrant." *The Polish Peasant in Europe and America,* Volume 2. New York: Alfred A. Knopf, 1927. p. 1831-2244.

H. G. Wells, *Experiment in Autobiography.* New York: Macmillan Co., 1934. xi + 718 p.

23 G. W. Allport, J. S. Bruner, and E. M. Jandorf, "Personality Under Social Catastrophe: Ninety Life-Histories of the Nazi Revolution." *Character and Personality* 10:1-22; September 1941.

24 F. G. Speck, *Penobscot Man:* The Life History of a Forest Tribe in Maine. Phila-delphia: University of Pennsylvania Press, 1940. xx + 325 p.

25 Arnold Gesell, *Wolf Child and Human Child.* New York: Harper and Bros., 1941. xvi + 107 p. See the next chapter for comment on this narrative.

understanding of his own life.[26] Sincere diaries may disclose interests, desires, tensions, and conflicts not revealed in the more formal autobiography, although the persons who keep diaries are not a representative group, and those who permit use of their diaries are even more highly selective. In general, the principles of historical research discussed in another chapter of this book apply in the analysis and interpretation of life-history documents such as autobiography, biography, diaries, and letters.[27] (These topics include sources, criticism of data, and historiography.)

**Illustrative life-history and biographical studies and procedures.** The literature of education, psychology, and sociology contains many other examples of life-history and biographical studies, as well as illustrations of the forms and procedures used in securing the data.[28] Bogardus in particular outlines a series of guides for securing the life histories of Orientals and other immigrants, native Americans, teacher-pupil relations, racial intermarriage, boys with problems, the boys' gangs, the boys' work leader, the boys' welfare agency, and the boy in relation to the church.[29]

The purposes and procedures of the autobiography or life history of a Hopi Indian are particularly helpful in securing an understanding of this approach.[30]

1. To prepare a relatively full and reliable account of an individual's experience and development from birth on, or a comprehensive life history emphasizing personality problems

2. To accumulate and arrange in natural order a socially and culturally oriented record of an individual in a "primitive society" for the purpose of developing and checking certain hypotheses in the field of culture

3. To attempt at least a partial interpretation of the individual's development and behavior

4. To utilize the investigation for the formulation of generalizations and the testing of theories in the field of individual behavior with respect to society and culture (reserved for further study).

[26] Ruth Strang, *Counseling Techniques in College and Secondary School.* New York: Harper and Bros., 1937. p. 113-14.

[27] Michael Kraus, *A History of American History.* New York: Farrar and Rinehart, 1937. Chapter 16.
Allan Nevins, *The Gateway to History.* Boston: D. C. Heath and Co., 1938. Chapter 12.

[28] Ruth Strang, *op. cit.,* Chapter 7.
Pauline V. Young, *Scientific Social Surveys and Research.* New York: Prentice-Hall, 1939. Chapter 10. Also see the 1949 edition.
Willard C. Olson, "Techniques and Instruments of Mental Hygiene," in "Mental Hygiene and Adjustment." *Review of Educational Research* 6:457-63; December 1936.
Percival M. Symonds, "The Autobiography and Life History," Chapter 4-E in "Pupil Personnel, Guidance, and Counseling." *Review of Educational Research* 9:143-252; April 1939.

[29] Emory S. Bogardus, *Introduction to Social Research.* Los Angeles: Suttonhouse, 1936. Chapter 10.

[30] Quoted from Leo W. Simmons, Editor, *Sun Chief:* The Autobiography of a Hopi Indian. New Haven: Yale University Press (for the Institute of Human Relations), 1942. xii + 460 p.

To use as an example the autobiography of an educator, Spaulding has written what is substantially his life history up to the completion of his graduate study in Europe and at Clark University, including his early life on a farm in New Hampshire, schooling in the district and college-preparatory schools in New England, four years at Amherst College, a doctoral program at the University of Leipzig, and a post-doctoral year at Clark University. Spaulding has prepared at least two additional volumes describing the application of his philosophy to the five public-school systems in which he served during a period of twenty-five years. The individual probably is not fully aware of the pattern and sources of his own philosophy, until he attempts what Spaulding has done in his autobiography and life history.[31]

Other interesting and helpful illustrations [32] may be listed from the fields of sociology and anthropology, and from psychology and psychoanalysis.

## STEP 3: DIAGNOSIS AND IDENTIFICATION OF CAUSAL FACTORS

**Functional relationships of diagnosis.** The structural pattern of diagnosis is the formulation of a theory or hypothesis of causation.[33] From causation, diagnosis looks toward the possibilities for growth and adjustment of the individual as a personality and as a social being who shares experiences with others.[34] For example, a large number of children and youth require special diagnostic study in the solution of their educational and social problems. This group includes: (1) the mentally and physically handicapped; (2) those who are maladjusted socially, morally, or emotionally; (3) those who perform below their level of learning capacity; and (4) others whose latent talents and special aptitudes because of inade-

---

[31] Frank E. Spaulding, *op. cit.*

[32] W. T. Brannon, *op. cit.*

Arthur Keith, *op. cit.* An eminent pioneer among anthropologists tells of his life and work.

Clellan S. Ford, *Smoke from Their Fires:* The Life of a Kwakiutl Chief. New Haven: Yale University Press, 1941. xiii + 248 p.

Chiang Monlin, *Tides from the West: A Chinese Autobiography.* New Haven, Conn.: Yale University Press, 1947. 282 p.

Emil A. Gutheil, Editor, *The Autobiography of Wilhelm Stekel:* The Life Story of a Pioneer Psychoanalyst. New York: Liveright Publishing Corporation, 1950. ix + 293 p.

Harry L. Hollingworth, *Leta Stetter Hollingworth:* A Biography. Lincoln: University of Nebraska Press, 1943. 228 p.

Carl Murchison, Editor, *A History of Psychology in Autobiography.* Worcester: Clark University Press, 1930, 1932, 1936. 3 vols. xviii + 516, xx + 407, xx + 327 p.

Herbert S. Langfeld and Others, Editors, *A History of Psychology in Autobiography,* Vol. 4. Worcester: Clark University Press, 1952. xii + 356 p.

[33] The development and testing of hypotheses are discussed and illustrated in the chapters on formulation of the problem and on the historical method.

[34] Ada E. Sheffield, *op. cit.,* Chapter 4.

quate stimulation are never given expression.[35] Groups with such varied problems require equally broad types of diagnosis, to be followed by corrective measures in the form of remedial instruction or by developmental opportunities in the form of well balanced educative experiences.

From this point of view, diagnosis and treatment at times are interwoven; diagnosis frequently parallels treatment and does not simply precede adjustment procedures, however desirable an orderly sequence of steps may seem to the logical mind.[36] Diagnosis is prognostic in pointing toward remedial treatment or developmental opportunities, and, when adjustment procedures are applied without reasonable success, further search for causal factors is necessary. Even in the last step of follow-up, if cases of unsuccessful adjustment are discovered, further diagnosis and treatment are desirable. It is obvious that diagnosis is closely related to and dependent upon the examination procedures used and the data collected in the second step of case study.

Attention should be directed to the comparatively recent development of client-centered therapy, a discipline which questions the need for psychological diagnosis in advance of psychotherapy (although recognizing the basic necessity for physical diagnosis in dealing with organic disease). According to the non-directive or client-centered view of psychological diagnosis, there are even certain objections to diagnosis before treatment or therapy: (1) the very process of psychological diagnosis in placing the evaluation so definitely in the hands of the expert may increase the dependent tendencies in the client, thereby causing him to feel that the responsibility for adjustment rests in the hands of another person; (2) certain social and philosophical implications are seen in the therapeutic control of the many clients by the few experts. For such reasons client-centered therapists have minimized the diagnostic process as a basis for therapy.[37]

**Criteria for successful diagnosis.** The essential characteristics of satisfactory diagnosis of difficulties, with particular reference to educational diagnosis, have been outlined at some length by Tyler and may be abbreviated as follows: [38]

[35] Carter V. Good, "Problems and Techniques of Educational Diagnosis and Adjustment," *op. cit.*

[36] An interesting case illustrating the interrelationships between diagnosis and treatment is reported in Fern Lowry, Editor, *Readings in Social Case Work, 1920-1938.* New York: Columbia University Press, 1939. p. 254-56. Also see:
Cora Kasius, Editor, *A Comparison of Diagnostic and Functional Casework Concepts.* New York: Family Service Association of New York, 1950. 169 p.
Robert I. Watson, *The Clinical Method in Psychology.* New York: Harper and Bros., 1951. p. 21-153, 527-761.

[37] Carl R. Rogers, *op. cit.,* p. 219-28.

[38] Ralph W. Tyler, "Characteristics of a Satisfactory Diagnosis." *Educational Diagnosis.* Thirty-fourth Yearbook of the National Society for the Study of Education. Bloomington, Ill.: Public School Publishing Co., 1935. Chapter 6.

1. Must concern itself with worth-while objectives; for example, discovery of the major generalizations in natural science incompletely understood by the learner rather than to emphasize search for the particular animal or plant structures that the student cannot name, in diagnosing the inability of the learner to interpret new scientific phenomena coming to his attention.

2. Must provide valid evidence of strengths and weaknesses related to the objectives; inspection of children's test papers in arithmetic indicates the types of examples solved correctly or not solved, but does not reveal the mental processes employed; in diagnosing the pupil's difficulties in methods of work it has been found necessary to interview each learner and to have him do his work aloud in solving the examples.

3. Must be reasonably objective, to permit other competent investigators to reach similar conclusions in employing the same diagnostic techniques; eye-movement photography has rendered objective the diagnosis of reading difficulties associated with number of fixations, duration of fixations, number of regressive movements, and accuracy of return sweeps.

4. Must be reliable, so that repeated diagnoses of other samples from the same learners will give similar results; analysis of several dozen themes rather than of two or three short compositions is necessary in determining the grammatical errors that a particular pupil is likely to make.

5. Must be carried to a satisfactory level of specificity; diagnosis in handwriting may be particularized to the extent of indicating deficiencies in movement, body and arm-hand position, manner of holding pen, and formation of particular letters of the alphabet.

6. Must provide comparable data; measurement of progress at intervals requires equivalent test forms or procedures adequately standardized and controlled.

7. Must provide sufficiently exact data; for diagnostic purposes, measuring instruments should be discriminating enough to indicate progress in units of weeks or months rather than limited to units of a semester or year.

8. Must be comprehensive or complete; in a particular subject, deficiencies in memorization of facts frequently are analyzed, without determining the ability to use these facts in reflective thinking or problem solving.

9. Must be appropriate to the desired program of instruction; any type of measurement or investigation that involves highly individual rivalry, anti-social motivation, or excessive introspection may have undesirable psychological, emotional, or social effects, and as such is open to question in the light of modern educational philosophy.

10. Must be practicable in terms of the conditions, time, personnel, equipment, and funds available in the particular school or situation; apparatus for eye-movement photography is available at present in only a very limited number of schools.

11. Must be conducted by adequately trained students of educational diagnosis; in increasing numbers such technically trained persons are to be found among teachers, supervisors, and administrators in the field, where their efforts supplement with increasing effectiveness the work of clinics, laboratories, research agencies, and psychological and educational specialists. (In the bibliography of this chapter are a number of related references.)

**Techniques of diagnosis.** Most of the data-gathering instruments and procedures named in discussing the preceding steps of case study contribute to diagnosis, in that the resulting data contain the clues for identifying causal factors. Techniques that have contributed especially to diagnosis include: [39]

1. Tests of general intelligence, aptitude, personality, and achievement
2. Observation of the pupil's study habits, attitudes, and reactions
3. Analysis of the pupil's written work
4. Analysis of the oral responses and reactions of the learner
5. Objective devices to determine the nature and significance of faults, as illustrated by diagnostic handwriting charts
6. The interview
7. Laboratory procedure.

Psychological and educational laboratory procedures have included a variety of approaches to diagnosis: [40]

1. Laboratory studies of school activities involving skill, as illustrated by the handwriting investigations made to determine the part contributed by each finger and by the movements of the hand, wrist, and arm
2. Time records, as in studying the rhythmic grouping of words in reading by securing time records on a kymograph drum
3. Photographing of eye movements during such activities as reading, reading of music, studying spelling, and looking at pictures
4. Motion and sound films, as used to determine the effect of various kinds of distraction upon pupils taking an examination or to record the behavior of a class during recitation, discussion, or study
5. Voice records, as used to compare the singing of one person with another and in diagnosing a particular difficulty in pitch, amplitude of sound, time, rhythm, and timbre
6. Measures of emotional tension, as revealed through use of types of apparatus to determine blood pressure, heart beat, breathing rate, amount of perspiration, and other physiological responses that may identify the mainsprings of emotional behavior.

**Causation.** In addition to the discussions of causal relationships in other chapters concerned with descriptive study, experimentation, and historical research, a brief statement should be made with respect to identification of causal factors in diagnosis. The major factors associated with learning difficulty are physical, intellectual, pedagogical, emotional, social, and environmental.[41] To use difficulty in reading as an example, before locating the cause of the poor performance it may be necessary to study

[39] Leo J. Brueckner, "Techniques of Diagnosis." *Educational Diagnosis, op. cit.,* Chapter 8. Also see:

Leo J. Brueckner, "Diagnosis in Teaching." *Encyclopedia of Educational Research.* Revised Edition. Edited by Walter S. Monroe. New York: Macmillan Co., 1950. p. 314-21.

Harold H. Anderson and Gladys L. Anderson, Editors, *An Introduction to Projective Techniques.* . . . New York: Prentice-Hall, 1951. xxiv + 720 p.

Robert I. Watson, Editor, "Diagnostic Methods." *Readings in the Clinical Method in Psychology.* New York: Harper and Bros., 1949. p. 183-443.

John E. Bell, *Projective Techniques:* A Dynamic Approach to the Study of the Personality. New York: Longmans, Green and Co., 1948. xvi + 533 p.

[40] G. T. Buswell, "The Place of the Psychological Laboratory in Educational Diagnosis." *Educational Diagnosis, op. cit.,* Chapter 9.

[41] "Factors Associated with Learning Difficulty." *Educational Diagnosis, op. cit.,* p. 17-92.

a wide range of factors: perceptual (visual and auditory), motor, intellectual, linguistic, emotional, and methodological.[42]

Rogers' "component-factor" method of diagnosis recognizes eight interacting forces and elements both within and without the individual child that must be considered in analyzing the behavior of the problem child: heredity, physical factor, mentality, family environment, economic and cultural forces, social factor, education and training outside the home, and the child's own insight into his present situation.[43]

Causation may be primary, secondary, tertiary, or contributory.[44] Diagnosis of the difficulties of a seventh-grade boy who is retarded, low in achievement, a behavior problem, and a truant may reveal a marked deficiency in reading ability as the primary cause of his maladjustment. Inability to use reading as a tool for study leads to failure in the school subjects of the seventh grade, which means that such failure is only a secondary cause of the boy's difficulties. His truancy results from learning difficulties and in turn adds to his deficiencies in the school subjects, although truancy itself in this case is only a tertiary cause of maladjustment. Cheerless and negligent home conditions may constitute a handicap that contributes to the maladjustment, but probably not as a direct or specific cause of failure, truancy, and misbehavior. The illustration cited suggests that in many instances successful diagnosis must identify more than one causal factor to explain a particular situation. This is especially true in determining what pattern of elements or combination of circumstances is most favorable to development of talent in such areas as music, art, and literature or in identifying the factors associated with and constituting the wholesome personality of a socially well adjusted, emotionally mature person.

**Illustrative cases, diagnosis, and interpretations.** The principles of diagnosis outlined in this section may be rendered more concrete by reading the parts of case studies concerned with diagnosis. A series of case studies of adolescent girls dealing with self-distrust, superiority, physical disability, exhibitionism, volitional retardation, depression, insecurity, environmental pressure, parental dominance, shame, and inferiority fear includes diagnosis of primary, secondary, tertiary, and contributory causes in reporting the cases.[45]

Hamilton shows by means of extracts from case records how diagnosis or interpretation has progressed from decade to decade of the present

[42] Marion Monroe, "Diagnosis and Treatment of Reading Disabilities." *Educational Diagnosis, op. cit.,* p. 206-16.
[43] Carl R. Rogers, *The Clinical Treatment of the Problem Child.* Boston: Houghton Mifflin Co., 1939. Chapter 3.
[44] Henry C. Morrison, *op. cit.,* p. 661-63.
[45] Elsie L. Smithies, *op. cit.,* p. 25-253.

century toward such standards of diagnosis as those summarized in this section.[46] The same author has made available in another source other examples [47] of diagnosis in social work.

For illustrative purposes, two especially extensive treatises on the principles and procedures of diagnosis, as applied to particular areas, may be cited. A treatment of educational diagnosis devotes separate chapters to reading, English, arithmetic, social studies, science, health, behavior, speech, vocations, music, art, leisure-time activities, and creativeness.[48] A volume on developmental diagnosis is addressed to physicians, but should also prove useful to psychological and educational specialists; it covers diagnosis of the following defects and deviations of development: amentia, endocrine disorders, convulsive disorders, neurological defects, cerebral injury, special sensory handicaps, prematurity, precocity, and environmental retardation, together with many illustrative cases.[49]

From the extensive literature of diagnosis only a few additional references, concerned especially with principles of interpretation in selected fields, can be cited: social research in general,[50] social work,[51] counseling,[52] personality,[53] and the life history.[54]

## STEP 4: ADJUSTMENT, TREATMENT, AND THERAPY

**Functional relationship between diagnosis and adjustment.** If the time and effort spent in reaching a diagnosis of causal factors are to be fully justified, an appropriate adjustment of conditions should be effected. As pointed out earlier in this chapter, the stages of treatment and follow-up usually are described as case work, ordinarily following case-study investigation. In numerous instances these complementary phases of case sequence are illustrated by the types of diagnosis and treatment carried out by the general practitioner in medicine. In many other medical situations, a specialist

---

[46] Gordon Hamilton, *Social Case Recording*. New York: Columbia University Press, 1936. Chapter 4.

[47] Gordon Hamilton, *Theory and Practice of Social Case Work, op. cit.,* Chapter 7. Also see the 1951 edition.

[48] *Educational Diagnosis, op. cit.,* p. 201-498.

[49] Arnold Gesell and Catherine S. Amatruda, *Developmental Diagnosis.* New York: Paul B. Hoeber, 1941. p. 118-291. Also see the 1947 revised edition.

[50] Emory S. Bogardus, *op. cit.,* Chapter 12.

[51] Florence Hollis, *Social Case Work in Practice.* New York: Family Welfare Association of America, 1939. p. 264-94.

[52] Ruth Strang, *op. cit.,* p. 47-49. Also see the 1949 edition.
John G. Darley, "Student Personnel Work-Techniques of Diagnosis." *Encyclopedia of Educational Research, op. cit.,* p. 265-68. Also see the 1950 edition.

[53] Percival M. Symonds, *Diagnosing Personality and Conduct, op. cit.,* p. 560-69.

[54] Manuel C. Elmer, *Social Research.* New York: Prentice-Hall, 1939. p. 105-7.
George A. Lundberg, *Social Research.* New York: Longmans, Green and Co., 1929. p. 204-8. Also see the 1942 revised edition.

administers the treatment, as exemplified by the work of the surgeon who performs the operation dictated by the diagnosis. It follows that, if a specialist is employed, he will check up the earlier diagnosis before treatment begins.

As emphasized throughout this chapter, a sharp line of demarcation cannot be drawn between the earlier steps of case procedure and the adjustment phase; for example, it was pointed out that in securing the life history certain therapeutic values might result for the subject in terms of release of tensions and increased understanding of his own life. The case conference is valuable in planning the treatment of the problem child, with the participants chosen from such workers and agencies as the clinic staff, school, visiting teacher, court, probation officer, child-placing agency, family agency, and children's institution; however, it is important to remember that treatment begins, consciously or unconsciously, when the child or his parents first enter the office of the professional worker in question and that refinements in diagnosis may well continue until the case is closed.[55]

Rogers' analysis of the process of therapy, in terms of non-directive or client-centered concepts, includes certain hypotheses that are based on an increasingly large body of experience:

1. Change or movement in therapy, as revealed in the type of verbal comment presented by the client; for example, from talk about his problems and symptoms, to insightful statements showing some self-understanding of relationship between his past and current behavior, to discussion of new actions in accord with his new understanding of the situation.

2. Change in the client's perception of and attitude toward self: (a) sees himself as a more adequate person, with increased worth and greater possibility of meeting life; (b) draws on more experiential data, thus achieving a more realistic appraisal of himself, his relationships, and environment; (c) tends to place the basis of standards or values within himself rather than in the experience or perceptual object.

**Preventive measures.**[56] The subsequent analysis of adjustment procedures is made with full recognition of the fact that "an ounce of prevention is worth a pound of cure," as illustrated by the emphasis of recent

[55] Carl R. Rogers, *The Clinical Treatment of the Problem Child, op. cit.,* p. 367-69.

Carl R. Rogers, *Client-Centered Therapy, op. cit.,* p. 131-96. This treatment of nondirective therapy assigns to diagnosis a much smaller role than is found in the same author's 1939 book, *The Clinical Treatment of the Problem Child.* Also see:

Robert I. Watson, *The Clinical Method in Psychology, op. cit.,* p. 21-153, 527-761.

[56] Carter V. Good, "Problems and Techniques of Educational Diagnosis and Adjustment," *op. cit.* Also see:

Sheldon Glueck and Eleanor Glueck, *Delinquents in the Making:* Paths to Prevention. New York: Harper and Bros., 1952. viii + 214 p.

Pauline V. Young, *Social Treatment in Probation and Delinquency:* Treatise and Casebook for Court Workers, Probation Officers, and Other Child Welfare Workers. Revised Edition. New York: McGraw-Hill Book Co., 1952. xxvi + 536 p.

decades on preventive medicine. Periodical physical and health examinations often reveal defects, the early correction of which may prevent later maladjustments. Correctly fitted glasses may prevent the appearance of deficiency in reading, and in turn of failure in the school subjects whose mastery depends on reading skill. The audiometer may identify hard-of-hearing children for whom deficiencies in reading and in other learning activities may be prevented by appropriate attention. Stimulating teaching and learning attitudes, methods, and materials are effective in keeping pupils of whatever ability working up to capacity and in preventing the development of behavior cases.

Varied sociological studies of preventive programs have been made.[57] A published symposium on preventive work includes samples of school programs, coördinated community work, police programs, intra- and extra-mural guidance activities, boys' clubs, and recreation programs.[58]

In spite of current emphasis on preventive measures, many individuals are still physically, mentally, or emotionally handicapped; others learn below the level of their capacities; and yet others possess undiscovered or undeveloped aptitudes. These conditions make necessary the use of such remedial and developmental procedures as are described in this section.[59]

**Tentative character of adjustment programs.** Before proceeding to a discussion of principles of remedial and developmental treatment, the tentative character of most adjustment procedures, like diagnosis, should be recognized. Obviously, techniques of demonstrated value should be employed whenever possible, as tested by experience and investigation. However, there are many questions of instructional procedure for which definitive answers have not yet been provided; for example, problems relating to reading readiness, manuscript writing, fusion, workbooks, book format, learning units, supplementary materials, laboratory methods, visual aids, sound equipment, adult needs, child interests, grade placement, time allotment, maturation, acceleration, enrichment, grouping, and individual differences. Therefore, treatment frequently represents the testing of an adjustment hypothesis formulated on the basis of the diagnosis reached. Follow-up, last step in the case-study and case-work sequence, should reveal the validity of the hypothesis or the effectiveness of the treatment.

[57] Walter C. Reckless, "The Clinical Approach and Delinquency Research in Educational Sociology," Chapter 4 in "Educational Sociology." *Review of Educational Research* 7:1-112; February 1937.

Dorothy Cason, "Experiment in Preventive Casework." *Journal of Social Casework* 28: 137-44; April 1947.

[58] Sheldon Glueck and Eleanor Glueck, Editors, *Preventing Crime:* A Symposium. New York: McGraw-Hill Book Co., 1936. 509 p.

[59] An especially helpful analysis is Leo J. Brueckner, "The Principles of Developmental and Remedial Instruction." *Educational Diagnosis, op. cit.,* Chapter 11.

It may be necessary to try a number of treatment procedures and even to formulate new diagnoses in complex or obstinate cases before appropriate adjustment has been accomplished.

**Objectives.** This chapter has stressed, as the major objective of case study and case work, development of the potentialities of the individual for growth. Applied to school activities, this means the focusing of attention on the pupil and on the learning situations that require attention rather than on the subject of instruction as such. Comprehensive study of the individual pupil in relation to difficulty in reading should reveal the presence of one or more causal factors—perceptual, motor, intellectual, linguistic, emotional, or methodological. Analysis of the learner's common errors in English usage indicates the focal points for remedial attention, in preference to distributing the instructional time with equal impartiality among the various units of grammar.

In planning a program of developmental and remedial instruction, the relative worth of objectives must be considered. All knowledge is worth something, but life is too short and time is too fleeting to cover more than a small portion of existing knowledge, even within a lifetime. Of the 600,000 entries in an unabridged dictionary, only some 4000 of the most common words can be used as the spelling program of the first eight grades. In geography, knowledge of man's relation to his environment in terms of securing food, clothing, and shelter takes precedence over places and political units. An understanding of movements in history and of cause and effect is of relatively greater importance than memorization of dates. The need for remedial and developmental opportunities in certain of the newer fields should not be overlooked; in additon to the areas of reading, English, arithmetic, social studies, and science, there are significant objectives to be attained in health, speech, vocations, music, art, leisure-time activities, creativeness, and conduct.

To use an illustration from another field, the objectives of the treatment process in social case work are concerned with reducing environmental pressures and inner pressures on the part of the client.[60] The ways in which the case worker relieves external pressure or encourages the client himself to bring about changes are by giving financial assistance, seeking employment for a client, facilitating health plans, taking a frightened client to a clinic, arranging for entrance of a boy or girl into an appropriate group activity, giving information and advice, encouraging the client in his own efforts, thinking things through together, and by modifying the attitudes of a friend, teacher, or relative. Treatment processes directed

[60] Florence Hollis, *Social Case Work in Practice, op. cit.,* p. 294-307.

toward decreasing internal pressures include: (1) bringing about modification of an inadequate or an over-restrictive conscience; (2) lessening the need for repression; (3) reducing feelings of anxiety, inadequacy, and defeat; and (4) helping the individual to see more clearly the nature of outer reality and his own relationship to it.

Another way of expressing the objectives of social treatment is to say that the case worker is concerned with preventing social breakdown, conserving strength, restoring social function, making life more comfortable or compensating, creating opportunities for growth and development, and with increasing the capacity for self-direction and social contribution.[61] Yet another analysis of the objectives of adjustment in social case work is in terms of the level of service rendered to meet the needs of the individual: (1) mere relief-giving in the form of cash, groceries, or medical aid; (2) service-giving, as illustrated by health care, vocational training, or recreational opportunity; (3) assistance toward self-understanding and self-direction on the part of the client; and (4) identification of the need-situation together with its related factors as a situation-centered unit of attention rather than a client-centered way as such of viewing the case.[62]

**Self-help and self-activity.** In the preceding analysis of the objectives of social treatment, self-help is emphasized in such expressions as encouraging the client in his own efforts, thinking things through together, and increasing the capacity for self-understanding and self-direction. It is essential in social case work to keep in mind the client's right to determine the course of his own life, to make choices in adjusting to the social order, and to employ self-diagnosis and treatment to the maximum degree possible. Physicians frequently say that the will of the patient to recover may be as effective in producing the desired result as the medicine administered. Educational and psychological workers have long recognized the doctrine of self-activity on the part of the learner in choosing goals, content materials and activities, instructional methods, evaluative procedures, and plans of organization and control. This type of pupil participation should possess definite transfer value in dealing with situations outside the school and in solving the problems of adult life.

**Attitudes.** The imparting of a diagnosis, preliminary to the inauguration of adjustment procedures, may require quite as much skill as the making of the diagnosis itself, if a favorable mental attitude is to be preserved or

[61] Gordon Hamilton, *Theory and Practice of Social Case Work, op. cit.,* p. 167-69. Also see the 1951 edition.
[62] Ada E. Sheffield, *op. cit.,* p. 278-79.
Carl R. Rogers, *Client-Centered Therapy, op. cit.* A contrasting view in its emphasis on the nondirective or client-centered approach.

developed for the persons concerned. The mental hygiene of the father and mother is especially affected when the grave developmental defect of a child brings a sense of frustration to their family life.[63]

The patient whose mental attitude is one of determination to recover has won at least half the battle. Causal factors precede the development of attitudes and definite effects follow. The boy who had never learned to read effectively failed in the subjects of the seventh grade, developed a dislike for school and his teachers, and became a behavior problem and truant. Faulty attitudes in school may be corrected by removing the cause, and desirable attitudes may be promoted by use of stimulating materials, methods, and activities. For the most effective remedial or developmental treatment, it is essential that the teacher or case worker have a genuine concern for the well-being of the pupil or client, and a feeling of warmth and liking toward him as a person. Treatment begins only when mutual confidence is established, when mutual interest is felt and expressed between worker and client or teacher and pupil. All of these individuals have prejudices and emotional reactions to understand and control. Through the process of interaction in treatment interviews and contacts there are opportunities for interstimulation and deepening of insight on the part of case worker and client or teacher and pupil. The engendering of favorable initial attitudes is doubly important in short contacts, as in large school systems and social transient work, where there may be only one or two brief interviews in which to determine a course of action, meet a crisis, or redefine loyalties and values.[64]

**Individual differences.** The emphasis of this chapter is that the capacity of the individual for growth should first be determined, that causal factors conditioning development should be diagnosed, and then an appropriate adjustment or treatment applied. This point of view recognizes the wide range of individual differences in physical, intellectual, pedagogical, emotional, social, and environmental factors; such differences require an equally wide range of diagnostic procedures and flexibility of treatment programs. A cardinal principle of treatment procedure is to make a specific attack on the particular difficulty at the actual level of the learner.

Several examples may be cited. Considerable work has already been done toward organization of remedial programs for inferior pupils and provision of developmental opportunities for superior pupils.

Attention has already been directed to the differences between the cor-

[63] Arnold Gesell and Catherine S. Amatruda, *op. cit.*, p. 312-15. Also see the 1947 revised edition.

[64] Robert S. Wilson, *The Short Contact in Social Case Work*, Vols. I and II. New York: National Association for Travelers Aid and Transient Service, 1937. x + 201, vii + 219 p.

rective case, which is susceptible of treatment within the regular program of the pupil, and the remedial case, which requires some formality in handling along with detailed investigation and treatment (appropriate therapy or developmental opportunities).

Variations in the treatment of children with problems of adjustment include: (1) change of environment through the foster home or institutional placement; (2) modification of environment through adjustments in the family, school, clubs, groups, and camps; and (3) treatment of the individual through a variety of therapeutic approaches,[65] including psychoanalysis, non-directive interviewing and therapy, group psychotherapy, projective techniques, play therapy, psychodrama, sociodrama, and hypnodrama. A somewhat similar analysis of treatment procedures in the area of mental hygiene and adjustment emphasizes: (1) parent education, family relationships, and the home; (2) educational adjustment; (3) in-

[65] Lawrence E. Abt and Leopold Bellak, Editors, *Projective Psychology:* Clinical Approaches to the Total Personality. New York: Alfred A. Knopf, 1950. xvii + 485 + xvi p.

Harold H. Anderson and Gladys Lowe Anderson, *op. cit.*

Virginia M. Axline, *Play Therapy: The Inner Dynamics of Childhood.* Boston: Houghton Mifflin Co., 1947. xii + 379 p.

John E. Bell, *op. cit.*

Kenneth M. Colby, *A Primer for Psychotherapists.* New York: Ronald Press Co., 1951. viii + 167 p.

John Dollard and Neal E. Miller, *Personality and Psychotherapy:* An Analysis in Terms of Learning, Thinking, and Culture. New York: McGraw-Hill Book Co., 1950. xiii + 488 p.

V. E. Fisher, *The Meaning and Practice of Psychotherapy.* New York: Macmillan Co., 1950. xv + 411 p.

Frieda Fromm-Reichmann, *Principles of Intensive Psychotherapy.* Chicago: University of Chicago Press, 1950. xv + 246 p.

L. Gorlow, E. L. Hoch, and E. Telschow, *The Nature of Nondirective Group Psychotherapy.* New York: Bureau of Publications, Teachers College, Columbia University, 1952. viii + 143 p.

Robert B. Haas, Editor, *Psychodrama and Sociodrama in American Education.* New York: Beacon House, 1950. xii + 251 p.

M. D. Hinckley, Robert G. Hermann, and Lydia Hermann, *Group Treatment in Psychotherapy.* Minneapolis: University of Minnesota Press, 1951. x + 136 p.

J. W. Klapman, *Group Psychotherapy.* New York: Grune and Stratton, 1946. ii + 344 p.

J. L. Moreno, *Group Psychotherapy.* New York: Beacon House, 1945. xiv + 305 p.

J. L. Moreno and J. M. Enneis, *Hypnodrama and Psychodrama.* New York: Beacon House, 1950. 56 p.

Clark E. Moustakas, *Children in Play Therapy:* A Key to Understanding Normal and Disturbed Emotions. New York: McGraw-Hill Book Co., 1953. ix + 218 p.

Otto Pollak and Others, *Social Science and Psychotherapy for Children;* Contributions of the Behavior Sciences to Practice in a Psychoanalytically Oriented Child Guidance Clinic. New York: Russell Sage Foundation, 1952. 242 p.

E. H. Porter, Jr., *An Introduction to Therapeutic Counseling.* Boston: Houghton Mifflin Co., 1950. xi + 223 p.

Carl R. Rogers, *Client-Centered Therapy, op. cit.* Includes chapters on play therapy and on group-centered psychotherapy.

Carl R. Rogers, *The Clinical Treatment of the Problem Child, op. cit.*

Samuel R. Slavson, *Analytic Group Psychotherapy with Children, Adolescents, and Adults.* New York: Columbia University Press, 1950. ix + 275 p.

Samuel R. Slavson, *Child Psychotherapy.* New York: Columbia University Press, 1952. 332 p.

Robert I. Watson, Editor, "Methods of Treatment." *Readings in the Clinical Method in Psychology, op. cit.,* p. 447-731.

Werner Wolff, Editor, *Success in Psychotherapy.* New York: Grune and Stratton, 1952.

stitutional treatment; (4) child management, training, and instruction; (5) physical treatment; and (6) occupational therapy.[66]

In urging that remedial and developmental treatment be provided to meet the needs of the individual, it seems desirable to correct a false popular notion that the handicapped individual compensates for his defect by strength in some other quarter or that the talented person is lacking in such respects as physical development and emotional or social adjustment. Although the evidence is not yet complete, it appears that similar traits usually go together, so far as ability, performance, and adjustment are concerned. The evidence is against deducing compensating abilities for the blind in the form of keener senses of hearing, smell, and touch or to ascribe sharper vision to the deaf, except for the results of training and use.

**Coöperation and coördination in treatment.** As a rule, case work involves situations in which several factors operate. This means that the physician will face more than a problem of ill health, the relief worker will encounter other deficiencies along with economic need, and the psychiatrist will meet more than emotional maladjustment. Complex causation, or even a single major factor basic to maladjustment, may result in a diagnosis that requires the coöperation of a number of specialists and agencies for successful treatment.

This type of coöperation is illustrated in the field of medicine by the joint efforts of the general practitioner, specialist, surgeon, nurse, laboratory technician, other hospital employees, and sometimes the social worker. Many of the contributions to the adjustment of problem and delinquent children through child-guidance clinics and mental-hygiene programs have been the result of pooling the resources of psychiatrists, physicians, psychologists, and social workers, with a more recent part played by sociologists. The therapy of clinical psychology depends on the coöperation of a number of agencies—foster homes, institutions for defectives and delinquents, social service, and child-placement organizations. The effectiveness of the synthesis and program of treatment in child guidance requires joint utilization of the resources of clinic, community, home, school, case-working organization, recreational program, and child-placement agency.[67]

The problem of coöperative relationships has been treated at length in an anthology of readings dealing with social case work in such professional fields and special areas as [68] sociology, psychology, psychiatry, public welfare, old age assistance, family welfare, home economics, child care, foster home, mental hygiene, medicine, hospital, school, visiting teacher, legislation, juvenile court, parole, community welfare, and housing.

[66] Willard C. Olson, "Techniques and Instruments of Mental Hygiene," *op. cit.*
[67] Paul L. Schroeder and Others, *op. cit.*, Chapter 10.
[68] Fern Lowry, Editor, *op. cit.*, p. 357-804.

Remedial treatment and developmental instruction should be organized as an integral part of a well rounded program of education, with one person responsible, preferably the teacher, for coördinating such special assistance as may be available for the treatment of an individual pupil. It has already been suggested that the usual corrective case may be adjusted within the resources of the pupil's regular program of courses. For obstinate remedial cases, the joint efforts of teacher, supervisor, principal, psychologist, psychiatrist, physician, visiting teacher, social worker, and even other specialists may be necessary.

A description of the administration of the Baltimore program of diagnosis and remedial instruction deals with problems that are essentially those of coöperation and coördination: leadership, organization of personnel, diagnostic services of the research department, administrative measures for diagnostic teaching, special classes and schools, and records.[69]

**Illustrative cases of treatment and references.** Additional references dealing with the following factors or aspects of treatment are cited below: treatment and relationships in social case work,[70] an anthology of readings on treatment processes in social case work,[71] extended extracts from case records illustrating adjustment procedures in social work,[72] case studies of adolescent girls with a section of each case report devoted to the treatment applied,[73] a descriptive summary of sociological studies of treatment programs,[74] principles of remedial teaching,[75] case and clinical approaches in relation to remedial work in reading,[76] and juvenile delinquency.[77]

[69] John L. Stenquist, "The Administration of a Program of Diagnosis and Remedial Instruction." *Educational Diagnosis, op. cit.,* Chapter 25.

[70] Virginia P. Robinson, *A Changing Psychology in Social Case Work.* Chapel Hill: University of North Carolina Press, 1930. Chapters 10-12.

[71] Fern Lowry, *op. cit.,* p. 281-353.

[72] Gordon Hamilton, *Theory and Practice of Social Case Work, op. cit.,* Chapters 8-10. Also see the 1951 edition.

Gordon Hamilton, *Social Case Recording.* New York: Columbia University Press, 1936. Chapter 4.

[73] Elsie M. Smithies, *op. cit.*

[74] Walter C. Reckless, *op. cit.*

[75] Leo J. Brueckner, "Diagnosis and Remedial Teaching." *Encyclopedia of Educational Research, op. cit.,* p. 392-98. Also see the 1950 edition.

Grace M. Fernald, *Remedial Techniques in Basic School Subjects.* New York: McGraw-Hill Book Co., 1943. 330 p.

[76] Emmett A. Betts, *The Prevention and Correction of Reading Difficulties.* Evanston, Ill.: Row, Peterson and Co., 1936. Chapter 14.

Luella Cole, *The Improvement of Reading:* With Special Reference to Remedial Instruction. New York: Farrar and Rinehart, 1938. 338 p.

E. W. Dolch, *A Manual of Remedial Reading.* Second Edition. Champaign, Ill.: Garrard Press, 1945. 460 p.

D. D. Durrell, *Improvement of Basic Reading Abilities.* New York: World Book Co., 1940. 407 p.

Grace M. Fernald, *op. cit.*

A. I. Gates, *The Improvement of Reading:* A Program of Diagnostic and Remedial Methods. Third Edition. New York: Macmillan Co., 1947. 657 p.

A. J. Harris, *How to Increase Reading Ability:* A Guide to Individualized and Remedial

## STEP 5: FOLLOW-UP PROGRAM

To complete the cycle of case study and case work, it is necessary to check on the validity of the remedial treatment. After medication or surgery the physician follows the convalescence of the patient to determine whether recovery takes place. In instances of failure to make reasonable progress, a new diagnosis and a modified treatment may be required (a procedure employed generally in case work).

Only through careful analysis is it possible to identify the factor that produces the changes observed. A patient may recover because of a strong constitution rather than as the result of medicines administered. Glasses correctly fitted during the summer months may fail to produce improvement in reading when school opens because of the faulty instructional methods employed by the pupil's new teacher. The evaluation of treatment leans heavily on the techniques of experimentation, as described in another chapter.

Useful work has been done in following normal children through the school years, and especially after leaving school, to evaluate the effectiveness of the educational program in relation to civic and social efficiency and to vocational adjustment, although such investigations have employed survey techniques more commonly than case study. A series of large-scale investigations of bright children has used case study as one instrument in following the subjects over a period of years through school into ma-

Methods. Second Edition, revised and enlarged. New York: Longmans, Green and Co., 1947. 582 p.

James M. McCallister, *Remedial and Corrective Instruction in Reading*. New York: D. Appleton-Century Co., 1936. Chapter 6.

C. M. McCullough, R. Strang, and A. E. Traxler, *Problems in the Improvement of Reading*. New York: McGraw-Hill Book Co., 1946. 406 p.

Marion Monroe, *Children Who Cannot Read*. Chicago: University of Chicago Press, 1942. 205 p.

Marion Monroe and Bertie Backus, *Remedial Reading*. Boston: Houghton Mifflin Co., 1937. Chapter 4.

H. M. Robinson, *Why Pupils Fail in Reading*. Chicago: University of Chicago Press, 1946. 257 p.

Staff of the Reading Clinics of the University of Chicago, *Clinical Studies in Reading, I*. Supplementary Educational Monographs, No. 68. Chicago: University of Chicago Press, 1949. 173 p.

Paul Witty and David Kopel, *Reading and the Educative Process*. Boston: Ginn and Co., 1939. x + 374 p.

[77] Kate Friedlander, *The Psycho-analytical Approach to Juvenile Delinquency:* Theory, Case-studies, Treatment. New York: International Universities Press, 1947. vii + 296 p.

Sheldon Glueck and Eleanor Glueck, *Unraveling Juvenile Delinquency*. New York: Commonwealth Fund, 1950. 416 p. Based on five hundred matched pairs of delinquent and non-delinquent boys rather than on case studies.

Sol Rubin, "Unraveling Juvenile Delinquency: I, Illusions in a Research Project Using Matched Pairs." *American Journal of Sociology* 57:107-14; September 1951.

Albert J. Reiss, Jr., "Unraveling Juvenile Delinquency: II, An Appraisal of the Research Methods." *American Journal of Sociology* 57:115-20; September 1951.

turity.[78] However, much remains to be done by way of tracing the after-school history of the physically handicapped, of those with personality and behavior maladjustments, of others who learn below capacity, and of yet others especially talented in a particular field, if appropriate adjustments are to be made in the instructional and treatment programs for such groups.

Many of the case reports to which reference is made in this chapter include statements of the follow-up phase of the work. For purposes of further illustration, specific mention may be made of: (1) follow-up statements in a series of case studies of adolescent girls; [79] and (2) a summary of appraisal investigations dealing with the effects of treatment in the area of mental hygiene.[80]

## CASE RECORDING[81]

**Purposes and attributes.** If the five phases of case study and case work outlined in this chapter are accepted as both a logical and a functional sequence of steps toward adjustment, extended comment is hardly necessary to emphasize the need for adequate records of evidence secured and of procedures employed. Even broader purposes than treatment are served by such records, as indicated by the following analysis of the functions of social case records.[82]

1. To facilitate treatment by providing an aid to the memory of the case worker, and by bridging the gap when the regular worker is transferred or a substitute is serving, when the client moves to another locality, or when a previously closed case is reopened
2. To serve as a medium for study of social problems, looking toward social reform
3. To provide materials for training students and for general instructional purposes
4. To educate the community concerning its social needs, with an indication of the possible contribution of social case work.

Essential attributes of well balanced records are accuracy and objectivity, conciseness and clarity, ease of reference and visibility, and uniformity and "up-to-dateness." Provision should be made for cumulative

[78] Lewis M. Terman and Others, *Genetic Studies of Genius,* Volumes I, II, and III. Stanford University, Calif.: Stanford University Press, 1925, 1926, 1930. xvi + 648, xxiv + 842, xiv + 508 p.

Lewis M. Terman and Melita H. Oden, *The Gifted Child Grows Up:* Genetic Studies of Genius. Stanford University, Calif.: Stanford University Press, 1947. xiv + 450 p.

[79] Elsie M. Smithies, *op. cit.*

[80] Willard C. Olson, "Techniques and Instruments of Mental Hygiene," *op. cit.*

[81] Gordon Hamilton, *Principles of Social Case Recording, op. cit.*

K. R. Hammond and J. M. Allen, *Writing Clinical Reports.* New York: Prentice-Hall, 1953. 288 p.

[82] Margaret C. Bristol, *op. cit.,* p. 4-14.

Gordon Hamilton, *Social Case Recording, op. cit.,* p. 3-6.

recording of interviews, the narrative, letters, anecdotal information, summaries, and interpretation and treatment. Certain of these characteristics will be discussed briefly.

**Accuracy and objectivity.**[83] A limited interpretation of the term *accuracy* refers to the correct reproduction in the record of information as received, without regard to the reliability of the source or the accuracy of the testimony in relation to the truth. A far more important concept of accuracy involves the correctness of the data in the absolute sense, although absolute accuracy is possible only in such concrete details as: names, addresses, relationships, dates, ages, marriage status, school grades, height, weight, and test scores. The discussion of criticism in the chapter on the historical method has applications to case recording, with respect to the reliability of witnesses and the accuracy of evidence.

Among the possible causes of inaccuracy in case recording are failure or neglect: (1) to keep the forms up to date; (2) to record accurately the information as received; (3) to express clearly in the record the meaning intended; and (4) to secure accurate information from the source. These four items may be rephrased to represent recommendations for increasing the accuracy of recording.

Since the emphasis of this book is on objective methods of investigation, other chapters dealing with techniques sometimes used in combination with case study may appropriately be examined to note the principles of objectivity discussed. Especially pertinent are the sections on historical, appraisal, questionnaire, observational, interview, genetic, and analytical procedures.

**Conciseness, ease of reference, and uniformity.**[84] Effective recording or reporting in any area of research must be an active process of attention and selection from a relatively large mass of available materials. Case-study recording is no exception. However, there is a balance to strike between the completeness necessary for objectivity and the brevity essential for clarity.

With respect to ease of reference to case records, many of the comments of the chapter on the reporting of research are applicable. Especially suggestive are the recommendations concerning main headings, subheadings, introductory statements, transitional paragraphs, and summaries. In other words, observation of the principles of effective reporting in general will go a long way toward guaranteeing ease of reference in the use of case records. In case recording, marginal notes for purposes of reference and

[83] Margaret C. Bristol, *op. cit.*, Chapters 2-3.
[84] Margaret C. Bristol, *op. cit.*, Chapters 4-9.
Gordon Hamilton, *Social Case Recording, op. cit.*, Chapters 2, 7, 8.

emphasis have frequently proved helpful. When used, however, such marginal notes should conform to the rules for construction of well organized outlines.

There are possible advantages for research, interchange of information, and functional use when reasonable uniformity of records prevails within the agency, institution, or school system, as well as between similar social services in different territories.

**Recording of interviews.**[85] Since the technique of interviewing is outlined at some length in another chapter, only a brief summary statement of recording of interviews is appropriate at this time, with illustrations drawn especially from the area of social work. Electronic (tape and wire) recorders are widely used for interviews, although they involve special problems of rapport.

In social case recording, the narrative usually begins with the first interview, although in certain instances the record may open with information concerning the prospective client, as supplied by a source of referral who may have sent a letter, telephoned, or made a personal visit to the agency. The first interview in a social-work agency is usually conducted by the intake department of the office or by an appropriate case worker in the office, except in instances of old age, illness, or other circumstances where it may be necessary to conduct the interview in the home. The importance of the first interview is such, in terms of initiating wholesome working relationships, that some of the best case workers may well be assigned to this task.

When conditions are favorable, with respect to the training of the case worker and the willingness of the client, the first interview should be reasonably complete, including for a public relief agency at least the minimum information regarding identity, address, legal residence, financial status, reason for application, and the nature and urgency of the problem. To record such items is relatively simple and brief, as is true of expressed needs in terms of given units of food, shelter, education, or convalescent care, but both interviewing and recording become more complicated in dealing with human relationships, and with the process and movement within the interview.

**The narrative and summaries.**[86] As in historical writing, the narrative

[85] For a discussion of principles and for illustrative interview records see:
Margaret C. Bristol, *op. cit.,* Chapter 10.
Gordon Hamilton, *Social Case Recording, op. cit.,* p. 87-113, 151-62.
Also see Virginia M. Axline, *op. cit.*
[86] For illustrative extracts from case records see:
Margaret C. Bristol, *op. cit.,* Chapters 11, 13.
Gordon Hamilton, *Social Case Recording, op. cit.,* Chapter 3.
Virginia M. Axline, *op. cit.,* p. 3-374.

or running record may be entered either chronologically or topically, or by some appropriate combination of the two plans of organization. According to the chronological method, the contacts and interviews between the agency and the individual are recorded in diary fashion as they occur, although marginal or topical headings within an interview may give at least a superficial appearance of topical recording. Large subdivisions of the chronological narrative correspond roughly to the five major steps in case study and case work, with the qualification that certain of these steps at times may be parallel or interwoven. The several phases of study, diagnosis, and treatment also represent large topical headings appropriate for thematic organization of data.

In topical recording, information from several contacts or interviews is combined under major themes, such as family and home setting, neighborhood and group life, cultural background, education, recreational activities and interests, health, mental attitude, occupation, and income and resources. Advantages in topical arrangement include conservation of space and emphasis on major issues, with minor details relegated to a position of comparative insignificance or shown as only small parts of the larger pattern of facts. To counteract certain undesirable tendencies in topical recording, the worker should be on guard against overemphasizing his own interpretation, to the neglect of including the evidence, and should indicate the source of the information recorded.

Topical recording may be differentiated from the various types of summaries, in that it presents original data (organized according to subject matter rather than chronological sequence), whereas the summary brings together and reviews material that has previously appeared in some form in the record.[87] The various types of summaries are: (1) "periodic," to cover material between given dates or at the end of certain episodes in the case history, or to begin a new volume or folder; (2) "transfer," to assign complete responsibility for a case to another agency or to refer a case to a coöperating agency; (3) "findings," to reveal data significant for diagnosis and treatment; (4) "records," to summarize the records in the files of other agencies; and (5) "closing," to show the status of the case at the time it is closed.[88] Topical rather than chronological form is recommended for summaries. Extended case histories are relatively unreadable unless supported at intervals by appropriate summaries.

The discussions of chronological and of topical organization of materials, as outlined in the chapter on the historical method, in earlier sections of the present chapter on the steps of case study, and in the chapter on

[87] Margaret C. Bristol, *op. cit.*, p. 119, 168.
[88] *Ibid.*, p. 168-71.

the reporting of research are generally applicable to the writing of the narrative in case recording.

**Letters and reports.**[89] Letters and written reports are an important part of case recording, since they frequently must serve as substitutes for personal visits and interviews. When viewed as necessary substitutes for direct contacts, the function and significance of effective writing in terms of communicating and requesting essential information become apparent. Letters and reports represent an especially important medium of communication between social-work, medical, clinical, legal, and educational agencies, including the individual workers represented. Letters should be written, however, only when communicating or requesting essential facts not otherwise readily available. The trivial character of letters in general has led to the statement that, if many letters remained unanswered for a month, no reply would be necessary, although this is not a true picture of written communications in case study and case work.

As to details of content, letters and reports now tend to stress the immediate situation and the treatment or adjustment measure applied (the information of most interest to the correspondent) rather than to present an extended summary of the entire case. Workers should be cautioned against making diagnoses, interpretations, or statements that go beyond their training; for example, a teacher may communicate certain objective facts covering a problem pupil's health, mental level, or behavior, but as a rule must leave diagnosis and treatment to the physician, psychologist, or psychiatrist. Letters and reports to agencies or individuals should be so worded or labeled as to indicate their confidential character. In certain routine types of communication, forms or blanks are usable, as between public schools and public-welfare agencies.

**Ethics of recording.**[90] As a background for consideration of the ethical

[89] For numerous illustrative letters and reports see:
Margaret C. Bristol, *op. cit.*, Chapter 12.
Gordon Hamilton, *Social Case Recording, op. cit.*, Chapter 5.
[90] For a statement of principles and for illustrative cases see:
Margaret C. Bristol, *op. cit.*, Chapter 15.
Gordon Hamilton, *Theory and Practice of Social Case Work, op. cit.*, p. 341-43. Also see the 1951 edition.
Many illustrations of problems, incidents, and principles of ethics in the clinical, consulting, professional, research, writing, and publication activities or relationships of the psychologist have been prepared by a committee of the American Psychological Association:
Nicholas Hobbs and Others, "Ethical Standards in Clinical and Consulting Relationships." *American Psychologist* 6:57-64, 6:145-66; February 1951, May 1951.
Nicholas Hobbs and Others, "Ethical Standards for Psychology (Professional Relationships, Research, and Writing and Publishing)." *American Psychologist* 6:427-52; August 1951.
Nicholas Hobbs and Others, *Ethical Standards of Psychologists.* Washington: American Psychological Association, 1953. xv + 171 p.
*Ethical Standards of Psychologists:* A Summary of Ethical Principles. Washington: American Psychological Association, 1953. 19 p.
Also see A. M. Lee, "Responsibilities in Sociological Research." *Sociology and Social Research* 37:367-74; July-August 1953. Ethics of sociology.

implications of case recording, the primary functions of records should be kept in mind: (1) to render study, diagnosis, and treatment of the case more effective in terms of the adjustment of the client; and (2) to serve community interests in the treatment of social problems and in planning programs of prevention.

Since a major purpose of records is to serve the interests of the client, critical judgment must be exercised with respect to including strictly personal or confidential information that may have little or no bearing on the case, facts that might be misused by politically minded individuals and persons of inadequate training with access to the records. In compiling case records of efficient and inefficient teachers, information concerning religion and political preference ordinarily would have little if any bearing on instructional efficiency and should be omitted; such facts might be distorted or misused by prejudiced school-board members or others. It even is probably unwise to enter the results of tuberculin tests of pupils and teachers in the individual records, if members of the local parent-teacher organization insist on examining and discussing such records as their right because of having sponsored the testing program. In addition to omitting strictly personal or nonessential confidential information from the records, other alternatives are to inform the client of the nature and use of case records before he gives confidential information, to label such material as "confidential," or to include such data with the assumption that all case records are confidential. (See the references in footnote 90 for ethical standards in psychology and sociology.)

An ethical problem arises in deciding what disposal to make of evidence that casts grave doubt on the efficiency of fellow workers or the policies of the agency or institution. A reasonable course is to record the objective facts, which usually speak for themselves. Case studies of deficiency in reading among second-grade pupils may reveal evidence pointing to the inefficiency of a first-grade teacher or to unsatisfactory materials and methods advocated by the administrative-supervisory staff, without making the case records a deliberate criticism of colleagues or school system. In compiling the facts of case study, diagnosis, and treatment (whether in medicine, social work, psychology, or education), the purpose of recording is not to fix blame on some person or agency for what did or did not happen; to fix blame is a function of the courts or of some appropriate administrative agency.

A question of ethics involves the integrity of the worker in recording his mistakes, such as inaccurate diagnoses or errors in treatment. The temptation is to omit errors of commission and omission from the record, just as scientists tend to omit the fallacious hypotheses tested and the blind alleys traversed in reporting their research. However, in the interests of both accuracy and self-discipline, the mistakes of the worker should be entered in the record; for example, loss of temper in disciplining a problem pupil or haste and irritation in interviewing the same pupil's parents.

Use of case records by professional workers has certain ethical implications. Social, psychological, educational, and medical workers will not ordinarily use either the pathos or the humor of life histories for purposes of mere entertainment at social gatherings. Difficulties and deficiencies of individual teachers or pupils in relation to discipline, achievement, mentality, or personality are professional problems of a confidential character rather than information for public consumption. Caution must be observed with respect to interpreting or transmitting data collected by another agency, especially a clinic or a hospital. Usually it is the responsibility of the medical agency to inform the patient of his physical condition, in so far as it is deemed wise for the patient to have the facts. Only in extraordinary instances do professional workers take case records outside the office where filed, since the risk of losing or misplacing records or of having them fall into the hands of persons outside the agency places a heavy responsibility on the person who removes records from the office. (As is generally known, protection of the records and documents of our federal government has been a crucial problem during recent decades.)

## CUMULATIVE AND ANECDOTAL RECORDS[91]

**Uses of cumulative records.** A cumulative record is one maintained for an individual pupil or client over a period of years, with successive additions to the record at relatively frequent intervals, as when entering marks in the school subjects at the end of a semester.

Case study and counseling in the schools to a large extent are dependent on the type of information found in the modern cumulative record; for example, record-data important in case study relate to school attendance, marks and scholarship, educational and general aptitude test scores, social and character ratings, health, home conditions and family history, extracurricular activities, vocational-interest and aptitude-test scores, and atti-

[91] Wendell C. Allen, *Cumulative Pupil Records:* A Plan for Staff Study and Improvement of Cumulative Pupil Records in Secondary Schools. New York: Teachers College, Columbia University, 1943. 69 p.

Eugene R. Smith and Others, *Appraising and Recording Student Progress.* Progressive Education Association, Commission on the Relation of School and College. New York: Harper and Bros., 1942. 550 p.

Carter V. Good, "Case and Cumulative Records." *Journal of Exceptional Children* 10: 78-84; December 1943.

tudes. Such records are especially important in making longitudinal studies through which a developmental view of the individual or the group may be secured. While use of cumulative records for case study and counseling implies analysis of the entire life history, there are many other occasions when only a single item of information, such as a test score, is taken from the record by the teacher, counselor, supervisor, or administrator.

Specific uses of cumulative records at the elementary and junior high school levels relate to: (1) study of the needs of pupils in an instructional field, (2) discovery of causes of behavior difficulties and failures, (3) identification of gifted pupils, (4) discovery of special abilities, and (5) advice to a pupil who wishes to leave school during or at the end of the junior high school period. Uses at the high school and college levels relate to: (1) selection of the program most appropriate for the learner, (2) choice of schools after graduation or when transferring, (3) efficient use of leisure time, and (4) placement. Certain relationships have been discovered between one or more items of knowledge concerning a pupil and his later behavior, a fact which attaches a prognostic value to many of the measurements recorded in cumulative records.[92]

**Format and structure of cumulative records.** The preceding discussion of the cumulative record assumes that all pertinent information concerning the individual will be filed in one place as a unit. An individual folder is necessary for filing subjective impressions, extended comments, samples of school work, test forms, behavior deviations, and adjustment procedures employed. To use medical-social work as an example, the unit record includes data from physicians, social workers, nurses, and technicians. Adequate school records depend on the coöperation of parents, teachers, principals, directors of special activities, and a number of technicians. Child-guidance clinics especially have sought to integrate into a unit record the medical, psychological, social, and psychiatric evidence discovered. Even though it may prove simpler to collect a single type of data in a given investigation, it is imperative to view the child in toto when planning adjustment or developmental procedures. A complete picture of the child as a unified personality depends largely on the details found in a cumulative, unit record system.

In addition to the suggested outlines for collecting data, as listed under the second step of case study and case work, a number of other sources

---

[92] David Segel, *Nature and Use of the Cumulative Record.* Office of Education Bulletin No. 3, 1938. Washington: Government Printing Office, 1938. vi + 48 p.

Anna R. Hawkes, "The Cumulative Record and Its Uses." *The Public School Demonstration Project in Educational Guidance.* Educational Records Bulletin, No. 21. New York: Educational Records Bureau, 1937. p. 37-64.

may be named. In most instances the titles of the references [93] listed indicate whether the emphasis is on case-study outlines as such or on cumulative-record forms.

**Characteristics of anecdotal records.** Anecdotal materials concerning behavior have come to play a significant part in rounding out the cumulative record. A type of continuing individual record with emphasis on items and episodes of behavior that are important in the development of character or personality is known as the anecdotal behavior journal.[94] In its most complete form, such a behavior journal may contain as varied types of data as are included in a detailed case study. Its anecdotes are not limited to the maladjustments of problem pupils, but report positive and constructive episodes, as well as the admirable behavior and outstanding achievements of especially talented or well adjusted pupils.

As originated at the Rochester Athenaeum and Mechanics Institute, the anecdote is a record of some significant item of conduct, a revealing episode in the life of the student, a word picture of the student in action, a verbal snapshot taken at the moment of an incident, or any narrative of an event significant for revealing personality.[95] Such anecdotes should possess the following characteristics: [96]

1. Objectivity, in the sense that a motion picture is objective as it presents a series of snapshots or frames; a series of anecdotes, like a cinema, also represents a flow of events and the dynamic characteristics of the behavior of the individual.

[93] Charles C. Cowell, "Records of Developmental Growth." *Educational Research Bulletin* 19:223-30, 244; April 10, 1940.

R. B. Embree, "The Cumulative-Record Card as an Aid to Research." *School Review* 47:425-30; June 1939.

Charles D. Flory, "Cumulative Records for Research Purposes." *Journal of Educational Research* 30:157-68; November 1936.

Gordon Hamilton, *Social Case Recording, op. cit.*, p. 9-16, 138-43.

Gordon Hamilton, *Principles of Social Case Recording, op. cit.*

K. R. Hammond and J. M. Allen, *op. cit.*

C. M. Louttit, *op. cit.*, p. 12-44. Also see the 1947 revised edition.

G. A. Lundberg, *op. cit.*, p. 188-95. Also see the 1942 revised edition.

Henry C. Morrison, *op. cit.*, Chapter 30.

P. L. Schroeder and Others, *op. cit.*, p. 40-159.

David Segel, *op. cit.*, p. 5-34.

Elsie M. Smithies, *op. cit.*, p. 18-22.

A. E. Traxler, "A Cumulative-Record Form for the Elementary School." *Elementary School Journal* 40:45-54; September 1939.

[94] L. L. Jarvie and Mark Ellingson, *A Handbook on the Anecdotal Behavior Journal.* Chicago: University of Chicago Press, 1940. xii + 71 p.

Willard C. Olson, *Child Development.* Boston: D. C. Heath and Co., 1949. p. 389-97.

J. A. Randall, "The Anecdotal Behavior Journal." *Progressive Education* 13:21-26; January 1936.

Judith I. Krugman and J. Wayne Wrightstone, *A Guide to the Use of Anecdotal Records.* Educational Research Bulletin of the Bureau of Reference, Research and Statistics, No. 11. New York: Board of Education, May 1949. 33 p.

[95] J. A. Randall, *op. cit.*, p. 22.

[96] *Ibid.*, p. 25.

A. E. Traxler, *The Nature and Use of Anecdotal Records.* Revised Edition. Educational Records Supplementary Bulletin D. New York: Educational Record Bureau, 1949. p. 4-8.

2. Subjectivity, to the extent that an artistically composed photograph is subjective; both are sharply limited to a center of attention, with inconsequential details subordinated.

3. Factual emphasis, limited to portrayal of behavior observed (raw data), with any interpretation or recommendation clearly separated from the incident.

4. Clarity, so as to insure complete understanding on the part of readers other than the recorder.

**Uses of anecdotal records.** Among the varied uses of anecdotal records and of the anecdotal behavior journal is provision of essential data and illustrative materials for: [97]

1. Increased faculty understanding of pupils, in terms of basic personality patterns of individuals
2. Counseling relationships and techniques, including self-appraisal on the part of pupils
3. Increased understanding of pupils by persons outside the school
4. Curriculum development and adjustment of the program to the individual
5. Appraisal of outcomes in terms of observable behavior
6. Assisting in the interpretation of quantitative records of achievement
7. Case instruction in textbooks and in professional programs.

Hamalainen found that anecdotal records were used by teachers to study the social relationships of their pupils, attitudes, worth-while activities, interests, and patterns of behavior, particularly for purposes of guidance.[98] Certain limitations in the use of anecdotal records were related to instruction of an unusually large number of classes by an individual teacher (particularly the "special" teacher), attitude of the teacher toward a formal academic program, type of curriculum made available to the pupil, background of the teacher in mental hygiene and child development, and skill in methods of observation.

**Steps in anecdotal-record planning.** While the nature of anecdotal recording is such as to be of most value when standardized or formalized procedures are avoided, certain steps are essential in making and using anecdotal records, whatever the modifications and adjustments to meet local needs. Among the more or less sequential stages represented when introducing the plan into a school are: [99]

1. Enlisting the coöperation of the faculty, including counselors, and development of an understanding and acceptance of the ideal of individualized education.

[97] J. A. Randall, op. cit., p. 23-25.
Arthur E. Traxler, The Nature and Use of Anecdotal Records, op. cit., p. 26-29.
Judith I. Krugman and J. Wayne Wrightstone, op. cit., p. 2-3, 21-22.
[98] A. E. Hamalainen, An Appraisal of Anecdotal Records. Contributions to Education, No. 891. New York: Teachers College, Columbia University, 1943. 88 p.
[99] Arthur E. Traxler, The Nature and Use of Anecdotal Records, op. cit., p. 9-22.
Judith I. Krugman and J. Wayne Wrightstone, op. cit., p. 8-14, 23-24.

2. Deciding how much should be expected of observers who write anecdotes, possibly a reasonable minimum number per week.

3. Preparing forms, which are usually very simple, as illustrated by forms in current use; [100] an outline adapted to most situations provides blank spaces for identifying the pupil, class, and observer, with separate columns for date, incident, and comment.

4. Obtaining the original records, including a plan for jotting down the name of the pupil and an appropriate catch word at the time of the incident, with a period set aside toward the end of the day for recording the anecdotes concerning significant behavior episodes observed during the day; a reasonable, although not equal, distribution of anecdotes among the pupils is desirable.

5. Central filing, as emphasized in the earlier discussion of cumulative records, in order that incidents described by different observers over a period of time may be assembled and compared to note trends.

6. Periodic summarizing, preferably under topical headings, as recommended earlier in the section on case recording.

**Precautions and problems in the preparation and use of anecdotes.** [101] Certain limitations and difficulties inherent in the preparation of anecdotes may be minimized by observing reasonable precautions: [102]

1. Accuracy and objectivity in observation and in recording are imperative, as emphasized in the discussion of case recording; statements of opinion must be separated from the report of the incident itself.

2. Anecdotal records should not be used as a defense mechanism by the teacher to justify some action on his part, such as, loss of temper or harsh discipline.

3. In many instances, a brief description of the background against which a behavior incident occurred is necessary, since there is grave danger of misinterpretation in isolating an episode from its social setting.

4. In summarizing and interpreting anecdotal records, one must be on guard against acceptance of a relatively small number of anecdotes as a valid picture of the total behavior pattern of the pupil; an understandable picture is based on some degree of repetition of similar behavior reported from a number of situations in different areas of conduct.

5. As in case study in general, anecdotal records must have professional and confidential treatment, in order that unfortunate behavior incidents may not prejudice the future adjustment and success of the pupils represented.

6. A workable plan for handling the load of clerical work and for summarizing anecdotes is necessary before a school commits itself to the writing of anecdotes.

[100] Arthur E. Traxler, *The Nature and Use of Anecdotal Records, op. cit.,* p. 10-14.
C. F. McCormick, "The Anecdotal Record in the Appraisal of Personality." *School and Society* 53:126-27; January 25, 1941.
[101] For examples of sample anecdotes see:
L. L. Jarvie and Mark Ellingson, *op. cit.*
J. A. Randall, *op. cit.,* p. 22-23.
Arthur E. Traxler, *The Nature and Use of Anecdotal Records, op. cit.,* p. 22-26.
Judith I. Krugman and J. Wayne Wrightstone, *op. cit.,* p. 1-29.
[102] Arthur E. Traxler, *The Nature and Use of Anecdotal Records, op. cit,* p. 22-26.
L. L. Jarvie, "Some Factors Bearing Upon the Use of Observational Records," *Official Report of 1940 Meeting.* Washington: American Educational Research Association, 1940. p. 35-39.
Judith I. Krugman and J. Wayne Wrightstone, *op. cit.,* p. 3-5, 15-20.

7. Urgent needs for adjustment, as revealed through anecdotes, should not encourage hasty generalizations and should not be used as excuses for short-cuts in personality adaptation, which is usually a long-term process.

8. Observers should strive to record evidence of growth and favorable adjustment even more diligently than instances of undesirable behavior.

9. Teachers must be on guard against overemphasizing inconsistencies in behavior or incidents that are not at all typical of the behavior of the particular pupil; sometimes behavior at the beginning of the school year is atypical, although anecdotes recorded during the first few weeks may possess some significance as single incidents for understanding the pupil; however, without repetition episodes give little insight for determining developmental patterns of behavior, and deviations cannot be recognized until the usual patterns have been established through a repetition of incidents in different situations.

The problems encountered at the Rochester Athenaeum are typical of the questions for which answers are being sought from an increasing reservoir of anecdotal materials.[103]

1. Are there patterns of behavior which may be considered as normal?

2. Is it possible to isolate symptomatic patterns antecedent to crises in behavior?

3. What techniques for discovering and understanding students in terms of their needs, abilities, and aspirations have been of value?

4. What techniques for diagnosing and improving normal behavior and behavior disorders have value?

5. To what extent can we classify behavior disorders in terms of overt patterns and of antecedent causation?

6. What procedures have been worthwhile in evaluating the development of personality as a whole in individual students?

7. What form of administrative organization has been most efficient in facilitating a program of personalized education?

## ILLUSTRATIVE CASE HISTORIES

Discussion of the principles and techniques of case study and case work cannot take the place of first-hand contact with field situations and with the resulting case histories. Therefore, illustrative sources reporting case histories from varied types of case study and case work should be cited, with the area of application indicated: social work;[104] guidance, counsel-

[103] L. L. Jarvie, "A Quantitative Study of Behavior Records," *Research on the Foundations of American Education*. Washington: American Educational Research Association, 1939. p. 106-11.

Judith I. Krugman and J. Wayne Wrightstone, *op. cit.*, p. 5-7.

[104] Margaret C. Bristol, *op. cit.*

Elizabeth S. Dixon and Grace A. Browning, Editors. *Social Case Records:* Family Welfare. Chicago: University of Chicago Press, 1938. x + 312 p.

M. R. Gomberg, Ruth E. Fizdale, and Meyer Brown, *Studies in the Practice of Family Case Work*. Brooklyn: Jewish Family Welfare Society, 1942. 93 p.

Gordon Hamilton, *Social Case Recording, op. cit.*

Gordon Hamilton, *Theory and Practice of Social Case Work, op. cit.* Also see the 1951 edition.

Florence Hollis, *Social Case Work in Practice, op. cit.*

ing, and therapy; [105] behavior problems and delinquency; [106] child development; [107] and interviewing methods.[108] To render more concrete the types of case histories reported in the educational, social, and psychological literature, a number of sources will be characterized in some detail.

Seven brief case histories of maladjusted teachers are identified as problems of mental hygiene: [109]

1. A conscientious and successful teacher with heavy afterschool responsibilities
2. A mean, sarcastic teacher who is not interested in children
3. An unattractive teacher with hypochondriacal tendencies
4. An incompetent, irritable teacher not interested in children
5. An exceptionally able teacher who compensates for inferiority feelings and seeks to dominate others

---

J. W. Madden and W. R. Compton, *Cases and Materials on Domestic Relations.* St. Paul, Minn.: West Publishing Co., 1940. 901 p.

Ada E. Sheffield, *op. cit.*

R. S. Wilson, *op. cit.*

Helen L. Witmer, *op. cit.*

Pauline V. Young, *Social Case Work in National Defense:* A Cultural Approach to the Problems of Enlisted Men and Their Families. New York: Prentice-Hall, 1941. xxi + 292 p.

[105] Clifford E. Erickson, *Counseling Interview.* New York: Prentice-Hall, 1950. 174 p.

Milton E. Hahn and Malcolm S. MacLean, *General Clinical Counseling in Educational Institutions.* New York: McGraw-Hill Book Co., 1950. xi + 375 p.

C. T. Holman, *Getting Down to Cases:* A Case and Method Manual for Personal Counseling. New York: Macmillan Co., 1942. 207 p.

E. H. Porter, Jr., *op. cit.* Extracts from cases are used as a test for counselors.

William C. Reavis, *Pupil Adjustment in Junior and Senior High Schools.* Boston: D. C. Heath and Co., 1926. xviii + 348 p.

Carl R. Rogers, *Client-Centered Therapy, op. cit.*

Mary B. Sayles, *Child Guidance Cases.* New York: Commonwealth Fund, 1932. xxiii + 584 p.

P. L. Schroeder and Others, *op. cit.*

Samuel R. Slavson, *Analytic Group Psychotherapy with Children, Adolescents, and Adults, op. cit.*

Elsie M. Smithies, *op. cit.*

W. U. Snyder, Editor. *Casebook of Nondirective Counseling.* Boston: Houghton Mifflin Co., 1947. viii + 339 p.

[106] Norman Cameron, *The Psychology of Behavior Disorders.* Boston: Houghton Mifflin Co., 1947. xxi + 662 p.

Arthur Burton and R. E. Harris, Editors, *Case Histories in Clinical and Abnormal Psychology.* New York: Harper and Bros., 1947. 680 p.

Sheldon Glueck and Eleanor Glueck, *Criminal Careers in Retrospect.* New York: Commonwealth Fund, 1943. xiv + 380 p.

A. C. Kinsey and Others, *Sexual Behavior in the Human Male.* Philadelphia: W. B. Saunders Co., 1948. xvi + 804 p.

C. M. Louttit, *op. cit.* Also see the 1947 edition.

Carl R. Rogers, *The Clinical Treatment of the Problem Child, op. cit.*

C. P. Stone, *Case Histories in Abnormal Psychology.* Stanford University, Calif.: Stanford Bookstore, 1943. v + 98 p.

Pauline V. Young, *Social Treatment in Probation and Delinquency, op. cit.*

[107] Arnold Gesell and Catherine S. Amatruda, *op. cit.* Also see the 1947 edition.

Arnold Gesell and Others, *op. cit.*

Robert J. Havighurst, *Human Development and Education.* New York: Longmans, Green and Co., 1953. p. 177-253.

Lewis M. Terman and Melita H. Oden, *op. cit.*

[108] Burleigh B. Gardner, *Case Studies for Interviewing Methods and Techniques.* Chicago: University of Chicago Bookstore, 1944. 101 p.

[109] Norman Fenton, *op. cit.*

6. A good teacher, very aggressive toward other teachers, and bad for school morale
7. An efficient teacher, irascible with boys, resistive to school regulations, yet demanding strict obedience and conformity from students.

Fink illustrates the several fields of social work by rather full case studies, including family-welfare work, child-welfare services, the child-guidance clinic, visiting-teacher work, the court, probation and parole, medical social work, public welfare and public assistance, social group work, and community organization.[110]

A group of social cases referred for psychiatric service represents the following problems: [111]

1. A boy of normal intelligence with no organic basis for facial tic and "nervousness"
2. A child with cardiac condition and peculiar eating habits
3. A boy of superior intelligence, difficult to control and self-willed
4. A mentally defective boy whose condition was not understood by his father
5. A girl with no organic basis for her physical symptoms
6. A young woman with periods of serious illness affected by frustrated achievement strivings
7. A young boy thought by his mother to have chorea and a "vicious disposition."
8. A boy of normal intelligence with no organic basis for his physical symptoms
9. A boy with no organic basis for his symptom, enuresis, whose mother revealed deep antagonism toward him
10. An adolescent boy with osteomyelitis and a delinquency record
11. A young woman in an acute anxiety state obsessed with the idea that her baby was dying or that some harm would befall him
12. A young woman with acute fears.

A collection of cases of child delinquency represents the following problems and procedures: [112]

1. Intelligence and adjustment
2. Parental rejection
3. Rigid parental control
4. Poverty and low social status
5. Bravado, a compensatory reaction
6. Unmoral, childish attitudes toward stealing
7. Development of a criminal career
8. Parental overprotection
9. Emotional immaturity
10. Conflict of loyalties

[110] A. E. Fink, *The Field of Social Work.* New York: Henry Holt and Co., 1942. x + 518 p.
[111] Charlotte Towle, *Social Case Records from Psychiatric Clinics.* Chicago: University of Chicago Press, 1941. xii + 455 p.
[112] Maud A. Merrill, *Problems of Child Delinquency.* Boston: Houghton Mifflin Co., 1947. xxiii + 403 p.

11. Maintaining self-esteem by stealing
12. Egocentrism and delinquency
13. Feeblemindedness and personality
14. Intelligence and recidivism
15. Failure to integrate motives
16. Delinquent behavior and feelings of inferiority
17. Private worlds
18. The play interview
19. Recidivism and adjustment
20. Evaluation of component factors as a basis for determining treatment
21. Family pattern of delinquency
22. Rebellion against authority.

Rogers' case history of Herbert Bryan is unique, in that it was the first time a complete account of the counseling process with one individual was recorded phonographically, including all the material of a series of eight counseling interviews, both the counselor's and the client's statements.[113]

Ten psychiatric cases of children and youth, as characterized briefly below, are reported at length by Witmer.[114]

1. A seven-year-old boy whose fearfulness was found to be a direct reaction to his parents' behavior toward him, and whose inability to read resulted from his depending entirely upon his unusually good visual memory in trying to learn words. The therapeutic relationship was used to further the learning process and to enable the child to express his feelings about his parents and about his reality situation.

2. A seventeen-year-old boy, isolated, rather confused, inadequate but not neurotic. The home situation was very trying, the mother being a sensitive, unstable person and the father very domineering. Since the home situation was unlikely to change, treatment aimed at "tiding the boy over" until maturity. The relationship was used to help the boy to express his feelings of dissatisfaction, of which he was already aware, to get a new perspective on his actions and those of his family, and thus to feel less alone and less different from others.

3. A typical five-year-old boy in difficulty over emancipating himself from his mother, establishing his masculinity, and dealing with castration fears. The therapeutic relationship was used to relieve anxiety and to secure resolution of emotional conflict by permitting the expression of his impulses and supporting his helpful identifications.

4. An alert, imaginative, docile eight-year-old girl whose crying spells appeared to represent fear of loss of her mother's love if she were not continually good. In the relationship with the therapist she expressed, largely through drawings, her desire to disobey, and then worked out a satisfactory solution to her emotional conflict about this matter.

5. A fifteen-year-old girl who engaged in petty, perhaps compulsive, stealing as a means of expressing her resentment of her mother's treatment of her. The emotional conflict resulted from the contrast between her real feelings and her desire to follow religious precepts. The relationship was used to give

[113] Carl R. Rogers, *Counseling and Psychotherapy*. Boston: Houghton Mifflin Co., 1942. p. 261-437.
[114] Helen L. Witmer, Editor, *Psychiatric Interviews with Children*. New York: Commonwealth Fund (Harvard University Press), 1946. v + 443 p.

the girl an opportunity of confessing her stealing to a person she trusted, of reëxperiencing the hurt of her first punishment for such a deed, of expressing her conscious resentment of her mother's actions, and of fostering her positive feelings for her mother.

6. A shy, timid, friendless thirteen-year-old boy suffering from anxiety attacks that were found to be attributable to emotional conflict between strong sexual tensions and fear of the consequences of relieving them. Since he was the kind of patient whose conflicts are near to consciousness and who is eager for help, it was possible to use the relationship to aid the boy in verbalizing his fears and guilt feelings and then to give him assurance that his desires and actions were neither abnormal nor sinful. The therapeutic results were reenforced by the boy's attending the therapist's summer camp.

7. A nine-year-old girl who used a neutrotic device as a means of stubborn, compulsive struggle with her nagging, discouraged parents. The therapeutic relationship was used to develop in the child new standards of conduct that would secure love and approval for her and would enable her to carry out her socially acceptable desires.

8. An eight-year-old girl whose normal development was hindered by a too close mother-child relationship and who expressed her struggle and her anxiety in wilful insistence on her timidity and in physical symptoms that were without organic basis. The relationship with the therapist was used to help the child to experience her anxiety herself as an independent human being who could assert her own desires and allow others to assert theirs.

9. A neurotic boy, nine years old, with a speech defect that was part of general motor symptoms and extreme perfectionist tendencies. These symptoms and his repression of all affect were judged to be a reaction to chronically unfavorable attitudes on the part of the mother. The therapeutic relationship and the therapist's tolerance of aggressive impulses and anal tendencies helped the child to relax his repressions and his reactions against dirtiness, to verbalize his real feelings, and to bear the anxiety and guilt that their expression occasioned.

10. A nine-year-old boy with ever-present bizarre and terrifying phantasies that served to protect him from awareness of the anxiety aroused by the discrepancy between his own and his parents' sexual behavior and the teaching of his church, as well as by his fear that his parents would separate and abandon him. Treatment in this case was of episodic character, for the child was apparently too disturbed to enter into the kind of treatment that involves progressive revelation of basic difficulties. The therapeutic relationship was used to lessen the pressure of the patient's anxiety by having him describe his phantasies and discover that the therapist considered them harmless. With anxiety decreased, the child's ego became stronger and he was enabled to function more effectively in the reality situation.

## LIMITATIONS AND RESOURCES OF CASE STUDY

**Limitations of case study.** The difficulties of case study are represented in the precautions emphasized throughout this chapter. These limitations are the same as for scientific method in general, whatever the field of application, and relate to clear-cut definition of the problem, formulation of shrewd hypotheses, invention of accurate and objective instruments of measurement, skillful use of such tools, adoption of standardized units of measurement and uniform terminology, adequate sampling, sound techniques for classification and analysis of data, and well organized systems of recording and reporting.

The argument that case study does not lend itself to statistical treatment need not prove too disquieting. Case study and statistical techniques are not necessarily antagonistic or mutually exclusive, since statistical concepts are employed when cases are combined and classified to reveal frequencies, types, trends, uniformities, or patterns of behavior. However, in one's zeal to collect and use quantitative evidence, it is especially important in educational, psychological, historical, and other social research not to overlook qualitative interpretations.

Early in the history of social research, able investigators recognized the supplementary and complementary uses of case study and statistical evidence. A French social reformer and economist, LaPlay (1806-82), in certain of his monographs on family standards of living a century ago combined the case-study approach and statistical measurement. Charles Booth (1840-1916) in England utilized his extensive statistical training to compile impressive masses of evidence in case study of community life. From the days of the introduction of life-history materials, a long series of volumes has combined statistical, case-study, and field-observation procedures.

Although more easily administered quantitative techniques have tended to replace case-study techniques in certain areas of investigation, especially when prediction must be made quickly for a large number of individuals, case-study materials will continue to serve as a valuable and even indispensable supplement to the techniques of statistics for purposes of prediction. A good illustration is the procedure of life-insurance companies in supplementing their actuarial tables by a medical examination (a case approach). The statistician and case-study worker may profit by borrowing from each other rather than by quarreling over the merits of their respective techniques. It remains to be proved that so-called scientific or statistical methods are superior to, or even equal to, the insights of trained workers especially gifted in understanding of human behavior and child development. Careful study is needed to determine the most fruitful way in which statistical and case-study methods of prediction may be used to supplement and complement each other.[115]

[115] Emory S. Bogardus, "Sociology and Social Philosophy." *Sociology and Social Research* 37:260-64; March-April 1953.

E. W. Burgess, "An Experiment in the Standardization of the Case-Study Method." *Sociometry* 4:329-48; November 1941.

S. A. Stouffer, "Notes on the Case Study and the Unique Case." *Sociometry* 4:349-57; November 1941. Also see:

To cite another example of the value of case materials, the sixty-nine case studies or case reports published over a twelve-year period in the *Journal of Abnormal and Social Psychology* are conveniently listed in a cumulative index of case reports. An editorial note points out that good case material has been a rarity in the fields of interest represented by the *Journal of Abnormal and Social Psychology* (suitable descriptions of clinical types, of individual "normal" personalities, and of significant social episodes such as crowds, panics, and rumors). Lack of adequate case materials in these areas handicaps both teachers and psychological theorists. Allport has asked significant questions concerning the value of the case approach: [116]

> May it not be . . . that the ultimate datum of psychological science is always the single case in all its uniqueness of pattern? Does one really know that the general laws we are gradually evolving will in fact overspread the structure and the dynamics of the single personality or the single social event? Or, alternatively, may it turn out that scientific psychology is both a nomothetic discipline (devoted to the discovery of general laws) and an idiographic discipline (destined to probe the internal structure of the single event—especially the dynamic patterning of a unique personality or a historical social event)?

In summary, many statisticians are likely to think of case studies as only the raw data for a later statistical study. While this is one possibility, it is by no means the chief contribution made by case knowledge. This tendency to seek laws may prove a barren use of the rich pictures produced by case studies; it may be something like analyzing the paintings of great artists to ascertain how many tubes of red paint were used by the various artists. While statistical studies are essential and defensible, in a social field they must be looked upon as the lesser rather than the major influence. Statistical and experimental studies do not play the role in education and in the various social areas that they do in the physical sciences. This is because the social sciences represent, by comparison, not only the scientific aspects of a problem or undertaking, but also the managerial, judicial, legislative, and various other practical aspects of putting science to work in the interest

---

L. S. Cottrell, "The Case-Study Method in Prediction." *Sociometry* 4:358-70; November 1941.

F. N. House, "Statistical Methods and Case Studies." *Development of Sociology*. New York: McGraw-Hill Book Co., 1936. p. 367-76.

George A. Lundberg, "Case Studies vs. Statistical Methods: An Issue Based on Misunderstanding." *Sociometry* 4:379-83; November 1941.

William J. Goode and Paul K. Hatt, *Methods in Social Research*. New York: McGraw-Hill Book Co., 1952. p. 330-31.

Pauline V. Young, *Scientific Social Surveys and Research, op. cit.,* p. 5-17, 265-85.

[116] "Cumulative Index of Case Reports—1938-1949." *Journal of Abnormal and Social Psychology* 44: vii-viii; October 1949. Also see the editorial note by Gordon Allport, p. 440-41.

of our social institutions. The field for future research [117] in case study and case work is as broad as the principles, techniques, and areas outlined in this chapter.

**Resources for case study and case work.** At various points in this chapter the resources available for coöperative attack on the problems of case study and case work have been indicated. Child-guidance clinics and mental-hygiene programs, in dealing with problem and delinquent children, pool the efforts of psychiatrists, physicians, psychologists, social workers, and sociologists, and utilize the resources of clinic, community, home, school, case-working organization, recreational program, and child-place-ment agency. These resources, as well as the varied principles and tech-niques outlined in this chapter, suggest the breadth of training desirable for effective case study and case work.

## CONCLUDING STATEMENT

Case study is essentially intensive investigation of the particular unit represented, whereas case work refers especially to the remedial, corrective, or developmental procedures that appropriately follow diagnosis of the causes of maladjustment or of approved behavior. Case study and case work, therefore, are complementary processes, even though they may not be performed by the same person or agency. The objectives of case study and of case work are no longer limited to investigation and correction of situations or conditions of maladjustment, but also include consideration of normal or well adjusted children, of effectively functioning institutions, and of well organized communities.

The complementary processes of case study and case work represent a logical continuity or sequence in study, diagnosis, and treatment—a series of steps that may be differentiated intellectually, although in an actual life situation these steps may weave in and out shuttle-like, to the distraction of the narrowly logical mind. The cycle of steps is: (1) recognition and determination of the status of the phenomenon to be investigated; (2) col-lection of data relating to the factors or circumstances associated with the given phenomenon; (3) diagnosis or identification of causal factors as a basis for remedial or developmental treatment; (4) application of remedial or adjustment measures; and (5) subsequent follow-up to determine the effectiveness of the treatment applied.

The first step in case study is the identification of the need-situation,

[117] Leo J. Brueckner, "Diagnosis and Remedial Teaching." *Encyclopedia of Educational Research, op. cit.* Also see the 1950 edition.
Howard W. Odum and Katharine Jocher, *op. cit.*
Ruth Strang, *op. cit.* Also see the 1949 edition.

aspect of behavior, or phase of the life process as the unit for investigation, with the case centered typically on the need-situation as the unit of attention rather than on the individual or client as such. (The comparatively recent development of non-directive therapy and counseling is client-centered.) In many instances, direct observation can be verified or supplemented by use of data-gathering and recording procedures and instruments, in order to determine more accurately the extent or degree of the deficiency, maladjustment, or ability in question.

The second step in case study represents a continuation of the data-gathering begun in the first stage of the investigation, but with emphasis on facts that may serve later as a basis for diagnosis or identification of the causal factors operating. Numerous research tools are available. In addition to the procedures and instruments useful in the first step of case study—including records, tests, questionnaires, check lists, scorecards, rating scales, interviews, and clinical and laboratory techniques—such materials as the life history, biography, autobiography, letters, and diaries frequently prove valuable sources of information.

Diagnosis, as the third step in case study, seeks to formulate a theory or hypothesis of causation, from which it looks toward the possibilities for growth and adjustment. (Non-directive or client-centered therapy minimizes diagnosis as a basis for treatment or therapy.) Diagnosis is not only prognostic in pointing toward remedial treatment or developmental opportunities, but also looks backward in its dependence upon the examination procedures used and the data collected in the second step of case study. To use learning difficulty as an illustration of the complexity of causation, the major factors contributing to maladjustment may be physical, intellectual, pedagogical, emotional, social, and environmental.

Treatment or adjustment, as the fourth step, is commonly characterized as case work. Appropriate adjustment of the conditions discovered through case-study investigation is essential, if the time and effort spent in reaching a diagnosis of causal factors are to be fully justified. In spite of current emphasis on preventive measures, remedial or developmental treatment is necessary for many handicapped individuals, for others below their level of learning capacity, and for yet others in possession of undiscovered or undeveloped aptitudes.

The fifth step, a follow-up program after treatment, completes the cycle of case study and case work. If determination of the effectiveness of the remedial or developmental measure reveals that reasonable progress toward adjustment has not been made, a new diagnosis and a modified treatment may be required. Only through careful analysis is it possible to identify the causal factor that produces the changes observed; a patient may recover because of a strong constitution rather than as a result of medicine administered, or through a combination of the two.

Effective recording, like effective listening, skillful interviewing, and discriminating writing in general, is an active process of attention and selection from a relatively large mass of materials. Well balanced records possess the essential attributes of accuracy, objectivity, conciseness, ease of reference, and uniformity. Special recording skills are essential in dealing with interviews, the narrative, summaries, and letters and reports. Recording problems with ethical implications arise with respect to: (1) strictly personal or confidential information that might be distorted or used against the client; (2) evidence that casts doubt on the efficiency of fellow workers or the policies of the agency or institution; (3) mistakes made by the worker himself; and (4) appropriate use of records by professional workers.

A cumulative record is one maintained for an individual over a period of years, with successive additions at relatively frequent intervals. The detailed uses of cumulative records are varied in such areas as case study and counseling. It is essential that all pertinent information concerning the individual be filed in one place as a unit. Anecdotal materials concerning behavior are significant for rounding out the cumulative record. An anecdote is a meaningful item of conduct, a revealing episode in the life of the student, or a word picture of any event helpful in revealing personality. If the varied potential uses of anecdotal records are to prove fruitful, certain steps in planning must be followed and definite precautions must be observed.

The difficulties of case study are those of science in general. The methods of case study and statistics are complementary rather than mutually exclusive, although in the attempt to secure and analyze quantitative data for case records the investigator should not overlook helpful qualitative interpretations. The varied resources available, as well as the multiplicity of problems for research, suggest the breadth of training desirable for effective case study and case work. One of the most important elements in this background is first-hand contact with field situations and with the resulting case histories.

## SELECTED REFERENCES

ABBOTT, Edith. "Twenty-One Years of University Education for the Social Services." *Social Service Review* 15:671-705; December 1941.

ABT, Lawrence E., and BELLAK, Leopold, Editors. *Projective Psychology: Clinical Approaches to the Total Personality.* New York: Alfred A. Knopf, 1950. xvii + 485 + xiv p.

ALLEN, Frederick H. *Psychotherapy with Children.* New York: W. W. Norton and Co., 1942. 311 p.

ALLEN, Wendell C. *Cumulative Pupil Records:* A Plan for Staff Study and Improvement of Cumulative Pupil Records in Secondary Schools. New York: Teachers College, Columbia University, 1943. 69 p.

ALLPORT, G. W., BRUNER, J. S., and JANDORF, E. M. "Personality under Social Catastrophe: Ninety Life-Histories of the Nazi Revolution." *Character and Personality* 10:1-22; September 1941.

ANDERSON, Harold H., and ANDERSON, Gladys L., Editors. *An Introduction to Projective Techniques. . . .* New York: Prentice-Hall, 1951. xxiv + 720 p.

ANDREWS, T. G., Editor. *Methods of Psychology.* New York: John Wiley and Sons, 1948. 604 p.

APA Committee on Test Standards. "Technical Recommendations for Psychological Tests and Diagnostic Techniques: Preliminary Proposal." *American Psychologist* 7:461-75; August 1952.

APTEKAR, H. H. *Basic Concepts in Social Case Work.* Chapel Hill: University of North Carolina Press, 1941. ix + 201 p.

ASSUM, Arthur L., and LEVY, Sidney J. "Analysis of a Nondirective Case with Follow-up Interview." *Journal of Abnormal and Social Psychology* 43:78-89; January 1948.

AUSTIN, Lucille N. "Trends in Differential Treatment in Social Casework." *Journal of Social Casework* 29:203-11; June 1948.

AXLINE, Virginia M. *Play Therapy:* The Inner Dynamics of Childhood. Boston: Houghton Mifflin Co., 1947. xii + 379 p.

BACH, George R. *Intensive Group Psychotherapy.* New York: Ronald Press Co., 1954. xi + 446 p.

BAKER, H. J., and TRAPHAGEN, Virginia. *The Diagnosis and Treatment of Behavior-Problem Children.* New York: Macmillan Co., 1935. 393 p.

BARR, Arvil S., DAVIS, Robert A., and JOHNSON, Palmer O. *Educational Research and Appraisal.* Philadelphia: J. B. Lippincott Co., 1953. p. 188-201.

BARTLETT, F. C., and Others. *The Study of Society:* Methods and Problems. London: Kegan Paul, Trench, Trubner and Co., 1939. xiv + 498 p.

BEIER, E. G. "Client-Centered Therapy and the Involuntary Client." *Journal of Consulting Psychology* 16:332-37; October 1952.

BEIER, E. G. "Problem of Anxiety in Client-Centered Therapy." *Journal of Consulting Psychology* 15:359-62; October 1951.

BELL, Hugh M., and Others. "Counseling, Guidance, and Personnel Work." *Review of Educational Research* 18:121-215; April 1948.

BELL, John E. *Projective Techniques:* Dynamic Approach to the Study of the Personality. New York: Longmans, Green and Co., 1948. 533 p.

BELLAK, Leopold, and JAQUES, Elliott. "On the Problem of Dynamic Conceptualization in Case Studies." *Character and Personality* 11:20-39; September 1942.

BENNETT, Margaret E., and Others. "Counseling, Guidance, and Personnel Work." *Review of Educational Research* 15:97-192; April 1945.

BERG, Charles. *The Case Book of a Medical Psychologist.* New York: Norton and Co., 1948. 260 p.

BERG, I. A. "Measures Before and After Therapy." *Journal of Clinical Psychology* 8:46-50; January 1952.

BERG, I. A. "The Use of Human Subjects in Psychological Research." *American Psychologist* 9:108-11; March 1954.

BERRIEN, F. K. *Comments and Cases on Human Relations.* New York: Harper and Bros., 1951. xi + 500 p. Applies the case method to undergraduate and graduate courses concerned with human relations.

BIBRING, Grete L. "Psychiatric Principles in Casework." *Journal of Social Casework* 30:230-35; June 1949.

BIBRING, Grete L. "Psychiatry and Social Work." *Journal of Social Casework* 28:203-11; June 1947.

BIESTEK, Felix P. "The Principle of Client Self-Determination." *Social Casework* 32:369-75; November 1951.

BLENKNER, Margaret. "Obstacles to Evaluative Research in Casework." *Social Casework* 31:54-60, 97-105; February, March 1950.

BLENKNER, Margaret, and Others. "A Study of Interrelated Factors in the Initial Interview with New Clients." *Social Casework* 32:23-30; January 1951.

BOEDECKER, Karl A. "The Case Method of Instruction." *Collegiate News and Views* 5:1-6; March, 1952.

BOGARDUS, E. S. *Introduction to Social Research.* Los Angeles: Suttonhouse, 1936. Chapters 10-12.

BOND, H. M. "Education as a Social Process: A Case Study of a Higher Institution as an Incident in the Process of Acculturation." *American Journal of Sociology* 48:701-9; May 1943.

BOWERS, Swithun. "The Nature and Definition of Social Casework." *Journal of Social Casework* 30:311-17, October 1949; 369-75, November 1949; 412-17, December 1949.

BOWES, Fern H. "The Anecdotal Behavior Record in Measuring Progress in Character." *Elementary School Journal* 39:431-35; February 1939.

BOYD, Gertrude, and SCHWIERING, O. C. "Remedial Instruction and Case Records: A Survey of Reading Clinical Practices." *Journal of Educational Research* 44:443-55; February 1951.

BOYD, Gertrude, and SCHWIERING, O. C. "A Survey of Child Guidance and Remedial Reading Practices." *Journal of Educational Research* 43:494-506; March 1950.

BRANNON, W. T. *"Yellow Kid" Weil:* The Autobiography of America's Master Swindler. Chicago: Ziff-Davis Publishing Co., 1948. 297 p.

BRISTOL, Margaret C. "Basic Concepts in Case Work Practice." *Sociology and Social Research* 23:447-54; May-June 1939.

BRISTOL, Margaret C. *Handbook on Social Case Recording.* Chicago: University of Chicago Press, 1936. xii + 219 p.

BROWER, Daniel, and ABT, Lawrence E., Editors. *Progress in Clinical Psychology.* New York: Grune and Stratton, 1952. 340 p.

BROWN, Andrew W. "Methods and Techniques in Clinical Psychology." *Methods of Psychology.* Edited by T. G. Andrews. New York: John Wiley and Sons, 1948. Chapter 19, p. 569-94.

BROWN, C. A. P. "Social Status As It Affects Psychotherapy." *Journal of Educational Sociology* 25:164-68; November 1951.

BRUECKNER, L. J., and Others. *Educational Diagnosis.* Thirty-fourth Yearbook of the National Society for the Study of Education. Bloomington, Ill.: Public School Publishing Co., 1935. x + 564 p.

BRUNNER, E. deS. "How to Study a Community." *Teachers College Record* 42:483-92; March 1941.

BRUNO, Frank J. *Trends in Social Work.* New York: Columbia University Press, 1948. xvi + 387 p.

BRUNO, Frank J. "Twenty-Five Years of Schools of Social Work." *Social Service Review* 18:152-64; June 1944.

BUGENTAL, James F. T. "Clinical Approach to the Guidance of the Superior Adult." *Peabody Journal of Education* 25:268-82; May 1948.

BÜHLER, Charlotte B. "Techniques for Studying Individual Children." *California Journal of Elementary Education* 21:58-63; February 1953.

BURGESS, E. W. "An Experiment in the Standardization of the Case-Study Method." *Sociometry* 4:329-48; November 1941.

BURTON, Arthur, and HARRIS, R. E., Editors. *Case Histories in Clinical and Abnormal Psychology*. New York: Harper and Bros., 1947. 680 p.

BUTLER, John M. "On the Role of Directive and Non-Directive Techniques in the Counseling Process." *Educational and Psychological Measurement* 8: 201-9; Summer 1948.

BYCHOWSKI, Gustav, and DESPERT, J. Louise, Editors. *Specialized Techniques in Psychotherapy*. New York: Basic Books, Inc., 1952. xii + 371 p.

CABOT, P. S. de Q. *Juvenile Delinquency:* A Critical Annotated Bibliography. New York: H. W. Wilson Co., 1946. 166 p.

CAIN, Leo F., MICHAELIS, John U., and EURICH, Alvin C. "Prognosis." *Encyclopedia of Educational Research*. Revised Edition. Edited by Walter S. Monroe. New York: Macmillan Co., 1950. p. 874-94.

CAMERON, Norman. *The Psychology of Behavior Disorders*. Boston: Houghton Mifflin Co., 1947. xxi + 662 p.

CARNES, Earl F., and ROBINSON, Francis P. "The Role of Client Talk in the Counseling Interview." *Educational and Psychological Measurement* 8: 635-44; Winter 1948.

CARR, Lowell J., and STERMER, James E. *Willow Run:* A Study of Industrialization and Cultural Inadequacy. New York: Harper and Bros., 1952. xxii + 406 p.

CASTORE, George F. "Attitudes of Students Toward the Case Method of Instruction in a Human Relations Course." *Journal of Educational Research* 45:201-13; November 1951.

CHAPIN, F. S., and Others. "The Main Methods of Sociological Research." *Sociology and Social Research* 33: 3-19; September-October 1948.

CHARNOW, John. *Topics for Research Concerning Public Assistance Programs*. Washington: Committee on Social Security, Social Science Research Council, 1941. 72 p.

CHOPE, H. D. "Case Method in Teaching Public Health Administration." *American Journal of Public Health* 34:605-10; June 1944.

CLARK, Elizabeth W. "The Challenge of Transplanted People for Casework." *Journal of Social Casework* 29:14-17; January 1948.

CLARK, Kenneth E. "The APA Study of Psychologists." *American Psychologist* 9:114-16; March 1954.

CLARKE, Helen I. *Principles and Practice of Social Work*. New York: Appleton-Century-Crofts, 1947. 450 p.

CLIFTON, Eleanor, and HOLLIS, Florence, Editors. *Child Therapy:* A Casework Symposium. New York: Family Service Association of America, 1948. 217 p.

COFFEY, Hubert, and Others. "A Technique of Group Psychotherapy." *Journal of Social Issues* 6:25-36; 1950.

COLBY, Kenneth M. *A Primer for Psychotherapists*. New York: Ronald Press Co., 1951. viii + 167 p.

COLEMAN, JULES V. "Distinguishing between Psychotherapy and Casework." *Journal of Social Casework* 30: 244-51; June 1949.

COLLIER, Rex M. "A Basis for Integration Rather Than Fragmentation in Psychotherapy." *Journal of Consulting Psychology* 14:199-205; June 1950.

COMBS, Arthur W. "Phenomenological Concepts in Nondirective Therapy." *Journal of Consulting Psychology* 12:197-208; July-August 1948.

Committee on Training in Clinical Psychology of the American Psychological Association. "Recommended Graduate Training Program in Clinical Psychology." *American Psychologist* 2:539-58; December 1947.

CONN, Jacob H. "Play-Interview as an Investigative and Therapeutic Procedure." *Nervous Child* 7:257-86; July 1948.

CONRAD, Dorothy C. "An Empirical Study of the Concept of Psychotherapeutic Success." *Journal of Consulting Psychology* 16:92-97; April 1952.

CORRELL, Malcolm. "Case Study in Scientific Inquiry: Atmospheric Pressure, Including Baliani's Ignored Letter." *Journal of General Education* 6:280-91; July 1952.

COTTRELL, L. S. "The Case-Study Method in Prediction." *Sociometry* 4:358-70; November 1941.

COWELL, Charles C. "Records of Developmental Growth." *Educational Research Bulletin* 19:223-30, 244; April 10, 1940.

COYLE, Grace. *Group Experience and Democratic Values.* New York: Women's Press, 1948. 185 p.

COYLE, Grace. *Studies in Group Behavior.* New York: Harper and Bros., 1937. x + 258 p.

CREEGAN, Robert F. "Case Methods 'Unlimited' " ? *School and Society* 74:214-16; October 6, 1951.

CUSTANCE, John. *Wisdom, Madness and Folly:* The Philosophy of a Lunatic. New York: Pellegrini and Cudahy, 1951. 254 p. Mostly written in a mental hospital by a manic-depressive patient. Compare with Beers, *A Mind That Found Itself.*

DALY, Dorothy B. *Case Work Practice in Public Assistance Administration.* Chicago: American Public Welfare Association, 1942. 158 p.

DARLEY, J. G. *Testing and Counseling in the High School Guidance Program.* Chicago: Science Research Associates, 1943. 212 p.

DARLEY, J. G. "The Structure of the Systematic Case Study in Individual Diagnosis and Counseling." *Journal of Consulting Psychology* 4:215-20; November-December, 1940.

DAY, Florence R. "Problems of Collaboration between the Clinic Center and the Psychology Department in Providing Clinical Experience." *Journal of Consulting Psychology* 13:272-78; August 1949.

DE GRAZIA, Sebastian. *Errors of Psychotherapy.* New York: Doubleday and Co., 1952. 288 p.

DERI, Susan, and Others. "Techniques for the Diagnosis and Measurement of Intergroup Attitudes and Behavior." *Psychological Bulletin* 45:248-71; May 1948.

DEJOGHN, Jan F. "A European Experiment in Casework Teaching." *Social Casework* 34:9-17; January 1953.

DE SCHWEINITZ, Karl, and Others. *Teaching Social Case Work.* New York: Family Welfare Association of America, 1940. 51 p.

DEMICHAEL, Salvatore G. "Characteristics of a Desirable Psychological Report to the Vocational Counselor." *Journal of Consulting Psychology* 12:432-37; November-December 1948.

DIMOCK, Hedley S., and TRECKER, Harleigh B. *Supervision of Group Work and Recreation.* New York: Association Press, 1949. xv + 280 p.

DITTMANN, Allen T. "The Interpersonal Process in Psychotherapy: Development of a Research Method." *Journal of Abnormal and Social Psychology* 47:236-44; April 1952.

DIXON, Elizabeth S., and BROWNING, Grace A., Editors. *Social Case Records: Family Welfare.* Chicago: University of Chicago Press, 1938. x + 312 p.

DOLLARD, John. *Caste and Class in a Southern Town.* Second Edition. New York: Harper and Bros., 1949. xvi + 502 p.

DOLLARD, John. *Criteria for the Life History.* New Haven: Yale University Press, 1935. vi + 288 p. Reprinted in 1949 by Peter Smith.

DOLLARD, John, AULD, Frank, and WHITE, Alice. *Steps in Psychotherapy.* New York: Macmillan Co., 1953. 222 p.

DONHAM, Wallace B. "Why Experiment? The Case System in College Teaching of Social Science." *Journal of General Education* 3:145-56; January 1949.

DRAKE, Frances, and DRAKE, Charles. *A Human Relations Casebook for Executives and Supervisors.* New York: McGraw-Hill Book Co., 1947. 187 p.

DREIKURS, Rudolf. "Psychotherapy through Child Guidance." *Nervous Child* 8:311-28; July 1949.

DYMOND, Rosalind F. "A Preliminary Investigation of the Relations of Insight and Empathy." *Journal of Consulting Psychology* 12:228-33; July-August 1948.

EDWARDS, A. L., and CRONBACH, L. J. "Experimental Design for Research in Psychotherapy." *Journal of Clinical Psychology* 8:51-59; January 1952.

ELLEDGE, Caroline H. *The Rehabilitation of the Patient:* Social Casework in Medicine. Philadelphia: J. B. Lippincott Co., 1948. xii + 112 p.

ELMER, M. C. *Social Research.* New York: Prentice-Hall, 1939. Chapters 7-8.

EMBREE, R. B. "The Cumulative-Record Card as an Aid to Research." *School Review* 47:425-30; June 1939.

EMBREE, R. B. "Developments in Counseling Bureaus and Clinics." *Educational and Psychological Measurement* 10:465-75; Autumn 1950.

ENGLISH, Horace B. "The Counseling Situation as an Obstacle to Non-directive Therapy." *Journal of Consulting Psychology* 12:217-20; July-August 1948.

ENGLISH, Horace B., and RAIMY, Victor. *Studying the Individual School Child.* New York: Henry Holt and Co., 1941. 131 p.

ERICKSON, Clifford E. *Counseling Interview.* New York: Prentice-Hall, 1950. 174 p.

*Ethical Standards of Psychologists:* A Summary of Ethical Principles. Washington: American Psychological Association, 1953. 19 p.

EVANS, Jean. "Case Reports: Miller." *Journal of Abnormal and Social Psychology* 45:359-79; April 1950.

EYSENCK, H. J. "The Effects of Psychotherapy: An Evaluation." *Journal of Consulting Psychology* 16:319-24; October 1952.

EYSENCK, H. J. "Training in Clinical Psychology: An English Point of View." *American Psychologist* 4:173-76; June 1949.

FAATZ, Anita J. *The Nature of Choice in Casework Process.* Chapel Hill: University of North Carolina Press, 1953. vii + 141 p.

FENLASON, Anne F. *Essentials in Interviewing:* For the Interviewer Offering Professional Services. New York: Harper and Bros., 1952. xi + 352 p.

FENLASON, Anne F., and HUFF, Mary L. "The Follow-up: The Client's Own Story of Social Case Treatment." *Social Forces* 16:372-80; March 1938.

FENLASON, Anne F., and LEAHLY, Alice M. "A Study of the Content of Social Case Work." *Social Forces* 14:538-46; May 1936.

FENLASON, Anne F., and Others. "Some Concepts of Social Case Work." *Social Forces* 16:75-83, October 1937; 17:372-79, 522-26, March, May, 1939.

FENSTERHEIM, Herbert, and BIRCH, Herbert G. "A Case Study of Group Ideology and Individual Adjustment." *Journal of Abnormal and Social Psychology* 45:710-20; October 1950.

FENTON, Norman. *The Counselor's Approach to the Home.* School Case Work Manuals, No. 1. Stanford University, Calif.: Stanford University Press, 1943. 32 p.

FENTON, Norman. *The Counselor's Interview with the Student.* School Case Work Manuals, No. 2. Stanford University, Calif.: Stanford University Press, 1943. 36 p.

FENTON, Norman. *Mental Hygiene in School Practice.* Stanford University, Calif.: Stanford University Press, 1943. xvi + 455 p.

FENTON, Norman, and LOUTTIT, C. M. "Child-Guidance Clinics." *Encyclopedia of Educational Research.* Revised Edition. Edited by Walter S. Monroe. New York: Macmillan Co., 1950. p. 197-99.

FENTON, Norman, and LOUTTIT, C. M. "Problem Children and Delinquents." *Encyclopedia of Educational Research.* Revised Edition. Edited by Walter S. Monroe. New York: Macmillan Co., 1950. p. 868-74.

FERGUSON, Leonard W. *Personality Measurement.* New York: McGraw-Hill Book Co., 1952.

FERNALD, Grace M. *Remedial Techniques in Basic School Subjects.* New York: McGraw-Hill Book Co., 1943. xv + 349 p.

FESTINGER, Leon, and KATZ, Daniel, Editors. *Research Methods in the Behavioral Sciences.* New York: Dryden Press, 1953.

FIEDLER, Fred E. "The Concept of an Ideal Therapeutic Relationship." *Journal of Consulting Psychology* 14:239-245; August 1950.

FINK, A. E. *The Field of Social Work.* New York: Henry Holt and Co., 1942. x + 518 p.

FISHER, V. E. *The Meaning and Practice of Psychotherapy.* New York: Macmillan Co., 1950. xv + 411 p.

FLORY, Charles D. "Cumulative Records for Research Purposes." *Journal of Educational Research* 30:157-68; November 1936.

FORD, Clellan S. *Smoke from Their Fires:* The Life of a Kwakiutl Chief. New Haven: Yale University Press, 1941. xiii + 248 p.

FOREMAN, Paul B. "The Theory of Case Studies." *Social Forces* 26:408-19; May 1948.

FRAIBERG, Selma "Some Aspects of Casework with Children: Part I, Understanding the Child Client." *Social Casework* 33:374-81; November 1952.

FRAIBERG, Selma. "Some Aspects of Casework with Children: Part II, Helping with Critical Situations." *Social Casework* 33:429-35; December 1952.

FREEMAN, Lucy. *Fight Against Fears.* New York: Crown Publishers, 1951. 332 p. A personal account of a woman's psychoanalysis.

FRENCH, David G. *An Approach to Measuring Results in Social Work.* New York: Columbia University Press, 1952. xiv + 178 p.

FRENCH, Lois M. *Psychiatric Social Work.* New York: Commonwealth Fund, 1940. xvi + 344 p.

FRIEDLANDER, Kate. *The Psycho-analytical Approach to Juvenile Delinquency:* Theory, Case-studies, Treatment. New York: International Universities Press, 1947. vii + 296 p.

FRINGS, John. "What About Brief Services?—A Report of a Study of Short-Term Cases." *Social Casework* 32: 236-41; June 1951.

FROMM-REICHMANN, Frieda. *Principles of Intensive Psychotherapy.* Chicago: University of Chicago Press, 1950. xv + 246 p.

FULLER, R. C., and MYERS, R. R. "The National History of a Social Problem." *American Sociological Review* 6:320-29; June 1941.

FURFEY, Paul H. *The Scope and Method of Sociology:* A Metasociological Treatise. New York: Harper and Bros., 1953. xii + 556 p.

CASE AND CLINICAL STUDIES    783

GARDNER, Burleigh B. *Case Studies for Interviewing Methods and Techniques.* Chicago: University of Chicago Bookstore, 1944. 101 p.

GARRETT, Annette. "Historical Survey of the Evolution of Casework." *Journal of Social Casework* 30:219-29; June 1949.

GARRETT, Annette. "The Professional Base of Social Case Work." *Family: Journal of Social Case Work* 27:167-74; July 1946.

GAW, Esther A. "Case-Study Techniques." *Journal of Higher Education* 14: 37-40, 58; January 1943.

GEE, Wilson. *Social Science Research Methods.* New York: Appleton-Century-Crofts, 1950. p. 230-51.

GESELL, Arnold. *Studies in Child Development.* New York: Harper and Bros., 1948. x + 224 p.

GESELL, Arnold. *Wolf Child and Human Child:* A Narrative Interpretation of the Life History of Kamala, the Wolf Girl. New York: Harper and Bros., 1941. 107 p.

GESELL, Arnold, and AMATRUDA, Catherine S. *Developmental Diagnosis:* Normal and Abnormal Child Development, Clinical Methods and Practical Applications. Revised Edition. New York: Paul B. Hoeber, 1947. xvi + 496 p.

GESELL, Arnold, and Others. *Biographies of Child Development.* New York: Paul B. Hoeber, 1939. xvii + 328 p.

GINZBERG, Eli, and BRAY, Douglas W. *The Uneducated.* New York: Columbia University Press, 1953. xxv + 246 p. Case histories from civilian and military life.

GIOSEFFI, William. "The Relationship of Culture to the Principles of Casework." *Social Casework* 32:190-96; May 1951.

GLADFELTER, Millard E. "Community College Case History." *School and Society* 71:353-56; June 10, 1950.

GLUECK, Sheldon, and GLUECK, Eleanor. *Criminal Careers in Retrospect.* New York: Commonwealth Fund, 1943. xiv + 380 p.

GLUECK, Sheldon, and GLUECK, Eleanor. *Delinquents in the Making:* Paths to Prevention. New York: Harper and Bros., 1952. viii + 214 p.

GLUECK, Sheldon, and GLUECK, Eleanor. *Unraveling Juvenile Delinquency.* New York: Commonwealth Fund, 1950. xv + 399 p.

GOLDBERG, H. L. *Child Offenders:* A Study in Diagnosis and Treatment. New York: Grune and Stratton, 1948. 215 p.

GOMBERG, M. R.; FIZDALE, Ruth E.; and BROWN, Meyer. *Studies in the Practice of Family Case Work.* Brooklyn, New York: Jewish Family Welfare Society, 1942. 93 p.

GOOD, Carter V. "Case and Cumulative Records." *Journal of Exceptional Children* 10:78-84; December 1943.

GOOD, Carter V. "Case Study of Exceptional Children." *Journal of Exceptional Children* 10:35-40, 56; November 1943.

GOOD, Carter V. "The Sequence of Steps in Case Study and Case Work." *Educational Research Bulletin* 21:161-71; September 16, 1942.

GOOD, Carter V. "Problems and Techniques of Educational Diagnosis and Adjustment." *School and Society* 48:261-67; August 27, 1938.

GOOD, Carter V., BARR, A. S., and SCATES, Douglas E. *The Methodology of Educational Research.* New York: Appleton-Century-Crofts, 1936. p. 565-75, 589-92.

GOODE, William J., and HATT, Paul K. *Methods in Social Research.* New York: McGraw-Hill Book Co., 1952. p. 330-40.

GORLOW, L.; HOCH, E. L.; and TELSCHOW, E. *The Nature of Nondirective Group Psychotherapy.* New York: Bureau of Publications, Teachers College, Columbia University, 1952. viii + 143 p.

GRECO, Marshall C. *Group Life:* The Nature and Treatment of Its Specific Conflicts. New York: Philosophical Library, 1950. xvi + 357 p.

GREENLEAF, W. J. "Sociodrama as a Guidance Technique." *California Journal of Secondary Education* 26:71-75; February 1951.

GREENWOOD, Ernest, and MASSARIK, Fred. "Some Methodological Problems in Social Work Research." *American Sociological Review* 15:546-550; August 1950.

GREGORY, Jean L. "The Generic and Specific Aspects of a Family Casework Program." *Social Casework* 31:284-291; July 1950.

GRIFFITHS, Daniel E., and HOBDAY, Arthur F. "A New Kind of Case Study." *Educational Research Bulletin* 31:19-21, 28; January 16, 1952.

GRUMMON, Donald L., and GORDON, Thomas. "The Counseling Center at the University of Chicago." *American Psychologist* 3:166-71; May 1948.

GUTHEIL, Emil A., Editor. *The Autobiography of Wilhelm Stekel:* The Life Story of a Pioneer Psychoanalyst. New York: Liveright Publishing Corporation, 1950. ix + 293 p.

HAAS, Robert B., Editor. *Psychodrama and Sociodrama in American Education.* New York: Beacon House, 1949. xii + 251 p.

HAHN, Milton E., and MACLEAN, Malcolm S. *General Clinical Counseling in Educational Institutions.* New York: McGraw-Hill Book Co., 1950. xi + 375 p.

HAIGH, Gerard, and KELL, Bill L. "Multiple Therapy as a Method for Training and Research in Psychotherapy." *Journal of Abnormal and Social Psychology* 45:659-66; October 1950.

HAMALAINEN, A. E. *An Appraisal of Anecdotal Records.* Contributions to Education, No. 891. New York: Teachers College, Columbia University, 1943. 88 p.

HAMILTON, Gordon. "Helping People—The Growth of a Profession." *Journal of Social Casework* 29:291-99; October 1948.

HAMILTON, Gordon. *Principles of Social Case Recording.* New York: Columbia University Press, 1946. vii + 142 p.

HAMILTON, Gordon. *Psychotherapy in Child Guidance.* New York: Columbia University Press, 1947. 340 p.

HAMILTON, Gordon. "The Role of Social Casework in Social Policy." *Social Casework* 33:315-24; October 1952.

HAMILTON, Gordon. *Social Case Recording.* New York: Columbia University Press, 1936. vii + 190 p.

HAMILTON, Gordon. *Theory and Practice of Social Case Work.* Revised Edition. New York: Columbia University Press, 1951. vii + 328 p.

HAMMOND, Kenneth R., and ALLEN, Jeremiah M. *Writing Clinical Reports.* New York: Prentice-Hall, 1953. 288 p.

HANDLEY, Katharine N. "Social Casework and Intercultural Problems." *Journal of Social Casework* 28:43-50; February 1947.

HARMS, Ernst. "Play Diagnosis; Preliminary Considerations for a Sound Approach." *Nervous Child* 7:233-46; July 1948.

HARRIS, Joseph P. "The Senatorial Rejection of Leland Olds: A Case Study." *American Political Science Review* 45:674-92; September 1951.

HARRIS, William W. "Bas Relief Projective Technique." *Journal of Psychology* 26:3-17; July 1948.

HARROWER, Molly R., Editor. *Recent Advances in Diagnostic Psychological Testing*. (American Lecture Series, Publication No. 81.) Springfield, Ill.: Charles C. Thomas. x + 120 p.

HAVIGHURST, Robert J., and MORGAN, H. Gerthon. *The Social History of a War-Boom Community*. New York: Longmans, Green and Co., 1951. xix + 356 p.

HAWKES, Anna R. "The Cumulative Record and Its Uses." *The Public School Demonstration Project in Educational Guidance*. Educational Records Bulletin, No. 21. New York: Educational Records Bureau, 1937. p. 37-64.

HECK, Arch O., and Others. "Pupil Personnel Work." *Encyclopedia of Educational Research*. Revised Edition. Edited by Walter S. Monroe. New York: Macmillan Co., 1950. p. 909-48.

HEISER, Karl F. "Survey of Departments Giving Instruction in Clinical Psychology." *American Psychologist* 5:610-19; November 1950.

HENDRY, C. E. *Decade of Group Work*. New York: Association Press, 1948. 189 p.

HERZOG, Elizabeth G. "One Research Project— A Case History." *Social Casework* 34:191-98; May 1953.

HERZOG, Elizabeth G. "What Social Casework Wants of Social Science Research." *American Sociological Review* 16:68-73; February 1951.

HILL, G. W. "The Use of the Culture-Area Concept in Social Research." *American Journal of Sociology* 47:39-47; July 1941.

HILL, Reuben. *Families Under Stress*. New York: Harper and Bros., 1949. x + 443 p.

HINCKLEY, Robert G., and HERMANN, Lydia. *Group Treatment in Psychotherapy*. Minneapolis: University of Minnesota Press, 1951.

HOBBS, Nicholas. "Group Psychotherapy in Preventive Mental Hygiene." *Teachers College Record* 50:170-78; December 1948.

HOBBS, Nicholas, and Others. "Ethical Standards in Clinical and Consulting Relationships." *American Psychologist* 6:57-64; February 1951.

HOBBS, Nicholas, and Others. "Ethical Standards in Clinical and Consulting Relationships." *American Psychologist* 6:145-66; May 1951.

HOBBS, Nicholas, and Others. "Ethical Standards for the Distribution of Psychological Tests and Diagnostic Aids." *American Psychologist* 5:620-26; November 1950.

HOBBS, Nicholas, and Others. "Ethical Standards for Psychology (Professional Relationships, Research, and Writing and Publishing)." *American Psychologist* 6:427-52; August 1951. Includes problems, incidents, and principles of ethics.

HOBBS, Nicholas, and Others. "Ethical Standards for Psychology: Ethical Standards and Public Responsibility, and Ethical Standards in Teaching." *American Psychologist* 6:626-61; November 1951.

HOBBS, Nicholas, and Others. *Ethical Standards of Psychologists*. Washington: American Psychological Association, 1953. xv + 171 p.

HOCHWALD, Hilde L. "The Use of Case Records in Research." *Social Casework* 33:71-76; February 1952.

HOEY, Jane M. "Social Work: Its Basc, Skills, and Relation to Other Fields." *Social Casework* 31:399-410; December 1950.

HOFSTEIN, Saul. "A Casework Approach to Camp Intake and Follow-up." *Journal of Social Casework* 28:261-69; July 1947.

HOLLINGWORTH, Harry L. *Leta Stetter Hollingworth: A Biography*. Lincoln: University of Nebraska Press, 1943. 228 p.

HOLLIS, Ernest V., and TAYLOR, Alice L. *Social Work Education in the United States:* Report of a Study Made for the National Council on Social Work Education. New York: Columbia University Press, 1951. xviii + 422 p.

HOLLIS, Florence. "The Relationship between Psychosocial Diagnosis and Treatment." *Social Casework* 32:67-74; February 1951.

HOLLIS, Florence. *Social Case Work in Practice:* Six Case Studies. New York: Family Welfare Association of America, 1939. v + 313 p.

HOLLIS, Florence. "The Techniques of Casework." *Journal of Social Casework* 30:235-44; June 1949.

HOLLIS, Florence. *Women in Marital Conflict:* A Casework Study. New York: Family Service Association of America, 1949. 236 p.

HOLMAN, C. T. *Getting Down to Cases:* A Case and Method Manual for Personal Counseling. New York: Macmillan Co., 1942. 207 p.

HOLT, Robert R. "Some Statistical Problems in Clinical Research." *Educational and Psychological Measurement* 10:609-27; Winter 1950.

HORNER, Francis J. *Case History of Japan.* New York: Sheed and Ward, 1948. xviii + 260 p.

HOUSE, F. N. "Statistical Methods and Case Studies." *Development of Sociology.* New York: McGraw-Hill Book Co., 1936. p. 367-76.

HUMPHREY, N. D. "The Concept of Culture in Social Case Work." *Sociology and Social Research* 26:53-60; September-October 1941.

HUNT, Howard F. "On Goals, Methods and Tactics in Psychotherapy." *Journal of Consulting Psychology* 12:68-75; March-April 1948.

HUNT, J. McV. "Measuring Movement in Casework." *Journal of Social Casework* 29:343-51; November 1948.

HUNT, J. McV., Editor. *Personality and the Behavior Disorders.* New York: Ronald Press Co., 1949. 1242 p. 2 vols.

HUNT, J. McV. "A Social Agency as a Setting for Research—The Institute of Welfare Research." *Journal of Consulting Psychology* 13:69-81; April 1949.

HUNT, J. McV. "Toward an Integrated Program of Research on Psychotherapy." *Journal of Consulting Psychology* 16:237-46; August 1952.

HUNT, J. McV., and KOGAN, L. S. *Measuring Results in Social Casework.* New York: Family Service Association of America, 1950. 79 p.

HUNT, J. McV., BLENKNER, Margaret, and KOGAN, L. S. *Testing Results in Social Casework.* New York: Family Service Association of America, 1950. 64 p.

HUNT, William A. "Clinical Psychology—Science or Superstition," *American Psychologist* 6:683-87; December 1951.

HUSTON, P. E. "An Orientation for Clinical Psychology." *Journal of Consulting Psychology* 12:221-27; July-August 1948.

HUSTON, P. E. "Some Observations on the Orientation of Clinical Psychology." *American Psychologist* 8:191-96; May 1953.

HSU, Francis L. K. *Under the Ancestors' Shadow.* New York: Columbia University Press, 1948. xiv + 317 p.

INGHAM, Harrington V., and LOVE, Leonore R. *The Process of Psychotherapy.* New York: McGraw-Hill Book Co., 1954.

IVES, Kenneth. "The Preparation of Case Balance Sheets." *Journal of Psychology* 35:45-58; January 1953.

JACKSON, Lydia, and TODD, Kathleen M. *Child Treatment and the Therapy of Play.* Second Edition. New York: Ronald Press, 1950. xii + 159 p.

JARVIE, L. L. "A Quantitative Study of Behavior Records." *Research on the Foundations of American Education.* Washington: American Educational Research Association, 1939. p. 106-11.

JARVIE, L. L. "Some Factors Bearing Upon the Use of Observational Records." *Official Report of 1940 Meeting.* Washington: American Educational Research Association, 1940. p. 35-39.

JARVIE, L. L., and ELLINGSON, M. *A Handbook on the Anecdotal Behavior Journal.* Chicago: University of Chicago Press, 1940. xii + 71 p.

JENNINGS, Helen H. *Leadership and Isolation:* A Study of Personality in Interpersonal Relations. New York: Longmans, Green and Co., 1950. xvii + 349 p.

JOEL, Walther, and SHAPIRO, David. "Some Principles and Procedures for Group Psychotherapy." *Journal of Psychology* 29:77-88; January 1950.

JONES, Harold E., and Others. *Development in Adolescence:* Approaches to the Study of the Individual. New York: Appleton-Century-Crofts, 1943. xviii + 166 p.

JONES, M. E. S. "Case Work and Social Work: The Function of Social Service." *Social Forces* 15:377-83; March 1937.

JONES, Maxwell. *The Therapeutic Community.* New York: Basic Books, 1953. 727 p.

JOSSELYN, Irene M. "The Caseworker as Therapist." *Journal of Social Casework* 29:351-55; November 1948.

KARDINER, Abram, and OVESEY, Lionel. *The Mark of Oppression:* A Psychosocial Study of the American Negro. New York: W. W. Norton and Co., 1951. xvii + 396 p. Case histories of 25 American Negroes.

KARSH, Bernard, and Others. "The Union Organizer and His Tactics: A Case Study." *American Journal of Sociology* 59:113-22; September 1953.

KASIUS, Cora. "Casework Developments in Europe." *Social Casework* 32:281-88; July 1951.

KASIUS, Cora, Editor. *A Comparison of Diagnostic and Functional Casework Concepts.* New York: Family Service Association of New York, 1950. 169 p.

KEITH, Arthur. *An Autobiography.* New York: Philosophical Library, 1950. vi + 721 p. An eminent pioneer among anthropologists tells of his life and work.

KELLY, E. Lowell, and Others. "Annual Report of the Committee on Training in Clinical Psychology: 1950." *American Psychologist* 5:585-93; November 1950.

KELLY, E. Lowell, and Others. "Standards for Practicum Training in Clinical Psychology: Tentative Recommendations." *American Psychologist* 5:594-609; November 1950.

KENDALL, Katherine A. "International Social Work: Plans and Prospects." *Social Casework* 32: 275-81; July 1951.

KENT, Grace H. *Mental Tests in Clinics for Children.* New York: D. Van Nostrand, 1950. xii + 180 p.

KINSEY, A. C., and Others. *Sexual Behavior in the Human Female.* Philadelphia: W. B. Saunders Co., 1953. xxx + 842 p.

KINSEY, A. C., and Others. *Sexual Behavior in the Human Male.* Philadelphia: W. B. Saunders Co., 1948. xvi + 804 p.

KLAPMAN, J. W. *Group Psychotherapy.* New York: Grune and Stratton, 1946. ii + 344 p.

KLEHR, Harold. "Clinical Intuition and Test Scores as a Basis for Diagnosis." *Journal of Consulting Psychology* 13:34-38; February 1949.

KLEIN, Philip. "The Social Theory of Professional Social Work." *Contemporary Social Theory.* New York: D. Appleton-Century Co., 1940. p. 754-92.

KLEIN, Philip. "Social Case Work." *Encyclopedia of the Social Sciences.* New York: Macmillan Co., 1934. Volume 14, p. 173-83.

KLINE, Draza, Overstreet, Helen M., and Others. "Maintaining Foster-Homes through Case-Work Skills." *Social Service Review* 22:324-39; September 1948.

KOGAN, Leonard S. "The Electrical Recording of Social Casework Interviews." *Social Casework* 31:371-78; November 1950.

KOGAN, Leonard S., and others. "Validation of Caseworker Impressions by Verbatim Interview Recording." *Social Casework* 32:376-81; November 1951.

KONOPKA, Gisela. *Therapeutic Group Work with Children.* Minneapolis: University of Minnesota Press, 1949. 134 p.

KOPEL, David, and Geerdes, Harold. "A Survey of Clinical Procedures in the Diagnosis and Treatment of Poor Reading." *Journal of Educational Psychology* 35:1-16; January 1944.

KORNER, Anneliese F. "Theoretical Considerations Concerning the Scope and Limitations of Projective Techniques." *Journal of Abnormal and Social Psychology* 45:619-27; October 1950.

KRAUS, Hertha. "The Role of Social Casework in American Social Work." *Social Casework* 31:3-11; January 1950.

KRUGMAN, Judith I., and WRIGHTSTONE, J. Wayne. *A Guide to the Use of Anecdotal Records.* Educational Research Bulletin of the Bureau of Reference, Research and Statistics, No. 11. New York: Board of Education, May 1949. 33 p.

KUBIE, Lawrence S. "Research in Psychiatry Is Starving to Death." *Science* 116:239-43; September 5, 1952.

LANE, Lionel C. " 'Aggressive' Approach in Preventive Casework with Children's Problems." *Social Casework* 33:61-66; February 1952.

LANGFELD, Herbert S., and Others, Editors. *A History of Psychology in Autobiography.* Vol. 4. Worcester: Clark University Press, 1952. xii + 356 p.

LAW, Stanley G. *Therapy through Interview.* New York: McGraw-Hill Book Co., 1948. xiii + 313 p.

LAZARSFIELD, Paul F., and ROBINSON, W. S. "The Quantification of Case Studies." *Journal of Applied Psychology* 24:817-25; December 1940.

LEBO, Dell. "The Present Status of Research on Nondirective Play Therapy." *Journal of Consulting Psychology* 17:177-83; June 1953.

LEFEVER, D. Welty, and Others. "Guidance and Counseling." *Review of Educational Research* 21:71-167; April 1951.

LEVINE, Rae A. "Case Work's Stake in Research." *Family: Journal of Social Case Work* 27:151-55; June 1946.

LEWIS, Oscar. "An Anthropological Approach to Family Studies." *American Journal of Sociology* 55:468-75; March 1950.

LEWIS, Oscar. "Urbanization without Breakdown: A Case Study." *Scientific Monthly* 75:31-41; July 1952.

LIEBERMAN, Joshua, Editor. *New Trends in Group Work.* New York: Association Press, 1938. xii + 229 p.

LINDNER, R. M. *Rebel Without a Cause:* The Hypnoanalysis of a Criminal Psychopath. New York: Grune and Stratton, 1944. 310 p.

LITTLE, Roger W. "The Social Side of Casework." *Social Casework* 31:162-64; April 1950.

LITTLE, Ruby. "Diagnostic Recording." *Journal of Social Casework* 30: 15-19; January 1949.

LORAND, Sandor. *Clinical Studies in Psychoanalysis.* New York: International Universities Press, 1951. 272 p.

LOUTTIT, C. M. *Clinical Psychology.* Revised Edition. New York: Harper and Bros., 1947. xviii + 661 p.

LOWRY, Fern. "Case-Work Principles for Guiding the Worker in Contacts of Short Duration." *Social Service Review* 22:234-39; June 1948.

LOWRY, Fern, Editor. *Readings in Social Case Work, 1920-1938.* New York: Columbia University Press, 1939. xiii + 810 p.

LUCHINS, Abraham S. "Patients View the Therapist: A Training and Research Device." *Journal of Consulting Psychology* 15:24-31; February 1951.

LUCHINS, Abraham S. "Problem-Centered Training in the Development of the Clinician." *American Psychologist* 3:203-5; June 1948.

LUCHINS, Abraham S. "Specialized Audio-Aids in a Group Psychotherapy Program for Psychotics." *Journal of Consulting Psychology* 12:313-20; September-October 1948.

LUCHINS, Abraham S. "Towards an Experimental Clinical Psychology." *Journal of Personality* 20:440-56; June 1952.

LUNDBERG, G. A. *Social Research:* A Study in Methods of Gathering Data. Second Edition. New York: Longmans, Green and Co., 1942. xxi + 426 p.

LUNDBERG, G. A. "Case Studies vs. Statistical Methods: An Issue Based on Misunderstanding." *Sociometry* 4:379-83; November 1941.

LUNDIN, William H. and ARONOV, Bernard M. "The Use of Co-therapists in Group Psychotherapy." *Journal of Consulting Psychology* 16:76-80; February 1952.

MAAS, Henry S., and VARON, Edith. "The Case Worker in Clinical and Socio-Psychological Research." *Social Service Review* 23:302-14; September 1949.

MADDEN, J. W., and COMPTON, W. R. *Cases and Materials on Domestic Relations.* St. Paul, Minn.: West Publishing Co., 1940. 901 p.

MADGE, John. *The Tools of Social Science.* New York: Longmans, Green and Co., 1953. 308 p.

MAGARET, Ann. "Generalization in Successful Psychotherapy." *Journal of Consulting Psychology* 14:64-70; February 1950.

MARCUS, Grace F. "Family Casework in 1948." *Journal of Social Casework* 29:261-79; July 1948.

MARZOLF, S. S. *Studying the Individual:* A Manual on the Case Study for Guidance Workers and Psycho-Clinicians. Minneapolis: Burgess, 1940 vii + 181 p.

MAXFIELD, F. N. "The Case Study." *Educational Research Bulletin* 9:117-22; March 5, 1930.

McCORMICK, C. F. "The Anecdotal Record in the Appraisal of Personality." *School and Society* 53:126-27; January 25, 1941.

McCORMICK, Mary J. *Thomistic Philosophy in Social Casework.* New York: Columbia University Press, 1948. 148 p.

McDONAGH, E. C. "An Approach to Clinical Sociology." *Sociology and Social Research* 28:376-83; May-June, 1944.

"Medical Psychotherapy (Psychiatry) and Non-Medical Psychotherapy." *Nervous Child* 8:375-83; July 1949.

MEIER, Elizabeth G. "Interrelationship of Social Causes and Casework in Child Welfare." *Social Casework* 31:105-112; March 1950.

MELTZER, H. "Approach of the Clinical Psychologist to Management Relationships." *Journal of Consulting Psychology* 8:165-74; May-June, 1944.

MENNINGER, William C. "The Relationship of Clinical Psychology and Psychiatry." *American Psychologist* 5:3-15; January 1950.

MENSH, Ivan N. "Statistical Techniques in Present-Day Psychodiagnostics." *Psychological Bulletin* 47:475-92; November 1950.

MERRILL, Maud A. *Problems of Child Delinquency.* Boston: Houghton Mifflin Co., 1947. xxiii + 403 p.

MILES, A. P. "Changing Concepts in Social Case Work." *Southwestern Social Science Quarterly* 24:36-45; June 1943.

MILLARD, Cecil V. *Case Inventory for the Study of Child Development.* Minneapolis: Burgess Publishing Co., 1950. 29 p.

MINER, Roy W., Editor. *Current Trends in Clinical Psychology.* Annals, New York Academy of Sciences, Vol. 49, 1948. 62 p.

MONLIN, Chiang. *Tides from the West:* A Chinese Autobiography. New Haven: Yale University Press, 1947. 282 p.

MONROE, Ruth L. "Diagnosis of Learning Disabilities through a Projective Technique." *Journal of Consulting Psychology* 13:390-95; December 1949.

MORENO, J. L. *Group Psychotherapy.* New York: Beacon House, 1945. xiv + 305 p.

MORENO, J. L., and ENNEIS, J. M. *Hypnodrama and Psychodrama.* New York: Beacon House, 1950. 56 p.

MORRIS, Cherry, Editor. *Social Case-work in Great Britain.* London: Faber and Faber, 1950. 223 p.

MORRISON, Henry C. *The Practice of Teaching in the Secondary School.* Revised Edition. Chicago: University of Chicago Press, 1931. Chapter 30.

MOUSTAKAS, Clark E. *Children in Play Therapy:* A Key to Understanding Normal and Disturbed Emotions. New York: McGraw-Hill Book Co., 1953. ix + 218 p.

MOWRER, O. H., and Others. "Annual Report of the Committee on Training in Clinical Psychology." *American Psychologist* 6:612-17; November 1951.

MOWRER, O. H., and Others. *Psychotherapy:* Theory and Research. New York: Ronald Press Co., 1953. 700 p.

MUDD, Emily H., and FROSCHER, Hazel Bazett. "Effects on Casework of Obtaining Research Material." *Social Casework* 31:11-17; January 1950.

MUENCH, George A. *An Evaluation of Non-Directive Psychotherapy.* Stanford University, Calif.: Stanford University Press, 1947. 163 p.

MURCHISON, Carl, Editor. *A History of Psychology in Autobiography.* Worcester: Clark University Press, 1930, 1932, 1936. 3 vols. xviii + 516, xx + 407, xx + 327 p.

NEWSTETTER, W. I.; FELDSTEIN, M. J.; and NEWCOMB, T. M. *Group Adjustment.* Cleveland: Western Reserve University, 1938. xv + 154 p.

NICOLS, J. Ernest. *Normal and Abnormal Personality.* New York: Macmillan Co., 1948. viii + 96 p.

ODUM, H. W., and JOCHER, Katharine. *An Introduction to Social Research.* New York: Henry Holt and Co., 1929. Chapter 15.

OLSON, W. C. "Case Study." *The Scientific Movement in Education.* Thirty-seventh Yearbook of the National Society for the Study of Education, Part II. Bloomington, Ill.: Public School Publishing Co., 1938. p. 329-32.

OLSON, W. C. "The Case Method," Chapter 6 in "Methods of Research in Education." *Review of Educational Research* 9:449-672; December 1939.

ORMSBY, Ralph. "Group Psychiatric Consultation in a Family Casework Agency." *Social Casework* 31:361-65; November 1950.

ORMSBY, Ralph. "Interpretations in Casework Therapy." *Journal of Social Casework* 29:135-41; April 1948.

PAGE, James D. *Abnormal Psychology:* A Clinical Approach to Psychological Deviants. New York: McGraw-Hill Book Co., 1947. xvii + 441 p.

PANZER, Joseph J. "Cumulative Record, Tool of Good Administration." *Catholic Educational Review* 47:315-18; May 1949.

PARADISE, Viola. *Toward Public Understanding of Casework.* New York: Russell Sage Foundation, 1948. 242 p.

PASCAL, G. R., and Others. "Prognostic Criteria in the Case Histories of Hospitalized Mental Patients." *Journal of Consulting Psychology* 17:163-71; June 1953.

PATTERSON, C. H. "Is Psychotherapy Dependent Upon Diagnosis?" *American Psychologist* 3:155-59; May 1948.

PENNINGTON, L. A., and BERG, I. A., Editors. *An Introduction to Clinical Psychology.* New York: Ronald Press Co., 1948. xv + 595 p.

PEPINSKY, Harold B. *The Selection and Use of Diagnostic Categories in Clinical Counseling.* Stanford University, Calif.: Stanford University Press, 1948. 140 p.

PERLMAN, Helen H. "Case-Work Services in Public Welfare." *Social Service Review* 21:190-96; June 1947.

PERLMAN, Helen H. "The Caseworker's Use of Collateral Information." *Social Casework* 32:325-33; October 1951.

PERLMAN, Helen H. "Content in Basic Social Case Work." *Social Service Review* 21:76-84; March 1947.

PERLMAN, Helen H. "Generic Aspects of Specific Case-Work Settings." *Social Service Review* 23:293-301; September 1949.

PERLMAN, Helen H. "The Lecture as a Method in Teaching Case Work." *Social Service Review* 25:19-32; March 1951.

PERLMAN, Helen H. "Teaching Case Work by the Discussion Method." *Social Service Review* 24:334-46; September 1950.

PICKFORD, Ralph W. "Personality and the Interpretation of Pictures: New Projection Technique." *Journal of Personality* 17:210-20; December 1948.

POLANSKY, N. A. "How Shall a Life-History Be Written?" *Character and Personality* 9:188-207; March 1941.

POLLAK, Gertrude K. "The Contribution of Casework to Family Life Education." *Journal of Social Casework* 30:362-68; November 1949.

POLLAK, Otto. "Cultural Dynamics in Casework." *Social Casework* 34:279-84; July 1953.

POLLAK, Otto. "Relationships Between Social Science and Child Guidance Practice." *American Sociological Review* 16:61-67; February 1951.

POLLAK, Otto. *Social Adjustment in Old Age:* A Research Planning Report. New York: Social Science Research Council, 1948. xi + 199 p.

POLLAK, Otto, and Others. *Social Science and Psychotherapy for Children.* New York: Russell Sage Foundation, 1952. 242 p.

POOLE, Florence. "An Analysis of the Characteristics of School Social Work." *Social Service Review* 23:454-59; December 1949.

PORTER, E. H., Jr. *An Introduction to Therapeutic Counseling.* Boston: Houghton Mifflin Co., 1950. xi + 223 p. Extracts from cases are used as a test for counselors.

PORTER, E. H., Jr. "On the Nature of Psychotherapeutic Interpretation." *Journal of Consulting Psychology* 16:343-46; October 1952.

PORTEUS, Stanley D. *The Practice of Clinical Psychology*. New York: American Book Co., 1941. 589 p.

POTTER, Muriel. "The Use of Limits in Reading Therapy." *Journal of Consulting Psychology* 14:250-255; August 1950.

POTTER, Van R., Editor. *Methods in Medical Research*. Vol. 1. Chicago: Year Book Pub., 1948. xiii + 372 p.

POWDERMAKER, Florence B., and FRANK, Jerome D. *Group Psychotherapy:* Studies in Methodology of Research and Therapy. Report of a group psychotherapy research project of the U. S. Veterans Administration. Cambridge: Harvard University Press, 1953. xv + 615 p.

PRESTON, Malcolm G., and Others. "An Experimental Study of a Method for Abstracting the Content of Social Case Records." *Journal of Abnormal and Social Psychology* 45:628-46; October 1950.

PRESTON, Malcolm G., MUDD, Emily H., and FROSCHER, Hazel B. "Factors Affecting Movement in Casework." *Social Casework* 34:103-11; March 1953.

PREU, Paul W. *Outline of Psychiatric Case-Study*. New York: Harper and Bros., 1939. 154 p.

QUAIN, Buell. *Fijian Village*. Chicago: University of Chicago Press, 1948. xvii + 459 p.

RABIN, Albert I. "Doctoral Dissertations in Clinical Training Programs: 1948-1953." *American Psychologist* 9:114-16; March 1954.

RAIMY, Victor C., Editor. *Training in Clinical Psychology*. New York: Prentice-Hall, 1950. xix + 253 p.

RALL, Mary E. "The Effective Use of Case-Work Principles in the Family Agency." *Social Service Review* 24:327-33; September 1950.

RANDALL, J. A. "The Anecdotal Behavior Journal." *Progressive Education* 13: 21-26; January 1936.

RASKIN, Nathaniel J. "The Development of Nondirective Therapy." *Journal of Consulting Psychology* 12:92-110; March-April, 1948.

RECKLESS, Walter C. "Juvenile Delinquency." *Encyclopedia of Educational Research*. Revised Edition. Edited by Walter S. Monroe. New York: Macmillan Co., 1950. p. 643-47.

REDFIELD, Robert. *A Village That Chose Progress:* Chan Kom Revisited. Chicago: University of Chicago Press, 1950. xiv + 187 p.

REDFIELD, Robert. "The Natural History of the Folk Society." *Social Forces* 31:224-28; March 1953.

"Research Design in Clinical Psychology; Symposium." *Journal of Clinical Psychology* 8:3-98; January 1952.

REYNOLDS, Rosemary; POWELL, Amy S.; and ZELDITCH, Morris. "Symposium: Casework and the Aging Population." *Journal of Social Casework* 30: 58-65; February 1949.

RICE, S. A., and Others. *Methods in Social Science*. Chicago: University of Chicago Press, 1931. xiv + 822 p.

RICHARDS, T. W. *Modern Clinical Psychology*. New York: McGraw-Hill Book Co., 1946. xi + 331 p.

ROBINSON, Helen. "Technics of Case Study in Reading." *Improving Educational Research*. Washington: American Educational Research Association, 1948. p. 23-28.

ROBINSON, Joseph F. "Current Trends in Child-Guidance Clinics." *Mental Hygiene* 34:106-16; January 1950.

ROBINSON, Virginia P. *A Changing Psychology in Social Case Work*. Chapel Hill: University of North Carolina Press, 1930. xviii + 204 p.

ROBINSON, Virginia P. *Supervision in Social Case Work*. Chapel Hill: University of North Carolina Press, 1936. 199 p.

ROBINSON, Virginia P., Editor. *Training for Skill in Social Case Work*. Philadelphia: University of Pennsylvania Press, 1942. 126 p.

ROE, Anne, and Others. "Training Needs of Psychologists in Practice." *American Psychologist* 4:407-9; October 1949.

ROGERS, Carl R. *Client-Centered Therapy*. Boston: Houghton Mifflin Co., 1951. xii + 560 p.

ROGERS, Carl R. *The Clinical Treatment of the Problem Child*. Boston: Houghton Mifflin Co., 1939. xiii + 393 p.

ROGERS, Carl R. "Coördinated Research in Psychotherapy: Non-objective Introduction." *Journal of Consulting Psychology* 13:149-53; June 1949.

ROGERS, Carl R. *Counseling and Psychotherapy*. Boston: Houghton Mifflin Co., 1942. xiv + 450 p.

ROGERS, Carl R. "A Current Formulation of Client-Centered Therapy." *Social Service Review* 24:442-50; December 1950.

ROGERS, Carl R. "The Interest in the Practice of Psychotherapy." *American Psychologist* 8:48-50; January 1953.

ROGERS, Carl R. "Some Implications of Client-Centered Counseling for College Personnel Work." *Educational and Psychological Measurement* 8:540-49; Autumn 1948.

ROGERS, Carl R. "Where Are We Going in Clinical Psychology?" *Journal of Consulting Psychology* 15:171-77; June 1951.

ROONEY, William S., and Others. "Psychiatric Casework in an Army Setting." *Social Casework* 32:31-7; January 1951.

ROSE, Alvin W. "Projective Techniques in Sociological Research." *Social Forces* 28:175-183; December 1949.

ROSENBERG, Morris, and LAZARSFELD, Paul F., Editors. *Reader in Social Research*. Glencoe, Ill.: Free Press, 1953.

ROSENTHAL, Leslie. "Group Psychotherapy in a Child Guidance Clinic." *Social Casework* 32:337-42; October 1951.

ROSENZWEIG, Saul. *Psychodiagnosis:* An Introduction to Tests in Clinical Psychology. New York: Grune and Stratton, 1949. xii + 380 p.

ROSS, Helen, and JOHNSON, Adelaide M. "The Growing Science of Casework." *Journal of Social Casework* 27:273-78; November 1946.

RUESCH, Jurgen. "Experiments in Psychotherapy: II, Individual Social Techniques." *Journal of Social Psychology* 29:3-28; February 1949.

SACKHEIM, Gertrude. "Suggestions on Recording Techniques." *Journal of Social Casework* 30:20-25; January 1949.

SACKS, Patricia. "Establishing the Diagnosis in Marital Problems." *Journal of Social Casework* 30:181-87; May 1949.

SARGENT, Cyril G., and FLOWER, George E. "The Case Method in Education for Administration: An Addendum." *School and Society* 78:33-36; August 8, 1953.

SAYLES, Mary B. *Child Guidance Cases*. New York: Commonwealth Fund, 1932. xxiii + 584 p.

SCHAFER, Roy. *The Clinical Application of Psychological Tests:* Diagnostic Summaries and Case Studies. Menninger Foundation Monograph Series No. 6. New York: International Universities Press, 1948. 346 p.

SCHAFER, Roy. "Psychological Tests in Clinical Research." *Journal of Consulting Psychology* 13:328-34; October 1949.

SCHARY, Dore. *Case History of a Movie*. New York: Random House, 1950. xix + 242 p.

SCHEIDLINGER, Saul. "Group Therapy—Its Place in Psychotherapy." *Journal of Social Casework* 29:299-304; October 1948.

SCHEIDLINGER, Saul. "The Uses of Social Case-Work Services in Group-Work Agencies." *Social Service Review* 21:208-18; June 1947.

SCHROEDER, P. L., and Others. *Child Guidance Procedures:* Methods and Techniques Employed at the Institute for Juvenile Research. New York: D. Appleton-Century Co., 1937. 358 p.

SCHWEINITZ, Karl de, and Others. *Teaching Social Case Work.* New York: Family Welfare Association of America, 1940. 51 p.

SEARS, Robert R. "Influence of Methodological Factors on Doll Play Performance." *Child Development* 18:190-97; December 1947.

SEEMAN, Julius. "A Study of Preliminary Interview Methods in Vocational Counseling." *Journal of Consulting Psychology* 12:321-30; September-October 1948.

SEGEL, David. *Nature and Use of the Cumulative Record.* Office of Education Bulletin No. 3, 1938. Washington: Government Printing Office, 1938. vi + 48 p.

SELLS, S. B. "Problems of Criteria and Validity in Diagnosis and Therapy." *Journal of Clinical Psychology* 8:23-28; January 1952.

SELLS, Saul R. "Observational Methods of Research," in "Methods of Research and Appraisal in Education." *Review of Educational Research* 18:424-47; December 1948.

SHAFFER, G. Wilson, and LAZARUS, Richard S. *Fundamental Concepts in Clinical Psychology.* New York: McGraw-Hill Book Co., 1952. 540 p.

SHAKOW, David, and Others. "Doctoral Training Programs in Clinical Psychology: 1949." *American Psychologist* 4:331-41; August 1949.

SHAW, Franklin J. "The Role of Reward in Psychotherapy." *American Psychologist* 4:177-79; June 1949.

SHAW, Franklin J. "Some Postulates Concerning Psychotherapy." *Journal of Consulting Psychology* 12:426-31; November 1948.

SHEFFIELD, Ada E. *Social Insight in Case Situations.* New York: D. Appleton-Century Co., 1937. xii + 283 p.

SHERIF, Muzafer, and WILSON, M. O. *Group Relations at the Crossroads.* New York: Harper and Bros., 1953. viii + 379 p.

SHOBEN, Edward J. "Psychotherapy as a Problem in Learning Theory." *Psychological Bulletin* 46:366-92; September 1949.

SHOOBS, Nahum E., and GOLDBERG, George. *Corrective Treatment for Unadjusted Children.* New York: Harper and Bros., 1942. 236 p.

SIKKEMA, Mildred. "An Analysis of the Structure and Practice of School Social Work Today." *Social Service Review* 23:447-53; December 1949.

SIMMONS, Leo W., Editor. *Sun Chief:* The Autobiography of a Hopi Indian. New Haven: Yale University Press, 1942. xii + 460 p.

SLAVSON, Samuel R. *Analytic Group Psychotherapy with Children, Adolescents, and Adults.* New York: Columbia University Press, 1950. ix + 275 p.

SLAVSON, Samuel R. "Authority, Restraint and Discipline in Group Therapy with Children." *Nervous Child* 9 No. 2:187-95; 1951.

SLAVSON, Samuel R. *Child Psychotherapy.* New York: Columbia University Press, 1952. 332 p.

SLAVSON, Samuel R. "Group Psychotherapy in Delinquency Prevention." *Journal of Educational Sociology* 24:45-51; September 1950.

SLAVSON, Samuel R., and Others, "Children's Activity in Casework Therapy." *Journal of Social Casework* 30:136-42; April 1949.

SLAVSON, Samuel R., Editor. *Practice of Group Therapy*. New York: International Universities Press, 1947. 271 p.

SLAWSON, John. "Case Work in an Authoritarian Setting." *Mental Hygiene* 23: 70-79; January 1939.

SMITH, Eugene R., and Others. *Appraising and Recording Student Progress*. Progressive Education Association Commission on the Relation of School and College. New York: Harper and Bros., 1942. 550 p.

SMITH, John C. "Casework on the Campus." *Social Casework* 33:423-29; December 1952.

SMITHIES, Elsie M. *Case Studies of Normal Adolescent Girls*. New York: D. Appleton and Co., 1933. x + 284 p.

SNYDER, W. U., Editor. *Casebook of Non-directive Counseling*. Boston: Houghton Mifflin Co., 1947. viii + 339 p.

SNYGG, Donald, and COMBS, Arthur W. *Individual Behavior*. New York: Harper and Bros., 1949. ix + 386 p.

SPECK, F. G. *Penobscot Man:* The Life History of a Forest Tribe in Maine. Philadelphia: University of Pennsylvania Press, 1940. xx + 325 p.

SPICER, Edward H., Editor. *Human Problems in Technological Change:* A Casebook. New York: Russell Sage Foundation, 1952. 301 p.

Staff of the Reading Clinics of the University of Chicago, *Clinical Studies in Reading, I*. Supplementary Educational Monographs, No. 68. Chicago: University of Chicago Press, 1949. 173 p.

STEIN, Harold. "Preparation of Case Studies: The Problem of Abundance." *American Political Science Review* 45:479-87; June 1951.

STEPHAN, F. F. "Training for Research in Social Welfare." *Journal of Educational Sociology* 9:284-90; January 1936.

STEVENS, G. D. "Suggested Criteria for the Selection of Items for a Cumulative Case Study Record for the Mentally Retarded." *Journal of Educational Research* 39:201-209; November 1945.

STONE, C. P. *Case Histories in Abnormal Psychology*. Stanford University, California: Stanford Bookstore, 1943. v + 98 p.

STONE, G. Raymond. "Prediction in Clinical Psychology and Behavior Theory." *Psychological Review* 59:95-97; March 1952.

STONE, Olive M. "What Can Social Case Work Contribute to the Social Sciences?" *American Sociological Review* 15:66-73; February 1950.

STOUFFER, S. A. "Notes on the Case Study and the Unique Case." *Sociometry* 4:349-57; November 1941.

STRANG, Ruth. *Counseling Techniques in College and Secondary School*. Revised and Enlarged. New York: Harper and Bros., 1949. xi + 302 p.

STRANG, Ruth. "Techniques and Instruments of Mental Hygiene Diagnosis and Therapy," Chapter 7 in "Mental Hygiene and Health Education." *Review of Educational Research* 10:403-504; December 1940.

STRANG, Ruth, and Others. "Pupil Personnel, Guidance, and Counseling." *Review of Educational Research* 12:1-136; February 1942.

STRANG, Ruth, and PANSEGROUW, Debora. "Studies of Individuals," in "Methods of Research and Appraisal in Education." *Review of Educational Research* 18:382-95; December 1948.

STRODE, Josephine. *Introduction to Social Case Work*. New York: Harper and Bros., 1940. xvi + 219 p.

STRODE, Josephine, and STRODE, Pauline R. *Social Skills in Case Work*. New York: Harper and Bros., 1940. x + 195 p.

SULLIVAN, Dorothea F., Editor. *The Practice of Group Work*. New York: Association Press, 1941. x + 230 p.

SWARD, Keith. "Are Psychologists Afraid of Therapy?" *American Psychologist* 5:50-54; February 1950.

SYMONDS, P. M. *Adolescent Fantasy:* An Investigation of the Picture-Story Method of Personality Study. New York: Columbia University Press, 1949. xi + 397 p.

SYMONDS, P. M. *Diagnosing Personality and Conduct.* New York: Century Co., 1931. 602 p.

SYMONDS, P. M. *The Dynamics of Parent-Child Relationships.* New York: Bureau of Publications, Teachers College, Columbia University, 1949. 197 p.

SYMONDS, P. M. "Education and Psychotherapy." *Journal of Educational Psychology* 40:1-32; January 1949.

SYMONDS, P. M. "New Directions for Projective Techniques." *Journal of Consulting Psychology* 13:387-89; December 1949.

SYMONDS, P. M. *Psychological Diagnosis in Social Adjustment.* New York: American Book Co., 1934. 362 p.

SYMONDS, P. M., and HESSEL, Martha G. "Development and Educational Significance of Projective Technics in Personality Measurement." *Review of Educational Research* 20:51-62; February 1950.

SYTZ, Florence. "The Unit of Attention in the Case Work Process." *Family: Journal of Social Case Work* 27:135-39; June 1946.

SYTZ, Florence. "The Development of Method in Social Casework." *Journal of Social Case Work* 29:83-88; March 1948.

SYTZ, Florence. "Teaching Recording." *Journal of Social Casework* 30:399-405; December 1949.

TABA, Hilda, BRADY, Elizabeth H., and ROBINSON, John T. *Elementary Curriculum in Intergroup Relations:* Case Studies in Instruction. Washington: American Council on Education, 1950. xiii + 248 p.

TAFT, Jessie. "A Conception of the Growth Process Underlying Social Casework Practice." *Social Casework* 31:311-18; October 1950.

TAFT, Jessie, Editor. *Family Casework and Counseling:* A Functional Approach. Philadelphia: University of Pennsylvania Press, 1948. x + 304 p.

TAFT, Jessie, Editor. *Social Case Work with Children.* Philadelphia: University of Pennsylvania, 1940. 237 p.

TAPPAN, Paul W. *Juvenile Delinquency.* New York: McGraw-Hill Book Co., 1949. x + 614 p.

TAYLOR, Alice L. "Case Recording: An Administrative Responsibility." *Social Casework* 34:240-46; June 1953.

TEAGARDEN, Florence M. "The Principles of Heredity as Applied to the Case Load." *Child Psychology for Professional Workers.* New York: Prentice-Hall, 1940.

TERMAN, Lewis M., and ODEN, Melita H. *The Gifted Child Grows Up:* Genetic Studies of Genius. Stanford University, Calif.: Stanford University Press, 1947. xiv + 450 p.

THEMAN, Viola, and WITTY, Paul. "Case Studies and Genetic Records of Two Gifted Negroes." *Journal of Psychology* 15:165-81; April 1943.

THOMAS, Dorothy V. "The Relationship between Diagnostic Service and Short-Contact Cases." *Social Casework* 32:74-81; February 1951.

THOMPSON, Clare W., and BRADWAY, K. P. "Teaching of Psychotherapy through Content-Free Interviews." *Journal of Consulting Psychology* 14:321-3; August 1950.

THOMPSON, Laura. *Culture in Crisis:* A Study of the Hopi Indians. New York: Harper and Bros., 1950. xxiv + 221 p.

THORNE, F. C. "A Critique of Nondirective Methods of Psychotherapy." *Journal of Abnormal and Social Psychology* 39:459-70; October 1944.

THORNE, F. C. "Principles of Directive Counseling and Psychotherapy." *American Psychologist* 3:160-65, 159; May 1948.

THORNE, F. C. "Rules of Evidence in the Evaluation of the Effects of Psychotherapy." *Journal of Clinical Psychology* 8:38-41; January 1952.

THORPE, Louis P., and KATZ, Barney. *The Psychology of Abnormal Behavior.* New York: Ronald Press Co., 1948. 877 p.

TOWLE, Charlotte. "Case-Work Methods of Helping the Client to Make Maximum Use of His Capacities and Resources." *Social Service Review* 22: 469-79; December 1948.

TOWLE, Charlotte. "Client-Centered Case Work." *Social Service Review* 24: 451-58; December 1950.

TOWLE, Charlotte. "The Contribution of Education for Social Casework to Practice." *Social Casework* 31:318-26; October 1950.

TOWLE, Charlotte. "Selection and Arrangement of Case Material for Orderly Progression in Learning." *Social Service Review* 27:27-54; March 1953.

TOWLE, Charlotte. *Social Case Records from Psychiatric Clinics.* Chicago: University of Chicago Press, 1941. xii + 455 p.

TRAXLER, A. E. "Case-Study Procedures in Guidance." *School Review* 46: 602-10; October 1938.

TRAXLER, A. E. "A Cumulative-Record Form for the Elementary School." *Elementary School Journal* 40:45-54; September 1939.

TRAXLER, A. E. *The Nature and Use of Anecdotal Records.* Educational Records Supplementary Bulletin D. Revised Edition. New York: Educational Records Bureau, 1949. 41 p.

TRAXLER, A. E. "Nonprojective Technics in the Appraisal of Personality." *Growing Points in Educational Research.* Washington: American Educational Research Association, 1949. p. 324-30.

TRECKER, Harleigh B. *Social Group Work:* Principles and Practices. New York: Woman's Press, 1948. vi + 313 p.

TRECKER, Harleigh B. *Group Process in Administration.* New York: Woman's Press, 1946. 127 p.

TREUDLEY, Mary B. "Psychodrama and Social Case Work." *Sociometry* 7: 169-78; May 1944.

WAELDER, Elsie M. "Casework with Marital Problems." *Journal of Social Casework* 28:168-74; May 1947.

WALKER, Charles R. *Steeltown:* An Industrial Case History of the Conflict between Progress and Security. New York: Harper and Bros., 1950. Pp. xv + 284. Case study of an industrial town, done with relation to a decision of the steel company to abandon the town and the plant; one of a series of studies on decision-making.

WALLIN, J. E. W. *Children with Mental and Physical Handicaps.* New York: Prentice-Hall, 1949. xxii + 549 p.

WALLIN, J. E. W. *Personality Maladjustments and Mental Hygiene.* Revised Edition. New York: McGraw-Hill Book Co., 1949. 522 p.

WARNER, W. Lloyd, and Associates. *Democracy in Jonesville:* A Study in Quality and Inequality. New York: Harper and Bros., 1949. 313 p.

WATSON, Robert I. "A Brief History of Clinical Psychology." *Psychological Bulletin* 50:321-46; September 1953.

WATSON, Robert I. *The Clinical Method in Psychology.* New York: Harper and Bros., 1951. xii + 779 p.

WATSON, Robert I., Editor. *Readings in the Clinical Method in Psychology.* New York: Harper and Bros., 1949. xi + 740 p.

WATSON, Robert I. "Research Design and Methodology in Evaluating the Results of Psychotherapy." *Journal of Clinical Psychology* 8:29-33; January 1952.

WATSON, Robert I., and MENSH, Ivan N. "The Evaluation of the Effects of Psychotherapy: I, Sources of Material." *Journal of Psychology* 32:259-73; October 1951.

WATSON, Robert I., and MENSH, Ivan N. "The Evaluation of the Effects of Psychotherapy: II, A Case Study." *Journal of Psychology* 32:275-91; October 1951.

WATSON, Robert I., MENSH, Ivan N., and GILDEA, Edwin F. "The Evaluation of the Effects of Psychotherapy: III, Research Design." *Journal of Psychology* 32:293-308; October 1951.

WATTENBERG, William W., and REDL, Fritz. "Mental Hygiene." *Encyclopedia of Educational Research.* Revised Edition. Edited by Walter S. Monroe. New York: Macmillan Co., 1950. p. 733-45.

WELLS, F. L. "Clinical Psychology in Retrospect and Prospect." *Journal of Psychology* 27:125-42; January 1949.

WERTHEIMER, Rita, and McKINNEY, Fred. "A Case History Blank as a Projective Technique." *Journal of Consulting Psychology* 16:49-60; February 1952.

WHITE, Robert W. *The Abnormal Personality.* New York: Ronald Press Co., 1948. 613 p.

WHITE, Robert W. *Lives in Progress:* A Study of the Natural Growth of Personality. New York: William Sloane Associates, 1952. Presents, interprets, and compares the lives (case studies) of three normal people.

WILLIAMSON, E. G., Editor. *Trends in Student Personnel Work:* Collection of Papers Read at a Conference Sponsored by the University of Minnesota to Celebrate a Quarter Century of Student Personnel Work and to Honor Professor Donald G. Paterson. Minneapolis: University of Minnesota Press, 1949. 417 p.

WILLIAMSON, E. G., and DARLEY, J. G. *Student Personnel Work:* An Outline of Clinical Procedures. New York: McGraw-Hill Book Co., 1937. 306 p.

WILLIAMSON, E. G., SARBIN, Theodore R., and Others. "Student Personnel Work." *Encyclopedia of Educational Research.* Revised Edition. Edited by Walter S. Monroe. New York: Macmillan Co., 1950. p. 1290-1362.

WILSON, Clara O. "Evaluation of Child Growth: An Anecdotal Record." *Educational Method* 20:178-81; January 1941.

WILSON, Gertrude. *Group Work and Case Work:* Their Relationship and Practice. New York: Family Welfare Association of America, 1941. v + 107 p.

WILSON, Gertrude, and RYLAND, Gladys. *Social Group Work Practice:* The Creative Use of the Social Process. Boston: Houghton Mifflin Co., 1949. xii + 687 p.

WILSON, Logan, and KOLB, William L. *Sociological Analysis:* An Introductory Text and Case Book. New York: Harcourt, Brace and Co., 1949. 866 p.

WILSON, R. S. *The Short Contact in Social Case Work,* Vols. 1, 2. New York: National Association for Travelers Aid and Transient Service, 1937. 201, 219 p.

WINDLE, Charles. "Psychological Tests in Psycho-Pathological Prognosis." *Psychological Bulletin* 49:451-82; September 1952.

WITMER, Helen L. *Psychiatric Clinics for Children.* New York: Commonwealth Fund, 1940. xix + 437 p.

WITMER, Helen L. *Social Work:* An Analysis of a Social Institution. New York: Farrar and Rinehart, 1942. xvi + 540 p.

WOLFF, Werner, Editor. *Projective and Expressive Methods of Personality Investigation.* New York: Grune and Stratton, 1950. 76 p.

WOOD, Austin B. "Transference in Client Centered Therapy and in Psycho-analysis." *Journal of Consulting Psychology* 15:72-5; February 1951.

WOOD, Ben D., and HAEFNER, Ralph. *Measuring and Guiding Individual Growth.* New York: Silver Burdett Co., 1948. viii + 536 p.

WRIGHT, Herbert F., and BARKER, Roger G. *Methods in Psychological Ecology:* A Progress Report. Field Study of Children's Behavior. Lawrence: University of Kansas, 1950. ix + 273 p.

YOUNG, Erle F. *Dictionary of Social Welfare.* New York: Social Science Publishers, 1948. vi + 218 p.

YOUNG, Kimball. "Social Psychology and Social Casework." *American Sociological Review* 16:54-61; February 1951.

YOUNG, Pauline V. *Interviewing in Social Work:* A Sociological Analysis. New York: McGraw-Hill Book Co., 1935. xvi + 416 p.

YOUNG, Pauline V. *Scientific Social Surveys and Research.* Second Edition. New York: Prentice-Hall, 1949. Chapters 12, 17-20.

YOUNG, Pauline V. *Social Case Work in National Defense:* A Cultural Approach to the Problems of Enlisted Men and Their Families. New York: Prentice-Hall, 1941. xxxi + 292 p.

YOUNG, Pauline V. *Social Treatment in Probation and Delinquency:* Treatise and Casebook for Court Workers, Probation Officers, and Other Child Welfare Workers. Second Edition. New York: McGraw-Hill Book Co., 1952. xxvi + 536 p.

YUEH-HWA, Lin. *The Golden Wing.* New York: Oxford University Press, 1948. xv + 234 p.

ZACHRY, Caroline B. *Personality Adjustments of School Children.* New York: Charles Scribner's Sons, 1929. xiii + 306 p.

ZNANIECKI, Florian. *Cultural Sciences:* Their Origin and Development. Urbana: University of Illinois Press, 1952. viii + 438 p.

# 9

# Genetic, Developmental, and Growth Studies

## INTRODUCTION

This chapter opens with an outline of the factors that have contributed to the genetic approach in psychology and education, followed by an analysis of the purposes and problems of genetic research. Next is a characterization of two major methods of investigation (cross-section and longitudinal) used in growth studies, and of other research techniques frequently associated with the genetic approach. Analysis and interpretation of genetic data are discussed in terms of nine aspects of genetic processes. Finally, the contributions of genetic research and problems for future study are outlined briefly, including comment on the extensive summaries of the literature.

The greatly accelerated interest of the present century in genetic psychology is related to the rapid development of biology; in fact, some universities classify psychology as a biological science. This relationship explains in part the early emphasis of genetic research on physical and anatomical development. Other factors [1] that have contributed to development of the genetic approach in psychology and education include:

1. Recognition of the importance of the child as an individual, as emphasized by Comenius, Rousseau, Pestalozzi, Herbart, and Froebel.
2. Formulation of evolutionary theories by Darwin, Spencer, Huxley, and Hobhouse.
3. Observations of the early development of children, and utilization of the techniques of the baby biography and questionnaire, reported by Darwin, Taine, Preyer, Shinn, J. M. Baldwin, Stern, and Stanley Hall. Hall was the leader of the first stage of the child-study movement, which extended over the last decade of the nineteenth century and the first two decades of the present century.
4. The psychological movements known as functionalism (sponsored by John Dewey), behaviorism, psychoanalysis, and Gestalt psychology.
5. Invention of measuring and recording instruments, especially mental tests, adapted to use in growth studies. These tools have played a prominent part in freeing the second or modern stage of child-development research of many of the errors commonly found in studies prior to 1920.

[1] N. L. Munn, *Psychological Development*. Boston: Houghton Mifflin Co., 1938. p. 1-8. Gordon Hendrickson, University of Cincinnati, unpublished notes.

The comparatively recent interest in studies of growth is illustrated by the measurement of mental development in childhood and youth.[2] Prior to World War I, the topic of mental growth and its measurement received little attention in psychological and educational literature. It is true that during the last decade of the nineteenth century and early in the present century a number of movements contributed to the devising of mental tests as practical instruments to meet some specific social need. These early developments included Cattell's energetic leadership in devising tests, the work of Binet in France in the measurement of individual differencs in mental ability, Goddard's English translation of the Binet-Simon scales, Ayres' study of school retardation, scientific interest in problems of juvenile delinquency and the establishment of the first juvenile court, Goddard's investigations of the cost of mental defect in terms of delinquency and of related educational problems, rapid increase in organized agencies for social welfare, group testing during World War I, and the rise of the mental-hygiene movement with its emphasis on the establishment of behavior clinics for children.

## PURPOSES AND PROBLEMS OF GENETIC RESEARCH

**Purposes of genetic research.** Genetic study is ideally long-term investigation of origin, direction, trend, rate, pattern, limit, and decline of growth. Genetic research should identify causes, interrelationships, and patterns of development among such factors as [3] experiential background, including both formal and informal teaching and learning, physiological age, mental age, degree of social maturity (or social age), interests, needs (personal and social), socio-economic status, motivation, attitudes, methods of instruction, materials of instruction, length and intensity of instruction, learning procedures, modifiability of native ability, aims and objectives, reading ability, habits and procedures in thinking and in problem solving behavior, adjustment status, and inherent difficulty of the material to be learned. The relationships between and pattern of development for mentality, emotional stability, and physical growth are far more significant than separate consideration of data for each phase of growth. This conception is much broader than that of many earlier investigators who considered growth data valuable per se, without practical applications. The trend today

---

[2] Florence L. Goodenough, "The Measurement of Mental Growth in Childhood." *Manual of Child Psychology.* Edited by Leonard Carmichael. New York: John Wiley and Sons, 1946. p. 450-54. Revised, 1954.

[3] Kai Jensen, "Needed Research." *Child Development and the Curriculum.* Thirty-eighth Yearbook of the National Society for the Study of Education, Part I. Bloomington, Ill.: Public School Publishing Co., 1939. p. 423-24.

in genetic studies to emphasize causal relationships, however, still leaves a place for determination of developmental norms, for use in the prediction and control of behavior.

The purposes of the genetic approach in relation to interpretation of behavior must include consideration of direction of growth, rate, and optimal development. The stage of development or level of maturity reached offers no adequate basis for prediction, since direction is not indicated—whether the child is moving forward, is stationary, or even may be slipping backward. Even when the direction of growth is known, it is essential to study the rate of development, whether progress is slow or rapid. Another problem is to determine whether the particular level reached represents optimal growth in relation to ability, a matter of especial importance in the instruction of gifted children. These maturity levels may shift with changes in the socio-economic status or interests of the individual, or with variations in instructional procedures, making it necessary to revise some earlier concept of optimal development for an individual or a group.

**Problems of genetic research.** As to locale, investigation of genetic problems is not limited to the classroom, laboratory, nursery school, and child clinic, but may be carried forward in the church school, home, child-care agency, camp, playground, or discussion group. As to scope of problems, to the earlier interest in physical and anatomical growth are now added phases of mental, social, and personality development as profitable areas for research. The breadth of the field is indicated by the contents of a treatise that traces the development of psychological processes in animals ranging from unicellular organisms to man and, in human individuals, from conception to senescence.[4] It is true that a particular research study, by way of delimitation, must concentrate on one level or one aspect of behavior at a time rather than to attempt simultaneously an investigation of all levels and phases of development.

As further evidence of the breadth of the genetic approach, investigations of mental and physical growth have sought answers to the following problems: [5]

1. The general nature of growth curves—their inception, shape, and point of cessation
2. Individual, age, maturity, sex, and ethnic differences in growth
3. The nature of growth curves of various structures
4. The nature, causes, and results of abnormal growth
5. Relationships between mental and physical growth
6. The relationship of physical growth to abnormalities of behavior

[4] N. L. Munn, *op. cit.*
[5] W. F. Dearborn and J. W. M. Rothney, *Predicting the Child's Development.* Cambridge, Mass.: Sci-Art Publishers, 1941. p. 340-42.

7. The relation of growth to environmental changes
8. The study of effectiveness of methods and techniques for obtaining the above information.

There are certain fields to which the genetic method could be applied more readily (the gifted, insane, criminal, and maladjusted in general), if adequate methods were available for identifying such individuals at an early age so as to permit a forward movement of observation from the beginning, in other words, a longitudinal type of study. In most instances of genius, insanity, criminality, and departure from normality it is necessary to work backward to origins through use of the case-study method or life history, since certain stages of development usually have been reached before discovery of the particular case.

## CROSS-SECTION VERSUS LONGITUDINAL APPROACH [6]

The preceding discussion of the purposes and problems of genetic research and the present analysis of two major techniques of investigation (cross-section and longitudinal) appropriate for growth studies may suggest that genetic research represents a point of view or approach to problem-solving rather than a special method distinct from other research procedures. This close relationship between developmental methods and other investigational techniques will be indicated in a subsequent section of this chapter. However, the extent to which growth studies combine a variety of research procedures into a sequence and developmental pattern of problem-solving seems to justify consideration of the genetic method on a basis coördinate with the historical, survey, experimental, and case methods.

**Cross-section technique.** Genetic research deals with a particular cross section of growth, not for its own sake, as in the normative-survey procedure, but seeks to discover sequences and principles of development in relation to other cross sections of growth. Cross-section data require at least a single measurement for each individual within certain groups, as when the weight or height for every pupil in each age group of a public-school system is determined and the average for each age group calculated. Comparisons between the averages (norms or standards) of the successive age groups indicate trends in the form of annual gains in weight or height

[6] John E. Anderson, "Methods of Child Psychology." *Manual of Child Psychology, op. cit.,* p. 6-9. Revised, 1954.
Raymond G. Kuhlen, *The Psychology of Adolescent Development.* New York: Harper and Bros., 1952. p. 14-25.

for the groups as a whole, with which individuals can be compared, although these central trends are not accurate for an individual child.

Many developmental norms, as reported in the psychological and educational literature, are for rather unusual performance of the laboratory type not directly related to life situations. It would be helpful to have norms for such every-day activities as dressing habits, ordinary motor performances, and virtually all practical skills (except those already available for achievement tests).

Cross-section data have a special advantage in providing new samples drawn from the population at each age level that will provide a cross-check upon the data at other age levels, although many such studies cover only a limited age range and fail to articulate with similar investigations at younger and older age levels. This type of genetic research presents special difficulties in sampling and in statistical procedure. As a rule, relatively large numbers of subjects are involved in cross-section studies, in contrast to the much smaller numbers followed over a period of time in longitudinal investigations. In recent years cross-section growth studies have been extended to wider age ranges and are being supplemented or replaced by longitudinal investigations of development.

**Longitudinal technique.** The longitudinal approach to investigation of the weight of school children is to follow a particular group of pupils or the same individual year after year through repeated measurements. The resulting series of measurements, therefore, represents growth sequences for the same group of children or same individual. Expressed otherwise, such a longitudinal study is a series of rather closely spaced cross sections for the particular group or individual. Ideally, development should be studied in this manner, as it takes place, although actually the majority of developmental investigations employ the cross-section technique (simultaneous measurement of different age groups) for reasons discussed later. Wider use of the longitudinal method has been urged, even as early as 1895, emphasizing that growth investigations of the same subjects should be conducted with the measurements made seriatim.

Uniform sampling criteria, as employed in cross-section studies, cannot be set up and applied for longitudinal data, since unpredictable and uncontrollable selective elimination almost inevitably occurs, because of the casualties of death, illness, moving of families, and changes in the coöperation of children and parents with the investigator in a longitudinal study. On the other hand, the genetic-longitudinal approach provides a significant picture of growth not present in curves based on averages at successive cross sections of development. Normative cross sections do not necessarily represent the genetic pattern of an individual child, since children grow at different rates and reach similar developmental levels at different ages. Individual curves for vocabulary growth, for example, as reported in baby biographies, differ markedly from the usual growth curves based on cross-section studies. As another illustration, the cross-section approach, on an age basis, groups together at the thirteen-year level girls who are well past puberty and other girls who are some months away from puberty. It is misleading to say that the average increment in height for this group of thirteen-year-old girls is typical, since a preadolescent girl at this age will have a much smaller gain in height than an adolescent girl who is passing through her stage of most rapid growth. Growth curves for adolescent groups tend to "smooth" this period and to conceal the spurt in height that usually takes place during adolescence, whereas individual curves of adolescent development reveal a rapid increment in growth.

Longitudinal study of child development frequently deals with the interrelations of many variables in growth through the coöperation of specialists in a variety of fields, as in the Stanford *Genetic Studies of Genius* and in the Berkeley Growth Study of mental, motor, and physical development from birth to maturity.[7] With adequate sponsorship and financial support, the longitudinal method may produce significant findings from a single investigation or a cluster of genetic studies—results not ordinarily obtainable through use of the cross-section method. The data of the Harvard Growth Study have been utilized in a pattern of genetic research concerned with [8] accelerated growth of boys during adolescence, the growth spurt in relation to the menarche, grouping on the basis of the period of maximum growth, prediction of individual growth, constancy of physical size, prediction of child weight, mental lag and accelerated growth, correlation between mental and physical development, the later period of continued mental growth, use of verbal and non-verbal materials in intelligence tests over a period of years, constancy of the I.Q., ossification of carpal bones as a growth index, effect of environment on intelligence, and growth of twins.

The preceding discussion and the literature of genetic research advocate wider use of the longitudinal method, in order to avoid the shortcomings of cross-section studies of growth. Longitudinal investigations of develop-

[7] Lewis M. Terman and Others, *Genetic Studies of Genius,* Vol. 1. Stanford University, Calif.: Stanford University Press, 1925. xvi + 648 p.
Barbara Stoddard Burks, Dortha Williams Jensen, and Lewis M. Terman, *Genetic Studies of Genius,* Vol. 3. The Promise of Youth: Follow-Up Studies of a Thousand Gifted Children. Stanford University, Calif.: Stanford University Press, 1930. xiv + 508 p.
Lewis M. Terman and Melita H. Oden, *The Gifted Child Grows Up:* Genetic Studies of Genius. Stanford University, Calif.: Stanford University Press, 1947. xiv + 450 p.
Harold E. Jones and Nancy Bayley, "The Berkeley Growth Study." *Child Development* 12:167-73; June 1941.
[8] W. F. Dearborn and J. W. M. Rothney, *op. cit.,* p. 345-57.

ment, however, should be undertaken only after thoughtful consideration of errors that may be present unless adequate precautions are taken. Cross-section studies involve some of the same difficulties.[9]

1. Difficulties in population sampling, such as the selective elimination of many of the original subjects during the course of a long-term investigation.

2. Maintenance of satisfactory working relationships among subjects, parents, schools, and investigators, particularly as personnel changes take place with the passing of time.

3. Motivation of children to demonstrate full rather than perfunctory performance, a real challenge in the case of repeated testing over a period of months or years.

4. Systematic errors of measurement in the administration or scoring of tests, mental or physical.

5. Non-comparability or uncertain psychological equivalence of tests used at different age levels, especially when the time span is from early childhood to adolescence.

6. Unequal experience of groups in terms of factors affecting the results of the measurement used, but not affecting the trait itself; for example, variation in previous experience with standardized tests.

7. Recording and manipulation of data; for example, graduate students probably are not as accurate and efficient as a highly trained permanent staff of skilled punch-card operators and statistical clerks.

8. Mistakes of interpretation resulting from failure to take account of the principle of regression, particularly in its effects on measurements of gain or loss.

## RELATIONS BETWEEN THE GENETIC APPROACH AND OTHER RESEARCH MATERIALS AND METHODS

As indicated earlier in this chapter, there are close relationships between genetic techniques and other materials and methods of problem-solving. In subsequent paragraphs are outlined the ways in which genetic research utilizes or builds upon the sources and procedures of historical, normative-survey, experimental, and case research.

**Sources of genetic data.** Sources of material [10] for study of child development include the following:

1. The present behavior of the child, including verbal output, as based on observations, measurements, and records in test or experimental situations, or on direct observation of behavior in play and social settings

2. Products of the child in the form of permanent records, including drawings, letters, and compositions

---

[9] Florence L. Goodenough, "Some Special Problems of Nature-Nurture Research." *Intelligence: Its Nature and Nurture.* Thirty-ninth Yearbook of the National Society for the Study of Education, Part I. Bloomington, Ill.: Public School Publishing Co., 1940. p. 367-84.
W. F. Dearborn and J. W. M. Rothney, *op. cit.,* p. 58-79.
[10] John E. Anderson, *op. cit.,* p. 13-14.

3. Records on file at home, school, and in a variety of agencies, covering school achievement, birth certificates, and health records

4. Introspections of the child

5. Memories of the child, or of the adult of his own earlier life, a based on the recording of conscious memories or of getting at more deeply buried memories by a free-association process or projective methods

6. Memories of the child's life as retained by those who have been associated with him

7. Measures of the parents, siblings, and other relatives of the child or of the environment, culture, or background in which he develops—a source that actually does not provide direct information concerning the child.

**Historical and biographical materials.** Both genetic and historical studies deal with the sequence and unfolding of events. The genetic approach, however, centers attention on events relating to individual growth and current developmental sequences, and usually employs a forward movement of research, with the investigator recording development as it takes place. The scope of historical research embraces the entire range of human events, and the movement is backward, with documents and remains utilized to reconstruct the scenes of the past in the form of an integrated narrative. The genetic and historical methods most nearly meet in the use of certain types of biography and autobiography to trace the development of the individual, as in the flowering of genius for characters who lived many years ago; for example, Cox attempted to estimate the I.Q.'s of three hundred geniuses [11] born between 1450 and 1849. As another illustration, an almost incredible biography or narrative interpretation of the developmental life history of Kamala,[12] the wolf girl, is based on a missionary's diary account and photographs of a child who apparently was reared by a wolf over a period of some seven years and then lived for nine years in an orphanage in India. Although the story may be a hoax or a case of credulity on the part of a missionary untrained in objective observation, testing of evidence, and research procedure, this developmental narrative makes fascinating reading.

Biographical data,[13] although subject to certain limitations, frequently present vivid descriptions of many factors that influence the development of the child; for example (1) the account of the early development of Leta

---

[11] Catharine M. Cox, *Genetic Studies of Genius*, Vol. II. Stanford University, Calif.: Stanford University Press, 1926. xxiv + 842 p.

[12] Arnold Gesell, *Wolf Child and Human Child*. New York: Harper and Bros., 1941. xvi + 107 p.

[13] Harry L. Hollingworth, *Leta Stetter Hollingworth*. Lincoln: University of Nebraska Press, 1943. 204 p.

Leta S. Hollingworth, *Children Above 180 I. Q. Stanford-Binet:* Origin and Development. Yonkers-on-Hudson, N. Y.: World Book Co., 1942. 332 p.

Hollingworth, as reported by her husband, with many of the characteristics of the life history; (2) Leta Hollingworth's study of children above 180 I.Q., including a long-time genetic investigation of twelve very gifted children; and (3) genetic records of two gifted Negroes, together with the effect of attitude and motivation on achievement.[14]

Autobiographical materials have proved useful in studying the development of behavior patterns in school situations. Although the school has been considered primarily as an agency for the formal education of the child, it is also of major importance in his social development, with its complex of social situations in which pupils live, compete, perform, develop attitudes, form response patterns, and fail or succeed in the process of social relationships.

(1) Memories of school life, viewed as a series of social situations, constitute a significant proportion of the childhood recollections of the authors of twenty-one unselected autobiographies. This fact suggests the possible importance of such situations in the study of behavior. (2) The references made by the authors tend to group themselves into areas of concentration, implying preponderances of problems and influences for future study. (3) It is significant that both the relative emphases given by the authors to the importance of school situations and the areas of concentration identified were made by authors of unrelated interests and backgrounds, and without promptings from a duly organized research project.[15]

**Survey instruments.** Genetic investigation makes extensive use of the varied data-collecting and recording tools of normative-survey methods, including developmental examinations, growth schedules, behavior records, anecdotal journals, anthropometric measuring instruments, standard tests, rating scales, check list, questionnaires, interviews,[16] and direct observations. The types of resulting data may include information concerning sociological, anthropological, psychological, educational, economic, and medical phases of growth. These survey instruments are essential for measuring and recording the level of growth reached at each stage of a series of repeated measurements, observations, or cross sections of development. Conditions and procedures for observation have been greatly

---

[14] Viola Theman and Paul Witty, "Case Studies and Genetic Records of Two Gifted Negroes." *Journal of Psychology* 15:165-81; April 1943.

[15] Quoted from James H. S. Bossard and Eleanor S. Boll, "School Situations in Behavior Studies: An Autobiographical Analysis." *Sociology and Social Research* 31:423-28; July-August, 1947.

[16] A. C. Kinsey and Others, *Sexual Behavior in the Human Male.* Philadelphia: W. B. Saunders Co., 1948. xvi + 804 p. A striking example of an elaborate technique of interviewing in a difficult investigational area.

A. C. Kinsey and Others, *Sexual Behavior in the Human Female.* Philadelphia: W. B. Saunders Co., 1953. xxx + 842 p. The sampling, statistical, and interpretative procedures of both reports have encountered sharp criticisms.

improved through use of the one-way vision screen, infant cabinet or clinical crib with movable cameras mounted on a glass observation dome, motion-picture photography, electroencephalograms, x-rays, stenographic records, time-sampling of behavior, situational analysis of behavior to note changes in different settings, and use of the parent as a participant-observer concerned with both the training and study of the child.

**Experimental techniques.** The genetic approach frequently is used in combination with the experimental method, as when employing parallel groups to study the effect on growth of variation in a nutritional factor. An especially apt illustration of the complementary relationship of genetic and experimental methods is the co-twin type of control, as in the stair-climbing study by Gesell and Thompson,[17] where the variable for the identical twins was in terms of training to climb the stairs. In this manner, experimental modification of developmental behavior took place.

**Case studies.**[18] Genetic and case methods have a common meeting ground in diaries, biographies, and life histories of child development, although typically the genetic approach has moved forward as normal growth sequences unfold, while the majority of case studies have looked backward *ex post facto* to diagnose conditions of maladjustment. Biography and the life history are concerned more nearly with total behavior, whereas the typical genetic study delimits in advance the aspects of development to be observed.

The Yale Clinic of Child Development provides good illustrations of the common interests of genetic and case methods in clinical techniques, as developed by Gesell and associates. One example is a ten-year study of the mental growth careers of eighty-four infants and children, with their case studies or biographies of development classified under such headings

[17] Arnold Gesell and Helen Thompson, *Learning and Growth in Identical Infant Twins.* Genetic Psychology Monographs, Vol. 6, No. 1. Worcester: Clark University Press, 1929. 124 p.

[18] Arnold Gesell and Others, *Biographies of Child Development.* New York: Paul B. Hoeber, 1939. xviii + 328 p.

Arnold Gesell and Catherine S. Amatruda, *Developmental Diagnosis.* New York: Paul B. Hoeber, 1947. xvi + 496 p.

W. E. Blatz, *The Five Sisters.* New York: William Morrow and Co., 1938. 209 p.

Robert W. White, *Lives in Progress:* A Study of the Natural Growth of Personality. New York: William Sloane Associates, 1952. Presents, interprets, and compares the lives (case studies) of three normal people.

Margaret Mead, *Coming of Age in Samoa.* New York: William Morrow and Co., 1928. xv + 297 p.

Margaret Mead, *Growing Up in New Guinea.* New York: William Morrow and Co., 1930. x + 372 p.

Margaret Mead, *Male and Female.* New York: William Morrow and Co., 1949. xii + 477 p.

Robert J. Havighurst, *Human Development and Education.* New York: Longmans, Green and Co., 1953. p. 177-253.

as: normal and retarded development, acceleration and superiority of equipment, atypical and pseudo-atypical growth complexes, physical asymmetry, glandular and nutritional factors in mental growth, prematurity and postmaturity, language problems, reading disabilities, twinship, and foster care and child adoption. A second illustration is a series of cases concerned chiefly with diagnosis of defects and deviations of child development in such clinical areas as amentia, endocrine disorders, convulsive disorders, neurological behavior, cerebral injury, special sensory handicaps, prematurity, precocity, and environmental retardation.

Blatz, a psychologist, has reported a developmental study of the Dionne quints. White has compared and interpreted the growth in personality of three normal persons. Mead, an anthropologist, has studied adolescent development in primitive cultures, as compared with Western civilization.

**Statistical techniques.** Genetic research utilizes statistical and correlation techniques to study the relationships between mental and physical factors, environment and growth of intelligence, heredity and mental development, race and mental growth, sex and growth, dentition and development, and between various anatomical, physiological, motor, and metabolic factors.

**Social change.** In the areas of education and sociology there are certain studies of social changes and processes that resemble genetic investigations of growth and development, when the emphasis is on change as a process, as in studying process or progress in some phase of growth. To cite an example, a series of investigations has as one of its purposes the identification of elements or influences that may be employed to exercise control over the direction of change in factors related to adaptability, in order that the community setting of the school system may be improved.[19]

## ADAPTATION OF TECHNIQUES TO DIFFERENT ASPECTS AND STAGES OF DEVELOPMENT

In the larger aspects of organization and design for research, growth investigations include at least three possibilities: (1) experimentation through the techniques of the control group and co-twin control, (2) the behavior survey, and (3) individual case study. Studies of different phases of growth

[19] Paul R. Mort and Francis G. Cornell, *American Schools in Transition.* New York: Teachers College, Columbia University, 1941. xxviii + 546 p.

Paul R. Mort and Francis G. Cornell, *Adaptability of Public School Systems.* New York: Teachers College, Columbia University, 1938. xii + 146 p.

Philo T. Farnsworth, *Adaptation Processes in Public School Systems.* New York: Teachers College, Columbia University, 1940. viii + 136 p.

Metropolitan School Study Council, *Administration for Adaptability.* Edited by D. H. Ross. New York: The Council, Teachers College, Columbia University, 1951. 3 vols.

—intellectual, emotional, and physical—involve corresponding variations in the techniques employed.[20]

The most noticeable shift in technique and emphasis during more recent years in studying the intellectual growth of children has been the increasing use of projective methods and particularly of drawing and painting as a means of exploring the more subtle changes in the child's inner world of thoughts and feelings; for example, the doll-play technique and spontaneous drawings and paintings have been utilized successfully in studying the emotional experiences and personality development of children. The investigation of personality development has included a variety of projective techniques (for example, word association, story telling, play, psychodrama, picture methods, drawing, and painting), observation of behavior, interviews, questionnaires, personal documents, rating scales, and other psychometric and sociometric instruments. Certain of these techniques have been treated at some length in earlier chapters.

Recent investigations of physical growth have emphasized longitudinal studies of the same children over a period of time, patterns of morphological variations among individuals (and of the relationships between physique, temperament, disease, and physical capacity), and integration of research findings from various sources.

Interesting variations of research methods have been applied in studying the growth of primitive children: the natural-history approach, recording of verbal behavior, the cross-section method of constructing a picture of the observed behavior of groups of children at each age level, the life history and the retrospective life history, longitudinal studies, and projective methods, including children's drawings and play techniques.[21]

[20] Lawrence E. Abt and Leopold Bellak, Editors, *Projective Psychology:* Clinical Approaches to the Total Personality. New York: Alfred A. Knopf, 1950. xvii + 485 + xiv p.
   Harold H. Anderson and Gladys L. Anderson, Editors, *An Introduction to Projective Techniques....* New York: Prentice-Hall, 1951. xxiv + 720 p.
   Virginia M. Axline, *Play Therapy:* The Inner Dynamics of Childhood. Boston: Houghton Mifflin Co., 1947. xii + 379 p.
   Nancy Bayley and Others, "Growth and Development." *Review of Educational Research* 17:301-403; December 1947.
   John E. Bell, *Projective Techniques:* A Dynamic Approach to the Study of the Personality. New York: Longmans, Green and Co., 1948. xvi + 533 p.
   Robert J. Havighurst, *op. cit.* The concept of developmental tasks.
   Lydia Jackson and Kathleen M. Todd, *Child Treatment and the Therapy of Play.* Second Edition. New York: Ronald Press, 1950. xii + 159 p.
   Willard C. Olson, *Child Development.* Boston: D. C. Heath and Co., 1949. p. 3-16, 389-97.
   Carl R. Rogers, *Client-Centered Therapy:* Its Current Practice, Implications, and Theory. Boston: Houghton Mifflin Co., 1951. xii + 560 p.
   Samuel R. Slavson, *Analytic Group Psychotherapy with Children, Adolescents, and Adults.* New York: Columbia University Press, 1950. ix + 275 p.
   P. M. Symonds, *Adolescent Fantasy:* An Investigation of the Picture-Story Method of Personality Study. New York: Columbia University Press, 1949. xi + 397 p.
   [21] Margaret Mead, "Research on Primitive Children." *Manual of Child Psychology, op. cit.,* p. 677-700. Also see:
   Margaret Mead, *Male and Female, op. cit.*

Studies of growth involve variation in technique with age.[22] Study of prenatal behavior is based on use of experimental and laboratory techniques with animal fetuses, together with limited experiments and extensive observations on premature human infants. The chief source of data for infants is from experiments, direct measurements, and observations, including ingenious techniques such as one-way vision screens, cinema recording, the Gesell observation dome, and the stabilimeter. Direct observation and experiments are prominent in studying preschool children, since many tests and measurements suitable for older children cannot be used with the younger child who has not learned to read and write. With older children and adolescents, paper-and-pencil tests and indirect measurement techniques to a large extent supplant direct observation. It is true that in more recent years observation of the older child has come to be used in natural or controlled situations, including the one-way vision screen and recording of individual behavior as it changes in a social setting, as well as sociometric techniques in dramatic-play situations and in diagramming social relationships.

These pages on developmental sources and techniques may well end with the restatement that genetic investigation, in terms of research techniques, is an eclectic approach to problem-solving. A similar statement can be made concerning genetic research in relation to the fields of knowledge on which it draws, including mathematics, statistics, physics, chemistry, biology, zoölogy, anatomy, physiology, medicine, psychiatry, psychology, sociology, anthropology, and education.

## ANALYSIS AND INTERPRETATION
## OF GENETIC DATA

Although problems of sampling and of analysis of evidence are discussed elsewhere in this book, it is appropriate to outline briefly in this chapter certain emphases in the treatment and interpretation of genetic data. The Harvard Growth Study [23] may be cited as illustrative of the special problems of sampling encountered in longitudinal studies, including initial selection of subjects, progressive decline in number of subjects, mutilated distributions, and time of year in which measurements are taken.

**Principles of child development.** A genetic approach to understanding of children and of the function of education is based on major principles of child development in relation to the curriculum.[24]

---

[22] John E. Anderson, *op. cit.,* p. 35-36.
[23] W. F. Dearborn and J. W. M. Rothney, *op. cit.,* p. 68-77.
[24] Arthur T. Jersild and Charlotte Fehlman, "Child Development and the Curriculum: Some General Principles." *Journal of Experimental Education* 12:130-42; December 1943.

1. Developmental objectives
2. Levels of maturity
3. Differential rates of maturing
4. Variability in rate of maturing
5. Variability in differential rates of maturing
6. Differential developmental preeminence at various stages of growth
7. "Wholeheartedness and gradation" in emotional development
8. Indigenous motivation or spontaneous use, as a feature of growing ability
9. The principle of anticipation
10. "Laying by" or shedding as a feature of development
11. Developmental revision of habits
12. Differentiation and integration
    a. Individuation
    b. Progression from generalized to more localized response
    c. Incorporation of separately practiced operations into larger activity systems
13. Priority of "large" over "small" muscular activities in certain sections of the body
14. Interaction between various aspects of growth
15. Vicarious extension of experience
16. Early establishment of some of the basic features of personality structure
17. The play of complementary and potentially conflicting forces
    a. Dependence—independence
    b. Self-centered and "outgoing" tendencies.

For present purposes, in analyzing and interpreting development and growth, nine aspects of the genetic processes will be considered.[25]

**Initiation or beginning of growth.** It is essential to identify the initial stage of development for a particular phase of behavior. For the infant, the beginning of certain types of behavior is usually as follows: in the first quarter of the first year he gains control of the muscles that move his eyes; second quarter, reaches out for things; third quarter, sits; fourth quarter, stands upright; second year, walks and runs, and articulates words and phrases; and in the third year he speaks in sentences, using words as tools of thought.[26]

**Augmentation versus qualitative change.** Both quantitative and qualitative phases of development are significant. Increased speed and legibility

[25] H. S. Conrad, "Child Development—General Aspects." *Encyclopedia of Educational Research.* Edited by W. S. Monroe. New York: Macmillan Co., 1941. p. 128-32. Also see the 1950 edition.
Arnold Gesell and Helen Thompson, *The Psychology of Early Growth.* New York: Macmillan Co., 1938. p. 193-205.
Arnold Gesell and Others, *Biographies of Child Development, op. cit.,* p. 108-9.
Carter V. Good, "Child Development and the Genetic Method of Research." *Elementary School Journal* 43:577-85; June 1943.
Robert J. Havighurst, *op. cit.* The concept of developmental tasks in education.
[26] Arnold Gesell and Others, *The First Five Years of Life.* New York: Harper and Bros., 1940. p. 13. Also see:
Arnold Gesell, *Infant Development: The Embryology of Early Human Behavior.* New York: Harper and Bros., 1952. 108 p.

of handwriting in the upper elementary grades probably are the result of both repetition or practice of former habits (quantitative emphasis) and relatively qualitative changes in the form of decreased tensions, improved nerve-muscle adjustments, and favorable concentration of effort and attention. Growth in vocabulary includes both the total number of words used and the effectiveness of such usage (a relatively qualitative aspect of development). Qualitative changes frequently are expressed in descriptive formulations rather than in precise quantitative terms; for example, at different stages an infant commonly responds to the mirror situation as follows: at forty weeks, smiles at his mirror image; at fifty-two weeks, approaches his mirror image socially and even vocalizes; and at fifty-six weeks, brings his face close to his image, sometimes kissing it.[27]

**Rate of growth in terms of trends, patterns, irregularities, and fluctuations.** Possibly all growth and development are basically gradual rather than sudden, when consideration is given to the long period or background of preliminary preparation, as in the case of the child's first cry, the first spoken word, and walking without aid. The child's first cry is preceded by a period of development of chest, thorax, and neural pathways. The stages of the behavior pattern that commonly precedes walking without aid include: at thirty-two weeks in sitting the infant leans forward passively, although he sits erect for a brief period, and standing he supports his entire weight, although he leans forward with considerable hip flexion; at forty weeks, when prone he pushes with his hands and regresses, and when standing supports himself by holding the crib side rail; at forty-eight weeks, when prone he creeps, and unaided pulls himself to standing, cruises sidewise holding on the crib rail, and may even walk forward if both hands are held; and at fifty-six weeks, he stands alone at least momentarily.[28]

It is true that there are occasional periods of rapid development, such as the growth spurt at adolescence. Also, there are some reversals in growth; for example, the neck girth shows a decrease during the infant's first year. In addition, a subsequent paragraph of this section points out the individuality of growth careers. It is with full recognition of the qualifications of the preceding sentences that attention is now directed to the available growth and developmental norms: [29] motor, adaptive, language, personal-social, and anthropometric. Of particular interest as a

---

27 Arnold Gesell and Helen Thompson, *The Psychology of Early Growth, op. cit.,* p. 158-63.

28 *Ibid.,* p. 156-62.

29 Arnold Gesell and Helen Thompson, *The Psychology of Early Growth, op. cit.,* p. 97-189, 265-68.

Arnold Gesell and Others, *The First Five Years of Life, op. cit.,* p. 16-261, 319-47.

Arnold Gesell and Catherine S. Amatruda, *Developmental Diagnosis, op. cit.,* p. 23-90, 378-99.

photographic technique is a systematic delineation of the forms and early growth of human behavior patterns, illustrated by 3200 action photographs.[30]

**Levels of maturity in terms of configuration of behavior and integrated growth.** There is reasonable harmony or unity in development at a particular stage of growth; for example, a minimum level of intelligence is necessary for growth of understanding in written language and arithmetic. Persons of high intelligence usually are talented in a number of areas of activity and as a rule are well adjusted generally. Individuals with special ability in such fields as music and art commonly possess relatively high general intelligence. These illustrations suggest that at a particular level of maturity the concept of integration may be represented in the form of a constellation of related characteristics or a configuration of similar responses. However, as an extreme exception to the concept of unity in development, the vestibule of the ear is of adult size at birth, whereas the heart has not fully completed its growth at the age of twenty. Retrogression in children's behavior is a frequent occurrence.

The concept of integrated growth is particularly significant in tracing mental development, since the changing nature of the individual under study frequently renders inappropriate the materials and techniques used at an earlier age. This makes it necessary to modify procedures from one age level to another, in order to meet the shifting phases and emphases in growth. Therefore, developmental reference points are not to be regarded as "norms" in the sense of successive steps on a scale, but as stages or "growth gradients" through which development progresses. Information concerning such stages of growth or development will be of aid to child guidance only if used in relation to the total growth "complex." Various attributes of development tend to cluster around a "center of gravity of growth" for the particular individual.

Jones, using longitudinal data for children ten to eighteen years of age, traced the development of one boy (John) over a period of seven years as compared with the norms for the group.[31] John was handicapped by a variety or "cluster" of maladjustments rather than by great severity of any single difficulty. The case study of John includes home background, entry into adolescence, reactions of teachers and classmates, membership in social groups, physical development, motor and mental abilities, inter-

---

[30] Arnold Gesell and Others, *An Atlas of Infant Behavior*. New Haven: Yale University Press, 1934. 922 p. Two volumes.

[31] Harold E. Jones, *Development in Adolescence*. New York: Appleton-Century-Crofts, 1943. 161 p.

For a highly detailed, contrasting study of behavior covering only one day see Roger G. Barker and Herbert F. Wright, *One Boy's Day: A Specimen Record of Behavior*. New York: Harper and Bros., 1951. x + 435 p.

ests and attitudes, John's view of himself, John's "drives" or motivational tendencies, and his struggle for maturity.

**Individuality of growth careers.**[32] While there are sequences of maturation and behavior patterns that account for the general similarities and basic trends of development, no two children grow up in exactly the same way, with the partial exception of identical twins. Individuality of behavior in motor activity relates to such items as output of energy, bodily activity and fatigability, and postural demeanor, with the latter noted to determine whether it is tense, relaxed, poised, steady, or variable. Adaptive behavior varies in terms of insight, inquisitiveness, originality, decisiveness, and initiative. Language is characterized by individual differences in articulation, flow of speech, inflections, inhibitions, conversational rapport, and expressiveness. Personal-social behavior reflects variations in emotional vitality; motivation; reaction to success, failure, and fatigue; reaction to novelty and surprise; and sense of humor. Illustrations of such differences are available in a ten-year study of the mental development of eighty-four infants and children.[33]

**Limits of growth.**[34] The terminal points of physical growth can be determined with much greater precision than mental development, as in the case of height or speed of running. To say that the chances are remote for running one hundred yards in nine seconds, whereas many athletes have done so in ten seconds, is to predict with some exactness the limits of one phase of physical performance. Relatively little is known concerning the possibilities for maximum mental development. An early position was that quantitative growth of intelligence ceases at approximately sixteen years of age, while later views held that development of intelligence continues until eighteen or nineteen years or even later. Only meager evidence is available concerning the upper limits of qualitative and functional aspects of intelligence in terms of vocabulary, information, and insight or power in contrast to speed of reaction, although such development probably continues well beyond the age of twenty.

**Maturity, old age, and deterioration.** As to physical and physiological changes, the human life span may be divided roughly into three periods: (1) from conception until past the age of twenty, when adulthood is attained; (2) a brief time span during which the individual is at the peak of his physical efficiency; and (3) the period of physical deterioration which

---

[32] Arnold Gesell and Others, *The First Five Years of Life, op. cit.,* p. 296-308.
Arnold Gesell and Others, *Biographies of Child Development, op. cit.,* p. 303-9.
[33] Arnold Gesell and Others, *Biographies of Child Development, op. cit.,* p. 13-302.
[34] P. L. Boynton and L. G. Humphreys, "Intelligence and Intelligence Tests." *Encyclopedia of Educational Research.* New York: Macmillan Co., 1950. p. 600-610.
Floyd Ruch and Irving Lorge, "Adult Intelligence." *Encyclopedia of Educational Research, op. cit.,* p. 32-35.

actually begins as early as the late twenties and accelerates with the passage of time, eventually taking the form of senility and dissolution. In a sense, physical maturity and physiological equilibrium are lost, at least in part, almost as soon as attained.[35]

Senescence or disease frequently brings about marked changes in behavior and even disintegration of personality. Such deterioration during later maturity and senescence is attributable to the physical changes of glandular involution, smoothing of cerebral convolutions, impairment of sense organs, hardening of arteries, and wasted musculature, with the psychological concomitants of a general decrement in sensory, motor, and symbolic function.[36] However, the earlier and more prominent deterioration of the anatomical and physiological functions may be offset by complex patterns of imagination, enriched experience, and sage judgment, with the result that the intellect operates in a socially effective manner.

Investigations of intellectual changes during maturity and old age definitely indicate that, with age, test performances change. A significant conclusion is that qualitative aspects of intellectual performance are fully as important as quantitative variations. A helpful direction for future research on the problem of aging is to study personality changes revealed by longitudinal studies, with a thorough analysis of cultural attitudes toward aging and of changing values, motives, and adjustment problems with increased age.

Increased interest in the problems of maturity and old age [37] is evi-

[35] W. W. Greulich, "Physical Changes in Adolescence." *Adolescence.* Forty-third Yearbook of the National Society for the Study of Education, Part I. Chicago: Department of Education, University of Chicago, 1944. p. 8.

[36] N. L. Munn, *op. cit.,* p. 518-23.

[37] Social Science Research Council. Sub-Committee on Social Adjustment in Old Age (Robert J. Havighurst, chairman). *Social Adjustment in Old Age:* A Research Planning Report. New York: The Council, 1946. 232 p. Also see:

Symposium on the physiological, psychological, sociological, and administrative aspects of the age problem in relation to research: N. W. Shock and Others, "The Age Problem in Research Workers." *Scientific Monthly* 72:353-67; June 1951.

Elizabeth L. Breckinridge, *Effective Use of Older Workers.* Chicago: Wilcox and Follett Co., 1953. xiv + 224 p.

Ernest W. Burgess, Editor, "Aging and Retirement." *American Journal of Sociology* 59:301-390; January 1954.

Paul L. Essert, Irving Lorge, and Jacob Tuckman, "Preparation for a Constructive Approach to Later Maturity." *Teachers College Record* 53:70-76; November 1951.

Jeanne G. Gilbert, *Understanding Old Age.* New York: Ronald Press Co., 1953. 442 p. Detailed treatment of gerontology; important physical aspects of the aging process and the intellectual, emotional, and psychosexual changes that take place in later years; normal and abnormal aging; twenty-six case histories based on the author's professional experience.

Robert J. Havighurst and Ruth Albrecht, *Older People.* New York: Longmans, Green and Co., 1953. xvi + 415 p.

Harvey C. Lehman, *Age and Achievement.* Princeton: Princeton University Press, 1953. xi + 358 p.

Geneva Mathiasen, Editor, *Criteria for Retirement:* A Report of a National Conference on Retirement of Older Workers. New York: G. P. Putnam's Sons, 1953. xix + 233 p.

T. Lynn Smith, Editor, *Living in the Later Years.* Gainesville: University of Florida Press, 1952. x + 176 p.

denced by the establishment of two journals dealing with aging, *Geriatrics* and *Journal of Gerontology,* as well as by a comprehensive report on social adjustment in old age, prepared by a subcommittee of the Social Science Research Council. The Division of Maturity and Old Age of the American Psychological Association stated recently that few university centers were offering instruction on the aging process for the benefit of professional workers with older clients or to stimulate research on the problems of mature and older persons. The medical sciences have conducted the most extensive research in this area, although psychology departments are interested in the possibilities of developing courses dealing with the problems of aging. As late as the middle of the twentieth century departments of education had done little in this field except for an occasional course in adult education.

**Developmental diagnosis and causation.** Earlier in this chapter the discussion of the purposes of genetic research has emphasized the importance of identifying causal factors in developmental studies. This interest in developmental diagnosis represents a considerably higher level of research skill and interpretative insight than is found in most investigations limited to determination of growth norms or sequences.

Errors in identifying causal factors have been frequent; for example, at one time the common lack of emotional stability among adolescents of Western civilizations was attributed primarily to physiological changes, but study of primitive societies has directed attention to the importance of such cultural factors as sexual repression in the Western world in producing emotional imbalance. A common error is failure to recognize the joint effects of two or more causal factors that are interrelated functionally, as in the case of heredity and environment. It is difficult to separate the influence of nature versus nurture on achievement, because of the interrelationships between superior heredity and favorable environment; persons of considerable ability tend to gravitate toward a good environment, which in turn provides a helpful setting for developing superior minds. To use another illustration,[38] learning and maturation probably are essentially alike as factors associated with development, although there is a tendency to characterize measurable changes as learning and in the case of more elusive factors to speak of maturation.

The factors that have been found to affect growth and development include [39]

---

Clark Tibbitts and Wilma Donahue, "Developments in Education for Later Maturity." *Review of Educational Research* 23:202-17; June 1953.

Jacob Tuckman and Irving Lorge, *Retirement and the Industrial Worker:* Prospect and Reality. New York: Teachers College, Columbia University, 1953. xvi + 105 p.

[38] Kai Jensen, *op. cit.,* p. 424-25.
[39] Quoted from H. S. Conrad, *op. cit.,* p. 130.

race; age; sex; familial heredity; prenatal conditions; birth trauma; birth order; maternal age at pregnancy; endocrine factors; nutritional factors; health factors; disease and infections; seasonal conditions; atmospheric conditions (temperature, humidity, pressure, etc.); national-racial culture; socioeconomic status; educational agencies; social pressure; family and neighborhood; acquaintances and friends; intelligence; knowledge; experience, exercise, and training; interests and motivation; and emotional adjustments.

Other details of diagnosis and of identification of causal factors are outlined in the chapter on the case-study method. In other sources are an extended treatment [40] of the diagnosis of defects and deviations of child development, and a diagnostic study [41] of the mental growth of eighty-four infants and children. The former volume discusses in detail a wide range of diagnostic problems: techniques for the developmental examination of behavior and norms of development; diagnosis of the defects and deviations of development (amentia, endocrine disorders, convulsive disorders, neurological diagnosis of infant behavior, cerebral injury, special sensory handicaps, prematurity, precocity, environmental retardation, and clinical aspects of child adoption); and protection of early child development, as related to diagnosis, guidance, and developmental supervision. Specialists in education, psychology, and sociology may well be familiar with such deviations, even though the diagnosis itself is reserved for experts with medical training.

**Developmental prognosis and prediction.**[42] The preceding discussions of the individuality of physical and mental growth careers, and of the variety of causal factors affecting development, imply that it is difficult to predict future development. Accurate prediction is possible only to the extent that: valid techniques of measurement are available, early development provides a stable base from which later growth proceeds, and later development is determined by the same causes as operated in earlier stages of growth. Prediction of growth is particularly hazardous for the period of adolescence. The marked individual differences among any age, sex, ethnic, or maturity group and the pronounced variability in individual growth curves are basic to consideration of such problems as the constancy of the I.Q., use of height-weight tables, prediction of time of maturity, and prediction of age at which growth will cease.

[40] Arnold Gesell and Catherine S. Amatruda, *op. cit.*
[41] Arnold Gesell and Others, *Biographies of Child Development, op. cit.*
[42] H. S. Conrad, *op. cit.,* p. 131-32.
  W. F. Dearborn and J. W. M. Rothney, *op. cit.,* p. 340-47.
  A. C. Eurich and L. F. Cain, "Prognosis." *Encyclopedia of Educational Research, op. cit.,* p. 838-60. Also see the 1950 edition, p. 874-94.
  Arnold Gesell and Others, *Biographies of Child Development, op. cit.,* p. 303-9.
  Kai Jensen, "Genetic Method," in "Methods of Research in Education." *Review of Educational Research* 9:493-94; December 1939.

## COMPLETED GENETIC STUDIES AND
## NEEDED RESEARCH

**Summaries of genetic research.** The volume of developmental investigations is so large that it is possible in this brief discussion only to cite selected sources in which thousands of genetic studies are summarized. More than 4000 such references are represented in the eight issues of the *Review of Educational Research* devoted to growth and development,[43] although there probably are some duplications in these bibliographies. Additional summaries and bibliographies concerned primarily with genetic research [44] may be cited at this time, and yet others are listed in the bibliography of this chapter. The chapter on the case-study method includes varied illustrations of the developmental approach, as applied to individuals, social institutions and agencies, and communities.

This large volume of genetic research has been partially centralized and coördinated through such university centers as California, Columbia, Chicago, Harvard, Iowa, Michigan, Minnesota, Stanford, and Yale. However, even the sponsorship, technical resources, and financial support of child-study divisions within higher institutions, plus some support from the foundations, are inadequate for the expensive and complicated procedures of long-range or longitudinal genetic studies, which suggests the need for enlisting public interest and support. The coöperation of teachers, supervisors, administrators, and parents is essential to the successful prosecution of child-development investigations, whether cross section or longi-

---

[43] "Growth and Development." *Review of Educational Research* 11, 14, 17, 20, 22: 475-618, 365-468, 301-403, 341-440, 387-525; December 1941, 1944, 1947, 1950, 1952.

"Mental and Physical Development." *Review of Educational Research* 3, 6, 9: 81-181, 1-152, 1-141; April 1933, February 1936, February 1939.

[44] Dorothy E. Bradbury and Esther L. Skeels, *A Bibliography of Nursery School Education, 1935-39.* Detroit: National Association for Nursery Education, 1939. iv + 64 p.

Marian E. Breckenridge and E. Lee Vincent, *Child Development:* Physical and Psychological Growth Through the School Years. Second Edition. Philadelphia: W. B. Saunders Co., 1949. viii + 622 p. Includes an extensive bibliography.

W. W. Greulich and Others, *A Handbook of Methods for the Study of Adolescent Children.* Monographs of the Society for Research in Child Development, Vol. III, No. 2, Serial No. 15. Washington: Society for Research in Child Development, National Research Council, 1938. xviii + 406 p.

Kai Jensen, "Genetic Method," *op. cit.*

A. G. Mitchell, *Pediatric Bibliography.* Monographs of the Society for Research in Child Development, Vol. VI, No. 1. Washington: Society for Research in Child Development, National Research Council, 1941. vii + 119 p.

N. L. Munn, *op. cit.*

Carl Murchison, Editor, *A Handbook of Child Psychology.* Second Edition, Revised. Worcester: Clark University Press, 1933. xii + 956 p.

Leonard Carmichael, Editor, *Manual of Child Psychology.* New York: John Wiley and Sons, 1946. viii + 1068 p. Revised, 1954. 1295 p.

"Child Development." *Encyclopedia of Educational Research, op. cit.,* p. 127-85. Also see the 1950 edition.

*Child Development and the Curriculum, op. cit.*

*Intelligence:* Its Nature and Nurture, *op. cit.*

tudinal in approach. Coördination of genetic research on a national basis has been facilitated by the Society for Research in Child Development, which publishes the journal, *Child Development,* as well as a periodical series of abstracts and a series of monographs.

**Needed research.** While available sources [45] have enumerated detailed series of problems in child development that touch the interests of education, psychology, and sociology, only a selected list of major problems for genetic investigation can be presented here:

1. Increased observation of development and behavior changes in relation to classroom activities (especially in the partially neglected intermediate grades), nursery school, playground, camp, home, museum, discussion groups, and even adult behavior

2. In addition to growth investigations of individuals and of relatively broad samples, study of developmental aspects of homogeneous groups

3. Developmental study of experimental modification or alteration of behavior

4. Invention of improved instruments suitable for measuring mental development in the late teens and early twenties

5. Publication of research programs undertaken and of the raw data of comprehensive longitudinal studies, to stimulate other workers: (a) to utilize such information and (b) possibly to assist in analysis and interpretation

6. Further emphasis on developmental studies that seek to secure a reasonable picture of the "total child;" for example, to identify interrelationships between mental, physical, and social-emotional factors, and the antecedents or underlying causes of observed growth sequences

7. A complete description of how individual children acquire certain social attitudes, ideals, interests, and modes of behavior, going considerably beyond what is usually possible in the life history or case study by way of tracing developmental sequences

8. Increased interest in the dynamics of origins of behavior and its control, as well as in rate, direction, patterns, and termination of development

9. Comparative sociological studies of children growing up under clearly defined social levels and backgrounds of different types

10. Evaluation of the effectiveness of social and institutional programs for child welfare, in terms of the wholesome development of children

11. Appraisal of the effects of periods of depression and war on the development of children.

## CONCLUDING STATEMENT

The interests of genetic research have now extended far beyond the early emphasis on physical and anatomical growth to mental, social, and personality development, and also include study of causal factors, as well as growth norms and developmental sequences. The scope of genetic inquiry

[45] Kai Jensen, "Needed Research," *op. cit.,* p. 423-37.
Mapheus Smith, "Suggestions for Sociological Research in Child Development." *Journal of Educational Sociology* 9:105-10; October 1935.
Also see the issues of the *Review of Educational Research* listed in footnote 43.

for human individuals includes growth and developmental processes from conception to senescence.

Cross-section data require at least a single (simultaneous) measurement for each individual within selected age groups, with the averages for the groups used for comparative purposes and to indicate trends. The longitudinal approach follows a particular group of subjects or the same individual through repeated measurements made seriatim over a period of time; this method has distinct advantages over the cross-section technique. Genetic research also utilizes or builds upon the procedures of the historical, descriptive-survey, experimental, and case methods.

Nine aspects of growth processes require consideration in the analysis and interpretation of genetic data: (1) initial stage of development, (2) quantitative versus qualitative changes, (3) rate and trends of growth, (4) unity in development at a particular level of maturity, (5) individuality of growth, (6) terminal points of growth, (7) decline or deterioration, (8) developmental diagnosis and causation, and (9) prognosis or prediction of growth.

The volume of genetic research is large, with a measure of coördination provided through the child-study divisions of certain university centers, although adequate resources and financial support are seldom available for long-term longitudinal studies. With several thousand genetic investigations completed, child development still remains one of the most fruitful and important fields for future research.

## SELECTED REFERENCES

ABT, Lawrence E., and BELLAK, Leopold, Editors. *Projective Psychology: Clinical Approaches to the Total Personality.* New York: Alfred A. Knopf, 1950. xvii + 485 + xiv p.

ANDERSON, Harold H., and ANDERSON, Gladys L. Editors. *An Introduction to Projective Techniques.* . . . New York: Prentice-Hall, 1951. xxiv + 720 p.

ANDERSON, John E. *The Psychology of Development and Personal Adjustment.* New York: Henry Holt and Co., 1949. xvi + 720 p.

ANDREWS, T. G., Editor. *Methods of Psychology.* New York: John Wiley and Sons, 1948. 604 p.

ARRINGTON, Ruth E. "An Important Implication of Time Sampling in Observational Studies of Behavior." *American Journal of Sociology* 43:284-95; September 1937.

ARRINGTON, Ruth E. "Time Sampling in Studies of Social Behavior: A Critical Review of Techniques and Results with Research Suggestions." *Psychological Bulletin* 40:81-124; February 1943.

BAKER, G. A. "Graduation of Human Growth Curves." *Growth* 9:299-301; December 1945.

BARKER, Roger, KOUNIN, Jacob S., and WRIGHT, Herbert F. *Child Behavior and Development.* New York: McGraw-Hill Book Co., 1943. 652 p.

BARKER, Roger G., and WRIGHT, Herbert F. *One Boy's Day:* A Specimen Record of Behavior. New York: Harper and Bros., 1951. x + 435 p.

BARR, Arvil S.; DAVIS, Robert A.; and JOHNSON, Palmer O. *Educational Research and Appraisal.* Philadelphia: J. B. Lippincott Co., 1953. p. 313-17.

BARTLETT, F. C. and Others. *The Study of Society:* Methods and Problems. London: Kegan Paul, Trench, Trubner and Co., 1939. p. 70-114.

BAUM, Mable P., and VICKERS, Vernette S. "Anthropometric and Orthopedic Examinations, A Technique for Use with Children." *Child Development* 12:339-45; December 1941.

BAYLEY, Nancy, and FREEMAN, Frank N. "Child Development." *Encyclopedia of Educational Research.* Revised Edition. Edited by Walter S. Monroe. New York: Macmillan Co., 1950. p. 137-39.

BAYLEY, Nancy, and Others. "Growth and Development." *Review of Educational Research* 17:301-403; December 1947.

BERNARD, Jessie. "Normative Collective Behavior: A Classification of Societal Norms." *American Journal of Sociology* 47:24-38; July 1941.

BEVERLY, Burt I. *A Psychology of Growth.* New York: McGraw-Hill Book Co., 1947. xv + 235 p.

BIBER, Barbara, and Others. *Child Life in School:* A Study of a Seven-Year-Old Group. New York: E. P. Dutton and Co., 1942. 658 p.

BLAIR, Arthur W., and BURTON, William H. *Growth and Development of the Preadolescent.* New York: Appleton-Century-Crofts, 1951. viii + 221 p.

BLATZ, W. E. *The Five Sisters.* New York: William Morrow and Co., 1938. 209 p.

BOSSARD, James H. S. *The Sociology of Child Development.* Revised Edition. New York: Harper and Bros., 1953. 788 p.

BOSSARD, James H. S., and BOLL, E. S. "Role of the Guest: A Study in Child Development." *American Sociological Review* 12:192-201; April 1947.

BRADBURY, Dorothy E., and SKEELS, Esther L. *A Bibliography of Nursery School Education, 1935-39.* Detroit: National Association for Nursery Education, 1939. iv + 64 p.

BRECKENRIDGE, Marian E., and VINCENT, E. Lee. *Child Development:* Physical and Psychological Growth Through the School Years. Second Edition. Philadelphia: W. B. Saunders Co., 1949. viii + 622 p.

BROWNELL, William A. "Problem Solving." *The Psychology of Learning.* Forty-first Yearbook, Part II. Chicago: National Society for the Study of Education, 1942. p. 415-33.

BUHLER, Charlotte. *Testing Children's Development from Birth to School Age.* New York: Farrar and Rinehart, 1935. 191 p.

BURLINGTON, Dorothy. *Twins:* A Study of Three Pairs of Identical Twins. New York: International Universities Press, 1953. x + 92 p. + 30 developmental charts.

BURTON, Arthur, and HARRIS, R. E., Editors. *Case Histories in Clinical and Abnormal Psychology.* New York: Harper and Bros., 1947. 680 p.

CARMICHAEL, Leonard, Editor. *Manual of Child Psychology.* New York: John Wiley and Sons, 1946. viii + 1068 p. Revised, 1954. 1295 p.

CHAMPNEY, Horace. "The Measurement of Parent Behavior." *Child Development* 12:131-66; June 1941.

CHAMPNEY, Horace. "The Variables of Parent Behavior." *Journal of Abnormal and Social Psychology* 36:525-42; October 1941.

"Child Development." *Encyclopedia of Educational Research.* Edited by W. S. Monroe. New York: Macmillan Co., 1941. p. 127-85. Also see the 1950 edition.

*Child Development and the Curriculum.* Thirty-eighth Yearbook of the National Society for the Study of Education, Part I. Bloomington, Ill.: Public School Publishing Co., 1939. x + 442 p.

"Child Development and Sociological Research." *Journal of Educational Sociology* 9:67-118; October 1935.

COLE, Luella. *Psychology of Adolescence.* Fourth Edition. New York: Rinehart and Co., 1954. xvi + 712 p.

COTTERMAN, C. W. "Relatives and Human Genetic Analysis." *"Scientific Monthly* 53:227-34; September 1941.

COWELL, Charles C. "Records of Developmental Growth." *Educational Research Bulletin* 19:223-30, 244; April 10, 1940.

CRUZE, Wendell W. *Adolescent Psychology and Development.* New York: Ronald Press Co., 1953. 584 p.

CURETON, T. K. "Elementary Principles and Techniques of Cinematographic Analysis." *Research Quarterly of the American Association for Health, Physical Education, and Recreation* 10:3-24; May 1939.

DEARBORN, W. F., and ROTHNEY, J. W. M. *Predicting the Child's Development.* Cambridge, Mass.: Sci-Art Publishers, 1941. 360 p.

DENNIS, Wayne, Editor. *Readings in Child Psychology.* New York: Prentice-Hall, 1951. xi + 624 p.

DERI, Susan, and Others. "Techniques for the Diagnosis and Measurement of Intergroup Attitudes and Behavior." *Psychological Bulletin* 45:248-71; May 1948.

DEWEY, John. "Evolution and Ethics." *Scientific Monthly* 78:57-66; February 1954. A reprint of a published lecture delivered near the beginning of the twentieth century.

DEWEY, Richard, and HUMBER, W. J. *The Development of Human Behavior.* New York: Macmillan Co., 1951. 832 p.

DUDYCHA, George J. "A Bibliography on Careers in Psychology." *American Psychologist* 2:376-83; September 1947.

DUDYCHA, George J., and DUDYCHA, Martha M. "Childhood Memories: A Review of the Literature." *Psychological Bulletin* 38:668-82; October 1941.

DUNCAN, Marie C. "Recording Descriptive Data and Observer Reliability." *Pedagogical Seminary and Journal of Genetic Psychology* 78:159-64; June 1951.

DUNN, L. C., Editor. *Genetics in the 20th Century.* New York: Macmillan Co., 1951. xi + 634 p.

EMERSON, Alfred E. "Dynamic Homeostasis: A Unifying Principle in Organic, Social, and Ethical Evolution." *Scientific Monthly* 78:67-85; February 1954.

ENGLISH, H. B. *Child Psychology.* New York: Henry Holt and Co., 1951. xiv + 561 p.

ENGLISH, H. B., and Raimy, Victor. *Studying the Individual School Child.* New York: Henry Holt and Co., 1941. 131 p.

ERIKSON, Erik H. *Childhood and Society.* New York: W. W. Norton and Co., 1950. 397 p.

ESSERT, Paul L., LORGE, Irving, and TUCKMAN, Jacob. "Preparation for a Constructive Approach to Later Maturity." *Teachers College Record* 53: 70-76; November 1951.

ESSERT, Paul L., and Others. "Adult Education." *Review of Educational Research* 23:191-283; June 1953.

FESTINGER, Leon, and KATZ, Daniel, Editors. *Research Methods in the Behavioral Sciences.* New York: Dryden Press, 1953.

FLEMING, D. M. *Adolescence.* New York: International Universities Press, 1949. vii + 262 p.

FOSTER, R. G. "Objective Methods of Sociological Research Generally Applicable to Child Development Studies." *Journal of Educational Sociology* 9:79-87; October 1935.

FREEMAN, Frank S., and MILES, Catharine C. "Sex Differences." *Encyclopedia of Educational Research.* Revised Edition. Edited by Walter S. Monroe. New York: Macmillan Co., 1950. p. 1201-08.

FROEHLICH, Gustav J., and Others. "Growth and Development." *Review of Educational Research* 20:341-440; December 1950.

FULLER, R. C., and MYERS, R. R. "The Natural History of a Social Problem." *American Sociological Review* 6:320-29; June 1941.

GARDNER, D. E. M. *Testing Results in the Infant School.* London, Eng.: Methuen and Co., 1948. x + 158 p.

GARRISON, Karl C. *Growth and Development.* New York: Longmans, Green and Co., 1952. xii + 559 p.

GARRISON, Karl C. *Psychology of Adolescence.* Fourth Edition. New York: Prentice-Hall, 1951. 510 p.

GESELL, Arnold. "Growth Potentials of the Human Infant." *Scientific Monthly* 68:252-56; April 1949.

GESELL, Arnold. *The Guidance of Mental Growth in Infant and Child.* New York: Macmillan Co., 1930. xii + 322 p.

GESELL, Arnold. *Infant Development:* The Embryology of Early Human Behavior. New York: Harper and Bros., 1952. 108 p.

GESELL, Arnold. "The Method of Co-Twin Control." *Science* 95:446-48; May 1, 1942.

GESELL, Arnold. "Scientific Approaches to the Study of the Human Mind." *Science* 88:225-30; September 9, 1938.

GESELL, Arnold. *Studies in Child Development.* New York: Harper and Bros., 1948. x + 224 p.

GESELL, Arnold. *Wolf Child and Human Child:* A Narrative Interpretation of the Life History of Kamala, the Wolf Girl. New York: Harper and Bros., 1941. 107 p.

GESELL, Arnold, and AMATRUDA, Catherine S. *Developmental Diagnosis:* Normal and Abnormal Child Development, Clinical Methods and Practical Applications. New York: Paul B. Hoeber, 1947. xvi + 496 p.

GESELL, Arnold, and ILG, Frances L. *Child Development.* New York: Harper and Bros., 1949. xii + 403, xxxii + 475 p.

GESELL, Arnold, ILG, Frances L., AMES, Louise B., and BULLIS, Glenna E. *The Child From Five to Ten.* New York: Harper and Bros., 1946. 475 p.

GESELL, Arnold, and THOMPSON, Helen. *Learning and Growth in Identical Infant Twins.* Genetic Psychology Monographs, Vol. 6, No. 1. Worcester: Clark University Press, 1929. 124 p.

GESELL, Arnold, and THOMPSON, Helen. *Twins T and C from Infancy to Adolescence:* A Biogenetic Study of Individual Differences by the Method of Co-Twin Control. Genetic Psychology Monographs, Vol. 24. Provincetown, Mass.: Journal Press, 1941. p. 3-121.

GESELL, Arnold, and Others. *An Atlas of Human Behavior.* Vols. 1 and 2. New Haven, Conn.: Yale University Press, 1934. 922 p.

GESELL, Arnold, and Others. *Biographies of Child Development:* The Mental Growth Careers of Eighty-four Infants and Children. New York: Paul B. Hoeber, 1939. xviii + 328 p.

GESELL, Arnold, and Others. *The First Five Years of Life:* A Guide to the Study of the Preschool Child. New York: Harper and Bros., 1940. xiii + 393 p.

GESELL, Arnold, and Others. *Infant and Child in the Culture of Today:* The Guidance of Development in Home and Nursery School. New York: Harper and Bros., 1943. xiv + 399 p.

GESELL, Arnold, and Others. *The Psychology of Early Growth:* Including Norms of Infant Behavior and a Method of Genetic Analysis. New York: Macmillan Co., 1938. x + 290 p.

GILBERT, Jeanne G. *Understanding Old Age.* New York: Ronald Press Co., 1953. 442 p.

GOOD, Carter V. "Child Development and the Genetic Method of Research." *Elementary School Journal* 43:577-85; June 1943.

GOOD, Carter V., BARR, A. S., and SCATES, Douglas E. *The Methodology of Educational Research.* New York: Appleton-Century-Crofts, 1936. p. 575-82, 592-93.

GOODENOUGH, Florence L. *Developmental Psychology.* New York: Appleton-Century-Crofts, 1934. xx + 619 p.

GOODENOUGH, Florence L., and MAURER, Katharine M. *The Mental Growth of Children from Two to Fourteen Years:* A Study of the Predictive Value of the Minnesota Preschool Scales. Institute of Child Welfare Monograph, No. 20. Minneapolis: University of Minnesota Press, 1942. xv + 130 p.

GREULICH, W. W., and Others. *A Handbook of Methods for the Study of Adolescent Children.* Monographs of the Society for Research in Child Development, Vol. 3, No. 2, Serial No. 15. Washington: Society for Research in Child Development, National Research Council, 1938. xviii + 406 p.

HAMALAINEN, A. E. "Evaluating Growth of Individual Children." *Elementary School Journal* 41:359-67; January 1941.

HAMALAINEN, A. E. "Existing Practices in the Evaluation of Pupil Growth in the Elementary School." *Elementary School Journal* 42:175-83; November 1941.

HAMILTON, Gordon, *Psychotherapy in Child Guidance.* New York: Columbia University Press, 1947. 340 p.

HAVIGHURST, Robert J. *Human Development and Education.* Revised Edition. New York: Longmans, Green and Co., 1953. ix + 338 p.

HILGARD, Ernest R., and MARQUIS, Donald G. *Conditioning and Learning.* New York: Appleton-Century-Crofts, 1940. 429 p. A critical survey of the literature.

HOLLINGWORTH, Harry L. *Leta Stetter Hollingworth.* Lincoln: University of Nebraska Press, 1943. 204 p.

HOLLINGWORTH, Leta S. *Children Above 180 IQ Stanford-Binet:* Origin and Development. Yonkers-on-Hudson: World Book Co., 1942. x + 332 p.

HOROWITZ, Ruth, and MURPHY, Lois B. "Projective Methods in the Psychological Study of Children." *Journal of Experimental Education* 7:133-40; December 1938. Predicts the rapid development of both the free and controlled toy and play approaches.

HORROCKS, John E. *The Psychology of Adolescence:* Behavior and Development. Boston: Houghton Mifflin Co., 1951. 614 p.

HURLOCK, Elizabeth B. *Adolescent Development*. New York: McGraw-Hill Book Co., 1949. x + 566 p.

HURLOCK, Elizabeth B. *Child Development*. Second Edition. New York: McGraw-Hill Book Co., 1950. xvi + 669 p.

HURLOCK, Elizabeth B. *Developmental Psychology*. New York: McGraw-Hill Book Co., 1953.

HUXLEY, Julian. *Evolution in Action*. New York: Harper and Bros., 1953. 182 p.

HUXLEY, Julian. *Heredity East and West:* Lysenko and Word Science. New York: Henry Schuman, 1949. 246 p.

"Improving Anecdotes of Behavior." *Childhood Education* 22:232-39; January 1946.

*Intelligence:* Its Nature and Nurture. Thirty-ninth Yearbook of the National Society for the Study of Education, Parts I and II. Bloomington, Ill.: Public School Publishing Co., 1940. xviii + 471, xviii + 409 p.

JACKSON, Lydia, and TODD, Kathleen M. *Child Treatment and the Therapy of Play*. Second Edition. New York: Ronald Press, 1950. xii + 159 p.

JARVIE, L. L., and ELLINGSON, Mark. *A Handbook on the Anecdotal Behavior Journal*. Chicago: University of Chicago Press, 1940. xii + 71 p.

JENKINS, Gladys G., and Others, *These Are Your Children:* How They Develop and How to Guide Them. Chicago: Scott, Foresman and Co., 1949. 192 p.

JENSEN, Kai. "Genetic Method," in "Methods of Research in Education." *Review of Educational Research* 9:491-97, 602-7; December 1939.

JERSILD, A. T. *Child Psychology*. Third Edition. New York: Prentice-Hall, 1947. xi + 623 p. Revised, 1954.

JERSILD, A. T. "Self-Understanding in Childhood and Adolescence." *American Psychologist* 6:122-6; April 1951.

JERSILD, A. T., and Others. "Growth and Development." *Review of Educational Research* 11:475-618; December 1941.

JERSILD, A. T., and Others. *Training and Growth in the Development of Children*. Child Development Monographs, No. 10. New York: Teachers College, Columbia University, 1932. 73 p.

JONES, Harold E. *Development in Adolescence*. New York: Appleton-Century Co., 1943. 161 p.

JONES, Harold E. "The Problems of Child Development." *Journal of Consulting Psychology* 6:123-27; May-June 1942.

JONES, Harold E., and BAYLEY, Nancy. "The Berkeley Growth Study." *Child Development* 12:167-73; June 1941.

JONES, Harold E., and Others. *Adolescence*. Forty-third Yearbook of the National Society for the Study of Education, Part I. Chicago: Department of Education, University of Chicago, 1944. x + 358 p.

JOYAL, Arnold E. "Research on Growth and Development." *Phi Delta Kappan* 29:292-94; March 1948.

KAWIN, Ethel. "Records and Reports; Observations, Tests, and Measurements." *Early Childhood Education*. Forty-sixth Yearbook of the National Society for the Study of Education, Part II. Chicago: University of Chicago Press, 1947. p. 281-314.

KINSEY, A. C., and Others. *Sexual Behavior in the Human Male*. Philadelphia: W. B. Saunders Co., 1948. xvi + 804 p.

KINSEY, A. C., and Others. *Sexual Behavior in the Human Female*. Philadelphia: W. B. Saunders Co., 1953. xxx + 842 p.

KOCH, Helen L. "Methods of Studying the Behavior and Development of Young Children." *Methods of Psychology*. Edited by T. G. Andrews. New York: John Wiley and Sons, 1948. Chapter 21, p. 624-63.

KUHLEN, Raymond G. *The Psychology of Adolescent Development*. New York: Harper and Bros., 1952. xvii + 675 p.

KUHLEN, Raymond G., and THOMPSON, George G. *Psychological Studies of Human Development*. New York: Appleton-Century-Crofts, 1952. 533 p.

LANDIS, Paul H. *Adolescence and Youth:* The Process of Maturing. Second Edition. New York: McGraw-Hill Book Co., 1952. xii + 461 p.

LEFEVER, D. Welty, and Others. "Guidance and Counseling." *Review of Educational Research* 21:71-167; April 1951.

LERNER, Eugene, and MURPHY, Lois B., Editors. *Methods for the Study of Personality in Young Children*. Monographs of the Society for Research in Child Development, Vol. 6, No. 4. Washington: National Research Council, 1941. 289 p.

LIGHT, N. Searle, and Others. *Early Childhood Education*. Forty-sixth Yearbook of the National Society for the Study of Education, Part II. Chicago: University of Chicago Press, 1947. xii + 390 p.

LOUTTIT, Chauncey M. *Clinical Psychology of Children's Behavior Problems*. Revised Edition. Edited by G. Murphy. New York: Harper and Bros., 1947. 661 p.

MARTIN, William E., and STENDLER, Celia B. *Child Development:* The Process of Growing Up in Society. New York: Harcourt, Brace and Co., 1953. xxii + 519 p.

McCLOY, C. H. *Appraising Physical Status:* Methods and Norms. University of Iowa Studies in Child Welfare, Vol. 15, No. 2. Iowa City: University of Iowa, 1938. 260 p.

McCLOY, C. H. *Appraising Physical Status:* The Selection of Measurements. University of Iowa Studies in Child Welfare, Vol. 12, No. 2. Iowa City: University of Iowa, 1936. 126 p.

McGRAW, Myrtle B. "Basic Concepts and Procedures in a Study of Behavior Development." *Psychological Review* 47:79-89; January 1940.

McGUIRE, Carson, and SMITH, Sidney B. "Child Development in Periodical Literature." *Child Development* 19:112-24; March-June, 1948.

McKINNON, Katherine M. *Consistency and Change in Behavior Manifestations:* As Observed in a Group of Sixteen Children During a Five Year Period. Child Development Monograph No. 30. New York: Bureau of Publications, Teachers College, Columbia University, 1942. xii + 144 p.

MEAD, Margaret. *Coming of Age in Samoa*. New York: William Morrow and Co., 1928. xv + 297 p.

MEAD, Margaret. *Growing up in New Guinea*. New York: William Morrow and Co., 1930. x + 372 p.

MEAD, Margaret. *Male and Female*. New York: W. Morrow and Co., 1949. xii + 477 p.

"Mental and Physical Development." *Review of Educational Research* 9:1-141, February 1939; 6:1-152, February 1936; 3:81-181, April 1933.

MERRY, Frieda K., and MERRY, Ralph V. *The First Two Decades of Life:* A Revision and Extension of *From Infancy to Adolescence*. New York: Harper and Bros., 1950. xiii + 600 p.

MEYER, Mrs. Eugene. "The Social Responsibilities of the Scientists for Child Care." *Child Development* 19:9-14; March-June, 1948.

MILLARD, Cecil V. *Case Inventory for the Study of Child Development*. Minneapolis: Burgess Publishing Co., 1950. 29 p.

MILLARD, Cecil V. *Child Growth and Development in the Elementary School Years.* Boston: D. C. Heath and Co., 1951. xiv + 511 p.

MITCHELL, A. G. *Pediatric Bibliography.* Monographs of the Society for Research in Child Development, Vol. 6, No. 1. Washington: Society for Research in Child Development, National Research Council, 1941. vii + 119 p.

MOHR, Clara L. "Child Development as an Approach to a Social Studies Curriculum." *Elementary School Journal* 44:388-95; March 1944.

MUNN, N. L. *Psychological Development:* An Introduction to Genetic Psychology. Boston: Houghton Mifflin Co., 1938. xx + 582 p.

MURCHISON, Carl, Editor. *A Handbook of Child Psychology.* Second Edition, Revised. Worcester: Clark University Press, 1933. xii + 956 p.

MURPHY, Gardner. *Personality:* A Bio-social Approach to Origins and Structure. New York: Harper and Bros., 1947. 999 p.

MURPHY, Gardner, and Others. *Experimental Social Psychology.* Revised Edition. New York: Harper and Bros., 1937. xi + 1121 p.

MURPHY, Lois B. "Social and Emotional Development." *Review of Educational Research* 11:479-501; December 1941.

NEUBAUER, Peter B., and STEINFRT, Joseph. "The Significance for Social Workers of the Multidiscipline Approach to Child Development." *Social Service Review* 24:459-68; December 1950.

Ohio State University. *Institute of Genetics.* Columbus: The University, 1954. 16 p.

OJEMANN, R. H., and Others. "Growth and Development." *Review of Educational Research* 14:365-468; December 1944.

OLSON, Willard C. *Child Development.* Boston: D. C. Heath and Co., 1949. xiii + 417 p.

OLSON, Willard C., and HUGHES, Byron O. "Concepts of Growth—Their Significance to Teachers." *Childhood Education* 21:53-63; October 1944.

OLSON, Willard C., and HUGHES, Byron O. "The Concept of Organismic Age." *Journal of Educational Research* 35:525-27; March 1942.

ORLANSKY, Harold. "Infant Care and Personality." *Psychological Bulletin* 46: 1-48; January 1949.

PENNINGTON, L. A., and BERG, I. A. *An Introduction to Clinical Psychology.* New York: Ronald Press Co., 1948. 600 p.

PRESTON, M. G. "Psychophysical Measurement Methods." *Psychological Bulletin* 35:63-83; February 1938.

RECKLESS, W. C. "As Sociologists Enter Child-Development Study." *Journal of Educational Sociology* 9:111-18; October 1935.

ROBINOW, Meinhard; LEONARD, Verna L.; and ANDERSON, Margaret. "A New Approach to the Quantitative Analysis of Children's Posture." *Journal of Pediatrics* 22:655-63; June 1943.

ROGERS, Carl R. *Client-Centered Therapy:* Its Current Practice, Implications, and Theory. Boston: Houghton Mifflin Co., 1951. xii + 560 p.

ROTHNEY, J. W. M. "Recent Findings in the Study of the Physical Growth of Children." *Journal of Educational Research* 35:161-82; November 1941.

SANFORD, R. Nevitt, and Others. *Physique, Personality and Scholarship.* Monographs of the Society for Research in Child Development, Vol. 8, No. 1. Washington: National Research Council, 1943. 705 p.

SCOTT, J. P. "Genetics as a Tool in Experimental Psychological Research." *American Psychologist* 4:526-30; December 1949.

SELLS, Saul R. "Observational Methods of Research," in "Methods of Research and Appraisal in Education." *Review of Educational Research* 18:424-47; December 1948.

SHOCK, N. W., and Others. "The Age Problem in Research Workers." *Scientific Monthly* 72:353-67; June 1951.

SLAVSON, Samuel R. *Analytic Group Psychotherapy with Children, Adolescents, and Adults.* New York: Columbia University Press, 1950. ix + 275 p.

SMITH, Eugene R.; TYLER, Ralph W.; and the Evaluation Staff. *Appraising and Recording Student Progress.* New York: Harper and Bros., 1942. 550 p.

SNYDER, Laurence H. "The Genetic Approach to Human Individuality." *Scientific Monthly* 68:165-71; March 1949.

Social Science Research Council. Sub-Committee on Social Adjustment in Old Age (Robert J. Havighurst, chairman). *Social Adjustment in Old Age: A Research Planning Report.* New York: The Council, 1946. 232 p.

STEPHENS, J. M. *Educational Psychology:* The Study of Educational Growth. New York: Henry Holt and Co., 1951. xxiii + 692 p.

STEVENS, G. D. "Studying the Child by Means of a Standardized Autobiography." *Elementary English* 24:220-24; April 1947.

STODDARD, George D. "Contributions to Education of Scientific Knowledge about Mental Growth and Development." *The Scientific Movement in Education.* Thirty-seventh Yearbook of the National Society for the Study of Education, Part II. Bloomington, Ill.: Public School Publishing Co., 1938. p. 421-34.

STODDARD, George D. *The Meaning of Intelligence.* New York: Macmillan Co., 1943. 504 p.

STODDARD, George D. "Methods of Research in Child Psychology," in "Methods and Technics of Educational Research." *Review of Educational Research* 4:65-71; February 1934.

STODDARD, George D., and WELLMAN, Beth L. *Child Psychology.* New York: Macmillan Co., 1934. xii + 419 p.

STOKE, Stuart M., and Others. "Growth, Development, and Learning." *Review of Educational Research* 22:387-525; December 1952.

STRANG, Ruth. *Introduction to Child Study.* Third Edition. New York: Macmillan Co., 1951. xi + 705 p.

TERMAN, Lewis M. "Psychological Approaches to the Biography of Genius." *Science* 17:293-301; October 4, 1940.

TERMAN, Lewis M., and ODEN, Melita H. *The Gifted Child Grows Up:* Genetic Studies of Genius. Stanford, Calif.: Stanford University Press, 1947. xiv + 450 p.

TERMAN, Lewis M., and Others. *Genetic Studies of Genius,* Vols. 1, 2, and 3. Stanford University, Calif.: Stanford University Press, 1925, 1926, 1930. 648, 842, 508 p.

THEMAN, Viola A., and WITTY, Paul. "Case Studies and Genetic Records of Two Gifted Negroes." *Journal of Psychology* 15:165-81; April 1943.

THOMAS, Dorothy S.; LOOMIS, Alice M.; and ARRINGTON, Ruth E. *Social Behavior Patterns.* New Haven: Institute of Human Relations, Yale University, 1933. 217 p.

THOMPSON, George. *Child Psychology.* Boston: Houghton Mifflin Co., 1952. xxxiii + 667 p.

TILDESLEY, M. L. "Choice of the Unit of Measurement in Anthropometry." *Man* 47:72-78; May 1947.

TORGERSON, Theodore L. *Studying Children:* Diagnostic and Remedial Procedures in Teaching. New York: Dryden Press, 1947. x + 230 p.

TRIMBLE, Harold C., and Cronbach, Lee J. "A Practical Procedure for the Rigorous Interpretation of Test-Retest Scores in Terms of Pupil Growth." *Journal of Educational Research* 36:481-88; March 1943.

TRYON, Caroline. "Studying the Behavior of Children." *Elementary School Journal* 42:241-54; December 1941.

VALENTINE, C. W. *Psychology of Early Childhood:* Study of Mental Development in the First Years of Life. Third Edition. New York: Methuen, 1946. 522 p.

VAN DE WATER, Marjorie. "Problems Faced by a Writer in Communicating Research Findings in Child Development." *Child Development* 19:67-75; March-June, 1948.

WAGONER, L. C. *Observation of Young Children.* New York: McGraw-Hill Book Co., 1935. 297 p.

WAGONER, L. C., and CASTELLANOS, J. M. *Observation of Young Children, Their Behavior, Their Teaching.* Revised Edition. Oakland, Calif.: L. C. Wagoner, Mills College, 1951. 142 p.

WALKER, K. F. "Sociology and Psychology in the Prediction of Behavior." *Psychological Review* 48:443-49; September 1941.

WALTER, H. E. *Genetics:* An Introduction to the Study of Heredity. Revised. New York: Macmillan Co., 1938. xviii + 412 p.

WASHBURNE, Carleton, and Others. *Child Development and the Curriculum.* Thirty-eighth Yearbook of the National Society for the Study of Education, Part I. Bloomington, Ill.: Public School Publishing Co., 1939. x + 442 p.

WATSON, Ernest H., and LOWREY, George H. *Growth and Development of Children.* Chicago: Year Book Publications, 1951. 260 p.

WERNER, Heinz. "Process and Achievement—A Basic Problem of Education and Developmental Psychology." *Harvard Educational Review* 7:353-68; May 1937.

WETZEL, Norman C. "Assessing the Physical Condition of Children: I, Case Demonstration of Failing Growth and the Determination of 'Par' by the Grid Method." *Journal of Pediatrics* 22:82-110; January 1943.

WILES, Kimball, and Others. "The Educational Program: Adolescence." *Review of Educational Research* 24:1-104; February 1954. Chapter 11 lists needed research.

WINN, Ralph B., Editor. *Encyclopedia of Child Guidance.* New York: Philosophical Library, 1943. 456 p.

WITMER, Helen L., Editor. *Psychiatric Interviews with Children.* New York: Commonwealth Fund (Harvard University Press), 1946. viii + 444 p.

WITTY, Paul, and PARKER, Beryl. "The Whole of Childhood—Some Suggestions for Research." *Childhood Education* 16:408-13; May 1940.

WOOD, Ben D., and HAEFNER, Ralph. *Measuring and Guiding Individual Growth.* New York: Silver Burdett Co., 1948. viii + 535 p.

WOODCOCK, Louise P. *Life and Ways of the Two-year-old:* A Teacher's Study. New York: E. P. Dutton and Co., 1941. 267 p.

WOODWORTH, R. S. "Psychology." *Research in the Social Sciences.* Edited by Wilson Gee. New York: Macmillan Co., 1929. p. 151-77.

# 10

# The Reporting and Implementing of Research[1]

EARLIER CHAPTERS have discussed the analysis and interpretation of data in terms of certain quantitative and qualitative concepts. This chapter deals with the preparation of the technical report as the communicatory stage in research. Careful outlining and note-taking are emphasized as preliminary steps essential to the development of logical subdivisions of the major parts of the research report. The larger divisions of the report are described at some length. Details of presentation of data, bibliographical and footnote form, and style are illustrated by numerous examples. Evaluation, preparation for possible publication, and implementation of the findings are discussed as the culminating stages of problem-solving (particularly in action research or operational research).

## REPORTING AS THE COMMUNICATORY STAGE IN RESEARCH

The research report represents the exposition type of composition and, as such, differs from description, narration, and argumentation. It is true that historical writing employs narration to an extent not found in other types of research; however, this type of composition has been discussed at length in the chapter on the historical method and need not be explored further at this time. The function of exposition, and of the technical or research report, is to communicate ideas in such form as to be readily understandable and usable by the reader. This concept emphasizes the ideas or evidence to be communicated, as well as the guiding purpose of the investigator in making the study and in preparing the report, rather than form and style of expression as such. In other words, the scientific

---

[1] Many of the procedures and recommendations of this chapter have been developed in the guidance of graduate students at the University of Cincinnati, and have been adapted for the purposes of this book and for the Cincinnati *Guide* listed below. The advice of Dr. Gordon Hendrickson of the Cincinnati staff has been particularly helpful.

Faculty of Teachers College, University of Cincinnati, with the assistance of Ora E. Smith, *A Guide for the Preparation of Dissertations, Theses, and Field Reports.* Cincinnati: University of Cincinnati, 1952. iii + 55 p.

For an extended discussion of technical writing see J. R. Nelson, *Writing the Technical Report.* New York: McGraw-Hill Book Co., 1940. xiv + 388 p. Also see the 1947 edition.

Other manuals are listed later in the footnotes and the bibliography of this chapter.

character of the data presented and the insight with which evidence is interpreted should be the major considerations in the evaluation of reports. Fortunately, there appears to be a definite relationship between clear thinking, logical organization of materials, sound interpretation, and an effective style of writing. On the other hand, carelessly prepared reports frequently represent loose thinking, faulty interpretation, and even errors in citations and calculations. It is difficult for the reader to give undivided attention to content if organization, form, and style are faulty or ineffective. Therefore, this chapter includes consideration of certain details of form, usage, style, and readability.

The preparation of the report should be viewed as a stage in the progress of the research project rather than as a process separate from the analytical steps of formulation of the problem, selection of the data-gathering procedure, collection of data, and analysis and interpretation of the evidence. Just as analysis is necessary from the very beginning of the investigation, careful notes covering the same stages are essential to preparation of an effective and complete report. First drafts of the introductory chapters or sections on the formulation of the problem and on the review of related studies can be prepared even before the data are collected.

## PURPOSES OF STYLE MANUALS

The primary purpose of this chapter is to help the graduate student place his written work in acceptable, well organized, attractive form in order that its true worth may be disclosed and that the material may be displayed to the best possible advantage. In accomplishing this purpose, the high standards of quality and style naturally expected of written work at the graduate level will be met.

To insure maximum usefulness to the student, this chapter first describes and explains the various parts of a thesis, after which it illustrates by specimen pages these same elements. As the student reads an explanation he is apt to become bewildered by the multitude of details which contribute to a well written thesis, but an examination of the specimen pages frequently reveals that what at first seems complicated is really simple. In thesis writing, as is true for almost any type of technical reporting, the main consideration is for the student's report to be consistent with a set of principles.

Although this chapter is designed to provide information for the student as he begins to write his thesis, dissertation, field report, or various papers related to regular class work, the manual has not been written that will answer every question arising in the mind of the student, and this chapter is no exception. If, after diligent search, the reader cannot find the answer to his question, he should consult his adviser and the references found in this chapter.

## GENERAL REQUIREMENTS AS TO FORM

**Typing.** All manuscripts submitted to the adviser, reading committee, or editor should be neatly and clearly typed on white bond paper, 8½ by 11 inches, 16-pound weight. The original and the first three carbon copies of theses and dissertations are frequently required by a particular university for reading and for filing in the library. Black ribbon and black carbon paper should be used. Either elite or pica type is acceptable, although the same style of type should be used throughout the thesis or report.

All margins should be reasonably wide, approximately one to one and one-fourth inches on all four edges of the page, in order to present a pleasing, balanced appearance and to facilitate trimming and binding of the thesis. The same width for margins should be left on pages containing charts, maps, graphs, or statistical tables. Double spacing should be used throughout the thesis or report, except as otherwise recommended for certain purposes such as quotations, headings, footnotes, bibliographies, and tables.

**Pagination.** Every page in a thesis is assigned a number. Introductory material (including acknowledgment, table of contents, list of tables, and list of figures) should be numbered in small Roman numerals at the bottom of the page, using "ii" for the acknowledgment, "iii" for the first page of table of contents, and omitting "i" on the title page. All other pages of the body of the thesis (including the bibliography and appendix) are numbered in Arabic numerals at the top of the page (right hand corner) with the exception of the first page of each chapter, which has the number placed in the center of the page at the bottom.

**Syllabification, spelling, numerals, and verb tense.** Unnecessary division of a word at the end of a line should be avoided. If it is necessary to divide a word, the conventional rules should be followed according to the natural divisions in correct pronunciation.

"Simplified" spelling is not yet generally used in academic and scientific writing. *Webster's New International Dictionary,* Second Edition, unabridged, is recommended as a guide.

Numbers below one hundred and round numbers such as five hundred, ten thousand, and one million should be spelled out, as well as any number at the beginning of a sentence. Spell out "per cent" rather than use the symbol %. Decimals such as those used in expressing money and per cent, and enumerations going as high as five or six separate items, should be expressed in figures.

To maintain consistency of verb tense throughout a paragraph or a section of the report has proved difficult for many students and writers. It is correct to use the past tense consistently when speaking of steps or procedures already completed. However, the present tense is in order when discussing a table or evidence immediately under the eye of the reader, as presented by the writer of the particular report. When referring to the data of an earlier investigator, the past tense is appropriate.

## OUTLINING AND BRIEFING

Certain skills in outlining and in preparing the brief are essential to the development of logical subdivisions of the major parts of the research report. To be of functional value, the outline must be developed before the thesis or technical report is written rather than afterward, so as to serve as a framework and guide in organizing the report. A valuable device in preparing a logical outline is the use of separate cards or slips of paper for the different headings and subheadings. This procedure enables the writer to vary the arrangement of headings at will until the most effective sequence and grouping of topics have been discovered.

A more advanced stage of thinking and outlining is represented by the brief, which expresses concisely the principal statements to be developed under each topic. If only one of these statements is placed on a card or slip of paper, it facilitates further revision of the outline and brief. A unifying theme is present in most good outlines, and especially in well written briefs and reports. Illustrations of the principle of synthesis or central thesis are found in the chapter on historical research.

## HEADINGS

Both the organization and reading of most research reports and theses are facilitated through use of both center and paragraph headings. Chapter titles are centered on the page and typed in full caps. Major headings within the chapter are centered on the page and typed in caps and lower case. Such center headings are set off from the body of the report by triple spacing. Paragraph headings, run in as a part of the paragraph, are underlined, and the initial letter only of the first word is capitalized. An exception to this principle of capitalization would occur when a proper noun or a proper adjective is a part of the paragraph heading. (See subsequent examples in this chapter.)

Noun rather than verb forms, and phrases rather than sentences, should be used for headings. The phrasing should be coördinate in structure. A heading is not necessary for each paragraph, but each heading should be adequate to cover all the material up to the next coördinate heading. A new paragraph heading is required only when showing the transition in thought to a new unit. There are definite advantages in keeping the length of a heading within a single line.

## LISTS OF ITEMS

The handling of several types of enumerations or lists of items is illustrated at various places in this chapter and in the book as a whole, with appropriate capitalization, indentation, and coördinate form indicated. As a general rule, the major headings are typed in single capitals (except chapter titles in a table of contents), with subordinate items capitalizing only the first letter of the first word. When an item in a list is not a sentence, no period or punctuation is required at the end of the item, except a period at the end of the last item of the enumeration.

## NOTE-TAKING

**Value.** Close relationships exist between the skills of reading, note-taking, outlining, and selection of headings, with a high level of comprehension in reading essential as the foundation on which the other techniques rest. A certain amount of preliminary reading and note-taking is necessary before the major topics of the outline begin to stand out in relief. In turn, the provisional outline and its headings serve as a guide for further reading, study, and note-taking, as emphasized in the chapter on the historical method. Therefore, the preparation of an effective report depends primarily upon the accuracy and completeness of the notes taken at the several stages of the project. Without adequate notes, one ordinarily cannot recall enough facts to organize logically, to interpret soundly, and to write smoothly. From this point of view, skillful note-taking is an important preliminary step, or series of steps, preceding the actual writing of the research report or thesis.

**Suggestions.** There are also interrelationships between expansion of the bibliography, analysis of content, and gathering of notes; in many instances these processes continue until the actual writing of the report begins, and even beyond. In most instances it is desirable to skim rapidly the contents of the chapter or article before attempting any note-taking, since a concise summary or series of points may be discovered near the end, so as to simplify greatly the task of note-taking. The listing of these major points on separate cards or slips of paper is a helpful device in the development and revision of the outline, and supplies the provisional headings for the report itself. As a matter of fact, when the notes have been carefully filed, the guide cards or major headings parallel closely the topics of the working outline and the titles of sections of the report.

Good examples [2] of note systems should be consulted for more complete guidance in note-taking, but the following brief suggestions may be helpful. The chapter on the historical method includes a discussion of note-taking and note-systems with special applications to historical research, although most of the suggestions hold for note-taking in other types of investigation.

As to the physical materials for note-systems, there is a range of choice in size of paper or card. The important considerations are to place only one note on a sheet of paper and to have large enough slips or cards to meet the needs of the particular study. Especially in historical work (and elsewhere), the flexibility of the loose-leaf system has been pointed out, in contrast to the rigidity of the older bound note-books once used by historians and others. Some writers find paper of different colors helpful; for example, varying the color for each type of note (bibliographical, subject, or method), or even using different colors for the main divisions of the subject notes.

Ideas or important observations frequently come to scholars, scientists, and students outside the library, study, or laboratory, as illustrated in the chapter on formulation of the problem. This suggests the desirability of carrying a small loose-leaf note-book or a package of cards for recording such ideas before they escape. Thomas Edison is said to have jotted down almost every thought that occurred to him, even though it may have appeared insignificant at the moment. Leonardo da Vinci's notes are an unusual illustration of recording in several areas of the arts.[3]

**Cautions.** One extreme in note-taking, especially in the early stages, is to include too much material for fear of omitting something important. This may be due in part to haziness in delimiting the problem or to lack of skill in selecting key statements from the material read. This shortcoming

---

[2] Carter Alexander and Arvid J. Burke, *How to Locate Educational Information and Data.* Third Edition. New York: Bureau of Publications, Teachers College, Columbia University, 1950. p. 179-193.

E. W. Dow, *Principles of a Note-System for Historical Studies.* New York: Century Co., 1924. vi + 124 p. plus numerous illustrations.

H. C. Hockett, *Introduction to Research in American History.* Second Edition. New York: Macmillan Co., 1948. p. 10-23, 46-55.

Cecil B. Williams and A. H. Stevenson, *Research Manual for College Studies and Papers.* Revised Edition. New York: Harper and Bros., 1951. p. 85-95.

[3] W. I. B. Beveridge, *The Art of Scientific Investigation.* New York: W. W. Norton and Co., 1950. p. 77.

is less harmful than the other extreme of ending up with such sketchy notes that connected writing and meaningful interpretation are impossible. A number of practices render notes unnecessarily verbose. In particular, the copying of long quotations is questionable when it is possible to return readily to the source when necessary. Matters of common knowledge based on the general store of information or on the general literature of the field represented, rather than on a particular investigation, may not require documentation in the notes or report, although this is a decision to be made with care. Distraction from the central theme by interesting but unrelated side lights in such sources as school-board minutes or newspapers renders some notes and reports tediously wordy and illogically organized, as illustrated in the examples cited in the chapter on the historical method.

**Types of notes.** As to content, notes are of three types. One type, the bibliographical entry, in addition to full reference information, may well include an annotation concerning the nature of the content and the usefulness of the document. The form for an annotated bibliographical note is illustrated as follows:

Ellwood, Charles A. *The Story of Social Philosophy*. New York: Prentice-Hall, 1938. 581 p.
A thorough study of the social theories developed in Italy, France, Germany, Great Britain, and the United States.

The subject note (and the majority of notes are of this type) includes one item of information on a topic, with the source of the note indicated. The subject heading is placed at the top of the paper, with a margin sometimes used for indexing or cross-reference. Subject notes concerned with investigations or experiments usually deal with the problem, sources, procedure, conclusions, limitations, applications, and recommendations. The form of the subject note may be the précis (a brief summary true to the original in content and style), rough summary, paraphrase, or direct quotation. A subject note might take the following form. (Information concerning the publisher and date need not be given in this type of note, since these details are available in the bibliography.)

Review of the Literature
Voelker, Paul F. *The Functions of Attitudes and Ideals in Social Education*, p. 86.
Voelker, in attempting to measure the effect of Boy Scout training on various phases of behavior, directly approached the problem of the detection of dishonesty when he tested eleven groups of boys in a series of specific situations. Various opportunities to overstate the extent of their knowledge were offered. He concluded that: "The results of the experiment do not warrant the general conclusion that it is unnecessary to train children in the formation of specific habits of morality."

The critical or method note is concerned with problems of evaluation and interpretation. An example follows:

Steinmetz, Roland P. *The Absence of Teachers in the Public Schools of Cincinnati, Ohio.*
In analyzing the reasons (p. 61) why women were absent almost twice as much as were men for personal illness, the author does not take into account the fact that elementary-grade teachers are almost exclusively women, and hence a greater percentage of women than men come into more intimate contact with their pupils. Thus they are more susceptible to the common colds of their pupils than are the men who, for the most part, teach on the junior high and secondary levels.

**Documentation and bibliographies.** The chapters on the formulation of the problem and on the survey of related literature have emphasized the necessity for identifying the related studies in the area under investigation. Throughout this book there is exemplified the desirability of documenting the major conclusions reached and the procedures described. In this respect, psychology has set an excellent example; a canvass of 144 periodicals in psychology and related fields, from 1900 to 1927, revealed 2134 bibliographies.[4] A discussion of the scientific use of available literature in conducting research characterizes bibliographical work as the pilot of research.

In spite of the importance and wide use of references in educational, psychological, and social-science literature, careless forms of citation are all too frequent. A sharp criticism of a book of psychological content calls attention to bibliographical lapses that violate most of the recommendations of this chapter.[5]

A far worse situation is the existence of a type of intellectual dishonesty known as plagiarism, which is appropriation of the ideas of another without giving recognition to the source employed. As a rule, the source plagiarized is some form of publication, although in some instances the source may be an unpublished document or even the ideas of an associate not committed to paper at the time. As a matter of intellectual honesty, the creative worker should receive full credit for his ideas, whether he is in the public school, higher institution, business, or industry. This concept does not preclude joint publication of a thesis or report where a faculty member and a student have worked in especially close coöperation. Numerous illustrations of literary piracy have been described in the literature; for example, lapses involving wholesale theft of ideas, use of figures or drawings without

[4] C. M. Louttit, "The Use of Bibliographies in Psychology." *Psychological Review* 36: 341-47; July 1929.
W. A. Hamor and L. W. Bass, "Bibliochresis: The Pilot of Research." *Science* 71:375-78; April 11, 1930.
[5] H. B. English, "On Citations to Scientific Literature." *Psychological Bulletin* 35:305-6; May 1938.

credit lines, and reproduction of large portions of copyrighted works for distribution without securing permission from the publisher or author.[6]

## QUOTATIONS

**Direct quotations.** Each direct quotation should be acknowledged by an accurate citation of the source by means of a footnote or by cross-reference to the bibliography. Direct quotations require care to see that the meaning is not distorted by separation from the context. Equal care is necessary in summarizing or paraphrasing. A break in a quotation is illustrated by the ellipsis mark, three points similar to periods, plus any punctuation ( ... ). Any interpolation or explanatory comment placed within a quotation requires brackets to distinguish it from the original text. Errors made by the original author are not corrected in direct quotation, but are indicated by *sic,* in brackets, immediately following the error; for example, quoting from the minutes of a school board meeting in 1880: "The trustees authorized hiring of a janiter [*sic*] to build fires and sweep the building." If the typewriter does not have a symbol for brackets, a pen may be used.

Long quotations of prose (four or more typewritten lines) should be typed without quotation marks and even with the margin of the page, as a paragraph or paragraphs, single spaced within the paragraph and double spaced between paragraphs. For a quotation within a single spaced quotation, double quotation marks are used. It is possible that many plagiarisms are unconscious, owing to failure in note-taking to use quotation marks for quoted material or to omission of the source.

Shorter quotations may be introduced into the paragraphs of discussion, enclosed in double quotation marks. A quotation within one of these short double spaced quotations is enclosed within single quotation marks. Quoted poetry is indented appropriately.

**Indirect quotations.** Paraphrasing and borrowing of ideas, sometimes referred to as an indirect quotation, should be acknowledged by appropriate documentation, although quotation marks are not used. There is a body of common knowledge in educational history and elsewhere, however, that may not require documentation; for example, the date of the founding of the first Latin grammar school, or first academy, or first high school in

[6] Nicholas Hobbs and Others, "Ethical Standards for Psychology (Professional Relationships, Research, and Writing and Publishing)." *American Psychologist* 6:427-52; August 1951. Includes problems, incidents, and principles of ethics.

W. D. Matthew, "Credit or Responsibility in Scientific Publication." *Science* 71:662-63; June 27, 1930.

Ralph R. Shaw, "Coypright and the Right to Credit." *Science* 113:571-73; May 18, 1951.

C. W. Stiles, "Absent-Mindedness as a Factor in Professional Ethics." *Science* 71:100-101; January 24, 1930.

G. M. Whipple, "Does a Coypright Mean Anything?" *Nation's Schools* 12:21-24; August 1933.

this country. Likewise, there is a body of commonly acknowledged fact in each major discipline that does not require documentation; for example, it is generally known by students of psychology that the lower threshold for sound is about twenty cycles. It is a frequent occurrence that investigators with extensive experience in a particular field of specialization absorb many facts and theories without recalling the specific origins; for example, the concept that, as skill in the performance of a complex activity develops, the individual becomes decreasingly aware of the separate acts, or that, under these conditions, performance becomes increasingly automatic.[7]

**Authorization to quote.** Permission to quote is not necessary in preparing an unpublished thesis or similar typewritten report. When quoting more than a few lines for publication from a copyrighted source, the safest plan is to secure permission from the copyright holder, in most instances the publisher but sometimes the author. Usually such authorization is granted without charge, unless the quotation runs into a matter of paragraphs or pages rather than a few sentences. Since an extended discussion of plagiarism, copyright law, and publication is beyond the scope of this book, the reader interested in these problems is referred to other sources.[8]

## FORMAT

The term *format* refers to the mechanical makeup of the thesis or technical report. The standards of publishing over the years have evolved a definite order of parts which are listed and described in this section of the chapter. The student's thesis, dissertation, or field report should conform to these several parts in the sequence listed.

In addition to examination of this book and other printed volumes, as well as typewritten theses in the local library, in order to secure illustrations of the major parts of research reports, reference may be made to other sources[9] that contain numerous sample pages, style sheets, or outlines for preparation of the book or thesis.

[7] Norman L. Munn, "The Ethics of Textbook Writing." *American Psychologist* 3:88-90; March 1948.

[8] W. E. Spahr and R. J. Swenson, *Methods and Status of Scientific Research*. New York: Harper and Bros., 1930. p. 328-58. Also see Nicholas Hobbs and Others, *op. cit.*

[9] E. M. Allen, *The Author's Handbook*. Scranton, Pa.: International Textbook Co., 1938. p. 76-87.

*A Manual of Style*. Tenth Edition, Revised. Chicago: University of Chicago Press, 1943. p. 11-20. Also see the 1949 edition.

W. G. Campbell, *A Form Book for Thesis Writing*. Boston: Houghton Mifflin Co., 1939. p. 7-13, 65-115.

Kathleen Dugdale, *A Manual of Form for Theses and Term Reports*. Bloomington: Indiana University, 1950. vi + 58 p.

Marjorie E. Skillin, Robert M. Gay, and Others, *Words into Type*. New York: Appleton-Century-Crofts, 1948. xx + 585 p.

Kate L. Turabian, *A Manual for Writers of Dissertations*. Chicago: University of Chicago Bookstore, 1937. p. 7-11, 58-61.

## MAJOR DIVISIONS OF THE REPORT

Relatively short reports or papers of less than fifty pages hardly lend themselves to the chapter form of organization, but can be divided into appropriate sections, with center and paragraph headings. The parts of the extended research report or thesis and the usual sequence are commonly as outlined below.

Title Page
Acknowledgment (if any)
  (The terms *Preface* or *Foreword* ordinarily are used in printed books, and sometimes an *Editor's Introduction* is included.)
Table of Contents
List of Tables (if any)
List of Figures (if any)
Formulation and Definition of the Problem
  (One or more chapters dealing with such items as the problem, sources, procedure, and related literature)
Presentation and Interpretation of Data
  (Commonly divided into several chapters)
Summary and Conclusions
  (Restatement of problem, sources, and procedure; conclusions and their limitations; application and recommendations; needed research)
Bibliography
Appendix (if any)
Index (if any)
  (Customary only in printed volumes)

**Title and title page.** The title page of a thesis should be concise and adequately descriptive. Beginners in the art of writing sometimes have to be reminded that the report cannot be made in the title; in other words, no sufficiently lengthy title has been devised to describe adequately the problem, sources, procedure, and results of a study. Sometimes a subtitle is employed in the interest of clarification, although this purpose is not always served, since the subtitle is frequently omitted from references and guides. Therefore, a single comprehensive title is recommended.

Certain forms of expression and phrasing are to be avoided. "Some Aspects of . . ." and "Comments on . . ." are vague generalities unsuitable for inclusion in the title of a research report. "A Study of . . .," "A Scientific Study of. . .," "An Investigation of . . .," "An Inquiry into . . .," and "An Analysis of . . ." are usually superfluous words that can be eliminated in view of the fact that the graduate thesis or report presupposes study, investigation, inquiry, or analysis of an objective character. Exceptions to this recommendation include quite legitimate attempts to indicate the research method employed; for example, "An Experimental Investigation of . . .," "A Genetic Study of . . .," or "Factor Analysis of . . . ." If the title of the report can be made so interesting as to arrest the attention of the reader, so much the better, although the importance of research and of the graduate school cannot permit the type of catchy, bizarre, and misleading title so frequently coined for novels, journalistic writing, and the movies.

It is usually possible to rephrase effectively a long, involved title; for example, to recast "A Plan Which Will Enable the State of Vermont to Reduce the Existing Inequalities of Educational Opportunity, to Distribute More Equitably the Financial Burden of Education, and to Provide More Adequate Support for the Schools of the State," so as to read "Reduction of Inequalities of Educational Opportunity and Support in Vermont." The following list of Doctor of Education projects, as worded below, is subject to certain of the foregoing criticisms, especially the length of the titles. The use of the infinitive to introduce the title is questionable, as found in the following titles.

To assist in the development, organization, and administration of a new coordinated program for the preparation of teachers of the arts at George Peabody College for Teachers with special reference to preparation of teachers of industrial arts.

To formulate plans as a guide in developing at Silliman University a program to educate teachers for leadership in the movement to make the schools better serve the needs of their communities in the Philippines.

To devise a type schedule better adapted to the needs of secondary schools that attempt to develop curricula which promote integration, particularly one better adapted to the needs of certain secondary schools of Tulsa, Oklahoma.

To formulate and introduce a plan for the organization and development of a program of art education for the junior college at San Luis Obispo and to integrate that work with the art program of elementary and secondary schools of that city.

Many other illustrations of reasonably satisfactory and of questionable research topics are given in the chapter on formulation of the problem. The exact form of the title page and of the several parts of the thesis usually is specified by the local graduate department, with illustrative style sheets supplied to the students. Therefore, examples of the title page and of other parts of the thesis, as presented in this chapter, should be regarded only as suggestive.

It should prove helpful to observe the capitalization and spacing of the title page illustrated on page 854. (The term *dissertation* is customarily reserved for the doctoral study.) It will be noted that the "inverted pyramid" or "hour-glass" of typed lines on the title page is pleasing to the eye and that a "block" arrangement of lines also presents a pleasing appearance. Balance, proportion, and centering should be considered by the typist in arranging titles and headings.

**Acknowledgment.** For all practical purposes in thesis writing and technical reporting, the terms *acknowledgment, preface,* and *foreword* are synonymous, although printed volumes frequently make distinctions between such terms as preliminary parts of a book and sometimes include an editor's introduction. The expression *acknowledgment* is the commonly used label for the page following the title of the research report. However, this section should be included only when substantial assistance and coöperation of a non-routine character require public recognition. The wording should be simple, concise, temperate, tactful, and modest. Bestowal of praise or expression of indebtedness in effusive, sentimental, or extravagant language may cause the reader to question the sincerity of the investigator or the soundness of the study. The listing of well known names, whether on the faculty of the local institution or elsewhere, to court favor or to enhance the value of the study by lending to it a fictitious authority, is a form of intellectual and professional dishonesty. Types of acknowledgment that have become stereotyped and may well be avoided are those referring to the patience and tolerance of a spouse during the pursuit of the graduate degree, exaggerated tributes to the advisory committee, contributions of the graduate classes attended, librarians from whom books were borrowed or references secured, efforts of the typist, clerks assisting in the scoring of tests or tabulation of data, operators of calculating machines, and casual or occasional interviews or letters. If these recommendations (by the process of elimination) leave the impression that the acknowledgment may well be simple and brief, the purpose of this discussion has been accomplished.

Dedications are ordinarily in questionable taste, and are especially inappropriate for thesis work. The relationships involved are usually of a personal nature and as such hold little interest for the public; the obligation to spouse, parents, professors, or students might better be expressed in private. In some instances the quality or character of the work may even be such as to embarrass the person to whom dedicated.

**Table of contents.** An adequate table of contents serves as a synopsis or headline display of the design or structural pattern of the body of the report. If the working outline is logical and the appropriate topical headings are parallel in phrasing, the table of contents should prove equally meaningful and satisfactory. The relationship between major headings and subtopics can be shown by variations in capitalization and by appropriate indentation.

A reasonably comprehensive table of contents is essential for the typed report or thesis, with the pages indicated, since ordinarily no index is prepared. In most instances, all the center and paragraph headings for a single chapter will not extend in length beyond one page in the table of contents. For the majority of chapters, the space per chapter in the table of contents probably will not exceed one-half page. Occasionally the synopsis is so detailed as to create the impression that an attempt has been made to write the report through the medium of the table of contents. In such an instance it is better to use only the major or center headings in the table of contents. A heading that is confined to one line in the body of the report, and in the table of contents, usually is advantageous in terms of brevity, clarity, and readability; to go beyond two lines seems inexcusable. Headings in the table of contents must duplicate exactly the subdivisions of the chapter and must be checked carefully against the manuscript, especially after each revision and retyping, when rephrasing of headings or renumbering of pages may have taken place.

The table of contents of this book may serve illustrative purposes. In addition, the reader may return in this chapter to the outline of the major divisions of a report, which present the parts and sequence of the table of contents, with the exception that "title page" and "table of contents" would not be set down as such in the actual table of contents. The table of contents on page 855 illustrates capitalization and spacing for the typed report. Workers especially interested in educational journalism may wish to examine a survey and series of recommendations concerned with use of the table of contents in periodicals.[10]

**Dealing with tables and figures.** A separate page or pages should be devoted to a listing of the tables presented in the report, a recommendation that holds for the list of figures. The essential information is the number of the table or figure, exact title, and page where found in the body of the report. Consecutive Arabic numerals are recommended for identifying the tables. A consecutive series of Arabic numerals is used to number the figures. The first letters of the principal words (except articles, prepositions, and conjunctions) in the titles are capitalized in the list of tables and in the list of figures. For practical purposes and in the interest of simplification, figures may include all types of illustrations, whether known as graphs, charts, diagrams, maps, or photographs. In mounting photographs or similar illustrative materials, paper of the same size as the sheets of the typed manuscript should be used, to facilitate binding of the thesis. The candidate may save time and effort by having the typist prepare accurate lists of tables and of figures after the manuscript has been completely typed, inserting the appropriate page references. It is imperative to check the titles and numbers in the lists against the manuscript after any revision

[10] H. Stoutemyer, "The Psychology of the Table of Contents." *Journal of Educational Research* 24:227-30; October 1931.

ςr retyping. Observe the capitalization and spacing in the illustrative list of tables and list of figures shown on page 856.

The following eleven recommendations cover the principal points to be observed in construction of tables. The student would do well to observe the structure, ruling, capitalization, and spacing of the illustrative tables found in this chapter. Walker and Durost have provided an especially helpful manual on the characteristics of a good table, analysis and criticism of illustrative tables, and steps in making a table.[11]

1. Each series of items that involves frequencies should be presented in the form of a table with an appropriate title and number. When a table lacks either title or number, both author and reader may have difficulty in referring to or locating readily the desired data.

2. The table heading should not be divided into separate clauses or sentences, but should express adequately in a continuous title the nature of the data included. To begin the title with such words as "showing," "table showing," and (usually) "distribution of" is superfluous. Ordinarily, titles of tables should answer questions relating to who, what, when, where, and how many, although in such studies as learning experiments, factors of time and place are not emphasized. Also, when all of the data have been gathered from a particular school system or school, at the same time, it may not be necessary to repeat in the titles the time and place. However, one cannot go far wrong in making identifying labels consistently complete for both tables and figures.

3. Horizontal and vertical rulings should be inserted as needed, and care should be taken that the heading above each particular section applies only to that section. Rulings are not necessary on the right and left margins of the table.

4. Uncommon abbreviations should be explained in footnotes below the table. In general, abbreviations are to be avoided, if possible.

5. Footnotes in connection with the table should be referred to by daggers (†), asterisks (*), or letters (a) rather than by figures. Otherwise, confusion of numerals with the data of the table might result.

6. If possible, confine each table to a single page. Unwieldy tables in many instances may be broken up into separate tables, in order to prevent use of a large sheet that has to be folded. Folded tables and graphs involve difficulties in binding the report, are easily lost or torn, and wear through where creased. When a table must be continued on a second page, the box headings should be repeated at the top of each column of data, so as to facilitate ready use of the material; the table number, but not the table

---

[11] Helen M. Walker and Walter N. Durost, *Statistical Tables:* Their Structure and Use. New York: Bureau of Publications, Teachers College, Columbia University, 1936. v + 76 p.

title, should be repeated, thus, TABLE 2 (Continued). It is sometimes necessary to turn unusually wide tables sidewise on the page, with the top of the table toward the margin to be bound.

7. A table should be placed in the manuscript as near the point of first reference as possible and should be centered in the page for the balanced appearance that results. Ordinarily a table should appear on the page immediately following the first reference to the data represented, or as soon thereafter as possible. If an initial reference to more than one table is made on a single page, these tables should be placed as a group on the pages immediately following the citation of the tables. In general, a table or a figure that occupies more than one-half page of space appears to better advantage when centered on a separate page without accompanying text on that particular page.

8. Too many groups or columns of data should not be shown in one table. It is better to select for each table the data needed to establish clearly a limited number of points, in some instances only one or two, than to invite confusion as the result of too complicated a table.

9. It may be advisable to place in the appendix a long table of several or more pages, using a shorter summary table in the body of the thesis.

10. Always refer to a table by its number. It is not necessary to cite the page on which a particular table appears, except when referring to data in the appendix.

11. A practical test of the effectiveness of a table or a figure is in terms of whether it is so complete as to be understandable apart from the text of the thesis or report.

With respect to figures, note that the legend is placed beneath the figure (single capitals). Use figures only when they make a real contribution to interpretation of the data or tables. Always refer to the figure by its number. Useful suggestions for the preparation of figures, graphs, diagrams, charts, and maps are as follows: [12]

1. The general arrangement of a diagram should proceed from left to right.
2. Where possible, represent quantities by linear magnitude, as areas or volumes are more likely to be misinterpreted.

[12] Quoted from *Report of the Joint Committee on Standards for Graphic Presentation.* New York: American Society of Mechanical Engineers, 1918. 50 p. Also see:
*Engineering and Scientific Graphs for Publications.* New York: American Society of Mechanical Engineers, 1943.
Herbert Arkin and Raymond R. Colton, *Graphs:* How to Make and Use Them. New York: Harper and Bros., 1936. xvi + 224 p. Also see 1940 edition.
R. R. Lutz, *Graphic Presentation Simplified.* New York: Funk and Wagnalls, 1949. xx + 202 p.
Rudolf Modley, *How to Use Pictorial Statistics.* New York: Harper and Bros., 1937. xviii + 170 p.
John L. Ridgway, *Scientific Illustration.* Stanford University, Calif.: Stanford University Press, 1938. xiv + 173 p.

3. For a curve, the vertical scale, whenever practicable, should be so selected that the zero line will appear in the diagram.

4. If the zero line of the vertical scale will not normally appear in the curve diagram, the zero line should be shown by the use of a horizontal break in the diagram.

5. The zero lines of the scales for a curve should be sharply distinguished from the other coördinate lines.

6. For curves having a scale representing percentages, it is usually desirable to emphasize in some distinctive way the 100 per cent line used as a basis of comparison.

7. When the scale of the diagram refers to dates, and the period represented is not a complete unit, it is better not to emphasize the first and last ordinates, since such a diagram does not represent the beginning and end of time.

8. When curves are drawn on logarithmic coördinates, the limiting lines of the diagram should each be of some power of ten on the logarithmic scale.

9. It is advisable not to show any more coördinate lines than necessary to guide the eye in reading the diagram.

10. The curve lines of a diagram should be sharply distinguished from the ruling.

11. In curves representing a series of observations, it is advisable, whenever possible, to indicate clearly on the diagram all the points representing the separate observations.

12. The horizontal scale for curves should usually read from left to right and the vertical scale from bottom to top.

13. Figures for the scale of a diagram should be placed at the left and at the bottom or along the respective axes.

14. It is often desirable to include in the diagram the numerical data or formulas represented.

15. If numerical data are not included in the diagram, it is desirable to give the data in tabular form accompanying the diagram.

16. All lettering and all figures in a diagram should be placed so as to be easily read from the base as the bottom, or from the right-hand edge of the diagram as the bottom.

17. The title of a diagram should be made as clear and complete as possible. Subtitles or descriptions should be added if necessary to insure clearness.

**Formulation and definition of the problem.** One or more chapters may be required for an adequate introduction to, or overview of, the investigation, depending on how fully it seems necessary to follow up details of defining the problem, such as analysis of the problem into its constituent elements, limits or scope of the investigation, orientation and related literature, sources of data and method, need for the study, technical terminology, and initial assumptions. Up to this point the pages of the report commonly are numbered at the bottom of the page in small Roman numerals to indicate the preliminary character of the material presented. With the introductory chapter, the Arabic numerals for pages begin.

In effect, a well organized report tells the reader where he is going, takes him there, and then tells him where he has been. The wife of Josiah Royce

whimsically makes a similar comment, in more complicated sentence structure, about her husband's method of lecturing at Harvard.[13]

> Oh, Professor Royce's method of lecturing is quite simple. He always tells
> his students at the beginning of the hour just what he is going to tell them, and
> how he is going to tell it to them; then he tells them exactly what he told he
> would tell them in exactly the way he told them he would tell them; then, at
> the end of his lecture hour, he always takes time to tell them that he has told
> them what he told them he would tell them.

In agreement with the foregoing sequence, the introductory chapter or
portion of the research report looks forward (and to some extent backward, through the related literature and the historical background). The
body of the thesis presents the data and interpretation. The chapter of summarization and conclusions looks backward (and forward, through discussion of applications, recommendations, and needed research).

The straightforward procedure is to state the purpose of the study in the
opening paragraph. Many readers are annoyed and confused when several
pages devoted to reasons for undertaking the investigation, the importance
of the problem, and the historical setting precede the statement of what the
problem actually is. One way of focusing attention on the major function
of the introductory chapter is to use such a title as "Formulation and
Definition of the Problem" or "The Problem and Its Setting" rather than
the vague general title, "Introduction." Certain of the more detailed explanatory materials sometimes found in the introductory chapter could
more appropriately be placed in the text or footnotes of later chapters.

It is recommended that the candidate prepare a first draft of the overview section early in the course of the investigation, before details are forgotten, and secure criticism of this introduction in time to modify procedure,
if necessary. This plan should also result in developing additional background and insight useful in rewriting the introductory chapter. As a
measure of the adequacy of the definition of the problem, the investigator
should ask himself whether one who had never heard of the study could
secure through this statement an adequate overview of purpose, sources,
and procedure. An even more challenging test is to ask the same question
with respect to the reader of fifty years hence, when all of the persons
connected with the investigation will have been removed from the immediate scene of action.

The earlier chapter on formulation and definition of the problem includes
illustrative statements of purposes, sources, and procedures. For additional

[13] J. R. Nelson, *op. cit.*, p. 30.
Also see J. R. Shannon, "Art in Writing for Educational Periodicals: The Introduction."
*Journal of Educational Research* 44:599-610; April 1951.

information concerning the introductory section of the technical report and for helpful models of style, there is available an extensive treatise.[14]

**Presentation of evidence.** If the introductory section of the report meets the standards outlined above, the transition to presentation and interpretation of the data should prove smooth and unified. A factor that frequently lies back of a disconnected report is the inexperience of the young writer who forgets that the typical reader has had no previous experience with the substance of the particular study. He leaves gaps in his organization of ideas, partly because the missing links have become so commonplace in his thinking and experience that he overlooks their importance for the reader. Such lapses can be prevented to some extent through a logical outline, a brief of key statements, well organized notes, and carefully worded headings.

In the first draft of the thesis it usually is expedient to place each table on a separate page and to begin a major heading on a new page. This procedure leaves room for insertion of transitional or connecting statements. Judicious use of scissors and paste in the work of revision makes unnecessary the recopying of the entire manuscript, before sending it to the typist. Advisers and members of reading committees are expected to read only consecutively typed, clean pages of text. In any draft of the report submitted for official or editorial reading full pages are typed in the conventional fashion.

The chapters that make up the body of the report vary in content and organization with the type of research method employed. In historical writing the narrative is told through a series of chronological or topical chapters; sometimes both forms of organization appear in a single study. The survey type of report consists of appropriate tables and their interpretation picturing the status of the current conditions investigated. An experimental study usually has a series of chapters dealing with details of equipment, procedure, and results. Actual case studies (appropriately grouped) frequently make up the bulk of the report when the case method has been used.

Within the chapter itself much can be done to insure unity through use of introductory, transitional, and summary paragraphs and sentences. When a series of points is to be discussed in detail, preliminary enumeration of them serves as a helpful introduction. Cross-references to other parts of the chapter or report are evidence of structural design and aid in avoiding unnecessary repetition, although overuse of this device may become irritating to the reader. The effectiveness of the paragraph organization is one of the best single measures of careful planning in the report.

[14] J. R. Nelson, *op. cit.*, p. 38-67.
Also see J. R. Shannon, *op. cit.*

Certain types of material tend to break the continuity of thought in the body of the text. In many instances long tables, questionnaires, tests, legal documents, and other essential exhibits can be placed in the appendix with an appropriate cross-reference in the text. Long or partially irrelevant quotations frequently have a distracting effect on the reader. In such instances, a shorter quotation or effective paraphrasing, with appropriate recognition of the source, will prove advantageous. A long series of quotations, apparently compiled under the misapprehension that every statement included must be supported by citation of some "authority," is more likely to annoy the reader than to impress him as evidence of the candidate's scholarship. The use of footnotes for references and for certain types of comments is a device to facilitate continuity of thought in the body of the page.

In certain types of theses and reports, there is danger of overloading the text with statistical details—an overemphasis that increases the difficulty of reading the reports of educational, psychological, and social research. Better and more intelligent use of statistical techniques is needed, with increased understanding of the assumptions and limitations of statistics.[15] Methods and results should be interpreted in keeping with the probable level of statistical sophistication of the reader. In the several chapters on research methods certain special problems of interpretation have been considered in some detail.

**Summary and conclusions.** The last chapter or section of the body of the manuscript is the summary and conclusions. This is an overview of the entire study, of particular value to many readers who may not go outside the final chapter for information concerning problem, sources, method, conclusions and their limitations, applications and recommendations, and needed research. It is not the place for introduction of new data or for encyclopedic enumeration of details reported earlier in the manuscript, but for final synthesis of the whole study. As such, it is the most frequently used part of the report. Chapter summaries are useful in preparing this section, although the mere process of adding them together falls short of synthesis.

The report begins with a statement of purpose and, at least by implication, with the formulation of a working hypothesis. The chapters concerned with presentation of data are the testing grounds for the hypothesis. The last chapter recapitulates the answer to the opening question of the investigation.

The statement of conclusions does not require the repetition of the data

---

[15] Harry J. Baker, "The Fetish of Statistics." *Journal of Educational Research* 34:458-59; February 1941.

or evidence on which they are based. Skillful grouping and appropriate subordination of conclusions under major headings are essential in avoiding encyclopedic enumeration of dozens of individual statements. Any discussion of limitations or qualification of results should avoid both an apologetic attitude and overconfidence. If applications or recommendations are made, based on the judgment and insight of the investigator rather than directly on the data, they must be plainly labeled as such. The probability of application of the results in practice will be increased, if nontechnical language is used in this concluding chapter. It is better to suggest a few carefully identified problems for future investigation, springing directly from the study reported, than to enumerate a large number of miscellaneous topics for further study.

Useful examples of the terminal section of the technical report may be found in the studies and theses on local library shelves, and in published handbooks.[16]

**Bibliography.** The practice in research reports is to place a complete bibliography of all references used immediately after the last chapter, with continuous page numbering, although textbooks commonly print chapter bibliographies. The references are alphabetically arranged in one list by surnames of authors, unless it seems advantageous to group the materials of a long bibliography by topics (not form of publication), with the alphabetical arrangement preserved under each heading. It makes for completeness and convenience of reference to include in the bibliography all the items to which the footnotes refer. It may even be desirable to list certain materials not examined, such as unpublished theses known to be directly related to the particular problem. The typical thesis bibliography is selective rather than exhaustive; for example, a study of the public vote on issues of school finance in a large city cannot list all of the available references on voting or on school costs and educational finance.

Annotations, to the extent of a sentence or a short paragraph for each reference, make the bibliography more meaningful, unless a relatively full review of the related literature has been given earlier in the report. The references must be numbered consecutively, if a cross-reference system of citation from the body of the report to the bibliography is used in place of footnotes. Models of style for footnotes and for the bibliography are given later in this chapter and in this volume as a whole.

**Appendix.** All cumbersome or voluminous material not essential to

---

[16] R. P. Baker and A. C. Howell, *The Preparation of Reports.* Revised Edition. New York: Ronald Press Co., 1938. p. 43-50, 489-95.

J. R. Nelson, *op. cit.,* p. 111-17. Also see the 1947 edition.

J. R. Shannon, "Art in Writing for Educational Periodicals: The Ending." *Journal of Educational Research* 46:333-45; January 195?.

the understanding of the text, but useful as supporting evidence, may be placed in the appendix of the report. Types of exhibits that tend to break the continuity for the reader (and therefore should be placed in the appendix) include long tables and raw data, questionnaires and schedules, form letters and even important personal communications, test forms, extracts from curriculum documents such as catalogues and courses of study, and formulas. A summary table or a short quotation in the body of the report frequently is sufficient, with a cross-reference to the full tabulation or complete document in the appendix. The materials of the appendix should be grouped into homogeneous parts, provided with numbers and appropriate headings, and listed in the table of contents. The appendix should never be made a dumping ground for miscellaneous or irrelevant materials that are placed there as a convenient method of disposal.

**Index.**[17] In view of the fact that the typical reader of this book is not preparing his report or thesis for publication, a detailed discussion of the index will not be attempted at this time. As a rule, the typed manuscript depends on a detailed table of contents rather than on an index for the guidance of the reader in locating desired information. The worker who expects to prepare an index for a published report may examine the index of this volume and of other well indexed books as illustrations of form. Some publications with heavy bibliographical content compile separate author and subject indexes. The usual plan in preparation of an index is to transfer from page proof to cards the key topics, names, and authors (only one item per card) with the pages indicated. Cards relating to the same topic or author can be combined, so as to transfer the page notations to a single card under the appropriate heading. The person inexperienced in this type of work should be cautioned that effective indexing is not as simple as it sounds and that, unless he is willing to expend the necessary energy in acquiring this skill, it may be better to employ a specially trained worker to prepare the index. The publisher usually has such a specialist available.

## FIELD REPORTS AND SPECIAL THESES

The organization suggested earlier in this chapter is suitable for a research report employing one or more of the generally recognized techniques of investigation (historical, survey, experimental, case study, or genetic). With some variations, the same organization can be used in

---

[17] Walter V. Bingham, "How to Make a Useful Index." *American Psychologist* 6:31-34; January 1951.

L. H. Warren, "Practical Suggestions for Reducing the Labor of Indexing a Textbook." *Science* 92:217-18; September 6, 1940.

REDUCTION OF INEQUALITIES OF
EDUCATIONAL OPPORTUNITY AND SUPPORT IN VERMONT

A field project)
A thesis      ) submitted to
A dissertation )

The Graduate Faculty of the Teachers College
of the University of Cincinnati

in partial fulfillment of the
requirements for the degree of

MASTER OF EDUCATION)

DOCTOR OF EDUCATION)

1952

by

John Smith Jones
B. S., University of Kentucky, 1950
B. E., University of Cincinnati, 1951

**Sample page of a thesis**

# TABLE OF CONTENTS

iii

**Sample page of a thesis**

# LIST OF TABLES

# LIST OF FIGURES

## Sample page of a thesis

CHAPTER II

HISTORICAL BACKGROUND OF READING INSTRUCTION

This chapter presents the historical background essential
to an understanding of effective appraisal in reading. Through tracing
the development of modern concepts of reading, it provides the setting
in which test construction in reading operates today.

### Statements of Reading Authorities

An early point of view.--In 1838, Horace Mann wrote in his
Second Annual Report of the Secretary of the Board of Education,
State of Massachusetts:

> Entertaining views of the importance of this subject
> [reading], ... I have devoted especial pains to learn with some
> degree of numerical accuracy, how far the reading, in our schools,
> is an exercise of the mind in thinking and feeling, and how far it
> is a barren action of the organs of speech upon the atmosphere....
> The result is that more than eleven-twelfths of all the children in
> the reading classes, in our schools, do not understand the meaning of
> the words they read [in spite of major emphasis on the tool subjects
> in the schools of Horace Mann's day].... It would hardly seem that
> the combined efforts of all persons engaged could have accomplished
> more in defeating the true object of reading.[1]

A modern point of view.--Charles H. Judd gives credit to
this criticism by Horace Mann for being the first of the many inquiries into reading that today have produced a complete change in
the current concept of reading.[2] It is not the purpose here to

-------------------

[1] G. C. Mann and Mary Tyler Mann, Life and Works of Horace
Mann, p. 508. Boston: Lee and Shepard, 1891.

[2] Charles H. Judd, Reading: Its Nature and Development,
p. 4. Supplementary Educational Monographs, Vol. 2, No. 4. Chicago:
Department of Education, University of Chicago, 1918.

4

**Sample page of a thesis**

## TABLE 7

ACTIVITIES OF TWELVE RURAL SUPERVISORS IN OHIO, 1942, AND THE
NUMBER OF HOURS DEVOTED TO EACH ACTIVITY

| Activity | Number of Hours | Rank |
|---|---|---|
| 1. Office Activities: | | |
| Preparing suggestions for teachers .. | 253.2 | 1 |
| Records and reports ................... | 241.3 | 2 |
| Correspondence ...................... | 164.7 | 3 |
| Conference with teachers ........... | 130.9 | 4 |
| Preparing for visits--collecting materials, reports, etc. .......... | 94.7 | 5 |
| 2. Miscellaneous Activities: | | |
| County meetings ..................... | 355.2 | 1 |
| Sectional meetings .................. | 247.3 | 2 |
| Fair-exhibit work ................... | 138.5 | 3 |
| Recreational institutes, play days, community clubs, etc. ............. | 38.3 | 4 |
| Preparing for professional meetings .. | 16.5 | 5 |

## TABLE 10

CHRONOLOGICAL AGES, MENTAL AGES, INTELLIGENCE QUOTIENTS, AND
READING SCORES OF SIX PUPILS IN GRADE IV, CINCINNATI, OHIO, 1942

| Pupil | Chrono-logical Age | Mental Age | I.Q. * | Monroe Silent Reading Test | | T-Score-Thorndike-McCall Reading Scale |
|---|---|---|---|---|---|---|
| | | | | Rate | Compre-hension | |
| 1 ......... | 10-2 | 8-8 | 85 | 131 | 7 | 35 |
| 2 ......... | 10-1 | 8-10 | 88 | 106 | 7 | 35 |
| 3 ......... | 11-3 | 10-3 | 91 | 44 | 4 | 38 |
| 4 ......... | 10-5 | 9-4 | 90 | 81 | 7 | 36 |
| 5 ......... | 10-4 | 9-11 | 96 | 72 | 5 | 45 |
| 6 ......... | 10-2 | 10-11 | 107 | 128 | 8 | 43 |
| September Standard | .... | ...... | ... | ... | 7.7 | 39.6 |

* Haggerty Intelligence Examination, Delta 2.

**Sample page of a thesis**

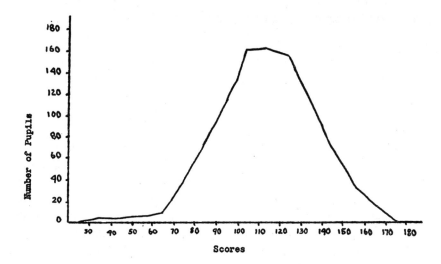

Figure 1.-- Gross Scores of 949 University of Cincinnati Freshmen
on the 1940 American Council on Education Psychological Examination.

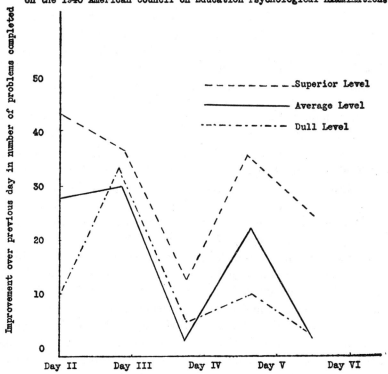

Figure 6.-- Amount of Daily Improvement at Three Levels of
Intelligence Under Conditions of Individual Competition.

**Sample page of a thesis**

many theses and field reports that do not follow one of these patterns of research, but make some other type of contribution to education. The special problems of organization in such theses and field projects are discussed in the following pages, with particular reference to the field of education, and based especially on extensive experience with graduate students at the University of Cincinnati and elsewhere.

**The field project.** Field reports may be varied in style, length, and organization. Some may resemble the research type of thesis in formal organization, impersonal style, and use of tabular data. However, many project reports may break away from research patterns, may be written in the first person, may call attention to the specific steps taken by the writers in working with their classes, with parents, with administrators or teachers, or with a school board, and may be illustrated by photographs, samples of work done by pupils, anecdotal records, and detailed accounts of teacher-pupil discussions.

A typical project develops out of problems characteristic of the regular professional responsibilities of the student. Generally some persistent phase of the student's work, or a problem which will engage much of his time over a period of several months, should be selected for attack. The project begins after the student has had a conference with his adviser, at which, among other things, the importance is pointed out of keeping careful records of the steps by which he advances toward his objective. Materials helpful in preparing oral reports for the sessions of a field-project seminar and for the final written report may include diary entries, a file of pertinent documents with dates and other identifying information, specially planned photographs, collections of pupil products (such as pictures, written reports, test papers, and school publications), minutes of committee meetings, correspondence files, first drafts of committee reports and courses of study as well as the final products, and detailed records of interviews, faculty meetings, and class discussions.

**Analysis of the literature.** A report or thesis (usually at the Master's level) may be an extended analysis of the literature in a selected field of education. For many educational problems that have inspired extensive discussion or prolonged and varied investigation, adequate summaries and evaluations of the literature are not available. Such a review should not be attempted without a careful canvass of the literature: (1) to insure that the review being undertaken is not a mere repetition of one already available, and (2) to guarantee that important sources are not overlooked.

A review of this type requires an introduction stating the problem, defining with precision the scope of the literature summarized, presenting a justification for the study, and indicating the organization of the report.

Definite information should be provided concerning the extent to which the literature has been canvassed. Analytical tables classifying the references by topics and/or by dates of publication may be useful. Such tables may be included as part of an introductory chapter, or may be presented as the major content of a special chapter.

Within the body of the report, a topical organization rather than a chronological one is more likely to lead to the type of critical and interpretative analysis that is the chief function of such a report. Reviews published in the *Encyclopedia of Educational Research, Review of Educational Research,* and *Psychological Bulletin,* although usually more condensed than summaries in a thesis of this type, furnish many examples of integration and interpretation of extensive bodies of literature. A review of the literature on a selected topic should avoid compilation of a series of isolated paragraphs or sections; that is, a running-bibliography type of treatment where each paragraph abstracts only a single study. The relative significance of the various materials reviewed should be reflected in the space allotted to their treatment. In summaries of this type, pertinent unpublished research, often available by interlibrary loan, should be given special attention. A critical review of the literature should close with a chapter of general summary and interpretation. This chapter will usually include suggestions for direct applications to educational problems and for further research.

**A textbook or course of study.** A report, project, or thesis presenting a textbook or course of study should include a careful analysis of the sources of information, related literature, local or other backgrounds, comparable texts or courses already available, detailed procedures, and problem-solving processes that served as a foundation for or entered into the work. In many instances the text or course can be given a trial in a teaching situation before the thesis is written. If such a trial is made, it should be reported. A well reasoned and carefully written account of the problem-solving approaches employed is at least as important at the graduate level as is the end-product in the form of the text or course of study. In general, a text or course of study, to be acceptable as part of a thesis, should be of such quality as to meet publication standards.

In some instances, a course of study may be presented as an extended chapter within the thesis, preceding the summary chapter (or in the appendix). A textbook, on the other hand, should generally be presented separately from the discussion of its basis, its organization, and similar topics. A course of study may be similarly treated. In order to present the text or course separately, the thesis should be divided into two parts: Part I, under some such title as "Development of a Course of Study in _____ for the Elementary Schools of _____"; and Part II, the completed course or text, under its own appropriate title. The title for Part I will ordinarily serve as the general title for the entire thesis. Textbooks submitted as a part of a thesis usually will bear distinctive titles, which would not be included in the general title of the thesis (for example, a thesis title may read: "A Series of Supplementary Readers on Art for a Junior High School Course"; and the titles of the readers themselves: *"Invitation to Look"; "The Story Back of the Picture"*; and *"Artists at Work"*). Pagination is usually continuous from the beginning of Part I through Part II. The bibliography (and appendix, if any) for Part I should be included immediately following this part. Part II may contain all the parts of a book (including front matter) and be in form suitable for publication; accordingly, it offers opportunity for more individuality in plan, style, illustrations, and the like than is desirable in a thesis of the research type. The general table of contents for a thesis organized in two parts should cover both divisions.

**Development and evaluation of a plan.** A thesis or project that reports the development and evaluation of a teaching, administrative, or supervisory plan should include a critical treatment of the sources or factors (current practice or conditions, authoritative opinion, educational theory, related literature or evidence, or careful observation) which led to the formulation of the given plan. Evaluation is obviously an important aspect of this type of report, including criteria deduced from such sources as historical background, best practice, expert judgment, investigational evidence, pertinent educational literature, and experimental tryout. The particular plan under consideration may be presented in a series of chapters within the body of the report, or separately, as in the case of a textbook or course of study. In the latter instance the suggestions in the preceding paragraph should be observed.

**Creative work.** A thesis or project may present a piece of creative work, possessing both intrinsic merit and educational significance. Such a piece of work may be in any of the fields of artistic creation, provided that it is in keeping with the student's program of courses and teaching specialization, and that it is presented with an accompanying essay descriptive of its development and its significance for education. Such an essay will serve the function of interpreting the creative production and of justifying it in terms of its educational contribution. A high standard of excellence is required for the acceptance of a piece of creative work. The faculty may secure the judgment of experts in the given artistic field in determining whether work submitted is worthy of acceptance.

Examples of creative work such as might be acceptable, together with the accompanying essay, are: (1) the score of a choral work for children's voices, suitable for a music festival; (2) a group of mural friezes appropriate for a high-school classroom used for the teaching of Latin; (3) a series of radio sketches interpreting in dramatic form the problems of parental education; and (4) a collection of short stories based upon the experiences of a teacher in a school located in an underprivileged area.

A piece of creative work in written form should be presented as Part II of the thesis. Detailed suggestions for organizing a thesis in such fashion are given above in the paragraphs concerned with reports presenting a textbook or course of study.

If the creative work consists of one or more musical compositions, the score(s) should constitute Part II. It may be necessary to use pages larger than 8½ x 11″ in the case of an orchestral score. These pages can be bound separately from the rest of the thesis. Since oversized volumes are usually filed in a special place in libraries, the use of large pages should be avoided if possible. An operetta may require a third part, for the libretto.

Some creative productions cannot be bound between the covers of a book; for example, a painting, a work of sculpture, or a motion-picture film. In such cases, the original production or a replica may be held by the graduate school for its permanent collection. Photographs of works of art, of scenes from motion pictures, and of steps or procedures in the development of the final production should be used in the thesis wherever they can contribute significantly to the exposition. If the project is a motion picture, a complete script should be presented in the thesis, usually as Part II.

The topics to be included in a thesis or project of the creative type will vary with the field and with the individual project. The term *related literature* should not be interpreted too narrowly. A psychological analysis of the creative activity itself may prove valuable. Discussion of the educational significance of the project is always expected as part of the interpretation and application. The relationship of one art form to others may be canvassed. The sources of inspiration and the procedure utilized in carrying through the idea are appropriate topics for analysis. In general, the essay part of the thesis is intended to interpret the creative project, from as many angles as possible, as a contribution to education.

## CONSISTENCY IN FOOTNOTE AND
## BIBLIOGRAPHICAL STYLE

The footnotes at the bottom of the pages and the chapter bibliographies throughout this book, including the present chapter, may serve as illustrations of the various types of references. This style has been developed by the National Education Association for its educational publications, particularly the *Review of Educational Research*. Except for minor variations and the use of abbreviations, the *Encyclopedia of Educational Research* has employed the same footnote and bibliographical style. (The illustrative footnotes in the body of the pages of this chapter represent another style for citation of references.)

Many other publication agencies have developed their own variations in style for footnotes and bibliographies. The American Psychological Association has adopted a bibliographical style for its journals.[18] The *Education Index* and similar guides use their own abbreviated forms of citation. This chapter and book have not attempted to demonstrate that one style is better than another, but urge that completeness and consistency be observed in following the forms recommended by the particular institution or publisher.

In the examples found in the body of the pages that follow, another well known type of footnote and bibliographical style is presented, with the thought that certain graduate schools or individuals may have a preference for it or may have adopted this style. These illustrations follow the form employed by the University of Chicago Press for its educational publications, including the *School Review, Elementary School Journal,* and the *Supplementary Educational Monographs.*

As outlined below, there are certain general recommendations that apply to all types of references, including books, monographs, articles in periodicals, and even other forms of citation.

1. For the sake of uniformity and completeness of information, the adopted bibliographical or footnote style should be followed rigorously, even though the student thinks he knows of a better system or believes he can improve on the forms recommended.

2. It is necessary to translate references of different styles from a variety of sources into the forms adopted by the particular graduate school or publisher.

3. It is imperative that complete references be entered when taking notes;

---

[18] *Publication Manual of the American Psychological Association.* Washington: American Psychological Association, 1952. 61 p.

John E. Anderson and Willard L. Valentine, "The Preparation of Articles for Publication in the Journals of the American Psychological Association." *Psychological Bulletin* 41:345-76; June 1944.

J. A. McGeoch, "Forms of Citation Adopted by the Board of Editors of the American Psychological Association." *Psychological Bulletin* 36:25-30; January 1939.

otherwise, difficulty and delay will result in looking up incomplete items for the second time.

4. As a general rule, the title of a part of a publication is placed within double quotation marks; for example, an article in a journal, a chapter in a book, or some other part of a work. The title of the entire publication is underscored on the typewriter.

5. Listing of titles, degrees, or positions should be avoided; scientific writing does not require this type of support or information.

6. Abbreviation of the names of journals, organizations, institutions, monograph series, and the months is awkward and confusing, and should be avoided. The possibility of saving a small amount of space in a typed thesis or technical report is relatively unimportant.

## FOOTNOTE USAGE

On the accompanying pages are certain general recommendations concerning use of footnotes, followed by explanations and illustrations of different types of footnote citations. The student should study carefully these recommendations, explanations, and illustrations, in order to identify the type and form of footnote citation appropriate for any particular type of reference material encountered.

1. As a rule, all bibliographical information such as title of book, publisher, and name of journal should be placed in footnotes rather than included in the body of the page.

2. A raised Arabic numeral calling attention to the appropriate footnote is placed after the key noun or major statement, but not after a verb or possessive. The usual recommendation is for the numeral to come at the end of a direct quotation, although it may be placed at the end of the last statement preceding the quotation.

3. To avoid confusion, asterisks (*) and daggers (†) instead of numerals should be used in tables, formulas, and mathematical materials.

4. A short line should be typed part way across the page to separate footnotes from the text. (On the printed page a different size of type usually sets off the footnotes from the body of the page.)

5. Footnotes are paragraphed separately and single spaced within a footnote, with a double space between footnotes.

6. Footnotes should be numbered consecutively in Arabics throughout each chapter of the report, beginning the numbering anew with each chapter. If it proves necessary to insert one or more citations in a long numbered series of completed footnotes, a letter of the alphabet may be added to the appropriate numerals. Thus, a reference inserted just after the sixteenth footnote would read 16a.

7. The name of the author appears in normal order in a footnote, followed by a comma.

8. In the footnote forms that follow it is customary to cite only the specific pages used (following the title except in the case of a journal), although some writers also include the total number of pages (at the end) for the particular reference. See the subsequent illustrations of this practice, and the variations in the footnotes and bibliographies of this book.

9. *Ibid.,* an abbreviation of *ibidem* ("in the same place"), is used when succeeding uninterrupted citations of a work occur on the same page. It is appropriate to give the work in full or to identify it properly when first cited on the page.

10. When other references intervene between different citations of a particular work, the author's name followed by *op. cit.,* the abbreviation of *opere citato* ("in the work cited"), and the pages may be used. If it has been more than four or five pages since the particular work was cited in full, it may be advisable to repeat the complete reference.

11. In lieu of numerous footnotes, some writers prefer a system of cross-reference to a consecutively numbered bibliography. For example, in the body of the page, John Doe's investigation (15:97-103) would mean that pages 97-103 of item 15 in the bibliography contain the material cited. The reference number usually follows the author's name, or another proper noun such as an institution or an organization, but does not come after other parts of speech or a possessive form. Unless cited earlier, a cross-reference follows at the end of a quotation, but is not enclosed in quotation marks; to use a hypothetical example, "The trend in measurement is toward evaluation" (95:114-15). When this plan is employed, it is essential that the bibliography be complete when the writing begins, although in case of necessity in a completed report a bibliographical entry can be inserted as 16a, 16b, or 20a without renumbering the entire list of references and the corresponding cross-references in the text. Many illustrations of this plan may be found in the *Encyclopedia of Educational Research, Review of Educational Research, Psychological Bulletin, American Journal of Sociology,* and *American Sociological Review.*

**Books not identified with a series.** The essential information for listing a book reference, with the exception of pagination, can be obtained from its title page. The name of the author should be entered exactly as given on the title page, especially in the case of a publication written by a woman. Subtitles may be listed as illustrated in this chapter. If a publishing house has more than one branch, the main office, which is given first on the title page, should be named. If the name of a printer employed by the publisher is given on the back of the title page or elsewhere, this information is not germane to bibliographical work and should not be entered as a part of the reference. The date to be given is the most recent year of copyright, which usually appears on the back of the title page. Publishers sometimes place the date of a reprinting on the title page without having made changes or revisions in the text, which gives a spurious impression of newness or recency to the work. A genuine revision is accompanied by a new copyright. The succeeding illustrations are accompanied by brief explanatory notes. The forms of punctuation and capitalization represented should be observed and followed closely in footnote citations.

The majority of book footnotes, as illustrated in the following references, cite particular pages or chapters, immediately following the title, rather than the total pagination. This example is the simplest and probably the most frequently used type of book reference. The necessary information is author's name in normal order, title (underlined), pages cited, place of publication, publisher, and date.

[3] Viktor Lowenfeld, Creative and Mental Growth, p. 4. New York: Macmillan Co., 1947.

A more complicated footnote citation is illustrated in the following reference. The essential information is the author's name in normal order, title (underlined in typing and italics in print), subtitle (not underscored), edition, place of publication, publisher, date of publication, and pagination (in this instance the total number of pages, front matter and text). Pp. is the abbreviation for the plural, pages; p. is the singular. Front matter or preliminary material in a book frequently is numbered in small Roman numerals. Only when a book has gone beyond the first edition is a reference made to the number of the edition or revision.

[4] Louis Shores, Basic Reference Books: An Introduction to the Evaluation, Study, and Use of Reference Materials with Special Emphasis on Some 300 Titles. Second Edition. Chicago: American Library Association, 1939. Pp. xiv + 472.

In the following citation, certain specifically designated pages follow the title, as is customary in footnotes, while the total pagination comes last. Most writers do not give the total pages when citing specific pages or quoting from a reference.

[5] Cecil B. Williams and Allan H. Stevenson, A Research Manual: With a Bibliographical Guide to College Studies and Interests, pp. 12-42, 113-98. New York: Harper and Bros., 1940. Pp. xvi + 264.

When a number of authors have contributed to a work, under a general editorship, the citation is as listed below for an encyclopedia. In this instance, the sponsoring organization also is given.

[6] Walter S. Monroe, Editor, Encyclopedia of Educational Research. Revised Edition. Prepared under the auspices of the American Educational Research Association. New York: Macmillan Co., 1950. Pp. xxvi + 1520.

When the reference is to an entire set of books, such as a multiple-volume encyclopedia, the total number of volumes is given, as illustrated below. This particular citation is to a fifteen-volume encyclopedia, prepared by many authors and edited by two men, with the publication dates of the different volumes in the set spread over several years. Note the manner in which the total number of volumes is expressed.

[7] Edwin R. A. Seligman and Alvin Johnson, Editors, Encyclopaedia of the Social Sciences. New York: Macmillan Co., 1930-1934. Fifteen volumes.

When the citation is to a specific article within a particular volume of a set, complete information should be given, as illustrated in the reference below. The information listed is the author and title of the article, title of the encyclopedia, volume number, pages covered by the article, editors, place of publication, publisher, and copyright date for the particular volume.

⁸ Margaret Mead, "Woman, Position in Society," Encyclopaedia of the Social Sciences, Vol. 15, pp. 439-42. Edited by Edwin R. A. Seligman and Alvin Johnson. New York: Macmillan Co., 1934.

When the original source of a reference is not available, and has to be cited through the medium of another publication, the form illustrated below may be used. Instead of the connecting expression, "as found in," it may be appropriate in certain instances to say "as quoted in" or "as summarized in."

⁹ Louis Shores, Basic Reference Books: An Introduction to the Evaluation, Study, and Use of Reference Materials with Special Emphasis on Some 300 Titles. Second Edition. Chicago: American Library Association, 1939. Pp. xiv + 472. As found in Pauline V. Young, Scientific Social Surveys and Research, Chapter 5. Second Edition. New York: Prentice-Hall, 1949.

In some instances a professional organization or institution is responsible for the authorship, as in the example below, where the professional organization is the author and serves as its own publisher.

¹⁰ National Education Association, Educational Policies Commission, Deliberative Committee Reports, 1939. Washington: The Commission, National Education Association, January, 1940. Pp. 54.

**Publications identified with a series.** References for monographs, yearbooks, catalogues, courses of study, annual reports, and bulletins follow the style for books, as illustrated above, with the addition of information concerning the title of the series, volume (if given), and number. For example, in the illustration below, the identifying number and year in the series of Office of Education bulletins follow immediately after the title. The Government Printing Office is the publisher and distributor.

¹¹ Ruth A. Gray, Bibliography of Research Studies in Education, 1939-1940. Office of Education Bulletin 1941, No. 5. Washington: Government Printing Office, 1941. Pp. xiv + 404.

The next example has more series-identification than is usually found on a title page. Sometimes the volume number on the title page is a Roman numeral, but in the interest of consistency for the references used in the thesis or research report the corresponding Arabic numeral may be used.

¹²Edgar Dale and Norma Vernon, Propaganda Analysis: An Annotated Bibliography. Bureau of Educational Research, Series 1, Vol. 1, No. 2. Columbus, Ohio: Ohio State University, 1940. Pp. ii + 30.

When more than three authors are involved, the method of indicating authorship is as illustrated below. In this instance, a particular page is cited, after the title. The listing of the total pagination is optional, and probably is not necessary in most footnotes when specific pages are cited.

¹³Henry W. Holmes and Others, Educational Research: Its Nature, Essential Conditions, and Controlling Concepts, p. 85. Council Studies, No. 10, Series 1. Washington: American Council on Education, 1939. Pp. viii + 186.

Yearbook references, as illustrated below, sometimes present special problems in listing complete information concerning: the author of the cited section of the yearbook, title of the particular section, yearbook title, pages covered by the designated section, editor of the volume, place of publication, publisher, and date.

¹⁴Carter V. Good, "Recent Graduate Theses in School Law," Ninth Yearbook of School Law, pp. 180-97. Edited by M. M. Chambers. Washington: American Council on Education, 1941.

Another complete citation to a section within a yearbook, as listed below, includes information concerning: the author of the particular section, title of his contribution, title of the entire yearbook, pages of the particular section, number of the yearbook in the series, place of publication, publisher, and date.

¹⁵Charles H. Judd, "Contributions of School Surveys," The Scientific Movement in Education, pp. 9-20. Thirty-seventh Yearbook of the National Society for the Study of Education, Part 2. Bloomington, Illinois: Public School Publishing Co., 1938.

In the following example the National Education Association is credited with the authorship, since two of its departments were responsible for the preparation of the yearbook. Note the manner in which departmental credit has been given.

¹⁶National Education Association, The Implications of Research for the Classroom Teacher. Joint yearbook of the American Educational Research Association and the Department of Classroom Teachers. Washington: National Education Association, 1939. Pp. 318.

In certain instances, no author or editor can be listed for a reference, since a number of unnamed persons may have aided in the compilation of the report, without a supervising editor being identified. This is especially true of the several examples below, in which catalogues, courses of study, and annual reports are represented. In some cases the general responsibility for authorship can be inferred from the agency of publication.

17 Selected References in Education, 1938. Supplementary Educational Monographs, No. 47. Chicago: Department of Education, University of Chicago, February, 1939. Pp. x + 221.
18 Announcement of the College of Applied Arts, University of Cincinnati, 1948-1949. University of Cincinnati Bulletin, Vol. 44, No. 4. Cincinnati, Ohio: The University, 1948. Pp. 57.
19 The Primary Manual. Curriculum Bulletin, No. 95. Cincinnati, Ohio: Cincinnati Public Schools, 1947. Pp. 577.
20 Report of the President for the Academic Years, 1949-1950 and 1950-1951. University of Cincinnati Bulletin. Cincinnati, Ohio: The University, 1951. Pp. 171.

**Journals.** In terms of frequency of publication, journals range from the weekly *Science* to the monthly (now bimonthly) *Psychological Abstracts,* the bimonthly *American Journal of Sociology,* and the *North Central Association Quarterly.* The student familiar with the format and content of journals distinguishes them readily from yearbooks, occasional bulletins, reports, proceedings, and monographs that usually belong to a series. The references below and the accompanying explanatory comments illustrate complete form for listing articles that appear in journals.

The essential information is author, title of article in quotes, name of journal underscored, volume number in Arabics, date, and pagination. In the case of a quotation, it may be that only a single appropriate page is cited. If some students strongly prefer the more cumbersome Roman numerals for the volume number, this practice is acceptable, provided the usage is consistent throughout the particular report.

21 Elizabeth M. Newton, "I Want to Color," School Arts, 41 (January, 1942), 153.

It is important to include the date of the month in the case of a biweekly such as *School and Society.*

22 A. R. Mead, V. A. Hines, and Ida Ruth McLendon, "Proposals to the American Educational Research Association for the Improvement of Educational Research," School and Society, 67 (February 28, 1948), 160-63.

No author is listed in the journal as the compiler in the following reference.

23 "Higher Degrees in Sociology Conferred in 1946," American Journal of Sociology, 53 (July, 1947), 43-48.

The entire issue of the following journal is regularly devoted to a central problem or theme, as in the case of the title in quotation marks. In most instances, especially in the bibliography, it is desirable to assign the authorship to the National Education Association, Research Division.

24 National Education Association, Research Division, "The Legal Status of the Public-School Pupil," Research Bulletin of the National Education Association, 26 (February, 1948), 1-38.

The article occupies the consecutive pages 12-19 and is concluded on page 29.

25 Louis Foley, "The Anatomy of a Paragraph," Phi Delta Kappan, 23 (September, 1940), 12-19, 29.

The journal appears bimonthly, which explains the listing of the two months.

26 Mapheus Smith, "An Approach to a Systematic Social Psychology," Sociology and Social Research, 32 (September-October, 1947), 507-12.

In the next example are given the authors of a particular section within the journal, the title of their contribution, the title of the entire issue, the pages of the particular section, the name of the journal, volume number, month, year, and total pages in the issue. The titles of both the particular section and the central theme of the entire issue are enclosed in quotation marks. This form shows the pages occupied by the particular section, as well as the total pages, and avoids the impression that the author listed is responsible for the entire issue.

27 Florence L. Goodenough and Dale B. Harris, "Intellectual Growth in Childhood," in "Growth and Development," pp. 306-16, Review of Educational Research, 17 (December, 1947), 301-403.

**Newspapers.** A reference from a newspaper should include a classification of the reference, the name of the newspaper, volume, date of publication, and page or pages cited.

28 Editorial in the Cincinnati Enquirer, 111 (February 1, 1952), 4.
29 News item in the Christian Science Monitor, 44 (January 8, 1952), 1.

**Unpublished material.** The titles of unpublished materials such as theses, minutes of a meeting, interviews, letters, and addresses are enclosed in quotation marks. Mimeographed reports and materials issued by similar methods of duplication follow the form for printed reports, except that the word mimeographed or some other process of reproduction is given at the end of the reference. Published theses frequently belong to a monograph series or may appear as separate publications, in the latter instance being listed like a book. The examples below illustrate optional forms for listing unpublished graduate theses.

The information given is author, title in quotes, degree toward which thesis is offered, school, date, and pages.

<sup>30</sup> Walter J. Wuerdeman, "A Comparison of Ratings by High-School Pupils and Teachers on Topics in Basic Business Education." Unpublished Master's Thesis, University of Cincinnati, 1948. Pp. vii + 166.

Below is an optional form for use in indicating the location of the school granting the degree. Pagination should be given when available.

<sup>31</sup> Charles L. Gary, "A History of Music Education in the Cincinnati Public Schools." Unpublished Doctor's dissertation. Cincinnati: University of Cincinnati, 1951. Pp. x + 291.

Footnote form for the unpublished minutes of a board of education is as illustrated below. The form for published minutes is the same as for annual reports and catalogues that belong to a series. The essential information for such unpublished material is: the name of the educational agency, place, date, and page citation.

<sup>32</sup> "Minutes of the Sycamore Township Board of Education, Blue Ash, October 9, 1951," p. 26.

An interview or letter should be cited so as to cover the persons represented, position (if helpful), place, and date; for example:

<sup>33</sup> Interview between the writer and Claude V. Courter, superintendent of the Cincinnati, Ohio, schools, at Cincinnati, October 8, 1951.
<sup>34</sup> Letter to the writer from Raymond Walters, president of the University of Cincinnati, Cincinnati, Ohio, dated October 8, 1951.

A public address, whether before a visible audience or by radio or television, should include information concerning the name of the speaker, position (if helpful), topic (in double quotation marks), audience represented, place, and date. Below are hypothetical examples.

<sup>35</sup> John Smith, dean of Teachers College, University of Walla Walla, "Youth and the Future," address before the Washington Education Association at Tacoma, Washington, December 29, 1951.
<sup>36</sup> Emery Brown, "Democracy and Education," address over Station WLW, Cincinnati, Ohio, October 8, 1951.

## BIBLIOGRAPHICAL USAGE

An earlier section of this chapter recommends that the bibliography be reasonably complete, including footnote references and even significant publications not examined, although references not directly used may well be marked by some symbol such as an asterisk. The possibility of organizing long bibliographies by topics, with an alphabetical arrangement of references under each heading, and the use of annotations also were discussed. Notes or annotations are unnecessary when a detailed review of the related literature, covering the items of the bibliography, has been given.

The illustrations below and the references listed in other chapters of this book indicate that there are few differences between style for footnotes and for bibliography. The bibliography is alphabetically arranged according to authors, with the surname listed first. References without an individual as an author may be alphabetized under the name of the institution, agency, commission, or school system that prepared the report. In the event that there is no indication whatever of authorship, as in the case of many editorials, the first significant word (excluding *a, an,* and *the*) of the title determines the alphabetizing. Some bibliographical styles place all references lacking a person as an author in a second alphabetical list at the end of the bibliography proper, which is an acceptable practice for the thesis or research report, if observed consistently.

If more than one reference is listed for the same author, his name should be repeated in full rather than to substitute some symbol for his name. When the cross-reference system is employed instead of footnotes, the bibliography must be alphabetized and numbered. In the event that references must be inserted after the numbering of a long bibliography is completed, a letter may be added to the appropriate numeral; for example, 16a, 16b, or 20a. The total pages of a work are cited more commonly in the bibliography than in a footnote, although listing of both specifically cited and total pages may be considered important for some references. A footnote citation frequently is to specific pages rather than to the total publication. The references may be typed single space, with a double space between items and indentation in the form of a hanging paragraph or hanging indentation, to make the surname of the author stand out.

The punctuation of the authors' names and capitalization should be carefully noted. Semicolons are used when there are three or more authors. For additional examples of footnote and bibliographical style in education, psychology, and the social sciences, numerous sources are available, some of which are listed below for illustrative purposes in the form of a bibliography rather than as a footnote (in the optional style described in this chapter).

Alexander, Carter, and Burke, Arvid J. How to Locate Educational Information and Data, pp. 126-53. Third Edition. New York: Bureau of Publications, Teachers College, Columbia University, 1950.
Appel, Livia. Bibliographical Citation in the Social Sciences. Second Edition. Madison: University of Wisconsin Press, 1946, Pp. 30.
Campbell, W. G. A Form Book for Thesis Writing, pp. 19-39, 101-15. Boston: Houghton Mifflin Co., 1939.
Conner, Martha. Practical Bibliography Making with Problems and Examples. New York: H. W. Wilson Co., 1938. Pp. 31.
Good, Warren R. An Introduction to Thesis Writing, pp. 19-25, 33-36. Ann Arbor, Michigan: Ann Arbor Press, 1937.
Hockett, H. C. Introduction to Research in American History, pp. 116-30. New York: Macmillan Co., 1932. Also see the 1948 edition.
Joughin, G. L. Basic Reference Forms: A Guide to Established Practice in Bibliography, Quotations, Footnotes, and Thesis Format. New York: F. S. Crofts, 1941. Pp. xi + 94.
A Manual of Style, pp. 123-32. Tenth Edition, Revised. Chicago: University of Chicago Press, 1943. Also see the 1949 edition.
Skillin, Marjorie E.; Gay, Robert M.; and Others. Words into Type: A Guide in the Preparation of Manuscripts; for Writers, Editors, Proofreaders and Printers. New York: Appleton-Century-Crofts, 1948. Pp. xx + 585.
Turabian, Kate L. A Manual for Writers of Dissertations, pp. 14-33, 49-52. Chicago: University of Chicago Bookstore, 1937.

## STYLE AND READABILITY OF THE REPORT

This brief discussion of style must leave to the handbooks of English usage and of manuscript writing the details of rhetoric, grammar, paragraph construction, sentence structure, punctuation, and spelling. The graduate student has covered these areas in high-school English classes, and usually has taken instruction in composition at the college level, although all too frequently he has not acquired the skill necessary to write an accurate and effective report. A number of helpful handbooks of usage are listed for the guidance of the graduate student.[19] The current edition of a particular manual should be consulted.

[19] Ralph M. Albaugh, *Thesis Writing:* A Guide to Scholarly Style. Ames, Ia.: Littlefield, Adams and Co., 1951. 149 p.
E. M. Allen, *op. cit.,* p. 23-71.
Richard D. Altick, *Preface to Critical Reading.* New York: Henry Holt and Co., 1946. xix + 321 p.
John Benbow, *Manuscript and Proof.* New York: Oxford University Press, 1937. p. 75-99.
Francesco Cordasco and Elliott S. M. Gatner, *Handbook for Research and Report Writing.* New York: Barnes and Noble, 1951. vii + 142 p.
Robert T. Fitzhugh, *Handbook of Writing.* New York: Appleton-Century-Crofts, 1946. viii + 156 p.
Rudolf Flesch and A. H. Lass, *The Way to Write.* Revised Edition. New York: Harper and Bros., 1949. x + 342 p.
Norman Foerster and J. M. Steadman, Jr., *Writing and Thinking:* A Handbook of Composition and Revision. Revised Edition. Boston: Houghton Mifflin Co., 1941. viii + 448 p.
Carl G. Gaum, Harold F. Graves, and Lyne S. S. Hoffman, *Report Writing.* Third Edition. New York: Prentice-Hall, 1950. xv + 384 p.

**Diction and phraseology.** Diction, the choice and use of words, is essential to precision of statement and to clarity of vocabulary and technical terminology. Scientists are alternately accused of being inarticulate or of expression in a language that few can understand. A forceful, simple, and direct vocabulary is more effective for purposes of communication than scientific jargon and worship of polysyllables. The quality of science resides in its content rather than in a language that is baffling.

George R. Harrison of the Massachusetts Institute of Technology tells a classic story of the pitfalls of scientific jargon, as compared with the effectiveness of a straightforward statement in simple English: [20]

A New York plumber of foreign extraction with a limited command of English wrote the National Bureau of Standards and said he found that hydrochloric acid quickly opened drainage pipes when they got clogged and asked if it was a good thing to use.

A Bureau scientist replied:

Garland Greever, E. S. Jones, and Agnes L. Jones, *The Century Collegiate Handbook.* Third Edition. New York: Appleton-Century-Crofts, 1950. xv + 460 p.

Eugene F. Grewe and John F. Sullivan, *The College Research Paper.* Revised Edition. Dubuque, Ia.: William C. Brown Co., 1950. xi + 109 p.

J. H. Hanford and Others, *The Nelson Handbook of English.* New York: Thomas Nelson and Sons, 1932. 344 p.

Florence M. A. Hilbish, *The Research Paper.* New York: Bookman Associates, 1952. 292 p.

J. C. Hodges, *Harbrace College Handbook.* New York: Harcourt, Brace and Co., 1946. xxii + 442 p.

Ellen Johnson, *The Research Report:* A Guide for the Beginner. New York: Ronald Press, 1951. vi + 141 p.

A. C. Jordan, *How to Write Correctly.* New York: Reynal and Hitchcock, 1941. xii + 194 p.

J. M. Kierzek, *The Macmillan Handbook of English.* Revised Edition. New York: Macmillan Co., 1947. xvi + 527 p.

*A Manual of Style, op. cit.*

A. H. Marckwardt, *Scribner Handbook of English.* New York: Charles Scribner's Sons, 1940. xii + 408 p.

C. O. S. Mawson, *Style Book for Writers and Editors.* New York: Thomas Y. Crowell Co., 1930. 213 p.

J. R. Nelson, *op. cit.*

Raymond W. Pence, *Style Book in English.* New York: The Odyssey Press, 1944. xiii + 545 p.

Porter G. Perrin, *Writer's Guide and Index to English.* New York: Scott, Foresman and Co., 1942. xii + 800 p.

Charles W. Roberts and Others, *A Handbook of English.* New York: Oxford University Press, 1944. xii + 292 p.

Marjorie E. Skillin, Robert M. Gay, and Others, *Words into Type:* A Guide in the Preparation of Manuscripts; for Writers, Editors, Proofreaders and Printers. New York: Appleton-Century-Crofts, 1948. xx + 585 p.

Richard Summers and David L. Patrick, *College Composition:* With Grammar Review and Repetitive Exercises. New York: Ronald Press Co., 1946. xvi + 294 p.

George Summey, Jr., and John P. Abbott, *A Manual for College English.* New York: Ronald Press Co., 1947. vi + 432 p.

Kendall B. Taft and Others, *English Communication:* A Handbook of Writing and Speaking. New York: Farrar and Rinehart, 1943. x + 435 p.

Cecil B. Williams and A. H. Stevenson, *op. cit.*

E. C. Woolley, F. W. Scott, and Frederick Bracher, *College Handbook of Composition.* Fifth Edition. Boston: D. C. Heath and Co., 1951. x + 344 p.

[20] F. Barrows Colton, "Some of My Best Friends Are Scientists." *Scientific Monthly* 69:156-60; September 1949.

"The efficacy of hydrochloric acid is indisputable, but the corrosive residue is incompatible with metallic permanence."

The plumber wrote back thanking the Bureau for telling him the method was all right. The scientist was a little disturbed and showed the correspondence to his boss—another scientist. The latter wrote the plumber:

"We cannot assume responsibility for the production of toxic and noxious residue with hydrochloric acid and suggest you use an alternative procedure."

The plumber wrote back that he agreed with the Bureau—hydrochloric acid works fine. A top scientist—boss of the first two—broke the impasse by tearing himself loose from technical terminology and writing this letter:

"Don't use hydrochloric acid. It eats h____ out of the pipes!"

Variety in the choice of words and judicious use of synonyms prevent monotony of expression. For assistance in promoting lucid diction, the handbooks and dictionaries should be consulted. Technical dictionaries [21] in education, psychology, and the social sciences are available and should be used as needed; these aids are listed at greater length in the chapter dealing with library techniques.

Phraseology, the arrangement of words in groups, is another important problem in writing, one that is fully treated in the handbooks of English usage. Variation in the structure and length of clauses, sentences, and paragraphs makes for a more readable style.

**Style in technical and research reporting.** Style is a more inclusive term than diction or phraseology, and is concerned with certain more general characteristics of writing, particularly individuality of expression. The technical or professional report is not an oration or a literary essay; therefore, its style should be natural, straightforward, and businesslike. This means simplicity, clarity, and directness rather than journalistic writing or literary embellishments. In the absence of real substance, no amount of ornateness, flowery language, or rhetoric can produce more than a literary clothes horse. To be avoided are trite or hackneyed phrases, over-worked literary illustrations or proverbs, slang, colloquialisms, titles and degrees, the first person, and the editorial "we." Lest he swing to the other extreme, in avoiding a "literary" or ornate style, the inexperienced writer, and even the more mature author, should be reminded that there is plenty of room for exercise of whatever skill in language he possesses. There is no obligation to be dull or monotonous, and the research report is no better because it is heavy reading. Scientific writing need not be

[21] Carter V. Good, Editor, *Dictionary of Education*. New York: McGraw-Hill Book Co., 1945. xl + 495 p. Scheduled for revision in 1956.

Philip L. Harriman, *New Dictionary of Psychology*. New York: Philosophical Library, 1947. 364 p.

H. C. Warren, *A Dictionary of Psychology*. Boston: Houghton Mifflin Co., 1934. x + 372 p.

H. P. Fairchild, Editor, *Dictionary of Sociology*. New York: Philosophical Library, 1944. viii + 342 p.

dull, but often is. It is neither good science nor common sense to write in monotonous or stolid fashion.

It is granted that publication in scientific journals and thesis writing involve a certain dignity of reporting, yet dignity is not synonymous with dullness. The scientist need not be afraid to exhibit a saving sense of humor, which may relieve what otherwise might be monotony or stolidity in reporting. Writers in scientific and professional journals and authors of graduate theses are individuals, who may even permit themselves an individual style of writing, rather than to attempt complete formality or stiffness in reporting. Fortunately, no matter how hard he may try, a writer cannot wholly conceal his individuality of expression. Sometimes it seems that authors willfully suppress every vestige of spontaneity and emphasis in their writing, in the mistaken conviction that they are proving their devotion to science. There appears to be something about "reporting an experiment" that freezes the pen of many an author, with the result that he becomes merely dull rather than scientific and scholarly in the presentation of his findings. Much would be gained by way of effective writing, if the investigator could carry over into his written report something of the enthusiasm (restrained, if necessary) that he usually reveals in describing orally an experiment to some colleague or advanced group of students.

Able scientists have varied greatly in style of writing.[22] Ebbinghaus produced work in Germany that was scientifically rigorous, yet lucid, interesting, and readable, with a human personality revealed through his pen, as was true of the books of William James in the United States. On the other hand, Wundt overwhelmed his reader with a host of facts, arguments, and dicta. With James, and probably for many others, effective scientific writing has been a matter of rewriting rather than a sheer gift or a sudden inspiration. James said that on the average he rewrote every page of his famous *Psychology* at least six times. It is significant to note the manner in which great documents have been painstakingly revised; for example, Jefferson's first draft of the Declaration of Independence (of course in long hand).

Gibbon says that he experimented extensively before he could strike a middle ground between a dull chronicle and a rhetorical declamation. He wrote the first chapter three times, and prepared two drafts of the second

[22] E. G. Boring, *A History of Experimental Psychology*. New York: Century Co., 1929. p. 383-84. Also see the 1950 edition.

H. C. Hockett, *Introduction to Research in American History*. New York: Macmillan Co., 1932. p. 137. Also see the 1948 edition.

James W. Thompson and Bernard J. Holm, *A History of Historical Writing*. New York: Macmillan Co., 1942. Vol. 2, p. 80.

Also see J. R. Shannon, "Tips to Writers from Seventy-Five Editors of Educational Periodicals." *Journal of Educational Research* 44:241-68; December 1950.

and third chapters of his *Decline and Fall of the Roman Empire* before he was reasonably well satisfied with the result. The fifteenth and sixteenth chapters were reduced by three successive revisions from a large volume to their present size. The first volume was written three times. In the earlier chapter of this book on the formulation of the problem are other illustrations of the care with which scholars and scientists have reworked and rewritten their materials.

On the other hand, the labor of literary composition sometimes is eased by a flash of inspiration. It is said that Rose Hartwick Thorpe wrote "Curfew Must Not Ring Tonight" during an arithmetic lesson in school, and that Munro Leaf completed "Ferdinand the Bull" in twenty-five minutes.

Style varies in certain respects with the type of research, according to whether the historical, experimental, survey, case, or some other method is used. The chapter on the historical method includes a discussion of style that has pertinent applications to reports of other types of research. Other analyses of special problems of reporting [23] deal with standards for psychological writing and reading difficulty of psychological materials, and the case method and the style of the case record.

**Principles of readability.** An excellent summarizing statement of principles of readability in reporting research may appropriately be quoted at some length: [24]

> If research is worth doing at all, it is worth reporting so that it will be read. Eventually it must "get into the minds of men who stir abroad"; it must be readable.
>
> Some investigators stop writing English when they begin reporting research. They have difficulty in getting down to the truth of the matter. They neglect the fundamental principles of composition: coherence, unity, and emphasis. By applying these and other principles of readability, research workers will more often write and be read.
>
> *The principle of appeal.*—Interest increases readability. If the reader sees that the report has meaning and use for him, he will put forth the effort that effective reading requires. It is the writer's job to make clear the purpose of his research and to suggest applications. In effect, he says to the reader: "Look, this is something new to you; this is something you can do."

[23] J. E. Anderson and W. L. Valentine, *op. cit.*
Katherine F. Bruner, "Of Psychological Writing: Being Some Valedictory Remarks on Style." *Journal of Abnormal and Social Psychology* 37:52-70; January 1942.
R. F. Flesch, *The Art of Plain Talk.* New York: Harper and Bros., 1946. xiii + 210 p.
S. S. Stevens and Geraldine Stone, "Psychological Writing, Easy and Hard." *American Psychologist* 2:230-35; July 1947.
Gordon Hamilton, *Social Case Recording.* New York: Columbia University Press, 1936. p. 114-37.
[24] Quoted from Ruth Strang, "Principles of Readability Applied to Reporting Research." *Improving Educational Research.* Washington: American Educational Research Association, 1948. p. 41-43. Also see:
John W. Hill and James E. Payne, "Scientists Can Talk to the Layman." *Science* 117: 403-405; April 17, 1953.

*The principle of personalization.*—This means putting human interest into the report of research. Cases are people. Even after they have been dehumanized by statistical treatment, they can still be used to personalize the report. Here are several ways in which the report can be personalized:

1. The writer can review the previous investigations as a story of other persons' success and failure, leading up to the need for the present study.
2. He can tell how he collected and treated the data. There is drama in methodology.
3. He can use illustrative cases to make concrete the generalizations derived from statistical treatment.
4. He can describe and explain deviations from central tendencies.

*The principle of patterning.*—Every research has a design that should be made plain to the reader. Out of his experience and study the writer has formulated certain hypotheses. These should be stated. He should then describe his plan for testing the hypotheses. The results of his study naturally follow, with their interpretation and the generalizations or conclusions that are warranted. Both the research and the report of research should have a design. To write such a report requires a sense of structure of sentences, of paragraphs, and of the chapter or article as a whole. The clear sentence offers to the reader a straight road or thought, with no detours. In research reports, we find many examples of "tangled sentences." We also find many incoherent paragraphs and illogical organization of the whole report. If the writer does not have a sense of structure, how can he expect the reader to get a pattern of thought?

*The principles of emphasis.*—The writer should make certain that the reader gets the important points. Too frequently the main ideas are submerged in a welter of words. This principle has been well expressed by a French author: *"L'art de ne pas tout dire"*—the art of not saying everything—at least in one sentence. This is particularly hard for the meticulous research worker to do because he wishes, quite rightly, to point out all the possible factors that may be influencing his results. For this reason he piles up one limiting phrase and clause after another. The result is that the reader is caught up in a thicket of details. What he wants is a straightforward path to comprehension. Research reports are too often cluttered with "it would seem," "it should be recognized," "it was demonstrated," "one might judge," and other round-about expressions. They are addicted to the passive tense. Translation of this cumbersome kind of writing into terse, active, subject-predicate form would vitalize many research reports.

*The principle of dilution.*—A report of research can be too concentrated. Too great density of ideas makes reading difficult. Brevity may be puzzling. This principle leads to expansion instead of deletion. The writer should space his ideas so that the reader has time to grasp them. What fills the space between main ideas is of the utmost importance. As suggested in the previous paragraph, irrelevant details may distract the reader's attention, while apt illustrations and supporting details build up the main ideas. Research workers often have protocols that they never use to illumine and clarify their main points and lighten the report as a whole.

*The principle of plain words.*—Choice of words is important in making a report readable. First, the writer should avoid "empty words"—fillers-in that do not carry essential ideas. Second, he should use short, simple, concrete words, whenever possible. One measure of readability is the number of prefixes and suffixes per hundred sentences. Flesch says that easy prose does not have more than thirty-one affixes per hundred words.[25] Another measure of

[25] Rudolf Flesch, *op. cit.*, p. 43.

difficulty of a passage is the number of unfamiliar words. This is one of the factors used in the Lorge readability formula. The writer should not use technical words with which the reader is unfamiliar when one or two simple root words will convey the thought. If difficult technical words are necessary— and they often are—the writer should use them in a context that makes their meaning clear, or define or illustrate the word the first time he uses it.

Profound and technical concepts obviously cannot be written so that anyone can comprehend them without difficulty. But the reader will grasp even essentially difficult material more easily if these principles are applied.

## EVALUATION, IMPLEMENTATION, AND ACTION PROGRAMS

**Evaluation of research.** Evaluation should accompany each stage in research, as well as follow completion of the report. The contents of this chapter and of other sections of this book provide the background for such evaluation. It probably is impossible to prepare a satisfactory rule-of-thumb check list of criteria for use in appraising research, although attempts have been made to compile such standards. Information is available concerning a variety of activities pointed toward the evaluation of current literature, manuscripts submitted to journals, theses, textbooks, and courses of study through the media or instruments of jury judgment, book reviews, and check lists.[26] (Some of these references include check lists for evaluation of research.)

**Implementation of findings.** A major obligation that accompanies the several stages in research, and follows the preparation of the report, is the application or implementation of the findings. As Thoreau has said: "It takes two to speak the truth; one to speak and one to listen."[27] The generally recognized stages in the cycle of problem-solving and implementation are:[28]

[26] H. H. Abelson, *The Art of Educational Research.* Yonkers-on-Hudson, New York: World Book Co., 1933. p. 308-9.

Carter V. Good, A. S. Barr, and Douglas E. Scates, *The Methodology of Educational Research.* New York: Appleton-Century-Crofts, 1936. p. 679-707.

B. R. Haynes and C. W. Humphrey, *Research Applied to Business Education.* New York: Gregg Publishing Co., 1939. p. 128-33.

W. S. Monroe and M. D. Engelhart, *The Techniques of Educational Research.* Bureau of Educational Research Bulletin, No. 38. Urbana: University of Illinois, 1928. p. 58-61.

F. L. Whitney, *The Elements of Research.* New York: Prentice-Hall, 1942. p. 415-23. Also see the 1950 edition.

G. M. Wilson, "Research: Suggested Standards for Summarizing and Reporting Applied to Two Recent Summaries of Studies in Arithmetic." *Journal of Educational Research* 28: 187-94; November 1934.

[27] C. L. Fry, *The Technique of Social Investigation.* New York: Harper and Bros., 1934. p. 223.

[28] E. D. Grizzell, *Educational Studies and Their Use:* An Exploratory Study of the Processes of Implementation in Secondary Education. Council Studies, Series 1, Vol. 4, No. 11. Washington: American Council on Education, January, 1940. p. 54-55.

Also see Leon Festinger and Daniel Katz, Editors, *Research Methods in the Behavioral Sciences.* New York: Dryden Press, 1953. p. 579-646.

1. Identifying the problem and the potential publics
2. Devising a plan to solve or throw light on the problem
3. Reporting the findings and recommendations in appropriate scientific language
4. Appraising the desire and readiness of the potential publics, lay and professional, for the findings and recommendations
5. Translating the findings and recommendations into usable form and language for the various publics
6. Disseminating and interpreting the findings through appropriate media
7. Advising the various publics in the use of the findings
8. Evaluating the effectiveness of the recommendations
9. Locating problems that develop from the implementation process and call for special attention.

Basic principles of implementation are as follows: [29]

1. Implementation is essentially the process of giving effect to the findings and recommendations of study-producing agencies. The process varies with the character of the findings and publics concerned and may be conceived as ranging from the discovery of truth to its use as a means of satisfying human wants.

2. It is essential to the preservation of democratic ideals and processes that enlightened public opinion shall determine educational policies and that no authority shall usurp the rights of the public in deciding major issues concerned with the education of youth.

3. Freedom of investigation by individuals or organizations shall be preserved and no authoritative central agency shall assume responsibility for selecting the studies or findings to be placed before the general public or the various special publics.

4. It is imperative that the general and professional publics be made constantly aware of data available for the solutions of problems in the education of youth.

5. A service agency shall be developed to render impartial aid and advice to the general public, to professional service groups, and to study agencies alike.

6. The function of promoting cooperative action among all parties concerned is the major responsibility of any agency for implementation of studies in a democracy.

Promising channels of communication for use in the translation of findings and recommendations are: [30]

1. Those depending mainly upon the spoken word—conversation; lectures and speeches; national, regional, and local conferences; study groups and institutes; radio [and television] programs; and the theater, including plays and pageants

2. Those depending mainly upon the written word—newspapers; magazines; correspondence; special publications such as pamphlets, bulletins, monographs, and house organs; annual reports; preparation of bibliographies and provision of library facilities to stimulate reading; and advertising

3. Those depending mainly upon the use of graphic techniques, either alone or in combination with the written or spoken word—motion pictures [and television] and lantern slides, cartoons, posters, snapshots and photographs, pictorial statistics, and exhibits.

[29] E. D. Grizzell, op. cit., p. 57-59.
[30] Ibid., p. 22-23.

Supplementary details of implementation, stressing particularly the obligations of science and of research workers to deal with the vital problems of society, may be found in other sources.[31] Many scholars and scientists during World War II and in the post-war period have felt an almost overwhelming concern about the social relations of science and research. It should not be taken for granted that this is primarily a physical world, or that physical science and physical might are in and of themselves important and self-sufficient, since the importance of science depends upon the values that a given society assigns to it.[32] The policies of a social world even determine whether the scientist is permitted to work.

In a world where invention, technology, and physical science have outrun the controls of social science, psychology, and education, the challenge is the greatest of all time to create a democratic society and to discover the coöperative processes necessary to maintain it. If we discard as a way of life the choices of isolation and imperialism, only one choice remains: that of coöperation in world understanding and good citizenship. The

[31] Ruth N. Anshen, Editor, *Science and Man.* New York: Harcourt, Brace and Co., 1942. viii + 494 p.

Bernard Barber, *Science and the Social Order.* Glencoe, Ill.: Free Press, 1952. xxiii + 288 p.

J. D. Bernal, *The Social Function of Science.* New York: Macmillan Co., 1939. xvi + 482 p.

J. Bronowski, *The Common Sense of Science.* Cambridge: Harvard University Press, 1953. 154 p.

John E. Burchard, Editor, *Mid-Century:* The Social Implications of Scientific Progress. Cambridge: Massachusetts Institute of Technology Press, 1950. xx + 549 p.

James B. Conant, *Science and Common Sense.* New Haven: Yale University Press, 1951. xii + 371 p.

James B. Conant, *On Understanding Science:* An Historical Approach. New Haven: Yale University Press, 1947. xv + 145 p.

J. G. Crowther, *The Social Relations of Science.* New York: Macmillan Co., 1941. p. 600-652.

William J. Goode and Paul K. Hatt, *Methods in Social Research.* New York: McGraw-Hill Book Co., 1952. Chapters 3, 4.

John A. Irving, *Science and Values:* Exploration in Philosophy and the Social Sciences. Toronto: Ryerson Press, 1952. xi + 148 p.

Ralph Linton, Editor, *The Science of Man in the World Crisis.* New York: Columbia University Press, 1945. 532 p.

George A. Lundberg, *Can Science Save Us?* New York: Longmans, Green, and Co., 1947. 122 p.

*Physical Science and Human Values:* A Symposium. Princeton; Princeton University Press, 1947. vii + 181 p.

Bertrand Russell, *The Impact of Science on Society.* New York: Columbia University Press, 1951. 64 p.

B. F. Skinner, *Science and Human Behavior.* New York: Macmillan Co., 1953. x + 461 p.

Roger J. Williams, *The Human Frontier.* New York: Harcourt, Brace and Co., 1946. ix +314 p.

Florian Znaniecki, *The Social Role of the Man of Knowledge.* New York: Columbia University Press, 1940. viii + 212 p.

[32] Douglas E. Scates, "How Wrong Are Educators?" *Journal of Educational Research* 35:705-12; May 1942.

Douglas E. Scates, "Not By Physical Might Alone." *Phi Delta Kappan* 29:352-54; February 1948.

Douglas E. Scates, "The Parallel Roles of Physical and Social Science." *Scientific Monthly* 64:14-20; January 1947.

methods of coöperation are dependent in large part on a sound program of education, which in turn must look to research for guidance. (This point of view recalls the central theme of our opening chapter.)

**Action programs.** Several terms have been employed to label the use of group dynamics and related concepts in the implementation of research findings, including action research, educational engineering, and operational research. The social psychology of action-research programs is based on the concept of bringing about change step-by-step through group participation. In the early stage of the project, the role of objective observer separates study of the problem from possible fear of any change that may be required by the findings. In later stages of the action program, participation as a group identifies the individual members with the project and develops attitudes or behavior favorable to approval and support by way of implementation or application of the findings. Identification of staff members of a school system or of participating members from other groups with a particular investigational project is one of the strongest forces for applying in practice the results of research.[33]

Certain differences in emphasis characterize so-called fundamental research as compared with action studies.[34] Up to the middle of the twentieth century the great majority of educational investigators were primarily interested in fundamental research, as described below.

1. Formulation of new generalizations, explanatory principles, and scientific theories or laws that go beyond the populations and situations represented, with the expectation that some other person will bring about improvement in practice.

2. High value placed on sampling procedures as a basis for generalizations.

3. Careful planning in advance of the investigation and adherence to the design of the study throughout the project, with the reporting done in sufficient detail to permit repetition of the study.

4. Desirability of technical training or equipment that frequently involves statistical, sampling, testing, or experimental procedures.

5. Judgment of the quality of the investigation based on the possibility of generalizing the methods and findings beyond the sample and situation studied, thus adding to the body of knowledge in the particular field.

The contrasting major emphases in action research are as follows:

1. Usually stemming from an urgent practical or felt need, with a goal of application of results and improvement of practice in the particular setting where the group or investigator works, through processes of group planning,

---

[33] J. Wayne Wrightstone, "Research-Action Programs for Research Bureaus." *Journal of Educational Research* 42:623-29; April 1949.

[34] Stephen M. Corey, "Fundamental Research, Action Research and Educational Practices." *Growing Points in Educational Research.* Washington: American Educational Research Association, 1949. p. 261-65.

Herbert A. Thelen, "Engineering Research in Curriculum Building." *Journal of Educational Research* 41:577-96; April 1948.

execution, and evaluation (by both research specialists and volunteer or lay participants).

2. Interest in the particular subjects investigated rather than in the total theoretical population represented by the sample under study.

3. A developmental design, with the hypothesis and method subject to modification during the course of the action program, and with due consideration of all interdependent groups concerned in any changes to be made.

4. Desirability of training in concepts of group dynamics as background for coöperative study of practical problems, with the guiding theory that of human interaction by which change is either facilitated or resisted, and with frequent difficulties of interaction with the particular community by way of choice of problem areas, specific formulation of the problem, selection of procedures, presentation of findings, and application to practices. The scientists or scholars in their role of democratic leaders stimulate and develop the talents of the group, and train and supervise the participants in the project.

5. Determination of the value of the action project in terms of the extent to which methods and findings make possible improvement in practice in a particular situation and realization of social and educational purposes.

Although action studies are more commonly of the survey, case-diagnostic, or experimental type, it is possible and sometimes desirable for programs of implementation and application of research to include the historical or genetic approach. One analysis of action programs includes four types of investigation: [35]

1. The diagnostic type, designed to lead to action, as in studying existing community tensions, sources of tensions, and available community resources for dealing with stress and strain, together with recommendations for remedial measures.

2. The participant type, with the central idea of involving in the research process from the beginning the persons who are to take the action; for example, a Mayor's Committee on Human Relations in a large city.

3. The empirical type, as exemplified by a boys' club, a settlement house, or other community project, including a record of what happens in accumulating experience from day to day.

4. The experimental type, with controlled procedures.

A good example of an extensive program of action research in anthropology and sociology deals with the American Indian: [36]

The Indian Personality and Administration Research was an interdisciplinary coöperative project, initiated and financed by the United States Office of Indian Affairs and directed by the University of Chicago's Committee on Human Development and the Society for Applied Anthropology. It was designed to illuminate the practical problem of how Indian Service policy and program might be improved in order to meet more effectively the needs of the Indians and to enhance their welfare. The project began in 1941 and was terminated

[35] Isidor Chein, Stuart W. Cook, and John Harding, "The Field of Action Research." *American Psychologist* 3:43-50; February 1948.

[36] Quoted from Laura Thompson, "Action Research Among American Indians." *Scientific Monthly* 70:34-40; January 1950.

in 1947. During the six years of its formal existence, eleven communities were investigated in five Indian tribes: Hopi, Navaho, Papago, Sioux, and Zuni. The major findings of the project are being presented in a number of tribal monographs, including *The Hopi Way* (Thompson and Joseph, 1944), *Warriors without Weapons* (Macgregor, 1946), *The Navaho* (Kluckhohn and Leighton, 1946), *Children of the People* (Leighton and Kluckhohn, 1947), *The Desert People* (Joseph and others, 1949); in numerous articles; and in a terminal report entitled "Personality and Government" (Thompson, *America Indigena, January,* 1950).

A variety of additional references to the literature of action research, educational engineering, and operational research may appropriately be listed to indicate the interest in such projects or programs as a medium for implementation of research findings.[37]

[37] Mark Abrams, *Social Surveys and Social Action.* London: William Heinemann, Ltd., 1951. 153 p.

Read Bain, "Action Research and Group Dynamics." *Social Forces* 30:1-10; October 1951.

Walter R. Borg, "Teachers as Intelligent Consumers of Research." *School and Society* 73:357-59; June 9, 1951.

John E. Brewton, "Educational Research in the South Related to Action Programs." *Peabody Journal of Education* 25:195-203; March 1948.

John E. Burchard, *op. cit.*

Veronica E. Casey and S. M. Corey, "Parents and Teachers Practice Action Research to Cope with Mutual Problems." *Educational Administration and Supervision* 38:333-41; October 1952.

W. W. Charters, "The Era of the Educational Engineer." *Educational Research Bulletin* 30:230-237, 246; December 12, 1951.

W. W. Charters, "Idea Men and Engineers in Education." *Educational Forum* 12:399-406; May 1948.

Isidor Chein, Stuart W. Cook, and John Harding, *op. cit.*

Stephen M. Corey, "Action Research, Fundamental Research, and Educational Practices." *Teachers College Record* 50:509-14; May 1949.

Stephen M. Corey, "Action Research by Teachers and the Population Sampling Problem." *Journal of Educational Psychology* 43:331-38; October 1952.

Stephen M. Corey, *Action Research to Improve School Practices.* New York: Bureau of Publications, Teachers College, Columbia University, 1953. xii + 161 p.

Stephen M. Corey, "Curriculum Development Through Action Research." *Educational Leadership* 7:147-53; December 1949.

Adam Curle, "A Theoretical Approach to Action Research." *Human Relations* 2:269-80; 1949.

H. A. C. Dobbs, *Operational Research and Action Research.* Washington, D. C.: Institute of Ethnic Affairs, 1947. 21 p.

Jessie Elliff and A. W. Foshay, "Action Research Means Cooperation; From the Viewpoint of Consultant and Principal." *Educational Leadership* 7:167-70; December 1949.

A. O. Felix, "Research By the People and For the People." *Nation's Schools* 47:69-71; March 1951.

Arthur W. Foshay, "Considerateness and Aggression: An Action Research Study." *Educational Research Bulletin* 32:85-112; April 8, 1953.

Arthur W. Foshay and M. R. Goodson, "Some Reflections on Coöperative Action Research." *Educational Leadership* 10:411-18; April 1953.

James W. Green and Selz C. Mayo, "A Framework for Research in the Actions of Community Groups." *Social Forces* 31:320-27; May 1953.

Robert G. Gunderson, "This Group-Dynamics Furor." *School and Society* 74:97-100; August 18, 1951.

Kenneth F. Herrold, "Evaluation and Research in Group Dynamics." *Educational and Psychological Measurement* 10:492-504; Autumn 1950.

L. Thomas Hopkins, "Dynamics in Research." *Teachers College Record* 51:339-46; March 1950.

John E. Ivey, Jr., "A University Experiments in Research Translation." *Educational Record* 31:383-404; October 1950.

**Implementation through publication.** A frequent criticism of professional and scientific writing is that of hurrying into print, which has made for too frequent duplication in research, unnecessary waste of effort and expense, and even the retardation of scientific progress. In the chapter on the formulation of the problem, a number of examples are cited, indicating the care and time prior to publication that went into the writing of such persons as Copernicus, Galileo, John Locke, Darwin, and William James. In recent years the scientist probably has had too much rather than too little freedom of the press, as measured in terms of adequate standards of professional reporting and publication, and in terms of the social functions or obligations of science.[38]

In the chapter on formulation of the problem certain related factors of problem-solving and implementation are discussed, including consideration of existing practices and needs as a source for locating research problems, significance for the field involved, timeliness, and practical value in terms of application of the results.

A detailed presentation of the various channels of implementation, including printed media, is outside the scope of this chapter and book. For preparation and handling of printed materials, in particular, adequate hand-

---

Marie Jahoda, Morton Deutsch, and Stuart W. Cook, *Research Methods in Social Relations*. Part 1, Basic Processes. New York: Dryden Press, 1951. Chapter 10.

George T. Renner, "Research as Educational Experience." *Teachers College Record* 53: 366-74; April 1952.

Arnold M. Rose, "Where Social Action and Social Research Meet." *Sociology and Social Research* 36:283-90; May-June, 1952.

D. C. Rucker and Alice Pittman, "Action Research Means Cooperation; From the Viewpoint of School Supervisors." *Educational Leadership* 7:164-67; December 1949.

Douglas E. Scates, "We're in a New Era of Public School Research." *Nation's Schools* 47:31-33; April 1951.

Stanley E. Seashore and Rensis Likert, "Action Research for Better Community Programs in International Affairs." *Adult Leadership* 2:23-25; July-August 1953.

Mary N. Smith, "Action Research to Improve Teacher Planning Meetings." *School Review* 60:142-50; March 1952.

M. W. Tate, "Operationism, Research, and a Science of Education." *Harvard Educational Review* 20:11-27; January 1950.

Herbert A. Thelen, *op. cit.*

Herbert A. Thelen, "Interaction Research Methodology." *Journal of Social Issues* 6:56-76; 1950.

Laura Thompson, "Action Research Among American Indians." *Scientific Monthly* 70: 34-40; January 1950.

John G. Withall, "Social Engineering: Selected References." *Progressive Education* 26: 220-22; May 1949.

J. Wayne Wrightstone, "Research-Action Programs for Research Bureaus." *Improving Educational Research*. Washington, D. C.: American Educational Research Association, 1948. p. 29-34. Also *Journal of Educational Research* 42:623-29; April 1949.

[38] Herbert S. Bailey, Jr., "The University Presses and the Popularization of Science." *Scientific Monthly* 64:416-20; May 1947.

Ralph Coghlan, "The Need for Science Writing in the Press." *Scientific Monthly* 62: 538-40; June 1946.

T. S. Harding, "The Sad Estate of Scientific Publication." *American Journal of Sociology* 47:593-601; January 1942.

books are available.[39] It is reasonable to suggest that, if the recommendations of this chapter are followed closely in the preparation of the technical report, few changes will be necessary to meet the standards of even the most exacting publishing house or journal.

## CONCLUDING STATEMENT

The preparation of the report represents the communicatory stage in research, in agreement with Thoreau's aphorism that "it takes two to speak the truth; one to speak and one to listen." This is a stage in the progress of the research project and not a process separate from the earlier steps in problem-solving. The research report is typically exposition rather than description, narration, or argumentation.

The materials of an extended report, such as a thesis, may well be organized into the major divisions described in this chapter. The logical arrangement and structure of these divisions depend on the care with which the outlining and note-taking have been done.

References in the form of footnotes and bibliographies are widely used in the educational, psychological, and social sciences, yet careless practices in citation are numerous, with even more regrettable instances of unmistakable plagiarism. Many illustrations of correct form and usage for references have been given in the preceding pages.

The preparation of an adequate research report takes time. "Good literature is not written, it is rewritten."[40] The style should be natural and straightforward, without exaggerated rhetoric or unnecessary literary artifices. A report of real substance requires only simplicity, clarity, and directness to be effective. It should be added, however, that there is every reason to exercise any skill in language one possesses; there is no premium on dullness or monotony in scientific writing.

Appraisal should attend each stage of problem-solving, including the process of application of findings or implementation. It is probably impossible to reduce the background and insight for evaluation of research to any rule-of-thumb check list of criteria.

Scientists and scholars have a grave responsibility to report their studies, to apply their knowledge to the crucial problems of society, and to use

[39] E. M. Allen, *op. cit.*
John Benbow, *op. cit.*
R. C. Binkley, *Manual on Methods of Reproducing Research Materials.* Ann Arbor, Michigan: Edwards Brothers, 1936. xiv + 207 p.
*A Manual of Style, op. cit.*
*Words into Type, op. cit.*
[40] C. L. Fry, *op. cit.*, p. 202.

their wisdom for the benefit of mankind. On the proper relationship between science, technology, implementation, society, and a system of values depend the welfare and even the very existence of science, research, and democratic society.

## SELECTED REFERENCES

ABELSON, Harold H. *The Art of Educational Research:* Its Problems and Procedures. Yonkers-on-Hudson, New York: World Book Co., 1933. Chapter 19.

AGG, T. R., and FOSTER, W. L. *The Preparation of Engineering Reports.* New York: McGraw-Hill Book Co., 1935. 192 p.

ALEXANDER, Carter, and BURKE, Arvid J. *How to Locate Educational Information and Data.* Third Edition. New York: Bureau of Publications, Teachers College, Columbia University, 1950. xix + 441 p.

ALLEN, E. M. *The Author's Handbook.* Scranton, Pa.: International Textbook Co., 1938. ix + 150 p.

ALMACK, J. C. *Research and Thesis Writing.* Boston: Houghton Mifflin Co., 1930. Chapters 9, 10.

American Association for Health, Physical Education, and Recreation. *Research Methods Applied to Health, Physical Education, and Recreation.* Revised Edition. Washington: The Association, N.E.A., 1952. p. 478-517.

ANDERSON, J. E. "The Preparation of Book Reviews." *Psychological Bulletin* 40:423-26; June 1943.

APPEL, Livia. *Bibliographical Citation in the Social Sciences:* A Handbook of Style. Second Edition, Revised. Madison: University of Wisconsin Press, 1946. 30 p.

BAKER, R. P., and HOWELL, A. C. *The Preparation of Reports.* New York: Ronald Press Co., 1938. xvi + 578 p.

BARKER, R. G. "Difficulties of Communication Between Educators and Psychologists: Some Speculations." *Journal of Educational Psychology* 33:416-26; September 1942.

BARR, Arvil S., DAVIS, Robert A., and JOHNSON, Palmer O. *Educational Research and Appraisal.* Philadelphia: J. B. Lippincott Co., 1953. p. 335-43.

BENBOW, John. *Manuscript and Proof.* New York: Oxford University Press, 1937. x + 118 p.

BERGLUND-GRAY, Gunborg. "Methods Used in Preparing Manuscripts for Publication in Psychology and Education." *Journal of Educational Research* 29:212-15; November 1935.

BIDDICK, Mildred. "This Business of Writing for Teachers." *Curriculum Journal* 11:56-60; February 1940.

BIERSTEDT, Robert. *"What Price Criticism?*— Continued." *American Association of University Professors Bulletin* 37:276-80; Summer 1951. Concerns more adequate compensation for services rendered publishers by members of the teaching profession.

BINGHAM, Walter V. "How to Make a Useful Index." *American Psychologist* 6:31-34; January 1951.

BINKLEY, R. C. *Manual on Methods of Reproducing Research Materials.* Ann Arbor, Mich.: Edwards Brothers, 1936. xiv + 207 p.

BIXLER, H. H. *Check Lists for Educational Research.* New York: Teachers College, Columbia University, 1928. Chapter 6.

BLOOMFIELD, Leonard. *Linguistic Aspects of Science.* International Encyclopedia of Unified Science, Vol. I, No. 4. Chicago: University of Chicago Press, 1939. viii + 59 p.

BOGARDUS, E. S. *Introduction to Social Research.* Los Angeles: Suttonhouse, 1936. Chapter 14.

BORG, Walter R. "Teachers as Intelligent Consumers of Research." *School and Society* 73:357-59; June 9, 1951.

BORING, E. G. "The Lag of Publication in Journals of Psychology." *American Journal of Psychology* 49:137-39; January 1937.

BRADFORD, S. C. *Documentation.* Washington: Public Affairs Press, 1948. 146 p.

BREWTON, John E. "Educational Research in the South Related to Action Programs." *Peabody Journal of Education* 25:195-203; March 1948.

BRIELAND, Donald M. "The Psychologist as Speaker." *American Psychologist* 5:409-11; August 1950.

BRISTOL, Margaret C. *Handbook on Social Case Recording.* Chicago: University of Chicago Press, 1936. xii + 219 p.

BRONK, Detlev W. "Science and Humanity." *Science* 109:477-82; May 13, 1949.

BROWN, Charles H. "Scientific Publishing in Continental Europe: Notes on Its War and Postwar Status." *Science* 106:54-58; July 18, 1947.

BURCHARD, John E., Editor. *Mid-Century:* The Social Implications of Scientific Progress. Cambridge, Mass.: Massachusetts Institute of Technology Press, 1950. xx + 549 p.

CAMPBELL, W. G. *A Form Book for Thesis Writing.* Boston: Houghton Mifflin Co., 1939. iv + 145 p.

CARTER, Boyd G. "The Modern Martyr." *American Association of University Professors Bulletin* 34:505-16; Autumn 1948.

CHARTERS, W. W. "Idea Men and Engineers in Education." *Educational Forum* 12:399-406; May 1948.

CHASE, Francis S. "Education Research by State Governments Confirms the Need for Action." *Nation's Schools* 43:23-25; April 1949.

CHASE, Stuart. *The Tyranny of Words.* New York: Harcourt Brace, 1938. xiv + 396 p.

Chicago, University of. *A Manual of Style.* Revised and Enlarged. Chicago: University of Chicago Press, 1949. x + 498 p.

CHISHOLM, George B. "Social Responsibility." *Science* 109:27-30, 43; January 14, 1949.

CLELAND, Ralph E. "Possible Advantages of Coöperation Between Societies in Publication." *Science* 105:567-68; May 30, 1947.

COLBY, Vineta. "The Nephew of William Hamilton Sutton (A Story)." *American Association of University Professors Bulletin* 37:372-87; Summer 1951. The life history of a doctoral dissertation, with a dash of humor and irony.

COLE, A. H., and BIGELOW, K. W. *A Manual of Thesis-Writing.* New York: John Wiley and Sons, 1935. x + 51 p.

COLTON, F. Barrows. "Some of My Best Friends Are Scientists." *Scientific Monthly* 69:156-60; September 1949.

CONDON, Edward U. "Science and the National Welfare." *Journal of Engineering Education* 38:522-31; April 1948.

CONE, Carl B. "Major Factors in the Rhetoric of Historians." *Quarterly Journal of Speech* 33:437-50; December 1947.

CONFREY, Burton. *Initiating Research in Catholic Schools.* Manchester, N. H.: Magnificat Press, 1938. Chapters 7, 8.

CONNER, Martha. *Practical Bibliography Making with Problems and Examples.* New York: H. W. Wilson Co., 1938. 31 p.

"Content of a Good Occupational Monograph—The Basic Outline." *Occupations* 19:20-23; October 1940.

COREY, Stephen M. "Action Research in Education." *Journal of Educational Research* 47:375-80; January 1954.

COREY, Stephen M. *Action Research to Improve School Practices.* New York: Bureau of Publications, Teachers College, Columbia University, 1953. xii + 161 p.

COREY, Stephen M. "Fundamental Research, Action Research and Educational Practices." *Growing Points in Educational Research.* Washington: American Educational Research Association, 1949. p. 261-65.

CORNELL, Francis G. "Getting Action by Means of the School Survey." *Growing Points in Educational Research.* Washington: American Educational Research Association, 1949. p. 62-67.

CUNNINGHAM, W. K., and PATRICK, B. M. *Typing Academic Papers.* Durham, N. C.: Duke University Press, 1937. 118 p.

DALE, Edgar, and HAGER, Hilda. "How to Write to Be Understood." *Educational Research Bulletin* 27:207-16; November 10, 1948.

Dartmouth College, Amos Tuck School of Administration and Finance. *Manual on Research and Reports.* New York: McGraw-Hill Book Co., 1937. x + 140 p.

DAVIS, R. A. "Writing a Thesis in Education." *Peabody Journal of Education* 27:285-95; March 1950.

DENNIS, Wayne, and GIRDEN, Edward. "Do Psychologists Read? The Case of the Psychological Bulletin." *American Psychologist* 8:197-99; May 1953.

DESING, Minerva F. "Suggestions to the Novice in the Mechanics of Research." *School Review* 49:206-12; March 1941.

DiMICHAEL, Salvatore G. "Characteristics of a Desirable Psychological Report to the Vocational Counselor." *Journal of Consulting Psychology* 12:432-37; November-December 1948.

DUGDALE, Kathleen. *A Manual of Form for Theses and Term Reports.* Bloomington: Indiana University, 1950. vi + 58 p.

DUTCHER, G. M. "Directions and Suggestions for the Writing of Essays or Theses in History." *Historical Outlook* 22:329-38; November 1931.

EELIS, Hasting. *Writing a Thesis.* Yellow Springs, Ohio: Antioch Press, 1947. v + 41 p.

EELLS, Walter C. "Publication of Educational Research." *Journal of Educational Research* 33:31-42; January 1931.

ELLIS, Albert. "The Application of Scientific Principles to Scientific Publications." *Scientific Monthly* 66:427-30; May 1948.

Faculty of Teachers College, University of Cincinnati, *A Guide for the Preparation of Dissertations, Theses, and Field Reports.* Cincinnati: University of Cincinnati, 1952. iii + 55 p.

FAIRCHILD, H. P., Editor. *Dictionary of Sociology.* New York: Philosophical Library, 1944. viii + 342 p.

FATOUT, Paul. "This Publishing Business." *Educational Forum* 15:359-62; March 1951.

FAULKNER, Donald. "Generalization through Condensation: A Research Technique." *Educational Research Bulletin* 19:492-93; November 20, 1940.

FAULKNER, Donald. "Logical Consistency as a Research Technique." *Educational Research Bulletin* 20:42-44, 54; February 12, 1941.

FELIX, A. O. "Research By the People and For the People." *Nation's Schools* 47:69-71; March 1951.

FESTINGER, Leon, and KATZ, Daniel, Editors. *Research Methods in the Behavioral Sciences.* New York: Dryden Press, 1953. p. 579-646.

FLESCH, Rudolf. *The Art of Readable Writing.* New York: Harper and Bros., 1949. xvi + 237 p.

FLESCH, Rudolf, and LASS, A. H. *The Way to Write.* Revised Edition. New York: Harper and Bros., 1949. x + 342 p.

FRY, C. L. *The Technique of Social Investigation.* New York: Harper and Bros., 1934. Chapters 11, 12.

GATNER, Elliott S. M., and Cordasco, F. G. M. *University Handbook for Research and Report Writing.* Brooklyn, N. Y.: The Authors, Long Island University, 1947. 154 p.

GAUM, C. G., and GRAVES, H. F. *Report Writing.* New York: Prentice-Hall, 1935. 319 p.

GOOD, Carter V., Editor. *Dictionary of Education.* New York: McGraw-Hill Book Co., 1945. xl + 495 p. Scheduled for revision in 1956.

GOOD, Carter V.; BARR, A. S.; and SCATES, Douglas E. *The Methodology of Educational Research.* New York: Appleton-Century-Crofts, 1936. Chapters 13, 14.

GOOD, Warren R. *An Introduction to Thesis Writing.* Ann Arbor, Mich.: Ann Arbor Press, 1937. 48 p.

GOODE, William J., and HATT, Paul K. *Methods in Social Research.* New York: McGraw-Hill Book Co., 1952. Chapters 3, 4, 21.

GOODRICH, Dorris W. "An Analysis of Manuscripts Received by the Editors of the *American Sociological Review* from May 1, 1944 to September 1, 1945." *American Sociological Review* 10:716-25; December 1945.

GOODSON, Max R. "Action Research in Education." *Graduate School Record* 1:3-6; July 1948.

GREEVER, Garland, and JONES, E. S. *Century Handbook of Writing.* Fourth Edition. New York: Appleton-Century-Crofts, 1942. xvii + 364 p.

GUNDELL, Glenn. *Writing—From Idea to Printed Page.* Garden City, N. Y.: Doubleday and Co., 1949. ix + 374 p.

GUNDERSON, Robert G. "This Group-Dynamics Furor." *School and Society* 74:97-100; August 18, 1951.

HAMILTON, Gordon. *Social Case Recording.* New York: Columbia University Press, 1936. vii + 190 p.

HARRIMAN, Philip L. *New Dictionary of Psychology.* New York: Philosophical Library, 1947. 364 p.

HART, Hornell. "Some Methods for Improving Sociological Definitions." *American Sociological Review* 8:333-42; June 1943.

HAYNES, B. R., and HUMPHREY, C. W. *Research Applied to Business Education.* New York: Gregg Publishing Co., 1939. Chapter 6.

HEBB, D. O., and BINDRA, Dalbir. "Scientific Writing and the General Problem of Communication." *American Psychologist* 7:569-73; October 1952.

HEMENS, Rollin D. "The University Presses: Their Function." *Scientific Monthly* 64:412-15; May 1947.

HERROLD, Kenneth F. "Evaluation and Research in Group Dynamics." *Educational and Psychological Measurement* 10:492-504; Autumn 1950.

HOCKETT, H. C. *Introduction to Research in American History.* New York: Macmillan Co., 1932. Chapter 3. Also see the 1948 edition.

HODGSON, James G. "Bibliographical Citations for Modern Scholars." *School and Society* 73:289-91; May 12, 1951.

HOGREFE, Pearl. *The Process of Creative Writing.* New York: Harper and Bros., 1947. x + 369 p.

HOLT, Robert R., and Others. "Publication Problems in Psychology." *American Psychologist* 8:235-42; June 1953.

HOLY, T. C. "Getting the Value Out of Research Through Applications." *Improving Educational Research.* Washington: American Educational Research Association, 1948. p. 37-41.

HOOK, Lucyle, and GAVER, Mary V. *The Research Paper.* New York: Prentice-Hall, 1948. 80 p.

HOPKINS, L. Thomas. "Dynamics in Research." *Teachers College Record* 51: 339-46; March 1950.

HOPPER, Robert L., and Others. *Interdisciplinary Research in Educational Administration.* Bulletin of the Bureau of School Service, Vol. 26, No. 2. Lexington: University of Kentucky, December 1953. 56 p.

HURT, Peyton. *Bibliography and Footnotes:* A Style Manual for College and University Students. Revised and enlarged by Mary L. H. Richmond. Berkeley: University of California Press, 1949.

IVEY, John E., Jr. "A University Experiments in Research Translation." *Educational Record* 31:383-404; October 1950.

JOHNSON, Loaz W. "Educational Research and Its Dissemination." *Educational Leadership* 10:423-27; April 1953.

JONES, W. Paul. *Writing Scientific Papers and Reports.* Dubuque, Iowa: William C. Brown Co., 1946. ix + 115 p.

JOUGHIN, G. L. *Basic Reference Forms:* A Guide to Established Practice in Bibliography, Quotations, Footnotes, and Thesis Format. New York: F. S. Crofts, 1941. xi + 94 p.

JURGENS, Marion A. "Research Publication: A Federal Responsibility?" *Science* 110:209-12; August 26, 1949.

KELLER, A. G. "Terminology." *American Sociological Review* 8:125-32; April 1943.

KERR, Chester. *A Report on American University Presses.* Washington: Association of American University Presses, 1949. 302 p.

KIDD, John W. "Check-List for Doctoral Research." *Journal of Educational Research* 47:555-57; March 1954.

KIERZEK, John M. *From Reading to Writing.* New York: Macmillan Co., 1946. vii + 319 p.

LEAL, Mary A. "Difficulties Encountered in Writing a Thesis." *Education* 52: 214-19; December 1931.

LINSTEAD, Hugh. "Scientist and Politician as Partners: The British Parliamentary and Scientific Committee." *Science* 108:47-50; July 16, 1948.

LONG, J. A. *Conducting and Reporting Research in Education.* Bulletin No. 6, Department of Educational Research. Toronto: University of Toronto, 1936. 77 p.

MAASKE, Roben J. "Preparation of Articles by School Practitioners." *Journal of Educational Research* 39:682-86; May 1946.

MCATEE, W. L. "On Scholarly Writing and Critical Reviewing." *Scientific Monthly* 51:77-79; July 1940.

MCCLELLAND, E. H. "Slips That Pass in the Night: A Plea for Accuracy in Printed Material." *Journal of Chemical Education* 20:546-53; November 1943.

McCormack, Eric D. "Scientist and the Common Good." *American Journal of Physics* 16:295-300; May 1948.

Mellon, M. G. "Publications: Pitfalls and Problems." *Journal of Chemical Education* 20:534-37; November 1943.

Merrill, Paul W. "The Principles of Poor Writing." *Scientific Monthly* 64: 72-74; January 1947.

Merton, Robert K. "The Role of Applied Social Science in the Formation of Policy: A Research Memorandum." *Philosophy of Science* 16:161-81; July 1949.

Mess, Henry A. "On Terminology." *Sociological Review* 32:50-63; January-April 1940.

Michels, Walter C. "Limits of the Scientist's Responsibility." *American Journal of Physics* 16:289-94; May 1948.

Minton, Arthur. "Style in Education Periodicals." *English Journal, College Edition* 24:724-27; November 1935.

Monroe, W. S., and Engelhart, M. D. *The Scientific Study of Educational Problems.* New York: Macmillan Co., 1936. Chapter 13.

Monroe, W. S. and Engelhart, M. D. *The Techniques of Educational Research.* University of Illinois Bulletin, Vol. 25, No. 19. Urbana: University of Illinois, 1928. 84 p.

Morgan, David H. *A Manual for Master's Theses and Reports.* Fort Collins: Colorado Agricultural and Mechanical College, 1948. 126 p.

Morphet, Edgar L., and Others. *Citizen Cooperation for Better Public Schools.* Fifty-third Yearbook of the National Society for the Study of Education, Part I. Chicago: University of Chicago Press, 1954. xvii + 304 p.

National Education Association, Research Division. "The Codification of School Laws." *Research Bulletin* 32:1-47; February 1954.

Nelson, J. R. *Writing the Technical Report.* Second Edition. New York: McGraw-Hill Book Co., 1947. xiv + 388 p.

Newsom, N. W., and Walk, G. E. *Standards for Thesis Writing.* Scranton, Pa.: International Textbook Co., 1936. 31 p.

Nichols, Frederick G. "Lag between Research Results and Practice." *National Business Education Quarterly* 17:19-23; March 1949.

Odum, H. W., and Jocher, Katharine. *An Introduction to Social Research.* New York: Henry Holt and Co., 1929. Chapter 23.

Parten, Mildred. *Surveys, Polls, and Samples:* Practical Procedures. New York: Harper and Bros., 1950. Chapter 17.

Paterson, Donald G. "Publication of Date of Receipt of Manuscript by Journals in Psychology and Allied Fields." *American Psychologist* 3:419-21; September 1948.

Perry, J. W. "The Utilization of Scientific Knowledge." *Scientific Monthly* 66:413-17; May 1948.

Pfiffner, J. M. *Research Methods in Public Administration.* New York: Ronald Press Co., 1940. Chapter 16.

*Publication Manual of the American Psychological Association.* Washington: American Psychological Association, 1952. 61 p.

Redford, Grant H. "Publish or Else." *Amerian Association of University Professors Bulletin* 38:608-618; Winter 1952-53.

Reid, Chandos. "Involvement Is Important in Research." *Educational Leadership* 10:438-43; April 1953.

Riker, A. J., and Others. "Advice to Newcomers: A Report on Releasing the Results of Research to the Public." *Scientific Monthly* 66:499-501; June 1948.

SANDERS, Chauncey. *An Introduction to Research in English Literary History.* New York: Macmillan Co., 1952. p. 277-315.

SCATES, Douglas E. "We're in a New Era of Public School Research." *Nation's Schools* 47:31-33; April 1951.

SCHMITZ, R. M. *Preparing the Research Paper.* New York: Richard R. Smith, 1931. vi + 94 p.

SEBOYAR, G. E. *Manual for Report and Thesis Writing.* New York: F. S. Crofts and Co., 1929. 58 p.

SEIDELL, Atherton. "The Publication of Scientific Research." *Science* 92:345-47; October 18, 1940.

SELLTIZ, Claire, and COOK, Stuart W. "Can Research in Social Science be Both Socially Useful and Scientifically Meaningful?" *American Sociological Review* 13:454-59; August 1948.

SHANNON, J. R. "Art in Writing for Educational Periodicals: The Introduction." *Journal of Educational Research* 44:599-610; April 1951.

SHANNON, J. R. "Art in Writing for Educational Periodicals: The Main Body." *Journal of Educational Research* 47:489-504; March 1954.

SHANNON, J. R. "Tips to Writers from Seventy-Five Editors of Educational Periodicals." *Journal of Educational Research* 44:241-68; December 1950.

SHAW, Ralph R. "Copyright and the Right to Credit." *Science* 113:571-73; May 18, 1951.

SHEFFIELD, Edward F. "That Thesis Outline." *Educational Forum* 17:355-364; March 1953.

SHILS, E. A. "Social Science and Social Policy." *Philosophy of Science* 16:219-42; July 1949.

SKILLIN, Marjorie E.; GAY, Robert M.; and Others. *Words into Type:* A Guide in the Preparation of Manuscripts; for Writers, Editors, Proofreaders and Printers. New York: Appleton-Century-Crofts, 1948. xx + 585 p.

SMITH, H. L. *Educational Research:* Principles and Practices. Bloomington, Ind.: Educational Publications, 1944. p. 205-44.

SOAR, Robert S. "Readability of Typography in Psychological Journals." *Journal of Applied Psychology* 35:64-7; February 1951.

SPAHR, W. E., and SWENSON, R. J. *Methods and Status of Scientific Research.* New York: Harper and Bros., 1930. Chapters 12-14.

SPENCE, Ralph B. "Research and Practice: The Case for Impure Research." *Growing Points in Educational Research.* Washington: American Educational Research Association, 1949. p. 297-302.

STEVENS, Neil E. "The Moral Obligation to Be Intelligible." *Scientific Monthly* 70:111-15; February 1950.

STEVENSON, Earl P. "Creative Technology." *Scientific Monthly* 76:203-6; April 1953.

STEWARD, Julian J. *Area Research:* Theory and Practice. New York: Social Science Research Council, 1950. xix + 164 p.

STRANG, Ruth. "Principles of Readability Applied to Reporting Research." *Improving Educational Research.* Washington: American Educational Research Association, 1948. p. 41-43.

SUPER, Donald E., and Others. "Ethical Standards for the Distribution of Psychological Tests and Diagnostic Aids." *American Psychologist* 4:495-501; November 1949.

SYMONDS, Johnnie P. "Ten Years of Journalism in Psychology, 1937-1946: First Decade of the Journal of Consulting Psychology." *Journal of Consulting Psychology* 10:335-40; November 1946.

SYMONDS, P. M., and STEWART, Richard A. D. "Educational Planning." *Teachers College Record* 49:510-19; May 1948.

TATE, M. W. "Operationism, Research, and a Science of Education." *Harvard Educational Review* 20:11-27; January 1950.

TAYLOR, Mary. "Popularizing Research Findings." *Journal of Home Economics* 31:524-29; October 1939.

*Textbooks in Education.* New York: American Textbook Publishers Institute, 1949. xi + 139 p.

THELEN, Herbert A. "Engineering Research in Curriculum Building." *Journal of Educational Research* 41:577-96; April 1948.

THELEN, Herbert A. "Interaction Research Methodology." *Journal of Social Issues* 6:56-76; 1950.

THOMPSON, James S. "Technical Book Publishing in Europe, 1947: Impressions from Visits to Eleven Countries." *Science* 106:47-53; July 18, 1947.

TRELEASE, Sam F. *Scientific Paper, How to Prepare It, How to Write It;* A Handbook for Students and Research Workers in All Branches of Science. Second Edition. Baltimore: Williams and Wilkins Co., 1951. 163 p.

TURABIAN, Kate L. *A Manual for Writers of Dissertations.* Chicago: University of Chicago Bookstore, 1937. vi + 61 p.

ULMAN, Joseph N., Jr. *Technical Reporting.* New York: Henry Holt and Co., 1952. xiv + 289 p.

VANCE, Silas. "What Price Publication?—University Presses." *American Association of University Professors Bulletin* 37:711-16; Winter 1951-52.

VAN DE WATER, Marjorie. "Problems Faced by a Writer in Communicating Research Findings in Child Development." *Child Development* 19:67-75; March-June, 1948.

VAN TIL, William A., and Others. "Research on Human Relations and Programs of Action." *Review of Educational Research* 23:285-385; October 1953. Chapter 4.

VERDOORN, Frans. "The Development of Scientific Publications and Their Importance in the Promotion of International Scientific Relations." *Science* 107:492-97; May 14, 1948.

WALKER, Helen M., and DUROST, W. N. *Statistical Tables:* Their Structure and Use. New York: Teachers College, Columbia University, 1936. viii + 76 p.

WALL, Florence E. "The Importance of Technical Writing in Chemical Education." *Journal of Chemical Education* 20:580-86; December 1943.

WARNER, Sam B. "Copyrights and the Academic Profession." *American Association of University Professors Bulletin* 35:251-58; Summer 1949.

WARREN, H. C. *A Dictionary of Psychology.* Boston: Houghton Mifflin Co., 1934. x + 372 p.

WARREN, L. H. "Practical Suggestions for Reducing the Labor of Indexing a Textbook." *Science* 92:217-18; September 6, 1940.

WATERMAN, Alan T., and Others. "Scientific Research and National Security." *Scientific Monthly* 78:214-24; April 1954.

WEISS, Paul. "Biological Research Strategy and Publication Policy." *Science* 101:101-4; February 2, 1945.

WELD, Walter E. *How to Chart:* Facts From Figures with Graphs. Norwood, Mass.: Codex Book Co., 1947. xiv + 218 p.

WHITNEY, F. L. *The Elements of Research.* Third Edition. New York: Prentice-Hall, 1950. p. 404-35, 485-519.

WILES, Kimball. "Can We Sharpen the Concept of Action Research?" *Educational Leadership* 10:408-10; April 1953.

WILLIAMS, C. B., and STEVENSON, A. H. *A Research Manual for College Studies and Papers.* Revised Edition. New York: Harper and Bros., 1951. 194 p.

WITHALL, John G. "Social Engineering: Selected References." *Progressive Education* 26:220-22; May 1949.

WOOLLEY, Edwin C., SCOTT, Franklin W., and BRACHER, Frederick. *College Handbook of Composition.* Fifth Edition. Boston: D. C. Heath and Co., 1951. x + 344 p.

WRIGHTSTONE, J. Wayne. "Research-Action Programs for Research Bureaus." *Improving Educational Research.* Washington: American Educational Research Association, 1948. p. 29-34. Also *Journal of Educational Research* 42:623-29; April 1949.

YOUNG, Erle F. *Dictionary of Social Welfare.* New York: Social Sciences Publishers, 1948. vi + 218 p.

# Index